D1309068

Gay & Lesbian
BIOGRAPHY

Gay & Lesbian
BIOGRAPHY

Editor

Michael J. Tyrkus

Consulting Editor

Michael Bronski

With a Preface by

Jewelle Gomez

Endorsed by the Gay, Lesbian, and Bisexual Task Force,
American Library Association

ST. JAMES PRESS

AN IMPRINT OF GALE

DETROIT • NEW YORK • TORONTO • LONDON

Michael J. Tyrkus, *Editor*
Michael Bronski, *Consulting Editor*

Laura Standley Berger, Peg Bessette, Joann Cerrito, David Collins,
Nicolet V. Elert, Miranda H. Ferrara, Janice Jorgensen, Margaret Mazurkiewicz, *Contributing Editors*
Peter M. Gareffa, *Managing Editor, St. James Press*

Mary Beth Trimper, *Production Director*
Shanna Heilveil, *Production Assistant*
Cynthia Baldwin, *Art Director*

Victoria B. Cariappa, *Research Manager*
Julia Daniel, Jennifer Lund, *Research Specialists*

∞™ The paper used in this publication meets the minimum requirements of American National Standard for Information Sciences—Permanence Paper for Printed Library Materials, ANSI Z39.48-1984.

This book is printed on recycled paper that meets Environmental Protection Agency Standards.

Gay & lesbian biography / introduction, Jewelle Gomez; consulting editor, Michael Bronski; editor, Michael J. Tyrkus.
p. cm.
Includes bibliographical references and indexes.
ISBN 1-55862-237-3 (alk. paper)
1. Gays—Biography—Dictionaries.
I. Tyrkus, Michael J., 1970-.
HQ75.2.G39 1996
305.9'0664'0922-dc20 96-27123
CIP

Printed in the United States of America
Published simultaneously in the United Kingdom

St. James Press is an imprint of Gale

10 9 8 7 6 5 4 3 2 1

CONTENTS

PREFACE *page* vii

CONSULTING EDITOR'S INTRODUCTION ix

EDITOR'S NOTE xi

ADVISORY BOARD xiii

CONTRIBUTORS xv

LIST OF ENTRANTS xix

GAY & LESBIAN BIOGRAPHY 1

NATIONALITY INDEX 475

OCCUPATION INDEX 481

GENERAL SUBJECT INDEX 489

NOTES ON CONTRIBUTORS 507

PHOTO ACKNOWLEDGMENTS 515

PREFACE

As you open this volume of *Gay & Lesbian Biography* a first question might be: Why a book such as this one? That question, sure to be on the lips of some, is better approached by framing another query: What is a lesbian or gay man? This has been debated by psychiatrists, politicians, doctors, parents, theologians, and talk show hosts for so long the question has ceased to have meaning. We might as well ask: Who is a person in a crowd? The answer will be as different as each individual, different from decade to decade, different from one culture to another. Social, literary, and media images of who lesbians and gay men are have been of little or no assistance is answering the inquiry. Each new representation of lesbians and gay men is embraced or rejected as representing (or not representing) the whole group, leaving in its wake a cacophony of images: the shy, sensitive student, flamboyant drag queen, flannel-shirted "woodsbian," ice-pick wielding siren, universal earth mother, bikeless leatherman, effete opera buff, repressed librarian, golfer, skater, waiter.... Lesbians and gay men are, of course, all of these things and more.

It wasn't until relatively recently that the question could even be formed. Social historian Dennis Altman pointed out in his book *The Homosexualization of America* (Boston: Beacon Press, 1982): "the existence of large numbers of women and men whose self-definition is homosexual, and who regard homosexual relationships as the primary ones in their lives, is largely confined to modern Western societies, and it seems to be possible only under the particular social formations of urbanization and industrialization." First the Industrial Revolution, then World War II helped to increase the mobility of the population, irrevocably altering the idea of the norm in society. The subsequent development of more extensive systems of national communications, the burgeoning economic independence of women, and growth of more urban areas continued to change the face of life in the United States. One of the things these developments provided was to offer individuals an opportunity to pursue same-sex relationships not as simply stolen moments but as defining elements of a social life. Lesbians and gay men could begin to establish the symbols and signals that would make them known to each other and begin to create social circles. Although it was still safer to maintain a discreet silence within a "special friendship," lesbians and gay men began to see the first crack in the wall of isolation and invisibility.

Even with this societal shift the time still had not (and has not) arrived when lesbian/gay life is looked upon without comment or judgement by some segments of the population. But from the very first stirrings for lesbian/gay rights in the U.S. in the 1950s the movement toward an open life as a homosexual has been steady and consistent. But why is it important to know who is a lesbian or gay man?

When we enter a room and see an apple on a table, what do we see? Some would just say "an apple." Others would say a "rome," or "gravenstein," or "baking apple." But it is often the context which gives depth of meaning to a concept. If the apple sits on a table that has seen very little food, an apple might mean saving someone's life. If it is on a table in a palatial estate it might mean a snack for the maid, or a dieting patriarch. It could be one person's entire dinner, or the beginning of a pie. For those with a Christian heritage that apple might suggest something much more significant than it does to those who adhere to Native American spiritual beliefs, or to a Buddhist. Looking at the context tells us so much more than just "an apple."

The same is true of people. If there were no hunger in the world, maybe just "an apple" would have all the resonance it needs. If there were no fear of, or discrimination against, lesbians and gays, maybe just "a person" would do. But our social instinct is to name, to define, even when those appellations become confining or negative. And the designee, in turn, often learns to cling to the name, in order to create space to exist in the world.

In making that safe place the naming has often created a box many individuals fight to escape. So there will always be those who would never consider calling themselves lesbian or gay even though their lives fit such a description. So it may be time to shed the traditional view that "labeling" a person as lesbian or gay diminishes them as individuals or taints their accomplishments. It can just as easily be suggested that adding the information about an individual's homosexuality opens a door, taking us further into that person's experience. As we learn each new facet of a personality we see the individual as more whole, complete. What do we know when we know that Edward Albee is gay? Or that Alan Turing, Elizabeth Arden, Countee Cullen, or Federico García Lorca are lesbians or gay men? By acknowledging the homosexual orientation of individuals we, by implication, refute the ironclad assumption of the heterosexual nature of society and history. That refutation makes the individual and our world not smaller, but bigger.

Whether their accomplishments are directly related to or obviously reflect their lives as lesbians or gay men is not the core issue. To examine the plays of Christopher Marlowe or to read the work of Susan Sontag, acknowledging their gayness, gives an added context for their lives and their work which can deepen the appreciation for their accomplishments. When we learn of Hans Christian Andersen's homosexual orientation does it make us shun his classic fairytales? Or make us more curious about who this creator of legends was? If we are able to consider the diverse music of Aaron Copland, Alix Dobkin, and Johnny Mathis in light of their mutual gayness we can expunge some of the empty stereotypes that limit our thinking and postulate the infinite variety of ways that gayness is manifest in culture and society.

For example, singer Alberta Hunter entertained audiences for over sixty years with her ladylike delivery of suggestive lyrics. Recording her first song in 1921, Hunter's mellow blues voice delighted listeners from Harlem's Apollo Theatre to Chez Florence in Paris back to the Cookery in New York City's Greenwich Village where she performed until her death in the 1984. She recorded the sound track for Robert Altman's 1977 film, *Remember My Name,* which included much of her own original music and brought her talents to the attention of a new generation of fans.

Despite her impish performance persona Hunter was also known to be a tough business woman. This ease with contrasts is also evidenced in Hunter's projection of a demure (and always heterosexual) playfulness in counterpoint to the sometimes racy implications of the lyrics of her songs. Her carefully constructed lady-like image and the layers of sexual innuendo take on a deeper resonance in light of her long-term lesbian relationships.

The complexities of individual identity are labyrinthine. Whether an individual has been in the position (historical, financial, or political) to be openly lesbian or gay is not an issue in this compilation. As always, what must be held most significant is how a person lives and contributes to the society. And in many cases it has been difficult or impossible for individuals to either allow sexual orientation to be openly acknowledged or to make it an overt element in his/her accomplishments. The opportunity for such openness is directly influenced by class, ethnicity, history, profession, acculturation, etc., all the variables that help make us who we are. This volume places within a valuable social/historical context many well-known citizens of the world for whom such a book would have been beyond their imagination. This contextualization allows us to see more than just an apple.

But to create such a book means that some people will, of practical necessity, be left out. The committee of advisors pored over lists of names for almost a year with the resulting conclusion (the same as the chant at every Lesbian/Gay Pride March): "We Are Everywhere." Consequently many people—well-known pioneers, significant historical figures, local leaders, do not appear here. What *is* here is a glimpse at the spectrum that lesbian/gay life and accomplishment encompasses. The book stands as a reference point, a place to begin, a door to open.

Other readers might wonder about some individuals they would define as bisexual, or question how transsexuals fit in. Again, this volume is meant to illuminate the discussion of lesbian/gay life, not set the definitive parameters for that discussion. The term "bisexual" has changed in implication over time and the bisexual movement, which has taken shape through the 1990s, will continue to help refine how we identify ourselves, as will transsexual and transgender activists. Because the discussion of identity is still being framed, included in this book are some individuals who will also be grouped, under other circumstances, with bisexuals or transsexuals. These inclusions do not dismiss the unique position of bisexuals or ignore the complex discussions raised by transsexual identity; they, again, suggest a place to begin.

In this way *Gay & Lesbian Biography* offers the fullest possible historical spectrum of what has been lesbian and gay life over the centuries.

—Jewelle L. Gomez
San Francisco State University, 1996

CONSULTING EDITOR'S INTRODUCTION

The World Split Open

Biography has traditionally been viewed as a sort of map of history. The lives of the great and the near great were seen as the locations in which history happened. Presidents, generals, statesmen, and writers were the fixed points—the geographic sites—where the overwhelming march and morass of "history" could be defined, delineated. Biographies were composed of facts and details that dovetailed with the historical record, the way a map corresponds to terrain and roadway. The problem with this was twofold: the proper subject of biography was assumed to be (for the most part) white men, and the proper method of writing biography was simply to relate the facts of public life. This all changed with Lytton Strachey who, in his studies of Florence Nightingale, Cardinal Newman, and Queen Victoria, among others, invented the radical ideas that the private life was as important as—perhaps even more important than—the public, and that men were not the only people who could change the world. If biography was a map to history Strachey insisted that much of the map was, up until then, an invisible one.

The notion that the lives of non-white men might be important was a tremendous shift in how biography, and history, was conceptualized; we now realize that such a limitation is wrongheaded and inaccurate. The notion that the personal life was as vital as the public, however, was downright revolutionary. The privatization of emotions and sexuality has been a primary form of social regulation. What happened in the public sphere was history, what happened in private was, well, private. When Strachey claimed the "private" as within the reach of biography he seriously disrupted how the world was ordered. The "private" realm of feelings, emotions, and sexuality were now seen as relevant not only to the individual subjects of biography, but to how they lived in the world. In a poem about German artist Kathe Kollwitz, Muriel Rukeyser has written: "What would happen if one woman told the truth about her life?/The world would split open." By simply discussing, openly and honestly, the sexuality of noted women and men, *Gay & Lesbian Biography* presents us, quite frankly, with a world split open.

The biographies here are a map to history. Reading them locates us in time and place, pinpointing moments of historical conflict and surveying movements of change and upheaval. But because they deal openly with the sexuality of their subjects, they present us with an increasingly visible map: what has been, in many cases, hidden, is now manifest. It is possible to divide the subjects in *Gay & Lesbian Biography* into two groups. The first are women and men who are acknowledged, historical figures such as Leonardo da Vinci, Virginia Woolf, Christopher Marlowe, and Anne Lister, among many others. By discussing the often complex sexual identities of these subjects, *Gay & Lesbian Biography* is attempting to shed new light on how we examine and understand the past. The second group of subjects are contemporary people who are living now, or have recently lived, as openly lesbian or gay, some of whom are active members in a broad range of political and cultural activities that constitute the gay liberation movement: Audre Lorde, Roberta Achtenberg, Harry Hay, Essex Hemphill, to name only a few. These women and men have already made themselves visible, their lives and accomplishments established on the visible map of history.

It would be a mistake to read *Gay & Lesbian Biography* as a standard volume of historical, political and cultural biographies that happens to mention its subjects' sexual orientation. That new information—while interesting—would simply be another, more or less consequential, fact. The reality is that sexual orientation is integral to identity and activity. What is interesting is not that Leonardo da Vinci had homosexual desires (and acted upon them) but how this affected his thinking and work. The importance of sexual desire on the private and public life is enormous. In her diaries, Virginia Woolf wrote "women alone stir my imagination." The profundity of sexuality and desire shapes how we all view the work, how we work, what we create. What would Langston Hughes's work have been like if he were not a homosexual? What did her lesbianism have to do with how Eleanor Roosevelt saw her role in the world and politics? Who would the women and men who create contemporary lesbian and gay culture be today if they were heterosexual? The experience of being lesbian or gay is not simply a sexual one that exists in the realm of the private, but one that affects how lesbians and gay men view and change the world in which they live. *Gay & Lesbian Biography* attempts to not only give new and more honest "facts" about its subjects, but allows its readers a new way to interpret these lives and the culture in which they live. It provides us with a new map—now visible—of the world split open.

—Michael Bronski

EDITOR'S NOTE

This first edition of *Gay & Lesbian Biography*—endorsed by the Gay, Lesbian, and Bisexual Task Force of the American Library Association—provides biographical information on 275 gays and lesbians. The entrants were selected by an advisory board consisting of six members, in conjunction with the consulting editor and myself. An initial list of over 600 influential gays and lesbians was created and then whittled down to the 275 names the user will find within these pages. The entrants cover all time periods and many parts of the globe—ranging from ancient Greece to modern-day San Francisco—and include a variety of vocations—from poets to psychologists. Gay men and lesbians are represented in roughly equal numbers.

Gay & Lesbian Biography will be of use to adults and young adults who are seeking a fuller knowledge of the lives of important individuals in history and an introduction to those who are currently active in the gay and lesbian communities. Entries provide complete biographical information, including a boldfaced heading that lists birth, death, nationality, and occupation information for quick reference. The essays, written by scholars in the field, discuss the entrant's life and importance to the gay and lesbian community. The views expressed in the essays are wholly those of the writer and should not be construed as those of St. James Press or the editors. Many entries feature a portrait of the entrant.

Users will also find of value the indices found at the back of the volume, including:

- *A Nationality Index,* alphabetically listing entrants according to country of origin, lengthy residences, and/or country of citizenship.

- *An Occupation Index,* alphabetically listing the entrants according to their various vocations.

- *A General Subject Index,* an alphabetical listing of nearly 200 relevant subject terms covered in the entries.

I would like to thank the entire St. James Press staff for their tireless efforts and diligence during the production of this volume; the members of the advisory board for their generous expertise; Michael Bronski for his boundless efforts; Michelle Pilarski and Amy Marcaccio Keyzer for their last-minute copyediting.

—Michael J. Tyrkus
Editor

ADVISORY BOARD

CONTRIBUTORS

Ronald C. Albucher
Andrew A. Anderson
Shelley Anderson
Lee Arnold
Cecily M. Barrie
Edith J. Benkov
Cynthia A. Bily
Sandra Brandenburg
Margaret Soenser Breen
Ira N. Brodsky
Peter Burton
Lara Bushallow-Wilbur
Liz Cannon
Joann Cerrito
Peter G. Christensen
Mary C. Churchill
Laurie Clancy
Elizabeth Hutchinson Crocker
Renee R. Curry
Susie Day
Joseph E. DeMatio
Danielle M. DeMuth
Peter Dickinson
Paul A. Doyle
Wayne R. Dynes
Joseph M. Eagan
Carolyn Eckstein-Soule
Jean Edmunds
Nicolet V. Elert
C. Frederick Farrell, Jr.
Edith R. Farrell
Laurie Fitzpatrick
Brian Francis
Jill Franks
Ronie Garcia-Johnson
David Garnes
Michelle Gibson
Chris Gilmore
Craig M. Goad
Marian Gracias
R. Ellen Greenblatt
Diane E. Hamer
Judith E. Harper
Laura Alexandra Harris
Loie B. Hayes
Karen Helfrich
Seán Henry
Debora Hill
Jon Hodge
Robert F. Jones
Jane Jurgens
Beth A. Kattelman
Judith Katz
Nicola King
Judith C. Kohl
Jelena Krstović
David Levine
Ray Anne Lockard
Lisa W. Loutzenheiser
Michael A. Lutes
Jacquelyn Marie
James P. McNab
Dianne Millen
D. Quentin Miller
Robert N. Mory
Tom Musbach
Catherine Nelson-McDermott
Caryn E. Neumann
Michael E. O'Connor
Ekua Omosupe
Teresa Ortega
William Armstrong Percy III
Andrea L.T. Peterson
Annmarie Pinarski
Joanna Price
Robert B. Marks Ridinger
Susan L. Rochman
Shawn Stewart Ruff
Sue Russell
Geoff Sadler
Lynda Schrecengost
Marvin S. Shaw
Charles Shively
Jack Shreve
Bryan D. Spellman
Claude J. Summers
Fraser Sutherland
Lucya Szachnowski
Jerome Szymczak
Alex Robertson Textor
Nicolas Tredell
Douglas Blair Turnbaugh
Michael J. Tyrkus
Richard Voos
Jonathan Wald
Sarah Watstein
Gary Westfahl
Tracy White
Catherine A. Wiley
Anna Wilson
Les K. Wright

Gay & Lesbian
BIOGRAPHY

LIST OF ENTRANTS

Berenice Abbott
Roberta Achtenberg
Peter Adair
Jane Addams
Alvin Ailey
Chantal Akerman
Edward Albee
Alexander the Great
Paula Gunn Allen
Dorothy Allison
Pedro Almodovar
Dennis Altman
Hans Christian Andersen
Margaret Anderson
Susan B. Anthony
Gloria Anzaldua
Virginia M. Apuzzo
Gregg Araki
Elizabeth Arden
Reinaldo Arenas
Dorothy Arzner
W. H. Auden

Francis Bacon
Sara Josephine Baker
James Baldwin
Benjamin Banneker
Ann Bannon
Djuna Barnes
Natalie Clifford Barney
Deborah A. Batts
Joseph Beam
Bishop Carl Bean
Sir Cecil Beaton
Alison Bechdel
Arthur Bell
Miriam Ben-Shalom
Ruth Benedict
Michael Bennett
Gladys Bentley
Nancy K. Bereano
Ruth Bernhard
Leonard Bernstein
Elizabeth Bishop
Emily Blackwell
Marc Blitzstein
Rosa Bonheur
Anne Bonny and Mary Read
Kate Bornstein
John Boswell
Beth Brant
Susie Bright
Benjamin Britten
Romaine Brooks
Rita Mae Brown
Ron Buckmire
Charlotte Bunch
Glenn Burke
Charles Busch
Lady Eleanor Butler *see* Ladies of Llangollen
Paul Cadmus
John Cage
Pat Califia
Michael Callen
Margarethe Cammermeyer
Truman Capote
Caravaggio
Edward Carpenter
Willa Cather
June Chan
Debra Chasnoff
George Chauncey
Meg Christian
Christina
Chrystos
Roy Cohn
Colette
Blanche Wiesen Cook
Aaron Copland
Tee A. Corinne
Midge Costanza
Quentin Crisp
Margaret Cruikshank
George Cukor
Countee Cullen
Merce Cunningham

Mary Daly
Mercedes de Acosta
Samuel R. Delany
John D'Emilio
Barbara Deming
Michael Denneny
Sergei Diaghilev
Emily Dickinson
Divine
Melvin Dixon
Judy Dlugacz
Alix Dobkin
Martin Duberman

Melissa Etheridge

Lillian Faderman
Rainer Werner Fassbinder
Harvey Fierstein
E. M. Forster
Michel Foucault
Barney Frank
Frederick II
Marcia Freedman
Anna Freud

Greta Garbo
Federico García Lorca
Sally Gearhart
Jean Genet
André Gide
Elsa Gidlow
Sir John Gielgud
Allen Ginsberg
Barbara Gittings
Gluck
Jewelle Gomez
Marga Gomez
Paul Goodman
Judy Grahn
Duncan Grant
Barbara Grier
Angelina Emily Weld Grimke

Marilyn Hacker
Hadrian
Radclyffe Hall
Dag Hammarskjold
Barbara J. Hammer
Lorraine Hansberry
Keith Haring
Bertha Harris
Harry Hay
Essex Hemphill
Gilbert Herdt
Magnus Hirschfeld
David Hockney
Rock Hudson
Holly Hughes
Langston Hughes
Alberta Hunter

Christopher Isherwood
James Ivory *see* Ismail Merchant

Henry James
Derek Jarman
Karla Jay
JEB
Sarah Orne Jewett
Elton John
Jasper Johns
Bill T. Jones
Cleve Jones
Sor Juana Inés de la Cruz
Isaac Julien

Frank Kameny
Arnie Kantrowitz
Jonathan Ned Katz
John Maynard Keynes
Willyce Kim
Billie Jean King
Irena Klepfisz
David Kopay
Sharon Kowalski and Karen Thompson
Larry Kramer
Sheila James Kuehl

k. d. lang
Eva Le Gallienne
W. Dorr Legg
Leonardo da Vinci
Edmonia Lewis
Liberace
Lisa Ben
Anne Lister
Ladies of Llangollen
  Lady Eleanor Butler
  Sarah Ponsonby
Audre Lorde
Greg Louganis
JoAnn Loulan
Susan M. Love
Amy Lowell
Charles Ludlam
Phyllis Ann Lyon and Del Martin

Robert Mapplethorpe
Christopher Marlowe
Del Martin *see* Phyllis Ann Lyon
Johnny Mathis
Leonard P. Matlovich, Jr.
Carson McCullers
Sir Ian McKellen
Herman Melville
Gian Carlo Menotti
Ismail Merchant and James Ivory
Michelangelo Buonarroti
Harvey Milk
Edna St. Vincent Millay
June Millington
Yukio Mishima
Agnes Moorehead
Cherrie Moraga
Dee Mosbacher

Martina Navratilova
Holly Near
Joan Nestle
Florence Nightingale
Simon Nkoli
Elaine Noble
Rudolf Nureyev

Jean O'Leary

Pat Parker
Michelle Parkerson
Pratibha Parmar
Walter Pater
Reverend Troy D. Perry
Charles Pierce
Plato
Sarah Ponsonby *see* Ladies of Llangollen
Deb Price
Marcel Proust
Manuel Puig

Gertrude "Ma" Rainey
Mary Read *see* Anne Bonny

Toshi Reagon
Mary Renault
Adrienne Rich
Marlon Riggs
Arthur Rimbaud and Paul Verlaine
Eleanor Roosevelt
Gayle Rubin
Muriel Rukeyser
Jane Rule
RuPaul
Vito Russo
Bayard Rustin

Vita Sackville-West
Assotto Saint
George Santayana
Sappho
José Sarria
May Sarton
Sarah Schulman
Carol Seajay
Randy Shilts
Charles Shively
Michelangelo Signorile
Barbara Smith
Bessie Smith
Dame Ethel Smyth
Stephen Sondheim
Susan Sontag
Gertrude Stein
Lytton Strachey
Gerry E. Studds
John Addington Symonds
Peter Ilich Tchaikovsky
Martha Carey Thomas
Karen Thompson *see* Sharon Kowalski
Alice B. Toklas
Daniel C. Tsang
Kitty Tsui
Alan Turing

Karl Heinrich Ulrichs

Urvashi Vaid
Carl Van Vechten
Paul Verlaine *see* Arthur Rimbaud
Gore Vidal
Rosa von Praunheim

Tom Waddell
Andy Warhol
John Waters
Edmund White
Walt Whitman
Oscar Wilde
Gale Wilhelm
Tennessee Williams
Cris Williamson
Jeanette Winterson
Monique Wittig
Merle Woo
Virginia Woolf

Marguerite Yourcenar

Babe Didrikson Zaharias
Franco Zeffirelli

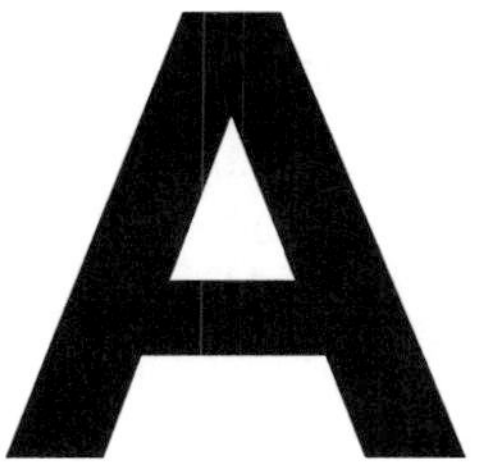

Berenice Abbott

1898-1991

American photographer

After exploring the fields of journalism and sculpture, Berenice Abbott found her calling with photography. Had she not, the world would not only be without the telling portraits of some of the literary and artistic figures of Abbott's day and her objective chronicle of the fascinating changes taking place in New York City earlier in this century, but also without the work of French photographer Eugène Atget as well as the vivid photographs of scientific phenomena Abbott began taking later in her life.

Berenice Abbott was born in Springfield, Ohio, on 17 July 1898 to Charles E. and Alice Abbott, who divorced soon after her birth. Abbott's childhood, which she described as an unhappy one, was spent apart from her three older siblings, and she had little contact with her father. Abbott credited these early experiences with forging her self-reliance and her independent nature. At various times during her youth, she wanted to be a farmer and an astronomer but finally decided on a career in journalism.

At the age of 19, Abbott entered Ohio State University in order to study her chosen field. A year-and-a-half later she went to New York City to visit a former schoolmate who was active in the productions at the Provincetown Playhouse. Restless and dissatisfied with her coursework, Abbott felt at ease in Greenwich Village's burgeoning bohemian atmosphere and decided to stay. After a short-lived attempt to resume her studies at Columbia University—she managed to last only about a week, stating in *Recollections: Ten Women of Photography* that it "seemed like a hell of a sausage factory"—Abbott left behind altogether her aspirations of becoming a journalist.

For the next three years she eked out a living, supporting herself by working in an office, modelling, waiting tables, and occasionally taking roles in theatrical productions. During this time, Abbott became interested in art and began to study sculpting. She was also beginning to meet some of the leading figures in arts and letters, including poet Djuna Barnes, critic Malcolm Cowley, the painter Marcel Duchamp, and his friend, photographer Man Ray.

The Expatriate in Paris

In 1921 Abbott bought a one-way ticket to Paris, intent on being a part of the growing cultural scene that was drawing artists and writers in large numbers. "I thought I may as well be poor there as poor here," Abbott recalled in *Recollections.* She continued sculpting, receiving instruction from Antoine Bourdelle, and working odd jobs. Two years later Abbott decided to travel to Berlin in order to study at the city's art school. It was there that it finally became apparent that success as a sculptor would continue to elude her.

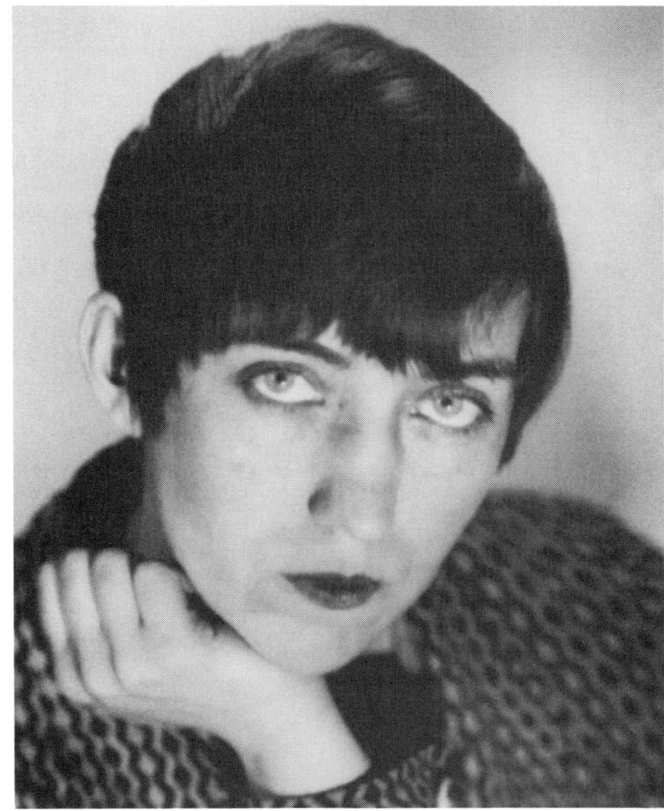

Berenice Abbott

She returned to Paris, leaving her last stone sculpture on the platform in Cologne in order to avoid a delay due to a mix-up of train schedules. Abbott became reacquainted with her friends there, including Man Ray, who in 1924 took her on as an apprentice and later a darkroom assistant when she dared him to make good on his desire to hire someone in his portrait studio who was completely ignorant of photography.

Abbott quickly took to the work, becoming adept at the technical aspects of the photographic process, and gradually started taking photographs on her own. Abbott did not begin to think seriously of photography as a career, however, until she realized that the majority of the photos she was taking were quite good. In 1925 with the aid of, among others, Peggy Guggenheim, Abbott opened her own portrait studio and was soon taking photos of some of the most celebrated figures in Paris at that time, among which were Jean Cocteau, Janet Flanner, André Gide, and Ernest Hemingway. Probably her most well-known portrait is that of James Joyce. A year after opening her studio, Abbott had her first solo exhibition at Au Sacre du Printemps, followed two years later by a group exhibition at the First Salon of Independent Photographers, which also included the work of Man Ray and André Kertész.

Atget's Work Is a Profound Influence

The person primarily responsible for influencing Abbott's work was the aged Parisian photographer Eugène Atget, who had been working in near total obscurity for years. Wanting to see more than just the few photos with which she had become familiar while working for Man Ray, she began visiting Atget's studio and found inspiration in his many photographs of Paris, which he had begun taking in 1899. Abbott responded to the realism she saw in the photos and developed a deep respect for the photographer, who had managed to make a living by selling prints to archives and artists. The only surviving portrait of Atget is the one taken by Abbott just days before his death. Wanting his work to receive the recognition she felt it deserved and intending to promote his reputation, Abbott managed to acquire the 8,000 prints and 1,500 glass-plate negatives from the friend to whom Atget had bequeathed them.

Abbott traveled to New York for a visit in 1929 but was so fascinated by the changes that had taken place in the city that she decided to return permanently. She set up a portrait studio, reserving at least one day a week just for photographing Manhattan and its environs, much as Atget had recorded the streets of Paris. Abbott also devoted much of her time to arranging print sales and exhibits of Atget's work. Thanks to her, a volume of his photos was published in 1930, and much later, in 1964, Abbott compiled her own book, *The World of Atget.* In 1968 the Museum of Modern Art purchased Abbott's collection of the photographer's work.

Abbott had been photographing New York for five years, while at the same time trying to get funding in order to concentrate full-time on her project and compile the resulting work for publication. In addition to her portraiture, Abbott would take on commercial work when necessary. Her response to those who might have criticized this was unapologetic, as she declared in *Recollections,* "There's nothing wrong with good, honest commercial work. It's good technical experience." Friends would often chide her for taking too long to make a portrait, explaining that she could make more money if she were to take more sitters and charge less. But Abbott would not hear of compromising her very high standards and took only one sitter a day in order to allow people to relax and be themselves, thereby producing a better photo.

"I'm No Lady. I'm a Photographer."

Funding was a difficult thing to come by at the height of the Depression, and Abbott's applications for monies were rejected. In addition, she was forced to realize that New Yorkers were not as willing as the Parisians had been to accept her particular eccentricities. Abbott endured comments concerning the trousers she wore, and, according to *Annual Obituary,* she is said to have replied to a truck driver who told her that taking photos outdoors wasn't ladylike, "I'm no lady. I'm a photographer." Her photographs of the city did not go unrecognized, however; some had been published as early as 1930 and the Museum of Modern Art and the Museum of the City of New York had both held exhibits that included some of her photos. It was at the first solo New York exhibit of her work, which was held in 1934 at the latter museum, that Abbott became acquainted with her lifelong friend, art critic Elizabeth McCausland.

In the meantime, Abbott did not strictly confine her work outside the studio to photographing New York and the surrounding area. The architectural historian Henry Russell Hitchcock, Jr., asked her in 1933 to provide the photographs for two of his projects. Abbott initially traveled along the Eastern seaboard, photographing representative works of the American architect, Henry Hobson Robinson. Then, in 1935, she and McCausland took a trip through Ohio, Pennsylvania, and the southeastern United States so that Abbott could take the photos for Hitchcock's series on architecture prior to the Civil War.

In the fall of 1935 Abbott began teaching photography at the New School for Social Research, where she would remain for more than 20 years. Later that year, Abbott received the news that the Federal Arts Project of the Works Progress Administration had granted her enough funds to allow her to concentrate on her New York work for the next four years. Ultimately, nearly 100 of Abbott's New York photos were collected into a volume entitled *Changing New York.* The book, which included an historical perspective written by McCausland, was published by E. P. Dutton in 1939.

Abbott Turns Her Lens on Science

Abbott would have liked nothing more than to continue focusing her efforts on photographing New York, but such an endeavor was just not economically feasible. Instead, she turned her attention elsewhere. In 1941 her *Guide to Better Photography* was published. Less instructional than ideological she wrote that "technic for technic's sake is like art for art's sake—a phrase of artistic isolationism, a creative escapism.... In short the something done by photography is *communication.*" And communication was exactly what Abbott hoped to accomplish with her next project. As she stated in *Recollections,* "It was an age of science and I decided to know more about the subject myself. I wanted to learn by photographing it."

She also wanted to share what she learned, so while Abbott set about initially photographing electricity—a challenge she certainly could not resist after encountering doubt that it could be done—and building the necessary equipment, she began the tedious process of trying to convince the scientific community that such photos were valuable instructional tools. Finally in 1958 Abbott was asked to take part in the Physical Science Study Committee sponsored by the Massachusetts Institute of Technology. The group was revamping the high school physics curriculum, and being familiar with her work, the committee chairman, Dr. E. P. Little, requested that Abbott provide the photographic illustrations for a new textbook.

Abbott threw herself into the project, developing even more photographic equipment—including several pieces for which she was awarded patents—and photographing such phenomena as magnetism, the pattern produced by the interference of two sets of waves, and, among her best, the refraction of light. *Physics* was published in 1960, but Abbott's photographs were not just confined to the text's pages. In addition to an exhibit that traveled to schools and science museums across the country, these photographs were used in other books for young adults as well.

Abbott had purchased a house in Maine in 1956 after seeing the state during two photographic trips made along US 1 to Florida two years before. She moved there permanently in 1966 and continued to work, finding a renewed interest in portraiture late in her life. Although the photos from her journeys the length of the pre-interstate highway have yet to be published, Abbott did produce the 1968 publication *A Portrait of Maine,* a collection of photos she had taken of her new home state.

It was at her home in Monson, Maine, that Berenice Abbott died at the age of 93 from congestive heart failure. However, the photographer lives on through the pictorial legacy she left behind. Abbott described her life's work in the November 1951 *Infinity:* "Living photography builds up, does not tear down. It proclaims the dignity of man. Living photography is positive in its approach; it sings a song of life."

References:

Abbott, Berenice. *A Guide to Better Photography.* New York: Crown Publishers, 1941.

———. "It Has to Walk Alone," in *Infinity,* November 1951.

Annual Obituary, 1991. Detroit: St. James Press, 1992: 715-19.

Berenice Abbott. New York: Aperture Foundation, Inc., 1988: 5-12, 88-92.

Current Biography, 1942. New York: H. W. Wilson, 1943: 1-2.

Hagen, Charles. "Berenice Abbott, 93, Dies; Her Photographs Captured New York in Transition," in the *New York Times Biographical Service,* December 1991: 1350-51.

Mitchell, Margaretta K. *Recollections: Ten Women of Photography.* New York: Viking Press, 1979: 12-13.

—Nicolet V. Elert

Roberta Achtenberg

1950-

American politician

Although the lesbian and gay community would likely hail Roberta Achtenberg for such achievements as being the first lesbian—in fact, the first openly gay person—ever to be nominated by the president and confirmed by the U.S. Senate (she was appointed to the position of Assistant Secretary for Fair Housing and Equal Opportunity by President Bill Clinton in 1993) or for being the supervisor of the San Francisco Board of Supervisors, Achtenberg sees her own accomplishments in a much different light.

Although Achtenberg readily acknowledges that her appointment by President Clinton—and the Senate's confirmation—was "a milestone for the [gay and lesbian] movement," she does not feel that the appointment itself was the most significant thing. This reasoning comes about because she measures her own successes by a different standard: "The most important thing about being the Assistant Secretary for Fair Housing," she says, "is being the best Assistant Secretary that ever was—not for the sake of being the best," but for affecting change and for being effective in the position.

"Doing the job right," she reiterates, "is more important than being the first" to hold the position. It is this outlook that she brings to life's challenges and it appears that it is this philosophy which drives her to accomplish and enables her to see success where others might not.

Roberta Achtenberg was born on 20 July 1950 to Beatrice and Louis Achtenberg. The Achtenbergs, a family of six, lived in Los Angeles and owned a small store. Achtenberg learned at home what would serve as the foundation for a lifetime of accomplishment: respect "for the values of family, hard work, and community."

Influenced by her brother's struggle to be independent in spite of his being confined to a wheelchair, she vowed early on to help those in need. Her career to date has been about precisely this ambition—helping those in need by challenging and changing the status quo, and by making legal and governmental protections available and accessible to those requiring them. To date, the measure of her own success has been based on how well she has effected change; how many people have had the circumstances of their lives changed, for the better, because of her work.

Achtenberg and her partner, former San Francisco Municipal Court Judge Mary C. Morgan—the first openly lesbian judge—have been together since 1983. Morgan, who is currently a Deputy Assistant Attorney General at the Department of Justice, has temporarily relocated to Washington, D.C., with Achtenberg and their son, Benji, where they will remain until both of them complete their tenure with the Clinton Administration.

Achievements and Career Milestones

Prior to the 1992 presidential election, Achtenberg was one of the first elected officials in California to endorse Clinton. In fact, she campaigned extensively for the candidate, serving as national co-chair of the campaign and later as Clinton's appointee to the prestigious platform drafting committee. She was also selected to address the Democratic National Convention in defense of that platform. Shortly after Clinton took office, Achtenberg was appointed Assistant Secretary for Fair Housing and Equal Opportunity and one of the most grueling Senate confirmation hearings followed.

As Assistant Secretary of Fair Housing and Equal Opportunity Achtenberg was the chief enforcement officer of the federal Fair Housing Act and of civil rights laws governing Department of Housing and Urban Development (HUD) programs. Among the many things she has accomplished, she ranks her work with housing at the top of the list: "integrating housing, restructuring the bureaucracy, housing people." Among other things, she took on the Ku Klux Klan to successfully integrate the public housing in one Texas community; she helped more than 13,000 low-income families find new homes after the 1994 earthquake in Northridge, Los Angeles; and even developed the first ever national Best Practices Fair Lending Agreement with the Mortgage Bankers of American and a Best Practices Agreement with the National Association of Home Builders. According to HUD Secretary Henry G. Cisneros, under whom Achtenberg worked, she "made a substantial difference in the lives of many Americans who might otherwise have faced housing discrimination."

Also high up on her own list is her work as legal director for the Lesbian Rights Project of Equal Rights Advocates (1984-1988)—fighting for "family rights of gay and lesbian people"; and the publication of her book, *Sexual Orientation and the Law,* which she calls a resource "very much needed ... for lawyers representing lesbian or gay clients." Of providing this essential volume, Achtenberg says, "I was glad to have done it."

As county supervisor in San Francisco, Achtenberg was an advocate for "basic things": families, children, a cleaner environment, crossing guards, etc. "Someone needs to do that stuff," she says. "I got to do it." She also penned the city's original "Sunshine" ordinance that allowed full public scrutiny of virtually every aspect of

Roberta Achtenberg

city government. She later drafted legislation to improve water recycling, promote ground water reclamation, and to require city agencies to protect the environment by reducing the use of wasteful paper products.

Chief among her concerns as supervisor was child-care for low income families. During her time on the San Francisco Board of Supervisors she worked for legislation that would require developers either to build child-care facilities or to contribute to a child-care fund for low income families. Her efforts resulted in legislation providing monthly child-care subsidies to graduates of job training programs as well as a guaranteed $10 million annual allocation to establish and administer a children's budget. But one of her proudest accomplishments while on the Board is her legislation establishing the San Francisco Commission on National Service, which has made substantial progress in promoting and directing the work of young people in San Francisco's neighborhoods.

Before her tenure on the San Francisco Board of Supervisors, Achtenberg had already distinguished herself as one of the country's leading civil rights attorneys. She has taught at the Stanford Law School, served as Dean at the New College of California School of Law, and as a member on the Board of Directors of the San Francisco Neighborhood Legal Assistance Foundation.

In 1989, Achtenberg was selected by the United Way of the Bay Area as Management Volunteer of the Year and in 1993 she was the California Senate's Woman of the Year for the Third Senate District. She has also received much recognition and many honors for her efforts on behalf of women's and gay and lesbian rights. Among them is the Lifetime Achievement Award which was presented to her by the Lambda Legal Defense and Education Fund in 1990.

She also received, during her time as Assistant Secretary for Fair Housing and Equal Opportunity, the National Performance Review's Golden Hammer Award from Vice President Gore for "streamlining her office's grant-making program, for saving the federal government millions of dollars, and for improving the quality of service to the public."

Losing or Winning?

Although the greatest challenge of her career might appear to have ended in failure, Achtenberg says of her attempt to win the 1995 San Francisco mayoral race: "I thought I did extremely well. I was wildly successful. The only thing I didn't do was win."

In a campaign where she was severely out-financed by her opponents, Achtenberg did do extremely well. So, will she run again? "We'll see," she says. More important than whether she won or lost, or whether she'll run again, she says, is what she took away from the campaign—the realization that "there is life after loss," something she says, "many [political hopefuls] don't realize."

The belief in a "life after loss" is clearly evidenced by her return in February 1996, after the San Francisco mayoral race, to HUD where she continues to chip away at the endless layers of bureaucracy, seeking to eliminate redundancy within the agency, and working for a more efficient, effective system.

Upon returning to HUD, Achtenberg assumed the position of senior advisor to HUD Secretary Cisneros. In that capacity she works to develop and implement Clinton administration and departmental policy on housing, home ownership, and community-based economic development. When emergencies arise, it is her job to quickly formulate and implement effective solutions.

Achtenberg maintains that she has no ultimate career goals. "That's not how I do my [life]. I don't do something [in order] to do something else," she maintains. Nor does she have any short term goals aside from returning to California because, as she says, "my son needs to start middle school back in San Francisco" in the fall. "It is important," she adds, "for him to spend his adolescence and high school years at home."

It is safe to say that whatever lies ahead will be a continuation of her commitment to eradicate discrimination, to make the basics readily available to the average person, and to continue to fight for change in government.

A Giant Step or Two for the Movement

Clearly her greatest contributions to the gay and lesbian movement are the publication of her book, *Sexual Orientation and the Law,* and her appointment as Assistant Secretary for Fair Housing and Equal Opportunity—controversial, she says, only because the radical right made it so.

"You don't know what it's going to be like," Achtenberg says of the ordeal of going through the historic, grueling senate confirmation of her appointment where she endured not only the routine questioning of the Senate committee, but also withstood the attacks on her character by Jesse Helms and others. "You [draw from] other burdens you have borne" when you face something this difficult and you get through it. Achtenberg maintains the process wasn't nearly the big deal for her, however, that it was for the public.

"Doing a good job," she stresses, "is exceedingly important ... wanting to lead your city ... [tapping into] people's best instincts not their worst fears." These are the things that Achtenberg considers more important than all of the firsts she has accomplished.

Current Address: HUD Fair Housing & Equal Opportunity, 451 7th St. SW, Room 5100, Washington, D.C. 20410.

References:

Achtenberg, Roberta. Interview with Andrea L.T. Peterson, March 1996.

Achtenberg, Roberta, with others. *Sexual Orientation and the Law.* New York: Clark Boardman, 1985.

(Additional biographical information provided by Roberta Achtenberg's campaign office in San Francisco).

—Andrea L.T. Peterson

Peter Adair

1943-1996

American filmmaker

Adair was a groundbreaking documentary filmmaker whose works deal with contemporary issues in an intelligent manner. "My movies," he asserted, "have always been a way of exploring subjects of personal interest. When I wondered about religion, I made a film about it. When I realized I was gay, I made a film about it." The latter film, *Word Is Out,* is widely considered the best documentary on the subject of homosexuality, and has been credited with changing attitudes both within and outside the gay community.

The son of an anthropologist, Adair spent his early years in New Mexico. He later observed that he very quickly became aware of being different from his mostly Native American and Hispanic peers, developing the outsider's perspective that characterizes his films. He subsequently lived in Santa Monica and graduated from Antioch College, but his film career had begun before he entered the university, when his parents gave him a movie camera as a high-school graduation present. Thereafter, Adair noted, he became obsessed with filmmaking, and he completed his first feature-length film, *Holy Ghost People,* when he was just 21. The film subsequently received a graet deal of attention when the noted anthropologist Margaret Mead gave it a glowing review.

After graduating from college, Adair worked in the film industry, but he eventually struck out on his own in order to make films about subjects that interested him. The subject that interested him at that point was homosexuality, and in order to accomplish the enormous task of documenting the multifaceted story of gay life, he formed the six-member Mariposa Group, which also included his sister Nancy. *Word Is Out* took five years to produce and upon its release in 1978 was hailed as a breakthrough, humanizing the faces of the gay community and documenting their struggles against irrational prejudices.

Adair subsequently produced *Stopping History* (1984), which examines the ethical questions surrounding the use of nuclear weapons, and *The AIDS Show: Artists Involved with Death and Survival* (1986). He also made *Modern Selling,* a tongue-in-cheek industrial film done in a mock-1940s style that purports to show bank loan officers how to treat their female clients.

Later, after he was diagnosed with HIV, Adair made *Absolutely Positive,* an upbeat look at twelve men and women—including himself—and their individual methods for coping with the virus. The film's participants discuss the issues of receiving "the quintessential bad news" of testing HIV positive, as one puts it, of breaking the news to family and friends, and of learning to go on living in the shadow of death.

Adair remained free of AIDS symptoms for 4½ years. In late 1995, he was felled by a series of opportunistic diseases: non-Hodgkin's lymphoma, cryptococcal meningitis, pneumonia and phlebitis. He died on 27 June 1996.

On Monday, 8 January 1996, Frameline, the nation's only non-profit organization exclusively dedicated to the distribution, funding, promotion, and exhibition of lesbian and gay film and video, presented Adair with its 1996 Frameline Award. Adair's response upon hearing that he was going to be honored with a retrospective career tribute, was "I was very relieved. I was hoping something like this would happen, frankly. You're not supposed to say that, but I'd been making films since 1959 or something. They've all been recognized to one degree or another, but never as a body of work."

References:

Burress, Charles. Obituary in the *San Francisco Chronicle,* 29 June 1996: A21.

Dunlap, David W. Obituary in the *New York Times,* 30 June 1996: 32.

—Sarah Watstein

Jane Addams

1860-1935

American social reformer and author

From the moment pioneering social reformer, social worker, sociologist, leader in the settlement movement, pacifist, intellectual, and author Jane Addams burst into public prominence following the founding of Hull House until her death, she was constantly in the public eye. As one of the great innovators in the settlement movement of the late nineteenth century, Addams and her Hull House associates revolutionized the way social reformers, philanthropists, and the public viewed poverty. And through her active role in society, Addams helped forge a radically new identity for women emerging from the repression of the nineteenth century—as active, committed citizens dedicated to improving the quality of human life.

Addams was born 6 September 1860, the eighth of nine children, into a prosperous upper-middle-class family in Cedarville, Illinois. Her early childhood was filled with tragedy and hardship. Her mother, Sarah Weber Addams, died when Jane was two years old. Four years later her sister Martha died. As a young child, Addams also suffered from tuberculosis of the spine, which caused a permanent curvature. Her health remained precarious through young adulthood. Her father, John Huy Addams, a prominent businessman, civic leader, and state senator, remarried when Jane was eight years old. Her stepmother, Anna Haldeman Addams, was a domineering woman who brought discipline and culture to the Addams household. Addams was very close to her father, who instilled in her a fascination for history, literature, philosophy, and national and foreign affairs.

The Quest for a Social Mission

When she was 17 years old, Addams entered Rockford Female Seminary. Although higher education for women was rapidly changing, Rockford operated according to Principal Anna Sill's Victorian conviction that the purpose of a woman's education was to enable her "to elevate and purify and adorn the home," and to "give oneself fully and worthily for the good of others." Yet Addams, true to an upbringing that encouraged independent thinking, envisioned an expanded role for modern women. In a speech at Rockford in 1880, she boldly presented a new vision of women as active providers, who could contribute much to society, through "good labor and honest toil."

But the years following Addams'ss graduation from Rockford were filled, not with purpose and good works as she had hoped, but with depression and self-doubt. Though her education had prepared her to fully engage in society, society still did not recognize women as viable participants. She briefly attended Philadelphia's Women's Medical College, but withdrew when she realized that she was ill-suited to medical training. Following this failure, Addams'ss health deteriorated, leaving her bedridden. As she regained her strength, she resisted her stepmother's efforts to have her marry and made two extended trips to Europe during the 1880s. The highlight of the second trip, made with Ellen Gates Starr, her close friend from Rockford, was a visit to Toynbee Hall in London in 1888, where Addams eagerly observed the British social reform movement's efforts to bridge the gulf between the wealthy and the poor.

Toynbee Hall was a social experiment, a prototype of what would come to be known as a settlement house. Its community consisted of university-educated young men, all dedicated to working and living among the poor. Addams was most impressed by the fact that the men served the poor without the paternalism and sense of "noblesse oblige" which she so disliked about traditional charity and philanthropy.

Building a Model Settlement at Hull House

Addams and Starr returned to the U.S. to initiate their own social experiment in the heart of Chicago. In 1889, after months of studying the city, Addams rented Hull House, a dilapidated mansion in the center of Chicago's 19th Ward, a squalid, tenement-ridden neighborhood teeming with European immigrants. Although Addams and Starr had their own plans for Hull House, they soon discovered the key to Hull House's future success: they allowed the community to instruct them about its needs. Guided by this principle, they opened a day nursery to help working mothers, and later added a dispensary, cooking and sewing classes, adult high school classes, the first public playground, and a cooperative boarding house for working girls. Hull House, which eventually grew to encompass thirteen buildings, also functioned as a community center and as a mediator between the government and 19th-Ward residents.

Jane Addams

Although Hull House was not the first settlement house in the United States, it soon gained a reputation for being the model. This was partly the result of Addams's intuitive understanding of how to manipulate the media to Hull House's benefit and partly due to her engaging personality which attracted people from all over the world. Addams had no trouble encouraging extraordinarily talented women and men to become part of Hull House. Young social reformers were eager to participate in the open, supportive, intellectual environment that Addams created at Hull House.

As the years passed, Addams became increasingly aware that although settlements like Hull House could ameliorate the conditions of the poor, they were ineffective at grappling with the causes of poverty. From the early 1890s on, Addams and other Hull House specialists initiated projects to effect social change. Florence Kelley led a State Bureau of Labor Statistics investigation of Chicago's garment industry, which employed thousands of children who labored 12-14 hours for six days a week. The results of the investigation, strengthened by the Hull House team's lobbying, led to the passage of the Illinois Factory Act of 1893, which regulated sweatshops and outlawed the employment of children under age 14. Other Hull House reformers included Alice Hamilton, pioneer in industrial medicine, who pressured factory owners to improve safety, Julia Lathrop, public welfare expert, who helped enact a law instituting the first juvenile court system in the U.S., and Mary Kenney, a tough, successful organizer of women laborers.

In 1895, Addams and Kelley led a large group of social workers in the production of a comprehensive sociological study entitled *Hull House Maps and Papers.* This ground-breaking document was the product of the first effort to intensively study an American working-class neighborhood. By scrutinizing the conditions contributing to the neighborhood's increasing poverty, *Hull House Maps and Papers* provided social reformers with the data necessary to lobby persuasively for legislative reforms.

The "Delivering Love" of Mary Rozet Smith

As the years passed, Addams and Starr slowly drifted apart. What had begun as an intensely romantic, intellectual union culminating in the founding of Hull House had gradually failed to meet each woman's needs. As Starr became increasingly engrossed in the book-binding trade, militant socialism, and medieval Christianity, Addams was busy administering Hull House and its many projects. Addams discovered the perfect companion in Mary Rozet Smith, a wealthy, college-educated Hull House worker and benefactor. Quiet and unassuming, Smith adored Addams, and eventually committed herself to loving, caring, and emotionally supporting her.

Throughout her teen years and young adulthood, Addams appears to have had no interest in pursuing heterosexual relationships. She resembled many first-generation women college graduates, 50 percent of whom did not marry and many of whom chose same-sex relationships and living arrangements. And, as is true of most nineteenth century romantic female friendships, although Addams's correspondence reveals her emotional and spiritual connection with both Starr and Smith, there is no evidence to suggest that either relationship was sexual in nature. As Jill K. Conway emphasizes in her study *The First Generation of Women College Graduates,* Addams and her fellow settlement workers renounced most Victorian conventions, but when it came to expressions of love, they did not challenge the Victorian dichotomy of "romantic love as spiritual and physical love as lustful." Although late nineteenth century women were frustratingly silent on the subject of sex, there is no question that Addams preferred the love and affection of other women and chose to be involved in exclusive, mutually supportive love relationships with them.

From Social Reform to Political Action

Once secure in the relationship with Smith, Addams entered a profoundly productive period during the early 1900s. Buoyed with self-confidence, she wrote a succession of highly acclaimed articles and books. Her book *Democracy and Social Ethics,* published in 1902, stressed how a tolerant understanding of immigrants from diverse cultures could strengthen democracy in an industrial society. *The Spirit of Youth and the City Streets* (1909) discussed the problems of young people growing up in the industrial age. And, in 1910, Addams published her autobiographical memoir, *Twenty Years at Hull House,* which quickly became a best-seller.

As leader of the National Conference of Charities and Correction (NCCC) and as vice president of the American Woman Suffrage Association (AWSA), Addams was drawn into the political arena during the 1912 presidential election. When the Republican party rejected the NCCC's proposals, which included an 8-hour work day, 6-day work week, ban on child labor, and national system of unemployment, accident, and old-age insurance, third-party candidate Theodore Roosevelt's Progressive Party accepted the entire platform and also agreed to support woman suffrage. Addams enthusiastically campaigned for Roosevelt, traveling and speaking all over the country. Despite his defeat at the polls, Addams's campaign efforts were successful in drawing national attention to social and industrial reform issues.

Sacrifices for Pacifism

Addams, long interested in pacifism, became completely engrossed in the quest for peace with the outbreak of World War I in 1914. Convinced that the United States should exercise its role as peacemaker, Addams organized 3,000 women in Washington, D.C., to form the Women's Peace Party (WPP) in 1915. She led a group of WPP delegates to the Hague Congress in the Netherlands, where she and other delegates were chosen to meet with the leaders of the seven warring nations. Although they were unsuccessful in their efforts to promote peace in Europe, they did open dialogue with European leaders regarding a future league of nations.

Upon her return to the U.S., Addams described her pacifist efforts in a speech at Carnegie Hall which triggered a massive attack on her patriotism. As the weeks passed, her repeated efforts to clarify her views failed as the press continued to misquote and vilify her. The woman who had been lauded in 1910 as a "Joan of Arc ... sacrificing all for the masses" was now dismissed as a "silly, vain, impertinent old maid." By the time the U.S. entered the war in 1917, she realized that publicizing her beliefs was counterproductive to the cause of peace. She also acknowledged in her book *Peace and Bread in Time of War* (1922), that the wartime political climate made it "impossible for the pacifist to obtain an open hearing."

Addams quietly continued her peace efforts by organizing the Second Women's Congress at Zurich in 1919 where the delegates formed a new peace organization, the Women's International League for Peace and Freedom (WILPF). Addams, who served as WILPF president until 1929, delivered the Zurich resolutions to the diplomats working on the Versailles Treaty. At home in the U.S., the public's antagonism toward pacifists did not end with the Armistice in 1918. Anxieties created by the war's aftermath, including fears of Bolshevism and Communism, intensified the American patriotic frenzy during the Red Scare of 1919-20. When immigrants, feared because of their foreignness, were persecuted and their rights violated, Addams found she could not be silent. Her outspoken defense of immigrants was perceived as being un-American and communist, and led to her being popularly branded as "the most dangerous woman in the world."

Throughout the 1920s and early 1930s, Addams persevered with her pacifist work, spending much of her time in Europe where she had never lost her popularity. Then, in 1931, at the height of the Great Depression, Addams's decades of pacifist activism were acknowledged when she was awarded the Nobel Peace Prize. At the Twentieth Anniversary Congress of the WILPF, in May of 1935, she was honored for her decades of contributions toward world peace. Ten days later, on 21 May 1935, Addams died at the age of 74 and was laid in state at Hull House where thousands gathered to mourn her.

John C. Farrell in his biography *Beloved Lady: A History of Jane Addams's Ideas on Reform and Peace* maintains that underlying all of Addams's achievements—the decades of social and industrial reform, the protection of the world's children, the defense of immigrants, and the struggle for world peace—were two ideals motivating all her actions, "the nurture of human life, [and] the defense of the weak and helpless." Throughout the 1920s and early 1930s, Addams continually emphasized that the problems of the twentieth century were humanitarian, not political. She never ceased communicating her vision of society as a humane community that strives to improve itself, not by the tyranny or exploitation of industrial capitalism, but by a sweeping affirmation of the values of human life—justice, peace, democracy, freedom, and the creative, life-affirming power of individual achievement.

References:

Conway, Jill Kathryn. *The First Generation of American Women College Graduates.* New York: Garland Publishing, Inc, 1987.
Davis, Allen F. *American Heroine: The Life and Legend of Jane Addams.* New York: Oxford University Press, 1973.
Deegan, Mary Jo. *Janes Addams and the Men of the Chicago School, 1892-1918,* New Brunswick, New Jersey: Transaction Books, 1988.
Farrell, John C. *Beloved Lady: A History of Jane Addams's Ideas on Reform and Peace.* Baltimore: Johns Hopkins Press, 1967.
Hovde, Jane. *Jane Addams.* New York: Facts on File, 1989.
Scott, Anne Firor. "Jane Addams," in *Notable American Women 1607-1820: A Biographical Dictionary,* edited by Edward T. James. Cambridge, Massachusetts: Belknap Press of Harvard University Press, 1971.
Woloch, Nancy. *Women and the American Experience.* New York: Knopf, 1984.

—Judith E. Harper

Alvin Ailey
1931-1989
African-American dancer and choreographer

Alvin Ailey was perhaps the greatest black modern dancer-choreographer in the United States. He was the founder of the Alvin Ailey Dance Theater and was influential in dance circles, especially to young black—but also white and Asian—dancers and choreographers. He grew up in southern Texas in the 1930s and 40s, moved to Los Angeles at age 12, and started studying modern dance with Lester Horton when he was 18. He studied off and on at various California colleges, majoring in languages, from 1949 to 1953 but finally quit to devote full time to dance. He formed his dance company in New York and went on international tours starting in the 1960s. He and his troupe were extremely well-received, particularly in Europe, Africa, and Asia. He choreographed many dances from black spiritual to jazz to classical themes. Many were tributes to important people in his life: Lester Horton, his first teacher, Duke Ellington, or most especially, his mother, to whom he dedicated *Cry*. His company had its financial troubles, often foundered but continued after his death in 1989, under the tutelage of premier dancer Judith Jamison.

Born in Rogers, Texas on 5 January 1931, Ailey grew up in poverty-stricken, rural, segregated Texas towns, picking cotton with his mother, Lula Elizabeth (Cliff) Cooper. His father, Alvin Ailey Sr., gave him a name but nothing else; he left when young Ailey was six months old. As a young boy, he moved to Los Angeles with his mother, who found work in an aircraft company. He was athletically built but preferred gymnastics to football. In high school he had a love for languages and literature and was soon reading Spanish classics.

The Los Angeles schools gave him a much better education than the segregated schools of the south. He was taken on a school trip to the Ballet Russe de Monte Carlo and soon roamed the theatre district himself. There he saw dance films, popular singers and bands like Billie Holiday and Duke Ellington, and his first black dance troupe, that of the influential Katherine Dunham. He later brought some of Dunham's dances out of retirement and restaged them with his dance company.

When Ailey saw Carmen de Lavallade, a black student, dance a Mozart piece in high school, he was enchanted and convinced to try dancing classes with her at the Lester Horton studio. Horton was a white, gay male, an innovator in dance, who was a pivotal force in Ailey's life. Horton's dance was eclectic, outside traditional dance forms, using influences ranging from Japanese theatre to American Indian dances in his school. This style attracted the shy young Ailey and started him visualizing his own dance forms.

When Lester Horton died in 1953, Alvin took over the company whose principal dancers were Carmen de Lavallade and James Truitte, both important people in Alvin's life. He started dancing duets with Carmen and went on with her to work with Jack Cole in Hollywood. However he had started choreographing his own material and needed to create his own style.

Ailey Finds His Niche on Broadway

In 1954, Ailey went to New York as a featured dancer in the Broadway show *House of Flowers* and stayed on to dance in Harry Belafonte's *Sing Man Sing* and with Lena Horne in *Jamaica* in 1957. He acted in plays such as *Carefree Tree* and had the starring role in the short-lived Broadway play, *Tiger, Tiger, Burning Bright* in 1962. Meanwhile, he studied dance with a series of teachers including Martha Graham, Hanya Holm, and Karel Shook but was never completely happy with their styles.

Ailey's first choreographed pieces (in 1954) were *According to St. Francis* (an homage to Horton) for James Truitte and *Mourning, Mourning* (from Tennessee Williams writings) for Carmen de Lavallade.

Ailey painstakingly put together a troupe, rehearsing in out of the way places, and gave his inaugural concert on 30 March 1958. His guest artist was the black dancer and later well-known choreographer, Talley Beatty, from Katherine Dunham's troupe. The dances were all choreographed by Ailey: *Ode and Homage, Redonda* with Latin music and themes, and the durable *Blues Suite* from his experience of Southern honky-tonk bars. The audience was enthusiastic.

The second concert, 21 December 1958, premiered *Arriette Oubliee* to Debussy music. It was danced by Ailey and de Lavallade and showed Ailey's versatility as a dancer and choreographer. In the third concert, *Revelations,* Ailey's masterpiece based on the Southern Baptist traditions and using black spirituals and gospel songs, was premiered. Since then, *Revelations* has been the dance most asked for and expected in concerts.

Ailey continued to choreograph pieces for other companies: *Ariadne* for the Harkness Ballet with Marjorie Tallchief in the title role, *Carmen* for the Metropolitan Opera in 1973, and *Precipice* for the Paris Opera in 1983. His *Knoxville: Summer of 1915* has been called his most autobiographical work. Its theme from James Agee's *Death in the Family* concerned a child who is loved but not understood.

The dance company found a home at the Clark Center for Performing Arts in the YWCA in New York. From 1958 to 1965 Ailey danced with the company as well as choreographing and generally holding the company together. His company was primarily black as he felt it important that black dancers were given a chance to dance (they were not accepted in most dance and ballet companies). As he stated in an interview on the video, *An Evening with the Alvin Ailey American Dance Theatre*, he had "grown up in a country which is intensely racist" and was making a "social and political statement" with a primarily black company. He wanted to continue the "black tradition which started with his black forefathers"; he wanted a "popular" company that his family and people in Texas could relate to. Later in the more militant 60s, he was chastised for allowing white and Asian dancers into his black troupe.

In the early years, Ailey's company often found Europeans more receptive than Americans; one audience in Germany applauded for an hour. His company was often asked to represent the United States at foreign festivals, such as the Paris Festival of Nations and the Premiere Festival Mondial des Arts in Dakar, Senegal, in 1966. In 1963 for their first international tour, they traveled first to Rio for a festival and then on to London and Paris. In 1965, they toured nine European countries for three months. In 1970 they were the first American dance troupe to tour the Soviet Union.

Ailey Releases Reins of His Dance Company

Finances were always difficult and Ailey often felt that he would have to disband the company, sometimes actually disbanding them but always pulling them together again. Dancers came and left, looking for more secure jobs, often disgruntled with Ailey. As one of his colleagues recalls in the book, *Judith Jamison: Aspects of A Dancer*, "Alvin came to New York with a Southern Baptist conscience, a prim idea of right and wrong. He was idealistic and committed, and that made him hard to work with, and for. Alvin did not spare himself. He saw no reason to spare other people."

In 1965, Ailey stopped dancing and turned the running of the business—the dance theater, with its training company, the Alvin Ailey Repertory Ensemble, and the Alvin Ailey American Dance Center, a school for young, talented, and often urban poor youngsters—over to other people, such as Ivy Clark, his general manager, and a board of directors.

Also in 1965, Judith Jamison made her debut. As Jamison said later in her autobiography, the company, even after Ailey stopped dancing, was "still very patriarchal. The concentration was on the men." However in a *Dance Magazine* article by Sylviane Gold, Jamison recognized Ailey's greatness as a teacher who "made sure that your influence was eclectic but that you realized what your roots were." Ailey designed the beautiful and mesmerizing *Cry*, dedicated to his mother and all black women everywhere, especially for Jamison; it became her signature piece.

In the late 1970s, Ailey lost close friends and associates to illness and death and became depressed, turning to drugs. The deaths of Duke Ellington (with whom he had collaborated on *The River* which Ellington did not have a chance to see before his death) and his old friend and dancer from the Horton days, Joyce Trisler, affected him greatly. He thought he might end up like Trisler dying a lonely death at an early age; her body lay for several days in her apartment before being found. He felt he might die immediately so he decided to, as he tells it in *Revelations*, "live quickly and get all that I could from what time I had left."

He connected with Abdullah, an Arab boy he had met earlier in Paris. "We found the best hashish and the best cognac in town and began to smoke and drink like two wild people—and to enjoy each other." Then he started on cocaine, spending four hundred dollars a week on the drug. In a drug-induced state, he still choreographed, particularly *Memoria* for Trisler to the music of Keith Jarrett.

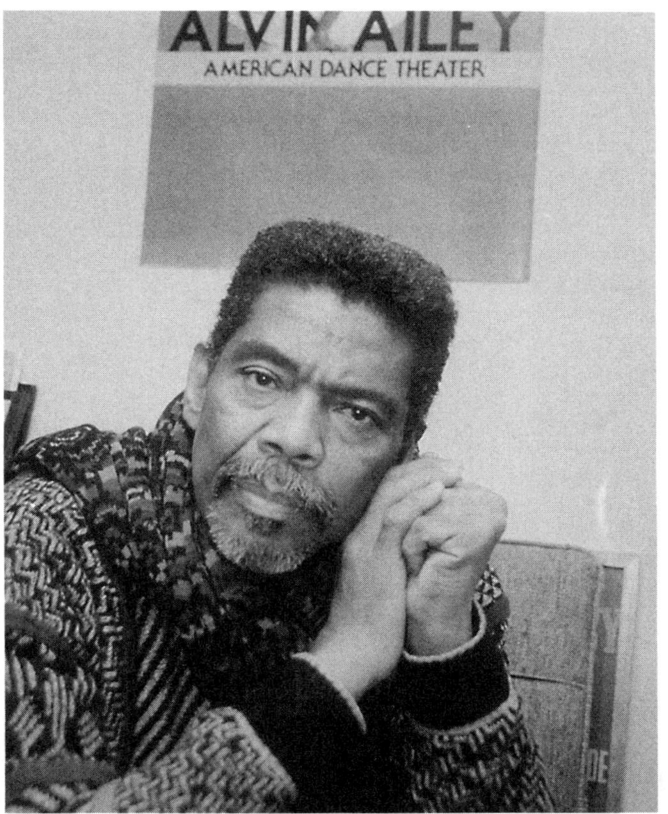

Alvin Ailey

Finally things became too much for his young lover, and Abdullah left him. Ailey describes his manic state as he raised a ruckus looking for the young man he thought he would have a "perfect relationship" with. He was apprehended and taken to Bellevue Hospital. In 1980 he ran through an apartment house yelling "fire" and broke into a woman's apartment; again he was hospitalized. After weeks of care, he went on lithium, stopped taking drugs and drinking, lost weight and, most importantly, started choreographing again.

His first post-hospital piece was *Phases* to music by Max Roach for Masazumi Chaya. Ailey went on to choreograph other pieces and keep his dance troupe going into the 1980s.In 1984, he and his troupe enjoyed a tremendous success at their twenty-fifth anniversary at the New York City Center, where 80 Ailey dancers gathered together. Ailey called this event in an article in *Ebony*, "a wonderful family gathering. It was one of my most memorable experiences."

In 25 years, the Alvin Ailey Dance Theater had been seen by 15,000,000 people in 48 states and 44 countries on 6 continents. They had been first in many areas, including the first black modern dance company at the Metropolitan Opera, the first American modern dance company in the Soviet Union and China, and the first American dance company to be awarded a National Endowment of the Arts long-term residency. Ailey was also awarded the 1975 *Dance Magazine* award, the 1979 Capezio award, and the 1976 NAACP Spingarn medal. In 1976, Ailey organized an Ellington festival for the Bicentenary of the American Revolution and specially composed the light-hearted *Pas de Duke* for the interesting duet of Judith Jamison and Mikhail Barishnikov.

Throughout his life, Ailey was a private person, often not even inviting friends or associates to his apartment. His relationships were part of this private life but seemed to come second to his overpowering creativity as a choreographer and his devotion to his dance theater. Ailey stated in *Revelations* that, at an early age, he knew all the gay youth in school and had "a lot of homosexual fantasies before I ever got into doing anything actually physical." Once when he was fifteen he found himself dressing in his mother's clothes to go to a party in drag. His friends at the time were having sex with an older man but he did not participate. Later in his autobiography he was somewhat open about his affair with Abdullah, but only as it related to his breakdown. He did state that he seemed to get involved with younger men throughout his life, often ones who robbed him. Few, if any, articles, obituaries, or biographies ever mentioned his sexual preference. However in an *Advocate* review of *Revelations*, John Weir opines that, "the book is coy about Ailey's homosexuality and indeed about the whole course of his romantic and sexual life." The 1996 biography *Alvin Ailey: A Life in Dance* uses new material, especially Ailey's poems and short prose pieces from the Black Archive of Mid-America in Kansas City, Missouri, to discuss his sexuality more completely. A piece from his younger years begins, "He had always clung to the thought that the thin boy would someday return to him, and that they together would find something more beautiful and real." A poem from the 1960s has these lines, "several hard-hipped hustlers and more I am I will always be queers gazing at the crotches of small thick-thighed magazines-sighing-'oh'." Again, these were private pieces not known to his friends until after his death.

In the end, Alvin Ailey was primarily a lover of dance and insisted that dance should come from the people and be delivered back to the people. The credo that best sums up Alvin Ailey and his philosophy of dance was written for the Alvin Ailey Dance Theater program in London in 1964:

> The cultural heritage of the American Negro is one of America's richest treasures. From his roots as a slave, the American Negro—sometimes sorrowing, sometimes jubilant, but always hopeful—has created a legacy of music and dance which has touched, illuminated, and influenced the most remote preserves of world civilization.
>
> I and my dance theatre celebrate, in our programme, this trembling beauty. We bring to you the exuberance of his jazz, the ecstasy of his spirituals, and the dark rapture of his blues.

Though Alvin Ailey died 1 December 1989 of HIV complications, this "exuberance, ecstasy, and rapture" lives on in his dances and the Alvin Ailey Dance Theater now under the capable leadership of Judith Jamison and Masazumi Chaya.

References:

Ailey, Alvin. *Revelations: The Autobiography of Alvin Ailey*. Secaucus, New Jersey: Carol Publishing Group, 1995.

"Ailey, Alvin, Jr. (obituary)" in *Current Biography Yearbook 1990*: 63.

Ailey Dances, produced by ABC Video Enterprises. Long Branch, New Jersey: Kultur, 1982.

"Alvin Ailey" in *Obituary Annual, 1989*: 749-751.

"Alvin Ailey at the Met Celebrating 25 Years of Dance" in *Ebony* (Chicago), October 1984: 164.

Barnes, Clive. "Burning Bright" in *Ballet News* (New York), November 1983: 13-15.

———. "Remembering Ailey" in *Dance Magazine* (New York), February 1990: 138.

Cook, Susan. *The Alvin Ailey American Dance Theater*. New York: Morrow, 1978.

Dixon, Brenda. "Black Dance and Dancers and the White Public: A Prolegomenon to Problems of Definition" in *Black American Literature Forum*, April 1990: 117-121.

Dunning, Jennifer. *A Life in Dance*. Reading, Massachusetts: Addison-Wesley Publishing, 1996.

Estell, Kenneth. *African America: Portrait of a People*. Detroit: Visible Ink, 1994.

Gold, Sylviane. "Thirty Years with Alvin Ailey: The Ailey Generations" in *Dance Magazine* (New York), December 1988:40.

Gresham, Jewell Handy. "Dance of Life" in *Nation*, January 8, 1990: 40.

Grimm, Thomas, producer. *An Evening with the Alvin Ailey American Dance Theater*. Denmark: Danmarks Radio/ZDF/RM Arts, 1986.

Hackney, C. "Ailey, Alvin—In Memoriam" in *Black Perspective in Music*, 1990: 214.

Hering, Doris. "Alvin Ailey Dance Theater at Clark Center" in *Dance Magazine* (New York), February 1962: 60.

In Black and White. Detroit: Gale, 1985: 9-10.

Ipiotis, Celia and Jeff Bush, producers. *Alvin Ailey*. New York: ARC Videodance, 1989.

Latham, Jacqueline Quinn Moore. *A Biographical Study of the Lives and Contributions of Two Selected Contemporary Black Male Dance Artists: Arthur Mitchell and Alvin Ailey*. Denton, Texas: PhD Dissertation, 1973.

Maynard, Olga. *Judith Jamison: Aspects of a Dancer*. Garden City, New York: Doubleday, 1982.

Mazo, J. H. "Ailey, Alvin (1931-1989)—In Memoriam" in *Dance Magazine* (New York), February 1990: 111.

Moore, W. "Ailey, Alvin (1931-1989)" in *Ballet Review*, Winter 1990: 12-17.

Pinkney, Andrea Davis. *Alvin Ailey*. New York: Hyperion Books for Children, 1993.

Weir, John. "*Revelations: The Autobiography of Alvin Ailey*" in *Advocate*, 7 March 1995: 61-62.

—Jacquelyn Marie

Chantal Akerman

1950-

Belgian filmmaker

Avant-garde, experimental, alternative, and feminist are terms frequently associated with the style and themes of Chantal Akerman's films. Her work runs the gamut of cinematography, from short subjects produced independently on a shoestring budget to full-length studio-produced feature films, from video to 16 mm to 35 mm, from color to black-and-white, from documentaries to musical comedies.

Akerman was born in Brussels, Belgium, to a Polish-Jewish immigrant family, her early years marked by the aftermath of the Holocaust. Her mother, herself an artist, experienced the horrors of Auschwitz, and returned to face life as a survivor. Her father, who had been a rich man in Poland, had to rebuild his life in Brussels as well. The family started out in relative poverty but gradually made its way back to middle-class comfort. Until the age of eight, Akerman was raised and educated by her maternal grandfather, a cantor, with whom Akerman studied the Talmud. After his death, she went on to study Latin, Greek, and literature in school. At fifteen, she saw Jean-Luc Godard's *Pierrot le fou,* a film that determined her choice of career. Akerman has often said that without Godard she would have probably become a writer. However, it was through Godard that she learned that cinematography could create a work at once personal and experimental.

From that time, the cinema became such a passion that she left high school to study it. Her education included a year at the INSAS film school in Brussels (1967-68), after which she moved to Paris where she attended the Université International du Théâtre (1968-69). It was during this period that Akerman completed her first short subject, *Saute ma ville,* financed through temporary jobs. Seen at a number of film festivals, that film brought her to the critics' attention, although it was not considered an unqualified success. Formal schooling, however, did not hold her interest for long. She soon left Europe for New York (1972-73) where, despite financial difficulties, she completed a number of short subjects and learned from the work of such American avant-gardists as Michael Snow and Stan Brakhage. Akerman acknowledges that the stay in New York (where she would return many times) was perhaps the most crucial in her development. After returning to Brussels, she moved back to Paris, in part to be further away from her family. She again worked temporary jobs to raise funds for her first full-length film, *Je, Tu, Il, Elle* (1974). With the release the following year of *Jeanne Dielman, 23 quai du Commerce, 1080 Bruxelles,* Akerman's reputation as one of Europe's premier experimental filmmakers was established. That film marked her a feminist director, a label which she judged too confining. Nonetheless, it is the female voice that more often than not dominates her films of the 1970s. While Akerman's early films are perhaps somber, by the 1980s, with *Toute une nuit* (1982), touches of comedy began to appear. Even musicals (for example, *Golden Eighties,* 1986) entered into her repertoire. Her most recent film, *Un Divan à New York* (1996), is a romantic comedy written for Juliette Binoche. Recently, Akerman has added another dimension to her work: the museum installation piece treating the breakup of the Eastern European block. "Bordering on Fiction: Chantal Akerman's *D'Est*" combines her film *D'Est* with video montage of the film itself and scenes of Eastern Europe, with Akerman reading from the Hebrew Bible and from her own writings.

Like other experimental filmmakers, Akerman often does not set out primarily to tell a story; rather, she exploits the possibilities of the medium. Among the trademarks of her cinematic language, depending upon the type of film she is making, are a pseudo-documentary style; a static camera; choreographed, highly stylized scenes; fragmented narratives; lingering shots after a scene has "ended;" and shooting a scene in real time. The plot, or more accurately, the development of a coherent, linear, traditional story rarely plays an important role in the film. Akerman has been known to say, "the important thing is the style, the form."

Nonetheless, Akerman is not an abstract filmmaker. Autobiographical elements run through much of her work as do certain key places (again grounded in the autobiographical)—New York, Brussels, Paris, Germany—and themes—solitude, alienation, mother-daughter relationships, sexual relationships, World War II—that are linked through transformations of Akerman's own experiences. Thus, *American Stories/Food, Family and Philosophy,* filmed in New York in 1988, reworks her Jewish heritage and her family's experience of World War II through stories told by Jewish-American immigrants in Brooklyn. Akerman has also not shied away from including lesbian and bisexual characters in her films. In one of the stories that thread their way through *Toute une nuit,* a woman leaves her husband to begin a liaison with another woman. *Je, Tu, Il, Elle* ends with a long sequence of Julie (played by Akerman) and "elle" making love while in *Les Rendez-vous d'Anna* (1978) the filmmaker-heroine reveals to her mother that she has begun an affair with a woman she met on a promotional tour. On the other hand, films such as *Un Divan à New York* or *Nuit et jour* (1992) trace the vagaries of heterosexual relationships.

Akerman's work for the past quarter century has earned her the status of one of the most important and innovative European filmmakers. Her stylistic explorations combined with her insightful portraits of women, both lesbian and heterosexual, clearly make Akerman one of the most significant woman filmmakers of the late twentieth century.

References:

Butler, Kristine. "Bordering on Fiction: Chantal Akerman's *D'Est,*" in *Postmodern Culture*, vol. 6, no. 1, September 1995.

Delavaud, G. "Les Chemins de Chantal Akerman," in *Cahiers du Cinéma* (Paris), April 1981.

"Fragments bruxellois," in *Cahiers du Cinéma* (Paris), November 1982.

Philippon, A. "Nuit Torride," in *Cahiers du Cinéma* (Paris), November 1982.

Riou, Alain. "Au nom de la mémoire," in *Le Nouvel Observateur* (Paris), 28 September 1989.

—Edith J. Benkov

Edward Albee

1928-

American playwright

With his first play, Edward Albee caught the attention of the theatrical world. He soon followed this success with the wildly popular *Who's Afraid of Virginia Woolf?* as well as several other award-winning plays. On the whole, Albee's work is substantial and includes: eight full-length plays, nine one-act plays, and five theatrical adaptations of novels. But, critical backlash against Albee has also been considerable, most notably a homophobic attack that has been leveled against him throughout his career. Regardless, as Michael Bronski writes, Albee "has maintained his position as one of the most important playwrights of the contemporary theater."

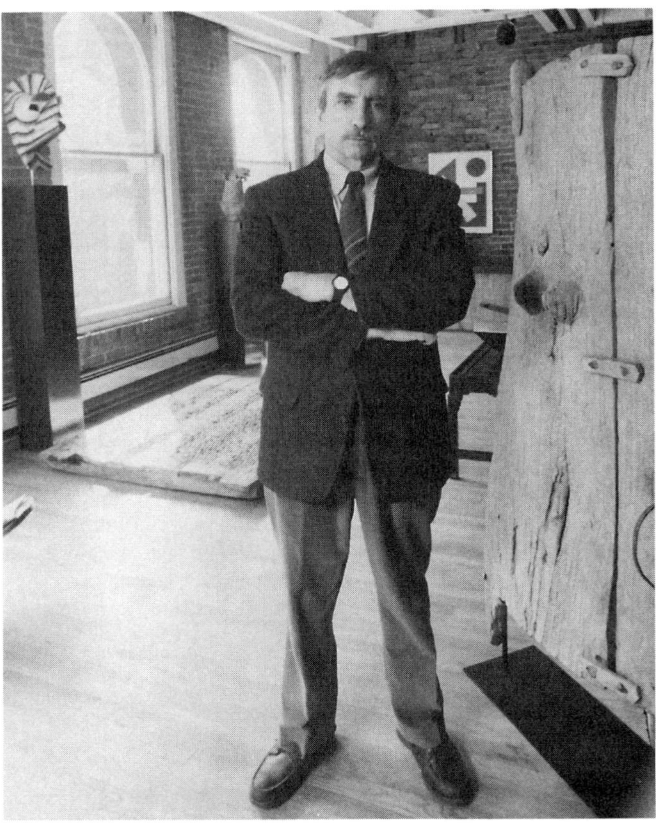

Edward Albee

Edward Franklin Albee was born, probably somewhere in Virginia although his official place of birth is listed as Washington, D.C., on 12 March 1928. Within just a few weeks he was adopted by Reed and Frances Albee. Though he wasn't born "in a theater," he was clearly born to it, as his later career would prove. Albee's father was, at the time, part owner of the Keith-Albee vaudeville circuit, which had been started by Albee's grandfather, Edward Franklin Albee II, whom the young Albee was named after. Albee's childhood, spent primarily among the well-to-do in Larchmont, New York, was filled with horses, toys, pets, and rolling landscapes, but his education was frequently interrupted by winter vacations to warmer climates and his emotional well-being was routinely challenged by his mother's constant reminders that he was adopted. It was fortunate for Albee that his maternal grandmother lived with the family. She was the ally, who in later years encouraged him and set up a trust fund for him. Albee's grandmother died in 1959, and the following year he dedicated his play *The Sandbox* to her.

An Uneasy Relationship with School

School and Albee were not the best of friends. Not only were his early studies at Rye Country Day School in Westchester interrupted by vacations, but he would also frequently cut classes. By the age of 11 he was enrolled in the first of several boarding schools—Lawrenceville School in New Jersey, from which he was eventually expelled for failing to attend classes. He also attended the Valley Forge Military Academy in Pennsylvania and Choate School in Connecticut. While he did not do well academically at any of them, he enjoyed his time at Choate where his teachers encouraged his writing (primarily poetry at this time). By the age of 12 Albee had written his first play, *Aliqueen,* a three-act sex farce. But it was his poetry that got Albee the most attention. In 1947, one of his poems was published in *Kaleidoscope,* a Texas-based literary magazine.

Albee attended Trinity College in 1946, but lack of interest and commitment led him to drop out after only a year-and-a-half. He returned home and took a writing job at the local radio station. After leaving home in 1950 he settled in Greenwich Village and spent the next ten years living in a series of places and working at a variety of jobs. Among these vocations, the job Albee liked most was messenger for Western Union. In the early 1950s Albee spent some time in Italy, where he wrote a novel, before returning to New York. During this time he met W. H. Auden, received advice from Thornton Wilder, and was greatly influenced by the work of Tennessee Williams. William Flanagan, the composer, was Albee's closest friend and roommate during these years.

Turning Thirty and Achieving Success

Living on the cusp of his third decade was apparently motivational for Albee and he quit his job with Western Union just before his birthday. In just three weeks, he wrote *The Zoo,* the play that would gain him entry into the world of drama. *The Zoo,* however, was rejected across the board by several New York producers until it eventually found its first audience at the Schiller Theater Werkstat in Berlin on 28 September 1959.

But *The Zoo,* Albee's first social commentary attacking individual and social apathy, failed to firmly establish him as a playwright. He soon followed-up his first play with *The Sandbox, The American Dream,* and *The Death of Bessie Smith.* With his new plays, Albee came down hard on "the substitution of artificial for real values" in American society, and tried to illustrate how relationships in society are valued primarily in commercial terms. Following the promise of his first offering, these three plays helped to solidify Albee a reputation as a promising new playwright. Albee once observed, "Fearful personalities utilize power to destroy and not to heal." He hoped to demonstrate these things on stage. Albee had been applauded in Europe, Turkey, South America, and several places in the United States, but it wasn't until *Who's Afraid of Virginia Woolf?,* in 1962, that he became recognized as a major New York playwright. The play was an unparalleled success and it catapulted Albee to fame. The following year, *Who's Afraid of Virginia Woolf?* won a Tony award.

Albee, who maintains that he intended to entertain as well as offend, could not have been surprised to find that the play that brought him due recognition as a playwright and a handful of awards also garnered harsh criticism. Although gay themes are conspicuously absent from Albee's work, he makes no secret of his own homosexuality. Some critics have maintained that his sexuality has influenced his understanding of heterosexuality as portrayed in his plays. Still others have argued that the characters in *Who's Afraid of Virginia Woolf?* closely resemble squabbling gay male couples. In fact, in 1961 Howard Taubman attacked what he saw as an overpowering homosexual influence on American theater. According to Bronski, this article was primarily concerned with "three unnamed playwrights who attacked marriage and women but were really writing about dysfunctional gay relationships." The playwrights were of course William Ing, Tennessee Williams, and Albee. This type of criticism is the kind usually levelled against Albee. But, as Bronski points out, criticism of Albee has always been hostile towards his homosexuality in two extremes: "As a somewhat closeted writer, Albee was attacked for artistic inauthenticity; as an openly gay writer he was attacked for his sexuality."

Nearly a dozen plays followed *Who's Afraid of Virginia Woolf?*, but none was such a sweeping success—nor were any quite so controversial. Among them have been: *Tiny Alice* (1964), *A Delicate Balance* (1966), *Everything in the Garden* (1967), *Seascape* (1975), and *The Man Who Had Three Arms* (1983); Albee won Pulitzer prizes for both *A Delicate Balance* and *Seascape*.

The Theatre of the Absurd

Albee has long been identified with the "Theatre of the Absurd," an identification Albee himself might consider absurd. In a 1962 *New York Times Magazine* article he posed the question "Which Theatre Is the Absurd One?" With this question, he posits the sentiment that the so-called real theater which panders to the public's illusory self-images might, in fact, be the truly absurd one. This is very much in keeping with Albee's contempt for misguided American values and misplaced priorities.

Albee is living proof that—as there was life well before Broadway—there is, for him, also life after Broadway. Since his *The Man Who Had Three Arms* in 1983, Albee has directed numerous productions in countless cities and he has taught a playwriting course in search of new writers who can "contribute something to the theater as an art form." His recent play, *Three Tall Women,* won the Pulitzer prize as well as numerous other awards. Throughout his career, the importance of Albee's body of work has been soiled by homophobic critics. As Bronski puts it, it has become "fashionable to dismiss much of Albee's work for a variety of reasons." Albee's work must eventually be reevaluated without the hurtful and ignorant approach that has been used in the past.

Current Address: 14 Harrison St., New York, New York 10013-2842.

References:

Albee, Edward. "Which Theatre Is the Absurd One?," in *New York Times Magazine,* 25 February 1962: 30-31, 64, 66.

Bronski, Michael. "Edward Albee," in *Gay & Lesbian Literature.* Detroit, Michigan: St. James Press, 1994: 3-5.

Current Biography Yearbook. New York: H. W. Wilson Co., 1963.

MacNicholas, John and Stephen M. Vallillo. "Edward Albee," in *Concise Dictionary of American Literary Biography: The New Consciousness, 1941-1968.* Detroit: Gale Research, 1987: 11-30.

New York Times Biographical Service. Ann Arbor, Michigan: University Microfilms International, vol. 24, nos. 1-12, 1993.

Rood, Karen L., ed. *Dictionary of Twentieth Century Culture: American Culture After World War II.* Detroit: Gale Research, 1994.

Taubman, Howard. "Not What It Seems: Homosexual Motif Gets Heterosexual Guise," in *New York Times,* 1961.

—Andrea L.T. Peterson

Alexander the Great

356 B.C.-323 B.C.

Macedonian ruler

Alexander the Great is one of the colossal figures in world history, arguably the most influential and fabled person of the ancient world. King of Macedon, Alexander in fact espoused Greek culture and established in many ways a single Hellenic world spanning much of Europe and Asia. Pharaoh of Egypt and Great King of Asia, Alexander also figures as a saint in Arabic-Persian tradition, a mythic figure in Israelite legend, and a hero of Christian tales in medieval and Renaissance lore. Circumstances of his recorded life have also placed him prominently within the gay pantheon.

In considering Alexander, one needs to be aware of the obstacles faced by modern historians. Accounts of his life are derived principally from five writers—Plutarch, Diodorus, Arrian, Curtius, and Justin—all of whom lived at least 300 years after his death. No contemporary chronicles of Alexander survive. Sorting out the facts of his life, especially those aspects of his personality not documented by historical record, is an exercise in separating probable truth from likely fiction, unwarranted surmise from reasonable conjecture.

Alexander was born in Pella, Macedonia, in 356 B.C., the son of King Philip II and Olympias, a princess of the kingdom of Epirus. For several years beginning in 343, Alexander was a pupil of Aristotle, heir of Plato and teacher of Hellenic traditions of philosophy, politics, and science. By the age of 16, Alexander had already established a military reputation, and at 18 was instrumental in the Macedonian victory at Chaeronea over the quarrelsome Greek city states. He succeeded to the throne as Alexander III on the assassination of Philip in 336.

Conquering the World

Although the Persian army was Alexander's greatest threat, he initially had to subdue a revolt within the Panhellenic states. His destruction of Thebes in 335 strengthened Macedonian control, and Alexander was able to turn his attention to the powerful Persian empire, ruled by Darius III.

In a series of battles in Asia Minor beginning in 334, Alexander, relatively inexperienced and far surpassed in troop strength and wealth, led his victorious army through Troy, Issus, Tyre, and into Egypt. In 331 he founded Alexandria, the first of the 60 Alexandrias he would establish at key trade route intersections throughout his empire. Darius was assassinated in 330, and Alexander solidified his power in Asia Minor, establishing himself as absolute Great King.

The conquest of India was the next challenge for Alexander, now at the command of a retinue estimated by Plutarch at over 120,000 soldiers and followers. Over the next several years, Alexander's armies marched as far east as the Khyber Pass. More cities were founded, including Samarkand and Bucephala (named for the king's legendary black horse Bucephalus). During this period Alexander married the first of his three wives, the princess Roxane, mother of his son Alexander IV (born after Alexander's death and executed in 310 B.C. at the age of 13).

Alexander's campaign in India faltered, and he was severely wounded in 325. He retreated in a disastrous march over the

Alexander the Great

Gedrosian Desert and returned to Persepolis. In a feast at Susa in 324 Alexander and 80 of his officers took Persian wives, further consolidating his Persian empire. He became ill the following year with what has been variously described as fever, pneumonia, wound complications, the effects of poisoning, and excessive drinking. Alexander died in Babylon in 323 B.C. at the age of 33.

The Nature of Alexander

While his accomplishments and public life as king and conqueror are well-documented, less is known for certain about Alexander the man. Accounts of his appearance agree on the smallness of his stature, and representations in plaster and on coins, in both his early and later life, have in common a certain intensity of expression. His physical stamina is attested to by the rigor and hardships of his campaigns.

Alexander's sexuality has been a subject of speculation and debate throughout the ages, often reflecting the social mores and biases of the particular commentator. Use of the modern terminologies heterosexuality, homosexuality and bisexuality may further complicate discussion of Alexander in this regard, connoting more of an alternative behavior to the societal norm than was true in earlier societies.

What must be considered in the case of Alexander is the nature of the culture in which he lived, specifically the pre-Christian, Athenian society by which he was influenced and to which he was attached. In his book *Greek Homosexuality*, K. J. Dover writes: "The Greeks neither inherited nor developed a belief that a divine power had revealed to mankind a code of laws for the regulation of sexual behavior; they had no religious institution possessed of the authority to enforce sexual prohibitions."

By every account, the most intense relationship in Alexander's life was that with Hephaestion, his boyhood friend and lifelong companion. Hephaestion figures in several incidents in Alexander's history, which, apocryphal or not, are significant for his presence. At Troy in 334, Alexander and Hephaestion laid wreaths at the tombs of, respectively, Achilles and his companion Patroclus, in likely acknowledgment of their parallel relationships. In 333, after the battle of Issus, Sisygambis, the queen mother of the defeated Darius, mistook Hephaestion for Alexander, who reportedly told her she had committed no wrong, "for Hephaestion is Alexander."

Hephaestion's untimely death in 324 occasioned an extraordinary outpouring of grief by Alexander. He fasted for three days over the corpse and proclaimed a period of mourning throughout the empire. A funeral pyre five stories high was constructed in Babylon, and plans for an immense monument were abandoned only after Alexander's own death a few months later.

Another figure in the life of Alexander, more historically elusive and problematic than Hephaestion, is the Persian eunuch, Bagoas. Cited by several early chroniclers, Bagoas, reputedly a favorite of Darius, first appears as a prize of war accepted by Alexander. A full six years later he is mentioned again in several accounts of a banquet, where he is acclaimed for his dancing and receives a public kiss from Alexander. He is also subsequently described as instrumental in causing the execution of a powerful Persian governor, Orxines. What is significant in these chronicles is the specific, repeated naming of Bagoas, as well as the implications of his influence over the king.

Myth and Reality

Mary Renault, whose fictional accounts of Alexander have enjoyed great popular success, writes in her biography *The Nature of Alexander*: "Filtered and refracted by layers of fable, history, tradition and emotion—a thing inseparable from him alive and dead—the image of Alexander has come down to us." Reflected in that image is a complex human being whose emotional life and sexual identity almost certainly bridge any so-called heterosexual/homosexual dichotomy.

In the end, the specifics of Alexander's personality can only be surmised, examined as they must be from the relatively dim perspective of over two millennia. What is indisputable is the personal power and charisma that carried him to his vast successes. In the words of Peter Green (*Alexander of Macedon*): "The proof of his immortality is the belief he inspired in others ... his greatness defies a final judgment."

References:

Bosworth, A. B. *Conquest and Empire: The Reign of Alexander the Great*. New York: Cambridge University Press, 1988.

———. *From Arrian to Alexander: Studies in Historical Interpretation*. Oxford: Clarendon Press, 1988.

Dover, K. J. *Greek Homosexuality*. Cambridge: Harvard University Press, 1978.

Duberman, Martin Bauml, Martha Vincinus, and George Chauncey, Jr., eds. *Hidden from History: Reclaiming the Gay and Lesbian Past*. New York: New American Library, 1989.

Ehrenberg, Victor. *Alexander and the Greeks*. Oxford: Basil Blackwell, 1938.
Green, Peter. *Alexander of Macedon, 356-323 B.C.: A Historical Biography.* Berkeley, University of California Press, 1991.
Hammond, N. G. L. *Sources for Alexander the Great: An Analysis of Plutarch's "Life" and Arrian's "Anabasis Alexandrou."* New York: Cambridge University Press, 1993.
Renault, Mary. *The Nature of Alexander.* London: Allen Lane, 1975.

—David Garnes

Paula Gunn Allen

1939-

Native American writer and scholar

Paula Gunn Allen is one of the most important Native American writers and intellectuals of the twentieth century. She is perhaps most highly regarded for her poetry, though her renown as a novelist and literary scholar cannot be denied. Her scholarship on American Indian understandings of gays and lesbians ("two-spirits") represents some of the most significant work on the subject, and it has laid the groundwork for more accurate and culturally relevant research in this area.

Allen was born Paula Marie Francis, 24 October 1939, in Cubero, New Mexico, a Spanish land grant town near Laguna Pueblo. Laguna, Lakota, and Scottish on her mother's side and Lebanese on her father's, Allen is one of five children born to Ethel Gottlieb Francis and E. Lee Francis, a former Lieutenant Governor of New Mexico. Growing up in a rural environment, she attended mission school locally then continued her Roman Catholic education in Albuquerque, where she attended a convent boarding school.

As an undergraduate at the University of Oregon, Allen earned her BA degree in literature in 1966. Two years later, she completed a Master of Fine Arts degree in creative writing at the same institution. She went on to attain a PhD in American studies from the University of New Mexico in 1975.

While Allen never planned on becoming a Native American scholar, she has nonetheless made her mark on academia. She has taught at several universities, most notably, the University of California, Berkeley. She presently is a professor of English at the University of California, Los Angeles. Her curricula span a variety of fields, including Native American studies, women's studies, literature, and philosophy.

As a scholar, Allen is probably best known for two groundbreaking books: *Studies in American Indian Literature: Critical Essays and Course Designs*, which she edited, and *The Sacred Hoop: Recovering the Feminine in American Indian Traditions.* The former is a foundational work in the area of teaching and interpreting Native literature. In the latter, a collection of essays, Allen argues for and engages in a "gynocentric," or woman-centered, understanding of American Indian traditions and cultures.

While her scholarship has always been accessible and intelligible to non-academics, she has initiated a series of books that appear directed to a broader audience. These works include *Spider Woman's Granddaughters: Traditional Tales and Contemporary Writing by Native American Women, Grandmothers of the Light: A Medicine Woman's Sourcebook*, and *Voice of the Turtle: American Indian Literature 1900-1970.* The anthologies demonstrate the existence of a rich and enduring body of literature written by Native American writers, whose works have been excluded from the American canon. The sourcebook, relying on a traditional method of teaching—storytelling—attempts to educate a non-Indian audience deluded by romantic portrayals of Native American spirituality.

Allen has written one novel, *The Woman Who Owned the Shadows,* and seven collections of poetry. Only beginning to receive the critical attention it deserves, the novel powerfully depicts the cycle of spiritual death and recovery of Ephanie Atencio, a Native woman of mixed heritage. Allen skillfully situates Ephanie and her struggle not only in modern urban American Indian life but also in the time of the grandmothers, the mythic matrix that fundamentally structures her consciousness. Allen's poetry, however, reveals most deeply the multitudinous reality that is the heart of her creative thought. Her words are soundings of the complex and beauteous universe that Allen both points to and evokes in her writing. She draws on and articulates the power of thought and language, understood by Lagunas since long ago. She has been recognized for her writing with grants from the Ford Foundation and the National Endowment for the Arts.

In various genres, Allen has addressed Native American lesbian and gay ways of life. Her essay "*Hwame*, *Koshkalaka*, and the Rest: Lesbians in American Indian Cultures" (*The Sacred Hoop*) remains an important contribution to the field. She also has written several poems with lesbian and gay themes, including, "Koshkalaka, Ceremonial Dyke" and "Never Cry Uncle" (both in *Wyrds*) and

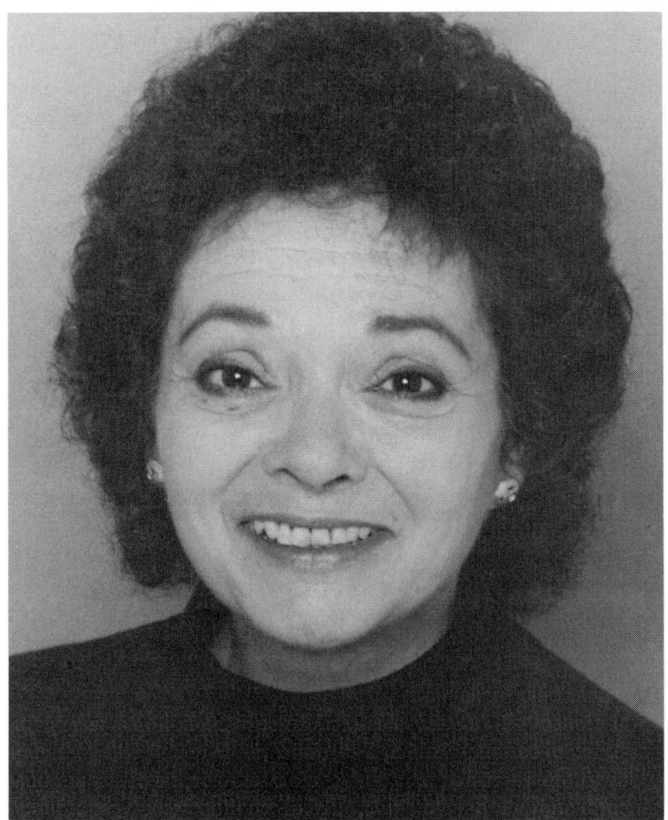

Paula Gunn Allen. ***Photograph by Tama Rothschild.***

"Some Like Indians Endure" *(Living the Spirit). Raven's Road*, a novel in progress, also features a Native American lesbian character. Chapters of this novel have appeared as "Deep Purple"*(Spider Woman's Granddaughters)*, "Selections from *Raven's Road*" (*Living the Spirit*), and "The Medicine Song of Allie Hawker" (*Intricate Passions*).

That Allen has been married during the course of her life with persons of the opposite sex and same sex is not surprising in light of the cultural understandings of many Native communities. As she herself has written, "I am not especially defined by my sex life, nor complete without it" (*Intricate Passions*). She has three grown children. Allen is important not only because of her writing on two spirits, but also because of her participation in gay and lesbian communities on the West Coast, where she has lived on and off for many years.

Current Address: Department of English, University of California-Los Angeles, 405 Hilgard Ave., Los Angeles, California 90024.

References:

Allen, Paula Gunn. "Beloved Women: Lesbians in American Indian Culture," in *Conditions* 7 (spring 1981): 67-87.

———. *The Blind Lion*. Berkeley: Thorp Springs Press, 1974.

———. "'Border' Studies: The Intersection of Gender and Color," in *Introduction to Scholarship in Modern Languages and Literatures*, 2d ed., edited by Joseph Gibaldi. New York: Modern Language Association of America, 1992: 303-19.

———. *A Cannon Between My Knees*. New York: Strawberry Press, 1983.

———. *Coyote's Daylight Trip*. Albuquerque: La Confluencia, 1978.

———. *Grandmothers of the Light: A Medicine Woman's Sourcebook*. Boston: Beacon Press, 1991.

———. "The Medicine Song of Allie Hawker," in *Intricate Passions: A Collection of Erotic Short Fiction*, edited by Tee Corinne. Austin: Banned Books, 1989: 119-23.

———. *The Sacred Hoop: Recovering the Feminine in American Indian Traditions*. Boston: Beacon Press, 1986.

———. "Selections from *Raven's Road*," in *Living the Spirit: A Gay American Indian Anthology*, edited by Will Roscoe. New York: St. Martin's Press, 1988: 134-52.

———. *Shadow Country*. Los Angeles: American Indian Studies Center, University of California, Los Angeles, 1982.

———. *Skins and Bones: Poems 1979-87*. Albuquerque: West End Press, 1988.

———. "Some Like Indians Endure," in *Living the Spirit: A Gay American Indian Anthology*, edited by Will Roscoe. New York: St. Martin's Press, 1988: 9-13.

———, ed. *Spider Woman's Granddaughters: Traditional Tales and Contemporary Writing by Native American Women*. Boston: Beacon Press, 1989.

———. *Star Child*. Marvin, South Dakota: Blue Cloud Quarterly, 1981.

———, ed. *Studies in American Indian Literature: Critical Essays and Course Designs*. New York: Modern Language Association of America, 1983.

———, ed. *Voice of the Turtle: American Indian Literature 1900-1970*. New York: Ballantine Books, 1994.

———. *The Woman Who Owned the Shadows*. San Francisco: Spinsters, Ink, 1983.

———. *Wyrds*. San Francisco: Taurean Horn Press, 1987.

—Mary C. Churchill

Dorothy Allison

1949-

American writer

Since the 1970s Dorothy Allison has written for feminist, lesbian, and gay newspapers and periodicals, but it was the publication of her first novel in 1992 that pushed her into the national spotlight. *Bastard Out of Carolina*, which Allison described to Alexis Jetter as "a heroic story about a young girl who faces down a monster," was a finalist for a National Book Award and won both the Ferro Grumley and Bay Area Book Reviewers Awards for fiction. While not wholly autobiographical nor explicitly lesbian, the novel explores the dramatic effects of emotional, physical, sexual, and psychic violence on personal identity from a lesbian-feminist point of view. These themes shape Allison's entire body of writing and, at the same time, have engendered both critical acclaim and controversy.

Dorothy Allison was born in 1949 in Greenville, South Carolina, to Ruth Gibson Allison, a poor 15-year-old who dropped out of school in the seventh grade to work as a waitress. Allison fondly remembers the women of her family—her aunts and grandmothers—as dazzling and outrageous storytellers. Yet, her childhood and adolescence are marked most painfully by the physical and sexual abuse she endured at the hands of her stepfather from the time she was five years old. While Allison told Jetter that she "has made peace" with her stepfather, her mother's complicity in the abuse has been much more difficult to reconcile. Despite the pained ambivalence that characterizes her feelings, Allison credits her mother with instilling in her a defiant pride and strong sense of self. Although she died of cancer in 1990 at the age of 56, just three months before the completion of *Bastard*, Ruth Allison remains a strong presence in her daughter's life and writing.

Much of Allison's writing directly addresses her abusive upbringing as well as her class background. Her parents worked in a series of blue collar jobs—her mother as a cook, fruit packer and clothes launderer, her stepfather as a route salesman. In her essay "A Question of Class," Allison explains that, for a time, she was able to "run away from [her] own life" and the myths she had internalized about growing up poor. In the late 1960s, she literally escaped her family life by attending Florida Presbyterian College in St. Petersburg on a National Merit Scholarship. There, she embraced feminism and the women's movement, lived in lesbian-feminist collectives, and attended consciousness raising sessions. She credits feminism with saving her life. In the essay "Believing in Literature," she writes that feminism offered her "a vision of the world totally different from everything [she] had ever assumed or hoped."

After earning a bachelor's degree in 1971, Allison worked in a series of jobs as a salad girl, substitute teacher, and maid, finding steady employment but long hours at the Social Security Administration. In addition, she helped publish a feminist magazine, volunteered in a child-care center, and answered the phones at a rape crisis center. Allison managed to stay away from her family for almost a decade and eventually moved north to New York City in 1979. There she attended the New School for Social Research and earned a master's degree in anthropology. At the same time, she worked at *Conditions*, a small feminist magazine, where she wrote grant applications, raised funds, edited other people's writing, and finally published some of her own work. Although writing was an act of resistance and a means to understand her past, Allison admits that until 1974, when she published her first poem, she built a ritual fire each year and burned every word she produced—journals as well as short stories and poetry.

Publishes First Book and Stirs Controversy at Barnard

In 1983, Long Haul Press published Allison's first book, *The Women Who Hate Me*, a collection of poetry which was expanded and reprinted in a 1990 edition by Firebrand Books. With razor sharp precision and exactitude, these poems explore love, sexual desire, betrayal, and bitterness. The first poem, "Dumpling Girl," establishes Allison's method for the entire volume, weaving memory and metaphor together with specific experience. Here, food is the catalyst for memory. The speaker of the poem celebrates her Southern heritage by identifying herself simultaneously as a "southern dumpling child, biscuit eater, tea sipper, okra slicer, [and] gravy dipper." Quickly, this catalogue is transformed into a meditation on lovemaking, a testament to the "butterfat shine" of her lover's thighs and the sweet, rock-salt taste of her belly. While similar themes of hunger, appetite, and desire run through the volume, the playful eroticism of "Dumpling Girl" is replaced in other poems by anger, regret, or sadness. In the book's title poem, for instance, Allison emphasizes the stinging ambivalence of desire, writing that

Dorothy Allison. ***Photograph by Jill Posener.***

> [t]he women who hate me cut me
> as men can't. Men don't count.
> I can handle men. Never expected better
> of any man anyway.

The poems as a collection are driven by Allison's pursuit of the truth about the vicissitudes of her sexual desires. Her poem "She Plays it Tight," for example, describes the object her desire with provocative language suggesting sadomasochism:

> A woman I love
> really thinks she can
> make of herself
> a boy
> a lean-hipped
> hard-eyed
> cold-hearted
> piece of
> rough trade.

A self-proclaimed "transgressive lesbian," Allison has always written and spoken candidly about sexuality, exploring taboo topics such as promiscuity and butch/femme role playing. Indeed, in an interview with the *Kenyon Review*, Allison affirms that she belongs to a "perverse" literary tradition of "iconoclasts" and "queers." This unwavering point of view has placed her at odds with certain segments of the feminist and lesbian communities and in the spotlight of the corrosive sex wars of the 1980s.

As Lillian Faderman explains in *Odd Girls and Twilight Lovers*, the sex wars saw cultural feminists and sex radicals divided over the issue of what constituted responsible, feminist expressions of lesbian sexuality. On the one hand, cultural feminists maintained that images of violence, domination and control are not only harmful ut anathema to lesbian ethics. On the other hand, sexual radicals encouraged lesbians to enjoy "freewheeling sexuality" and to reappropriate lust as a positive virtue. Allison's commitment to sexual freedom linked her to the sex radicals and provoked some feminists to label her work "pornographic."

In 1982, as the sex wars were developing, Allison was picketed by anti-pornography feminists at a symposium on sexuality at Barnard College where she was scheduled to speak. At the time, Allison was an outspoken founding member of the Lesbian Sex Mafia, "an old-fashioned consciousness raising group whose whole concern would be the subject of sex." The group championed free sexual expression and, as Allison explains in the essay "Public Silence, Private Terror," "concentrated on attracting members who primary sexual orientation was s/m, butch/femme, fetish specific, or otherwise politically incorrect." In this same essay, Allison recounts how her affiliation with the Lesbian Sex Mafia and the Barnard incident disrupted her life. Mainstream feminists and colleagues alike labeled her an antifeminist writer and a pawn of the patriarchy; anonymous phone callers urged her boss to fire her; and she was expelled from the Sex Mafia. In an interview with the *Advocate*, she claims that the worse accusation "was that I was guilty of child sexual abuse because of the writing I was doing."

Allison's Fiction Wins Acclaim

Despite the Barnard controversy, Allison remained convinced that sexuality was a vital issue both in political organizing and in her literary vision. "Public Silence, Private Terror" clarifies that for Allison "the struggle came down to an inner demand that [she] again look at sexual fear from [her] own perspective, without giving in to the impulse to hide, deny, or wall off desire itself." The 1988 collection *Trash*, published by Firebrand, testifies to this commitment. The preface succinctly explains that Allison's motives for writing are "to put on the page a third look at what I've seen in life—the condensed and reinvented experience of a cross-eyed working class lesbian, addicted to violence, language, and hope, who has made the decision to live." The voice of the first-person fictional narrator in *Trash* clearly expresses this motivation and unifies the volume.

The stories in *Trash* are variously focused on childhood experiences, physical violence, poverty, class politics and lesbian sexuality. The themes of personal, sexual, and physical violence emerge in myriad settings. In "Mama," the narrator recounts her stepfather's beatings, disclosing the survival tactics she learned to master. She writes: "When my stepfather beat me I pulled so deeply into myself I lived only in my eyes, my eyes that watched the shower sweat on the bathroom walls, the pipes under the sink, my blood on the porcelain toilet seat, and the buckle of his belt as it moved through the air." In other stories, violent imagery merges with graphic depictions of sexual desire. In "Her Thighs," for example, the narrator explores her dangerous attraction to Bobby, "a wild-eyed woman, proud of her fame for running women ragged," candidly revealing that "Bobby loved to beat my ass, but it bothered her that we both enjoyed it so much."

While *Trash* won two Lambda Book Awards for lesbian fiction and lesbian small press book, *Bastard Out of Carolina* gained national recognition for Allison. Like *Trash*, the novel relies on the perspicacity of its first person narrator to drive the story. The voice in the novel belongs to Ruth Anne Boatwright, nicknamed Bone, who tells the story of her life and her world until she is 13 years old. Beside Bone, a host of characters populate a deftly drawn setting recalling rural South Carolina in the 1950s. The novel's focus on Southern family life has evoked literary comparisons to Flannery O'Connor and William Faulkner. Bone's poor, white working-class Southern family is stubborn, violent, and, at the same time, fiercely loving. Bone worships her cadre of uncles—hard-drinking, wide-shouldered men who terrorize the county yet are protective and affectionate toward Bone and her cousins; her Aunt Raylene is also of special importance, an independent woman who once worked the carnivals and who had a female lover. However, Bone's most unforgettable and pernicious relationship is with "Daddy Glen," her stepfather, who abuses her in every conceivable way. Her mother knows about the abuse but fails to stop it.

The novel thus chronicles the treachery, intimacies, and hateful paradoxes of family love and Bone's attempts to understand the cruelty she endures. One of the hard-learned lessons which looms over the novel and into Bone's consciousness is "that we do terrible things to the ones we love sometimes." Randall Kenan, a gay novelist and book reviewer for the *Nation*, addresses the potential problems with the material of family drama that the novel presents. However, he argues that when *Bastard* succeeds, it does so by eluding the trap of Southern stereotypes and rendering Bone's milieu with devastating realism. To the *Kenyon Review* Allison speculates about the reasons for the novel's success with wide and varied audiences. She suspects that "an enormous range of people [can] relate emotionally to Bone's experience.... The level of emotional brutality that a lot of us have survived is appalling. The book is useful for in some ways it's a mirror you can look into." *New York Times* book reviewer George Garrett concurs that the novel's emotional authenticity coupled with its "living language" and "cumulative lyricism" signal the arrival of "a wonderful work of fiction by a major new talent." Presently *Bastard Out of Carolina* is being made into a Hollywood movie directed by Anjelica Huston. Allison is at work on her second novel, *Cavedweller*.

***Skin* Talks About Sex, Class, and Literature**

Allison revisits many of the themes of *Trash* and *Bastard Out of Carolina* in her first published collection of nonfiction essays, performance pieces, and autobiographical narratives entitled *Skin*. Some of the pieces are updated versions of earlier material while other essays were written especially for this volume. The subject matter ranges from details of Allison's lifelong commitment to feminist activism, to personal recollections of her experiences with pornography, to memories of her friend and mentor, the novelist Bertha Harris. Probably the most poignant essay echoes the title of the volume. "Skin, Where She Touches Me" remembers the two most important women in Allison's life—her mother and her first lover. Both have died, but Allison maintains she "cannot stop talking about them, retelling their stories, turning their jokes to parables and their stubborn endurance to legend." Allison admires and desperately loves both women, crediting them for shaping who she has become.

Allison continues to pay tribute to the women in her life with the publication in 1995 of *Two or Three Things I Know For Sure*, originally written for performance in the months following the completion of *Bastard Out of Carolina*. This multi-media piece was first performed in 1991 in San Francisco and has been substantially revised for publication. While it is dedicated to her sisters, Allison claims that the characters are composites, "creations based on friends, family, and acquaintances." Moreover, family snapshots intermittently illustrate the written text. The title is Allison's touchstone throughout, a credo adapted from the words of an aunt whose declaration, "There's only two or three things I know for sure," offered the women of the family comfort in times of hardship.

Two or Three Things I Know For Sure details the molestation by her stepfather and its effects on her life. The "sweaty power of violence" and "the sweet taste of desire" merge for Allison in the image she conjures of her stepfather during target practice. The rendition of this memory, among others, captures Allison's power as a storyteller who uses fiction not as therapeutic indulgence but as a method to save lives. The lives she elucidates here, including her own, are resilient and determined; the stories here, like the ones which distinguish her previous fictional efforts, are passionate and desperate. Yet, they "all have to be told in order not to tell the one the world wants." Indeed, Dorothy Allison's work attempts to come to terms with a host of experiences that the world would rather keep silent.

Current Address: P.O. Box 14474, San Francisco, California 94114.

References:

Faderman, Lillian. *Odd Girls and Twilight Lovers: A History of Lesbian Life in Twentieth Century America.* New York: Columbia University Press, 1991.

Garrett, George. "No Wonder People Got Crazy as They Grew Up" in *New York Times Book Review,* 5 July 1992: 3.

Huston, Bo. "A Storyteller out of Hell" in *Advocate,* 7 April 1992: 70-72.

Jetter, Alexis. "The Roseanne of Literature" in *New York Times Magazine,* 17 December 1995: 54-57.

Kenan, Randall. "Sorrow's Child" in *Nation,* 28 December 1992: 815-16.

Megan, Carolyn. "Moving Toward Truth: An Interview with Dorothy Allison" in *Kenyon Review 16,* 1994: 71-83.

—Annmarie Pinarski

Pedro Almodovar

1951-

Spanish filmmaker

Pedro Almodovar is a Spanish film director who takes full advantage of the artistic freedom in his country which followed the death of Francisco Franco. Under Franco's dictatorship, 36 years of cultural repression and censorship stifled progress in the arts. Almodovar began his career as a filmmaker in 1980 when he produced his first feature film. His work marks the beginning of a new era for Spain. Throwing caution to the wind, he is garish and outlandish in style, openly homosexual, and flaunts bizarre sex in his films. A favorite theme is relationships among women, whom he finds more interesting than men. Explicit sex, disregard for conventional morality, and twisted personalities mix with satire and bathroom humor in controversial productions.

Almodovar was born in 1951 and spent his earliest childhood in the small, poor village of Calzada de Calatrava. His father was a bookkeeper and gas station attendant who made wine on the side for some extra income. His mother, Francisca Caballero, ran the home. Pedro had two sisters and one brother. When he was eight, the family moved to Caceras, in the province of La Mancha. It was an isolated, cold region, where he never felt he belonged. Even though he was close to his family, he longed to leave and explore the big cities. He began school at age ten, when he was given a scholarship by some Salesian priests who found him teaching villagers how to read.

When Almodovar was 17 he left Caceras for Madrid, intending to become the most modern hippie in the city. He adopted hippie clothing and earned a living selling crafts on the street. He went to work for the national telephone company two years later. While he was employed, he pursued creative ventures on the side. He began filming a series of short, silent films with a Super-8 camera. He attracted quite a cult following, showing his creations in schools, bars, or parties, and providing his own commentary to make up for their lack of sound. During this time he also performed with a punk-rock band known as Almodovar and McNamara. He joined an avant-garde theatre group, Los Goliardos. One of the actresses in the group, Carmen Maura, would later star in several of his films.

Underground Contract

A contract from an underground newspaper propelled him on the road to notoriety. Almodovar produced an outrageous, brazen film called *Pepi, Luci, Bom y otras chicas del monton* [*Pepi, Luci, Bom and Other Girls on the Heap*]. It took a year and a half to make, resulting in a bizarre lack of continuity. For example, characters sometimes appeared with different hair lengths in the same scene. It is a raw, sexual production, violating good taste at every turn. Appearing at the San Sebastian Film Festival in 1980, it received an angry reaction from audiences. This film is the only one never released in the United States.

Almodovar's second film is a pop musical, *Laberinto de pasiones* [*Labyrinth of Passion*]. Its cast includes far-fetched characters from the fringes of society—punk rockers, transvestites, and the bisexual son of a deposed Iranian emperor. It takes a humorous look at a section of society that cares more about instant gratification than traditional mores. Released in 1982, it remained popular up through 1990 in Madrid.

Until 1982, Almodovar was popular mostly in his own region. His international reputation grew with the release of *Dark Habits* in 1983. It played at the Venice and Miami film festivals in 1984, creating a name for him as an outlandish, garish director. *Dark Habits* satirizes the work of an imaginary order of nuns called the Humble Redeemers. The subversive portrayal of the nuns as drug

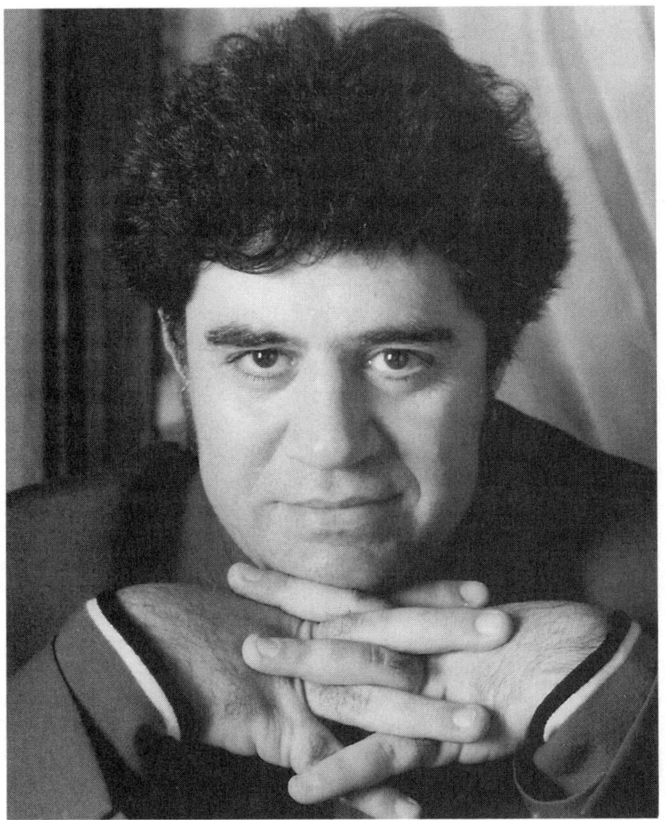

Pedro Almodovar

addicts, murderers, and delinquents is, nevertheless, presented with humor. The sisters come across as crazy but likable. Almodovar often depicts Catholicism in an unfavorable light, growing out of early unpleasant memories from his school years. In both this film and others, the special effects and lighting are especially notable. He uses neon color, grotesque close-ups, dramatic music, and a fast pace to enhance his defiance of convention in subject matter.

Controversial Career—Conventional Success

Almodovar featured Carmen Maura in *What Have I Done to Deserve This?* It was his first commercial success in Spain. The film depicts the life of a frenzied housewife in Madrid, satirizing the growing pains of modern Spain in 1985. While it carries undertones of Almodovar's idealism, still there is no attempt at using a different technique to make his statement. Almodovar returns to his same combination of ribald humor and dirty talk. His next film was less successful. His intent with *Matador* was a commentary on the glamourization of death in traditional Spanish culture. However, most people who viewed it missed that message amidst the story of a disreputable matador, whose student attempts to rape the matador's mistress. *Matador* was shown at the Rio International Film Festival in 1986 and released in the United States in 1988, but it never did well at the box office in Spain.

Frustrated by disagreements with the financial backers of *Matador,* Almodovar put together his own production company, El Deseo, with his brother. Together they produced *La ley del deseo* [*Law of Desire*] with financial assistance from Spain's Ministry of Culture. This homosexual love story was Spain's biggest moneymaker in 1986. It became an international cult favorite, appealing to both gay and straight audiences with its romance and humor.

He proceeded from there to produce his most acclaimed film, *Women on the Verge of a Nervous Breakdown,* which received an Oscar nomination for best foreign film in 1988. The New York Film Critics Circle cited it as the best foreign film, and Almodovar received a screenwriter's award at the Venice Film Festival. Carmen Maura starred in the role of an unmarried, pregnant television actress recently abandoned by her lover. *Women on the Verge of a Nervous Breakdown* is modeled on American comedies of the 1950s, such as *How to Marry a Millionaire.* But it is a comedy with a message about female loneliness. The characters are beautiful women in plush surroundings, with funny situations happening all around them. But meanwhile, the women are alone, and it is evident that beautiful things cannot make up for sadness within.

The contrast between this film and his next one, *Tie Me Up! Tie Me Down!* (1990) deserves note. *Tie Me Up! Tie Me Down!* departs from all of his previous work by actually turning in the direction of convention, sentiment, and optimism. It's the controversial story of a former mental patient who kidnaps a porn star, ties her to a bed, and waits for her to fall in love with him. Many feminists criticized the film for its depiction of violence against women. Almodovar insists that is not the case, that the ropes are symbolic only of the difficulty of two people getting to know each other. Critical reaction was much the same, with many critics feeling the film was uninspiring and devoid of substantial meaning while others praised it as Almodovar's best work yet.

Whatever the case may be, filmmaking is Pedro Almodovar's obsession. He lives for the intensity and excitement of bringing his dreams alive. He even enjoys the challenge of limited budgets, which he says stimulate his creativity. He's a demanding director, praised by his actors for the excellence he pushes them to achieve. His films are about today, what is happening now, and he records a viewpoint of society that challenges the mainstream.

Current Address: El Deseo SA, Ruiz Perello 15, Madrid 28028, Spain.

References:

Current Biography Yearbook, 1990. New York: H. W. Wilson Co., 1990.

International Who's Who, 57th ed., 1991-92. London: Europa Publications, 1991.

Thomson, David. *Biographical Dictionary of Film.* New York: Alfred A. Knopf, 1994.

—Carolyn Eckstein-Soule

Dennis Altman

1943-

Australian writer

Dennis Altman was born in Sydney on 16 August 1943, the son of Assia and Andy Altman, refugees from Europe. His father was Austrian, his mother Russian, and they met in Australia. He spent the years between 1950 and 1964 in Hobart, Tasmania; he was educated at the Friends' School, Hobart, before going on to the University of Tasmania, where he took an honours degree in 1964. Between 1964 and 1966 Altman studied on a Fulbright Scholarship in the United States, earning a Masters degree from Cornell University in 1966. Since then he has worked in a number of academic positions both in Australia and overseas and currently holds a chair at La Trobe University in Melbourne. He lives with his companion Anthony Smith and three cats in the inner Melbourne suburb of Clifton Hill.

Altman achieved national and international recognition with his groundbreaking *Homosexual: Oppression and Liberation.* First published in 1971, the book has been repeatedly reprinted and in 1991 was named as one of the all-time best 101 Australian books in a selection by the National Centre for Australian Studies at Monash University. This thoughtful, analytic account of the gay movement anticipated and set the agenda for much of the discussion through the 1970s and 80s. Writing of the book's effect on himself and his friends, Jeffrey Weeks has said that "what we needed was a framework that would pull all these experiences together, giving them a theoretical structure and some sense of history, which in turn could feed back into practice. Altman's book was the first full-scale work to try to do that."

For all its limitations (which the author has subsequently acknowledged and attempted to remedy) such as the relative neglect of female homosexuality, *Homosexual* was a profoundly pioneering work in its insistence on the normative nature of homosexuality and its fierce rejection of attempts to ghettoise the homosexual, even when those attempts took the comparatively benign form of pitying tolerance. Its emphasis is on the positive value of homosexuality, on the communal nature of the gay movement and on the connections between homosexuals and other oppressed groups in society, such as blacks.

The book was followed by a collection of essays, *Coming Out in the Seventies* (1979), which developed and reconsidered many of the themes of its predecessor, and then *Rehearsals for Change* (1980). More recently, Altman has extended his interest in the theories and practices of sexuality to the social, political and cultural impact of the AIDS epidemic and to political culture and its representations in Australia and the United States. He has said that "My contact and fascination with the United States persist," both in his periods of residence in America and his teaching of courses in American studies to his Australian students. These interests led to the publication of *The Homosexualization of America, the Americanization of the Homosexual* (1982), *AIDS in the Mind of America* (1986) which was also published in England and Australia as *AIDS and the New Puritanism,* and *Power and Community: Organisational and Cultural Responses to AIDS* (1994). More recently he has published *Paper Ambassadors: The Politics of Stamps* (1991), and a novel, *The Comfort of Men* (1993). Set in Altman's native Tasmania, one of the last democratic states to maintain its ban on homosexual practices in private between consenting adults, this is a disconcerting but original mixture of political fantasy and a straightforward, partly autobiographical account of the protagonist's growing up to discover and accept his sense of his own identity as a homosexual. It postulates a Tasmania which has cut itself off from the mainland of Australia in 1971 and declared its independence, under the leadership of far right demagogues.

Altman has written prolifically and with authority over a wide range of cultural, social and sexual issues, in venues ranging from relatively little-known gay magazines to government reports on issues such as AIDS and universities and intellectual life. His writing is consistently lucid, persuasive, passionate without being strident. He has said ruefully of the perils of being a "public homosexual": "I found myself criticized for hogging the limelight—the media tended to turn to me too often—and just as often for refusing to support the movement if I refused to speak." But he is in great demand as a speaker and commentator on many social and intellectual issues. He is one of the very few Australian intellectuals who probably has a larger reputation overseas than in his native country, but he has chosen to remain in Australia: "In the end I decided I had little talent as an expatriate."

Current Address: c/o Politics Department, La Trobe University, Bundoora, VIC 3083, Australia.

References:

Altman, Dennis. *Homosexual: Oppression and Liberation.* New York: New York University Press, 1993.

———. *The Homosexualization of America, the Americanization of the Homosexual.* New York: St. Martin's Press, 1982.

—Laurie Clancy

Hans Christian Andersen

1805-1875

Danish writer

Hans Christian Andersen remains one of the most revered children's writers. His plots are simple, but he combined a marvelous eye for detail with total mastery of the telling phrase. No one will ever forget the dog "with eyes as big as saucers" from *The Tinderbox*, nor the pathos of the little match girl, dying of hunger and exposure and afraid to go home lest her father beat her. She is barefoot, because her one slipper has been stolen by a little boy for a doll's cradle—which perfectly encapsulates the difference between his home and hers. It is shameful that his stories are often now "re-told" (i.e., falsified) in a sentimental and debased form with no unhappy endings, for they are all about the struggles of losers and outsiders (often successful, but often not), from which stems their pathos and their drama.

Andersen's origins couldn't have been more suitable for a teller of fairy tales had he chosen them himself. He was born at Odense, on the Danish island of Funen, the son of a poor shoemaker who mended more shoes than he made. As a child he spoke the local dialect, of which the inhabitants immodestly say: "It's the language the angels speak on Sundays."

Every circumstance of his early life reinforced a taste for the dramatic: his father (also named Hans) was a free-thinker, to the distress of Anne-Marie, his superstitiously pious mother; his grandfather had the sort of disposition which is regarded as charmingly eccentric in the rich and harmlessly mad in the poor; he himself was invited to visit both the prison and the poorhouse (which doubled as a madhouse) where he observed, respectively, public executions and the effects of tertiary syphilis.

The Bailiff with the Whip

He never lost the great charm he possessed as a child, for he never ceased to be childlike. He recorded in his autobiography that he and his mother sometimes went gleaning in fields where there was "a notoriously ill-natured bailiff." They ran, but once he was caught when his clogs came off.

> Already he had raised his whip; I looked at his face and said spontaneously: "How dare you strike me, when God can see it?" And the stern man at once grew quite mild, patted me on the chin, and asking my name gave me money. When I showed this to my mother, she said to the other people: "He's a strange child, my Hans Christian! Everybody is good to him, and even the wicked man has given him money!"

Friends among the Famous

This episode has doubtless benefited from Andersen's literary skill, but from his earliest struggles in Copenhagen he was never short of patrons to offer him food, finance, favours and, especially, friendship.

The young Andersen's chief delight was the theatre. His ambition was to be an actor, and at the age of 14, equipped with his lifesavings of 13 rigsdaler (which he had kept in a piggy bank) he took the coach to Copenhagen, determined to make his mark on the stage. His natural charm brought him patronage, initially from Mme Schall the ballerina, but for as long as he needed it kindly people, often of great distinction, made sure that he didn't starve.

Nonetheless, his early life was not easy. He had some talent as a boy soprano, but his broken voice had no potential; he lacked the physical presence of an actor, and was too ungainly to be a dancer. As a last resort he turned to writing for the stage. Here his potential was obvious; his plays contain many good lines, but they lack dramatic tension, and are rarely revived. But they were good enough to win him a royal grant, first to complete his secondary education (which meant attending at 17 a class full of 12-year-olds), then to attend university. There he first gained public favour with his poems and travel writing, and the story of his struggles effectively ended.

Lasting Fame

There followed more plays and novels, which struck a chord with the public although they seem overly autobiographical and linear today. His future was secure, but he would now be remembered only as a minor poet had he not produced, as an incidental effort, his first set of stories for children.

Thereafter his fame was assured and rapidly became international, not least through the patronage of Dickens. Much of his life thereafter was passed in travel, and he was received as Denmark's unofficial ambassador at large. At his death, he was one of the most renowned men in Denmark, and the king was chief mourner at his funeral. Yet was he truly happy? And was he fulfilled?

The Sexual Enigma

The assumption that Andersen was homosexual is based on the analysis of Albert Hansen, who took the simple but reasonable view that a man who displayed such a constellation of gay behaviour patterns could be nothing else. Nielsen cites Dr. Hjalmar Helweg as having "disproved" that "pure invention", but in fact neither side has any proof whatever; for Andersen was an intensely sociable man, living by choice very much in the public eye, to whom no sexual scandal of any kind ever attached. Everyone sees in him what they want to see. Monica Stirling, for instance, quotes a passage from his Italian diary in which he laments a "powerful lust" which he must control; yet she presumes that he was tempted, not by youthful flesh of both sexes available in such profusion, but by the desire to masturbate!

The evidence that he proposed marriage to a number of obscure and famous beauties, most notably Jenny Lind, is hardly disproof of bisexual tendencies; as a man of honour (and one with the lifelong fear of appearing ridiculous in public which he turned to such good account in "The Emperor's New Clothes") he must have known himself to be capable of consummation had he been accepted, but he may well have taken their refusals with some measure of relief.

The Orang-utang

Every portrait of Andersen shows a man with friendly and engaging features to which it is impossible not to warm; yet he was by no means handsome, and surely knew it, for he had exquisite aesthetic refinement. All his famous vanity was for his prosperous turn-out and social triumphs, none for his looks or physique. When he had his portrait painted, or allowed himself to be photographed, it was not to record his beauty but to demonstrate his high social standing—Hans Christian Andersen, condescending to sit for a society portraitist!

Hans Christian Andersen

Indeed, in his latter years he acquired the nickname of "the orang-utang", and with his thinning red hair, long bony limbs, protruding jaw and sharply receding forehead, one can see why—his later photographs put one in mind of Abraham Lincoln, a fellow-sufferer from Marfan syndrome.

This hereditary disorder varies markedly in severity but is characterized by long limbs and fingers. It may be accompanied by mild or severe weaknesses of any thoracic organ, and gave rise to the many references to chronic ill health in Andersen's letters (which are often cited as evidence of hypochondria). It is probable that his natural dignity and decency prevented him from either pursuing very strenuously people of either sex who were much more beautiful than himself, or addressing at all those whom he regarded as in any way second best.

Friendship is for all ages, but sexual love is for adults. Andersen feared the adult world where adult emotions demand adult toughness, the more so as the insecurity of his childhood never really left him. He was always careful with money, living well within his means (whether ample or strait), and never failing to put a little by—still a careful child with a piggy bank. In later life a more eccentric manifestation was his habit of travelling with a stout coil rope which he took to bed with him, so that should the building ever catch fire he could escape through the window. And while childlike friendships served him so well, financially and emotionally, why should he be in such a hurry to grow up?

These traits tended to reinforce each other in a man whose extreme romanticism combined with rather meagre sex-drive, perhaps exacerbated by Marfan syndrome.

References:

Andersen, Hans Christian. *Fairy Tales*. New York: Macmillan, 1963.
Nielsen, Erling. *Hans Christian Andersen*. Copenhagen: Royal Danish Ministry of Foreign Affairs, 1983.
Spink, Reginald. *Hans Christian Andersen and His World*. New York: G. P. Putnam's Sons, 1972.
Stirling, Monica. *The Wild Swan*. London: Collins, 1965.

—Chris Gilmore

Margaret Anderson

1886-1973

American publisher and writer

During the years beginning in 1914 when Margaret Anderson founded the *Little Review* and her death in 1973, she created an enviable literary legacy. Not only did she publish many of the most notable and avant garde writers of the first half of the twentieth century, she also authored several important works.

Margaret Carolyn Anderson was born in Indianapolis on 24 November 1886, to Arthur Aubrey Anderson and Jessie Shortridge. Anderson's childhood in Youngstown, Ohio, where the family had relocated after her birth, was not an especially happy one. Although Aubrey was loved by his children, there seemed to be a neverending struggle between Anderson's father and mother, whose frustrations over her own aborted musical career caused her to become something of a tyrant at home.

Anderson was 27 when she founded and began editing the *Little Review*—an innovative literary magazine based in Chicago, where Anderson soon met one of the greatest influences on her life: Jane Heap. Anderson was intrigued by Heap's mind, and was forced by Heap to consistently exercise her own. Before the *Little Review* folded in 1929, Anderson and Heap had published works by Amy Lowell, Sherwood Anderson, Djuna Barnes, Emma Goldman, and a handful of other literary greats of the day. In addition to these publishing endeavors, Anderson also published many influential works of her own, including: *My Thirty Years' War* and *The Fiery Fountains,* which comprise her autobiography; and *Forbidden Fires,* a strongly autobiographical novel that, thanks to the work of Mathilda Hills, was located, edited, and published in 1996 by Naiad Press.

Meanwhile, the private relationship between the two women, begun in 1915, remained unstable to say the least. While they appeared together often in public, it wasn't long before Anderson sought the company of another woman. When she left the United States to live in France in 1924, Anderson essentially turned the *Little Review* over to Heap.

As the publisher of the *Little Review,* Anderson was daring. The publishing of James Joyce's *Ulysses* resulted in the arrest of both Anderson and Heap. In 1921 the two women were found guilty of sending obscene literature through the U.S. mail. Both women were fingerprinted and fined, and later found little support for their cause—*Ulysses* wouldn't pass censorship for more than a decade. By that time, the *Little Review,* which constantly struggled to be ahead of its time and, it seems, to fight financial disaster, almost folded.

Shortly after the *Ulysses* verdict, Anderson found her affections transferred not only from literature to music—her first love—but from Heap to the French actress/singer Georgette Leblanc as well. According to Mathilda Hills in her introduction to *Forbidden Fires,* Anderson found in Leblanc "what real love is like—a bond of mutual understanding"—in spite of Anderson's decade's long romantic obsession with Josephine Plows Day (known as Tippy) and her passionate affair with Solita Solano.

The relationship between Anderson and Leblanc spanned 20 years, until Leblanc's death from breast cancer in 1941. On her return to America at this time, Anderson met her last great love, Enrico Caruso's widow, Dorothy, with whom she shared her life until the latter's death in 1955. Anderson then returned to France, where she spent her the remainder of her life. She died on 19 October 1973 from emphysema and is buried in Le Cannet, France, beside Georgette Leblanc.

References:

Hills, Mathilda. Interview with Andrea L.T. Peterson, Spring 1996.
———. "Introduction," in *Forbidden Fires* by Margaret Anderson. Tallahassee, Florida: Naiad Press, 1996.

—Andrea L.T. Peterson

Susan B. Anthony

1820-1906

American activist

Susan B. Anthony, leading nineteenth-century feminist activist, devoted almost all of her adult life to social reform. As a leader of the women's rights movement for more than 50 years, she formed a dynamic partnership with fellow activist Elizabeth Cady Stanton. Together they focused primarily on advancing the cause of women's suffrage. Anthony was convinced that without the vote, women would never achieve the political power necessary to ensure their personal safety, financial security, and equality in the workplace and in the home. Her achievements are all the more remarkable because they occurred in an era that was singularly repressive to women. Her constant traveling, lecturing, and grass-roots organizing violated nearly every standard of Victorian propriety. Any woman who dared to speak in public or to create a public role for herself was considered outrageously indecent, unnatural, and unsexed. Because Anthony refused to be limited by society's rules, she was free to develop her superior powers of organization, to capitalize on her phenomenal energy, and to single-mindedly focus on one goal: to organize women into a dynamic movement that would revolutionize society.

The second of Daniel and Lucy Read Anthony's eight children, Susan Brownell Anthony was born in Adams, Massachusetts, on 15 February 1820. The tightly knit, liberal Quaker family soon moved to Battenville, New York, in 1822, to live at the site of Daniel's new textile mill. Throughout Anthony's childhood, her parents actively encouraged her education. When she was 17 years old she briefly attended a Quaker boarding school near Philadelphia but left when her father experienced a severe financial failure following the Panic of 1837. She was then forced to help support the family by teaching at a local school. In 1839, she became a teacher at a Quaker boarding school in New Rochelle, New York, and in 1846, became headmistress at an academy in Canajoharie, New York.

The Search for a Career in Social Reform

After ten years of teaching, Anthony grew restless and sought new outlets for her energy and imagination. While managing her father's farm, she became involved in the local chapter of the Daughters of Temperance, her first active membership in a social reform movement. Temperance reformers advocated total abstinence from alcohol because they believed that alcohol abuse (particularly men's) was at the root of society's ills. Yet the more Anthony became involved in temperance work, the more she realized that abolishing alcohol would not remedy the problems caused by women's powerlessness in society. She soon became convinced that only political change could force the government to recognize women as viable citizens with the same rights as men.

In 1849, at the time Anthony delivered her first speech to the Daughters of Temperance, she was also investigating the anti-slavery movement and women's rights issues. Though she had wanted to meet the women's rights activist Elizabeth Cady Stanton from the time Stanton and Lucretia Mott had organized the first women's rights convention in 1848, it was not until 1851 that Anthony and Stanton met. Despite their dissimilarities (Stanton was five years older than Anthony and a wife and mother), they soon discovered their common goals and their intellectual compatibility which formed the foundation of their enduring, intimate bond.

In 1852 when the Sons of Temperance refused to permit Anthony and other Daughters of Temperance to speak at a joint meeting, Anthony withdrew and, with Stanton, formed the Woman's State Temperance Society. After they organized the society's first convention, Anthony was launched in her career in social reform. In 1854, with Stanton's advice and assistance, the two women spearheaded a campaign to repeal New York State's Married Woman's Property Law that prevented married women from owning or inheriting property in their own names. In 1860, after years of grass-roots organizing, canvassing, petitioning door-to-door, and coordinating women's rights conventions, the state legislature finally enacted a new law. For the first time, married women won the right to own property and to earn wages in their own names, to own businesses, to enter into contracts, to sue and be sued, and to be the joint guardian of their children.

A Relationship between Equals

Although Anthony received several offers of marriage in her youth, she did not accept any, though she asserted she never ruled out the possibility of marriage. By the time she formed her friendship with Stanton, Anthony had by and large resolved herself to her single status. In an 1896 interview in the *San Francisco Chronicle* she reflected on her single status: "Simply this, I never found the man who was necessary to my happiness. I was very well as I was." But most historians agree that Anthony's single existence was not entirely due to a lack of worthy marital opportunities. Kathleen Barrie, author of *Susan B. Anthony: A Biography of a Singular Feminist,* points out that "underlying Anthony's critique of marriage was an analysis and awareness of sex as domination." Indeed, Anthony was vehemently critical of an institution she believed to be essentially inegalitarian. She often quoted feminist reformer Lucretia Mott's vision of the ideal marriage: "In the true marriage relation, the independence of the husband and wife is equal, their dependence mutual and their obligation reciprocal." Despite her single status, Anthony was by no means alone. She had many close friendships with other women, but none rivalled the intensity of the profound mutual admiration and love she shared with Stanton. Theirs was a unique partnership, in which both work and love were inextricably intertwined and in which each woman's strengths complemented the other's. Stanton was the brilliant writer and rhetorician, and Anthony, the savvy strategist who provided the organizational genius, the grit, and the boundless energy necessary to execute their ideas.

As is true of most well-documented romantic female friendships of the nineteenth century, it is impossible to discern to what extent sexual attraction was a factor in Anthony's and Stanton's relationship from their correspondence. What is known is that the two women's love found expression in physical closeness, including long, warm embraces. Yet such physical demonstrations of affection between women were extremely common in the nineteenth century and did not necessarily signify a sexual bond or even a deep, emotional attachment. Based on her landmark study of nineteenth-century romantic female friendships in *Surpassing the Love of Men: Romantic Friendship and Love between Women from the Renaissance to the Present,* Lillian Faderman defined lesbianism as "a relationship in which two women's strongest emotions and affections are directed toward each other," a definition which encompasses the essence of Anthony's and Stanton's mutual love and respect.

From Abolitionism to Women's Suffrage

In 1856, Anthony became more involved in the abolitionist cause, as did many feminists, when she became the principal New York agent for William Lloyd Garrison's American Anti-Slavery Society. Garrison's radicalism appealed to her, particularly his refusal to compromise on the issues of slavery. Anthony's radical egalitarianism—her demand for universal equality regardless of race or gender—made her message unique among abolitionists, the majority of whom advocated only the abolition of slavery.

During the Civil War, in 1863, Anthony and Stanton won the respect of male Republican abolitionists when they formed the Women's Loyal National League which organized thousands of women to press for legislation prohibiting slavery. After the war, Anthony and Stanton continued their collaboration with male abolitionists by joining the American Equal Rights Association. Although its male Republican leaders vowed to secure the rights of all people, they soon sacrificed women's suffrage to gain citizenship and suffrage for black men. Angry and disillusioned, Stanton and Anthony withdrew and formed the National Women's Suffrage

Association (NWSA), an organization to be led only by women and to be devoted solely to the cause of women's suffrage.

Lucy Stone and her husband Henry Blackwell, both former New England abolitionists and women's rights advocates, formed the rival American Woman Suffrage Association (AWSA) in 1869. They proclaimed the AWSA the foremost women's rights organization, protesting that the NWSA's agenda was too radical and had strayed too far from the mainstream culture. Despite the AWSA's popularity, Anthony and Stanton never wavered from the NWSA's mission to organize women to obtain a national suffrage amendment. Not until 1890 would the two groups overcome their differences and unite their efforts.

In 1868, Anthony and Stanton fulfilled their dream of publishing a national women's journal. The *Revolution,* a militant, no-holds-barred feminist newspaper discussed suffrage issues and boldly addressed nearly every taboo topic related to women's political powerlessness, including prostitution, infanticide, divorce, rape, and women's labor unions. Despite their efforts to stay solvent, the *Revolution* failed in 1870, leaving Anthony deeply in debt.

In the 1872 presidential election, Anthony, frustrated by the slow progress toward women's suffrage, voted with fourteen other women for the Republican candidate Ulysses S. Grant. Recent women's rights conventions had argued that the 14th Amendment enfranchised women, based on a liberal interpretation of the amendment's first sentence, "All persons born or naturalized in the United States ... are citizens of the United States and of the State wherein they reside." Anthony and other leading feminists argued that this sentence superseded all other clauses or laws which specifically restricted suffrage.

A few weeks after Anthony cast her ballot in Rochester, New York, she was arrested. At her trial, the judge ordered the all-male jury to declare her guilty and demanded that she pay a $100 fine. Anthony refused to pay the fine in the hopes that she would again be arrested, thus giving her the opportunity to plead her case before the U.S. Supreme Court. But the judge stymied this plan by refusing to enforce the sentence. Anthony was disappointed, but the entire experience proved to be a public relations boon as she used the miscarriage of justice as the focus of a successful lecture tour.

Laboring for a Women's Suffrage Amendment

From the 1880s onward, Anthony developed close, interpersonal working relationships with a number of young women dedicated to the suffrage cause. These friendships developed out of Anthony's deep-seated concerns about the future of the movement and her realization that national women's suffrage probably would not be fulfilled in her lifetime. Anthony allied herself with Rachel Foster Avery, Carrie Chapman Catt, and Anna Howard Shaw, whom she trusted to propel the movement to its final conclusion. Anthony was impatient with the younger generation of women, especially the college-educated social reformers who were more interested in social change than in political reform. She kept insisting that suffrage must be the prerequisite agenda. "All we can do is agitate, agitate, agitate," she exhorted in an interview published in the journal *Kate Field's Washington* in 1890. And in an 1899 London *Times* interview she explained, "When men know that women can vote their heads off, then officials and office-seekers will attend to women's wants."

"I have been as a hewer of wood and a drawer of water to the movement," Anthony is quoted as saying in *The Life and Work of Susan B. Anthony* by Ida Harper, and throughout the 1870s, 1880s,

Susan B. Anthony

and 1890s, with Stanton by her side, Anthony labored indefatigably for the cause. She lectured throughout the country, lobbied for a 16th Amendment to guarantee women's suffrage, organized women's rights conventions, and agitated on behalf of women's labor unions. From the late 1870s on, Anthony collaborated with Stanton and Matilda Joslyn Gage in the writing of *The History of Woman Suffrage.* The first volume was published in 1881, followed by three more volumes published in 1882, 1886, and 1902, respectively. Two subsequent volumes, detailing the final years of the suffrage battle, were published in 1922. In 1888, Anthony founded the International Council of Women, which culminated in 1904 in the formation of the International Woman's Suffrage Alliance, for which she was named honorary president. Even as late as 1895-96, at the age of 75, Anthony traveled throughout California, lecturing on behalf of its state suffrage campaign. Although she never retired from suffrage work, after suffering a mild stroke in 1898, she began to curtail her travel and lecturing. Stanton died in 1902, leaving Anthony almost paralyzed with grief. But by 1903, she was back at work. In 1905, at age 85, when she traveled to a conference in Oregon she observed in a letter to a cousin, "I feel that it would be just as well if I reached the end on the cars or anywhere else as at home." For Anthony, the end came at the home she shared with her sister in Rochester, New York, on 13 March 1906.

In the 1890s, when Anthony finally won respect for her achievements, she was as unaffected by the adulation as she had been by the decades of ridicule. Perhaps more than any other nineteenth-century reformer, Anthony's absolute absorption in her work was what enabled her to ignore society's restraints and push on toward achieving her goals. At the last women's suffrage convention she attended, a month before her death, Anthony stood up and declared, "Failure is impossible." And although the nineteenth Amendment would not become law for fourteen more years, the momentum Anthony created by a half-century of grueling effort not only resulted in national women's suffrage, but in the creation of a new consciousness—of women actively asserting their power and claiming their place in society.

References:

Barrie, Kathleen. *Susan B. Anthony: A Biography of a Singular Feminist.* New York: New York University Press, 1988.

———. "Susan B. Anthony," in *Women Public Speakers in the United States, 1800-1925: A Bio-Critical Sourcebook,* edited by Karlyn Kohrs Campbell. Westport, Connecticut: Greenwood Press, 1993.

Campbell, Karlyn Kohrs. "Elizabeth Cady Stanton," in *Women Public Speakers in the United States, 1800-1925: A Bio-Critical Sourcebook,* edited by Karlyn Kohrs Campbell. Westport, Connecticut: Greenwood Press, 1993.

Lutz, Alma. "Susan B. Anthony," in *Notable American Women 1607-1950: A Biographical Dictionary,* edited by Edward T. James. Cambridge, Massachusetts: Belknap Press of Harvard University Press, 1971.

Pellauer, Mary D. *Toward a Tradition of Feminist Theology: The Religious Social Thought of Elizabeth Cady Stanton, Susan B. Anthony, and Anna Howard Shaw.* Brooklyn, New York: Carlson Publishing, 1991.

Sherr, Lynn. *Failure Is Impossible: Susan B. Anthony in Her Own Words.* New York: Times Books/Random House, 1995.

—Judith E. Harper

Gloria Anzaldua

1942-

Hispanic-American writer and activist

Gloria Anzaldua's strength as a Chicana lesbian writer and activist has long been based on a certain defiance of what is expected of her, a rejection of what popularly constitutes political correctness, and a steadfast refusal to accept any of the labels applied to her. In all her writing, from her poetry to her more political essays, she stresses the potential for unity among varying cultures, divergent sexualities, and both genders. Much to the dismay of both her literary lesbian counterparts and her less politicized Mexican-American cohorts, she refuses to rank her various identifiers, refuses to elevate or denigrate her lesbianism above or below that of her other identities, and argues in the end that she (and all of us) should belong to no one but ourselves.

"What am I?" she asks in the autobiographical essay "La Prieta," included in the groundbreaking 1981 anthology *This Bridge Called My Back: Writings by Radical Women of Color* which she co-edited with writer Cherrie Moraga. "A third-world lesbian feminist with Marxist and mystic leanings," she concludes.

In short, "queer" for Anzaldua goes well beyond sexual identity. In *This Bridge*, she wrote that "Third-world women, lesbians, feminists, and feminist-oriented men of all colors are banding and bonding together to right (the) balance.... We are the queer groups, the people that don't belong anywhere, not in the dominant world nor completely within our own respective cultures." For Anzaldua, it is the full embrace of their ambiguity that will allow oppressed people "of all stripes" to survive, thrive, and create a truly broad-based political movement for change.

Humble Beginnings

Anzaldua was born on 26 September 1942 on a settlement ranch of migrant workers in south Texas called Jesus Maria of the Valley. By all accounts, life was far from easy. Both parents worked the fields and made barely enough to feed the family, but still encouraged their children to pursue the education neither of them had enjoyed. Anzaldua's mother was sixteen when she gave birth to Anzaldua, and when Gloria was fifteen her father died, leaving mother and children with little choice but to continue to travel and work the fields, from south Texas to Arkansas and back again. The dream was to have the boys, especially, finish school in Texas, but it was Gloria alone who ended up getting a college education, still working the fields every weekend and summer. "[I was] not just the only woman," she told Elizabeth Baldwin in a 1988 interview in *Matrix,* "but the only person from the area who ever went to college."

She received her Bachelors degree in English, secondary education, and art from Pan American University in Edinburg, Texas, in 1969, and almost immediately began teaching among the people she had grown up with, the people who needed her the most: bilingual, preschool education; special education to emotionally and mentally challenged students; English at the high-school level; and instruction to administrators and teachers in methods for educating migrant workers and Mexican-American students in general.

In 1972, Anzaldua earned her Masters degree in English and education from the University of Texas in Austin, and embarked on teaching feminist studies, Chicano studies, and creative writing in Texas and on both coasts. When her graduate dissertation work on Chicano and feminist studies was rejected by the University of Texas in 1975, she (wisely) transferred to the University of California in Santa Cruz, where she still lives, writes, teaches, serves on various editorial boards, and is a popular public speaker.

A New Language

While working for a national feminist writers' group in 1978, Anzaldua met Cherrie Moraga, another Chicana lesbian writer, and the two embarked on co-editing *This Bridge.* The book was quickly termed a landmark event in feminist publishing because it was the first systematic collection of writings against racism by women of color that utilized, according to *The Gay and Lesbian Literary Heritage*, "full engagement with lesbian concerns and voices, and the non-tokenistic presence of lesbian writers." "We want to express to all women," Anzaldua and Moraga wrote, "the experiences which divide us as feminists. We intend to explore the causes and sources of, and solutions to, these divisions. We want to create a definition that expands what 'feminist' means to us." After being rejected by dozens of squeamish publishers, Moraga and African-American lesbian activist Barbara Smith co-founded Kitchen Table/ Women of Color Press to publish it. The book went on to win the American Book Award from the Before Columbus Foundation and still enjoys widespread acclaim among both women of color and in women's studies courses across the country.

It is in communicating the contradictions and complex identities of people of color that Anzaldua seems to hit her most resonant, moving chord. In 1990, Anzaldua edited a follow-up collection, *Making Face/Making Soul: Creative and Critical Perspectives by Women of Color,* which focused on the complexities of self-identification and the strain of differences between women of color. Yet, it is this very focus on ethnic complexity that has distanced her from other lesbian/feminist writers, Moraga included, who feel that her work fragments the lesbian-of-color agenda. "The first rule that I break," she writes in *Borderlands* (1987) "is the rule that says that there is a cohesive, coherent, self-directed self." In her short stories and poetry, Anzaldua speaks even more intimately of her conflicting cultural traditions, and of the spiritual and physical boundaries that define her life and that of so many others. In *Borderlands,* for example, she writes of the land between and within genders, genres, cultures, and the self as inhabited by "the prohibited and the forbidden." "*Los atravesados* live here: the squint-eyed, the perverse, the queer, the troublesome, the mongrel, the mulatto, the half-breed, the half dead, those who cross over, pass over, or go through the confines of the 'normal'." In *Borderlands,* she likewise seeks to create a new language, weaving text and poetry in Chicano Spanish, Tex-Mex, Nahuatl, and Pachoco in a combination of historical documentation and autobiography.

According to critics on both sides, Anzaldua redefines and elevates "queerness" to a political pedestal not merely sexual in nature. Yet, Anzaldua's value both as a creative and political writer and thinker lies in the very fact that her devaluation is multi-pronged. She represents, according to critic Shelley Fishkin, "people who were dismissed and devalued because they had the 'wrong' race class, gender, ethnicity, or sexual preference." Gloria Anzaldua has lived with a lot of strikes against her, and she strives not only to embrace all of them equally in her struggle, but to remind us that it is this very oppression, the very ambiguity of who we are, that underscores our unity and our strength.

Current Address: 126 Centennial St., Santa Cruz, California 95060.

References:

Anzaldua, Gloria. *Borderlands/La Frontera: The New Mestiza.* San Francisco: Spinsters/Aunt Lute Press, 1987.

———, ed. *Making Face/Making Soul: Creative and Critical Perspectives by Women of Color.* Spinsters/Aunt Lute Press, 1990.

Anzaldua, Gloria and Moraga, Cherrie, eds. *This Bridge Called My Back: Writings by Radical Women of Color.* Watertown, Massachusetts: Persephone Press, 1981.

Baldwin, Elizabeth. "Interview with Gloria Anzaldua." *Matrix,* May, 1988: 1-33.

Pollack, Sandra and Knight, Denise D., eds. *Contemporary Lesbian Writers of the United States.* Westport, Connecticut: Greenwood Press, 1993.

Summers, Claude J. *The Gay and Lesbian Literary Heritage.* New York: Henry Holt, 1995.

—Jerome Szymczak

Virginia M. Apuzzo

1941-

American activist

Virginia Apuzzo emerged from an unlikely background as a nun in the 1960s to become one of the foremost feminists and gay and lesbian rights activists in the 1970s and 1980s. In the post-Stonewall era largely dominated by gay men, Apuzzo represented one of the most forceful and compassionate lesbian influences. She was particularly active in New York State Governor Mario Cuomo's administration, serving as his official liaison to the lesbian/gay community from 1986 to 1989 and as vice-chair of the New York State AIDS Advisory Council from 1985 to 1995. A glance at Apuzzo's resume conveys her commitment to civil rights and gay-related issues, including her work with the National Gay and Lesbian Task Force. She has also served as executive director for the Fund for Human Dignity, a public education foundation organized to educate the American public on the contributions of homosexual men and women to American society.

Virginia M. Apuzzo was born on 26 June 1941 in the Bronx, New York, to an Italian, working-class family. Her father owned a gas station, and her mother, who would later suffer a nervous breakdown, worked at various jobs—including waitress, factory worker, and sales clerk—out of financial necessity. The eldest daughter in her family, Apuzzo was an excellent student from elementary school to Catholic high school. Her passion for justice as an adult strongly reflects her upbringing and education.

Entered Convent after Successful Teaching Career

Apuzzo received a Bachelor of Science in History and Education from the State University of New York, College of New Paltz, in 1963; a Master of Science in Urban Education from Fordham University in New York City in 1973; and amassed 33 credits toward her Ed.D. in Urban Education from Fordham University in 1974. In June of 1988, Queens College, City University of New York Law School, conferred upon Apuzzo an Honorary Doctor of Law Degree "in recognition of inspired contributions to law in the service of human needs."

While only in her twenties, she became the tenured teacher/chairperson of the Social Studies Department (kindergarten through 12th grade) for the Marlboro Central School District in Marlboro, New York. In the late 1960s, realizing the need to ponder the future direction of her life, Apuzzo entered a convent and became a nun in the Sisters of Charity Order. In *Lesbian Nuns: Breaking Silence,* Apuzzo wrote that although there was no identifiable gay movement at the time, she was:

> Fully aware of my homosexual identity when I joined the Sisters of Charity, and I stayed three years searching for answers to fundamental questions.... I thought of my religious life as temporary. I didn't know whether it would take one year or twenty years to explore the morality of my homosexual identity. Being a nun was painful but productive. I couldn't be doing all the work I do now for gay liberation without having learned to channel my energy.

During her period in the convent, Apuzzo continued to teach at two schools: Cathedral High School in New York City; and College of Mount St. Vincent in Riverdale, New York. In 1969, Apuzzo departed the convent and took a teaching position in the school of education at Brooklyn College, City University of New York. Responsible for placement, field supervision, and evaluation of social science majors apprenticing in public secondary schools, she worked with many educational leaders representing public school personnel (e.g., United Federation of Teachers, and Council of Supervisors and Administrators). Apuzzo went on to become a tenured lecturer at Brooklyn College, where she continued to teach until 1986.

In the early 1970s, Apuzzo codeveloped and copiloted the Undergraduate Performance-Based Field-Centered Teacher Education Program, which became a prototype for competency-based teacher education programs in New York State. From 1973 to 1974, she worked on three grants: the Danforth Foundation Grant; the Summer Innovative Grants Program; and the Department of Health, Education and Welfare Grant. During her 17 years at Brooklyn College, Apuzzo took three leaves of absence: two to accept public service positions and the third to serve as executive director of the National Gay Task Force and as executive director for the Fund for Human Dignity.

In the 1970s, Apuzzo served on the Coordinating Committee of the Manhattan Women's Political Caucus. She also coordinated the National Gay Task Force's efforts to obtain a gay rights plank in the Democratic party platform. She made an abortive attempt to get elected to the New York State Assembly in 1978. By 1979, she had taken a leave from Brooklyn College to become assistant commissioner for operations in the New York City Department of Health, a position which entailed operating six bureaus, including the District Health Services—the largest ambulatory health care operation in the United States. At the request of Anne Wexler, special assistant to President Carter, Apuzzo began the 1980s with an effort to coordinate the lesbian/gay political factions in support of the Carter/Mondale presidential ticket.

Explored Link Between Sexism and Racism

In the summer of 1976, Apuzzo and Betty Powell—a co-chair of the National Gay Task Force Board of Directors and an activist in the National Black Feminist Organization—both served as facilitators in a three-day, feminist conference of workshops, lectures, and discussion groups. The conference, sponsored by the National Black Feminist Organization and Sagaris—an independent institute for the study of feminist politics—explored the linkage between racism and sexism. Dorothy Allison, who went on to become a very successful author with a lesbian cult following, interviewed Apuzzo and Powell for the spring 1977 issue of *The Quest.* Apuzzo commented, "In that workshop, I really saw some women taking their own responsibility for their racism.... This conference took all the assumptions regarding black and white feminists working together and smashed them."

Achieving her greatest visibility in the late 1970s and the 1980s, Apuzzo often lectured on civil rights at such schools as Yale, Harvard, Princeton, Columbia, and the Kennedy Institute for Policy Studies; and appeared on such television programs as *Nightline, The McNeil-Lehrer Report, CBS Morning News, 20/20,* and the *Phil Donahue Show.* Among her literary achievements, Apuzzo contributed to the book *Our Right to Love: A Lesbian Resource Book* and wrote the chapter "Grace to Empower" for *Lesbian Nuns: Breaking Silence.*

Wanted $100 Million for AIDS Funding

By 1982, she was one of the few openly gay delegates to the midterm Democratic party convention in Philadelphia. Apuzzo's commitment to the National Gay and Lesbian Task Force continued throughout the 1980s; she became its executive director from 1983 to 1985.

Apuzzo addressed the topic of AIDS on many occasions in the 1980s; in January of 1983, she held a press conference in which 50 gay community groups attended to define a national blood donor policy. Here, she emphasized the significance of screening blood rather than preventing high-risk populations from donating blood. In May of 1983, she testified before a Federal House Appropriations Subcommittee on the funding and priorities of the departments of Labor, Health and Human Service, and Education, asking that $100 million be appropriated by Congress to combat AIDS. It was the first of many times that Apuzzo would testify before Senate and House subcommittees to encourage increased AIDS funding.

In September of 1984, Apuzzo collaborated with the Lambda Legal Defense and Education Fund and the American Association of Physicians for Civil Rights to successfully negotiate a model consent form for AIDS-related research funded by the Public Health Service. Dr. Edward Brandt, assistant secretary of health, went on to recommend the form for national use.

Governor Cuomo's Rising Star

Throughout the 1980s, Apuzzo urged U.S. Health and Human Services Secretary Margaret Heckler to organize a federal plan to combat AIDS and to protect the confidentiality of research subjects. She lobbied for federal monies for direct grants to community-based organizations to promote education among groups at high risk for AIDS. She also successfully negotiated with the head of the Social Security Administration to secure Social Security/disability benefits for persons with AIDS without the usual two-year waiting period. To achieve her ambitions, Apuzzo often collaborated with the Lambda Legal Defense and Education Fund, a national nonprofit organization that promotes the protection of civil rights for gays, lesbians, and people with HIV.

Explaining the passion of her commitment to combat AIDS, Apuzzo said in a *New Republic* article (2 November 1987): "For a long time gays' objective was to get the government off our backs. With the advent of AIDS it became very clear that there were some problems the government had to be involved in."

By June of 1984, New York Governor Mario Cuomo had taken notice of Apuzzo's civil rights achievements and appointed her on a panel to investigate discrimination against homosexuals in New York State in the areas of state employment, services, and benefits.

Honors in the 1980s and 1990s

In 1985, Governor Cuomo appointed Apuzzo as the executive deputy of the New York State Consumer Protection Board. Among her responsibilities, Apuzzo initiated state investigations into the cost of FDA-approved drugs and products that fraudulently promoted themselves as panaceas for HIV or AIDS. In the mid 1980s, Cuomo also named Apuzzo vice-chair of the New York AIDS Advisory Council.

Since she began on the National Gay Task Force in the 1970s, Apuzzo has received numerous honors and citations from all over the United States. A chronological sampling follows:

**1982:* Apuzzo received the first Human Rights Campaign Fund Award.

**October 1983:* The New York State Executive Chamber recognized her work as a founding member of the Lambda Independent Democrats of Brooklyn.

**August 1984:* Apuzzo received the San Francisco Board of Supervisors Certificate of Honor.

**September 1984:* Apuzzo received a citation from the Alice B. Toklas Democratic Club of San Francisco.

**October 1984:* Houston, Texas, proclaimed Virginia M. Apuzzo Day.

**April 1985:* The Gay Men's Health Crisis (GMHC) presented Apuzzo with a special citation.

**December 1985:* Apuzzo received the New York State Center for Women in Government Award.

**January 1986:* The New York Civil Liberties Union presented Apuzzo with a special citation.

**October 1986:* The California State Assembly Resolution honored Apuzzo.

**June 1987:* Apuzzo received the Greater Gotham Business Council Award.

**June 24, 1989:* Apuzzo served as the keynote speaker in Central Park, New York City, at the commemoration of the twentieth anniversary of the Stonewall Rebellion, the 1969 police raid on a Greenwich Village bar which triggered the gay rights crusade.

**June 24, 1994:* Apuzzo received the Victory Fund Award for her contribution to the lesbian and gay community.

**May 8, 1995:* The Hedrick Martin Institute in New York City gave Apuzzo an award for outstanding contribution to lesbian and gay youth.

Commissioner of Civil Service Commission

Over the course of the Cuomo Administration, Apuzzo worked with the governor, his counsel unit, and the New York State Lesbian and Gay Lobby, to pass inclusive, language-specific legislation to combat bias-motivated acts of violence. Apuzzo believes that despite the governor's and state assembly's support, the state senate did not pass the bill because it made some references to gays and lesbians. After three terms as New York governor, Cuomo lost the 1994 election to Republican opponent George Pataki.

Although Apuzzo's commitment to civil rights hasn't waned in the 1990s, her work has expanded beyond gay-related and AIDS-related topics. From 1985 to 1991, she was the deputy executive director of the New York State Consumer Protection Board; from 1991 to 1994, she was the executive deputy commissioner of the New York State Division of Housing and Community Renewal.

Since 1994, Apuzzo has been working for the New York State Civil Service Commission; starting as the organization's president, she has been its commissioner since January 1995. Begun more than a century ago and the oldest organization of its kind in the nation, the commission adopts and modifies rules governing a wide range of state and local civil service matters and hears and determines examination and classification appeals. In her current position, she serves as one of three members appointed by Governor Pataki and confirmed by the State Senate. Her decisions on titles, salary levels, and minimum qualifications for classified service positions affect 189,000 state employees and 350,000 municipal employees.

As president of the commission, Apuzzo re-examined and redirected commission standards for approval of waivers allowing retired state employees to simultaneously draw government salaries and pensions. As commissioner, Apuzzo initiated the "Workforce 2000" campaign to raise awareness of the government and the public about challenges and issues facing the state government workforce in the twenty-first century. Utilizing the powers conveyed by executive order, Apuzzo convened the Governor's Executive Council on Affirmative Action for the first time in six years. Of course, Apuzzo has tackled some gay issues with the Civil Service Commission. For example, she has been working to expand the New York State Health Insurance Program (NYSHIP) eligibility to include domestic partnerships.

Throughout Apuzzo's long and varied career, she has shown a remarkable commitment not simply to gay and lesbian rights but also to basic civil rights and dignity for all Americans. Her optimism is borne out in having worked on so many AIDS-related projects; she believes that the AIDS epidemic has united many seemingly disparate factions of the gay and lesbian community. Apuzzo anticipates that many of the legislative gains that gays and lesbians have reaped in the last two decades are transferable to other oppressed groups (e.g., disabled, elderly). Without her force and clarity of vision, those developments might not have been possible.

Current Address: State of New York, Department of Civil Service, The W. Averell Harriman State Office Building Campus, Albany, New York 12239.

References:

Allison, Dorothy. "Confrontation: Black/White (Interview with Ginny Apuzzo and Betty Powell)," in *Quest 3* (Spring 1977): 34-46.

Apuzzo, Virginia. "Grace to Empower," in *Lesbian Nuns: Breaking Silence,* edited by Rosemary Curb and Nancy Manahan. Tallahassee, Florida: Naiad, 1985.

Blow, Richard. "Those Were the Gays: What Now for the Gay Movement," in *New Republic,* 2 November 1987: 13-16.

Hardy, Gayle J. *American Women Civil Rights Activists: Bibliographies of 68 Leaders.* New York: McFarland & Co., 1993.

Vida, Ginny, ed. *Our Right to Love: A Lesbian Resource Book.* Englewood Cliffs, New Jersey: Prentice-Hall, 1978.

—David Levine

Gregg Araki

1959-

Asian-American filmmaker

Gregg Araki is to contemporary gay cinema what Dennis Cooper is to contemporary gay writing. Like Cooper, Araki's work is steeped

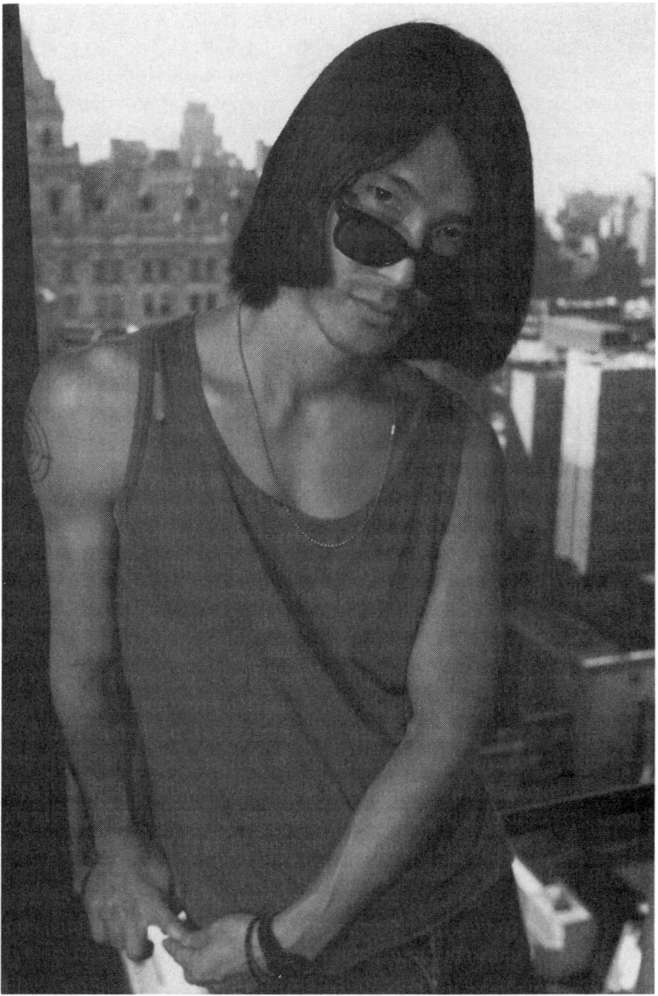

Gregg Araki

within the idioms of punk, porn, and B-grade splatter films. Refusing to shy away from recording supposedly incorrect representations of homosexuality, Araki's movies brilliantly capture the growing disaffection among a Los Angeles subculture that has never known sex without the association of death, a group of late adolescent and twentysomething gays and lesbians that Araki has referred to as both "the alienation generation" and "the doom generation."

The son of a machinist and an optometrist's assistant, Gregg Araki was born in Los Angeles, California in 1959. While he was still a young boy, his Japanese-American parents moved the family to the predominantly white suburb of Santa Barbara, where, despite his ethnic heritage and a growing awareness of his sexuality, he learned to fit in.

Before discovering punk music, Araki's spare time as a teenager was taken up mostly with collecting comic books. According to Pat Blashill, in a December 1995 *Details* article, Araki's "youthful obsession with comics as a graphic storytelling form" goes a distance toward explaining "the lurid surrealism of his films" (123). Comics also help explain both the hyper-erotic and anti-mythic qualities of the gay characters he portrays on screen. The naked sculpted torsos of actors Mike Dytri (in *The Living End*) and Jonathon Schaech (in *The Doom Generation*) are certainly suggestive of superheroic virility; but these men are not interested in saving the world, only themselves.

After graduating from the University of California at Santa Barbara with a film studies B.A. in 1982, Araki went on to collect an M.F.A. in film production from the University of Southern California in 1985. It was just two years later that Araki wrote, directed, and produced his first feature, a short entitled *Three Bewildered People in the Night*. Focusing on the triangular relationship between a female video artist, her sexually ambivalent boyfriend, and her best friend, a gay male performance artist, the film earned Araki a slew of honours, including the Bronze Leopard Critics' Prize and Young Cinema Award at the Locarno International Film Festival in Switzerland. This early triumph was followed, in 1989, by *The Long Weekend (o' Despair)*, which tells the story of three couples—one lesbian, one gay, and one straight—getting together for a holiday reunion filled with anxious conversation and general inactivity. Shot in grainy black-and-white, and financed on a shoestring budget, it received the L.A. Film Critics' Prize for Best Independent Feature. In both of these early films, narrative and sexual expectations remain deliberately unfulfilled as Araki deftly cross-cuts from one ennui-laden character to another. According to critic Daryl Chin, this "intentional stylistic roughness" allows Araki "to emphasize the qualities of grit, contrast, and disfunction that underscore his characteristic portrayal of a generation adrift" (106). Araki reached an even wider audience with 1992's *The Living End*. Trading cross-cuts for jump-cuts, and taking the action out of dark, cramped apartment buildings and onto the road, he gives the stock tale of doomed love enacted in this film a tense, kinetic energy. Against the backdrop of a disintegrating urban wasteland of endless freeways and 7-11 stores, HIV-positive lovers Jon and Luke careen violently and passionately, toward an inevitably foreshortened future and an increasingly apocalyptic horizon. With *Totally F***ed Up* (1993) Araki tackles the issue of suicide among gay and lesbian teens, introducing us to six club-hopping, pill-popping alienated and underemployed L.A. adolescents through video fragments that break up the already highly elliptical 16mm narrative. In this iconoclastic look at the new gay youth culture, Araki's protagonists are just as much at odds with mainstream gay and lesbian lifestyles as they are with the straight world.

While premiering the movie at the Toronto International Film Festival, Araki met and fell in love with a local man. The relationship, although intense, did not seem destined to survive the move to L.A., and after a tumultuous year and a half of living together in a tiny Hollywood Hills apartment, Araki's lover moved back to Toronto.

It is a measure of Araki's success during his gritty apprentice years making independent features that for his most recent release, *The Doom Generation* (1995), he secured his first big budget (one million dollars) and his first major distribution deal (with Trimark Pictures). In a typically subversive move, however, Araki took the money and made what he refers to facetiously as "a heterosexual movie," a reverse allegory of the American wet dream in which reluctant fugitives Xavier Red, Jordan White, and Amy Blue stop driving only long enough to eat junk food, have sex, and occasionally knock over a convenience store. As Blashill sums up the film (and this is a description that applies equally well to almost all of Araki's work), "*Doom* is a generational coming-of-age film, but once the heroes and heroines cum, there's nothing left. No epiphanies, just a bag of Doritos in the backseat" (120).

Araki has earned his share of criticism, from both inside and outside the gay community. The violent, nihilistic, and occasionally misogynist images that dominate his cinema are frequently seen as symptomatic of a gay exploitation aesthetic. But as Araki puts the finishing touches on *Nowhere*, his sixth picture, and the final installment in the "Teen Apocalypse" trilogy that started with *Totally F***ed Up*, he would be the first to admit that the characters in his movies believe in the redemptive power of love. Araki, the quintessential L.A. cynic, is really a romantic at heart.

Current Address: c/o Steven Pegner, Inc., 248 W. 73rd St., New York, New York 10023.

References:

Blashill, Pat. "Doom with a View" in *Details*, December 1995: 119-25.

Chin, Daryl. "Girlfriend in a Coma: Notes on the Films of Gregg Araki" in *Queer Looks: Perspectives on Lesbian and Gay Film and Video*, eds. Martha Gever, John Greyson, and Pratibha Parmar. New York: Routledge, 1993: 103-107.

—Peter Dickinson

Elizabeth Arden

1884-1966

Canadian entrepreneur

Thirty years after her death, Elizabeth Arden is still remembered for the feminine presence she created in early-twentieth-century American society. She made a place for herself near the top of two male-governed domains—business and horse-racing—and while doing so, she guided other women, from Fortune 500 matrons to shop girls, toward self-empowerment.

Arden was born Florence Nightingale Graham in Woodbridge, Ontario, Canada on New Year's Eve. Too poor to complete high school, Arden moved restlessly from one job to another in Ontario until, at age thirty, she decided to follow her brother to New York City. It was there, while working as a secretary to a cosmetician, that Arden developed her talent for facial massage and foresaw the enormous business potential if high-society women could be assured that it was their right to look the best they could; Arden, of course, would provide them the means. After ending a short-lived partnership, Arden opened her first salon in 1910, on Fifth Avenue, under her business name, Elizabeth Arden. She worked tirelessly to provide high-quality products and services to her high-quality customers. In a cover article published in *Time* a writer points out that Arden "has one mighty asset besides well-publicized vitality: a native shrewdness at hiring smart people to work for her. Says she: 'I only want people around me who can do the impossible.' She rarely hires anyone who is out of job."

Arden accomplished several firsts. By inventing cosmetic creams and astringents to supplement facial massage, she opened the door to beauty treatments for "respectable," wealthy women in an age when make-up was considered unladylike and fit only for women of questionable morals. After this innovation, Arden introduced the idea that an acceptable beauty treatment was not complete without lipstick, in a colour that would enhance the wearer's complexion tone and wardrobe. This concept of accentuating the positive then expanded to concealing the negative features of the customer's appearance. Within fifteen years, Arden convinced American women that beauty aids were not only acceptable but also an essential means by which every women could look young, beautiful, and even glamorous. Arden's business genius was to sell the idea before she sold the product, and then to provide a multitude of products which she knew women would buy. Eventually, her company's cosmetic line included 450 products in 1500 shades which were sold all over the world.

Offered Women Opportunity to Re-create Themselves

Once she made beauty fashionable, Arden was ready to open even more doors. Beyond the superficial changes made by cosmetics, Arden offered women the opportunity to re-create themselves. Over the years she always kept her New York headquarters on Fifth Avenue, and from the first two-room shop to the final seven-story salon, Arden demanded elegant decor, well-trained staff, and an atmosphere of luxurious intimacy from which, as *Time* describes it, prominent women would emerge "emotionally as well as physically restored." Arden pioneered the concept that beauty aids were only a part of a holistic program designed to instill women with self-confidence. She wrote a self-help booklet and urged a regimen of healthy diet, good posture, yoga, and exercise routines accompanied by popular music, preferably while attired in pink silk.

In order to provide these services in an exclusive environment, Arden opened the first health and beauty spa in the U.S., called Maine Chance Farm, in Mount Vernon, Maine. At this facility, and later at the winter version in Phoenix, Arizona, well-to-do women were encouraged to cultivate their individuality while being assured that beauty and life began at forty. She reinforced this with indi-

Elizabeth Arden with Bobby Permane

vidually prescribed diets and by offering the women several enjoyable forms of exercise—horseback riding, bowling, swimming, tennis, and badminton.

Arden was described as five feet and four inches of determined energy, her petite figure swathed in pink, her hyacinth-coloured eyes twinkling with infectious laughter or flashing with the strange blue light of an impending storm. She was labelled a perfectionist and fanatical in her belief in herself and her products. Albro Martin states in *Notable American Women: The Modern Period* that "Elizabeth Arden fits the classic model of the entrepreneur as closely as any other man or woman in the history of American business.... Although she mastered the pose of the demure little girl who wanted everything to be in pink, she drove home her message with the force of a steel executive."

As her business flourished and expanded, even during the Depression of the 1930s, Arden began to indulge her passion for horses. She raised them at first on her Maine Chance farm for sport, but in typical Arden fashion, within fifteen years her thoroughbreds were dominating the yearling and 2-year-old classes. Arden, who used her real name in racing circles, was the winningest owner of 1945 with purses totalling over one half million dollars, and in 1946 her horse Jet Pilot won the Kentucky Derby. Thus, few argued when Arden brought her holistic beliefs to the stable, believing that "a beautiful horse is like a beautiful woman." She would order her jockeys not to use the whip and her trainers to keep a close eye on whether flies were bothering the horses or if the horse-shoes fit properly. Arden used some of her creams to personally massage swellings on sore equine joints and ordered that all her horses have their legs massaged before and after races. Interestingly, she would bet no more than $5 on a race and never on her own horses.

In her personal life, Arden loved not only horses but also dogs, flower and landscape gardening, interior decorating, and fine art. Her collection included works by O'Keefe, Cassatt, Laurencian, and Chagall, and her penthouse garden was a favourite haven for Garden Club members. A staunch Republican and Episcopalian, she occupied a solid and uniquely feminine status in American society. Her influential role was recognized with an honorary doctor of laws degree from Syracuse University and a Great Lady Award from Theta Sigma Phi national sorority which thanked Arden for "having made beauty attainable to all American women."

Two Marriages End in Divorce

Arden was married twice, the first time to Thomas Lewis. Hambla Bauer reports in the *Saturday Evening Post* that "the wedding took place one afternoon at five. Miss Arden was back at work at five-thirty." Arden's marriage to Lewis automatically gave her American citizenship and also a talented business manager, for Lewis, after he returned from the war, worked for her in that capacity until Arden's chief competitor, whom she called "that woman," Helena Rubenstein, lured him away in the late 1930s. Arden married a Russian immigrant, reportedly a prince, in 1942. This marriage served the purpose of "cementing her position in high society" reports a writer in *Mothers of Invention,* and lasted fifteen months.

Arden's comments are recorded in the Hambla Bauer article: "In a sad little voice, Miss Arden says, 'I pick good women, but I haven't had any luck with my men.'" Bauer also reveals one of the few portraits of Arden's private life—Arden adored entertaining and loved being followed around by people. She kept paid confidantes who sometimes lived at her apartment and suited their mood to hers. She was inclined to complicate life for her female executives by including them in this group. Some did not mind the 24 hour assignment. "You go to lovely dinners; she takes you to the opera; she might even suddenly take you off to Europe," one observed. "It's fun while it lasts." "She prides herself on the personal interest she takes in her employees, whom she calls, "my family." Included in it were salesgirls, for in the cosmetic business the girls behind the department-store cosmetic counters usually were employed by the manufacturers, not the store. An ex-Arden executive and long-time companion told of "the intimate and thoughtful" presents Miss Arden sent these girls.

Why Florence Graham chose Elizabeth Arden as her business name may also shed more light on this exceptional woman who once said in an interview in *Saturday Evening Post,* "There's only one Elizabeth like me and that's the Queen." Although, biographers agree that "Arden" came from Tennyson's poem, "Enoch Arden," Arden may have appreciated the title's pun rather than the poem's lyricism, for she loved gardens. In fact, the "Elizabeth" is said to have come from her reading *Elizabeth and Her German Garden,* a turn-of-the-century diary about the restorative power women may find by retreating alone to a beautiful country setting. The optimistic sensuality may have infected Arden for she remarked in the *Saturday Evening Post:* "Brought back my childhood with a rush and all the happy days I spent in a garden.... It was the beginning of my real life, my coming of age as it were, and entering into my kingdom.... I vowed myself then and there to nature, and have been happy ever since." Of course, another theory, equally believable, is that Arden chose "Elizabeth" simply because that name was already on the door of her recently purchased shop and she refused to pay the extra cost to have it removed and another name applied.

Arden's bold presence in American society opened many doors for women. She proved that it is possible to play by one's own rules and succeed. She understood what her customers needed and wanted, sometimes even before the customers themselves knew, and she understood that what millions of American women wanted was to feel beautiful.

References:

Bauer, Hambla. *Saturday Evening Post,* 24 April 1948.
Cover article in *Time,* 4 May 1946.
Mothers of Invention, New York: William Morrow, 1989.

—Cecily M. Barrie

Reinaldo Arenas

1943-1990

Cuban novelist

Reinaldo Arenas, from an impoverished background, found his voice as a novelist within the Cuban Revolution. In turn he tried to use that new strength to transform and liberate homosexuality inside literature, inside Cuba, and throughout the world.

Born 16 July 1943, on a farm between Holguín and the port of Gibrara in eastern Cuba, Arenas remembered as a child seeing his father (Antonio Arenas) only once and being reduced to eating dirt out of hunger. His mother, Oneida Fuentes, lived with her father. In 1958 Reinaldo joined the revolutionary forces who captured Gibrara. After Castro took power, the boy received a scholarship to study agriculture, worked on a chicken farm and, in 1962, won a scholarship to the University of Havana.

In 1964 Arenas took a job at the National Library where he could write. He soon completed his first novel, *Celestino antes del alba,* which received a prize in 1965 and publication in 1967. (It was revised in 1980 as *Cantando en el pozo* and translated as *Singing from the Well*, 1987). While the government published Arenas' writing, his style, like that of his mentor José Lezama Lima, ran counter to socialist realism. After the notorious Congress on Education and Culture (1971) harassment against writers and homosexuals increased.

Refused publication, Arenas illegally smuggled manuscripts abroad. His second novel *El mundo aluciante* (1969; published as *Hallucinations*, 1971; revised and retitled *The Ill-Fated Peregrinations of Fray Servando*, 1987) appeared in Mexico, Barcelona and Paris and received the *Le Monde* prize for the best foreign novel in 1969. In 1973, arrested for "ideological divergence," Arenas went to prison but escaped and became a fugitive until thrown into the notorious Morro Castle. His novel *Arturo, La estrella más brillante* (1984, "The Brightest Star" in *Old Rosa, A Novel in Two Stories*, 1989) recounts the contradictions of concentration camps for homosexuals in revolutionary Cuba. After accepting a "Political Rehabilitation Plan," he received probation. Arenas cleverly managed to escape Cuba by falsifying his papers. On 5 May 1980, he joined refugees who left the Cuban port of Mariel for Florida.

After leaving Cuba, Arenas spent ten hectic years gathering scattered manuscripts, rewriting them and writing more. His most ambitious project, the *Pentagonía (Pentagon)* cycle of five novels marks one of his many triumphs. The Pentagon cycle traces the peregrinations of a constantly resurrected hero. The cycle begins with *Singing from the Well,* which offers harsh details of rural poverty. Censors objected to the second Pentagon novel—*El palacio de las blanquísimas mofetas* (published 1975 in French translation; 1980 in Spanish; *The Palace of the White Skunks*, 1990). The portrait of Batista resembled Castro and the work celebrated sex between men. Cuban officials destroyed the first version of the *Palace* manuscript. Later volumes appeared only after the 1980 exile. The third Pentagon novel (*Otra vez el mar*, 1982, *Farewell to the Sea,* 1986) followed Ishmael down to the sea in search of tricks. The final two Pentagon novels—*El color del verano* (1991, *The Color of Summer*) and *El asalto* (1991; *The Assault*, 1994)—appeared posthumously. *The Assault* ends with sexual congress between Arenas and Castro who turns into the virgin Mary on the eve of her immaculate conception.

Arenas committed suicide 7 December 1990, in New York City. In a press release, he wrote: "Cuba will be free. I already am."

Reinaldo Arenas' remarkable novels may have overshadowed his other writings. Arenas wrote many poems, collected in *Leprosorio: Trilogía poética* (1990). The Gay Sunshine Press translated three of his short stories in *This Deep Dark Pain Called Love* (1983); many more have been published in Spanish in *Con los ojos cerrados* (1972) republished as *Termina el desfile* (1981). Likewise his plays await translation and study. His anti-Castro writings have received considerable attention outside Cuba: *Necessidad de libertad* (1986); *Voluntad de vivir manifestándose* (1989), and *Un plebiscito a Fidel Castro* (1990). The latter challenged Castro to hold a plebiscite (like that in Chile) to determine the future of Cuba.

Arenas' sexual politics rests on an ironic view of history. The energy relieved in the revolution actually increased sexual activity between men. In *El color del verano (The Color of Summer)* Arenas shows how sexualities can unfold inside restrictive environments. Within the sexual liberation of the United States, Arenas found that homosexuals had less sex, less fun, and more isolation than in Cuba. He rejected the simple notion that AIDS developed from sexual promiscuity and argued that the disease originated (if it was not invented) in the United States. Some of his most explicitly sexual work has not found ready publication in English.

Ante que anochezca: Autobiografía, (1992; *Before Night Falls: A Memoir,* 1993) dramatically capped his career. Arenas weaves together his political, sexual, intellectual, and magical history. Naked, brutal and uncompromising, he leaves the reader gasping, astonished, and grateful for the illumination of his life. Opposing Castro, Arenas, nonetheless, carried within himself revolutionary ideals. He declared, "I have always considered it despicable to grovel for your life as if life were a favor."

References:

Epps, Brad. "Proper Conduct: Reinaldo Arenas, Fidel Castro, and the Politics of Homosexuality" in *Journal of the History of Sexuality,* October 1995: 231-283.

Lumsden, Ian. *Machos, Maricones and Gays: Cuba and Homosexuality.* Philadelphia: Temple University Press, 1996.

Paulson, Michael G. *The Youth and The Beach: A Comparative Study Of Thomas Mann's Der Tod In Venedig (Death In Venice) and Reinaldo Arenas' Otra vez el mar (Farewell To The Sea).* Miami: Ediciones Universal, 1993.

Soto, Francisco. *Reinaldo Arenas: The Pentagonía.* Gainesville: University Press of Florida, 1994.

—Charles Shively

Dorothy Arzner

1900-1979

American filmmaker

Dorothy Arzner was one of the top film directors of her time and the only woman director in Hollywood during the 1930s. Beginning her career as the era of silent films was coming to a close, Arzner smoothly made the transition to sound films, directing for Hollywood studios and working with many of the industry's biggest stars, including Clara Bow, Katharine Hepburn, Merle Oberon, and Rosalind Russell. According to Ally Acker, author of *Reel Women,* "Dorothy Arzner was, and still is, the only American woman to develop a substantial body of work in the mainstream Hollywood system. What's more remarkable is that Arzner never sold herself, or the integrity of her screen characters, short in order to accomplish her remarkable task."

Dorothy Arzner

Born on 3 January 1900 in San Francisco, Arzner grew up in Los Angeles, where her father owned a restaurant frequented by many Hollywood celebrities. After finishing high school, she enrolled at the university of Southern California with the hope of becoming a doctor. During World War I, she left school to work for an ambulance corps but was never sent into the field. When the war ended, she decided against returning to her studies and, after a visit to a film studio, decided to pursue a career as a film director.

"Sometimes," Arzner told interviewers a number of years later, "I think pride is the greatest obstacle to success. A silly false pride, that keeps people from being willing to learn, from starting at the bottom no matter how far down it may be, and learning every step of the way up. When I went to work in a studio, I took my pride and made a nice little ball of it and threw it right out the window."

Arzner did indeed start at the very bottom of her profession: she went to the noted, flamboyant film director Cecil B. De Mille and applied for a job as a script girl. De Mille hired her, and within six months she was reassigned to work as a film cutter at a Paramount subsidiary, a job she later maintained taught her more about filmmaking than any other she held. She was then promoted to film editor at Paramount, her first assignment being the renowned classic *Blood and Sand,* starring Rudolph Valentino. As before, she quickly mastered the job and was soon receiving accolades for the quality of her work. During this period, Arzner also began writing film scripts, sometimes in collaboration with others.

Ambitious and energetic, Arzner always took the initiative to make things happen. In 1927 she was ready to make things happen by accepting an offer from another studio. When De Mille heard that she was planning to leave Paramount, he offered her the the job of director on the melodrama *Fashions of Women.* Arzner later joked, "I had not directed anything before. In fact, I hadn't told anyone to do anything before."

Nevertheless, *Fashions* was a hit. One paper's headline read: "Triumph for Star and Woman Director." Arzner had learned her craft inside and out and, with her directorial debut, was able to demonstrate her prodigious skills. *Fashions for Women* won first prize for directing at London's International Festival of Women's Films. Arzner directed twenty more films and, despite her gender, garnered respect within the filmmaking community. Some say her androgynous appearance helped her fit in as "one of the boys," but Arzner was fully aware that whether she was accepted by them or not, she would never fully have the support that the male directors gave each other.

In 1929 Arzner made Paramount's first sound film, *Wild Party,* with Clara Bow and Frederic March. The film is also notable for its depiction of supportive female friendships. Within the confines of traditional film genres and plots, Arzner sought to undo stereotypes of women and to present them as autonomous, rational creatures. In the 1933 film *Christopher Strong,* for example, Katharine Hepburn plays a fiercely independent aviator. Another of Arzner's notable films is *Craig's Wife,* in which she directed Rosalind Russell in a highly acclaimed performance as a frustrated, vengeful housewife.

Arzner insisted on doing her films her own way. She would sooner pass a film along to another director than be influenced—or pressured—to direct it a certain way. The freedom to reject of accept a film, and the assurance that, once she accepted it, she could do it her way was made certain when she left Paramount in 1933 to pursue a freelance directing career.

After working on the 1943 film *First Comes Courage,* in which Merle Oberon plays a member of the Norwegian underground working to defeat Nazi troops, Arzner retired from directing. She subesquently became involved in the production of training films for WACs and later established the first filmmaking course at the Pasadena Playhouse. She also filmed Pepsi commercials at the request of Joan Crawford and taught in the University of California's film department. She died at the age of 82 in her desert home in La Quinta, California.

Although respected by her peers, Arzner did not receive the recognition many felt she deserved for several decades. However, as the accomplishments of women were reassessed in the 1970s, Arzner's work was rediscovered. In 1972, *The Wild Party* was featured at the First International Festival of Women's Films in New York City. The second festival featured a full retrospective of her works. Also, in June 1975, four years before her death, the Director's Guild of America in staged a tribute to Dorothy Arzner.

References:

Acker, Ally. "The Sound Era: Dorothy Arzner," in her *Reel Women: Pioneers of the Cinema 1896 to the Present.* New York: Contiuum, 1992.

—Andrea L.T. Peterson

W. H. Auden

1907-1973

British writer

W. H. Auden quickly established himself as the leading British poet of the 1930s, and during and after the Second World War he won a reputation in the United States as well. In his work, he rejected the fragmented Modernism of T. S. Eliot's celebrated poem *The Waste Land* (1922) and employed regular verse forms, often with rhyme; but he nonetheless achieved, in the 1930s, a distinctively modern style, rhythmically vibrant, resourceful in its fusion of colloquial and erudite terms, and knowing and witty in tone. His poems in that decade were alert to the contemporary world and to the current concerns of the young intelligentsia; he created an imaginative landscape, made up of elements like frontiers, railways, helmeted airmen, abandoned mines, and rusting machinery, which seemed appropriate to a period of technological advance and economic depression; he registered the political turmoils of the period, drew upon Marx and Freud, and engaged, in a coded way, with the emotional complexities of gay relationships. From the end of the 1930s up to his death, however, Auden's poetry took on a more cautious and Christian tone, stressing what he saw as human limits and repudiating the socially and politically activist attitude which he and his fellow poets had held in their youth.

Wystan Hugh Auden was born in the ancient cathedral town of York, England, on 21 February 1907, the third and last son of a doctor and a pious Anglo-Catholic mother. In 1908, when Auden was one and a half, the family moved to Birmingham in the industrial Midlands, where Auden's father had been appointed as the city's first School Medical Officer. Auden's parents sent their eight-year-old son to St. Edmund's preparatory school, Surrey, in 1915; there, he befriended a fellow pupil who was later to become known as the novelist Christopher Isherwood. At the age of 13, in 1920, Auden moved on to Gresham's School at Holt in Norfolk. While the ethos of some English schools unofficially encouraged homosexuality, Gresham's induced sexual guilt; nonetheless, in his fifteenth year, Auden began to feel attracted to a schoolmate, Robert Medley, although they became friends rather than lovers. Auden also found a mentor in a 26-year-old newspaper subeditor, Michael Davidson, who fell for him passionately. Auden rejected his advances, later claiming that this was because he found Davidson unattractive, but Davidson continued to give Auden books and provide constructive criticism of his youthful poetry; Auden recalled him as a valued mentor.

Auden had originally intended to study science at Oxford but soon switched to English. He quickly established a reputation as a poet and personality among his contemporaries, who included Stephen Spender, Louis MacNeice and Cecil Day-Lewis, all to become well-known poets themselves. It was Spender who privately printed Auden's first collection of poems in 1928. At Oxford, Auden was twice co-editor of the student anthology *Oxford Poetry;* he also took a particular interest in Anglo-Saxon and Middle English poetry, the robustness of which informed his own work. In contrast to Gresham's, the climate of Oxford was favourable to homosexuality at this time, and licensed Auden to gratify his desires; for a time, he promiscuously pursued sexual adventures and experiments with fellow students and casual pick-ups. Despite his newfound freedom, however, he still felt some guilt about his sexuality.

Having taken a third-class degree, Auden left Oxford in 1928 and stayed for a time in Berlin, where Isherwood was making a living as an English teacher. Together they explored the erotic and cultural excitements which the German city had to offer. In 1929, however, Auden came back to England to look for work as a schoolmaster and to try to make his name as a poet.

Auden and the 1930s

In 1930, the prestigious publishing house of Faber, where T. S. Eliot was poetry editor, brought out Auden's *Poems.* This was followed by *The Orators* (1932), *The Dance of Death* (1933), and *Look, Stranger!* (1936). These volumes secured Auden's reputation as England's most notable young poet. Among the most memorable poems from the 1930s are "A Summer Night, 1933," in which the sensuous evocation of warmth and friendship contrasts with an apprehension of impending violence; and "Lay your Sleeping Head," a lyric in which love is affirmed in full awareness of its transience. Although the lover for whom the poem was written was a teenage boy, the poem itself contains no indication of the gender of the person whom it addresses. This was characteristic of Auden's approach to love poetry, which he maintained should be universally applicable, irrespective of sexual preference.

Throughout the 1930s, Auden continued to visit Isherwood in Germany, where their pleasures were overshadowed by their awareness of the growth of Fascism. In this period, the two men were often lovers, but their relationship was based more on close friendship and literary collaboration than on intense emotional attachment. Together they wrote *The Dog beneath the Skin* (1935), *The Ascent of F6* (1936), and *On the Frontier* (1938), plays which combine verse, songs, and prose, and show the influence of the early work of Bertolt Brecht and Kurt Weill. Rupert Doone's Group Theatre, with which Auden had become linked in 1932, put these plays on the stage.

Auden's visit to Germany in 1935 led to his marriage of convenience to Erika Mann, the eldest daughter of the novelist Thomas Mann, in order to provide her with a British passport so that she could escape the Nazis. In the same year, Auden began to work for the film unit of the British GPO (General Post Office) and got to know the composer Benjamin Britten. Auden's most famous contribution to the work of the film unit was the rhythmically compelling poem *Night Mail,* for the classic 1936 documentary of the same name; Britten wrote the score, and was to set many of Auden's poems to music. Auden later wrote the libretto for Britten's opera *Paul Bunyan,* first performed in 1941. With Louis MacNeice, Auden went to Iceland in 1936, and they produced the book *Letters from Iceland* (1937); this includes Auden's long, witty poem *Letter to Lord Byron,* written in the style of Byron's *Don Juan* (1819-24), but updated to the modern world. The Spanish Civil War, a key event for many writers in the 1930s, took Auden to Spain for two months in 1937, where he worked as an ambulance driver; though sympathetic to the Republicans, their repression of religion shocked him, and, on his return, he wrote the poem "Spain," a complex meditation on politics, commitment, and violence, which he later revised and, for a time, tried to suppress. A visit with Isherwood to China in 1938, at the time of the Japanese invasion, resulted in their joint book *Journey to a War* (1939).

Auden in America

In January 1939, Auden and Isherwood set sail for the United States. Some people in Britain saw their departure as an act of

W. H. Auden

desertion and their reputation would suffer for some time to come. Two poems written in this year, "In Memory of W. B. Yeats" and "September 1st, 1939," were significant both for their technical accomplishment and for the way in which they signalled Auden's changing view of the poet's role, from that of political activism to the celebration of human life in the face of death and despair.

At first, Auden and Isherwood lived in New York; but soon Isherwood set off for California, where he was to meet Don Bachardy and spend the rest of his life. At a New York literary discussion in April 1939, Auden had met the 18-year-old Chester Kallmann, who was to become his own partner, although their relationship was not always easy. Between 1946 and 1947, Auden also had an affair with a woman, Rhoda Jaffe; this seems to have been his last heterosexual excursion, though he continued to get on well with women in other ways. Auden found the United States friendly and rich: he earned his living by journalism, giving readings, and university teaching.

Wartime collections of poetry by Auden included *Another Time* (1940), and *The Double Man* (1941), published in the United Kingdom as *New Year Letter;* this verse missive reiterated Auden's rejection of political activism and expressed his growing sense of human frailty. *For the Time Being: A Christmas Oratorio* (1944) was dedicated to his mother, who had died in 1941; the volume also contained *The Sea and the Mirror,* a complex and fascinating set of dramatic monologues based on Shakespeare's play *The Tempest.* In these years, Auden began to move back to his mother's Christian faith and to attend church regularly; he was aware of a contradiction between the edicts of his religion and his sexual preference, but he did not let this inhibit his sexual activities.

Auden built up his American reputation, receiving a Guggenheim Fellowship in 1942 and the Poetry Prize of the American Academy of Arts and Letters in 1945. Despite his departure from England, he had always made it clear that he was ready to help the war effort, and in 1945 he obtained a job, which carried the honorary rank of Major, with the Morale Division of the US Strategic Bombing Survey. He went to Germany to write a report for the Pentagon on the psychological effects of bombing on the civilian population. Returning to America, he moved into an apartment in Greenwich Village with Kallmann and, in May 1946, he became a U.S. citizen. The year 1947 saw the publication of a dramatic work combining verse and prose, *The Age of Anxiety: A Baroque Eclogue.* Reviewers received it poorly, but it won a Pulitzer Prize and prompted Leonard Bernstein to write a symphony with the same title. Auden continued to live in America in the early 1950s, and to produce collections of poems such as *Nones* (1951) and *The Shield of Achilles* (1955); the latter has often been seen as his finest single volume. He also wrote a number of librettos, most notably, with Kallmann, for Stravinsky's *The Rake's Progress* in 1951.

England Again

As the 1950s progressed, and Auden consolidated his reputation as a poet, the stigma of his wartime absence started to fade in England. His reentry into the English literary scene was confirmed when he became Professor of Poetry at Oxford in 1956, a part-time office achieved by winning an election in which all Oxford MAs can vote. He remained in the post for the statutory five years and was a popular figure at the university, holding court in a local cafe and giving readings and lectures. A further volume of poetry, *Homage to Clio,* appeared in 1960, while *The Dyer's Hand* of 1962 was a lively and wide-ranging collection of essays and lectures.

In the 1960s, however, Auden found himself out of sympathy with the libertarian, anarchic, and revolutionary currents which were swelling in that decade. He came to be seen as increasingly reactionary, a view reinforced by his *Collected Shorter Poems* (1966), *Collected Longer Poems* (1968), and *Collected Poems* (1976), over which he exercised strong editorial control, suppressing or extensively revising his earlier work to repress his radical past. *The English Auden,* which came out in 1977, provided a partial antidote, in that it contained the original versions of his early poetry and of some prose.

In contrast to his old friend and lover Isherwood, who vigorously supported gay causes and used the new freedoms to write frankly of his and Auden's amorous adventures in *Christopher and His Kind* (1977), Auden was ambivalent about gay liberation. When lecturing or giving readings at universities, he was always ready to talk to homosexual student societies; but he did not declare his sexual preference in the wider public sphere and he would not let one of his poems appear in an anthology of gay verse. He was very upset by the unauthorised publication in the mid-1960s of his gay pornographic poem "The Platonic Blow."

When Auden returned to Oxford in 1972, to live in a cottage provided by his old college, Christ Church, he seemed a sad and neglected figure, disliked by some dons and no longer much sought out by students and younger poets. Nonetheless, he spent much of his later life in Oxford; but he especially enjoyed staying with Kallmann at their house in Kirchstetten in Austria, and *About the House* (1965) is an homage to their life together there. The last volumes published in his lifetime were *City without Walls* (1969), *Academic Graffiti* (1971), and *Epistle to a Godson* (1972). On 28 September 1973, after giving a poetry reading in Vienna, he returned to his hotel and went to bed; the next morning, Kallmann found him dead, of a heart attack.

Since Auden's death, critics have brought a range of fresh perspectives to bear on his work, and his reputation has revived. The increased interest in modern criticism in the relationship between politics and literature has brought about an upward estimate of his 1930s work. He has also been read in poststructuralist terms, as a poet whose work puts into play the idea of the fixed, stable self. Recent biographies by Charles Osborne, Humphrey Carpenter, and H. P. T. Davenport-Hines have dealt frankly with his sexuality, and literary criticism can no longer ignore it as it once did; although there is still intense debate as to how far it should affect the interpretation of his poems, as can be seen from the 1991-92 dispute between Laurence Lerner and Alan Sinfield in the journal *New Literary History*. Auden has also, unexpectedly, found a wide popular audience, through the inclusion of "Funeral Blues," one of his lyrics from the 1936 play *The Ascent of F6,* in the hit film *Four Weddings and a Funeral* (1994)—a film which places the lyric in an explicitly homoerotic context, since it is read aloud by a gay man at the funeral of his partner. As a result of the interest aroused by the film, Auden's publishers brought out a booklet of his 1930s poems and songs, *Tell Me the Truth about Love,* which has enjoyed extensive sales. Auden's complete works are now being published in eight volumes, and it seems likely that interest in him will continue into the next century; but his position as one of the twentieth century's most vivid and provocative poets is already secure.

References:

Carpenter, Humphrey. *W. H. Auden: A Biography.* Oxford: Oxford University Press, 1992.

Clark, Thekla. *Wystan and Chester: A Personal Memoir of W. H. Auden and Chester Kallmann.* London: Faber, 1995.

Cunningham, Valentine. *British Writers of the Thirties.* Oxford: Oxford University Press, 1988.

Davenport-Hines, H. P. T. *Auden.* London: Heinemann, 1995.

Hynes, Samuel. *The Auden Generation: Literature and Politics in England in the 1930s.* London: Bodley Head, 1976.

Isherwood, Christopher. *Christopher and His Kind: 1929-1939.* London: Eyre Methuen, 1977.

Kermode, Frank. *History and Value: The Clarendon Lectures and the Northcliffe Lectures 1987.* Oxford: Clarendon Press, 1989.

Lerner, Laurence. "A Response to Alan Sinfield," in *New Literary History* (Charlottesville, Virginia), vol. 23, 1992: 214-16.

———. "Unwriting Literature," in *New Literary History* (Charlottesville, Virginia), vol. 22, 1991: 795-815.

Osborne, Charles. *W. H. Auden: The Life of a Poet.* London: Eyre Methuen, 1980.

Sinfield, Alan. *Cultural Politics—Queer Reading.* Philadelphia: University of Pennsylvania Press, 1994.

———. *Literature, Politics and Culture in Postwar Britain.* Berkeley: University of California Press, 1989.

———. "'Reading Extraneously': A Reply to Laurence Lerner," in *New Literary History* (Charlottesville, Virginia), vol. 23, 1992: 213-14.

Smith, Stan. *Auden.* London: Northcote House, 1995.

—Nicolas Tredell

Francis Bacon

1909-1992

British artist

Francis Bacon is the most powerful and controversial painter to emerge from postwar Britain. His images of distorted, mutilated, melting, bleeding, screaming, caged, and confined flesh are potent incarnations of the human condition in the 20th century, modern versions of the Crucifixion in a world without resurrection or redemption. The terrible beauty of his paintings both repels and allures. Their contradictory nature echoes what Bacon himself once called, in a telegram reproduced in Daniel Farson's 1993 biography, his "gilded gutter life." Even though his postwar rise to fame brought him great wealth and enabled him to indulge his tastes for good clothes, gambling, oysters, and champagne, he continued to live like a bohemian, working in cramped, chaotic studios and spurning possessions and honours; for instance, he refused to accept the Queen's offer of both a knighthood and an Order of Merit.

Francis Bacon was born in Dublin, Ireland, on 28 October 1909. A descendant of the celebrated Elizabethan essayist and philosopher whose name he shared, he was the second of five children of English parents. His father, a former soldier who had fought in the Boer War and still held the title of Honorary Major, was a breeder and trainer of racehorses; his mother was heiress to a steelworks and a coal mine. When war broke out in 1914, the Bacon family went to London, where his father joined the War Office. They did not settle into a permanent home, however, but continued to move between Britain and Ireland, changing houses every year or so. World War I, and the armed struggle for independence in Ireland, contributed to a climate of violence in Bacon's formative years.

As a child, Bacon suffered badly from asthma, which was to plague him throughout his life and sharpen his sense of the proximity of death. His formal education was sparse; his parents sent him to only one small school, in Cheltenham, but he kept running away. Andrew Sinclair's 1992 biography quotes Bacon's claim that he "read almost nothing as a child" and was "hardly aware that [pictures] existed." The lads and grooms in his father's stables, however, handled his sexual initiation. He did not get on with his parents, who saw him as an effeminate drifter, and in 1925, when his father discovered him dressing in his mother's underwear, he turned him out of the house.

With an allowance of £3 a week from his parents, the 16-year-old Bacon lived a bohemian life in London; he moved from one rented room to another, sometimes leaving with the rent unpaid, and worked for brief periods as a solicitor's manservant, and in an office. In 1927, he went to Berlin for about three months, where he found the combination of sexual freedom, and emotional and sometimes physical violence, both stimulating and shocking. According to Sinclair, it was in Berlin that Bacon first saw Eisenstein's film *Battleship Potemkin* (1925), and he would later acknowledge the impact on his imagination of the close-up of the screaming nurse on the Odessa Steps, of whom he was to paint a *Study* in 1957. From Berlin, he moved on to France in 1928; at the Musée Condée in Chantilly, he encountered another harrowing scream, in Poussin's painting *The Massacre of the Innocents*. A secondhand medical textbook picked up on the Paris *quais* impressed him with its beautiful handcoloured plates of mouth diseases. It was, however, a Picasso exhibition at the Paul Rosenberg gallery in 1928 that made him feel that he himself might become an artist. He started to make drawings and watercolours, but at this time he was more actively studying interior decoration and furniture design, for which he received occasional commissions.

Bacon came back to London in 1929, and held an exhibition, in his Queensbury Mews studio, of furniture and rugs he had designed. He started to paint in oils, taking no formal instruction, but learning by trial and error. Roy de Maistre, an Australian artist and designer who was four years Bacon's senior, but who shared with the younger man a horse-breeding background and a lack of schooling, became Bacon's friend and mentor, and introduced him to potential patrons. In 1930, they set up an exhibition in Bacon's studio of furniture, paintings, and gouaches.

Bacon moved to the Fulham Road in 1931, and his work as a designer trailed off as he devoted his energy to painting; he survived financially by doing odd jobs, by gambling, and, in his own words as quoted in Sinclair's biography, by "petty theft" and by "living off people." His artistic career seemed likely to prosper when a reproduction of his painting *Crucifixion*, in Herbert Read's 1933 book *Art Now*, prompted Sir Michael Sadler to buy the picture by telegram. In the same year, Freddie Mayor included Bacon's work in two exhibitions at his new Cork Street gallery. Bacon himself followed this up with his first one-man exhibition in 1934, at what he called the Transition Gallery in the basement of Sunderland House in London. But attendance was poor and no pictures were sold. Further discouragement came with the rejection of work he had submitted to the 1936 International Surrealist Exhibition for which his work was judged insufficiently surreal. In 1937, he took part in an exhibition at London's Agnew Gallery, where his fellow exhibitors included Graham Sutherland, Victor Pasmore, and Ivon Hitchens, but only one of his pictures found a buyer. At the end of the 1930s, he remained an obscure and impoverished artist, who had not yet found a distinctive style of his own.

Postwar Breakthrough

Due to his asthma, Bacon was declared unfit for military service in World War II. He left London during the Blitz for a rented cottage in Petersfield, Hampshire, where he started to paint again. When the air raids eased in 1942, he came back to London, and took a studio in Kensington which had once belonged to Sir John Everett

Millais, the famous Victorian painter. Bacon served for a time as an Air Raid Warden, but made no other direct contribution to the war effort. His social and sexual life at this time was lived in the raffish, bohemian areas of central London known as Soho and Fitzrovia, where he drank in the Gargoyle Club and the York Minster (generally called the French Pub), and ate at Wheeler's Seafood Restaurant. While this ambience was congenial to him, he did not let it distract him from painting, which he began to focus on with more intensity; he destroyed most of his earlier work—only 10 of the paintings produced between 1929 and 1944 survived—and started to develop a distinctive manner of his own. It was in April of 1945, only a month before the end of the war in Europe, that London's Lefevre Gallery in London showed his triptych *Three Studies for Figures at the Base of a Crucifixion.* These images of grey, headless, screaming, bandaged mouths thrusting out from red backgrounds provoked distress and revulsion; they could be dismissed as products of a perverse imagination, but they could also appear to echo the anguish of a devastated Europe which was soon to see the horrors of Belsen in newsreels and photographs, and to learn of the dropping of the atom bomb.

Bacon had found his mature style; and his output and reputation started to grow. *Painting, 1946* showed the railings and carcasses which were to become keynotes of his art. His working methods were distinctive; in his crammed, untidy studio, he would paint on the unprimed back of the canvas rather than the front, using decorator's one-inch brushes and a plate for a palette. He believed in the crucial role of chance in painting. Both the Farson and Sinclair biographies quote Bacon's words in his introduction to the catalogue of Matthew Smith's 1953 retrospective exhibition: "painting today is pure intuition and luck and taking advantage of what happens when you splash the stuff down." Bacon also, however, affirmed the importance of formality and control and distanced himself from the American action painting of Jackson Pollock.

Bacon's dedication to painting did not inhibit his bohemian lifestyle; indeed, his new success encouraged it. With the £100 he received from the sale of *Painting, 1946*, he went to Monte Carlo, where he spent many nights gambling at roulette, sometimes winning large sums, sometimes losing everything. When in London, he continued to move in the Bohemian ambience of Soho and Fitzrovia, receiving £10 a week and free champagne for bringing wealthy patrons and friends to a drinking club called the Colony Room, which he would continue to frequent until his death.

In 1948 and 1949, Bacon started painting a series of heads, one of which, *Head VI* (1949), anticipated his famous "screaming pope" picture. The *Heads* were exhibited at a one-man show in 1949 at the Hanover Gallery in London, which acted as his agent for the next 10 years. In 1950, he taught briefly at the Royal College of Art, somewhat casually standing in for the artist John Minton, but otherwise he steered clear of any work other than painting. In his pictures of animal and human figures in this period, Bacon made use of the photographs by Eadweard Muybridge (1830-1904) collected in *Animals in Motion* and *Studies for the Human Figure in Motion*; a number of pictures of men wrestling, most notably *Two Figures* of 1953, doubled as coded images of men making love, in defiance of both the criminal law and the social and artistic codes of the time. It was also in 1953 that he produced his most memorable work: the *Study after Velazquez's Portrait of Pope Innocent X*, in which the Pope, sitting formally on his throne, is confined in a kind of glass cage, his face blurred by vertical brushstrokes, his mouth open in a scream. Among other notable work of this period was a series of portraits which pay tribute to an artist he much admired, Van Gogh.

It was in the 1950s that Bacon acquired an international reputation, exhibiting in New York, Venice, Paris, Turin, Milan and Rome. Confirmation of his status at home was provided by a retrospective exhibition at the Institute of Contemporary Arts in 1955. In 1958, he switched abruptly from the Hanover Gallery, which had handled his affairs since 1949, to Marlborough Fine Art. Marlborough's astute management of the sales of Bacon's increasingly valuable work were to make the painter a multi-millionaire.

Sadness and Success

Bacon's personal life in the 1950s had been marked by his passion for Peter Lacey, a gentlemanly ex-fighter pilot. Lacey introduced him to Tangiers, which Bacon liked for its sexual freedom and which he often visited between 1956 and 1959. Lacey's death in 1962 left Bacon grieving; but in the same year, Britain's premier gallery for modern art, the Tate, held a major retrospective of his work. In 1962 Bacon also painted his first large triptych, *Three Studies for a Crucifixion*, which New York's Guggenheim Museum bought. It followed this in 1963 with its own Bacon retrospective.

In 1963, Bacon began an affair with George Dyer, who became a model for many of his paintings. In 1964, he produced another large triptych, *Three Figures in a Room*, and a *Double Portrait* of the painters Lucian Freud and Frank Auerbach. A large *Crucifixion* followed in 1965. But personal sadness still shadowed professional success. In 1971, while a major Bacon retrospective was in progress at the Grand Palais, Paris, Dyer killed himself. His death prompted Bacon to paint a large *Triptych* in memory of him, and also influenced the three large pictures, sometimes known as the *Black Triptychs*, which he painted between 1972 and 1974. But his fame continued to grow. In 1977, when he attended a private view of an exhibition of his recent work in Paris, 7,000 people crammed the Galerie Claude Bernard and blocked the surrounding streets. Bacon was proud of his high standing in France, where two important studies of his work appeared: Michel Leiris's: *Francis Bacon ou la Vérité criante* in 1974, and Gilles Deleuze's *Francis Bacon: Logique de la Sensation* in 1981.

Bacon found a new and young love in the 1980s in John Edwards, the son of a London docker. Now in his seventies, he continued to produce notable paintings such as *Oedipus and the Sphinx after Ingres* (1983), *Study for Self-Portrait—Triptych* (1985-6), and *Study for Portrait of John Edwards* (1986). In the exhibition catalogue of the Tate Gallery's second retrospective in 1985, Director Alan Bowness, called Bacon "the greatest living painter," and Sinclair's biography quotes the claim of critic Brian Sewell, writing in the *Radio Times* of 10 November 1984, that "Bacon works in the tradition of a Renaissance master ... He deals with Renaissance themes of religious and temporal power, authority, corruption, conflict and lust." Not everyone shared Sewell's estimate; the Farson and Sinclair biographies both quote the former British Prime Minister, Margaret Thatcher, who reportedly once referred to Bacon as "that dreadful man who paints those horrible pictures." As it happened, Bacon shared many of Mrs. Thatcher's reactionary political views, but he did sign a protest against her government's Clause 28, a legislative measure designed to prevent local authorities from promoting homosexuality. He also made his contribution to Gorbachev's *glasnost*, agreeing to an exhibition of his work in Moscow in 1988, although he was annoyed that some of the more sexually explicit pictures were withdrawn.

Entering into his eighties, Bacon continued to live a bohemian life, though he became increasingly unwell. On 28 April 1989, he died quickly in Madrid, of a heart attack. According to Farson's biography, Bacon had once said: "[w]hen I'm dead, wrap me in a plastic bag and throw me in the gutter;" his cremation at Madrid's Almudena cemetery had a fitting simplicity. A few journalists were present, but no close friends; the only bouquet was of white and yellow roses from his drinking partners at the French Pub. His death hit the headlines worldwide, however, and brought many tributes—although, characteristically, acclaim was not universal.

Bacon's position as the most striking British painter of the later twentieth century is likely to stand. His only rival in terms of renown, David Hockney, has not, so far, tackled the themes of anguish and suffering with which Bacon was obsessed. Bacon's engagements with the torments, desires, cruelties and beauties of the flesh, and with the material substance of paint, still have the power to shock and compel, while his life remains exemplary in its dedication to art, chance, and the pursuit of pleasure.

References:

Ades, Dawn, and Andrew Forge. *Francis Bacon,* exhibition catalog. London: Tate Gallery and Thames and Hudson Ltd. New York: Abrams, 1985.

Deleuze, Gilles. *Francis Bacon: Logique de la Sensation*, 2 vols. Paris: Éditions de la Différence, 1981.

Farson, Daniel. *The Gilded Gutter Life of Francis Bacon*. London: Century Random House UK, 1993.

Gowing, Lawrence and Sam Hunter. *Francis Bacon*. London: Thames and Hudson, 1989.

Leiris, Michel. *Francis Bacon ou la Vérité criante*. Paris: Éditions Fata Morgana, 1974.

———. *Francis Bacon: Full Face and in Profile*. New York: Rizzoli, 1988.

Russell, John. *Francis Bacon*. London and New York: Thames and Hudson, 979.

Sinclair, Andrew. *Francis Bacon: His Life and Violent Times*. London: Sinclair-Stevenson, 1993.

Sylvester, David. *The Brutality of Fact: Interviews with Francis Bacon,* 3rd ed. London and New York: Thames and Hudson, 1987.

—Nicolas Tredell

Sara Josephine Baker

1873-1945

American physician and public health administrator

Sara Josephine Baker was a true public health pioneer. The first woman to receive a Ph.D. in public health, she became director of New York City's first child hygiene department. Her innovations in education for parents and preventive medicine for children drastically reduced infant mortality rates. Many of her methods were adopted around the world.

Sara Josephine Baker was born in Poughkeepsie, New York, on 15 November 1873, into a wealthy Quaker family. Her mother, Jenny Harwood Brown Baker, had been one of the first women to study at Vassar College; Orlando Daniel Mosser Baker, her father, was a lawyer. Baker (she used the name "S. Josephine" in later life, to avoid confusion with the famous dancer, Josephine Baker) was encouraged to develop her intellect and social conscience, but was also brought up to expect a conventional life as wife, mother, and homemaker. When she was 16, her father and brother both died in a typhoid epidemic, and Baker decided to study medicine.

After graduating from New York Women's Medical College in 1898, Baker interned in Boston at the New England Hospital for Women and Children. Here she had her first experience working with poor women and children, and found her life's work. She also found her first partner, Florence M. Laighton, another intern. Later, the two moved to New York City and set up a private medical practice, but women physicians were not widely accepted and they were not able to attract enough patients to earn a living. Baker went to work for the city department of health as a medical inspector in Hell's Kitchen, one of the city's worst slums.

Her job was to visit the tenements, looking for cases of infectious diseases including typhoid fever, smallpox, and dysentery. The tenements were filthy and poorly ventilated, the parents were ignorant of basic hygiene, and the babies were dying at a rate of 1500 per week. Baker and a team of nurses spread out over the area, teaching young mothers how to feed and clean their babies, encouraging breastfeeding, distributing pasteurized milk, and explaining the importance of proper ventilation. In one summer, the infant mortality rate in her area dropped to only 300 deaths per week.

Her success led to the establishment of an official Bureau of Child Hygiene, with Baker as director. It was the first tax-sup-

Sara Josephine Baker

ported child hygiene department in the world, and Baker had to develop programs and techniques with no models to follow. She also had to persuade the men in her department to take orders from a woman. (In protest of her first supervisory position with the department of health, her male staff had resigned *en masse* her first day on the job.) Nevertheless, the Bureau quickly established standards and practices for midwives, produced and distributed public health information pamphlets, instituted school tests for infectious diseases, and organized foster care for orphans. Baker invented the first foolproof container for the eye drops placed in newborn babies' eyes to prevent infant blindness; the standard containers then in use tended themselves to spread infection from one child to the next. She also designed patterns for sensible and hygienic infant clothing that were distributed by the hundreds of thousands by the McCall pattern company.

In 1915 she was invited to lecture at the New York University-Bellevue Hospital Medical School. She agreed only on the condition that she be allowed to enroll as a student as well. Her terms were refused—the School would not enroll a woman. A year later, having been unable to find another lecturer of her caliber, the University agreed to allow women into its doctor of public health program. Baker lectured for 15 years, in spite of a hostile reception from several of her male students. She earned her doctorate, and co-founded the College Equal Suffrage League.

Later in her life she served on the health committee of the League of Nations, and advised the U.S. Children's Bureau. She shared a home with the writer Ida Wylie and another physician, Louise Pearce. By the time she died in 1945, her procedures were credited with saving the lives of hundreds of thousands of babies.

References:

Baker, S. Josephine. *Fighting for Life*. New York: Krieger, 1939.

Peavey, Linda, and Ursula Smith. *Women Who Changed Things*. New York: Scribner's, 1983.

Russell, Paul. *The Gay 100: A Ranking of the Most Influential Gay Men and Lesbians, Past and Present*. New York: Citadel Press, 1995.

Vare, Ethlie Ann, and Greg Ptacek. *Mothers of Invention: From the Bra to the Bomb, Women and Their Unforgettable Ideas*. New York: William Morrow, 1987.

—Cynthia A. Bily

James Baldwin

1924-1987

African-American writer

It is nearly impossible to overestimate James Baldwin's importance as a public figure, a visionary, and a storyteller. The author of some two dozen books, Baldwin employed a wide range of voices and genres to tell his personal story and the story of his nation over the course of his prolific career. His six novels, seven collections of essays, and scattered short stories, plays, and poetry all attest to the value of a struggle. For his country, this struggle was the challenge to live up to its promise of liberty for all of its citizens. For Baldwin, it was the challenge to forge an identity as a gay, black man within this conflicted nation and to tell other beleaguered Americans not to lose sight of their nation's promise.

James Baldwin was born to Berdis Jones on 2 August 1924 in New York City's Harlem Hospital. His biological father left Berdis before James was born. His stepfather, David Baldwin, was a preacher and laborer who moved north from New Orleans in the early 1920s. One of nine children in the Baldwin household, James learned at an early age that the world was not always going to be fair to him. Growing up in Harlem during the Depression, he learned that, in fact, the world was going to be quite unfair to him. But, his strong sense of spirituality, his renowned talents as a writer, and the support of his family and friends enabled him to forge ahead in his search for the elusive promise of social equality and acceptance.

Educated initially at New York's P.S. 24 and later at Frederick Douglass Junior High School, Baldwin was singled out at a young age for his talents: oration, singing, and writing. At the age of 14 he discovered a talent for public speaking and gained notoriety as a young minister in several Harlem churches. Baldwin moved away from the impoverished community of his childhood when he was accepted to the mostly white, largely Jewish De Witt Clinton High School in the Bronx where he became active on the school's literary magazine. He tried to work through his divided loyalty between church and school in the poems, plays, and stories that he contributed to the magazine. His budding awareness of his homosexuality and his growing love of the arts caused Baldwin to leave his church in 1940.

Guided by two notable mentors—the poet Countee Cullen and the painter Beauford Delaney—Baldwin began to discover that possibilities existed in the arts for a black man to locate his identity. After graduating from Clinton, he eventually gravitated to Greenwich Village where he was able to experiment with his writing and with his sexuality. Throughout the late 1940s he pursued sexual experiences with both men and women, but few of these encounters led to long-term relationships. He also experimented with his writing; he published a handful of essays and reviews and a short story, but he stopped short of "facing his 'demons' head-on," as David Leeming points out in his biography of Baldwin.

The Artist in Exile

To face these *demons,* notably his sexuality and his troubled relationship with his stepfather, Baldwin did what many American writers had done a generation before: he went to Paris in 1948. There he wrote his first meditation on homosexuality in an essay entitled "The Preservation of Innocence" in which he writes of "the presence and passion of human beings, who cannot ever be labeled." It was also in Paris where he met Lucien Happersberger, a Swiss street boy of 17 who Baldwin later described as the love of his life. Over the next few years Baldwin came as close as he would ever come to fulfilling his dream of a domestic life and a monogamous relationship with a male lover. During this time, he was finally able to address his identity crisis in a prolific outburst of writing; he published a number of essays and completed his first novel, *Go Tell It on the Mountain.* The protagonist of this novel, John Grimes, strongly resembles the young Baldwin wrestling with his paternal and religious demons and emerging from the struggle as a strong, vital man ready to face more challenges. This powerful novel reflects Baldwin's claim in his 1955 essay "Autobiographical Notes" that: "One writes out of one thing only—one's own experience. Everything depends on how relentlessly one forces from this experience the last drop, sweet or bitter, it can possibly give."

Although it enabled him to resolve some personal conflicts through writing, his relationship with Lucien was far from perfect, as one can see from its fictional rendition in his second novel, *Giovanni's Room.* Virtually all of Baldwin's novels treat the topic of homosexuality to one degree or another, but *Giovanni's Room* is his most moving and extended meditation on the subject. Between his idyllic time with Lucien in Paris and Switzerland from 1949 to 1952 and the publication of *Giovanni's Room* in 1956, Baldwin traveled back and forth across the Atlantic, enjoying a reputation as a young writer of great renown from his first collection of essays, *Notes of a Native Son,* as well as from his first novel. His relationship with Lucien tapered off, and although some of his long-term attempts with subsequent lovers were somewhat successful, he never quite got over Lucien. Mirroring this difficulty in Baldwin's life, *Giovanni's Room* is a novel about the risks and vulnerabilities of love. Its protagonist, David, is an American living in Paris who leaves his fiancée for Giovanni. When he tells her of his plans to leave her, she tells him about love in a forceful manner reminiscent of Baldwin's days as a preacher:

> You never have loved anyone, I am sure you never will! You love purity, you love your mirror—you are just like a little virgin.... You will never let anyone *touch* it—man *or* woman. You want to be *clean.* You think you came here covered with soap and you think you will go out covered with soap—and you do not want to *stink.*

Unlike David, Giovanni is not afraid of "the stink of love," a quality which makes him a superior lover. Love requires risks, Baldwin believed, and it can only work if people aren't afraid of it. Baldwin's realization of the fact that love requires a willingness to open up had much to do with his own identity crises as a gay man in a straight world, as an unwanted stepson in a large family, and as an African American in a country dominated in every sense by its white majority population.

Baldwin and the Civil Rights Movement

In 1957 Baldwin returned for an extended time to the United States in order to confront directly the racial problems that plagued his native country. He traveled through the American South, visiting such landmarks as the Tuskegee Institute and meeting such notable figures as Martin Luther King, Jr. The Civil Rights Movement at this time was moving to the front burner, and Baldwin found his own anger coming to a slow boil. His struggle to determine his role in the movement is apparent from the title of his next collection of essays, *Nobody Knows My Name.* Race is a more prevalent topic than homosexuality in this book, but the two are related; as Baldwin himself writes in the introduction, "the question of color ... operates to hide the graver questions of the self."

The theme of the struggle for identity is present throughout his work, but it is especially evident in his writings from the early 1960s, notably his widely acclaimed novel *Another Country.* On one level, this book seems to do what his essay "Many Thousands Gone" had done a dozen years earlier—it readdresses the way that Richard Wright had written about racial injustice in his influential 1940 novel *Native Son.* Baldwin writes in this essay, "*Native Son* finds itself at length so trapped by the American image of Negro life and by the American necessity to find the ray of hope that it cannot pursue its own implications." Baldwin's goal in *Another Country* was to pursue these implications, by employing his victim Rufus Scott not as a "social symbol" like Wright's victim Bigger Thomas, but as a real person whose death allows the novel's other characters to examine their own identities. The other country of the title exists within all of us; Americans must go there in order to address the problems which plague their nation.

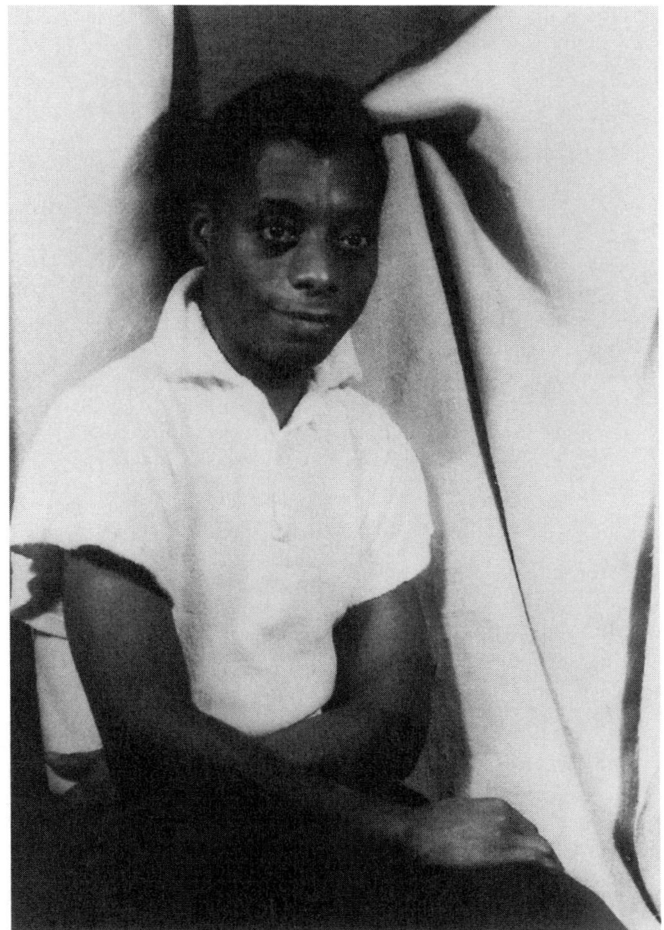

James Baldwin

Baldwin was justly famous by this point; his literary fame brought him in contact with writers like William Styron and Norman Mailer, actors like Sidney Poitier and Marlon Brando, and Civil Rights leaders like Malcolm X. Like Malcolm, Baldwin traveled to Africa in order to get a clearer sense of the movement, and when he returned he was prepared to throw himself into the thick of it as an activist both in the South and in New York. His new role as a spokesman landed him on the cover of *Time* on 17 May 1963; six days later he met with Attorney General Robert Kennedy to discuss the rising crisis of racial strife in America. His literature, notably his play "Blues for Mister Charlie," which was produced on Broadway in 1963, also addressed the most controversial racial issues of the time. Race and homosexuality were part and parcel of his nation's identity crisis because, Baldwin felt, Americans were plagued by their tendency to label everything and everyone and to stigmatize an Other.

Ironically, some members of the Civil Rights Movement were uncomfortable with Baldwin's homosexuality; Eldridge Cleaver attacked Baldwin's sexual preference in his best-seller *Soul on Ice*. Such attacks did nothing for Baldwin's confusion about his place within his country and within the Civil Rights Movement. On one level he craved acceptance; on another level he had to remain true to his own sense of self. At times he allied himself with Cleaver, the Black Muslims, and the Black Panthers; at other times he associated with King's non-violent approach to the problem. Baldwin was a writer who rejected labels on every level, and his refusal to be tied to any group within the Civil Rights Movement is not unlike his restlessness in his relationships. He created a character named Black Christopher in his 1968 novel *Tell Me How Long the Train's Been Gone* who seems to embody both his political and sexual interests. Yet Baldwin is more like the flawed protagonist of the novel, Leo Proudhammer, than he is like the idealized Black Christopher. The distance between Baldwin and his characters such as Black Christopher are testimony to his capacity for self-evaluation.

Different Directions

In the late 1960s and early 1970s Baldwin gradually became disillusioned with both his role in the Civil Rights Movement and his personal relationships. His health was also in decline; hepatitis and years of drinking had damaged his liver considerably. He was worn down both mentally and physically. He shuttled continuously between Paris, Istanbul, and New York, and the title of his next collection of essays, *No Name in the Street,* indicates that he remained aware of his identity crisis and his displacement. Some negative reviews of it contributed to his depression, which was also fueled by the death or deterioration of a few close friends. His next novel, *If Beale Street Could Talk,* was his most involved fictional depiction of the tribulations of Black America. He gained some comfort through this period from his relationship with the artist Yoran Cazac, to whom he dedicated *Beale Street.* By the time of his 50th birthday party in 1974, he was proud of his accomplishments and ready to move forward.

The next few years saw him complete *The Devil Finds Work,* an extended essay on America focusing on film history, and his ambitious final novel *Just Above My Head.* This novel begins, like *Another Country,* with the decline and death of a character and continues with other characters' reactions to this death. But *Just Above My Head*'s Arthur Montana is a celebrity and a homosexual, more obviously like Baldwin than *Another Country*'s Rufus Scott. Despite his failing health and the demands of this novel, Baldwin remained energetic through this period. He began and ended more personal relationships and embarked on a second career as an academic; he taught at Bowling Green University and at the five colleges in and around Amherst, Massachusetts well into the 1980s. His final work of nonfiction, *The Evidence of Things Not Seen,* focuses on the race problems that continued to haunt America in the 1980s. Although it was not as well received as earlier works, the intensity of *Evidence* proves how committed Baldwin was to social change even in his final years. When his health began to rapidly deteriorate in the mid-1980s he returned to the village of St.-Paul-de-Vence where he died of liver cancer in 1987. A whole nation mourned his passing at his funeral at the Cathedral of Saint John the Divine in New York, but they also celebrated his life. Like a blues song, the funeral was at once a record of sadness and an expression of both joy and hope for the future.

Many have paid tribute to Baldwin's courage, his vision, and his art. In a collection of essays entitled *James Baldwin: The Legacy,* edited by Quincy Troupe, Toni Morrison writes to Baldwin: "You knew, didn't you, how I needed your language and the mind that formed it? How I relied on your fierce courage to tame wildernesses for me?" Chinua Achebe adds: "As long as injustice exists ... the words of James Baldwin will be there to bear witness and to inspire and elevate the struggle for human freedom." Witness to a nation's errors, prophet of its future, and teller of its troubled stories, Baldwin remains one of the most inspirational authors of the twentieth century. In "Autobiographical Notes," Baldwin stated his simple goal: "I want to be an honest man and a good writer." He was all that and much, much more.

References:

Leeming, David A. *James Baldwin.* New York: Knopf, 1994.

Troupe, Quincy, editor. *James Baldwin: The Legacy.* New York: Simon and Schuster, 1989.

—D. Quentin Miller

Benjamin Banneker

1731-1806

African-American mathematician and astronomer

Benjamin Banneker is popularly known as the first African-American man of science, but he was a man of firsts in an even broader context. His passion for mathematics and fascination for time led to publication of one of the country's first almanacs. His early mechanical abilities led him to build a famous wooden clock. His penchant for astronomy paved the way for him to accurately predict a solar eclipse. His keen eye and problem-solving abilities had him assisting in the early surveying of what was to become Washington, D.C. And his drive for the abolition of slavery earned him a reputation worldwide as one of the first African-American men of letters to be accepted by the white establishment.

Banneker was born in Ellicott's Mills, Maryland with both black and white blood in his veins and what might be termed an "inherited predestiny" for speaking out against slavery. His maternal grandmother was an Englishwoman who, after purchasing a small plantation in America, bought two African slaves, liberated one, and married him. Her daughter, Benjamin's mother, likewise married a slave who assumed her surname. Benjamin was their only son.

He was instructed in reading and religion by his grandmother, attended one of the first integrated schools, and early on displayed an amazing aptitude for mathematics and all things mechanical. Although he was forced to cut his formal education short when he was old enough to work the family farm, he nonetheless pursued a youthful desire to better himself by reading any books he could get his hands on. "All his delight was to dive into books," biographer Silvio Bedini quotes classmate Jacob Hall as remembering.

As a young man of 22, he constructed a wooden clock with no previous training or instruction, thus signaling a passion for the workings and measurement of time that were to be reflected in his later almanacs. He applied his natural mechanical and mathematical abilities to diagrams of wheels and gears, and converted these into three-dimensional wooden clock-parts he carved with a knife. "His fame spread rapidly through the valley," Bedini noted, and "Banneker's own pleasure in it was equaled only by the wonder and astonishment of people who visited the farmhouse and saw it."

He took part all his life in a popular gentlemen's game of exchanging difficult math problems, and in 1773, began making astronomical calculations for almanacs at the urging of mill-owner George Ellicott. In the spring of 1789, he accurately predicted a solar eclipse, and in that same year, he was publicly recognized for his efforts by being appointed to the President's Capital Commission, the first African-American to receive such an honor.

Pungent Stings and Guilty Passions

Throughout his life, Banneker never married, and there is no evidence of his ever being romantically involved with a woman, a fact which has led many historians to speculate that he may have been homosexual. Some unwitting self-revelation is evident between the lines of some of his early essays, including one cited by Bedini where Banneker claims that poverty, disease and violence are more tolerable than the "pungent stings ... which guilty passions dart into the heart."

Banneker's self-isolation and love of drink is sometimes cited as at least a partial explanation for his lifelong bachelorhood. But his grandmother, parents, and sisters were known to be people of considerable Christian dominance, and he always lived under their supervision. His father died when Banneker was 28 years old, leaving him as the sole caretaker of farm and family. The responsibility, says Bedini, "he assumed with his customary seriousness [at] an age when he would have been seeking a wife." As he grew older, his reliance on the Bible as a daily guide to living may have hindered any natural homosexual tendencies.

Because Banneker was also familiar with the science of surveying, another completely self-taught discipline, he was enlisted in 1789 to assist Ellicott and Pierre Charles L'Enfant in laying plans for what was to become Washington, D.C. He made copious notes and calculations as required, and even used astronomical instruments he had helped design to establish base markers. Here he was, almost 60 years old, with no education beyond what he had arduously gleaned from borrowed books, participating in one of the greatest surveying projects in the new republic. It was also the first time he had wandered more than 50 miles from his birthplace, a trip which must have excited him. Alexandria, Virginia was one of the country's largest commercial centers, a rendezvous for sailors, merchants and travelers of all stripes. "The city," Bedini notes, "brought to life the magic world of history which he had found in his books, and his eyes and ears and mind were filled with a multitude of exciting impressions."

The Astronomer and Abolitionist

In 1790, Benjamin Banneker sold the carefully tended farm he had inherited from his father and devoted the rest of his life to publishing his works on astronomy, mathematics, and the abolition of slavery. Because Banneker was black and so obviously gifted, according to *The Alyson Almanac*, "the abolitionist movement often focused attention on him to emphasize the human potential that was suppressed by slavery." In 1791, he defended the intellectual equality of African-Americans in groundbreaking correspondence with then Secretary of State Thomas Jefferson.

Benjamin Banneker, 1980 commemorative stamp.

By the end of 1791, Banneker was publishing his almanac, which was greatly admired by Jefferson and was even sent to Paris for inclusion at the Academy of Sciences. The "African astronomer" as he was now popularly known became famous throughout Europe, though he remained characteristically humble and stayed close to home.

It was also during this period that the growing abolitionist societies, spurred on by the English Quakers, were desperately seeking candidates to demonstrate the Negro's intellectual achievements as justification for the legal establishment of equal rights. Banneker was a natural for the cause, and with the publication of his almanac assured, he began a correspondence with Thomas Jefferson on the politically explosive subject of the abolition of slavery. "He appears to have been the pioneer in the movement in this part of the world, towards the improvement of his race," biographer Bedini quotes from the papers of Banneker's neighbor Mary Ellicott Tyson, "at a period of our history when the negro occupied almost the lowest possible grade in the scale of human beings."

Benjamin Banneker continued to publish his works through the end of the century, producing a dissertation on bees, a study of locust-plague cycles, and more letters on segregationist trends in America. By the time it was sold in 1802, his almanac, based on a lifetime's study of the mathematical calculations he loved, was still going strong. He died in Boston in 1806, to the end a respected, yet humble, pioneer in matters of equal rights.

References:

The Alyson Almanac. Boston: Alyson Publications, 1994-95.

Bedini, Silvio A. *The Life of Benjamin Banneker.* New York: Charles Scribner's Sons, 1972.

Webster's New Biographical Dictionary. Springfield: Merriam-Webster, 1988: 74

White, James T. (ed). *The National Cyclopedia of American Biography,* 1894: 36.

Who Was Who in America—Historical Volume (1607-1896). Chicago: Marquis Publications, 1967.

—Jerome Szymczak

Ann Bannon

1932-

American novelist

Ann Bannon. ***Photograph by Tee A. Corinne.***

Ann Bannon is a pseudonym for one of the most popular "lesbian pulp" writers of the late 1950s and early 1960s, a period that saw a spate of drugstore novels with lesbian themes—some 350 titles by 1965. Most of these novels perpetuated self-destructive stereotypes and attracted heterosexual men with their lurid covers, but Bannon struggled to create characters who rose above their "tragic fate" to find identity and community. Her books (*Odd Girl Out, I Am a Woman, Women in the Shadows, Journey to a Woman, The Marriage, Beebo Brinker*) thus became prized possessions for lesbians looking for positive portraits of "all-American girls" who happened to prefer each other's company.

Kate Millett remembers treasuring her Bannon collection because, as she tells Andrea Weiss in *Before Stonewall,* "they were the only books where one woman kissed another." Bannon's stories are also notable for pioneering real characters and themes, such as a lesbian of color and a supportive relationship between a gay man and a lesbian who eventually raise a child conceived by artificial insemination.

Ann Bannon was born in September of 1932 in Joliet, Illinois and was raised in Hinsdale, a western suburb of Chicago. In 1954, she graduated Phi Beta Kappa from the University of Illinois with a major in French. She married that same year and moved with her husband to Philadelphia, where she began writing *Odd Girl Out.* In 1956, she and her husband moved to California, where a busy Bannon wrote five more books and had two daughters over the next several years.

In the mid-1960s, Bannon stopped writing and returned to college—first for a teaching credential, then for a Master of Arts degree from the California State University in Sacramento (CSUS), and finally for a Ph.D. in Linguistics from Stanford University in 1975. She started her hard-earned teaching career as a professor of linguistics in the English Department at CSUS in 1974, became a Program Coordinator in Liberal Studies in 1985, and is today an Associate Dean for Curriculum in the School of Arts and Sciences. In the midst of all this activity, has Bannon had time for any serious relationships since separating from her husband? "Yes, but they have been few ... and private," she recently told this writer.

Bannon's writing stands out because her pre-Stonewall portrayals helped establish a sense of lesbian community since their approach was more wholistic than others of the genre. Her six early works created an ongoing series of stories that scores of women could identify with. These were women who, according to Cathy Davidson in *The Oxford Companion to Women's Writing in the United States,* were "struggling against the restrictions placed on white middle-class girls of the 1950s ... they have illicit lesbian affairs and heterosexual sex without birth control, and try desperately to combat the pressure to fulfill traditional gender roles."

As Bannon's characters moved from scandalous college affairs to the bars of Greenwich Village and through troubled marriages, they became a tapestry of prototypes and feminist struggles a myriad of women could empathize with. Outgoing, vivacious Beth meets shy Laura in college; Laura moves to New York and falls in love with the young, butch Beebo Brinker; Beebo is brutally assaulted and raped; Laura meets a gay man, marries him, and has a baby by artificial insemination; Beth is trapped in an unhappy marriage and struggles to leave it; Beth seeks out Laura and, in the end, gets together with Beebo.

Some critics have faulted Bannon for what they feel are negative images of lesbians. "Titillating trash," Leigh Rutledge labels the books in *The Gay Decades,* "but indispensable reading to the nation's lesbians." Most critics, however, agree that Bannon's work underscores the legitimacy of the various and very difficult choices faced by women—leaving a family, coming out, creating a new family—in the context of tightly-closeted 1950s America. In the final analysis, Bannon's novels evidence one of the earliest challenges to "standard" sexual and gender identities by portraying butch/femme sensibility, "queer" families, and the sometimes brutal honesty of lesbian life as it was "back then." "Looking back from the mid-80s to the distant 50s and 60s," Bannon said in the forward to the reissue of *I Am a Woman* (1983), "the books as they stand have 50s flaws. But they speak truly of that time and place as I knew it ... if Beebo is really there for some of you—and Laura and Beth and the others—it's because I stayed close to what felt real and right."

All of Bannon's novels were reissued in the early 1980s by Tallahassee, Florida-based Naiad Press. "This is fantastic," Rutledge quotes one of Bannon's grown daughters as exclaiming when she realized her mother had been writing underground novels all those years. "Her other daughter—a born-again Christian—," Rutledge adds, "was not nearly as pleased over the revelation." Bannon has completed a new novel—still in need of reworking, she says—designed to carry Beebo Brinker into a more contemporary lesbian orbit. Her plans are to retire from academia in 1997 and finish the necessary editing. "Also in the works," she notes with enthusiasm, "is a fictionalized account of the life of Aphra Behn, the brilliant and spunky playwright and novelist of the Restoration period in England." Like Beebo and Beth, Bannon has come a long way from 1950s suburbia and the bars of Greenwich Village.

Current Address: c/o Naiad Press, P.O. Box 10543, Tallahassee, Florida 32302.

References:

Bannon, Ann. *I Am a Woman.* Tallahassee, Florida: Naiad Press, 1983.

Buck, Claire, ed. *The Bloomsbury Guide to Women's Literature.* New York: Prentice-Hall, 1992.

Davidson, Cathy N., ed. *The Oxford Companion to Women's Writing in the United States.* New York: Oxford University Press, 1995.

Rutledge, Leigh. *The Gay Decades.* Boston: Alyson Publications, 1992.

Weiss, Andrea. *Before Stonewall.* Tallahassee, Florida: Naiad Press, 1988.

—Jerome Szymczak

Djuna Barnes

1892-1982

American novelist, playwright, poet, and journalist

Djuna Barnes, who often described herself as "the most famous unknown in the world," was in fact a well-known writer in the bohemian communities of Greenwich Village and Paris from 1910 to 1930. Barnes was recognized for her sharp wit and quirky journalism, as well as her strange, dark fiction, plays, and poetry. She was also an illustrator, drawing ink or charcoal portraits of such illustrious models as James Joyce and Getrude Stein. Many of her colleagues deemed her writing the product of genius, but the general reading public often found it difficult and a bit morbid and perverse. Her most celebrated novel, *Nightwood,* which tells the story of betrayal between lovers Nora and Robin, has been described as a modernist masterpiece. This novel, like much of her work, has its roots in autobiography. In a 1971 interview with James B. Scott, Barnes admitted that "every writer writes out of his life." At the same time, however, Barnes was intensely private, resisting or refusing most attempts at interview or biography. She also resisted being classified in either her work or her personal life—a resistance that may account for her conflict with critics, scholars, and admirers who embraced her as a lesbian writer.

Djuna Chappell Barnes was born 12 June 1892 in Cornwall-on-Hudson, New York, to Wald Barnes and Elizabeth Chappell Barnes. The family's life was complex. Zadel Barnes, Wald's mother, lived in and financed the household of her talented, self-indulgent son, who kept his wife, his mistress, and the children of each under the same roof. This unconventional family situation created a kind of resentment in Barnes that later surfaced in her creative work as often unfavorable and satirical portraits of family life. As Andrew Field commented in his 1983 biography of Barnes, "Her weak English mother, strong-willed American grandmother and spoiled American father were inept eccentrics. That was her misfortune, but it was also the wellspring of all her art."

Zadel Barnes, the "strong-willed American" grandmother, was a great influence on Djuna. Zadel, a journalist and creative writer, also advocated many progressive causes, spiritualism, and the philosophy of free love. Her book of verse entitled *Meg: A Pastoral* received some attention after its printing in Boston in 1878. London became Zadel's home base in 1880, when sent there by *McCall's* magazine. When she moved back to America in 1889, Zadel convinced her son Wald and his fiance Elizabeth Chappell to emigrate as well; they all shared visions of artistic successes. Wald's philandering and inability or unwillingness to work, however, created financial problems, as he fathered more children than their resources could handle. Elizabeth gave up her artistic endeavors to take care of their children, and Zadel supported the family, often requesting money from acquaintances, including Jack London. When Djuna was five years old, Fanny Faulkner moved into the household and became Wald's mistress; her children, Djuna's half-siblings, also began to fill their house. The entire brood eventually moved to a farm in Huntington, Long Island.

Educating a Writer

The children did not attend school regularly, but were tutored by their parents in an eclectic education, including art and music and a

Djuna Barnes

philosophy of sexual freedom. Barnes received extra attention from Zadel, who shared her interest in literature. Barnes's favorite literary works included Chaucer, Shakespeare, Dante, Restoration drama, and Robert Burton's *Anatomy of Melancholy.* Her love of the history of the English language informed her own writing, with its fondness for archaic usage and complex syntactical structures. Bawdy humor was encouraged, a fact made evident by the surviving letters between Barnes and Zadel.

The family's sexual openness may have also had its darker side: studies of Barnes's relationships with family suggest possible sexual abuse. Some researchers make reference to Barnes's father arranging his daughter's sexual initiation by a man several times her age, although it is not certain whether Wald was directly involved in the incident. Scholars have also pointed to evidence in Barnes's letters and private papers suggesting that the intense relationship between Barnes and her grandmother may have had a sexual element. Although Barnes explores incest in her work, it is not clear to what degree it was a part of her own background. Nonetheless, we do know that her active sexual life began at least as early as 18, when Zadel encouraged her common-law marriage to Percy Faulkner, then 52; the match only lasted a few months.

In 1912, amid financial difficulties, Zadel urged her son to make a choice between his two families. He chose to make the illegitimate family legitimate, and Elizabeth and her children were turned out. This act had a profound effect on Barnes: she was forced to go to work in order to help support her family. This fact, while it hastened her entry into her profession, created a pressure that denied a more relaxed approach to her creative work. Elizabeth and her children moved to New York City, where Barnes took art classes at Pratt Institute for a year, then at the Art Students League. These were her only instances of formal training.

Barnes Impresses Newspaper World

Barnes began her writing career in 1913 as a freelancer for the *Brooklyn Daily Eagle.* She was soon writing for the *New York Press, New York World Magazine,* and *New York Morning Telegraph.* The kinds of stories Barnes wrote varied greatly, from pieces on the "bohemians" in Greenwich Village to participatory "stunt" journalism. When, for example, many activists for the women's suffrage campaign were being force fed in jail, Barnes opted to undergo the ordeal in order to write a piece on "How It Feels to Be Forcibly Fed."

While writing journalism, Barnes was also publishing her poems, short stories, drawings, and one act plays in many newspapers and small press magazines such as *Smart Set,* and *Little Review.* In 1915, Bruno's Chap Books series printed her volume *The Book of Repulsive Women,* which consisted of eight "rhythms" and five stylized Aubrey Beardsley-influenced drawings. A few of the poems and the drawings were lesbian in content, but the imagery was obscure enough to thwart censorship. In "From Fifth Avenue Up," for example:

> Someday beneath some hard
> Capricious star—
> Spreading its light a little
> Over far,
> We'll know you for the woman
> that you are.
> ...
> See you sagging down with bulging
> Hair to sip,
> The dappled damp from some vague
> Under lip.
> Your soft saliva, loosed
> With orgy, drip.

Field credited the pamphlet with being "the first modern literary work in English to bring the theme of woman's 'bitter secret' (it is never named) to the misty fore"—a full decade before Radclyffe Hall's *The Well of Loneliness.* But, as he pointed out, many readers, including American censors, were "either incapable of recognizing or of articulating what that 'vague under lip' from which the repulsive woman sags down to sip was." In later years Barnes regretted the volume, especially when she could not prevent pirated copies from circulating.

In her Greenwich Village years the beautiful and stylish Barnes had many love affairs with both men and women. Phillip Herring, in his 1995 biography of Barnes, wrote that "When she arrived in Paris in the early twenties, she told her friend the poet Mina Loy that she had had nineteen lovers, and that women were better in bed than men." Some of these lovers included Ernst "Putzi" Hanfstaengl, a German who later became Hitler's chief minister of the foreign press; Courtney Lemon, a socialist academic; and Mary Pyne, a writer involved with the Provincetown Players (as was Barnes) whose death of tuberculosis in 1919 devastated Barnes. Some of Barnes's melancholy poems in *A Book* (1923) are dedicated to Pyne. Barnes's beloved grandmother Zadel had died of uterine cancer only two years earlier in 1917.

Gay Paris and the Expatriates

Like her grandmother before her, Barnes's success as a journalist in New York led to her assignment in Europe in 1921 for *McCall's*. She stayed for over 10 years. Her Paris years were some of her most important, personally as well as professionally. Soon after arriving in Paris, following a brief stint in Berlin, Barnes met Thelma Wood, a sculptor and silverpoint artist from St. Louis, whose previous lovers included Edna St. Vincent Millay and the photographer Berenice Abbott. The difficult relationship and cohabitation that ensued between Barnes and Wood lasted nearly a decade and was the impetus behind *Nightwood*.

Barnes lived and wrote as part of the expatriate literary enclave in Paris' fashionable Left Bank. She was part of Natalie Clifford Barney's lesbian literary salon, and her work was supported by the patronage of Barney as well as Peggy Guggenheim. She also continued to write journalism. One notable piece is her famous 1922 interview of James Joyce for *Vanity Fair*. In 1923, Barnes put together a manuscript of her short stories, poems, plays, and drawings; Boni and Liveright, a prestigious press that took risks with new writers and experimental work, published the collection by the title *A Book*. With this volume, Barnes established herself as a serious artist.

Her next book, *Ladies Almanack*, a parody of Natalie Barney and her circle, was first privately published in 1928. Barnes wrote the book to amuse Wood during an illness—rather than for sales. Only 1050 copies were printed, financed by Barnes's friends, and Barnes hand colored 50 copies before hawking them all in the streets of Paris. Given the explicitly lesbian subject matter, Barnes did not put her name on the volume, instead attributing authorship to "A Lady of Fashion." The wealthy Barney, featured as the lesbian mock-heroine and "as fine a Wench as ever wet Bed," loved the book—so much so that it may have secured her patronage of Barnes's future work. Susan Sniader Lanser, in her introduction to the 1992 reissue of *Ladies Almanack*, wrote that the book "is now recognized as both a brilliant modernist achievement and the boldest of a body of writings produced by and about the lesbian society that flourished in Paris between the turn of the century and the Second World War." Barnes, though, in an author's foreward to Harper and Row's 1972 reissue, dismissed it as one of her less serious works, "a slight satiric wigging." She feared attention to it might overshadow *Nightwood*.

Censored *Ryder* Hits Best Seller List

Barnes's first novel, *Ryder*, also appeared in 1928, published by Boni and Liveright. Barnes wrote the obviously autobiographical work in a bawdy, mock-Elizabethan style and supplemented the prose with poems and illustrations. In an afterword to the 1990 Dalkey Archive Press reissue of the novel, Paul West commented on the literary taste of New York in 1928 that put the book on the *New York Times* best-seller list: "*Ryder* was briefly a best-seller among those who could hardly have guessed they were reading a guyed, lurid version of Barnes's family history. They bought it for its prose, its dangerousness." *Ryder* faced censorship when it reached the New York Post Office. Barnes and her editor were forced to delete some drawings and text, among them passages that referred to bodily fluids. Furious at the violation of her work, Barnes demanded that asterisks replace the deleted material so that the reader could see "where the war, so blindly waged on the written word, has left its mark."

Nightwood tells "Her Life with Thelma"

After the eight-year relationship with Wood ended in 1929 as a result of Wood's repeated infidelities and alcohol abuse, Barnes spent the next several years exorcising that relationship by writing the novel that became *Nightwood*. She returned to New York in the early 1930s, though she made visits to England and Paris. After Wood, Barnes's lovers were mostly men, though none of the relationships lasted long. As Barnes told her friend Emily Coleman in a letter, "I have *had* my great love, there will never be another."

Nightwood was published by Faber and Faber in 1936, after several years of difficult revision by Barnes and rejections from several different publishing companies. But the novel had its supporters, including T. S. Eliot, who endorsed publication of the novel after Coleman persuaded him to read it. Harcourt and Brace published the American edition in 1937. Eliot's introduction attributes to the novel "the brilliance of wit and characterisation, and a quality of horror and doom very nearly related to that of Elizabethan tragedy." At the center of the tragedy is the broken relationship between Nora and Robin. Doctor Matthew O'Connor, a grand gay transvestite character who philosophizes in witty monologues, counsels and consoles Nora in the painful reality of her betrayal by a woman who is "a beast turning human" and who "lives in two worlds—meet of child and desperado." Nora's love cannot tame Robin, and Robin leaves her for another woman.

Wood's reaction to *Nightwood* was not favorable—she was angered by Barnes's portrayal of her as the selfish, nearly inhuman Robin. Barnes knew the risks involved in this public indictment of Wood's betrayal. While writing the novel she wrote to Coleman: "Had a letter from Thelma, possibly the last in my life if the book does get printed ... She will hate me so. It's awful—God almighty what a price one pays for 200 pages." But, as Cheryl Plumb asserted in her article "Revising *Nightwood*: 'a kind of glee of despair,'" for Barnes "writing is the recompense, the resurrection." Plumb quoted from a letter dated 22 July 1936 from Barnes to Coleman: "I come to love my invention more—so I am able—perhaps only so able—to put Thelma aside—because now she is not Robin."

The next several years after the publication of *Nightwood* were difficult for Barnes, who battled depression, alcoholism, and illness. Relations with her surving family members were also strained, especially when her brothers and mother conspired to send her to a sanitorium. In general, her family did not appreciate her creative work and pressured her to get a steady job. In 1940 Barnes moved into a tiny flat at 5 Patchin Place in Greenwich Village, where she was to live for the next 42 years. In disgust at what she had become, Barnes stopped drinking and smoking in 1950. Her strength returned and she was ready to begin her next major work, *The Antiphon*, a verse drama that turns its sharp artistic eye on the troubled relationship between a daughter and her weak mother. Since her mother had died in 1945, Barnes was free to explore further the troubled past that she had parodied in *Ryder*. Her father had already died in 1934.

The Dramatics of Family History

The Antiphon, first published in 1958 and revised in 1962 for *The Selected Works of Djuna Barnes*, is a densely poetic drama of family strife and consequence. "May God protect us! I wonder what you'll write / When I am dead and gone!" says Augusta in Act III to her daughter Miranda. Indeed, like Barnes's earlier work, this play presents the past with a spirit of revenge. It is a difficult and subtle piece, and its initial audiences had mixed reviews. Some readers were utterly perplexed. It had the support of T. S. Eliot and the poet Edwin Muir and the admiration of Dag Hammarskjold, then United Nations secretary-general. Its only full production was in Stockholm, Sweden in 1961.

In the last 20 years of her life Barnes wrote mostly poetry. She had been elected to the National Institute of Arts and Letters in 1959 and saw the publication of her *Selected Works* as well as reissues of some of her earlier books, but she no longer published a great deal of new work. The poems she did publish, though, appeared in such prestigious magazines as the *New Yorker* and *Grand Street*. These late poems explore themes of time turning backwards, "de-evolution," and mortality. Her last poem, "Rite of Spring," appeared in *Grand Street* in 1982. She received a National Endowment for the Arts grant to finish her last collection of poems, a bestiary titled *Creatures in an Alphabet*, which was also published in 1982. Barnes, who had outlived most of her friends, died a few days after her 90th birthday in June 1982.

Barnes and her work received renewed attention in her last few decades, especially from scholars and critics interested in feminist and gay and lesbian themes in her writing. Barnes was resistant to this attention, partly out of a desire for privacy, but also out of bitterness about what she saw as a limited audience. Nonetheless, her courage in writing openly about same-sex relationships and painful family realities has been inspirational to many; her vision, invaluable.

References:

Allen, Carolyn. "The Erotics of Nora's Narrative in Djuna Barnes's *Nightwood*," in *Signs* (Chicago, Illionois), Autumn 1993: 177-200.

Curry, Lynda. "'Tom, Take Mercy': Djuna Barnes's Drafts of *The Antiphon*," in *Silence and Power: A Reevaluation of Djuna Barnes*, edited by Mary Lynn Broe. Carbondale: Southern Illinois University Press, 1991: 286-298.

Eliot, T. S. "Introduction," in *Nightwood*, by Djuna Barnes. New York: New Directions, 1961: xi-xvi.

Field, Andrew. *Djuna: The Life and Times of Djuna Barnes*. New York: Putnam, 1983.

Herring, Phillip. *Djuna: The Life and Work of Djuna Barnes*. New York: Viking, 1995.

Kannenstine, Louis F. *The Art of Djuna Barnes: Duality and Damnation*. New York: New York University Press, 1977.

Lanser, Susan Sniader. "Introduction," in *Ladies Almanack*, by Djuna Barnes. New York: New York University Press, 1992.

Levine, Nancy J. "Works in Progress: The Uncollected Poetry of Barnes's Patchin Place Period," in *The Review of Contemporary Fiction* (Elmwood Park, Illinois), Fall 1993: 187-200.

Messerli, Douglas. "Foreward," in *New York*, by Djuna Barnes, edited by Alyce Barry. Los Angeles: Sun and Moon Press, 1989: 11-12.

O'Neal, Hank. *"Life is Painful, Nasty and Short ... In My Case It Has Only Been Painful and Nasty": Djuna Barnes 1978-1981; An Informal Memoir by Hank O' Neal*. New York: Paragon, 1990.

Plumb, Cheryl J. *Fancy's Craft: Art and Identity in the Early Works of Djuna Barnes*. Selinsgrove, Pennsylvania: Susquehanna UP, 1986.

———. "Revising *Nightwood*: 'A Kind of Glee of Despair,'" in *Review of Contemporary Fiction* (Elmwood Park, Illinois), Fall 1993: 149-159.

Ponsot, Marie. "A Reader's *Ryder*," in *Silence and Power: A Reevaluation of Djuna Barnes*, edited by Mary Lynn Broe. Carbondale: Southern Illinois University Press, 1991: 137-154.

Scott, James B. *Djuna Barnes*. Boston: Twayne, 1976.

West, Paul. "Afterword: 'The Havoc of this Nicety,'" in *Ryder*, by Djuna Barnes. Elmwood Park, Illinois: Dalkey Archive Press, 1990: 243-250.

—Karen Helfrich

Natalie Clifford Barney

1876-1972

American poet

A beautiful, unconventional—even notorious—wealthy expatriate, famous for her warm, open personality, Natalie Clifford Barney spent most of her life in Paris, France. Her renowned international salon at 20, rue Jacob brought together intellectuals and writers, and often was the site for readings and performances. Known in Paris as "l'imperatrice de lesbiennes," Barney, with her lover Renée Vivien, prompted the early-twentieth-century recovery of Sappho and organized the Academie des Femmes. Many writers, especially women, portrayed her in their novels. Unashamed of her lesbianism, as most were at the time, she recorded her love affairs in her own writings, thus attesting to her credo that art and life are inseparable. Her life itself was a work of art. She claimed, according to George Wickes in *The Amazon Letters*, "my life is my work, my writings are but the result."

Born 13 October 1876, in Dayton, Ohio, Natalie Clifford Barney was the elder daughter of Alice Pike Barney, a painter and whiskey heiress, and Albert Clifford Barney. Sometime in the early 1880s, Albert sold Barney Car Works, the family's railroad car business, to the Pullman Sleeping Car Company and, when Natalie was 10, relocated the family from Cincinnati to Washington, D.C., where they moved in influential social circles which Natalie disdained; they summered in Bar Harbor, Maine. Early on, young Natalie recognized the hypocrisy of her parents' unhappy marriage cloaked in Victorian convention and the stifling patriarchal authority of her father. According to Shari Benstock in *Women of the Left Bank*, Barney found intolerable her father's "social snobbery, authoritarianism, arbitrariness, the inability to control one's temper, and an insistence on seeing women as possessions." She also was aware of her lesbianism by adolescence. Never forced into open rebellion against her father, Barney's discretion and evasive tactics permitted her sexual freedom while she resisted her father's insistence on her marrying. However, in 1899 he discovered her love affair with the Parisian courtesan Liane de Pougy (Anne-Marie Chassaigne). His rage intensified upon his daughter's publication in 1900 of *Quelques portraits—sonnets de femmes*, a volume of erotic lesbian poems illustrated with portraits of Barney's lovers by her mother, who, Benstock suggests, was probably then unaware of her daughter's sexual orientation. Albert Barney bought up all the copies and destroyed the plates.

Defined by French Culture

In 1886, Barney and her sister Laura, who, according to Wickes, took after their "stuffy" father, accompanied their mother to Paris where she studied painting with Whistler and Duran. The girls enrolled at les Ruches, the famous boarding school at Fontaineblue whose co-headmistress was Madame Marie Souvestre, the ardent feminist and founder of Allenswood in Wimbledon, England, which Eleanor Roosevelt attended. Influenced by her French-speaking great-aunt Louisa and French governesses, Barney already spoke French and in her 18 months at the French finishing school became completely bilingual. Her studies included French poetic form as well as other social arts. In 1893, she completed her education at Miss Ely's School for Girls in New York City where she met Eva Palmer, heiress to the Huntley and Palmer biscuit fortune, who introduced her to Sappho's poetry and probably lesbian love. During the summer of 1894, Natalie traveled in Europe with two friends chaperoned by Miss Ely and then studied German and violin in Dresden for seven months. In 1897, a properly "finished" young woman, she was presented to society.

Over the next few years, the sisters and their mother returned to Paris several times, while Albert Barney traveled to London devoting his time to alcohol and mistresses. Barney's trips, under the guise of self-improvement, and unacceptable suitors aided her evasion of marriage. At one point to her father's consternation, she suggested marriage to Alfred, Lord Douglas; nevertheless she enjoyed the flirting with numerous suitors. Meanwhile, despite her camouflage engagement to Freddy Manners-Sutton (there would be others), she fell in love with the famous *belle époque* actress/courtesan Liane de Pougy planning to support her using money from her trust fund. Soon, in addition to her father, all of Paris would know of their love affair, for in 1901, encouraged by Barney herself, de Pougy published the bestselling autobiographical novel *Idylle saphique.* Barney appears as the experienced American seductress Florence Temple-Bradford (the pseudonym Natalie herself used), or "Flossie," opposite a worldly courtesan. Passionate, but inconstant, the now notorious Barney had already moved on to other lovers. But Barney's misreading of the "independence and power" of the women of the *demi-monde* helped shape her conviction that love of Beauty would shape her life.

Other Books and Other Lovers

"Miss Flossie" reappeared in Colette's *Claudine s'en va* in 1903, although Colette knew Barney then only by reputation and by an earlier brief encounter in the Bois du Bolougne. They eventually became good friends. Barney and Renée Vivien also appeared in Colette's *Le pur et l'impure* (1932) in a slave-master relationship. In 1901, Barney published *Cinq petits dialogues grecs* under the pseudonym Tryphê. Written in French, as most of her writing, the poems exalt Sappho and virginity's preservation of women's bodies and praise love and art, sensuality and beauty, topics which Barney studied with another lover. In 1899, she began a love affair with Renée Vivien (1877-1909), born Pauline Mary Tarn in Paddington, England, but raised in France. After vacationing in Bar Harbor, the two young women briefly studied classical Greek at Bryn Mawr College where Eva Palmer was enrolled. Several years later, Palmer joined them in Paris, but eventually married. Upon their return to Paris they continued to study with the classical scholar Charles Brun who quickly identified Vivien's talent. In 1901, Vivien published her first of many volumes of poetry, *Etudes and Preludes.* Under Brun's tutelage, Barney and Vivien wrote poetry in the style of Sappho and Vivien translated Sappho's fragments into modern French. They imagined forming a contemporary colony of women in honor of Sappho where women, rather than the patriarchy, would be able to define themselves. Their collaboration, and especially Vivien's translations, began the twentieth century recovery of Sappho's works, spurred by interest in recently discovered fragments of Sappho's poetry. Thus, Barney and Vivien are credited with providing lesbians with their poetic roots and reviving what some call the archetypical lesbian. They also took the lead in returning lesbianism to the female community and rescuing it from male pornographers. As part of the "Sapho 1900" movement, Barney wrote *Equivogue* using fragments of Sappho's poetry in 1906. She rewrote Sappho's legend by depicting Sappho's death as suicide for the unrequited love of Timas, bride of Phaon. Vivien's inability or unwillingness to accept Barney's infidelities cooled their affair, although Barney tried to revive it in 1904 with a trip on the Orient Express via Constantinople to Lesbos itself. Vivien recounts their affair in her autobiographical novel *Une Femme m'apparut* where, as Karla Jay points out, she obsessively portrays Barney as Lorely, a seductress who betrays the suffering poet. In 1909, the self-destructive Vivien died of anorexia and alcoholism. Barney later established the Renée Vivien literary prize in her memory.

Meanwhile, Albert Clifford Barney died in 1902 in Monte Carlo. Natalie and her sister each inherited $2,500,000. According to Benstock, their mother took on the role of patroness of sometimes risque amateur theatricals and built Studio House in Washington, D.C. Upon Alice's marriage to one of her male models, the sisters each inherited another $1,500,000. Now 26 years old, Barney, following her mother's Bohemian lead, moved permanently to Paris, a city in which she moved with ease and where she knew she could live and express herself as she pleased.

Despite Barney's insistence on non-monogamy and freedom to love as she chose, many of her former lovers valued her continuing, devoted friendship. Now her former lover, Lucie Delarue-Mardus facilitated her introduction to aristocrats such as Elisabeth de Gramont, Duchesse de Clermont-Tonnere, yet another lover. Immediately, Barney began inviting French writers and intellectuals to lawn parties at her Neuilly house. Early visitors included Paul Claudel, Andre Gide, Marcel Proust, and Paul Valéry. Delarue-Mardus wrote passionate poems to Barney and later portrayed her as Laurette in her novel *L'Ange et les pervers* (1930).

20, rue Jacob

Just before Vivien's death in 1909, perhaps in an effort to win her back, Barney moved to the Left Bank into a *pavillon* at 20, rue Jacob not far from the Boulevard St. Germain in the intellectual and artistic quarter of Paris. This small house surrounded by a spacious garden was the site of the famous international salon where Barney would be "at home" on Friday evenings for the next 60 years. By 1913, most of Paris knew Barney as *l'Amazone* from the epistolary essays the Symbolist literary critic Remy de Gourmont addressed to her and published in the *Mercure de France,* later collected in *Lettres à l'Amazone* and *Lettres intimes à l'Amazone.* That de Gourmont, a recluse, was so taken with Barney attests to her magnetic charm. Barney used the sobriquet in her *Pensées d'une Amazone,* a collection which includes her forthright views on sapphic love, observations on war as excessive male combativeness, descriptions of wartime Paris, and witty epigrams possibly sifted from salon conversation. Frequented by French intellectuals and expatriates, the salon's heyday withstood World War I extending through the 1930s and, albeit outmoded even in the late 1920s, continued nearly until Barney's death. She held her last "at home" during the student riots of May 1968.

The Fridays were formal; tea and cucumber sandwiches were served. Many thought them boring, but most prized an invitation. Over the years, attendees included Andre Gide, Jean Cocteau, Colette, Paul Valéry, Ernest Hemingway, F. Scott Fitzgerald, Ranier Maria Rilke, Sherwood Anderson, Thornton Wilder, William Carlos Williams, Gabriele D'Annunzio, Ford Madox Ford, James Joyce, Edith Sitwell, T. S. Eliot, Olga Rudge, Ezra Pound, and in its later days Truman Capote. Often as a patron of the arts, Barney arranged special programs. Through Pound, in 1926, the American experimental musician George Antheil premiered his First String Quartet. Barney also supported Pound's "Bel Esprit" scheme to subsidize poets such as T. S. Eliot. Radclyffe Hall's influential, but banned, lesbian novel *The Well of Loneliness* includes descriptions of the house and salon and the famous portrayal of Barney as Valerie Seymour, an unapologetic lesbian:

> She was not beautiful nor was she imposing, but her limbs were very perfectly proportioned, which gave her a fictitious look of tallness. She moved well ... Her face was humorous, placid and worldly; her eyes were very kind, very blue, very lustrous. She was dressed all in white, and a large white fox skin was clasped round her slender and shapely shoulders ... she had masses of thick fair hair, which was busily ridding itself of its hairpins.

The description succeeds in capturing Barney's dedication to a highly feminized womanhood.

Academie des Femmes and Other Writings

By 1927, Barney had formed the Academie des Femmes. In addition to publishing subsidies, the Academie fostered recognition of women writers. Barney's circle included *New Yorker* columnist Janet Flanner; drama editor for the *New York Tribune* Solita Solano; dancer Isadora Duncan; poet Mina Loy; Esther Murphy of the wealthy American family; Djuna Barnes; Lucie Delarue-Mardus; Dolly Wilde, Oscar's niece; Elisabeth de Gramont, Duchess de Clermont-Tonnerre; Una, Lady Troubridge; and the aforementioned Radclyffe Hall; more than several were Barney's lovers. In 1915 the bisexual painter Romaine Brooks became, at first, Barney's lover and then companion for nearly 50 years. Brooks painted the women's portraits, including one of Barney costumed as an Amazon. Barney organized evenings for these serious women writers to gather for discussion. With Ford Madox Ford, she arranged an evening to introduce Djuna Barnes, author of *Ladies Almanack,* a novel often described as a satire on Barney and her circle, but which celebrates female sexuality in its depiction of a community where women are not defined in patriarchal terms. Barney appears as Dame Evangeline Musset, a woman committed to rescuing her gender from the perils of heterosexuality who eventually achieves sainthood. Most of the other characters are less thinly veiled. The book was privately printed and sold by subscription. Another evening featured the work of Virgil Thomson and Gertrude Stein, who eventually became a friend although she disapproved of Barney's behavior. In 1934, Edna St. Vincent Millay attended a reading of translations of her poetry. The garden at 20, rue Jacob contained a Doric temple inscribed "À l'Amitié." Here, lesbian women gathered for what Benstock calls evenings of "attic abandonment." They staged ritual celebrations invoking female empowerment in honor of Sappho or goddesses of the moon, such as Diana, goddess of the hunt. Photographs from Barney's collection show they often dressed in Greek or nymphlike costumes which accented their femininity. Barney wrote at least one theatrical set for production in the garden, *Actes et entr'actes;* its theme is patriarchal constraints, a leitmotif for all of Barney's writing and life.

Barney published three volumes of memoirs which focus on her literary friendships. *Aventures de l'esprit* focuses on the first twenty years of the salon and the Academie des Femmes. In *Souvenirs indiscrets,* Barney serves as literary historian with personal sketches of her most intimate friends. In both she preserves a record of the Parisian lesbian and gay lifestyles during the first half of the twentieth century. Less keen are the between the war memories in *Traits et portraits.* Her only piece written in English is a collaboration with Romaine Brooks, who illustrated *The One Who Is Legion or A. D.'s Afterlife,* a limited edition Gothic novel in which, Benstock argues, Barney encoded her affair with Vivien as well as her own life and work.

When the outbreak of World War II forced Barney to temporarily close the salon in autumn 1939, she and Brooks fled to Florence, Italy. In March of 1940 she visited Rapallo and left a radio with the ill-fated Ezra Pound who had often served as Barney's personal literary critic. She wanted Pound to listen to anti-British broadcasts by Lord Haw-Haw (William Joyce), for despite her pacifism in World War I, like Pound, Barney came to approve fascism, value anti-Semitism and thought Mussolini an admirable leader. When they returned to Paris, Barney reopened the salon, now more than ever an anachronism. Ever loyal, she entertained a silenced Pound in 1965. Brooks and Barney remained together until shortly before the former's death in 1970; they broke over yet another of Barney's infidelities. Barney spent the last year of her life a near invalid and died in Paris on 2 February 1972, at the age of 95. Her papers are collected at the Fonds Litteraire Jacques Doucet, Paris, and at the Beinecke Rare Book and Manuscript Library, Yale University.

Described by her biographer Wickes as the "most daring and candid lesbian of her time," Natalie Clifford Barney boldly urged women to celebrate their sexuality and express themselves through their bodies. Her Academie des Femmes supported women as intellectuals and serious writers. Even today, her inspiration continues; she appears in Anna Livia's *Minimax* (1992), a comic portrayal of vampire life, and some works have recently been published in translation. Characteristically, Barney wrote her own epitaph: "She was the friend of man and the lover of woman, which, for people full of ardor and drive, is better than the other way around."

References:

Barnes, Djuna. *Ladies Almanack.* Paris: privately printed by Robert McAlmon, 1928.

Barney, Natalie Clifford. *Actes et entr'actes.* Paris: Sansot, 1910.

———. *A Perilous Advantage: The Best of Natalie Clifford Barney,* translated by Anna Livia. Norwich, Vermont: New Victoria, 1992.

———. *Aventures de l'esprit.* Paris: Emile Paul, 1929; as *Adventures of the Mind,* New York: New York University Press, 1992.

———. *Cinq petits Dialogues grecs.* Paris: La Plume, 1901.

———. *Nouvelles Penseés de l'Amazone.* Paris: Mercure de France, 1939.

———. *The One Who Is Legion.* London: Eric Partridge, 1930.

———. *Pensées d'une Amazone.* Paris: Emile Paul, 1920.
———. *Quelques Portraits—Sonnets de Femmes.* Paris: Ollendorf, 1900.
———. *Souvenirs indiscrets.* Paris: Flammarion, 1960.
———. *Traits et portraits.* Paris: Mercure de France, 1963.
Benstock, Shari. *Women of the Left Bank: Paris, 1900-1940.* Austin: University of Texas Press, 1986: 180, 274, 277, 301.
Chalon, Jean. *Portrait of a Seductress: The World of Natalie Barney,* translated by Carlo Barko. New York: Crown, 1979.
Colette. *Claudine s'en va.* Paris: Ollendorft, 1903.
———. *Le pur et l'impur.* Published as *The Pure and the Impure,* translated by Herma Briffault. New York: Farrar, Straus & Girous, 1967.
de Gourmont, Remy. *Lettres à l'Amazone.* Paris: Cres, 1914.
———. *Lettres intimes à l'amazone.* Paris: La Centaine, 1926.
de Pougy, Liane. *Idylle saphique.* Paris: Plume, 1901.
Delarue-Mardrus, Lucie. *L'Ange et les pervers.* Paris: Ferenczi, 1930; as Lucie Delarue Mardrus, *The Angel and the Perverts,* translated by Anna Livia, New York: New York University Press, forthcoming.
Hall, Radclyffe. *The Well of Loneliness.* New York: Doubleday, 1928; reprint, 1990: 244.
Jay, Karla. *The Amazon and the Page: Natalie Clifford Barney and Renée Vivien.* Bloomington: Indiana University Press, 1988.
Russell, Paul Elliott. *The Gay 100.* New York: Citadel Press, 1995.
Vivien, Renée. *Une femme m'apparut.* Paris: Alphonse Lemerre, 1904; as *A Woman Appeared to Me,* translated by Jeannette H. Foster, Tallahassee, Florida: Naiad Press, 1979.
Wickes, George. *The Amazon of Letters: The Life and Loves of Natalie Barney.* London: Allen, 1977: 48.
———. "Natalie Barney," in *Dictionary of Literary Biography, Volume 4: American Writers in Paris, 1920-1939,* edited by Karen Lane Rood. Detroit: Gale Research, 1980.

—Judith C. Kohl

Deborah A. Batts

1947-

African-American judge

Deborah A. Batts was thrust into history in 1994, when she was appointed by President Bill Clinton to serve as a district-court judge in New York City, making her the nation's first openly gay African-American federal jurist. Clinton's nomination of Batts, recommended by Senator Daniel Patrick Moynihan of New York, was confirmed by the U.S. Senate with no opposition.

The quick confirmation was somewhat surprising in light of the strong opposition to Clinton's earlier nomination of another lesbian attorney, Roberta Achtenberg, for the post of under-secretary in the Department of Housing and Urban Development. But, unlike, Achtenberg, Batts was not know for being particularly active in the gay-rights movement; on the other hand, she never made a secret of her sexual orientation and had, according to Peter Freiberg of *Frontiers* magazine, been prepared to answer "any question that was raised" by the Senate Judiciary Committee prior to her confirmation. In the end, the Committee never even brought up the issue. Another reason for the relatively easy Senate confirmation is that Batts was obviously very well qualified for the job.

Batts was born in Philadelphia on 13 April 1947, and graduated from Radcliffe College (with a B.A. in government) in 1969 and Harvard Law School in 1972. After receiving her J.D., she served as a clerk to Lawrence W. Pierce, a District Court judge in Manhattan. "It was apparent to me," Judge Pierce told Frances A. McMorris of the *Wall Street Journal*, "that she was very bright, very energetic, and very personable. Those factors combined to make me select her as one of my clerks."

Batts went on to become an associate at Cravath, Swaine & Moore, a prominent New York corporate law firm. There she handled general cases involving securities law, antitrust, and libel. In 1979, she left private practice to become assistant U.S. attorney in the Criminal Division of the Southern District of New York, the major anti-crime unit of the Manhattan Federal Prosecutor's office. As a prosecutor, she served as lead attorney in cases ranging from armed robbery to international art theft.

In 1984, Batts accepted a position as associate professor of law at Fordham University, making her the first African-American member of the Fordham Law School faculty. At Fordham, she taught courses in property law and domestic relations and was affiliated with the Corporation Counsel Trial Advocacy Program. After her appointment to the Federal bench in 1994, she continued to serve as adjunct professor of law at the university.

With such credentials, there can be little doubt as to Batts's qualifications for the Federal judiciary. Still, in a profession not particularly well known for its diversity, Batts tends to stand out. McMorris of the *Wall Street Journal* stated that "gay legal groups are hailing the appointment of Judge Batts ... as a historic ... breakthrough. Many in the legal profession say her appointment marks a turning point in attitudes toward gay men and lesbians." And Freiberg of *Frontiers* magazine proclaimed, "Another lavender ceiling has been shattered."

For her part, Batts, who is divorced and the mother of two children, tries to downplay the fanfare. According to Freiberg, she told the *New York Law Journal* that she does not want to become known as "the gay judge," and she generally shies away from discussions about her personal coming-out process. McMorris quotes her telling the *Washington Blade*: "Being a lesbian is definitely part of my life.... It is also one of many parts of my life. I am also a very devoted mother, I'm an attorney, a former prosecutor, and I'm an African American. If people assume any one of these aspects is going to predominate it would create a problem."

Nevertheless, despite the fact that, as Jim Williams, president of the Lesbian and Gay Law Association of Greater New York, told McMorris, "Debbie has always been very low key," neither has she shied away from her own brand of activism. Freiberg cites her remarks to the 1994 graduating class of Fordham Law School in which she "appealed to them to work for the civil rights of minorities, and ended with a plea for laws to protect lesbians and gay men from discrimination."

Current Address: U.S. Courthouse, 40 Centre St., Foley Sq., Rm 2904, New York, New York 10007.

References:

Almanac of the Federal Judiciary, Volume 1. Aspen Law & Business, 1996.

Freiberg, Peter. "Lesbian Federal Judge Makes History," in *Frontiers*, 26 August 1994.
McMorris, Frances A. "Judge Adds Diversity to Federal Bench," in *Wall Street Journal* (New York), 13 September 1994: 816.

Joseph Beam

1954-1988

African-American writer and activist

Although Joseph Beam was a leading gay African-American author, lecturer, and activist during the 1980s, his highest accomplishment was serving as editor of *In the Life: A Black Gay Anthology*. It is considered the first literary anthology to focus exclusively on the experiences of black, gay men.

Joseph Fairchild Beam was born in Philadelphia on 30 December 1954. His father, Sun Fairchild Beam, was employed as a bank security guard, and mother, Dorothy Saunders Beam, worked as a teacher and school counselor in the Philadelphia public schools. Raised in Philadelphia throughout his childhood, Beam began his education in the city's public schools. He then attended St. Joseph School for Boys in Clayton, Delaware, and the Malvern Preparatory School in Paoli, Pennsylvania. He returned to Philadelphia, to graduate with honors from St. Thomas More High School in 1972. After high school, Beam moved to Franklin, Indiana, where he attended Franklin College, earning a B.A. in 1976. It was during college that Beam acknowledged his sexual orientation to his parents, as explained by Dorothy Beam to Carol Horner in the *Philadelphia Inquirer*. Mrs. Beam recalled her response, "I love you even though you are gay, and anything I can do to make your life happier, I will do." Following the completion of his education, Beam returned to Philadelphia to begin his career and spend the remaining years of his life.

During the next 12 years, Beam had several jobs as both a waiter and a bookseller, including a position at Giovanni's Room, a gay, lesbian, and feminist bookstore. He also served on the board of directors of the National Coalition of Black Lesbians and Gays.

Beam had also begun to write about African-American gay life in a variety of genres. His work eventually appeared in several lesbian and gay publications, including the *Advocate, Blackheart, Gay Community News,* the *New York Native,* the *Painted Bride Quarterly,* the *Philadelphia Gay News,* and the *Windy City Times.* He was a founding editor of *Black/Out,* a publication of the National Coalition of Black Lesbians and Gays. He also served as a contributing editor of the magazine *Blacklight* and as a columnist for *Au Courant.*

In April of 1984, Beam contacted Alyson Publications with his proposal for an anthology by gay black male authors. Frustrated that gay writing as a genre had excluded African-American male authors, characters and issues, he sought a voice for a silent minority. Although his initial solicitation produced only a few manuscripts, he was eventually inundated with materials and was consumed with his task as editor. But, as he explained in his introduction to *In the Life,* "Not only was I an editor, but often a confidant and friend to the brothers who submitted their work." The book, which was published in October of 1986, was favorably reviewed by the gay and lesbian press and widely praised by African-American gay men. After the book's publication, Beam's popularity rose as he gave lectures and poetry readings and made appearances at bookstores nationwide.

Beam died in Philadelphia of complications from AIDS on 27 December 1988, three days before his 34th birthday. His friend, the Reverend Darlene C. Garner of the Metropolitan Community Church of Philadelphia, officiated at his memorial service on 5 January 1989. The Joseph F. Beam Scholarship Fund, designed for minority students interested in gay and lesbian writing and research, was established at Temple University in Philadelphia following his death. On 28 December 1991, Unity, Inc., a Philadelphia organization, sponsored a conference, "In the Life," that paid tribute to Beam by addressing issues important to African-American lesbians and gay men. Beam's personal papers are held by the Schomburg Center for Research in Black Culture in New York City.

Prior to his death, Beam had collected manuscripts for a sequel to *In the Life.* His friend Essex Hemphill, the writer and poet, completed the project with the assistance of Dorothy Beam. *Brother to Brother: New Writings by Black Gay Men,* edited by Essex Hemphill (1991), was a critical and commercial success and provided yet another lasting tribute to Joseph Beam.

References:

Beam, Joseph, ed. *In the Life: A Black Gay Anthology.* Boston: Alyson, 1986.
Dahir, Mubarak S. "Joe Beam Honored at Unity, Black Gay Talks," in *Au Courant* (Philadelphia), 10 January 1992: 3-4.
Horner, Carol. "A Son's Work and a Mother's Love," in the *Philadelphia Inquirer,* 4 February 1992: C1, 7.
St. George, Donna. "Joseph Beam, Writer and Gay Activist," in the *Philadelphia Inquirer,* 31 December 1988: B5.

—Joseph M. Eagan

Bishop Carl Bean

1944-

African-American religious leader

The Rev. Carl Bean is a living example of how despair can lead to hope, and how hope can then lead to determined action. By overcoming the prejudice and rejection which he suffered as a young boy, and steadfastly clinging to his belief in a compassionate and universal Christianity, Bean has provided a haven for those who suffer prejudice because of their race or sexual orientation.

As a 12-year-old in Baltimore, Bean suffered an emotional trauma so devastating that it prompted him to attempt suicide. After he professed his homosexuality to his foster parents, they took him to a minister for counselling. The meeting was not a success. Bean returned home and swallowed whatever medications he found in the bathroom medicine cabinet in an attempt to escape permanently the rejection he felt from his family and from the church which had meant so much to him. After this, Bean was sent away for psychological evaluation, and later reunited with his birth mother.

Bishop Carl Bean

Her acceptance of his homosexuality helped make the next few years very happy ones.

Although the church which he had loved as a child had offered him little support when he had needed it, Bean did not reject Christianity, and religion played a vital part in his life even after he left home at 16. Bean performed as a singer on the gospel circuit for 15 years and had roles on Broadway in *Don't Bother Me, I Can't Cope* and *Your Arm's Too Short to Box with God.* His career as a singer and performer culminated in the mid-1970s, when he moved to Los Angeles and recorded a gay-themed disco-beat tune titled "I Was Born This Way" for Motown Records.

Although Bean had incorporated his religious convictions with his identity as a black homosexual, he felt he was being called to do more. Carol Chastang, in her article about Bean for the *Los Angeles Times,* quoted him as remembering, "I dreamed I was in the inner city, and the people were crying out for help and support. I was hesitant, but a voice was telling me to go."

As a gay man, and a Christian, Bean felt drawn to offer others the support that he had needed so desperately as an adolescent, and that had been so woefully lacking. Also, Bean was aware of the special needs of black gays and lesbians, who suffer from a double stigma of being both a racial and a sexual minority. Bean was ordained a minister in 1982, and founded the Unity Fellowship Church in 1985. The church began as a small bible-study group that met in the home of one of the members. As its ranks swelled, the church moved to its present location in a warehouse on Jefferson Boulevard in Los Angeles. Bean's original calling, to serve and support black gays and lesbians, quickly broadened to embrace other minorities as well. Latino, Native American, and white homosexuals and heterosexuals alike were also attracted by the church's openness and lack of the homophobia and hypocrisy which they had encountered in other churches.

Also in 1985, Bean founded the Minority AIDS Project to help meet the special needs of members of minorities who found themselves suffering not only from the effects of racism and homophobia, but from AIDS as well. The staff of the Minority AIDS Project includes health professionals, social workers, and outreach workers; HIV-testing is available, as well as nursing care, counselling and even financial assistance. Homeless AIDS sufferers also receive assistance and temporary housing through Dignity House. In 1991, the Minority AIDS Project was threatened with closure due to lack of funds. In an appeal for public and corporate support, Bean vowed to fast until the funds needed for the operation of the project were raised.

In 1993, the Unity Fellowship Church received the Prophetic Witness Award from the Southern Christian Fellowship Conference of Greater Los Angeles and the Martin Luther King Legacy Association. Southern Christian Fellowship Conference spokesman Kevin C. Spears is quoted by Larry Stammer in the *Los Angeles Times* as stating that the presentation of the award "is intended as a signal to mainstream churches in the black community ... the African-American church needs to recognize there are persons in our community that represent alternate lifestyles." Bean himself best sums up his continuing work in Chastang's article: "My ministry ... will always be a continuum of dealing with the disenfranchised, providing for the poorest of the poor, the undocumented person, persons who can't speak the language, persons in and out of the prison system, kids out of the gangs ... to touch those who are considered the untouchables."

Current Address: c/o Minority AIDS Project, 5149 West Jefferson, Los Angeles, California 90016.

References:

Chambers, Veronica. "Bishop Carl Bean: Ministry for All," in *Essence* (New York), June 1994.

Chastang, Carol. "Good News at Unity," in *Los Angeles Times,* 5 October 1992.

Jones, Charisse. "Minority AIDS Project May Fold, Appeals for Cash," in *Los Angeles Times,* 9 January 1991.

Stammer, Larry B. "SCLC to Honor Founder of Church for Minority Gays," in *Los Angeles Times,* 1 January 1993.

—Jean Edmunds

Sir Cecil Beaton

1904-1980

British photographer, diarist, and designer

Cecil Walter Hardy Beaton, the eldest of four children, was born in Hampstead, a middle-class section of London, on 14 January 1904. His mother was Esther Sisson, whose forebears had been millers or poultry farmers in Westmorland. His father, Ernest Beaton, though the son and grandson of pharmacists, made his livelihood as a timber merchant. Before his marriage to Esther Sisson, Ernest had been a good amateur actor and was a passionate cricket player well into middle-age. The fact that Cecil was born in the Edwardian era was to influence much of his work. He had an uncanny ability to seek out detail. Nothing escaped his notice. He remembered being mesmerized at the age of three when looking at a picture postcard of a famous stage heroine, thus anticipating his lifelong interest in photography and fashion. His early classmates later recalled that he had a beautiful face, some even thinking he was too beautiful to be a boy, which caused them to steal a glance in the boys' room just to be sure.

School at Harrow for young Beaton was mostly a struggle. He showed no academic slant whatsoever, eventually devoting his time to painting, drawing, acting, and photographing. He was admitted to Cambridge, where he often skipped lectures but was soon a member of the Theatre Club and busy with all aspect of stage production from acting to designing costumes and decor. It was here that he started his diary writing, which he would pursue the rest of his life. While it appears that he had his share of sexual encounters with other boys at Harrow, he gives the impression, then and later, of not being sexually forward. At Cambridge University, smarting from rumors at Harrow, he rebuffed several suitors, determined to forego romantic involvements in the interest of an impeccable reputation. Instead, he devoted his time to designing theatrical productions—taking female leads in several of them. When he left Cambridge in 1925, he had no degree, but several "connections." He already showed a strong penchant for achieving visibility and pursuing publicity. He had photographs of himself taken in plays and in his rooms, which he would send to newspapers. Later, with flair and daring, he did the same thing with his sisters and mother, a strategy that was sometimes successful.

Becoming a Photographer

Beaton became a professional photographer by accident and never really considered it his life's work. Gradually, as he became immured in an expensive lifestyle, it was photography that paid the bills. A big influence on Beaton was his wealthy friend, Stephen Tennant, a homosexual aesthete with brilliant, if often outrageous, ideas in decorating, dressing, and grooming. He provided Beaton with early entrée into upper-class circles. Through Tennant, he met the Sitwells and Edith Olivier, who was to become a mentor and important supporter.

By the time he was 25, Beaton had held his first exhibition and was already in demand in London as a photographer of unconventional poses. That same year, he set out for the United States, where he began a long association with Condé Nast, publisher of *Vogue*, contributing fashion sketches and portraits caricatures of well-known London hostesses and actresses. Soon even in the United States, Cecil had the necessary connections to gain access to the glittering world of the illuminati, whose social life he aspired to. His ambition, easy wit, and natural self-assurance were assets that favored his climb. The managing editor of *Vogue* said of him much later, "Now Cecil may have been born from the middle classes but he didn't have a middle class bone in his body." Still, he had ambivalent feelings toward the rich: "He needed them and he liked being in their company, and their way of life. But if he was given a good enough pew, be would have gladly witnessed their execution." Within a few years he was an arbiter and connoisseur of taste, and on the list of the world's best-dressed men.

By 1939 Beaton became the favored photographer of the British royal family, which assured his renown and social ascendancy. Except for Prince Philip and Princess Anne, the Windsors apparently loved his sense of humor, which could easily convulse them with giggle, and which prevented his royal portraits from turning out sullen and stiff. In fact, he may be credited with enhancing the royal family's image by giving them a more glamorous and popular look. He spent the war years in Egypt, India, and China, on photographic assignments for the British government. He made himself useful and left a good impression on many of the people he met, often showing bravery and courage. Though he could easily put himself across as the grand *seigneur*—George Cukor said much later that Beaton found it hard to give orders to an English milord—he was gifted with the ability to be as at home with a dressmaker as with a duchess, with a boxer as with a general.

Beaton's war photographs with their sincere and clear cut approach are a sharp contrast to his gauze-like fashion poses. He produced several wartime books, including *Air of Glory* (1941), *Winged Squadrons* (1942), *The Near East* (1943), and *The Far East* (1945). "His knowledge," writes photographic historian Gail Buckland, "of how to light a face, create a dramatic background, spot a symbolic action, humanize a sitter, see beauty, use abstraction, arouse sympathy and compose a picture ensured that this body of work was varied and stimulating."

Back to the Theater and an Extravagant Lifestyle

Along with Cornelia Otis Skinner, Beaton acted in the 1946 San Francisco production of Oscar Wilde's *Lady Windermere's Fan* for which he did the sets and costumes. It was his first appearance as a professional actor. Back in London, he turned increasingly to the theater, doing the stage design for, among other plays, *Return of the Prodigal* (1948), *Charley's Aunt* (1949), and *Aren't We All* (1953). His sets and costumes for the Metropolitan Opera's 1961 production of Puccini's *Turandot* won rave reviews for their use of bold colors and original designs. Another great success was his decor for Balanchine's 1950 New York production of *Swan Lake*.

Beaton's strong penchant for high visibility went hand in hand with his extravagance. The homes he chose—eighteenth-century Ashcomb on the edge of the Wiltshire Downs and, later, Reddish House in Queen Anne style near Salisbury—had gardens and were large enough to require a staff of domestic help: four full-time servants and three part-time by 1958. In addition, there was Eileen Hose, Beaton's secretary and the mainstay of his life from 1953 on. As early as 1934, his earnings just from *Vogue* guaranteed him $17,000 per year, money which he quickly lavished on travels and entertaining. In October of 1958 he could command $6,000 for a morning's work at Londonderry House, and in one long day at Broadchalke he earned a record $15,000, reports Hugo Vickers in his biography.

His friendship with Truman Capote sheds light on Beaton's ability to appreciate genius for how else would he have been able to get along so well with the irascible Capote? They must have cut an extraordinary figure together on their 1957 trip to Japan, where, in Kyoto, they were to meet Helena Rubinstein and her travelling secretary Patrick O'Higgins, who later told this story. For their initial meeting, Beaton and Capote arranged to wait for them in the bar of the Miyako Hotel. Just in advance of their meeting, the concierge advised O'Higgins: "Two very fine English ladies waiting for you in the bar. Both dressed like gentlemen."

Sir Cecil Beaton

Beaton met and kindled, in varying degrees, friendship in a number of celebrities, including Audrey Hepburn, Christopher Isherwood, Mick Jagger, Baron Philippe and Pauline Rothschild, Noel Coward, the Duchess of Windsor, Mrs. Ian Fleming, Clarissa Churchill, Jean Cocteau, Mrs. Kenneth Clark, Lady Diana Cooper, Elizabeth the Queen Mother, and Gertrude Stein. And, over his long career as photographer of the famous and glamorous, there were few notables who did not sit for him. He was fond of pointing out that only Virginia Woolf and Queen Mary had refused to face his shutter.

"The Surface of Things"

While his romantic life has been well documented, little is known of his sexual life. His romance with Greta Garbo had sincere dimensions, but Beaton was so attracted to the surface of things that none of his relationships attained any depth. His diary accounts of his relationship with Garbo lead the reader to infer intimacy—certainly not impossible since Beaton seems to have been capable of sexual arousal with women. Yet, as publicity-minded Beaton wrote his diaries, he could not help having one eye on eventual publication. He lived in an age when homosexual acts were viewed as criminal. He cannot be judged harshly for wanting a cover especially since his career depended on his being conspicuously visible. It seems that his libido did not torture him unduly. Hugo Vickers opines that, for Beaton, "Sex was often an item to be fitted into a crowded day. Occasionally when working in New York he would receive a young man in his room, sent to him by a friend. Usually his visitor had departed within twenty minutes." When the Wolfenden Report appeared in 1966, Beaton wrote in his diary: "Of recent years the tolerance towards the subject has made a nonsense of many of the prejudices from which I myself suffered acutely as a young man.... Selfishly I wish that this marvelous step forward could have been taken at an earlier age It is not that I would have wished to avail myself of further license, but to feel that one was not a felon and an outcast could have helped enormously during the difficult young years." "I don't really feel that I am going to come into my own, and justify myself and my existence by some last great gesture. I am likewise certain that nothing I have done is likely to live long after me."

One of Beaton's two great frustrated ambitions was to become a playwright, but he found dialogue hard to make convincing. He wanted badly to be viewed as a serious artist. Later, he was even to hire a gifted American intellectual, Waldemar Hansen, to be his ghost-writer for revisions of his only play, *The Gainsborough Girls*, which he started in 1945 and did not abandon until 1974. It flopped in 1951 in its sole production. His other great obsession was the doomed love of his life, Peter Watson (1908-56), a tortured playboy type, who inherited his father's margarine fortune. Vickers describes him as suffering from "a deeply cruel and masochistic streak which made him an unpredictable friend." Watson and Beaton met in Vienna in 1930. Together, they went sightseeing and browsing in antique shops without taking any special notice of each other. Then, one day, coming down in an elevator together, it happened, as Beaton writes: "He shot me a glimpse of sympathy, of amusement it may have been a wink—but it did its work—it went straight to my heart—and from that moment I was hypnotized by him; watching every gesture of his heavy hands, the casual languid way he walked." For the next four years, in particular, Beaton's professional and social life took back seat to this unweening obsession, from which he never entirely delivered himself and which was never apparently consummated. It is rather clear that Beaton was quite simply not Watson's type, and Beaton lacked the analytical powers to transcend his passion and transform it into mere friendship, which was all that Watson wanted from Beaton. In short, his professional success was not mirrored by personal emotional success: "That I have not inspired love in anyone enough to take me under their wing and insist on my mending my frivolous ways is a serious self condemnation. That I have not inspired real love at all is a very pitiable lacuna, and that is the awful realization I must face. I wasn't able to inspire enough feeling in Peter and certainly Greta only superficially was intrigued—not enough ... and others have merely been phenomena of the flesh."

Beaton's monolithic interest in the surface of things caused him to neglect general knowledge, for which he was to chide himself in later years and which no doubt accounted for his feelings of inadequacy. "Just as he liked to inspire envy, so he suffered from it ... it does not take the form of envying people their particular talent so much as envying them the success their talent brings them." Much of Beaton's attraction to the young six-foot-four-inch-tall American, Kin, was based on his admiration for Kin's broad knowledge of history and art. Twenty years later Kin still described Beaton as "the most honorable man I've ever met." A Princeton graduate and art historian, born in 1934, Kin was exactly half Beaton's age when they met in 1963 while Beaton was in Hollywood doing the costumes for the film version of *My Fair Lady*. He came to England to spend two years at Beaton's and attend London's Courtaauld Institute but ended up spending only one year. He commented many years later, "I knew that to many people to be under Beaton's protection and share his exciting life would appear enviable. I too recognized the quality of the gift I had been given but it was not what I needed.... It was as though he had given me the world's most beautiful cat for a pet, but I loved only dogs." His exit from Beaton's life left a profound void never again to be filled.

Beaton Triumphs over Oscar

My Fair Lady was the play that Beaton could, and should, have written. With its Edwardian backdrop and its heavy reliance on visual effects, it was the perfect vehicle for his expertise. Already drawing Ascot fashions as a child, he was a perfect choice for costume designing, as he was for *Gigi*, about which Stanley Kauffman wrote: "*Gigi* is consistently pleasant but is extraordinary in only one way. Do not be deceived by the advertising. The real star is Cecil Beaton, who designed the scenery and the costumes and scenery.... His work in this film is gorgeous." Beaton won Academy Awards for *Gigi* and *My Fair Lady*, on both of which he also served as production designer.

Beaton designed scenery and costumes for opera, ballet and theatrical productions, and was a leading arbiter in taste and fashion for much of the twentieth century. Harry Yoxall wrote in his memoirs that Beaton made a greater contribution to *Vogue* than any other artist. The epitome of the self-made man, with considerable talents founded on nothing firmer than instinct, and with even greater stamina and panache, Cecil Beaton stayed in the British limelight for nearly sixty years, through his innovative portraiture photography, bold set and costume designs, and by publishing over 30 works that chronicled twentieth-century fashion and design as well as his own impact on them. Repository of the latest gossip and scandal of the *beau monde*, he was a pioneer jet-setter with *entrees* in the homes of the rich and famous long before these terms were coined. As Waldemar Hansen noted: "He had an unerring instinct for what was chic and fashionable; he knew whom to cultivate. He was the right kind of snob. He had his stethoscope on the heart of society."

When Beaton was knighted in 1972 at the age of 68, he wrote, "But I felt suddenly a good deal more elderly and eminent. Still it is a very nice tribute and I feel I have deserved it, not for my talent, but for character, tenacity, energy and wide-reaching efforts." He died in Broadchalke, England, 18 January 1980.

References:

Vickers, Hugo. *Cecil Beaton: A Biography.* Boston: Little, Brown and Company, 1985.

—Robert F. Jones

Alison Bechdel

1960-

American cartoonist and writer

In 1983, when Alison Bechdel published her first *Dykes to Watch Out For* cartoon in the lesbian pride issue of New York City's feminist paper, *WomaNews,* a kind of history was made. That single panel-slice of urban lesbian life would eventually evolve into a series of posters and postcards, eight *Dykes to Watch Out For* calendars, and six collected volumes of *Dykes to Watch Out For* comic strips. With each image that Bechdel has created, she invites the lesbian community, both in the United States and internationally, to gaze into a mirror that reflects its passions, politics, and idiosyncrasies.

Alison Bechdel was born on 10 September 1960, the oldest of three children, in Lock Haven, Pennsylvania, and grew up in Beech Creek, Pennsylvania. Her parents, Helen Fontana Bechdel and Bruce Bechdel, were both high school English teachers and encouraged her drawing as a child. As she told Dwight Garner in a *Boston Globe Magazine* interview, "When I was little, my father would bring me big stacks of typing paper, and I'd fill them up with 60 or 70 pages of my cartoon stories."

Bechdel had a range of models before her as a child, many of them macabre and most from pop culture. *Mad Magazine* was one, and, as she told Anne Rubenstein when she was interviewed for *Comics Journal,* others were "Norman Rockwell and certain children's book illustrators. We had some books of children's poetry that Edward Gorey illustrated.... I also loved Hillary Knight's work, the guy who did the *Eloise* books. And Dr. Seuss. And Richard Scarry's picture books."

Bechdel left high school a year early to attend Simon's Rock College, an "early" college in Great Barrington, Massachusetts, from 1977 to 1979. She transferred to Ohio's Oberlin College in 1979, where she continued to draw cartoons, although her professors were more interested in her "serious" studio work. Bechdel graduated from Oberlin with a BA in studio arts and art history in 1981.

Alison Bechdel views her biggest college accomplishment not as the art she made and studied there, but her coming out as a lesbian. "That's the main thing I'm grateful to Oberlin for," she told Rubenstein. A rendition of Bechdel's coming out story appears in an early *Dykes to Watch Out For* strip entitled "Mo Phones Home," although that version was fictionalized. One closer to the truth can be found in the autobiographical cartoon story that appeared in a *Gay Comix* issue devoted entirely to Bechdel in 1993. Here, our heroine is depicted surreptitiously purchasing lesbian literature at the college bookstore and sneaking peeks at her straight roommate's collection of sexually explicit lesbian lore before coming out herself.

After college, Bechdel moved to New York City, where she pursued a variety of jobs and avocations. "I did a lot of menial publishing industry kinds of jobs," she told Rubenstein. "Proofreading, word-processing. And I started volunteering at a feminist newspaper called *WomaNews,* where I did paste-up and production and wrote an occasional review." Bechdel also became involved in martial arts, studying karate four times a week; the skill would later make an appearance in her comics.

Dykes to Watch Out For Is Born

Dykes to Watch Out For was born during this time, in the margin of a letter Bechdel was writing to a friend. As she told Rubenstein, "I drew this whacked-out lesbian holding a coffee pot, and called it 'Marianne, dissatisfied with her breakfast brew: Dykes to Watch Out For, plate number 27.' Even though it was the first one I ever drew. But something about it really held my interest, and I started doing a series of drawings of these whacked-out lesbians."

One of Bechdel's co-workers at *WomaNews* persuaded her to submit some of the drawings for publication. The paper ran two of

Alison Bechdel. ***Photograph by Martha Tormey.***

them in their 1983 Lesbian Pride issue, and a piece of lesbian cultural history began. The *WomaNews* collective handed out copies of the paper at the Pride march. "I was so elated that my work was getting passed around, and getting read," Bechdel told Rubenstein. "It was really thrilling to actually see people react to my cartoons, to laugh. I was so happy. I knew that was something I wanted." The event inspired her to turn a hobby into a serious career pursuit.

Bechdel drew one-panel cartoons for *WomaNews* for a year before expanding to a whole strip. "I'd been hesitant to do a strip because it meant you had to draw the same characters more than once," she told Rubenstein. "When I finally tried it, I found that you really didn't have to make them exactly the same from panel to panel, you could just sort of fake it. And I really liked doing a strip much better. I ran out of fuel very quickly with the one panel format.... It's so much more difficult to say something in one panel." Writing to and engaged in a highly political community, Bechdel had plenty of motivation to make her work "say something."

Bechdel thought that other people might be interested in her cartoons, so she began to self-syndicate by writing letters to other gay and lesbian papers. "I've really just made it up as I've gone along," she told Rubenstein. "I started with two or three papers. Gradually, over the years it's grown to about four dozen." Nonetheless, Bechdel has remained engaged at a grassroots level with gay and lesbian publishing, even as she's moved around the country.

Bechdel moved from New York City to Northampton, Massachusetts, where she lived from 1985 to 1986. After Northampton, she moved to Minnesota, living for a year in St. Paul, and then to Minneapolis, where she lived until 1991. While living in the Twin Cities, Bechdel did layout for the gay/lesbian community paper *Equal Time,* which also featured her strip.

First *Dykes to Watch Out For* Collection Published

In the mid-1980s Bechdel received a fan letter from independent feminist publisher Nancy K. Bereano, who was just then leaving the Crossing Press and starting her own publishing house, Firebrand Books. As Bechdel told Rubenstein, "I met with her, and she was very encouraging. I didn't have a vast audience at the time. She really had a lot of faith in me, to seek me out like that and publish me." The feeling was mutual—Bereano has declared Bechdel "The Patron Saint of Poetry," because the cartoonist's work sells so well that Firebrand is able to fund the publication of fiction and poetry that do not have a broad market. Bechdel's work, however, quickly accumulated a large following, both among newspaper readers and book buyers.

Since the first volume of Bechdel's cartoons, *Dykes to Watch Out For,* appeared in the fall of 1986, Firebrand Books has published five other collections: *More Dykes to Watch Out For* (1988), *New Improved Dykes to Watch Out For* (1990), *Dykes to Watch Out*

For: The Sequel (1992), *Spawn of Dykes to Watch Out For* (1993), and *Unnatural Dykes to Watch Out For* (1995). In addition, Firebrand has been publishing *Dykes to Watch Out For* calendars since 1990.

In 1987, after four years of drawing, syndicating, and publishing *Dykes to Watch Out For,* Bechdel decided to create a recurring cast of characters for her strip, as well as an ongoing story line. The first of these characters was Mo, a socially responsible, serious-to-a-fault white lesbian who Bechdel readily acknowledges as somewhat autobiographical. As Garner remarked, "Mo is easily frazzled; an extended glance at the evening news is enough to set her nerves atwitter for a week. Bechdel and Mo look alike—they share the same close-cropped brown hair, slight build, and dead-on directness." Bechdel does warn against too literal a reading, however: "I don't want to identify too much with Mo," she told Garner, "because it's not an autobiographical strip.... But I'm a lot like her."

She also informed Garner that the same insight applies, to some degree, to all of the characters who have become known to readers over the years: "In a way, the characters are all aspects of me. Together, they form this composite of myself." She further broke it down for Garner, explaining that the sexually mischievous Lois represents her sensuous side; lawyer/activist Clarice plays out her efficiency; lesbian mom Toni is her romantic, domestic alter ego; academic Ginger over-intellectualizes as Bechdel believes she sometimes does; and 12-step advocate Sparrow represents her spiritual side.

Characters Create Community

By using the same cast of characters Bechdel has been able to create a cartoon lesbian community—a fictional world that encapsulates the issues facing lesbians across the country on a daily basis. In the course of her strip, and through certain characters concerns, Bechdel has dealt with lesbian romance (monogamy, non-monogamy, fidelity), lesbian parenthood, disability rights, racism, and breast cancer—to name only a few. Such topical concerns are also reflected in Bechdel's efforts to make her strip inclusive of a diverse lesbian community, including characters of different ethnicities, differently-abled lesbians, women with differing sexual identities and, recently, gender identities. Bechdel has also infused her strips with a consciousness about national and international topical and political concerns, such as the O. J. Simpson trial and the Persian Gulf War.

All of these elements contribute heavily to Bechdel's creative process, often determining the direction of a strip as she's working. Bechdel explained to Rubenstein: "First, I procrastinate until the last possible minute. Then I go to the huge stack of magazines and newspapers I get every month and skim through them, making notes about what's going on in the world, and in the community, what the latest issue is, what people are wearing.... I just feed all this stuff into the hopper. Then I get out my big chart. I have all my episodes listed on one axis, and all my characters on the other so I can track what's happening to whom and whose story needs attention ... then I try to mesh the lives of the characters with what's happening in the world at large. The plot kind of creates itself from the tension between these two things."

Other Projects

Despite the success of *Dykes to Watch Out For*—which has remained undiminished over the years—Bechdel has also put energy into new projects. In 1988, the *Advocate* commissioned her to develop a new strip. The result was *Servant to the Cause,* which features gay men as well as lesbians and focuses on the lives and struggles of a gay/lesbian community newspaper collective. The *Advocate* published the strip until 1990.

Since 1991, Bechdel has lived in Duxbury, Vermont, where she works full-time a cartoonist. Occasionally, she travels the country presenting a slide show in which she talks about her own work as an artist and a lesbian. She also discusses the representation of women in popular American culture, using cartoons as examples. As she told Rubenstein, "I talk about how as a child I never drew women or girls, I always drew men." As she has since perceived, that choice was influenced by the way men and women were represented in the comics she saw around her. She explains in her lecture that male characters appeared "normal" and female characters, "different"—or, as she told Rubenstein, "Men get represented as 'universal' and women get represented as a sexualized subset, an aberration. Cartoons are such a good place to explore this stuff, because it's all so transparent." She also told Rubenstein that "changing that," she commented to Rubenstein, "not just in the comics, but in the world, is my mission in life."

In addition to her slide show, Bechdel has produced posters on commission for issues ranging from sexual harassment to the support of gay and lesbian youth. Her work has appeared in *Ms. Magazine,* the *Village Voice,* and *American Splendor,* as well as on several book covers.

In 1994, Bechdel was approached to develop a mainstream strip for Universal Press Syndicate, but she turned them down. "I thought about it for a couple of weeks," she told Rubenstein,"but eventually I came to my senses.... I'm really happy doing what I'm doing. And I have less than no interest in speaking to the mainstream. I mean, if my work ever got banal enough to make it into a mainstream newspaper, I hope someone would just put me out of my misery."

Even publishing with an independent press, Bechdel has sold over 100,000 *Dykes to Watch Out For* books and calendars. Off the beaten path or not, she has a large and eager audience. More importantly, Alison Bechdel has created a vision of a strong, struggling, and funny lesbian community and has made it accessible to everyone.

Current Address: P.O. Box 703, Waterburg, Vermont 05676.

References:

Bechdel, Alison. *Dykes to Watch Out For.* Ithaca, New York: Firebrand Books, 1986.

———. *Dykes to Watch Out For: The Sequel.* Ithaca, New York: Firebrand, 1992.

———. *Gay Comix.* Ithaca, New York: Firebrand, 1993.

———. *More Dykes to Watch Out For.* Ithaca, New York: Firebrand, 1988.

———. *New Improved Dykes to Watch Out For.* Ithaca, New York: Firebrand, 1990.

———. *Spawn of Dykes to Watch Out For.* Ithaca, New York: Firebrand, 1993.

———. *Unnatural Dykes to Watch Out For.* Ithaca, New York: Firebrand, 1995.

Brown, Katie. "A Dyke to Watch Out For: Alison Bechdel," in *Deneuve* [now *Curve*], January/February 1993.

Garner, Dwight. "Strip Artist," in *The Boston Globe Magazine,* 15 August 1993.
Rubenstein, Anne. "Alison Bechdel Interview," in *The Comics Journal* (Seattle, Washington), August 1995.

—Judith Katz

Arthur Bell

1939-1984

American journalist and activist

Arthur Bell was one of New York City's most widely recognized gay men in his time. As a journalist, author and activist, he helped shape the gay male cultural and political outlook that emanated from Greenwich Village in the post-Stonewall era.

Arthur Irving Bell was born on 6 November 1939, in Brooklyn, New York. His father, Samuel Bell, worked as a successful clothing manufacturer, while his mother, Claire (née Bodan) Bell, designed clothing. When he was in junior high school, Bell moved to Montreal with his family. Bell's early homosexual experiences began in a movie theater at the age of 17 and quickly increased when he discovered some of the Manhattan bars and bathhouses where gay men congregated in the 1950s.

Returning to New York City permanently in 1960, Bell worked in publicity for Viking Press until 1968, when he became publicity director for children's books at Random House. In 1964 he began his long relationship with Arthur Evans, a film distributor who later pursued a Ph.D. in philosophy at Columbia University.

After the Stonewall riots of June 1969, Bell and Evans began attending meetings of the newly formed Gay Liberation Front (GLF), a radical group of homosexuals concerned with a variety of progressive issues. Dissatisfied with GLF's purpose, organization and tactics, Bell joined GLF dissidents Jim Owles, Marty Robinson and other activists at a 24 November 1969 meeting to begin a group solely dedicated to homosexual liberation. On 21 December 1969, a group that included Evans, Owles, and Robinson met in Bell's Greenwich Village apartment to formally adopt the Gay Activists Alliance (GAA) constitution and to elect its first officers. The new group's intention combined the activism of the GLF with the focus of the homophile groups founded prior to Stonewall.

Bell became a pivotal GAA member in the early 1970s. Because of his flexible schedule at Random House, he could participate in many of GAA's New York City "zaps"—confrontations with politicians such as Mayor Lindsay and media figures such as talk show host, Dick Cavett. He championed the rights of all homosexuals—including street transvestites such as Stonewall veteran Ray "Sylvia" Rivera—to participate in GAA. Most importantly, Bell served as GAA's first publicity chair, helping to build the organization's exposure and membership utilizing the skills and contacts that he had developed in publishing. For several months he wrote a column—using the pseudonym "Arthur Irving"—publicizing GAA in *Gay Power,* a New York City biweekly newspaper. His media attention heightened when WOR-TV interviewed him as an openly gay man and homosexual rights activist for a three-segment profile that was aired in November of 1970. Although he gradually lessened his commitment to GAA, his influence on the organization was profound.

Arthur Bell

In late 1970 Bell's relationship with Evans ended, although the two would remain lifelong friends. Bell also resigned his position at Random House, intending to devote himself full-time to writing and gay activism. He wrote film reviews for *Gay,* and began writing feature articles for the *Village Voice,* beginning with a front-page article about gay politics on 13 August 1970. His account of his first year as a gay activist, *Dancing the Gay Lib Blues: A Year in the Homosexual Liberation Movement,* became one of the first books about gay liberation published by a mainstream publisher.

Touching another form of gay activism, Bell began covering the gay crime beat in early 1973, beginning with a *Village Voice* story about the murders of four gay men in New York City. When "Little John" Wojtowicz robbed a Brooklyn bank to finance a sex change operation for his lover (later portrayed in the film *Dog Day Afternoon*), Bell was called in to act as his mediator. He also reported about the sadistic serial killer Dean Corll and Felix Melendez, who killed newspaper heir John Knight III. The latter slaying became the subject of Bell's second book, *Kings Don't Mean a Thing: The John Knight Murder Case,* which received mixed reviews after its publication. By this time, Bell was writing about crime, entertainment, politics and gay liberation for several publications, including *Cosmopolitan, Esquire, Playboy,* and the *New York Times.* "Bell Tells," his weekly column which began in 1976 in the *Village Voice,* focused on the New York City entertainment and nightlife scene.

Bell died in New York City on 2 June 1984, of complications from diabetes. The *Village Voice,* in a 26 June 1984 article, provided an opportunity for his friends, including Arthur Evans, Harvey Fierstein, Arnie Kantrowitz, Merle Miller, Vito Russo, James M. Saslow, and Liz Smith to share their memories of Arthur Bell.

References:

"Arthur Bell, 51, a Columnist, Homosexual Rights Activist," in *New York Times,* 4 June 1984: IV, 18.

"Arthur Bell: Two or Three Things We Loved About Him," in *Village Voice* (New York), 26 June 1984: 10-11.

Bell, Arthur. *Dancing the Gay Lib Blues: A Year in the Homosexual Liberation Movement.* New York: Simon and Schuster, 1971.

———. *King's Don't Mean A Thing: The John Knight Murder Case.* New York: Morrow, 1978.

Contemporary Authors. Detroit: Gale Research, vols. 85-88, 1980.

Contemporary Authors. Detroit: Gale Research, vol. 112, 1985.

Duberman, Martin. *Stonewall.* New York: Dutton, 1993.

Ortleb, Charles. "Arthur Bell," in *Christopher Street,* February 1979: 61-3.

Schneiderman, David. "A Death in the Family," in *Village Voice* (New York), 12 June 1984: 3.

Teal, Donn. *The Gay Militants.* New York: Stein and Day, 1971.

—Joseph M. Eagan

Miriam Ben-Shalom

1948-

American Army reservist and activist

On 3 May 1948 the woman who would later become Miriam Ben-Shalom was born in Waukesha, Wisconsin. One of six children, she began grade school in Big Bend, then later moved to East Troy where she attended and graduated from East Troy Community High School.

After high school, in 1967, she was married. During her brief marriage, she had a daughter, Hannah Devorah. Like so many others, Ben-Shalom says that she "couldn't have told you" she was gay at the time she married. Ben-Shalom then spent five years in Israel, where she developed a strong tie with the country and a strong identification with its culture. She also became an Israeli citizen and fought in the Israeli army.

It was during this period that she chose for herself a new name that reflected her identification with that culture—Miriam Ben-Shalom. Miriam, she says, was the sister of Moses, reputed to have been so uppity that God had to smite her with leprosy to calm her down—the name itself comes from the word "bitter." Ben-Shalom is the house of Solomon or house of peace. "Bitter things," she says, come from these two places.

When Ben-Shalom returned to the United States, she attended the University of Wisconsin at Milwaukee with the intention of eventually becoming a rabbi and received her bachelor's degree with honors. She then went on to earn her M.A., also with honors.

In 1974, she joined the Army Reserves where she excelled, becoming one of the first two female drill sergeants in her division. It was Sgt. Leonard Matlovich's face on the cover of *Time* magazine in 1975 that got her into trouble. Ben-Shalom could not understand why the gay Air Force Sergeant had been discharged and began asking questions. Those questions, and her frank admission of her lesbianism led to an "honorable discharge."

"I realized my lesbian identity," she says in *My Country, My Right To Serve* "without the benefit of a lover." So, without the benefit of a charge of any kind of misconduct and with only verbal statements about being a lesbian made by Ben-Shalom, the Army sent her packing.

Ben-Shalom had been active in the gay community since coming out in 1973 and was determined to fight the discharge. "In May of 1980 I was the first to win my case," she says emphatically, noting the importance of her victory four months before Matlovich's. She then adds, "It was not a white, gay, male, but a Jewish lesbian to first win such a case." From August of 1987 until February of 1990 she was the "only openly acknowledged homosexual in any branch of service."

In 1988, when her tour of duty was complete, Ben-Shalom wanted to reenlist for another six years. The army, using the same arguments as it had used in 1976, refused to let her do so. In August of 1989, the Seventh U.S. Circuit Court of Appeals reversed the lower court decision allowing Ben-Shalom to rejoin the reserves. However, in October of 1989, she was informed of a stay of the lower court's decision and filed a writ of certiorari with the U.S. Supreme Court. But, in February of 1990, the Supreme Court refused to consider her challenge to the military's policy on gays, effectively ending her military career.

The need for an organization for gay and lesbian veterans quickly became apparent to Ben-Shalom. In 1990, she founded the Gay, Lesbian, & Bisexual Veterans Association (GLBVA), and served as the organization's first president. She is still a member of GLBVA and, in 1993, served as veteran's coordinator for the Campaign for Military Service.

Ben-Shalom is currently an openly gay high-school teacher in the Milwaukee, Wisconsin, public school system where she works with at-risk children. "It is profoundly ironic," she says, "that I'm trusted to teach children, to teach English, but I'm not trustworthy enough to serve my country!"

Teaching and gay activism are not the extent of Ben-Shalom's community involvement. A published writer with poetry, short stories, and other work to her credit, she is very involved with the Gay republican group, the Log Cabin Club. She worked very closely with the Pride Fest committee to put on one of the finest, three-day festivals in the Midwest. Ben-Shalom is also one of the founders of her local community's business association—the Vliet Street Business and Resident's Association. She has worked with the city to get federal and state funding to eliminate drug houses and improve the quality of life in her community.

In 1994, Ben-Shalom received the Anderson Award for her activist work within the gay community. For her work in her local community, she has received the Lisbon Area Neighborhood Development Award for community activism. In addition, she has received civil rights awards, the 1988 Soldier of the Year Award, human rights awards, public service awards, merit awards, and community service awards for her contributions to her local as well as to the gay and lesbian community. She has also won fellowships and grants, and received awards for her poetry.

References:

Ben-Shalom, Miriam. Interview with Andrea L.T. Peterson, August 1996.

Humphrey, Maryann. *My Country, My Right to Serve.* New York: HarperCollins, 1990.

Shilts, Randy. *Conduct Unbecoming.* New York: St. Martin's Press, 1993; CD-ROM version, ApolloMedia Corporation.

—Andrea L.T. Peterson

Ruth Benedict

1887-1948

American anthropologist

Ruth Benedict's rejection of the restrictive Victorian cultural milieu into which she was born led her to break personal and professional boundaries as she forged a place for herself as a woman and an intellectual to become the leading anthropologist of her generation. Personally alienated, Benedict applied her writing, research, and teaching beyond anthropology to contemporary social problems and thereby transformed the values and beliefs of American society, particularly in regard to race, deviancy, and the importance of culture in shaping personality. Her classic *Patterns of Culture* (1934), through specific examples, established that individuals could indeed change their lives if so desired.

Ruth Fulton Benedict was born in New York City on 5 June 1887 to Beatrice Shattuck Fulton, an educator and librarian, and Frederick Samuel Fulton, a surgeon and homeopathic physician. Because of Frederick's failing health, the family moved to the Shattuck dairy farm in Chenango County near Binghamton, New York. Frederick's subsequent death and Beatrice's "cult of grief" profoundly affected the 21-month-old Ruth. In "The Story of My Life," Benedict wrote: "Certainly from my earliest childhood I recognized two worlds ... the world of my father, which was the world of death and which was beautiful, and the world of confusion and explosive weeping which I repudiated." This Apollonian-Dionysian juxtaposition, religion, and death became recurrent themes in some of Benedict's most influential anthropological work.

Genteel Poverty and Scholarships

The young widow Fulton stayed on her parents' farm and raised Ruth and her sister Margery, eighteen months Ruth's junior. Fulton soon returned to teaching, first near the farm, then in Missouri and Owatonna, Minnesota, as Lady Principal of the Pillsbury Academy, finally becoming, in 1899, Superintendent of Circulation at the Buffalo Public Library. Amid genteel poverty, the sisters attended St. Margaret's Episcopal Academy for Girls from 1900 to 1905 on scholarship. Subsequently, Mrs. F. F. Thompson sponsored both sisters' four year scholarships to their mother's alma mater, Vassar College, where Ruth read the works of Walter Pater, Nietzsche, Whitman, Santayana, Charlotte Perkins Gilman, and the naturalist John Burroughs (she met the latter two on their visits to the campus); later she would incorporate many of their theories into her own work. The sisters graduated in 1909, and Ruth was inducted into Phi Beta Kappa.

After their graduation from Vassar, Margery married Rev. Robert Freeman and Ruth embarked on a year's sponsored trip to Europe, eventually joining the Freemans in California, where she taught high school for several years. In June 1914, after some vacillation, she married Stanley Rossiter Benedict, a 1908 Yale graduate, the brother of Vassar acquaintances, and soon-to-be professor of biochemistry at Cornell Medical School in New York City.

After a stormy childhood, marked by partial deafness from a bout with measles that was not discovered until she was five, the shy, stammering adolescent Ruth had turned to writing as an outlet. She had begun a journal while teaching in California. Now, as a suburban housewife with free time and a strong need for something more, she continued; instead of short stories Benedict eventually turned to biography and mapped out a project for essays on the freethinkers Mary Wollstonecraft, Margaret Fuller, and Olive Schreiner, from whose strong lives she drew inspiration. No essays were published; however, she also began writing poetry in earnest, first using the name Ruth Stanhope and then Anne Singleton, the pseudonym under which she published many poems during the next decade. In 1918, still dissatisfied at the age of 31, Benedict returned to school. She studied the educational philosophy of John Dewey at Columbia University and then in 1919 at the New School for Social Research discovered anthropology in courses with Elsie Clews Parsons and Alexander Goldenweiser. Shortly thereafter, Benedict met two people who would change her life.

Life-Changing Mentors

In 1921, upon enrolling in the Ph.D. program at Columbia, Benedict became the student of Franz Boas, the university's influential first professor of anthropology who insisted on field work, for data collecting through keen observation of "living cultures." Within a year, Benedict became Boas's assistant and over the next seven years, often unsalaried, held temporary year-to-year appointments at Barnard or Columbia. In 1924, Boas arranged her appointment as first assistant editor and then editor of the *Journal of American Folklore;* she served until removed in 1939. In 1931, now separated from Stanley, who disapproved of her having a career, Benedict was appointed assistant professor at Columbia, becoming a full professor in the department of anthropology in 1941. Meanwhile, in 1922 while lecturing in Boas's seminar, Benedict met Margaret Mead, 15 years younger and a student at Barnard College. Mead became Benedict's first student.

Although Mead married three times, the two women formed an intimate physical relationship. Benedict's biographer Margaret M. Caffrey writes that they were lovers by the summer of 1925, before Mead went to Samoa. At first, student and teacher comforted each other over the suicide of a Barnard student, but their discussions soon included anthropology, and under Benedict's influence, Mead also enrolled as Benedict's and Boas's student. During the next few years the two women attended seminars together despite Benedict's having already earned a Ph.D. in 1923 with her dissertation "The Concept of the Guardian Spirit in North America."

Mead introduced Benedict to her Barnard roommate Leonie Adams and, with Louise Bogan, they formed a poetry support group. By 1925, under the Singleton pen name, Benedict published her first poems in the New York magazine the *Measure.* Other poems were published in Harriet Monroe's *Poetry,* the *Nation,* and *Palms.* De-

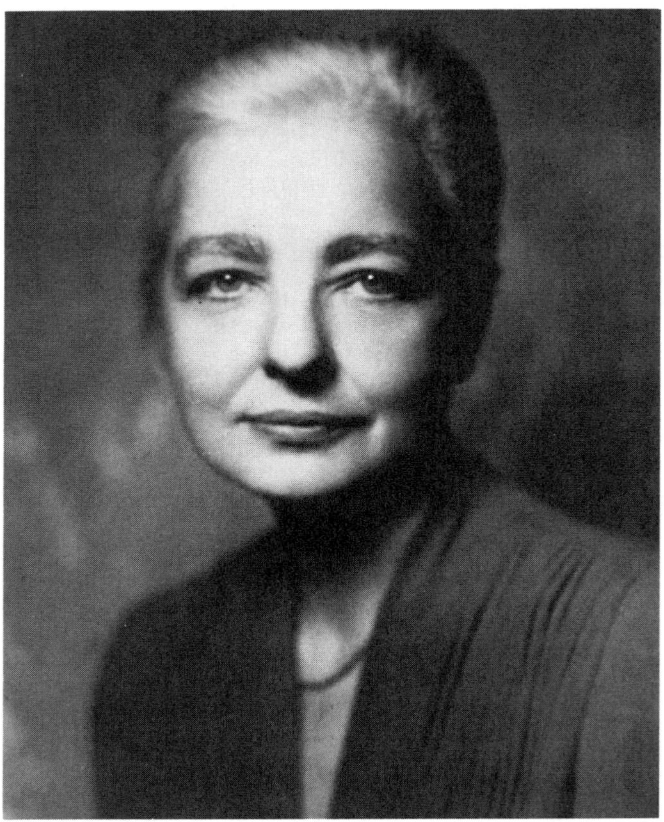

Ruth Benedict

spite this success, Benedict kept the poet and the anthropologist separate; only as she gained confidence did the public and the private personalities begin merging. By the early 1930s, Benedict was no longer using a pseudonym. Several of her poems, letters, and journal entries from this period attest to her happiness. Caffrey sees Benedict's intimacy with Mead "as a revelation" which "affected her so deeply that from that time forward she became a woman-loving woman." Consequently, after Mead, according to Caffrey a "true bisexual," married Rao Fortune, Benedict shared a New York apartment with the Californian Natalie Raymond who came east to attend Cornell Medical School, but seldom finished things. Nevertheless, they lived, according to Benedict, in the "happiest of conditions" until 1938 when Raymond, financed and accompanied briefly by Benedict, left to write a travel account of Guatemala, but the relationship was over. After their breakup, an exhausted Benedict suffering from pleurisy visited her sister in California. While recuperating Benedict moved to the home of Ruth Valentine, a clinical psychologist; thereafter, in the early 1940s "Val" moved to New York as Benedict's companion until the latter's death.

Changing Homophobic Attitudes

Meanwhile, although their physical intimacy waned, Benedict and Mead solidified a lifelong professional collaboration. Following Boas's dictum, both engaged in field work: Mead in Samoa (1925) and Benedict with the Serrano (1922), the Zuni (1924, 1925), and the Pima in Arizona (1927). Their journals and letters record countless hours of discussion as they hammered out their theories. Within the context of their intimate physical relationship, not surprisingly one concern was deviancy within a culture. In an application of Benedict's theory that culture could change, the two set out to change homophobic attitudes. Their discussions resulted in several, now classic, essays and books.

In 1928, Mead published *Coming of Age in Samoa;* its Chapter 11, "The Girl in Conflict" written in 1926, offers their "alternative standard" tenet which argues that unconventional behavior if coupled with a healthy self-respect may be considered undesirable within a culture, but not delinquent. Mead has written that the chapter stems from the question "Ruth Benedict taught me to ask: 'Were there no conflicts, no temperaments which deviated so markedly from the normal that clash was inevitable?'" Benedict furthered the discussion in "Anthropology and the Abnormal" where she shows how one culture's "abnormal" functions with "ease and with honor" in another's. *Patterns of Culture* (1934) brought their argument to a large audience.

In 1928, at the Twenty-third International Congress of Americanists, Benedict created a stir when she delivered "Psychological Types in the Cultures of the Southwest," in which she applied Nietzsche's Apollonian-Dionysian labels to the Zuni and Pima cultures. The paper laid the foundations of *Patterns of Culture,* a volume which compares the results of her field research of the Pueblo, with that of Rao Fortune's of the Dobu of New Guinea and Boas's of the Kwakiutl of Vancouver Island. The book opens with clear definitions of anthropology and culture, presents Benedict's case for studying primitive cultures using the Pueblos, Dobu, and Kwakiutl and explains the "great arc of possible human behaviors" from which a culture selects its valued behaviors and, thus, configures itself. This "culture provides the raw material of which the individual makes his life." The final chapter again takes up Benedict's concern with, according to Mead, how "narrow definitions of normal behavior penalize or give preference to certain innate capacities." Benedict concludes that "those who function inadequately in any society are not those with certain fixed 'abnormal' traits, but may well be those whose responses have received no support in the institutions of their culture ... they are individuals whose native responses are not reaffirmed by society." Widely read and translated into 14 languages, *Patterns of Culture* succeeded in one of Benedict's ongoing goals of popularizing cultural studies and, according to fellow anthropologist Dorothy Lee in Caffrey's biography of Benedict, introduced "a new approach to studying society" by emphasizing culture over biology and employing a world view that prefigures late twentieth century intercultural interests. In fact, in 1939, Benedict assisted the Bureau for Intercultural Education in bringing "cultural diversity" to schools as students ate ethnic food and met foreign born relatives. Without doubt, *Patterns of Culture* placed Benedict at the cutting edge of anthropology.

Applying Anthropology to the War Effort

In 1932, *Science* selected Benedict as one of five top United States anthropologists. The next year *American Men of Science* named her one of the country's three leading women scientists. Meanwhile, Benedict continued reviewing, consulting, teaching and advising at Columbia, and her research on her two-volume work *Zuni Mythology* (1935). In 1939, the American Anthropological Association placed Benedict as the first woman ever in line for its presidency; she held the office from 1947 to 1948. In the late 1930s, Benedict, following the lead of Boas, whose books were burned in Germany, worked at undermining Nazi theories of inferior races and anti-semitism. By 1937 she was secretary and membership chair of the University Federation for Democracy and Intellectual Freedom. She served on many boards and relief committees, some of which were attacked as Communist fronts. Her anti-Fascist activities, combined with her impeccable Revolutionary War and Mayflower heritage, led to the offer to write *Race: Science and Politics* (1940), a scholarly tract analyzing race and racism. While *Race* itself never reached a wide readership, its arguments were distilled over several collaborative projects which did.

The first was a resource unit for teachers: *Race and Cultural Relations: America's Answer to the Myth of A Master Race* (1941), which frankly identified racial prejudice in America towards blacks, Orientals, and Jews and offered solutions to the problem. In 1943, the pamphlet *The Races of Mankind,* sponsored by the Columbia Public Affairs Committee, cost a dime and, thanks to protests by a southern Congressman, sold almost a million copies in the next decade. The popular pamphlet became a comic book, an educational cartoon, and the children's book *In Henry's Backyard,* in 1948.

During World War II, Benedict continued her militant activities for racial equality by speaking out against racism through public lectures and articles, many collected in Mead's *An Anthropologist at Work;* she also often wrote letters to newspapers and magazines defending persecuted groups. Her efforts for peace continued the call for acknowledging and respecting differences. By 1943, Benedict had moved to Washington, D.C., to become the head of the Basic Analysis Section, Bureau of Overseas Intelligence, Office of War Information (OWI), a one-woman office. Using applied anthropology, Benedict wrote a series of short papers on Rumania, Thailand (then the Kingdom of Siam), Germany, and Holland. Then, in 1944 as a Social Science Analyst in the Foreign Morale Division of OWI, she began her study of Japan which influenced the government's long range policies. With the publication of *The Chrysanthemum and the Sword: Patterns of Japanese Culture* in Fall 1946, Benedict also influenced the American public's attitude toward Japan, for the enthusiastically received book helped to explain the heretofore unfathomable Japanese behavior. That same year Benedict won the American Design Award; conferred for giving "the world understanding of its different citizens through her studies of various civilizations of all races." She also won the Achievement Award from The American Association of University Women, and announced she would use the $25,000 she was given for student awards in her newly organized European seminar at Columbia.

Nationally Funded Human Behavior Studies

Benedict always believed that lasting peace would come through cultural understanding, hence her enthusiasm for her final enormous undertaking. In 1942, Mead and her husband, Gregory Bateson, organized the Council on Intercultural Relations—an early "think tank" for the study of human behavior. By 1947, the reorganized council formed the Columbia University Research in Contemporary Cultures (RCC), a study of national character funded by the Office of Naval Research with a yearly budget of nearly $100,000. With Benedict as director, Ruth Bunzel, Valentine, and Mead shaped the non-hierarchical organization and enlisted the participation of most of the anthropologists committed to cultural relativity; its purpose was to study foreign origin groups in the United States. Its theories and techniques unsupported by the scientific school of anthropology, the RCC had limited immediate impact, but its organization served as a model for future projects. Mead saw RCC to its conclusion in 1951.

In May 1948, Columbia University finally promoted Benedict to full professor. She was the first woman to hold the rank in the faculty of political science. That summer she lectured in the UNESCO seminar on childhood education in Czechoslovakia, since child-rearing and family had been long-time interests. Her energetic participation in the seminar and European travel exhausted her. Two days after her return, Benedict suffered a heart attack and died on 17 June 1948—her father's birthday.

Benedict's work influenced an entire generation of anthropologists as she helped transform anthropology from an esoteric science. Contemporary descriptions sketch a shy, elegant, civilized, tolerant woman whose high standards, compassion, and dedicated leadership helped destroy female academic stereotypes and shape contemporary American attitudes.

References:

Bateson, Mary Catherine. *With a Daughter's Eye.* New York: William Morrow and Co., 1984.

Benedict, Ruth. "Anthropology and the Abnormal," in *An Anthropologist At Work: Writings of Ruth Benedict,* by Margaret Mead. Boston: Houghton Mifflin, 1959; New Foreward, 1966; Greenwood Press Edition, 1977: 262-283.

———. *Patterns of Culture.* Boston: Houghton Mifflin, 1959: ix, 252, 270.

———. "Psychological Types in the Cultures of the Southwest," in *An Anthropologist At Work: Writings of Ruth Benedict,* by Margaret Mead. Boston: Houghton Mifflin, 1959; New Foreword, 1966; Greenwood Press Edition, 1977.

———. "The Story of My Life," in *An Anthropologist At Work: Writings of Ruth Benedict,* by Margaret Mead. Boston: Houghton Mifflin, 1959; New Foreword, 1966; Greenwood Press Edition, 1977: 97-112.

Caffrey, Margaret M. *Ruth Benedict: Stranger In This Land.* Austin: University of Texas Press, 1989: 188, 202, 263.

Current Biography. New York: H. W. Wilson, 1941.

Feminist Companion to Literature in English: Women Writers From the Middle Ages to the Present. New Haven, Connecticut: Yale University Press, 1990.

Howard, Jane. *Margaret Mead: A Life.* New York: Simon and Schuster, 1984.

Kunitz, Stanley J., ed. *Twentieth Century Authors: A Biographical Dictionary of Modern Literature.* New York: H. W. Wilson Co., 1955.

Mead, Margaret. *An Anthropologist at Work: Writings of Ruth Benedict.* Boston: Houghton Mifflin, 1959; New Foreword, 1966; Greenwood Press, 1977.

———. *Blackberry Winter: My Earlier Years.* New York: William Morrow, 1972.

———. *Ruth Benedict.* New York: Columbia University Press, 1974.

Modell, Judith Schactner. *Ruth Benedict: Patterns of A Life.* Philadelphia: University of Pennsylvania Press, 1983.

Wenner-Gren Foundation for Anthropological Research. *Ruth Fulton Benedict: A Memorial.* New York: Viking Fund, 1949.

—Judith C. Kohl

Michael Bennett

1943-1987

American choreographer, director, and writer

Michael Bennett DiFiglia was born on 8 April 1943 in Buffalo, New York, the son of Salvatore Joseph DiFiglia, a factory worker for General Motors, and Helen (Ternoff) DiFiglia, a secretary at Sears Roebuck. Bennett began his dancing career at the age of three, and he attended numerous dance schools throughout his childhood, including Beverly Fletcher's Dance School in Niagara Falls, New York, Mrs. John Dunn's Little Stars of Tomorrow in Buffalo, and, during the summer of 1955, Sylvia Fort's School of Theater in New York City, where he began to work with professionals such as Aubrey Hitchins and Matt Mattox. He danced at weddings and other events, using some of the money he earned to help pay for dance shoes and lessons. By the age of 12, Bennett was studying tap, modern, and folk dancing as well as ballet. By the age of 14 he was choreographing and directing high school productions, appearing in community theater (he played Puck in *A Midsummer's Night Dream* at the Studio Arena in Buffalo, New York) and appearing on local radio and television shows. Eventually he became an apprentice in summer stock at the Melody Fair Theater in North Tonawanda, New York.

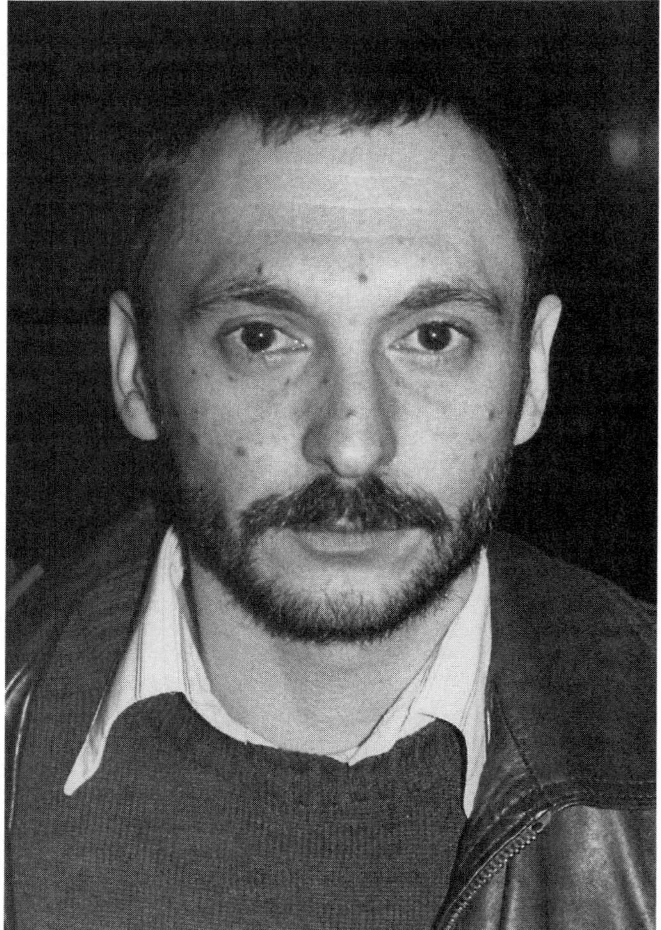

Michael Bennett

In September of 1957, Bennett decided to enroll at Hutchinson Central Technical High School for Boys to study architectural design as a career to fall back on. Although he was a member of the student council, a cheerleader, and active in school thatrical productions at Central, he was not much interested in his studies there, and after being asked to repeat his sophomore year at Hutchinson Tech, he decided to transfer to Bennett High School in the fall of 1959. By the end of his junior year, Bennett lost interest in school altogether, and he dropped out officially to pursue a career in the theater in September 1960.

On to Broadway

Bennett's first major role was that of Baby John in Melody Fair's production of *West Side Story* in 1959. This helped him land the same role for the European tour the following year. After returning from Europe, Bennett taught dancing at the June Taylor Studios in New York City. He made his Broadway stage debut in 1961 in *Subways Are for Sleeping,* but his career as a dancer was short-lived; he had only two more Broadway shows to his credit: *Here's Love* (1963) and *Bajour* (1964). He claimed to prefer choreography over performing, even as a child.

A Joyful Noise was the first Broadway musical Bennett choreographed solo. It opened at the Mark Hellinger Theater in 1966 but closed after just 12 performances. Despite the short run of the play, critics were enthused about Bennett's choreography, and he was nominated for a Tony Award for his work in the play. *Henry, Sweet Henry* was the next Broadway show Bennett choreographed. Like *A Joyful Noise,* the play had a short run, but Bennett was once again singled out for praise and received a second Tony nomination.

In 1968 Bennett had his first big hit, *Promises, Promises,* which was based on the film *The Apartment* by Billy Wilder and I. A. L. Diamond and ran for over two years. His next show, *Coco* (1969), a musical based on the life of Coco Chanel, starred Katharine Hepburn. Although critics were unimpressed, the play was popular and showcased Bennett's inceasingly innovative style. By 1970, Bennett had built a reputation and had quickly become known as a talented contemporary choreographer. The musical *Company,* which was the fifth Broadway show he choreographed, ran eighteen months; it was with this production that Bennett decided he wanted to be a director as well choreographer.

In 1971 Bennett produced and directed *Twigs.* In that same year he choreographed and co-directed, with Harold Prince, the musical *Follies,* which garnered Bennett his first Tony Award for choreography. Two years later, Bennett was called in to save the ailing show *Seesaw* just six weeks before it was to open. He accepted under the condition that he would have creative control of the production, and he ultimately served as director and co-choreographer along with Grover Dale and Tommy Tune. *Seesaw* closed after ten months with decent reviews and won two Tony Awards. Bennett began, but never completed, two more musicals after *Seesaw*: *Space* and *Pin-Ups*. *Space* was never completed due to casting problems and *Pin-Ups* ran into financial problems.

A Chorus Line

Despite his burgeoning success, Bennett became unhappy and frustrated with himself, Broadway, and American society in general. He began looking back on his own theatrical experiences and decided that he wanted to do a show about the lives of dancers. Late one night in January of 1974, Bennett invited eighteen dancers he knew to the Nickolaus Exercise Center in New York City to discuss their lives and experiences. They sold their stories to Bennett for $1. Later, some would regret selling out, but others were thankful to be involved this once-in-a-lifetime experience. What grew from that session, and one other in February, was unquestionably the greatest accomplishment of Bennett's career—*A Chorus Line*.

After some difficulty in securing backers, *A Chorus Line* officially opened at the Shubert Theater on Broadway on 25 July 1975. It became the longest running Broadway show in history on 23 September 1983 and finally closed on 28 April 1990. Bennett directed, co-produced, co-authored and co-choreographed *A Chorus Line* and won nine Tony Awards for his work.

Bennett's next play, *Ballroom,* was disappointing, receiving mediocre reviews and eventually causing Bennett to lose money. His last play was *Dreamgirls,* a rollicking homage to girl-groups of the 1960s which he produced, directed, and co-choreographed with Michael Peters.

Bennett's other credits include choreography for the television programs *Hollywood Palace* from 1964 to 1970, *Hullabaloo* from 1965 to 1966, the *Ed Sullivan Show* from 1968 to 1971, the *Dean Martin Show,* and the film *What's So Bad About Feeling Good?* in 1968. It was while working on Hullabaloo that he met the dancer Donna McKechnie, whom he married in 1976. The marriage lasted less than two years, but the two maintained a close friendship for many years. Bennett also had romantic relationships with both men and women. It was his intimate understanding of both sexes that enabled him to become so successful as a director.

Following the success of *A Chorus Line,* Bennett sought to give something back to the community that had afforded him such great success. He purchased a building at 890 Broadway, which he renovated and maintained as studio and performance space for dancers, writers, producers, set designers, costume makers, and directors. His goal was to provide a forum for untested work that might fail to attract backing from mainstream theaters.

A Theatrical Legacy

Bennett died from AIDS-related lymphoma on 2 July 1987, in Tucson, Arizona, and his death was mourned as a great loss by the theatrical community. Respected for his theatrical genius, he could be demanding and controlling but also inspirational. A perfectionist, he liked to be in charge and often times manipulated people to get what he wanted. He sometimes paid the price with broken relationships. Yet Bennett's main source of satisfaction and pride was his work, and given his enormous stage successes, he had much to be proud of.

References:

Buffalo News, 9 February 1990; 22 November 1987; 3 February 1987; 8 March 1979; 21 February 1976.

Contemporary Authors, vol 101. Detroit: Gale, 1984.

Contemporary Theater, Film, and Television, vol. 5. Detroit: Gale Research, 1981.

Current Biography Yearbook. New York: H.W. Wilson Co., 1981, 1987.

Kelly, Kevin. *One Singular Sensation: The Michael Bennett Story.* New York: Doubleday, 1990.

Kroll, Jack and Constance Guthrie. "Gotta Dance ... Gotta Dance" in *Newsweek* (New York), 9 June 1975: 85-6.

Kroll, Jack and Constance Guthrie. "Broadway's New Kick" in *Newsweek* (New York), 1 December 1975: 66-70.

Mandelbaum, Ken. *A Chorus Line and the Musicals of Michael Bennett.* New York: St. Martin's Press, 1989.

Philip, Richard. "Michael Bennett and the Making of *A Chorus Line*" in *Dance Magazine* (New York), June 1975: 62-65.

Saal, Hubert. "The Dance: Broadway Rhythm" in *Newsweek* (New York), 13 December 1971: 76-77.

Viagas, Robert, Baayork Lee, and Thommie Walsh. *On the Line: The Creation of "A Chorus Line."* New York: William Morrow, 1990.

—Lara Bushallow-Wilbur

Gladys Bentley

1907-1960

African-American blues singer

Gladys Bentley is one of the bolder and more enigmatic figures of classic blues and lesbian history. Reaching the zenith of her popularity during the 1920s and 1930s, she was a renowned singer and piano player in the underground sporting life of rent-parties and Harlem clubs such as the Mad House, Clam House, and Cotton Club, where she was infamous for her roguish appearance and naughty twists on popular lyrics. Bentley began a more traditional female blues recording career in August of 1928 with the Okeh recording company. Accompanying herself on the piano she recorded blues songs such as "How Long, How Long Blues" and "How Much Can I Stand?" In 1945 she recorded five discs on the Excelsior label. Bentley was also known for her extraordinary public lesbian persona, which was portrayed in the character of Sybil in Blair Nile's gay novel *Strange Brother* (1931). Her later career included a move to the West Coast where she performed at Hollywood's Rose Room.

Bentley's life is not well documented. She was born the first of four children on 12 August 1907, to George L. Bentley and Mary C. Mote. Living in Philadelphia, Bentley's family faced the economic discrimination with which many African-American families struggled. In addition to her poor and inauspicious origins, Bentley claimed in an autobiographical essay for *Ebony* magazine to have been aware that she was different in terms of her gender and sexuality at an early age: "It seems I was born different.... I never wanted a man to touch me.... I began to feel more comfortable in boy's clothes than in dresses." Bentley depicts her childhood as one of marked difference due to her weight, color, and gender non-conformity. As a young adolescent she became aware of her attraction to women after a sustained crush on a schoolteacher. Enduring many types of pressure to change, from the ridicule of peers to her parents consulting doctors about her so-called sexual problem, Bentley avoided further trauma by escaping her hometown of Philadelphia at the age of 16 to take up residence in Harlem.

Sporting Life Days to Hotspot Headliner

Arriving in Harlem, Bentley gravitated towards the lively sporting life that was not condoned by black middle-class imperatives of moral rectitude informing the Harlem Renaissance. "Sporting life" refers to the social activity which took place on the economically illicit side of Harlem, one that abounded with gambling, rent-parties, female impersonators, sex shows, drugs, and alcohol. For Bentley, and many others, this subcultural arena offered acceptance and approval of gay and lesbian identities. Performing at private parties and other all-night venues, Bentley became a popular figure in the socially marginal Harlem nightlife.

Bentley's first nightclub chance came when she was hired to perform at the Mad House on 133rd Street in "Jungle Alley," an area between Lenox and Seventh Avenues. Her salary in the beginning was $35 a week but was increased to $100 a week when downtowners such as Carl Van Vechten began patronizing her shows. Becoming popular with the fashionable audiences, Bentley performed at the Cotton Club and Harry Hansberry's Clam House, places where the culturally sophisticated and white patrons came to applaud her talents. Headlining at the Clam House for several years, Bentley became a unique event in Harlem nightlife. In his memoir, *The Big Sea,* Langston Hughes recalls that Bentley was "something worth discovering in those days." Hughes describes the magic of Bentley's performance:

> For two or three amazing years, Miss Bentley sat, and played a big piano all night long, literally all night, without stopping ... Miss Bentley was an amazing exhibition of musical energy—a large, dark, masculine lady, whose feet pounded the floor while her fingers pounded the keyboard—a perfect piece of African sculpture, animated by her own rhythm.

Bentley thus built her career as a notorious Harlem performer and overt lesbian—one who proudly displayed the "bulldagger" image. In "Gladys Bentley: The Bulldagger Who Sang the Blues," Eric Garber writes that this image was "the one identifiable black lesbian stereotype of this period: the tough-talking, masculine acting, cross-dressing, and sexually worldly 'bull dagger.'" Bessie Smith sang about "mannish acting women," and Ma Rainey enjoyed "wearing a collar and a tie" in "Prove It on Me Blues," but Bentley made the black bulldagger role the center of her performance. Bentley performed in tuxedos and top hats, sang to women in the audience, exulted in being the object of sexually suggestive gossip, and married her female lover in a much publicized wedding. So compelling was Bentley's cross-dressing performance that decades later the artist Romare Bearden mistook her for a female impersonator.

West Coast Blues

In the early 1930s, Bentley survived the repeal of prohibition, the onset of the Depression, and the slump in the craze for black female blues singers. She moved with New York's jazz scene to 52nd Street to perform at the Ubangi Club, where she shared billing with Jackie Mabley, Bill Bailey, and a chorus line of female impersonators. By the late 1930s the vogue for Harlem was gone. Bentley relocated to the West Coast to live with her mother and perform at local clubs where she had moderate success.

Ultimately, Bentley's cross-dressing style brought difficulties. Garber reports that in February of 1940 her employers at Jaoquin's El Rancho in Los Angeles were forced to obtain a special police permit "to allow Gladys Bentley, 250-pound colored entertainer, to wear trousers instead of skirts during her act." Morevoer, although Bentley had spent a lifetime cultivating her queer audience, she later denounced her lesbian past, as in "I Am a Woman Again," in which she claimed to be cured of her homosexuality and happily married to a man. In the 1950s she appeared on the Groucho Marx show and recorded a disc with the Flame label. During her remaining years, she performed in Hollywood, volunteered as a churchworker at the *Temple of Love in Christ,* and cared for her aged mother. Bentley died at the age of 52 during a flu epidemic.

Although she never became a popular recording star, Bentley carved out her own niche with a musical career that challenged negative stereotypes of black female sexuality. Her musical prowess defines Bentley as one of the most fascinating, witty, richly imaginative, and influential performers of the Harlem Renaissance.

References:

Bentley, Gladys. "I Am a Woman Again," in *Ebony* (Chicago), August 1952: 7, 92-98.

Carby, Hazel. "It Jus Be's Dat Way Sometime," in *Feminisms,* edited by Robyn R. Warhol and Diane Price Herndl. New Brunswick: Rutgers University Press, 1991: 746-758.

Garber, Eric. "Gladys Bentley: The Bulldager Who Sang the Blues," in *Outlook 1*, Spring 1988: 52-61.

———. "A Spectacle in Color: The Lesbian and Gay Subculture of Jazz Age Harlem," in *Hidden from History,* edited by Martin Bauml Duberman, Martha Vicinus, and George Chauncey, Jr. New York: Penguin Books, 1989: 318-331.

Hughes, Langston. *The Big Sea.* New York: Thunder's Mouth Press, 1986: 226.

Willis-Braithwaite, Deborah. *VanDerZee: Photographer 1886-1983.* New York: Harry N. Abrams, Inc., 1993: 110.

—Laura Alexandra Harris

Nancy K. Bereano

1942-

American publisher and editor

As an editor at Crossing Press, and later as publisher and editor of Firebrand Books, Nancy K. Bereano has consistently produced quality works by a broad spectrum of lesbian and feminist writers in a variety of genres.

Nancy Kirp Bereano was born 17 August 1942 in New York City to Adele Relis Kirp and Herman "Hy" Kirp. Bereano's mother was a homemaker, and her father owned a small wholesale food company that distributed canned fish. Of her parents, Bereano says: "My father is very comfortable around language and words and so I think I got from my dad a real sense of pleasure in language. Also an enormous drive, for better or worse, to do something significant in life. From my mother, I got a sense of aesthetics which is

Nancy K. Bereano. ***Photograph by Jill Posener.***

helpful when putting books into the world, and a sense of what it means to survive."

Growing up in New York, Bereano attended public school. Describing her childhood, Bereano says simply: "I read a lot and I was a *painfully* good girl." She auditioned successfully on the piano for entrance into the School of Music and Art where she learned to play the cello. Bereano stayed in New York to attend Queens College, and shortly after graduating with a B.A. in English in 1963, married Philip L. Bereano. In 1968, after a two-year tour of duty in Washington, D.C., the couple moved to Ithaca, New York, where Philip attended Cornell University. The next year Bereano gave birth to her only child, Joshua. The couple divorced several years later.

In those days of the anti-Viet Nam war movement, the university was a politically charged environment and it was not long until Bereano became active in grassroots organizing. Throughout the 1970s, she was engaged in various progressive movements, including anti-war activism, women's liberation, and welfare organizing. The skills and connections she acquired during these years provided a solid foundation for her upcoming career in publishing.

In 1980, Bereano took a part-time position at Crossing Press as editor of its Feminist Series. "At the time, I thought editing meant putting in commas," comments Bereano, and although she has since discovered differently, "it has turned out to be my right work." During her five years at Crossing Press, Bereano developed a penchant for acquiring manuscripts of such seminal feminist works as Audre Lorde's *Sister Outsider* and Marilyn Frye's *The Politics of Reality*, and attracting such noted authors as Charlotte Bunch, Michelle Cliff, Judy Grahn, Valerie Miner, Pat Parker, and Jane Rule.

It was shortly before starting work at Crossing Press that Bereano came out. "I didn't come out until I was 38. I was able to be a lesbian because of the feminist and lesbian movement," Bereano reflects. "Once I came out I felt like I had been given another opportunity in my life. I wouldn't have been able to come close to realizing whatever potential I have without living in a lesbian world."

While at Crossing Press, Bereano attended the second Women in Print Conference, an event that was to resonate strongly throughout her life, both professionally and personally. "It was mind boggling. I met everyone involved in lesbian and feminist publishing," she recounts. She made valuable connections at the conference and became a key player in the Women in Print movement, drawing upon her political organizing and publishing skills. On a personal note, Bereano met Janis Kelly, one of the conference organizers and a member of the *off our backs* collective. The two quickly became lovers, forming a relationship that lasted ten years.

In October of 1984, Bereano was fired from Crossing Press because of creative differences. Drawing upon "a certain amount of anger and revenge" in addition to her considerable publishing skills and connections, Bereano started Firebrand Books the very next month. By April of 1985, Firebrand had published its first three books. Over the years, Firebrand has gone on to publish over 80 books documenting the rich diversity of the lesbian and feminist experience and has won 11 Lambda Literary Awards and four American Library Association Gay, Lesbian, and Bisexual Book Awards. Among the prominent authors that Firebrand has published are: Dorothy Allison, Alison Bechdel, Beth Brant, Cheryl Clarke, Leslie Feinberg, Jewelle Gomez, Judith Katz, Audre Lorde, Joan Nestle, Pat Parker, Cindy Patton, Minnie Bruce Pratt, Ruthann Robson, Barbara Smith, and Kitty Tsui. Bereano herself was awarded the 1996 Publisher's Service Award by the Lambda Literary Awards, which declared her "at the forefront of lesbian and small press publishing."

Bereano resides in Ithaca with novelist Elisabeth Nonas, her lover since 1995. Reflecting on publishing, she says: "I really do believe that books have a power to help change the world and that has been true in my life. At the times in my life when there were momentous changes, books have been the way I've expanded my horizons. I feel like doing this is a kind of payback, helping to put back in the world lots of what I got out."

Current Address: c/o Firebrand Books, 141 The Commons, Ithaca, New York 14850.

References:

Bereano, Nancy. Interview with R. Ellen Greenblatt, 1996.

—R. Ellen Greenblatt

Ruth Bernhard

1905-

American photographer

Ruth Bernhard is a pioneering photographer of the twentieth century. Throughout six decades of photography she combined a successful commercial photographic career with her pursuit of photography as an art.

Bernhard was born in Germany on 14 October 1905 to a family with an artistic tradition—her father was a commercial artist whose distinctive work was everywhere in their home country. Bernhard was educated at the Akademie der Kunst in Berlin from 1925 to the time of her emigration to the United States in 1927, becoming a citizen in 1935. She learned the craft of photography under Ralph Steiner at the popular magazine the *Delineator* after her arrival from Germany and struck out on her own in the early 1930s.

Bernhard met photographer Edward Weston in 1934. "That was the first time I saw a photographer who was an artist," she told Liz Lufkin. It took a year after their meeting until Bernhard was prepared to pick up her own work (as opposed to her commercial work) again.

Bernhard's photographs of female nudes bring her the most renown. Asked why these studies are so distinctive, she said: "I was always interested in life forms, and seed pods ... To me, the nudes were only a progression of that kind of thinking. I think we are seed pods, human seed pods. We are the past, the present, and also the future..." "I wasn't aware that it was unusual to photograph nudes. I didn't even know it was unusual to be a woman photographer." Coincidence brought her to the photography of nudes and into the avant garde of the 1930s art world. She worked in New York in advertising, architectural, and industrial photography. "I was living on Lexington Avenue and above me lived a man who was in charge of a catalog for the Museum of Modern Art called 'Machine Art'.... So I got the job to shoot the catalog. One day they sent me a large stainless steel bowl for making salads in hotels. My friend Peggy came by, and I said, 'Why don't you get in this bowl?' She said, 'Great,' took off her clothes and jumped in."

Bernhard's move to Southern California brought her into the heart of the Los Angeles artistic community. Her commercial work moved toward the realm of California's industry, Hollywood.

Bernhard committed to the World War II effort by joining the Women's Land Army, charged with contributing to sustaining the civilian and army work forces. Illness during the late 1940s and early 1950s restricted her creative efforts.

In April of 1953 she finally settled on Clay St. in San Francisco where she has since remained. Her studio attracted students and she began teaching there. Bernhard's special gift for the female form was recognized by the director of the Berkeley extension school: she taught the art of photographing the nude there. She also taught at the University of California Extension in San Francisco, Utah State University in Logan, and a master class at Columbia University in New York.

Bernhard's work is in the San Francisco Museum of Modern Art, the Museum of Modern Art in New York, the Center for Creative Photography, the Bibliotheque Nationale in Paris; the George Eastman House in Rochester, New York; and the Massachusetts Institute of Technology, among others.

Her first solo exhibition was in 1936 at the Pacific Institute for Music and Art in Los Angeles. Her most recent was at the San Francisco Museum of Modern Art in 1986. Bernhard also exhibited in local and traveling group shows at, among other places, the Metropolitan Museum of Art, New York; the International Center of Photography in New York; and in a traveling show that included the Corcoran Gallery, Washington, D.C., and the Centre Pompidou in Paris.

Bernhard's published work includes the volumes *The Big Heart* (1957), *Collecting Light: the Photographs of Ruth Bernhard* (1979) *The Eternal Body: Photographs by Ruth Bernhard* (1986), and *Gift of the Commonplace* (1996).

References:

Evans, Martin Marix, ed. *Contemporary Photographers*, 3rd ed. Detroit: St. James Press, 1996.

Lufkin, Liz. "Ruth Bernhard," in *American Photographer*, April 1988.

Who's Who in American Art, 1995-96. 21st ed. New York: R.R. Bowker, 1996.

—Richard Voos

Leonard Bernstein

1919-1990

American composer and conductor

Musical Renaissance man Leonard Bernstein is the most protean figure worldwide in twentieth-century music, with an unmatched flair for showmanship and popular appeal. He had classic good looks with a compact physique, deep-set hazel eyes, aquiline nose, and athletic coordination. By nature he was good humored, personable, and generous. With his ebullient theatricality and his verve, erudition, and magnetic allure, he seemed one of life's darlings. Not an innovator, he was Shakespearean in his ability to assimilate what others had invented and to set upon it the stamp of his own unique genius.

Louis (later Leonard) Bernstein was born in Lawrence, Massachusetts, 25 August 1918, to first-generation American citizens, Samuel Yosef and Jennie Resnick Bernstein, from the Jewish pale of the Ukraine. Samuel started life cleaning fish in the Fulton Street Market in New York, then, thanks to a stint in a barbershop, became associated with a supplier of hair and beauty products. By 1930 he was the owner of the Samuel Bernstein Hair Company with a staff of 50. This was the springboard to middle-class prosperity. It was thanks to this affluence that the younger Bernstein would have access to good teachers and a superior education.

A Musical Upbringing

Leonard's tastes for music asserted themselves when he was ten years old with the arrival of a mahogany upright piano, a gift from an aunt. His connection to the instrument was immediate and spontaneous. He soon asked for lessons, and within one year his teacher was assigning him Chopin nocturnes and preludes. He met his lifelong friend, Sid Ramin, at the age of 12. Ramin later reported to biographer Humphrey Burton that he had no recollection of 14-year-old Bernstein having a regular girlfriend. "He held back from committing himself physically with either sex."

By the age of 13, Bernstein had outgrown his local piano teacher, so his family chose a teacher at the New England Conservatory of Music. At about the same time, Bernstein was admitted to the Boston Latin School. His classmates, who considered him a good first baseman, could not deter him from his 5:30 departure to practice his piano and do his homework even by cat calls of "fruit, fruit, sissy." There are no stories of his sexual leanings from this period of his life. His next piano teacher, Helen Coates, who started working with him when he was 16 and eventually became his private secretary, was to enjoy with him a relationship that lasted 50 years.

Bernstein graduated with honors in 1931 and was admitted to Harvard. "The seventeen-year-old Leonard Bernstein was a good-looking, debonair young man, five feet eight and slim, with a thick shock of wavy dark hair; he dressed smartly, usually sporting a bow tie and a cigarette in an elegant holder." Two years later, he met the famous Greek conductor, Dimitri Mitropoulos, aged 40, who was honored at Harvard at a function during which Bernstein was invited to play. The conductor was so impressed by the young man's musical passion that he invited him to attend his rehearsals of the Boston Symphony Orchestra. Bernstein was profoundly affected by Mitropoulos' expressive style that had recourse to flamboyant body language articulated by magnetism and physical power. It was he who persuaded Bernstein that he had the makings of a fine conductor. Along with Serge Koussevitzky, Mitropoulos discerned quite early Bernstein's prodigious potential and promoted him as a wunderkind.

Another early influence on Bernstein was Aaron Copland, whom he met while still at Harvard. Despite the 20-year age gap, they enjoyed a close friendship over the next six years, and there is some evidence that they even became lovers, as Mitropoulos and Bernstein had also presumably done—though neither relationship was long-lasting. Copland gave his young friend invaluable advice as he took his first halting steps in composition and conducting. By the time of his senior year at Harvard, he began to confront his sexuality after discovering the New York gay colony, where guilt was apparently not a problem.

Choosing Music as a Career

Even with a Harvard diploma now in his hand, Bernstein faced an uncertain future. He turned down his father's offer to join the family firm at $100 a week. Instead he joined a group of five unknown performers who sublet a New York apartment with a Steinway grand piano. Continued encouragement from Mitropoulos and Copland steered him toward conducting. It was perhaps through Copland's contact with Fritz Reiner that Bernstein was admitted to the Philadelphia Curtis Institute of Music, which attracted both aspiring performers and composers. It was Mitropoulos—not Samuel Bernstein—who offered to pay the $75 a month that was not covered by the scholarship.

It was in the summer after his first year at Curtis that Bernstein had his introduction to the Berkshire Music Center at Tanglewood, a famous Massachusetts site of musical activities since 1937. Serge Koussevitzky, reigning director of the Boston Symphony, held court there. It began as a festival but soon included a vigorous training center for some 300 students every summer. Along with four other students, Bernstein, had been singled out to participate in Koussevitzky's conducting class and was selected to conduct the first concert of the season. In the audience were his parents along with sister Shirley, a student at Mount Holyoke, and brother Burtie, who was then eight. In a letter to Copland, who was also present at Tanglewood that summer, Bernstein wrote, "Not seeing you is something of a shock, you understand. The summer was a revelation in that regard: neither of us (I hope) tired of the other (I had feared you might), and I came, in fact, to depend in many ways on you. I've never felt about anyone before as I do about you, completely at ease, and always comforted with you. This is not a love letter, but I'm quite mad about you."

H. Burton concludes that Bernstein had no great love affair during his student days other than *his* love affair with music. More revealing, perhaps, is an observation of Bernstein's to Shirley Gabis, a Curtis student with whom he became close during his second year: "I have a canker in my soul."

Bernstein's first big break came when he was asked by Artur Rodzinski to become his assistant conductor at the New York Philharmonic. His duties entailed sitting in on all rehearsals and learning each score sufficiently well to substitute for the maestro at a moment's notice. He rented his first apartment in Carnegie Hall itself. Later that season, when he had to replace Bruno Walter, who had become ill, he became the youngest person ever to direct a Philharmonic concert as well as the first American-born conductor to head a major orchestra. Though he had not even had time to rehearse with the orchestra, at the end of the nationally broadcast concert, the audience brought him back four times, and the critics covered him with bouquets in all the major New York newspapers.

Soon he was invited to appear with the Pittsburgh and Boston orchestras, and he was on his meteoric rise to international celebrityhood. Much of Bernstein's leap to fame is a study in timing. The following season three of his compositions had premieres in New York: his first musical, *On the Town*; his first symphony, *Jeremiah*; and his first ballet, *Fancy Free*. *Jeremiah* was selected by the New York Music Critics Circle as the outstanding classical work of the season. *Fancy Free*, a masterpiece of American vernacular, claimed a new role for dance in musical comedy. Soon, he was besieged by numerous offers to conduct.

In 1945, Bernstein was guest conductor with 14 different symphonies. From 1945 to 1948 he was conductor of the New York City Orchestra. In 1953 he became the first American to conduct at Milan's acclaimed La Scala with Maria Callas singing the starring role. Not one to concentrate only on work, he gives a glimpse of his personal life in a letter to Copland. "I miss you terribly and need your cynical ears for my latest tales of love and limb—from Montreal to San Francisco. Oh, what a divine one in San Francisco!"

Felicia Montealegre, born in Costa Rica in 1922 of a Chilean mother and American father, was 24 and in New York studying to be an actress when she met Bernstein. She was slim, even delicate, educated by British Catholic nuns, and every inch a lady. According to some, it was love at first sight. They soon became engaged. But the engagement dragged on so long that Montealegre finally called it off and plunged headlong into her own career, which soon had her in important television dramatic roles. By the end of 1949, she was elected as the female Most Promising Star of Tomorrow by members of the industry. Bernstein and Montealegre finally married within four years of their first meeting, Montealegre aware of Bernstein's attraction to men but confident that he would change. There were three children.

The 1950s, when Bernstein was in his 30s, were his most productive years. In 1956 *Candide* received the New York Theater Critic award. *The Serenade for Violin and String Orchestra with Percussion* won high critical praise in 1954. The previous year *Wonderful Town* was a long-run hit, but it was *West Side Story* in 1957 that spoke most eloquently the language of contemporary music. Exploding with energy, animation, and feeling, it is a prodigious amalgamation of American musical strains, including jive and big-band jazz, and, with its highly lyrical love songs and Latino dance rhythms, it is a blend of opera, choreography, and musical comedy.

Bernstein's first season with the New York Philharmonic, where he was director from 1957-69, ushered in a new age in the explora-

Leonard Bernstein

tion of American music. Sometimes as pianist-soloist conducting from the keyboard, he commanded a vast repertory. He gave music lovers the opportunity to hear a new generation of composers: George Chadwick, Lukas Foss, Ned Rorem, and Gunther Schuller. He drew on his talents as an educator in TV appearances and phonograph recordings, the most notable of which were some 50 "Young People's Concerts" and his educational programs on the PBS cultural series "Omnibus."

"A Bitter and Lonely Old Man"

With his children nearly grown, Bernstein became deeply involved with Tom Cothran, a relationship which threatened the equilibrium of his marriage. Cothran even accompanied him as a "traveling secretary" in 1976 on a cross-country tour as part of the bicentennial celebrations.

Of Irish descent, Tom Cothran was 24 and music director of a San Francisco radio station. Bernstein was 53, his hair now gray and the lines in his face quite conspicuous. During his 20-year marriage Bernstein had had his share of homosexual encounters. (No affairs with women are ever referred to by his biographer though his sister Shirley declared him bisexual.) Cothran's entry into his life marked the beginning of a strong emotional relationship with a man and the end of an intimate relationship with Montealegre, who was to die two years later of inoperable lung cancer. Bernstein believed himself responsible for his wife's death, a belief that cast its shadow over the 12 years that remained to him. He never forgot her whispered curse when he told her he was leaving her for Cothran: "You're going to die a bitter and lonely old man."

Bernstein's biographer, Humphrey Burton, speculates that when Cothran became stricken with AIDS in 1980, Bernstein lost the "only person who might have filled the void left by Felicia." He now became noisy about the need to come out of the closet. Once, when he egged on Aaron Copland, in his 80s, to "come out," he got this curt reply: "I think I'll leave that to you, boy." During his final decade, he explored relationships with dozens of men, easily becoming enamored with the young conductors he worked with each year. At his daughter's wedding reception at the Waldorf-Astoria, with 400 guests present, he ended his toast with a list of his new son-in-law's virtues, adding this boast in conclusion: "and he's *straight*."

By now, whenever he went abroad, Bernstein was courted by monarchs and presidents and often the guest of honor at public receptions and private parties, and he received prestigious awards. In France he was honored with the title of Commander in the Legion d'Honneur. The Germans gave him the coveted Hartmann medal. By 1985, with Karajan ailing, he had become the leading conductor in the German-speaking world. The $250,000 he received as part of the Siemens Prize he gave away to music colleges. Whenever he was invited to perform in Israel, he gave his fee back to the Israel Philharmonic. In London and Vienna, he was only paid half his international fee. He had become music's spokesman to the world and gave himself generously to a myriad of musical projects. In 1987 Bernstein, who apparently never tested HIV-positive, was part of the first "Music for Life" AIDS benefit at Carnegie Hall, which raised $1.7 million for patient care.

Even at the age of 70, Bernstein was falling in love with young protegees. Mark Stringer, a conducting student from Georgia who fell under his charm, wrote this tribute: "He was the most important man in my life, intellectually and emotionally.... He was an incredible intellectual stimulus.... No other human being had ever given me total trust, looking past all my emotional insecurities.... No one believed in me more.... So I poured every ounce of dedication into my work for him."

Bernstein's Legacy

The violinist Isaac Stern predicted that Leonard Bernstein would be remembered as the man who taught America what classical music was. He is remembered too for his willingness to take risks in his excursions into avant-garde music and his preview talks to audiences. Bernstein used religious themes in his important non-theatrical works that treat a crisis in faith. Several vocal pieces follow biblical texts. Among his 14 works for the theater, the most notable are the operetta *Candide* (1956), his Oscar-nominated film score for *On the Waterfront* (1954), and his musicals, *On the Town* (1944), *West Side Story* (1957), and *1600 Pennsylvania Avenue* (1967). Of his 17 orchestral works for the concert hall, the most outstanding are his three symphonies *Jeremiah* (1944), *The Age of Anxiety* (1949), and *Kaddish* (1963). *Chichester Psalms* (1965) is a work for chorus and orchestra. *Mass* (1971), Bernstein's most original work, represents the synthesis that he sought between Broadway and the concert hall. A theater piece for singers and dancers, it was commissioned at the suggestion of Jacqueline Kennedy for the opening of the John F. Kennedy Center for the Performing Arts in Washington, D.C. He also authored five books, all of which are currently in print: *The Joy of Music* (1959), *Leonard Bernstein's Young People's Concerts* (1962), *The Infinite Variety of Music* (1966), *The Unanswered Question* (1976) drawn from his lectures at Harvard when he was the Charles Eliot Norton Professor of Poetry (1972-73), and *Findings* (1982). He also recorded over 100 albums.

Joseph Machlis states: "He has a real flair for orchestration. The spicy and balance of sonorities, the use of the brass in high register, the idiomatic writing that displays each instrument to its best advantage—all these show his deftness. His harmonic idiom is spicily dissonant, his jazz rhythms have vitality. The formal structure tends to be diffuse, as is natural with a temperament that is lyrical and prone to improvise."

Bernstein's attraction to the music of Copland and Stravinsky coupled with his reverence for Gustave Mahler and Richard Strauss gave his style a blend of neo-classic and post-Romantic elements, though, in the final analysis, he is a maverick who does not fit categories. We are left to speculate whether he would have become one of the four B's—as opposed to the three Bach, Beethoven, Brahms—had he committed himself to serious composition for which he was brilliantly gifted rather than to the stunning, rich variety of musical endeavors that won for him fame, though likely to be ephemeral fame.

Leonard Bernstein died at his New York home in 1990 of a heart attack brought on by a pleural tumor, emphysema, fibrosis, and a series of pulmonary infections. He was buried next to his wife in the Greenwood Cemetery in Brooklyn.

References:

Burton, Humphrey. *Leonard Bernstein.* New York: Doubleday, 1994.

Machlis, Joseph. *Introduction to Contemporary Music.* New York: W. W. Norton & Co., 1961.

Peyser, Joan. *Leonard Bernstein.* New York: Ballantine, 1988.

Siegmeister, Elie, ed. *The New Music Lover's Handbook.* Harvey House, Inc., 1973.

—Robert F. Jones

Elizabeth Bishop

1911-1979

American poet

In the years since Elizabeth Bishop's death in 1979, her poetry, praised by her peers during her lifetime, has gained steadily in popularity with a general audience as well. Although she was extolled most frequently for her "famous eye," contemporary readers are quick to note that the scope of her talent went far beyond a gift for mere description. Bishop was a perfectionist whose poetic output was relatively small—only 101 published poems during her lifetime—but quantity was irrelevant for this "poet's poet's poet." Robert Lowell, a close friend and major influence, said in *Elizabeth Bishop and Her Art,* "When we read her, we enter the classical serenity of a new country."

Bishop was born in 1911 in Worcester, Massachusetts, the first and only child of Gertrude Boomer and William Bishop. Her father died during her infancy, and her mother, who suffered from bouts of mental instability, was permanently committed to an asylum when Bishop was five years old. Bishop spent her early childhood with maternal relatives in Great Village, Nova Scotia. Her recollections of life there are captured in such poems and prose pieces, respectively, as "First Death in Nova Scotia" and "In the Village."

Eventually, her paternal grandparents expressed concern about the limited resources available for the child's education in Nova Scotia. Bishop went to live with them in Massachusetts and was sent to Walnut Hills School for Girls and later to Vassar College. Her relationship with the Bishop family was not particularly warm. During her college years she spent vacations and summers mostly with friends from school.

The years at Vassar (1930-1934) were important for Bishop both intellectually and socially. In student essays, she expressed her affinity for the poets whom she would favor throughout her career, including George Herbert and Gerard Manley Hopkins. She cited Hopkins for his ability to capture "the mind thinking," a quality she hoped to emulate in her own poems, which she was already sending out to small magazines and competitions with some success. Also significant was the beginning of her lifelong friendship with Marianne Moore.

After graduation, Bishop lived in New York, traveled for an extended period in France, and eventually settled in Key West, where she stayed from 1938 until 1944. Many poems from her first book, the Pulitzer Prize-winning *North and South* (1946), are set there. It took the next nine years for Bishop to bring out a new volume. *A Cold Spring* (1955) was supplemented with the poems from her earlier collection to give the appearance of a full-length book.

By this time, Bishop had begun her long sojourn in Brazil, where she lived for 14 years in the mountain town of Pétropolis with her lover Lota de Macedo Soares. Her journey to Brazil began as a vacation that would include a visit with the aristocratic Lota, whom she had met in New York. During that visit, Bishop suffered an extreme allergic reaction to the cashew fruit. Lota helped nurse her back to health and then invited her to stay. Bishop, deeply moved by this offer, surprised herself by saying yes. Her third book, *Questions of Travel,* dedicated to Lota, came out in 1966. Half the poems are set in Brazil. Lota, whose health had begun to fail in their last years together, committed suicide in 1967.

After Lota's death, Bishop maintained a Brazilian residence in the seaside town of Oûro Preto, but she also spent time in New York and San Francisco. In 1970, she accepted a teaching position at Harvard, replacing Robert Lowell, then on leave. She remained in Boston for the last nine years of her life, graced with the companionship of a young woman, Alice Methfessel, now executor of her literary estate. Her fourth book, *Geography III,* came out in 1976. That year she received the Books Abroad-Neustadt International Prize for Literature, judged by John Ashbery.

Bishop was deeply reticent about her personal life. She also took a strong stance against anthologies limited to female poets, feeling that this exclusivity would make the quality of the poetry secondary to other concerns. The provisions of her literary estate still honor this policy, which extends to gay and lesbian collections as well. Consequently, Bishop's name becomes a footnote in volumes that contain the work of other important poets of her generation who also happen to be lesbians, such as Muriel Rukeyser and May Swenson. These roadblocks make it difficult for readers interested in the lesbian aspects of her poetry to trace a scholarly path for future generations. Nevertheless, we have the work to guide us, like these lines from "The Shampoo," written for Lota de Macedo Soares:

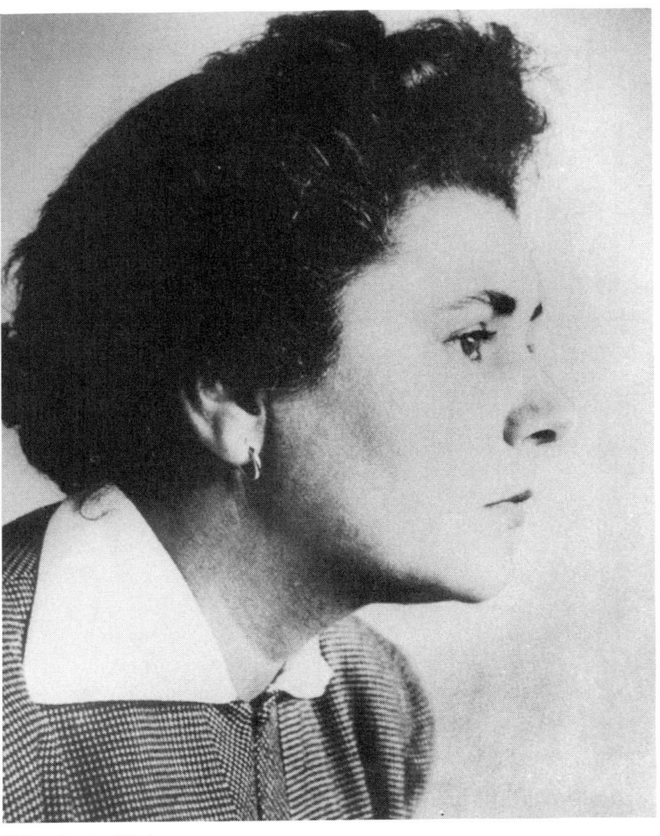

Elizabeth Bishop

The shooting stars in your black hair
in bright formation
are flocking where,
so straight, so soon?
—Come, let me wash it in this big tin basin,
battered and shiny like the moon.

References:

Bishop, Elizabeth. *The Collected Prose*, edited by Robert Giroux. New York: Farrar, Straus and Giroux, 1984.

———. *The Complete Poems: 1927-1979*. New York: Farrar, Straus and Giroux, 1983.

———. *One Art: Letters*, selected and edited by Robert Giroux. New York: Farrar, Straus and Giroux, 1994.

Fountain, Gary, and Peter Brazeau. *Remembering Elizabeth Bishop: An Oral Biography*. Amherst: University of Massachusetts Press, 1994.

Goldensohn, Lorrie. *Elizabeth Bishop: The Biography of a Poetry*. New York: Columbia University Press, 1992.

Miller, Brett C. *Elizabeth Bishop: Life and the Memory of It*. Berkeley: University of California Press, 1993.

Schwartz, Lloyd, and Sybil P. Estes, eds. *Elizabeth Bishop and Her Art*. Ann Arbor: University of Michigan Press, 1983.

—Sue Russell

Emily Blackwell

1826-1910

American physician

Emily Blackwell enjoyed a long and successful career as a physician, surgeon, hospital administrator, mother, reformer, and professor. Although less famous than her sister Elizabeth Blackwell—the first woman of modern times to receive her medical degree and practice medicine—Emily worked alongside Elizabeth, administering the programs and institutions she founded. She also, like many women of her era, shared her home with another woman in what was then known as "romantic friendship." Since women were generally assumed to be asexual in Victorian culture, such intimacies rarely prompted comment or suspicion, although they may have in many cases masked what we would today call a lesbian relationship.

Emily Blackwell was born in Bristol, England, the sixth of nine children of Samuel Blackwell and Hannah Lane. Samuel Blackwell, a sugar refiner, preacher, and reformer, raised his children in an educated, liberal home. When Emily turned five, Samuel moved his family to America, eventually settling in Ohio. He supported many burgeoning, idealistic, liberal, American institutions, most notably the Abolitionist Movement.

When Samuel died of malarial fever, the family opened a school, for which Emily—age 13—taught. In this way, the tightly knit Blackwells could afford to maintain the household for their younger siblings and mother. When Emily was 18, her older sister Elizabeth left home to pursue her medical education.

All the Blackwell sisters defied the traditions of the women of their times. In the 1910 article "The Reminiscences of Dr. Emily Blackwell," she described the professional climate for ambitious nineteenth-century women: "No one who was not alive 60 years ago can realize the iron wall hemming in on every side any young woman who wished to earn her living or to do anything outside of the narrowest conventional groove. Such a woman was simply crushed. Those who were of a character not to be crushed without resistance had to fight for their lives, and their fight broke the way through for the others to follow."

Emily's Struggle to Attain Education

Emily described teaching as the "most detestable occupation," but it supported her financially during her early medical studies. In 1848 she began a course of medical reading and dissection with Dr. Davis, a demonstrator of anatomy in the Cincinnati College. By 1850, she had decided to follow her sister Elizabeth into medical practice. Applying to college after college, Emily was turned down despite the fact that other women had received medical degrees since Elizabeth succeeded in obtaining hers.

During the summer of 1852, through the intervention of Horace Greely, Emily was permitted to work at Bellevue Hospital in New York, accompanying doctors on their ward rounds and attending operations. That fall, she was accepted at Rush Medical College in Chicago, but when patients objected to her presence in the doctor's office, she had to leave. A year later she was admitted into Western Reserve Medical School. In February of 1854, she graduated with high honors, at last a doctor.

A nineteenth-century medical education was rather superficial, even for men. The average student need only complete three years of study, two of which could be spent in private study with an experienced doctor. Because the Blackwell sisters stood for thorough and scientific training, Emily went to Europe to gain more extensive experience in medicine, giving up her rather fanciful, albeit long contemplated idea of going to Paris disguised as a man to get the training she needed. In England, she became an assistant to Dr. James Simpson—one of the first to use anesthesia in surgery—and gained surgical experience in his practice in female diseases, then studied with Dr. Jenner at the Children's Hospital and at St. Bartholomews. In Paris, Emily worked with Dr. Pierre Huguier, then entered the cloistered confines of La Maternite to learn midwifery. After two years in Europe, she returned to America as one of the best-trained physicians of her time.

Medical Career with Elizabeth Blackwell

Emily returned to New York in 1856 and began working with Elizabeth in her New York Dispensary for Poor Women and Children, a one room clinic in a slum near Tompkins Square. Initially, women were afraid to come, but driven by need, they soon arrived in significant numbers.

Three years later, Elizabeth opened the New York Infirmary for Indigent Women and Children in a house at 64 Bleeker Street. Emily organized the hospital and arranged the dispensary on the model of London's Children's Hospital. Elizabeth's idea was to provide medical care from women physicians for poor women and their children. The infirmary also provided medical training for women who had recently graduated from medical schools. Despite dire predictions of failure from skeptics, and two small riots after deaths occurred in the infirmary, the Blackwell's new hospital prospered.

When the lease for the infirmary expired in 1859, the sisters found a larger building at 126 Second Avenue, and persuaded the trustees of the infirmary to buy it. The Blackwell's sold their boarding house on 69th Street and moved into the attic of the new building. Shortly thereafter, Emily traveled to Albany, met with state representatives, and secured $1,000 a year stipend for the infirmary from the state of New York. The funding represented not only financial gain, but the stamp of legitimacy from state legislature.

When the Civil War broke out, Elizabeth and Emily called a committee meeting of women associated with the nfirmary to develop plans to help Union soldiers. The *New York Times* advertised the meeting, and unexpectedly, hundreds of women showed up. To satisfy demands for training, the Blackwells founded the Women's Central Association of Relief. The work of this small organization inspired a movement that spread throughout the North—by June of 1860 it was re-established by President Lincoln as the United States Sanitary Aid Commission and given government funding. Known as "The Sanitary" by grateful soldiers, the organization included the U.S.O., the Red Cross, and the hospital unit of the Civil War.

In 1868, Elizabeth opened the Women's Medical College. Emily served on the faculty as the professor of obstetrics and diseases of women, while Elizabeth taught hygiene. Shortly thereafter, the Women's College became one of the first medical schools to require a four-year program of study.

In 1869, Elizabeth moved to England, leaving the dispensary, the infirmary, and the college to Emily to administer alone. The Women's College trained women physicians for 30 years, until 1899 when it was decided that the college would close due to declining enrollment and Emily's poor health. At the College's 31st annual commencement, Emily explained that the Women's College had opened because other medical schools would not enroll women. Because John Hopkins and Cornell University had begun admitting women, the mission of the Women's College had been fulfilled.

Establishing a Family Of Her Own

The Blackwell sisters were fond of taking in orphans. At the age of 44, Emily adopted a baby girl as she had more time and greater financial stability to enable her to care for a child. Of all the children adopted by the Blackwells, only Emily's daughter Nannie called her adoptive mother "Mamma."

In 1883, Emily moved into a house on 20th Street with Dr. Elizabeth Cushier, Emily's former roommate at the infirmary. Cushier had been listed as a resident physician at the infirmary since 1974. Eleven years younger than Emily, Cushier was a tall, handsome, dark-haired woman who, unlike most of the doctors, went out of her way to wear traditionally feminine clothes. Quoted by biographer Elinor Hays in *Those Extraordinary Blackwells,* Emily's niece Alice Blackwell described her aunt's reaction to a visit by Cushier, in which Emily went to the gate to greet her friend "with a hop skip and jump of exultation ... actually capering, in spite of her avoirdupois." Cushier and Emily lived together for 27 years, until Emily's death.

After Emily closed the College, she and Cushier (who gave up her practice) spent their remaining winters together in either California or Southern Europe, as the warmer climates were better for Emily's health. In the late summer of 1910, Emily became ill again, and on 7 September she died. In her aunt's obituary in *Women's Journal,* Alice Blackwell described Emily as having "a warm and tender heart, though it was hidden under a reserved manner which made her rather awe-inspiring to strangers."

References:

Blackwell, Alice Stone. "An Early Woman Physician," in *Women's Journal* (Boston), 6 October 1906.

———. "Obituary for Emily Blackwell," in *Woman's Journal* (Boston), 10 September 1910.

———. "Reminiscences of Dr. Emily Blackwell," in *Women's Journal* (Boston), 17 September 1910.

Hays, Elinor. *Those Extraordinary Blackwells.* New York: Harcourt, Brace and World, Inc., 1967.

—Laurie Fitzpatrick

Marc Blitzstein

1905-1964

American composer

"Marc is dead and I've lost an arm," Leonard Bernstein wrote to his sister Shirley in London in 1964. "It's open season for Kaddish. Do you realise that we have loved Marc for twenty-five years?"

Although the composer Marc Blitzstein was intent on writing for the popular theatre and produced perhaps his finest, and certainly his most widely known piece, *The Cradle Will Rock*, in 1937, its success was never repeated and to a large extent his life and work have been overshadowed by that of his protegé Bernstein and, to a lesser degree, by the Broadway scores of Stephen Sondheim. Blitzstein's adaption of Bertholt Brecht and Kurt Weill's *The Threepenny Opera* was that show's first successful American production and ran at the Theatre De Lys in New York City from 1954 to 1961.

Blitzstein used to say that he was the victim of "three strikes"—utilizing the baseball rule that stipulates three strikes and you're out. He has said, "Number one I'm a Jew. Number two I'm a communist. Number three I'm a homo composer." Yet he never tried to disguise these facts and consequently, when he should have been hitting the peak of his career, he was marginalised because he embodied almost everything that America in the grip of McCarthyism felt it was defending itself against.

Marc Blitzstein

Proactive Anti-Capitalist Music Dramas

Marc Blitzstein was born on 2 May 1905, scion of a Philadelphia banking family whose fortunes were controlled by his matriarchal grandmother. Blitzstein began studying music at the age of three and by the age of five was playing the piano in public. By the age of seven he had started composing. He went to the University of Pennsylvania at the age of 16 and by the time he was 21 was in Europe, studying with Nadia Boulanger in Paris (1926) and Arnold Schoenberg in Berlin (1927). He composed a piano sonata in 1927, which premiered in New York in 1928.

Blitzstein was drawn towards composing for the stage, as a result, his first opera *Triple-Sec* (1928) was a deliberately surreal piece seen through the eyes of a drunk. It was staged as part of a Broadway revue, but its less than enthusiastic reception caused the composer to declare opera "rotten nineteenth-century trash" and turn his attention towards more populist music theatre.

This musical transition was due in part to Blitzstein's political conversion which came about in the mid-1930 after he attended a series of lectures in New York given by the German Marxist composer, and Brecht collaborator, Hans Eisler. Eisler's lecture, entitled "The Crisis in Music," propounded the view that the role of creative artists was essentially political and that they had to translate themselves from being parasites on society to fighters on its behalf. A meeting with Brecht further fuelled Blitzstein's enthusiasm for radical politics and under the influence of the song-plays of Brecht and Eisler and Brecht and Weill, he embarked upon a series of proactive anti-capitalist musical dramas which combined traditional arias and recitatives with elements from jazz and popular idioms.

Of these the most successful was *The Cradle Will Rock*, produced by John Houseman and directed by Orson Welles, the show ran in New York for 108 performances. Set in mythical Steeltown, U.S.A., *The Cradle Will Rock* tells the story of a bitter struggle between bosses and workers who are trying to form a union. *Cradle* became front page news when on the opening night in June of 1937 the entire company—led by Blitzstein, Houseman, and Welles—outwitted a U.S. Government ban imposed for political reasons and marched 20 blocks from the padlocked theatre in which they were due to open to an entirely different venue. Blitzstein became a national figure and was recognised as the leading exponent of American music theatre.

In 1938, Bernstein saw a production of the play on Broadway and decided to present it at Harvard. This was the beginning of a relationship that was to have far-reaching consequences for American music theatre. It is quite possible to state that without Blitzstein and *The Cradle Will Rock* there would have been no *Candide* or *West Side Story*, and that without Bernstein's contribution, there may have been no *Pacific Overtures* or *Assassins*. In this way, the musical line of descent from Blitzstein to Bernstein and from Bernstein to Sondheim is clearly evident.

Regina and *The Threepenny Opera*

The success of *The Cradle Will Rock* was unfortunately never to be repeated. But, Blitzstein's association with Brecht and Weill was to prove a productive one. Weill's wife, Lotte Lenya, made her American radio debut in 1937 in a small but significant role in Blitzstein's *I've Got The Tune* and it was his adaption of Brecht and Weill's *The Threepenny Opera* which established it as a music theatre classic.

During World War II, Blitzstein served with the U.S. Air Force in England and composed his *Airborne Symphony* (premiered in 1946), a monumental work about the history of flight which is marred by the pretensions of the spoken text. As the British music critic Jeremy J. Beadle so succinctly put it:

> Although Blitzstein's interest in his subject arose from his own position as a corporal (later sergeant) in the 8th Air

Force, his text has the same ambiguous attitude to flight and air forces as Auden's early poem "The Orators," as well as similar homoerotic glamorising of "Airborne Men."

Regina premiered in 1949, and was based upon Lillian Hellman's play, *The Little Foxes.* The original version of the opera achieved some success, but for many people it was neither opera nor musical and it wasn't until John Mauceri's superb Decca recording (1992) that the power and range of *Regina* was fully recognised. Here indeed is a precursor to Sondheim's *A Little Night Music*—some of Regina Gitting's most vociferous schemings are set in a kind of ballroom dance form. Yet after *Regina,* Blitzstein's career went into decline. There were other interesting music theatre pieces—*Reuben, Reuben* (about a suicidal artist) and *Juno* (an account of Sean O'Casey's *Juno and Paycock*). In 1960, he was re-united with Hellman when he composed the incidental music for her play *Toys in the Attic.*

While wintering in Martinique to compose an opera based upon Bernard Malamud's story "Idiots First," Blitzstein picked up three Portuguese sailors who robbed him and beat him to death. Bernstein was appointed musical executor, but he never fulfilled his duties. It has been only recently that Blitzstein's work has been re-evalued and its place in American music theatre acknowledged.

References:

Beadle, Jeremy J. "Marc Blitzstein: Mister Three-Strike," in *Gay Times* (London), 1995.

Blier, Steven. *Zipperflys & Other Songs.* Koch International Classics, 1991.

Burton, Humphry. *Leonard Bernstein.* London: Faber & Faber, 1994.

Capote, Truman. "Music for Chameleons," in *Music for Chameleons.* London: Hamish Hamilton, 1981.

Higham, Charles. *Orson Welles: The Rise and Fall of an American Genius.* Sevenoaks, Kent: New English Library, 1986.

Kennedy, Michael. *The Oxford Dictionary of Music.* Oxford: Oxford University Press, 1985.

Krasker, Tommy. "*Regina* restored," in *Regina.* Decca, 1992.

Ledbetter, Steven. "Blitzstein's *Airborne Symphony.*" RCA Victor, 1995.

O'Connor, Patrick. "Blitzstein, Hellman and *Regina.*" Decca, 1992.

Peyser, Joan. *Leonard Bernstein.* London: Bantam Press, 1987.

Spoto, Donald. *Lenya: A Life.* London: Viking, 1989.

—Peter Burton

Rosa Bonheur

1822-1899

French painter

Marie-Rosalie Bonheur was the oldest daughter of an impoverished but artistic French family who went on to experience phenomenal success for a woman of her time, largely because of the encouragement of both her parents to hone her talent for painting and drawing above all else. From childhood on, Bonheur was seldom pressed to pursue conventional schooling, which bored her anyway, and was instead encouraged to roam the countryside and nearby stables to draw and paint animals, which became her lifelong claim to fame. In 1887, her masterpiece *The Horse Fair* was bought by Cornelius Vanderbilt, and today it hangs in the Louvre.

As Bonheur began to enjoy worldwide acclaim (and some disapproval) from European royalty, art critics, and other eccentrics (like Wild Bill Cody, whom she painted), she started to indulge her own "eccentricities" by dressing in men's clothing and playing the part of a "gentrified gentleman" in her chateau in the Fontainbleau Forest, where she would smoke cigarettes and tend to her exotic menagerie of animals, including a pet tiger. Throughout her life, Bonheur also treasured what she termed a 45-year "sisterly" relationship with childhood friend, Nathalie Micas (who nonetheless played the passionate role of "wife" to Bonheur's "husband," by all accounts). In her later years, after Micas' death, Bonheur savored another close friendship with a young American artist named Anna Elizabeth Klumpke, who also lived with her. Though she was formally coy about her lesbianism all her life, Bonheur did refer to Klumpke as "my wife" to intimate friends and made her the sole heir to her estate when she died, over vociferous family opposition.

"Feel ... Think ... Act"

Rosa Bonheur was born on 16 March 1822 in Bordeaux, France. Because her father Raimond was an artist and an art teacher, and her mother Sophie was a musician, Bonheur was encouraged from a young age to pursue a career as an artist. Even the two brothers and a sister who followed her eventually became artists. What was perhaps even more fortunate for Bonheur was the fact that her father was a follower of the French social philosopher Saint-Simon, who advocated the full and complete emancipation of women and the erasure of conventional sex roles. In this way, Bonheur was taught to "first feel, then think, then act," in the manner of all Saint-Simoneans. Unfortunately, her father's zealousness for such tight fraternity and ideology often made for a quixotic childhood where she, as the oldest, felt forced to fulfill his dreams before formulating her own. "Despite her ambivalence about his character," notes biographer Dore Ashton in *Rosa Bonheur: A Life and a Legend,* "Rosa Bonheur remained in her own mind a product of her father's intense ambition."

Although it was Raimond who encouraged her to go to the Louvre and copy the old masters, it was her mother, Sophie, whom Bonheur recalled as being inspirational and self-sacrificing on a more down-to-earth basis. Sophie had willingly given up a promising musical career and a certain life of luxury and success to be the struggling wife of a poor artist. She was kind, loving, and encouraging to all her children, but was also a woman who was often exhausted and frustrated from following her restless and volatile husband. She was determined to raise her children with the same gentility she had known, in spite of their poverty. And, according to Bonheur, she did it all for love.

Sophie had two children within two years of her marriage to Raimond, gave music lessons to local children to supplement their income, and all the time encouraged young Bonheur to paint, draw, and roam the local stables and hillsides as it became evident that she had a fondness and a talent for drawing animals. When Bonheur showed signs of having trouble reading, for example, Sophie en-

Rosa Bonheur

couraged her to draw an ass opposite the A, a cow opposite the C, and so on. "I was allowed to run about everywhere," Bonheur remembered. Not surprisingly then, she was to specialize in drawing wild animals throughout her life and, according to writer Paul Russell, it became "an academic genre whose conventions she honed to perfection."

Given the love, patience, and encouragement Sophie showed, it's no wonder 11-year-old Bonheur suffered nearly unbearable grief when her mother died in 1833. Such grief, as well as dreams of her mother appearing to her and offering encouragement, were to haunt Bonheur all her life. According to Ashton, she "identified her own emotional difficulties with the early loss of her mother and seemed to recognize that her attachments to women rather than men had in some way been affected by her perception of her parents' troubled life."

Following Sophie's death, Raimond bravely kept all his children with him while struggling to give them the best formal and artistic education possible. For a brief time, he tried to push Bonheur toward more practical endeavors, even apprenticing her with a local dressmaker. When it was discovered she was spending more time in the husband's shop helping him make shotguns than she was in the dress shop, such foolish notions were abandoned. She was also sent for a short time to a formal boarding school, but was quickly sent home when it was discovered she was something of an "instigator." "My tomboy manners had an unfortunate influence on my companions," Ashton quotes Bonheur as remembering. "One day I proposed as a game a sham fight in the garden [with] wooden sabers and ... a cavalry charge. The result was the destruction of [her host's] fine rosebed ... [and they] sent me back home in disgrace."

"Permission de Travestissement"

Raimond sent Bonheur, at the age of 14, to the Louvre for formal training in painting and sculpture. She was not the only female, but was by far the youngest student there. By all accounts, she was her father's dutiful pupil—following his instructions in her daily routine, taking his criticism of her work in the evenings and, because he still feared for her "real" education, reading the history of France every evening after dinner. Soon, her brothers and sisters followed in Bonheur's footsteps and, according to Ashton, the family "seemed to have formed a strong unit, quite independent of outside resources, and Bonheur's memories abound in harmonious scenes of everybody drawing and painting."

Bonheur went on to study with Leon Cogniet at the Ecoles des Beaux Arts, and continued to excel in her formalized paintings and drawings of animals. By 1841, when she was only 19, her work was being shown in all the official Paris salons. She began frequenting the slaughterhouses and horse fairs in and around Paris for subjects and, largely because of these visits, obtained official police sanction—"Permission de Travestissement"—to wear male clothing.

Renewable every six months, the permit was originally given "for reasons of health" and in order for her to avoid being "bothered" by the workers when she was trying to paint. The permit likewise had to be signed by her doctor and prohibited attendance, according to Ashton, at any "spectacles, balls, or other public meeting places." Men's clothes soon became Bonheur's informal preference, which perhaps explains her general look of discomfort when sitting for photographs or self-portraits in full-blown, layers-thick skirts and high collars. She also smoked cigarettes at a time when "cultured" women simply did not do such a thing, or at least did not publicly admit to such "gentlemanly" habits.

"You Can Do What You Like"

Bonheur's work was as quickly a popular success as it was a critical one. In 1848, when she was only 26, she was awarded her first gold medal for her painting *Ploughing the Nivernais* (now in the Louvre). According to Russell, such an honor is doubly impressive when one considers the fact that such prizes were juried by artists like Corot, Delacroix, and Ingres. In 1865, Bonheur became the first woman to receive the Grand Cross of the Legion d'Honneur from the French government for her outstanding work. In that same year, a smaller version of her famous painting *The Horse Fair* was hung in the National Gallery, and her work began selling at record-setting prices. Given the rumors surrounding Queen Victoria's lesbianism, it is perhaps not surprising that she befriended Bonheur, which resulted in her works were sought after by scores of English gentry.

Bonheur took to all the notoriety, fame, and wealth quite readily and, as writer Russell notes, even commented in "words that presage Virginia Woolf's feminist prescription of the next century. 'I mean,' [Bonheur wrote,] 'to earn a good deal of filthy lucre for it is only with that that you can do what you like.'"

"She Alone Knew Me"

When Bonheur was 14, three short years after her mother's death, she had met and quickly bonded with a sickly girl whom her father had been commissioned to paint because her parents feared she would not live much longer. Twelve-year-old Nathalie Micas easily accepted Bonheur's friendship and self-defined role as the stronger child and protector. As for Bonheur, she just as readily allowed Micas to "mother"

her in exchange. Micas busied herself with all those tasks—sewing, looking after the studio—that Bonheur found difficult.

The two girls lost touch in their teens, but when they were reunited in their early 20s, they began a decades-long relationship that lasted until Micas' death in 1889 at the age of 65. Though never openly acknowledged as a love relationship (Bonheur always characterized it as "sisterly"), they nevertheless lived together in a chateau Bonheur was able to purchase near Fontainbleau in 1860. Micas continued as the "femme" to Bonheur's "butch"—which also allowed Bonheur more time to paint. During this rather exotic period in their lives, the boot-clad Bonheur would stroll the grounds of the chateau and, when asked, elusively protest to friends that she had no time for marriage—that she had yet to meet anyone who loved her enough.

Though the intimacy of their connection was never verbalized, it is interesting to note how much can be gleaned from Bonheur's letters, and how much we can surmise from the savvy of family members around them. When Micas' father was on his deathbed in 1836, for example, both women were in their mid-20s. The breadth of their need for each other must have been obvious to the dying man, even if it had not quite yet dawned on the young women. According to Ashton, he "summoned the two young women and admonished them to stay together, giving them his blessing as if they were about to marry."

Likewise, in a letter written by Bonheur to a friend just weeks after Micas' death, the depth of her emotional loss is evident, as is the notion that the two of them felt quite alone and frustrated in their struggle against closet doors that were euphemistically "bolted" from the outside as well. Editor Theodore Stanton quotes Bonheur as writing: "you can well understand how hard it is for me to be separated from a friend like my Nathalie, whom I loved more and more as we advanced in life; for she had borne, with me, the mortifications and stupidities inflicted on us by silly, ignorant, low-minded people, who form the majority on this terrestrial ball.... She alone knew me, and I, her only friend, knew what she was worth."

The Divine Affection of Friendship

After Micas' death in 1889, Bonheur was grief-stricken. But later that same year, she met 33-year-old Anna Elizabeth Klumpke when Klumpke's mother brought her to Paris to experience European culture. Like Micas, Klumpke was delicate and in fragile health, having been lame since childhood. According to Russell, Klumpke "took up where Micas had left off." Klumpke moved into the chateau and, in 1898, just a year before her own death, Bonheur wrote a bold letter to Klumpke's mother announcing that the two women had decided to "share their lives." Bonheur made Klumpke her sole heir and, according to Russell, "all three women are buried together in Paris' Pere Lachaise Cemetery beneath the inscription 'Friendship is divine affection'."

Rosa Bonheur died in May of 1899 near Fontainbleau, still one of the most celebrated artists of her time. Her life as well as her work is a study in contrasts. On the one hand, her paintings are painstakingly academic and "respectable," with every stroke a study in control. On the other hand, her life was lived as she saw fit, with all the bold eccentricity and thinly disguised lesbianism fully intact. If she chose to live her life with another woman, however, it was by the "rules" of conventional Victorian modesty—by the strictures that dictated one be the "husband" and the other the "wife." It was, above all, her financial success and popular notoriety that gave her any leeway in her life-choices. (Remember, this was a time when women could be arrested for wearing pants!) Bonheur was steadfast and determined enough to at least get official approval to dress as she preferred.

According to Russell, Bonheur knew quite well the nature of her "divine affection" for women, even though she never officially termed it lesbianism. When the scholar Magnus Hirschfeld surveyed Bonheur late in her life, as part of his study of "indeterminate sexual types," Russell claims Bonheur identified herself as a "contrasexual," a member of the "third sex," a "masculinized woman." Through such candid characterizations, through the strength of her work, through the courage of her unconventional lifestyle, Bonheur is an inspiration for woman artists down through the decades. By exploring all the options open to women in the nineteenth century, both personal and professional, Rosa Bonheur threw open doors for all independent-minded women determined to make their own way—in their art and their lives. The quality of "dignified realism" often used to describe her best work might also be applied to the way she lived and loved.

References:

Ashton, Dore. *Rosa Bonheur: A Life and a Legend.* New York: Viking Press, 1981.

Russell, Paul. *The Gay 100: A Ranking of the Most Influential Gay Men and Lesbians, Past and Present.* Secaucus, New Jersey: Citadel Press, 1995.

Stanton, Theodore, ed. *Reminiscences of Rosa Bonheur.* New York: D. Appleton, 1910.

—Jerome Szymczak

Anne Bonny

1700-17??

British pirate

Mary Read

1692-1720

British pirate

Anne Bonny and Mary Read are famous because of their colourful careers as pirates, both choosing to flout social and sexual conventions of the era, disguising their sex and dressing as men and often acting with greater bravery than their male shipmates. Their colleagues respected them as fierce, fearless fighters with great leadership skills.

Mary Read

Mary Read lived and dressed as a boy from an early age. She was born in England, the second child of Polly Read whose husband,

Alfred Read, disappeared at sea, leaving Polly with their first child, a son. Mary was illegitimately conceived later. When her son died, Polly appealed to her husband's mother for money, disguising Mary as the boy, and received a crown a week for the "boy's" maintenance.

Polly's mother-in-law died when Mary was 13 but Mary continued to live and dress as a boy, being entered as a footboy to serve on a French lady. Not liking this, she left and joined the crew of a man-of-war, on which she served some time before going to Flanders to serve as a cadet, first in a foot regiment and later in a horse regiment. She managed to conceal her true sex until deciding to take a fellow soldier, Corporal Jules Vosquon, as her lover. They married after the campaign, receiving gifts from their regiment and a discharge from service. For several years Mary chose to adopt a more conventional female role while she and her husband ran an eating house called The Three Horseshoes near Breda castle.

In 1716, after her husband's death and when trade began to decline at the inn, Mary once again chose to dress as a man and sign on as a soldier. However, there was little chance of promotion in peacetime and she embarked on a dutch ship bound for Jamaica. When the ship was apprehended in the Caribbean by pirates, Mary joined the crew and from then on made her name as one of them. She sailed with Captain Jennings, a famous buccaneer from the pirate city of New Providence.

In 1718 Read was one of 600 pirates who took advantage of a pardon granted by King George I of England via an official proclamation to pardon any pirates who surrendered by the end of September of that year. The English Captain Woodes Rogers became the official Governor of the Island of Providence and Mary signed on with him as a privateer to fight against the Spanish. However, many of these privateers returned to piracy as did Mary.

Anne Bonny

Anne Bonny (or Bonn) was born near Cork, Ireland on 8 March 1700. She was the illegitimate daughter of William Cormac, an attorney, and Peg Brennan, a maid. The maid was sacked by Cormac's wife after she discovered Peg had stolen some spoons. Cormac left his wife after Brennan had given birth to Anne. He tried to bring Anne up himself, disguising her as a boy and pretending that she was a relative's son who he was training to be a clerk.

When the scandal broke, Anne's parents embarked for Charles Town, Carolina, where the family became prosperous in trade. The two best-known stories from Anne's life at this time are that she stabbed and killed a servant during an argument and that she managed to beat up a young man who tried to rape her.

Anne met sailors and pirates, including Captain Raynor, while in Charles Town. Captain Raynor introduced her to James Bonny, a seaman from Bristol, whom she decided to marry against her parents' wishes. In 1716 Anne and her husband eloped to the pirate haven of New Providence in the Bahamas, but the two separated shortly afterwards and Anne began her career as a pirate, joining the crew of Captain Rackam and becoming his mistress.

Like Mary, Anne took advantage of the 1718 proclamation of amnesty and shortly after that Anne gave birth to a girl, but the child did not survive. By July of 1719 Anne had returned to piracy with Captain Rackam and, according to some accounts, was looked upon as one the leaders on the ship, suggesting that the crew swore on a hatchet rather than a bible and that they flew a flag drenched in blood.

Anne and Mary Meet

Mary Read and Anne Bonny met while both were members of Rackam's crew, both disguised as men. Anne discovered Mary's real sex when she tried to seduce her. Apparently, she was surprised to learn that Mary was female but afterwards, according to *A General History of the Pyrates* by Daniel Defoe, the two women "became intimate." However, both women also took lovers from among the male members of the crew and Mary once fought a sword and pistol duel with another pirate in place of her male lover, because she believed that she had a better chance of winning the fight than her lover. In fact, she killed the opponent on the spot.

Both women's careers ended in 1720 when Rackam's crew were apprehended by Captain Charles Barnet. Mary, Anne, and Mary's lover were the only three of the crew to stand and fight to resist arrest, the rest remaining below deck despite Mary firing a pistol into the hold, killing one man and wounding another, to try and stir them to action.

The trial of the pirates took place on 28 November 1720, at the Court of Vice Admiralty, St Jago de la Vega, Jamaica. Anne and Mary both dressed as men at the trial. During the trial Mary claimed that she never wanted to be a pirate and was only forced to by lack of money, but several of her companions declared under oath that "in times of action no person amongst them was more resolute, or ready to board or undertake anything that was hazardous than she and Anne Bonny." The two women were found guilty but their execution was delayed by the discovery that both were pregnant.

On 28 November the male pirates were hanged. Anne visited Captain Rackam before his death, but only to tell him, "that she was sorry to see him there, but if he had fought like a Man, he need not have been hang'd like a Dog."

Mary died of a fever on 4 December while still in prison, her fate undecided. Anne gave birth to her child while in prison but was eventually released following a personal, unofficial letter from Governor Woodes Rogers. Anne's records are untraceable after that and it is not known what happened to her or when or where she died.

The place of Anne Bonny and Mary Read in a book of gay and lesbian is perhaps anomalous. There is no evidence that Anne or Mary were lesbians, and accounts that they both enjoyed relationships with the opposite sex, their story shows how women have adopted roles that are generally considered to be male. Both defeated men in physical combat and impressed men with their martial prowess, bravery and skills of leadership.

References:

Carlova, John. *Mistress of the Seas.* Jarolds Publishers Ltd. 1965.

Defoe, Daniel. *A General History of the Pyrates.* N.p., n.d.

Gosse, Philip. *The History of Piracy.* Longman, Green and Co, 1932.

Johnson, Captain Charles. *Lives of the Most Notorious Pirates.* (Folio Society Edition). First published 1724.

Rush, P. *Mary Read, Buccaneer.* T.V. Boardman & Co Ltd, 1945.

Shay, Frank. *Mary Read, the Pirate Wench.* Hurst and Blacket Ltd, 1934.

—Lucya Szachnowski

Kate Bornstein

1948-

American writer, performer, and activist

"Transgendered dyke" (her self-description), Kate Bornstein is passionate on the subject of gender. "The way I see it," she writes in "Transsexual Lesbian Tells All!" first presented at the Out/Write '90 conference, "the gay and lesbian community is as much oppressed for gender transgressions as for sexual distinction. We have more in common, you and I, than most people are willing to admit." As a playwright, actor, frequent guest on television talk shows, and a presence on the Internet and World Wide Web, Bornstein keeps the dialogue about gender and the fluidity of sexuality open, lively, and accessible.

Born 15 March 1948, in Neptune, New Jersey, the former Albert Herman Bornstein sensed something was "deeply, terribly wrong" from early childhood. In an interview with the *Chicago Tribune,* Bornstein explains the trauma she experienced in nursery school when instructed to get in line, "girls here, boys over there." She recalls, "I literally looked around to see where I should go." Her first choice was the girls' line, but the shaming look of the adults told her she had made a terrible mistake. "I skulked over to the boys' line," Bornstein reported, "where I stayed for the next 17 years."

While outwardly seeming to conform to expected male behavior, Bornstein fantasized a sex-change machine that would transform him. "Being raised as a male," she told the *Chicago Tribune,* "I never experienced what it meant to be female in this culture, so I built a repertoire of female gestures, phrases, body language and outfits in my head and practiced them at night when everyone was asleep."

Bornstein went on to study drama at Brown University in Rhode Island, where her roles included everything from King Lear to the king in the musical *The King and I.* It was during this troubled period that Bornstein lived in a kind of frantic blur. "I hid out in medical textbooks, pulp fiction, drugs and alcohol," she explained to the *Chicago Tribune.* "I numbed my mind with everything from peyote to Scientology. I buried my head in the sands of television, college, lovers and spouses." In fact, Bornstein was married three times and fathered a daughter. Her association with Scientology, described the *Chicago Tribune* as a "self-proclaimed applied religious philosophy," was long lasting and, according to Bornstein, a damaging experience. Bornstein explained in an interview with the *San Diego Union-Tribune* that "it was a safe place for me to be when I was in my early 20s. And I was very good at it." However, she became disillusioned with the organization and in 1981, decided to leave this increasingly popular religious faction. at the same time, her then eight-year-old daughter, as Bornstein told the *Union-Tribune,* was "forbidden, under penalty of excommunication, to contact me," and therefore, was left to live with her mother and stepfather.

It wasn't until the period from 1985 to 1986 that Bornstein, at the age of 37, actually underwent the series of sex-reassignment surgeries. It is at this point in her life, as a postoperative transsexual, that Bornstein's philosophy of gender, and the art derived from her experiences, strikes out in new and unexpected directions. This surgery, rather than setting free the woman inside, had, in fact, jettisoned Bornstein out of the gender loop altogether. "Now I know I'm not a man," Bornstein told the *Chicago Tribune,* "and I've come to the conclusion I'm probably not a woman, either, at least not according to a lot of people's rules."

Bornstein's first "transsexual" play was *Hidden: A Gender,* presented in San Francisco in 1989. This two-act comedy-drama blends two stories, one autobiographical and the other historical, about a 19th-century hermaphroditic French schoolteacher. The two tales are narrated by a reactionary talk-show host, originally played by Bornstein, who harangues against the danger of "gender blur" and peddles a Gender Defender elixir, guaranteed to cure the problem. The review in the *San Francisco Chronicle* considered the play "merely a rough sketch" for a similar play to come, while crediting it for its "important, moving statements" and "funny parody scenes."

For Bornstein's first one-person show "The Opposite Sex ... Is Neither," she created, what Ben Brantley in the *New York Times* called "a series of mystically connected monologues in which [Bornstein] embodies a host of characters on different levels in the twilight zone of sexual identity" including a male impersonator and a "she-male" drag queen. Brantley praises Bornstein's expertness "in conveying the pain and disorientation of people who belong nowhere in the established social order" and "the warm mantle of empathy" of her impersonations.

Her 1994 one-person show "Virtually Yours" has strong autobiographical resonances, while exploring what happens to a relationship when the female lover of a female transsexual is in the processing of switching genders. This actually happened to Bornstein and the relationship ultimately ended, though the two remain close friends.

Kate Bornstein. ***Photograph by Dona Ann McAdams.***

Bornstein is also the author of a book *Gender Outlaw: On Men, Women and the Rest of Us,* which Heather Little in the *Chicago Tribune* calls "part stream-of-consciousness autobiography, part sexual-political manifesto." Her first novel, *Nearly Roadkill, an infobahn erotic adventure* (1996) co-written with Caitlin Sullivan, explores love and gender play in cyberspace as well as the importance of the Internet as a meeting ground for marginalized people.

Today, Bornstein no longer calls herself a lesbian, stating that lesbian implies "woman-loving-woman," and that she is not a woman. She refers to herself as an "omnisexual, omnivorous, sadomasochistic transgendered dyke." Her importance to gay and lesbian life and thought goes far beyond being "out" as a transgendered person and beyond even the warmth and intelligence and humor she brings to the dialogue about gender and sexuality in her art. Her life and work are striving to rethink the base assumptions and definitions of what is a man and what is a woman. "Let's reclaim the word 'transgendered' so as to be more inclusive," she writes in *Gender Outlaw.* "Let's let it mean 'transgressively gendered.' Then, we have a group of people who break the rules, codes, and shackles of gender.... It's the transgendered who need to embrace the lesbians and gays, because it's the transgendered who are in fact the more inclusive category."

Current Address: c/o Random House, 201 E. 50th St., New York, New York 10022.

References:

Bornstein, Kate. *Gender Outlaw: On Men, Women, and the Rest of Us.* New York: Vintage, 1994.

Brantley, Ben. "Review/Theater: Exploring Sexes and Identities," in the *New York Times,* 30 August 1993: C, 13.

Jones, Welton. "Transsexual Sees Gender as a Freedom-of-Choice Issue," in *San Diego Union-Tribune,* 26 July 1994: E-4.

Little, Heather M. "Bornstein Again: Despite Life of Gender Confusion, Feminism Comes Through Clearly," in *Chicago Tribune,* 10 September 1995: Womanews section, 3.

Weiner, Bernard. "Curtain Calls: Reviews," in *San Francisco Chronicle,* 5 December 1989: Daily Datebook, E-4.

—Ira N. Brodsky

John Boswell

1947-1994

American historian

Historian John Boswell addressed seemingly recondite medieval subjects in a way that captured the attention of both the scholarly community and a general audience. He was also a pioneer of gay visibility, especially in academia. Before his time, prestigious American universities had employed a good many closeted professors—who were expected to maintain a low profile as a tacit condition of continued employment. Exceptionally, Boswell seems to have been hired and promoted at Yale University in full knowledge not only of his orientation but in recognition of his contributions to the field of homosexual history. A convert to Catholicism, he sought more than scholarship, for he intended, in the spirit of the Second Vatican Council (1962-65), to move the Roman Catholic Church away from its antihomosexual stance back to what he regarded as the tolerant views of an earlier period.

John Eastburn Boswell was born in Boston on 20 March 1947. The offspring of a military family, he had the benefit of residing in the several foreign countries where his father was posted: hence his interest in languages and in Islam, the subject of his Harvard doctoral dissertation (published as a book, *The Royal Treasure: Muslim Communities Under the Crown of Aragon in the Fourteenth Century,* in 1977). Appointed an assistant professor in the history department at Yale in 1975, he rose to the rank of full professor, also enjoying election as head of the Department.

From the beginning of his Yale years, it had been known that he was working on a book on medieval homosexuality. Few were prepared, however, for the phenomenal success of his *Christianity, Social Tolerance and Homosexuality: Gay People in Western Europe from the Beginning of the Christian Era to the Fourteenth Century,* which the University of Chicago Press published in 1980. Not only did this monograph earn the American Book Award in History, together with other distinctions, but it made its author a celebrity in great demand as a speaker. His concern with gay history yielded further publications. Instrumental in setting up a system of annual conferences on the subject, he nonetheless failed to establish an institute of gay and lesbian studies at Yale, perhaps because of increasing ill health. Boswell died on 24 December 1994, of complications of AIDS.

Boswell's magnum opus remains the 1980 *Christianity, Social Tolerance and Homosexuality.* Citing original texts, he sought to show that, contrary to common belief, before the fourteenth century the Church had no fixed policy of opposition to homosexual behavior. Although Boswell deserves credit for bringing the debate into the limelight in a way it hadn't been before, his argument was not entirely new. He was preceded by book-length studies by Canon Derrick Sherwin Bailey (*Homosexuality and the Western Cultural Tradition,* 1955) and Michael Goodich (*The Unmentionable Vice: Homosexuality in the Later Medieval Period,* 1975). Nonetheless, the amplitude and self-confidence Boswell displayed convinced many lay readers that his presentation is the last word. As is generally the case in scholarship, however, the issues he raised—and made prominent—are still under discussion.

While it bristles with a formidable apparatus of citations, some readers have found that this book ranks less as objective and balanced account than as a kind of lawyer's brief, persuading through selective use of evidence. Boswell's depiction of the flourishing gay subculture of twelfth-century Europe is basically accurate, but that is no more an attestation of tolerance than the similar development in Victorian England. Although he was acquainted with some 15 ancient and modern languages, Boswell's abilities in this sphere rarely sufficed to meet the exacting canons of philology. Detractors of his work have found this problem especially evident where he seeks to interpret the original Greek wording of antihomosexual passages in the New Testament. Errors appear to encumber his expositions, but it is hard to determine whether these are honest mistakes or conscious distortions designed to buttress his case.

Boswell may have stepped beyond the bounds of purely objective scholarship because the larger social ramifications of a successful argument could be so great: large-scale reform of the Catholic church's treatment of homosexuality. But the times were not favorable. Growing conservatism in the hierarchy (though not among

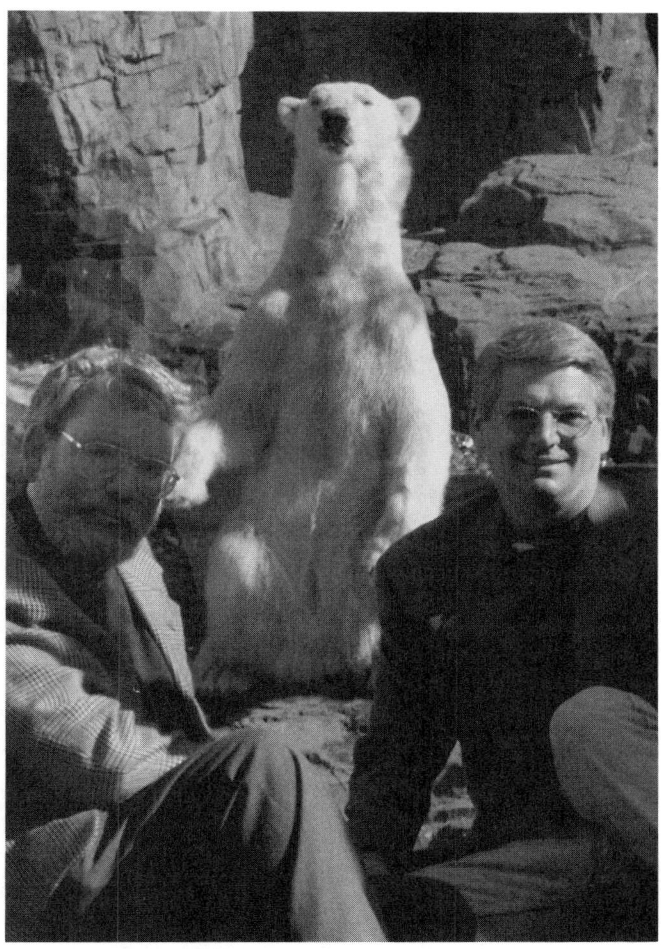

John Boswell (right) with Henry Beard.

many communicants) shifted Church policies away from reform, as seen in Vatican opposition to women clergy, clerical marriage, and contraception. In this increasingly chilly climate, Boswell's ambitious goal—the eradication of antihomosexualism from the doctrine and practice of his Church—was not destined to succeed, though it is arguable that the effort was worth making. Indeed, his ideas may have had their most significant impact among other denominations, as in some sectors of the American Episcopal Church. Not surprisingly, his conclusions have found favor among gay and lesbian groups, such as the Metropolitan Community Church. On the other hand, his efforts to "detoxify" Scriptural passages long acknowledged as antihomosexual have not generally been accepted by mainstream Bible scholars.

After publishing a study of the treatment of foundlings (*The Kindness of Strangers: The Abandonment of Children in Western Europe from Late Antiquity to the Renaissance,* 1988), Boswell produced a final book, *Same-Sex Unions in Premodern Europe* (1994). Here he cannily addressed the historical evidence for a social issue that was becoming urgent at the time of publication. A decade before, when he first began to study the pertinent Church rituals, Boswell interpreted them as documents of gay marriage. Further consideration indicated the need for qualification, so that when it came time to publish the book he termed these pacts "same-sex unions." After an initial flurry of interest, the book faded into relative obscurity, possibly because of this last minute emendation. If these rituals were simply partnerships without intended sexual content, as it appears they were, they are of little interest. Contrary to what one might expect, his findings have not figured significantly in the current debate over gay marriage.

The problem of a possible conflict between Boswell's gay (and ecclesiastical) activism, on the one hand, and his duty as an objective scholar, on the other, remains unresolved. Was he simply telling the truth—setting the historical record straight—in the expectation that the Roman Catholic hierarchy would alter its policies accordingly? Or did he begin with the goal of social change, and then tailor the evidence he gathered to suit that purpose?

In person John Boswell, or Jeb as he was known to his many friends, had a winsome, though fragile quality. His vulnerability, together with his public success, seemed to capture much of the complexity of the attainment of some gay men and lesbians to highly visible roles in American society following the watershed marked by the Stonewall riots of 1969.

References:

Greenberg, David F., and Marcia H. Bystrin. "Christian Intolerance of Homosexuality," in *American Journal of Sociology* (Chicago), no. 88, 1982: 515-48.

Johansson, Warren et al. *Homosexuality, Intolerance and Christianity: A Critique of John Boswell's Work.* New York: Gay Academic Union, 1985.

Shaw, Brent D. "A Groom of One's Own? The Medieval Church and the Question of Gay Marriage," in *New Republic* (New York), 18/25 July 1994: 33-41.

—Wayne R. Dynes

Beth Brant

1941-

Native American writer and editor

"I am a Mohawk lesbian," Beth Brant proudly states in *Writing as Witness,* "These two identities are parts of who I am." Although she did not begin writing professionally until the age of 40, Brant has emerged over the past decade as a powerful voice in contemporary Native-American and lesbian literature. Combining indigenous oral storytelling traditions with modern feminist politics and a playful butch-femme aesthetic, Brant has produced an impressive body of work—including stories, poems, and essays. All address the effects of racism and colonialism on native peoples, the frequent physical and emotional abuse of women by men, and, above all, the triumphant lessons of family history and community survival.

Beth Brant was born in her paternal grandparents' house in Detroit, Michigan on 6 May 1941, to an Irish-Scots mother, Hazel Smith Brant, and a Mohawk father, Joseph Brant. As a child, Brant would often accompany her family on trips to the Tyendinaga Mohawk Territory near Deseronto, Ontario, her father's birthplace,

Beth Brant. ***Photograph by Denise Dorsz.***

and home to her ancestors from the Bay of Quinte Turtle Clan. Now, a mother and grandmother, Brant divides her time between Melvindale, Michigan and Walpole Island, Ontario, where she and her partner of 20 years, Denise Dorsz, have a small cottage.

Brant began reading at the age of four, taught by Grandpa Joseph and her father. Her father, who took night classes at college while working days in an auto factory, also instilled in his daughter the importance of a formal education. After becoming pregnant at the age of 17, Brant was forced to drop out of high school and marry the child's father. The 14 years she spent with her husband, a white navy cadet, were punctuated by drunken rages and physical abuse, and the only happiness Brant received during this time came from her three daughters, Kimberley, Jennifer, and Jill. After divorcing her husband in 1973, Brant supported herself and her family by working as a salesclerk, waitress, and cleaning woman. In 1976 she met Dorsz, a Polish-American woman 12 years her junior. They have been together ever since.

As Brant explains, her interest in writing began as an impulse during a 1981 camping trip with Dorsz in the Mohawk Valley. A journey that also began as a quest for the spirit of Molly Brant, an ancestral Clan Mother, and elder sister of Chief Joseph Brant, who fought alongside the British in the American War of Independence. Returning to Michigan, the couple decided to take a detour through some old growth forest, where they were soon transfixed by a magnificent bald eagle that flew in front of their car and then perched on the branch of a nearby tree. Brant took this as a sign, and began to write as soon as she got home. The results of these initial efforts were eventually published in *Sinister Wisdom,* a feminist journal then edited by Michelle Cliff and Adrienne Rich. Two years later, in 1983, Cliff and Rich approached Brant about editing a special issue of the journal, to be devoted exclusively to Native-American women's writing and art. This became the ground-breaking *A Gathering of Spirit,* the first anthology of its kind to be edited by a Native-American woman. It was also remarkable in another manner—of the 60 contributors to the volume, ten were openly lesbian.

The year 1985 saw the publication of Brant's first book, *Mohawk Trail.* As its title suggests, many of the stories and poems that make up this collection show Brant on the trail of her lost Native-American heritage, writing for and about her family and community. Addressing painful memories and subjects through autobiography became a form of healing for Brant. Humour contributed to this process as well and, as a result, the book is filled with wonderful comic touches, as portrayed in the lesbian seduction scene concluding the ribald "Coyote Learns a New Trick." *Mohawk Trail* was followed, in 1991, by a second collection of short fiction, *Food and Spirits,* and, in 1994, by a volume of essays, *Writing as Witness.* Most recently, she has published *I'll Sing Til the Day I Die* (1995), a compilation of oral histories from Tyendinaga elders. Brant's stories have been widely reprinted and anthologized across North America, and she has received numerous awards for her work, including an Ontario Arts Council Award, a Canada Council Grant, and a National Endowment for the Arts Literature Fellowship. She is currently completing *Testimony from the Faithful,* another volume of essays.

Brant has, on more than one occasion, referred to writing by Native-American lesbians as a gift or "giveaway." As she states in a *Signs* article, "We write not only for ourselves but also for our communities." This generosity of spirit extends to Brant's work as a teacher of creative writing and a lecturer on Native-Americans and women's issues as well. Having had no models for her writing when she began her career, Brant has become just such a model for a whole new generation of Native-American lesbians.

Current Address: 18890 Reed, Melvindale, Michigan 48122.

References:

Brant, Beth. "Giveaway: Native Lesbian Writers," in *Signs: Journal of Women in Culture and Society* (Chicago, Illinois), vol. 18, no. 4, 1993: 944-47.

———. *Writing as Witness: Essay and Talk.* Toronto: Women's Press, 1994: 76.

—Peter Dickinson

Susie Bright

1958-

American writer, activist, and sexologist

Susie Bright is a writer, performer, sex-positive educator, pornographer, and political activist. An "X-rated intellectual," as Alice Walker dubbed her in the *San Francisco Chronicle,* Bright brings intelligence and humor to her analyses of sex, pleasure, and repression. Her essays, reviews, and commentaries have been featured in publications as diverse as the *New York Times Book Review* and *Penthouse Forum,* and her candid and insightful attitudes have inspired a new public discussion of eroticism and sex.

Susie Bright was born on 25 March 1958, in Arlington, Virginia, and grew up in California and Canada. Bright's iconoclasm became evident during her association with the longest-lasting underground high school newspaper in the United States, the *Red Tide;* then when, as a young adult, she worked as a community and trade union organizer. In 1981, after receiving a Bachelor of Arts degree in Community Studies from the University of California, Santa Cruz, she took a string of short-lived jobs in San Francisco, including: dishwasher, book clerk, and waitress. Finally, she was hired at Good Vibrations, a sex-positive vibrator and sex toy shop, and she found her calling.

At Good Vibrations Bright created the first feminist erotic video library for the store. She also dispensed advice and, by listening to their questions, learned about other women's sex lives. She later applied the information she was acquiring to the role that would first bring her national attention—as co-founder and editor of *On Our Backs,* the magazine for "adventurous lesbians." Bright began writing a regular column, called *Toys For Us,* for the magazine to combat, she says in the introduction to her book *SexWise* (1995), "the biggest lie ever told since the world was proclaimed flat: lesbians don't have sex." In 1987, these same concerns were addressed in Bright's first book, *Herotica*—the first woman-authored collection of erotica, which was a huge success and eventually became a series of which Bright edited the first three volumes. Bright's alter-ego, Susie Sexpert, emerged from her columns for *On Our Backs.* Bright later collected these writings into the book, *Susie Sexpert's Lesbian Sex World* (1990), a combined how-to manual and cultural analysis of the state of women's sex. *Susie Sexpert's Lesbian Sex World* was an enormous success among readers of all genders and sexualities.

Even in the face of heated resistance from some feminists, Bright has always been vocally pro-pornography. While criticizing the male-dominated porn industry, Bright celebrates the right of women to make and enjoy erotic images. She became *Penthouse Forum*'s female x-rated film critic in 1986, and was immediately dubbed "the Pauline Kael of porn" by the *San Francisco Examiner,* in recognition of the seriousness with which she looked at the way women and men enjoy themselves. In 1987, Bright created her live performance, "How to Read a Dirty Movie," in which she shows clips from gay and straight pornography in order to explore the successes and failures of American erotic cinema. In 1989, she staged "All-Girl Action: The History of Lesbian Erotica," which examines lesbian images in films of all ratings. Both shows have toured around the world.

Bright's other books all blend personal stories with incisive cultural criticism, and they're known for their sense of humor. *Susie Bright's Sexual Reality: A Virtual Sex Reader* (1992) includes Bright's musings on the internet and on her own pregnancy; *SexWise* features her take on subjects as diverse as Dan Quayle, Stephen King, Madonna, and the Black Panthers. She has also edited two series, *Best American Erotica* (1993-1997) and *Herotica* (1988, 1992, 1994), as well as numerous other erotica collections, and her writing has been featured in the *Village Voice,* the *New York Times Book Review, Playboy, Esquire,* the *San Francisco Review of Books, Future Sex,* and *Out.* She has collaborated on two feature screenplays, *Bound* (1995) and *Erotique* (1994), and been interviewed or written about frequently. Her charm and sense of humor have made Bright a highly sought-out speaker: she has delivered speeches at every Ivy League College and a keynote address for the Modern Languages Association, and she has been a frequent guest on television talk shows, including *The Joan Rivers Show* and *The Phil Donahue Show,* before which she was instructed not to talk about nipples.

Bright's sexual openness has made her both a popular and a controversial figure. For example, at the same time as *Newsweek* named her one of America's new power-brokers of gay clout and the *Utne Reader* deemed her one of the "100 visionaries who could change your life," the Canadian border authorities stopped her during a visit, searched her luggage and all of her safe sex supplies, and questioned whether she was really the mother of her 5-month-old daughter.

Despite the controversy, Bright's work continues to make life easier for pleasure-seekers of all genders and sexualities—including Bright herself. As she notes optimistically in *SexWise,* while considering the changes in social attitudes towards sex over the last 30 years: "For sexual discussion to move so quickly from the criminal and pathological to the realm of the creative and political is phenomenal, a triumph of honesty and democracy over hypocrisy and elitism."

Current Address: c/o Cassell Publishing, 215 Park Avenue South, New York, New York 10003.

References:

Bright, Susie. *Herotica.* Burlingame, California: Down There Press, 1987.

———. *SexWise.* Pittsburgh, Pennsylvania: Cleis Press, 1995.

———. *Susie Bright's Sexual Reality: A Virtual Sex Reader.* Pittsburgh, Pennsylvania: Cleis Press, 1992.

———. *Susie Sexpert's Lesbian Sex World.* Pittsburgh, Pennsylvania: Cleis Press, 1990.

—Jonathan Wald

Benjamin Britten

1913-1976

British composer

One of the most prolific of this century's composers (also pianist and conductor), Edward Benjamin Britten (Lord Britten of Aldeburgh) is undoubtedly one of the greatest British composers. He has also, coincidentally, profoundly influenced British gay cultural life—not least because he worked closely with gay librettists (W. H. Auden, E. M. Forster, William Plomer) on operas which were taken from substantially gay texts (Melville's *Billy Budd,* James' *The Turn of the Screw,* Mann's *Death in Venice*) and in tandem with his lover of almost 40 years, (Sir) Peter Pears (*Seven Sonnets of Michelangelo*).

That pervasive influence can also be discerned in the work of a younger generation—notably of gay writers, who have utilized Britten's work to make points within their novels. Two noteworthy instances of this are Alan Hollinghurst's *The Swimming-Pool*

Library and Patrick Gale's *The Facts of Life*. References to Britten are littered throughout the work of novelist David Rees—whose essay "Britten in the Darbies" is a notable contribution to gay studies of the composer; Gale's "Death to *Death in Venice*" is an astringent retake on "this gay cultural phenomenon" and the playwright Michael Wilcox has completed a study of the operas (*Benjamin Britten,* 1997) which makes some highly original decodings.

A gay man whose long-term relationship was acknowledged by the British Establishment (Elizabeth, the Queen Mother, sent a telegram of condolence to Pears after Britten's death) and a conscientious-objector during World War II (much of which was spent in America), Britten himself was to become an Establishment figure. His operas joined the international repertoire and he was feted and honoured around the world to a degree that has never been accorded Britten's friend and close contemporary, Sir Michael Tippett—a more openly gay composer, imprisoned in Britain during World War II for *his* conscientious objections, whose work has probably suffered in comparison because of his insistence on providing his own libretti for his operas. Britten's persistent use of already existing literary source material in adaptations by writers who were themselves distinguished has served him well. The difference between Britten and Tippett is similar to the difference between (for example) the operas of Puccini and Wagner: The words have it.

The Sea, the Sea

Benjamin Britten was born 22 November 1913, the feast day of St Cecilia, the patron saint of music (celebrated in his *Hymn to St Cecilia*, 1942). The importance and influence of his birthplace in a house overlooking the North Sea in the resort town of Lowestoft in Suffolk on the English East Coast cannot be overestimated. "No composer has written finer sea music than Britten, and the sea is inescapably present in every bar of *Peter Grimes* and *Billy Budd*," David Rees wrote. "Water, indeed, is his element: *Curlew River*, *Noye's Fludde*, *Death in Venice*.... He never lived far from it and it seems to pervade everything he wrote...."

From an ordinary middle-class family (his father was a dentist, his mother was a keen amateur singer with no training but a sweet voice), Britten grew up with the ever audible twin sounds of music in the family home and the sea breaking on the sandy beach but a hundred yards from that home. No wonder then that in the years to come, the latter was so often to inform the former. But the sea was not the only abiding influence and theme which percolated through the whole of Britten's life and music. He shared (along with those other quintessential English composers Holst, Parry, and Vaughan Williams) an intense interest in the work of amateurs and children (brilliantly combined in *Noye's Fludde*, his masterly setting of the Chester miracle play, 1957).

"I am first and foremost an artist—and as an artist I want to serve the community.... It is not a bad thing for artists to try to serve all sorts of people," Britten commented in 1952. "That is why I personally enjoy writing pieces for special occasions—music for children or amateurs ... trying to pour into these restricted bottles my best wine."

Unpalatable Skeleton

Yet there may have been a further dimension to this interest in composing for children. The music critic Tom Sutcliffe has suggested that there may be a "few unpalatable skeletons in the cupboard."

Benjamin Britten

> Britten was a bit of a monster, as well as being a charming little boy to the day he died. He was a brilliant composer, with devastating flaws....
>
> Two hints throw up intriguing possibilities for Britten research in the future. What was it that Ronald Duncan said Britten had told him, of something that had happened to Britten in childhood, that was so dreadful it could never be repeated?...
>
> We uncovered a story that Britten once confessed his own father had been a pederast who played with the little boys the young Britten brought home (an implicit procurer). A suicide note was found amongst Britten's father's papers when he died (of natural causes) a standby, use-if-necessary, suicide note....
>
> There was also the strange rumour ... that around the time of *Turn of the Screw* an adolescent boy, with whom Britten and Pears were in some sense involved, committed suicide—though the case was hushed up.

However, Sutcliffe concludes with a comment from Britten's biographer Humphrey Carpenter that he had found no evidence Britten ever did more with his boys than "kiss and cuddle."

That said, it has to be concluded that Britten and Pears shared an interest in boys and used their own relationship as a mask for desires which may not have been fulfilled but which were clearly evident in their lives and work. Towards the end of his biography of Pears, Christopher Headington describes the books on the shelves of Pears' bedroom:

> There are also some books with what may crudely be called "gay themes": Martin's *Aubade* (an account by a teenage author of a first homosexual love), Montherlant's *The Boys*, James Hanley's disturbing sea story *Boy* (admired by E. M. Forster and T. E. Lawrence), and Robin Maugham's *The Wrong People*....

Rather than gay-themed, these novels, presumably enjoyed by Britten as well as Pears, were specifically pederastic in theme and, interestingly, three are set either by, or on, the sea.

Therefore it can be confidently stated that in Britten's beginnings were all the materials from which he would construct his life and work to the extent that the final major work—*Death in Venice* (1973)—completed the circle by returning (in a metaphorical sense) to those very beginnings.

"*Death in Venice* was Britten's last opera, written in circumstances of great stress and later revised here and there in circumstances that were scarcely serene," Donald Mitchell has written.

> It is tempting to read into the work, and perhaps especially because of the coincidences between Britten's personal history and the history of the protagonist, a particular awareness on the composer's part of mortality, of the possibility (somewhat nearer that hitherto) of his own death....
>
> The opera, as it happened, turned out to be a kind of last statement, at least in terms of Britten's contribution to the musical theatre, because of his untimely death and because of the strange parallels that sometimes run between life and art.
>
> In one respect, however, the opera was undeniably a "testament" (though it need not have been a last one) and also autobiographical in character. *Death in Venice* embodies unequivocally the powerful sexual drive that was Britten's towards the young (and sometimes very young) male.

Awareness of Mortality

Essentially a vocal composer (the operas and song cycles are the most widely known of his compositions), Britten also wrote one full-length ballet, the rarely-seen *The Prince of the Pagodas* (1956); the orchestral works (including the popular *Young Person's Guide to the Orchestra,* 1946); concertos, choral works (including *War Requiem*, 1961, using poems by Wilfred Owen, which opened the rebuilt Coventry Cathedral); works for brass, piano and solo voice. He also composed incidental music for films, plays and radio—including *The Ascent of the F6* by Auden and Christopher Isherwood and *The Sword in the Stone* by T. H. White.

The first real intimation of the shape of things to come came with the composition of *Paul Bunyan* (1940-41). Based on an American folk tale and with a libretto by Auden, this operatic piece came as a direct result of American exile—Britten and Pears had followed Auden and Isherwood to America in 1939. Written with an eye to Broadway and using idioms which suggest that Britten had quickly assimilated the American musical theatre form, *Paul Bunyan* had its premiere in New York in May of 1941—but it was clear to composer and librettist that revisions were needed. These were put in by hand, but because Britten and Pears returned to Britain in 1942, were not completed and the opera had to wait until 1975 for its European premiere.

One of the reasons Britten had been distracted from the revisions of *Paul Bunyan* was his discovery in a Los Angeles bookshop of Thomas Crabbe's poem *The Borough*, which became the inspiration for Britten's first mature opera, *Peter Grimes*, which premiered at Saddler's Wells in London with Pears in the title role in 1945.

Peter Grimes is the first of what may be considered a cycle of powerful operas the themes of which encompass variously the exposure of young males to adult experience, the inexorable pull of the sea, and awareness of mortality (the third of Britten's abiding themes). Grimes, the bad-tempered, anti-social workaholic fisherman whose apprentices are prone to accidents becomes a tremendously sympathetic character due to Britten's ability to present him as an archetypal outsider (ie: a gay man) who is persecuted, hunted and ultimately propelled to suicide by a prurient and insensitive mob who, like all mobs, misunderstands and whose morality is more than suspect.

Britten's reputation as a composer of opera rests chiefly on *Peter Grimes* and *Billy Budd* (1951) and Rees argues convincingly that "they are arguably the two finest operas since Verdi's *Otello* and *Falstaff*." It is certainly the first of these which is most consistently revived and which has been most reinterpreted on record.

The themes of innocence destroyed and persecution (the autobiographical well-spring is obvious) continued with *Billy Budd*, *The Turn of the Screw*, and *Owen Wingrave* (both of the latter with libretti by Myfanwy Piper out of Henry James). These and the incomparable *War Requiem* make manifest the darker side of Britten's musical personality and intellect and somewhat overshadow the rather more celebratory or comic works: *Gloriana*, written for the Coronation of Queen Elizabeth II in 1953 and initially regarded as a failure; his lively account of Shakespeare's *A Midsummer Night's Dream* (1960); and the highly diverting comic opera *Albert Herring* (1947).

Britten's interest in chamber opera and his ambitions for a festival rooted in English village life (allied to his interest in working with amateurs and children) provoked him to found the Aldeburgh Festival in 1948. Aldeburgh, just along the Suffolk coast from his birthplace, had become Britten's home after World War II and thereafter he became a kind of artistic lord of the manor, the community's most prominent citizen and a lure for musical celebrities from around the world eager to appear at the annual festival (which continues to this day) and tourists fascinated by a famous British composer.

Appointed a Companion of Honour in 1953 and awarded the Order of Merit in 1965, Benjamin Britten was created a life peer (Lord Britten of Aldeburgh) in 1976. His activities had been much diminished after a severe and not entirely successful heart operation and he died in 1976. Peter Pears died ten years later, in 1986.

References:

Carpenter, Humphrey. *Benjamin Britten: A Biography.* London: Faber & Faber, 1992.

Gale, Patrick. "Death to *Death in Venice,*" in *Gay Times* (London), May 1992.

———. *The Facts of Life.* London: Flamingo, 1995.

Headington, Christopher. *Peter Pears: A Biography.* London: Faber & Faber, 1992.

Hollinghurst, Alan. *The Swimming-Pool Library.* London: Chatto & Windus, 1988.

Kennedy, Michael. *The Oxford Dictionary of Music.* Oxford: Oxford University Press, 1988.

Mitchell, Donald and Philip Reed. *Letters from a Life: The Selected Letters and Diaries of Benjamin Britten 1913-1976; Volume 1 - 1923-1939* and *Volume 2 - 1939-1945.* London: Faber & Faber, 1991.

Palmer, Christopher. *The Britten Companion.* London: Faber & Faber, 1984.

Rees, David. "Britten in the Darbies" in *Words & Music.* Brighton: Millivres Books, 1993.

Sutcliffe, Tom. "Unmasking Britten," in the *Guardian* (London), 26 February 1991.

—Peter Burton

Romaine Brooks

1875-1970

American painter

The long life of Romaine Brooks reads simultaneously like a Gothic nightmare and a French fantasy—elements of which are reflected in her sometimes ghoulish drawings and paintings. Though she died quite eccentric and in obscurity in 1970 at the age of 96, her work endures as a testament to both her tortured childhood and her stylish life of lesbian independence in Paris, Capri, and the south of France in the first half of this century. She moved within, and chose to remain just outside of, artistic and literary circles that included Gertrude Stein, Alice B. Toklas, Somerset Maugham, Ezra Pound, André Gide, Jean Cocteau, and Constance Mackenzie. She also painted many of the women in her intellectual constellation, some of whom were also her lovers, and later shunned most of these fellow expatriates when she tired of their social "demands." As biographer Meryle Secrest quotes Brooks as saying in *Between Me and Life:* "One should be a slave to nothing except one's toothbrush."

Brooks' drive to be a "genuine invert" was stalled, sanctioned, and spurred all at once by her 50-year love affair with American heiress, poet, and writer Natalie Barney. Both women believed that true rebellion against convention went beyond merely thumbing one's nose at it, and that it required steadfast determination to be true to one's self. When Brooks first moved to Paris in her early 20s, for example, she was among the first women to cut her hair short and dress in men's clothes—a statement that was soon mimicked by dozens of Parisian "wannabes," whether truly gay or just "mildly amused."

In Barney, Brooks found a soulmate in what Secrest terms such "scandalous unorthodoxy." The two women shared a home they built together, opened joint bank accounts, and made arrangements to be buried together—all quite daring steps for same-sex lovers, even in the "roaring" 1920s. Though the relationship was challenged from the beginning by Barney's distaste for monogamy, (which is why an unstable Brooks finally refused to have anything to do with Barney near the very end of their lives), the emotional bonds and domesticity that took root over the years were a welcome counterpoint to the unstable hell that had haunted Brooks' childhood.

"Almost Supernatural Evil"

Romaine Brooks was born on 1 May 1874 in a hotel room in Rome, Italy, where her mother happened to be traveling at the time. By all accounts, both of her American parents were extremely wealthy and had enjoyed all the comforts of a genteel nineteenth-century upbringing. But Brooks' alcoholic father disappeared shortly after her birth, and her unstable, sadistic mother is said to have treated Brooks like a servant while she lavished all her attention on Brooks' sickly, mentally-fragile older brother, St. Mar. Secrest claims that this situation created a childhood of "almost supernatural evil that reflected itself in the recurring themes of Brooks' paintings and drawings." Not only was the mother unstable, unloving, and obsessed by St. Mar, but the boy increasingly adored his sister, even as he drifted toward madness. Any perusal of Brooks' gaunt, haunting paintings and simple, introspective drawings—often pleadingly saddled with titles like "Asking the Way" and "Time Separates"—point toward the melancholy no doubt bred during these years. "To be caught in the vicious circle of another's life is to revolve perilously in another's perils," she wrote of her rejection by her mother in her unpublished autobiography *No Pleasant Memories.* "My dead mother gets between me and life," Secrest quotes Brooks as saying in a notebook discovered only after her death.

Not surprisingly though, such rejection also created in Brooks a fierce drive for independence. At the age of 17, she was sent to a girl's finishing school in Geneva, Switzerland, where she experienced the usual crushes on several of her classmates and teachers. Because she showed considerable talent for both music and art, she headed for Paris at the age of 19 and lived with a French family for two years while she studied voice. To be an artist was to most likely starve to death, she surmised, so why not pursue a singing career? Besides, it all meant she was able to get that much further away from her mother.

For any single girl of her class—even in the "gay" 1890s—life was much more confining, much more about preparing for marriage than anything else. A life of true independence was simply unthinkable. Yet, largely because her childhood had prepared her well for loneliness, Brooks set out to pursue a life of "artistic poverty" in Paris—and later in Rome and Capri—rather than, as biographer Secrest puts it, "forever caper around the ring to the commands of a mad ringmaster. All her strength and pride and all her courage were gathered to make that single-minded leap of desperation."

"Thief of Souls"

The island of Capri was, by the end of the century, quite the bohemian haven for artists, eccentrics, and the usual high concentration of gay men and lesbians that fill these ranks. It was here that Brooks maintained a painting studio after studying in Rome, and it was here that she met—and later briefly married—John Ellington Brooks, a known homosexual who had fled England following the trial of Oscar Wilde. She also claims to have had affairs with Wilde's ex-lover, Lord Alfred Douglas, and with the Italian writer Gabriele d' Annunzio as well as his mistress Ida Rubinstein, who became the model for many of Brooks' more androgynous female nudes.

In 1902, Brooks inherited the family fortune when her mother and brother died within months of each other. In 1905, she left her ex-husband with a generous "settlement," cropped her hair short, and returned to Paris to begin painting the portraiture and nudes that remain her signature work. She had an uncanny, otherworldly ability to depict a wan truth in people's appearances—especially in her thin, bloodless, almost ghostly female portraits and nudes—and she soon earned a beguiling reputation as "the thief of souls." "You have not beautified me," writer Paul Russell notes one wealthy subject as telling Brooks. "No, but I have ennobled you," came Brooks' reply. Her fame was further solidified by a highly successful show of her work in Paris in 1910.

While Brooks' drawings in particular reflect the artistic climate in Paris at the turn of the century, they also somehow transcend all influences to make their own unique statement. Her beautiful curves attest to long, singular, and thoughtful strokes on the paper, as if following the same muse who may have influenced Aubrey Beardsley or any of the other Symbolists. Moreover, as Secrest notes, an Art Nouveau influence is evident, and there is a striving for perfection not unlike that of the Japanese print. And yet, her depictions of bizarre beings, psychic manifestations of death, and otherworldly fantasies occupy an artistic space of sentiment all their own, no doubt born of some alchemy between her "real" existence and a more ethereal, inner, artistic life.

"Eroticism with Symbolism"

In 1915, Brooks met writer and lesbian expatriate Natalie Barney in Paris. The two women quickly fell in love and maintained a relationship that would last for 50 years. Barney had a notorious reputation as "the wild girl from Cincinnati," and Brooks is said to have liked her immediately, if only at first because Parisian society was wary of her. They traveled together, collaborated on Barney's book *The One Who is Legion* (with Brooks doing the quirky and uncharacteristically comical illustrations which attest to her happiness), and enjoyed Parisian "salon life" with the likes of Stein, Maugham, Cocteau, Pound, Gide, and Colette.

Brooks was not particularly fond of the Parisian "social whirl," but Barney maintained her salon in the same house at 20, rue Jacob till her death there in 1972 at the age of 72, and Brooks painted many of the lesbians who frequented the place, including Lady Una Trowbridge and Barney herself as an "Amazon." Her paintings showed the influence of Whistler, but are better defined as displaying a more humanistic modernism—"eroticism with symbolism," as some critics have described it—that broke away from the modernism and abstraction popular at the time. She contemplated painting Stein for decades, according to biographer Secrest, but Stein always declined. Nonetheless, Toklas, Stein, and Brooks and Barney remained fast friends for years.

"Romaine was happiest when she could have Natalie all to herself," notes Secrest, which was not always an easy task given Barney's love for gatherings. The strength of their love affair was probably based on their opposing temperaments. Barney said many times that she considered her life to be her art, while her poetry and other writings were just by-products. Brooks was more practical, working toward her goal of living for her art with a determination that Barney had great respect for. An ever-confident Barney hated to be alone and surrounded herself with quick-witted friends and confidants. The self-conscious Brooks, on the other hand, detested crowds and was generally distrustful of others—a notion that manifested itself in paranoia later in her life.

In spite of—and maybe because of—their differences, the two women knew each other like no one else was allowed to. It is Brooks' "Amazon" painting of Barney, for example, that is said to embody the writer in a light uncharacteristic of the way she was known to others. Wearing furs and sitting beside a small jade horse that Brooks owned, Barney has an ethereal look in her eyes, a contemplative face her more animated "social self" seldom let the outside world see. As Secrest says, "Perhaps Romaine was trying to express a fundamental aspect of their psyches. They shared a view that life had frustrated them, and looked elsewhere: to art, to poetry, to philosophy ... to the other sex inside themselves for fulfillment." It's as if Brooks was trying to display this inner haunting in much of her work.

The Hyphenated Villa

In the mid-1920s, Brooks and Barney built a house together near Beauvallon, France—far from the fashionable world of Paris that Brooks was growing increasingly disenchanted with. Because it was connected by a common dining room, they called it the Villa Trait d'Union—the hyphenated villa. According to Russell, "this architectural detail tells us much about their relationship: they were often physically apart but emotionally connected, despite Barney's many affairs over the years."

This arrangement seemed to work well for both of them, at least until the house burned down during World War II. Barney carried on a "country version" of her Paris salons, and Brooks continued to draw, paint, swim, and work on her memoirs. They also opened a joint bank account in Geneva, and requested that they be buried together. It was Barney's aversion to monogamy that fueled any discord, according to Secrest, but "[the villa] was physical proof of a relationship both ... believed would last till the end of their lives." And the ongoing arrangement was not without its high comedy. Over the years, Brooks also enjoyed a few "extramarital" affairs, and she even shared some of the details with Barney. If, however, one of Barney's many flirtations became "onerous," according to Secrest, "[Romaine] would contact Natalie with good-natured exasperation and say 'Do send me a telegram saying that someone is dying'."

In the end, it was Barney's infidelities that destroyed the union, even after 50 years of physical and emotional roots. In 1968, only two years before her death at the age of 96, (and four years before Barney's death at the age of 95), what Russell calls "an increasingly paranoid and eccentric" Brooks ended their relationship and refused to have anything to do with Barney. "It was jealousy that led to the final break," notes Secrest, "violent, irrational, inevitable."

Pre-Dating Lipstick Lesbianism

After World War II, and indeed until the end of her life, Brooks lived in relative obscurity. Ironically, she died just a year before a major revival of her work was staged in New York, amid a growing interest in "overlooked" female painters of this century. As a more sophisticated sense of "lesbian style" came into vogue in the 1970s, Brooks' paintings served as a reminder that such style was not without precedent. "The lipstick lesbians of the 1980s," notes Russell, "may, in fact, owe some of their glamour to the Romaine Brooks revival."

Today, the drawings and paintings of Romaine Brooks—like her nineteenth-century counterpart Rosa Bonheur and fellow Francophile Mary Cassat—stand out as a talented testament of perseverance against male-dominated histories of art. "Romaine never knew where the line would go," notes Secrest, "and followed with mingled pride and astonishment the way it would become a form; the way its sure sweep would give shape to the most inchoate emotion." Her own place in history—as an artist, as an out lesbian among a courageous, talented, and visionary lesbian expatriate community, as a chronicler of her times—is secured by even the most cursory look at her work and her life.

References:

Russell, Paul. *The Gay 100: A Ranking of the Most Influential Gay Men and Lesbians, Past and Present.* Secaucus, New Jersey: Citadel Press, 1995.

Secrest, Meryle. *Between Me and Life: A Biography of Romaine Brooks.* Garden City, New York: Doubleday, 1974.

—Jerome Szymczak

Rita Mae Brown

1944-

American writer and activist

Jane Rule writes that *Rubyfruit Jungle*, Rita Mae Brown's novel about a Southern lesbian feminist, is the contemporary literary lesbian Bible, performing the same function that Radclyffe Hall's *The Well of Loneliness* did for earlier generations. Brown is best known for this 1973 bestseller, although her contributions to grass roots women's activism are equally important. Her relationship and breakup with tennis star Martina Navratilova caused national publicity as well.

Rita Mae Brown was born 28 November 1944 and adopted by Ralph and Julia Brown in Hanover, Pennsylvania, near the Mason-Dixon line. Her father died when she was 15, but it was her mother and aunt who were the strongest influences in her life. Brown appreciated their working-class candor and toughness, saying in *Current Biography* that they "didn't give a rat's ass what anybody thought" because nobody cares what poor people do. Brown did well in high school, but tried to hide her talent because she wanted to be socially popular. Describing herself as "pansexual," she already knew that she liked both boys and girls. Since *Rubyfruit Jungle* is partly autobiographical, we get the idea that her early sexual experiences with boys were not as good as those with girls.

Trouble Over Her Lesbianism

Like her novelistic character, Brown was expelled from the University of Florida for her lesbianism. According to Carol Ward, she boldly stated to her sorority sister that she didn't care whether she fell in love with "a black or a white or a man or a woman or an old or young person. I just care that they have a good heart" (Ward 3). This statement finished her matriculation.

Brown continued her education at New York University, taking a degree in English and classics in 1968. She also studied cinematography at the School of Visual Arts in Manhattan. After working for a year as a photo editor for Sterling Publishing Company, Brown moved to Washington, D.C. She found the film industry particularly sexist, and she hated the ugliness and bad manners of New York City. In Washington, Brown lectured in sociology at Federal City College and was a research fellow at the Institute for Policy Studies, where she received a Ph.D. in political science and English.

At this time, Brown tried to align herself with various feminist groups, but learned a series of lessons about the divisiveness within "the" movement. Women's rights was not a single movement, but a set of split-off groups with different agendas. In particular, NOW (National Organization for Women) was not accepting of Brown's lesbian identity and politics. NOW members ostracized Brown and other lesbians because they perceived lesbianism as a threat to the potential for gaining equal rights from the patriarchal sources of power, as they assumed that lesbianism was the most fundamental threat to men's self-image.

Brown co-authored the essay "Woman Identified Woman" for the group Radicalesbians, which defined a lesbian as "the rage of all women condensed to the point of explosion." Such a strong position perforce creates separatism. Brown also tried a communal living experiment with separatist lesbians called Furies Collective, but once again she was expelled from a group for her trenchant expression of different opinions.

Her Own Ideology

Brown no longer believes in separatism, for, as she says in *Plain Brown Rapper,* it is just what patriarchy wants: "I don't want to be separate from anyone—that just keeps the Big Man on top of all of us." Brown's version of lesbian politics stresses homosexuality as a means to self-knowledge and personal freedom. She writes that women making love with women means confronting themselves, without the protective device of a socially-prescribed role.

Brown has tried to keep her own sex life private since the publicity surrounding her relationship with Navratilova. That two-year relationship (1979-81) took place in a shared home in Charlottesville, Virginia, and is described in Navratilova's biography, *Martina.* Both women have admitted to an imbalance in their relationship, between Navritilova's one hundred percent dedication to sports and Brown's dedication to culture, writing, and the intellect. Navratilova's intense tennis-circuit schedule conflicted with Brown's self-imposed writing schedule, leaving each feeling neglected at various times. Although Navratilova left Charlottesville to move in with another woman, basketball player Nancy Lieberman, in Dallas, their relationship was not a sexual one, according to Navratilova. Navratilova has publicized the fact that anger and fighting between herself and Brown existed at the time of the breakup, while Brown comments on her broken heart and shock, because of her inexperience in long-term relationships. She characterizes herself as a loner, but after Navratilova's departure, Brown kept company with Judy Nelson, Navratilova's ex.

When Navratilova left in 1981, Brown took her broken heart to Los Angeles to try to make money by screenwriting. She could not afford the Charlottesville house without Navratilova's salary. Brown's one singly-authored screenplay that was produced is considered by some an embarrassment to the lesbian movement, as it is in the super-sexist genre of horror flick. Brown explains that the all-female cast save themselves from the electric-driller killer without

Rita Mae Brown

male intervention, but she bemoans the fact that, in Hollywood, "to assume that a screenwriter has any power over the process of filming is naive in the extreme".

Other screenwriting achievements include a co-authored remake of Faulkner's *The Hamlet* and a story of lesbian self-discovery, *My Two Loves,* both for television. She also narrated a documentary, *Before Stonewall*, about the history of homosexuality in America. At the time, she was researching the Civil War for a novel, *High Hearts* (1986), which tells of a woman who dresses in drag so that she can accompany her husband into the fray of the Civil War.

Moving back to Charlottesville in 1982, Brown tried new genres. *Starting from Scratch* (1988) is a writer's manual and *Wish you Were Here* (1990) is a murder mystery in a series called *Kitty Crime*. Two teleplays, "I Love Liberty" and "The Long Hot Summer" were nominated for Emmys in 1981 and 1984. She has been publishing one novel a year for the last five years, all with Bantam Books. Nevertheless, 1973's *Rubyfruit Jungle* remains Brown's most popular work, perhaps because of its shock value to its 1973 audience and its consequent launching as a manifesto of lesbian freedom, as well as its appeal to "straights" as an American novel of one person's success against great odds. Her other novels have been variously criticized. *Newsweek* critic Richard Boeth felt that the characterization in *Six of One*, a novel about Brown's female ancestors, was flat, shallow, and unfunny: "These aren't human beings talking; it's 310 pages of 'Gilligan's Island.'" *Sudden Death*, a novel about life on the women's tennis circuit, lacked the characteristic voice—laidback, comedic, and loose—that Brown had become known for. *New York Times Book Review* critic Elisabeth Jakab wrote that this novel "tends to read like the casebook of an anthropologist stranded in the midst of a disappointingly boring tribe." Brown comments that there is a double standard being applied to fiction by lesbians: "often the lesbian is reviewed, not the book."

Brown's signature quality, and the one that she self-consciously strives to maintain in her work, is her sense of humor in the face of the misery that lesbians can feel. In contrast to most works about lesbian life, *Rubyfruit Jungle* celebrates lesbian sexuality and, more importantly, self-realization regardless of sexual preference. Brown is aware of the stigma of overseriousness that lesbian fiction carries. She commented in *Contemporary Authors* that "most lesbians are thought to be ugly, neurotic and self-destructive and I just am not." She resents being categorized as a lesbian writer because she feels it marginalizes her and obscures her worth as a writer. She described in an interview with Ward how she would prefer to be known: "I'm a writer and I'm a woman and I'm from the South and I'm alive, and that is that."

Current Address: American Artists Inc., P.O. Box 4671, Charlottesville, Virginia 22905-4671; c/o The Wendy Weil Agency, 232 Madison Avenue, New York, New York 10016.

References:

Brown, Rita Mae. Letter to the author. 27 March 1996.

———. *A Plain Brown Rapper*. Oakland, California: Diana Press, 1976.

Contemporary Authors: New Revision Series. Vol 35. Detroit: Gale Research, 1992.

Current Biography Yearbook. Ed. Charles Moritz. New York: H. W. Wilson, 1986.

Navratilova, Martina, with George Vecsey. *Martina*. New York: Ballantine Books, 1985.

Ward, Carol. *Rita Mae Brown*. New York: Twayne, 1993.

—Jill Franks

Ron Buckmire

1968-

West Indian-born mathematician and activist

Gay computer activist and mathematician Ron Buckmire is the founder of the Queer Resources Directory (QRD), the largest and oldest repository of gay, lesbian, bisexual, transgender, and AIDS information available on the Internet.

Ron Buckmire was born on 21 May 1968 in Grenville, Grenada, to Rose Henry and Reginald Buckmire. The next year his father brought the family to the United States while he attended graduate school at the University of Massachusetts at Amherst working towards a Ph.D. in food science and nutrition. Buckmire's parents divorced in 1974, and in 1978 the family returned to the Caribbean, this time to Barbados, where Dr. Buckmire worked for the Caribbean Development Bank.

While in Barbados, Buckmire developed an avid interest in chess, becoming an international-level youth player from 1981 to 1986 and participating in championship competitions in Finland, England, Scotland, and the United States. He was also Barbados Junior Champion for four consecutive years from 1982 to 1986 as well as a three-time Barbados National Champion from 1983 to 1986. Buckmire's interest in chess continues today; currently he is a United States Chess Federation Senior Master ranked in the top 250 in the nation.

In 1986, Buckmire returned to the United States to attend college. Just three years later he earned his bachelor's degree in mathematics magna cum laude at Rensselaer Polytechnic Institute in Troy, New York. He went on to get his masters in mathematics in 1992 and his Ph.D. applied mathematics in 1994 at the same institution.

It was during his college days that Buckmire came out. In 1988, he began to question his sexuality. Buckmire consulted what many at that time would have thought a surprising source of information—the Internet: "I came out pretty quickly, with the aid of computer-mediated communication." It didn't take long for Buckmire to turn into an activist. When asked what drew him to queer activism, Buckmire: "It just seemed like the obvious thing to do. I read a lot of books on gay history (*The Mayor of Castro Street*, etc.) and found out how few rights gays and lesbians had and was shocked. The arguments against equal rights for gays and lesbians are so illogical and internally inconsistent that it was completely natural to join the fight. Civil rights for all just makes sense." Asked what drew him to computer activism in particular, he says simply: "Because that was what I knew, and there wasn't much of it going on at the time."

During his years at Rensselaer Polytechnic Institute, Buckmire served as president of the Rensselaer Gay/Lesbian/Bisexual Association from 1991 to 1993, and co-creator and executive producer of HomoRadio, the local queer radio show from 1992 to 1994. He was also a member several campus advisory committees and even co-founded the Women Students Association in 1992.

But his most enduring contribution has been the creation of the Queer Resources Directory (QRD) in the spring of 1991. Originally begun as an electronic archive for Queer Nation (QN), Buckmire realized that "a more extensive resource than just an archive for QN would be useful for the queer Internet community" and began the process of transforming the QRD into its current status as the premier queer site on the Internet whose "function is to provide as much information as possible on every facet and issue relating to sexual minorities." Comments Buckmire, who currently serves as executive director of the QRD: "Creating the QRD and seeing it used by people all over the world in numerous situations is extremely rewarding."

In January of 1991, Buckmire met his partner, Dean Elzinga. Asked how they met, Buckmire answered: "Through the Internet! I came to Los Angeles to visit my sister (attending USC) and a number of soc.motss [USENET newsgroup for members of the same sex] gatherings were thrown together for me. At the third one it was just Dean and me and that was the beginning." Still together, the couple celebrates 13 January as their anniversary.

Currently, Buckmire has just completed a Minority Scholar-In-Residence Postdoctoral Fellowship and now serves as assistant professor in the department of mathematics at Occidental College in Los Angeles, California. His field of study centers around mathematical modelling and applied mathematics. Most of his work has been in theoretical aerodynamics and computational fluid dynamics.

Active in the queer immigration rights movement, Buckmire is a founding member of the Los Angeles Chapter of the Lesbian and Gay Immigration Rights Task Force. Buckmire comments: "I have spent 18 of my 28 years in the USA as a 'non-immigrant resident' but I hope to become a permanent resident soon."

Buckmire also works as contributing producer for *This Way Out*, an award-winning weekly international lesbian and gay radio magazine currently airing on almost 100 stations in seven countries. He remains active on the Internet. Remembering its importance in his coming out process, Buckmire assures safe space on the Internet for gays, lesbians, bisexuals, transgendered and questioning people throughout the world by administering several queer electronic discussion lists, including: GGBB ("girl-girl-boy-boy") for gay and lesbian couples; GLBMATH for queer mathematicians; GLBPOC for queer people of color; HOMORADIO for those involved in radio programming for queers; MARRIAGE for activists working to gain the right of same-sex couples in the United States to marry; QI (Queer Immigration) to discuss the impact of immigration policies on queers; QUEERLAW for discussion of queer legal theory; and, QUEERPLANET to enable queer activists and organizations the world over to network.

The Internet has become a vital tool in queer organizing, the "silicon solution" as Michelangelo Signorile terms it in his book *Queer in America*, due in large part to the efforts of Buckmire. Buckmire has chiselled out "queer space" on the Internet by generously giving of his time and resources to ensure that lesbians, gays, bisexuals, and transgendered persons can access and disseminate all types of information on the Internet. Buckmire continues to protect the rights to this information by being a part of the lawsuit challenging the Communications Decency Act which seeks to censor such information.

Current Address: Department of Mathematics, Occidental College, 1600 Campus Road, Los Angeles, California 90041. Email: ron@abacus.oxy.edu.

References:

All the information in this essay was found on the Internet. Much of the information can be found on Ron Buckmire's home page: http://abacus.oxy.edu/~ron/ or in the Queer Resources Directory: http://www.qrd.org/QRD/

Quotes are taken from email correspondence with Ron Buckmire and from the QRD FAQ (Frequently Asked Questions).

—R. Ellen Greenblatt

Charlotte Bunch

1944-

American educator, writer, and activist

For 30 years, Charlotte Bunch has worked as a lesbian feminist educator on global feminism, personifying the contemporary saying, "Think globally, act locally."

Charlotte Bunch was born in 1944 in West Jefferson, North Carolina, the third child of Charles Pardue and Marjorie King Bunch. The family, which eventually included her two sisters and brother, moved to Artesia, New Mexico that same year. She was raised in a Methodist family that regularly attended church, and instilled in the children a strong sense of community responsibility and quiet activism.

Moving back to North Carolina to attend Duke University in 1962, Bunch immediately began working within the civil rights movement, going quickly from thinker to activist. Her early religious involvement stayed with her throughout her college career as she participated in the civil rights movement and it continued to influence her life, especially as she chose to be an activist as well as an academic, theorist, and educator. After graduation, Bunch moved to Washington, D.C. intending to organize in the black community but soon realized that, as a white person, her energies would be put to better use educating whites about racism.

Bunch's years in Washington were hectic: she continued for a few years to be active in the radical Christian movement, married a man (Jim Weeks) she'd met within that movement, and continued to be active in radical politics. She also joined a leftish think tank, the Institute for Policy Studies (IPS) and it was here that she first felt the sting of sexual discrimination. With another woman from IPS, Marilyn Salzman Webb, Bunch started a woman's group. This being 1968, Bunch was right in line with the developing women's liberation movement sweeping across the United States. She quickly met women from across the country who were linking work for peace with fighting other forms of oppression. Soon, groups began whittling down those developing ideas about women's oppression into ones distinct from other forms of oppression. Bunch began writing about women's liberation in the liberal Methodist publication, *Motive.* She was soon being published and anthologized, lecturing, and labeling her politics as feminist.

By 1970, IPS began to recognize the women's movement and Bunch rejoined IPS. After a short time in Cleveland where her husband was doing graduate work, Bunch went back to Washington, D.C. At this point, women's liberation was in full-swing and by luck, Washington was crowded with young feminists who would one day be the leading names of the movement. Bunch began to recognize lesbianism as a choice that made sense for her both politically and personally. She left her marriage and came out in 1971. The gay/straight split in the women's movement led to the formation of a group called the Furies that included Joan Biren, Ginny Berson, Rita Mae Brown, and Sharon Deevey among others. The Furies Collective published a newspaper called the *Furies* and, as Bunch writes in *Passionate Politics: Feminist Theory in Action, Essays 1968-1986,* devoted itself to "developing a lesbian-feminist political analysis, culture and movement." After a year, internal struggles led to the group's demise, but the seeds it planted and the work the women did are still felt in the movement today.

After the Furies dissolved, Bunch traveled widely in Africa and it was this experience that led to her re-interest in global feminist issues. This in turn led to her working with other similar-minded women and they founded the journal *Quest: A Feminist Quarterly,* one of the first women's liberation periodicals that looked at the global oppression of women while incorporating class and race perspectives. Throughout the 1970s, Bunch worked on *Quest,* edited anthologies, and participated in conferences. In 1979, she founded a consulting firm called Interfem, and worked closely with other organizations including the International Women's Tribune Centre. Her work was increasingly international in focus, and she always brought a lesbian feminist perspective to her work. This international work led to organizing for United Nations conferences on women in Copenhagen (1980), Nairobi (1985), and Beijing (1995). Along the way, Bunch established links with women such as Peggy Antrobus, Claudia Hinojosa, and Betty Powell, all working together in the international sphere.

Charlotte Bunch. ***Photography by Terry Lorant.***

In 1987, Bunch took a chair in women's studies at Rutgers University, New Jersey, and in 1989 established the Douglass College Center for Women's Global Leadership. The Center builds on the 30 years of work that Bunch has done, establishing world-wide links between women and policy makers (as well as the function of women as such), to recognize, as the Center writes in its Global Center News, that "global issues are interconnected and have both local and international dimensions."

Bunch's contribution to the lesbian feminist movement, expressed through action and theory, cannot be separated from her contributions to the international feminist movement. Her early work in analyzing women's oppression and heterosexism gave way to an expanding analysis of world-wide oppression. Through her efforts at educating the public she has brought a feminist analysis to people and places who might not otherwise be exposed to these ideas or better yet, put these ideas into action. Her work spurs action. Her commitments to justice and human rights, to always including a lesbian feminist perspective, and to bringing a gentle, effective voice to enact change, will surely have everlasting impact.

Current Address: c/o Center for Women's Global Leadership, 27 Clifton Ave., New Brunswick, New Jersey 08901.

References:

Bunch, Charlotte. *Passionate Politics: Feminist Theory in Action, Essays 1968-1986.* New York: St. Martin's Press, 1987.

Reilly, Niamh, ed. *Global Center News.* New Brunswick, New Jersey: Center for Women's Global Leadership, vol. 1., no. 1, Fall 1994.

—Diane E. Hamer

Glenn Burke

1952-1995

African-American baseball player

Glenn Burke's legacy is that he was the first and, to date, the only major league baseball player to publicly acknowledge his homosexuality. By his own accounting, it was management's inherent homophobia that inevitably drove him from the game he loved—the only vocation for which he had ever prepared. Though at the age of 27, he was termed "the new Willie Mays" because of his size and speed, he was driven from the game at the age of 29, after only three short professional seasons. He slid into a life of despair and drugs, hastening his death from AIDS complications at the age of 42. Ironically, he is also credited with inventing the "high five" salute that has become a celebratory fixture on the field.

Burke began life with the odds stacked against him. His father, a sawmill worker, left the family when Glenn was just a year old. His mother struggled to support seven children by working as a nursing-home aide, moving her family around their native Oakland and nearby Berkeley, California neighborhoods in search of ever-dwindling affordable housing. "She was a strong woman," Burke told *People Weekly* with classic understatement in one of his last interviews.

As a teenager, Burke excelled in baseball and basketball at Berkeley High School. He befriended local jock Michael Hammock, now sport's coordinator for Oakland's parks and recreation department, and spent all of his spare time at nearby Bushrod Park. In 1970, he won a scholarship to the University of Denver, but dropped out after just a few months, blaming the cold weather. He was actually back home playing baseball at Bushrod in 1971 when his sister Lutha—who also took care of him in the last year before his death—pedaled by to tell him that Los Angeles Dodger scouts were at the house looking for him.

He spent five challenging years in the minor leagues before being picked up by the Dodgers in 1976. At a solid 220-pounds, he was soon nicknamed "King Kong" by his teammates, an image he enhanced by likewise becoming a speedster, leading three minor leagues in stolen bases.

"I Wasn't No Sissy"

Even while Burke was lighting up the scoreboard professionally, he was personally in turmoil. He had come out to family and friends in 1975, but was adamant that management, his fellow players, and the general public never find out. "I'm sure he played in fear," teammate Davey Lopez told Jennifer Frey, "the fear of the fact that it's going to get out that he's gay and once it comes out, you're going to take abuse." Burke himself told Frey that he "got used to the 'fag' jokes. You heard them everywhere then. I knew who I was. I wasn't no sissy. I was a man. It just so happened that I lived in a different world."

Dodgers' manager Tommy Lasorda had trouble with Burke right off, citing Burke's lack of training discipline. But Burke claimed he made Lasorda uncomfortable because he hung out with Lasorda's gay son, a contention echoed by many of Burke's teammates. (Lasorda Jr. died of AIDS in 1991, according to close friends, but the senior Lasorda has never publicly addressed the issue.) Burke even maintained that Dodgers management offered him a paid honeymoon if he would only get married. Whatever the root cause, Burke was traded to the Oakland Athletics in 1978—a move that was to facilitate the downward fizzle of his career.

By the late 1970s, Burke was an athletic hero to the local gay community, despite his "official closet." As longtime friend and former sport's editor of the *San Francisco Sentinel*, Jack McGowan, told Frey, "It was not so much that he was masculine, but that he was superbly athletic, and we were proud because he showed the world that we could be gay and be gifted athletes." All of which did not sit well with the notoriously homophobic Oakland A's manager Billy Martin, who regularly referred to Burke in public as "the faggot" and did his best to get him off the team, despite his speed and promise (Burke hit .237 and stole 35 bases in his brief career).

Dejected and frustrated, Burke left the team in 1979 after appearing in only 23 games. He had a change of heart in 1980, but injured his knee in spring training and quit baseball for good in 1981, convinced that he had been blackballed. He was 29 years old.

The 1980s signaled Burke's downward spiral of drug abuse. Without exception, friends and family have said that Burke never really figured out what he would do without baseball—so when that was finished, his life began to revolve around drugs. In October of 1982, he came out officially in *Inside Sports* and was still a figure of pride for the gay community, a position which sustained his flagging self-confidence through the 1986 Gay Games.

But the drugs were proving it was indeed a long way down. Gay softball teammates would see him less and less and, when they did, he would sometimes be carrying his clothes in a paper bag after sleeping in the rough the night before.

Prejudice (and Drugs) Win Out

Following a series of odd jobs and a hit-and-run accident in San Francisco that shattered his leg, Burke's downward spiral quickened. He had a falling-out with his family and started going from friend to friend, then stranger to stranger, in the Castro. In 1991, he pleaded guilty to grand theft and possession of drugs, and served six months of a 16-month sentence. He was subsequently incarcerated two more times for parole violation, and was finally reduced to panhandling to survive.

"Glenn went downhill so fast," longtime friend McGowan told Frey. "All he had were his professional abilities, and once he hurt his leg, people stopped glorifying him." Finally, in May of 1994, McGowan was stepping out of a cab and caught sight of a yet another gaunt, shaking soul with "the death look" standing in a doorway. It was his buddy Glenn Burke.

Burke deteriorated quickly, succumbing to AIDS complications in June of 1995. "My mission as a gay ballplayer was to break a stereotype," Burke told *People Weekly* in late 1994. "I think it worked." When asked if he had any regrets, he said only that perhaps he should have played basketball. Prejudice just won out, is how Burke called the play—how he explained his exile—a bias based on his sexual orientation and not on the color of his skin. "But no one can say I didn't make it," he said in his 1982 coming out article. "I played in the World Series. I'm in the book, and they can't take that away from me. Not ever."

Even if it shuns responsibility, the world of professional sports should certainly take heed of Burke's short, tragic life and career. As former teammate Dusty Baker, the man Burke first saluted with the now-emblematic "high five" nearly 20 years before, said in *Sports Illustrated* shortly after Burke's death: "We'll never know how good he could have become."

References:

The Alyson Almanac. Boston: Alyson Publications, 1994-95.
Frey, Jennifer. "A Boy of Summer's Long, Chilly Winter" in *New York Times* 18 October 1994: 13-15.
Inside Sports, 1 October 1982: 19.
Jet Magazine, 19 June 1995: 50.
People Weekly, 21 November 1994: 151-152.
Sports Illustrated, 12 June 1995: 15.

—Jerome Szymczak

Charles Busch

1954-

American actor and playwright

Charles Busch

Ben Brantley has called actor-playwright Charles Busch "arguably the most beloved drag performer in the New York theater." That classic of high camp, *Vampire Lesbians of Sodom,* of which Busch was the author and star—and a string of gleeful, wicked comedies have built his reputation on a surefire show-biz formula of high heels, heart, and happy endings.

The young Busch was raised in a Jewish family in Hartsdale, a middle-class suburb outside of New York City. Busch grew up with two older sisters, Meg and Betsy (now, respectively, a producer of promotional spots for Showtime and a textile designer).

But when Busch was seven, his mother died, and for the next seven years, he "sort of got lost in this world of old movies and trivia to block out the real world," he told Lisa Anderson in an interview for the *Chicago Tribune.* "I had this completely overblown sense of the romantic."

"He was saved by his Aunt Lillian—Lillian Blum—his mother's oldest sister and a former schoolteacher, who, with his father's permission, moved him to Manhattan and got him into the High School of Music and Art," reports Alex Witchel in the *New York Times.* "Chuck was always special," Blum, at the age of 85, related to Witchel. "But he was so shy it was almost pathological.... Before he moved in with me, I would pick him up in Hartsdale on a Friday afternoon, and he would be like a zombie. But the minute we crossed the river to New York he was absolutely a new boy."

His aunt's love and strong personality made all the difference. She insisted, for example, that he read the front page of the newspaper every day just to help him keep at least one foot in the real world. "I didn't do drugs," Busch explained to Witchel, "I did Warner Brothers movies." Thanks to Aunt Lillian, Busch graduated high school and went on to study drama at Northwestern University, in Evanston, Illinois.

While in some ways a frustrating experience, college helped Busch define his own strengths as a performer. "I was dealt a strange hand," he told Witchel, "Too thin, too light, which is the euphemism for gay. I was never cast at Northwestern for basically these reasons, and finally, I thought maybe what's most disturbing about me is what is most unique: my theatrical sense, my androgyny, even identifying with old movie actresses." So Busch began writing his own material, including a play, *Sister Act,* in 1976 about Siamese twin showgirls. "It made a big sensation at Northwestern," Busch told Anderson. "They'd never seen anything like it."

After college, from 1978 to 1984, Busch toured the country in a one-person non-drag show he wrote called *Alone with a Cast of Thousands.* Between bookings he would come back to New York where he cleaned apartments, scooped ice cream, gave the odds on a betting line, or did whatever he could to make ends meet.

But by 1984, the bookings had all but dried up and Busch was ready to throw in the towel. His last hurrah was going to be a little skit—with Busch in drag—that he arranged to put on at the Limbo Lounge, a gay bar in Manhattan's East Village. The skit, which eventually became *Vampire Lesbians of Sodom,* turned out to be a great hit, and Busch and his collaborators, who called themselves the Theatre-in-Limbo, created a series of drag spectacles at the bar, including *Theodora, She-Bitch of Byzantium* and *Times Square Angel.*

With his usual indomitability of spirit, Busch decided to mount a commercial production of *Vampire Lesbians,* and after going "to every friend, family member, and ex-lover to raise the money," the show opened at the Provincetown Playhouse in Greenwich Village (c. 1985), where it received nearly unanimous raves. "The audience laughs at the first line and goes right on laughing at every line to the end, and even at some of the silences," wrote D. J. R. Bruckner in a career-changing *New York Times* review.

Vampire Lesbians established the characteristics that typified Busch's comedies over the next nine years: manic energy, bigger-than-life female roles, fabulous and funny costumes, and sharp and knowing parodies of old film and fashion styles. In *Vampire Lesbians,* Busch spoofed the antics of 1920s silent pictures and their stars. *Psycho Beach Party* (1987) had its fun with 1960s beach-party movies while *The Lady in Question* (1989) targeted 1940s wartime dramas. *Red Scare on Sunset* (1991) used the conventions of film noire to tell a tale of Communist-baiting in Hollywood of the 1950s.

With his 1994 play *You Should Be So Lucky,* Busch gave himself his first non-drag role since hitting it big. The play is an updated Cinderella story in which Cinderella is a pathologically shy gay man, an electrologist yet, who through the intervention of a fairy godmother—the enigmatic, elderly businessman Mr. Rosenberg—not only gets to go to the ball where he meets the man of his dreams, but is left Mr. Rosenberg's fortune, too.

Busch's upcoming projects include *Queen Amarantha,* with a juicy new over-the-top drag role for himself, for the 1996-97 New York season. In a telephone interview, he said he hoped to reassemble his usual collaborators, at least, "whoever is alive and still speaking to me." He has also written the book for a musical, *The Green Heart* in development at the Manhattan Theater Club.

Through the medium of his own plays, Busch both spoofs and lovingly inhabits an outsized and glamorous world that captivated and charmed him and many other gay men as children. "Drag is being more, more than you can be," he told Witchel. "When I first started drag I wasn't this shy young man but a powerful woman...." In a *New York Times* interview with Patrick Pacheco, Busch said of appearing in drag: "It liberated within me a whole vocabulary of expression. It was less a political statement than an aesthetic one. He finishes the thought with "I look kinda pretty in a dress," which may just be an attempt to dispel any air that there's something serious going on under all that Max Factor.

Current Address: c/o Jeffrey Melnick, Harry Gold Agency, 3500 West Olive, Suite 1400, Burbank, California 91505; c/o Marc Glick, Glick and Weintraub, 1501 Broadway, Suite 2401, New York, New York 10036-5503.

References:

Anderson, Lisa. In *Chicago Tribune,* 10 November 1993.
Brantley, Ben. In *New York Times,* October 1993.
Bruckner, D. J. R. "Stage: 'Vampire Lesbians of Sodom'," in *New York Times,* 20 June 1985.
Busch, Charles. Interview with Ira Brodsky. 11 April 1996.
Current Biography, June 1995. New York: H. W. Wilson, 1995: 11.
Pacheco, Patrick. In *New York Times,* 23 July 1989.
Witchel, Alex. "Shopping with: Charles Busch; After Divas, It's a Challenge to Play a Man," in *New York Times,* 19 October 1994: C1.

—Ira N. Brodsky

Paul Cadmus

1904-

American artist

"Sailor Beware—Artist with Camera" blared the headline in a *Time* piece on artist Paul Cadmus, referring to such paintings as *The Fleet's In, Shore Leave,* and *Sailors and Floosies,* all of which depicted sailors doing what comes most natural to them when they are off ship and at liberty—trying to pick up some willing girls they hope will be easy sex. An admiral's influence got *Sailors and Floosies* removed from the American painting section of the Golden Gate International Exposition in San Francisco in 1940. It was re-hung soon afterward because the director of the Palace of Fine Arts at the Exposition, Timothy Pflueger, stated, "If every picture to which some may object was removed, none would remain."

It is a wry but appropriate footnote to the progress of acceptance of the subjects of art—and to Cadmus's status as a premier American artist especially—that *The Fleet's In* now hangs in the Naval Historical Center in Washington, D.C. Still, one wonders how much of the Navy's supposed wrath might have really been aroused by one striking detail: at the upper left, a sailor accepts a cigarette from a blonde civilian who is looking intently at him. Much the same kind of detail can be found in *Shore Leave,* in which a sailor is being picked up by a similar civilian, who has markedly swishy characteristics.

It was such satiric depiction that earned Cadmus his reputation as an "enfant terrible" before he was out of his twenties. But actually, it is Cadmus's repeated drawing and painting of the vital, fresh young male in all his splendid proportions that demonstrates the artist's love of such a subject best and most idealistically. Though Cadmus has never stated directly in any public medium that he is gay, nor has such a careful biographer as his friend Lincoln Kirstein ever so indicated explicitly, the presumption that Paul Cadmus is gay is general and solidly believed. His close association with such obviously gay men as the poet W.H. Auden and the novelist E.M. Forster is further substantiation. Cadmus's long co-habitation with the singer and dancer Jon Anderson, many times his model as well, affirms his sexual orientation.

Portrait of the Artist

Some have made the erroneous assumption that the artist's name indicates a Greek origin, but there is no connection between the artist's lineage and the mythic Cadmus, founder of Thebes, grandfather of Labdacus, and great grandfather of Oedipus. Actually, the family name is Dutch, and the artist's mother was from a Spanish family. Both parents were artists. Paul was born on 17 December 1904, when the family was living on 103rd St. in New York. He has one sister, Fidelma, who has posed for him.

Paul Cadmus

Paul Cadmus entered the National Academy of Design when he was 15 and rapidly acquired skills in drawing and printmaking. From 1928 to 1931, he worked as a commercial illustrator. Then, in 1931, he and close friend Jared French went to Europe, bought bicycles, and toured in France and Spain. After they had visited Madrid's Prado Museum, the two went to Mallorca, where they lived for two years. This period saw the genesis of Cadmus's style, with many drawings of Mallorcan seacoast scenes and bicyclists emerging. Ironically, some of his most famous works, such as *Shore Leave* and *Y.M.C.A. Locker Room,* were produced there.

While some of Cadmus's creations from the 1930s, with their emphases on the male form and/or satiric interpretations seemed entirely original with him, there were plenty of antecedents in both subjects. Thomas Eakens's *The Swimming Hole,* with its depiction of nude adolescent boys freely disporting, and George Bellows's *Stag at Sharkey's,* with the drama of a furious boxing match, both display a previously established enthusiasm for the robust male.

On the satiric side, William Gropper's *The Senate* makes fun of the windy politician, and Jack Levine's *The Feast of Pure Reason* skewers the cop, the ward heeler, and the plutocrat in solemn conference on the fate of humankind.

Satiric depiction continued to attract Cadmus, though such canvases contributed to his reputation as a troublesome rebel. One especially pungent example is *Coney Island,* which aroused the resentment of the businessmen of that resort with its clustering of lumpy show-offs supposedly enjoying themselves at the shore.

Some subjects were part of a series. Particularly biting was *Aspects of Suburban Life,* which was commissioned by the Treasury Relief Art Project in 1936, one more of the public works projects of the Roosevelt era designed to employ artists. The Marina dock, regatta, commuter rush, polo, and golf all got treatments that mixed colorful liveliness with realizations of shallow play.

Cadmus also produced an urban series, of which *Subway Symphony* is a prime example. The cacophony of big-city life, as Cadmus sees and hears it, is a phantasmagoria of near-freakish riders on the underground, some asleep, others listening to a boombox or blowing bubblegum, but all crammed together temporarily in all their idiosyncracies. It dates from the 1970s, indicating that Cadmus's interest in satirizing persisted long after his 1930s-era U.S. Navy depictions.

One example from his earlier period, *Greenwich Village Cafeteria,* however, has a significant example of his daring on gay subject matter. At one side of this crowded, raffish bunch of diners is a man looking over his shoulder provocatively as he is about to enter a men's restroom.

Another example from the 1930s is *Venus and Adonis,* a satire on a classical subject and a humorous depiction of a silly and sordid phenomenon of the time, the attempted seduction of the young male by a woman well past her age of attractiveness. In it, Adonis is shown as an athletic young man with tennis racket and balls trying to escape from a middle aged woman with bleached blonde hair holding on to him desperately. Off to one side is a squalling Cupid. Obviously, the young man would much rather be with the other young men on the court in the background. The gay suggestion is a strong part of the satire.

Cadmus's deeper interest in the human dilemma is represented too, though, in a 1940 work called *Herrin Massacre,* showing a brutal murder in the Illinois town of Herrin in 1925. A contract dispute had flared into a bloody riot, and 26 strike breakers hired by the coal company were killed by the union members. Though the massacre had actually occurred at the mine, Cadmus set his depiction in a cemetery, with the headstones as emphatic commentary. The painting was commissioned by *Life* magazine. Critical remarks in art periodicals called the work "just gory journalism," but Cadmus's love of the male body is evident in the partially stripped forms of the slain, and the circular, dramatic composition bespeaks the influence that the Italian masters of the Renaissance and following periods had on him.

Contrasting with such violence is the series Cadmus painted of ballet scenes in the late 1930s and early 1940s. The 1941 *Arabesque* captures the grace of both male and female dancers as they perfect their art in the rehearsal hall. Such studies emerged from daily observations Cadmus made at the School of American Ballet. He became even more involved with dance when he designed scenery and costumes for the ballet *Filling Station,* which was set to the music of the gay composer Virgil Thomson. The interior Cadmus designed for the set used some of the same kinds of figures the artist had put into the *Aspects of Suburban Life* series, here transformed into comic silhouettes. Cadmus's costume for Lew Christensen in the *"danseur noble"* lead role as the mechanic was cut from transparent plastic, which showed off the dancer's splendid build.

A Change of Medium

It was during this period of working on the ballet drawings and paintings that Cadmus was introduced to the egg tempera technique of painting, a method first evolved in the Italian Renaissance by Cennino Andrea Cennini. More modern means of producing egg tempera were advanced by Daniel V. Thompson of Yale University, and Cadmus adapted those to his own use. The result was a light, creamy emulsion which facilitated fastidious handling of all subjects and resulted in a porcelain finish which gave completed works a lifelike glow.

Soon after his development of his own style of egg tempera, Cadmus was to apply it to what Lincoln Kirstein, in *Paul Cadmus,* called the "capstone of Cadmus's career." The work in question is the seven-panel *Seven Deadly Sins.* While such a judgement could easily be thought of as premature, inasmuch as the artist is still living and working in his 92nd year and has been doing so steadily in the intervening fifty years since *Seven Deadly Sins* was painted, the very nature of the work, subject and technique both, mark it as highly distinctive.

Painted in the years 1945-49, *Seven Deadly Sins* once more shocked the public probably even more than Cadmus's earlier notorious works. Of course, classification of sins has used various terms: "capital," "mortal," and "venial" being some of the most frequently used. Cadmus is most likely to be thought of as a lapsed Catholic, the devoutly practiced faith of his mother. His father was apparently staunchly atheistic. It would be too much of a stretch to presume a really religious intention to this work, however.

Nonetheless, the seven venial sins Cadmus found to be most ubiquitous among humans, though not necessarily the most condemnatory, are Lust, Pride, Sloth, Anger, Envy, Avarice, and Gluttony. The representation of each demonstrates a command of imagination and skill which impresses the viewer that the series is a masterpiece.

For example, *Lust* is a bisexual (as are all the figures really) encased totally in a condom, the hands clasped across a vacant crotch, the face a combination of satisfaction and desperation. The bisexuality is most obviously shown first, a chest of full, ripe breasts, and, beneath that, an abdomen of masculine abdominal muscles. The overall effect is an obsessed creature trapped in a transparent casing of its own creation.

Anger is a furiously red monster bristling with black spines and thorns and surrounded by splatters of blood. The total effect is a roar of uncontrolled rage. *Gluttony* is a human being incredibly bloated but still stuffing itself, even while its guts are bursting out of an enormously distended abdomen. The viewer's realization is that this sin knows no satiation.

While this series does not include such sins as murder, idolatry, or adultery, which could be thought of as more definitely capital crimes, it is easy to see that those three, whose consequences are more deeply serious than the seven, are still linked. For instance, out of anger comes murder; out of lust comes adultery. So who is to say which "set" is the more important? W.H. Auden suggested to Cadmus that he produce a contrasting series on the Christian virtues, but the artist felt that the static, passive factors which are intrinsically present in the virtues did not lend themselves to any impressive representations.

During the same early 1940s period, Cadmus created many beach scenes, some of them from his sojourns at Fire Island, which was already a favorite as an artist's retreat but not yet the great gay magnet it was to become. Possibly the most famous of these is *The Shower,* with two nude male figures and, chastely draped nearby, a woman. The gay suggestion is there.

This period also includes another work in which satire reappears: *Fantasia on a Theme by Dr. S.* Its basis is a body-typing theory of a constitutional psychologist named Dr. William Sheldon, among whose ideas were the classifications of ectomorph (thinner than average), mesomorph (average body weight and proportions) and endomorph (heavier and stockier than average). In the center of the painting are three figures representing the three body types: a skinny queen in a nelly pose, a plump slob, and between them a gloriously developed young blonde in an athletic pose. On the right side of the painting come two young women in dark glasses just turning their gaze at the sexy mesomorph. Cadmus has certainly not been above making fun of gay stereotypes.

But more natural to his idealistic conceptions of human beings and his admiration of attractive and promising young men are such pieces from the 1950s as *The Inventor,* in which a young man has created a mobile of natural beach objects; *Aviator,* in which a youth has made a kind of box kite that could be his dream of flight; and *Architect,* a picture of an intent young man with the T-square and blueprint of his intended vocation.

However, the commenting creation was still showing up in Cadmus's later work. *Night in Bologna* (1958) shows a dramatic triangle of a pale (and probably gay) man alone at a cafe table in an arcade looking piercingly toward a virile soldier, who, in turn, is looking at the retreating, seductive form of a young woman.

But a work which is more likely the most characteristic of this later part of Cadmus's life is *Study of David and Goliath,* in which Cadmus's companion—performer—model Jon Anderson is posed, while Cadmus himself is in front of a sketch pad looking over at the viewer with a smile.

An Artistic Credo Fulfilled

With the collaboration of his early friend, fellow artist Jared French, Cadmus composed his credo as an artist in 1937. Among the more important statements is the following: "I believe that art is not only more true but also more living and vital if it derives its immediate inspiration and its outward form from contemporary life. The actual contact with human beings who are living and dying, working and playing, exercising all their functions and passions, demonstrating the heights and depths of man's nature, gives results of greater significance than those gained by isolation, introspection, or subjective contemplation of inanimate objects."

The accumulation of the creations of Paul Cadmus in the nearly sixty years since the statement of that credo bear it out powerfully.

Current Address: P.O. Box 1255, Weston, Connecticut 06883-0255.

References:

Davenport, Guy. *The Drawings of Paul Cadmus.* New York: Rizzoli, 1989.

Hunter, Sam, and John Jacobus. *American Art of the 20th Century.* New York: Abrams, 1973.

Kirstein, Lincoln. *Paul Cadmus.* New York: Imago Imprint, 1984.

Sutherland, David. *Paul Cadmus: Enfant Terrible at 80.* David Sutherland Productions, 1984.

—Marvin S. Shaw

John Cage

1912-1992

American composer

John Cage was the most influential American composer of the mid-twentieth century. His work challenged conceptions of music that had been dominant in the West since the Renaissance. His suspicion of harmony, his deployment of chance operations in composition, his challenge to the distinction between music and noise, his concern with silence, and his use of electronic technology provoked controversy and condemnation, but also opened up a range of new artistic possibilities. While his sexual preference was not an explicit part of his public profile, the example of his work and life helped to create more freedom for alternative practices in the personal, cultural, and social spheres.

John Milton Cage, Jr., his parents' only surviving child, was born on 5 September 1912 in Los Angeles. His father was a fertile but financially unsuccessful inventor in a range of fields from submarines to patent medicines; his mother, who had been married twice before, was active in women's clubs and later became a columnist for the *Los Angeles Times.* His parents' frequent moves meant many changes of school for Cage, but he was a good student, who ended as valedictorian of his class at Los Angeles High School and won first prize in the Southern California Oratorical Contest.

His interest in music developed early. When his mother took him to a symphony concert at the age of five, he stood in the aisle wholly absorbed for two hours. In the fourth grade at school, he started taking piano lessons, though he did not think himself very gifted. But one of his piano teachers, his Aunt Phoebe, taught him sight reading, and, according to Cage as quoted in Calvin Tomkins's *The Bride and the Bachelors* (1965), this "seemed to open the door to the whole field of music." The Los Angeles Public Library's large music collection helped him to explore that field. He also showed early signs of enterprise: at the age of 12, he persuaded a Los Angeles radio station to let him present a regular Boy Scout radio programme which proved very popular.

In 1930, at the age of 16, Cage moved from Los Angeles High School to Pomona College in Claremont. He abandoned his initial plan to follow his grandfather into the ministry of the Methodist Episcopalian Church. His academic performance declined, and after two years he left for Europe. In Paris, he worked for a time as an assistant to the modernist architect Erno Goldfinger and studied briefly with the leading piano teacher at the Paris Conservatoire, Lazare Levy. But a visit to a concert by the pianist John Kirkpatrick, which included the work of Stravinsky and Scriabin, aroused his interest in modern music.

Cage had proposed marriage to a girl before leaving America, but in Paris, he had gay relationships, first with John Goheen, the son of a Queen's College professor of music, then with an aspiring artist, Don Sample, who introduced him to modern art and literature. After six months, Cage left Paris with Sample, and they travelled through Europe, visiting Biskra, Madrid, Seville, Berlin, Italy, and North Africa. During these travels Cage painted and wrote poetry, and, in Majorca, tried to compose music for the first time.

New Musical Inventions

In the fall of 1931, Cage returned to the United States and worked as a gardener, cook, researcher, and freelance lecturer on modern art and music, while continuing to write, paint, and compose. He developed a complex and tightly structured 25-tone method of composition, and the pianist Richard Buhlig, who had become his teacher, encouraged him to send some of his pieces to Henry Cowell, the composer and concert promoter. Cowell advised Cage to study with the composer Adolph Weiss, a former pupil of Schoenberg, and then with Schoenberg himself. Cage went to New York in 1934 to study harmony and composition with Weiss and to become the assistant and student of Cowell, who was then teaching at the New School for Social Research.

Cage came back to California in 1935 and took Schoenberg's six-week summer course at UCLA. In that summer, he married the girl he had proposed to before leaving for Europe, Xenia Andreevna Kashevaroff, one of six gifted and spirited daughters of a Russian Orthodox priest. Cage's most significant composition of 1935 was a 20-minute *Quartet* for unspecified percussion instruments, the start of a concern with percussion which was unusual in 1930s America, but which Cage encouraged in other composers and musicians. In Richard Kostelanetz's book *Conversing with Cage* (1988), Cage recalls a further important development at this time; while working with the abstract filmmaker Oscar Fischinger, he was "set on fire" by Fischinger's axiom that "[e]verything in the world has its own spirit, and this spirit becomes audible by setting it into vibration." In Cage's own words, Fischinger "started me on a path of exploration of the world around me which has never stopped—of hitting and stretching and scraping and rubbing everything."

From the fall of 1937, Cage worked as an assistant in the UCLA elementary school and played as an accompanist and gave percussion classes. He became a member of the training school faculty at Westwood, where he improvised at the piano for the classes of a modern dance group and soon began to compose percussion pieces for their dances. Asked to write for the annual water ballet of the UCLA swimming team, he devised a way to mark time by dipping a vibrating gong into the water; the sound thus produced delighted him, and he often used it in later compositions. In the spring of 1938, with his Aunt Phoebe, he taught a UCLA extension course in which students experimented with a range of sounds from shaking rice-filled balloons to hitting radiators with tires. Cage also took off the piano lid and tied the strings with objects—an anticipation of the "prepared piano" which was to become one of his major innovations.

Late in 1938, Cage started to work for Bonnie Bird, a former dancer with Martha Graham's troupe who was now teaching at the Cornish School, Seattle. There, he met the dancer Merce Cunningham, who was to become a key figure in both his artistic and personal life. He held his first percussion concert in Seattle in December 1938 and in 1939, for a Seattle performance of Cocteau's *Marriage at the Eiffel Tower,* he wrote the *Imaginary Landscape No. 1,* a six-minute piece for muted piano, cymbal, and two variable-speed turntables—his first use of electronic technology in a composition.

Avant-garde Reputation Grows

Cage moved to San Francisco in 1939, where he taught in hospitals and community centres for the recreation project of the Works Progress Administration. In 1940, asked by the dancer Syvilla Fort to provide music for her dance solo *Bacchanale,* he produced his first fully fledged piece for prepared piano—a piano with objects such as bolts, screws, and nails inserted between the strings. In the same year, he wrote *Living Room Music,* for four performers who were to play whatever happened to be in the living room—furniture and other objects, and parts of the building itself. The Hungarian artist Laszlo Moholy-Nagy invited Cage to teach a class in experimental music at the Chicago School of Design, and Cage and Xenia moved to Chicago in 1941. At a local radio station, he devised an *Imaginary Landscape No. 2* and an *Imaginary Landscape No. 3,* and for CBS Radio he worked with Kenneth Patchen as writer to create a show called *The City Wears a Slouch Hat,* which was broadcast nationally and well-received.

In 1942, Cage and Xenia moved to New York. His main source of income was writing music for modern dancers. He avoided the draft as he was doing library research for his father, who was involved in wartime work on submarine detection and vision systems for aircraft. In February 1943, at New York's Museum of Modern Art, he held the first of a series of concerts and recitals which were to establish his reputation as a leading avant-garde artist. Personal crisis accompanied his increasing professional success and led in 1945 to his divorce from Xenia and the confirmation of Merce Cunningham as his personal as well as his artistic partner. Cage moved to New York's Lower East Side and began to learn from one of his students, Gita Sarabhai, about Indian music and its cultural and philosophical contexts. Cage also went regularly to D. T. Suzuki's lectures on Zen at Columbia University. This concern with Eastern music and philosophy fed into his compositions of the later 1940s, especially the *Sonatas and Interludes* (1946-48) for prepared piano, and the ballet *The Seasons* (1947).

During these years, Cage made several tours with the Merce Cunningham Company, which was gaining recognition as an innovative and exciting modern dance troupe. In 1948, the company performed at Black Mountain College, where Cage organized a festival of the music of Erik Satie, which had interested him for many years. But his hope that the college would publish his talks on Satie was scotched when his claim that Beethoven's influence had been lamentable outraged some faculty members. January 1949, however, saw the first performance in Carnegie Hall of Cage's *Sonatas and Interludes,* which were hailed by the composer Virgil Thomson. The National Academy of Arts and Letters gave Cage a $1,000 award, and the Guggenheim foundation came up with a grant of $2,400. He went to Europe for three months, gave concerts and dance recitals with Cunningham in Paris, and got to know the avant-garde composer and conductor Pierre Boulez.

Chance, Controversy and TV Triumph

In 1950, Cage began to draw up charts to assist his composition and to employ chance operations to eliminate the subjective element from his music. In 1951, he discovered the *I Ching,* the Chinese *Book of Changes,* and used charts derived from this to determine the pitches, durations, and timbres of the long piano work *Music of Changes.* His use of chance was his most controversial move, even leading to a breach with Boulez. In 1952, he produced the *Imaginary Landscape No. 4,* which uses 12 radios with two

John Cage

performers at each, one turning the tuning knob, the other the volume control: the results vary according to what is being broadcast at any given time.

In the summer of 1952, Cage returned to Black Mountain College. With David Tudor, the artist Robert Rauschenberg, and the poets Mary Caroline Roberts and Charles Olsen, he staged what he called a "concerted action," a prototype of the 1960s "Happening" and the 1990s multimedia event which combined readings, dance, painting, still pictures, and movies. In August 1952, at the Maverick Concert Hall in Woodstock, New York, the premiere took place of Cage's most famous, or notorious, piece—*4' 33"*, with David Tudor sitting silently at a piano for precisely four minutes and thirty-three seconds.

Between 1952 and early 1954, Cage spent much time touring America with the Cunningham Dance Company, which was consolidating its high reputation. In the summer of 1954, while living with David Tudor and others in a cooperative community in Rockland County, he began to take an interest in mycology, the study of mushrooms. Later that year, he and Tudor made a concert tour of Europe which provoked a largely hostile response but aroused the interest of the German composer Karlheinz Stockhausen. May 1958 saw a retrospective concert of Cage's music at the NewYork Town Hall which culminated in an uproar in the audience recalling that which had greeted the 1913 performance of Stravinsky's *Rite of Spring.*

In the summer of 1958, Cage taught, lectured, and gave concerts in Europe. Invited to Milan by the composer Luciano Berio, he spent four months working in the tape studio of Milan Radio and produced the tape piece *Fontana Mix.* His most notable Italian exploit was a series of appearances on the television quiz show *Lascia o Raddoppia,* where he presented works such as *Water Walk* and *Sounds of Venice* and answered increasingly difficult questions on mushrooms, eventually winning $6,000.

Cage and the Counterculture

From 1960 to 1961, as a Fellow at the Center for Advanced Studies at Wesleyan University, Cage completed his book *Silence.* He developed his interest in mushrooms by confounding the New York mycological society in 1962. In that year, he and David Tudor also undertook a six-week concert tour of Japan. But the attempt by Leonard Bernstein to present Cage's *Atlas Ellipticals* at New York's Lincoln Center in 1964 provoked the hostility not only of most of the audience but also of the orchestra. The cultural tide, however, was turning in Cage's favour. The 1960s counterculture shared his concern with chance, anarchy, and Eastern religion and philosophy. He also won further academic recognition. In 1967, he was composer in residence at the University of Cincinnati and from 1967 to 1969 an associate of the Centre for Advanced Study of the University of Illinois, where he presented, with Lejaren Hiller, Jr.,

HPSCHD, a multimedia event combining harpsichords, computers, tapes, amplifiers, films, slides, and coloured lights. The year 1968 saw Cage's election to the National Institute of Arts and Letters, and in 1969 he became artist in residence at the University of California, Davis.

In the 1970s and 1980s, Cage suffered increasingly from health problems, especially arthritis. This did not stem his creative output, but works such as *Cheap Imitation* (1971-72) and *Etudes Australes* (1974-75) did employ more conventional instrumentation and notation, while the *Thirteen Harmonies* of 1984 even began to show a concern for harmony. His interest in Joyce's *Finnegans Wake* culminated in the *Roaratorio* of 1979, while his *Europeras I and II* (1987) mixed together fragments of European opera to provocative and sometimes hilarious effect. In the 1980s he produced some series of etchings at the Crown Point Press in California, and in the fall of 1988 he received the further academic accolade of an appointment as Norton Professor of Poetry at Harvard. As he moved into the 1990s, he looked set to join the writer William Burroughs as an octogenarian survivor of the American avant-garde. In anticipation of his eightieth birthday on 5 September 1992, worldwide plans were made for celebrations, concerts, symposia, and exhibitions, but Cage died suddenly on 12 August 1992.

Cage was a distinctively American artist in his rejection of European tradition and his desire to find new aesthetic and philosophical principles and practices. But his concern with indeterminacy and chance, with the elimination of the subjective element, and with the use of electronic media, make him the precursor and prophet of the global culture of postmodernism and of advanced computer technology. His life and work will remain controversial: but the approach of the twenty-first century is likely to enhance their resonance and relevance.

References:

Cage, John. *Empty Words.* London: Marion Boyars, 1980.

———. *For the Birds: John Cage in Conversation with Daniel Charles.* Boston and London: Marion Boyars, 1981.

———. *M.* London: Marion Boyars, 1973.

———. *Silence: Lectures and Writings.* London: Calder and Boyars, 1968.

———. *X.* Corrected second edn. London: Marion Boyars, 1987.

———. *A Year from Monday: New Lectures and Writings.* London: Calder and Boyars, 1968.

Fleming, Richard, and William Duckworth, eds. *John Cage at Seventy-Five.* Lewisburg, Pennsylvania: Bucknell University Press, 1989.

Hamm, Charles. "John Cage," in *The New Grove Dictionary of Music and Musicians,* edited by Stanley Sadie. London: Macmillan, vol. 3, 1980: 597-603.

Kostelanetz, Richard, ed. *Conversing with Cage.* New York: Limelight Editions, 1988.

———. *John Cage.* London: Allen Lane, 1971.

Perloff, Marjorie, and Charles Junkerman, eds. *John Cage: Composed in America.* Chicago, Illinois: University of Chicago Press, 1994.

Revill, David. *The Roaring Silence: John Cage: A Life.* London: Bloomsbury, 1992.

Tomkins, Calvin. *The Bride and the Bachelors: The Heretical Courtship in Modern Art.* London: Weidenfeld and Nicolson, 1965.

—Nicolas Tredell

Pat Califia

1954-

American writer and activist

Pat Califia is a writer, activist, and self-proclaimed troublemaker. Since the early 1970s she has advocated for the rights of those individuals perceived by the mainstream as perverts and outcasts. She has eloquently railed against sexual repression and repression in general. Her twelve books and many articles and stories run the gamut from cultural criticism to pornographic fiction to sexual how-to guides, and she is widely regarded as an expert on sadomasochistic relationships. Califia's work has provided both the impetus for and a chronicle of the sex-radical movement in the United States.

Califia often writes about herself, and her writing provides the main source of information about her difficult growing up. Pat Califia was born in 1954, into a Mormon family. She came out in 1971, when she was 17, in her first year of college in Utah; the process was extremely difficult for her. The woman she desired, a fellow student, insisted on maintaining a purely platonic friendship. Califia's family disapproved of her sexuality, and school pressures mounted. Califia, distraught, wrote poetry and took drugs to cope, but ultimately a nervous breakdown forced her out of school.

She went on public assistance and quickly realized that, as she writes in the introduction to the third edition of *Sapphistry,* "There simply was not any room in the system for women, especially lesbians. I had to become involved in political activity or I would not survive." Moving into a women's center to heal, she became involved with a range of feminist causes. She participated in consciousness-raising for the Equal Rights Amendment and founded a women's center. She became active in movements addressing self-health, peace in Vietnam, and housing for poor people and minorities. Despite these activities, she felt unhappy in Utah; by the end of 1973, Califia had quit her $1.60-an-hour job at a bindery and moved to San Francisco.

Califia dove into feminist politics in San Francisco. She joined the Daughters of Bilitis, Del Martin and Phyllis Lyon's pioneer lesbian organization. She worked on the San Francisco Sex Information switchboard and became a sex educator. Discouraged that lesbians never called the switchboard, Califia began to lead groups on lesbian sexuality. *Sapphistry* (The Naiad Press, 1980), her first book, came out of these workshops.

Sapphistry was a straightforward yet revolutionary guide to lesbian sex and sexuality. *Sapphistry* became enormously successful and eclipsed the few previous sex manuals written by lesbians (such as the *Joy of Lesbian Sex*). Columbia University's department of English and comparative literature recently listed *Sapphistry,* along with Sigmund Freud's *Theory of Sexuality* and Margaret Mead's *Coming of Age in Samoa,* as a book that shaped 20th century ideas about sexuality.

> Where many texts had assumed that women intuitively knew how to perform sexually with each other, Califia recognized that many women felt unsure of their erotic abilities or embarrassed by their desires, and emphasized communication and openness in sex. Completely unfazed by the variety of sexual fantasies and practices among women, Califia's attitude throughout the book is an explicitly feminist combination of unabashed celebration and cool report-

Pat Califia. ***Photograph by Marc Geller.***

> age of lesbian desire. For the first time many lesbians—those with disabilities, women growing older, teenage lesbians, women whose sexual activities included sadomasochism, group sex or role-playing—saw their sexuality discussed in a nonjudgmental, common sense way.

Sapphistry quickly found a large audience, and has been reprinted three times and translated into German.

With the success of her first endeavor, Califia branched out, writing about women's culture and feminist politics; she also began writing erotica and about erotica. Her articles appeared in various venues, including *Vector, Sisters, Focus, Black Maria,* the *Lesbian Tide, Heresies,* and the *Advocate,* for which she wrote a regular column. In addition, Califia's research on lesbian sex was published in the *Journal of Homosexuality.*

Califia has become known as a powerful voice for the freedoms of social outsiders, sexual and otherwise. She supports anyone who addresses social and economic inequity in society, whatever their specific subject, and her definition of radical embraces a diverse range of people. As she writes in *Public Sex:*

> Being a sex radical means being defiant as well as deviant. It means being aware that there is something unsatisfying and dishonest about the way sex is talked about (or hidden) in daily life. It also means questioning the way our society assigns privilege based on adherence to moral codes. If you believe that inequities can only be addressed through extreme social change, then you qualify as a sex radical, even if you prefer to get off in the missionary position and still believe there are only two genders.

She has often focused on communities previously underrepresented, and her stances have not always been popular with mainstream feminists and lesbians. She strongly supports pornography, sex clubs, deviant sex of all kinds—including NAMBLA, the National Man-Boy Love Association, despite its disavowal by every major lesbian and gay rights group in America.

Two of her most common topics are working-class lesbians and lesbians who have sadomasochistic sex, outcast communities that she regards as anti-assimilationist. Califia is widely regarded as an expert on sadomasochism in general and on lesbian s/m relationships in particular. Her book *Sensuous Magic* is a how-to guide to sadomasochism for beginners, and she has served as editor on numerous collections of leather erotica and instructions. Her popular novel *Doc and Fluff* (Alyson Publications, 1990) deals with these communities; an often violent and over-the-top science-fiction novel about a pair of outlaw women, it is filled with tough love and rough sex.

Califia's most recent book is *Public Sex* (Cleis Press, 1994), a collection of essays examining sex, feminism, censorship and economics in the United States, Canada, and Great Britain. Califia's other books include a collection of her *Advocate* columns published as *The Advocate Adviser: America's Most Popular Gay Columnist Tackles the Questions That the Others Ignore* (Alyson Publications, 1991). She has written two collections of erotic fiction, *Macho Sluts* (Alyson Publications, 1988) and *Melting Point* (Alyson Publications, 1993), contributed to many other collections, and edited collections, including *Doing It for Daddy* (Alyson Publications, 1994) and *The Lesbian S/M Safety Manual* (Lace Publications, 1988).

Most recently Califia has become a speaker for lesbian safe sex, openly discussing the previously taboo subject of lesbian drug use. Her work against censorship is ongoing: she has campaigned actively against anti-pornography laws, from child pornography cases to the 1996 Communications Decency Act, which attempts to eliminate pornography on the World Wide Web. In 1995 she contributed to *Forbidden Passages: Writings Banned in Canada* (Cleis Press, 1995), published to raise funds for Canada's Little Sister's Book and Art Emporium in its lawsuit against a section of the Canadian Customs Acts that allowed Customs officers to seize books, video and other materials as they entered the country.

In 1994, Califia said, on the publication of *Public Sex,* "Today, at the amazing age of forty, I am trying to cause as much trouble as I did when I was twenty-five." She is also solidifying her stance with professional training—she is currently completing her M.A. in counseling psychology at the University of San Francisco. Her continued dedication to sexual, political, and informational freedom has earned her the respect of activists and deviants around the world.

Current Address: 2215R Market St. #261, San Francisco, California 94114.

—Jonathan Wald

Michael Callen

1955-1993

American performer, songwriter, and AIDS activist

"I was diagnosed with AIDS before the term AIDS even existed.... According to the best estimate, of the 1,049 Americans diagnosed with AIDS during 1982, twenty-five are still alive.... I am one of the lucky ones." In 1990, Michael Callen began his highly autobiographical book, *Surviving AIDS,* with those words. A devout atheist, he did not believe in providence, only luck. But, he had a lot more going for him than luck in the relatively short period he was alive. He was a soloist and lead singer with the Flirtations (a five-man *a cappella* group), a legal secretary, writer, and composer; yet, it was his role as an AIDS activist which many will remember most.

Of Native American and Pennsylvania Dutch stock, Callen was born in 1955 in Rising Sun, Indiana, and raised in Hamilton, Ohio. He attended Boston University on a musical scholarship and graduated in 1977. He moved to New York, working by day as a legal secretary and singing on the side. From *Surviving AIDS:* "At that time, I had been transformed from a silly, immature, lonely Midwesterner into a silly, immature, lonely urban gay man ... I only halfheartedly pursued singing. There were too many other distractions—mostly sex." He took up sex with militant zeal. He further explained: "Some of us believed that we could change the world through sexual liberation and that we were taking part in a noble experiment ... Unwittingly, and with the best of revolutionary intentions, a small subset of gay men managed to create disease settings equivalent to those of poor third-world nations in one of the richest nations on earth." He was diagnosed with GRID (Gay-Related Immune Deficiency) in 1982. Influenced by his physician Dr. Joe Sonnabend's multifactor theory (i.e., that repeated assaults on the immune system by many common sexually transmitted diseases and drug use result in a suppressed immune system), he became an AIDS activist.

Michael Callen

In 1983 Michael Callen wrote, with Richard Berkowitz and Richard Dworkin, *How to Have Sex in an Epidemic: One Approach.* In that same year he, with other AIDS activists, created an AIDS self-empowerment movement and instituted the term "People with AIDS" (PWA) in lieu of "victim." He helped found the PWA Coalition and became the founding editor of its *Newsline.* He edited two volumes under the title *Surviving and Thriving with AIDS:* volume one, *Hints for the Newly Diagnosed* (1987), and volume two, *Collected Wisdom* (1988). He wrote and co-wrote several articles, testified before Congress, and appeared on national and local talk and interview shows. He was well known for his disdain for several AIDS drugs, especially AZT, which he routinely referred to as toxic. He devoted a whole chapter to AZT in *Surviving AIDS* and summed up: "I consider AZT to be Drano in pill form—pure, lethal poison. Anyone who takes AZT without examining all the evidence is a fool."

In 1991, *U.S. News & World Report* featured 12 personal narratives on HIV/AIDS; Michael Callen's was one of them:

> I'm still alive thanks to luck, Classic Coke and the love of a good man [Richard Dworkin].... I want to devour every drop of life's preciousness. I'm determined to compress my life into a few years, and that impatience has made me take greater risks, say what's really on my mind, write more songs than ever. I'm happier now than I've ever been. I don't mean to reduce AIDS to an Est seminar and recommend everyone should get it, but when humans are faced with catastrophe, they can either give in or fight. I've chosen to maintain an exhausting schedule as a singer and activist. I challenge the image that all people with AIDS are incapacitated. For me, it's more like having the flu for the rest of my life.

Callen became a tireless proponent of safer sex and took that message wherever he could. Even his singing was political. The song "Living in War Time" is a sobering summation of the lack of government and national resolve to adequately confront the epidemic. Callen and the Flirtations had a cameo spot in the AIDS-themed film *Philadelphia* (1993), and Callen himself played Miss HIV in the musical comedy film about AIDS, *Zero Patience* (1993). According to Jim Merrett, writing in the *Advocate,* "Callen appears as a drag Miss HIV in a role that apparently appealed to him because he got to hold a note longer than Barbra Streisand." And hold that note he did.

Michael Callen's solo album *Purple Heart* came out in 1988. With the Flirtations, which also formed in 1988, he released two albums: *The Flirtations* (1990) and *Live, Out on the Road* (1992).

Again, from *Surviving AIDS:* "AIDS forced me to take responsibility for my own life—for the choices I had made and the choices I could still make. For better or worse, AIDS has made me the man I am today." Michael Callen died 27 December 1993. He was 38.

References:

Berkowitz, Richard, and Michael Callen. *How to Have Sex in an Epidemic: One Approach.* New York: News from the Front Publications, 1983.

Callen, Michael. *Purple Heart.* New York: Significant Other Records, 1988.
———. *Surviving AIDS.* New York: Harper Perennial, 1990.
———, ed. *Surviving and Thriving with AIDS: Hints for the Newly Diagnosed.* New York: People With AIDS Coalition, 1987.
———, ed. *Surviving and Thriving with AIDS: Collected Wisdom.* New York: People With AIDS Coalition, 1988.
Demme, Jonathan, dir. *Philadelphia.* TriStar Pictures, 1993.
Dunlap, David W. "Michael Callen, Singer and Expert on Coping with AIDS, Dies At 38," in *New York Times,* 29 December 1993: D19.
Flirtations. *The Flirtations.* New York: Significant Other Records, 1990.
Flirtations. *Live, Out On the Road.* N.p.: Flirt Records, 1992.
Folkart, Burt A. "Composer Callen Loses 12-Year Fight with AIDS," in *Los Angeles Times,* 29 December 1993: B1, B4.
Gottlieb, Michael et al. "Speaking of the Plague...," in *U.S. News & World Report* (Washington, D.C.), 17 June 1991: 23-4.
Greyson, John, dir. *Zero Patience.* Zero Patience Productions Ltd., 1993.
Merrett, Jim. "Take My HIV, Please," in *Advocate,* 22 March 1994: 72-73.

—Lee Arnold

Margarethe Cammermeyer

1942-

American nurse and political activist

In 1989, after a brilliant military career, Margarethe (Grethe) Cammermeyer distinguished herself further when she became the nation's highest-ranking officer to challenge the United States' longstanding policy prohibiting gays and lesbians from serving in the armed forces. In the years since, Cammermeyer has become an ardent though somewhat reluctant activist. Her life and legal battles are documented in her 1994 autobiography *Serving in Silence,* which served as the basis for an acclaimed film produced by Barbra Streisand and starring Glen Close as Cammermeyer.

Examples of Courage

Cammermeyer was born 24 March 1942 in Oslo, which was at that time occupied by Nazi forces. Her father was a Norwegian doctor who had grown up in Africa, where his father operated a clinic, and her mother was a nurse and the daughter of a prominent psychiatrist. The example of patriotic courage and opposition to tyranny came early in Cammermeyer's life: both her parents actively aided the Norwegian underground. They frequently sheltered members of the resistance movement in their apartment, which was across the street from Nazi headquarters, and in Cammermeyer's autobiography she recounts an incident in which her mother used her baby carriage to transport weapons to resistance fighters.

After the war, Cammermeyer's father's career as a neuropathology researcher required that he move frequently, and his family occupied a series of residences as Cammermeyer was growing up. In 1951, believing that the most challenging opportunities were to be found in the United States, he moved his family there. Cammermeyer was nine years old at the time, and she later noted that the transition was a difficult one. Throughout her adolescence, she was embarrassed by her foreignness and felt, for the most part, alienated from her classmates.

Cammermeyer was nevertheless an excellent student, interested in particular in science and math, and at the age of 15 was invited to join a semiprofessional baseball team. Throughout her childhood and adolescence, she planned to become a physician, like her father. However, after a disastrous first semester at the University of Maryland, her self-confidence was shaken, and she transferred to the nursing program. She subsequently made up for her earlier poor performance, excelling at her studies, performing volunteer work in her free time, and working to pay her own expenses.

During her sophomore year, Cammermeyer discovered that if she agreed to join the army upon graduation, her remaining college tuition would be paid. Remembering the heroism of the American military during World War II, she also viewed serving as a nurse in the army as a way of augmenting what she viewed as the inferior status of her profession. In order to compensate for her failure to become a doctor, she hoped to become Chief Nurse of the Army Nurse Corps. Cammermeyer joined the army in July of 1961, before beginning her junior year at the university. After completing her degree, she was assigned to active duty at Fort Sam Houston in Texas, where she completed basic training and further instruction in practical nursing techniques.

Distinguished Service

After serving at Fort Houston and later Fort Benning, Cammermeyer applied for and was granted assignment to Germany, where she worked in a variety of nursing positions for the next two years. It was also in Germany that she met and married a young military officer named Harvey Hawken, despite some misgivings on her part about their compatibility. The couple subsequently served together in Vietnam in 1967 and 1968, with Cammermeyer receiving the Bronze Star for her excellent performance at the 24th Evacuation Hospital in Long Binh.

Near the end of her assignment in Vietnam, Cammermeyer became pregnant with her first child, and she was forced by regulations to resign from the army one month before her son was born. Her husband also left the service, and the couple settled near Hawken's hometown of Seattle, where they had purchased land a few years before. For the next several years, they worked toward a goal of self-sufficiency, building their own home, growing their own food, and raising a family which eventually included three more sons.

Shortly after the birth of her first child, Cammermeyer returned to nursing on a part-time basis. Then, in 1972, when the law prohibiting mothers with dependent children from serving in the military was repealed, she joined the Army Reserves and was assigned to be the nursing supervisor at the reserve hospital at Fort Lawton, Washington. She later wrote in her autobiography: "For the first time since my marriage, I felt that my dream to become a national chief nurse might one day be realized." Cammermeyer later accepted the post of Chief Nurse of the Washington State National Guard, and in 1987 she was promoted to the rank of colonel.

A Growing Awareness

Cammermeyer recounts in her autobiography that while she felt different from her peers at an early age, the idea that she might be

Margarethe Cammermeyer. ***Photograph by Lee T. Anderson.***

homosexual did not occur to her until many years later. Nevertheless, she believes her feelings manifested themselves in a sense of alienation from her husband from the very beginning of their marriage. In addition, Hawken held traditional views of the role of women, resenting greatly Cammermeyer's professional ambitions, and, after several years of marital strife, the couple divorced in 1980. During the 1980s Cammermeyer devoted herself to her nursing career, moving in 1981 to San Francisco to work in the neuro-oncology unit of the Veterans Administration Hospital. In 1986 she returned to Washington State to be closer to her sons, who lived with their father, and to work at the Veterans hospital in Tacoma.

It was in 1988, when she met and fell in love with an artist and teacher named Diane Divelbess, that Cammermeyer fully acknowledged her lesbianism. Shortly after their meeting, Cammermeyer and Divelbess developed a committed relationship, although Divelbess continued to maintain her own residence in California. The following year, still working toward her goal of becoming national Chief Nurse, Cammermeyer applied for the increased level of security clearance that would be necessary for her to attend the military's War College, and it was during the interview for this clearance that Cammermeyer revealed that she was a lesbian. She later noted that while she was aware of regulations against homosexuals in the military, she was not aware of the stringency of the rules, and she moreover believed that her rank and long record of achievements would make her an exception. "I didn't think that in America I would have to choose between being honest and serving my country," she wrote.

The Battle for Justice

The regulations concerning homosexuals in the military were, however, specific and not subject to appeal; Cammermeyer's admission was cause for immediate discharge, and the Army promptly instituted proceedings against her. Within a few months, she was informed that she would be the subject of an investigation, and in 1991, when the investigation was finally completed, she was offered two options: she could resign from the military or request a hearing. Cammermeyer chose the latter, and sought help from the most prominent attorneys in the fields of civil rights and military law. Nevertheless, her appeal at the hearing was unsuccessful, and on 11 June 1992, she was discharged from the National Guard.

Although the exposure of the most intimate aspects of her life to wide public and media scrutiny was distasteful to Cammermeyer, she had come to believe that the military's policy must be challenged and defeated. As a result, she refused to accept the army's decision, and promptly filed suit in civil court, seeking to challenge the constitutionality of the military's ban on homosexuals. At the same time, she began making public appearances to rally support for her cause and rapidly moved to the forefront of the movement for gay and lesbian rights. In 1994, a federal judge ruled against the army, but the government has appealed the case. It may take a supreme court decision to finally return Cammermeyer to her position.

Meanwhile, Cammermeyer has become a most effective advocate for the civil rights of homosexuals. With her unblemished military record and professional credentials, which include a Ph.D. in nursing, she commands great respect among military officials, legislators, and the public at large. In 1992 she was awarded the Feminist of the Year Award by the Feminist Majority Foundation, and that same year she was named Woman of the Year by the National Organization of Women. In 1994, she was nominated for Woman of the Year by the American Biographical Institute, and she has since received a variety of other awards from political and professional organizations as well as the gay and lesbian community.

Current Address: 1715 S. 234th St., Seattle, Washington 98198-7522; American Lake VA Medical Center, Department of Neuroscience, Tacoma, Washington 98493.

References:

Cammermeyer, Margarethe with Chris Fisher. *Serving in Silence.* New York: Viking, 1994.

—Joann Cerrito

Truman Capote

1924-1984

American writer

In 1966, Truman Capote was probably the most famous writer in America. His picture appeared on the cover of *Newsweek, Life,* and *Saturday Review;* his "nonfiction novel," *In Cold Blood,* topped the best-seller lists and received praise from both popular and academic critics; the "black and white ball" he gave in honor of publisher Katharine Graham (which was more a coronation party for Capote than a celebration of Graham) attracted a celebrity guest list unrivaled in the decade, perhaps in the century. The dimensions of Capote's overnight fame (for which he had been preparing and toward which he had been laboring since the mid-1930s) seemed likely to make him a major figure on the national literary scene for many years to come. But, when he died eighteen years later, Capote had produced no further major work and had instead become a figure of either fun or pity, depending on whether he was being viewed by his many enemies or his few remaining friends. Dorothy Parker's comment about the dead Scott Fitzgerald could as easily have been said of Capote: "The poor son of a bitch."

The person who would become Truman Capote was born 30 September 1924, in New Orleans, Louisiana, and named Truman Streckfus Persons. His father, Arch Persons, was a salesman with a smooth line and little substance; his mother, Lillie Mae Faulk Persons, had married Arch when she was seventeen and would divorce him by the time she was twenty-four. For a time Capote traveled around the South with his mother, who would go out for the evening, as Capote told his biographer, Gerald Clarke, locking him in her hotel room and ordering the staff to ignore him. Capote told Clarke that his mother's tyrannical actions left him with permanent free-floating anxiety: "She locked me in and I still can't get out." Capote was eventually stashed with relatives in Monroeville, Alabama, where he experienced the tender care of an aging cousin, Sook Faulk, memorialized in the story "A Christmas Memory"—probably the most famous and widely reprinted of Capote's stories. Another important connection Capote formed in Monroeville was with a next-door neighbor, Nell Harper Lee, who achieved her own literary eminence with *To Kill a Mockingbird;* the character Dill in that novel is based on the young Capote.

In 1932 Capote's mother, by now divorced and living in New York, married Joseph Garcia Capote, a well fixed Cuban-American businessman. Capote adopted his new wife's only child in 1935 and renamed him Truman Garcia Capote. The child then spent the rest of his childhood and adolescence in the Northeast, in New York City and in Greenwich, Connecticut, returning only occasionally to the rural South, where he probably had been happier. Troubles multiplied for Capote in his adolescent years, for it was soon clear that he was not the "manly" boy his mother expected him to be. Indeed, as Capote told Gerald Clarke, his homosexual orientation was apparent early on: "I always had a marked homosexual preference." Capote's mother tried various methods to force him toward at least the pretense of heterosexuality, including sending him to a military school, where he was acutely miserable. But, her endeavors were to no avail. By the time he was in high school Capote was as overtly out as it was possible to be in those times, and he never afterward made any pretenses about his sexual orientation. Although he had a famous series of friendships with beautiful women—Marilyn Monroe, Jacqueline Kennedy, Lee Radziwill, Babe Paley—his romantic life was altogether homosexual.

Childhood Practice, Early Success

Capote told various interviewers several stories about how old he was when he began working diligently toward being a writer. It is reasonable to suppose that he was writing fairly seriously by age twelve; the stories and poems printed in Greenwich school publications show that he was doing derivative but skilled work at fifteen. When his parents moved back to New York, Capote attended and graduated from the Franklin School, although in later years he liked to say that he had quit high school without a diploma. His first national publication came when he was only nineteen, in *Decade of Short Stories.* At about the same time, Capote became an office boy at the *New Yorker.* He tried to sell his stories to that magazine without success, but in 1945 he received considerable attention when *Mademoiselle* printed "Miriam"—a story of loss, isolation, and a need so powerful it leads toward madness. These were themes which would occupy Capote's attention for many years.

Buoyed by acceptances from important magazines, Capote left the *New Yorker* and began to write full-time. Between the real successes he experienced as a writer and the publicity about himself that he proved skillful in generating, Capote became one of the best-known of the younger generation of writers, without having published a novel. That lack was remedied in 1948 with the printing of *Other Voices, Other Rooms,* a book which soon became a *cause celebre,* in part because the central character's search for a father ends with his acceptance of and salvation through a homosexual relationship and in part because the dust jacket photo of Capote showed him reclining on a settee and looking (or so some thought) like a degenerate child. The review of the book in *Time* said that its theme was "calculated to make the flesh crawl," and *Newsweek* called the book "a deep, murky well of Freudian symbols." Other critics praised the book, especially the virtuoso quality of its prose style. Academics like Carvel Collins writing in *American Scholar,* and Frank Baldanza in *Georgia Review,* took the book quite seriously, with the former finding the myths of the quest for the Holy Grail worked into its structure, and the latter identifying Platonism in the novel. In later life Capote liked to deride academic critics, but he was intensely sensitive to their opinions and to his standing with intellectuals. A love affair with Newton Arvin, the noted scholar and university teacher, helped Capote overcome his lack of formal education. The complex prose style of *Other Voices, Other Rooms* demonstrated that Capote had learned the lessons of Modernism well.

As the critics debated the merits of Capote's first book, the young author went into exile. Capote spent most of the years between 1949 and 1958 in Europe, chiefly in Sicily. With him during those years was the one enduring love of his life, Jack Dunphy, a former Broadway dancer and an aspiring novelist. Despite dramatic differences in temperament (Capote was endlessly gregarious, an excellent listener, and a raconteur; Dunphy was withdrawn, anti-social, and dour) the two remained a couple for more than thirty years. Their homes became stopping places for a variety of international celebrities. Guest lists included Tennessee Williams, W. H. Auden, Cecil Beaton, Noel Coward, and Peggy Guggenheim.

Although Capote stayed busy as a host, he was not deflected from his writing. A collection of stories, *A Tree of Night,* appeared in 1949, and a second novel, *The Grass Harp,* was published in 1951. Capote also began what would be a year-long association with the film industry, writing dialogue for the David Selznick-produced film *Indiscretion of an American Wife* and then screenplays for *Beat the Devil* and *The Innocents* (based on the Henry James novella *The Turn of the Screw*). Capote also branched out into the playwright's trade and wrote a Broadway version of *The Grass Harp,* which received some good notices but was not a popular success. A later musical comedy, *House of Flowers,* based on a Capote short story, ran for 155 performances in 1955. Unfortunately, plagued by artistic conflicts of various sorts, the play never achieved the success many of its admirers thought it deserved.

Journeys to the Edge: Russia and Western Kansas

Capote stayed on the move for most of the rest of the 1950s, traveling to the Far East, where a late-night interview with Marlon Brando turned into an extended profile for the *New Yorker,* "The Duke in His Domain," regarded by many as the most revealing study ever done of Brando's character. Probably more important was when Capote arranged to accompany the *Porgy and Bess* touring company on a landmark visit to the Soviet Union. His report of the rather bizarre goings-on was published first in the *New Yorker* and then as a book, *The Muses Are Heard.* Although the book achieved less acclaim than did Capote's next publication, *Breakfast at Tiffany's,* it pointed the direction Capote's career was about to take—almost exclusively into nonfiction.

On Monday, 15 November 1959, Capote read a *New York Times* story about the murder of a wealthy Kansas farmer, his wife, and their two children. Within days Capote was on his way to the high plains of western Kansas to begin what would be a nearly six-year-struggle with the story of those murders and the murderers. *In Cold Blood,* the nonfiction novel which emerged from those years, became the most talked-about book of its time. Using all the skills he had accumulated in a quarter of a century of writing, Capote developed a portrait of the Clutter family, the victims, as the quintessential American family: successful, loving, morally rigid; then balanced against that picture the images of Dick Hickock and Perry Smith, the killers: damaged, rootless, amoral. The book's real hero, Kansas Bureau of Investigation special agent Alvin Dewey, in heroic fashion, pursues the killers, brings them to justice, and watches them hang.

In Cold Blood offers close-up portraiture of fascinating characters (especially Perry Smith, with whom Capote developed an intense rapport, finding in the killer's tortured childhood echoes of his own life), the excitement of a detective story as the killers are tracked down, the slow but inexorable grinding of the machinery of justice, and at least something of a meaning in what might otherwise seem to be merely random violence. Some critics loved it: George Garrett, writing in the *Hollins Critic,* called it "a frank bid for greatness"; Rebecca West, in *Harper's,* asserted that "nothing but blessing can flow from Mr. Capote's grave and reverend book." Dissenting critics, though a numerical minority, attacked *In Cold Blood* savagely. In the *Nation,* Sol Yurick described Capote's thinking in the book as "cheap, shallow, sentimental"; Kenneth Tynan attacked Capote so bitterly that Capote replied angrily and in print. Whether good or bad, the attention the book received helped it climb the best-seller lists. Capote made huge amounts of money and made, as well, the transition from minor writer admired for his sensuous prose to major literary figure. In 1965, Capote was a highly specialized taste. By the end of 1966, anybody who did not know about Truman Capote obviously had not been paying attention.

The Long Slide Down Begins

Capote was physically and emotionally drained after his *annus mirabilis* in 1966, and did not move immediately to consolidate his gains. Having written a long work about a multiple murder and the execution of the killers, Capote came to be regarded as an expert on crime and punishment; he was not shy about making known his views on these subjects. He became something of a regular on the talk shows. His wit, his curious, childlike voice, and his willingness to make outrageous statements and take extreme positions made him a consistently memorable guest. When he talked about his work, the one constant was reference to *Answered Prayers,* a book which he claimed he had been working on since the 1950s and which would assure him a place among the literary immortals. Capote had, in fact, been working very diligently since the 1950s to insinuate himself among the rich and famous, to make himself their confidante, and thus to gather material for a book that he meant to rival Proust's *Remembrance of Things Past.* The book was almost ready to be published, Capote kept claiming as the 1960s ended and the 1970s advanced, but somehow publication was continually postponed.

Truman Capote

Instead of gaining greater fame as a writer, Capote began to earn notice as a substance abuser and for a series of physical ailments and injuries that seemed nearly self-inflicted. In 1975, Capote inflicted on himself a psychological wound as destructive as any he had suffered since his mother's nightly abandonments when he agreed to *Esquire*'s publication of pieces of *Answered Prayers.* The first, "Mojave," appeared in June and stirred very little interest. The second, "La Cote Basque, 1965," was published in November and caused a major furor in the society into which Capote had wormed his way. The story named names, embarrassed a number of powerful people, possibly caused a suicide, and made Capote unwelcome in most of the places where he had been happiest. "I must just as well have killed the Lindbergh baby," Capote told Anne Taylor Fleming. Although Capote said he was unaffected by the rejection he experienced, in truth he was deeply wounded and rendered vulnerable to further injury.

The disasters continued to pile up, both personally and professionally. Capote became involved in a love affair with a married man, a relationship that would prove both financially draining and physically abusive. He had a near-fatal automobile accident. His drinking and drug taking increased. Not even the publication, in 1980, of *Music for Chameleons* could slow significantly the downward spiral of Capote's career. The book received generally polite reviews and one part of it, "Handcarved Coffins," which was alleged to be another nonfiction account of a series of murders, was sold to the movies for a reported $300,000. But the book was not the tell-all *Answered Prayers* for which those interested in Capote's work had been waiting.

Indeed, the reading public had to wait until after Capote's death to read *Answered Prayers.* In August 1984, Capote retreated to the home of his old friend Joanne Carson (one of Johnny's several ex-wives), and there, on the 25th of the month, a little more than a month before his sixtieth birthday, he died. An autopsy revealed liver disease, complicated by emphysema and phlebitis, as the cause of death. When *Answered Prayers* was published in 1987, it set off no shock waves and required no reassessment of the whole body of Capote's work, for it consisted solely of stories previously published in *Esquire,* with only minor editorial changes. If Capote had written more of *Answered Prayers* (as he told everyone he had), he had apparently destroyed the manuscripts, so that what was published during his lifetime would remain what he would be judged by. It is an imposing body of work, capped by the now-classic *In Cold Blood.* Few of Capote's contemporaries wrote with more intensity or stylistic brilliance, and none could surpass his genius for attracting attention. Writing about himself in a self-interview in 1980, Capote said: "I'm an alcoholic. I'm a drug addict. I'm homosexual. I'm a genius." It was an accurate summary of Capote's life.

References:

Baldanza, Frank. "Plato in Dixie," in *Georgia Review* (Athens, Georgia), vol. 12, 1958: 151-167.

Capote, Truman. *Music for Chameleons.* New York: Random House, 1980.

Clarke, Gerald. *Truman Capote: A Biography.* New York: Simon and Schuster, 1988.

Collins, Carvel. "Other Voices," in *American Scholar* (Washington, D.C.), vol. 25, 1955-56: 108-116.

Fleming, Anne Taylor. "The Private World of Truman Capote," in *New York Times Magazine,* 9 July 1978: 22-25; 16 July 1978: 12-13, 15, 44.

Garrett, George. "Crime and Punishment in Kansas: Truman Capote's *In Cold Blood,"* in *Hollins Critic* (Hollins-College, Virginia), vol. 3, 1966: 1-12.

"Other Books: 'Other Voices, Other Rooms,'" in *Newsweek* (New York), 26 January 1948: 91.

"Spare the Laurels," in *Time* (New York), 26 January 1948: 102.

West, Rebecca. "A Grave and Reverend Book," in *Harper's* (New York), February 1966: 108, 110, 112-114.

Yurick, Sol. "Sob-Sister Gothic," in *Nation* (New York), 7 February 1966: 158-160.

—Craig M. Goad

Caravaggio

c.1571-1610

Italian painter

Few artists have exercised such powerful influence as the short-lived and impassioned Caravaggio, and few revolutions in art have been quite so easy to document. Reacting against the extravagance of the Mannerist style which stressed intellectual preconception over visual perception, and the archeological romanticism of the Classicists, Caravaggio gave to Italian art the theatrical intensity of realism and the fresh technique of orchestrating the interplay between bright light and almost impenetrable shadow. His best paintings rely on the tension between commonplace detail and sublime lighting.

Caravaggio's instinctive naturalism fit comfortably with the mystical, evangelical and austerely penitential mood of the Counter-Reformation that he encountered at the Papal Court. Painting the saints and the persons who appeared with them in his compositions as ordinary people admirably fulfilled the official requirement to encourage worshippers to identify with the mysteries depicted on the canvas. This gave rise to masterpieces that portrayed the apostles as coarse peasants, the executioners of St. Peter as thugs, the feet of the faithful as dirt-spattered in the *Madonna of Loreto* and the corpse of Mary already swollen by decomposition in *Death of the Virgin.*

It must be borne in mind that dates and motives for many of the vicissitudes of Caravaggio's tempestuous life are speculatory and subject to further research in the vast repository of Italian archives. This is especially true for the daunting and arduous task of dating each of Caravaggio's paintings, for his six earliest biographers (see Hibbard under references) give no dates and are of limited value in determining the chronology of his paintings. An additional complication for non-Italians is the multiplicity of names by which his works are sometimes known in translation (e.g., *Lute Player* and *Lutenist*).

Early Life

Michelangelo Merisi (Merigi, Amerigi and many other variants of the surname appear in records) was born between September and December 1571 in either Milan or nearby Caravaggio just south of Bergamo in Lombardy, Italy. Although he was formerly believed to have been born in 1573, this new date of birth is calculated on the basis of a document of sale dated 25 September 1589 in which Caravaggio declared himself to be eighteen years old. His father, Fermo Merisi, was the majordomo and possible architect for the Marquis of Caravaggio, and his mother, Lucia Aratori, was his father's second wife, whom he married on 14 January 1571. When Fermo Merisi died intestate in 1578, Lucia assumed the guardianship of their four children, and the family of five left Milan and moved back to Caravaggio.

In 1584 the young painter was apprenticed to Milanese painter Simone Peterzano, a follower of Titian and friend of art theorist Giovanni Paolo Lomazzo (1538-1600). Although the apprenticeship was supposed to last four years, it is not known whether Caravaggio stayed with Peterzano the entire time or even extended his term. Giulio Mancini, an early biographer, states that due to his quick temper and high spirits, the four or five years of his apprenticeship in Milan were turbulent ones. In May 1592, after the death of his mother, Caravaggio claimed his inheritance, only a modest portion of the estate, mostly in cash, in contrast to his younger brother who came to possess the family homestead in Caravaggio. By the latter half of the same year, Caravaggio was living in Rome, where he had an uncle who was a priest.

Career in Rome

From about 1596 to 1600 Caravaggio worked under the patronage of Cardinal Francesco Maria del Monte (1549-1626), who at one time had in his possession ten paintings by Caravaggio. A connoisseur of music, alchemy, and young boys, Cardinal del Monte helped Caravaggio obtain his first public commission in 1597—to decorate a chapel in San Luigi dei Francesi, the French church in Rome, with three scenes from the life of St. Matthew that were to be among his most influential creations. In the same year occurs the first reference to the contemporary reputation of Caravaggio, when the Abbot of Pineroli bequeathed to his nephew in his will a painting of St. Francis "executed with great diligence by the famous painter Caravaggio."

In October 1600 his name made its first appearance elsewhere—in police records as a witness to a street brawl. In the following month he himself was accused of unprovoked assault.

Soon afterwards even his patron Cardinal del Monte was referring to Caravaggio as "strange" or "odd" (*stravagantissimo*, quoted in a letter of 24 August 1605 from Fabio Masetti to Count Giovanni Battista Laderchi) in a context that implied the artist was unreliable. According to court proceedings and newspaper accounts between October 1600 and September 1605, on eleven separate occasions Caravaggio was brought to trial on charges ranging from beating an acquaintance with a stick to throwing a plate of artichokes at a waiter whom he considered insolent.

In 1603 the painter Giovanni Baglione, an artistic rival and future biographer of Caravaggio, initiated a libel suit against Caravaggio and others for writing and distributing defamatory verses about him. It was during this lengthy trial (28 August 1603) that Mao Salini claimed that one of the persons who circulated the satirical verses, a young man named Giovan Battista, was Caravaggio's *bardassa*. This word, which is the ultimate source of the anthropological term *berdache* (catamite or kept boy), is our primary contemporary evidence for the homosexuality of Caravaggio.

In 1606 after a tennis game he killed an opponent named Ranuccio Tommasoni by knifing him in the groin, and although badly wounded himself, his friends spirited him away before the police arrived. Derek Jarman in his film *Caravaggio* (1985) used clues he gleaned from Caravaggio's paintings to piece together a theory that Ranuccio was killed not in a scuffle over a tennis match but in the heat of sexual jealousy. For Jarman, Ranuccio is the street fighter of whom Caravaggio becomes enamored, and Lena, Ranuccio's female lover, becomes involved with both men. Since Lena, who seems to have been a prostitute, is in fact referred to in contemporary testimony (by Mariano Pasqualone, 29 July 1605) as "Caravaggio's girl," there may be some grounds for the contention of many critics that Caravaggio was bisexual.

Earliest Homoerotic Works

At the beginning of his career Caravaggio produced a half dozen paintings of effeminate young men or groups of effeminate young men adorned with fruits, flowers, or musical instruments. These figures with their dark curly hair, alabaster skin, and rich thick lips speak so strongly to modern gay observers that even without the actual archival testimony that exists, Caravaggio is immediately recognized as a homosexual of pederastic tastes.

Predictably, many art historians have attributed these homosexual aspects of his early work to the influence of Cardinal del Monte. Yet even among the paintings not executed for del Monte the artist persisted in portraying figures (the boys in *Fortune Teller* and *Calling of St. Matthew* or the angel violinist in the *Rest on the Flight to Egypt* or the angel cradling the saint of Assisi in the *Stigmatization of St. Francis*) that while more masculine and muscular, still preserve some of the homosexual allure conveyed in his paintings made for Cardinal del Monte. In fact, one of his most sensuous *John the Baptist* paintings (Galleria Borghese, Rome) is now thought to be among the very last works that he painted—long after he left the influence of the Cardinal. Although the religious nature of his artistic commissions required him to depict women subjects as well, they are often, like the penitent Magdalene and the dead Virgin Mary, represented in comparatively unappetizing postures.

The first of the homoerotic paintings, the lost *Boy Peeling Fruit,* known from four copies, is considered the earliest of Caravaggio's paintings for which there is visual evidence. The mood is lyrical and the boy is delicate, but the boy does not yet solicit the observer since his eyes are fixed intently on his task of peeling. In contrast, the languorously gazing and garlanded young *Bacchus* (Uffizi, Florence), posing behind a tempting basket of fruit, dares to solicit the spectator's attention and even offers a glass of wine. His cloak has already fallen from one of his shoulders and with his right hand he clutches whatever part of the garment still covers him as if to free it from restraint.

In the third and fourth paintings, the *Concert* (Metropolitan Museum, New York) and the *Lute Player/Lutenist* (Hermitage, St. Petersburg), Caravaggio's youths frankly proffer music as prelude to love. Two of the four face the observer directly, and one of the two young musicians not facing forward seems to be painted from the same model who posed for *Boy Peeling Fruit.* The Hermitage lutenist is so sexually ambiguous that Caravaggio's early biographer Bellori genuinely mistook it for a girl. According to Baglione, Caravaggio considered it the most beautiful work that he ever produced.

It has been similarly argued that the *Fruit Vendor* (Borghese Gallery, Rome) is female. His tousled hair, impassioned gaze, and the smooth flesh of his bare rounded shoulder can scarcely be intended as attributes to help advertise the basket of fruit that he holds a little too tightly. Conversely, the fruit, which is frequently symbolic of sexual gluttony, seems instead to adorn the boy and to intimate the delicious pleasures that await the lucky taker of the boy. At least one critic (A. Czobor) has seen the *Fruit Vendor* as one of Caravaggio's many idealized youthful self-portraits.

The sixth of Caravaggio's homoerotic paintings, *Boy Bitten by a Lizard* (Longhi Collection, Florence), is the most complex and the most suggestive. At the very moment that a small lizard, concealed among the fruits on a table, bites the finger of the elaborately coiffed youth who is about to grasp a delicacy, the subject recoils with striking squeamishness and effeminacy. His helpless hand hangs limply, his grimace suggests a womanish whimper rather than a masculine oath, and he fixes his stunned gaze, not at his injured finger but at the observer, as if in accusation for causing the mishap by the rejection of his overture.

In our own times the sexuality of Caravaggio has fascinated writers who have chosen to recreate his life in fiction. Robert Payne's novel *Caravaggio* (1968) emphasizes the artist's homosexuality and the giddy succession of patrons, lovers, and intrigues that characterized the later years of his short life. In *The Dark Fire* (1977), however, art historian Linda Murray challenges the legend of Caravaggio's homosexuality and gives him a heterosexual relationship and two illegitimate children. Almost as a compromise, Michael Straight in his play, *Caravaggio* (1979), suggests that human relationships, homosexual as well as heterosexual, may not have played such an important role in the life of someone as intensely egocentric as Caravaggio.

Last Years in Exile

Forced to flee Rome in the wake of his murder of Ranuccio Tommasoni, Caravaggio sought refuge in Naples where he painted feverishly. The following year in pursuit of the Cross of Malta, which was characteristically awarded as a honor to persons of merit and stature, Caravaggio appeared on the island of Malta, where he produced two portraits of the French Grand Master of the Order, Alof de Wignacourt (1547-1622). When the Maltese apparently discovered the reasons for Caravaggio's flight from Rome, they imprisoned him in the impregnable Castel Sant'Angelo in Vittoriosa, but he made a daring escape and fled northward to Sicily, where he made a hasty landing at Syracuse. There he met an old friend from his Roman days, Mario Minniti, who helped convince the Senate of Syracuse to give Caravaggio the commission for his altarpiece commemorating the burial of Saint Lucy.

Never feeling safe from the vengeance of the knights of Malta, he went from Syracuse to Messina to Palermo, leaving masterpieces behind in each city. According to his early biographer Susinno, he was forced to leave Messina because he had wounded a schoolteacher who objected to the excessive interest which Caravaggio seemed to be taking in some of his boys.

By 1609 Caravaggio was back in Naples, where he suffered stab wounds so severe that news of his possible death arrived at Rome. During this time efforts were being made at the Papal Court to obtain a remission of the sentence of banishment from Rome that had been levied upon him, and the pardon seemed to be within reach.

Whether aware of the pardon or not, in July of 1610 he boarded a felucca for Porto Ercole, a Spanish enclave between Tuscany and the Papal States. Upon landing, he was arrested by mistake and by the time he was released, he could not find the felucca with his belongings. Thrashing about wildly under the merciless rays of the sun, he contracted a fever from which he died in late July. His Papal pardon had been granted, but by then it was useless.

Contributions as Artist

Even more than the technique of chiaroscuro (the effect created by the interplay of light and shadow in painting) which Caravaggio adopted as a religion and whose name came to typify the phenonemon as it spread throughout Europe, he cherished reality in painting. Because he wished to restore corporeal density to the unstable figures of Mannerism, he avoided models of formal aristocratic perfection, choosing instead for his subjects average people and ordinary things.

Another distinguishing characteristic of his mature religious art that first appeared in such of his early works as the *Boy Bitten by a Lizard* and *Lute Player,* was a diagonal shaft of light slanting across the back wall. This probably meant that there was in his studio a high window from which light came streaming in as he worked, and that he cultivated the resource as a means to indicate or "highlight" the important and/or divine elements of a composition.

In addition, Caravaggio is distinguished from his Mannerist and Renaissance predecessors because he executed most of the detail of his paintings without the help of assistants and painted directly on the canvas without first making tentative sketches. His oeuvre, produced within a span of twenty years, consists of some forty works and approximately twenty attributions or copies. But this number is continuously expanding because works previously thought of as copies are being certified as his own. Their recovery is due as much to modern methods of cleaning and restoration as to the rigorous scrutiny of dedicated art historians.

Within Italy Caravaggio's influence was primarily felt by his follower and imitator, the Mantuan Bartolommeo Manfredi (c. 1580-1620/1) and by members of the Neapolitan School such as Giovanni Battista Caracciolo (c. 1570-1637). Another Italian, Orazio Gentileschi (1563-1639), spread "Caravaggism" to France, Spain and England. Although he was popular during his own lifetime and for several decades thereafter, he faded into oblivion and it was not until about 1900 that interest in his work began to revive. This was due partly to a renewed appreciation of Baroque art, the style that followed Mannerism and lasted well in the eighteenth century, which employed illusionism, color, light, and movement to overwhelm the spectator, and partly to a new sympathy for the ideas that informed his art.

References:

Cinotti, Mia. *Immagine del Caravaggio.* This catalogue, prepared for what was assumed to be the quatercentenary of the artist's birth in 1973, was republished with additions in Mia Cinotti's *Novità sul Caravaggio.* Milan: Regione Lombardia, 1975.

Derek Jarman's Caravaggio: The Complete Film Script and Commentaries. London: Thames and Hudson, 1986.

Friedlander, Walter F. *Caravaggio Studies.* Princeton: Princeton University Press, 1955.

Gash, John. *Caravaggio.* London: Bloomsbury Books, 1988.

Gash, John. "Caravaggio" in *The Dictionary of Art,* ed. Jane Turner. New York: Grove's Dictionaries, 1996.

Hibbard, Howard. *Caravaggio.* New York: Harper & Row, 1983. An appendix includes primary excerpts from the six original sketches of Caravaggio's life in their original languages as well as in English translation, those by Giulio Mancini (written about 1620) in Italian, Carel Van Mander (1604) in Dutch, Giovanni Baglione (1642) written in Italian, Giovanni Pietro Bellori (1672) written in Italian, Joachim von Sandrart (1675) written in German, and Francesco Susinno (1724) written in Italian.

Hinks, Roger. *Michelangelo Merisi da Caravaggio: His Life, His Legend, His Works.* New York: Beechhurst Press, 1953.

Kitson, Michael. *The Complete Paintings of Caravaggio.* New York: Harry N. Abrams, 1967.

Mariani, Valerio. "Caravaggio" in *Encyclopedia of World Art.* New York: McGraw-Hill, 1960.

Moir, Alfred. *Caravaggio.* New York: Harry N. Abrams, 1989.

Moir, Alfred. *The Italian Followers of Caravaggio.* 2 volumes. Cambridge: Harvard University Press, 1967.

Murray, Linda. *The Dark Fire.* New York: Morrow, 1977.

Payne, Robert. *Caravaggio.* New York: Little, Brown, 1968.

Posner, Donald. "Caravaggio's Homo-erotic Early Works" in *Art Quarterly* (Metropolitan Museum of Art) 34 (1971): 301-324.
Straight, Michael Whitney. *Caravaggio: A Play in Two Acts.* London: Devon Press, 1979.

—Jack Shreve

Edward Carpenter

1844-1929

British writer

In late Victorian England, Edward Carpenter made himself a spokesperson for uncompromising, progressive politics in many spheres. A disciple of Walt Whitman, Carpenter set a courageous example of honesty and truth to one's own sexual nature during the Oscar Wilde scandal of the 1890s and the repression that it unleashed. Carpenter also firmly believed in the reconciliation of social classes and in socialism as he understood it. He took interest in the religions of India, which he perceived as fostering universal solidarity. The reputation engendered by his visionary approach had great appeal during the years of his maturity, only to decline later. In the England and America of his day, when the general public had access to only a few publications on sexual subjects, his daring yet accessible writings won him a large public. Carpenter also enjoyed considerable influence on the European continent, especially in Germany.

On the centenary of his birth, in 1944, even his admirer E. M. Forster conceded that he was "rather forgotten." Carpenter's reputation revived, however, after the Stonewall Rebellion of 1969, when the gay left hailed him as a forerunner.

A Varied Life

Edward Carpenter was born into upper middle-class comfort in the English seaside town of Brighton on 29 August 1844. The family fortunes derived from naval connections and civil service in India. The boy spent many long hours gazing at the sea, and the sense of wholeness endowed by this experience never left him. This effect is seen in his prose poem of 1883, "The Ocean of Sex." Carpenter's father was devoted to German idealist writers, such as Fichte and Hegel, and this interest probably lay at the heart of his son's later attraction to mysticism.

On trips to the continent the teenage Ted Carpenter learned French and German. He was exceptionally well prepared to enter Trinity Hall in Cambridge, where he was awarded a fellowship. This led to his appointment as a don, or instructor, which at that time required that he profess clerical orders in the Church of England. His early academic career was characterized by several major crushes on young men, but he remained sexually frustrated. It was clear to him that he had no physical attraction to women, though he later championed women's causes.

After a long mental struggle, in 1874 Carpenter abandoned his post at Cambridge and took an appointment as University Extension lecturer in the north of England. He was particularly taken by the possibilities of speaking to young workmen, perhaps with the hope of finding a companion among them. At this time, however, his sexual needs were mainly discharged through unsatisfactory encounters with prostitutes during his visits to Paris.

Through these many stages in his working and intellectual life, Carpenter was moving toward a reconciliation between his youthful idealism and his new belief in the importance of the body. This evolution prepared him to receive what was to become his most important intellectual experience. In 1874 he wrote a long, passionate letter to Walt Whitman, whose poems he had studied in an English edition edited by William Michael Rossetti. Three years later Carpenter visited the American sage in Camden, New Jersey. Carpenter thoroughly enjoyed America, rounding out his stay with a visit to Ralph Waldo Emerson in Concord and a view of Niagara Falls. He continued to correspond with Whitman until the poet's death in 1892.

Whitman's counsel, combined with his own inclinations, led Carpenter to experiment with living on a farm. He also began to have gratifying sexual relations with men he met in that setting. Around this same time, he first took interest in Eastern religions, prompted by a translation of the Bhagavad Gita that he received from a Sri Lankan friend. He published the first version of his Whitmanesque prose poem *Towards Democracy* anonymously in 1883. The comparison to Whitman was one he made himself, later remarking that his book was like a moon compared to the sun of Whitman's *Leaves of Grass.*

In that same year an inheritance enabled him to acquire a market farm, Millthorpe, near industrial Sheffield. Here, with the assistance of several working-class hands, he successfully practiced agriculture. In this hermitage he also received a stream of admirers. Among them were Goldsworthy Lowes Dickinson, a closeted Cambridge don who nonetheless exercised a beneficent influence over generations of homoerotic students, and Charles Robert Ashbee, who influenced the arts and crafts movement through his Guild and School of Handicraft.

Carpenter threw himself into the vortex of socialist politics, though he never adopted a doctrinaire theoretical approach. Much influenced by the cooperative anarchism advocated by Peter Kropotkin, Carpenter's political views were always strongly tinged with individualism. He held that the redemption of a deeply flawed society must come less from external reorganization—as advocated by socialism—than from individual self-realization, which would lead to the development of cosmic consciousness. Nonetheless, to help the causes with which he was in sympathy he wrote and composed the music for the hymn "England Arise! A Socialist Marching Song."

In 1889-90 he went to see for himself the birthplaces of the Eastern philosophy that attracted him. At the invitation of a friend he visited Sri Lanka and then traveled the length and breadth of India. He recorded the trip in his book *From Adam's Peak to Elephanta: Sketches in Ceylon and India* (1892).

During this same period he met the man who was to become his life partner. George Merrill, of working-class origins, was both muscular and feminine in his traits—a combination Carpenter liked very much. As their relationship deepened, Merrill came to share the Millthorpe establishment as a full partner. Like John Addington Symonds, Carpenter believed that such relationships could serve as a powerful solvent to break down class barriers, and thus open the way to a new era of human happiness, which would be cooperative rather than competitive. His return to the simple life—which included vegetarianism and casual dress, as well as a general anticipation of today's counter-culture styles—was part of his program of

Edward Carpenter

"exfoliation," a deliberate discarding of the husks of the old society in preparation for the dawning New Life.

In 1892 Henry Havelock Ellis, acting in concert with J. A. Symonds, asked Carpenter to contribute an account of his sex life for a study on homosexuality. Eventually, this account, an important source for Carpenter's biography, was published in Ellis' book *Sexual Inversion* (1897).

Although his influence as a progressive thinker waned some with the turn of the century, Carpenter's political views remained just as adamant. Unlike the majority of the British public, Carpenter spoke out against World War I. He condemned the carnage, which he viewed as the natural consequence of the destructive traits of civilization that he had castigated.

George Merrill's death in 1928 dealt Carpenter a blow that he could not surmount. He died the following year at Guildford on 29 June.

Carpenter's Views

All of Carpenter's stances on particular issues fit into the broader context of his views about society and history. Carpenter's ideas about social transformation derive from ancient millenarian traditions that regard the present era as bad, while looking forward to its imminent transformation. In this context Carpenter habitually uses the term "civilization" in a pejorative sense. Nurtured by Indian sources, Carpenter's mysticism also drew on contemporary psychology with its pre-Freudian concept of a "subliminal self." He advocated cosmic consciousness as a state "in which the contrast between the *ego* and the external world, and the distinction between subject and object, fall away." He was also interested in hypnotism and speculations about the fourth dimension. These ideas struck a responsive chord in artists like Max Weber and Marsden Hartley, who attempted to give them visual realization, and the writer D. H. Lawrence.

Despite early discouragements from publishers and a malicious campaign of defamation waged against him, Carpenter produced books discussing homosexuality openly. While *Towards Democracy* discusses many matters, it had room for a commendation of passionate love for one's own sex. Carpenter even describes approvingly a visit to the room of a male prostitute. In 1895 he produced the pamphlet *Homogenic Love, and Its Place in a Free Society* for private circulation. Eventually, as his books on other subjects gained support he was able to publish openly and at length on same-sex love.

Carpenter rejected the term "homosexuality," because it combined Latin and Greek roots, preferring "homogenic," which is entirely Greek. He sometimes used the terms "Uranian" and "Urning," invented by the German scholar Karl Heinrich Ulrichs (1825-1895), a pioneer in studies of homosexuality. As Carpenter freely acknowledged, many of his ideas on the subject were derived from Central European researchers, who had been making important contributions since the 1860s. Following these thinkers, Carpenter advocated the idea of sexual intermediacy, holding that there were no sharp contrasts between the poles of male and female, but rather a gradual transition. He insisted that one could not say in any general way that these intermediate types were good or bad, high or low, worthy or unworthy. Rather some perhaps exhibit "through their double temperament a rare and beautiful flower of humanity."

Carpenter's society, however, did not in general share his views. On the one hand, most "homogenic people" felt it prudent to mask their feelings, which facilitated the mistaken impression that same-sex attraction was rare. On the other hand, the life stories that did become known stemmed from interviews by psychiatrists, who for obvious reasons tended to see disturbed individuals. Carpenter spoke against this misperception, though he acknowledged that the stress of their lives might induce nervous excitability in individuals of this kind.

To counteract further the skewed image of homosexuals in his time Carpenter recalled the names of distinguished people who had been attracted to their own sex from the Greeks onwards. He believed that society stood on the brink of a major change in cultural evolution, which would result in greater esteem for homogenic love. He believed that his own pattern of attraction to workingmen was part of the emergence of a new sense of universal social solidarity. "Eros is a great leveler," he wrote. "Perhaps the true Democracy rests, more firmly than anywhere else, on a sentiment which easily passes the bounds of class and caste, and unites in the closest affection the most estranged ranks of society."

Carpenter's *Ioläus, an Anthology of Friendship* (1902) was modeled on a similar German work prepared by Elisar von Kupffer. This collection included work from ancient Greece and Rome, the Middle Ages, and leading figures of modern times. Appropriately, the anthology concludes with selections from Whitman's *Leaves of Grass. Ioläus* enjoyed considerable popularity among those in the know. This work, together with Carpenter's own copious writings, helped to reinforce a sense of positive self-identity in a period of profound antihomosexual backlash in English-speaking countries in the wake of the Oscar Wilde trials.

Probably Carpenter's most important scholarly contribution is his cross-cultural monograph *Intermediate Types among Primitive*

Folk: A Study in Social Evolution. The final version, which appeared in book form in 1919, collected separate studies that had begun to appear in 1911. In this work Carpenter distinguished two different types of homosexual behavior. First there was the gentle side of same-sex love, as seen today in those attracted to the arts as well as those active in the helping professions, such as nursing. This mode had roots in the historic types of the berdache and the shaman. In addition, Carpenter recognized a more virile type, stressed in the military cultures of ancient Greece and later times, as well as in the Samurai of traditional Japan.

Sadly, the significance of Carpenter's intellectual and political work has met with neglect for some time. With the exception of recognition from democratic socialists and some gay intellectuals, his legacy has faded. Fortunately, however, most of his books are once again available, and readers can gauge his contribution for themselves. Carpenter was the hero of a play widely performed in England, Noel Greig's "The Dear Love of Comrades" (1981). Thanks to the writings of such gay scholars as John Lauritsen and David Thorstad his contribution to homosexual emancipation is secure.

References:

A Bibliography of Edward Carpenter. Sheffield: Sheffield Central Libraries, 1949.

Delavenay, Emile. *D. H. Lawrence and Edward Carpenter: A Study in Edwardian Transition.* New York: Taplinger, 1971.

Greig, Noël. "Introduction," in *Selected Writings,* by Edward Carpenter. London: Gay Men's Press, 1984: 9-77.

Henderson, Linda Dalrymple. "Mysticism as the 'Tie That Binds': The Case of Edward Carpenter and Modernism," in *Art Journal* (New York), 1987: 29-37.

Lauritsen, John, and David Thorstad. *The Homosexual Emancipation Movement in Germany.* New York: Times Change Press, 1975.

Rowbotham, Sheila, and Jeffrey Weeks. *Socialism and the New Life: The Personal and Sexual Politics of Edward Carpenter and Havelock Ellis.* London: Pluto Press, 1977.

Tsuzuki, Chushichi. *Edward Carpenter, 1844-1929: Prophet of Human Fellowship.* Cambridge: Cambridge University Press, 1980.

—Wayne R. Dynes

Willa Cather

1873-1947

American writer

Willa Cather was famous in her lifetime as the author of *My Antonia* and *O Pioneers!*, novels that celebrate and invoke the lives of the pioneer settlers of the Nebraska prairie. A prolific, successful journalist and drama critic for 20 years before writing her first novel, she also wrote movingly in *The Song of the Lark* of the challenges and choices facing the woman artist. Cather guarded her privacy with great care, burning all correspondence she could find, and stipulating in her will that any letters which escaped destruction could never be quoted in print. The direct evidence for her affective practices is thus lacking, but Cather has nonetheless been persuasively claimed as a lesbian, on the evidence of both life and work, by many recent interpreters.

Willa Cather was born the eldest of seven children in Back Creek, Virginia, on 7 December 1873. In 1883, her father followed other members of his family to Nebraska. After 18 months of farming on the prairie, the Cathers moved to the small town of Red Cloud, then a busy stop on several intersecting railroads, where Charles Cather worked in real estate and insurance. The young Willa felt the transition from the lush, cultivated farmland of Virginia to the bleak, open prairie as an assault, describing it as "the end of everything ... a kind of erasure of personality," according to a 1913 newspaper interview. Yet Cather soon found compensations in her new environment, immersing herself in the stories told by the immigrant women of the plains, a community that included recent arrivals from Sweden, Germany, Denmark and Bohemia; these kitchen tales provided the seed material for many of her later works.

The Cross-Dressing Vivisectionist

Cather was a precocious, flamboyant child. Her first ambition was to be a surgeon, a goal she pursued both by experimenting in vivisection, and by accompanying the local doctors on their rounds, even adopting the name of the doctor who delivered her, Love, as a middle name. Her manipulations of self soon became more pronounced, and more clearly cross-gendered; either in 1886 or in 1888 (accounts vary), Cather took herself to the barber's for a crew cut, and began referring to herself as "William Cather, Jr." and "William Cather, M.D." She now appropriated "Sibert" as a middle name, claiming to have been named for an uncle, William Sibert Boak, who died as a Confederate soldier. She cross-dressed for several years, acquiring notoriety for her "masculine" garments, voice, and hair style both in Red Cloud and at the University of Nebraska at Lincoln, where she began five years of study in 1890.

Cather's impact on the university was intellectual as well as sartorial; a professor was so impressed by her essay on Carlyle that he sent it secretly to the *Nebraska State Journal*, where it was published in 1891 to general acclaim. Cather was soon producing reviews, columns, and drama criticism regularly. From 1893 on, she supported herself through her journalism, working first for the *Journal* and then for the *Courier*, acquiring a reputation as an outstanding—and for visiting stage companies, terrifying—drama critic.

In 1896, Cather left Lincoln for Pittsburgh, recruited to become the editor of a new women's magazine, *Home Monthly*, which it was hoped would grow to rival the immensely popular *Ladies Home Journal*. Under a series of pseudonyms, Cather wrote vast chunks of each issue. Most of her production was resolutely genteel, but it does include a mildly subversive short story, "Tommy, the Unsentimental," which features a rather butch, capable heroine who rescues her ineffective fiance from ruin and then contrives to ensure that he marries someone else of more suitable feminine type, leaving Tommy unencumbered.

Fame as the Voice of the Prairie

After a few years as a high school teacher, Cather was recruited by the magazine tycoon S.S. McClure to edit *McClure's*. She moved

Willa Cather

to New York City, where she lived for the remainder of her life, apart from excursions to Europe, visits to her family out West, and summer retreats to New Hampshire and an island off New Brunswick. While working full-time in journalism, Cather had published a few stories in national magazines, a volume of poetry, *April Twilights* (1903), and a collection of stories, *The Troll Garden* (1905). It was only after meeting the established writer Sarah Orne Jewett in 1908, who acted as a mentor, encouraging Cather to devote herself to her writing, that Cather abandoned journalism for fiction, producing *Alexander's Bridge* in 1912. This novel, still written in the Jamesian manner of many of Cather's early stories, was politely received. With *O, Pioneers!* (1913), however, Cather achieved critical success; her depiction of the rugged inhabitants of the prairie was hailed as a authentic new American voice. Although Cather wrote many novels set elsewhere, it is as author of *My Antonia* (1918) and as nostalgic invoker of a lost realm of purity and struggle, that Cather is most remembered. Her many subsequent novels brought her fortune and status. She won the Pulitzer Prize for *One of Ours* (1922), but this same novel marked the beginning of Cather's bad critical press. H. L. Mencken, after applauding dismissed this World War I story as romantic slush, a dismal failure to reflect the mood of the times caught so memorably by John Dos Passos, or by e.e. cummings' *The Enormous Room*, while Hemingway damningly described her battle scenes as "catherized." Cather went on to produce, among others, *A Lost Lady*, (1923), *The Professor's House* (1925), and *Death Comes for the Archbishop* (1927), but her critical reputation, although not her popular appeal, never recovered its original glory.

While James Woodress claimed in his 1970 biography that Cather was "married to her art," more recent interpreters have emphasized the passionate nature of Cather's attachment to the women in her life. A few letters survive which strongly suggest that as an undergraduate Cather was in love with a fellow student, Louise Pound (who went on to become a distinguished academic). In Pittsburgh, Cather met Isabelle McClung, who moved her into her parents' house despite some familial opposition; Cather lived there for five years, and whatever their sexual practices (there are contradictory reports as to whether or not they shared a room), McClung would seem to have been the emotional center of Cather's life. Cather often returned to the house in Pittsburgh to write, and the two women vacationed together for years. When McClung married unexpectedly, in 1916, Cather admitted in letters that this was a devastating loss. In New York, meanwhile, Cather moved into a Washington Square apartment with Edith Lewis, whom she met at *McClure's*. They lived together until Cather's death, and were reunited thereafter; Lewis is buried beside her near their summer retreat in New Hampshire. Lewis seems to have fulfilled the literary wife's traditional role, silently and self-effacingly enabling Cather's work.

Politically reactionary, Cather had no truck with feminism, but she nonetheless offers a valuable model to women writers, having successfully inserted herself into a male pastoral tradition; she claimed ground first staked out by Walt Whitman, producing an elegiac account of pioneer experience that is sensitive to the lives of ordinary people, both female and male. Although she shunned publicity and would hate to be labelled a lesbian, Cather's youthful cross-dressing and her appropriation of masculine privilege and desire have provided subsequent generations with ways of imagining a lesbian past.

References:

Bennett, Mildred. *The World of Willa Cather*. Lincoln: University of Nebraska Press, 1951.

Bohlke, L. Brent. *Willa Cather in Person: Interviews, Speeches, and Letters*. Lincoln: University of Nebraska Press, 1986.

Brown, E.K. *Willa Cather: A Critical Biography*. New York: Knopf, 1953.

Fryer, Judith. *Felicitous Space: The Imaginative Structures of Edith Wharton and Willa Cather*. Chapel Hill: University of North Carolina Press, 1986.

Lee, Hermione. *Willa Cather: Double Lives*. New York: Pantheon Books, 1989.

Lewis, Edith. *Willa Cather Living*. New York: Knopf, 1953.

O'Brien, Sharon. *Willa Cather: The Emerging Voice*. New York: Oxford University Press, 1987.

Sergeant, Elizabeth Shepley. *Willa Cather—A Memoir*. Philadelphia: J.B. Lippincott, 1953.

Woodress, James. *Willa Cather: Her Life and Art*. New York: Pegasus, 1970.

——. *Willa Cather: A Literary Life*. Lincoln: University of Nebraska Press, 1987.

—Anna Wilson

June Chan

1956-

Asian-American neurobiologist and activist

When queried about her political activism in the Asian lesbian community, June Chan expressed her dismay that she is singled out as one activist when there are dozens of other Asian American lesbians doing similar work. Chan is a founding member of the Asian Lesbians of the East Coast (ALOEC)—co-founded with Katherine Hall in 1983—one of the first organizations of its kind to advocate on the behalf of Asian American lesbians in the United States.

June Chan was born in Manhattan on 6 June 1956, the second of six children. Her father, Frank Chan, owned a print shop in Chinatown that produced Chinese and English newspapers, where all of the children worked while growing up. Her mother, Tim How Chan, co-owned a small store where she worked six days a week. As a girl, Tim How Chan had survived years of starvation and war as a refugee of the Japanese invasion of China. June Chan attended New York public schools, and in 1973 she enrolled in the City College of New York, majoring in biology. Graduating with a bachelor's degree in science in 1977, Chan continued her graduate studies in biology at the State University of New York at Buffalo, and received her MA in 1980. Today, Chan conducts research in neurobiology at Cornell Medical College in Manhattan.

Chan's interest in political activism began when she was a child, after she witnessed a demonstration held in Chinatown in which Asian Americans protested racist attitudes of tourists who visited her neighborhood. Residents objected to the degrading imposition of having their photographs taken with tourists. Years later, as an undergraduate at City College, Chan participated in a large student demonstration that protested the introduction of tuition at the historically free City University of New York. Despite their dramatic takeover of the administration building, tuition was imposed. Nonetheless, Chan felt empowered by her first real contact with the power of political organizing.

June Chan

Asian Lesbians Seek Identity and Visibility

As she pursued her studies, Chan remained politically active in the women's movement of the early 1970s, working primarily for the Committee for Abortion Rights and Against Sterilization Abuse. Despite her commitment to women's activism, Chan understood there were few ethnic lesbians involved with the groups she supported. She began searching for other Asian lesbians who were likewise interested in forming a group of their own. In 1983, Chan met Katherine Hall, a woman of mixed Asian descent, and together they founded ALOEC.

ALOEC was envisioned by Chan and Hall as a source of support and information for other Asian lesbians, while providing a separate identity within a gay community that was predominantly white and male. ALOEC also strove to break stereotypes about Asians in American culture through organized political activism.

ALOEC began as a small discussion group that rapidly grew within one year into an organization boasting some 80 members. One of their first tasks was to establish a group identity through researching the history of Asian lesbians. Politically, ALOEC worked to promote a more visible Asian lesbian presence at the 1989 lesbian and gay march on Washington for civil rights. Chan's organizing effort led her to other grassroots Asian groups that were active across the country, unbeknownst to each other, primarily from the West Coast. Together these groups formed the Asian Pacific Bisexual Lesbian Network. The establishment of this national network led to the creation of the Asian Lesbian Network in Asia. As a result, ALOEC and other groups now enjoy international connection, recognition, and support.

ALOEC Mobilized Against Broadway

In December 1990, ALOEC and GAPIMNY (Gay Asian and Pacific Islander Men of New York) learned that two major lesbian and gay organizations—the Lambda Legal Defense and Education Fund and New York City's Lesbian and Gay Community Center—planned to use the Broadway show *Miss Saigon* as their annual fund raiser. The Asian groups criticized the institutional racism of *Miss Saigon* that depicted Asian women as submissive and self-effacing, and Asian men as asexual and contemptible. In the spring of 1991, after much debate, the larger gay groups proceeded with their fund raiser, and the ALOEC and GAPIMNY staged their protest. Two activists managed to get into the show and heckle Jonathan Pryce (a Caucasian British actor playing an Asian pimp) as he sang his opening number.

The combined effort of ALOEC and GAPIMNY and their protest of *Miss Saigon* led to criticism of the leadership structure of the larger gay organizations in New York City, which are well funded and predominantly headed by white males. Despite the protest, *Miss Saigon* plays on Broadway today and is touring in other major U.S. cities.

June Chan currently lives in Manhattan with her life partner Marianna Romo-Carmona, a writer and activist, and Carmona's son.

References:

Henry, Jim. "June Chan," in *Notable Asian Americans,* edited by Helen Zia and Susan B. Gall. Detroit: Gale Research, 1995: 32-33.

Sherman, Phillip. "June Chan, Marianna Romo-Carmona," in *Uncommon Heroes—A Celebration of Heroes and Role Models for Gay and Lesbian Americans.* New York: Fletcher Press, 1994.

Yoshikawa, Yoko. "The Heat Is on Miss Saigon Coalition," in *The State of Asian American Activism: Activism and Resistance in the 1990s.* Boston: South End Press, 1994: 275-95.

—Laurie Fitzpatrick

Debra Chasnoff

1957-

American filmmaker

Debra Chasnoff. ***Photograph by Irene Young.***

The day after she won the 1992 Academy Award for Best Documentary, and made film history at her acceptance speech by publicly thanking her lesbian lover, Debra Chasnoff finally decided that filmmaking was "what I should do." Chasnoff had spent years before this, working for an assortment of progressive organizations, only sporadically stopping to make movies. She's now a dedicated filmmaker, producing powerful documentaries that address a variety of social issues, from environmental crises to lesbian and gay rights.

Born 12 October 1957 in Philadelphia to Sue Prosen, a psychologist, and Joel Chasnoff, an attorney, Debra Chasnoff grew up in Maryland's liberal Montgomery County, where her father was elected to the Maryland State Legislature. Although her family was politically moderate, Chasnoff remembers being keenly aware of and sympathetic to the civil rights and the anti-war movements as a child.

Graduating a year early from high school, Chasnoff entered Wellesley College where she majored in economics. She also helped organize a boycott, led by the human rights group INFACT, of the Nestle company, whose profits were soaring due to its sales of nutrition-poor infant formula to developing countries. In her sophomore year, Chasnoff fell in love for the first time—with a woman—and came out as a lesbian.

Chasnoff graduated from Wellesley in 1978 and moved to Somerville, Massachusetts, where she landed a job in a prestigious consulting firm, some of whose clients were telecommunications companies that promoted nuclear power. But Chasnoff, having become a part of the anti-nuclear movement, felt torn, and soon quit. By her own admission, she has not had a "straight" job since. She became an editor and co-publisher at *Dollars and Sense,* a progressive economics magazine, and went on to organize, administrate, and fund-raise for other periodicals and for groups such as 9 to 5, an advocacy organization for clerical workers. About 1980, Chasnoff met Kim Klausner, then a union organizer at Boston University. The two began a primary relationship—and, on Klausner's suggestion, made a movie.

Choosing Children, a film about lesbians deciding to have children, was three years in production and was released in 1984 to positive reviews and top awards. In 1985, Chasnoff and Klausner moved to San Francisco, where Chasnoff was associate producer for *Acting Our Age,* an hour-long documentary on women and aging; advised Roberta Achtenberg on her campaign for state assembly; and became co-founder and executive editor of the lesbian and gay quarterly *OUT/LOOK.* In 1988, the couple's first son, Noah Klausner Chasnoff, was born.

In 1990, INFACT hired Chasnoff to write and direct a documentary about its second corporate responsibility campaign, a boycott of the General Electric Company (GE). According to INFACT, GE, then a leader in the production and sale of nuclear weapons, had failed to clean up its Hanford Nuclear Reservation site in Washington state, and had knowingly poisoned its Knolls Atomic Power Plant workers in Schenectady, New York, with asbestos and nuclear radiation.

With a budget of only $65,000, Chasnoff finished her film in a little over nine months. *Deadly Deception: General Electric, Nuclear Weapons and Our Environment* lasts a mere 29 minutes, yet its impact is harrowing, due to Chasnoff's decision to juxtapose scenes of birth defects and cancer suffered by citizens and GE workers, with the blithe corporate jingle: "GE: We bring good things to life." At the last minute, Chasnoff entered her film in the Academy Awards competition for Best Documentary Short Subject—and was astounded when it was nominated.

On 30 March 1992, Debra Chasnoff accepted her Oscar, and told a billion people worldwide to "boycott GE." She also thanked her "life partner," Kim, and their son Noah, "who reminds me on a daily basis why it is so important to keep working for peace and justice." Although GE assured the public that INFACT's boycott, *Deadly Deception,* and Chasnoff's speech had no effect on its earnings, the company nevertheless announced less than a year later that it was pulling out of the nuclear weapons industry.

Chasnoff won over 25 more awards for her film, then went on to direct *A Day in the Life of Continuum* (1993), a film about an HIV treatment center, and *Reflections through a Social Change Prism* (1994), about progressive activists who gather to assess the state of their movements. In 1994 Chasnoff's and Klausner's second son, Oscar Chasnoff Klausner (named not for Chasnoff's Academy Award but for her great grandfather and Klausner's great uncle), was born.

It's Elementary, Chasnoff's latest project, is a feature-length documentary about elementary through middle school teachers addressing lesbian and gay issues with their students. The project was motivated, says Chasnoff, by the anti-gay rhetoric of the 1992 Republican convention and by the prospect of her own son entering school, "where the family he adores would be invisible." She is also developing a film about the Karen Thompson/Sharon Kowalski gay and disability case.

Whatever her project, Chasnoff is committed to building a world of equality and compassion. "It's very important," she says, "that my work be politically useful." With her intelligence, her artistry, and her political commitment, Chasnoff looks forward to many more years of provocative, insightful filmmaking. So can we.

Current Address: Women's Educational Media, 2180 Bryant Street, #203, San Francisco, California 94110. E-mail: WEM DHC@aol.com.

References:

Chasnoff, Debra. Interview with Susie Day. 19 April 1996.

"Dykes' Night OUT at the Oscars," in *OUT/LOOK* (San Francisco), Summer 1992: 31-4.

Herman, Ellen. "Academy Award-Winning Lesbian Speaks," in *Gay Community News* (Boston), 9-21 May 1992: 8-9.

———. "Oscar Springs Filmmaker into the Spotlight," in *The Boston Globe,* 9 April 1992: 1, 78.

Malkin, Marc S. "One Woman General Electric Won't Soon Forget," in *Bay Windows* (Boston), 9-15 April 1992: 1, 10.

Rosenfeld, Megan. "Bringing Bad Things to Light: GE Expose Gets Debra Chasnoff an Oscar ... and Maybe Even a Second Phone," in *Washington Post,* 23 April 1992: A1, D10.

—Susie Day

George Chauncey

1954-

American historian

With the publication of *Gay New York: Gender, Urban Culture, and the Making of the Gay Male World 1890-1940* (Basic Books, 1995), George Chauncey was thrust into prominence in the field of gay history. Several well-received papers, along with *Gay New York* and a myriad of academic accomplishments have made Chauncey an extremely influential member of the gay community and he has become one of the more important historians of gay life in America.

George Austin Chauncey, Jr., was born in Brownsville, Tennessee, to George Austin Chauncey, a Presbyterian minister, and Barbara (Davis) Chauncey. Chauncey, Sr., was active in the civil rights movement in the 1950s and 1960s, so the family, according to Chauncey, "went from one conservative little church to the next." Consequently, Chauncey, older brother to Carolyn and Leslie, grew up in a handful of small towns in Tennessee, Arkansas, and Kentucky—as well as Atlanta, Georgia, and Richmond, Virginia, where he lived from the time he was about 12 years old until he graduated from high school.

Chauncey wasn't conscious of his gayness until after his first year at Yale. He ultimately became very active at Yale fighting for, among other things, a lesbian and gay hotline on campus and, in 1977, organizing the first week long Gay Rights/Gay and Lesbian Awareness Days. "I discovered in college," says Chauncey, "how much I really loved history. And I realized that it is important politically—historical analysis is required to understand present social arrangements, and how they can be changed."

But the idea of gay or gay and lesbian history was foreign to Chauncey. His undergraduate focus of study was African history, and after graduation a John Courtney Murray Traveling Fellowship enabled him to go to Zambia for a year to research the labor and women's history of that nation's mining industry. Chauncey then returned to Boston where he wrote for the *Gay Community News* before continuing graduate work at Yale. He received his M.A. in 1981. In the Fall of 1984, after completing the course work for his Ph.D., Chauncey moved to New York to focus on his dissertation. In 1995, that research would eventually become his first book—*Gay New York.* He spent seven years in New York, living for the last five with David Hansell, the director of legal services, and then deputy executive director for policy at New York's GMHC.

After receiving his Ph.D. in 1989, Chauncey accepted two one-year positions—first as a fellow at Rutgers' Center for Historical Analysis, then as an assistant professor of history at New York University. In 1991 he went to the University of Chicago as an assistant professor. He is currently a tenured, associate professor of history at Chicago. Over the past seven years Chauncey has published nearly a dozen articles, co-edited *Hidden from History: Reclaiming the Gay and Lesbian Past* with noted historians Martin Duberman and Martha Vicinus (New American Library, 1989), and written *Gay New York* in 1995.

Gay New York garnered several awards, including: the Frederick Jackson Turner Award, the Marle Curti Social History Award, the *Los Angeles Times* Book Prize for History, the Lambda Literary Award for Gay Men's Studies, the John Boswell Award, and a *New York Times* Notable Book Award. Translations and plans for a film based on the book are also underway.

Chauncey's articles have appeared in dozens of collections, professional journals, and gay and lesbian publications. "Christian Brotherhood or Sexual Perversion: Homosexual Identities and the Construction of Sexual Boundaries in the World War One Era," which first appeared in the *Journal of Social History* (Winter 1985), has been reprinted in a half dozen collections. He has contributed essays to reference volumes, served as historical consultant to "Becoming Visible: The Legacy of Stonewall," a 1994 New York Public Library exhibit, and has been co-chair of the University of Chicago Workshop on Lesbian and Gay Studies since 1991.

George Chauncey. *Photograph by Stuart Michaels.*

Chauncey testified as an expert witness on the history of anti-gay discrimination and gay political participation at trials deliberating the constitutionality of Colorado's Referendum Two (October 1993) and Cincinnati's Issue Three (June 1994), both of which had overturned local gay rights laws. Closer to home, as chair of the University of Chicago's Lesbian and Gay Faculty Organization (LEGFASO) Chauncey led the campaign that resulted in Chicago becoming one of the first universities to adopt a comprehensive domestic partnership policy.

During his academic endeavors Chauncey has received fellowships from the Guggenheim Foundation and the National Humanities Center in North Carolina to support work on his next book, *American Culture and the Making of the Modern Gay World.* Chauncey plans to spend the 1996-1997 academic year in North Carolina with his partner, film historian Ron Gregg, working at the Center, and then return to the University of Chicago.

Current Address: c/o George Borchardt, 136 E. 57th St., New York, New York 10022.

References:

Chauncey, George. Interview with Andrea L.T. Peterson, 1 September 1996.

—Andrea L.T. Peterson

Meg Christian

1946-

American singer and songwriter

Meg Christian was a pioneer in the women's music industry and one of the founders, with Cris Williamson and others, of Olivia Records, where women produced, engineered, and marketed women's music. Her albums were extremely popular and influential in the early 1970s women's movement. In 1984 she left Olivia Records and touring to devote herself full-time to Siddha Yoga. In the process, she learned Indian instruments and wrote and recorded her songs to Gurumayi as well as Indian bhajans (religious songs).

Christian was born in Lynchburg, Virginia, in 1946. She was educated in Virginia and then graduated from the University of North Carolina with a double major in English and music. Trained as a classical guitarist, she soon discovered folk musicians such as Joan Baez, Buffy Sainte Marie, and the Limelighters. When she moved to North Carolina, she became aware of Appalachian songs and guitar styles. Later, women songwriters became important as she started learning and performing the music of Joni Mitchell, Laura Nyro, and Carole King. It was 1969 when Christian discovered the women's movement in her first consciousness-raising group.

The primary influence in Christian's life was probably Cris Williamson, another lesbian songwriter/singer. Early on Christian heard Williamson's songs and felt a kindred spirit. She learned all of the songs on Williamson's first album, *The Changer and the Changed* and when she met Williamson in 1973 in Washington, D.C., Williamson, as Christian phrases it, "nearly fell off the piano bench" when Christian and her friends knew all the words and sang along.

In 1973, Christian started concentrating on performing and writing women's/lesbian music and particpated in the founding of Olivia Records. Christian and Olivia were closely intertwined. The first Olivia single featured a cover version of King's "Lady" performed by Christian and "If It Weren't for the Music" by Williamson. Christian's *I Know You Know* album was released by Olivia in 1975. All of her subsequent albums, *Face the Music,* 1977, *Turning It Over,* 1981, and *From the Heart,* 1984, were also produced by Olivia. Olivia Records grew in those years to be a 15 member, all-women's collective which sold one and one-half million records. A lively and exciting concert at Carnegie Hall in 1982, celebrating ten years of Olivia was recorded and issued by Olivia and was a bestseller. Olivia Records, the music it produced, and the concerts were all an unqualified success.

In an interview in *Off Our Backs,* March 1981, Christian explains her view of music: "All my life I've been a musician. When I got involved in the women's movement ... I used my music to ... express what I was learning about my life in this world, as a woman and as a lesbian." She came out as a lesbian through her songs such as her humorous "Ode to a Gym Teacher," on her *I Know You Know* album:

> She was a big time woman the first to come along that showed me being female meant you still could be strong and though graduation meant that we had to part, she'll always be a player on the ballfield of my heart.

In 1977, after drinking for fourteen years, Christian realized she was, in her own words, "dying of alcoholism" and changed her life to include recovery programs and women's support groups such as the Alcoholism Center for Women in Los Angeles. She also began an exploration of her own spirituality that would ultimately lead her to embrace Eastern mysticism. Her album, *From the Heart,* explores her newfound inner spiritual experiences. A most important component of the recovery for Christian was learning to relax her expectations of herself as the perfect feminist/lesbian, doing/being everything for everyone. She had an extreme sense of responsibility to her audience as well as the women's music community who had supported her for years. As Judy Dlugacz describes the situation in *Hot Wire,* "Not only did Christian devote herself to Olivia night and day but she was really the person we depended on to bring home the money."

Since leaving Olivia, Christian has not been inactive in music but has recorded two CDs for the Siddha Yoga Foundation. One, *The Fire of My Love,* issued in 1986, contains Indian devotional songs and original compositions by Christian. *Songs of Ecstasy* (1995) shows the breadth of Christian's musical knowledge and talent. She plays the harmonium and sings Indian religious songs, Bhajans in Hindi and Abhangas in Marathi; she also produced the album.

Christian has meant much to the women's community as a singer, as a songwriter, as a lesbian feminist. Her music has been widely praised for its sensitivity and candor, and a 1990 Olivia reissue of her songs, *The Best of Meg Christian,* is still selling in music stores. As Mary Pollock writes in her *Frontiers* article, "Meg Christian has been one of the creators of contemporary women's culture; in fact, without her, contemporary women's music as we know it might not exist."

Current Address: c/o SYOA, P.O. Box 600, South Fallsburg, New York 12779.

—Jacquelyn Marie

Christina

1626-1689

Swedish queen

One of the enduring images in motion picture cinematography is the extended close-up of Greta Garbo at the end of Rouben Mamoulian's *Queen Christina.* As the ship carrying the abdicated queen leaves Sweden, the camera tracks slowly to the Sphinx-like face of Garbo (Christina) at the prow, then freezes in a frame of lingering ambiguity. While the film abounds in flights of fancy characteristic of the Hollywood dream factory of the 1930s (the beauty of Garbo versus the physical appearance of the real Christina, for example), this shot is true to the historical persona of the queen. Vilified and praised for her religious beliefs, scorned and admired for her intellectual pursuits, described variously as a lesbian, hermaphrodite, bisexual, and transvestite (but rarely as a heterosexual), Christina is one of the most enigmatic and fascinating figures in history.

Christina was born in Stockholm on 17 December 1626, the daughter of Gustavus Adolphus and Maria Eleonora of Brandenberg. As king and military leader, Gustavus Adolphus had brought Sweden to a position of political power in a Europe embroiled in the protracted tumult of the Thirty Years' War. With the death of the king on the battlefield in 1632, Christina, his sole heir, became ruler-elect at the age of six. During her minority, Christina—and the political affairs of Sweden—were guided by her father's chancellor, Count Axel Oxenstierna, who continued to exercise influence throughout her reign.

"Minerva of the North"

Even before her father's death, Christina had begun a regime and education more typical of a prince than a princess, a deliberate and unusual effort by Gustavus Adolphus to prepare her for the throne. Comments by the adult Christina, cited by M. L. Clarke in "The Making of a Queen: The Education of Christina of Sweden" in *History Today*, are illuminating regarding her father's wishes: "My inclinations were wonderfully in agreement with his intentions. I had an aversion and an invincible antipathy to all that women are and say." An expert horsewoman, Christina also excelled with the sword, hiked long distances, and hunted game with the eye of a sharpshooter. In the classroom, her schooling was exceptionally disciplined and rigorous. Besides Greek and Latin, she learned French, German, Italian, Flemish, and later some Hebrew and Arabic.

Christina's appearance at this time reflects her "princely" endeavors and confirms the general impression she made on observers throughout her life. In her biography *Queen Christina*, Georgina Masson cites a Spanish envoy, Pimentel, a member of Christina's inner circle: "There is nothing feminine about her but her sex. Her voice and manner of speaking, her walk, her style, her ways are all quite masculine ... Though she rides side-saddle she holds herself so well and is so light in her movements that, unless one were quite close to her, one would take her for a man."

In her childhood and adolescence, Christina formed close attachments to her cousin, Charles Gustavus—later seen as a likely husband to the young queen—and to her lady-in-waiting, Ebba Sparre. Christina's relationship with the beautiful "Belle" Sparre, discussed in contemporary written accounts, was intense and long-lasting, fueling much speculation concerning the nature of her sexuality.

After Christina was crowned queen in 1644, she continued her intellectual pursuits, inviting foreign scholars to her court, most notably Descartes (who died in Stockholm in 1650, when Christina was 24). She supported, to an extravagant degree, literature, music, and art, becoming known throughout Europe as a munificent "Minerva of the North." It is during this period that Christina may have also begun to question the strict Calvinist beliefs of her Lutheran upbringing, a spiritual journey that resulted in her eventual conversion to Roman Catholicism.

In 1654, Christina stunned her country and, indeed, all Europe, when she formally abdicated, naming Charles Gustavus (her would-be consort) as successor. Speculation as to why Christina relinquished her throne was rampant at the time and continues to this day. Certainly her secret but widely rumored embracing of the Catholic faith was incompatible with ruling a rigidly Protestant Sweden. Other reasons suggested by biographers and historians include Christina's own views concerning the superiority of men in the political arena; possible health problems that would have precluded producing an heir; a desire to flee the rigors and barrenness of life in the north for the warmer climes and aesthetic riches of Rome; and widely held, substantive opinions concerning the queen's lesbianism.

The Road to Rome

Christina left Sweden immediately following a formal ceremony of abdication. Her road to Rome was similar to a royal progress, made all the more celebratory by a public declaration of her conversion to Catholicism. She was greeted by mobs and emissaries as she travelled with her entourage through Flanders, France, Innsbruck, and the kingdoms of Italy. Her arrival at the border of the Papal States was met with elaborate ceremony, and she completed her journey in the carriage of Pope Alexander VII. For her official state entry into Rome, Christina passed the Porta del Popolo, embellished in her honor by no less than the sculptor Bernini, and as she entered the Vatican she was welcomed by the entire College of Cardinals.

For the next 34 years, Christina lived in lavish exile, assembling in her palazzo on the Tiber a vast collection of paintings, books, drawings, sculptures, and manuscripts. She maintained correspondence with figures as diverse as Cardinal Mazarin, Louis XIV's Prime Minister, and La Rochefoucauld, whose *Maxims* she emulated in a series of philosophical writings. Christina became the patron of a variety of musicians and writers, including Scarlatti, Corelli, Baldinucci, and Bernini. She also established salons and academies, whose activities were viewed with disapproval by a succession of reigning popes. In this respect, Christina's heralded presence in Rome was not quite the religious coup originally envisioned by the Vatican hierarchy.

Although her sphere of influence in Sweden had ended with her abdication, Christina had political ambitions regarding other thrones. An attempt to become queen of Naples failed, resulting in the scandalous murder in France of Christina's equerry, Monaldeschi, by her own orders, a crime she freely admitted and defended as her royal right. A second try for the throne of another Catholic country, Poland, was also unsuccessful.

Christina's later years in Rome were marked by an increasingly close relationship with Decio Azzolino, an influential cardinal who became her confidant, financial advisor, and, according to wide speculation, her lover. Christina died in Rome at the age of 63 in 1689, probably of congestive heart failure resulting from a succession of infections and chronic illnesses. In a funeral of great pomp and splendor, Christina, dressed uncharacteristically in gold and ermine, was buried in the crypt of the basilica of St. Peter's. Cardinal Azzolino, who outlived the queen by only a few months, was named in her will as sole heir.

In this final public gesture to Azzolino, Christina once again displayed both a willfulness and ambiguity of nature evident in her behavior throughout her life. Even taking into account her privileged royal status, Christina's unusually independent, dominant personality defined virtually all her relationships. Judging from her many letters to Azzolino, however, her feelings towards him ranged from nearly obsessive passion to sardonic rage to, finally, a highly atypical subservience. Sven Stolpe, in *Christina of Sweden*, cites a letter written to Azzolino in 1667, when Christina was 41: "I beg you to believe that you have unlimited power over me and that being obliged to you in the way that I am, your will shall be an eternal law to me against which I shall never demur." In another letter she writes: "All your coolness cannot stop me from worshipping you until death."

The general assumption that Christina and Azzolino were lovers is a reasonable one. In addition to the evidence of the letters, their relationship, begun soon after her arrival in Rome, was sustained at a level of unusual intimacy for over 30 years. Whatever the exact nature of their bond, there is no question that he was the master in her life and the recipient of her deepest feelings in her mature years.

The Queen and Her Lady-in-Waiting

If Azzolino dominated Christina's emotional life during her exile in Rome, Ebba ("Belle") Sparre inspired an equal devotion from the time of their adolescence in Sweden to Sparre's death a few years after Christina's abdication. Notwithstanding the passionate nature of friendships common among blue-stockings of the time (Sparre was of the nobility, and well-educated), Christina's love for Belle, noted by contemporaries and documented in a series of authenticated letters, argues strongly for a lesbian relationship.

Belle Sparre appeared at Christina's court in 1645, when both she and the queen were 19. As Christina's lady-in-waiting, Sparre accompanied Christina everywhere, including the sharing of her bed (admittedly, a not uncommon practice for unmarried monarchs at that time). Sparre's personality and appearance were exceptional, according to comments in many letters and documents by diplomats and other visitors to the Swedish court. In *Queen Christina*, Georgina Masson quotes from the extensive journal of Oliver Cromwell's ambassador to Sweden, Bulstrode Whitelocke, who was much taken by Belle: "She was modest, virtuous, witty, of great beauty, and excellent behavior." He also reported that "the queen sayd: 'Discourse with this lady, my bed-fellowe, and tell me if her inside be not as beautiful as her outside'." Allowing for Christina's acknowledged love of the scandalous *bon mot*, the remark is nonetheless revealing.

Although Belle married and left the court a year before Christina abdicated, it was she who continued to be the recipient of Christina's intimate thoughts and passionate sentiments. Letters that Christina wrote to Belle during the early years of her self-imposed exile reveal a deeply felt love. Sven Stolpe records in *Christina of Sweden* a note sent from Rome in 1656:

> How happy I should have been, Belle, had it been granted to me to meet you. But I am condemned for ever to love and adore you without being allowed to see you. The envy which the stars have of human happiness prevents me from being entirely happy, for happy I cannot be so long as I am far from you. Do not doubt the truth of my words, and believe me when I say that, wherever I may find myself in the whole world, in me you will find one who is as devoted to you as ever.

This and other love letters to Belle Sparre offer evidence of Christina's lesbian nature that is convincing far beyond the many contemporary accounts and editorial commentary concerning her "unfeminine" and "masculine" demeanor. If only those stereotypical descriptions existed, one would have to balance speculation about her sexuality against the unique situation in which she found herself: a princess already raised as a prince who might have reasonably felt that *playing* the part of "king" rather than "queen" would ensure greater success as monarch.

Nevertheless, in the centuries following her death, Christina's unconventional physical appearance and demeanor have in themselves continued to feed additional rumors. As recently as 1965, as part of a commemorative exhibition, the queen's body was removed from its sarcophagus in St. Peter's, ostensibly for analysis of her burial clothes and silver death-mask. In fact, her corpse was also deliberately and exhaustively examined at this time for signs of hermaphroditism. The results of this bizarre effort were inconclusive, however, and Christina was once again laid to rest in her Vatican tomb.

Christina and the Varieties of Sexual Identity

In an article in *Feminist Studies* entitled "'A Girton Girl on a Throne': Queen Christina and Versions of Lesbianism, 1906-1933," Sarah Waters comments on what she calls Christina's *liminality*: "her resistance to categorization, her tendency, in fact, to cross category, whether national, religious, sexual or sartorial." Indeed, Christina's sexuality does remain ambiguous and confusing if one's goal is to define it precisely, to categorize it, to label it with sociological terms, most of which did not even exist in her lifetime. In the words of Waters: "it is the inconsistencies *within* versions of sexual identity, as well as the contention between them, to which ... portraits of Queen Christina must, ultimately, direct us." Perhaps Christina's sexuality may best be seen as illustrative of the multiplicities of sexual identity that can find expression over an individual's lifetime.

As a person of wealth and privilege, Christina had the advantage of being able to bend societal mores throughout her tumultuous life. She also bore the burden, however, of spending her years as princess and queen under the intense scrutiny of her rigidly Protestant subjects, a situation that continued—to an extent, at her own instigation—after she abdicated and became a Catholic exile in Rome. In both venues and in each personification, her rigorous, impassioned search for self-expression made her then, as it does now, a figure of exceptional and lasting interest. In the words of one of Christina's contemporaries, quoted in Georgina Masson's *Queen Christina*: "She freely followed her own genius in all things and car'd not what anybody said."

References:

Akerman, Susanna. *Queen Christina of Sweden and Her Circle: The Transformation of a Seventeenth-Century Philosophical Libertine.* New York: E. J. Brill, 1991.

Anderson, Bonnie S. and Judith P. Zinsser. *A History of Their Own: Women in Europe from Prehistory to the Present. Volume II.* New York: Harper & Row, 1988.

Clarke, M. L. "The Making of a Queen: The Education of Christina of Sweden," in *History Today,* April 1978, no. 28: 228-35.

Goldsmith, Margaret. *Christina of Sweden: A Psychological Biography.* London: Arthur Barker, 1933.

Masson, Georgina. *Queen Christina.* New York: Farrar, Straus & Giroux, 1969.

San Juan, Rose Marie. "The Queen's Body and Its Slipping Mask: Contesting Portraits of Queen Christina of Sweden," in *Reimagining Women: Representations of Women in Culture,* edited by Shirley Neuman and Glennis Stephenson. Buffalo: University of Toronto Press, 1993.

Steegmuller, Francis. "The Return of Christina," in *New Yorker,* 17 September 1966, no. 42: 160-68.

Stolpe, Sven. *Christina of Sweden.* New York: Macmillan, 1963.

von Platen, Magnus, ed. *Queen Christina of Sweden: Documents and Studies.* Stockholm: Kungl. Boktryckeriet P. A. Norstedt & Soner, 1966.

Waters, Sarah. "'A Girton Girl on a Throne': Queen Christina and Versions of Lesbianism, 1906-1933," in *Feminist Review* (London), Spring 1994, no. 46: 41-60.

—David Garnes

Chrystos

1946-

Native American writer and activist

Self-described as an "Urban Indian," Chrystos is an unflinchingly political poet and activist whose memories of her troubled childhood and years of struggle with mental illness, drugs, and alcohol permeate her work. "Make words, not war!" is the credo Chrystos recommends in her second collection of poems titled *Dream On* (1991). It is a defiantly activist stance that weaves itself throughout her work like a heavy mist of rage as she writes about the murder of indigenous people, the treatment of the institutionalized, the rape and victimization of women, child abuse, and society's general disregard for the eccentric. "Make war with words!" seems to be the profound and justifiable undercurrent of her plea.

Although Chrystos is perhaps best known for her angry poems and violent style, she also writes erotic lesbian verse that is both lusty and celebratory. "With frequent allusions to all the senses," notes Barbara Dale May in *Contemporary Lesbian Writers of the United States,* "but especially to those of taste, smell, and touch, these poems can quite fairly be described as delicious reading." In short, the motivation and lyrical sense behind her non-political poems provides the sensation of joyous flight, a soaring over the earthly confines and prejudices against lesbian lovemaking. "I roll in you like first snow melt shocking my blood," Chrysto says in "Na Natska" *(Dream On)*, "with this glistening new river of humming birds between us."

Chrystos was born on 7 November 1946 in San Francisco. Her father was a Menominee Indian and her mother was part Lithuanian and part French. The hard-hitting, painful accounts of her childhood, largely contained in her first collection of verse *Not Vanishing* (1988), drive home the realities of too many indigenous peoples' lives spent in self-hate and subsequent self-destruction. Her mother suffered from severe depression, causing Chrystos to conclude that she was more burden than joy to her. Her father evidenced lifelong shame at his ethnicity, causing the young girl to grapple with whatever fleeting ethnic pride she could muster for herself. Add to this her sexual abuse by an uncle, and her own early pattern for self-destruction becomes all too predictable. "You've hit me with that irresistible deadly weapon," she writes painfully in "What Did He Hit You With? The Doctor Said" *(Dream On)*. "Hatred dressed in the shoes and socks of the words I love you."

"The Women Who Love Me"

Even with all this baggage, Chrystos managed to educate herself, both as a poet and artist (a handful of her illustrations appear in her collections). She has lived on Bainbridge Island in Washington State since 1980, and has also worked vociferously for various indigenous peoples' land and treaty-rights causes, the freedom of activist Leonard Peltier, and the rights of the Dine and Mohawk nations among them.

Chrystos credits the efforts of her first lesbian lover in the 1960s for saving her from what writer May terms "a life of drugs, prostitution, suicide attempts and the revolving door of mental institutions." In both *Not Vanishing* and *Dream On,* Chrystos pays homage to the loving inspiration of women in her life, and stresses the importance of maintaining solid relationships, however trying they might sometimes be. It was Kate Millett who, in the early 1970s, encouraged Chrystos to write for publication and gave her renewed hope, and she dates her life of sobriety back to October of 1988, just after publication of *Not Vanishing.* "The Women Who Love Me," she writes in the poem of that name in *Dream On,* "know how to write fuck paint kiss dance hate & love how to leave a woman and how to stay."

Chrystos's work has appeared in various anthologies, most notably the groundbreaking works *This Bridge Called My Back: Writings by Radical Women of Color* (1981), *A Gathering of Spirit: Writing and Art by North American Indian Women* (1983), and *Living the Spirit: A Gay American Indian Anthology* (1988). *Bridge* was the first collection where lesbian and feminist women addressed each other as well as "outsiders" on issues of racism and stereotyping, *Gathering* was the first anthology of Native writing edited entirely by a Native person, and *Living* was the first specifically gay and lesbian collection of Native writings. "Now we are rare and occasionally cherished as Eagles," Chrystos writes of her people in "Winter Count" *(Dream On)*, "(but) Never forget america is our hitler."

"Offensive and Intriguing"

Critics on both sides of Chrystos's work have pointed to a vague political agenda and her sometimes alienating anger as what both draws and repels. She occasionally speaks of "legion white lesbians" and the "white plague" in her work, which has prompted some critics to agonize over her own allegiance to feminist and/or lesbian causes. "Not to recognize the existence of these hurtful components," says May, "would be to ignore a key element in her writing, which, oddly, is at once offensive and intriguing."

Yet, it is her troubled childhood memories and ongoing identification (or lack thereof) with her parents that holds the key to her rage. And it is the reflection of this rage that points a finger at the atrocities of European culture, which the mother represents, visited upon anyone non-white and any whites foolish enough to diverge from rigid norms. In short, she completely identifies with her idealized paternal heritage, a Menominee "fathertongue" never recognized by him because of his shame. And she rejects the other half or her identity, the "mothertongue."

In this sense, Chrystos's work speaks to the problems of an indigenous generation coming of age in fits and starts, and it is only in her erotic poetry that one finds respite. "She is desperate for my pretense that she was a good mother," Chrystos says of her mother in "Burning Up" *(Dream On),* "I am desperate for her acknowledgment that my childhood was a painful chaos of beatings and her emotional absence ... I'm a figment of her sentimental guilt ... It is desperation She wants me to comfort her before she dies."

Two-Spirit Revival

Chrystos was among the first writers to deal with the combined issues of homosexuality and marginalization of indigeneous peoples, reflecting what writer Will Roscoe in *The Gay and Lesbian Literary Heritage* calls "a wide range of ethnographic and literary references to two-spirit (homosexual) roles ... and an optimistic prediction of their restoration." When Chrystos received a National Endowment for the Arts grant to write *Dream On*, poet Adrienne Rich noted that this was a sign "of the power not only of (her) work, but of the current of resistance running beneath the inertia and pseudo events that have constituted public life for two decades."

Nevertheless, and perhaps not surprisingly given the often-brutal honesty and loving lesbian erotica evident in her work, Chrystos has gone largely unnoticed by the mainstream current of critical reviews. In the end, Chrystos is content to listen to more ethereal voices. Of *Dream On,* she notes: "This title came in a dream I believe if we begin to listen to our dreams, which are spirits speaking to us when we aren't as rude as usual, we could solve many of our troubles Let us honor our different, sacred paths & work to transform our anger and grief to change our world so all may live, without hunger or hatred, in peace."

Current Address: 3900 Pleasant Beach Dr. NE, Bainbridge Island, Washington 98110-3215.

References:

Chrystos. *Dream On.* Vancouver: Press Gang Publishers, 1991.

Chrystos. *Not Vanishing.* Vancouver: Press Gang Publishers. 1988.

Pollack, Sandra and Knight, Denise D., eds. *Contemporary Lesbian Writers of the United States.* Westport, Connecticut: Greenwood Press, 1994.

Summers, Claude J., ed. *The Gay and Lesbian Literary Heritage.* New York: Henry Holt, 1995.

—Jerome Szymczak

Roy Cohn

1927-1986

American attorney

> By impersonating the aggressor, assuming his attributes or imitating his aggression, the child transforms himself from the person threatened into the person who makes the threat. (A. Freud)

Roy Cohn's life evokes a long list of paradoxes fueled by the idea that power is essential at any price. In fifty-nine years Roy Cohn lived the life of a liberal and an arch-conservative, a Jew who fraternized with anti-Semites, and a man who hobnobbed with the elite but died a pauper. He was also a gay man who flaunted his homosexuality while frantically lobbying to block gay civil rights.

Getting Established

Born in the Bronx in 1927, Roy Marcus Cohn was the only child of the unhappy marriage of Al Cohn and Dora Marcus. Roy's

Roy Cohn

father was a renowned liberal judge appointed by then-Governor Franklin Roosevelt. Democratic power politics surrounded young Roy, but did not prevent the prosecution of Roy's favorite uncle, Bernard Marcus, who was sentenced to Sing-Sing for a bank failure. Communists were blamed for the bank run, and the case had a major impact on Roy.

Roy was a loner most of his early life and bit of a prodigy. He attended school at Horace Mann, Columbia College, and graduated Columbia Law School by the time he was 20. By 1948 he became an assistant U.S. Attorney. Within three years Cohn convicted the Rosenbergs of treason and then underhandedly arranged the death penalty for both of them. By age 26 he beat out Bobby Kennedy for the position of chief counsel to Senator Joseph McCarthy.

Seeing "Red"

In 1947, the House Committee on Un-American Activities began questioning people's allegiance before Congress. The government persecuted its citizens for what they thought, not their conduct. Initially the public broadly supported these efforts, but in the end not a single communist would be found.

Gay men and lesbians were as much targets as communists. The 1952 presidential campaign promised to remove the "lavender lads" from government (von Hoffman, p. 127). The Republican National Chairman stressed the need to work the "homosexual angle," since they were "perhaps as dangerous as the actual Communists" (von Hoffman, p. 128).

Roy Cohn, already acknowledging his own homosexuality, could never defend gays in the public realm; it would be a death blow to any hope at real power. However, instead of remaining neutral, he sided completely and for the rest of his life with those committed to harming the homosexual community.

The government's witch hunting ended as a result of the Army-McCarthy hearings, when the military accused McCarthy and Cohn of keeping David Schine (Cohn's suspected lover) from performing difficult military service. By the end of 1954, McCarthy's approval rating fell through the floor and the Senate censured him. McCarthy drank himself to death by 1957, leaving Cohn alone to defend their legacy.

After McCarthyism

Roy Cohn returned to New York City and over several decades expanded his power base to include such contacts as Cardinal Spellman, Ronald Reagan, Donald Trump, and Jesse Helms. He set up a private legal practice that operated on IOUs—employees and creditors never knew if they would be paid. Yet Roy continued to attract an impressive list of clients due to his authority and reputation.

Not everything went smoothly, however. Bobby Kennedy became attorney general in 1961 and sought his revenge against Roy. Mail intercepts, phone taps and twenty-three years of IRS investigations complicated the rest of Roy's life.

With the death of his mother in 1967, Roy became very promiscuous, entertaining on his yacht or at Studio 54 in New York. As one friend put it, "He did all kinds of things that he never believed he was doing.... I think he would completely, in one part of his mind, separate from his homosexual self, so that, that's like someone else doing it." (von Hoffman, p. 316)

Despite his outrageous behaviors, some in the company of arch-conservatives who merely looked the other way, Roy continued to oppose any advances in gay civil rights. When a group of gay schoolteachers asked him to represent them, his reply was, "I believe that homosexual teachers are a grave threat to our children—they have no business polluting the schools of America." (Zion, p. 236)

Near the End

With his AIDS progressing rapidly, Roy Cohn connived his way into the National Institutes of Health for treatment with the then-experimental drug, AZT. Cohn continually denied the accusations that he contracted HIV but also used his power to increase funding for AIDS research within the Reagan administration.

In his last weeks, the Disciplinary Committee of the American Bar Association began disbarment proceedings against Cohn over a $100,000 debt he owed to a client twenty years prior. It came at a bad time for him; his illness was in its end stages and the treatments clouded his ability to think clearly. Roy Cohn died six weeks after his disbarment in 1986.

Although despised by most of the gay community, Roy Cohn illustrates some provocative realities, leaving an unexpected legacy for us to ponder. His experience leads us to question politicians' true motives. How our own struggle for power can redefine us in unflattering ways unless we are careful. Or how difficult it is to be consistently true to ourselves. While Roy Cohn's solution to these problems may not be palatable, the questions raised by his particular approach must be answered.

References:

Freud, Anna. *The Ego and the Mechanisms of Defense*. International University Press, 1966.

New York Times Biographical Service, various issues.

von Hoffman, Nicholas. *Citizen Cohn: The Life and Times of Roy Cohn*. New York, Doubleday, 1988.

Zion, Sidney. *The Autobiography of Roy Cohn*. Secaucus, NJ: Lyle Stuart, Inc., 1988.

—Ronald C. Albucher, M.D.

Colette

1873-1954

French writer

Sidonie Gabrielle Colette, influential and controversial French author, is acclaimed in Lynne Huffner's *Another Colette* as the "first woman in French literature to write as a woman." Colette wrote extensively in many genres: novels, short stories, plays, essays, literary and theater reviews, newspaper articles, and letters. Her writings, cited as "laying the foundations of feminist writings in France after 1968," continue to influence women's writing and the current feminist movement.

Colette was born on 28 January 1873 in Saint-Sauveur-en-Puisaye, France, the youngest daughter of Adele-Eugenie-Sidonie Landoy (Sido) and Jules Joseph. Colette's older siblings included two brothers, Achille and Leo and one sister, Juliette. At 19 she married literary critic Henri Gauthier-Villars ("Willy"). Between 1900-1907, while married to Willy, Colette wrote the famous Claudine novels all under the pen name "Willy." The novels, which created a sensation in Paris, depict the sexual awakening and slowly evolving lesbian consciousness of the heroine from adolescence to married woman. The series includes *Claudine à l'école* (trans. *Claudine at School*, 1900), *Claudine à Paris* (trans. *Claudine in Paris*, 1901), *Claudine en ménage* (trans. *Claudine Married* or *The Indulgent Husband*, 1902), *Claudine s'en va* (trans. *Claudine and Annie* or *Journal of Annie* or *The Innocent Wife*, 1903) and *La Retraite Sentimentale* (*Retreat from Love*, 1907).

Colette's marriage to Willy was an unhappy one and she writes in her 1936 *Mes Aprentissages* that "working for him, near him, taught me to distrust him, not to know him better." While married to Willy, Colette was introduced to the Natalie Barney circle, the celebrated "women of the left bank," a diverse group of lesbian writers and other artists that included Renee Vivien , Djuna Barnes, Sylvia Beach, Janet Flanner, Gertrude Stein, and Alice B. Toklas. Colette and Barney became close friends. After her separation from Willy in 1906, Colette moved to an apartment on the Right Bank in the area of Paris known as Passy. She began earning her living as a dancer and a mime in the marginalized world of the music hall theater in Paris. From 1906-1912, she lived with her lover, the Marquis de Belbeuf ("Missy"). Colette and Missy were a well-known pair in Parisian society. They created a sensation one evening in 1907 when they exchanged a passionate kiss while performing in a pantomime at the Moulin Rouge in Paris. Colette's marriage to Willy ended on 21 June 1910, and she began to publish under her own name of "Colette." The writings during her "vagabond" years included *Les vrilles de la vigne* (*The Tendrils of the Vine*, 1908), *La Vagabonde* (*The Vagabond*, 1911), *L'Entrave* (*The Shackle*, 1913), and *L'Envers du Music-Hall* (*Music-Hall Sidelights*, 1913).

Colette married Henri de Jouvenal on 19 December 1912. Her only child, Colette-Renee de Jouvenal, was born on 3 July 1913. She divorced Jouvenal in 1924, and in 1925 married Maurice Goudeket. The marriage lasted until Colette's death on 3 August 1954.

Themes in the Works of Colette

In her writings, Colette explores the entire range of sexual attitudes and behaviors between the sexes and between members of the same sex. The variety of roles that women play as mothers, daughters, sisters, friends, and lovers are central to her themes. Colette is concerned with female independence and the degree to which women will pursue of their own identities. The writer explores the range of sexual behaviors and attitudes that exist among women without the domineering presence of men. Thematically, female friendships and bonding are as important as sex. As she questions traditional gender roles, Colette engages in gender-bending; many of her characters appear as androgynous—outcasts on the margins of society. Women are frequently represented as strong while the men appear weak. Colette's work is also concerned with how women represent and define themselves in their own language.

Colette

Colette and the Lesbian Image

Colette's powerful depictions of lesbians continue to influence the way lesbians are perceived. In an essay entitled "Lesbian Intertextuality," author Elaine Marks notes that Colette never uses the word "lesbian" in her writings. "Homosexual" is a term applied to men. Women are treated as individuals and their nature cannot be encompassed with a single label. Lesbian relationships bear witness to the complex physical and cultural realities of women, who often seek out other women as a refuge from the indifference, exploitation, and cruelty of male domination. The image of a tender, caring relationship that is reminiscent of the maternal bond between mother and daughter is a powerful theme that continues to surface in her writings. In the prose poem "Nuit blanche," published in the 1908 collection entitled *Les vrilles de la vigne,* (1908), she writes:

> Because I know that then you will tighten your embrace and that if the rocking of your arms does not calm me, your kisses will become more tenacious, your hands more loving, and that you will give me pleasure as an aid, as a supreme exorcism which will drive out the demons of fever, of anger, of unrest ... You will give me pleasure, leaning over me, your eyes full of maternal solicitude, you are seeking in your passionate friend, for the child you never had.

Women who love other women is central to Colette's most ambitious statement on sexuality, *Le Pur et l' impur* (*The Pure and Impure*, first published as *Ces plaisirs*, 1932, reedited in 1941). Colette hoped that this work would "perhaps be recognized one day as [her] best work." The novel is considered unique among Colette's other works in its exhaustive treatment of a range of lesbian identities and relationships. She describes a group of lesbians which includes older women of the aristocratic classes "baronesses of the empire, canoness, lady cousins of Czars, illegitimate daughters of grand-dukes, exquisites of the Parisian bourgeois and some aged horsewomen of the Austrian aristocracy, hand and eye of steel" who meet secretly and, adopting the manner and dress of men, advise and otherwise groom younger female protégés. The central figure of this group of women is the powerful figure La Chevaliere, a woman reminiscent of Colette's lover Missy. Other lesbian figures emerge such Renee Vivien, the "vulgar femme de lettres," the wise and reflective Amalia X, the mannish La Lucienne and the Ladies of Llangollen, the aging lesbian couple who only appear to be successful in living together as man and wife. In this novel, women give authentic voice to their own feelings and communicate in their own unique language.

Due in part to her concern with women's roles and the realities of the female condition, as well as her acceptance of the naturalness of sex, Colette's honest and sensitive depictions of the sexual and emotional responses of women endure.

References:

Benstock, Shari. *Women of the Left Bank.* Austin: University of Texas Press, 1986.

Eisinger, Erica Mendeson and Mari Ward McCarty, eds. *Colette: The Woman, the Writer.* University Park: Pennsylvania State University Press, 1981.

Huffer, Lynne. *Another Colette.* Ann Arbor: University of Michigan Press, 1992.

King, Adele. *French Women Novelists: Defining a Female Style.* New York: St. Martin's Press, 1989.

Mitchell, Yvonne. *Colette: A Taste For Life.* New York: Harcourt Brace Jovanovich, 1979.

Sartori, Eva Martin, and Dorothy Wynne Zimmerman, eds. *French Women Writers: A Bio-Bibliographical Source Book.* New York: Greenwood Press, 1991.

Stambolian, George and Elaine Marks, eds. *Homosexualities and French Literature: Cultural Contexts/Critical Texts.* Ithaca: Cornell University Press, 1979.

Summers, Claude J., ed. *The Gay-Lesbian Literary Heritage.* New York: Henry Holt & Company, 1995.

—Jane Jurgens

Blanche Wiesen Cook

1941-

American historian

An international activist for peace, human rights, and the environment, Blanche Wiesen Cook energetically uses historical research and journalism to reinforce her activism for personal freedoms and the revelation of truth. Working with a wide network of committed women, Cook's campaigns include gaining public access to classified documents, anti-militarism, women's rights, global pollution, and sexual freedoms. Her personal commitments often replicate the passions and convictions of the subjects of her research—the social reformer and feminist Crystal Eastman, Henry Street Settlement founder Lillian Wald, President Dwight David Eisenhower, and first lady Eleanor Roosevelt.

Peace Research Focus of Early Activism

Born 20 April 1941 in New York City to Sadonia Ecker, an educational and legal secretary, and David Theodore Wiesen, a food importer and later a bus driver active with Mike Quill's New York Transport Worker's Union, Cook grew up in a nonpolitical home with her younger sister, Marjorie. She attended New York City schools, graduating from Flushing High School in 1958, where she excelled in sports. Her political activism began at Hunter College, where she was elected president of the student council, and student affairs vice-president of the National Students Association (NSA). Subsequently, her dissatisfaction with the NSA's stand on racial issues led her to help found Students for a Democratic Society (SDS). Cook continued her political activities as a graduate student at Johns Hopkins University, where in 1964 she and her dissertation supervisor, American historian Charles Barker, helped found the Council of Peace Research in History (now the Peace History Society); Cook served on its board, holding several offices, until 1989. Cook credits her time at Hopkins and the encouragement of Barker and historians Alfred Chandler and Frederic C. Lane with fostering her liberal vision. Her doctoral dissertation "Woodrow Wilson and the Antimilitarists," accepted with distinction unanimously in 1970, complemented her civil rights and anti-Vietnam activities as did her *Bibliography on Peace Research in History* (1969).

Educator, Broadcaster, Writer

Cook's concerns are wide-ranging. As an educator she has taught at Hampton Institute (1963-64), Stern College of Yeshiva University (1964-1967), and since 1968 at John Jay College of Criminal Justice, City University of New York. She was appointed professor of history and of women's studies at the graduate center, CUNY, in 1987, and is now distinguished professor. She has held visiting professorships at West Point, UCLA, and Hunter. Her seminars cover women in politics; women and social change; twentieth-century international politics; biography and autobiography; and history, literature and politics of the gay and lesbian experience. Her articles appear in *Chrysalis, Radical History Review, Women's Studies Quarterly, Signs,* and *Feminist Studies.* From 1991-94, Cook served as vice-president for research of the American Historical Association, and she served as a member of the board of directors of the Institute for Media Analysis.

As a journalist, Cook contributes frequently to a number of periodicals, including *Women's Review of Books, New Directions for Women, Ms, New York Times, Los Angeles Times,* and *Newsday.* From 1974-77 she contributed to the syndicated feature "One Woman's Voice." Recent columns and addresses have covered the legacy and future of the United Nations and criticism directed at first ladies Eleanor Roosevelt and Hilary Rodham Clinton. Beyond print, during 1975-76 Cook appeared as a panelist on William F. Buckley's televised *Firing Line.* In 1979, she began producing and broadcasting her own radio show for Radio Pacifica (WBAI in New York and KPFK in Los Angeles); her show "Women and the World in the 1980s" subsequently became "Activists and Agitators" from 1986-1989, then "Women and the World in the 1990s" and "Broadsides" in 1996. Her film consultancies include *Cold War: USA; Women Make Movies;* the Emmy-winner *Before Stonewall;* David Brubin's *FDR; Transcending Silences: the Life and Poetic Legacy of Audre Lorde;* and the Arts & Education channel's *Eleanor Roosevelt.*

Concurrently, Cook continued her "hard history" research on two twentieth-century figures: President Dwight David Eisenhower and lawyer Crystal Eastman, co-founder of the Woman's Peace Party of New York. Cook's decade of research for *The Declassified Eisenhower: A Divided Legacy of Peace and Political Warfare* (1981), a *New York Times Book Review* Notable Book of 1981, led naturally to her participation in the Forty-Eighth American Assembly "The Records of Public Officials," whose work resulted in changes in federal law regarding presidential records. Her essay "The Dwight David Eisenhower Library: Manuscript Fiefdom at Abilene" (1977) was published by the Organization of American Historians, an organization for which Cook served as co-founder and co-chair of the Freedom of Information and Access Committee during the early 1980s. As senior editor (1970-1980) for the Garland Library of War and Peace, she wrote introductory essays for many volumes, including reprints of works by Helena Swanwick, Marie Degan, and Jane Addams. Simultaneously, Cook was completing work on her edition *Crystal Eastman: On Women and Revolution* (Oxford, 1978), an undertaking begun in the mid-60s before Cook was consciously a feminist and which reflects her keen attention to repossessing women's history and combating the historical denial of lesbianism.

Women's Support Networks

In "Female Support Networks and Political Activism," an essay which offers a broad definition of "lesbian," Cook wrote "the personal is the political: ... Networks of love and support are crucial to our ability as women to work in a hostile world ... Frequently the networks of love and support that enable politically and professionally active women to function independently and intensively consist largely of other women." Cook enjoys just such a feminist support network.

Central to that group is playwright and psychotherapist Clare Coss, Cook's partner of 27 years who, to use Cook's words, makes "my life crackle and leap" (interview). Indicative of their interests, they met, while Cook was briefly married to Sam Cook, a librarian, at a Vietnam protest meeting of the Women's International League of Peace and Freedom. While a student at Hunter, Cook met the poet Audre Lorde (1934-1992). These three form the nucleus of a nurturing academic, artistic New York intellectual support group which includes, among others, the historians Joan Kelly (1928-1982) and Alice Kessler-Harris, Carroll Smith Rosenberg, and Sandy Cooper. Mutually criticizing and cross-fertilizing one another's work, these women often publish, serve on committees, or travel to or organize meetings together. Cook remembers integrating eateries in Baltimore with Lorde, her children, and other friends in 1963. Along with working with Bella Abzug on environmental issues, in 1989 with Amy Swerdlow she represented the United States at a global conference on women, peace and the environment in Russia. Cook also serves on the board of the East End Gay Organization and belongs to the Gay Women's Alternative, the Biography Seminar of the New York Institute on the Humanities at New York University, and the Columbia University Seminar on Women and Society.

Best Seller on Eleanor Roosevelt Earns Honors

To "Why Eleanor?" Cook replied, "I've spent most of my vital youth with one dead general. Why not?" Actually, after her strong review of an unsympathetic book about Lorena Hickok, Eleanor Roosevelt's friend, others urged Cook to write about Roosevelt. At the Roosevelt Library in Hyde Park, Cook discovered an unknown Eleanor Roosevelt. Cook's national bestseller, *Eleanor Roosevelt, Volume One 1884-1933* (1992), offers an energized, provocative reading of ER's public and private lives, especially of the development of her concerned political activism and of her feminist associates and intimate friendships with bodyguard Earl Miller and journalist Lorena Hickok. In 1992, the "ardently feminist biography" won the *Los Angeles Times* Book Award for Biography, Feminist of the Year Award from the Feminist Majority Foundation, and the LAMBDA Literary Award. Volume two will carry the biography to 1945. Honored as the 1996 Scholar of the Year by the New York Council for the Humanities, Cook spoke on "Eleanor Roosevelt: Women and Power" at the recognition dinner.

An activist who employs her history and journalism for the empowerment of others, Cook's mandate, as she sees it, is "not *just* to tell a story. I'm telling a story out of a great sense of urgency so that people can make connections. I'm not an antiquarian. Like Marc Bloch, I'm interested in how things move and develop and involve people" (interview). When she wrote that Crystal Eastman believed that "women should seek and use power to transform society and to change the conditions of their private lives" (*Women in Culture and Politics,* 358-59), Cook was also writing of herself.

Current Address: Department of History, John Jay College of Criminal Justice, City University of New York, 445 West 59th Street, New York, New York 10019-1104.

References:

Contemporary Authors, Volumes 53-56. Detroit: Gale Research, 1975.

Cook, Blanche Wiesen, ed. *Bibliography on Peace Research in History.* Santa Barbara, Caliofornia: American Bibliographic Center, Clio Press, 1969.

———. *Crystal Eastman on Women and Revolution.* Oxford: Oxford University Press, 1978.

———. *The Declassified Eisenhower: A Divided Legacy of Peace and Political Warfare.* New York: Doubleday, 1981

———. "The Dwight David Eisenhower Library: Manuscript Fiefdom at Abilene," in *Access to the Papers of Recent Public Figures,* Alonzo Hamby and Edward Weldon, eds. Organization of American Historians, 1977.

———. *Eleanor Roosevelt: Volume One 1884-1933.* New York: Viking, 1992.

———. "Feminism, Socialism, and Sexual Freedom," in *Women in Culture and Politics: A Century of Change,* Judith Friedlander, Blanche Wiesen Cook, Alice Kessler-Harris, Carroll Smith-Rosenberg, eds. Indiana University Press, 1984.

———. Interview with Judith C. Kohl, 19 April 1996.

———. "The Historical Denial of Lesbianism," in *Radical History Review,* Spring/Summer 1979, no. 20: 60-66.

———. "The Life of Lorena Hickok: ER's Friend," in *Feminist Studies,* Fall 1980.

———. "One First Lady to Another," in *New York Times,* 17 January 1996.

———. "The Disunited Nations," *Los Angeles Times Book Review,* 11 February 1996.

———. "U.S. Risks Eleanor Roosevelt's Legacy," in *Newsday,* 7 July 1995.

———. "Women Alone Stir My Imagination: Lesbianism in the Cultural Tradition," in *Signs,* no. 40, 1979: 718-39.

———. *Women and Support Networks* (includes "Women Against Economic and Social Repression," a speech delivered at the international conference in women's history "Women and Power: Dimensions of Women's Historical Experience," 18 November 1979, College Park, Maryland, and "Female Support Networks and Political Activism: Lillian Wald, Crystal Eastman, Emma Goldman, Jane Addams," revised reprint from *Chrysalis,* Autumn 1977). Brooklyn, New York: Out & Out Books, 1979.

———. "Women, Peace and the Environment: A Review Essay," in *The Women's Review of Books,* 1991.

——— and others. *Passion: Women on Women.* Sound recordings, two cassettes; Cook reads excerpts from *Eleanor Roosevelt.* DoveAudio, 1995.

——— and others. Introduction, *Women, History, and Theory: The Essays of Joan Kelly.* Chicago: University of Chicago Press, 1984: xv-xxvi.

Harrison, Cynthia. Rev. of *Eleanor Roosevelt, Volume One 1884-1933,* in *American Historical Review,* February 1993, no. 98: 123-24.

Kennedy, David M. "Review of Cook, *Eleanor Roosevelt,* " in *New York Times Book Review,* 19 April 1992.

Ward, G. C. "Outing Mrs. Roosevelt," in *New York Review of Books* 24 September 1992: 49-52.

Who's Who in America, 49th edition, 1995. New Providence, New Jersey: Marquis Who's Who, 1994.

Who's Who of American Women, 17th edition, 1991-1992. Wilmette, Illinois: Marquis Who's Who, 1991.

—Judith C. Kohl

Aaron Copland

1900-1990

American composer

Aaron Copland, one of the United States' most honored cultural figures, created concert music uniquely American in sound and spirit. Several of his works—*Appalachian Spring, Lincoln Portrait, Fanfare for the Common Man*—have become national classics. Among his many honors were the Presidential Medal of Freedom, the Congressional Gold Medal, and the Kennedy Center Award. He won an Oscar for his movie score to *The Heiress,* a Grammy for the *Suite* from his opera *The Tender Land,* and the Pulitzer Prize for the ballet *Appalachian Spring.* Hailed as the "Dean of American composers," Copland was tireless in his support of American music and generous in his encouragement of others.

A Son of Brooklyn

Born in Brooklyn, New York, on 14 November 1900, Aaron Copland was the fifth and youngest child of Harris Morris Copland and his wife, Sarah Mittenthal Copland. Harris Copland was born in Lithuania in 1860. At the age of seventeen, like many European Jewish boys of his generation, he emigrated to America. Somewhere in the transition the family name, "Koplan" or "Kaplan," was translated as "Copland."

When Sarah Mittenthal was six or seven, her family came to America from a small village on the Russian-Polish border. She was raised in Chillicothe and Peoria, Illinois, and later in Dallas, Texas. The Mittenthals moved to New York City when Sarah was nineteen, and she married Harris Copland in 1885. By the time Aaron was born, his father was proprietor of H.M. Copland's department store on Washington Avenue in Brooklyn. The family lived above the store, and Mrs. Copland and the children helped out in the business.

Musical Beginnings

As a child, Copland heard violin-and-piano duets played at home by his oldest brother Ralph and sister Laurine. Aaron coaxed Laurine into teaching him piano, then moved on to private lessons. After youthful attempts at songwriting, Copland in 1917 began the study of musical composition with Ruben Goldmark, his first important influence. Goldmark gave Copland a solid grounding in the fundamentals, but to Copland's dismay his mentor was not fond of the new musical idioms and experiments of the day.

Copland studied with Goldmark until 1921. During this period he was an avid concert-goer, and read about the more controversial composers—Stravinsky, Schoenberg, Ornstein, Mahler, Sibelius—in Paul Rosenfeld's commentaries in the *Dial,* an avant garde monthly. By the time Copland graduated from Boys High School in 1918, he had already decided not to attend college, but to pursue a musical career instead. His studies were supplemented by various jobs playing piano, from Brooklyn's Finnish Socialist Hall to several hotels in the Catskills.

The Lure of Paris

Copland's good friend Aaron Schaffer was studying at the Sorbonne in Paris, and provided a steady correspondence detailing artistic life there, including accounts of contemporary musical events. When Copland read in *Musical America* magazine that the French government was planning to establish a summer school for American musicians at the Palace of Fountainbleau, he was the first to apply, and was awarded a scholarship.

Copland also arranged that at the end of the summer he would share an apartment in Paris with a distant cousin. Thus began a lifelong friendship with Harold Clurman, later known as a writer, critic, and one of the founders of the Group Theatre.

First Voyage: Paris 1921-1924

Copland sailed for France in June 1921. At Fountainbleau he made an important connection. Upon the urging of a friend, he reluctantly agreed to sit in on a harmony class. The instructor, Nadia Boulanger, so impressed Copland that he determined to study with her when he returned to Paris.

Copland's stay at Fountainbleau also yielded the first sale of his work. At the intermission of a student concert, he was approached by Jacques Durand—Debussy's publisher—who expressed interest in *Le Chat et la souris (The Cat and the Mouse)*. For the piece, Copland received the grand total of 500 francs ($32.50).

Nadia Boulanger's musical knowledge was vast and she had invaluable contacts. Her Wednesday teas would draw writers, painters, and the *creme de la creme* of composers: Stravinsky, Milhaud, Poulenc, Roussel, Ravel, Villa-Lobos, Saint-Saens. Copland flourished under her strict and caring discipline. Another of her American students, Virgil Thomson, became a longtime Copland colleague.

In 1924, when it was announced in Paris that the famous Russian conductor Serge Koussevitsky would be leading the Boston Symphony Orchestra the following season, "Mademoiselle" took Copland to see him. The composer was later fond of telling friends, including this author, that at the end of the meeting, the charismatic conductor declared with a flourish, "You vill write a concerto for organ, Mademoiselle Boulanger vill play it, and *I*, Koussevitsky, vill conduct!"

A Tumultuous American Debut

The Boston performance was preceded by the work's premiere with the New York Symphony in December 1924. As Copland noted in his autobiography (1984), conductor Walter Damrosch, aware that this modern piece might ruffle his audience's traditional sensibilities, declared from the stage: "If a gifted young man can write a symphony like this at twenty-three, within five years he will be ready to commit *murder!*"

Aaron Copland

Copland had made a sensational debut. But even in those early years, he was also interested in helping promote the cause of new music. In 1928, with composer Roger Sessions, he organized the Copland-Sessions Concerts of Contemporary Music. In the first of four successful seasons, works by eleven American composers were featured.

For several years in the 1930s, Copland wrote the "Scores and Records" column for *Modern Music* magazine. In 1937, his "opera for school children," *The Second Hurricane*, with libretto by Edwin Denby and directed by Orson Welles, was performed by a student cast at New York's Henry Street Settlement.

Songs of the People

Though certain of Copland's pieces (for example, *Piano Variations* and *Statements for Orchestra* both written about 1930) were considered "difficult," another characteristic of his music was also beginning to emerge—Copland's use of indigenous folk themes. *Vitebsk* (1929) incorporated Jewish folk tunes; *El Salon Mexico* (1937), written at the request of Copland's great friend, composer Carlos Chavez, used themes heard in Mexican cantinas; cowboy songs were the inspiration for *Billy the Kid* (1938), commissioned for Lincoln Kirstein's Ballet Caravan. More Western tunes were used for *Rodeo* (1942), choreographed and danced by Agnes de Mille with the Ballet Russe de Monte Carlo. Dance rhythms heard in Havana influenced *Danzon Cubano* (1942). Copland's *Clarinet Concerto* (1948), written for Benny Goodman, was inspired by American jazz.

Copland's most famous use of folk themes was his adaptation of the Quaker hymn "Simple Gifts" in *Appalachian Spring*, the ballet he wrote for dancer/choreographer Martha Graham in 1944. This is perhaps his most enduring and popular work.

Music and Politics

During the World War II years, Copland produced the dramatic *Lincoln Portrait* (1942), with its quotes from the Gettysburg Address, and the stirring *Fanfare for the Common Man* (1943). His important *Third Symphony* (1946) incorporated elements of *Fanfare*. Later quintessentially American pieces are two sets of *Old American Songs (Newly Arranged)* (1950 and 1952), as well as *Twelve Poems of Emily Dickinson* (1950).

Copland toured Latin America on behalf of the coordinator of inter-American affairs (1941) and the State Department (1947). William W. Austin noted in the *New Grove Dictionary of American Music* that Copland "in many ways ... exemplified the 'good neighbor policy' of Franklin Roosevelt—Copland's Americanism was always more neighborliness than chauvinism."

Though not a very political man, Copland was summoned in 1953 by the U.S. Senate Permanent Subcommittee on Investigations and interrogated by its chairman, Senator Joseph McCarthy, the infamous anti-communist. The committee took no action against Copland, but as a result of the publicity, several concerts, commissions and honors were cancelled, and his passport was tied up for some time.

Copland welcomed the opportunity to write for films, and enjoyed his brief stays in Hollywood working with the excellent studio orchestras. His feature-length scores, which set a new standard, were: *Of Mice and Men* (1939), *Our Town* (1940), *The North Star* (1943), *The Red Pony* (1948), *The Heiress* (1949), and *Something Wild* (1961).

Tanglewood, Koussevitsky, and Bernstein

One of Copland's longest affiliations was with the Berkshire Music Center at Tanglewood in Lenox, Massachusetts. This largest and most famous of American summer music festivals was founded by Serge Koussevitsky. Beginning in 1940, Copland spent twenty-one out of twenty-five summers at Tanglewood, teaching, lecturing, conducting and composing.

Also an integral part of Tanglewood was Copland's dear friend, composer and conductor Leonard Bernstein. They originally met in 1937 when Bernstein, a Harvard junior, had astonished Copland with a dazzling rendition of Copland's *Piano Variations*. They became close personal and professional friends. As a conductor, Bernstein championed Copland's music, and in the late 1960s when Copland's composing years were ending, Bernstein helped him establish a conducting career. In short, Bernstein adored Aaron, and Copland got a kick out of the flamboyant "Lenny."

In the 1960s, Copland's work took a new direction as he turned to serialism and a twelve-tone technique. His *Connotations for Orchestra* (1961-62) and *Inscape* (1967) have a harsher, more dissonant sound than his earlier works, and though not as popular, have been critically praised.

A Good Citizen of the Republic of Music

Copland served as president of the American Composers Alliance, the American Academy of Arts and Letters, and was an early and important member of ASCAP, the American Society of Authors, Composers and Publishers.

Teaching at the New School for Social Research in New York inspired Copland's first book, *What to Listen for In Music* (New York: McGraw-Hill, 1939). That was followed by *Our New Music* (New York: Whittlesey House, 1941), later revised and updated as *The New Music, 1900-1960* (New York: W.W. Norton, 1968). In 1951 Copland was appointed Norton Professor of Poetics at Harvard University, the first American composer to hold that position. His lectures there were later published as *Music and Imagination* (Cambridge: Harvard University Press, 1952). *Copland on Music* (New York: Doubleday, 1960) consisted of selected essays.

Copland also helped popularize serious music by appearing as speaker, pianist, or conductor on fifty-nine television programs between 1959 and 1972.

Moderation and Wit

Well-spoken, with an easygoing yet droll sense of humor, Copland was an even-tempered man, a gentleman. While musically and intellectually he was open to new ideas, his personal style was simple and unpretentious. "Home" was a utilitarian studio in New York City, then a converted barn in Ossining, New York. In 1960 he bought a comfortable yet rustic house overlooking the Hudson River in Peekskill, New York. There, at "Rock Hill," he spent the next thirty years.

His long-term composer colleagues included William Schuman, Elliott Carter, David Diamond, Ned Rorem and Paul Bowles. Boosey & Hawkes of London remained his music publisher from the day in 1938 when British composer Benjamin Britten introduced Copland to the firm. In his eighties, Copland published two volumes of autobiography, written with Vivian Perlis, director of the American music oral history project at Yale University.

A Private Life

Copland never officially came out, though he was quite relaxed and open with friends. His most important relationship was with photographer Victor Kraft, a younger, darkly handsome man who grew quite tempestuous. Kraft, who later married and fathered a son, died in 1976, after he and Copland had known each other for forty-four years. Copland's friend Paul Moor wrote in the *Advocate* (January 15, 1991), "One cannot question Victor's deep, lifelong love for Aaron and his sometimes fierce protectiveness of him. Over the years, Aaron did have other primary male relationships—in at least one, he even shared his house—but as long as Victor lived, he occupied a unique position in Aaron's cosmos."

Copland was a musical genius, perhaps the greatest composer the United States has ever produced. He traveled the world as an ambassador for new music, and was honored by many nations. Over forty colleges and universities granted him doctorates, and in 1982 Queens College of the City University of New York founded the Aaron Copland School of Music. Upon his death, his papers were presented to the Library of Congress. The bulk of his estate was used to establish the Aaron Copland Fund, for the support of young composers.

References:

"Aaron Copland." Brochure, London: Boosey & Hawkes, 1996.

Austin, William W. "Aaron Copland" in *The New Grove Dictionary of American Music*. London: Macmillan Press Ltd., 1986.

Copland, Aaron. Conversations with Michael E. O'Connor, 1983-87.
Copland, Aaron, and Vivian Perlis. *Copland: 1990 through 1942.* New York: St. Martin's/Marek, 1984.
Copland, Aaron, and Vivian Perlis. *Copland: Since 1943.* New York: St. Martin's, 1989.
Moor, Paul. "Fanfare for an Uncommon Man" in *Advocate* (January 15, 1991): 54-55.

—Michael E. O'Connor

Tee A. Corinne

1943-

American artist

Tee Corinne's career as an artist began in 1965 after she received her B.A. at the University of South Florida (Tampa) that same year. In 1968 she earned her M.F.A. at the Pratt Institute in Brooklyn, where she studied drawing with Calvin Albert and photography with John Civardi. The subject matter on which she primarily focuses her camera is fourfold: the alcoholic family (as in *Family: Growing Up in an Alcoholic Family* [North Vancouver, B.C.: Gallerie, 1990]), sexual molestation, lesbian identity, and erotica. Corinne has gained national attention as one of the first feminist artists to explore those issues. She has, throughout her career, been primarily dedicated to three tasks—creating images of lesbians for lesbians, documenting lesbian artists, and fostering the work of other lesbian artists. She has been exhibiting her works nationally since 1965 and publishing in the women's movement press since 1974.

Corinne was born to Marjorie Isabelle Meares and Thomas Barnes Cutchin on 3 November 1943 in St. Petersburg, Florida, and spent her childhood there as well as in Islamorada. She grew up using her innate artistic talent to create healing images for herself while convalescing from childhood tuberculosis and physical child abuse. By the time she had graduated from high school, she had won a school art award and a national journalism prize. Corinne then traveled to New York City where she studied drawing, printmaking, and photography at the Pratt Institute.

After a brief, unhappy marriage, Corinne divorced and moved to San Francisco. Corinne, who describes herself as "a feminist and woman interested in reclaiming sexual power," was a leader in feminism and women's art several years before lesbian sex magazines appeared. Sexually explicit images were not yet available to women in the 1970s. The art Corinne later created developed from her experiences working with the San Francisco Sex Education Switchboard. It was in such organizations that women of the time learned to talk about sexuality and explore and create images of their own bodies. Corinne began to draw and do photography for the project and has since become a pioneer in the field.

The Influence of Sex Education and a Relationship

Corinne readily acknowledges the influence of Betty Dodson's book *Liberating Masturbation* (New York: Dobson, 1974) and the author's slide shows of lovemaking and genital imagery presented at women's workshops during the 1970s. Corinne's *Cunt Coloring Book* (San Francisco: Pearlchild Productions, 1975) developed out of her own work with the Sex Education Switchboard, was encouraged by Dodson, and quickly became instrumental in the reclamation of women's bodies. The workshop, Feminism, Sexuality and Lesbianism, was another profound experience for Corinne as she used her early drawings of female genitalia and cofacilitated with lesbian leader Sally Gearhart. In the spring of 1975, Corinne created photographs for *Loving Women,* the first lesbian sex manual. Nine women photographed themselves and each other for this book and those works, in turn, led to Corinne's current work with solarized photographic images.

From 1975 to 1977, Corinne's relationship with the photographer Honey Lee Cottrell informed her art. In her book *The Sex Lives of Daffodils: Growing Up As an Artist Who Also Writes,* Corinne states that while the two women were together she and Cottrell "explored color photography [and] the vibrancy of [their] relationship [was] reflected in the images." Corinne's images at the time changed from black-and-white pieces to color slides of women's genitals, photographs and slides of her partner, and close-up images of flowers and other erotica. Few lesbians, with the exception of Marilyn Gayle and Barbary Katherine in *What Lesbians Do* (Eugene, Oregon: Godiva, 1975), were publishing lesbian art or literature at the time. After her partnership with Cottrell dissolved, Corinne began graduate study at the Institute for Advanced Study in Human Sexuality in San Francisco where notable faculty members included Phyllis Lyon (cofounder of the Daughters of Bilitis, the first national lesbian organization) and Wardell Pomeroy, who had interviewed the sexologist Alfred Kinsey. She also briefly studied at the Kinsey Institute in Indiana. Both experiences allowed her to research representations of lesbian erotica and encouraged her to continue her work.

Lesbian Art Exhibitions Begin

With the publication of a cover for *A Woman's Touch* (1979, 1982) and the 16 color plates in *I Am My Lover* (Burlingame, California: Down There Press, 1978), it was immediately apparent that Corinne's use of sexual imagery was revolutionary. The close-up images of female genitalia were simultaneously confrontational and empowering. In the more symbolic work, *Yantras of Womanlove* (Tallahassee, Florida: Naiad Press, 1982), solarized photographs of lovemaking and labia made visual the mystery of sexual feeling. Some of the works included in that publication also became part of the groundbreaking exhibition at the University of California, Berkeley, *In a Different Light: Visual Culture, Sexual Identity, Queer Practice.*

Living in Brooklyn from 1979 to 1981, Corinne showed works at the Womanart Gallery in Manhattan, but was excluded from an exhibition of lesbian art because of the "sexual nature" of her work. One of her images was, however, included in an exhibition of artists who had been published in a portfolio of the *Advocate* held at the Hibbs Gallery. Corinne and Dr. James Saslow (Queens College) delivered innovative lectures on homosexuality in erotic art during the exhibition. In 1980 Corinne was invited to participate in GALAS (the Great American Lesbian Art Show) held at the Women's Building in Los Angeles. At this exhibition, ten lesbians were honored for their work and willingness to share their sexual orientation with the public.

A Focus on Photography and Research

During 1979 and 1980 Corinne, Carol Newhouse, and lesbian photographer Joan E. Biren traveled cross-country teaching in the

Feminist Photography Ovulars, founded by Ruth and Jean Mountaingrove. The group's name was purposefully chosen over "seminar," the meaning of which derives from seminate or semen. This was, clearly, meant to be a woman's community in which feminist photographers camped in woodland settings, created their own images, and discussed their work. From 1981 to 1984 Corinne created works for *The Blatant Image: A Magazine of Feminist Photography,* which she had planned with the Mountaingroves and Caroline Overman since the autumn of 1980. It was designed to be accessible to all women, strongly feminist in nature, and its images were created to confront the viewer.

It was also at this time that Corinne began to conduct research on the American photographer Bernice Abbott at her home in Blanchard, Maine. Since Abbott did not want to discuss being a lesbian, Corinne could not explore her work honestly until after the older woman died in December of 1991. Corinne finally presented a paper on Abbott's photographs of other lesbians at the national conference of the College Art Association in 1996. Corinne's own research efforts on lesbian artists have led her to openly lament the absence of biographies, the inadequacies of the few that do exist, and the fragility of means for preserving our histories and artworks. In addition, her national reputation as a researcher on the lesbian aesthetic, lesbian photographers, and the lesbian artists of 1920s Paris have afforded her the opportunity to present other research in papers at the College Art Association (1991 and 1994-96) and the Women's Caucus for Art (1983, 1986, 1988, 1989, 1993, 1994), among others. Corinne cofounded the Lesbian/Bisexual Caucus of the Women's Caucus for Art in 1993 and the Gay and Lesbian Caucus, an affiliated society of the College Art Association, in 1989. She also served as cochair with Edward Sullivan of the latter from 1990 to 1992.

Out of concern for documenting the lives of lesbian artists and preserving their works, Corinne began to photograph lesbian authors when she attended conferences. She is also a founder of SO CLAP! (The Southern Oregon Country Lesbian Archival Project), which interviews and solicits materials from lesbians in the region. Those materials are then combined with published sources and deposited in lesbian and gay archives around the country. In addition, finding galleries unreceptive to lesbian-themed work and desiring to make both lesbian and female sexuality visible, Corinne has always decided to self-publish and used small women's presses to create a wide audience for her own work. She sends copies of her artist's books to the library of the Museum of Modern Art, the Lesbian Herstory Archives in New York City, the National Museum of Women in the Arts, the Gay and Lesbian Art Archives at Oberlin College, and the Gay and Lesbian Center of the San Francisco Public Library.

Current Address: P.O. Box 278, Wolf Creek, Oregon 97497.

References:

Corinne, Tee A. *The Sex Lives of Daffodils: Growing Up As an Artist Who Also Writes.* Wolf Creek, Oregon: Pearlchild Press, 1994.

———. *Wild Lesbian Roses: Essays on Art, Rural Living and Creativity.* Unpublished papers delivered at conferences and full versions of published, edited articles. Photocopy, 1996.

—Ray Anne Lockard

Midge Costanza

1934-

American politician

Midge Costanza, politician, activist and lecturer, the first woman to be in the inside circle of presidential advisers, was President Jimmy Carter's presidential assistant for public liaison, his "window to the nation." As John Mitchell of the Los Angeles Times noted, "She met with groups representing women, the young, senior citizens, veterans, minorities and the handicapped and she served as an advocate of federal funding for abortions and the equal rights amendment." Costanza held the first White House meeting with gay activists in March 1977.

Born in Rochester, New York, in 1934, Margaret (Midge) Costanza was one of four children. Her father owned a sausage company. "I didn't grow up in wealth, but we never starved. I went to school and had opportunities," she told the *Washington Post* in 1977.

Costanza entered politics in Rochester, setting up an office for Robert Kennedy. A Rochester reporter recalled: "It was a shoestring operation and she did everything from washing the walls ... to answering telephones and canvassing the voters. She's incredibly competitive, especially against men." She was elected to the Democratic National Committee in 1972, was vice-mayor of Rochester, served on Governor Carey's state task force on public authorities, was elected deputy mayor of Rochester in 1973 and ran unsuccessfully for the House of Representatives against longtime Republican Barber Conable, Jr. in 1974.

In an interview in 1985, Costanza recalled her introduction to Carter during her 1974 congressional campaign: "This man with a Southern accent called me on the phone and said, 'Hi, my name is Jimmy Carter. I'm the governor of Georgia and I've been looking over your position and I find that you and I are compatible.'" She continued, "I thought I had a nut on the phone. A Southerner compatible with me."

She was co-chair of Carter's 1976 New York campaign and gave the seconding speech for his nomination as the candidate for president at the 1976 Democratic National Convention. After Carter's election, Costanza was the only northerner to reach the inner circle of Carter advisers.

As presidential assistant for public liaison, Costanza and her staff of 10 (her predecessor in Gerald Ford's administration had had a staff of 21) "answered 68,000 letters, and reached nearly half a million people," she told *Parade Magazine*. "I made 400 personal appearances." Her outspokenness and her sharp sense of humor brought her into conflict with the administration. "The President advertised his Administration as being an open one, and I took the opportunity of exercising openness. I'm an advocate, but in the White House, only the President is allowed to be an advocate." Her comment in the first weeks of the Carter administration to the *Washington Post*, "Either I will function as a window for the President or I won't be in Washington" proved prophetic.

The controversial activities that eventually led to her resignation included the historic invitation of gay activists to the White House—at the time when administration was trying to ignore the gay rights issue brought to the fore by Anita Bryant's anti-gay campaign. Costanza also claimed she would like to "make bookends out of" Anita Bryant and anti-ERA activist Phyllis Schlafly. The National Gay Task Force, in a statement issued at the time, called the meeting "a happy milestone on the road to full equality under law for gay women and men."

Costanza has never left public life. She served as executive director of Shirley MacLaine's Higher Self seminars and as a vice president of a division of Alan Landsburg Productions (in 1985) producing films and advertisements for commercial clients, and as executive director of the American Task Force for the Homeless. She has served on the community board of Search Alliance, an AIDS research group, and on the board of the National Gay Rights Alliance.

Costanza has also not ceased her involvement in political life. She served as campaign coordinator for California Senator Barbara Boxer in 1992 and more recently as San Diego County campaign manager for Kathleen Brown's failed run for governor in California in 1994.

References:

Bachrach, Judy. "Midge Costanza: The View from the Ground Floor," in *Washington Post*, July 26, 1978.

Barbash, Fred. "Midge Costanza Resigns: Colorful, Outspoken Presidential Aide" in *Washington Post*, August 1, 1978.

Broder, David S. "N.Y. Woman to Be Named Carter Aide" in *Washington Post*, January 1, 1976.

De Witt, Karen. "Midge Costanza: President Carter's 'Window on the Nation'" in *Washington Post*, April 26, 1977.

"Former Carter aide seeks Higher self" in *USA Today*, May 27, 1987.

"Gay Rights Leaders Greeted in White House for 1st Time" in *Washington Post*, March 27, 1978.

Marelius, John. "Brown Wallops Wilson as Out-of-Touch Leader: Democrats Fired up by Coronado Speech" in *San Diego Union-Tribune*, September 11, 1994.

Mitchell, John L. "Midge Costanza, Carter Aide, Recalls Life in the Fishbowl" in *Los Angeles Times*, January 26, 1985.

Petrillo, Lisa. "Women 'Credit' Judge at Empowerment Seminar" in *San Diego Union-Tribune*, September 20, 1992.

Satchell, Michael. "Midge Costanza: It Was a Matter of Style" in *Parade Magazine*, March 25, 1979.

Stein, Jeannine. "Midge Costanza, NGRA Board Member Trio Honored for AIDS Work" in *Los Angeles Times*, April 17, 1989.

Walsh, Edward. "Costanza Defends Carter on Recruitment of Women" in *Washington Post*, January 28, 1977.

Wielawski, Irene. "Panel Says Insurance Plan Lacks Funding" in *Los Angeles Times*, December 9, 1990.

Wilkie, Curtis. "Read Her Lips" in *The Boston Globe*, October 25, 1992.

—Richard Voos

Quentin Crisp

1908-

British entertainer

Quentin Crisp has been the subject of many interviews, a documentary, as well as a song by Sting, "Englishman in New York;" he has authored countless articles, reviews, and opinion editorials (which could be said to define all of his writings regardless of their announced genre) as well as a series of books: *How to Have a Lifestyle*, *How to Go to the Movies*, and *The Naked Civil Servant*. In addition, he has appeared in Calvin Klein ads for CK1, in photographs published in the *Village Voice* and in the film *Philadelphia* as an extra. Most recently, at the age of 88, he has been interviewed about the history of cinema for the documentary *The Celluloid Closet*. From this epic catalogue of accomplishments, Crisp's most important contribution to literature must still be his 1968 autobiography *The Naked Civil Servant* which in itself merely chronicles his more important contribution to the twentieth century: his unwavering dedication to the "profession of being," a profession that requires the individual to cultivate a unique "style." Indeed, all these cameos, articles, and sound bytes return him to this central idea of witty/campy self-presentation.

Though he speaks endlessly about himself, Crisp provides little of the information from which biographies are written. Yet even though his writings are more philosophical than biographical, one can still piece together some of the more conventional aspects of biography. *The Naked Civil Servant* chronicles his life from 1908 to 1968, *An Evening with Quentin Crisp* (1979, available on CD) picks up from there, and Jonathon Nossiter's *Resident Alien* documents Crisp's life from 1982 to 1992. Quentin Crisp, whose first name was Denis before he (in his words) "dyed" it, was born in 1908 in Sutton, England. His family lived in debt and ultimately had to move to a smaller house and release the live-in servants during the First World War. He attended a small boarding school where he claims to have only learned that his "great gift was for unpopularity." Next, he briefly attended King's College, London, where he studied journalism.

Throughout his early twenties, Crisp felt the pressures of both finding a job and confronting his sexuality, two issues that simultaneously found resolution via each other while Crisp was wandering though the streets of London's West End. There he saw men, some of whom were prostitutes, who adopted a campy style of flamboyant dress and cosmetics as an expression of their homosexuality. Crisp immediately followed suit. He sat with these men at the Black Cat on Compton Street in Soho, compared lipstick and chatted the nights away. His effeminate dress should not be confused with drag though, for the effect of drag, he claims in his 1968 biography, would "make me look less feminine." Even as Crisp's career changed from prostitution to art, he maintained this flamboyant appearance. His subsequent professions have been various—architectural copying, advertising, free-lance commercial art, writing, criticism, and modeling—yet they all center on the world of images and representation, which, arguably, laid the groundwork for his life profession of being a stylist. For example, Crisp explains in *The Naked Civil Servant* that although he never had formal training for the theater, he nevertheless took to the stage effortlessly because his "whole life was an unsympathetic part played to a hostile audience." The meaningless drudgery of these jobs was brought to a halt with the television broadcast of *The Naked Civil Servant* which made Crisp an overnight sensation. From here, he entered the realm of celebrity, being asked to be a spokesperson on culture, style, art, and homosexuality, all of which he attacks, ironically, as impediments to style. The last significant moment in Crisp's biographical timeline is when he comes to live in New York City for the simple reason that people are friendlier there.

Crisp's Notion of Style

An Evening with Quentin Crisp can be listened to as a treatise on style. In it, he argues that since humanity cannot escape from some form of chains that bind, we must embrace chains of our own making: the chains of style. Style, most succinctly, is "an idiom arising spontaneously from the personality but deliberately maintained." That is to say, when Crisp began wearing cosmetics, he was only consciously presenting with pride a femininity which others had recognized in him as an unconscious tick. But style is not simply a deliberate presentation of what we are proud of; it must incorporate our deficits as well as our assets. Once one has polished up the raw identity into a lifestyle, one can do barter with the rest of the world. It was this bartering that got his life story on television and, as Crisp makes clear in *An Evening with Quentin Crisp*, television is the great adjunct of style. Style's main purpose, for Crisp, is to promote honest human contact. Socializing is his lifeline. He calls his social calendar "the sacred book" and he lists his number in the phone book with the expressed purpose of accepting any invitation out to lunch or dinner. He explains in *An Evening with Quentin Crisp* that when he is confronted with the line, "Now that you're rich and famous," he stops his interlocutor and responds: "I am not famous, I am notorious. And if I am rich it is because I have taken my wages in people. You are my reward."

Quentin Crisp

Crisp on Gay Lifestyle and Politics

Clearly, Crisp has to be seen as a forerunner of twentieth-century homosexual activism. As he writes in *The Naked Civil Servant*, by wearing cosmetics he "managed to shift homosexuality from being a burden to being a cause.... to a nature as dramatic as mine, not to deny rapidly became a protest." He also realized that having his autobiography on television would reach far more people than if it were at the cinema where "only homosexuals, and liberals wishing to be seen going to it" would learn about him. Basically, Crisp believes that the bored housewife will wade through two hours of Quentin Crisp sooner than 30 minutes of the nightly news. Yet, for all this "activism," Crisp seems rather disappointed in the gay movement. He cannot understand how a group of men so oppressed by convention and conformity would only arrive at another form of convention. Responding to the clone culture of the 1970s, Crisp notes that gay men all look exactly alike, a display that he reads as "conformity of the most absurd kind." Conversely, some of his advice to gay youth is ill-received by the gay community in that it sounds a bit too much like the military's "don't ask, don't tell" policy: "don't boast or conceal. Neither confirm nor deny."

The Profession of Being

According to Crispian philosophy, once one has cultivated one's style, one is ready to enter the profession of being. This rather slippery notion has allowed Crisp to be identified as a Philistine at large, a matriarch of manners, a doctor who is more ill than his patient, a mail-order guru, a court jester, and even a sort of tinted George Burns. All of these nominations bear up in relation to Crisp if for no other reason than his style, as he claims in *An Evening with Quentin Crisp*, intends for him to be not so much noticed, but recognized. And in that these names, some more accurate than others, perform the function of recognizing, they succeed in labeling Crisp. It is not so much the label he wears, but our need to label him, that makes Crisp's style.

Current Address: 46 East Third Street, New York, New York 10003.

References:

Crisp, Quentin. *The Naked Civil Servant.* Worcester, England: Duckworth, 1968.

———. *An Evening with Quentin Crisp.* DRG Records Incorporated, 1979. Compact Disc.

—Jon Hodge

Margaret Cruikshank

1940-

American educator

Margaret Cruikshank is recognized as a pioneer in the field of women's studies, as well as in the area of gay and lesbian studies.

As professor, author, editor, and reviewer, Cruikshank has been instrumental in attaining recognition and visibility for lesbians and lesbian studies within the women's movement and in academic settings.

Cruikshank was born in Duluth, Minnesota, on 26 April 1940. She attended Benedictine schools and ultimately received a degree in English from the College of St. Scholastica in 1962. She continued her education, receiving a Ph.D. in Victorian literature from Loyola University, Chicago, in 1969. She later returned to complete a masters degree in gerontology at San Francisco State. Cruikshank was the first woman post-doctoral fellow at St. John's Abbey in Minnesota, where she completed a biographical and critical study of historian Thomas Babington Macaulay. From 1970 to 1972, Cruikshank taught Victorian literature at Central College in Iowa.

Cruikshank was director of the women's studies program at Mankato State in Minnesota from 1975 to 1977. Her experiences resulted in the writing and publication of an autobiographical piece on lesbians in academia published in *Our Right to Love: A Lesbian Resource Book.* With this, and contributions to gay scholarship beginning in 1975, Cruikshank embarked upon a long writing career of bringing issues of importance to lesbians to the fore.

In the late 1970s and the 1980s, Cruikshank reviewed books for a wide variety of gay, lesbian, and women's studies publications, including *Gay Community News, Philadelphia Gay News,* the *Advocate,* and *Women's Review of Books.*

Cruikshank's first edited volume, *Lesbian Path,* broke new ground as one of the first collections of autobiographical tales written about the lives of lesbians. The work includes the writings of well-known artists, writers, and activists, as well as those not known until the book was published. These stories—many of which described the women's "coming out"—were of especially great importance in 1980, because many lesbians struggled with invisibility and isolation. The publication of the revised edition, just five years later, speaks to the continuing vitality and importance of the coming out stories, even as the assumption that increased media exposure lessens the need. In an Cruikshank edited anthology with Bonnie Zimmerman, *Lesbian Studies,* personal narratives are not only useful to decrease invisibility but they also chart the growth and development of the individual and the collective movement. *Lesbian Path* gives the interested reader the opportunity to see from whence we came.

According to Cruikshank, *Lesbian Studies* (1982) was conceived to record the history of the moment, as well as to clarify the origins, goals, and assumptions of lesbian studies. By including a variety of articles of interest to researchers and teachers alike, the writers hoped to replace ignorance with knowledge, add a political dimension to women's studies by insisting on the inclusion of lesbian-feminist issues, and to encourage a re-examination of the traditional ways of thinking. At the time of the book's development, the field of lesbian studies was very new and this anthology was an attempt to offer practical advice to teachers through the inclusion of syllabi, as well as to develop some conceptual frameworks for the continuing development of the field. A new edition of *Lesbian Studies,* edited by Zimmerman and Toni McNaron, was published by Feminist Press in the fall of 1996.

In recognition of the importance of lesbian research and scholarship, Stanford University Center for Research on Women named Cruikshank an affiliate scholar. She held this title from 1981 until 1988. Also in 1981, Cruikshank received an appointment to the faculty of the City College of San Francisco, where she continues to teach. City College is the home of the first gay and lesbian studies department in the country; while the department was not established until 1989, Cruikshank began teaching gay and lesbian literature at the college in 1982.

Margaret Cruikshank. ***Photograph by Barbara Giles.***

With the publication of *New Lesbian Writing* (1984), Cruikshank continued to encourage the publication of clearly "out" works by lesbians. This volume, edited by Cruikshank, contains fiction and non-fiction with entries from the United States, Canada, and a single entry from Australia. The collection includes writings by recognized and unpublished authors offering an opportunity for newer lesbian writers to gain the audience they deserve.

In the preface to *The Gay and Lesbian Liberation Movement,* Cruikshank states that the book is not a history of the struggle for gay and lesbian rights, but a personal and feminist interpretation of the movement by a writer who participated in it. She characterizes the movement for liberation as political, sexual, and as a movement of ideas. Within these frameworks, Cruikshank delves into the historical roots of the activist movements, and examines the forces inside and outside of the movement that contribute to its successes and failures. While the reader might wish for more personal recollections from Cruikshank, the book is an accessible overview which adds to a growing body of historical literature.

Cruikshank's latest editorial foray is *Fierce with Reality,* an anthology on aging. With this collection, Cruikshank applies her considerable editorial skills, and as she has with previous works on and about gays and lesbians, presents an issue not often talked about, thereby making it visible, and open for public discussion.

Current Address: City College of San Francisco, 50 Phelan Avenue, San Francisco, California 94112.

References:

Cruikshank, Margaret. In *Our Right to Love: A Lesbian Resource Book,* edited by Ginny Vida. Englewood Cliffs, New Jersey: Prentice-Hall, 1978, revised edition, 1996.

———. *Gay and Lesbian Liberation Movement.* New York: Routledge, 1992.

—Lisa W. Loutzenheiser

George Cukor

1899-1983

American film director

In a career that spanned half a century, George Cukor emerged as a major director, noted for crafting sophisticated films and eliciting excellent performances from actors. Several of his films—including *Dinner at Eight* (1933), *Camille* (1937), *The Philadelphia Story* (1940), *Adam's Rib* (1949), *Born Yesterday* (1950), *A Star Is Born* (1954), and *My Fair Lady* (1964)—are renowned as classics, while others, like the eccentric *Sylvia Scarlett* (1936), have become cult favorites. Although Cukor was known to be gay within the film community, his homosexuality remained a secret to the public until his death in 1983.

George Cukor was born in New York on 7 July 1899, to Victor and Helen Cukor, middle-class Jewish-Hungarian immigrants. Though his parents wanted him to become a lawyer, young Cukor fell in love with the theatre, and after briefly attending college he took several theatrical jobs in New York and Rochester, working his way up from assistant stage manager to stage manager, and finally, to director. By the late 1920s he had directed five Broadway plays, though none were great successes.

In 1929, he came to Hollywood as a "dialogue director," helping silent film directors cope with "talking pictures"; in that capacity, he contributed to Lewis Milestone's *All Quiet on the Western Front* (1930). Then, after co-directing three films, he graduated to solo directing assignments, the first being *Tarnished Lady* (1931) with Tallulah Bankhead. Other early Cukor films included: *What Price Hollywood?* (1932), later remade as *A Star Is Born,* and Katharine Hepburn's first film, *A Bill of Divorcement* (1932); but it was the following three remarkable films that established his reputation: *Dinner at Eight,* an all-star drama with John Barrymore, Lionel Barrymore, Wallace Beery, Marie Dressler, and Jean Harlow; *Little Women* (1933), with Hepburn; and *David Copperfield* (1933), effectively employing W. C. Fields as Mr. Micawber.

While little is known about his sexual activities in New York, Cukor in Hollywood settled into a homosexual lifestyle, enjoying innumerable brief affairs with anonymous young men without emotional attachments. He and his friends would cruise Los Angeles streets, looking for sexual partners, until an arrest—covered up by studio executives—led Cukor to stay home, relying on friends to bring attractive men to his weekend parties. In the 1960s, Cukor had a long-term relationship with George Towers, and while Towers later married, the men remained close friends.

George Cukor

It is hard to say exactly how Cukor's homosexuality affected his career. Although he declined to direct the film version of Tennessee Williams' *Cat on a Hot Tin Roof* because censors were removing the play's homosexual subtext, Cukor's films display little interest in gay characters or themes, except for the effeminate men in *Our Betters* (1933) and *Adam's Rib,* the shocking scene of two lesbians dancing in *A Woman's Face* (1941), and the spectacle of Hepburn dressed as a man in *Sylvia Scarlett.* The hallmarks of Cukor's direction—his sensitivity and skill in working with sometimes difficult actresses like Hepburn, Greta Garbo, Joan Crawford, and Judy Garland; his love for witty dialogue; and his concern for elegance in costumes and set decorations—have been attributed to a gay sensibility, but such comments may reflect stereotypical thinking. A tangible effect of his homosexuality was that Cukor was fired as director of *Gone with the Wind* (1939) because, according to Patrick McGilligan's *George Cukor: A Double Life,* the very masculine Clark Gable refused to be "directed by a fairy." Still, since a few of his scenes were used in the film, and since he continued to secretly coach Vivien Leigh and Olivia de Havilland, Cukor deserves some credit for the film's success.

Despite the unpleasant experience of *Gone with the Wind,* Cukor worked steadily in the 1930s and 1940s. Noteworthy achievements include: Garbo's finest film, *Camille;* two sparkling comedies with Hepburn and Cary Grant, *Holiday* (1938) and *The Philadelphia Story,* the latter also starring James Stewart in an Oscar-winning role; the all-female comedy *The Women* (1939); three films pairing Hepburn and Spencer Tracy, *Keeper of the Flame* (1943), *Adam's Rib,* and *Pat and Mike* (1952); and the Oscar-winning performances of Ingrid Bergman in *Gaslight* (1944), Ronald Colman in

A Double Life (1947), and Judy Holliday in *Born Yesterday.* During World War II, Cukor briefly served in the Army, but unable to obtain a prestigious, film-making position like other directors, he soon left military service.

In the 1950s, Cukor directed his first musical, *A Star Is Born,* with career-best performances by Garland and James Mason, but brutal, last-minute editing by the studio—a problem Cukor often faced—diminished its impact; the restored 1983 version better conveys the film's quality. He also directed two more films featuring Holliday, *The Marrying Kind* (1952) and *It Should Happen to You* (1954), the latter with Jack Lemmon in his first screen role. With Hollywood moving in new directions, Cukor's assignments became more eclectic: two more musicals, *Les Girls* (1957) with Gene Kelly and *Let's Make Love* (1960) with Marilyn Monroe; *Bhowani Junction* (1956), a romantic adventure set in India; *Heller in Pink Tights* (1960), a Western with Sophia Loren and Anthony Quinn leading a troupe of theatrical performers; and the lurid *Chapman Report* (1962) with a young Jane Fonda. In 1962, Cukor started another Monroe film, *Something's Got to Give,* but it was cancelled because of the actress's erratic behavior. Then came Cukor's greatest success: the musical *My Fair Lady* (1964), universally praised for its polish and fine performances, though plagued by controversy involving the casting of Audrey Hepburn as Eliza Doolittle instead of Julie Andrews, who had played the role on Broadway. Along with Oscars for Best Picture and Best Actor, for Rex Harrison, *My Fair Lady* also earned Cukor his only Oscar for direction.

Regardless of the triumph of *My Fair Lady,* the collapse of the studio system made it difficult for Cukor to find work, though he received growing critical attention and several honors, including an honorary degree from Loyola University in 1976. Five years after *My Fair Lady,* Cukor directed *Justine* (1969), a troubled production with actors Michael York and Anouk Aimée, whom Cukor disliked. *Travels with My Aunt* (1972) was better, though Maggie Smith seemed a poor substitute for Hepburn, who had withdrawn because she disliked the script. But Hepburn happily joined Laurence Olivier for Cukor's television movie *Love among the Ruins* (1975), a courtroom drama of autumnal romance that earned Emmys for Hepburn, Olivier, and Cukor; another television movie with Hepburn, *The Corn Is Green* (1979), proved less popular. The 1970s also brought Cukor's biggest disaster, *The Bluebird* (1976); though briefly involved with *The Wizard of Oz* (1939) as a possible director (he is credited with the decision to remove Garland's blonde wig), Cukor had never worked with fantasy or children's films, and the logistical problems of working in Russia with a multinational crew proved nightmarish. But his career ended with a nice flourish: *Rich and Famous* (1981), an elegant comedy that recalled Cukor's glory days in Hollywood and brought out Candice Bergen's comedic talents for the first time. He died in Hollywood of a heart attack on 23 January 1983.

Despite his successes, discussions of Cukor's career often drift to might-have-beens: films he never made, films he never should have made, films he lost control of, films that were butchered before release. Still, the films we have provide sufficient evidence of his enormous talents, and his lasting reputation as a superior director seems secure.

References:

Bernardoni, James. *George Cukor: A Critical Study and Filmography.* Jefferson, North Carolina: McFarland & Company, 1985.

Carey, Gary. *Cukor and Company: The Films of George Cukor and His Collaborators.* New York: Museum of Modern Art, 1971.

Clarens, Carlos. *George Cukor.* London: Secker & Warburg Limited, 1976.

Cukor, George. "The Director." In *Hollywood Directors: 1914-40,* edited by Richard Koszarski. New York: Oxford University Press, 1976: 355-68.

Estrin, Allen. *Capra, Cukor, Brown: The Hollywood Professionals,* Volume 6. South Brunswick: A. S. Barnes, 1980.

Gray, Beverly. "A Conversation with George Cukor," in *Performing Arts* (Los Angeles), August 1980: 12-18.

Lambert, Gavin. *On Cukor.* New York: G. P. Putnam's Sons, 1972.

Levy, Emanuel. *George Cukor, Master of Elegance: Hollywood's Legendary Director and His Stars.* New York: William Morrow and Company, 1994.

McGilligan, Patrick. *George Cukor: A Double Life.* New York: St. Martin's Press, 1991.

Overstreet, Richard. "George Cukor," in *Interviews with Film Directors,* edited by Andrew Sarris. New York: Avon Books, 1969: 92-126.

Phillips, Gene D. *George Cukor.* Boston: Twayne Publishers, 1982.

Powers, James. "Dialogue on Film: George Cukor," in *American Film* (Washington, D.C.), February 1978: 33-48.

—Gary Westfahl

Countee Cullen

1903-1946

African-American poet

Countee Cullen grew up in New York City and became the representative poet of the Harlem Renaissance. His writings overtly celebrated black consciousness and covertly expressed his love for men.

Early Career

As he wished, everything about his early years remains obscure. No record of his birthplace or the names of his natural mother or father survives. Cullen listed his date of birth as Saturday, 30 May 1903. His second wife remembered his going to Louisville, Kentucky, to bury his mother in the 1940s. His poem "Saturday's Child," claimed "Dame Poverty gave me my name,/ And Pain godfathered me." Another poem (dedicated to a lover, Eric Walrond) "Incident," suggests he lived in Baltimore from May to December, 1911 and remembered another boy there: "I smiled, but he poked out/ His tongue, and called me, 'Nigger.'"

Sometime after 1911, Countee appeared in Harlem and made the acquaintance of the Reverend Frederick A. Cullen, whose Salem Methodist Episcopal Church had grown from a storefront to a congregation of several thousand. A prominent member of the NAACP, Frederick Cullen met successfully with President Wilson along with W.E.B. DuBois and James Weldon Johnson in 1919 to save some condemned black soldiers.

The minister took a lively interest in the young men's boxing club, reportedly liked to use his wife's makeup, and unofficially

Countee Cullen

"adopted" Countee, who after 1918 identified himself as "Countee Cullen." Leaving his wife at home, Reverend Cullen took Countee (often accompanied by other male lovers) on trips to Jerusalem eleven times. In his poem "Fruit of the Flower," Cullen claimed that the man and the boy shared a "sacred sin."

With no other human were his ties so close as those with Frederick Cullen. When the elder man was in the hospital in 1945, his wife wrote Countee, "every thought of his has been for you." They both died in 1946 within a few months of each other—Countee on 9 January 1946, the Reverend Cullen in April.

In "Dark Tower," his regular column in the Urban League magazine *Opportunity*, Cullen wrote in 1928 that "there are some things, some truths of Negro life and thought, of Negro inhibitions, that all Negroes know, but take no pride in.... Every phase of Negro life should not be the white man's concern."

His adopted father enrolled Cullen in the DeWitt Clinton High School where he began a spectacular career. Only fourteen, he wrote "To the Swimmer;" *Modern School* published the Whitmanesque poem in May, 1918. Another precocious poem, "Life's Rendezvous," received first prize in a contest sponsored by the Federation of Women's Clubs. At New York University (1922-25), Cullen continued to write poetry, publish it, and win prizes; he graduated Phi Beta Kappa in 1925. Harper published *Color* that same year and he entered Harvard University where he received a M.A. in 1926.

Harlem Renaissance

Cullen's marriage to Yolande DuBois served as the apogee of the Harlem Renaissance. The only child of W.E.B. DuBois, Yolande joined in matrimony with Harlem's most celebrated poet, only child of the minister at the Salem Methodist Episcopal Church, 9 April 1928. Several thousand guests attended—the distinguished list of bridesmaids and ushers included Langston Hughes. When the marriage quickly ended in divorce, DuBois blamed his daughter and maintained a lifelong affection for Cullen, even delivering a eulogy at his funeral.

For DuBois, Cullen remained a preeminent representative of what he called "The Talented Tenth," who through their education could organize their people and gain respect from the general society. Cullen worked with other talented Harlem Renaissance figures to forge a respectable culture: Wallace Thurman, Gwendolyn Bennet, Richard Bruce Nugent, Langston Hughes, Claude McKay, and Allen Locke. They strayed a long way from what Cullen called the "Methodist parsonage" background, when they published the openly homoerotic *Fire!* in November, 1926.

While Cullen maintained a respectable front in society, he always felt free to find special friends. High school sweetheart Harold Jackman, a handsome West Indian, often traveled with Cullen, acted as his pallbearer, and received his papers. Dedicated to Jackman, Cullen's "Heritage" asks:

> What's your nakedness to me?
> Here no leprous flowers rear
> Fierce corollas in the air;
> Here no bodies sleek and wet,
> Dripping mingled rain and sweat,
> Tread the savage measures of
> Jungle boys and girls in love.

Later Career

Critics have often pondered Cullen's alleged "decline" after the 1920s. From being a celebrity he became a French teacher in the DeWitt Clinton school. A student in his French class, James Baldwin, interviewed him in 1942. Cullen explained that "poetry is something that few people enjoy and which fewer people understand."

Cullen tried his hand at writing a novel, but his *One Way to Heaven* (1932) struck the wrong note for the depression years. As in Carl Van Vetchen's *Nigger Heaven* (1926) the parties of A'Lelia Walker now seemed embarrassing. His children and cat books demonstrate his charm and cat/child-like grace, but never secured a large readership.

Cullen scored some success in the field of drama. Virgil Tompson set Cullen's translation of *The Medea* (1935) to music; rearranged in 1967 by Daniel Pinkham the work is still performed. Cullen wrote lyrics for *St. Louis Woman*, which became the vehicle for Pearl Bailey's great Broadway success, but only after his death.

Gay Art

For Cullen, art served as the ultimate redeemer of humankind—it uplifted the fallen and crude, the ugly and unhappy. His ideal of art resembled that of Oscar Wilde and the nineteenth century aesthetes. Art could purify not only blackness but also homosexuality as well as save one from the drabness of Methodism. While Cullen embraced such values, he shied away from Oscar Wilde or the French. Although a student at the Sorbornne and a French teacher, he never mentions Rimbaud, Gide, or Proust; he did, however, translate Verlaine, Baudelaire, and Bilitis.

Cullen was a superb lyricist and he admired John Keats but found little in American poetry—either black or white—that interested him. He seldom (if ever) mentions Walt Whitman, although his juvenile "To the Swimmer" echoes the solitary singer:

With an outward stroke of power intense your mighty arm goes forth,
Cleaving its way through waters that rise and roll, ever a ceaseless vigil keeping
Over the treasures beneath.

The possible sexual allusion to genitals ("treasures beneath") can be found in a poem for another boyfriend, John Gaston Edgar:

I have wrapped my dreams in a silken cloth,
And laid them away in a box of gold
Where long will cling the lips of the moth....

Many Harlem poets linked African paganism with their homosexuality. Answering the question "What is Africa to me?" Cullen dedicates "Heritage" to his lover Harold Jackman. The title poem from *The Black Christ and Other Poems* (1929) centers on the lynching of a stunningly beautiful Jim. This "Black Christ" parallels Melville's *Billy Budd*, published in 1924. "Spring's gayest cavalier," Jim appears inside "queerly capering shadows." And the strange fruit:

O Tree was every worthier Groom
Led to a bride of such rare bloom?
Did ever fiercer hands enlace
Love and Beloved in an embrace
As heaven-smiled-upon as this?

Perhaps covertly Cullen described his own poetry in "Atlantic City Waiter" (as a college student the poet had worked there during the summer).

Sheer through his acquiescent mask
Of bland gentility,
The jungle flames like a copper cask
Set where the sun strikes free.

References:

Early, Gerald. *My Soul's High Song: The Collected Writings of Countee Cullen, Voice of the Harlem Renaissance.* New York: Doubleday, 1991.
Reimonenq, Alden. "Countee Cullen's Uranian 'Soul Windows'" in *Critical Essays: Gay and Lesbian Writers of Color,* edited by Emmanuel S. Nelson. Binghampton, NY: Haworth, 1993.
Shucard, Alan R. *Countee Cullen.* Boston: Twayne Publishers, 1984.
Wagner, Jean. *Black Poets of the United States from Paul Laurence Dunbar to Langston Hughes,* translated by Kenneth Douglas. Urbana: University of Illinois, 1973.
Watson, Steven. *The Harlem Renaissance, Hub of African-American Culture, 1920-1930.* New York: Pantheon, 1995.

—Charles Shively

Merce Cunningham

1919-

American dancer and choreographer

New York of the 1940s presented an exciting time to be a young artist. Merce Cunningham had just arrived in the city to dance with Martha Graham. Shortly thereafter, he began promoting his startlingly unique dance aesthetic. Cunningham's early dances were attended by New York's avant-garde, including Max Ernst, Marcel Duchamp, Piet Mondrian, and Peggy Guggenheim. Embracing Duchamp's theories about chance and the acceptance of all forms as art, Cunningham and his partner John Cage invented processes through which traditional dance forms were taken apart, partially discarded, then rearranged and polished into infant examples of post-modern dance.

Merce Cunningham was born 16 April 1919, in Centralia, Washington, the second of three sons of Clifford and Marion Cunningham. Cunningham's father, a successful small town lawyer, encouraged his son's interest in dance. At age eight, Cunningham began performing simple vaudeville dances that were commonly taught in small dance schools across America. At thirteen he continued his lessons with Mrs. Maud Barrett, learning tap, waltzes, and soft shoe. Graduating from high school in 1937, Cunningham attended the University of Washington in Seattle for one year, then transferred to the Cornish School for Performing and Visual Arts. Taking dance classes with Bonnie Bird, Cunningham first encountered the

Merce Cunningham

choreography of Martha Graham. Bird had been a member of Graham's dance company. During his second year, Cunningham met John Cage, a pianist brought in to play for class. Cage began a percussion orchestra, which Cunningham joined, and taught dance composition classes in which he encouraged students to write their own music.

In 1939, Cunningham attended a second summer of dance classes at Mills College in Oakland, California. Martha Graham's entire Bennington School of the Dance was in residence and Cunningham worked with them, appearing in "Men's Dance," by Doris Humphrey. Graham invited Cunningham to dance with her company in New York. In *The Dancer and The Dance*, Cunningham recalls his parents' astonishment at Graham's invitation, "I said to my parents, I'm going to New York. My mother's mouth fell open. My father looked at me, then looked back at her and said, 'Let him go, he's going to go anyway.'"

Cunningham appeared at Graham's New York dance studio that fall, surprising her as she had not expected him to make the journey. He began performing with her right away, becoming a soloist in her company. The following year, Cage joined Cunningham in New York, and by 1944, they had premiered their own short programs. A year later, Cunningham left Graham, preferring Cage's ideas about structuring music and dance.

The first big success for Cunningham and Cage was in 1947, when the Ballet Society of New York (which later became the New York City Ballet) commissioned their work "The Seasons." The simple costumes and minimal sets were designed by Isamu Noguchi. A critical success, "Seasons" toured nationally the following year. By 1949, "Seasons" was included in the inaugural season of the New York City Ballet, and Cunningham and Cage began touring Europe.

In the summer of 1948, Cunningham and Cage brought their unique work to Black Mountain College in South Carolina, an arts school that followed the Bauhaus tradition of experiment and innovation. With students, they performed "The Ruse of the Medusa," the text and music written by Eric Satie, an early example of the Theater of the Absurd in America. In the summer of 1952, Cunningham and Cage performed "Theater Piece #1"—the first "happening" in America—and invented performance art. They returned to Black Mountain College every summer until it closed in 1957. Many of their students rose to prominence in the international art world of the 1950s and 60s, including Buckminister Fuller, Elaine and William de Kooning, Irving Penn, Robert Rauschenberg, Jasper Johns, Franz Klein, Mark Rothko, and Robert Motherwell.

During the summer of 1953, Cunningham rehearsed his newly formed dance company at Black Mountain College, then returned to New York to open their first season that winter. By 1955, the Merce Cunningham Dance Company toured nationally. The Company still operates today, performing works that are both new and revived Cunningham classics.

Aside from making new dances, Merce Cunningham devises material that fits his diminishing physical abilities, while making astute and poignant comments about his ageing as a dancer. He never pretends to be young for the sake of the spotlight, as the graceful wave of a hand has replaced the powerful leap. Always looking toward the future, Cunningham employs computers as choreographic tools.

Merce Cunningham's relationship with John Cage spanned 54 years. Cage was described by Pia Gilbert in "John Cage," *Dance Magazine*, as Cunningham's "partner in life and work." Although Cage separated from his wife Xenia in 1945 and never remarried, he and Cunningham did not share their first apartment until 1971. They lived together until Cage's death in 1992.

Cunningham's dances are included in the repertories of dance companies worldwide. He has received dozens of prestigious international awards for his contributions to modern dance, and was made Commander of the Order of Arts and Letters by the French Minister of Culture, inducted into the American Academy and Institute of Arts and Letters, and given the National Medal of Arts by President Bush. He received two Guggenheim fellowships, and for his 75th birthday, New York mayor Rudolph Giuliani declared 16 April 16 1994 as "Merce Cunningham Day."

Current Address: 55 Bethune Street, New York, New York 10014-1703.

References:

Barnes, Clive. "Merce Cunningham at 75" in *Dance Magazine*, May 1994, 112.

Belfond, Jacqueline Lesschaeve. *Merce Cunningham: The Dancer and The Dance.* Marion Boyers Inc., New York, 1985.

Gilbert, Pia. "John Cage" in *Dance Magazine*, March 1993, 46-48.

Klosky, James. *Merce Cunningham.* Proscenium Publishers, New York, 1986.

Martin, Leslie. "Black Mountain College and Merce Cunningham in *The Fifties: New Perspectives"* in *Dance Research Journal*, spring 1994, 46-48.

Sontag, Susan. *Cage, Cunningham, Johns: Dancers on a Plane: In Memory of their Feelings.* Alfred A. Knopf, Inc., New York, 1990.

Vreeland, Nancy. "Merce! Passages in a Performing Life" in *Dance Magazine*, March 1985, 50.

—Laurie Fitzpatrick

Mary Daly

1928-

American theologian and feminist philosopher

Mary Daly, a self-described radical feminist pirate, is also a well-respected philosopher and theologian. The author of numerous books, anthology contributions, and articles on (among other things) patriarchy and the misogyny of religion and society, her works have been crucial to the development of radical feminist theory.

Born on 16 October 1928, Daly, the daughter of Anna Catherine and Frank X. Daly, grew up during the years of the Depression and World War II. She spent her childhood in Schenectady, New York where she attended co-educational Catholic institutions from elementary school through high school. She completed her undergraduate studies at a small Catholic women's college and went on to Catholic University to earn a Master's in English. It was here she decided she wanted to study theology and philosophy, but in 1952 women were not admitted to theology programs. Daly found a theology school for women (the first of its kind) led by a fiery nun, and received her Ph.D. in religion at the age of twenty-five.

Daly found it difficult for a woman to find a tenure-track post at a four-year university or college. She finally found a position at Cardinal Cushing College in Brookline, Massachusetts, and taught for five years. Yet, Daly still wanted to complete a Ph.D. in philosophy. She entrolle at the University of Fribourg, Switzerland, where she earned doctorates in theology and philosophy. In the 26 February 1996 issue of the *New Yorker*, Daly explains why she pursued so many doctorates. She "went on and on pursuing doctorates because theology ... is a treasure chest containing archaic gems. By studying arduously, I equipped myself to reverse the reversals inherent in Christian dogma and decode its doctrines with precision." She finally obtained a position as an assistant professor at Boston College in 1966.

Soon after, Daly published a book on Jacques Maritain (1966), but soon began to delve into the position of women in the Catholic Church. Daly's next books, *The Church and the Second Sex* (1968; rev. eds., 1975, 1985), a response to Simone de Beauvoir, and the more philosophical *Beyond God the Father* (1973; 2nd rev.ed., 1985) were strongly worded critiques of the Catholic Church and its subjugation of women. The publication and subsequent publicity surrounding *The Church and the Second Sex* led Boston College to fire Daly, only to reluctantly rehire her after 2500 students protested.

With the publication of *Gyn/Ecology: The Metaethics of Radical Feminism* (1978) and *Pure Lust* (1984) Daly cemented her position as the leading voice of radical feminism. In *Gyn/Ecology*, Daly argues that patriarchy is the cause of women's subjugation, and that man is the subjugator. In these later books, Daly moved from not only critiquing the anti-woman, anti-feminist language within religion and society, in general, to developing or "claiming" a new vocabulary, which recaptures words such as "hag" and "crone" and uses them in praise of women.

Daly describes her latest book, *Outercourse* (1992), as "contain[ing] recollections from my logbook of a radical feminist philosopher." It is an autobiography filled with philosophic analysis, letters from readers, comments from reviewers, and anecdotes of Daly's life. All of this is accomplished in the language of new meanings developed in her books and explained in her 1987 *Websters' First New Intergalactic Wickedary of the English Language* written with Jane Caputi. In some ways, *Outercourse* seems a summing up or synthesis of her ideas and works to date. The definitions were created and developed in her works, rendered precise in the dictionary.

Daly is currently working on *Quintessence: Re-Calling the Outrageous, Contagious, Courage of Women*. According to Daly the book is "mystical, philosophical and about the Fifth Spiral Galaxy. A book which explores the fragmentation and Diaspora of feminism."

While Daly's contributions are undeniable, some critics of Daly have pointed out that the creation of new word meanings and the density of her writing style leave her writings inaccessible to many readers. Others have noted that while Daly attempts to refocus the use of language toward the more "woman-centered," she omits the voices and models of non-Western women.

Daly's rejection of male-dominated power structures both inside and outside of the religious realm is praised by many for offering a differing vision of spirituality and lesbian identity. Her works have offered some women a way in to spirituality, without the necessity of embracing a male dominated religious structure. Daly's refusal to be silenced, even at the cost of her job and advancement, as well as her public embrace of the controversies surrounding religion, women, and the roles of language are praiseworthy.

Current Address: Department of Theology, Carney Hall, Boston College, Chestnut Hill, Massachusetts 02167.

References:

Contemporary Authors. New Revision Series. Vol. 30. Detroit: Gale Research, 1987.

Daly, Mary. "Sin Big," in *New Yorker*, 26 February-4 March, 1996.

—Lisa Loutzenheiser

Mercedes de Acosta

1893-1968

American poet and playwright

All but forgotten today, Mercedes de Acosta was nonetheless a notorious lesbian, libertine, and bon vivant in 1920s and 1930s Hollywood. She is remembered little for her writings, but primarily for her brief, passionate affairs with Greta Garbo, Marlene Dietrich, and Isadora Duncan, to name a few. Later in life, she was a confidant of Andy Warhol and something of a darling on the New York social scene, though many found her demands on their friendship "excessive." "If sleep failed her," friend Kieran Tunney notes in his *Interrupted Autobiography*, "she thought nothing of calling at one or two or three in the morning to discuss the meaning of existence,... and if one were invited (away) for a weekend de Acosta expected one to arrange that she too was included even if the host had never met or heard of her."

De Acosta was the youngest of eight children, brought up in a magical, pre-World War I New York, when there were still organ-grinders with tethered monkeys working the streets, and immigrants of all stripes spilling out onto their stoops and hawking wares from horse-drawn carts. All her life, she claimed to be of Spanish descent, but it is generally accepted now that her family came from Cuba.

By all accounts, she did not have an easy life all-around. As a child, she suffered from depression, and as an adult was troubled by chronic insomnia and migraines. According to author Hugo Vickers in *Loving Garbo*, she often endured what she poetically termed "the dark night of the soul." She believed devoutly in "astral traveling," where "the spirit or ego leaves the body while one sleeps and yet remains connected to the life force." A sudden jerking awake would interrupt this precious travel and cause distress, she maintained.

She was also a scholar of eastern religions, a follower of Krishnamurti, and a strict vegetarian. "Meat eating makes a tomb out of our living bodies for the corpses of animals," Vickers quoted her as having said.

Not a Boy, Not a Girl, Maybe Both

Even as a child being raised as a Roman Catholic, she was sometimes over-the-top in her zealousness. "She put nails and stones into her shoes and walked till her feet bled," Vickers says, and she would often kneel for hours "with arms extended in the form of a cross." "I don't believe in dogmas," she reportedly once told actress Elsa Maxwell, "I believe in taking the essence from all religions in arriving at your own creed." Not surprisingly, she was also an ardent feminist, and an outspoken admirer of dancer Isadora Duncan for liberating women from corsets, stockings, and other extraneous layers of clothes.

Until she was seven years old, de Acosta was convinced she was a boy. Her mother had wanted a son, so her parents encouraged her to play with the boys. Then one day, as Vickers cited, what she called "the tragedy" occurred. One of her playmates took her behind a bath-house and showed her his penis. "Have you got this?" he asked. "If you are a boy and you haven't got this, you are deformed."

It was a crushing experience for her. "In that one brief moment," Vickers quoted her as saying "everything in my young soul turned monstrous and terrible and dark." She was subsequently whisked off to a convent to learn more "feminine" ways, but she kept running away, still insisting she was not a boy or a girl, but maybe both. Later in life, she claimed these early esoteric beliefs enabled her to view life in all its mystical and romantic half-tones. "I do not understand the difference between a man and a woman," she wrote, "and believing only in the eternal value of love, I cannot understand these so-called 'normal' people who believe that a man should love only a woman, and a woman love only a man ... it disregards completely the spirit."

"I Can Get Any Woman ..."

Like many 1920s New Yorkers, de Acosta loved the seedy speak-easies and drag clubs, and was involved with a number of women she met through contacts there and in more "upper-crust" social circles—the Russian actress Alla Nazimova, Duncan, Garbo, and Dietrich among them. "I can get any woman from any man," Vickers cited her as boasting to "Dickie" Fellowes-Gordon, lifelong friend of Elsa Maxwell. Apparently, there was an abundance of evidence to back her up.

Between 1920 and 1935, she was married to painter Abram Poole, and even claims to have taken a girlfriend with her on their honeymoon.

During the course of a lifelong friendship with Duncan, de Acosta arranged for payment of many of her bills and the editing and publishing of Duncan's memoirs, *My Life*. As Vickers noted, Duncan even composed a quite randy and revealing poem to their love in the last year of her life (1927), describing in detail her "hungry mouth" yearning for both "sprouting breasts" and "lower still a secret place" to "hide my loving face."

In early 1931, de Acosta met Greta Garbo and, by all accounts, was smitten in a manner her former lasciviousness had not prepared her for. By the summer, de Acosta was entranced and obsessed with Garbo, writing in length, according to Garbo biographer Barry Paris, about Garbo as being "of the elements" and of the "six perfect weeks out of a lifetime" their getaway to the Sierra Nevadas represented. By year's end, de Acosta was living next door to Garbo just outside Hollywood and writing a script for her, ironically titled *Desperate*, that was loosely based on Garbo's childhood. Because much of the action called for Garbo to be dressed as a boy, the studio quickly nixed the idea.

Alas Garbo, popularly and forthrightly dubbed the "the Swedish Sphinx," proved more asexual than truly lesbian. No one found this harder to accept than de Acosta who, according to Paris, wrote to friend and fellow Garbo-lover Cecil Beaton that "she isn't so far a lesbian, but might easily become one."

"The Best Card to Hold"

It is ironic that, for all her passion and connections, for all her living of life to the fullest, precious little attention ever came to de Acosta through her work. Her poems enjoyed limited popularity and none of her scripts ever made it to the screen, partly due to her sense of "purism." According to Vickers, for example, she was fired by Irving Thalberg in 1932 for refusing to write a scene in *Rasputin and the Empress* that describes a meeting between the Mad Monk and the Princess Irene Yusupov. Because the meeting had never taken place in real life, de Acosta asserted, she wasn't going to put it in.

Even when her memoirs, *Here Lies the Heart*, were published in 1960 (with a jacket photograph by Dietrich nonetheless), they were received with mixed reviews. Garbo was furious at de Acosta's candid descriptions of their affair and never forgave her. Others in their circle officially touted the book as a volume of lies, but privately admitted their accuracy and at least "essence" of truth. In the end, the book was released at a time when interest in Garbo and Dietrich was simply not as strong as it would later become. De Acosta is said to have made no money from it.

Mercedes de Acosta continued to be welcome in all sorts of literary, film, and social circles till her always-fragile health began to fail her in the mid-1960s. She died alone in 1968 after depleting much of her funds and selling most of her jewelry to pay medical expenses. Shortly after her death, Truman Capote—just one of her fans long fascinated by her sexual conquests—is quoted by Vickers as having remarked to art historian John Richardson that he "thought up a game he called International Daisy Chain, the point of which was to link people sexually, using as few beds as possible, [and] Mercedes was the best card to hold. You could get to anyone—from Cardinal Spellman to the Duchess of Windsor." She would have appreciated the epitaph.

References:

Paris, Barry. *Garbo.* New York: Alfred A. Knopf, 1995.

Tunney, Kieran. *Interrupted Biography.* London: Quartet Books, 1989.

Vickers, Hugo. *Loving Garbo—The Story of Greta Garbo, Cecil Beaton, and Mercedes de Acosta.* New York: Random House, 1994.

—Jerome Szymczak

Samuel R. Delany

1942-

African-American novelist, essayist, and critic

Samuel Delany's writing encompasses many genres, openly exploring and celebrating male homoeroticism. A professor of comparative literature, he has published science fiction works which incorporate surprising references to Foucault and postmodernism; he is also the author of the pornographic *Tides of Lust* (1973). Science fiction fans, especially gay and lesbian aficionados, claim him as one of their own, while literary critics argue as to whether his works should be classified as semiotic fantasy, science fiction or social commentary.

Born in Harlem on 1 April 1942, Delany grew up in New York City, attending Dalton School and Bronx High School of Science. He studied at City College, where he was poetry editor for *Promethean.* His attraction to words and imagination was clear from the beginning—he published his first novel, *The Jewels of Aptor,* in 1962, when he was 20 years old. There were other attractions during this period of his life, which he was struggling to identify and articulate. *The Motion of Light on Water: Sex and Science Fiction Writing in the East Village 1957-1965* (1988; an expanded version, *The Motion of Light on Water: East Village Sex and Science Fiction Writing 1960-1965, with The Column at the Market's Edge,* later appeared in the United Kingdom in 1990), gives a moving account of his developing sexuality. He became aware of his preference for homoeroticism at a young age, but he also engaged in sex with women, one such encounter resulting in the pregnancy which forced him into an unhappy marriage to the talented poet Marilyn Hacker. The marriage lasted for nineteen years, during which time Delany openly pursued homosexual liaisons.

The Jewels of Aptor foreshadowed elements that later appeared in Delany's works: the use of mythological symbols and images (frequently ancient Greek mythology, with its overtones of homosexuality); detailed background, and precise language. In 1963 the first novel in *The Fall of the Towers* trilogy, *Captives of the Flame,* appeared, followed by *The Towers of Toron* (1964) and *City of a Thousand Suns* (1965). In these novels Delany explored questions about multiple loyalties and ethnicities, questions to which his identity as an African-American man who loves other men made him particularly sensitive. His sophisticated writing style and the complexity of the issues he dealt with were a cut above most science fiction writers of the 1960s. This often led to his writing being heavily edited, though in later reprints many passages that had been excised were reinstated. Along with writers like Ursula K. Le Guin and Harlan Ellison, he helped move science fiction out of the clean-cut-hero-versus-evil-Martians mode and into social commentary.

Two novels were published in 1966: *Empire Star* and *Babel-17.* In this latter work, linguist and heroine Rydra Wong successfully learns to understand the alien by studying its attempts at communication. By this time Delany had earned a reputation as the thinking person's sci-fi writer. The respect of fellow science fiction authors won him the Nebula award in 1966—an award he was to win again in 1967 and in 1969. After winning the prestigious Hugo award in 1970, Delany published his epic novel *Dhalgren* in 1975.

Delany's best-known science fiction works are in his Nevèrÿon series: the novel *Nevèrÿona; or, The Tale of Signs and Cities* (1983); and short story collections *Tales of Nevèrÿon* (1979); *Flight from Nevèrÿon* (1985); and *The Bridge of Lost Desire* (1987, later revised as *Return to Nevèrÿon* in 1989). Sexuality and power are explored as the hero Gorgik is enslaved and slowly leads a rebellion which ends the institution of slavery. Homosexual desire is a key element in the series, as are other unorthodox sexual practices like sado-masochism and bondage. In *Flight from Nevèrÿon* Delany compares the response of the New York gay community to AIDS with the reactions of his fictional characters to a sexually transmitted disease.

Delany combined literary criticism with drama in his play *Wagner/Artaud: A Play of 19th and 20th Century Critical Fictions* (1988); and social commentary with popular culture in *Silent Interviews: On Language, Race, Sex, Science Fiction, and Some Comics: A Collection of Written Interviews* (1994). In a genre where many readers are young people, Delany has dared to discuss homosexuality, the intricacies of identity, imagination and longing. He has helped bring gays and lesbians into the mainstream and made a space for them in popular fiction.

Current Address: c/o Henry Morrison, Inc., P.O. Box 235, Bedford Hills, New York 10507.

References:

McAuley, Paul J. *St. James Guide to Fantasy Writers,* edited by David Pringle. Detroit: St. James Press: 151-153.

Slusser, George. *St. James Guide to Science Fiction Writers,* edited by Jay P. Pederson. Detroit: St. James Press: 237-240.

—Shelley Anderson

John D'Emilio

1948-

American historian, policy analyst, and activist

John D'Emilio was born in 1948 in New York City. He attended New York's Jesuit, all-male Regis High School. He did both his undergraduate and graduate work at Columbia University, and received his Ph.D. in history in 1982.

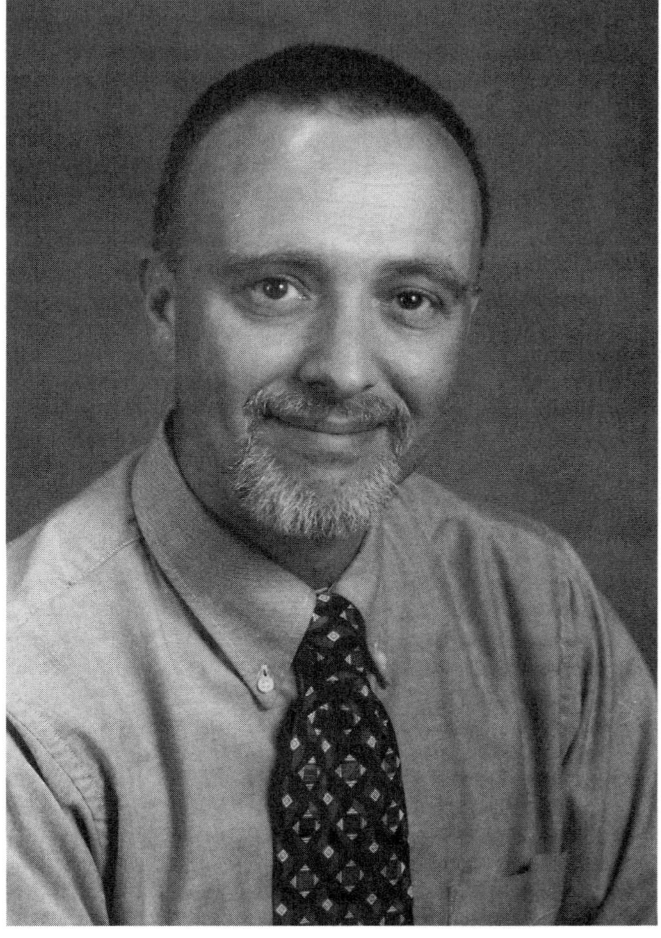

John D'Emilio

John D'Emilio's gay cultural activism has roots both deep and broad. He was founder and a key member of the Gay Academic Union, from 1973 to 1975. From 1975 to 1977, he was a member of the Gay Socialist Action Project, a small political group that organized zaps and demonstrations. Throughout the 1970s, D'Emilio's politics were often expressed through organizing and participating in demonstrations.

From 1978 through 1981, lesbian and gay historical research began to establish a national grassroots network. D'Emilio was a crucial part of that network's development. In 1979, while living in San Francisco, D'Emilio established friendships with a number of other historians and activists doing research on lesbian/gay topics. This circle included Allan Berubé (with whom D'Emilio has done joint research) and lesbian AIDS activist and cultural critic Amber Hollibaugh. D'Emilio's career as an academic writer began with this ground-breaking work on lesbian/gay historical studies. His early publications include work on gay community politics in San Francisco and sexuality in the military during the Cold War. Outside of sexuality within U.S. social history, D'Emilio's research has focused on the Civil Rights Movement. One of D'Emilio's current academic projects is an historical biography of Bayard Rustin.

As an historian and cultural critic, D'Emilio has published three books. The first, *Sexual Politics, Sexual Communities*, was a social history of lesbian and gay political organizing, from the homophile movement of 1940s through the post-Stonewall radical gay liberation movement. In 1988 he co-authored *Intimate Matters: A History of Sexuality in America* with Estelle Freedman, a professor of history at Stanford. In 1992, he published a collection of essays titled *Making Trouble: Essays on Gay History, Politics, and the University*. As a pioneer in the field of lesbian/gay social history, D'Emilio has been widely anthologized.

In the introduction to *Making Trouble*, D'Emilio provides a brief chronology of his life, discussing the nexus between progressive left politics, gay male sexual practices, gay community, and academia as it influences his intellectual, political, and cultural development. Of particular note in this introduction is the attention D'Emilio pays to the specific energies of the lesbian/gay community in the late 1970s San Francisco, and the sense of political possibility that this community strength precipitated. D'Emilio also writes about his romantic relationship with Freedman in the 1970s, prompting a rare discussion of eroticized relationships between gay men and lesbians.

Although his research and writing have always addressed lesbian/gay community needs, D'Emilio has also devoted considerable energy to activism beyond the academy. He began his association with the National Gay and Lesbian Task Force (NGLTF) in 1983, when he acted as a consultant for an NGLTF report on antihomosexual U.S. governmental policies in the 1950s. Outside of gay cultural activism, D'Emilio has worked as a program developer for the Bank Street College Day Care Consultation Service (1977-78), as a policy analyst on child care issues (1981-1993), and with a youth organizing project in East Harlem. In 1981, he was assistant director on a successful statewide New York campaign to defeat a prison construction bond.

In 1983, D'Emilio began teaching in the history department at the University of North Carolina-Greensboro. In 1992, he advanced to the position of full professor. D'Emilio remained at UNC-Greensboro through 1995. During the 1990-91 academic year, D'Emilio was a fellow at the Center for Advanced Study in the Behavioral Sciences at Stanford. Throughout the 1980s and 1990s, D'Emilio received a number of research grants and fellowships.

In the summer of 1995, D'Emilio left the University of North Carolina-Greensboro to assume the position of executive director of the National Gay and Lesbian Task Force's Policy Institute. D'Emilio's new position at NGLTF came out of his many years of work with the organization. D'Emilio joined the board of directors of NGLTF in 1988 and remained until 1993. From 1989 to 1991, he served as co-chair of the board. As director of NGLTF's Policy Institute, D'Emilio oversees a nationally coordinated effort to establish a dialogue between queer academics, movement activists, and social service providers.

John D'Emilio's entire career has been based on the possibility of radical social change. As a professor who has consistently written for lesbian/gay community papers as well as academic journals, D'Emilio has worked for several decades to link communities and coalitions toward a goal of social transformation. In this capacity, D'Emilio has fashioned himself as a contemporary, public intellectual.

References:

D'Emilio, John. *Making History: Essays on Gay History, Politics, and the University.* New York: Routledge, 1992.

—Alex Robertson Textor

Barbara Deming

1917-1984

American author and activist

Barbara Deming

A carefully educated woman of intellect and privilege, Barbara Deming spent her early life writing poems, essays, and short stories. In her mid-forties, however, Deming was startled into an awareness of the imminent need for radical social change. She dedicated the rest of her life to nonviolent activism in the civil rights and peace movements, and later in the lesbian feminist movement. Arrested and jailed many times for civil disobedience protests against racism, the Vietnam War, and U.S. military policies, Deming was a transformative figure in progressive circles, chronicling her struggles to distill a certain loving essence within the heart of any conflict. "We must certainly be frank with each other when we disagree," she said in a speech to the War Resisters League, "but my plea is that we not ... in a panic, try to wish any of us out of the picture.... We are all part of one another."

Born 23 July 1917, in New York City, Deming was the second of four children of Katherine Burritt and Harold Deming, a prosperous Republican lawyer. Early influenced by Quakerism, Deming attended the Friends School of Fifteenth Street Meeting in New York City from kindergarten through high school. During her teens, she became friends with the poet e.e. cummings and Bessie Breuer, one of the first successful women reporters in the U.S. Soon Deming was writing poetry and, at seventeen, began an affair with the much older Norma Millay, sister of poet Edna St. Vincent Millay.

Deming entered Bennington College in 1934, studied drawing with George Grosz, and started a seven-year relationship with Vida Ginsberg, the first of what were to be three significant lesbian partners in her life. In 1938, Deming received a B.A. in theater from Bennington, and in 1940, an M.A. in theater from Western Reserve in Cleveland, Ohio. In 1942, Deming was hired by the Library of Congress as a film analyst, and began her first book, *Running Away from Myself—A Dream Portrait of America Drawn from the Films of the '40s,* which was not published until 1969.

In the early 1950s, Deming toured Europe, where she began a series of short stories, published in the 1974 collection, *Wash Us and Comb Us.* She also commenced an autobiographical novel, *A Humming Under My Feet: A Book of Travail,* published in 1984. In 1954, Deming met artist Mary Meigs, and the two became lovers, moving to Wellfleet, Massachusetts, where Meigs painted and Deming submitted her writings to assorted periodicals. Although Deming published a few poems, short stories, and essays in the *Partisan Review* and *New Yorker*, she generally received more rejection slips than offers.

In 1959, Deming and Meigs traveled to India, where Deming was inspired to read the writings of Gandhi. Deming, who until then had been "vaguely liberal," became "radicalized," realizing that "I was in the deepest part of myself a pacifist." In 1960, Deming went to Cuba, where she spent an hour talking to Fidel Castro, who challenged her to look for herself at the poverty of his people, victims of U.S.-sponsored greed. "The shock of the trip began my liberation," she writes. It also liberated her writing. Deming returned to the U.S. committed to nonviolent revolutionary action, and immediately became involved with the Peacemakers, the Committee for Nonviolent Action, and the War Resisters League.

Having joined the peace movement, Deming was distressed at its distance from the burgeoning civil rights struggles, and with others, took pains to integrate peace walks through the southern United States. During the Quebec to Guantanamo Walk for Peace in 1963-64, Deming was arrested and later wrote in a book called *Prison*

Notes (1966) about the four weeks she spent in the Albany, Georgia jail. In 1971, she published *Revolution and Equilibrium*, a book of essays about anti-Vietnam War activism.

Deming also wrote patient, meticulously loving letters that sought to analyze and heal political wounds. In her 1971 letter to African-American activist Ray Robinson, Deming began to address her invisibility as a lesbian within their movements: "I haven't of course, Ray, been to the bottom ... that you have touched.... [A]s I write this, the tears begin to gush from my eyes.... The bottom I write about ... is of being a homosexual." By now, Deming was involved with her third partner, Jane Gapen, whose husband, in one of the first open lesbian custody cases, had threatened to take his and Gapen's two children.

During the 1970s, Deming turned increasingly toward the women's movement, and wrote on misogyny and violence against women in *We Cannot Live without Our Lives* (1974) and *Remembering Who We Are* (1981). She and Gapen moved to Sugarloaf Key, Florida, to cultivate a strong, nurturing women's community. In 1983 Deming was arrested as part of the Women's Encampment for a Future of Peace and Justice, an anti-military action near Seneca, New York. A year later, Deming was diagnosed with ovarian cancer and endured months of chemotherapy and radiation. On 2 August 1984, attended by her lover and friends, Deming died in her Florida home.

Deming is acknowledged to have been a rare and radiant presence in the women's community as well as in every political movement she touched. She worked to enlarge a radical perspective, not just intellectually, but spiritually. "Vengeance is not the point," she once wrote, "change is."

References:

Deming, Barbara. *Revolution and Equilibrium*. New York: Grossman Publishers, 1971.

———. *We Are All Part of One Another: A Barbara Deming Reader*. Philadelphia: New Society Publishers, 1984.

DiGia, Ralph. Interview with Susie Day, 14 March 1996.

McDaniel, Judith. "Barbara Deming," in *American National Biography*. Cary, North Carolina: Oxford University Press, 1998.

———. Introduction to *Prisons That Could Not Hold*. Athens, Georgia: University of Georgia Press, 1995.

—Susie Day

Michael Denneny

1943-

American editor

As an editor at St. Martin's Press and co-founder of *Christopher Street* magazine and the Publishing Triangle, Michael Denneny has worked tirelessly and successfully to bring gay literature into the mainstream.

Michael Leo Denneny was born 2 March 1943 in Providence, Rhode Island and was raised in Pawtucket, Rhode Island, where his mother Dorothy worked in a factory and his father, Leo, was a postman. Of his parents, Denneny said, "Both were avid readers when I was quite young, although neither had gone past high school, and this had an impact on me." Books were so important to the young Denneny that he spent his allowance joining eight book clubs. After attending public school, Denneny left Rhode Island in 1960 to attend the University of Chicago, where he spent the next decade, first as a student and later as an instructor. Denneny was greatly influenced by his mentors at the university's Committee on Social Thought, renowned scholars Hannah Arendt and Harold Rosenberg, to whom he attributes much of his success in later years.

Denneny has always been politically active. During his teenage years he protested nuclear testing, participated in Woolworth's lunch counter sit-ins, and picketed for civil rights. While at the University of Chicago, he became increasingly involved in the anti-Vietnam War movement. His political activism led to Denneny's disenchantment with academia: "I'd always thought I'd end up an academic and didn't know what else to do." Denneny eventually found a job at the University of Chicago Press, "after being convinced that this wasn't technically part of the university."

It was during this time that Denneny came out. "From my early teenage years on, I knew I responded to male erotica yet I led a straight life (mostly) ... until I was 27, when the events at Stonewall precipitated a crisis." To come to terms with his sexual identity, he

Michael Denneny

joined a consciousness raising group "which I learned to my surprise was being led by my last girlfriend," Denneny continued. "It was hard to be gay in Chicago. Most people just thought it was my latest political enthusiasm. So, in essence, I moved to N.Y.C. to try out being gay. (It worked!)"

When Denneny moved to New York City in 1972, he intended to work in the theater, but the only job he could find was as an editor at Macmillan. "I got into publishing by accident, to pay the rent," Denneny commented. While at Macmillan, Denneny worked with several notable authors, including Buckminster Fuller and Ntozake Shange. In 1975, Denneny published his first gay book, Allan Ebert's *The Homosexuals: Who Are What We Are,* a book of interviews with gay men. Around the same time, Denneny worked with Chuck Ortleb and others to found *Christopher Street,* a gay literary magazine modelled after the *New Yorker.* Finding material for the magazine was difficult at first: "Having no place to publish it, most gay writers we knew simply were not writing gay material. This we didn't figure out until we had done several issues and it created problems. I remember one issue where Ed White wrote something like five different articles under five different names to fill up the magazine," Denneny reminisces. "We had a great many friends who were (gay) writers and from the beginning *Christopher Street* was supposed to be a writers' magazine. It survived because this large and open-ended group of gay writers supported it."

A month after *Christopher Street* appeared, Denneny was fired from Macmillan. "When looking for jobs, I plopped the magazines down on the table, announced that I was involved with it and if that was a problem we should just enjoy the lunch (since this is a very expensive restaurant and you're paying)." "Although [the interviewers] said it didn't bother them, I only got one job offer, at St. Martin's (and none for the next 17 years)—which made me think being publicly gay had something to do with it."

During his 17 years at St. Martin's Press, Denneny published over 500 books, one quarter of which were concerned with gay. In 1987, Denneny launched Stonewall Inn Editions, the first trade paperback line to exclusively publish gay and lesbian books. Currently Stonewall Inn has 84 titles in print. While at St. Martin's Press, Denneny helped to found the Publishing Triangle "to encourage and support gay and lesbian writing in every way we could, as well as being a networking organization for gay/lesbian people in publishing." Denneny helped to establish the Bill Whitehead Award, honoring lifetime contribution to gay and lesbian writing, and to launch Gay and Lesbian Book Month, to encourage broader visibility for gay and lesbian titles. In 1994, the Lambda Literary Awards paid tribute to Denneny's immense contribution to gay and lesbian publishing by presenting him with the Publisher's Service Award. Later that year, Denneny moved to his current job as an editor at Crown Publishers, and shortly thereafter he was awarded the prestigious Literary Market Place Editor of the Year Award for 1994 for Individual Achievement in Trade Editorial.

Denneny's staunch dedication has contributed enormously to the phenomenal increase in gay and lesbian titles available today. Publishing gay books "was in effect like holding down a second job, since I also had to keep a regular publishing list running," reflects Denneny. "When I started it was a rare thing for a mainstream house to publish a gay book and it caused a great hullabaloo. I wanted to normalize the publishing of gay books. Originally I thought it would take three to five years, it actually took about 15, but the effort was finally successful. Every major publishing house in the country now does gay books and it isn't considered extraordinary."

References:

Denneny, Michael. E-mail interview with R. Ellen Greenblatt, 1996.

—R. Ellen Greenblatt

Sergei Diaghilev

1872-1929

Russian impresario

Although Sergei Diaghilev was neither a composer nor a choreographer, he was without equal in recognizing gifted artists and in securing their collaboration. From 1909 until his death in 1929, his Ballets Russes played an immense role in shaping and defining the cultural landscape of Europe. He did more than any other individual to gain wide acceptance for ballet, restoring its luster with season after season of dazzling productions. Many of his ballets, choreographed by Fokine, Nijinsky, Massine, Nijinska, and Balanchine, continue to be presented.

Diaghilev's gift for choosing choreographers was equalled by his musical foresight. When Stravinsky was practically unknown, Diaghilev commissioned *The Firebird.* Stravinsky went on to compose some of his most celebrated works for him. Diaghilev would later count European—especially French—composers among his collaborators. They included Ravel, Satie, and several of the group known as "The Six." Among the most brilliant of the painters who worked with him were Picasso, Braque and Gris, Matisse, and Chirico. Long after his death, Diaghilev's influence continues to be felt through former members of his company such as George Balanchine in the United States and Serge Lifar in Paris.

Three of Diaghilev's most influential choreographers, Nijinsky, Massine, and Lifar, were his lovers. With an eye for genius and a genius for creating a whole better than the sum of its superb parts, Diaghilev was also manipulative and unscrupulous, with an imperious need to control others, if necessary by pitting them against each other.

Sergei Pavlovich Dyagilev was born in Seleschev, in Novgorod, Russia, 19 March 1872, the first son of Pavel Pavlovich, a cavalry officer, and Evgenia Nicolaevna Essipov, of old provincial nobility. Although his mother died shortly after giving birth, his childhood was happy. His father was posted to Saint Petersburg and remarried there in 1874. His stepmother shared her husband's love of music, and came from a musically gifted family. Until the age of ten, Sergei grew up in Saint Petersburg. But Pavel Pavlovich, having run up debts, went home to the remote city of Perm, almost one thousand miles east of Saint Petersburg. While Perm had none of the brilliance of the capital, the family was affluent, and maintained an interest in music and the arts. Sergei's father would end his career as a lieutenant-general and aide-de-camp to the Emperor.

Saint Petersburg: The World of Art

At 18, Sergei went back to Saint Petersburg to study law. Though he completed his degree, he was more interested in the arts. Through

Sergei Diaghilev

his cousin Dmitri Filosofov, he was introduced to a gifted circle of friends that included the painters Alexander Benois and Leon Bakst. Diaghilev took singing lessons, but his baritone voice, though powerful, was unpleasant. Similarly, he was advised by Rimsky-Korsakov, with whom he studied composition, that he had no talent as a composer.

Diaghilev cultivated an intense interest in the graphic arts, becoming the cofounder and editor of the progressive art magazine the *World of Art*, which enjoyed an ephemeral but influential life. He was asked to edit the *Annals of the Imperial Theatre*. He transformed it, setting new standards in graphic design and typography, but overrunning his budget. He lacked tact and made enemies. His private life, especially his rather obvious homosexuality, was attracting unfavorable attention. An initial offer to stage an Imperial ballet, Delibes' *Sylvia*, was withdrawn. Out of spite Diaghilev resigned from the editorship of the *Annals*. Before long, however, he would regain the favor of the Emperor.

The Conquest of Paris

Although self-taught, Diaghilev also acquired sure taste as an arbiter of painting. He selected works to be displayed in several major exhibitions, including one of Russian historical portraits in Saint Petersburg in 1905, under imperial patronage, then an exhibit of Russian painting in Paris in the fall of 1906, with works loaned by the Emperor and major patrons. Diaghilev was successful in having Russian painting recognized abroad, and in awakening curiosity about the Russian cultural scene in general.

Having created an artistic demand, Diaghilev the impresario would then satisfy it. He was able to arrange for five major concerts at the Paris Opéra in 1907. These were a showcase for the talents of Glazunov, Rachmaninov, and Rimsky-Korsakov, who conducted their own works and brought to the Western public the music of Moussorgsky, Borodin, and Scriabin, including operatic excerpts sung by the bass Chaliapin, then at the start of his world career. The following year, a production of the opera *Boris Godunov*, staged by Diaghilev, with Chaliapin in the title role, enjoyed spectacular success in Paris. This was the first production of the opera outside Russia.

Questions of Identity: Impresario and Autocrat

The term "impresario," while an apt description for what Diaghilev did for the next twenty years, does him scant justice. To be sure he handled the challenges of any impresario, starting with the financing of his lavish productions. He took huge risks, dreaming up grandiose projects while bankrupt. The 1921 revival of *Sleeping Beauty* (renamed *The Sleeping Princess*) was a financial disaster, and threatened the very existence of the company, which was saved only by finding a permanent home in Monte Carlo the next year. Diaghilev worked with fellow impresarios in Paris and London. For example, he plotted both with and against Astruc, his first Parisian impresario. He cultivated the rich to generate their support. A notorious misogynist, he remained a good friend of Misia Sert who would persuade Parisian high society—"les chers snobs"—to back Diaghilev.

What distinguished Diaghilev was extraordinary taste and judgment, and knowledge of *all* of the arts. He loved the new, and working together, "his" artists were inspired to new levels of creativity. It is clear that Stravinsky, for example, was helped by his discussions with the painter Benois while composing *Petrushka* for the Ballets Russes, or with the painter Roerich, while working on *The Rite of Spring*. Such fruitful contacts were entirely due to Diaghilev.

Inseparable from Diaghilev's identity as impresario was a need to control others that brooked no opposition. A huge man, one in a continuous line of Russian nobles, he intimidated others by his very presence. This imperiousness defined him and especially shaped his sexual identity.

In his *Memoirs* (II, 75), Alexandre Benois describes a first meeting with Diaghilev when they were young men. Slight of build, he was astonished to find Diaghilev, on the slightest of pretexts, "on top of him," laughing and punching. Subsequently, he would often be "on top." When he came to Paris, Diaghilev became overnight the leader of the very influential homosexual elite. Cocteau, for example, while hoping for a dalliance with Nijinsky—which Diaghilev was determined to prevent—also tried to attract Diaghilev, making his "position" clear by wearing rouge and lipstick. Stravinsky joked that at the climax of *Afternoon of a Faun* Nijinsky made love to a scarf because Diaghilev would tolerate nothing else. Diaghilev in effect considered Nijinsky his personal chattel. This was a pattern often repeated, with scenes of jealous rage if any of his lovers or even ex-lovers made a commitment to another, as when his secretary Mavrine ran off with the dancer Olga Feodorova, or Nijinsky, from the safe distance of South America, got married.

The Ballets Russes

Beginning in 1909, Diaghilev offered European audiences ballets of unsurpassed beauty and excitement. Though at first more interested in opera than ballet, he responded willingly to an invitation to hold a Paris season of Russian ballet. French ballet of the period was uninspired. Diaghilev recruited his Russians. Three superb dancers, Michael Fokine, Anna Pavlova, and Vaslav Nijinsky, had recently emerged in Russia, but were unknown in Paris. Fokine, influenced by the free-flowing forms of Isadora Duncan, was a choreographer of genius. And Diaghilev obtained the collaboration of Benois, Bakst, and others for his costumes. The resulting spectacle, 19 May 1909, danced to the music of Russian composers, caused a sensation, the first of many.

In 1911, Diaghilev ended ties with the Imperial Theatre, and the Ballets Russes became his own. Many dancers, including Nijinsky, crossed over to his company. In Paris especially, but in other European capitals also, where his company performed from 1911 on, Diaghilev's artists stirred up a frenzy of enthusiasm. After Fokine left the company, Diaghilev promoted choreographers from within the company. Nijinsky, for example, invented a new style of movement for the highly controversial *Après-Midi d'un Faune* (1912) inspired by Mallarmé's poem, with music by Debussy. The premiere of Stravinsky's *Rite of Spring* (1913) caused even more of an uproar. The police ejected the most violent demonstrators, aligned for or against Stravinsky's percussive rhythms or Nijinsky's provocative choreography.

With the departure of Nijinsky after tours of North and South America in 1917, Diaghilev promoted Léonide Massine from inside the group. Increasingly, he turned to non-Russian—especially French—composers and painters. *Parade* (1917), a cubist ballet brought together by Jean Cocteau, combined the genius of Picasso, Erik Satie, and Massine.

Nijinska (Nijinsky's sister), Massine's successor, created many outstanding ballets in the early 1920s, especially *Les Noces* (1923) to music by Stravinsky. One of Diaghilev's greatest discoveries, George Balanchine, showed up in Paris in 1924. A Russian émigré dancer, he first displayed his genius in choreographing a revival of Stravinsky's *Le Chant du rossignol* and went on to compose *Apollo* in close collaboration with Stravinsky, then the poignant *Prodigal Son.*

In the last two years of his life, Diaghilev's interest in ballet waned as, in the company of his secretary Boris Kochno, he pursued a passion for first editions of Russian manuscripts. His collection became one of the finest in the world. Ever the aesthete, he was not interested in reading the works, but in their beauty. He fought a losing battle against diabetes, and his death came in Venice, on 19 August 1929, in the presence of his friends Kochno and Lifar, who, overcome by jealous rage, fought, as Misia Sert looked on in horror. Diaghilev's burial in the graveyard of San Michele in Venice marked the passing of an era, the end of the Ballets Russes as such. His artistic legacy remains.

References:

Benois, Alexandre. *Memoirs I, II,* translated by Moura Budberg. London: Chatto, 1964.

Buckle, Richard. *Diaghilev.* New York: Atheneum, 1979.

Kirstein, Lincoln. *Fokine.* London: British-Continental Press, 1934.

Kochno, Boris. *Diaghilev and the Ballets Russes,* translated by Adrienne Foulke. New York: Harper & Row, 1970.

Massine, Leonide. *My Life in Ballet,* edited by Phyllis Hartnoll and Robert Rubens. London: Macmillan, 1968.

Nijinsky. London: Weidenfeld and Nicolson, 1971.

Nijinsky Dancing. New York: Alfred A. Knopf, 1975.

Percival, John. *The World of Diaghilev.* New York: Harmony Press.

Sert, Misia. *Two or Three Muses.* London: Museum Press, 1953, rev. ed. 1979.

Sokolova, Lydia. *Dancing for Diaghilev,* edited by Richard Buckle. London: Murray, 1960.

Steegmuller, Francis. *Cocteau.* Boston: Little Brown, 1970.

—James P. McNab

Emily Dickinson

1830-1886

American poet

Emily Dickinson wrote nearly 1800 poems, but only seven were published in her lifetime. When the first posthumous collection of her work appeared in 1890, she was regarded as an interesting but idiosyncratic minor poet. As the twentieth century has progressed, however, her poetic achievement has won increasing recognition. Working for the most part with the conventional form of the rhymed four-line stanza, and seeming to observe the proprieties of her time, Dickinson nonetheless engages in an original and vibrant way with love, eroticism, nature, death, immortality and eternity. Her work is notable for its power, compression and complexity, its precise and startling phrasing, its inventiveness of rhythm and rhyme, and the exploratory daring which belies its apparent decorum.

Her life was also marked by apparent decorum. She always lived in her family home in Amherst, Massachusetts, and, from her thirties, she was virtually a recluse. Nonetheless, she was in touch through her father and brother, and through her correspondence and reading, with wider political, religious, and cultural currents in nineteenth-century America and Europe, and her poems and her letters show her capacity for ardent attachment both to men and women. Whereas critics and biographers in the past often played down her feelings for women, recent biography and criticism has stressed their importance and intensity. For example, Judith Farr's *The Passion of Emily Dickinson* (1992) traces what Dickinson herself called, in her *Letters* (1958), the "endless fire" of her love for Susan Gilbert, while Paula Bennett's *Emily Dickinson: Woman Poet* (1990) argues that Dickinson's "homoerotic and autoerotic commitment to women" is the basis of her "ability to transcend the limitations placed upon her gender and to pose female sexuality and female creativity as valid, autonomous *alternatives* to male sexuality and male creativity."

Emily Elizabeth Dickinson was born on 10 December 1830, in Amherst, Massachusetts. She was the second child of the lawyer and prominent local citizen, Edward Dickinson, and Emily Norcross Dickinson, who appears to have been a reticent and submissive wife. Dickinson's elder brother, Austin, had been born the previous year, and her younger sister, Lavinia, was to arrive in 1833. At the time of Emily's birth, the family was then living at the Homestead, a house which had been built in 1814 by Edward's father, Samuel Fowler Dickinson, who would move to Ohio in 1833. Edward's own rise in the Amherst community was signalled by his appointment in 1835 as treasurer of Amherst College, and in 1838 he began his first term in the Massachusetts General Court. He sold his half-share of the Homestead in 1840 and moved his family to a nearby house on Mount Pleasant Street. In September of that year, Dickinson and her younger sister entered the co-educational Amherst Academy.

Dickinson's first intense and intimate friendship was with Sophia Holland, whom she idolized but who died when Dickinson was 14. Dickinson's *Letters* record that she wrote of Sophia: "[s]he was too lovely for earth." In 1844, she began another intense friendship with Abiah Root, then herself a student at Amherst Academy. Although Abiah left after a year to go to Springfield Academy, Dickinson continued to write lovingly to her until 1856, the year in which Abiah married and stopped replying to Emily's letters. In 1846, Amherst experienced one of its periodic religious revivals, but Dickinson had already confided her doubts about faith to the more devout Abiah, and she kept her distance from the increased evangelical fervour. Her poetry was to display a strong fascination with faith, especially with the ideas of immortality and eternity, but it would combine this with agnosticism and with a subversive ambivalence towards the patriarchal aspects of Christianity.

In September 1847, Dickinson started to attend Mount Holyoke Female Seminary at South Hadley but her father withdrew her in August of the following year. From then on, she was to educate herself through her reading and correspondence. In 1849, Longfellow's popular prose romance *Kavanagh* was published and Austin Dickinson secretly gave his elder sister a copy. It was also in 1849 that she read Charlotte Bronte's *Jane Eyre* (1847) and found it impressive. She had already discovered the poetry of Elizabeth Barrett Browning, and Browning, the Brontes, George Eliot and George Sand were to become the key figures in her self-constructed pantheon of contemporary female writers.

Emily Dickinson

Dickinson's Private Passions

Between 1847 and 1850, Dickinson got to know Susan Huntington Gilbert, and became passionately attached to her—an attachment that remained when Susan and Austin Dickinson started courting. 1850 saw Dickinson's first publication, a prose valentine in the Amherst undergraduate magazine *The Indicator*. In the same year, there was another religious revival in Amherst, and Dickinson's father, sister, and Susan Gilbert, all joined the First Church of Christ. Dickinson, however, once more kept her distance, "standing alone in rebellion" as she says in her *Letters*. At around this time, the health of Dickinson's mother started to decline, but Dickinson and her sister were still able to travel to Boston in 1851. Their father campaigned for the U.S. House of Representatives as a conservative Whig Party candidate and was elected in 1852. On 20 February 1852, Dickinson published her first poem, "Sic transit gloria mundi," in the *Springfield Daily Republican*. The editor and part-owner of the *Republican* was Samuel Bowles, a Dickinson family friend, and he and Emily were to engage in a long correspondence. In 1853, her brother Austin entered Harvard Law School, and he and Susan Gilbert became engaged.

The Dickinson family visited Washington in 1854. Dickinson and her sister made a return visit by themselves the following year, and then went on to Mount Vernon and to Philadelphia. In 1855, Edward Dickinson repurchased the entire Homestead and brought the family back to the paternal property. He accepted the Whig nomination for Congress in October, but his election bid was defeated the following month, and he started a law partnership with his son. A further decline in her mother's health in November meant that Dickinson and her sister had to take over the management of the household. In January 1856, Austin joined his father, younger sister, and fiancee as a member of the First Church of Christ, and on 1 July he married Susan Gilbert. The newlyweds moved into the Evergreens, a house next to the Homestead which Edward Dickinson had built for them. Their first child, Edward, was to be born in 1861. Ralph Waldo Emerson stayed with Austin and Susan when he came to Amherst in 1857 to lecture on "The Beautiful in Rural Life," but Dickinson herself did not attend his lecture.

Dickinson was working hard on her poetry in 1858, and it was around this time that she started to bind her verses into homemade packets or "fascicles." In about 1859, she met a friend of Susan's, Catherine Scott, and for a time they had a passionate romantic association; their acquaintance seems finally to have ended in 1866, when Catherine married.

Between 1858 and early 1862, Dickinson wrote three intense and passionate letters to "the Master" which have prompted much speculation. Samuel Bowles has been seen as a likely candidate, but the identity of "the Master" has never been authoritatively established, and indeed it has been questioned whether he existed at all, except as an imaginative construction.

The Woman in White

In 1861, Dickinson's poem "I taste a liquor never brewed" was published, under the title of "The May-Wine," in the *Springfield Republican*. By this time, she was well on her way to becoming a recluse. Up to her mid-twenties, she had lived the kind of social life expected of the daughter of an eminent citizen, but as she moved towards her thirties, she started to withdraw from the outside world, and by the time she was approaching forty, her seclusion was virtually complete. Jay Leyda's *The Years and Hours of Emily Dickinson* (1960) quotes a letter written by Mabel Loomis Todd in 1881 which conveys the impression made by Dickinson's withdrawal: "I must tell you about the *character* of Amherst. It is a lady whom the people call the *Myth* ... She has not been outside of her own house in fifteen years ... She dresses wholly in white, & her mind is said to be perfectly wonderful. She writes finely, but no one *ever* sees her."

The *Springfield Republican* published a further Dickinson poem, "Safe in their alabaster chambers," in March 1862. The next month, an article called "To a Young Contributor," giving practical advice to aspiring authors, appeared in the literary magazine *Atlantic Monthly*. It was by Thomas Wentworth Higginson, an essayist, abolitionist, campaigner for women's rights, and former Unitarian minister, and it prompted Dickinson to write to him and send him some of her poems. A long correspondence resulted, but Higginson, like Charles Wadsworth, met Dickinson on only two occasions. He encouraged her to write, and acted, as she had requested, as her "Preceptor," but he did not try to get her work published. Higginson did, however, enable her to renew her acquaintance with Helen Hunt Jackson, a novelist and poet who was one of America's leading women writers, and a crusader for the rights of Native Americans. Jackson and Dickinson had known each other when growing up in Amherst, but it was only in the 1870s that they came into contact again, and another long correspondence ensued.

Two more of Dickinson's poems appeared in print in 1864—"Some keep the Sabbath going to church" in the New York *Round Table* and "Blazing in gold and quenching in purple" once again in the *Springfield Republican*. She found herself suffering, however, from the eye trouble which was a family affliction, and she had to spend seven months in Boston for treatment. Despite this, she had written, by the end of 1865, about 1000 poems. The poem "A narrow fellow in the grass" appeared in the *Springfield Republican* in 1866. At the end of the year, Austin and Susan's second child, Martha, was born. The continued devotion of Dickinson's brother and father to the First Church of Christ was demonstrated when Austin supervised the construction, opposite Evergreens, of a new Church building, and Edward Dickinson gave the dedicatory speech in 1868.

Thomas Wentworth Higginson came to Amherst in 1870 and met Dickinson for the first time. *The Letters of Emily Dickinson* record that he wrote to his wife: "I never was with any one who drained my nerve power so much." In that year a Dickinson family friend, Josiah Gilbert Holland, a part-owner with Samuel Bowles of the Springfield *Daily Republican*, became the founding editor of the influential literary magazine *Scribner's*, but, although he knew many of Dickinson's poems, he printed none. Edward Dickinson resigned as Treasurer of Amherst College in 1872, but his son was elected to the office the following year, confirming the prominence of the Dickinson family in the town. Near the end of 1872, Higginson gave a lecture in Amherst and paid his second and last visit to Dickinson. Her father was elected to the Massachusetts House of Representatives as an independent candidate in 1873, but in 1874, he died suddenly in Boston. The following year, his widow became bedridden with paralysis, six weeks before the birth of Austin and Susan's third child, Thomas Gilbert.

Jackson Sees Dickinson's Greatness

By 1878, Dickinson had written over 1400 poems. Helen Hunt Jackson had urged her to publish them, telling her, in an 1876 letter quoted in Cynthia Griffin Wolff's biography of Dickinson, that she was "a great poet" who should "sing aloud." Only one further song appeared in print in Dickinson's lifetime, however: "Success is counted sweetest" was published anonymously in *A Masque of Poets* in the "No Name" series in 1878. Many thought its author was Emerson.

Around this time, a potential new suitor for Dickinson appeared. Otis Phillips Lord, an eminent Massachusetts judge who was a family friend, often visited her in 1880 after the death of his wife, and the surviving rough drafts of 15 letters Dickinson wrote to Lord written between 1878 and 1882 suggest that her feelings for him were intense. But although marriage was discussed, nothing came of it. The year1880 also saw the Reverend Charles Wadsworth's second and last visit to Dickinson, an unexpected one prompted by his feeling that his death was imminent. He did indeed die two years later, in March 1882, and in November of that year, death finally came to Dickinson's invalid mother. A more shocking and unexpected loss was that of Dickinson's nephew, Austin, at the age of eight. This compounded the pain Susan was already suffering because of her husband's affair with Mabel Loomis Todd, the 28-year old wife of an astronomy professor at Amherst Academy, which had begun the previous year and would continue until Austin's death. In 1884, Otis Phillips Lord died, and Dickinson had her first bout of kidney trouble. The death of Helen Hunt Jackson occurred in 1885, and Dickinson herself died of Bright's disease on 15 May 1886. She was 55.

After her death, her sister Lavinia found over 1000 poems in her sister's room. Thomas Wentworth Higginson and Mabel Loomis Todd edited two selections of the poems which came out in 1890 and 1891, but they altered them considerably to try and bring them into line with current conventions. Further selections, by Alfred Leete Hampson and Dickinson's niece, Martha Dickinson Bianchi, appeared between 1914 and 1937, but these were also heavily and clumsily edited. In 1945, however, Todd and her daughter brought out *Bolts of Melody*, which kept closer to Dickinson's original texts and included many poems suppressed by her relatives, and in 1955, Thomas H. Johnson's variorum edition of all 1775 known poems laid the foundation of modern Dickinson studies.

It can now be seen that in nineteenth-century American literature, Dickinson stands as the great contrast and complement to Walt Whitman. Private where Whitman was public, restrained where he was rambunctious, she wrote in her *Letters* that she "never read his Book [*Leaves of Grass*]—but was told that he was disgraceful."

Dickinson was also, however, disgraceful in her way, and she shares with Whitman the credit of having widened the scope of modern poetry to take in a range of repressed experiences, including, in her own case, female autoeroticism and the passion of women for women. Her life and work remain exemplary because of the way in which, within the social and cultural constraints of her time, she opened up a distinctive space for women's creativity and desire.

References:

Bennett, Paula. *Emily Dickinson: Woman Poet*. New York and London: Harvester Wheatsheaf, 1990.

Farr, Judith. *The Passion of Emily Dickinson*. Cambridge: Harvard University Press, 1992.

Johnson, Thomas, ed. *Emily Dickinson: An Interpretive Biography*. Cambridge: The Belknap Press of Harvard University Press, 1966.

———. *The Letters of Emily Dickinson*. Cambridge: Harvard University Press, 1958.

Leyda, Jay. *The Years and Hours of Emily Dickinson*. New Haven: Yale University Press, 1960.

McNeil, Helen. *Emily Dickinson*. Virago Pioneers series. London: Virago, 1986.

Patterson, Rebecca. *The Riddle of Emily Dickinson*. Boston: Houghton Mifflin, 1951.

Rich, Adrienne. "Vesuvius at Home: The Power of Emily Dickinson" in *On Lies, Secrets and Silence: Selected Prose 1966-1978*. New York: W.W. Norton, 1979.

Sewall, Richard B. *The Life of Emily Dickinson*. 2 vols. New York: Farrar, Straus and Giroux, 1974.

Wolff, Cynthia Griffin. *Emily Dickinson*. New York: Alfred A. Knopf, 1986.

—Nicolas Tredell

Divine

1946-1988

American actor and female impersonator

By his own definition, Divine was an actor who was no different from any other person on stage or in film. His career playing female roles extensively, though, also earned him the titles of transvestite and drag artist. He created a name for himself in cult films during the 1960s through the 1980s playing grotesque and sometimes disgusting female roles. Divine was driven to challenge cultural and gender stereotypes with his acting.

Divine was born Harris Glen Milstead in Baltimore, Maryland, on 19 October 1945. He grew up on a large estate with his parents, Harris and Frances Milstead. A lonely, overweight boy, Divine entertained himself by dressing up in his mother's clothes and running about his home. In high school he became friends with John Waters. Waters nicknamed his friend "Divine" and as a film director later cast him in many of his films. For years, Divine's parents were estranged from him, but they reconciled by the time of his death on 7 March 1988 from heart disease.

Divine's first film was *Roman Candles* (1962), but the film that gave him his first real recognition was *Eat Your Makeup* (1963). In it he parodied two famous women, Jackie Kennedy and Elizabeth Taylor. His size, at over 300 pounds, made it a grotesque and bizarre portrayal. Directed by Waters, the film is the story of a crazy, violent woman who injects eyeliner and throws punches at people. His next film, also directed by Waters, was *Mondo Trasho* (1969). From there his roles grew by leaps in their shock value. In a calculated move by Waters designed to bring Divine notoriety, he actually consumed dog excrement in *Pink Flamingos* (1972), another cult film.

The films he starred in during the early 1970s had a common theme. They were satires of soap operas about victimized women or delinquent girls living in the suburbs. Typical of underground cult films during that time, they featured various forms of physical punishment, rape, murder, and even cannibalism. In *Female Trouble* (1974) Divine played dual roles of a man and a woman, and made love to himself in a trash dump. *Desperate Living* (1977) also employed the "problem women" theme.

As homosexuality gained more exposure during the 1970s, Divine appeared in films that were known outside of the film underground. He made two comedies in the mid-1980s, *Lust in the Dust* (1985) and *Trouble in Mind* (1986). His roles changed from vulgar and promiscuous women to women with huge personalities who lived extraordinary, outrageous lives. He injected glamour into these roles, in the style of his idols—Elizabeth Taylor, Bette Davis, and Joan Crawford. He based his characters on that type of polished, aggressive woman who knows herself and gets what she wants.

Divine's real goal during this time was to make people laugh and forget their troubles for a couple of hours. He modified his usual look of elaborate wigs and exaggerated makeup in the movie *Hairspray* (1988), which attracted a mainstream audience. *Hairspray*

Divine

was the story of Baltimore in the early 1960s, a nostalgic look at the world he knew during his teen years. It was a rapid critical and commercial success.

In addition to film acting, Divine's career included singing and nightclub entertaining. He had great stage presence, combining humor and charm. Several hit records grew out of his nightclub acts during the 1970s and 1980s. Two of the more well-known titles are "You Think You're a Man" and "Walk Like a Man." Naturally, they were self-parodies of his show characters. Not content to be known only for his outlandish film roles, Divine went in a new direction in the mid-1970s. He starred in a theatre production of *Women Behind Bars* (1976) in New York and London, to applauding audiences. Later he did additional serious acting. He was about to appear on television in an episode of the Fox series "Married ... with Children" when his sudden death occurred before the show was complete.

Divine made a name for himself as a coarse, crude character on film. But his approach to his work was the opposite. He always considered himself an actor, not an impersonator. He earned the respect of people in the production end of the business through professionalism and dedication to his roles. Considering that he died at the early age of 42, in a relatively short career his accomplishments were many. As an underground film star, nightclub entertainer, recording artist, television actor, and stage performer, he had no equal.

References:

Annual Obituary, 1988. Chicago: St. James Press, 1990.

Contemporary Theatre, Film, and Television, Volume 7. Detroit: Gale, 1989.

Newsmakers, 1988, Issue 3. Detroit: Gale, 1988.

New York Times Biographical Service. Ann Arbor, Michigan: University Microfilms International, 1988.

—Carolyn Eckstein-Soule

Melvin Dixon

1950-1992

African-American writer and educator

Melvin Dixon was a leading authority on African-American and West African literature. His second novel, *Vanishing Rooms* (1991), was his major legacy to the gay literary heritage.

Melvin Dixon was born in Stamford, Connecticut, on 29 May 1950. His father, Handy Dixon, was a house painter and contractor who was born in North Carolina. His mother, Jessie Dixon, was a nurse who came from South Carolina.

Dixon pursued a joint English/theater major at Wesleyan University in Middletown, Connecticut. While in college his first drama and film criticism was published. He was also a director of the University's Black Repertory Theater, which performed two of his own dramatic pieces under his direction. He received his BA degree from Wesleyan in 1971. He traveled in Europe prior to entering the graduate program in American civilization at Brown University in Providence, Rhode Island. From the fall of 1972 until the summer of 1974, he lived mostly in Paris. There, he researched the Parisian exile of the African-American author Richard Wright, and wrote poetry and an unpublished novel, *Let the River Answer*. He visited Senegal for a month in the summer of 1974 and spent the following winter in Paris.

After receiving his MA (1973) and his PhD (1976) from Brown University, Dixon was an assistant professor of English (1976-1980) at Williams College in Williamstown, Massachusetts. During the late 1970s he did research in Haiti and visited Paris three times to write, lecture, and give readings of his poetry. Dixon was appointed to the English faculty at the graduate center of Queens College, City University of New York, where he was successively associate professor (1980-1986) and full professor (1986-1992). He visited West Africa in 1980 and 1983, and was the Fulbright Professor of American Literature and Civilization at the Université de Dakar, in Dakar, Senegal, from 1985 to 1986. He received a National Endowment for the Arts poetry fellowship in 1984 and a New York Arts Foundation artist fellowship in fiction in 1988.

Dixon's highly acclaimed writings and translations encompassed many genres, but most remained rooted in West African and African-American experiences. His principal work of literary criticism, *Ride Out the Wilderness: Geography and Identity in Afro-American Literature* (1987), traced the creation of geographic and spatial metaphors in defining black identity from slave narratives and songs to the novels of Toni Morrison.

Dixon's poetry, which he considered among his greatest accomplishments, was published in leading American poetry reviews and compiled in *Change of Territory* (1983). His poetry often reflected his own experiences as a gay African-American. Fluent in both Parisian and West African French, he translated *The Collected Poetry* by Leopold Sedar Senghor (1991), thereby making the work of West Africa's leading poet accessible to English-speaking readers.

Critics often consider Dixon's two published novels to be his most innovative work. *Trouble the Water* (1989) used the birthplace of Dixon's father, Pee Wee, North Carolina, as the setting for a Southern Gothic tale that inverted several traditional African-American literary themes. The book won the 1989 Nilon Excellence in Minority Fiction Award. In his final novel, *Vanishing Rooms*, Dixon explored homophobic violence and interracial gay relationships through three interwoven first-person narratives. The book was widely praised in both the mainstream and gay press for its literary merits, and is often compared to James Baldwin's *Giovanni's Room*.

Dixon was concerned about racism in the gay and lesbian community and was an early member of Black and White Men Together, a gay group that addressed the issue. In a *Christopher Street* interview with Clarence Bard Cole in the May 1991 issue, he berated the gay media for ignoring gay black male authors.

Melvin Dixon died of complications from AIDS in Stamford, Connecticut, on 26 October 1992. He will be best remembered for his scholarship in the field of African-American literature, as well as the creativity of his poems and novels.

References:

Cole, Clarence Bard. "Other Voices, Other Rooms: An Interview With Melvin Dixon," in *Christopher Street* 14, May 1991: 24-7.

Contemporary Authors. Volume 132. Detroit: Gale Research, 1991.

Fabre, Michel. *From Harlem to Paris: Black American Writers in France, 1840-1980.* Urbana: University of Illinois, 1991.
Malinowski, Sharon, ed. *Gay and Lesbian Literature.* Detroit: St. James, 1994.
Nelson, Emmanuel S. *Contemporary Gay American Novelists: A Bio-Bibliographical Critical Sourcebook.* Westport, Connecticut: Greenwood, 1993.
Obituary in *New York Times*, 29 October 1992: B16.
Peterson, Bernard L., Jr. *Contemporary Black American Playwrights and Their Plays: A Biographical Directory and Dramatic Index.* Westport, Connecticut: Greenwood, 1988.

—Joseph M. Eagan

Judy Dlugacz

1952-

American businesswoman

Judy Dlugacz, entrepreneur and owner of Olivia Records and Olivia Cruises and Resorts, launched the women's music movement and almost single-handedly created the lesbian travel industry.

In 1973, 20-year-old Dlugacz left law school and formed Olivia Records with nine friends (including musician Meg Christian) in Washington, D.C. (Olivia is named after a French novel of a schoolgirl's love for her teacher.) Together they borrowed $4000. Christian and Cris Williamson were the label's first musicians.

"We were pretty radical feminists and lesbians in the early '70s, and we knew we wanted to start a business together," Dlugacz told the *Los Angeles Times* in 1993. "But when the others said they wanted to start a record company, I said, 'Are you crazy?' But they said it was all about creating a place for women in the music business, which was very closed."

Dlugacz's commitment to increasing the women's representation in music and in the music industry has not flagged for 25 years. "Fifteen percent of the low-level executives in the record business are women," she told the *San Francisco Business Times*' Patrick Danner. "Low level not even in the higher echelon of making real decisions.... Excuse me, but name five women drummers, five women bass players, five women guitar players and five women producers.... I've been doing that for 15 years and nobody has been able to name them."

Unable to find distribution through mainstream music industry channels, Olivia distributed their records at the concerts that drew larger and larger audiences. Olivia remains in the record and concert promotion industry, though the travel division of the corporation supports the record group, which remains committed to its vision of social change.

In 1993, celebrating the twentieth anniversary of Olivia, Dlugacz told the *Los Angeles Times,* "My experience in the last 20 years has been in creating visibility for women, and particularly for lesbians. There are now many role models that this is a healthy, normal way to be, and that there aren't stereotypical ways you have to look or be. These days are very exciting."

Danner suggests: "Dlugacz has been described as a visionary, whose creativity, earnesty, and vigor have helped elevate women up the music business ladder while pushing an untapped art form—women's music." Dlugacz has made a film of the early days of Olivia, with Frances Reid: "The Changer: A Record of the Times."

"We felt it was a very radical movement. We created a cultural alternative for women. Thousands of women came out of the closet because of our little band of renegades." Dlugacz moved to Los Angeles before settling in San Francisco, where in 1978 she met Rachel Wahba, a psychotherapist, now her partner. They share a home in Glan Park. Wahba's daughter works for Olivia.

The comment of a woman at a Seattle concert prompted Dlugacz to expand Olivia into the travel business. Beginning with the down payment for the first cruise and the commitment and pre-payment of 600 women from Olivia Records' mailing list, Olivia is now the largest company providing all-women's cruises.

The travel business has proved popular and profitable for Olivia. On one trip, one third of the travelers were repeat customers; the proportion can go as high as 50 percent. Overall, Olivia's travel business has a 40 percent return rate. The cruise business generates between $2.5 and $4 million dollars in sales each year.

References:

Adams, Jane Meredith. "A Vacation Paradise for Lesbians At Ixtapa," in *San Francisco Examiner*, 10 March 1996.
Burstiner, Marcy. "Gay Cruise Line Steams Ahead," in *San Francisco Business Times*, 12 August 1993: 12.
Danner, Patrick. "Dlugacz's Vision Revolutionized Recording Industry for Women," in *San Francisco Business Times*, 21 November 1988.
Greenberg, Peter. "The Journey Man: Gay Travelers Are Getting Out and About," in the *Seattle Times*, 6 June 1993: K6.
Hochman, Steve. "You've Come a Long Way, Olivia," in *Los Angeles Times*, 23 June 1993.
Levy, Dan. "Stonewall Riots' Legacy of Freedom to Come Out," in *The San Francisco Chronicle*, 27 June 1994.
Liveten, Sharon. "Olivia Records, a Healthy Gain in 15 Years," in *Los Angeles Times*, 14 May 1988.
Van Gelder, Lindsy and Pamela Robin Brandt. "Cruising Greek Isles With Daughters of Sappho," in *Los Angeles Times*, 28 March 1993.

—Richard Voos

Alix Dobkin

1940-

American singer, songwriter, and activist

If Alix Dobkin is known as a music-maker extraordinaire and a rabble-rouser par excellence, she comes by her reputation honestly. The descendant of working-class Russian Jewish immigrants who wanted to change the world through art, music, and the Communist Party, Dobkin became a singer, songwriter, and a lesbian separatist because she also felt the world needed changing. Dobkin is among the first, and still one of the few, major figures of women's music to sing openly about her politics and her lesbian consciousness. Described as "Mythic ... a foremother of women's music" by lesbian historian Lillian Faderman, Dobkin has delighted and incited audiences all over the world, and produced seven record albums. Up front and at times infuriating, says music critic Jim Fouratt, Dobkin has nevertheless "cleared the stage for the Tracys, the k.d.s, the Melissas, the Micheles, the Latifahs and all the other strong women making pop music."

The oldest child of William Dobkin and Martha Kunstlich was born on 16 August 1940 in New York City. She was given the name "Alix" in memory of her uncle Cecil Alexander Kunstlich, a fiery organizer for the National Maritime Union, who died a guerrilla fighter in the Spanish Civil War, his fist in the air before a Fascist firing squad, shouting, "¡Viva la Revolucion!" Back in the United States, Alix's father, Bill Dobkin, led a more conventional life as a professional fundraiser for a succession of Jewish organizations, while Martha Dobkin worked in their home, raising Alix and later her brother and sister. But behind these all-American scenes, both Bill and Martha were organizers for the Communist Party. As an infant, Dobkin would be wheeled out to the waterfront, her carriage crammed with union leaflets, then displayed prominently, as her parents explained the benefits of union membership to dockworkers who, they feared, might have beaten them up, were it not for the endearing presence of their baby.

Dobkin's family was loving and stable, yet her childhood was an unconventional blend of traditional lower middle-class values and radical left-wing politics. On one hand, her parents led clandestine lives as Party members, and during the dangerous McCarthy era, they taught their daughter the importance of holding fast to dearly held principles. On the other hand, Alix attended public school, got good grades, adored the Brooklyn Dodgers, saw the latest movies, and became infatuated with wholesome movie star Jane Powell—an excellent feminine role model for the 1950s.

Dobkin's early musical influences, therefore, swung all the way from the Red Army Chorus to Rogers and Hammerstein. Her parents loved music; Bill Dobkin singing, and Martha playing and teaching the piano. They bought records and filled their house with the sounds of Ray Charles, Paul Robeson, Pete Seeger, Louis Armstrong, Woodie Guthrie, Bach, Burl Ives, Broadway show tunes, and traditional Yiddish folksongs.

Dobkin was also heir to the vibrant New York Jewish culture that seems to flourish during peaks in radical left-wing activity. And, except for what Dobkin remembers as two stultifying years in Kansas City, the family managed to live in cities on what Dobkin calls the "radical, Jewish" East Coast. Gradually, however, Dobkin's parents became disillusioned with the Communist Party, and in 1956, summarily resigned, outraged and embittered by Kruschev's revelations of Stalin's atrocities. Meanwhile, Dobkin nursed her crush on Jane Powell, flirted with boys, and continued what appeared to be a normal trajectory for a girl coming of age in the Eisenhower years.

Beginnings as a Folksinger

Partly as a way of fitting in socially, and very much against her parents' wishes, Dobkin herself joined the Communist Party at 16. Along with thousands of students of the Beat generation, she was also drawn toward folksinging, and soon learned to play the guitar. Dobkin enrolled at Temple University's Tyler School of Fine Arts in Philadelphia, and joined the Jewish Young People's Chorus. She also began to spend time around the ethnic folk circles of Philadelphia, and to perform such folkie standards as "Pretty Peggy-O" and "Old Blue" at private parties, meetings, and progressive picnics.

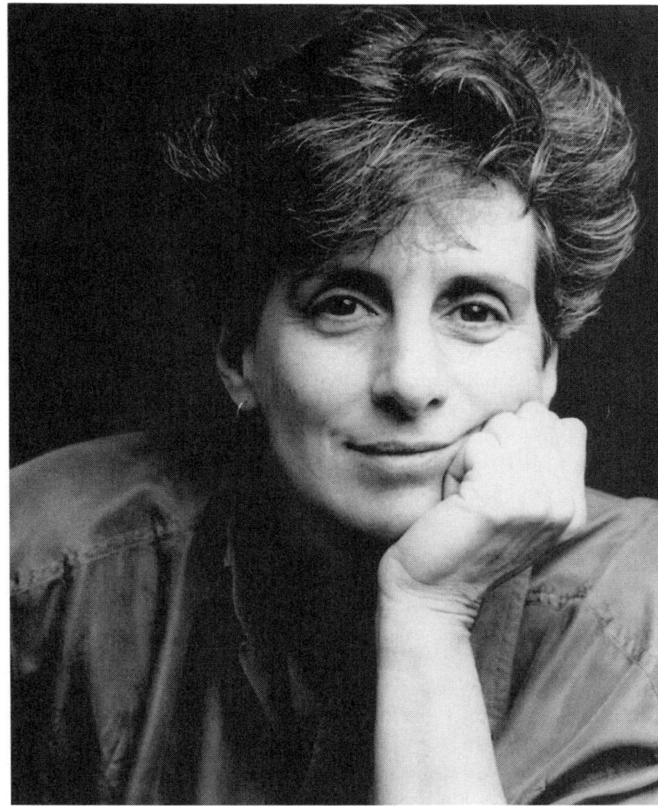

Alix Dobkin. ***Photograph by Joanne Giganti.***

One day, a man who hung around Dobkin and her revolutionary comrades suggested that she could get paid for performing in coffee houses—perhaps as much as $150 a week. Dobkin's first show was such a resounding success that the man became her manager on the spot. He went on to manage Bill Cosby and Buffy St. Marie, although at the time Dobkin and her friends didn't trust his politics. Years later, long after Dobkin had left the Communist Party, her manager sat her down and told her that during those early years, he had been an FBI informant. "We knew that," smiles Dobkin. "It was kind of satisfying to have our suspicions confirmed."

In the spring of 1962, Dobkin graduated *cum laude* with a BFA in painting, and moved to New York City, where she began performing professionally at the Gaslight Cafe in Greenwich Village. Billed as "Miss Alix Dobkin, International Folksinger," she also toured the country, singing standard folk songs. In 1965 she married Sam Hood, the son of the Gaslight's manager, and moved with him to Miami to open the Gaslight South. For two years, Dobkin appeared on the bill with the likes of Josh White, Simon and Garfunkel, Ronnie Gilbert, and Gordon Lightfoot. But the club couldn't make it financially, so the couple returned to New York. Here, Hood managed the Gaslight, and Dobkin became the only woman in a forgettable folk foursome called "Chester's Children." Dobkin soon returned to her solo act, and late in 1970, her daughter Adrian Hood was born. In 1971, Dobkin and Sam Hood separated and later divorced.

Early Feminism

By now, Dobkin had become alert to the emergence of feminism. She started to read the new feminist manifestoes and was particularly moved by the words of Germaine Greer. One evening, she heard Greer interviewed on a local New York radio show by a woman named Liza Cowan. Cowan later invited women songwriters to appear on her show, and Dobkin, having already written a few songs about women, tried them out on the air. She also fell deeply in love with Cowan. It was with Cowan on Valentine's Day, 1972, that Dobkin decided that—"sexually, politically, emotionally, culturally, socially, you name it"—she was a lesbian.

As her feminism grew, Dobkin began to turn away from what she now saw as the "typically woman-hating" lyrics of many of the songs she had sung for years. It was time, she realized, for "new songs and a new audience to sing them for." One of her first "new" songs is still perhaps her most popular: "The Woman in Your Life Is You" exults in the power of a woman to claim her own existence in the world. It was, says Dobkin, "my first fully conscious women's song." Moving from the leftist political to the feminist personal, Dobkin wrote songs celebrating the women in her life—her daughter, her lover, her crushes, even an occasional foe. She explored her developing feminist consciousness in such songs as "Fantasy Girl," and her lesbian sexuality in such songs as "A Woman's Love." Characteristically, Dobkin was never afraid to sing the word "lesbian" out loud: "Let's be in no man's land/Lesbian, Lesbian/Any woman can be a Lesbian" (from "Gay Head," 1973).

At this point in her career, Dobkin closed the door to mainstream success. Judy Collins's manager, having heard some of Dobkin's songs for and about women, arranged a meeting for Dobkin with a producer at Elektra Records. Producers at Columbia also asked her to sign a contract. But Dobkin, bolstered by her growing sense that lesbians were "going to save the world," told Elektra she wanted control of the advertising, and told Columbia that she wasn't sure if she wanted her music to be heard by men. Although somewhat surprised when both companies backed down, Dobkin shrugged and turned her attention to creating a women's culture.

About this time, in what could be called a Great Moment of Herstory, Dobkin met flutist Kay Gardner, who was to become another matriarch of women's music. Together they worked out simple musical arrangements and began playing them around New York City, soon adding a bass player to their duo. Dobkin and company decided to name their band "Lavender Jane Loves Women" after two significant Janes: political fugitive Jane Alpert, who had recently galvanized radical feminists with her indictment (written in hiding from the FBI for her part in protest bombings) of the Left's virulent sexism; and, of course, Jane Powell, who still occupied a warm spot in Dobkin's heart. The band's first record, also called *Lavender Jane Loves Women,* was a community project that took a few months to finance, but the overwhelmingly positive response to it made the effort worthwhile. Dobkin, Cowan, and Gardner, among others, formed the Women's Music Network, Inc., a short-lived prototype of women's music collectives to come. Then, with Cowan and a loose collective of other women, Dobkin moved to upstate New York, staked out a rural, separatist life, and released an album daringly titled, *Living with Lesbians.* For almost a decade following, Dobkin played and sang exclusively for women.

Women's Community, Women's Culture

The purposeful exclusion of males from many venues of women's culture became a central issue among lesbian feminists during the 1970s and much of the 1980s. Until the mid-1980s, Dobkin, as a performer and a public figure, held fast to what she saw as an essential need for consistent "women-only space." For this stance, she garnered enemies, ironically most of them women—yet there were also women who criticized Dobkin for not being separatist *enough.* As women's culture blossomed, Dobkin continued to write songs about her life and her feminist principles, and began to perform at a growing number of women's music festivals across the country. In 1975, the Michigan Womyn's Music Festival was born, and almost instantly became the crucible for the great lesbian feminist debates of the era. Not surprisingly, Dobkin became one of the great debaters there.

Held late in the summer each year in the Michigan countryside, the Womyn's Festival soon began to attract thousands of women from all over the world. At first, the music was relatively simple and unadorned: voices of such performers as Meg Christian and Maxine Feldman rang out against the mellow accompaniment of acoustic guitars. Over the years, however, as women's culture expanded, the festival also attracted the harsher and more sophisticated sounds of such groups as Tribe 8 and Girls in the Nose. But even this turbulent musical mix has been eclipsed at times by such polarizing issues as male children, sadomasochism, and transgendered people—and whether they should be allowed on "women's land."

Dobkin, in favor of preserving "safe space" for women, objected to what she saw as the intrusive presence of sadomasochistic activities and transgendered people. But, in a movement hungry for leaders, what are in fact Dobkin's opinions may well have been perceived as her edicts. Dobkin says that she has tried to express her "highest, best values" during the festival's controversies, hoping that other women would come forth in a mutually respectful manner to discuss their own values. Yet, perhaps owing to changing times and politics, Dobkin, having been a constant presence at the festival since its beginning, was not invited back for its twentieth anniversary in 1995.

Although her separatist ideology has received mixed reviews, there seems little disagreement that Dobkin's performances are strong, joyous, and professional. Dobkin has toured the United States and Canada, as well as Australia, New Zealand, Europe, Scotland, Ireland, England, and Wales. She's received several awards from the music magazine *Hotwire,* appeared in scores of television and radio interviews, and has written on women's music and women's culture for various music and feminist periodicals. In the 1980s, Dobkin launched a campaign, including magazine articles, lectures, and a slide show, to educate women about the sexist and racist lyrics taken for granted in such popular songs as "Brown Sugar" and "Under My Thumb." And she continued to produce more albums, including *XXAlix, Yahoo Australia,* and *Love & Politics.*

Revolution to Evolution

Over the years, Dobkin's politics have evolved. In the mid-1980s, she began opening some of her performances to men, not only for financial reasons, but also because she felt she needed political allies. "I've been perceived as an extremist," reflects Dobkin. "And that's often been correct. But what's correct for me has changed. I am still an anti-racist; I believe in the necessity for women-only space; I believe that, as a rule, male institutions keep women down." And gradually, Dobkin's idea of women's capabilities has stabilized: "With the exception of pissing over their shoulders," she says, "women can do anything men can do, and often better—including being oppressive or exploitative. I have, I hope, fewer illusions that all women are wonderful and all men stink." Yet through decades of change, Dobkin's essential belief that "each woman is her own final authority" remains as true today as it was when she wrote "The Woman in Your Life." "That's why feminism is so powerful for me," continues Dobkin. "Rather than being anti-male, it's pro-personal power."

Today, Dobkin is at work on her memoirs. She also leads vocal workshops and continues to perform, "educating" not just lesbians, but anybody "with a mind and a heart." In 1995, she moved from upstate New York to Oakland, California, to be with her partner, Sherry Booth. Dobkin's sister Julie, also a lesbian, lives nearby in Oakland, while her daughter Adrian remains in New York City, working with children and pursuing a Masters degree in social work.

Dobkin's friends and role models are legion and sometimes legendary. They include lesbian writers Bertha Harris, Jorjet Harper, and Sarah Schulman; ex-Michigan Festival producer Boo Price; Australian potter Suzanne Bellamy; Margaret Sloan Hunter, poet and founder of *Ms.* magazine; Jo Mapes, 1960s folksinger; and painter Louise Fishman. These and thousands of other women are part of a growing and vital women's community that Dobkin has helped to build. Although Dobkin may not have changed the world as much as she would have liked, she has imbued women's culture with her indelible zeal and integrity. Phranc, lesbian folksinger of a new generation, has called Dobkin *her* "perfect Lesbian role model."

Current Address: c/o Retts Scauzillo, 506½ Sanchez, San Francisco, California 94114; 415-552-DYKE [3953].

References:

Dobkin, Alix. *Alix Dobkin's Adventures in Women's Music.* Preston Hollow, New York: Tomato Publications, Ltd., 1979.

———. "Sexism and Racism in Rock 'n' Roll," in *Fuse,* Summer 1984: 55-58.

———. Telephone interview, 30 March 1996.

———. Unpublished, untitled memoirs.

Fouratt, Jim. "Growing Up Lesbian," in *OutWeek,* 23 December 1990: 54-55.

Harper, Jorjet. "Yahoo Michigan! Alix Dobkin Live on the MWMF," in *Girlfriends,* July 1995: 44.

Obejas, Achy. "The Cult of Alix Dobkin," in *Advocate,* 25 August 1992: 74-76.

Phoenix, Val C. "From Womyn to Grrrls, Finding Sisterhood in Girl Style Revolution," in *Deneuve,* January/February 1994: 40-43.

Smith, Jackie. "Women-Hating Words Fill Pop Music, Expert Says," in *Toronto Star,* 27 September 1983: 7.

—Susie Day

Martin Duberman

1930-

American writer and educator

Martin Duberman, a prolific and prize-winning historian, biographer, playwright, and critic, is one of America's most prominent gay scholars and educators. He emerged as a gay activist in 1973 after a twenty-five year struggle to suppress his homosexuality. He later became a pioneer in the fledgling field of gay and lesbian studies.

Duberman was born in New York City on 6 August 1930. His father, Joseph M. Duberman, was a Ukrainian Jew who emigrated to the United States and became a successful dress manufacturer. Duberman's mother, Josephine (née Bauml) Duberman, was a second-generation Austrian-American who became a homemaker after her marriage in 1923.

Competitive, intelligent, and linguistically gifted, Duberman steadily climbed the ladder of academic success. He graduated Phi Delta Kappa from Yale University (1952) and received his MA (1953) and PhD (1957) in history from Harvard University. He taught history at Yale for five years while he prepared his PhD dissertation for publication. *Charles Francis Adams, 1807-1886* (1961) won him the prestigious Bancroft Prize and a faculty appointment at Princeton University in 1962. He was successively assistant professor (1962-1965), associate professor (1965-1967), and full professor (1967-1971) at Princeton. He was the editor of, and a contributor to, *The Antislavery Vanguard: New Essays on the Abolitionists* (1965). His second biography, *James Russell Lowell* (1966), was a finalist for the National Book Award. He collected his writings for publication in *The Uncompleted Past: Collected Essays, 1961-1969* (1969). In 1971 he was appointed Distinguished Professor of History at Lehman College, City University of New York.

Meanwhile, Duberman had broadened his writings beyond the spheres of biography and history. He had been interested in the theatre since his teenage years and began earnestly writing plays in the early 1960s. The first, and most commercially successful, of his

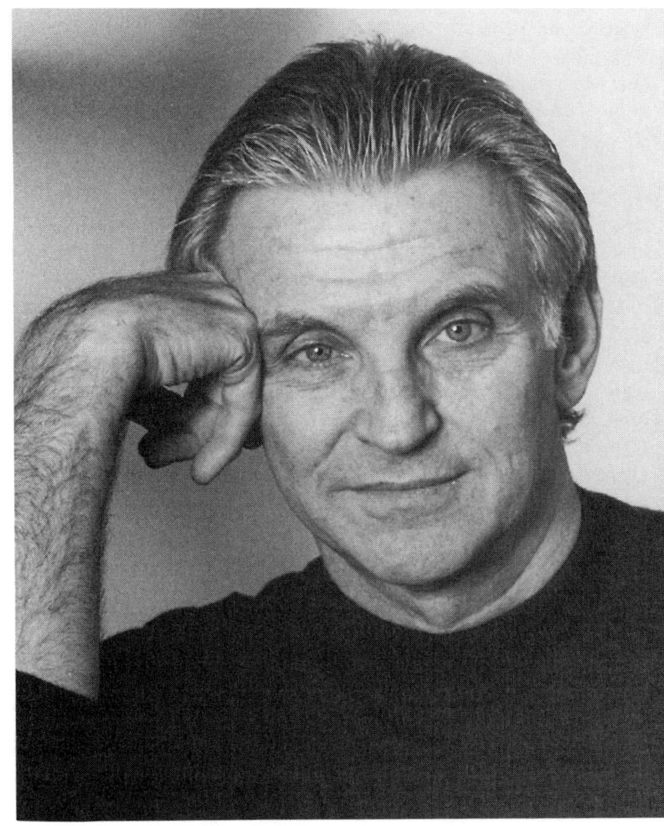

Martin Duberman. ***Photograph by Gene Bagnato.***

many plays was *In White America* (Produced New York, 1963; Houghton, 1964). This dramatic piece reflected his interest in race relations and the civil rights movement. It won the 1964 Vernon Rice/Drama Desk Award for Best Off-Broadway Production of the season. After enjoying a long run, it was filmed for television in 1970. The success of *In White America* opened further opportunities for Duberman. He began to write articles and reviews for several national publications, appeared on PBS, and became loosely affiliated with some New Left organizations. He collected many of his later plays in *Male Armor: Selected Plays, 1968-1975* (1975).

This period of growing acclaim, however, was marked by inner turmoil, as Duberman revealed in his memoir of his youth and early adult years, *Cures: A Gay Man's Odyssey* (1991). While still an undergraduate at Yale, he had begun to have sex with men. His discomfort with his homosexuality grew, even as he discovered the Boston—and later New York—parks, bars, bathhouses, and beaches where homosexual men congregated in the 1950s. His successive relationships were generally troubled and short-lived. In 1955 Duberman commenced fifteen years of intermittent therapy with a series of well-respected but homophobic psychotherapists to "cure" his "sickness." He explained in *Cures* that therapy only reinforced the societal homophobia that he had earlier internalized.

During the 1960s Duberman grew dissatisfied with academic life, particularly Princeton's smug milieu of privilege. Four factors contributed to an inseparable gulf that developed between him and his Princeton colleagues: his play-writing, his 1964 change of residence from Princeton to Greenwich Village, his sympathy for student radicals, and the university's rejection of his proposed education reforms.

Duberman gradually broke from his troubled past in the early 1970s. After his last therapist terminated his sessions in 1970, he never again turned to psychoanalysis to "cure" his homosexuality. Gay themes increasingly permeated his plays, books and essays. His 1971 play, *Payments* (produced in New York, 1971) for example, drew on his personal experiences with male hustlers. In *Black Mountain: An Exploration in Community* (1972), an innovative and controversial history of an experimental North Carolina college community, he publicly admitted his homosexuality. His essay on post-Stonewall gay male literature, one of the first of its kind to appear in a national publication, was published by the *New York Times Book Review* in its 10 December 1972 issue.

Duberman's emergence as an openly gay activist, writer, and scholar accelerated after the *Times* essay. In 1973 he was simultaneously on the originating boards of the Gay Academic Union, the Lambda Legal Defense and Education Fund, and the National Gay and Lesbian Task Force. He appeared as a gay spokesperson on television and on college campuses and frequently published articles on gay literature, theatre and news events. Frustrated by the commercial failure of his plays after *In White America*, Duberman redirected his energies in the late 1970s to researching gay and lesbian history. He published many historical documents that he discovered hidden in libraries and archives in a *New York Native* column that ran from 1981 to 1983. These documents, along with selections from his own writings and personal diaries, were published as *About Time: Exploring the Gay Past* (1986). Duberman was a co-editor of, and a contributor to, a ground-breaking collection of historical essays, *Hidden from History: Reclaiming the Gay and Lesbian Past* (1989). His widely praised *Stonewall* (1993), the first book-length examination of the watershed 1969 riots, traced the transformation of the homophile movement into gay liberation through the interlocking lives of six lesbians and gay men.

The research and writing of *Paul Robeson* (1989) drew on Duberman's lifelong interest in theatre, civil rights, and left-wing politics. This life of the African-American actor, singer, and political activist was critically acclaimed for its balance and documentation.

Duberman served as the Director of the Center for Lesbian and Gay Studies (CLAGS) at the Graduate Center, City University of New York in the early 1990s. Founded by Duberman in 1991, CLAGS is a model program which sponsors conferences and colloquia and provides research grants. He is also the general editor of two Chelsea House Publishers series of books, one on notable lesbians and gays and another on issues in gay and lesbian life, primarily aimed at teenagers. In 1996 Duberman's second autobiographical work, *Midlife Queer: Autobiography of a Decade, 1971-1981* (1996) appeared.

Duberman, who was chosen by Paul Russell for inclusion in his book *The Gay 100: A Ranking of the Most Influential Gay Men and Lesbians, Past and Present* (1995), has exerted a profound influence on gay and lesbian scholarship. His research, teaching, and writings have helped to shape a younger generation of queer academics, and CLAGS serves as a model for the integration of gay and lesbian studies into the higher education setting. Furthermore, Duberman's personal journey of liberation has inspired his readers in their individual lives.

Current Address: 475 W. 22nd St., New York, New York 10011.

Berney, K. A. *Contemporary Dramatists.* 5th ed. Detroit: St. James, 1993.

Contemporary Authors, New Revision Series. Vol. 2. Detroit: Gale Research, 1981.

Duberman, Martin. *Cures: A Gay Man's Odyssey.* New York: Dutton, 1991.

——. *Midlife Queer: Autobiography of a Decade, 1971-1981.* New York: Scribner, 1996

Malinowski, Sharon, ed. *Gay and Lesbian Literature.* Detroit: St. James, 1994.

Russell, Paul. *The Gay 100: A Ranking of the Most Influential Gay Men and Lesbians, Past and Present.* New York: Carol, 1995.

Who's Who in America, 1996. Vol. 1. New Providence, New Jersey: Marquis, 1995.

—Joseph M. Eagan

Melissa Etheridge

1961-

American singer and songwriter

One of the more popular rock and roll performers in the United States, Melissa Etheridge has been steadily building a loyal following throughout the 1990s. The return to grass-roots rock that Etheridge practices along with the raw emotion present in her music are responsible for much of her popular appeal. As she told David Wild, "I come from the heartland."

Melissa Lou Etheridge was born on 29 May 1961 in Leavenworth, Texas, to John and Elizabeth Etheridge. John Etheridge taught psychology and government in addition to coaching basketball at the Leavenworth high school. Elizabeth Etheridge was an Army computer specialist. Melissa was the couple's second child, and Etheridge's elder sister of four years is named Jennifer. Etheridge was raised by her parents to be self-sufficient. As she told Fred Schruers, "My father grew up in poverty ... it was sort of the same case for my mother.... My parents went through changes over time—they really evolved. But in the 1960s and 1970s, when I was growing up, they were hardworking, trying to just do good—but quite on their own." From an early age, Etheridge displayed a love of music. When Etheridge was three years old, as she told Patricia Smith, she was "hooked on radio." From there, it didn't take long for Etheridge to decide on a career.

Around the time of her eighth birthday, Etheridge's father gave her her first guitar. Shortly after, she began lessons with a local jazz musician named Don Raymond, and at the age of ten wrote her first song, "Don't Let It Fly Away (It's Love)." Two years later Etheridge began performing live at a variety of public functions, including bowling alleys, bars, and even supermarket openings. Etheridge began playing with her first band, a country-and-western group called the Wranglers, when she was 13. The group enjoyed a moderate amount of local success, performing in a variety of locales and situations. By this time Etheridge had become proficient not only on guitars but also on the saxophone, clarinet, and piano. Etheridge's father was extremely supportive of his daughter's endeavors during this period. As she told Maureen Littlejohn, "My father helped me when I was singing in bands. He took me around to the bars and sat there all night because I was underage."

It was around this time that Etheridge first made the discovery that she was a lesbian. "It wasn't until my seventeenth birthday that I kissed a girl and went, 'Whoa!'" she told Schruers. "All of a sudden everything just went boom inside. And then it was like, 'Oh, two plus two, that's it.' It added up. It made sense." But Etheridge's revelation only led to a continued sense of isolation at school. "Not only was I different because I was lesbian and had no interest in a lot of the things that the girls around me were interested in—boys, cheerleading—but I was a musician, and there were not too many of those around my high school either." Although her ability as a musician did bring her a few friends, Etheridge chose not to get too attached since she had no plans to spend the rest of her life, nor that much longer, in Leavenworth.

Melissa Etheridge

"Whatever I Wanted"

Upon graduation, Etheridge enrolled in the Berklee College of Music, in Boston. But, while hungering for the rock 'n' roll lifestyle, she dropped out after only her second semester. She supported herself for the next year by working part-time as a security guard at a Boston-area hospital while performing in local clubs in her off hours. Etheridge then returned to Leavenworth, where she worked at a restaurant for nine months to earn enough money to buy a car.

On her 21st birthday she moved to Los Angeles to pursue her own identity. As she told Schruers, "At lot of it was [that] I wanted to get away from what I was in that town ... and go to a place where I could make whatever I wanted to make and, yeah, be whoever I wanted."

For the next four years, Etheridge played the women's bar scene in Long Beach, California. During this period she played in various lesbian clubs and at local women's festivals, all the while developing her distinctive songwriting style (which has been described as Springsteenesque). She first heard the music of Joni Mitchell, Janis Joplin, and Joan Armatrading while playing in Long Beach and those influences figured prominently in establishing Etheridge's songwriting. Prior to this time, Etheridge's act consisted of primarily cover songs, but these artists, and the burgeoning sense of self-worth that she was herself cultivating, allowed Etheridge to begin writing songs. She soon began doing predominantly original music in her act and then hired a manager.

In 1986, Chris Blackwell, the founder and chairman of Island Records, signed Etheridge to a recording contract. Blackwell had come to see her play at a club called Que Sera Sera. After hearing only five songs, he approached her with his offer and she quickly began work on her first album. *Melissa Etheridge* was released in 1988 and received favorable reviews. Several of these early reviews, such as the one by Ralph Novak, praised Etheridge's energy and emotion: "[Etheridge's] music has a rigorous vitality, and there's an edge to it." This was indicative of the critical reception that Etheridge would enjoy throughout her career. Although *Melissa Etheridge* did not sell well initially the sales picked up after she appeared on the Grammy Awards show in February of 1989, eventually earning Etheridge her first gold record. Her next album, *Brave and Crazy,* was released in 1989 and the concert tour promoting the album prompted Jon Bream to write that Etheridge was "a remarkable, emotionally charged singer of the caliber of Bruce Springsteen and Janis Joplin." Etheridge continued that type of singer/songwriter approach to her music with her third album, *Never Enough,* in 1992. The album was immensely popular and even earned Etheridge a Grammy Award for best female rock vocalist. When she accepted the award, according to *Current Biography,* she dedicated the award to her father and thanked her lover, Julie Cypher."

Yes I Am

Etheridge had met independent filmmaker Julie Cypher while shooting the video for "Bring Me Some Water" (a single from *Melissa Etheridge*) in 1988. Cypher was working as assistant director on the shoot when the two met and eventually, after Cypher's separation from her husband, actor Lou Diamond Phillips, fell in love and decided to spend their lives together. The couple have been together since and have recently announced that Cypher is pregnant and expecting a child in early 1997.

Etheridge's announcement of her sexuality at the Grammys was not as shocking as it could have been since she had come out in January of 1993 at the National Press Club in Washington, D.C., during the first lesbian-and-gay inaugural celebration. As Etheridge told Rich Cohen in *Rolling Stone,* the announcement was spontaneous, "I had no plan to do it that night, no plan whatsoever. It was the atmosphere." Shortly after the announcement, Etheridge's next album, *Yes I Am,* was released. The title was widely, and wrongly, acknowledged as an affirmation of her lesbianism. It was rather, as Etheridge has stated in numerous interviews, simply the declaration of a lover's confidence of being the right partner for their lover. This double meaning in the album's title is indicative of the way in which all of Etheridge's work can be perceived. Her writing has always had a sort of androgynous style to it. As she has noted to Patricia Smith, "It's not a conscious effort on my part. I didn't realize I was doing a genderless thing, but then I saw how it made my music accessible to almost everyone."

Etheridge released her latest album, *Your Little Secret,* in 1995. The album came at the end of a triumphant year that saw performances at Woodstock, on MTV Unplugged with Bruce Springsteen, and at the grand opening of the Rock 'n' Roll Hall of fame in Cleveland, Ohio.

References:

Bream, Jon. In the *Minneapolis Star and Tribune,* 12 February 1990.
Cohen, Rich. In *Rolling Stone,* 29 December 1994/12 January 1995.
Current Biography Yearbook 1995. New York: H. W. Wilson, 1996: 154-157.
Littlejohn, Maureen. "Forever Etheridge," in *Modern Woman,* April 1996.
Lustig, Jay. "Melissa Etheridge: Impending Parenthood Leads to a Change in Attitude," in the *New Jersey Star-Ledger,* 27 August 1996.
Novak, Ralph. In *People,* 8 August 1988.
Schruers, Fred. "Melissa Etheridge," in *US,* December 1995.
Smith, Patricia. In the *Chicago Sun Times,* 5 August 1990.
Thomas, Elizabeth. "Melissa Etheridge," in *Contemporary Musicians.* Detroit, Michigan: Gale Research, vol. 4, 1991.
Warden, Steve. "Melissa Etheridge: Feeling Free," in *Access,* January/February 1996.
Wild, David. In *US,* January 1994.

—Michael J. Tyrkus

Lillian Faderman

1940-

American educator and writer

Lillian Faderman is the foremost experts on lesbian history in the United States. A professor of English at California State University, Fresno, Faderman was born in the Bronx, New York, on 18 July 1940. Her parents were immigrants from Latvia and Poland and she was raised by her unmarried mother, a garment worker. Faderman's first professional aspirations were in theater, because actresses provided a unique model of successful, independent women, and she took formal acting training at the Theatre Arts Workshop in east Los Angeles from 1951 to 1955. This experience would lead, indirectly, to one of her many books on the social history of lesbians.

As a teenager, Faderman was initiated into the mostly-underground gay world of the 1950s by a male friend who showed her the bar scene. She now considers herself fortunate to have interacted with such positive role models while she was still growing up. In a 1994 interview with *10 Percent* magazine, Faderman said: "[T]hose women dancing together, talking together, and being what I assumed to be independent of men—that vision was like an epiphany. It showed me what I could do with my life, that I could be as ambitious as I wanted. I didn't have to cut eroticism out of my life." Her provocative theory that independence from men constitutes the crucial element of lesbianism, rather than sexuality alone, is a central theme in all of her writing.

At the age of 17 Faderman married an older gay man as a way to escape from home. When the marriage ended, she enrolled at the University of California at Berkeley, where she received a B.A. in English in 1962. Continuing her resistance to convention, she earned money for school by working as a stripper in San Francisco. The pay for women was higher, she recalls, than waiting tables or clerking, and the labor less intensive.

Awards for First Book on Lesbian History

Faderman earned master's and doctoral degrees in English at UCLA, and an educational management certificate at Harvard. Her early academic publications include two co-edited volumes of American ethnic minority literature in 1969 and 1973, years before multiculturalism became popular on campuses nationwide. Her first book was *Lesbian Feminism in Turn-of-the-Century Germany* (1980), co-written with Brigitte Eriksson. Her next book, *Surpassing the Love of Men*, was more ambitious in scope, tracing same-sex loving women from the sixteenth century to the 1980s, in Europe and the United States. This book established Faderman as an important historian and theorist of lesbianism. When asked to take sides in the academic debate between essentialists, who credit heredity for sexual orientation, and social constructionists, who read history and culture as the forces shaping sexuality, Faderman identified with the latter. Despite its recognition with both gay and nongay publishers' awards, *Surpassing the Love of Men* was attacked by some essentialists because it appeared to de-sexualize love between women before the twentieth century. But according to Faderman in the *10 Percent* interview, essentialist theories that inflate biology's role in sexuality are simplistic and misleading. "They don't account for the fact ... that people often move in and out of sexualities; they could be heterosexual for one period of their lives and homosexual for another.... It seems to me the essentialists don't deal with the complexity of human sexuality."

In *Surpassing the Love of Men*, Faderman poses a significant question for lesbian history: why were passionate romantic friendships between women socially accepted before the twentieth century, and how did they come to be stigmatized? Before the 1910s, women's love affairs, sexual in a contemporary sense or not, were considered normal, but since then they have been mostly viewed as pathetic at best and destructive at worst. While Faderman argues that pre-twentieth century romances between women were generally devoid of genital sexual contact because women were taught to be passionless, she adds that "whether or not these relationships had a genital component, the novels and diaries and correspondence of these periods consistently showed romantic friends opening their souls to each other and speaking a language that was in no way different from the language of heterosexual love: They pledged to remain 'faithful' forever, to be in 'each other's thoughts constantly,' to live together and even to die together."

According to Faderman, the real challenge of lesbianism was economic rather than sexual: women who did not marry, for either financial security or love, threatened the patriarchal order that described women exclusively as mates for men. Either as titillation or dire warning, lesbianism of the kind we understand today has been around since at least the sixteenth century. In France, in the sixteenth and seventeeth centuries, lesbianism was considered a prelude to heterosexuality, not a threat but an aphrodisiac to men, as long as the women "lovers" did not take themselves seriously. All extant lesbian erotic literature before the eighteenth century was written by men. The typical formula was two conventionally beautiful women, the older of whom seduces the younger and whose relationship consists primarily of jealousy. Eventually a man rescues and converts the younger woman to her true heterosexual self.

For eighteenth and nineteenth century men, a woman who passed as a man was a greater criminal than a woman who merely loved another woman. Indeed, given conventions concerning women's great capacities for feeling over thinking, women were expected to love each other. But to dress, work, and live as a man was to appropriate masculine privilege in a radically unacceptable way. As Faderman writes, "Transvestites were, in a sense, among the first feminists. Mute as they were, without a formulated ideology to express their convictions, they saw the role of women to be dull and limiting. They craved to expand it—and the only way to alter that role in their day was to become a man." While many nineteenth century transvestites engaged in erotic lesbian relations, their significance as gender outlaws is as great as their sexual rebellion.

In *Surpassing the Love of Men*, Faderman blames the rise of sexologists in the late nineteenth century for pathologizing love between women. Combined with Victorian anti-feminism, the decadent movement's voyeuristic interpretation of female sexuality led to a new suspicion of women's romantic friendships. The sexologists, who were doctors, scientists, or social philosophers, created a third sex, the invert, who neurotically rejected women's prescribed, passive role. As soon as love between women earned a sexual connotation, romantic friendships and lesbianism would never be separated again.

Faderman controversially insists that lesbianism has more to do with affectional preference than with sex. Women loving women has been *made* a mostly sexual phenomenon by pseudo-science, not necessarily by lesbian experience. In her conclusion, Faderman imagines a time when all people will avoid the labelling performed by sexologists, and which has been so damaging to women who love women. She writes: "[In an ideal world] potential or actual bisexuality, which is today [1981] looked on by lesbian-feminists as a political betrayal and by heterosexuals as an instability, would be normal, both emotionally and statistically."

Faderman's next book, *Scotch Verdict*, elaborates on the theme of women's relationships in the nineteenth century by examining the transcript files of the court case which inspired Lillian Hellman's "lesbian" play, *The Children's Hour*. As a teen studying acting, Faderman played the role of "bad seed" Mary Tilford in Hellman's play and had her first serious crush on an adult, her drama coach. This experience gave Faderman a lifelong interest in the true story of the case, that of school-mistresses Marianne Woods and Jane Pririe, who sued Dame Helen Cumming Gordon for libel in Scotland in 1810. *Scotch Verdict* is an idiosyncratic rendering of Faderman's research in Scotland, combining a condensation of the trial transcripts and Faderman's own diary entries. Romantic friends desirous of financial independence, Woods and Pririe opened a girls' school, and seemed to have succeeded when a local aristocrat sent her granddaughter to them. But the girl (Mary Tilford in Hellman's play), a half-caste, illegitimate Indian child, told her grandmother of strange behavior between the two teachers and the school was immediately closed. Woods and Pririe sued for libel, since the veiled accusations of sexual misconduct between them appeared so ludicrous in 1810, and while they eventually won their case, their careers and life together were over.

Although Faderman believes it would have been unlikely for the two women to have engaged in genital sexual activity, she argues that the crux of the case was its challenge to the convention that women's romantic friendships were completely asexual. Lesbians simply did not exist in nineteenth century Scotland. As one of the judges put it, "God forbid that the time should ever arrive when a lady in Scotland, standing at the side of another's bed in the night time, should be suspected of guilt because she was invited into it." All of the judges found the case particularly difficult, not only due to its prurient nature, but also to their own frank disbelief in the accusations.

Faderman ultimately takes the case of the girl, Jane Cumming, who initiated the rumor, calling her as much of a victim of the Victorian class, race, and gender system as the two women whose lives she ruined. All of the women, but especially the servants, who participated in the trial (not a single man testified) were cross-examined for their veracity, emphasizing women's tenuous claims to citizenship, not to mention equality, at that time.

As Faderman puts it, "It must have been intimidating enough to be a woman examined and cross-examined by a room full of men—but to be examined and cross-examined on the subject of sex, and moreover a variety of sex that was not supposed to have existed, must have been terrifying." *Scotch Verdict* shows contemporary readers the price of invisibility for lesbians and all women living independently of men.

Odd Girls and Twilight Lovers Nominated for Pulitzer

In 1991, Faderman published another award winning title, *Odd Girls and Twilight Lovers: A History of Lesbian Life in Twentieth-Century America*, which picks up historically where *Surpassing the Love of Men* concluded. Beginning with romantic friendships and their perversion by sexologists in the 1920s, *Odd Girls* moves through each decade of our century, focussing especially on working-class lesbians and their distinctive culture, and the conflict between them and the lesbian feminists of the 1960s and 1970s.

Odd Girls begins by reminding the reader that when the book was written in the 1980s, lesbianism was more accepted than it ever was in this century, but it is still not as normal as romantic friendships were earlier. Faderman attributes four choices to the same-sex loving woman in the twentieth century: she could see lesbians as the experts initially had—women trapped in men's bodies—and thus consider herself normal because she had no desire to be male; repress her feelings and deny the attraction she felt for women; live as a closeted lesbian; or define herself as a lesbian and thus show independence and a certain social radicalism.

Feminism and radical struggle for women's rights and lesbianism have always been connected by the dominant culture, but the same women have not necessarily been feminists and lesbians. Working-class lesbians from the 1940s and 1950s, for example, felt betrayed by radical lesbian-feminists in the 1960s and 1970s who equated women's liberation with lesbianism and ignored the struggles of earlier lesbians who either passed as men or lived closeted. Lesbian feminists, mostly middle-class and college educated, often criticized non-feminist lesbians for their politics, without acknowledging the courage of merely surviving as a lesbian before the 1960s.

Such misunderstandings have occurred, and still do, based on ethnic as much as class background, and the splits over identity politics challenging the mainstream women's movement have been echoed in lesbian movements. But Faderman points out that the evolution of social acceptance, or at least tolerance, for lesbianism, has allowed more and more women to "come out" and be themselves regardless of politics. Thus butch-femme couples, once relegated to the working-class, can co-exist with high-powered lipstick lesbians in mini-skirts. They can even, fantastically enough, be the same woman according to her mood.

Chloe Plus Olivia Wins Faderman Second Lambda Literary Award

Perhaps Lillian Faderman's most important contribution to the growing documentation of lesbian realities is the manner in which she presents her findings. Meticulously researched and referenced, her books are accessible to the non-academic reader; she has tried and succeeded in giving lesbians, as she says, a "useable history." The utility of such practical scholarship cannot be overestimated, especially considering the influence working-class lesbians have had and continue to have in shaping lesbian cultures. All women, equipped with the latest gender theories or not, should have a chance to read their own histories. One thinks, for example, of working-class writer and historian Leslie Feinberg, author of *Stone Butch Blues* and *Transgender Warriors*, whose work on blue-collar women passing as men in the 1950s might not have been possible without Lillian Faderman's pioneering scholarship.

Faderman's latest contribution to lesbian history is an anthology of men's and women's writing about lesbians from the seventeenth to the late-twentieth centuries. In *Chloe Plus Olivia*, stories, poems, and essays document, first, how men viewed women-loving-women and, secondly how women viewed themselves both in fantasy and in their daily lives. *Chloe Plus Olivia* continues Faderman's project of providing scholarship and literature useful to many women, with a biography and bibliography of each author before the entry. Her selections range from the detailed nature imagery of Emily Dickinson to the sado-masochistic details of Pat Califia, placing, for the first time, all varieties of lesbians and lesbian desire together.

Lillian Faderman lives in Fresno, California, with her partner of many years, retired music professor Phyllis Irwin. Faderman's nineteen-year-old son, Avrom (she laughingly calls herself the first lesbian to use artificial insemination), is a doctoral student at Stanford.

Current Address: Professor Lillian Faderman, English Department, California State University, Fresno, California 93740.

References:

Faderman, Lillian, ed. *Chloe Plus Olivia: An Anthology of Lesbian Literature from the Seventeenth Century to the Present.* New York and London: Penguin, 1994.

———. *Odd Girls and Twilight Lovers: A History of Lesbian Life in Twentieth-Century America.* New York: Columbia UP, 1991.

———. *Scotch Verdict.* New York: William Morrow, 1983, reissue Columbia UP, 1993.

———. *Surpassing the Love of Men: Romantic Friendship and Love Between Women Sixteenth Century to the Present.* New York: William Morrow, 1981.

Schwartz, Arie. "Surpassing the Odds," in *10 Percent,* June 1994: 67-70.

—Catherine A. Wiley

Rainer Werner Fassbinder

1945-1982

German filmmaker

Rainer Werner Fassbinder has been called both the "cold statistician" and the "genius wunderkind" of modern German cinema. Yet, regardless of critique, most agree that he was the most brash, most original, most prolific, and most driven of writers/directors to emerge from the ashes and angst of post-war Europe. He directed, wrote most of the scripts for, and even acted in many of more than forty films in a too-short, thirteen-year career (tragically extinguished by an overdose of sleeping pills, alcohol, and cocaine in 1982).

Openly gay and quite sexually active since he was a teen, Fassbinder had two great homosexual loves—Algerian El Hedi Ben Salem (the Arab in his 1974 *Ali: Fear Eats the Soul*) and German Armin Maier—both of whom committed suicide shortly before Fassbinder's own untimely death. He also briefly married German actress Ingrid Caven in 1970.

As for any "responsibility" as a gay filmmaker, he was equally dichotomous. "Homosexuality is probably a factor in all of my films," author Raymond Murray quotes him as saying in the early 1980s. "Not all have a gay subject, but they all have the point-of-view of one gay man." Yet, just a few years previous, author Leigh Rutledge quotes Fassbinder as decidedly "off" the notion of a "gay sensibility" as pervasive or even necessary in his work. "I don't think homosexuality is a life-filling subject," he said. "It's not a subject I would choose for my films. I don't think homosexuality is even an evening-filling subject."

So although there are gay themes and characters in several of his films, their concerns as sexual human beings are always secondary to the notion of power, the idea of dominance, and/or the issue of betrayal—to name just a few classic Fassbinder preoccupations. Even in what are considered among his two masterpieces—the 1980 television mini-series *Berlin Alexanderplatz* and his 1982 feature *Querelle*—the overt homoeroticism is secondary to larger social issues of "who's on top" socially and economically.

Whether such an outlook spurs or impedes the gay and lesbian cause for rights and mainstream recognition must be left up to the individual movie-goer. Those who are able to overlook today's pervasive "political correctness" in support of his more generic outlook are convinced of his genius. Detractors argue against his too-strong "subjectivity." As writer James W. Jones observes in the *Encyclopedia of Homosexuality*, Fassbinder "shows that the failure of the relationships he depicts to survive or even to nurture does not stem from the nature of homosexuality itself. Rather, he makes evident that such love cannot succeed ... under conditions where human beings have lost their ability to form any relationships (not) based on objectification and exploitation."

Rainer Werner Fassbinder

Either Mad or a Genius

By his own admission, much of the despair and helplessness so prevalent in Fassbinder's films find their genesis in his turbulent childhood. He was born in Munich just three months after Germany's unconditional surrender following World War II, which meant sharing small rooms amongst the rubble with various relatives while both parents neglected him in their struggle to make ends meet. "I lived entirely on my own very early," he told biographer Ronald Hayman in 1985, "I was already what's called manic-depressive."

He was the only child of a father who was a doctor and a mother who worked as a translator of books as well as a nurse for her husband. His parents divorced when he was six, and all his life he blamed the chaos of his childhood on his father, who had two sons by a previous marriage and simply did not take much interest in him. His mother entered a sanitarium for a year when he was eight, and he was subsequently abandoned by most of his extended family (who had either died or since moved away). He filled the empty hours reading and viewing Hollywood films—all kinds of films—almost daily at the local cinema. His teachers began to report that he was either mad or a genius, for he chalked-up either the highest or lowest possible scores on tests. "I still bear the scars of that [time] so deeply," he told the *Washington Post* in 1976, "that I can never settle down in a stable home."

It is curious to note that his father regularly treated the local prostitutes, so although he was cautioned never to have anything to do with them, Fassbinder grew up entirely non-judgmental about the "profession." (Prostitution and other "sexual outlaws" figure largely in many of his films).

At the age of 16, he quit school and went to live with his father, who was now quite "mad" himself, but had gained the boy's respect by abandoning his medical practice to be a poet. Rainer had the task of collecting the rents in the run-down apartment house his father had purchased, and so he met more of Germany's "disenfranchised"—more prostitutes of both sexes, travestites, alcoholics, eccentrics, and foreign workers.

Boys Will Be Boys

It was also during this period that Fassbinder was just coming to terms with what he termed the "sensation" of his own homosexuality. "Listen," he told his father one day, according to Katz. "I found out something. I'm really happy. I don't want to have anything to do with girls. I want a man."

"Who is this 'man'?" asked the poet.

"He's a butcher, a butcher's apprentice," answered Fassbinder.

"Well, if you want to go to bed with men," said the father, "can't it be someone from the university?"

He was ecstatic about his newfound "gayness," and it was only after witnessing his mother's hysteria over the subject that he realized some people might have a problem with it. "But it wasn't [a problem] for me," he told Katz. "I never felt it as such, and I still don't."

It was also in his mid-teens that Fassbinder met and fell in love with "Dodo," a beautiful transvestite prostitute he began to both learn about the streets from and pimp for (after all, it was post-war Cologne). According to Katz, they both catered to the lowlife, the guest-worker trade, "for they had a cause: bringing love and affection to people in despair. Dodo stuffed his bra. Rainer stuffed his crotch. Boys will be boys."

Antitheater and Cool Applause

In 1965, Fassbinder made a half-hearted attempt to get into the Berliner Film Academy in West Berlin and made his first film, *Die Stadtstriecher*. The following year he sporadically attended the Fridl-Leonhard Drama School in Munich where he met lifelong friend and actress Hanna Schygulla and made his second short film, *Die Kleine Chaos* (The Little Chaos). By 1967, he followed Schygulla to the Munich Action Theater, from which he soon broke away to form the "Munich Antitheater," living communally with fellow-performers and staging productions in old movie houses and the back rooms of bars.

The Antitheater created quite the surprise sensation over the next several years, thanks largely to Fassbinder's boundless energy and ceaseless promotion. He would finish a script—most often an adaptation of Goethe, Sophocles, or some other classic—over a weekend. His efforts reflected, according to what a close friend told the *Washington Post*, "a critique of the cruelty of society ... in present-day, working-class Munich." At the same time, he was writing and performing a spate of original works for German radio.

In 1969, he wrote and directed his first feature-length film, *Love Is Colder Than Death*. It was screened at the Berlin Film Festival that same year to cool applause, although it has since been compared to Jean Luc Godard's classic first film *Breathless* in terms of social insight.

The pump thus primed, the filmmaker seemingly unaffected by praise or the lack of it, Fassbinder completed forty-two full-length features over the next 13 years—averaging a grueling 15-day shooting schedule per picture, and likewise writing most of the scripts. The majority of these films, according to author Raymond Murray in *Images in the Dark*, contain "not traditional heroes and great lovers, but losers and victims: battered people victimized by an oppressive economic system,... tormented with personal despair, anguished by love affairs gone dead, and betrayed by the people around them."

Cynicism ... and Sex ... and Power ... and Sex

Although Fassbinder's "gayness" can be read into most of these works, only *The Bitter Tears of Petra von Kant* (1972), *Fox and His Friends* (1974), *In a Year of Thirteen Moons* (1978), and *Querelle* (1982) have overtly gay themes. This is not to say, however, that these four films did not alienate some gay and lesbian audiences when they were released. *Tears*, focusing as it did on "lesbian mind games" and female jealousy, was labeled misogynist and even picketed by some lesbian groups. *Fox* was criticized because it presented, according to Andrew Britton in London's *Gay Left* magazine a "version of homosexuality that degrades us all, and should be roundly denounced." *Moons*, about the doomed life of an abandoned, unloved transsexual, was called by Vincent Canby in the *New York Times* a "grotesque, arbitrary, sentimental and cold as ice [work of] genius." Fassbinder's last and gayest film, *Querelle*, has been criticized by some as a too-campy, too-irreverent bastardization of Jean Genet's masterpiece, presenting as it does a swaggering Brad Davis, a swarthy Franco Nero, and a drooling Jeanne Moreau over-emphasizing the notion of sex as power as sex.

Yet, throughout his meteoric life and career, Rainer Werner Fassbinder, often termed the "Messiah" of modern German cinema, claimed his films remained true to his own outlook on life. "My work is cynical," Murray quotes him as telling writer Boze Hadleigh, "it is realistic. Pessimistic. Life is pessimistic in the end, because we die, and it is pessimistic in between." Love, manipulation, power, lost dreams, despair—all of these themes in all of their complex interactions were stylized by Fassbinder to give a voice to those traditionally denied one. Perhaps herein lies the true "gay sensibility" of his works.

References:

Dynes, Wayne R. *Encyclopedia of Homosexuality*. New York: Garland Publishing, 1990.

Hayman, Ronald. *Fassbinder—Film Maker*. New York: Simon and Schuster, 1985.

Katz, Robert. *Love is Colder Than Death: The Life and Times of Rainer Werner Fassbinder*. New York: Random House, 1986.

Murray, Raymond. *Images in the Dark-An Encyclopedia of Gay and Lesbian Film and Video*. Philadelphia: TLA Publications, 1994.

Rutledge, Leigh. *The Gay Decades*. Boston: Alyson Publications, 1992.

Washington Post, 19 December 1976.

—Jerome Szymczak

Harvey Fierstein

1954-

American actor and playwright

Playwright and actor Harvey Fierstein made American theatrical history in 1982 when he became the first "real live, out-of-the-closet queer on Broadway" (his description) with his play *Torch Song Trilogy*. His seriocomic collection of three one-acts about the life, loves, and growth to maturity of a drag queen won Fierstein two Tony awards, for best actor and best play of the season. In a 20 June 1983 *Newsweek* article, Jack Kroll called *Torch Song* "the first stage work that has made gays and straights laugh and cry at the upside-down similarities between the emotional and sexual hang-ups in both worlds." Gerald Clarke, writing in *Time* (20 June 1983) noted that "never before has an out-of the-closet play ... done so well with straight, middle-class audiences."

Fierstein went on to write the book for the musical *La Cage aux Folles,* a lavish $5-million spectacle that, in its own more modest way, was something of a ground-breaker. In *La Cage,* Fierstein and company put a long-term gay relationship front-and-center in a milieu where previously the gay presence had been expressed *sotto voce* in style and tone, but where the story line was always decidedly heterosexual.

From Playwright to Player

Since the late 1980s Fierstein has been in evidence more as an actor than playwright. With his justly famous gravel voice (a sound compared to everything from mating bull doves to a backed-up vacuum cleaner) and warmly fey persona, Fierstein has played lovable gay roles in major Hollywood movies like Robin Williams's *Mrs. Doubtfire* and sitcoms like "The Simpsons" and "Cheers," for which he won an Emmy nomination.

Fierstein grew up in Bensonhurst, Brooklyn, as one of two sons of Jewish parents who had emigrated from Eastern Europe. His father was a modestly successful handkerchief manufacturer, and his mother a homemaker. Fierstein came out to his parents at age 13. "We were brought up with the feeling that the family unit was everything," Fierstein told Michiko Kakutani in the 14 July 1982 *New York Times.* "Something as minuscule as my being gay was not going to disrupt that."

However, more problematic for Fierstein than his sexual orientation was his weight. Acknowledging himself to have been "a fat kid," Fierstein tipped the scales at close to 250 pounds. According to the *1984 Current Biography Yearbook,* Fierstein "turned to cross-dressing for self-protection as well as self-expression."

"In drag," Fierstein explained in a 22 August 1983 interview with *New York,* "I could completely become someone else. And guess what? I liked it." He began doing a comic drag act at an East Village bar, performing under names like Virginia Hamm, which led at age 16 to his playing an asthmatic lesbian cleaning woman in Andy Warhol's play *Pork* at La Mama theater in the East Village. While living at home and studying art at the Pratt Institute in Brooklyn, Fierstein traveled daily into Manhattan, where he developed his actor's chops in a string of Off-Off-Broadway plays.

According to the *1984 Current Biography Yearbook,* Fierstein began writing his own "raunchy chic" Off-Off-Broadway vehicles around the time he graduated from Pratt in 1973 with a fine arts degree. His titles included (most outrageously) *Freaky Pussy,* in which Fierstein played a transvestite hustler working out of a subway men's room, and *Flatbush Tosca,* an updated, drag version of the Puccini opera.

Inspiration for *Torch Song*

Torch Song Trilogy came about as a result of a breakup in 1976 of a two-year love affair with a bisexual schoolteacher. "When he left me," Fierstein told *Newsweek,* "I went to this therapist and said, 'What do I do?' She said, 'Well, you can commit suicide. You can go home and eat a lot of ice cream. Or you can write about it.'" Obviously, Fierstein wrote.

"International Study," "Fugue in a Nursery," and "Widows and Children First!"—the plays that make up *Torch Song*—were first presented individually during the 1978 and 1979 seasons at La Mama E.T.C. The Glines, a production group dedicated to gay-themed material, presented the complete *Trilogy* (with a running time of four-and-a-half hours) Off-Off-Broadway in 1981.

After glowing reviews in the *Times* and the *Village Voice,* a slimmed-down version of the play moved to a regular commercial Off-Broadway run at the Actors Playhouse in Greenwich Village and then five months later, in June of 1982, opened on Broadway at the Little Theatre. Gerald Clarke, in *Newsweek,* sums up the story

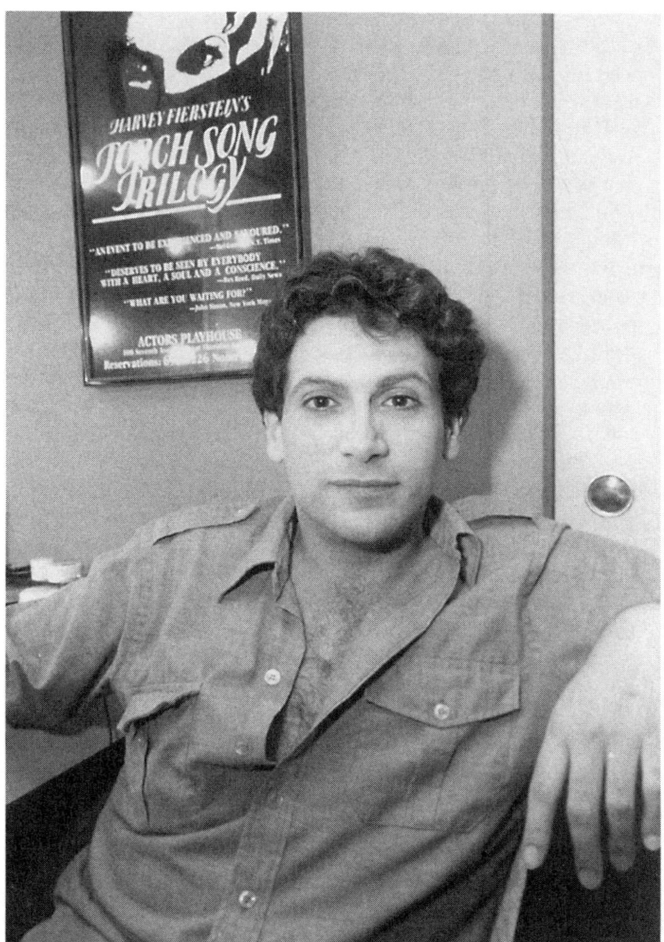

Harvey Fierstein

like this: "For 3 hours and 40 minutes [the audience] enters into the life of Arnold Beckoff, who makes his living performing as a drag queen in a New York City nightclub. He falls in love with a schoolteacher, loses him to a woman, then falls in love again, only to have that lover killed by a gang of gay baiters. What Arnold really wants is to have a family, like everyone else, and he winds up adopting a gay 15-year-old." Fierstein comments in the same article, "The basic theme is self-respect."

Interestingly, the greatest controversy over *Torch Song* developed within the gay community. Some gay people questioned Fierstein's attachment to middle-class conventions of marriage and monogamy and wondered if heterosexual marriage really could serve as the ideal paradigm for gay relationships. Fierstein's character Arnold says to his ex-lover Ed in the last, and best, of the three plays, "[My mother] thinks I hate her and everything she stands for. And I don't, for the life of me, know how to tell her that what I want more than anything is to have exactly the life she had. With a few minor alterations."

Torch Song played on Broadway for two years, and in 1988 was made into a film with Fierstein reprising his role and Anne Bancroft playing the role of Arnold's mother. The gay landscape had altered so completely as a result of AIDS that the movie had to be set in a specifically pre-AIDS New York. Though the movie maintained a good portion of the drama and some of the humor of the play, it seemed somewhat tame in light of the changes going on in both gay art and life.

As book writer for the musical of *La Cage aux Folles,* which opened on Broadway in August 1983 while *Torch Song Trilogy* was still playing, Fierstein is credited in *People* (23 December 1983) with giving the show "its surprisingly sentimental core." Based on a French farce, which was made into a film (and in 1996 was remade in Hollywood as *The Birdcage),* it is, according to Fierstein, "a musical about a marriage."

The story of two fiftysomething men (one a drag performer) who run a nightclub in St. Tropez and have raised a son, Jean-Michel, is by now familiar. Jean-Michel has gotten engaged and needs to bring his prospective in-laws to meet his family. Unfortunately for Jean-Michel, the father is a self-righteous and puritanical politician, and the son is more concerned about winning over the girl's father than honoring his own two fathers. "The villain of the original play is the father of the girl," Fierstein told *New York* in a 22 August 1983 interview. But in the musical, "the one who does the villainous deeds is the son—like asking Albin [the drag queen] not to be there when the parents of the girl come. He cannot see that this man who raised him is his mother." Interestingly enough, the wildly successful 1996 film adaptation was criticized by Bruce Bawer in a 10 March 1996 *New York Times* essay for missing this very point.

In 1987, Fierstein returned to Broadway as playwright and star in a new collection of three one-acts, *Safe Sex,* the first Broadway play to focus on AIDS. In a *New York Times* interview (5 April 1987) he said, "I didn't want to write a play about how a guy gets sick before your eyes and what happens to the people around him. This is not a play about disease, it's a play about life." Though *Safe Sex* ran only briefly on Broadway, an off-Broadway production was mounted a year later and the longest of the three plays, "On Tidy Endings," was filmed for HBO with Fierstein starring.

Fierstein Dubbed "Almost Mainstream"

In the 1990s, Fierstein has become "almost mainstream," according to a 21 September 1994 *Sacramento Bee* article, as the actor of first choice for the flamboyant gay character roles in movies and TV. As for those who are troubled by the kinds of characters he sometimes plays, for example the flamboyantly swishy fashion designer he played in *Daddy's Girls* (a short-lived 1994 sitcom starring Dudley Moore), Fierstein is of a different mind. "I have a real problem with people who talk about gay stereotypes," he told the *Sacramento Bee.* "You can find every kind of gay man, from flamboyant to conservative. There are even gay Republicans."

As a playwright and as an actor of his plays on stage, screen, and TV, Fierstein has broken ground at the highest levels of the entertainment world. He has given voice to types of gay characters who had previously been kept silent and told their stories in a true, loving, and funny way.

Current Address: c/o Green Siegel & Associates, 8730 Sunset Boulevard, Suite 470, Los Angeles, California 90069.

References:

Clarke, Gerald. "'No One Opened Doors for Me,'" in *Time,* 20 June 1983: 80.

Collins, Glenn. "In 'Safe Sex,' Harvey Fierstein Turns Serious," in the *New York Times,* 5 April 1987: 5.

Current Biography Yearbook 1984. New York: H. W. Wilson, 1984: 122.

"Harvey Fierstein," in *People,* 26 December 1983: 60.

Kroll, Jack. "His Heart Is Young and Gay," in *Newsweek,* 20 June 1983: 71.

Wolf, Jeanne. "Harvey Fierstein Brings a Gay Man to Prime Time," in *Sacramento Bee,* 21 September 1994: SC1.

—Ira N. Brodsky

E. M. Forster

1879-1970

British writer

Although E. M. Forster's literary voice is an individual and uniquely appealing one, his humanism was shaped by his immersion in two circles of friends: the humane college milieu at Cambridge and, after graduation, the Bloomsbury group in London. Both circles were characterized by the tolerant interaction of homosexuals and heterosexuals, in about equal proportion. Because of the repressive atmosphere that prevailed in England in the wake of the Oscar Wilde trials, Forster felt that he could not publish writing on gay subjects during his lifetime. Some have thought him excessively prudent, at least in his later years. That aside, Forster left behind valuable gay material that he kept in reserve, including his sixth novel, *Maurice*, published posthumously in 1971.

Edward Morgan Forster never knew his father, an architect, for he died less than two years after his birth. The boy was raised by a group of female relatives, who adhered to a stern evangelical sect. When he was 10, a great-aunt Marianne Thornton left him a trust fund of 8,000 pounds, which permitted him to obtain a good private education and to start his career as a writer.

Forster detested Tonbridge School, and developed a life-long aversion to the "manly values" imparted at British public schools. By contrast, he found King's College, Cambridge, where he went in 1897, a veritable paradise. At that time the atmosphere among students and faculty was strongly homoerotic. Forster formed an intense Platonic bond with another undergraduate, H.O. Meredith, who appears as "Clive" in *Maurice*. As had long been the case, Greek studies served as a vehicle for homoerotic interests, a potential subtly exploited by Goldsworthy Lowes Dickinson; Forster was to write a biography of this teacher in 1934. A figure of surpassing importance was the philosopher G. E. Moore, with his ethics of personal integrity. In 1901 Forster joined an elite secret society, the Apostles, fostering close ties with such Cambridge contemporaries as John Maynard Keynes, who was to become a noted economist, and Lytton Strachey, the biographer.

Post-Graduate Travels and Writings

At loose ends after graduation, he traveled in Italy for a year with his mother. A cruise to Greece followed. Not only did he find his vocation as a writer in those historic lands, but through the end of his life he was to cherish an ideal of Mediterranean tolerance and earthiness in contrast to the Protestant seriousness and commercialism of his native England. Returning to London in 1902, he offered a course at the Working Men's College, a connection he would retain for some 20 years.

Four novels appeared in quick succession: *Where Angels Fear to Tread* (1905), *The Longest Journey* (1907), *A Room with a View* (1908), and *Howards End* (1910). Forster spent several months in India in 1912-13. In 1915 he volunteered to serve with the Red Cross in Alexandria, Egypt. There he met the great modern Greek poet Constantine Cavafy, who was also gay and whose work Forster helped to publicize. He also encountered a young Egyptian streetcar conductor, Mohammed el Adl, who gave him his first satisfactory sexual relationship.

In 1921-22 Forster returned to India, serving as private secretary to the Maharajah of Dewas State Senior. Here he gathered the material for his novel *A Passage to India*, acclaimed as his masterpiece on publication in 1924.

Resettling permanently in England, in 1927 he gave the Clark Lectures at Trinity College, Cambridge; these were published as *Aspects of the Novel*. Civil liberties questions engaged him, and in the following year he rallied public opinion against the suppression of the lesbian novel of Radclyffe Hall, *The Well of Loneliness*. This period also saw the beginning of Forster's intense friendship with a heterosexual policeman, Bob Buckingham, which lasted for the rest of his life.

In 1946, forced to leave his home at Abinger, he accepted an offer to become an honorary fellow at King's College Cambridge, where he lived in tranquility for the rest of his life.

As noted above, Forster published a brilliant quartet of novels in the astonishing space of only five years (1905-10). This debut provided a lasting foundation for his fame and confirmed his centrality in the advanced Bloomsbury group. Discarding Victorian and Edwardian pieties, the novels espouse a humanistic ethics of psychic integration and fulfillment through caring and mutual concern. Although close scrutiny highlights elements of male-bonding, all these novels are overtly concerned with heterosexual relationships.

E. M. Forster

Breaking a novelistic absence of 14 years, Forster emerged with his most significant achievement yet, *A Passage to India*. Sharply critical of British imperialism, the novel affirms the viability of human connections as possible even across national and class lines. After 1924 Forster seemingly fell silent as a novelist. He kept in the public eye with reviews and essays.

Posthumous Controversy Surrounds *Maurice*

For the rest of his life he kept several cards close to his sleeve. In July 1914 Forster completed the first draft of a homosexual novel, *Maurice*. Maintaining that it was not publishable in the Britain that had persecuted Oscar Wilde, he shared the manuscript only with a few friends, including D. H. Lawrence, who seems to have used it as the model for his heterosexual novel *Lady Chatterley's Lover* (privately printed in 1928). Never losing sight of the work, Forster revised *Maurice* as late as 1960, but it did not appear until after his death, in 1971.

As he had feared, however, the publication of *Maurice*—even in the liberal climate of the "sexual revolution"—elicited dismay. Several critics who had formerly admired his work now began to speak of "homosexual bias," and the novel was generally relegated to a place inferior to the other five.

These criticisms are unjustified. While *Maurice* is not without flaws, it certainly stands comparison with his first four novels. Forster's homosexual novel has two parts. In the first part, the impressionable hero falls under the domination of his Cambridge friend, Clive, with his seemingly high-minded, but in reality shallow, Platonism. In the second, he finds his true destiny with a working-class boy, a gamekeeper employed on Clive's estate. At the end the two elope "into the greenwood." Although this idyll has struck some readers as sentimental and improbable, it is modeled on fact: the successful life of the homosexual theorist Edward Carpenter, who ran a market farm together with his proletarian lover, George Merrill.

At various times of his life Forster composed homoerotic stories, including the tragic "The Other Boat" (written 1957-58), which is also a critique of imperialism. The most important of these stories were collected in *The Life to Come* (1972).

With minimal changes the film version of *Maurice,* released by the Ivory-Merchant-Jhabvala team in 1987, emerged as fully credible. Apart from *The Longest Journey*, his novels have all been made into movies that sensitively recapture the age in which he lived.

In his novels Forster was a conservative modernist, rooted in the social comedy of Victorian times, but also showing affinities with the work of his more avant-garde friends D. H. Lawrence and Virginia Woolf. Although the revelation of Forster's homosexuality diminished him in the eyes of some critics, his acquaintance with the ideas of the early homosexual rights movement was actually a source of strength. He succeeded in forging the insights of Carpenter, John Addington Symonds, and others into more universal terms. As a result even readers who do not know the full background obtain the benefit.

References:

Beauman, Nicola. *E. M. Forster: A Biography.* New York: Alfred A. Knopf, 1994.

Furbank, P. N. *E. M. Forster: A Life.* New York: Harcourt Brace Jovanovich, 1978.

Summers, Claude J. *E. M. Forster.* New York: Frederick Ungar, 1983.

—Wayne R. Dynes

Michel Foucault

1926-1984

French historian, social philosopher, and activist

Foucault has proved one of the most influential and widely read thinkers of any country in the second half of the twentieth century. Unlike some other French intellectuals, such as Claude Lévi-Strauss and Pierre Teilhard de Chardin, famous in their day, Michel Foucault retains his persuasive power. And this interest is not limited to Western countries, but extends to Japan, India, and Brazil.

Unlike his leading French contemporaries, Foucault was not buoyed by previously existing loyalties. Thus Louis Althusser profited from his assertion that he pursued rigorous Marxism and Jacques Lacan claimed to be returning to the "original" Freudian core of psychoanalysis. Foucault distanced himself from any previous school or ideology. In a sense he built a "we" on his own—a world-wide community of adepts and researchers.

In his later years it was generally known that Foucault was gay, apparently exclusively so. It is not surprising that many of his followers are gay intellectuals and scholars; he has influenced, often to a great degree, their methods of work.

Still, it is safe to say that the majority of Foucaldians are heterosexual. Only recently have these admirers had to deal directly with the issues of his sexuality. Perhaps their loyalty will persist in the face of some unfair allegations.

A Brilliant French Academic Career

Paul-Michel Foucault was born in Poitiers on 15 October 1926. In 1946 he was admitted to the prestigious École Normale Supérieur in Paris, where he took degrees in philosophy and psychology. After beginning his teaching career in psychology at the University of Lille, he was appointed to teach French at the University of Uppsala in Sweden. It was in the excellent library of the latter institution that he conducted the research that formed the foundation of his studies on madness. In 1958 he became director of the French center at the University of Warsaw, from which, however, he was soon dismissed because of a homosexual affair. (He was entrapped by the Communist security forces). Through the sympathetic intervention of the French ambassador to Poland, he was able to take up a similar post in Hamburg, Germany, before returning to France to teach psychology at the University of Clermont-Ferrand.

In 1961 he received his doctorate for the thesis that became his major book *Folie et déraison: histoire de la folie a l'âge classique* (Paris, 1964; translated only in an abbreviated version: *Madness and Civilization*, New York, 1967). In this study he attacked the idea that madness is uniform across time. Rather, he argued that it was a changing historical phenomenon. In the period that he studied it was addressed by massive efforts by the state, which resulted in what he termed "the great confinement." This monograph revealed Foucault's characteristic ability to frame bold historical hypotheses and to give them literary form in gripping set pieces. During the student uprisings in Paris in May of 1968, Foucault was teaching in Tunisia, he followed the events closely over the telephone. He soon returned, and the ensuing period proved very propitious for Foucault's reputation both in France and abroad, especially in the United States where he taught on several occasions. He participated in the general climate of activism of the 1970s, showing concern about prisoners, mental patients, the Poles and the Iranians, the Afghan rebels, and human rights generally.

In 1969 Foucault was elected to the Collège de France, at the summit of French academia. Increasingly his lecturers concentrated on the history of sexuality. Foucault died in Paris on 25 June 1984 of AIDS complications.

A Truly Multifarious Thinker

Not only did Foucault contribute to many different fields, he also assumed different intellectual positions. For this reason it is not easy to pinpoint Foucault's philosophy. There were several Foucaults, as each dominant preoccupation yielded to the next. The pulsations of these changes can be monitored by segmenting his

Michel Foucault

career in periods of approximately five years: 1950-54 (apprenticeship, characterized by the sway of German thinkers: Hegel, Marx, Heidegger, Freud, Nietzsche); 1955-60 (exile—Sweden, Poland, Germany; preparation of his huge thesis); 1961-65 (preoccupation with madness and total institutions); 1966-70 (publication of the daunting grand theoretical works); 1971-75 (activism); 1976-80 (start of sex project; Northern California becomes his second home); 1981-84 (execution of the multivolume sex project on a new plan).

Many, even those well versed in the study of Foucault, neglect his complexity. Frustrating as this may be to the neophyte, Foucault studies demand almost total immersion, an invitation to which, by its nature, only a few can respond.

Speaking generally, one can detect a trajectory of affiliations—from Marxist to structuralist to skeptic and power analyst. The 1970s saw him increasingly involved with the problem of power, which he perceived as universally diffused though not in very different measures. The modern state in particular has learned to harness to its purposes such bodies of knowledge as medicine and the social sciences, which serve to colonize and subjugate the individual. The individual can confront this phalanx of domination with only a stubborn recalcitrance. At this time the concept of archaeology yielded to the more corrosive and dynamic "genealogy," derived from the German philosopher Friedrich Nietzsche, probably the most significant influence on Foucault's later thought. His increasing iconoclasm and skepticism led him to deny that historical record yields any evidence of a stable human subject, of a human "condition," or of human "nature."

In the mid-1970s he turned to the matter of sexuality, issuing a programmatic statement in 1976 (*La Volonté de savoir*, Paris, 1976; translated as *The History of Sexuality*, vol. I, New York, 1978). The five volumes that were to succeed this little book, treating the early modern period and the recent past, never appeared. Yet at the end of his life he surprised the world with two successor volumes with a different subject matter: the management of sexuality in ancient Greece and Rome. While completing these books he was already gravely ill, a fact that may account for their turgid, sometimes repetitive presentation.

The Personal Element

Foucault's personal style lacked the flamboyance of an Oscar Wilde. During his lifetime the French scholar sought to direct attention away from his personal circumstances. He wanted his admirers and detractors to concentrate on his work. There was also a factor of prudence, which favored controlling the amount and nature of information about his sexuality.

What is not well understood today is the difficulty presented in managing a homosexual identity in the France of Foucault's early maturity. Despite their distinguished homosexual literary tradition, ever since 1870 the French had obsessed with their declining demographics, especially in comparison with Germany. Homosexual activity did not contribute to repeopling the country. Also Foucault had several psychotic episodes as a student. Several times he contemplated suicide.

Foucault maintained that he did not want to be pigeon-holed as a gay thinker. No one, it is said, is ever out of the closet 24 hours a day. Foucault was both in and out, and he tried to walk a narrow line, keeping his renown as a universal thinker while not disappointing his gay following. Although this complicated dance of identity perception may be interpreted as a form of stigma management, it was probably sensible. Attacks after his death have, alas, confirmed the validity of some of his fears.

Two questions are of particular importance: 1) What is the relation of Foucault's work to his homosexuality? Clearly a Kinsey 6 with no heterosexual component, was he also oriented to S/M?; and 2) What is the value of Foucault's theory for gay studies and gay politics?

A controversial attempt to link the life and work has been made by heterosexual American biographer James Miller in *The Passion of Michel Foucault* (New York, 1993). Probably without intending to do so, Miller has furnished information of a salacious sort that is serving to undermine Foucault's reputation. Fascinated with Foucault's late interest in the baths of San Francisco's Folsom street, Miller presents these as places where hideous, death-defying acts were practiced on a daily basis. This lurid picture is false, for these places were not sources of immediate danger. One could contract the AIDS virus there, but that could occur in many other kinds of places. The one truly unworthy statement of Miller's is his assertion (which he makes only to partially withdraw it) that Foucault went to the baths knowing that he had AIDS with the intent of spreading it. Miller links this information (and misinformation) to Foucault's interest in Nietzsche and limit-experiences. In the writer's interpretation the boy Foucault was "imprinted" with a taste for S/M by his physician father's requiring him to witness an amputation.

The adult is supposed to have developed a death wish that suffused both his life and work. Hence the purported link between the recklessness of his life and the iconoclasm of his work. Ultimately it is probably impossible to form a conclusive opinion on such a purported link between the life and the work. As is generally the case in intellectual work, its value—if it has value—must assume a life independent of its creator. Time seems to be bearing this conclusion out. Nonetheless, one must register concern when some Foucault critics seem to wish to exploit the lurid material to discredit him.

Contribution to Gay Endeavors

What now is the contribution of Foucault to gay scholarship and gay activism? In the 1980s a methodological demand came to prominence in gay scholarly circles that seemed to sweep all before it: Social Construction. This approach emphasizes the historical variability of all same-sex expression, asserting that, as a transhistorical entity, the homosexual does not exist. Foucault was not the origin of Social Construction as he is sometimes thought to be. The approach has a number of sources, including an article by Mary Mackintosh and the symbolic interactionist approach of the Chicago sociologists. However, in a famous paragraph of his book *The History of Sexuality* (volume 1) about the 19th-century shift from the sodomite, a mere dabbler in homosexuality, to the fixed type of homosexuality, he seemed to lend support to Social Construction.

A broader support for Social Construction stems from the general framework of discontinuity (breaks, ruptures, thresholds, etc.) so central to his books *The Order of Things* and *Archaeology of Knowledge*.It is true that late in life Foucault denied being the philosopher of discontinuity, but some of his most influential works are saturated with it.

Devoted (as much of his early ground-breaking work was) to the history of medicine and psychiatry, Foucault lent support to the exaggeration among gay theorists of the role of medicine as the conceptual matrix out of which the concept of "homosexuality" developed. This "medicalization thesis" is ostensibly buttressed by the claim that the inventor of the word homosexual (in 1868), K. M. Kertbeny, was a physician. He was not.

Apart from his contribution to the study of history, what is the lesson of Foucault for gay activism? Here we must go back to the question of the common theme, if one can be pinned down, that underlies his diverse work. His French biographer Didier Eribon holds that Foucault was motivated by a kind of primordial rebelliousness, showing itself in his dislike of institutions. His activist role was not consistent throughout his whole mature life. Rather, it was limited to the period 1970-75, under the influence of his companion Daniel Defert. This was a time of great confusion in French society, a confusion that subsided as France became more prosperous and modern.

There are great problems with Foucault's notions of power and his equation of it with knowledge. For his concept of power as a kind of Brownian motion running in every direction all at once is in fact profoundly disconcerting. How can one take action against a corrupt and oppressive social system without recognizing its impact and envisioning something that might take its place? Critics, notably Jürgen Habermas, hold that Foucault's concept is, in effect, disempowering, counseling accommodation and resignation as the inevitable way of the world.

A Suspended Assessment

More than a decade after Foucault's death, his reputation has not settled down. The voices of his many admirers are countered by the discordant notes of almost as many skeptics. With a thinker who has been influential while at the same time controversial anyone undertaking a comprehensive "quality review" must meet the challenge of two questions. Why, despite all the favorable attention, have resistance and dislike persisted? Then there is the complementary question: why the continuing elevated levels of esteem? Why then, to combine the two questions, do both underestimation (and/or) extravagant admiration continue?

To be sure, this ambivalence, which if it lasts over a long time must count as a kind of cognitive dissonance, may be resolved. At various stages we can see this process of resolution at work in relation to other stellar intellects. Take the cases of Sigmund Freud and Arnold Toynbee; the reputation of the second has long since faded, and the first now seems in retreat. No one can predict that this fading will not be the lot of Michel Foucault, but no one can say that it won't, either. Still, one must hope that the final assessment will be based on his actual achievement and not on scandalous—and largely untrue—stories.

References:

Clark, Michael. *Michel Foucault: An Annotated Bibliography*. New York: Garland, 1983.

Eribon, Didier. *Michel Foucault,* translated by Betsy Wing. Cambridge, Massachusetts: Harvard University Press, 1991.

Gutting, Gary. *The Cambridge Companion to Foucault*. New York: Cambridge University Press, 1994.

Halperin, David M. *Saint-Foucault: Towards a Gay Hagiography*. New York: Oxford University Press, 1995.

Macey, David. *The Lives of Michel Foucault: A Biography*. New York: Pantheon Books, 1993.

Merquior, José C. *Foucault*. London: Fontana, 1985.

Miller, James. *The Passion of Michel Foucault*. New York: Simon and Schuster, 1993.

—Wayne R. Dynes

Barney Frank

1940-

American politician

Barney Frank has been involved in many key political issues during his eight terms in Congress. An outspoken liberal, he led the legislative struggle for the redress of Japanese Americans interned in camps during World War II. In 1990 Frank fought against provisions of the immigration law barring HIV-positive persons from entering the United States. He worked diligently and successfully for amendments to the Fair Housing Bill which included AIDS victims and HIV-positive persons under its provisions. During House debate on allowing gays and lesbians in the armed forces, Frank authored the "Don't ask, don't tell, and don't listen, and don't investigate" policy as a more inclusive alternative to Senator Sam Nunn's "Don't ask, don't tell" compromise. The proposal reflected Frank's propensity for matching liberalism with hard nosed pragmatism in order to move the legislative agenda. While Frank vigorously debated and voted against Nunn's "Don't ask, don't tell" it was adopted into law.

Colleagues on Capitol Hill describe Frank as a natural politician who has the instinct for effectively framing issues and accomplishing the task at hand. He is noted as a "sharp-tongued and quick witted debater" by fellow congressmen. Frank is also considered to be a brilliant, honest, and strong deal-maker. While he listens intently to arguments his rapid fire delivery of questioning and debate has disarmed many opponents. He is less rigidly partisan than many members of Congress, openly considering the intellectual merits of legislation above the political fray, and viewing himself as a pragmatic zealot.

Barney Frank was born on 31 March 1940, to Samuel and Elsie Frank in Bayonne, New Jersey. He has one brother, David, and two sisters, Doris Breay and Ann F. Lewis. Growing up in Bayonne he often helped his father at the truck stop he owned and managed, pumping gas. While Frank describes his parents as not well educated, they put a premium on education and reading for the family. Following graduation from high school in 1957, Frank attended Harvard University. He took a year's leave when his father died, and graduated with an A.B. degree from Harvard in 1962.

From 1963 to 1967 Frank worked at Harvard as a teaching fellow in government, and in 1966-67 served as the assistant to the director of the Institute for Politics at Harvard's John F. Kennedy School of Government. He worked on the Mississippi Summer Project in 1964, and various political races in the Boston area. He abandoned pursuit of a Ph.D. degree at Harvard to assist Kevin White's successful mayoral election in Boston. Frank served as Mayor White's executive assistant from 1968 to 1971, familiarizing himself with the Boston political scene and its vital players. He then worked for one year as administrative assistant to U.S. Congressman Michael J. Harrington, from Massachusetts. Frank revealed in a July 1987 interview with the *Washington Post* that during his tenure in Congressman Harrington's office he strongly believed he could never be an elected official because he was gay.

Elected to Massachusetts House of Representatives

In 1972 Frank ran for election to the Massachusetts House of Representatives for a vacated seat in Boston's Back Bay district. He was elected by plurality to the State House due in large part to Boston University students in the district, who also supported the presidential bid of George McGovern. As a state legislator Frank targeted issues of women's rights, gay rights, and social services in his policy programs. His strident liberal agenda caught the attention of Massachusetts and national politicos. Despite his confrontational and unorthodox behavior he won three more terms as state legislator. During his tenure in the Massachusetts state legislature Frank was selected as "Legislator of the Year" by several state and national groups. By 1977 he earned a law degree from Harvard University and in 1979-80 taught public policy courses at Harvard's Kennedy School of Government.

Following Pope John Paul II's 1980 reaffirmation of church doctrine which prohibited Roman Catholic clergy from serving or seeking public office, liberal Jesuit priest Robert F. Drinan declined to seek a sixth term in Massachusetts' fourth congressional district. Within days of the papal decree the prospective number of candidates for Drinan's seat swelled to 16, including Frank and John Kerry, a Middlesex prosecutor with no legislative experience. Frank was considered the "political heir apparent" for representative from

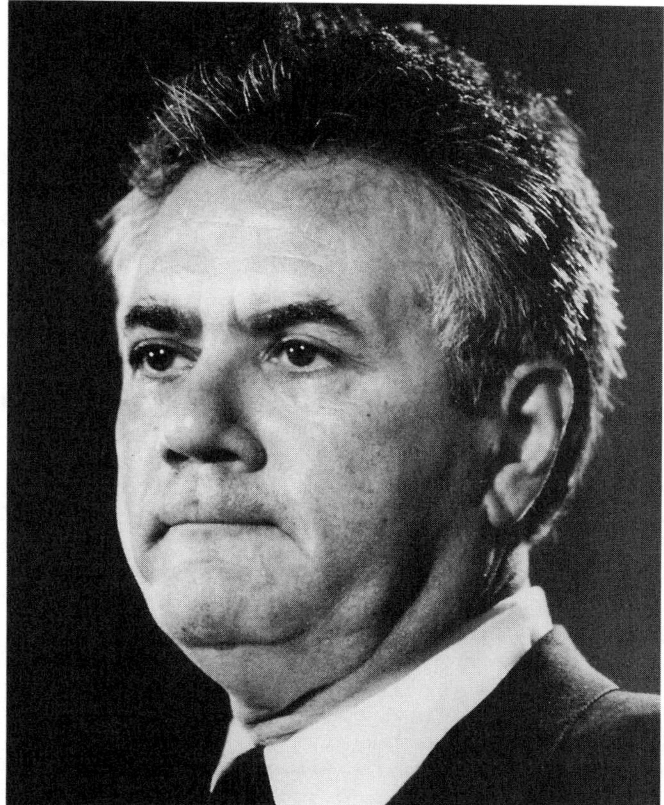

Barney Frank

the district, and Kerry quickly withdrew from the race. Frank declared his candidacy for the seat and moved from Boston's Back Bay neighborhood to outlying Newton. The archbishop of Boston, Humberto Cardinal Medeiros, warned parishioners of the fourth district's 400 Catholic churches not to vote for Frank or candidates who approved the legalization of abortion. With the support of Drinan and the endorsement of the *Boston Globe* he defeated the conservative, anti-abortion challenger, Mayor Arthur Clark of Newton by a small margin. In the general election he defeated Republican Richard Jones by a similar margin.

In his first term of office Frank was chosen to serve on the Government Operations Committee; Select Committee on Aging; Banking, Financing, and Urban Affairs Committee; and the Judiciary Committee. Frank rolled out a progressive program of action. He sponsored a bill to prevent new owners of low-income buildings from evicting current tenants. Frank vociferously fought the Reagan administration attempts to dismantle the Legal Services Corporation and budgetary cuts in elderly social services programs.

The politically configured fourth congressional district encompassed affluent suburbs, depressed factory towns, and rural farms alike. Following the 1982 redistricting Frank was left with a district which was 30 percent his own constituency and 70 percent from the district previously served by Representative Margaret Heckler. Heckler was a formidable and popular opponent. Most congressmen believed Frank would not survive this political battle.

Frank targeted Heckler's major weaknesses in the campaign. He exploited the considerable dissatisfaction of the low income, blue collar, and elderly voters with Heckler's term in Congress along with her support of President Reagan's economic policies. Overcoming political adversity Frank carried the district with 60 percent of the vote in the 1982 general election. This adverse experience helped coalesce the public and private lives of Frank. Soon after being reelected to his second term he began to tell his closest political allies and college friends he was gay. He was seen at Washington, D.C.'s Gay Pride Day festivities, and most of the Massachusetts delegation knew or surmised he was gay.

In the 1984 election Frank defeated his Republican opponent, Jim Forte by a wide margin. Two years later Republicans did not field a candidate and Frank defeated the American Party candidate Thomas D. DeVisscher by an even wider margin, receiving 89 percent of the vote.

Supporter of Needy

The liberal pragmatic side of Frank soon came to the forefront. While he vehemently supported obvious liberal measures such as legislation which would make it easier for low income and elderly persons to obtain generic drugs, he was on the opposing side on other liberal mainstays. Frank was among the few liberals who supported the Simpson-Mazzoli immigration reform bill and legislation which would give equal access to school facilities for student religious groups.

With the 1986 publication of former congressman Robert Bauman's autobiography, *The Gentleman from Maryland,* Frank was publicly outed. In the book Bauman refers to Frank as the "witty liberal who appears at Washington's annual Gay Pride Day in a tank top with a young companion." Many reporters called and asked Frank directly if he was gay. Frank refused comment because of the scurrilous content of Bauman's autobiography. He added that when he did talk about his life it would be through the *Boston Globe.*

During a May 1987 interview with the *Boston Globe* Frank publicly acknowledged he was gay. He stated: "I don't think my sex life is relevant to my job.... But on the other hand I don't want to leave the impression that I'm embarrassed by my life." Nearly 90 percent of the correspondence Frank received afterward were in his support. Further evidence of his constituents support came in his 1988 landslide reelection. Even in Fall River, the stronghold of blue collar Roman Catholicism, Frank carried a large vote plurality.

A 1989 Republican National Committee memo to 200 Republican leaders brought Frank's sexual orientation into the spotlight again. The memo compared the voting record of the newly elected House Speaker Thomas S. Foley to that of Frank's voting record. The memo contained the headline "Tom Foley: Out of the Liberal Closet," the memo was an attempt to depict Foley as a left wing liberal who might possibly be gay. Frank attacked the memo as a vicious unfounded attack, and if they didn't desist he would reveal names of Republican congressmen and other well-known Republicans who were in the closet. As a result Mark Goodin, who had written and distributed the memo, resigned as communication director of the Republican National Committee.

Plagued by Embarrassing Publicity

In less than three months Frank was again thrown into a whirlwind of embarrassing publicity. Stephen Gobie, a housekeeper and driver for Frank, revealed in a story in the *Washington Times* he had run a male prostitution business out of Frank's townhouse with the full knowledge of the congressman. A convicted felon, Gobie was on probation when Frank met him through a personal ad. The same day Frank held a news conference and admitted he knew Gobie was a prostitute, but hoped he could help rehabilitate him. While Frank acknowledged the truth in some of Gobie's claims, he stated he was unaware of the prostitution operation in his townhouse until the landlady reported to him suspicious activities, at which point Frank fired Gobie. Frank told *Newsweek* reporter Tom Morganthau: "Thinking I was going to be Henry Higgins and trying to turn him (Gobie) into Pygmalion was the biggest mistake I ever made. It turns out I was being suckered."

A number of congressmen and journalists rose to Frank's defense. Speaker of the House Thomas Foley issued a statement in which he asserted Frank had provided exemplary service to his constituency and the country, and would continue doing so long after the Gobie issue had been forgotten. Morton Kondracke, a journalist for the *New Republic,* dismissed the idea that Frank had become a deadly political burden for the Democrats and his legislative effectiveness had been destroyed. On the same date the *Nation* declared "What has been overlooked in all the to-do about his future is the true significance of his predicament, which is the predicament of all transgressors of our mythical sexual norms who desire to serve the government.... Nothing gets said about the intolerance ingrained in our culture that makes life hell for those like Frank who discover they are different."

Through the insistence of Herb Moses to fight the allegations, Frank called for an investigation by the House Ethics Committee. The committee launched an investigation into the Gobie charges. On 20 July 1990, five years after he met Gobie, the House Ethics Committee reported it found no evidence Frank knew of the prostitution ring being run in his townhouse, and extremely few facts to support Gobie's claim such activity occurred earlier. The committee further found several allegations by Gobie in support of this statement untrue, and there was no evidence to substantiate the claim. Frank was cited for misusing Congressional privilege in getting Gobie's parking tickets waived. Following four hours of heated floor debate, Frank accepted the committee's findings and apologized for his actions. The House of Representatives voted to reprimand Frank for his actions, following the failure by a vote of House members to expel or censure him.

Running for his sixth consecutive term in 1990, Frank was challenged by Republican nominee John Soto, an accountant and lawyer. Soto continually charged Frank with bad judgement, asked him to submit to an HIV test, and to make test results public. Soto's tactics were dismissed by constituents and Frank carried a resounding majority of the vote. Prior to the 1992 election the fourth district was again redistricted. Frank won reelection hands down. In seeking his eighth term of office Frank was challenged by minor party candidates and won easily. Frank's political comeback was due in large part to his perseverance, intelligence, and hard work.

Frank's political manifesto was published in 1992. The book, *Speaking Frankly: What's Wrong with the Democratic Party and How to Fix It,* argued the party had become to closely allied with the radical fringe, alienating mainstream voters. Liberal democrats suffered as a result of their close association and defense of the protestors in the 1960s and 1970s. That was why the Democrats had lost five of six presidential elections by 1992. Now it was time for the Democrats to expose the radical right politics of the Republicans along with the issue of class warfare.

Frank played a leading role in the 1993 debate concerning lifting the ban on gays and lesbians in the military. He believed Congress was not politically ready to completely lift the ban so he advocated a clear alternative to Senator Sam Nunn's policy whereby service people could lead an openly homosexual lifestyle off-base, but were forbidden to reveal their sexual orientation while on duty: the so called "Don't ask, don't tell, and don't listen, don't investigate" policy. After much political debate and rancor the controversial Nunn compromise, "Don't ask, don't tell," was approved by Congress, minus Frank's vote, and signed into law by President Clinton.

Following the Republican takeover of the U.S. House and Senate in the 1994 elections, Frank has served as the voice of the Democratic opposition. He declared that his mission is to shine the light where the Republicans don't want it shone.

While Frank describes himself as an often controversial, pragmatic liberal, he has consistently been a supporter of gay rights. He was one of the first Massachusetts legislators to sign a gay rights bill. He wrote a revision of the McCarran-Walter Act which removed homosexuality as grounds for denying entry by foreigners into the U.S. He has co-sponsored the Employment Non-Discrimination Act. Frank has also worked diligently for AIDS funding and housing programs for persons with AIDS. Working with the Clinton administration, Frank secured the establishment of non-discriminatory employment policies in all federal agencies. Further procedures were also instituted whereby gay, lesbian, and bisexual employees could file grievances for maltreatment. Most importantly, he was responsible for the recision of the federal security clearance ban for gays issued during the Eisenhower presidency. Frank continues to reside in Washington, D.C., with his longtime companion, economist Herb Moses.

Current Address: U.S. House of Representatives, 2210 Rayburn HOB, Washington, D.C., 20515.

References:

Congressional Directory, 104th 1995/96. Washington, D.C.: United States Government Printing Office, 1995.

Congressional Quarterly's Politics in America: 1996. Washington, D.C.: CQ Press, 1995.

Current Biography Yearbook 1995. New York: H. W. Wilson Company, 1995.

Frank, Barney. *Speaking Frankly: What's Wrong With the Democrats and How to Fix It.* New York: Times Books/Random House, 1992.

Hohler, Bob. "Brawler on the Hill," in *Boston Globe,* 21 May 1995.

Kaufman, Jonathan. "The Problem With Being Too Frank," in *Boston Globe,* 17 September 1989.

Kosova, Weston. "Frank Incensed: Outspoken Rep. Barney Frank; Interview," in *New Republic,* 6 March 1995.

Morganthau, Tom. "Barney Frank's Story," in *Newsweek,* 25 September 1989.

Romano, Lois. "Barney Frank, Out of the Closet," in *Washington Post,* 2 July 1987.

Wilkie, Curtis. "Barney Frank: Making of a Pragmatist," in *Boston Globe,* 10 June 1993.

—Michael A. Lutes

Frederick II

1712-1786

German monarch

History presents us with no dearth of military leaders who were gay: Alexander the Great, Julius Caesar, Richard I (the Lion Heart), to name a few. Even in the early Nazi hierarchy, before it was cleansed of impure elements, General Rohm practiced his type of homosexuality openly. But when the subject of scrutiny has been the brilliant Frederick the Great, who was not only a military leader but one of the great intellectuals and reformers of the Enlightenment, some writers and historians have "risen" to his defense and denied any involvement in homosexual activity. Because a great deal of evidence supports the contention that he was gay, such defenses have sometimes led to absurd contortions of logic and evidence.

In 1986, for example, on the occasion of the 200th anniversary of the death of Frederick II, both East and West German museums had exhibitions celebrating the many achievements of the monarch. But no mention was made, in discussions of his private life, of his sexual preference. James D. Steakley reports in his *Sodomy in Enlightenment Prussia* that visitors to Frederick's palace in Potsdam were told that Frederick never lived with his wife because he did not like people and preferred the company of his dogs. The truth is the opposite: Frederick delighted in the company of people with whom he shared some of his wide-ranging interests, including sexual.

Youth and Adolescence

Frederick's youth and adolescence consisted in large part of a contest (or perhaps "battle" is more apt) of wills with his father, Frederick William I. The king had early detected in the Crown Prince proclivities that he thought inappropriate. Prince Frederick was polite, delicate, intellectual, and musical. Frederick William was coarse, given to physical violence (his cane, applied to his children, was infamous), and anti-intellectual. One author refers to him as "loutish." Once, in his younger years, Prince Frederick persuaded his tutor Duhan to teach him Latin. When his father discovered them discussing a Latin text one day, he flew into a rage, brought out his cane and ordered them to stop. Such tantrums were frequent, along with the canings for the prince.

By the time Prince Frederick was in his late teens, the king suspected that some of the prince's friends and relationships were homosexual. And they probably were.

In 1730 the Prince formed an intense friendship with a lieutenant in the army, Hans Hermann von Katte, a handsome young man 26 years old from a distinguished family. It is almost certain they were lovers, but their correspondence was destroyed when King Frederick William began to look for evidence. Because of the constant torment and baiting by the king, von Katte and Frederick decided to flee the army and Germany and seek freedom in England.

Unfortunately, the plot to escape was discovered and both the prince and von Katte were thrown in prison. One morning, while the prince was still in solitary confinement, he was wakened at dawn by his jailers and ordered to look out of his cell window. Lieutenant von Katte was led into the courtyard. As von Katte bowed down to pray, he was beheaded by a saber blow. Having been told beforehand what was going to take place, Prince Frederick

Frederick II

fainted before the blow was struck. He lapsed into a coma and remained delirious for a day and a half.

That event seemed at last to break the prince's will. He informed his father that he would accede to his wishes totally. Frederick William's decision was to allow the prince a probationary period of undetermined length in the civil service, until he had proved himself worthy of a full pardon. In time he was given his pardon, along with a residence near Berlin at Rheinsberg. In 1733, without enthusiasm, he married Elizabeth Christine, daughter of the Duke of Brunswick-Bevern. Now withdrawn from the constant surveillance of his father, Prince Frederick assembled a court of like-minded people and indulged his tastes for discussion, reading, writing, and music—he was an excellent flutist and a good composer.

Frederick Becomes King

Frederick William I died on 31 May 1740. On becoming king, Frederick moved swiftly to make the changes that would finally honor him with a revered and respected position in the history of the Enlightenment. His civil reforms included the abolition of torture, press censorship, and religious discrimination. In cultural matters, he recalled exiled intellectuals and writers and began to restore the Berlin Academy to a position of international reputation and respect.

Another aspect of Frederick's character, hitherto unsuspected, began to reveal itself at this time. Using as an excuse a centuries old claim to three Silesian duchies, he conquered all of Silesia within seven weeks. The ensuing realignments (Silesia had been a part of Austria) upset the balance of power among the European powers, and led to a number of other conflicts. In the end Frederick got all of Silesia and earned the grudging respect of the European powers.

The longest of Frederick's military ventures was the Seven Years' War (1756-63). It began as a joint effort of Maria Theresa of Austria and Louis XV to regain Silesia for Austria and to conquer various parts of the Low Countries and the Rhineland for France. Ultimately, Sweden and Russia also joined the war on the side of France and Austria. Despite early heavy losses and numerical odds weighed against him, Frederick's military genius and his armies finally prevailed. At the war's end, there was no doubt that Prussia had attained the status of a world power.

The facts of Frederick's reign, political and military, as sketched above, are not in dispute. These are what made him such an important historical figure. The facts of his personal life are more problematical. His marriage to Elizabeth Christine of Brunswick was a fraud. He did not find her interesting in any way and wrote about her in a letter, "I wish her the best of luck and pray from the bottom of my heart that the Emperor of Morocco will fall in love with ... her charms, abduct and marry her. Empress of Morocco is worth twice as much as Crown Princess of Prussia." (Reiners). After the marriage, Frederick eventually gave her residences of her own. When he assumed the throne, he rarely saw her but he made sure all her needs were taken care of.

The presence of male company, very often young and handsome, as mentioned earlier, continued. His circle of male friends grew and included those of intellectual and musical accomplishment, including Voltaire and other luminaries of the period. This is not to say they were all, or mainly, homosexual, but some were. When Frederick built his residence in Potsdam, Sans Souci, that became the favorite gathering place of his entourage. In celebration of its completion, he wrote the following poem to his close friend, Count Kaiserlingk (James B. Steakley):

Dans ce nouveau palais de noble architecture
Nous jouirons tous deux de la liberte pure,
Dans l'ivresse de l'amitie!
L'ambition, l'inimitie
Seront les seuls peches taxes contre nature.

In this new palace of lofty build,
Both of us will sport in pure freedom,
In this intoxication of friendship!
Ambition, enmity
Will be the only sins denounced as against nature.

—trans. Mona Logarbo

Unhappily, Frederick's final years were lonely ones. Most of his close friends had died. He also suffered from gout and other ailments to the point where he sometimes could not think clearly. One ray of light, however, was a new friendship with a lively witted young Italian, the Marchese Lucchesini, whose conversation could keep up with Frederick's. Easy-going and tactful, and a person with no enemies, Lucchesini was rewarded with an ambassadorship when Frederick died on 17 August 1786 after a long illness.

References:

Asprey, Robert B. *Frederick the Great: The Magnificent Enigma.* New York: Ticknor & Fields, 1986.

Henderson, Susan W. "Frederick the Great of Prussia: A Homophile Perspective," in *Gai Saber 1* Spring 1977: 46-54.
Mitford, Nancy. *Frederick the Great*. New York: Harper & Row, 1970.
Reiners, Ludwig. *Frederick the Great,* translated by Lawrence P. R. Wilson. London: Oswald Wolff, 1960.
Steakley, James D. "Sodomy in Enlightenment Prussia," in *Journal of Homosexuality 16,* 1989: 163-176.
Zimmerman. "Select Views," in *Frederick the Great,* edited by Louis L. Snyder. Englewood Cliffs, New Jersey: Prentice-Hall, Inc., 1971: I, 45-58, 61-67.

—Robert N. Mory

Marcia Freedman

1938-

American-born Israeli author and activist

Marcia Freedman's pioneering efforts in the women's movement in Israel started a chain of actions improving the lives of women throughout the country. As a feminist and legislator in Israel in the 1970s, she introduced legislation to reform abortion and brought feminist issues to the floor of the Knesset for discussion. She helped open both the first battered women's shelter and the first feminist bookstore in Israel.

Marcia Freedman was born in the United States in 1938. Her father, Philip Prince, was a labor organizer and a Communist during the McCarthy era. Her father died in 1970. Her mother Anne died in 1993 at age 84.

Freedman, her husband Bill, and their daughter Jenny emigrated from the United States to Israel in 1967. During her time on the Knesset, she and her husband separated and eventually divorced.

Freedman's involvement with the modern feminist movement in Israel began during afternoon consciousness raising sessions at a sidewalk cafe in Haifa with several other women. The movement in Haifa grew and eventually supported a strike of women factory workers demanding equal pay, pursued abortion reform, and established a day care center at the university.

While teaching philosophy at Haifa University, Freedman taught an extracurricular seminar open only to women on the topic of Women's Liberation; the enrollment for her seminar quickly grew to 100 women.

On 14 January 1974, Freedman was sworn into the Knesset, the governing body in Israel. She was elected with Shulamit Aloni and the Citizen's Rights Movement Party. As an outspoken feminist, she did not expect to win the election, and she was asked by her party to resign after she did.

A particular source of inspiration to Freedman during her time on the Knesset was Rachel Kagan, a member of the first Knesset elected on an independent women's list. Kagan had proposed an Equal Rights for Women Act and her experiences proved similar and inspirational to Freedman as she worked for feminist reform in Israel.

As a result of Freedman's efforts, the Youth Ministry's budget for girls in distress was increased and wife-battering in Israel was investigated. Freedman also introduced abortion legislation which would have lifted all restrictions on abortions during the first trimester. At the time, doctors could only legally perform abortions when necessary to save a mother's life. Her bill did not pass, but another did which had fewer restrictions than what had been in place.

Because she spoke up frequently on the subject of a two state solution to the Israeli government's conflict with Palestinians, she was called a self-hating Jew. Her support of this solution brought her criticism in Israel, and it was at the heart of much her conflict with the Israeli feminist movement.

Freedman was elected to the Knesset with the Citizen's Rights Movement and finished her term with the Women's Party. At the end of her term, she decided not to run for reelection but rather to work for the support necessary to win at least one seat on the Knesset for the Women's Party. Although the campaign was not successful, it forced women's issues to public debate during the campaign.

In 1977 Freedman and four other women opened the first battered women's shelter in Israel. As a result of their work, a woman's legal right to leave her violent husband was recognized. They also created a network of support services for battered women which included financial support, police protection, and medical and social services. Eventually a budget to support the shelter was secured from the Welfare Ministry.

Marcia Freedman came out in 1977. She and her lover at the time opened a women's bookstore and center, Woman's Voice, in Haifa. Through their bookstore, they created a feminist community of lesbians and straight women in Haifa. They made extraordinary efforts to spread feminist books to women in their community and to women elsewhere in Israel.

Freedman left Israel for Berkeley in 1981. In Berkeley she is active in the Jewish women's peace movement, and she founded the Women's Computer Literacy Project. In 1985, she began working with the American Society on Aging and is the liaison to its Task Force on Lesbian and Gay Aging issues. She is a writer and has done book reviews for the *San Francisco Chronicle*. *Exile in the Promised Land*, the memoirs of her time in Israel, was published in 1990 by Firebrand books. The book offers sharp insight into Israeli and international feminism, government sexism, and politics, racism and homophobia found in the feminist movement.

References:

Freedman, Marcia. *Exile in the Promised Land.* Ithaca, New York: Firebrand Books, 1990.
———. "At the Edge of Old Age," in *Lambda Gray.* North Hollywood, California: Newcastle Publishing, 1993.

—Danielle M. DeMuth

Anna Freud

1895-1982

Austrian child psychoanalyst

Anna Freud's life was dedicated to increasing the happiness and self-understanding of others. She was thoroughly involved in the

Anna Freud

lives of her clients, friends, and father. After being exiled from her native Austria by the Gestapo, in 1940 she founded Hampstead Nurseries in London for children who had been separated from their families during World War II. She nursed her father through his cancer illness, which lasted for sixteen years. Although she did not marry, and had no children of her own, Freud helped raise the children of her dearest friend, Dorothy Burlingham, and also helped rear the children she taught in school, analyzed in her office, and matriculated in her nurseries.

Born in Vienna on 3 December 1895 to parents Sigmund and Martha Bernays Freud, Freud was the last of six children. Soon after her birth, Martha's sister, Minna, moved in to help care for the children. Freud sometimes felt left out from the family clan and developed an early attachment to her father, which lasted her entire life. Whereas her sister Sophie was beautiful and delicate, Freud was "plain," and developed her intellect. Sigmund Freud eventually developed the strongest of bonds with Anna, likening her to Cordelia, as the daughter most faithful to her father, and to Antigone, as the female archetype of loyalty to father and siblings.

The Freuds were upper middle class, so Freud went to good private schools. A woman was not expected to attend university, nor did Freud seriously consider doing so after graduating high school at the age of 15. Instead, she trained to be an elementary school teacher, and taught at the same grammar school, the Cottage Lyceum, that she had attended. After five years of teaching experience, Freud quit the profession to become a psychoanalyst. At 23 years old, she underwent psychoanalysis by her father, a practice unheard of today, but common in the early days of psychoanalysis.

In the 1920s, there were as yet no schools for training, only an enthusiastic group of psychoanalysts in Vienna who shared their findings and their hopes for the social ramifications of the discipline. One became a practicing psychoanalyst by attending Sigmund's lectures, reading the literature, and undergoing short sessions of psychoanalysis. The group was incestuous, not only in the strictest family sense, but also because this was a small group which "treated" its own members. When interviewed about those early days of the discipline, both Erik Erikson (an analysand of Freud) and Freud herself stress the atmosphere of enthusiasm and optimism for the idea that an ever-growing group of psychoanalyzed people could change the face of society. "We were all trying to harvest a great crop," said Freud. "This was a utopian moment," echoed Erik Erikson.

Began Life Long Relationships

Sigmund Freud exhibited a tendency to protect his daughter from the inevitable suitors who were attracted to her, many of them analysts and colleagues of Sigmund. On the other hand, her father encouraged Freud's friendships with women in the field. Thus began the two most notable and extended friendships in Freud's life: with Lou Andreas-Salome, analyst, writer, and *femme fatale* who had affairs with Nietzsche and Rilke; and with Dorothy Burlingham, who arrived in Vienna in 1925 as an American analysand.

Burlingham lived with the Freuds and stayed on with Anna for the rest of her life. Dorothy collaborated with Freud in every way: founding Hampstead Nurseries, co-authoring articles, traveling to Freud's many speaking engagements abroad, pursuing research projects and even sharing the bringing up of her own four children, whom Freud analyzed. Of course there is speculation about the nature of this partnership, but both women are so discreet in their correspondence that there is no reference to a possible sexual connection between them. Robert Coles, child psychiatrist at Harvard Medical School, biographer and acquaintance of Freud, writes that it doesn't take a "psychiatric wizard to figure out that Freud found it much easier and more appealing to get close emotionally to women than to men, and that her initially professional relationship with Mrs. Burlingham and her children became familial in nature—in a way that today would be certain to raise eyebrows among admission committees at psychoanalytic institutes." He adds that the relationship Freud had with her father—analysand, colleague, confidante—made him irreplaceable by any other man.

Apparently, this unconventional attachment and the absence of the more conventional attachment through marriage to a man did not negatively affect Freud's work or reputation. Perhaps it was understood and accepted as a less conventional but still honorable situation: that here was a woman who had devoted her life to a man who happened to be her father instead of her husband. Freud's reserved nature, her objectivity, diplomacy, and refusal to criticize other members of the field even when they attacked her, added to her persona as the Antigone type: "womanly" in her dedication to an important man and his career, yet "strong" in her pursuit of his field, albeit in a subspecialty that did not compete with his.

Some critics have read Freud's first published work, an article entitled "Beating Fantasies and Daydreams" (1922), as an illustration of how she became masochistically subservient to her father. One thing is clear: Freud was never very close to her mother, and her decision to become a therapist only furthered the alienation from her mother, who believed that the profession was "a form of pornography." Freud's professional role *vis-a-vis* her father was certainly a subservient one, as she frequently gave him credit for her achievements and recognized that several of the rewards she received after his death were really for him.

Made Mark in Fields of Psychoanalysis and Psychology

In May of 1936, Freud published her best-known book, *The Ego and the Mechanisms of Defense*. With it, she established some measure of independence from her father, at least insofar as its subject matter was different from his. While her father had been focussing on the *id*, Freud took up the ego, even naming new mechanisms of defense that her father had not previously discovered: *altruistic surrender* and *identification with the aggressor*. The familiarity of these terms today suggests the impact of the book, both on the field of psychoanalysis in 1936, and now, in lay, or "pop" psychology. Interestingly, "identification with the aggressor" was a mode of defense that Freud would, in three years' time, see in proliferation as she took up a practice for children who had been traumatized by war.

Freud's main contribution to the field is the idea that an analyst can use the same fundamental principles of psychoanalysis on children as on adults. Yet, children are in some ways easier patients to treat because they are more willing to share their thoughts and feelings. She stressed that the role of child psychoanalyst is a dual one: as therapist and educator. Children's behavior is more easily modified than that of adults, since they are generally more eager to please adults and have fewer or looser neurotic strategies for coping with their complexes.

Freud's gentle temperament, her dedication to not only her father's career but also to his visions of the good that can come from psychoanalysis, and her lifelong commitment to bettering the lives of children make her a well-known historical figure whose phrase, "the best interests of the child," rings through courtrooms today as the standard by which child custody dispositions are adjudicated.

—Jill Franks

Greta Garbo

1905-1990

Swedish actress

Greta Garbo was one of the few actors in Hollywood to achieve stardom in both silent and talking pictures. Her exotic beauty, her superb acting ability and professionalism, her androgynous sexuality, and her mysterious private life made her a star *and* a legend.

She was born Greta Louisa Gustafson in Stockholm, Sweden, on 18 September 1905. Her parents, Karl Alfred and Anna Louisa Gustafson, were so impoverished that they briefly considered allowing Karl's employer to adopt Greta, the youngest of their three children. Garbo's father dies when she was 14 years old.

Greta had been starstruck since she was a small child. She loved to sing and perform for her family, and dreamed of the theatre. But there was no money for theatre tickets. Soon after her father's death, Greta took her first job, as a lather-girl in a barbershop. A little later she became a clerk in the millinery department of a large department store, and then appeared in print ads modeling the store's hats. This led to her first film, *How Not to Dress* (1921), a short advertisement for the store.

Appearing in low-budget films, Greta received minor critical attention for her unusual beauty and comedic talent. By now her desire for a theatrical career was almost an obsession, although she also demonstrated the depression and craving for solitude that would mark her later life. She overcame her shyness to compete successfully for a scholarship to the Royal Dramatic Theater Academy. With a few years' maturity and training, she won her first important film role in 1924 in an adaptation of Selma Lagerlöf's *Saga of Gösta Berling*, which became a great European success. This was the first film in which she used her stage name, "Greta Garbo."

Garbo's first important Hollywood film was *The Torrent* (1926), from Metro-Goldwyn-Mayer. It made her a star, praised more for her talent than for her beauty. Over the next four years she appeared in ten more silent films, learned to speak English, had her teeth straightened, and took on a new image fashioned by MGM. By the time she made her first talking picture, *Anna Christie* (1930), Garbo was the embodiment of feminine passion and exotic beauty. She made several important films in the 1930s, including *Mata Hari* and *Grand Hotel* (1932), *Queen Christina* (1935), *Anna Karenina* (1935), *Camille* (1936) and *Ninotchka* (1939). In these films she played mysterious women in glamorous wardrobes; critics found her roles melodramatic, but audiences and other actors adored her.

Off-screen, Garbo was far different from the women she played. Although the studio arranged to have her photographed as often as possible on the arms of handsome male stars, she had had several relationships with women since the age of 14. Through the 1930s she was involved with Mercedes de Acosta, a former lover of

Greta Garbo as Mata Hari

Marlene Dietrich; Garbo and de Acosta would remain on-again-off-again lovers and friends for 40 years. When not working, Garbo wore wide-shouldered suits with trousers, an unusual look for women at the time. MGM would not permit her to wear pants in her films because it would counter the studio's carefully crafted feminine image. But the public became accustomed to seeing newspaper and magazine photos of her in pants, and found the combination of androgynous off-screen image and ultra-feminine on-screen image intriguing.

Among friends, Garbo enjoyed playing the role of a man, and being addressed as "sir." As her power at the studio increased, Garbo lobbied MGM for films in which she could play male characters, including Hamlet and Dorian Gray. But her efforts were unsuccessful.

In 1941 Garbo starred in the disastrous *Two-Faced Woman*. She was unhappy throughout the filming, and never acted again, in spite of several offers of choice roles. Retired at the age of 36, she became a recluse, almost as famous in subsequent decades for her mysterious isolation as for her films. In 1954 she was awarded a special

Academy Award by the Motion Picture Academy, but she did not attend the ceremony to accept it. After decades of stepping outside only in disguises and dark glasses, of signing into hotels under assumed names, of dodging curious reporters, she died alone in her New York apartment in 1990. Her death was not the end of speculation about her, but only the beginning of a new phase. That the elusive and mysterious sex symbol had never married, that the star loved by millions had died alone, only added to the legend.

References:

Collis, Rose. *Portraits to the Wall: Historic Lesbian Lives Unveiled.* London: Cassell, 1994.

Paris, Barry. *Garbo: A Biography.* New York: Knopf, 1995.

Vickers, Hugo. *Loving Garbo: The Story of Greta Garbo, Cecil Beaton, and Mercedes de Acosta.* New York: Random House, 1994.

—Cynthia A. Bily

Federico García Lorca

1898-1936

Spanish poet and playwright

Federico García Lorca ranks as Spain's most famous twentieth-century author. During his lifetime he achieved international recognition as both a poet and dramatist, and his death in the first weeks of the Spanish Civil War rapidly became an emblem of the brutality and anti-intellectualism of the Nationalist forces led by General Franco. Lorca was a leading light in the flowering of Spanish literature that occurred between 1918 and 1936, and he is generally counted as one of the most significant members of the so-called "Generation of '27," a group of writers, mainly poets (Jorge Guillén, Pedro Salinas, Rafael Alberti, Vicente Aleixandre, etc.), of roughly the same age who were all working and publishing over this period.

The oldest of Federico García Rodríguez and Vicenta Lorca Romero's four children, Federico García Lorca was born on 5 June 1898, in Fuente Vaqueros, a village outside the city of Granada in southern Spain. Fuente Vaqueros is located on the *vega,* a large, fertile, irrigated plain; Lorca's father, a well-to-do farmer and landowner, prospered there thanks to the sugar-beet boom that ensued when the supply of Cuban cane sugar was cut off after the Spanish-American war. Several years later they moved to another village close by, called Asquerosa (now Valderrubio).

García Lorca grew up in an essentially agricultural environment, tempered by the more cultured interests of his mother, a primary school teacher, who professed an enduring passion for literature. Information regarding his early childhood is relatively sketchy, but sources agree that García Lorca stood out from the rest of the village children, not only as the scion of a somewhat more refined and moneyed family but also as a rather delicate, sensitive, and impressionable child.

In 1909 García Lorca's parents moved to the city of Granada, motivated in part by the desire to give their growing family a sound secondary education. However, Federico was a mediocre student, daydreaming and inventing jokes and games rather than applying himself to his studies; nevertheless he managed to graduate high school and started courses in philosophy and law at the local university.

During these adolescent years García Lorca's main interest was music rather than literature, and he became an excellent pianist even dabbling with composition. He played the piano for pleasure throughout his life, but the idea of performance as a serious career stalled with the death, in 1916, of his venerated music teacher and his father's refusal to send him to a conservatory.

García Lorca Moves to Madrid's "Residencia de Estudiantes"

Other changes were occurring too. A literature professor at the University of Granada encouraged him to start writing, and in 1920 (after two exploratory trips in 1919), García Lorca transferred to the University of Madrid and secured a room at the Residencia de Estudiantes; there he would live, off and on, for the next ten years, returning home for the holidays and occasionally at other times of the year. In 1918 he published his first book, a travelogue (*Impresiones y paisajes—Impressions and Landscapes*), in 1920 he premiered his first play (*El maleficio de la mariposa—The Butterfly's Evil Spell,* a resounding flop), and in 1921 he brought out his first collection of poetry (*Libro de poemas—Book of Poems*), which went largely unnoticed.

If García Lorca did not emerge as a writer until he turned 20, he had nevertheless been an avid reader since childhood, and he was strongly influenced by many poets, among them the French Romantics and Symbolists and the Latin American *modernistas,* especially Rubén Darío. This post-Romantic mindset probably accounts for several late adolescent "crushes" on local Granada girls, always from afar, as well as a decidedly heterodox vision of Christianity which Federico expounded in his literary juvenilia. With the years, García Lorca's readings continued and widened, and among them we can now identify Plato (the *Symposium*), Verlaine, Wilde, Proust, Gide, and Cocteau (Whitman came rather later). In addition, his personal letters of the period (c. 1918-20) suggest that he was beginning to become aware of his real sexual orientation, a process accelerated by the move to the all-male Residencia de Estudiantes and by the many new friendships that he made there.

It is hard to overestimate the importance of the Resi, as it was known, in the course of García Lorca's life. Modelled after the colleges of Oxford and Cambridge, its goal was to provide students with adequate lodgings and at the same time to encourage intellectual contact and discussion. The comparison with British university life during the inter-war years is not inappropriate: a mixture of high jinks, pranks and hoaxes, in jokes and catch-phrases, cliques, elaborate tea parties, earnest conversations late into the night, concerts, amateur dramatics, lectures by international celebrities, all this and more constituted the fabric of everyday life at the Residencia.

Over García Lorca's first several years at the Resi a passionate friendship evolved between him and a fellow poet, Emilio Prados, though the latter seems to have invested the relationship with greater significance than García Lorca did. There too he met art student Salvador Dalí, another "residente," and their friendship grew and became increasingly intense over the period 1923-1927. It is clear that García Lorca fell in love with Dalí, beguiled both by his personality and artistic talent; Dalí's exact response, and the dynamics of their relationship, are still a matter for speculation, given the latter's notorious unreliability and his own complex sexuality in the 1920s. The relationship came to an end in 1928. Dalí fell increasingly under the (artistic) influence of Luis Buñuel (yet another famous "residente"), and together they went on to make the first Surrealist film, *Un Chien andalou* (1929), which has been interpreted by some as a veiled commentary on García Lorca's sexuality. García Lorca, meanwhile, had started an affair with a young sculptor, Emilio Aladrén.

These events need to be placed in context. In the 1920s Spain was still a strongly Catholic country, and from 1923 was ruled by a dictator, General Primo de Rivera, who modelled himself on Mussolini. Within artistic circles and restricted groups of friends homosexuality was easily accepted, but it was something discreetly hidden in society at large, and García Lorca did not make any attempt to diverge from this "norm."

On the literary front, this was a decade of considerable success. García Lorca published two more books of poetry, the second of which, *Romancero gitano* (*Gypsy Ballad-Book*) (1928), became an all-time best-seller and established his reputation on the literary scene; in the theatre, his second play to be staged, *Mariana Pineda* (1927), notable for its première in Barcelona with sets designed by Dalí, had a more modest success.

A Year in America

As the decade drew to a close, García Lorca was in a profound depression. The breakup with Dalí, Aladrén's cool yet exploitative response, the popularity of *Romancero gitano* based on what he felt was a fundamental misreading of the poems, a crisis of aesthetic direction, family pressure to think about a "serious" career, all contributed to his troubles. Thus, when the opportunity of a trip outside Spain presented itself, García Lorca leaped at the chance. He travelled by train and steamer to New York in June 1929 and registered for summer session English classes at Columbia University. García Lorca spent some eight months in the United States. Besides New York, he travelled to Vermont and the Catskills, and although he was notionally a student, he explored, observed, and socialized, met Hart Crane, read *Leaves of Grass*, toured Harlem with Nella Larsen, and he was on hand for the great Wall Street Crash of fall 1929. Out of this experience came one of his best-known collections of poetry, *Poeta en Nueva York* (*Poet in New York*) (written 1929-30, published 1940).

In March of the following year he travelled to Cuba to give a series of lectures. He warmed to the Latin atmosphere of the island immediately. While jazz-age New York had opened his eyes to a lifestyle and moral code quite different from that prevalent in Spain, it was the indulgent port city of Havana that afforded him the possibility of a more active sexual life than he had hitherto known, thus prompting him to seek to incorporate homosexual themes centrally and explicitly in his literary work. Hence the poem "Oda a Walt Whitman" (1930, privately printed 1933, later incorporated in *Poeta en Nueva York*), and the play *El público* (*The Audience*) (also 1930, but neither published nor staged in his lifetime).

García Lorca Heads Student Theater Troupe

Back in Spain by the summer of 1930, García Lorca had shed his depression and again threw himself into work and Madrid life. He rented his own attic apartment in the capital, and in the spring of 1931 he witnessed the ouster of Spain's King Alfonso XIII and the establishment of the Second Republic. Later that year he was asked

Federico García Lorca

to head one of the many cultural initiatives sponsored by the new government: a student theater group, to be called "La Barraca," which would perform plays from the Spanish "Golden Age" (sixteenth and seventeenth centuries) in Madrid during term and in the provinces during vacations. His directorship of the troupe lasted from 1932 to 1935, and during this time "La Barraca" toured successfully all over Spain.

Meanwhile, freed from the strictures of both family and dormitory living, García Lorca continued the more active sexual lifestyle that he had espoused in Cuba. His amorous involvements of this period are ill-documented, due in part to the discretion he still exercised. Several of his contemporaries in the "Generation of '27" were also homosexual, notably the poet Luis Cernuda, who also began writing, in only thinly veiled terms, about homosexual themes. In 1933 García Lorca met Rafael Rodríguez Rapún, an engineering student who had just been appointed secretary of "La Barraca" and who was to become the main love of García Lorca's last years.

The year 1933 was important also for the première in Madrid of *Bodas de sangre* (*Blood Wedding*), the first play of the so-called trilogy of rural tragedies; the commercial success of this work was such that it made García Lorca financially independent of his family for the first time in his life.

Top Billing in Buenos Aires

García Lorca's second and last foreign trip lasted from October 1933 to March 1934, and came about thanks to an invitation from a well-known Argentinian actress to participate in stagings of his plays in Buenos Aires. García Lorca enjoyed the new-found celebrity and the financial rewards that went with it. Operating out of a hotel room, he plunged into Buenos Aires literary life and barely found time to spend a couple of weeks across the River Plate estuary in Montevideo. The theater played to packed houses, *Bodas de sangre* was the sensation of the season, and several new editions of *Romancero gitano* were hurried into print.

His last full years—1934 and 1935—were ones of increasing literary fame and success. *Diván del Tamarit* (1931-34, published 1940) is the last major poetic collection; while it charts retrospectively the pains of a love affair and its breakup, the book's title and the poem's names ("Gacela," "Casida") serve as an invocation of, and homage to, Moorish Spain: Granada was the last city to fall during the Reconquest, marking the very end of the Arab occupation of Spain (711-1492), and García Lorca clearly sympathized with Moorish culture and its much more tolerant attitudes to sexuality. *Yerma,* the second play in the aforementioned trilogy, was premiered at the end of 1934, and *Doña Rosita la soltera* (*Doña Rosita the Spinster*) in late 1935, during a notable run of his plays in Barcelona. The relationship with Rapún continued, and its vicissitudes inform the cycle of late love sonnets, in some ways reminiscent of Petrarch, that are known as the "Sonetos del amor oscuro" ("Sonnets of Dark Love") (1935). In June 1936 García Lorca completed the first draft of what was to be his last play, and probably his best-known work, *La casa de Bernarda Alba* (*The House of Bernarda Alba*).

The Outbreak of Civil War

Political tensions that had been simmering ever since the advent of the Second Republic boiled over in the summer of 1936—*coup d'état* headed by Franco was only partially successful, and triggered the start of civil war. García Lorca found himself in the wrong place at the wrong time: Madrid remained staunchly Republican, but he was down in Granada, visiting his parents at their summer home, and Granada soon fell to the Nationalist forces. As in other cities that suffered the same fate, the army, Civil Guard, and impromptu death-squads launched a full-scale purge of liberal and leftist elements; in mid-August, some five weeks after the initial *coup,* García Lorca was arrested on trumped-up charges and shortly after shot. It has been estimated that, in Granada alone, a minimum of 5,000 individuals shared his fate.

For decades the nature and circumstances of García Lorca's violent and untimely death overshadowed his literary genius. Spanish Republicans and sympathizers seized on the act as a touchstone for Franco's barbarism, rapidly converting García Lorca into a martyr figure. Franco's victory and his subsequent regime, that lasted until 1975, obscured matters further. Official policy on his death, which had become something of an embarrassment, was a mixture of denial and professions of ignorance, until in the 1950s a theory was advanced that it was actually the result of a homosexual *crime passionnel.* This absurd notion served the regime particularly well, as imputations of homosexuality discredited the individual while the nationalist military forces could disclaim involvement in his death. Of course, the situation is much different today. Thanks to modern research, most of the historical facts have been established beyond doubt, and García Lorca's literary works are published, translated, read, and performed more widely than ever before.

García Lorca never became an active exponent of homosexual rights, although it is self-evident that he believed in them. The majority of his works do not have specifically homosexual themes, and generally tend to be existential in nature, dwelling on time, mortality and the many frustrations inherent in the human condition. In those compositions where homosexual themes are discernible, there is considerable stylistic variation: several works are oblique or "difficult," making their interpretation problematical, but some, such as the "Oda a Walt Whitman" and *El público,* are much more explicit, and this goes a long way to explain their delayed and checkered publication history. A major theme in *El público* is the equal acceptability or "legitimacy" of all forms of human sexuality, one of García Lorca's most deeply held ideas; the play was not published until 1976 and did not receive a commercial première until 1986-87 (the same production in Milan and then Madrid).

References:

Anderson, Andrew A. "Federico García Lorca," in *Dictionary of Literary Biography,* vol. 108, *Twentieth-Century Spanish Poets,* edited by Michael L. Perna. Detroit: Gale Research, 1991: 134-161.

———. "Federico García Lorca," in *Gay and Lesbian Literature,* edited by Sharon Malinowski. Detroit: St. James Press, 1994: 145-149.

Ash, John. "City of Night. García Lorca's Old-Fashioned Modernism," in *Village Voice* (New York), 26 July 1988: 52-53.

Binding, Paul. *Lorca: The Gay Imagination.* London: GMP, 1985.

Eisenberg, Daniel. "Federico García Lorca (1898-1936)," in *Encyclopedia of Homosexuality,* edited by Wayne R. Dynes. New York: Garland, 1990: 743-745.

———. "Lorca and Censorship: the Gay Artist Made Heterosexual," in *Angélica,* no. 2, 1991: 121-145.

Gibson, Ian. *The Assassination of Federico García Lorca.* London: W. H. Allen, 1979.

———. *Federico García Lorca. A Life.* New York: Pantheon Books, 1989.

Swansey, Bruce, & José Ramón Enríquez. "Homosexualidad en la Generación del 27. Una conversación con Jaime Gil de Biedma," in *El homosexual ante la sociedad enferma,* edited by José Ramón Enríquez. Barcelona: Tusquets, 1978: 193-216.

Sahuquillo, Angel. *Federico García Lorca y la cultura de la homosexualidad. Lorca, Dalí, Cernuda, Gil-Albert, Prados y la voz silenciada del amor homosexual.* Stockholm: University of Stockholm, 1986; 2nd ed., Alicante: Instituto de Cultura "Juan Gil-Albert"—Diputación de Alicante, 1991.

—Andrew A. Anderson

Sally Gearhart

1931-

American writer, educator, and activist

Sally Gearhart's life exemplifies an ongoing exploration of the twin identities "female" and "lesbian" and the radical changes in their definition through language and gender-based philosophy which occurred in the second half of the twentieth century. Through her careers as academic, gay rights activist, author, and feminist spiritual thinker, she brought a unique and vital perspective to public debate, drawing on her own evolving insights to assist and promote necessary social change.

Sally Miller Gearhart was born on 15 April 1931, in the rural Virginia town of Pearisburg. Raised by her mother and grandmother in a predominantly female environment, she became acquainted with the male universe through the lodgers of her mother's rooming house. She attended Sweet Briar College, acquiring a strong liberal arts education and discovering both her identity as a lesbian and a passion for religious and philosophical discussion which would surface in her later writings. Following degree work at Bowling Green State University and the University of Illinois in the fields of speech and theater, she taught at various institutions across the Midwest and in Texas (at one time considering entering the Lutheran clergy) and living a closeted life.

Her formal link with the feminist community began with a trip to study group encounter techniques at the Western Behavioral Sciences Institute in La Jolla in 1968. Following a summer of consciousness raising on feminist issues and expanding her knowledge of herself as a woman, she moved to San Francisco that autumn, becoming part of its energetic lesbian literary community. Settling in as a member of the speech faculty at San Francisco State University, she involved herself with a wide range of issues, most notably sharing her life nationwide as part of the 1977 documentary film *Word Is Out*. Her most public role came as a leader in the campaign against the proposed "Briggs Initiative" which would have barred homosexuals from teaching in California schools. Appearing as a spokeswoman for both the male and female homosexual communities in televised debates with state senator John Briggs, in company with openly gay city supervisor Harvey Milk, she utilized her skills as a public speaker (honed at many gay and lesbian pride events) to aid in educating voters toward the eventual defeat of the bill. Following Milk's assassination in 1978, she was asked to lead the memorial candlelight march in his honor, and continued to serve as an outspoken critic of the ways in which his political and theoretical heirs in the gay civil rights movement were addressing and defining the place of gender-related issues until her retirement from teaching in 1992. She also served as the narrator for a 1986 video describing an in-home hospice program for AIDS patients.

Gearhart's importance to the history of the American lesbian feminist community lies in her clear and persistent articulation of a powerful personal vision at a time when externally defined categories imposed on women of all sexual orientations were being sharply questioned. Her spiritual questing and curiosity made it inevitable that she would take part in the reevaluation of the male version of historically transmitted culture begun in the 1970s. In the introduction to her work *A Feminist Tarot*, she stated that "a consideration of both the 'material' and the 'psychic' is necessary to the growth of individuals and to the development of feminism as a global force," perhaps the clearest statement of her philosophy. The card suits in Gearhart's tarot deck were drawn subsequently on by lesbian poet Judy Grahn for the titles of her works *The Queen of Wands* and *The Queen of Swords*.

The most widely read expression of this call for a balanced approach to activism effective enough to recreate the world is the mosaic of tales (some previously published) comprising *The Wanderground: Stories of the Hill Women*, a work which is now standard reading in many women's studies courses. It depicts a future where a totally female society has been consciously crafted and maintained through feminine spiritual powers and values in opposition to a male-ruled culture where women are objectified. Three years after her withdrawal from public life, she penned an essay entitled "Notes of a Recovering Activist." In it, she continued exploring the most effective strategies for creating opportunities for dialogue and change, moving away from her former militancy while acknowledging valuable lessons learned over 25 years as she "crusaded and persuaded and brigaded."

References:

Gearhart, Sally. "Notes from a Recovering Activist," in *Sojourner*, vol. 21, no. 1, September 1995: 8-11.

Gearhart, Sally and Susan Rennie. *A Feminist Tarot*. Watertown, Massachusetts: Persephone Press, 1981.

Karr, M. A. "Sally Gearhart: Wandering—And Wondering—On Future Ground," in *Advocate*, 21 February 1980: 21-22.

Secor, Cynthia. "Sally Miller Gearhart," in *Contemporary Lesbian Writers of the United States: A Bio-Bibliographical Critical Sourcebook*, edited by Sandra Pollack and Denise D. Knight. Westport, Connecticut: Greenwood Press, 1993: 205-212.

—Robert B. Marks Ridinger

Jean Genet
1910-1986
French writer

Bastard, foster child, juvenile delinquent, soldier, petty thief, vagabond, pornographer, novelist, poet, literary genius, human rights activist, saint. Jean Genet was all of these and more, and also somewhat less. It is almost impossible to summarize a life as varied as Genet's in a brief essay. This is especially so in light of his penchant for mythologizing his autobiography. Like the characters in his novels and plays, Genet took elements of his life and enlarged them until they took mythic proportions, obscuring the more banal reality.

Genet was born in Paris on 19 December 1910, to 22-year-old Camille Gabrielle Genet and an unknown father. On 28 July 1911, Camille gave her child to the Hospice for Welfare Children in Paris, which almost immediately placed the child with a foster family, the Regniers, in the central French village of Alligny-en-Morvan. Shortly before his 14th birthday, Genet returned to Paris as an apprentice typographer, but ran away ten days later.

Between 1924 and 1929, Genet ran away from numerous state institutions and was jailed several times, eventually leading the judiciary to place him in reform school until his majority. In 1929, in order to escape the reform school, he joined the military, and rose through the ranks. His first tour of duty sent him to Syria where he formed the attachments to the Arab world he kept for the rest of his life. Despite an apparent penchant for military life (he re-enlisted three more times), in 1936 he missed roll call and was declared a deserter.

Jean Genet

Poet, Playwright, Vagabond, Thief

For the next year Genet wandered across Europe with falsified papers. Authorities arrested and deported him from Albania, Yugoslavia, Italy, Austria, Czechoslovakia, and Poland. On 16 September 1937, Genet was arrested in Paris for the theft of 12 handkerchiefs from the Samaritaine department store. Over the next seven years he was repeatedly arrested and imprisoned for vagrancy or petty thefts, usually involving pieces of cloth or books. This quintessential criminal, popularly thought to have spent most of his life in prison, served numerous terms ranging from a few days to eight months for the theft of history and philosophy books, pieces of silk, and a rare first edition of nineteenth-century French poet Paul Verlaine's *Fêtes galantes*.

Often judges overturned his convictions or released him from jail early, but in December 1943, his prison luck almost ran out. Instead of being released at the end of his term, he was transferred to the Camp des Tourelles in Nazi-occupied Paris, one of the centers which sent prisoners to the concentration camps. Through the intervention of his influential supporters he was finally freed on 15 March 1944, the last day he spent in prison.

During the first 35 years of his life, he met two of the most important (and homosexual) writers of twentieth-century France, André Gide and Jean Cocteau. Cocteau found Genet his first publisher. *Our Lady of the Flowers* appeared in 1943, *Chants secrets* (a collection of his poems) in 1945, *Miracle of the Rose* in 1946, two plays—*Deathwatch* and *The Maids* in 1947. That year also saw the clandestine publication of *Funeral Rites* and Gallimard's anonymous publication of *Querelle* and brought the première performance of *The Maids*, produced by Louis Jouvet. *Poems* appeared in 1948, as did a clandestine Swiss publication of *The Thief's Journal*. *Adame Miroir*, *The Criminal Child*, and a French edition of *The Thief's Journal* were published 1949. In 1950, Genet spent several months shooting *A Song of Love*, the only film that he directed in its entirety. The French publishing house Gallimard began publication of Genet's *Complete Works*, and devoted the entire first volume to Sartre's preface, *Saint Genet, Comedian and Martyr*, but not until 1955 did Genet's own artistic production resume with any intensity. *The Balcony* was published in 1956, "The High-Wire Artist," dedicated to his lover Abdallah Bentaga, in 1957, *The Blacks* in 1958, and *The Screens* in 1961. Meanwhile *The Maids, The Blacks,* and *The Balcony* were all produced on stage in France and abroad, by such notable directors as Louis Jouvet, Roger Blin, Tony Richardson, and Peter Brook. *The Screens* was the last of Genet's works to be published during his lifetime.

Travels in America (Illegally, Of Course)

In keeping with the spirit of the times, the American government prohibited the sale of Genet's works in the U.S. in 1951. While *The Balcony* was produced in New York in 1960 with great success, it was not until 1963 that Grove Press published *Our Lady of the Flowers* and George Braziller *Saint Genet: Comedian and Martyr*. In 1964, *Playboy* magazine published a long interview with Genet. In it the question of his homosexuality is raised. When he was asked, "Have you deliberately chosen to become a homosexual, traitor, thief, and coward...?" Genet replied, "I didn't choose. There never was a decision like that.... If I stole, it's simply because I was hungry. Later I had to justify this act, absorb it. As for my homosexuality, I know nothing about it. Who knows why he is homosexual.... As a child I was aware of the attraction other boys exerted over me. I've never been attracted by women. It was only after having felt this attraction that I 'decided,' *chose* my homosexuality freely in the Sartrean sense of the word *choose*."

In November 1965, the U.S. State Department refused Genet a visa. Entering the country illegally via Canada, Genet covered the 1968 Democratic convention for *Esquire* magazine. Again in 1970, the U.S. refused to grant Genet a visa, so he crossed the border from Canada and spent two months travelling across the country with the Black Panthers. In 1975, for the third time, the State Department denied him a visa.

Diagnosed with throat cancer in 1979, Genet continued writing, travelling, and speaking out on behalf of the downtrodden until his death on 15 April. His last major work, *Prisoner of Love*, was published on 26 May of that year.

The Creation of Self—The Writer as Drag Artist

Genet's work is important on many levels. Maurice Nadeau writes:

> Even in his novels ... Genet is, in effect, more poet than novelist. He possesses a sumptuous language, draped and hieratic, which transfigures, makes sublime the mud in which it covers itself. Whether he sings of abjection..., homosexuality..., the beauty of robbery..., his song, paradoxically, rises in a pillar of purifying flame.

Perhaps the most important aspect of Genet's work is his use of identity. In his novels, his characters assume the role of stereotype, or icon, where image is more important than reality—indeed where image becomes reality. His theatre is written as play within the play where characters assume the roles of others, i.e. the maids become their mistress, the blacks become whites. In *The Balcony*, set in a brothel, respectable citizens live out their fantasies as bishops, generals, political leaders.

Living as an outcast from society, Genet felt free to write his own legend, create his own persona, just as if he were one of the characters in his oeuvre. It is this outrageous sense of self-creation that resonates most with us today.

References:

Farmer, Amy. "Jean Genet," in *The Gay and Lesbian Literary Heritage*, edited by Claude J. Summers. New York: Henry Holt & Company, 1995: 308-312.

John, S. B. "A Theatre of Victims," in *French Literature and its Background, 6: The Twentieth Century*, edited John Cruickshank. London: Oxford University Press, 1970: 265-283.

Nadeau, Maurice. *Le roman français depuis la guerre*. Paris: Gallimard, 1963: 116-119.

Storzer, Gerald H. "The Homosexual Paradigm in Balzac, Gide, and Genet," in *Homosexualities and French Literature*, edited by George Stambolian and Elaine Marks. Ithaca, New York: Cornell University Pressm, 1979: 186-209.

White, Edmund. *Genet*. New York: Alfred A. Knopf, 1993: 33.

—Bryan D. Spellman

André Gide

1869-1953

French writer

One of the giants of modern French literature, André Gide had secured an international reputation several decades before he was awarded the Nobel prize for literature in 1947. Relying on the resources of a private income, he never had to work for a living, so he devoted his life to personal self-creation and examination, including acknowledgement of the social matrix—the many-leveled meshing of varied components that individual self-realization inescapably entails.

Gide's writing—flexing its wings during the highly self-conscious and formalistic era of Symbolism in the 1890s—demonstrated a supple elegance enlivened by flashes of lyrical intensity. The aesthetic approach of Symbolism favored suggestion rather than direct statement. This approach stood Gide in good stead when he began to write about sex, providing a certain distance that was reassuring to heterosexual readers. Gide rarely presents the physical facts of sexual contact directly. His courage and candor were nonetheless remarkable. During the 1920s, when he had much to lose, he emerged forthrightly as the pioneer defender of gay rights in France. In the following decade he incurred the wrath of the Left by criticizing Soviet communism on humanistic grounds. While Gide may never have quite merited, as some admirers asserted, the accolade of a twentieth-century Voltaire, his courage and honesty have made him a role model for a host of gay and lesbian intellectuals who came after him.

André (-Paul-Guillaume) Gide was born in Paris on 22 November 1869. Following the death of his father, a law professor, when he was 11, Gide was raised an only child in a chiefly female household. He perforce absorbed the narrow family ethos, grounded in puritanical Calvinism. While he always retained a love for the Bible, this religious orientation was tempered by an appreciation of the humanistic deposit of classical culture, especially the writings of his beloved Virgil, whose sexual tastes he must have intuited from his first exposure to Latin literature in the elite French schools in which he was (intermittently) educated. In their turn, these influences were remolded by the searing experiences obtained through his visits to North Africa between 1893 and 1896. The upshot was to foster a composite, largely neo-pagan outlook that eventually carried him forward to complete emancipation from the stifling moral and sexual conventions of his upbringing.

In 1895, still unsure of himself, he married his cousin Madeleine Rondeaux. For a good many years Gide sought to maintain a precarious distinction between love (for his wife) and passion (for his young male friends). This understanding of the matter finally broke down when Gide formed a liaison with the gifted Marc Allégret; in

André Gide

consequence he and his wife separated in 1918. At the start of his career, Gide forged close friendships with other French writers, including Paul Claudel and Pierre Louys. Different as these comrades were from him in temperament and sexual tastes, they provided sounding boards for his emerging self-consciousness. In keeping with this undertaking, it always seemed natural to him to keep a diary, addressing both personal and literary concerns. Much of this *Journal*, spanning the years 1889-1949, he gradually published. Appropriately, for a writer concerned with self-confession, this great canvas represents Gide's magnum opus.

In 1908 Gide joined a number of French writers to found a prestigious literary periodical, the *Nouvelle Revue Française*. In the 1930s, when the popular front enjoyed wide support among France's intellectuals, Gide gravitated to the left, frequently appearing as an honored speaker at political rallies. Yet after a study trip to the Soviet Union in 1936, he voiced his disillusionment with Stalin's regime in a book, *Retour de l'U.R.S.S.* (*Back from the USSR,* 1936). While other visitors were impressed by the selective vision offered by their Soviet hosts, Gide's experience as a gay man in a hostile society had taught him to look beneath the official face of society so as to detect the hidden reality. Not surprisingly, his honesty was met with vilification as a "dirty queer" in the French communist press, which had formerly been so eager to enlist his support. As a result, Gide withdrew from active participation in politics.

During World War II he lived in exile in Algiers. Returning to Paris after the Liberation, Gide savored the final fruits of his fame in the French capital, where he died of pneumonia on 19 February 1951, serenely confident that his mature views were well-founded. Ironically, he died when the homosexual liberation movement that was to vindicate a significant part of his life's work was just beginning.

After a period of obscurity in the period from about 1960 to 1990, the maturing gay and lesbian sensibility was of massive assistance in resorting his reputation.

Overcoming Asceticism

Gide's earliest prose writings are suffused with an ascetic self-denial reflecting his Calvinist background. Significantly, however, one of these, *Le Voyage d'Urien* (*Urien's Voyage,* 1893) contrasts heterosexual self-indulgence—concluding disastrously in the ravages of venereal disease—with chastity. At this stage, Gide knew better what repelled him than what attracted him. While it is easy to attribute the antisexual atmosphere of these early works to his narrow Calvinist background, it is important to note that his upbringing in a religious minority (Catholicism being the official religion of the majority of French people) prepared him for his future role as the spokesperson and defender for a sexual minority. In any event, Gide's habit of taking his vacations in North Africa decisively changed his outlook. This was especially true of his 1893 stay, when he had the singular experience of being tutored in the practice and values of pederasty by such notorious adepts as Oscar Wilde and Lord Alfred Douglas, who were visiting Algeria as enthusiastic sexual tourists.

In his literary work, Gide's first excursion into the realm of moral transgression was *Les Nourritures terrestres* (*The Fruits of the Earth,* 1897). The author exhorts the hero, the youth Nathanael, to free himself of the shackles of the Christian sense of sin and seek the path of self-realization through an honest acknowledgment of the life of the senses. His own experience, especially in North Africa, is more evident in the *L'Immoraliste* (*The Immoralist,* 1902). Michel, the hero, is torn between his fascination with young men and their natural sensuality, and his wife, to whom he is devoted, though with decreasing loyalty. She dies, and on the last page of the book, Michel seems to turn to a boy. Tantalizingly, Gide leaves the question open whether Michel's shift has a sexual component or not. The real theme of the book is the need to be true to one's sensual nature. The play *Saül* (1903; not performed until 1922) concerns a love triangle (not overtly consummated) among King Saul, David, and Jonathan.

Less overtly concerned with homoerotic sensibility, his satirical novel *Les Caves du Vatican* (*The Vatican Cellars,* 1914) features a picaresque young man, who "lives dangerously," committing a seemingly senseless murder as a psychologically liberating "gratuitous act."

Gide's Advocacy of Homosexuality

Although Gide did not serve in World War I, this massive bloodletting signaled a major shift in his approach: in his literary work he came out. This change is all the more remarkable because the period saw a renewed emphasis on heterosexualism in France, which was convinced that the population losses of the war must be made up by intense pronatalist activity, whatever the cost.

The vehicle for Gide's emergence as a homosexual theorist was a treatise, *Corydon*, cast in the form of four dialogues. As early as 1911 he had a short sketch privately printed. In 1920 he delivered an enlarged essay for private issue in March 1920. At this point a larger circle of his friends had got wind of his intentions. Some of them urged him to withhold publication, asserting that, in the prevailing homophobic climate, a defense of homosexual behavior would stir up a violent backlash. While they were—in the short run—proved correct, Gide felt that like Martin Luther four centuries earlier "he could not do otherwise," and proceeded with his plan. In accordance with his wishes, the final text of *Corydon* went on sale in May 1924, making the tabooed subject the talk of the salons of Paris. Gide's exposition, deriving in part from research published in other countries but not as yet well-known in France, nonetheless represented a remarkable accomplishment. Gide's eloquent text blended extensive personal experience, the established French toleration for the objective presentation of eccentric behavior, the traditional appeal to the glories of ancient Greece, and the emergent discipline of ethology—the comparative study of animal behavior as a context for human variation.

Like his older contemporary Marcel Proust, Gide had long meditated on discussions that had, however episodically, engaged the French public. These included the highly publicized events of the scandal of the homosexual Philipp Prince Eulenburg in Germany and a dispute over the homosexuality of Walt Whitman that had appeared in the French intellectual journal *Mercure de France*. Proust himself weighed in with a major segment of his life work, *Sodome et Gomorrhe* (*Cities of the Plain,* 1921), which dealt both with the theory of homosexuality and the exploits of several overtly homosexual characters. Although Proust's view was more negative than Gide's, it helped to prepare the way.

With a sure instinct, Gide directly confronted the medical point of view, for he deemed physicians the social group most firmly opposed to homosexuality in his own day. Curiously for someone so saturated in the Bible, Gide ignored religion—apart from remarks near the end criticizing the monastic suppression of the homosexual literature of antiquity and the Christian exaltation of asceticism.

Rejecting the idea of the unnatural, Gide argues at the outset that homosexual behavior is natural, appealing to sexual polarity and the statistical ratio between the sexes, while positing the independence of sexual pleasure from reproduction. In the second half of *Corydon*, Gide further affirms that homosexuality is a natural occurrence among human beings. Far from being a mere remnant of an earlier stage of our evolution, it is capable of bearing a major creative role, that of inspiring a resurgence of civilization.

Responding to the growing literature of his time on the subject of homosexual behavior, Gide boldly attacked two central issues. The first was the sociobiological status of the role of homosexual behavior in human evolution in the broadest sense. This question still remains unresolved today. The second issue—the more familiar one in his day—was the contribution of homosexuality to the erotic and cultural life of particular societies. Responding from his own experience, he argued that the achievements of the ancient civilizations of Greece and Rome stem from their approval of the institution of pederasty. He contrasted this pattern to the adult-adult homosexuality of modern times, and to "inversion," the passive-effeminate type of male homosexuality which he ungenerously disdained as unfortunate, perhaps even "degenerate."

For Gide's critics he was henceforth tainted with the stain of a "perverter of youth." For the writer himself, this was, however, no mean honor, since it paired him with Socrates.

Refusing to be silenced or stereotyped by the *Corydon* controversy, during the mid- and late 1920s Gide issued a wide variety of publications. In autobiographical studies he sought better to understand the conflict of his idealistic feelings for his wife with the urgency of his attraction to young males.

The outstanding achievement of this period is his greatest work of fiction, *Les Faux-monnayeurs* (*The Counterfeiters,* 1926). Taking his cue from the Cubist experiments of the modern art of his time, Gide employs a kaleidoscopic technique, embedding the varied rhythms of sexual and intellectual maturation of his characters in the complex texture of modern urban life. Presenting a variety of Parisian homosexual characters, this novel is Gide's first serious fictional consideration of the theme of intergenerational mentoring, whereby the older man bestows the benefit of his life experience with his young protégé. This was salient in the ancient Greek pederastic pattern, to which Gide had appealed in *Corydon*. However, in previous works of imagination Gide had presented a narrower vision, treating the adolescent (often a third-world youth) simply as a sexual object for the older man, while offering a self-centered analysis of the responses of the latter as part of a pattern of sexual maturation.

The depression years of the 1930s were problematic for Gide, as he was first attracted to and then repelled by the political movements of the Left. In 1946 he transcended politics in his *Thesée,* a hopeful parable about an ancient Greek hero, Theseus, who founded a society that came close to realizing an ideal in the actual world: ancient Athens.

In his last years André Gide, whose work elicited the sometimes grudging approval of the establishment, remained a beacon for lonely gay and lesbian people in many countries outside France, where acceptance of sexual variance had still not reached the qualified acceptance it had there. While their own authors in this realm might suffer marginalization as neurotic or pornographic, these foreign readers and writers take comfort in with the knowledge that at least one literary titan had had the boldness and perseverance to confront the issue of same-sex love. That confrontation would last, not only for himself, but for the world at large.

References:

Apter, Emily S. *André Gide and the Codes of Homotextuality* (Stanford French and Italian Studies). Saratoga, California: ANMA Libri, 1987.

Brée, Germaine. *André Gide*. New Brunswick: Rutgers University Press, 1963.

Ciholas, Karen Nordenhaug. *Gide's Art of the Fugue: A Study of "Les Faux-monnayeurs."* Chapel Hill: University of North Carolina Department of Romance Languages, 1974.

Cordle, Thomas. *André Gide*. Boston: Twayne, 1969.

Littlejohn, David, ed. *Gide: A Collection of Critical Essays*. Englewood Cliffs, New Jersey: Prentice-Hall, 1970.

Maurer, Rudolf. *André Gide et L'URSS*. Paris: Editions Jean Touzot, 1983.

O'Brien, Justin. *Portrait of Andre Gide: A Critical Biography*. New York: McGraw-Hill, 1953.

Pollard, Patrick. *André Gide: Homosexual Moralist*. New Haven: Yale University Press, 1991.

Raimond, Michel, ed. *Les critiques de notre temps et Gide*. Paris: Garnier, 1971.

Robinson, Christopher. *Scandal in the Ink: Male and Female Homosexuality in Twentieth-Century French Literature*. New York: Cassel, 1995.

Tolton, C.D.E. *André Gide and the Art of Autobiography: A Study of "Si le grain ne meurt."* Toronto: Macmillan, 1975.

—Wayne R. Dynes

Elsa Gidlow

1898-1986

Canadian poet

Elsa Gidlow was the first Canadian poet of the twentieth century to write from an openly lesbian perspective. Writing from the heart, and untouched by the poets of the day, her verse lacks the defensiveness often exhibited by other gay and lesbian poets.

One of seven children, Elsa Gidlow was born in Hull, Yorkshire, in December 1898 into a middle-class family. When she was six years old, her free-thinking parents moved to rural Quebec, where she grew up in a poor French-Canadian village. Her mother was an avid reader and it was her awareness of music and poetry that made young Elsa aware of such a world and of her own desire to find it. On the other hand, her hard-drinking, ambitious father found Elsa's interest in poetry impractical.

Elsa was a lonely child who early in life developed a poetic fantasy life and soon recognized the "need to voice the poetry seething in me."

When she was 16, the family moved to Montreal, where Gidlow discovered the library and bookshops. Her very first allowance went to the purchase of a collection of Samuel Taylor Coleridge's poetry. She took courses at McGill College and discovered the works of Baudelaire, Rimaud, and other liberated poets of the time. She was influenced by the classic literature of India.

Finding Sappho and Other Lesbians

Of her being different, Gidlow said: "In a land of apples, I am faithful to oranges." While she always knew she was different, she did not attribute that difference solely to her lesbianism—she felt she was set apart from others because she was a writer.

To meet more writers, Gidlow devised a clever scheme. She sent a letter under a pseudonym to a Montreal newspaper enquiring of the existence of a literary group. Under her own name, she sent a reply to her own query saying there was no such organization but "one is in the process of being formed." She included her name and address. Happily, she received quite a few responses which resulted in the formation of a bohemian literary group and the publication of a "little magazine" which eventually included much gay material.

Through the literary group, she met a young man who was gay. He introduced her to the work of Sappho. Gidlow knew she was not attracted to men, and at just 18, Sappho became her role model. Adventure had always seemed to Gidlow to be the prerogative of men, and the role of the non-heterosexual artist—in her case a poet—in the early 1920s was unexplored territory, her "adventure" as it was.

As a lesbian in the 1920s, one of the greatest challenges facing Gidlow was finding other lesbians. It was a lonely time, during which she knew no one else like herself. But it was not just the difference in sexual orientation that accounted for the isolation Gidlow felt. It was the poet in her that also separated her from others who were not poets, be they heterosexual or homosexual.

Although she fell passionately in love with a friend when she was 16, the friend never knew and there was never any question of a lesbian relationship between the two young women. A few years later she met a woman about 12 years her senior. "I felt extremely drawn to her," said Gidlow. The two shared a kiss that ignited incredible flames in Gidlow, but the other woman was heterosexual. Even so, the unconsummated relationship lasted for almost three years.

She finally met Violet Henry-Anderson who gave her her first love experience. Their relationship lasted 13 years, until Violet's death. Although there was no formal commitment, the two were virtually monogamous for the duration of the relationship.

A six-year relationship with a woman six years her junior followed. By that time she was nearing 40, and despite meaningful relationships and countless wonderful friends, Gidlow felt that the aloneness she experienced as a young girl never really left her. She was happy with friends, but least alone with nature.

Gidlow had been earning her own living since she was 16. She left Canada for New York to further her writing career when she was 21. When she arrived there, she sent a letter to Frank Harris, editor of *Pearson's* magazine enclosing some of her poetry and reviews. He hired her first as poetry editor, later as associate editor of *Pearson's*. She left *Pearson's* in 1926 to move to San Francisco where she was an editor then freelance writer for the remainder of her life.

Her first book of poetry, *On a Grey Thread*, a book of unreserved lesbian love verse, was published in 1923. She was "too ignorant and too courageous to know better" about producing so controversial a book.

Revolting against Injustice

Throughout her life, Gidlow was commited to fighting injustice. That commitment made her a visible and easy target in the early 1950s when the California Un-American Activities Committee was hunting for communists—which "I was not," said Gidlow. Just the same, the Tenney Committee accused her and her career as a freelancer and a journalist was threatened. However, as she ever had, Gidlow continued to use poetry to express the deepest emotions of her inner self.

By the time she died in 1986, Gidlow had to her credit a sizable body of work, including the poetry collections *Sapphic Songs* (1976) and *Moods of Eros* (1970), *Ask No Man Pardon* (1975), a short philosophical treatise on the importance and place of lesbianism in the larger culture, and her frank, sensitive autobiography, *Elsa: I Come With My Songs* (1986).

References:

Adair, Nancy and Casey Adair. *The Word Is Out: Stories of Some of Our Lives*, based on the film *The Word Is Out*.

Gay & Lesbian Literature, edited by Sharon Malinowski. Detroit: St. James Press, 1994.

—Andrea L.T. Peterson

Sir John Gielgud

1904-

British actor

Sir John Gielgud has been described by Ephraim Katz as the "leading exponent of the English theatre and one of the most eminent Shakespearean interpreters of his generation."

On 14 April 1904, one of the foremost Shakespearean actors of the century, Arthur John Gielgud, was born in South Kensington, London. The third child born to Frank and Kate-Terry Gielgud, Gielgud had a happy childhood growing up in London with his siblings Lewis, Val, and Eleanor. His mother's side of the family was not unfamiliar with the theatre; his mother was a niece of the actress Ellen Terry, and his mother's sister, Aunt Mabel, was an actress in her won right. While still quite young, Gielgud decided that a career in acting was for him, and Mabel (who had left the theatre to marry and then returned to it after her husband's death) was both encouraging and supportive of the young Gielgud's pursuits.

Gielgud began training for the stage in 1921 at Lady Benson's School, and then at the Royal Academy of Dramatic Art in London in 1922. In 1921, the man who would play the part of Romeo more than 500 times made his stage debut at the age of 17 at the Old Vic Theatre in London, performing in *Henry V.* Soon after making his debut, Gielgud began a career that included working with several acting companies, among which were the Oxford Repertory Company (1924-25) and the Old Vic Company, which he joined in 1929. Four years after making his motion picture debut in the 1924 film *Who Is the Man?,* Gielgud appeared in his first Broadway play. In 1950, after triumphs in numerous Shakespearean roles, Gielgud made his first appearance at Stratford-upon-Avon. In acknowledgement of the effect that Gielgud has had on drama throughout his career, London's Globe Theatre was renamed the Gielgud Theatre in 1994. Although he has not been an exclusively Shakespearean actor, he is without a doubt best known as such and

Sir John Gielgud

is often considered the best of his day. Gielgud has described the acting as well as the language of Shakespeare as follows, "There is sound and fury, tenderness and lyricism, humor and philosophy; and quite a number of platitudes as well."

Although a superb dramatic actor, Gielgud has also performed in comic roles. In 1930, he played John Worthington in Oscar Wilde's *The Importance of Being Earnest.* His first popular success came in *Richard Bordeaux* in 1932. Before joining the Queen's Repertory Company in 1937, Gielgud had many successful roles and produced as well as directed a few productions. Gielgud was, of course, aware that in any career, there are bound to be failures as well as triumphs and is quick to point out that an actor can still be successful in a part when the vehicle is a failure. Fortunately, his career has been marked consistently by his successes, possibly due to his continued devotion to the theatre.

Gielgud's homosexuality, possibly due to the circumstances of its declaration, isn't talked about much by either the actor nor anyone else. But, Gielgud has been "out" for more than 25 years. Coming out, however, was not entirely his own choice. In the mid-1960s he was arrested in a London lavatory on a morals charge. At his trial the following day a reporter recognized him and Gielgud consequently found his name in the papers accompanied by a call for him to give up the knighthood he had received in 1952. Gielgud did not surrender his knighthood, and the fuss over his unfortunate legal predicament soon subsided.

In his autobiography, *An Actor and His Time,* Gielgud states that he is "quite useless at about everything except where theatre is concerned and so I have always been completely occupied there ... I do not like all the things that occupy most people in their spare time. I am rather solitary in some ways and prefer to be, though I have had wonderful friends and associates in the theatre all my life."

Current Address: c/o International Famous Agency, Oxford House, 76 Oxford SE, London, W1R 1RB, England.

References:

Gielgud, John, John Miller, and John Powell. *An Actor and His Time.* London: Sidgwick and Jackson, 1979.

Katz, Ephraim. *The Film Encyclopedia.* New York: HarperCollins, 1994: 524-525.

Kitchin, Laurence. "John Gielgud," in *International Directory of Theatre, volume 3: Actors, Directors and Designers,* edited by David Pickering. Detroit, Michigan: St. James Press, 1996: 300-306.

—Andrea L.T. Peterson

Allen Ginsberg

1926-

American poet

In a public career of more than 40 years, Allen Ginsberg has been a pioneer in broadening the range of American poetry, opening it up to new influences, freeing it from convention and inhibition, and restoring its appeal to a large public. From his first reading of "Howl" before a wildly enthusiastic audience in San Francisco (1955) to the publication of his major *Collected Poems* (1985) and beyond, Ginsberg has championed individual freedom in his writing, performances, and appearances, proclaiming his defiance of all forms of control, conformity, or spiritless materialism. He probably did more than any individual to prepare the way for gay liberation, and as much as any when it organized. His poetry celebrates homosexuality in frank terms, and challenges discrimination against it. As one of the founders of the Beat Generation, Ginsberg combined elements of revolt, liberation, and idealism that still hold a strong appeal for youth not just in the United States, but throughout the world. He may well be the most widely traveled artist of all time. While his refractory message may now be blunted by the self-deprecating irony of old age: "Drink your decaf Ginsberg old communist/*New York Times* addict, be glad you're not Trotsky" ("Not Dead Yet" in *Cosmopolitan Greetings*, 1994), he has remained engaged with the world, adapting to meet its challenges, refusing any compromise with the establishment against the disestablished.

Irwin Allen Ginsberg, who was named for his paternal grandfather, S'rul Avrum Ginsberg, was born 3 June 1926, in Newark, New Jersey, the second son of Naomi and Louis Ginsberg. A poetic and artistic temperament was very much in evidence in the family. Naomi sang, played the mandolin, and made up stories colored by her communist sympathies. Louis, an accomplished poet, earned his living teaching English in Paterson, New Jersey. Allen's older brother, Eugene Brooks Ginsberg, eventually dropped his last name, and as Eugene Brooks, became a well known attorney and poet in his own right.

Questions of identity haunt Ginsberg's poetry, and, given his family background, this is hardly surprising. Many differences came between his parents. Naomi's family arrived in the United States in 1905, fleeing the Russian pogroms. Whereas Louis was a socialist, a lifelong liberal and agnostic, Naomi was a staunch communist and unrelenting atheist. Her passion for a workers' revolution and active part in local Communist Party politics fueled her aversion to Louis's liberalism and "bourgeois" poetry. Given Louis's modest income, money was always tight and caused tension. Above all, Naomi's health was precarious in the extreme. She had a first nervous breakdown before her marriage—a marriage opposed by his family—and another when Allen was three. She spent time in a private sanatorium that her husband could ill afford, causing him to go deeply into debt. Her delusions of persecution grew steadily worse and came to define her. The barbaric treatments she underwent, including some forty insulin shock treatments, did nothing to help. In 1948, by which time she and Louis had divorced, Allen had to sign the papers authorizing a prefrontal lobotomy. He had little choice, given her violent schizophrenic paranoia, but this action would haunt him for the rest of his life. Naomi died in a mental institution in 1956. Louis Ginsberg died twenty years later, in 1976.

While Allen Ginsberg was loved by both his parents, circumstances at home were painfully difficult. Even as a boy, he was increasingly called upon to look after Naomi. In his poem "Kaddish," a deeply moving commemoration of his mother, he describes an episode that occurred when he was fifteen. As she experienced an epileptic seizure in their bathroom at home, he could only stand by helplessly, a witness to her utter, hellish loss of bodily control.

In spite of the domestic arguments, the penury that led to frequent moves, the anti-semitism of other children, the frequent scenes of indignity at home, and the confusion and embarrassment caused by his awakening homosexuality, Ginsberg was a superior student. At East Side High School in Paterson, he was elected president of the Debating Society and the Talent Club, and when he was graduated in 1943, his excellent academic record earned him a university scholarship from the State of New Jersey.

Inevitably, Ginsberg's childhood marked him deeply. His willing acceptance of Naomi, and his attempt to understand and even identify with her, psychosis and all, fostered and forever shaped his extraordinary ability to identify with the victim or underdog—Australian aborigine, Indian pariah, or American homeless, for example—against the establishment, viewed as oppressive. Throughout the 1960s and 1970s, he played a major role in antiwar demonstrations and liberation movements. Having observed Naomi exposed in all her frailty and difference, he in turn elected to reveal himself and to try to understand himself more fully. Certainly his sense of personal identity was far from secure, with parents who placed different expectations upon him, a home environment that was anything but stable, and a sexual identity that for many years caused him shame and indeed self-rejection.

Columbia University, New York, and the Beginnings of Beat

Ginsberg enrolled at Columbia University. He soon gave up plans to become a labor lawyer to concentrate instead on literature. Lionel Trilling and Mark Van Doren, nationally renowned men of letters and professors at Columbia, saw in the son the literary gifts of the father, whose poetry they admired. But if Trilling and Van Doren represented the academic side of Columbia, Ginsberg also discovered a far different world.

He became friendly with, and indeed fell in love with, Lucien Carr, a brilliant classmate from St. Louis, worldly wise and widely read. Carr, a heterosexual, the first of many to whom Ginsberg would be attracted in a pattern of hopeless love, introduced him to a circle of friends that included William Burroughs, David Kammerer, Jack Kerouac, and others. Burroughs, a brilliant 30-year-old Harvard graduate in English, knew Carr from their hometown of St. Louis. Burroughs, a homosexual, had already embarked on his lifelong exploration of alternative visions ranging from Mayan civilization to Rimbaud's *Season in Hell* to a wide range of mind-altering drugs. He was fast becoming an authority on hallucinogens. Like Carr, he was fascinated by the low life of New York. David Kammerer, another of Carr's acquaintances from St. Louis, was obsessed with Carr and followed him to New York. Carr could offer Kammerer no satisfaction beyond tolerating his presence. Finally, in the summer of 1944, Carr, importuned and threatened by the jealous Kammerer, stabbed him to death. He received a light sentence.

The brilliance of Kerouac stood out, even in this remarkable group. In his quest for a New Vision, a literature of spontaneous expression, he had written by far the most. In addition, he combined athletic prowess (he had attended Columbia briefly on a football scholarship) with unusual sensitivity. Ginsberg fell in love with him. Out of friendship or open-mindedness, Kerouac had several sexual encounters with Ginsberg, but Ginsberg, recognizing the lack of reciprocity in these relations, was left far from satisfied.

In the company of his friends, Ginsberg discovered the hidden New York world of drifters, panhandlers, addicts, and outcasts, a counterculture that slipped through the net cast by mainstream society. In their own quest for a new vision and an alternative form of expression, Kerouac, Burroughs, and the neophyte Ginsberg, the nucleus of what became the Beat Generation, found in the New York netherworld inspiration and, ultimately, a perverse state of grace. In a flash of recognition, Kerouac grafted the notion of beatitude on to the earlier sense of beat as downcast.

The explosive mixture of artistic inventiveness, low-life experience, homosexual tension, and drug experimentation has no precedent in American literature, but it bears comparison with French precursors, in particular Rimbaud's affair with Verlaine around 1870, or, to a lesser extent, Cocteau's with Radiguet in the early 1920s. But, whereas Rimbaud stopped writing before he was 20, and Radiguet died at 20, Ginsberg found himself as a poet quite late, at close to thirty. By some miracle, he has been able not only to survive, but to keep on searching, to keep on finding, and to keep on writing into old age. Through it all, he maintained an extraordinary gift for friendship, even when that friendship was sorely tested, as by Kerouac's alcoholism or political conservatism, for example.

Coming to Terms with Homosexuality

Kerouac was the first person to whom Ginsberg revealed his homosexuality. Ironically, Ginsberg was dismissed from Columbia in 1945 over an incident that partly involved Kerouac. A dean of students entered his room at night to investigate obscene remarks Ginsberg had written in the grime of his window. He found Kerouac sharing his friend's bed in real innocence—Kerouac needed a place for the night—but perceived perversity. Ginsberg was expelled for a year, moved in with Burroughs, and immersed himself in the marginal life of the city under the homosexual and hallucinogenic guidance of the future author of *The Naked Lunch*. In 1948, after re-enrolling at Columbia, he completed his Bachelor of Arts degree with an A- average.

While at Columbia, Ginsberg was acutely embarrassed by his homosexuality and tried to conceal his feelings from Carr and Kerouac. As part of a course of psychotherapy he underwent in 1948, he admitted his sexual orientation to his father. Louis considered homosexuality a mental disorder and was especially upset when he learned of Allen's love for Neal Cassady. The two had met in 1947. Cassady, the prototype for Dean Moriarty of Kerouac's novel *On the Road*, became an icon of the Beat Generation, a legend for his nonstop talk, fast driving, sexual exhuberance, and boundless energy. Born on the road in Salt Lake City, he seemed to embody the broad spirit of the West. He and Ginsberg became lovers and Ginsberg experienced with him an unprecedented intensity of passion. Ginsberg made him the subject of many poems and dedicated the collection *Planet News 1961-1967* (1968) to him. In "Elegy for Neal Cassady," Ginsberg celebrated Neal's memory with a tenderness reminiscent of Walt Whitman's homoerotic subtlety in, say, "Song of Myself." But Ginsberg was also the poet of undisguised carnality and deliberate provocation, as may be seen from his poem "Please Master" (1968). Even allowing for the violence of the period the Vietnam War, demonstrations, counter-demonstrations and extremes begetting opposing extremes—the language of *this* elegy to Cassady was unprecedented in its presentation of the details of gay sex.

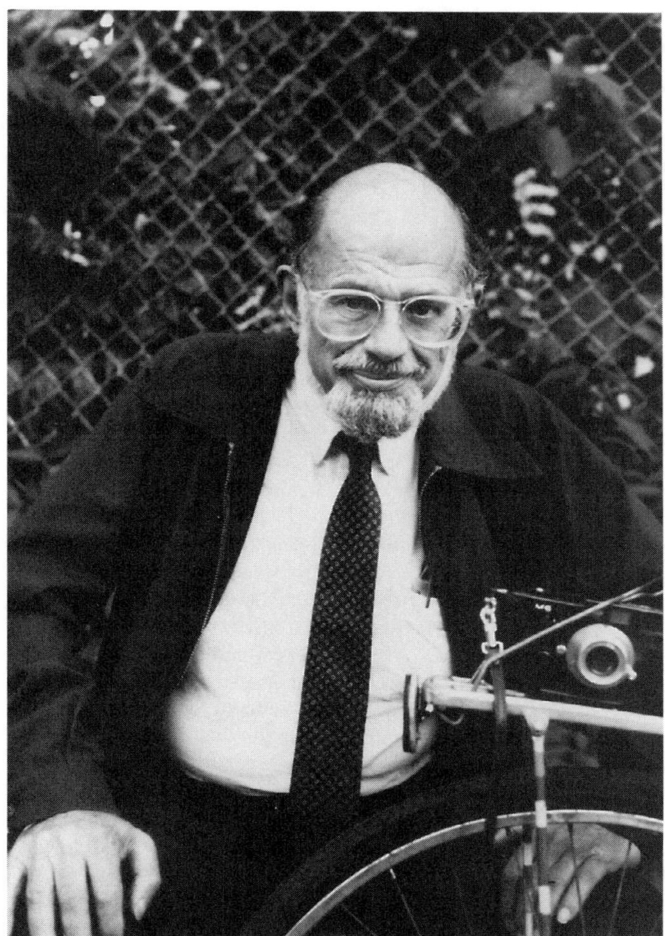

Allen Ginsberg. ***Photograph by Robert Frank.***

If the image we now have of Ginsberg, colored by "Howl" and later poems to Cassady and others, is of a man at ease with his sexual identity, it is worth recalling that the pressures to conform with the heterosexual majority were so great that in 1950 he announced to Kerouac, after being discharged from the Psychiatric Institute, that he would give up homosexuality and try to lead a "straight" life. He had spent eight months in the psychiatric hospital as a condition for avoiding prison after naively receiving stolen goods for some petty burglars in New York. For a while, he did try to live the heterosexual life.

If Ginsberg's courage in speaking out proved to be a catalyst for the gay liberation movement, the spirit and substance of his relationship with Peter Orlovsky served as a prototype for many gay couples. Ginsberg saw a painting of Orlovsky and asked to meet him. Orlovsky struck Ginsberg not just with his beauty, but his gentleness. In February 1955, in San Francisco, the two formally exchanged vows, in a mutual giving of self, an agreement to seek whatever salvation they could find together. In spite of Orlovsky's recurring mental illness, drug addiction, and problem drinking, Ginsberg has honored this relationship and stood by his friend.

The Vocation of the Poet

In 1948, in the first of several mystical revelations, hearing what he took to be the voice of William Blake, while reading Blake's "Ah Sunflower" after masturbating, Ginsberg saw himself as one in a line of visionary poets. His simple faith in poetry and in his role as a poet were strengthened, becoming quite exceptional in an unpoetic era. In the years immediately following, Ginsberg was far from inactive, accumulating life-experience and writing. But in many respects these were years of latency, maturation, and preparation. With "Howl," he and the Beat Generation found their poetic voice. In an evening organized by Ginsberg, he and Gary Snyder, Kenneth Rexroth, Michael McClure, Philip Lamantia, and Philip Whalen read to a capacity crowd at the Six Gallery in San Francisco, 13 October 1955. The event was of incomparable significance. With his one poem, Ginsberg crystallized the voiceless desperation of all those alienated by the materialism of American society, took pride in his own homosexuality, restored poetry's relevance to a large public, and re-inserted it in an oral tradition, while fulfilling the Beat dream of a free-flowing, spontaneous form of expression.

Howl and Other Poems (1956), published by San Francisco poet Lawrence Ferlinghetti's City Lights Books, reached a huge audience and enshrined Ginsberg as national poet and figure of controversy. Ferlinghetti was arrested and charged with publishing obscene material. Though he and Ginsberg won the trial and the volume was hailed by many as a groundbreaking work of genius, others condemned its lack of decorum. Not just "Howl," but companion poems such as "In the Baggage Room at Greyhound," "Sunflower Sutra," "America," and "A Supermarket in California," juxtaposing a critique of the U.S. with a search for beauty and meaning amid the shards of a debased reality have lost none of their appeal.

From the heartrending demise of many that opened "Howl": "I saw the best minds of my generation ... destroyed by madness...." Ginsberg turned to one, that of his mother, in "Kaddish" (*Kaddish and other Poems*, 1956), composed under the influence of hallucinogenic drugs. A terrible intimacy unites son to suffering mother. In other poems, as in the beautiful "At Apollinaire's Grave," a more tranquil intimacy prevails.

In his fascination with death and his pursuit of enlarged or altered consciousness—involving an astonishing range of experience from using the very potent hallucinogen yage in Peru, to living next to suffering, disease, and death in India, Ginsberg ran the risk of a complete loss of self in death or madness. But he came to turn away from this self-destructive bent. *Planet News, 1961-67* (1968) chronicles drug experiences with Kerouac and others and LSD "trips" with Timothy Leary, alongside an attack on the phantasmagoric jumble of images through which television conceals political realities and the horrors of the Vietnam war ("Television Was a Baby Crawling Toward That Deathchamber"), before outlining his ongoing search for expanded consciousness in the Orient. But in India, he met a Tibetan lama, Dudjom Rinpoche, who advised him to stop, renounce this search, accept his body, and look to himself. This reversal came into perfect focus on a train ride from Kyoto to Tokyo and is described in "The Change." At that point, Ginsberg understood that he must let go of Blake and Beat and the drug-induced hallucinations that were now hounding him, ghosts barring the way to the future. In the second half of *Planet News*, Ginsberg's contact with quotidian reality becomes firmly grounded and quite ironic, a pattern that continued into later poetry.

Buddhist and More

The very title *Mind Breaths: Poems 1972-1977* (1978) reflects Ginsberg's interest in Oriental meditation, the oneness of mind with breath as it is expelled and dissolves in space. The title poem "Mind Breaths," in which the "stanzas" are a series of breath units, is serene and effective. In 1971, after a year of Hindu sitting meditation, he met Tibetan lama Chogyam Trungpa Rinpoche, studied with him, and, in 1972 took formal vows as a Buddhist, assuming the name Lion of Dharma. At Trungpa's request, he became a cofounder of the Jack Kerouac School of Disembodied Poetics at Naropa Institute in Boulder, Colorado, a Buddhism-based university. Ginsberg was co-administrator of the school for ten years, and taught there regularly. Trungpa himself, who died in 1987, was very controversial.

Eclectically gifted as ever, Ginsberg also spontaneously composed, with encouragement from Bob Dylan, a number of blues songs that are included in *Mind Breaths*. He had sung them at his own recitals or during his long tour with the "Rolling Thunder Review" led by Dylan in late 1975. And, incorrigibly iconoclastic as ever, he includes in the collection "Sweet Boy, Gimme yr Ass," as forthright as the title suggests, and "Come All Ye Brave Boys," a homosexual *carpe diem* as explicit as any ever written.

Ginsberg's later collections, including *White Shroud, Poems 1980-1985* (1986) and *Cosmopolitan Greetings, Poems 1986-1992* (1994) continue to reflect his Buddhist studies and practice. But of course, however proud he is of helping bring Buddhism to the U.S., he cannot be defined by this alone. Dharma Lion, he is also "Yiddishe Kopf" (*Cosmopolitan Greetings)* and unrepentant Beat, bringing to his art a diversity of experience, a depth of compassion, and a power of indignation that assign him a unique position.

Current Address: c/o Bob Rosenthal, P.O. Box 582, Stuyvesant Station, New York, New York 10009-0582.

References:

Ginsberg, Allen. *Collected Poems: 1947-1980.* New York: Harper & Row, 1985.

———. *Cosmopolitan Greetings, Poems 1986-1992.* New York: Harper Perennial, 1994.

———. *Howl and Other Poems,* introduction by William Carlos Williams. San Francisco: City Lights Books, 1956.

———. *Kaddish and Other Poems. 1958-1960.* San Francisco: City Lights Books, 1961.

———. *Mind Breaths: Poems, 1972-1977.* San Francisco: City Lights Books, 1977.

———. *Planet News, 1961-1967.* San Francisco: City Lights Books, 1968.

Miles, Barry. *Ginsberg: A Biography.* New York: Simon and Schuster, 1989.

Schumacher, Michael. *Dharma Lion: A Biography of Allen Ginsberg.* New York: St. Martins Press, 1992.

—James P. McNab

Barbara Gittings

1932-

American activist

Barbara Gittings is one of the pioneers of gay and lesbian activism. Throughout her career, spanning four decades, she has worked resolutely towards achieving lesbian and gay civil rights.

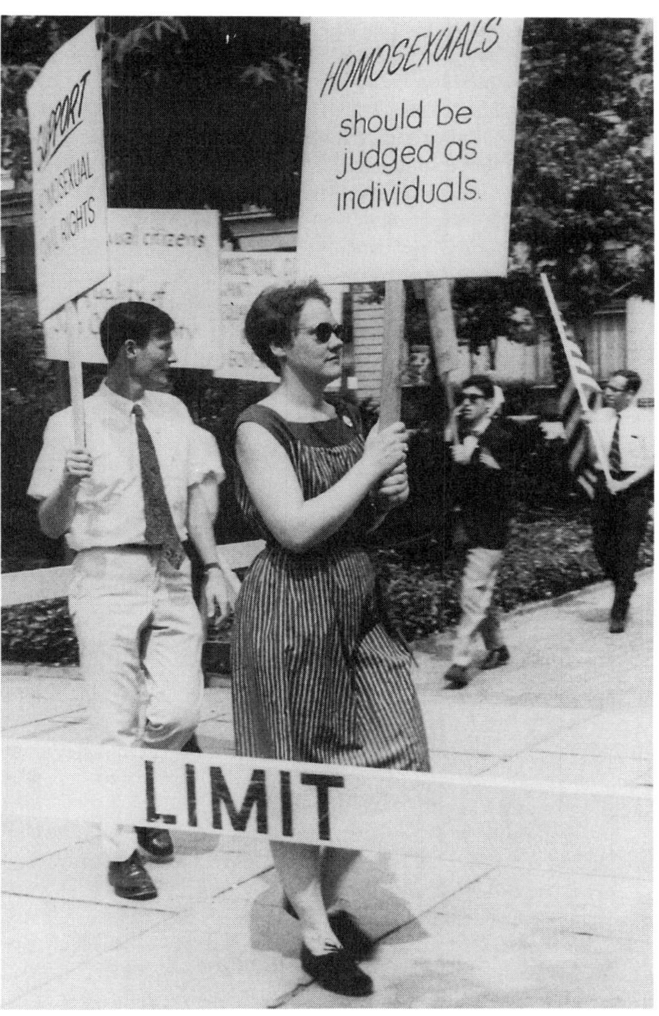

Barbara Gittings (center) picketing Independence Hall in Philadelphia on 4 July 1965. ***Photograph by Kay Tobin Lahusen.***

Barbara Gittings was born on 31 July 1932 in Vienna, Austria, to Elizabeth Brooks Gittings and John Sterett Gittings, who was in the American diplomatic service. Educated in the United States and Canada, Gittings attended Northwestern University in 1949. During her freshman year, she was falsely accused of having an affair with another female student. Although the rumor was untrue, it sparked a realization in Gittings, who soon spent all her time searching libraries throughout the Chicago area for information about homosexuality. She neglected her classes and flunked out of school. Explains Gittings: "My mission was not to get a general education but to find out about myself and what my life would be like. So I stopped going to classes and started going to the library. There were no organizations to turn to in those days, only libraries were safe, although the information they contained was dismal."

After briefly returning home, Gittings ran away to Philadelphia to continue exploring her new-found identity. She read all she could on the subject, and in 1953, came across Donald Webster Cory's *The Homosexual in America*. Upon finding his bibliography, she comments: "I was fascinated to find that there was more to read than I knew about." Inspired, she contacted the author to talk with him about identifying more gay literature. Gittings credits Cory with introducing her to the young homophile movement. Learning from Cory of the existence of ONE, Inc. in Los Angeles, Gittings journeyed to California to visit the organization. There she found out about the other two homophile organizations, the Mattachine Society and Daughters of Bilitis (DOB) in San Francisco.

Gittings marks her official association with the movement two years later, in 1958, when she was asked to help start the New York Chapter of DOB, even though she lived in Philadelphia. She spent two weekends a month "up the road," serving as the chapter's first president. In 1961, at a DOB social gathering, Gittings met her current companion and lover, Kay Tobin Lahusen. Their courtship took place in Boston and New York, but eventually Gittings persuaded Lahusen to join her in Philadelphia.

In 1963, Gittings became editor of the *Ladder,* the DOB magazine, a "temporary job" which lasted until mid-1966. "Once I started I found I really liked it. I liked the power of the editor to shape the content of the magazine and to shape the readers' attitudes. I found that this was a way I could make a real difference," Gittings reflects. Working on the *Ladder* was a family project: "Kay was really co-editor although her name didn't appear on the masthead." Together the couple implemented several changes in the magazine, slowly bringing the magazine itself out of the closet. They strove to "crack the cocoon of invisibility" by adding the subtitle "A Lesbian Review" and featuring photographs of real lesbians on the cover. They also began distributing the *Ladder* through bookstores. One Greenwich Village store displayed the magazine right by the cash register and sold over 100 copies a month. "It was a victory to have it publicly sold instead of only circulated by mail," Gittings comments, "It was important to do this because in the early '60s people had strange ideas of what lesbians were like. This way they could see lesbians as happy, healthy, wholesome human beings."

While still with the *Ladder,* Gittings became active with the East Coast Homophile Organizations (ECHO) and later the Homophile Action League, plunging into social activism and relentlessly staging pickets and protests. In 1971, she became involved in the effort to get the American Psychiatric Association (APA) to drop its listing of homosexuality as a mental illness. The campaign was successful and in 1973, the APA Board of Trustees voted to remove homosexuality from the list of mental disorders.

In 1970, Gittings began her 16-year association with the American Library Association (ALA). Books and libraries had played a significant role in Gittings' life, and so although she was not a professionally trained librarian, when she discovered ALA's new Task Force on Gay Liberation she joined immediately. Before long, she became the task force coordinator. Under her guidance, the task force promoted its annual Gay Book Award (the first gay literary award), issued increasingly larger bibliographies and reading lists, presented thought-provoking programs, and agitated for policy changes. The article, "Gays in Library Land," relates Gittings' experiences with the task force.

Since leaving the task force in 1986, Gittings has spent her time lecturing and conducting workshops. Asked about her plans for the future, Gittings responded: "Kay and I are encouraging the creation of gay retirement homes. We've built our social lives in the gay community, and we know lots of us wouldn't feel right in a hetero retirement setting. We want to be with our own gay-and-gray friends."

Current Address: P.O. Box 2383, Philadelphia, Pennsylvania 19103.

References:

Gittings, Barbara. "Gays in Library Land: The Gay and Lesbian Task Force of the American Library Association: The First Sixteen Years," in *WLW Journal,* no. 14, Spring 1991: 7-13.

———. Interview with R. Ellen Greenblatt, 1996.

Tobin, Kay, and Randy Wicker, eds. "Barbara Gittings," in *The Gay Crusaders.* New York: Paperback Library, 1972: 205-224.

—R. Ellen Greenblatt

Gluck

1895-1978

British painter

Any study of Hannah Gluckstein's life and work is a lesson in defiance and contrasts. She was proud and egotistical—always authoritative in men's clothes—and yet generally humble about her work, which she refused to exhibit except in solo shows. She rejected femininity as inappropriate for herself, yet was always dependent upon some other woman at each phase in her life. She fancied herself a visionary painter, yet did some of her best work on commission for the walls of the well-to-do. She claimed to have rejected her rich, snobbish family, yet always relied on them for her income. Her dedication to her work was total, she claimed, yet she was often obsessed with material concerns. She was a Jew who wanted to paint the crucifixion of Christ. She claimed to be unafraid of death, but was reportedly a hypochondriac. In the end, according to her biographer Diana Souhami, she was "mercurial, maddening, conspicuous and rebellious, (and) she inspired great love and profound dislike. Perhaps what she most feared was indifference—the coldest death."

"Please return in good condition to Gluck," Souhami says Hannah wrote on the back of prints of her paintings, "no prefix, no suffix, or quotes." To her servants she was Miss Gluck, and to her lovers and friends she was variously Darling Tim, My Black Brat, Dearest Grub, or even Peter, a Young English Girl, as she was in the 1924 portrait of her painted by Romaine Brooks. Her reasons for choosing the simple syllable Gluck were twofold: 1) it was the paintings that mattered, she righteously claimed, not the sex of the painter, and; 2) it was the paintings that mattered, not what family or school the painter came from.

A Traditional Family

Hannah Gluckstein was born in London in 1895. Her father was a wealthy businessman who had founded the J. Lyons and Company catering empire, and her mother (whom Hannah called "the meteor") was a talented musician. Gluck herself contemplated a career in music until, while still in her teens, she saw a painting by Henry Sargent, which suddenly made her just as determined to be an artist. As part of her traditional middle-class education, she attended St. John's Wood School of Art from 1913 to 1916. But as she began to slowly break away from her family, she had more lofty, independent plans for the future.

"No family could have been less attuned to rebellious displays of individualism than the Gluckstein's," notes Souhami. Gluck's entrepreneurial grandfather had come to England from Prussia and got his start in the tobacco business. He and his illiterate wife eventually had ten children and set each of them and their families up for generations with a kind of familial socialist experiment dubbed the Fund. In short, each family member was allowed access according to his or her needs (number of children, widows, boys who won scholarships, etc.). If one was willing to conform to the family's way of life—which for women meant total domestication— the Fund was truly cementing in every sense of the word. Unfortunately for Gluck, Souhami notes, "no clause was included for daughters who ran away with lesbian lovers to paint, smoke pipes and wear men's clothes."

In 1916, at the age of 21, Gluck left her family to study at the Newlyn artist's colony in Lamorna, Cornwall. Here, working with painters like Laura Knight and Dod Procter, she honed her visionary style, yet refused to associate herself with any one trend or school of teaching, which is also why she only did one-person shows. She thought of herself as an essentially British painter, and covered subjects that were part of her life: light-filled landscapes; formal flower groups, portraits of family, friends, and lovers; and her travels. Her work reflected changing styles—the "Odeon" in the 1920s and all-white interiors in the 1930s, for example—but it also showed an exacting harmony and musicality all its own as it seemed to link both to her inner feelings and those of her subject.

In her portraits especially, she used little color, preferring "black, white and grey to model the features," according to Dunford. It is generally accepted that her portraits of women are her best work, showing off their assertiveness and style in a series of hats, jewelry, and fancy clothes. "It used to annoy me when I was younger to be told how 'original' I was," Gluck remarked. "What is there so original in just being oneself and speaking one's mind."

A Stormy Career

Gluck had five exhibitions of her work: in 1924, 1926, 1932, 1937, and, after a gap of 36 years, in 1973. All of these were received with excitement and acclaim. The great battle which kept her from the easel for many years (roughly 1953-1964) was a fight with paint manufacturers in general, and the British Standards Institute in particular over what she termed the "greasy turbidity" of their oil paints. She wasted years of creative time, but in the end got the institute to formulate a standard for oils, and got manufacturers to produce specialized paints made with hand-ground pigments and cold-pressed linseed oil. Here again is the classic Gluck of contrasts, for as Souhami observes, "she fought it because she wanted her work to last forever; yet she seemed unconscious of the irony that not to produce paintings is the surest way to artistic oblivion."

No doubt Gluck could also afford to fight because she never completely cut herself off from the family fortune. Throughout her life, she maintained a studio in Cornwall, a home in Hampstead in the 1920s and 1930s, and a home with longtime lover and journalist Edith Shackleton Heald in Sussex from 1945 until her death there in 1978. Though she had always dressed in men's clothes, she made some concessions to convention in the 1940s and 1950s, partially for Edith's sake.

Gluck herself divided her life, loves and work—which were often inseparable—into three periods. Her rebellious years lasted until she was roughly in her early forties. During this period she divided her time between London and Cornwall with a female art student who used only her surname, Craig; fell in love with a journalist named Sybil Cookson; had a relationship with floral designer Constance Spry (whence came Gluck's love of painting flowers); and produced most all the work for her first four major exhibitions. During this time her mother decided she had "a kink in the brain" but hoped it would pass.

In 1936, according to Souhami, after meeting and falling in love with the "glittering and elusive" socialite Nesta Obermer, Gluck began burning all references to her past—diaries, letters, pictures of old lovers, and references to her family. "The reason for creation is the same as for destruction," Souhami has her telling a friend who witnessed some of the burning. "Anything even vaguely smelling of the past stinks in my nostrils," she told her new love. Later in life, Gluck would refer to this wholly unproductive time as the "YouWe" years.

The final period in her life was perhaps the most serene, comparatively speaking. From 1945 to 1978 she lived with her "last great love," the writer Edith Shackleton Heald in Sussex. She painted sporadically, experienced some frustration over her work and life, and fought the paint manufacturers. When she bravely (some say mercilessly) mounted one last solo exhibition at the age of 78, she simply said, according to Souhami, "I would like to go out with a bang."

Friends and Lovers

In each phase of her life, Gluck was reliant not only on her own boisterous strength, but on the quieter solidity of women around her, which may attest to just how vulnerable she was beneath the manly mannerisms. First and foremost, there was her mother, who never quite approved of Gluck's eccentricity. "Everything the Meteor touches," Gluck observed, "always seems to lead to confusion—even her kind acts." Then it was the haughty Nesta Obermer, who sapped all of Gluck's artistic energy for love, and whom Gluck was never able to capture on the canvas no matter how she struggled. Finally, there was Heald who, although by all accounts was trustworthy and loyal, nevertheless frustrated Gluck with her virtuousness.

In the end, biographer Souhami offers the best explanation for Gluck's drive and dissatisfaction, which certainly fueled each other. The three women were never "particularly separate in Gluck's psyche," Souhami suggests. "They merged, with other women, more peripheral to her life, in some unresolved desire for love and home." Perhaps this is the link through which her paintings persevere.

References:

Dunford, Penny. *A Biographical Dictionary of Women Artists in Europe and America Since 1850.* Philadelphia: University of Pennsylvania Press, 1989.

Souhami, Diana. *Gluck: Her Biography.* London: Pandora Press, 1988.

—Jerome Szymczak

Jewelle Gomez
1948-
African-American writer, activist, and educator

Jewelle Gomez, author and activist, has touched many lives through both her writing and her community involvement. The author of two books of poetry, a feminist vampire novel, and an autobiographical book of essays, Gomez's work often explores the complexity of identities and communities. She describes her own complex identity in her collection of essays, *Forty-Three Septembers,* as "African-American, Ioway, Wampanoag, Bostonian, lesbian, welfare-raised, artist, activist." Gomez connects her writing with her personal struggles; in a 1991 interview in *Ms. Magazine,* she says, "Audre Lorde says poetry is not a luxury; poetry for me is the embracing of the difficulty of struggle in my own personal life. Everybody can be doing that."

Jewelle Gomez was born on 11 September 1948 in Boston, Massachusetts, to John "Duke" Gomez, a bartender, and Dolores Minor, who would later become a nurse while in her fifties. Growing up, she lived with her great-grandmother, Grace A. Morandus, who had been born on an Indian reservation in Iowa of half-Ioway, half-African-American parents. Gomez traces her desire to write back to her childhood: "I wanted to write ever since I was a kid, growing up with my great-grandmother in a cold-water flat in Boston," she recalls in a 1994 volume of *Contemporary Authors.*

Gomez describes her extended family in *Forty-Three Septembers.* She writes affectionately of her father as a man known for his style and charm: "My father was magic." Duke maintained two households with two wives, neither of whom were Gomez's mother; as a child, Gomez visited these two homes each weekend. Gomez graduated from Northeastern University with a BA in 1971, and from Columbia University with an MS in 1973.

Gomez was employed as a production assistant for WGBH-TV in Boston on "Say Brother" from 1968-1971 and, in the 1970s, in New York City for Children's Television Workshop and WNET-TV. She also worked as a stage manager for various Off-Broadway theaters between 1975 and 1980. In *Contemporary Authors,* Gomez says, "My training in journalism was excellent grounding in writing for the feminist and gay press, and helped me to focus my own essay and fiction skills." In fact, she published her first book of poetry in 1980, *The Lipstick Papers,* with the lesbian press Firebrand Books.

Moving from her work in the theater and with television, Gomez worked as a New York State Council on the Arts program associate from 1983 to 1989. In 1989, she became the director of its literature program, a position she was to hold until 1993. Gomez also began teaching as a lecturer of women's studies and English at Hunter College in New York City from 1989 to 1990. She also became increasingly visible as a founding board member of the Gay and Lesbian Alliance against Defamation (GLAAD) in 1985, and as a member of the Feminist Anti-Censorship Taskforce (FACT). Gomez's public involvement also included her service as a member on boards of advisors for several organizations including the Cornell University Human Sexuality Archives, the National Center for Lesbian Rights, the *Multi-Cultural Review* magazine, Open Meadows Foundation, and the PEN American Center.

Gomez's second book of poetry, *Flamingos and Bears,* was published in 1986, also by Firebrand. Its title poem was later to be

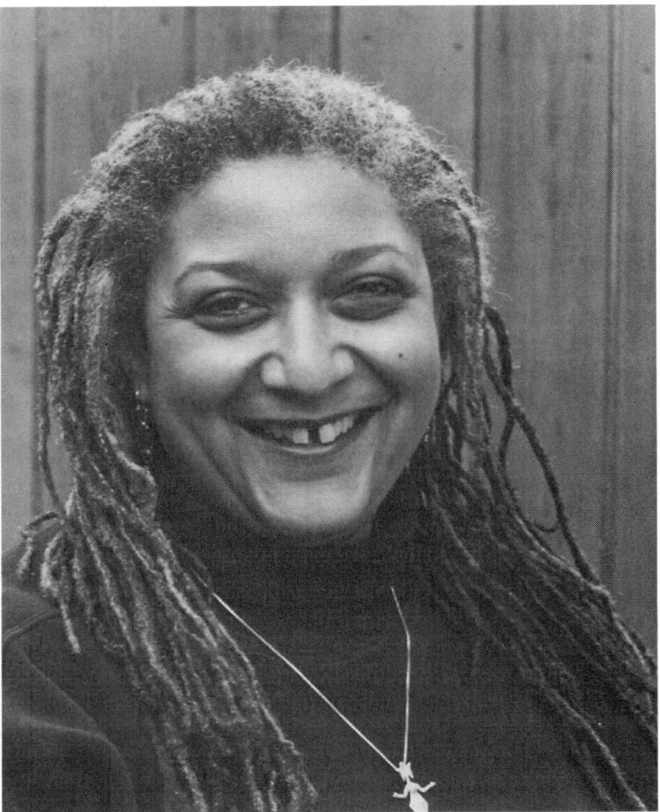

Jewelle Gomez. ***Photograph by D. Sabin.***

included in the 1992 anthology *The Persistent Desire: A Femme-Butch Reader.* Gomez won the Money for Women/Barbara Deming Award for fiction in 1990; her novel *The Gilda Stories* was published the following year and received an enthusiastic public reaction. In *Belles Lettres,* Karen Crowley calls *The Gilda Stories* "one of the most imaginative novels in lesbian fiction ... a rare reading experience." The novel traces a community of vampires from 1860s Louisiana to the twenty-first century, with a heroine whom Judith E. Johnson in the *Kenyon Review* appropriately describes as "a kind of American Everywoman engaged in a pilgrimage through our History, our society, and our changing ideas about life, love, responsibility, and the proper place of women." In her novel, Gomez set out to redefine the vampire, a mythological creature that exists in many cultures; in *Contemporary Authors,* Gomez reflects: "The novel is about the often overlooked interconnection between power and responsibility—how we create family for ourselves in extraordinary circumstances and how heroic any one of us can be." *The Gilda Stories* won Lambda Literary awards for both fiction and science fiction in 1991. *The Gilda Stories* was also adapted for the stage in a production entitled *Bones and Ash: A Gilda Story.* A collaborative effort between Gomez and the dance company Urban Bush Women, the production also featured music by lesbian composer Toshi Reagon and toured the United States during the 1996 season.

Central to Gomez's writing is "continuity, a link to a past and a future, to a people, to all people," writes Susan Sherman in *New Directions for Women.* This concern with "continuity" can be seen both in *The Gilda Stories* and in *Forty-Three Septembers,* which was published in 1993. In this book, Gomez writes her own history, and, in doing so, describes both her family history and a history of feminist and lesbian communities with which she has been involved. Gomez's third book of poetry, *Oral Tradition,* was published in 1995.

Gomez has recently moved from New York to San Francisco and has become an active, vocal, and visible member of many communities in this new city. Gomez taught creative writing at New College of California, San Francisco, and has been researching material for a biography of Audre Lorde. In *Contemporary Authors,* Gomez declares, "What do I hope to achieve by writing? Changing the world!"

Current Address: 206 Fairmount Street, San Francisco, California 94131.

References:

Crowley, Karlyn. "*The Gilda Stories,*" in *Belles Lettres: A Review of Books by Women* (North Potomac, Maryland), vol. 7, no. 3, Spring 1992: 60-61.

Findlen, Barbara. "Bold Types," in *Ms. Magazine* (New York), July/August 1991: 87.

Johnson, Judith E. "Women and Vampires: Nightmare of Utopia?," in *The Kenyon Review* (Gambier, Ohio), vol. 15, no. 1, Winter 1993: 72-80.

Olendorf, Donna, ed. *Contemporary Authors.* Detroit: Gale Research Inc., vol. 142, 1994: 159-160.

Sherman, Susan. In *New Directions for Women* (Englewood, New Jersey), November-December 1991.

—Elizabeth Hutchinson Crocker

Marga Gomez

Hispanic-American performer and writer

Successfully merging artistic genres and categories, Marga Gomez is a multitalented entertainer who has forged a career as a stand-up comic, actor, writer, and performance artist. The daughter of a Cuban comedian and a Puerto Rican exotic dancer, Gomez bills herself as an "exotic comedian"; like her comic idol, Lily Tomlin, Gomez is adept at creating a bevy of outrageous characters onstage. Gomez is known for her ability to shift easily from comic one-liners to dramatic disclosure, and has received critical acclaim in the 1990s as one of the outstanding practitioners of the dramatic monologue form. She is also a recognized leader in the growing field of gay and lesbian comedy.

Marga Gomez was born to two well-known New York City performers, Margo (who danced under the name Margo the Exotic) and Wilfredo Gomez (known onstage as Willy Chevalier). Growing up in the upper Manhattan neighborhood known as Washington Heights, she entered show business as a child performer, appearing onstage with her parents for the first time at age seven. The Latino theatrical world provided an unconventional and influential backdrop for Gomez's early years; she would later chronicle her formative childhood experiences in performance pieces such as *Memory Tricks* and *A Line around the Block.*

Gomez's parents divorced in the mid-1960s, at which time the fame and financial security they had previously earned in the theater began to dissolve. Gomez went to live with her mother in Massapequa, Long Island, and saw her father on weekends. Gomez had attended an inner-city Catholic school as a child; during her adolescence, she attended a high school where she was the only Latino student. Suburban Long Island felt isolating to Gomez and she became shy and introverted. On graduating from high school, Gomez went to Oswego State College in upstate New York, where she first came out as a lesbian. After studying English and political science for two years, Gomez flunked out of college and moved to Binghamton, New York, where she became involved in a lesbian feminist community.

Career Starts in San Francisco

Gomez moved to San Francisco in the early 1980s, where she attempted to get involved in acting. She joined Lilith, a feminist theater ensemble, and toured Europe and the West Coast extensively for three years. Gomez credits this experience with giving her theatrical monologues and stand-up material a feminist edge. Gomez also spent a season with the San Francisco Mime Troupe and was one of the original members of the Latino comedy group Culture Clash. During this time, Gomez developed her stand-up routine—a mixture of off-beat characterizations, quirky social commentary, and sexual politics.

By 1988 Gomez had acquired a loyal following and won the Cabaret Gold award as "Entertainer of the Year" from the San Francisco Council on Entertainment. Gomez has performed at countless events across the country and has been a featured performer on numerous television shows. In addition to her work for television, Gomez made a brief appearance in the feature film *Batman Forever.*

Performance Monologues Win Kudos

In 1991, as a result of an offer from the University of California San Diego Multi-Cultural Theater Festival, Gomez created the full-length performance monologue, *Memory Tricks,* the first in a series of performance pieces written and performed by Gomez, along with *Marga Gomez Is Pretty, Witty & Gay* and *A Line around the Block.* It is this body of work which has brought Gomez her greatest critical attention, including rave reviews, international media focus, honors and awards. The tragicomic story of Marga's relationship with her flamboyant mother, *Memory Tricks* traces the emotional path from her mother's days as a showgirl to her struggle with aging and Alzheimer's disease. Gomez probes the difficult emotions surrounding the mother-daughter relationship, in this case, a relationship in which the child must play mother to her own parent.

Following its six-week sold-out run at the Marsh Performance Space in San Francisco, *Memory Tricks* was twice chosen to be a part of the prestigious "Solo Mio" festival at Life on the Water Theater in San Francisco. Gomez was invited to perform a one-hour version of *Memory Tricks* as part of the New York Shakespeare Festival's Festival of New Voices in 1992, followed by a limited engagement of the complete piece in April 1993. It has since been performed all over the United States, Canada, and Europe.

Gomez's next performance piece, *Marga Gomez Is Pretty, Witty & Gay,* opened at Josie's Cabaret in San Francisco in October 1991 to packed houses. The work has played across the U.S. and in March 1993 it was included as part of the Whitney Museum's Biennial Performance Series. The work's title is a send-up of the song "I Feel Pretty" from *West Side Story;* it also marks the fact that Gomez has been an out performer for most of her career. Although Gomez's lesbianism is only indirectly mentioned in *Memory Tricks, Marga Gomez Is Pretty, Witty & Gay* is packed with lesbian humor, including a hilarious sketch describing a fantasy relationship between Anais Nin and Minnie Mouse. During the show, Gomez overturns a common stereotype of gays and lesbians with the line, "We do not recruit, we impress."

Latin Memories Form *A Line around the Block*

Gomez began performing *A Line around the Block,* a companion piece to *Memory Tricks,* in 1994. The work was co-commissioned by the Mark Taper Forum in Los Angeles and The New World Theater at the University of Massachusetts in Amherst. *A Line around the Block* had its creative beginnings in a sketch entitled "The 13 Minutos," which formed part of the theater group Culture Clash's show, *Carpa Clash,* at the Mark Taper Forum. Gomez won Theater LA's 1993-1994 Ovation Award as Best Featured Actress in a Play for her work in *Carpa Clash.*

A Line around the Block is a remembrance of Gomez's father, Willy Chevalier, as well as a bittersweet look back at the Latino theatrical world of the 1950s and 60s. Gomez has credited her father with giving her the desire and the determination to go into show business. In both *Memory Tricks* and *A Line around the Block,* Gomez pays tribute to her parents by showing the limits

Marga Gomez. ***Photograph by Linda Sue Scott.***

placed on their talents by discrimination against Latinos and Latinas. Despite her own assimilated background, the immigrant experience of her parents and Latino/a culture have been major influences on Gomez's work. Gomez sees the strength of her writing coming from being an outsider in two worlds: a queer in the Latino world, a Latina in the gay world.

Playhouse International optioned Gomez's screenplay of *Memory Tricks*, which has been expanded to include several players in order to be made into a feature film. Gomez has also contributed written material to several books: *Out, Loud, & Laughing*; *Out of Character*; and *Contemporary Plays by American Women of Color*. Currently, Marga Gomez is dividing her time between coasts as she continues with all her pursuits. With her many talents and powerful presence, this rising star—an inspiration to both the gay and lesbian and Latino/a communities—is just beginning to shine.

Current Address: c/o Irene Pinn, P.O. Box 460368, San Francisco, California 94146.

References:

Guthmann, Edward. "A Chip Off the Old Block," in *San Francisco Chronicle*, 5 November 1995.

Horowitz, Simi. "Marga Gomez," in *New York Native*, 10 May 1993.

Pollon, Zélie. "Marga Gomez Is Definitely Going Places," in *Deneuve*, October 1994: 24-27, 54.

Reser, Phil. "Marga Gomez Lifting Spirits, A Family Tradition," in *San Francisco Hot Ticket*, September 1988.

Troy, Patricia. "Marga Gomez," in *Venice*, April 1994.

Valdes, David. "Pretty Wonderful," in *Bay Windows*, 12 May/18 May 1994.

West, Blake. "Marga Gomez Goes Public," in *Metroline*, 2-15 February 1995.

—Teresa Ortega

Paul Goodman

1911-1972

American writer and educator

Paul Goodman often called himself "a Man of Letters," a term as good as any other for a man who was a novelist, playwright, literary critic, poet, educator, and activist. It is almost pointless to try to label someone who wrote the equivalent of at least one book a year for more than thirty years, someone who tackled so many different topics (e.g., Freudian theory, juvenile delinquency, anarchism, American education, architecture, his own bisexuality) in so many different literary forms (e.g., poetry, tragedy, farce, reportage, novel, essay, musical composition, short story, television column, and political manifesto). Despite Goodman's versatility, many critics do not consider him a good writer and happily catalog his numerous violations of style, point of view, tone, and pattern. Goodman often boasted of not qualifying as an expert on many of the topics he discussed; he took pride in his ignorance and naivete. Most of Goodman's critics do not consider him a literary artist, but do acknowledge him as an insightful critic of American society in the mid-twentieth century.

Grew up Fatherless

Paul Goodman was born on 9 September 1911, in New York City, to Augusta and Barnett Goodman. His German-Jewish father, having failed in business, abandoned the family before Paul's birth. Since Paul's mother frequently traveled as a salesperson, his older sister Alice and maternal aunts raised him. Paul also had a younger brother, Percival, with whom he later collaborated on *Communitas* (1947), a volume on urban design.

Paul attended Manhattan's public schools and impressed his teachers as a good student; he performed especially well in literature and language courses at Townsend Harris Hall High School and graduated in 1927. His scholastic success continued at the City College of New York, where Paul received his A.B. in philosophy in 1931. In college, Paul established many solid friendships, one of the most important with the philosopher Morris R. Cohen.

After graduation from college, Paul aspired only to become a writer. For the next five years, he lived with his sister, who supported him financially. With little desire to obtain a full-time job, Paul published a few poems, short stories, and a play; and audited graduate philosophy courses at Columbia University. Although far from famous and earning a just a minuscule income from writing, Goodman did receive some literary fan mail.

Fired Three Times for Sexual Behavior

From 1936 to 1940, Goodman was a graduate student in literature and philosophy at the University of Chicago. He worked as a research assistant from 1936 to 1937 and as a part-time instructor in "Ideas and Methods" from 1937 to 1939. Goodman became a perennial student, finally obtaining a Ph.D. in literature (his dissertation was called *The Structure of Literature*) from the University of Chicago in 1954.

In 1938, he entered into a common-law marriage to Virginia Miller, which would last about five years. His first child, Susan, was born in 1939. During this period, Goodman often cruised the local parks and bars for young men. This conduct upset his wife less than it did university officials, who ultimately fired Goodman for sexual impropriety. Toward the end of his life, Goodman would claim that he had been fired from jobs three times in his life, and all three dismissals were based on sexual orientation.

In 1940, Goodman moved back to New York and got published as a film critic for *Partisan Review*. His success with the latter turned out to be short-lived; after the Pearl Harbor bombing, *Partisan Review*'s editors stopped publishing Goodman's work when they discovered that he was a flamboyant bisexual who promoted draft-dodging.

For the next two decades, Goodman depended on friends with little printing presses to publish his work. He published his first novel, *The Grand Piano*, in 1942. David Dellinger put out Goodman's 1950 novel *Dead of Spring* (which Goodman considered his best fictional book). In 1943, he began teaching at Manumit, a progressive boarding school; less than a year later, he was dismissed for homosexual behavior.

In 1945, he entered into a common-law marriage with his occasional secretary, Sally Duchsten, a relationship that would last until the end of his life. His second child, Mathew Ready, was born in 1946. Goodman and his family mostly subsisted on his wife's secretarial salary until he published *Growing Up Absurd* (1960). Although he was prolific in the 1940s and 1950s and taught at such schools as New York University and Black Mountain College, the Goodman family often lived below the poverty line.

Life Irrevocably Changed after *Growing Up Absurd*

Goodman's most famous book is *Growing Up Absurd* (1960), which became a best-seller and remains in print today. Subtitled "The Problems of Youth in the Organized System," this long essay targets the topic of American delinquency in society. Here, Goodman captures the spirit of alienated American youth and encourages them to rebel against an establishment that restricts their sexual autonomy and does not provide them with substantial employment.

With the success of *Growing Up Absurd*, Goodman's money woes were over, and lecturing and publishing opportunities abounded. He bought a farm near North Stratford, New Hampshire, where he would live intermittently until his end of his life. While he still published in magazines such as *Liberation* and *Dissent*, he also pursued more mainstream, liberal-minded publications. In 1963, his wife had a daughter, Daisy.

Goodman became the first visiting fellow of the Institute for Policy Studies, a radical think-tank founded in 1963. He often lectured at colleges; the Berkeley campus particularly impressed him as an anarchist environment. The radical student movement's affection for Goodman began to wane in the mid-1960s, and he acquired something of a reputation for bourgeois individualism. Even so, in 1966, he became the first student-hired professor in the Experimental College at San Francisco State.

Pacifist Son Killed in Accident

By the late 1960s, Goodman was involved in the anti-Vietnam War movement; he, Grace Paley, and Karl Bissinger formed the New York branch of Resist, which counseled draft refusers. Goodman's son, Mathew, participated in the first mass burning of draft cards in New York. Mathew, who turned 21 in 1967, had not registered for the draft, and the Federal Bureau of Investigation was pursuing his case. Goodman wished his son would flee to Canada, but Matt never had the chance—he was killed in a mountain-climbing accident on 8 August 1967. Understandably devastated by such a loss, Goodman became more sympathetic to the many draft dodgers, often getting arrested in their demonstrations.

In his last years, Goodman continued writing and lecturing at colleges, but, depressed over the loss of his son and in increasingly poor health, Goodman may have known his life was nearing completion. He suffered his first heart attack in 1971, and was working on his *Collected Poems* when he died of a heart attack on 2 August 1972 in New Hampshire.

It would be an oversimplification to classify Goodman as a gay writer, although he often dealt off-handedly and overtly with homosexuality and bisexuality in his personal and professional life. He is too eclectic a writer to pigeonhole into such a label, although he experienced the sting of homophobia on many occasions in his life, particularly when he was unjustly dismissed from employment. Of his many works, the ones that dealt most directly with homosexuality are an essay entitled "The Politics of Being Queer" (1969), published in *Nature Heals: The Psychological Essays of Paul Goodman* (1977) and his notebook entries published as *Five Years* (1966). Ultimately, Goodman will be remembered for the enormous volume of his literary output and his energetic, intellectual role-playing.

References:

De Leon, David, ed. *Leaders from the 1960s: A Biographical Sourcebook of American Activism.* Westport, Connecticut: Greenwood Press, 1994.

Summers, Claude J., ed. *The Gay and Lesbian Literary Heritage.* New York: Henry Holt and Company, 1995.

Widmer, Kingsley. *Paul Goodman.* Boston: Twayne Publishers, 1980.

—David Levine

Judy Grahn

1940-

American poet, activist, and publisher

Judy Grahn has been called a pioneer in the field of gay cultural history—but the terms philosopher, shaman, historian, cultural theorist, and literary detective can be applied to her as readily. Like Gertrude Stein, Walt Whitman, or e.e. cummings, Grahn often uses techniques of repetition and ritual incantation to create rhythmic patterns in her poetry and prose, which enlivens her work all the more as a quest for gay and lesbian identity through empowering reassessment of gay myth and legend.

Throughout her endeavors, the common, working-class ethos is foremost. "[My generation] began wresting poetry from the exclusive clutches of the sons and daughters of the American upperclass and returning it to the basic groups from which it seeped and sprung," she observes in *The Gay and Lesbian Literary Heritage*. "I think it is important for people to know that an open, working-class lesbian poet who surfaced in 1970 with the word 'dyke' in the title of her first book is now considered literary canon," she adds in a quote from *Gay and Lesbian Literature*. "Now I feel capable of becoming a world class philosopher, using the best gifts of my communities and my spirits to help reshape the world."

Anger and Determination

Judith Rae Grahn was born on 28 July 1940 in Chicago, Illinois, and spent her childhood in a small town in New Mexico she described in her book *Another Mother Tongue* as "an economically poor and spiritually depressed [place] near the hellish border of West Texas." Her father was a cook and her mother was a photographer's assistant. Although Grahn began writing articles at the age of six and poetry by the time she was ten, she soon realized that in her small town, "virtually everything was prohibited except low-level wage slavery and mandatory, joyless marriage."

By the time Grahn was 16, she was identifying herself as lesbian, and at 18 she "eloped" with her first female lover Yvonnne, who was studying at a small college nearby. "Vonnie" introduced Judy to the "secret" homosexual world of the late 1950s—a world Grahn would observe unflinchingly and later chronicle in her work.

Though Grahn says she knew she was a poet by the age of ten, it was not until she was in her mid-twenties that she committed herself fully to her writing. At 19 she joined the Air Force, only to be given a less-than-honorable discharge two years later for being a lesbian—a charge that involved the seizure of notes implicating friends and the Air Force's notification of her parents as to her "crime." She spent the next few years at odd jobs in order to earn money for school, and experienced more homophobia when she was denied jobs, housing, and was even once beat up in public for looking to masculine. "These jolts ... taught me everything I would ever need to know about the oppression of Gay people," she says in *Tongue*.

Continuing her youthful self-exploration and research into the culture of homosexuality she was increasingly proud to be a part of, Grahn was further incensed by the "jail for books" syndrome she encountered when shown an off-limits series of studies on homosexuality at a Washington D.C. library. "They showed me a wire cage where [these] 'special' books were kept," she notes in *Tongue*. "Only professors, doctors, psychiatrists, and lawyers for the criminally insane could see them, ... material of which my own person was the subject.... [I became] angry and determined enough to use my life to reverse [this] perilous situation."

"Take Every Single Risk"

By 1963, Grahn was sufficiently politicized to be one of only 15 members of the fledgling Mattachine Society to picket the White House for gay rights. She also published a handful of poems in the *Ladder*—the groundbreaking and treasured lesbian newsletter put out by the Daughters of Bilitis—and in 1964 published an article in *Sexology Magazine* (under a pseudonym) arguing that lesbians were ordinary people. Suddenly, at age 25, while she was studying sociology at Howard University, Judy Grahn fell into a coma caused by a serious brain fever. When she came out of it, she came to terms with her calling, as she summarized in a speech to a *Women Writers of the West* conference in 1983: "I realized that if I was going to do what I had set out to do in my life, I would have to go all the way and take every single risk you could take.... I decided I would not do anything I didn't want to do that would keep me from my art."

Not surprisingly, Grahn's dedication and drive led to a blossoming in both life and career, and a position for her at the forefront of the burgeoning lesbian/feminist/women's poetry and prose renaissance of the late 1960s and early 1970s. In 1969, she founded the Women's Press Collective (WPC) with then-lover and artist Wendy Cadden. WPC began as a mimeograph operation in their basement and grew to publish thousands of volumes by over 200 women on a variety of subjects—rape, racism, classicism, multiculturalism, and women's spirituality—before it merged with Diana Press in 1977. Grahn was also a founding member of the first lesbian feminist collective—West Coast Lesbian Feminist Movement—and an originator of the country's first women's bookstore—A Woman's Place—in Oakland, California.

Disempowering Negativity

From the beginning, Grahn used her poetic gifts to repossess words and symbols of "dyke-dom" that were too-long and too-wrongly spun as derogatory by outsiders. In doing so, she also disempowered negative attitudes and their accompanying homophobia. In her first published volume of poetry, *Edward the Dyke*, for example (published by WPC in 1971, but actually written in 1964), Grahn satirically writes of doctors attempting to "cure" a lesbian of her "disease and depravity"—as if "illness" were solely in the eyes of the (heterosexual) majority. *She Who* (1972) might well be termed an experiment in feminist scripture, as Grahn writes of being "the wall with the womanly swagger ... the dragon, the bulldyke, the bulldagger." In *A Woman Is Talking to Death* (1974), Grahn hits a profound spiritual stride when she lists the times she failed to help a woman who needed her as the ultimate answer to the societal stigmata of a question: "Have you ever committed any indecent acts with women?" These three volumes were published together as *The Work of A Common Woman* in 1978.

Grahn strives to redefine the word "love" for lesbians, gay men, and the rest of society at large. It is never about mere romance in her eyes, but about reclaiming power to relate to one another spiritually, socially, emotionally, and politically. And it is increasingly open to new definitions of how "common" women (another word Grahn has rescued from the dustbin and elevated to its rightful place of honor) relate to one another—from baking bread to making love. When Grahn published her collection of poems in *The Common Woman* (1969), for example, she created portraits of seven women—only one of which is lesbian—in order to offer something to the reader "which described regular, everyday women without making us look either superhuman or pathetic." And, as in much of Grahn's work, women's power in everyday life is linked to those in nature—thunderstorms, new moons, rattlesnakes.

Some have commented on how Grahn strives for a "neo-mythology" in her work, most notably in *Queen of Wands* (1982) and *Queen of Swords* (1987), a series of poems based on the Tarot. In both texts, the character Helen (of Troy) travels from ancient Greece to Hollywood, to a factory, and into the underworld of a lesbian bar. Here, it is enlightening to see how Grahn seeks to re-mythologize women's common lives by spinning everyday experiences upward and back into their proper orbits of beauty, love, light, fire, and thought.

Culture as Everything

Between *Wands* and *Swords,* Grahn published what is perhaps her most ambitious and widely read work, *Another Mother Tongue* (1984). According to Diane Lund in *Contemporary Lesbian Writers of the United States*, the book "combines autobiography, history, legend, poetry, and etymology in order to discover women's history, gay history, and the language of gay culture."

"What gives any group of people distinction and dignity is its culture," Grahn observes in *Tongue*, "[including] a remembrance of the past and a setting of itself in a world context whereby the group can see who it is relative to everyone else." In *Tongue*, Grahn sets out to explore fully the origins of contemporary gay culture by researching the wealth of historical information about "gay" words like Amazon and bulldyke (related to female warriors like the Celtic Boadacea), faggot (pertaining to gay wizardry), and the deeper acknowledgment that women's history (if we must view it as apart) "parallels, crisscrosses, and influences Gay cultural ... and tribal history."

What one gets from *Tongue* is a sense that gay culture in its historical context not only meets but transcends standard spiritual functions. In short, lesbians and gay men must not be content to cower on some lower rung of contemporary society's strata. The word "dyke," according to Grahn, goes back to the goddess Dike, whose name was synonymous with balance. "One of the major homosexual/shamanic functions in any society," she writes in *Tongue*, "is to cross over between these two essentially different worlds [of male and female] and reveal them to each other."

"Healthy Doses of Common Sense"

Tongue likewise signaled a widening path in Grahn's career—one that, according to writers Martha Nell Smith and Stacy Steinberg in *The Gay and Lesbian Literary Heritage*, continues to imbue "all of our work and culture with healthy doses of common sense," and includes a novel (*Mundane's World*, 1988), and what they term her "recuperative literary criticism" (*The Highest Apple*, 1985 and *Really Reading Gertrude Stein*, 1989).

With *Apple*, Grahn wears the hat of critic and historian as she links the work of nine poets throughout history in search of a "lesbian poetic tradition with Sappho." It is interesting to note that she dedicates the book "to ALL lovers" in an effort to mainstream lesbian poetry through to our modern day. The poets (including herself) are: Paula Gunn Allen, Olga Broumas, Emily Dickinson, H.D., Audre Lorde, Amy Lowell, Adrienne Rich, and Gertrude Stein. With *Stein*, Grahn, according to Smith and Steinberg, "not only recovers little-known works by this lesbian writer but, as a map or rereading, energetically and profoundly urges readers beyond fascination with her celebrity and into appreciation of Stein's widely admired but little-read texts."

Grahn's first novel, *Mundane's World*, is both a mystery story and a portrait of a world before patriarchy. The culmination of this tale—centered around five "mostly brown" girls in the city of Mundane—is a ritual ceremony for them when they reach the age of menstruation. The structure of *Mundane's World* further reflects contemporary holistic theories in the natural sciences by creating a community of interconnected plants, people, and animals in both the world of the living and that of the dead.

As for the theme of menstruation, Grahn is implying that blood is at the center of our culture, and focusing on it is a call for women to reclaim science and religion as well as their other usurped energies. As she told the *Advocate* in a 1993 interview, "it doesn't have to be traumatic blood. It can be natural blood and the rituals that women have always performed that have given us all the things we treasure."

"Either, Both, or Neither of the Genders"

In 1993, Grahn published what, after 20 years in the making, was to prove her most controversial, uncommon work. "When I finished writing *Blood, Bread and Roses: How Menstruation Created the World*," she told the *Advocate*, "I felt at home in the world. I understood."

In *Blood*, Grahn strives to re-place women at the center of the culture and menstruation as a blood ritual back in its place at the beginning of all our origin myths, gay and straight. All of which, according to Grahn, puts women back at the center of religion. "We haven't been there for 2,100 years," she told the *Advocate*. "It's astonishing to me. I can't wait to see what kind of effect that's going to have."

It is wrong to assume, however, that *Blood* speaks only to women. "Because I have frequently identified with either or both or neither of the genders, I've been able to go back and forth and gain a perspective," Grahn further elaborates in the *Advocate* interview. What results, she claims, is an ability to see society through "dyke eyes" that made her the "ultimate other"—an and/or, neither/nor kind of vision that was tortuous until she learned how to put it to use in *Blood*. One would assume that such a perspective applies to how gay men view and are viewed by society as well. "I like Judy's willingness to think about origins," says author Felice Picano. "So much in gay writing today seems to be about the moment, about the surface. We've got to find out who we are—WHY we are."

In all her work, Judy Grahn has strived for the empowering larger picture—a gay cosmology for gay men and lesbian women that is ever expanding and, consequently, growing ever more inclusive. As she told the *Advocate*, "there is a dance—sometimes lovely and sometimes very violent—that goes back and forth between men and women as we exchange information and learn from each other." Let's hope Grahn will continue to hum the tune for us.

Current Address: Box 11164, Oakland, California 94611.

References:

Donnelly, Nisa. "An Uncommon Woman," in *Advocate*, 30 November 1993: 56-59.

Grahn, Judy. *Another Mother Tongue—Gay Words, Gay Worlds.* Boston: Beacon Press, 1984.

———. *Mundane's World.* Freedom, California: Crossing Press, 1988.

———. *The Work of a Common Woman.* Oakland, California: Diana Press, 1978.

Pollack, Sandra and Denise D. Knight, eds. *Contemporary Lesbian Writers of the United States.* Westport, Connecticut: Greenwood Press, 1994.

Russell, Paul. *The Gay 100—A Ranking of the Most Influential Gay Men and Lesbians, Past and Present.* Secaucus, New Jersey: Citadel Press, 1995.

Summers, Claude J., ed. *The Gay and Lesbian Literary Heritage.* New York: Henry Holt, 1995.

Yalom, Marilyn, ed. *Women Writers of the West.* Santa Barbara, California, 1983.

—Jerome Szymczak

Duncan Grant

1885-1978

British artist

Duncan Grant was one of the most versatile and innovative British artists of the twentieth century. A pioneer avant-gardist, he later turned to figurative representation. As Kenneth Clark wrote, "no one who loved life and visual experience as much as Duncan did could have remained an abstract painter for long, and very soon flowers began to appear on his canvases, and seductive nudes." These nudes were male, often portraits of his lovers. Grant's personal life was as iconoclastic, admirable and varied as his art work. He is remarkable as a celebrity who lived openly with a succession of lovers until his death at the age of 92.

Duncan James Corrowr Grant was born on 21 January 1985, at his family's great house at Rothiemurchus, in Inverness-shire, Scotland. He was the only child of Major Bartle Grant and Ethel McNeil Grant. Grant's early years were spent in India, where his father was stationed. He returned to England for his schooling and lived with his extraordinary relatives the Stracheys. There he had a relationship with his cousin, Lytton Strachey, five years his senior, followed by an intense love affair with Lytton's classmate from Cambridge, Maynard Keynes.

Thanks to his nurturing aunt Lady Strachey, Grant attended Westminster School of Art and thus found his vocation. Later he studied in Paris, at the school of Jacques-Emile Blanche, where he absorbed the latest art theories. In tune with modernists, Grant also found inspiration in the art of the past. He copied old masters in Italy, and studied Roman and Romanesque stone carvings and mosaics in Sicily and Tunisia.

In 1911, synthesizing all these influences, and with reference to Michelangelo, Grant painted two large murals, "Bathing" and "Football," which brought his first public success. As a subversive device to allow him to deal with the male body, Grant depicted modern athletes as heroic figures. These murals now hang in the Tate Gallery.

Grant believed that all surfaces were suitable for decoration. In 1912, he and the influential artist/critic Roger Fry formed the Omega Workshops, where artists designed household items. Many artists were employed until the outbreak of World War I.

In the years to come, Grant decorated houses, designed ceramics, china, fabrics, worked in ballet and theatre, did illustrations and printmaking, as well as easel painting and murals. His influence radically altered British taste in art and design.

Painter Vanessa Bell and her husband art critic Clive Bell folded Grant into the intellectual circle known as the Bloomsbury group, where his presence caused erotic havoc. Grant was good looking, good natured and witty, with a gift for friendship. "It was very easy to understand why so many people, men and women, loved him," wrote the Duke of Devonshire. "More striking even than his looks was his charm: a quality impossible to describe in words or paint." Vanessa Bell aggressively pursued the reluctant but finally acquiescent Grant. She claimed he was the father of her daughter. Although their sexual liaison was brief, they remained intimate friends and shared a country house with her husband and children until her death.

After World War II, as he began to paint in a more representational manner, Grant was shunned by the new art market, which abhorred figurative work. Still he had prestigious commissions, for example, from Queen Elizabeth for a painting at St. Paul's Cathedral, and in 1959, from Lincoln Cathedral for murals for the Russell Chantry. Grant took the opportunity to depict Christ the Good Shepherd as a handsome blond youth carrying a lost sheep. The model for the Christ was Paul Roche, who was not only a former Roman Catholic priest but also Grant's lover. Cathedral officials, alarmed by the cheerful homoerotic sensibility, closed the Chantry and for many years used it as a storeroom. It is now open to the public.

Today, Grant is considered by a new generation of art critics to be one of the most important British artists of the twentieth century, and the aesthetic precursor of David Hockney. Tragically, rehabilitation of Grant's reputation is in abeyance because his work is in copyright to a hostile and seemingly homophobic estate, which typically denies permission to reproduce his pictures or write about him until the copyrights expire in the year 2053.

Grant told this author that his moral attitudes reflected more of the sexual tolerance of the Regency period than the repressive Victorian age he was born into. Because he was a sexually active gay man, in terms of British law, Grant was a criminal throughout his very long life. After his death in 1978, he was given a memorial service at St. Paul's Cathedral, and now Charleston, his country house in Sussex, is now open to the public. By virtue of his courage in living an openly gay life in an age when this could be a life threatening risk, and through his unqualified depiction in his art of his love of men, Duncan Grant deserves his place in the pantheon of gay heroes.

References:

Roche, Paul. *With Duncan Grant in Southern Turkey.* Renfrew, Scotland: Honeyglen, 1982.

Shone, Richard. *Bloomsbury Portraits.* Oxford: Phaidon, 1976.

Turnbaugh, Douglas Blair. *Duncan Grant and the Bloomsbury Group.* Secaucus, New Jersey: Lyle Stuart, 1987; London: Bloomsbury, 1987.

———. *Private: The Erotic Art of Duncan Grant.* London: Gay Mens Press, 1989.

Watney, Simon. *The Art of Duncan Grant.* London: John Murray Publishers Ltd., 1990.

—Douglas Blair Turnbaugh

Barbara Grier

1933-

American publisher and editor

Barbara Grier has spent four decades on the frontline of lesbian publishing, originally as a contributor to and later editor of the first national lesbian magazine, the *Ladder,* and currently as the co-founder and publisher of Naiad Press, the world's largest publisher of lesbian books.

Barbara Grier was born on 4 November 1933, in Cincinnati, Ohio to Dorothy Vernon Black and Philip Strang Grier. Her father was a physician and her mother worked as a secretary. She has two older half brothers, William and Brewster, and two younger sisters, Diane (who is also a lesbian) and Penelope. Her parents separated when Grier was ten and divorced when she was 13.

Throughout her childhood and youth, Grier travelled extensively, visiting every state in the union and several foreign countries. According to Grier, the travel "took the place of formal education. To the extent I have been successful, I owe it to being extremely well-read and well-travelled."

Grier remembers being "madly in love with my babysitter" at the age of eight and having several other crushes on other young women before she came out at age 12. Relating her coming out process in the lesbian classic, *The Coming Out Stories*, Grier states: "When I discovered behavior patterns in myself that I could tell were different from behavior patterns in my friends ... I investigated it in quite a sensible way for a fairly bright child: I went to the library and started looking." In the video *Lesbian Tongues*, Grier tells what happened when she returned from the library and told her mother that she was a homosexual. "My mother answered, 'No, because you're a woman, you're a lesbian. And since 12 years old is too young to make such a decision, let's wait six months before we tell the newspapers.'"

From that time on, Grier has lived her life openly as a lesbian. "What's hard about being out?" Grier asks, and she answers immediately, "What's hard is *not* being out!" Grier credits her ease in coming out to her mother: "She was very supportive. She didn't consider it unusual or remarkable. She had come from a background in the performing arts and had been around gays and lesbians all her life. If all people coming out were as supported as I was by my parents, we would grow up without any vestige of emotional pain."

Shortly after graduating from high school in 1951, Grier met Helen Bennett in the literature and popular section of the Kansas City (Missouri) Public Library and began a relationship that was to last 20 years. The couple moved to Denver, Colorado, so that Bennett could attend library school. "It was there I began to write and began to collect lesbian literature. As it later turned out, that's what I was to spend my life doing," Grier reminisced in *Heartwomen*. Afterwards, they moved to Kansas City, Kansas, where they both got jobs at the local public library, Bennett as a librarian and Grier as a clerical worker in the cataloging department.

Barbara Grier

Grier Works on the *Ladder*

Grier became involved with the legendary lesbian publication the *Ladder* almost from its inception. The *Ladder*, the first national lesbian magazine, was begun by the Daughters of Bilitis in San Francisco, California, in 1956. In an interview with Kate Brandt, Grier reflects: "When I saw my first copy of an issue of the *Ladder* I realized what I was going to spend my life doing." From 1957 to 1972, she was involved in practically every aspect of the operation from reviewing books to contributing articles to writing columns to editing and eventually publishing the magazine.

Grier began her fifteen year association with the *Ladder* by submitting book reviews for its "Lesbiana" column. Since in the 1950s, there could be serious repercussions for women writing openly as lesbians, Phyllis Lyon, editor of the *Ladder* at that time, urged Barbara to write under a pseudonym. She did so, thinking it was "romantic and glamorous" and chose the name "Gene Damon: Gene, because I'd always liked and wanted the name, and Damon, because it means, literally, 'the devil' or 'demon' ..." Grier states in *Happy Endings*. She eventually took on several more pseudonyms, and wrote at least one entire issue of the *Ladder* herself "including letters both for and against a particular topic" using these various pen names.

She also submitted articles and reviews to other gay publications, including *ONE Magazine*, the *Mattachine Review*, and *Tangents*. Throughout her association with these publications and afterwards, Grier worked a series of clerical jobs to pay her expenses so she could devote herself to her lesbian volunteer work. She threw herself wholly into this work, spending all her free time writing and researching.

In 1967, Grier met Donna J. McBride who had just joined the staff of the Kansas City Public Library. McBride had been warned about "that woman who collects *those* books." Recognizing her own lesbian feelings, McBride recalls that she would read every book that Grier requested and later even started following her around the library. In 1971, McBride began to volunteer at the *Ladder* and soon became involved with Grier, who ended her 20-year relationship with Bennett. The couple moved in together on 22 January 1972. McBride continued working at the Kansas City Public Library, "rising through the ranks." She eventually abolished the literature department where both she and Bennett had met Grier. "She made certain that I couldn't hunt there anymore," quips Grier.

After taking on a succession of progressively more responsible positions at the *Ladder*, including fiction and poetry editor, Grier took over as editor-in-chief in 1968. The late 1960s was an era of social activism and Grier witnessed the birth of several liberation movements, most notably those demanding equality for women and gays. Reflecting on the times in *Heartwomen*, Grier comments, "as the new wave of the feminist movement became a powerful force it seemed obvious to me that that's where the magazine had to go." However, Grier's political activism ran contrary to the assimilationist philosophy of the Daughters of Bilitis (DOB). "In 1970, Rita [Laporte, national president of DOB] and I literally divorced the *Ladder* from DOB—i.e., we stole it. We took the magazine away and turned it into a very strong women's liberation magazine, although it stayed purely lesbian," Grier told Kate Brandt in *Happy Endings*. The takeover was short-lived, however, because without the DOB's financial backing "the *Ladder* simply ran out of money." Its last issue appeared in the fall of 1972.

Much of the content of the *Ladder* was republished in book form in 1976 including *The Lavender Herring: Lesbian Essays from the Ladder* (Diana Press), *Lesbian Lives: Biographies of Women from the Ladder* (Diana Press), and *The Lesbians Home Journal: Stories from the Ladder* (Diana Press), all of which Grier co-edited with Coletta Reid; and *Lesbiana: Book Reviews from the Ladder, 1966-1972* (Naiad Press), edited by Grier herself.

Grier Co-Founds Naiad Press

Shortly after the demise of the *Ladder,* Anyda Marchant and Muriel Crawford lent Grier and McBride money to start a lesbian publishing company. In January of 1973, Naiad Press was founded, publishing its first book, *The Latecomer* by Anyda Marchant, the following year. For the next eight years, both McBride and Grier worked full-time jobs in addition to running Naiad Press. In 1980, the couple moved Naiad from Kansas City to Tallahassee, Florida, where they ran the business out of their garage. Grier became Naiad's first full-time employee in January 1982 with McBride following as the second in June of that same year. From those modest beginnings, sole proprietors Grier and McBride have carefully cultivated Naiad Press, transforming it into the world's largest lesbian press, publishing altogether over 300 books. Commenting on Naiad's impressive growth in the video *Lesbian Tongues*, Grier says: "I love the idea that lesbian money literally is keeping Naiad Press growing like crazy."

Naiad Press, the oldest continuously publishing lesbian press in the United States, has supplied a generation of readers with romance, mystery, science fiction, fantasy, and humor books and has resuscitated many lesbian literary and pulp classics from past generations, including Margaret C. Anderson's *Forbidden Fires*, Gertrude Stein's *Lifting Belly,* Gale Wilhelm's *We Too Are Drifting*, and Ann Bannon's *Beebo Brinker* series. Additionally, Naiad has published such significant works of nonfiction as Clare Potter's *Lesbian Periodicals Index* and J.R. Roberts' *Black Lesbians: An Annotated Bibliography.*

Included among the diverse array of authors published by Naiad are Katherine V. Forrest, Jeannette Foster, Lee Lynch, Claire McNab, Isabel Miller, Jane Rule, Diane Salvatore, Ann Allen Shockley, Sheila Ortiz Taylor, and Valerie Taylor. Grier herself has contributed to Naiad's prolific output by co-editing several books herself, including *The Erotic Naiad* (1992), *The Romantic Naiad* (1993), and *The Mysterious Naiad* (1994), all co-edited with Katherine V. Forrest; and *The First Time Ever* (1995) and *Dancing in the Dark* (1996), both co-edited with Christine Cassidy.

Naiad Press books have been recognized in gay and lesbian literary circles, winning one American Library Association Gay, Lesbian, and Bisexual Book Award and six Lambda Literary Awards. Tribute has been paid to Grier as well for her unrelenting devotion to lesbian and gay concerns. In 1985, the prestigious Gay Academic Union paid homage to Grier by bestowing upon her its President's Award for Lifetime Service. And in 1992, both Grier and McBride were awarded the Publisher's Service Award at the fourth annual Lambda Literary Awards banquet.

Throughout her life Grier has been a avid collector and documenter of lesbian literature. She began "haunting" used bookstores as a teenager collecting books with lesbian themes, an activity that "began as a search, and then it became a dream, and then it became an obsession," according to her account in *Happy Endings*. She became friends with Jeannette Foster, author of *Sex Variant Women in Literature*, who helped Grier find even more ways to identify lesbian-themed literature.

Along the way, Grier documented what she found. Throughout the early 1960s, she (under the pseudonym of Gene Damon) and noted author Marion Zimmer Bradley together compiled what they termed "a complete, cumulative checklist of lesbian, variant, and homosexual fiction, in English, or available in English translation, with supplements of related material, for the use of collectors, students, and librarians." She went on to compile, with the help of Lee Stuart and later Jan Watson (a pseudonym of Donna McBride) and Robin Jordan, the renowned bibliography *The Lesbian in Literature*, originally published in 1967 and updated twice.

Her obsession with these materials has resulted in one of the largest collections of its type, including manuscripts, personal papers, photographs, and other memorabilia, as well as books and periodicals. Grier donated this collection, valued at over $400,000, to the newly opened James C. Hormel Gay and Lesbian Center at the San Francisco Public Library.

Currently, Grier and her partner, Donna McBride, live "terribly middle class" lives in Tallahassee, Florida. "We are very good neighbors, yet very publicly and explicitly lesbian. We do not hide it. In other words, the grass is green, the sky is blue, and we're lesbians."

What most concerns Grier today is the issue of gay and lesbian marriage: "In the eyes of the law a man and a woman who are legally married are one person, one body. When one person dies, their possessions pass seamlessly to the other, like siamese twins, and no inheritance tax is assessed. We are not similarly protected in our relationships. It is a privilege granted solely to heterosexual married couples—one that is used for social control. If the State were to eliminate this privilege totally, its coffers would be soon be empty. What politicians are voting against is not against marrying a mate—they don't want us to take advantage of social security or to have disability acts kick in. It all has to do with money. Money is the decision making factor in this country."

Grier continues: "Another aspect of this issue is that marriage creates visibility. When we are banned from marrying, we are kept from doing publicly the ordinary and rational things that people do anyway—marry, settle down, get jobs, and live like everyone else." Barbara Grier has brought lesbian culture and literature into the lives of two generations of lesbians. Through her work with the *Ladder* in the 1950s and 1960s and Naiad Press in the 1970s, 1980s, and 1990s, she has lived up to her goal of "making it possible that any lesbian, anywhere, any age, who comes out can walk into a bookstore and pick up a book that says 'of course you're a lesbian and you're wonderful!'"

Current Address: c/o Naiad Press, P.O. Box 10543, Tallahassee, Florida 32302-2543.

References:

Boucher, Sandy. "Clinging Vine," in *Heartwomen: An Urban Feminist's Odyssey Home.* San Francisco: Harper & Row, 1982: 212-230.

Grier, Barbara. "Climbing The *Ladder* to Success: Naiad Press," in *Happy Endings: Lesbian Writers Talk about their Lives and Work,* by Kate Brandt. Tallahassee, Florida: Naiad Press, 1993: 99-108.

———. "The Garden Variety Lesbian," in *The Coming Out Stories*, edited by Susan J. Wolfe and Julia Penelope Stanley. Watertown, Massachusetts: Persephone Press, 1980: 235-240.

———. Interview with R. Ellen Greenblatt, 1996.

Lesbian Tongues: Lesbians Talk about Life, Love, and Sex. Washington, D.C.: Pop Video, 1989.

Troxell, Jane. "Naiad Press Founders Celebrate 20 Years of Personal and Professional Triumphs," 3 (May/June 1992): 8.

—R. Ellen Greenblatt

Angelina Emily Weld Grimke

1880-1958

African-American writer

An African-American writer of poems, plays, and short stories, Angelina Weld Grimke suffered through a life of suppression. Battered by racism and muffled by homophobia, she never lived up to her early literary promise and died almost forgotten. Among the lesser lights of the Harlem Renaissance, the black cultural movement of the 1920s, Grimke wrote primarily about racial concerns and lost love before overwhelming despair stilled her pen.

One of the members of the famed interracial Grimke family, Angelina was born in Boston on 27 February 1880, the only child of Sarah E. Stanley, a white woman, and Archibald Grimke, a mulatto former slave. Named after her great-aunt Angelina Weld, nee Grimke, a fighter for abolition and women's rights, she is often confused by readers with the older woman. Grimke's parents separated shortly after her birth and she went to live with her mother for five years, until Sarah shipped the child back to Archibald in 1887. Angelina never saw her mother again.

A prominent lawyer and a diplomat, Archibald Grimke raised his daughter alone, educating her at a number of prestigious schools in Massachusetts and Minnesota. Grimke took a degree in physical education at the Boston Normal School of Gymnastics in 1902. In that same year, she began to pursue a career as a gym teacher, starting at the Armstrong Manual Training School in Washington, D.C. Amidst much turmoil with the principal, Grimke transferred to the more academic M Street High School in 1907, where she taught English until retiring to New York City in 1926. There is some question why the academically inclined Grimke took a degree in physical education in the first place, with Carolivia Herron suggesting in her introduction to *Selected Works of Angelina Weld Grimke* that, as a closeted lesbian, Grimke found gymnastics attractive because it provided sublimated contact with women.

The lesbian tone in much of Grimke's writings is unmistakable and it is perhaps for this reason that little of her work made it into print during her lifetime. The drama *Rachel* (1920) is her only published book, while just a few of her more than 300 poems, short stories, and nonfiction works (reviews and biographical sketches) appeared in the newspapers, magazines, particularly *Opportunity*, and anthologies of her day. Most of Grimke's works were written between 1900 and 1920, but she began writing verse with homosexual themes before the turn of the century and her sexual identity seems quite clear. Her love letters to women, found among her papers, date back to 1894 and, at her death, Grimke left behind 20 lesbian poems. Correspondence with Mamie Burrill in 1896, reprinted in Herron's collection, makes definite reference to a prior love affair and includes the passage:

> [I]f you only knew how my heart beats when I
> think of you and it yearns and pants to gaze,
> if only for one second upon your lovely face
> ... I hope, darling, that in few years you
> will come to me and be my love, my wife!

The writings that did appear in print show the impact of concealment upon a creative mind. Uniformly somber, these works deal mainly with the lynching and the subjugation of African-Americans. Crushed by both heterosexism and racism, Grimke could only publicly address the latter and she did so powerfully, becoming, with the play *Rachel*, one of the first to use the American stage to denounce social injustice. Appalled at the restricted world to which the United States confined its black citizens, Grimke advocated racial self-genocide as a method of protest. Both "The Closing Door" and "Goldie," published in the *Birth Control Review* in September 1919 and November 1920 respectively, encourage black women not to have children. Like "Goldie," many of Grimke's works contain promises of the violent revenge that African-Americans will someday take for the injustices that whites have long heaped upon them. In the poem "Beware When He Awakens," from the 10 May 1902 *Pilot*, Grimke lists various racist atrocities and warns:

> But mark! there may draw near
> A day red-eyed and drear,
> A day of endless fear;
> Beware, lest he awakes.

In the years after the end of the Harlem Renaissance, Grimke quietly drifted into obscurity. Stunned by her inability to find a lifelong partner and angry about being smothered by the restrictions of the larger culture, she stopped trying to publish. Her undated poem "An Epitaph" is likely autobiographical. It depicts the futility and despair of the narrator who first longs for joy, then for love, and is answered with pain and death. Alone, Angelina Grimke died in a New York City apartment on 10 June 1958, receiving an obituary in the *New York Times* for her teaching, not her writing. Grimke's unpublished works can be found in the manuscript collection of the Moorland-Spingarn Research Center, Howard University, Washington, D.C.

References:

Herron, Carolivia, ed. *Selected Works of Angelina Weld Grimke.* New York: Oxford University Press, 1991.

Hull, Gloria. *Color, Sex, and Poetry: Three Women Writers of the Harlem Renaissance.* Bloomington: Indiana University Press, 1987.

—Caryn E. Neumann

Marilyn Hacker

1942-

American poet

Marilyn Hacker has been writing poetry for thirty years. Since the private publication of *The Terrible Children* (1967), Hacker has written ten books of poetry. All of them concentrate on two relationships: 1) women's relationships with other women and their worlds, and 2) women poets' relationships to literary forms. Her work is also known for its graphic, yet lyrical, portrayals of women's bodies and for its frankness about lesbian love. According to Felicia Mitchell in *Dictionary of Literary Biography,* "Marilyn Hacker fits into the contemporary poetry scene because of her unusual critical perspective, which bridges the traditional and the feminist ... Hacker has insisted and shown that the traditional poetic forms are as much women's as they are men's." Hacker excels at writing the sonnet and the sonnet sequence. In her *Love, Death, and the Changing of Seasons* (1986), she brings the frankness of the forbidden—the love that should not speak its name as well as the vocabulary that should not make its presence known—to the sonnet:

Well, damn, it's a relief to be a slut
after such lengths of "Man delights not me,
nor woman neither," that I honestly
wondered if I'd outgrown it. Chocolate
or wine, a cashmere scarf, a cigarette,
had more to do with sensuality
than what's between my belly and my butt
that yearns toward you now unabashedly.
I'd love to grip your head between my thighs
while yours tense toward your moment on my ears,
but I'll still be thankful for this surprise
if things turn out entirely otherwise,
and we're bar buddies who, in a few years,
will giggle about this after two beers.

The head between the thighs nestled in the ninth line, especially designed to rhyme with "surprise," exemplifies Hacker's wit and impeccable sense of form. In Hacker's hands, this age-old form, a form that women have been using since its inception, makes way for lesbian lovemaking, twentieth-century style.

Ironically, what many critics refer to as her "graphic," "frank," or "honest" language, she refers to in an interview with Karla Hammond as "ordinary": "I like the tension in a poem that comes from the diction of ordinary speech playing against a form." Perhaps her lyrical strength and charm lie in her ability to assert the ordinariness of lesbian love language.

A Poet in the Making

Marilyn Hacker was born 27 November 1942 to Jewish immigrants Albert Abraham Hacker and Hilda Rosengarten Hacker. She grew up in the Bronx and attained most of her formal education in New York, culminating in a BA degree from New York University. Hacker tells Karla Hammond that her earliest education about women writers and feminism occurred through adolescent reading that she happened into on her own: "I've always been and continue to be a science fiction reader. When I was an adolescent, there wasn't very much science fiction by women.... Now, much of the most exciting new speculative fiction is being written by women.... Women writers are interested in writing about women enjoying all the human freedoms." Hacker's discovery of poetry also occurred quite early in her life: "When I was ten or eleven or twelve I thought of male poets as being "poets" and thought, as one thought then, that it was the women poets who needed the qualifying adjective.... I wish now that I had been aware of the work of H.D. [Hilda Doolittle] when I was in my teens. Yet her work was largely out of print."

In an interview with Annie Finch in *American Poetry Review*, Hacker reveals that her earliest memories of writing have her writing in fixed forms: "I wrote little quatrains when I was five years old. I like to think that somebody read me Blake's *Songs of Innocence*—I didn't though come from a family where poetry of any kind was read out loud.... The first poem I can remember writing which was a bit more than doggerel was a sonnet."

Similar to many successful writers, Hacker discusses her education about poetry and writing as synonymous with reading from an early age. Along with her formal education, Hacker considers the reading of poetry as a great influence on the formation of herself as a writer. In her interview with Finch, she emphasizes this point when she discusses her methods of conducting poetry workshops: "When I teach writing, I'm always teaching reading as well.... Too many students enroll in writing courses in American universities as an alternative—not an enhancement—to taking literature courses. They want to write, but they've never read anything. That offends and perplexes me as an inveterate reader—but it's also a damned shame for them."

When asked by interviewer Karla Hammond to name the writers that she read and who she felt most influenced her, Hacker immediately named women writers: "Adrienne Rich is the one who first comes to mind. I've been reading her with great interest since about 1972.... Another writer with whom I've felt a strong affinity is Judy Grahn. I was lucky enough to know about her work since 1968 or 1969 when we were both in San Francisco. Audre Lorde is awfully good: both on the page and to hear aloud." Hacker reads mostly women poets, though she admits in her interview with Finch that there have been some touchy moments when she has felt at odds with the women writers she has most admired: "Adrienne Rich's love-hate relation with fixed forms touches me more directly. I'm a writer who's a woman, Jewish, lesbian, feminist, urban, as she is herself: there's no way I could not have felt implicated by her decision, in the early 1970s, not only to reject traditional prosody, but to state that she was doing so out of feminist convictions, out of her relationship, as a woman, with the language and the canon. But my own self-examination, as much visceral as rational, did not produce the same recoiling."

Although Hacker voices and acts on her commitments to women throughout her life, she never confuses this commitment with deference to their politics. She strives to establish and maintain her voice among the many women writers she cherishes, rather than to echo their concerns.

In 1961, Hacker married the African-American novelist Samuel R. Delany. They had a child, Iva Alyxander Hacker-Delany, about whom Hacker writes continuously. Hacker, a lesbian, and Delany, a gay man, were married for thirteen years. Since their divorce, Hacker has had love relationships with women. She writes about these relationships with a range of emotion throughout her poetry. She currently lives with her lover, Karyn London.

With the publication in 1974 of *Presentation Piece,* for which she won the Discovery/The Nation Award, the Lamont Poetry Book Award, and the National Book Award, Hacker achieved immediate acclaim and has remained a significant figure in poetry from that moment. She has authored eleven books: *The Terrible Children* (1967); *Highway Sandwiches* (1970); *Presentation Piece* (1974); *Separations* (1976); *Taking Notice* (1980); *Assumptions* (1985); *Love, Death, and the Changing of Seasons* (1987); *Going Back to the River* (1990), which received a Lambda Literary Award; *The Hang-Glider's Daughter* (1990); *Winter Numbers* (1994), which received a Lambda Literary Award and the Academy of American Poets/The Nation Lenore Marshall Prize; and, *Selected Poems 1965-1990* (1994), which received the 1996 Poets' Prize. Poetry is central to Hacker's life as is commitment to women: "Right now, primary commitment to women, on every possible level, is central to my life: politically, in my personal relationships, and with respect to what I'm attempting to do in my work and with other writers" (Hammond). Hacker has not swayed in this vision from the moment she set out to write: To be a superb writer of fixed form poetry and to write women's lives into these forms.

Collection Establishes Voice, Wins National Book Award

Marilyn Hacker lived in London and worked as a book dealer throughout the early seventies. In 1974, she became both mother to Iva and a National Book Award winner. *Presentation Piece* immediately established Marilyn Hacker as one of the most significant writers of the day. This book brings together the graphic images and forthright language about love that would become Hacker trademarks. As well, it attends to fixed forms and the gathering of intriguing, time-bound quotes that have resonance for all people of this generation. Lines such as "Take another little/piece of my heart now baby," from the title poem "Presentation Piece" resuscitate Janis Joplin's scratchy voice as if it were fraught with prophetic meaning. Joplin provides one of the multiple quotes residing in this poem that serves as part of a presentation piece for the times, a piece that tells us "One of these messages may be for you."

Presentation Piece also includes feminist commentary. The female persona gazes at the male's inadequacies in "She Bitches about Boys":

> Girls love a sick child or a healthy animal.
> A man who's both itches them like an incubus,
> but I, for one, have had a bellyful
> of giving reassurances and obvious
> advice with scrambled eggs and cereal

This gaze constitutes a flash of knowledge and resistance to come.

In "Sestina," Hacker displays the graphic language of sexuality that will become part and parcel of her expressive system of poetics throughout her career. Hacker portrays male genitalia: "Your cock whispers/ inside my thigh that there is language/without memory."

She includes in this book a number of fixed forms including the sonnet sequence "A Christmas Crown." As well, she includes villanelles and sestinas. All of her skills are apparent and honestly delivered in this book. What comes thereafter is enhancement of these skills. Felicia Mitchell reminds us that "The images of the body, the harsh and honest sounds and words of common language, which are held by the form, and the sense of humor ensuring that disappointment never seems like despair constitute Hacker's mark." The book demanded attention for all the reasons that Hacker has proved worthwhile reading throughout her career.

In the years following publication of *Presentation Piece,* Hacker has moved back and forth between the United States and Paris. She has held a variety of visiting creative-writing professorships, has edited a number of literary magazines, including the feminist literary magazine *13th Moon* (State University of New York, Albany) in the mid-1980s, an issue of *Ploughshares,* and a four-year stint as editor of the *Kenyon Review,* and has been a single mother.

Passionate Lesbian Sonnet Sequence Finds Audience

Love, Death, and the Changing of the Seasons (1986) chronicles in sonnets the cycle of love between two lesbians. The cycle begins simply, with mere hugs: "Hug; hug; this time I brushed my lips/just across yours, and fire down below/in February flared," and ends one year—212 pages—later: "I drank our one year out in brine instead/of honey from the seasons of your tongue." Throughout the sequence, Hacker captures emotions in the slowest, most minute details: mundane intimacies, out-of-control moments, heartwrenching rejections, warnings unheeded, ensuing neediness and suffocating clinginess, cooling off, loneliness, loss, absence, anger, and ultimate acceptance of a love ended. It reads like a narrative of people about whom you care deeply. She creates people with stunning emotional capacities, capacities that we see in ourselves, capacities from which we want to protect ourselves, and capacities we want to enjoy again. At times you want to call out to the "I," "hold back," "be careful," and at other times, you want to say: "call her," "take a risk." It is an incredibly interactive piece of writing, an engaging, humble, loving text, a text about human beings at their most vulnerable: Human beings in love.

Hacker's sense of love and poetic form is that it is fraught with humor. In the beginning of the relationship between Hacker and Rachel, she quips:

> I venture it's a trifle premature
> to sign the china-pattern registry
> before you are, at least, at liberty
> to hang your PJ's on my bathroom door.

In another sonnet, she depicts fantasizing about Rachel, her new lover, and masturbating on a friend's couch:

> Which didn't deter, me then from lying down
> on Jackie's couch, for the first time in days,

to let my hands and mind go back a ways,
and forward, in, against, above, around,
until I said your name (what corn) and came.
(I didn't muck up the upholstery,
Jax).

This humor is one that catches her laughing at herself and at the melodrama of sexual fantasy. Moaning Rachel's name and joking about the love stains on the furniture demonstrate Hacker's determination to bring the beauty of the sexual imagination to the fixed form and prescribed rhythms of the sonnet—what better form to contain the rhythms of love.

Once the lovers both embrace coupledom and try living together, the sonnets become less humorous and more intensely loving:

Sweetheart, I'm still not getting enough sleep,
but I'm not tired, and outside it's spring
in which we sprang the afternoon shopping
after I'd been inside you, O so deep
I thought we would be tangled at the roots.
I think we are. (I've never made such noise.
I've never come so hard, or come so far
in such a short time.)

Hacker excels at depicting the intensity of the sexual experiences between two new lovers. She helps us to remember the experience and to delight in it again. She captures love in an eternal present. She permits us to share again in this private, mysterious world:

Sometimes, when you're asleep, I want to do
it to myself while I'm watching you. It
would be easy, two fingers along my clit,
back, in, back out. Your skin's heat comes into
me adjacent.

Hacker writes about her relationships with women, and she writes in fixed forms because it brings her pleasure. "I write the way I do because it's the way that gives me most pleasure, and which finds me my way into the poem" (Finch). When Hacker uses phrases such as "my way," she means more than just the simple "my" of a singular individual.

Hacker believes that "as a woman becomes more and more politicized, as a feminist, she realizes that her concerns are concrete, that while they apply to the world at large, her perceptions of them begin as perceptions of her own life. The political concerns express something that permeates her whole life, permeates *my* whole life" (Hammond). Hacker will continue to chronicle the process of women making changes and making connections in their own worlds and the world at large.

Selected Poems 1965-1990: A Lifetime of Women

Sometimes women are unable to connect with one another. Hacker is especially compassionate about this inability, and she is not afraid to use her own experience as grounds for poetic musing: In the last poem included in *Selected Poems,* "August Silence," Hacker painfully and courageously resurrects the relationship she had with her dying mother-in-law, Iva's grandmother:

Because you are
my only daughter's only grandmother,
because your only grandchild is my child
I would have wished you to be reconciled

to how and what
I live. No name frames our connection, not
"in-laws." I hoped, more than "your son's ex-wife."
I've known you now for two-thirds of my life.

Much of Hacker's life work has been to frame the nameless inside the names, to work on providing forms for the formless. She has already succeeded, and she has not yet run out of stamina for the future. Marilyn Hacker's importance to poetry is synonymous with her persistent contribution of her own life experiences and her own life's wisdom to the feminist lesbian canon.

Current Address: 230 West 105th Street, #10A, New York, New York 10025.

References:

Finch, Annie. "An Interview on Form," in *American Poetry Review,* vol. 25, no. 3, May/June 1996: 23-27.

Hacker, Marilyn. *Love, Death, and the Changing of the Seasons.* New York: Norton, 1986.

———. *Selected Poems 1965-1990.* New York: Norton, 1994.

Hammond, Karla. "An Interview with Marilyn Hacker," in *Frontiers,* vol. 3, 1981: 22-27.

Mitchell, Felicia. "Marilyn Hacker," in *Dictionary of Literary Biography,* vol. 120. Detroit: Gale, 1992: 102-08.

—Renee R. Curry

Hadrian

76 A.D.-123 A.D.

Roman Emperor

Hadrian was a lover of all things Greek. Chief among these loves was Antinous, the Greek boy from the bucolic town of Bithynia. Although scholars disagree, it is generally believed that Hadrian was born in Rome, and spent at least part of his youth in Spain. He was later educated in Greece, an idyllic period that firmly established him as a Grecophile. In spite of his overarching and determined ambition, Hadrian's political/military career was exemplary but unspectacular. His first speech before the Senate was greeted with guffaws due to his provincial dialect, a humiliation that prompted him to hire an actor to tutor him in speech.

In the early years of his reign, Hadrian was successful at placating the hard-to-please Senate and acquired a reputation for tolerance and generosity toward his provincial subjects. He was also a reformer who promulgated a new legal code and humanized the treatment of slaves. He was certainly the most well-traveled of the Roman emperors. The Empire is replete with examples of Hadrian's obsession for building things. Everywhere he went he initiated pub-

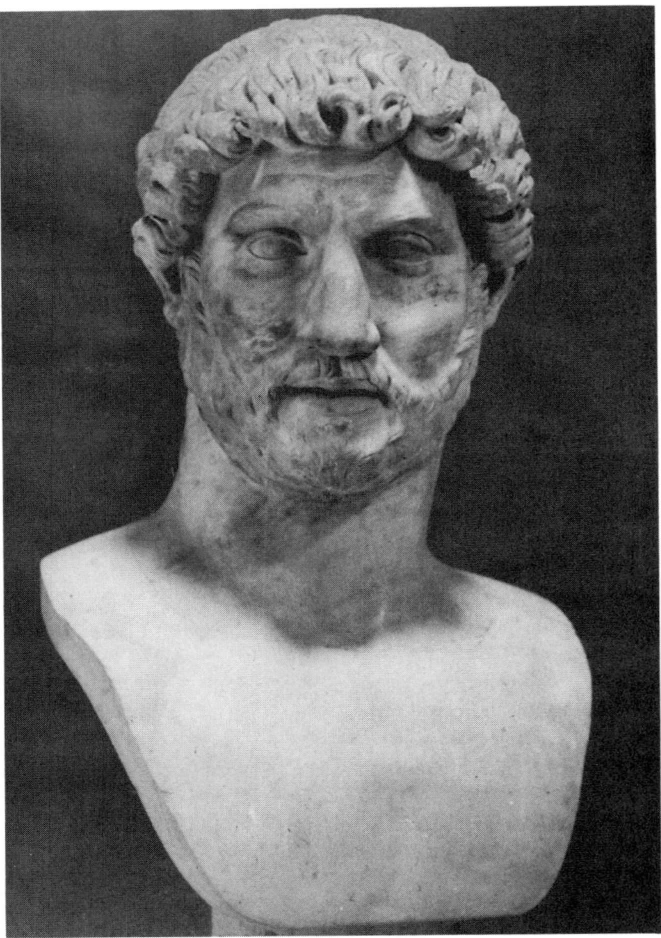

Hadrian

lic works projects, from bridges to temples to aqueducts. The peace and prosperity of Hadrian's rule are exemplified in his "Peace Under Rome" policy, a personal ideology that strove to unify Greek culture with Roman sovereignty.

Hadrian's country retreat, the villa at Tibur, reflected the many visages of his temperament: mercurial, eclectic, a melange of sights and souvenirs from his travels, a mix of artistic styles.

Historical evidence indicates that Hadrian developed an early attraction for members of his own sex, and there are accounts that reveal Hadrian and his predecessor Trajan competing for each other's lovers. Hadrian did marry (Trajan's great-niece Sabina) but it was a cold, childless relationship. Historians differ as to whether Sabina was a frigid harpy or Hadrian a neglectful leach—the truth probably lies somewhere in between. Hadrian was reputed to have had lovers of both sexes, but with women he seemed most comfortable in relationships that were maternal in nature. He was very close to Plotina, Trajan's wife, and it is believed she may have been instrumental in getting him named emperor. (No one knows for sure whether Trajan's death-bed "adoption" of Hadrian was authentic, and some historians suggest that, aided by Plotina, Hadrian claimed his succession under dubious circumstances.)

Antinous, the boy from Bithynia, was clearly the great and enduring love of Hadrian's life. Hadrian's relationship with Antinous is believed to have been his only truly intimate one. His obsession with the boy was extravagant and conspicuous even in a society tolerant of such relationships.

In his relationship with Antinous, Hadrian was acting within an established institution of pederasty. This practice honored the relationship between the *erastes*, an older man between 20 and 40, and the *eromenous*, a boy between the age of 12 and 18. Although sexual in nature, the relationship also took the form of mentor and novice, with the older man guiding the younger in physical and intellectual development as well as in civic responsibilities. Such relationships were intended to be short-lived, and generally ended with the onset of manhood, evidenced most clearly by a hirsute body, around the age of 18.

When Antinous drowned himself in the Nile at the age of 20 (some scholars say 18), Hadrian was inconsolable. The mystery surrounding his death continues to this day—the longest and least conclusive inquest in all of history. Some say Hadrian forced Antinous to kill himself as a means of prolonging his own life (one of the many quirky religious ideas of the time). Others suggest that Antinous died while undergoing voluntary castration in an effort to preserve his fading beauty. Still others surmise that Antinous' death was a ritual sacrifice ending with Hadrian inspecting his dead lover's entrails in order to ascertain omens, but there is no clear evidence of this. The more plausible explanation is that Antinous, fully aware of the limitations imposed upon his relationship with Hadrian and fearful of what his position was to be following its demise, opted for an escape that would be both beneficial to Hadrian and honorable to himself. Hadrian and Antinous would have been aware of the Egyptian belief that those who drowned in the Nile were sacred and would be deified. Antinous' sacrifice would not only guarantee Hadrian a longer life, but it would ensure Antinous' own immortality.

Hadrian was not the same man after Antinous' death. Illness and grief made him a harsher, more suspicious ruler. His sanctions against the Jews were particularly severe, earning him the title "Hadrian the Wicked." At his death he was generally reviled, his earlier munificence forgotten.

In the eight years left to Hadrian following Antinous' death, the Emperor made certain the world would not forget his beloved. Antinous came to signify the new classical ideal in Greek sculpture: sensual contours, low brow, heavy lips, dreamy eyes—the embodiment of beauty and youth. His likeness was venerated throughout the Empire; over 500 sculptures survive to this day. Antinous games were established in Athens, Argos, and Eleusis, and a city was founded in Egypt near the place where Antinous drowned, named Antinoopolis. Hadrian actively promoted the cult of Antinous-Dionysos, with its unique priests and rituals, and at his own villa at Tibur, surrounded himself with inadequate facsimiles of the boy he loved.

In the nineteenth century, the English poet Alfred Lord Tennyson, strolling among the Roman sculptures in the British museum, paused before Antinous' bust and declared, "Ah—this is the inscrutable Bithynian. If we knew what he knew, we would understand the ancient world."

References:

Grant, Michael. *The World of Rome*. Cleveland: World Publishing, 1960.

Lambert, Royston. *Beloved and God: The Story of Hadrian & Antinous*. New York: Meadowland Books, 1988.

Perowne, Stewart. *Hadrian.* London and Southampton: Hodder and Soughton by the Camelot Press, 1960.
Salmon, Edward T. *A History of the Roman World: 30 BC to AD 138.* London: Butler & Tanner, 1944.
Schmidt, Joel. *Hadrian: A Novel.* San Francisco, California: Gay Sunshine Press, 1984.
Time-Life editors. *Rome: Echoes of Imperial Glory.* Alexandria: Time-Life, 1994.
Wallace, Alexander. "The Genius of Hadrian," in *Archaeology,* March/April 1996: 68.
Yourcenar, Marguerite. *Memoirs of Hadrian.* New York: Random House, 1954.

—Lynda Schrecengost

Radclyffe Hall

1880-1943

British writer

Radclyffe Hall is best known as the author of the famous lesbian novel *The Well of Loneliness.* She was a successful writer by the time *The Well of Loneliness* was published and embarked upon it with the intention of creating, according to Una Troubridge in *The Life and Death of Radclyffe Hall,* "a book on sexual inversion, a novel that would be accessible to the general public who did not have access to technical treatises." It was published in 1928 and created much controversy. Court cases led to the book being banned in both the United Kingdom and the United States. The American verdict was overturned on appeal, but the book remained unpublished in the United Kingdom until 1949.

Radclyffe Hall was born Marguerite Radclyffe Hall on 12 August 1880, at Christchurch, Bournemouth, England; in later life she was called John by her friends and M. Radclyffe Hall or simply Radclyffe Hall in her books. Her mother, Marie, was American and her father, Radclyffe Radclyffe Hall—or Rat—was British. Her parents divorced in 1882 and Marie remarried a musician, Albert Visetti, whom Radclyffe Hall did not like.

Hall's first romantic attachment was to a singer called Agnes Nicholls who boarded with her mother. After she came of age and inherited her grandfather's considerable fortune, Hall visited her American family and developed close friendships with her cousins Jane Randolph and Dorothy Diehl. Hall claimed that she was never in the slightest attracted to men.

Hall wrote poetry from an early age, and her first volume of poems, *'Twixt Earth and Stars,* was published in 1906. However, at that time, her main interests were hunting and travel. On 22 August 1907, at the German spa of Homburg, Hall met Mabel Batten, a 50-year-old married woman with a grown daughter. Mabel, or Ladye as her friends called her, had been a renowned beauty and was a keen amateur singer. They became lovers and Batten influenced Hall greatly, encouraging her to pursue her poetry writing. The year 1908 saw the publication of Hall's second book, which included "Ode to Sapho," and her third volume came out a year later. When Batten's husband died in 1910, the two women made a home together. Hall's fourth poetry anthology was dedicated to Mrs. George Batten and more volumes of poetry followed.

Batten introduced Hall to lesbian society and to Catholicism, and Hall began to develop a masculine image, wearing tailored jackets and stiff collars. They both remained in England during World War I (1914-18) due to Batten's ill health, and Hall began to try writing fiction.

Early Troubles

In 1915, Hall met Una Troubridge and began a relationship with her that was to last the rest of her life. Troubridge was a professional artist with a young daughter named Andrea and was married to a naval captain, Ernest Troubridge. This affair caused an uneasy situation between Batten, Troubridge, and Hall until Batten died in 1916.

Afterwards, Hall and Troubridge developed an interest in spiritualism and began regular seances with a medium, Mrs. Osborne Leonard, believing that Batten's spirit advised them. Sir Oliver Lodge, a member of the Royal Society and former president of the Society for Psychical Research (SPR), encouraged the two women to write a research paper about their seances. However, Cara, Batten's daughter, complained to the SPR that the women's relationship affected their research methods.

In 1919, Troubridge and her husband agreed to a legal separation, allowing her and Hall to organize more settled domestic arrangements. Hall also returned to novel writing, starting the book that would be published as *The Unlit Lamp.* However, Hall's problems

Radclyffe Hall

were not over. In 1920 George Lane Fox Pitt of the SPR accused Hall and Troubridge of writing an "immoral" paper after talking with Troubridge's husband. Hall and Troubridge sued for slander and won a close victory.

Literary Success

In 1923, Hall acquired a literary agent, Audrey Heath, and began *The Forge,* published by Arrowsmith in 1924. This sold well and Cassell agreed to publish *The Unlit Lamp. A Saturday Life,* her third novel, was released on 1 April 1925 with a jacket designed by Troubridge. Hall started to write *Adam's Breed,* which the American publisher Russell Doubleday took on.

Adam's Breed was released on 4 March 1926 to great reviews. In early July, Hall completed the short story "Miss Ogilvy Finds Herself," which dealt with homosexuality, and 12 days later started writing *Stephen,* the novel that became *The Well of Loneliness.*

The Well of Loneliness

The Well of Loneliness, a tragic novel about the life of a lesbian, conveys the message that lesbians cannot help being what they are and are unfairly persecuted by society. Hall researched scientific theories about homosexuality, especially those of Havelock Ellis, an English sexologist who believed that homosexuality was "congenital." She had trouble finding a publisher, eventually persuading Jonathan Cape to take it on in the United Kingdom and Alfred Knopf in the United States.

The Well of Loneliness appeared in 1928 and initial sales and reviews were good. Then on Sunday, 19 August, the *Sunday Express* printed a damning article labelling it immoral; "I would rather give a healthy boy or a healthy girl a phial of prussic acid than this novel. Poison kills the body, but moral poison kills the soul." The book became headline news and sales rocketed. On Wednesday, 22 August, the Home Secretary instructed Cape to stop the book or face legal proceedings for obscenity. U.K. publication stopped, but Cape began printing it in Paris. Nevertheless, uneasy American publishers halted the scheduled U.S. October release.

On 4 October, Dover customs officers seized a shipment of the novel bound for London. They released the books on the 18th, but only so that the Metropolitan Police could use Lord Campbell's Obscene Publications Act of 1857 to confiscate and destroy copies in shops and at Cape's Bedford Square office.

The courts were packed for the trial. Hall was not asked to stand in the witness box and the presiding magistrate disallowed all but the first expert witness for the defense on the grounds that opinions were not evidence. He decided for the prosecution, saying that the book's subject matter was obscene. A December appeal failed to overturn the verdict.

However, the book continued to sell well in France. In America, the Covici Friede imprint was similarly seized by New York Police and charges brought. The verdict of the first trial was that the book was obscene, but an appeal reversed the verdict.

Despite her disappointment, Hall started work on a new novel, published in 1932 as *The Master of the House.* Hall's writing was heavily influenced by Catholicism and in this novel the hero dies by crucifixion. Oddly, while writing it, Hall claimed to have developed stigmata in her hands. The book sold well initially, but reviews were disappointing. In 1934, a collection of short stories called *Miss Ogilvy Finds Herself* was released but, again, reviews were slightly disappointing.

At this time Hall met Evgenia Souline, a Russian nurse hired when Troubridge contracted enteritis while on holiday. Hall and Souline embarked on an affair which lasted until shortly before Hall's death, causing unhappiness for Troubridge, who stayed with her throughout. Hall's health collapsed in 1943 and an examination revealed that she had cancer of the rectum. Operations were unsuccessful and she died on 6 October after several painful months, watched over by Troubridge, her faithful companion until the end.

References:

Baker, Michael. *Our Three Selves: A Life of Radclyffe Hall.* London: Hamish Hamilton Ltd., 1985.

Hall, Radclyffe. *The Well of Loneliness.* London: Jonathan Cape Ltd., 1928.

Troubridge, Una. *The Life and Death of Radclyffe Hall.* London: Hammond and Hammond 1961.

—Lucya Szachnowski

Dag Hammarskjold

1905-1961

Swedish diplomat

Dag Hammarskjold's position in world political history is secure. As the United Nation's Secretary General at the height of the Cold War, he created and shaped the role of the UN in its international peace-keeping efforts. It was a position to which he brought his own vigorous, yet patient style of activism, one characterized by unrelenting tenacity and seemingly boundless energy. His appointment to the UN followed a brilliant political career in Sweden. He had progressed from positions in the Treasury Department to the Foreign Ministry as secretary-general, then as Minister of State in the Foreign Office. In 1951 he was appointed vice-chairman of the Swedish delegation to the United Nations. By 1953, the position of Trygve Lie, the first secretary-general, had become untenable because of the Soviet Union's active opposition to him, and, simultaneously, mistrust of him in the United States right-wing press. A new secretary-general was needed, one who would be acceptable to both the Communist bloc nations, led by the Soviet Union, and to the western powers. After a large number of potential candidates had been proposed, and rejected, the name of Dag Hammarskjold was submitted and was found acceptable.

When the time came to announce the appointment, Matt Gordon, a press officer of the UN, gave a short biographical description of Hammarskjold's accomplishments. "And a fairy!" interrupted a voice from the audience. When told of this interruption and comment, Dag shrugged his shoulders and said nothing. (The incident is recounted in *Hammarskjold*, by Emery Kelen.)

Early Years

Dag Hammarskjold was born 29 July 1905, in Jonkoping, Sweden, the son of the statesman Hjalmar Hammarskjold, who was prime minister during World War I and who had achieved fame for keeping Sweden out of the war. He had had an illustrious political career previous to the war, but as food shortages developed during the course of the war he took the blame and resigned under pressure in 1917.

By all accounts, Hjalmar Hammarskjold was an austere, unemotional man, a disciplinarian and a severe judge. He was a person who took most seriously his sense of duty to his principles, born in large part of his background and his stern Lutheran Christianity. He was descended from an old Swedish family, one noted for the large number of military and governmental leaders it had produced. Dag Hammarskjold inherited from his family and his background a very large measure of a personal sense of duty, and, in his case, duty both to country and humanity as a whole.

Dag Hammarskjold was awarded his first degree from Uppsala University in 1925 and his law degree in 1930 from the same university. Almost immediately, he was appointed to a governmental position on a committee for unemployment, a post which he held until 1934. In 1934 he received a Ph.D. in political economy from Uppsala. After earning his doctorate, he held a number of offices in the Department of Finance and related governmental advisory boards.

International Statesman

In the international sphere, Hammarskjold served on several commissions dealing with economic matters between Sweden and other countries, primarily after World War II. These efforts culminated in his participation as Sweden's delegate at the Paris Conference in 1947, the organizational meeting for the Marshall Plan. Participation in other post-war economic meetings continued, until 1952 when he was sent to the United Nations as vice-chairman of the Swedish delegation, and again in 1953 as head of the delegation.

In his role as secretary-general, he showed himself to be an active, forceful leader, no doubt the most assertive of all the secretaries-general up until the present. This was the preconceived vision he had of the role of the secretary-general before his election, and the international conditions prevailing in the 1950s gave him ample opportunity to prove his mettle. The crises that involved UN action during those years are well known.

UN involvement in the Suez crisis of 1956, precipitated by Egypt's nationalization of the canal and subsequent refusal to allow passage of Israeli vessels, helped to avert what then threatened to become all-out war in the Middle East, possibly involving the super powers. Lebanon became another potential flash point of international armed hostility in 1958. Before then, Lebanon's government had reflected the more or less equal division between the Christian and Moslem populations. With the Moslem population growing larger, civil war threatened and the political parties began to draw foreign governments into the conflict. An American landing of armed forces did actually occur at one point. After lengthy negotiations, Hammarskjold persuaded all sides to withdraw in order to allow direct negotiations on the parts of Lebanese parties involved in the conflict. Although those measures prevented the crisis in 1958 from expanding, the subsequent history of the Middle East has continued to be turbulent and bloody. Still, the principles espoused and put into action then—that of a neutral UN presence with intense dialogue between adversaries—have continued to be a generally productive modus operandi.

Dag Hammarskjold

The first series of political crises in the Belgian Congo (now Zaire) presented Hammarskjold with some of the most difficult and dangerous problems of his secretariat. His involvement ended up costing his life, finally, under circumstances that are still suspicious.

The precipitous withdrawal of the Belgian civil service from the Congo in 1960, upon the granting of freedom to the country, eventually led to murderous rivalry for leadership among various Congolese factions. The ongoing crisis threatened to involve outside intervention from the Soviet Union, as well as from other countries, and once again Hammarskjold called upon the UN for peace-keeping forces. The UN had not finished its work when Dag Hammarskjold was killed in a plane crash in Ndola, Northern Rhodesian (now Zambia) on 18 September 1961.

Personal Life

Dag Hammarskjold was a very private person. His few close friends were very devoted. They would never have divulged anything of a personal nature, especially in the area of sexual matters, if Hammarskjold had not wished it. Still, even without a tell-tale letter or two, or the memoirs of some embittered lover, the evidence seems convincing that he was homosexual.

Conor Cruise O'Brien was a member of the Irish delegation during a part of the Congolese crisis; he served in the Congo as a member of the UN Secretariat and, for a time, as representative of the secretary-general in Katanga. He later wrote a play concerning this period in the Congo, *Murderous Angels*. Hammarskjold is depicted as homosexual in the play, though only, as O'Brien explains, because it makes for good drama. O'Brien is comfortable with the idea of homosexuality and certainly has no axes to grind. Nonetheless, O'Brien observes in the preface to *Murderous Angels* that at the UN (and outside) Hammarskjold was "generally reputed" to be gay. Sven Stolpe, Hammarskjold's long-term friend and admirer, wrote of him (in *Dag Hammarskjold: A Spiritual Portrait*) that "I sometimes felt that for all his polite talk at parties he never visually discriminated between a shapely woman and, say, a sofa or a chair." In an account from yet another observer, one time one of Hammarskjold's personal bodyguards, a new one at the time, asked him, "How about the girls, Mr. Secretary-General?" Hammarskjold replied that he would answer him some other time. Hammarskjold was later asked the same question, by the same bodyguard. He replied that when young, he had been interested in *a* girl, [my italics] "but then I began to study hard and had no more time for girls" (Emery Kelen, *Hammarskjold*). One wonders if this simple-minded answer is an example of Hammarskjold's well-known wit, delivered for his own pleasure if not for that of this ingenuous questioner.

Of the people who knew Dag Hammarskjold well, the consensus is that he probably was gay, though celibate, at least during the years at the UN when he had such a high, public profile. Of the younger years of his life, one can only wonder. We might ask, for example, if the following "memorial" poem, written by Hammarskjold in 1959, sounds like one written by a dedicated celibate?

A church spire, erect on the plain
Like a phallus.
The boy in the forest
Throws off his best Sunday suit
And plays naked.
***
Black shooting-stars,
The swallows utter shrill cries
As they mate in mid-air.
***
He lowered his eyes
Lest he should see the body
To lust after it.
***
Denied the Sought-After
He longed to deserve
To be the Sought-After.
***
Honey suckle
In a grey twilight
His sensuality awoke.

References:

Besko, Bo. *Dag Hammarskjold: Strictly Personal.* New York: Doubleday & Co., 1969.

Hammarskjold, Dag. *Markings,* translated by Leif Sjoberg and W. H. Auden. New York: Alfred A. Knopf, 1966.

Kelen, Emery. *Hammarskjold.* New York: G.P. Putnam's Sons, 1966.

O'Brien, Conor Cruise. *Murderous Angels.* Boston: Little, Brown and Company, 1968.

Stolpe, Sven. *Dag Hammarskjold: A Spiritual Portrait.* Trans. Naomi Walford. New York: Charles Scribner's Sons, 1966.

Urquhart, Brian. *Hammarskjold.* New York: Alfred A. Knopf, 1972.

—Robert N. Mory

Barbara J. Hammer

1939-

American filmmaker

Appropriately termed "the mother of lesbian film" for her ground-breaking experimental techniques and themes, Barbara Hammer is an award-winning auteur/spokesperson for both lesbian and independent, avant-garde film. She has made over 80 films and videos since 1968, consciously choosing to remain outside standard narrative forms, opting instead for a more somatic, poetic, and often highly erotic approach that involves the camera as "caresser." This prioritization of her own aesthetics over traditional patriarchal strictures has earned her films a reputation for being sensual, intellectually stimulating, and always challenging.

Born 15 May 1939 in Hollywood, California, Hammer traces her earliest artistic influences to her maternal grandmother, Anna Kusz. As Cathleen Rountree relates in her book *Coming into Fullness: On Women Turning Forty*, Barbara learned from Anna early on "that art is anything you say it is,... the most important decision is to keep making it."

Barbara's mother, Marian Hammer, was likewise an early influence, albeit from the other end of the spectrum. Marian's immigrant, Ukrainian, working-class background fostered a desire to rise above her class, and Barbara's freckle-faced precociousness pointed toward a financial way upward following the twinkling, tapping lead of Shirley Temple. Lack of money for the right acting classes squelched the fantasy, but the seed of Barbara's love for the theater was planted. "It would be very curious for her [Marian] to see that I am involved in film," Hammer told Rountree in 1991, "but on the other side of the camera."

In 1961, Hammer received a bachelor's degree in psychology from the University of California, Los Angeles, married the day after graduation, and moved to San Francisco with her husband, where she enrolled in the Master's Program in English at San Francisco State University. A series of what she calls "social jobs" followed which, according to Raymond Murray's *Images in the Dark*, included "counseling for emotionally disturbed teenagers, playground supervision, and even a bank job."

It did not take long for Barbara to realize that a vital, yearning, creative part of her was being neglected. "I wanted to stay home and *make things*," she told Rountree, "but I couldn't justify the self-indulgence." She was coming to terms with having overlooked that critically important period in a woman's life where, "she can make her own way in the world, earn money, travel, have an experience as a solitary individual, rather than as a child of a family, or the wife of a husband." A brief attempt to try to get pregnant proved unsuccessful—which in the end, according to Hammer, was lucky "because what I really wanted was to be an artist."

Barbara Hammer. ***Photograph by Glenn Halverson.***

Barbara Hammer did not come out as a lesbian or an artist until she was 30. Following a brief stint as a painter and a potter, she made her first Super-8mm short (*Schizy*) in 1968, a film that deals with an individual's conflicting masculine/feminine feelings. Her first 16mm film (*A Gay Day*) playfully satirizes marriage by showing two women, both in bridal gowns, rolling down a hill together. Next came the ground breaking *Dyketactics* (1974), a film encompassing how she feels her life changed once she began making love to women. It was hailed by many as the first truly erotic lesbian film to be made by a lesbian. *Superdyke* (1975) follows a gang of women in early guerilla-girl takeovers of San Francisco institutions, while *Menses* (1974) and *Women I Love* (1976) work to reclaim a celebratory femininity that has been buried in a society dominated by men.

According to Holly Willis in *Film Quarterly* (1994), her work "is both stridently lesbian and boldly experimental ... humorous stories which play with mythological images of women and critique the patriarchal world." At the same time, Hammer often forgoes formal filmmaking techniques with her disassembly of standard narrative, opting instead for animation, superimpositions, and optical printing techniques to appeal to a viewer's more experiential senses—like touch. "I began to connect touch and sight in my work in 1974 (*Dyketactics*)," Hammer told Willis. "I think that my sight is connected to my sense of touch.... It was Aldous Huxley who pointed out that children know the world through touching before they can ever see. We are touching even when we are sleeping!"

The year 1993 marked the premiere of Hammer's 51st feature-length film (*Nitrate Kisses*). It was termed by some critics (for example Canby and Ayscough) as a demanding, passionate, "heavy-hammering" documentary that examines the loss of queer history through the intercutting of newer and older experimental clips of lesbians and gay men—young and old—as they make love and talk of their experiences, both past and present. Most other reviews were less checkered, and *Nitrate Kisses* received acclaim at the Sundance Festival and won various awards at international festivals throughout 1993.

Hammer believes *Kisses* is her most intellectual film thus far. The experiential level of the camera caressing the couples throughout is still a major focus but, as Hammer told Willis, "I decided not to leave the research out of the film this time. I kept the quotes from the books that really influenced me ... and shot them. Some people feel like it breaks, but again, that's what I want it to do—break the continuity that is part of commercial cinema."

In 1995, Hammer's Making Visible Productions released *Out in South Africa*, Hammer's pastiche of interviews with lesbians and gay men throughout that country over several weeks in 1994—in the townships, at her film workshops, and at a retrospective festival of her films. True to form, the film is neither a linear narrative nor a straight documentary, and was met with reviews that reflected Hammer's ongoing artistic motivation to keep viewers examining the efficacy of traditional filmmaking/storytelling structure. Terms like "disturbing and exhilarating," "fascinating and frustrating" were used to describe the work, but always with the stipulation that it was a "must-see." In a review in the *Advocate* (7 February 1995), Victoria A. Brownworth called *Out in South Africa* "an uneven but intensely moving look at the personal and political struggles of an emerging lesbian and gay culture ... [held together] by Hammer's keen eye for complementary visual imagery."

In the end, Barbara Hammer's ongoing success as a filmmaker and an artist centers on a dual desire: a striving to make her films accessible to an ever-widening audience, and to maintain a visionary edge. The autobiographical *Tender Fictions* (winter 1995) reaches for this goal by broadening the future landscape for lesbian autobiography even as it challenges a younger gay/lesbian generation to carve their own identities from the Americana mold.

Hammer continues to promote and document lesbian visibility/sensibility by inviting women around the world to share their dreams, fantasies, and aspirations via her Web Page on the Internet. "We don't want to always be looking at our own cultural product, we want to contribute to the general culture," Hammer told Owen Levy in *Moving Pictures Berlinale* (February 1996). "Our work shouldn't be closed off to the world at large and the world shouldn't close itself off."

Current Address: E-mail: http://www.echonyc.com/~lesbians.

References:

Ayscough, Suzan. "Nitrate Kisses," in *Variety* (New York), 1 February 1993: 100.

Brownworth, Victoria A. "The Final Frontier," in the *Advocate*, 7 February 1995: 61-63.

Canby, Vincent. "Postwar Western Gay Culture," in *New York Times*, 9 April 1993: C-10.

Levy, Owen. "Hammer Aims to Break out of the Ghetto," in *Moving Pictures Berlinale*, 23 February 1996.

Murray, Raymond. *Images in the Dark: An Encyclopedia of Gay and Lesbian Film and Video.* Philadelphia: TLA Publications, 1994.

Rountree, Cathleen. *Coming into Our Fullness: On Women Turning Forty*. Freedom, California: The Crossing Press, 1991.
Willis, Holly. "Uncommon History: An Interview with Barbara Hammer," in *Film Quarterly* (Berkeley, California), Summer 1994: 7-13.

—Jerome Szymczak

Lorraine Hansberry

1930-1965

African-American playwright

Still regarded by most as America's leading black playwright and a major name in the dramatic world, Lorraine Hansberry made history with the runaway success of her play *A Raisin in the Sun*, the first drama by a black author to be shown on Broadway. Impressive as her achievement is in the field of literature, she has now becoming recognized as a pioneering defender of lesbian relationships, as part of a wider campaign to apply the principles of the U.S. Constitution to all disadvantaged groups.

A Chicago Childhood

Lorraine Vivian Hansberry was born in Chicago, Illinois on 19 May 1930, the youngest daughter of Carl Augustus Hansberry and Nannie Perry Hansberry. Her father was a wealthy real estate broker, and Hansberry enjoyed a privileged upbringing in comparison with most of her school classmates. Paul Robeson, Dr. W.E.B. DuBois, and Langston Hughes were all friends of the family, and visited the Hansberry home when Lorraine was in her teens. All three were later to prove important influences on her writing career. From her parents Hansberry inherited an awareness of her own worth as an individual, and a burning desire for freedom and justice. As she grew up, her wide reading helped her to obtain a detailed knowledge of black hero-figures and role models, notably Toussaint L'Ouverture, and of past African civilizations and their achievements.

Hansberry was exposed to the violence of racism at an early age. In 1938 Carl Hansberry, a determined challenger of ethnic segregation, moved his family to a house in a white neighborhood between 61st and Rhodes, and immediately came under attack by local racists. On one occasion a mob gathered and stormed the house, and eight-year-old Lorraine was narrowly missed by a flung brick that came through the window and embedded itself in a wall. Jewel LaFontant, a friend of Lorraine's elder sister, remembered witnessing this incident. Later, a law suit was brought to evict the family, but Carl Hansberry did not scare easily, and brought a counterclaim that was fought all the way to the Supreme Court. The court eventually found in his favor in 1940, after a lengthy legal battle. Although Carl Hansberry won his case, his experiences of race hate left him embittered. As Lorraine remarked in an interview with the *New Yorker* on 9 May 1959: "Daddy felt he still didn't have his freedom in this country." In fact, he later decided to move the family to Mexico, but, before the move was completed, he died suddenly in 1946. These early experiences of prejudice had a lasting effect on Lorraine, but made her more determined not to be intimidated. She also used some of these incidents later in her own writing.

Lorraine Hansberry

Lorraine attended public schools in Chicago before going on to Englewood High School, from which she graduated in 1948. It was here she first became aware of the attraction of drama through school plays, and later watched performances of *The Tempest* and *Othello*, starring family friend Paul Robeson at the height of his fame. This interest in the theater was not always obvious to those who knew her. Jewel LaFontant noted that Lorraine was regarded as rather spoiled, having known only wealth as a child, where her elder siblings had experienced hard times. "Lorraine was very smart," LaFontant recalled in *An Autobiography of Black Chicago*. "She was very quiet and a little stand-offish. I was shocked when she turned out to be a brilliant playwright. She always wanted to be a doctor. I never thought of her in the theater or being a writer."

Writer and Activist

Lorraine went on to enroll at the University of Wisconsin where she studied art, geology and stage design. This led to a more detailed examination of dramatic structure and content, and she was able to see the plays of Strindberg and Ibsen in performance for the first time. The works of these writers had a profound effect on her as did the plays of the Irish dramatist Sean O'Casey, who was later to prove another stylistic influence. Hansberry loved his ability to convey complex, many-sided characters in a positive way, avoiding the familiar stereotypes.

At the same time, Lorraine took her first steps into politics, working as an activist for Progressive candidate Henry Wallace, and as chairperson for the Young Progressives of America. In 1949, she attended a University of Guadalajara art workshop at Ajijic, in Mexico, where she finally decided that she was not cut out to be a painter. By the time she left the University of Wisconsin to settle in New York in 1950, she had already written three unfinished plays and a number of short stories, and was sure of her future direction.

Hansberry's writing was allied to a strong social and political commitment, and during the early 1950s she campaigned actively on behalf of all disenfranchised groups. As a schoolgirl, she recalled feeling distanced from her poorer black classmates, who regarded her as an outsider and on one occasion beat her up, but in later years she came to admire their daily battle against racism and segregation, and vowed to carry on the fight for them as well as for herself. In 1951 she joined *Freedom* magazine, a campaigning journal founded by her friend Paul Robeson, for which she worked full-time for the next two years, rising to associate editor in 1952. Hansberry wrote lively, provocative articles on a variety of topics from worker participation to colonialism to emergent African nationalism in modern Kenya. Hers was a broad raft of freedoms, not merely ethnic but also personal and sexual, and she worked closely with fellow female activists. She was one of a women's delegation to fly to Jackson, Mississippi, to protest at the execution of the black youngster Willie McGee, and that summer covered the Communist trials in Foley Square. Later in 1951 she attended the Sojourners for Truth Conference in Washington, D.C.

It was in the same year that she met her future husband, Robert Nemiroff, on a picket line at New York University, where he was then a student. From the beginning, they established a close rapport that was to ripen into love and a lasting relationship that outlived their marriage.

By 1952 Hansberry was teaching at Frederick Douglass School as well as working for *Freedom* magazine, an appropriate choice for her, as Frederick Douglass was a much admired role-model whose books she studied in detail. Perhaps the most important event of the year for her was her appearance in Montevideo, Uruguay, where at age 22, she delivered an impressive speech to a banned peace congress in place of Paul Robeson, whose passport had been revoked by the United States government (then in the throes of McCarthyism). It was a courageous act, in keeping with Hansberry's commitment to the oppressed. Sadly, it resulted in her own passport being revoked.

The Ladder and *A Raisin in the Sun*

Hansberry married Robert Nemiroff on 20 June 1953, and gave up her post with *Freedom* but not her activism. She wrote further articles for the journal, while exploring her ethnic roots by studying African history with W.E.B. DuBois and teaching black literature at Jefferson School of Social Sciences. When Nemiroff's song "Cindy, Oh, Cindy" became a popular hit in 1956, the money enabled Hansberry to become a full-time writer.

Hansberry began work on her play *A Raisin in the Sun*, and in 1957 read her first draft to publisher Philip Rose. At this point she realized that the play had taken on a life of its own. That same year she made clear her commitment to freedom of expression for lesbians in a letter to the *Ladder*, a pioneering lesbian periodical. Here Hansberry connected anti-lesbian attitudes to anti-feminism and the oppression of women, commenting that: "It is time that 'half the human race' had something to say about the nature of its existence." Rejecting the immoral nature of a sexist society, she demanded a new approach "as per marriage, as per sexual practices, as per the rearing of children, etc.," and went on to claim that: "In this kind of work there may be women to emerge who will be able to formulate a new and possible concept that homosexual persecution and condemnation has at its roots not only social ignorance, but a philosophically active anti-feminist dogma." This uncompromising libertarian stance, at once far-sighted and, in 1957, extremely courageous, marked Hansberry's strong commitment as feminist and pro-lesbian spokesperson. Only in recent years has this contribution been noted.

Hansberry's dramatic masterpiece, *A Raisin in the Sun* (1959), brought immediate and lasting fame. Taking its title from a Langston Hughes poem ("What happens to a dream deferred?/ Does it dry up/ Like a raisin in the sun?"), the play focuses on the black Younger family—sturdy matriarch Lena, student daughter Beneatha, son Walter Lee, his wife Ruth and their child Travis—in their ghetto home in Chicago. When Lena inherits $10,000 insurance money from her dead husband, conflicts arise between them. Walter Lee, trapped in a hum-drum job, schemes to set up a liquor store, and is thwarted by Beneatha's medical ambitions and Lena's eventual decision to buy a house in a white neighborhood with the money. Walter Lee's frustration and anger are destructive, one with Beneatha's dismissive sarcasm. For a time, it seems he will accept the bribe, offered to the family with veiled threats by Kinder, who represents the hostile neighbors-to-be, but at the play's climax Walter Lee finally asserts himself, the family unites to reject the offer, and moves to its new home. A strong, positive drama which matches the "male lead" of Walter Lee with three strong female characters, *Raisin* draws directly on Hansberry's own experiences, not least in the figure of Beneatha. It emphasizes the strength and endurance of the black family, and its triumph in the face of long odds. The first play by a black author on Broadway, *Raisin* proved a runaway success, winning the New York Drama Critics Circle Award, and made Hansberry a household name. Her screenplay, completed in 1960, won the Cannes Film Festival Award in 1961.

Hansberry continued to write steadily through the 1960s. Her plays *The Drinking Gourd* and *Les Blancs*, not published in her lifetime, present deep and unsentimental visions of American slavery and violent African revolution respectively. Both were written in 1960, while *What Use Are Flowers?*, a bleak fable of post-nuclear survival, appeared in 1962.

Hansberry's continuing activism did not falter. In television appearances she rebuked Otto Preminger for the stereotypes and "bad art" in his movie version of *Porgy and Bess*, and in 1961 sparred with Norman Mailer over his view of black Americans in a series of letters to the *Village Voice*. She became increasingly involved in supporting the civil rights movement, and produced a sequence of masterly captions for a photographic work on civil rights and racism, *The Movement*, published in 1964.

Last Days

Sadly for Hansberry, time had already begun to run out. In 1963 she became unwell and an exploratory operation revealed the presence of duodenal cancer. She underwent a second operation later in the year, but the threat was not averted. Still a fervent campaigner, she confronted Attorney General Robert Kennedy over his record on civil rights, and in the same year met Malcolm X. The strains of her many activities took their toll on her marriage, and on 10 March 1964 she and Robert Nemiroff obtained a Mexican divorce. Despite the separation, they remained friends and continued to collaborate artistically. Hansberry named Nemiroff her legal executor, and he was responsible for the publishing and performance of many of her works after her death.

The Sign in Sidney Brustein's Window (1964) was the last of Hansberry's works to appear in her lifetime and opened on Broadway on 15 October 1964. Originally titled *The Sign in Jenny Reed's Window* and intended to feature a female leading character, it is perhaps the most difficult of Hansberry's plays due to the multiplicity of its themes. The main thread of the story deals with Sidney's gradual and painful awakening to personal commitment in the face of the apathy all about him, but the play also comments on the role of women, gay and interracial relationships, political shenanigans, and the strains of modern urban life. It met a mixed reception from critics and the public, but won the approval of several leading figures in the theatrical world. Later published by Nemiroff, it remains a complex, many-layered text that rewards the careful reader.

Hansberry died on 10 January 1965, in her 35th year. In the years following her death, Robert Nemiroff completed her play *Les Blancs*, which appeared on Broadway in 1970, and published it together with *The Drinking Gourd* and *What Use are Flowers?* as *Les Blancs: Collected Last Plays of Lorraine Hansberry* (1972). From her diaries, journals, letters and extracts from her previous work, he constructed a moving dramatic documentary of her life: *To Be Young, Gifted and Black*, which opened in New York in 1969 and proved a smash hit, touring nationally in 1970-72. *Raisin*, his musical adaptation of *A Raisin in the Sun*, was staged in 1973, and won a Tony Award for best Broadway musical.

Lorraine Hansberry is rightly regarded as the foremost of African-American dramatists. *A Raisin in the Sun* celebrates the strength of the black American family in the face of adversity—its ability to endure and overcome. It is also a tribute to the women of those families and their role in the winning of civic and personal freedom. In her plays and in her actions, Hansberry fought tirelessly for such freedoms, sacrificing her marriage, her health, and ultimately her life. Freedom of sexual expression and choice was clearly one of her main aims, and her letter to the *Ladder* showed the extent of her commitment.

References:

Cheney, Anne. *Lorraine Hansberry*. Boston: Twayne, 1984.

Current Biography. New York: H. W. Wilson, 1959.

Hansberry, Lorraine. *A Raisin in the Sun*. London: Methuen, 1960.

Hull, Gloria T., and others. *All the Women Are White, All the Blacks Are Men, but Some of Us Are Brave*. New York: Feminist Press, 1981.

Travis, Dempsey J. *An Autobiography of Black Chicago*. Chicago: Urban Research Institute Inc., 1981.

—Geoff Sadler

Keith Haring

1958-1990

American artist

Keith Haring's distinctive style, coupled with the visibility of the streets and subways of New York City, which he often chose as the venue for his art, served to make his work instantly recognizable. His thickly outlined, featureless figures have a nearly universal appeal, a sort of "everyperson" quality that cuts across gender, social, and cultural lines. Haring was not one to create merely—if at all—for art's sake, choosing instead to use his art to break down barriers and publicize issues, a quality that would often garner him criticism for being too commercial. One of the issues about which Haring was most concerned was AIDS, the disease that ultimately took his life at the age of 31.

Born in Kutztown, Pennsylvania, on 4 May 1958 to Allen and Joan Haring, the artist showed talent even at a young age. Haring's father, a foreman at an electricity plant, especially encouraged his son's creative endeavors. Drawing cartoons was a pastime for him, and he urged the younger Haring to use his imagination to create stories and to illustrate them. According to Haring in an interview with David Sheff in *Rolling Stone*, "In my mind, though, there was a separation between cartooning and being a quote-unquote artist. When I made the decision to be an artist, I began doing these completely abstract things that were as far away from cartooning as you could go."

Haring decided on his career at about the age of 16, around the same time he began taking hallucinogens. The drugs made him see shapes that found their way into his drawings, and creative antidrug commercials depicting the kinds of visions seen by users fascinated, rather than discouraged, him. Taking drugs, Haring believed, was a way to resist conforming to the conservative norm in his small hometown.

Convinced by his parents that artists should have a business background, Haring was briefly enrolled in a commercial art school. He quit when he realized that taking a nine-to-five job too often meant sacrificing one's own art. Attending a Pierre Alechinsky retrospective at the Carnegie Museum of Art, Haring was gratified to see that someone whose work was similar to his own could thrive as an artist, and he concluded that that was the path he wanted to follow.

Early Success Prompts a Move to New York

Haring applied for work at a public employment agency during his six-month stay in Pittsburgh and coincidentally ended up with a maintenance job at what is now the Pittsburgh Center for the Arts, the most important venue, after the museum, for art in Pittsburgh. He was allowed to use the facilities to paint increasingly larger canvases, and, in another fortunate twist, when an artist cancelled an upcoming exhibition, Haring was invited by the Center to show his work in the space. With this taste of success, as he told Sheff, "I knew I wasn't going to be satisfied with Pittsburgh anymore or with the life I was living there.... New York was the only place to go."

Despite having a live-in girlfriend, Haring had begun sleeping with men. When his girlfriend said she was pregnant, he realized that settling down, being a local artist and family man, was definitely not what he wanted. He arrived in New York's East Village in 1978, just when that area's art community was beginning to flourish.

Haring's first foray into graffiti art stemmed from his fascination with the literary cut-up method employed by William Burroughs and Brion Gysin in their book *The Third Mind*. Using headlines from the *New York Post*, Haring would randomly cut out words then paste them together to create realistic yet perplexing announcements. He turned these into handbills, posting them on the streets in order to make people stop and wonder at the arresting headlines.

In 1979 Haring went back to school, this time attending the School of Visual Arts, where he stayed for a year. While there studying abstract expressionism, he became increasingly disillusioned with the elitist attitudes of those in the art world and realized that creating "high" art held no appeal for him. Working in front of the open studio doors, Haring discovered that passersby often made more astute comments about his art than did others at the school, and he realized that these were the people he wanted to reach. Haring hoped to make art that was more accessible, wanting his work to be understood by many, not just a few.

Haring had begun drawing on huge rolls of paper, initially sketching abstracts, but more and more often images were appearing in the drawings. Influenced by the semiotics course he had taken, Haring thought of the images as symbols, a pictorial "vocabulary." "Suddenly it made sense to draw on the street, because I had something to say," Haring told Sheff. Two of his most popular and recognizable figures evolved from those early sketches: The Radiant Baby, a crawling child emanating rays of light, which began as a person on hands and knees; and the Barking Dog, an open-mouthed dog with sharp, jagged teeth. However, as Haring asserted to David Galloway in *Art in America,* "Much of what I do is chance. I don't really invent figures so much as I tap into a common image bank." Haring also began to incorporate Hispanic and African elements into his drawings, giving them an ethnic feel.

Inspiration Hits on the Subway

Riding the subway one day, Haring saw one of the uncovered spaces where advertisements are placed and decided it would be the perfect spot for a drawing. He began to notice these spots more frequently, and, using chalk on the soft black paper, which provided a sort of natural "frame," he was surprised to discover that, despite the fact they could easily have been wiped away, people had a sense of respect for the drawings and left them alone. Haring felt the sketches provided people with a sense of empowerment, allowing them to choose not to deface the drawings and thereby sustaining the contrast between the fragility of the images and the violence that occurred around them in the subways.

In the meantime Haring had become involved with a group of underground artists that would hold exhibitions in such unusual places as abandoned buildings. In 1980, Collaborative Projects (COLAB) organized an exhibit of a number of outsider artists, including Haring, in the Times Square Show. The exhibition marked the first time that works of graffiti artists had received any real recognition from those in the art world, and along with the work of Jean-Michel Basquiat—whom he greatly admired—Haring's drawings were singled out for praise.

Small crowds of people were beginning to gather whenever Haring would start to sketch in the subways, making the work seem almost like performance art. Intrigued by the opportunity for interaction, he started handing out buttons with drawings on them. Not only did this provide him with a means to get to know his audience, but the many different people wearing the buttons now had something in common, something on which to base their own interactions, and Haring was proud that his art could promote such a thing.

While Haring had been drawing on the streets and in the subways, he was also using friends' studios to do more traditional work. In order to quit the odd jobs he'd been working and paint full time, he needed to sell his work, so, after getting a studio of his own, Haring began allowing collectors and dealers to come and buy paintings directly from him, eschewing the accepted gallery route.

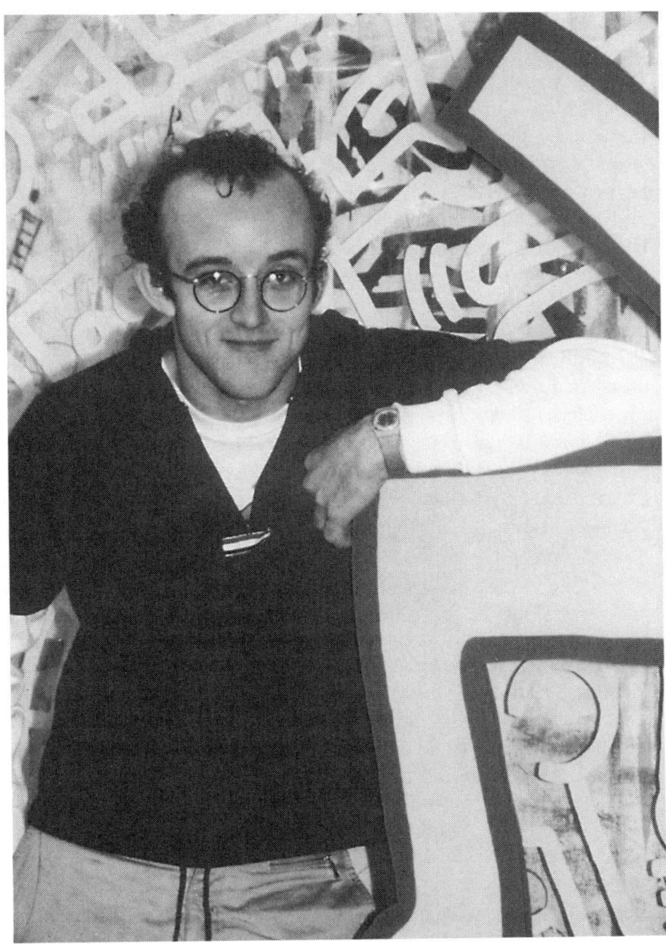

Keith Haring

He soon became disillusioned, however, with people constantly trying to bargain with him on prices he already considered quite reasonable. He decided that selling his work through a gallery would give him the distance he needed, and in 1982 Haring had his first solo show at a New York City gallery, the Tony Shafrazi Gallery in SoHo.

Haring's graffiti work was still important to him, though, and he continued to draw on the streets and in the subways, putting as much thought into these sketches as he did into a painting on canvas. However, while his work was popular with passersby and onlookers, the police were not quite as thrilled, and in 1982 he was arrested for criminal mischief. Undeterred by this and the death of graffiti artist Michael Stewart, who allegedly died as a result of a beating he received from the police, Haring continued to draw in public spaces. He was caught on a number of occasions and taken to the police station in handcuffs, but gradually even the police became fans, and he would end up being released. Sometimes the officers would actually ask for his autograph. Haring's "underground" work was collected in *Art in Transit, Subway Drawings by Keith Haring,* which was published in 1984.

Haring's Art Took Many Forms in Many Countries

Haring did not strictly stick to traditional drawing and painting but worked in other mediums as well. He painted Grace Jones's body for one of her performances; designed a jacket for his friend Madonna, whom he met soon after arriving in New York; made densely patterned totemic sculptures and brought his already kinetic two-dimensional figures even more to life by sculpting them in steel (three of these works are installed in the Dag Hammarskjöld Plaza Sculpture Garden at the United Nations building in New York); designed the sets for both an MTV show and a dance choreographed and performed by Arnie Zane and Bill T. Jones; and for a solid month in 1982 the Radiant Baby brightened the sky over Times Square, where it flashed on the Spectacolor billboard, providing a break from the normally incessant advertising.

In addition, Haring's work could be found in many countries other than the United States. Indeed, according to Galloway, "European critics, curators, and collectors generally treated the artist's achievements with a seriousness he rarely encountered at home." Among his works done abroad were a videotape commercial for a Swiss department store; the curtain he painted for the Ballet National de Marseille's 1985 performance of Roland Petit's *The Marriage of Heaven and Hell;* and three huge steel sculptures installed in public spaces in Düsseldorf, Germany. One of Haring's most ambitious projects was a monumental mural depicting the Ten Commandments, which was commissioned by the Musée d'Art Contemporain de Bordeaux in France. Haring admitted that he had to consult a Bible the night before starting the project to refresh his memory of the Commandments. In October of 1986 Haring used the colors of the East and West German flags—yellow, red, and black—to paint a mural the length of a football field on the Berlin Wall. For Haring, painting the chain of interlocked human figures was a socially conscious act, "an attempt to psychologically destroy the wall by painting it," he was quoted as saying in the 24 October 1986 *New York Times;* the wall came down three years later, just a few months before his death. Haring also had exhibitions around the world in such cities as Amsterdam, Basel, Milan, and Tokyo. The December 1989 exhibit of ten "Dancer" drawings held at the Hete Hünermann Gallery in Düsseldorf turned out to be Haring's last show of new, unique works.

While Haring worked hard, he also enjoyed being a regular on the club scene. In addition to Madonna, he counted among his friends Yoko Ono, Michael Jackson, Brooke Shields, and Andy Warhol. Haring had always been inspired by Warhol's work and was thrilled when photographer Christopher Makos took him to Warhol's studio, the Factory, and introduced them. Haring was somewhat intimidated by Warhol, who was not an easy person to get to know, but their friendship steadily grew.

Pop Shop Opens Amidst Controversy

Warhol's support helped Haring weather the storm of criticism that surrounded the opening of the Pop Shop, a New York City retail outlet for Haring products. Haring had noticed that his subway drawings were disappearing almost as fast as he made them, then turning up for sale. In the meantime his pieces had started to command higher prices, and he began increasingly to feel that access to his work was being sacrificed. Haring's solution was the Pop Shop. Opened in 1986 amidst accusations of commercialism and selling out, the store carried t-shirts, posters, mugs, and other items printed with Haring designs. The attitude of his critics was compounded by the fact that he had produced advertisements for such products as Swatch watches and Absolut vodka. However, as Haring explained to Sheff:

> [Opening the store] was all about participation on a big level.... If it was about money, I could have been the most successful commercial designer and illustrator in the world.... But the point wasn't to try to get rich. The money has been the least interesting [aspect of success] and, in some ways, the biggest drawback.... That's why it's the biggest insult of all when people talk about me selling out. I've spent my entire life trying to avoid that, trying to figure out why it happens to people.... How do you participate in the world but not lose your integrity?

One way that Haring answered this question was to become involved in projects that he felt gave something back to society. He loved children and often took on works that were directed at young people or in which they could participate, including designing playgrounds. Other such projects included painting a mural with 300 students from Chicago schools, providing the designs for the United Nations' International Youth Year in 1985, and completing a set of murals for the children's wing of New York's Mount Sinai Hospital. Haring also provided designs for such causes as the South African anti-apartheid movement, *Live Aid* in 1985, and the effort to end nuclear armament. Richard Lacayo summed up the seeming contradictions in Haring's life and art in *Metropolitan Home,* stating that "what Haring eventually became was a paradox, a second-generation Pop Artist with the social conscience of a WPA muralist."

In 1987 Haring learned that he was HIV positive. He actually had expected to contract AIDS, pointing out to Sheff, "I was here at the peak of the sexual promiscuity in New York.... I was major into experimenting. If I didn't get it no one would. So I knew. It was just a matter of time." This sentiment may well account for Haring's many images of figures being pursued by huge, menacing snakes or running from some unseen assailant.

Haring Presses on Despite AIDS

When he actually received the news, however, Haring admitted that he was "completely wrecked." But, he maintained, "you realize it's not the end right then and there—that you've got to continue, and you've got to figure out how you're going to deal with it and confront it.... You can't despair, because if you do, you just give up and you stop." Haring did not stop. Instead he threw himself into his work with even more urgency, explaining in the *Rolling Stone* interview, "That's the point that I'm at now, not knowing where it stops but knowing how important it is to do it now." He became involved with the gay AIDS awareness group ACT UP and contributed a mural to one of the organizations campaigns; to commemorate AIDS Awareness Day in 1989, he painted a mural at the Art Center College of Design in Pasadena, California; and he produced designs, including the recurring character Debbie Dick, for advertisements, t-shirts, and other products promoting safe sex. In Denise Hamilton's article in the *Los Angeles Times* Haring was quoted as saying, "When AIDS became a reality in my life, it started becoming a subject in my paintings. The more it affected my life the more it affected my work."

Haring's life ended on 16 February 1990, but his legacy continues through the work he left. His "vocabulary" of images has become a part of the world's universal language, a fact that Haring would celebrate. Indeed, that's what Keith Haring's life was all about, believing, as he stressed in an interview with Daniel Drenger in *Columbia Art Review,* that "the contemporary artist has a responsibility to continue celebrating humanity." Even in the face of his illness Haring felt happy, almost fortunate to have gained a new appreciation for life, a life with which he was at peace. He explained this sentiment to Sheff, stating, "I don't regret anything I've ever done. I wouldn't change anything.... [Death could happen] any time, and it is going to happen sometime. If you live your life according to that, death is irrelevant."

References:

Annual Obituary 1990. Chicago: St. James Press, 1991: 115-18.
Current Biography Yearbook, 1986. New York: H. W. Wilson Co., 1987: 197-200.
Drenger, Daniel. "Art and Life: An Interview with Keith Haring," in *Columbia Art Review,* Spring 1988.
Galloway, David. "Keith Haring: Made in Germany," in *Art in America,* March 1991: 118-122, 163.
Gruen, John. *Keith Haring: The Authorized Biography.* New York: Prentice Hall, 1991.
Hamilton, Denise. "Artist with AIDS Races the Clock to Spread His Message," in *Los Angeles Times,* 1 December 1989: 11, 20.
Lacayo, Richard. "Keith Haring: The Legacy Lives On," in *Metropolitan Home,* September 1990: 97-102, 150.
Sheff, David. "Just Say Know," in *Rolling Stone,* 10 August 1989: 58-66, 102.

—Nicolet V. Elert

Bertha Harris

1937-

American novelist

Bertha Harris was born in Fayetteville, North Carolina, on 17 December 1937, to Mary Zuleika Jones and John Holmes Harris, a salesman. She was raised in a home without books and did not discover the public library until she was 12 years old. In her 1993 introduction to her novel *Lover,* Harris writes, "I grew up in an excessively hick town" where she was "confined to the house and yard" and "dreamed of being kidnapped by a family with exquisite taste." Self-described as a "lonely, anxious, skinny child," Harris attended a small parochial school and eventually went to the Woman's College of the University of North Carolina (which is now the UNC-Greensboro), where she earned her BA degree in English in 1959.

While in college, at the age of 18, Harris came out. As a consequence, according to Harris, "she was confined to the college infirmary—except for classes, trips to the library, and attendance at some concerts." The 1960s found her in New York, where she worked at a variety of clerical jobs for several years. Harris had come to New York to "find lesbians," according to Ann Wadsworth in her biography of Harris. Instead, and in spite of her earlier coming out, Harris found herself married in 1963. The marriage lasted only a year, but also gave Harris her only child, a daughter named Jennifer Harris Wyland.

Harris remained in New York, where she worked to support her daughter before returning to North Carolina to pursue her master of arts degree in writing in 1967. She wrote her first novel, *Catching Saradove,* as the thesis for her MFA, in 1969. Harris would write two more novels: *Confessions of Cherubino* in 1972 and *Lover,* her most acclaimed work, in 1976. In 1977, Harris collaborated with Emily L. Sisley to co-write *The Joy of Lesbian Sex,* which became the first commercially published book of its kind. In 1993, Harris updated *Lover* with a spectacular introduction that reads like a fictional narrative itself. The new introduction offered insights into the characters of the key players in *Lover* and those in Harris's life that had influenced the work.

According to Wadsworth, Harris has stated that in *Catching Saradove* she was "trying to break through the warped rituals of love and hate that her parents have taught her." It is clear from Harris's introduction to *Lover* that much of the author's adult life has been plagued by, if not dominated by, a less than idyllic relationship with her mother. Among her most significant and most damaging relationships was the one she had with June Arnold and Parke Bowman, the two women who would publish her third novel. Arnold and Bowman, both now deceased, owned and ran Daughters, Inc. in Baltimore and Harris's relationship with them directly reflects the unrequited, unhealthy relationship she had with her mother.

A relatively apolitical creature, Harris became almost instantly political in the 1970s. She was dually motivated, she says in *Lover*'s introduction, by an unwillingness to disappoint one of the movement's most notable lesbians, Kate Millett, author of *Sexual Politics,* and by the desire to "have fun." Feminism seemed to Harris to promise a good time. "Back then," she says of feminism, "it still frightened the horses; it made most men foam at the mouth, and it got the best women horny." Harris taught writing, English literature, and women's studies in colleges and universities until the early 1970s. In 1972 she began teaching Women's Studies full time at Richmond College of the City of New York University. But, in 1976, not long after Daughters, Inc. published *Lover,* she left that position to take on all of the editorial responsibilities at Daughters, Inc., in effect, freeing Arnold to write full time. Although Harris doubted there was sufficient work to occupy her, she signed on and remained entangled in the business and emotional lives of Arnold and Bowman at least until Arnold's death in 1982, if not until Bowman's years later. In the fall of 1996 Harris completed her fourth novel, and began the search for a publisher.

References:

Blain, Virginia, Patricia Clements, and Isobel Grundy. *The Feminist Companion to Literature in English: Women Writers from the Middle Ages to the Present.* New Haven, Connecticut: Yale University Press, 1990.
Contemporary Authors. Detroit, Michigan: Gale Research, vol. 29-32, 1978.
Harris, Bertha. *Lover.* New York University Press, 1993.
Tipps, Lisa. "Bertha Harris," in *American Women Writers,* edited by Lina Mainiero. New York: Frederick Ungar Publishing Co., 1980: 250-252.
Wadsworth, Ann. *Bertha Harris.* Boston: Boston Athenaeum.

—Andrea L.T. Peterson

Harry Hay

1912-

American activist

Harry Hay not only helped found gay liberation in the United States but also provided some of the most creative and influential ideas for lesbians and gay men. After a bohemian life in Hollywood and labor activism during the Depression, in 1950 Hay organized (with four others) the Mattachine Foundation, which began the modern gay movement. In 1978 with a second wind he helped launch the Radical Faeries. Always struggling against conformities, Harry Hay continues developing further visions of sexual, social and spiritual liberation.

Discovering a Gay Vision

Born near Brighton Beach in Worthing, England, 7 April 1912, Henry "Little Harry" Hay, Jr., early gloried in the delights of nature, particularly of the sea and the wild woods. In 1914 his mother Margaret Neall (born in Arizona Indian Territory) moved the family to join Henry Sr.—"Big Harry"—in the mountains of Chile at the Atacama Desert Copper Mine. In 1916 Big Harry suffered a disabling accident. The family resettled in Orange County, California, and then in 1919 moved to Los Angeles.

Hay's mother, who possessed a magnificent, deep voice, taught him to sing before he was a year old. As a three-year-old in the icy Andean night, he could hear Quechua villagers singing the traditional four-octave Inca Hymns to the Sun. Through a Woodcraft Ranger Boys' Group in Los Angeles, his love of music expanded to include Monteverdi, Handel, Wagner, Bruchner, and Mahler.

The Rangers developed Hay's interest in the mountainous West (a lifetime love-affair). Learning horsemanship between ages eleven and thirteen, he had some preparation for work in the hayfields of western Nevada where his father sent him in the summer of 1925. An Indian teammate invited him to join his village feast day where the Sacred Ghost-Dance Prophet Wovoka (1856-1932) appeared. Known to Anglos as "Jack Wilson," Wovoka's songs, dances, and sacred vestments had terrified the United States Army between 1885 and 1891. Hay's maternal uncle had fought against the Sioux and received a decoration for the slaughter committed at Wounded Knee in 1890 against followers of Wovoka. In 1925 Wovoka looked "into his heart" and blessed the grand-nephew as one "who will someday be a Friend."

In the fall of 1930, Hay entered Stanford University's experimental independent studies but he pursued lovers, poetry, and drama more than medicine, law, or engineering. Hay had affairs at Stanford with fellow soloists in the Glee Club, a college actor, a swimming team diver, and filmmaker/poet classmate James Broughton. In the winter of 1932 a severe sinus infection forced him to leave school.

In the Hollywood of the 1930s he worked in many jobs: a "bit" part actor in B movies, in repertory stage companies, in portraying the first gay part in professional theater (May 1935), and ghost-writing the 1943 Academy Award winning *Heavenly Music.* His sometime lover Will Geer found him "very believable" as an actor. Some years after Geer's death in 1974, Hay said to his widow, "I had him first," to which she replied, "I had him longest."

Hay first learned about radical politics from the Wobbly (IWW) migratory workers during the Nevada summers of 1925-32. Geer encouraged Hay's political bent, which developed into a lifelong struggle against oppression. The Communist Party taught Hay every possible organizing technique. In the 1930s they represented a vital progressive force, promoting popular art, literature, music, and theater. Hay married another party member for whom he felt and would always feel immense affection.

Founding the Mattachine Society

Researching medieval music, Hay found references to confraternities of peasant monks who performed forbidden fertility songs and dances in the Vernal Equinox Festival Dance (now called "April Fools"). "Mattachine" was the name of one of the performing confraternities. "The Mattachine troupes conveyed vital information to the oppressed in the countryside of 13th-15th century France, and perhaps," Hay recalled, "I hoped that such a society of modern homosexual men, living in disguise in twentieth-century America, could do similarly for us oppressed Queers."

Lovers and acquaintances had brought stories of Magnus Hirschfeld's group in Berlin and of Henry Gerber's corporation in Chicago, but the former had been destroyed by the Nazis and the latter by the Chicago police. On 10 August 1948, Hay interested others in presenting an anti-entrapment plank for Henry Wallace's Progressive party platform. Nothing came of that proposal, but the "Bachelors for Wallace" provided a basis for further organization. On 11 November 1950, a group gathered to discuss Hay's call to form discussion groups on Alfred Kinsey's *Sexual Behavior of the Human Male* (1948). The five founders included Hay and his then lover Rudi Gernreich, Dale Jennings, Bob Hull and Chuck Rowland. From the *Kinsey Report* (1948), Hay had extrapolated that ten percent of the population was gay and from that he had argued that gays formed a cultural minority since there was a common language, "a psychological make-up in common, and in the cruise-necessities of the double entendres of CAMP ... a common culture." Most lesbian and gay organizations and culture even now continue to work through these ideas.

In February 1952, the Los Angeles police accosted Dale Jennings, arrested him, and charged him with "lewd and dissolute behavior." A defense committee quickly organized and in June the court dismissed all charges against Jennings after the jury deadlocked (eleven believed Jennings; one supported the policeman). In effect, the community had won the first U.S. court victory. In a single year the Mattachine grew from a few hundred to a few thousand members. Feeling the new awakening, the Los Angeles Mattachine Society Steering Committee sent a letter to city council candidates asking their views on the rights of homophiles.

The authorities struck back quickly. As part of the red-baiting of the times, a Los Angeles columnist charged that Mattachine represented a threat to the city: "a well-trained subversive could move in and forge [sexual deviates] into a dangerous political weapon." Another newspaper fingered Hay as a Marxist. Groups within Mattachine, meanwhile, organized to normalize the group. They attacked both the idea of a gay culture and any agitation. Hoping to paint themselves as acceptable, they praised the institutions of "home, church, and state." They threatened to turn anyone in to the F.B.I. who opposed such institutions. In 1955 the House Un-American Activities Committee visited Los Angeles and called Hay to testify. While his testimony seems to have successfully befuddled

Harry Hay (right) with John Burnside. ***Photograph by Daniel Nicoletta.***

the committee, he remained largely excluded from gay groups until the end of the 1950s.

Between July 1952 and May 1962, Hay lived with a beautiful young Danish hatmaker. He plunged himself into a multi-level historical materialist research into the roots of what is now called "gay consciousness." ONE Institute (an independent offshoot of Mattachine) published his "The Moral Climate of Canaan in the Time of Judges" in the premier issue of *ONE Institute Quarterly of Homophile Studies* (1958), the first scholarly lesbian/gay publication in the United States. Hay explored the mother goddess traditions of the Canaanites as an early expression of gay sensibility.

Radical Faeries

In 1963, Hay lived for four months with Jim Kepner, another of the great pioneers in the Los Angeles gay liberation struggle. In October 1963, he met John Burnside, who had invented the Teleidoscope, a wonderful instrument that made it possible for the viewer to perceive the world kaleidoscopically. Together Burnside and Hay developed a projector, called a symmetricon, which—using color-slides as well as bits of Venetian glass—could project "healing patterns" into an infinity of delight.

In 1965, they formed the Circle of Loving Companions in Los Angeles to provide at all lesbian and gay meetings an "open mike" for dissenters. Early in the Vietnam War, Hay and Don Slater in Los Angeles and others in San Francisco, set up networks of gay draft resistance. In 1966 Hay and Burnside helped establish the North American Committee of Homophile Organizations (NACHO). Meeting in San Francisco in May 1966, the Western branch inaugurated the first zap of the American Psychiatric Association.

In May 1970, Hay and Burnside moved their Teleidoscope Factory to New Mexico. They brought a small industry to the Tewa Indian Pueblo of Oke Owinge (known as San Juan Pueblo) and promoted gay liberation to both the Chicano and Tewa pueblos. Hay found gay life in Santa Fe and Albuquerque very conservative. The Circle of Loving Companions set about grass roots organizing and began self-examination workshops in the gay and lesbian group at the University of New Mexico. Together with Katherine Davenport, they got the Lambdas de Santa Fe organized in 1977, hosted the first openly Lesbian-Gay dance in Santa Fe and won first prize for the handsomest booth at the Santa Fe Fiesta. In 1976, the crew for the documentary *Word Is Out* (1978) caught the couple picking rosehips on the banks of the Rio Grande. In a 1989 "Valentine for Harry" Burnside wrote, "Hand in hand we walk, as wing tip to wing tip our spirits roam the universe, finding lovers everywhere. Sex is music. Time is not real. All things are imbued with spirit."

Jonathan Katz published a long interview with Hay in *Gay American History* (1976) and John D'Emilio featured him in *Sexual Politics, Sexual Communities* (1983). Hay in the meantime remained active with groups such as the Committee for Traditional Indian

Land and Life and worked with Rarihokwats of the Mohawk Nation *Akwesasne Notes*. Hay helped organize the Nation-Wide Friends of the Rio Grand that successfully stopped developers from diverting water from agriculture.

In New Mexico, Hay pursued his lifelong study of Native American life. His researches into the berdache (man/woman or more properly "Two Spirit") tradition have inspired and paralleled the works of Sue Ellen Jacobs, Judy Grahn, Arthur Evans, Mitch Walker, Walter Williams, Starhawk, Will Roscoe and many others.

In the fall of 1978, Don Kilhefner and Hay invited Mitch Walker to join them in hosting a workshop around these new sensibilities at the UCLA meeting of the Gay Academic Union. The workshop led to further organization. Hay and Burnside moved to Los Angeles the following July where with Kilhefner they issued "A Call to Gay Brothers" for "A Spiritual Conference for Radical Faeries." Over two hundred faeries answered the call Labor Day weekend, 1979, at a desert sanctuary near Tucson, Arizona. They explored "breakthroughs in gay consciousness," shared gay visions, and awakened "the spiritual dimensions of their lovely sexual gayness."

That gathering and subsequent ones both on local and national levels mushroomed much as the early Mattachine Society had. A wide network of rural communes already existed; *RFD: A Male Journal for Gay Brothers* begun in 1974 already provided communication among groups and individuals. In the summer 1975 issue of *RFD,* Hay and Burnside had contributed an essay on the emerging Faerie sensibility. The relationships among individuals and groups remained flexible and occasionally contentious. Nonetheless, together they sought to reassert a gay liberation overwhelmed by academics, politicians, business groups and others who sought to confine the movement to no more than a behavioral variation. In July 1995 the first Euro-faerie gathering convened, involving Faeries from eight countries.

Hay as Theorist

Some of Hay's original ideas have now become so accepted within the lesbian and gay movement that they seem commonplace such as the idea of gays being a cultural minority and the importance of organizing as a minority and fighting back with education, protest, litigation, and other strategies. Even activists who denounce what they call "essentialist" theory continue to attend conferences, offer courses, write books, develop lesbian/gay/bisexual study programs—all within the parameters set out by the early Mattachine Society.

Other of his ideas await further development—for instance, what he calls "the right to appreciation." Every lesbian or gay man feels a constant erasure of their lives by family, fellow workers, and society in general. That erasure is really a form of extermination. Hay has always argued that gays share a different consciousness, a consciousness that offers additional gifts to the rest of society, who do not share these gifts. Using a developed as well as inherited "gay window," queers can illuminate the whole society.

Hay has stressed the peculiar subject-subject nature of gay male relationships. For him homosexual love does not serve some exterior purpose as marriage, family, property, or reproduction. Instead, beyond the exuberances of the pleasure principle, we find a possibility of a new "love for fellows equally dedicated and devoted" to each other that carries with it a special consciousness "of transcendent sexual wholeness."

Hay has never rested on his many past triumphs or long mourned his losses. For the twenty-fifth anniversary of Stonewall in New York City in 1995, he was one of the organizers for the Spirit of Stonewall (SOS) counter-parade. At the Stonewall Inn, he joined representatives of drag queens, hustlers, sexologists, AIDS activists, boy lovers, and other liberationists to rally another parade in which the whole community could march. Arm and arm with Kepner and Burnside, Hay led off the demonstrators (estimated by the press as 70,000 as opposed to 700,000 at the official parade). With Hay, the Radical Faeries, Nambla, Act Up, the American Civil Liberties Union, and a vast assemblage of demonstrators marched from the original Stonewall site to Central Park. When he organized Mattachine in 1950 Hay was two decades before Stonewall. In 1995, he remained out of step—decades if not centuries ahead of the mainstream.

References:

Burnside, John. *Who Are the Gay People? And Other Essays.* (A Radical Fairy's Seedbed no.5). San Francisco: Vortex Media, 1989.

D'Emilio, John. *Sexual Politics, Sexual Communities: The Making of a Homosexual Minority in the United States, 1940-1970.* Chicago: University of Chicago, 1983.

Harry, Hay. *Radically Gay: The Story of Gay Liberation in the Words of its Founder.* Boston: Beacon Press, 1996.

Katz, Jonathan, ed. *Gay American History: Lesbians and Gay Men in the U.S.A.* New York: Crowell, 1976.

Timmons, Stuart. *The Trouble with Harry Hay: A Biography.* Boston: Aylson, 1990.

—Charles Shively

Essex Hemphill

c.1956-1995

African-American writer

When Essex Hemphill began his writing career, there was little if any voice credited to the gay community. Through his poetry and the compilation of various anthologies Hemphill was instrumental in bringing such issues as gay identity and community to the attention of mainstream society. Hemphill, however, was not content with merely establishing a gay voice in his writing, he also sought to create an African-American voice in his writing as well.

Essex Hemphill was born in Chicago but grew up in Washington, D.C.. The second of five children born to what he has called "very strong parents," Hemphill was very close to his mother. As he grew up, he found the racism around him to be all too apparent. Hemphill became equally aware of his homosexuality as an adolescent and the oppression of homophobia:

> My sexual curiosity would have blossomed in any context, but in Southeast Washington ... I had to carefully allow my petals to unfold. If I had revealed them too soon they would have been snatched away, brutalized, and scattered down alleys. I was already alert enough to know what happened

to the flamboyant boys at school who were called "sissies" and "faggots."

Seeking His Own Voice

While still in his twenties, Hemphill began searching for his identity. He was impressed by the black nationalist movement that was popular in the 1960s and 1970s, but as Hemphill got older, he found that the doctrine of that movement "proved too narrow a politic" for his interests. The politics of the gay and lesbian movement also proved too narrow for Hemphill who sought a comfortable space for his blackness and for his gayness.

Hemphill's search for a voice for the black gay male was made increasingly difficult by the effects slavery had had on the culture of America. According to Michael Broder in his essay on Hemphill in *Black Writers,* "Slavery and racism often encouraged white men to bolster their own sense of masculinity by asserting their dominance over black men. In response to this violent and abusive history, the black community placed a high premium on strong male images." Consequently, Hemphill understood that homosexuality, particularly effeminacy, was definitely taboo. Finding it difficult to be gay within the black community, and as equally difficult to be black within the racist gay community, Hemphill found the challenge to find his own identity compounded and his efforts to do so frustrated.

For Hemphill, the theme of "being a minority within a minority," was a recurring one. That much is clear not only from his own work, but from the selections he includes in works like *Brother to Brother,* the controversial anthology of black gay poets he agreed to complete when its editor, his dear friend Joseph Beam, died in 1988. The anthology succeeded in giving black gay and lesbian writers a literary identity. Not only did Hemphill support a distinct black voice, he also believed there was a need for a black gay sensibility. "There is a sensibility," he maintained in a 1988 *Village Voice* interview, "that heightens the flamboyance and drama of language, dance, and music."

In a continuing effort to identify a distinct black gay voice and a gay sensibility, Hemphill has noted the distinct gifts or blessings of individuals. "Take care of your blessings," he said in a 1990 interview. "Some of us bake wonderfully, write, paint, do any number of things, have facilities with numbers that others don't have. Those," he explains, "are your blessings ... Just be aware of what your particular things are and nurture them and use them toward a positive way of living. Take care of your blessings."

Black Gay Male Voices

The poet, who took very good care of his own blessings, in 1985 published two chapbooks, entitled *Earth Life* and *Conditions.* Selections from these, as well as more recent work are included in later anthologies. Hemphill's poetry has also been included in a number of anthologies, and a selection of his own poetry is included in *Brother to Brother.* The exploration of being a black gay man was continued in *Ceremonies,* an anthology of Hemphill's own writings, published in 1992. In a *Village Voice Literary Supplement* review of the book, David Trinidad explained Hemphill's quest for his identity in the following way, "[He] has forged—with few role models to emulate, and with little or no support from the white gay literary establishment—an identity and a style."

In addition, Hemphill wrote and performed his own monologues—gathered in the collection *So Many Dreams,* and then co-founded and, for a time, served as the publisher of *Nethula Journal of Contemporary Literature.* Hemphill, who also contributed to Isaac Julien's film *Looking for Langston Hughes* and Marlon Riggs's *Tongues Untied* was, according to Broder, "a key figure in the emergence of a distinctive African American perspective in the overall field of gay literature." He became very vocal about AIDS in his speaking and in his writing. He even voiced skepticism about the "natural" origins of the virus that has successfully left its mark on two minorities of which Hemphill, as a black gay man, was a member.

Hemphill died on 5 November 1995, from AIDS-related complications. He was very much aware that he had no closet to go back to, and he was unable to understand how once out anyone could try to go back. In his own writing, Hemphill tried to "be very real" with himself when "alone with that paper."

References:

Broder, Michael. "Essex Hemphill," in *Black Writers.* Detroit, Michigan: Gale Research, 1994: 299-301.

———. "Essex Hemphill," in *Gay & Lesbian Literature.* Detroit, Michigan: St. James Press, 1994: 180-181.

Hemphill, Essex. *Ceremonies: Prose and Poetry.* New York: New American Library, 1992.

Hemphill, Essex, ed. *Brother to Brother.* Boston: Alyson Publications, 1991.

Morse, Gary and Joan Larkin, eds. *Gay & Lesbian Poetry in Our Time: An Anthology.* New York: St. Martin's Press, 1988.

Poulson-Bryant, Scott. "New Faces," in *Village Voice* (New York), 28 June 1988: 24f.

Tarver, Chuck. *Network* (New York), December 1990.

Trinidad, David. In *Village Voice Literary Supplement* (New York), June 1992: 7-8.

—Andrea L.T. Peterson

Gilbert Herdt

1950-

American anthropologist

Gilbert Herdt is variously identified as a prolific writer, scholar, teacher, and social anthropologist, with far-reaching, long-term interests in the origins of sexuality, gay identity and community, the impact of AIDS, and gender roles and their development. He first gained notoriety primarily in academic circles for his groundbreaking studies in the idioms and rituals associated with gender and masculinity in New Guinea, and his work on ritualized homosexuality in Melanesia, all done in the 1980s. He is currently chairman of the Committee on Human Development and a professor of human development and psychology at the University of Chicago.

In the late 1980s and early 1990s, Herdt turned his attention to less esoteric and uniquely American topics: the ramifications of a changing gay/lesbian culture, the emerging identities of gay/lesbian youth in America, and the impact of AIDS. In the process, he gained a more mainstream readership and popularity. His books and studies now invariably draw praise from fellow academics and laypersons alike, who point up, as reviewer Michael Lutes notes, his "invaluable insight into the development of contemporary gay society and consciousness."

Gilbert Herdt was born on 29 February 1949 in Oakley, Kansas. He was educated at the University of Washington in Seattle, where he received his M.A. in anthropology in 1974, and at the Australian National University, where he received his Ph.D. in 1977. From 1974 through 1985, Herdt did fieldwork in New Guinea, which led to several fascinating and precedent-setting studies on sexuality, gender, and rituals of manhood. These include: *Guardians of the Flutes* (1981), *Rituals of Manhood* (1982), *Ritualized Homosexuality in Melanesia* (1982), and *Sambia: Ritual and Gender in New Guinea.*

In 1978, Herdt also began as an assistant professor of anthropology at Stanford University in California. He was a member of the Gender Identity Clinic at the University of California at Los Angeles, and is still a fellow with the American Anthropological Association, and a member of the Association for Social Anthropology in Oceania. He is currently in a long-term committed relationship with another man who is also a scholar.

In 1989, Herdt edited *Gay and Lesbian Youth,* a collection of contemporary ethnographic studies of lesbian and gay youth coming-of-age in various world cultures, including England, France, Brazil and Mexico. By presenting these studies—which include analyses of parental influence on self-esteem, identity confusion, and cultural identity and commitment—Herdt strived for a common ground of understanding for what he terms "four preconceptions (about) gay youth ... regarding their heterosexuality, inversion, stigma, and [homogeneity]." In short, gay and lesbian adolescents are first wrongly presumed to be heterosexual; are accused of being "inverts" when they face the fact that they are not; are then stigmatized; and finally, are subject to the assumption of homogeneity, or the belief that gays and lesbians everywhere experience the same "coming-out" experiences, the same cultural identification, and the same identity problems.

In 1992, Herdt edited a popular collection of eight essays titled *Gay Culture in America.* Probing, according to Lutes, "well beyond the stereotypes," this unique collection delves into issues of race, diversity within the gay community, the demise of the "male clone," and "coming out" as a rite of passage. "Our interest here," says Herdt, "lies in the legitimacy of the gay experience and the authenticity of gay culture, in both its public and personal dimensions." "What [we] have in common," Herdt concludes, is that being gay ... no longer depends on sex per se." Also in 1992, Herdt co-authored *Social Analysis in the Time of AIDS: Theory, Method, and Action* with Shirley Lindenbaum, a work designed to provide practical tools for assessing the impact of AIDS on an ever-changing gay society.

In 1993, Herdt co-authored, with sociologist Andrew Boxer, a study based on over two years of research with gay and lesbian youth at a social service agency in Chicago called Horizons. The result, *Children of Horizons,* is an honest, inside account of how gay and lesbian youth today are "leading a new way out of the closet" via modern rituals of their own. These encompass loss, acceptance, resocialization, and ultimately the destruction of myths about who this "invisible minority" is. Even though self-identified gay and lesbian youth are coming out for the first time in history—an "unprecedented cultural development" as Herdt righteously asserts—there has been almost no information available on their lives. *Horizons* finally fills the void. As reviewer James Van Buskirk notes, "This moving inquiry demonstrates that any confusion youth may experience is not about their sexual identity but about how to express themselves in an intensely homophobic society."

In 1996, Herdt edited another groundbreaking collection entitled *Third Sex, Third Gender: Beyond Sexual Dimorphism in Culture and History,* with studies suggesting that society is poised to move beyond the notion that sexuality is merely an "either/or" prospect. The ongoing work of "social-salvage" anthropologists like Gilbert Herdt is critical if "gay culture" is to reach any significant pinnacle of self-esteem and community as we approach the millennium still burdened with the specter of AIDS. Denial of same-sex orientation by gay youth is certainly easier in an era when hostility and stigma are compounded by the possibility of a terminal illness. As Herdt and his colleagues show us, denial of the self is brutally shadowed by the denigration of self-esteem. "The horizons of gay culture," Herdt concludes in *Gay Culture in America,* "have also been greatly expanded and will in time become even more diffuse, with new potentialities available for the self and the community of the future."

Current Address: E-mail: herdt@ccp.uchicago.edu.

References:

Boxer, Andrew and Gilbert Herdt, eds. *Children of Horizons: How Gay and Lesbian Teens Are Leading the Way Out of the Closet.* Boston: Beacon Press, 1993.

Herdt, Gilbert, ed. *Gay Culture in America.* Boston: Beacon Press, 1992.

———, ed. *Gay and Lesbian Youth.* New York: Harrington Press, 1989.

Lutes, Michael. Rev. of *Gay Culture in America,* in *Library Journal* (New York), December 1991.

Van Buskirk, James. Rev of *Children of Horizons: How Gay and Lesbian Teens Are Leading the Way Out of the Closet,* in *Library Journal* (New York), July 1993.

—Jerome Szymczak

Magnus Hirschfeld

1868-1935

German physician

A world-renowned figure in his day, Magnus Hirschfeld was responsible for founding and sustaining the German homosexual emancipation movement, which in his time was a model for the world. Hirschfeld correctly perceived that legal reform was the central issue to be confronted if the lives of gays and lesbians were to enter into the serenity and productivity he envisaged for them. He also understood that this reform depended on an enlightened state of public opinion; hence the need for solid, sustained scientific research and scholarship which would command the respect of the nongay public. In this realm, Hirschfeld was a prolific scholar, writing on many sexual topics. He wrote the first great synthesis on the subject in book form and launched the first truly scholarly periodical on the subject of homosexuality.

A Career in the Kaiserreich and the Weimar Republic

Magnus Hirschfeld was born of Jewish parents in Kolberg on the Baltic coast of Prussia (today Kolobrzeg in Poland) on 14 May 1868. His father, Hermann Hirschfeld, was a civic leader who distinguished himself by making the town a popular resort. The son followed the then-common pattern of studying at several German universities, first languages and philosophy at Breslau (now Wroclaw) and Strasbourg, then medicine at Munich and Berlin, where he took his degree.

Then he set out to see something of the world, traveling to the United States and North Africa. After living briefly in the town of Magdeburg in Saxony, he boldly settled in Charlottenburg, a fashionable quarter on the west side of Berlin, where he practiced medicine.

The suicide of one of his patients, a young officer who ended his life to avoid contracting a marriage arranged to please his family, stimulated the young physician's interest in the problem of homosexuality. International interest in the subject was in fact cresting, as publications by Arnold Aletrino, Edward Carpenter, H. Havelock Ellis, Richard von Krafft-Ebing, Cesare Lombroso, Marc-André Raffalovich, and John Addington Symonds, to cite only the major names, indicate. Hirschfeld judged it prudent to issue his first book under the pseudonym of Th. Ramien. Entitled *Sappho und Sokrates* (1896), after the two leading figures of female and male homosexuality in classical antiquity, this publication argued that same-sex love is an integral part of human sexuality. For this reason both its causes and its manifestations should be the object of scientific investigation. Finally, sounding the keynote of the movement he was to found, Hirschfeld recommended that the penal laws against homosexuality should be changed in society's own interest.

Hirschfeld founded the Wissenschaftlich-humanitäre Komitee (Scientific-Humanitarian Committee) on his 29th birthday, 14 May 1897. The first and foremost goal of the committee was legal reform. Following the establishment of the North German Confederation and then of the German Empire, a new penal code was adopted that went into force on the entire territory of the Reich on 1 January 1872. Its Article 175 criminalized lewd and unnatural acts between males, with a maximum penalty of two years. The repeal of this punitive provision was the committee's central objective during its 36 years of existence. For this purpose Hirschfeld and his associates drafted a petition "to the Legislative Bodies of the German Empire" that was ultimately signed by some 6,000 Germans prominent in all walks of life.

The committee realized that, before the aim of repeal could be achieved, educational work was necessary on several fronts. In 1899 the committee began the publication of the *Jahrbuch für sexuelle Zwischenstufen* (*Yearbook for Sexual Intermediates*), the world's first periodical devoted to scholarship on all aspects of homosexual behavior. Edited by Hirschfeld, its 23 volumes are a model collection of materials of all kinds on the subject, ranging from questionnaire studies and articles on homosexuality among tribal peoples to literary themes and biographies and analyses of theoretical problems in law and biology. The annual bibliographies were in effect the clearing house of all current research on the subject.

Magnus Hirschfeld

The committee was in practice the world's first center for the study of all aspects of homosexuality. Though ignored by academic scholars, Hirschfeld collected material from various sources on the frequency of homosexual behavior in the population and the psychological profile of the homosexual personality. In 1904 he reached the conclusion that 2.2 percent of the population was exclusively homosexual. Scarcely surprising today, the figure was greeted with incredulity.

Hirschfeld delved into the private lives of the individuals he examined from numerous aspects, in every one of which he found evidence that supported his theory of an innate third sex. Anticipating the later empirical work of Alfred C. Kinsey, Hirschfeld created a questionnaire with 130 separate items which was completed by more than 10,000 men and women. The data he collected served as the basis of major articles. Together with the historical research published in the *Jahrbuch,* this data was summarized in a monumental book of over 1,000 pages, *Die Homosexualitat des Mannes und des Weibes* (*Male and Female Homosexuality,* 1914). Only a few brief sections have been translated into English. Following a study of the historical terminology of the subject, the book presents a series of chapters from a medical and biological standpoint. The volume deals with such other matters as etiology and incidence, the history and worldwide phenomenology of homosexuality, and famous homosexuals. Contemporary problems are treated under the headings of legal disability, prostitution, and blackmail. The final chapter deals with organizations for homosexual emancipation. As a collection of current knowledge, this book was only surpassed by the 1990 *Encyclopedia of Homosexuality.*

After the end of World War I (1914-18) and the proclamation of the Weimar Republic, film censorship was suspended. In 1919 Hirschfeld and the committee began a new aspect of their educational work, accepting an offer from Richard Oswald to produce a film about homosexuality. The result was the somewhat melodramatic silent film *Anders als die Andern* (*Different from the Others*), which premiered in Berlin on 24 May 1919. A breakthrough in the dramatic presentation of a controversial subject, the movie elicited bitter opposition. Its purpose was to expose the evils of Article 175 of the penal code, especially the way that it encouraged blackmail. Today the film survives in a somewhat mutilated version.

In addition to outside attacks, there was dissension within the sexual research community itself. Hirschfeld did not accept Sigmund Freud's psychoanalysis, and Freud fought behind the scene to undermine his authority. From an entirely different camp, Hirschfeld's archenemy Albert Moll, also a physician of Berlin, had made sure that Hirschfeld was not invited to the 1926 International Congress for Sexual Research. Ostensibly Moll was opposed to the propagandistic element in the latter's activity.

Undeterred, Hirschfeld presided at four successive conferences of the World League for Sexual Reform on a Scientific Basis (Berlin, 1921; Copenhagen, 1928; London, 1929; Vienna, 1930). These international gatherings featured papers on the whole spectrum of problems of sexual life, together with vigorous pleas for the reform of repressive laws and practices. Major preoccupations were sex education, women's health, birth control, law reform, sexual anomalies, and eugenics.

Hirschfeld's German campaigns for homosexual emancipation were less successful. However, he did persuade the district attorneys in the larger German cities to refrain from enforcing Article 175 where private, consensual adult behavior was concerned. In the 1920s, Germany was the only country in the world with an extensive network of homosexual organizations and of bars, cafes, and other meeting places which individuals seeking partners of their own sex could casually frequent. In this way it prefigures the situation in the United States after 1969.

Law reform remained elusive. Under Hirschfeld's leadership the Committee followed a "top-down," elitist strategy, under the assumption that if the power structure could be won over, victory would be a formality. However, the committee itself never gained more than 1500 supporters. Toward the end of his life, Hirschfeld wearily conceded that the majority of homosexuals were unwilling to fight for their legal and political rights. In the absence of such support, the existing political parties felt no pressure to reform the penal law.

Nazis Destroy Institute

The growing anti-Semitic movement in Germany made Hirschfeld one of its targets. He was assaulted in Munich in 1920 and again in 1921; the second time he suffered a fractured skull and was reported dead. On the other hand, the Social Democrats and Communists supported the committee's demands in the German Parliament, and in 1929, a 15-13 vote of a committee approved the striking of the "homosexual article" from the draft penal code. However, this victory was premature, for no final action was taken by the Parliament. Driven by the coming of the world Depression, the mounting economic crisis not only made other issues more urgent, but led to the phenomenal rise of the National Socialist German Workers Party (Nazis). Despite the presence of a few homosexuals in their own ranks, the Nazis vociferously denounced the homosexual liberation movement, in part because it was identified with such Jewish figures as Hirschfeld and Kurt Hiller.

In November of 1931 Hirschfeld left Germany for a tour around the world, lecturing and gathering material for shipment to the Institute for Sexual Science in Berlin.

The Nazi assumption of power on 7 March 1933 was followed by the wilful destruction of the institute and its unique files and library. Of its own volition the Scientific-Humanitarian Committee dissolved in order to avoid further attacks by the new regime. Fortunately Hirschfeld had not returned to Germany at this point. He decided to settle in France, where he attempted to recreate his research institute on a smaller scale. However, the world depression and mounting dissension within the sexual reform movement restricted what he could accomplish. Magnus Hirschfeld died in Nice in the south of France on his 67th birthday, 14 May 1935.

Critical Evaluation

The truth of a number of scandals surrounding Hirschfeld is hard to estimate, for anyone taking a prominent role in the causes that he espoused would be subjected to innuendo and outright lies. His enemies made fun of the elaborate soirees held at his home in Berlin, dubbing him "Auntie Magnesia." He is reputed to have been a foot fetishist who solicited male prostitutes for the purpose.

Other criticisms apply to the public sphere. During the 1906 dispute between the journalist Maximilian Harden and Prince Philipp von Eulenburg, a closeted high official, his testimony as to the homosexuality of Count Kuno von Moltke indirectly played into the hands of homophobes who wished to equate sexual unorthodoxy with sedition. Curiously enough, it was the newspapers' widespread use of the term homosexual during the Harden-Eulenburg affair that made it a household word, displacing the medical coinages current until then in the specialized literature of the subject.

Hirschfeld's methods of raising moneys for the Institute for Sexual Science were sometimes questionable. They included endorsement of patent medicines, the value of which was uncertain. At the end of his life this practice proved an obstacle to establishing the institute in France, where such endorsements met disapproval.

In intellectual matters he might have perhaps avoided the breach with the school of thought represented by Benedict Friedlaender and Hans Blüher. Both were interested in intergenerational homosexuality. Originally a member of the Scientific-Humanitarian Committee, Friedlaender led a movement to secede from it. This led to the formation of a rival group, the Gemeinschaft der Eigenen (Community of the Exceptional), which focused on the virile homosexual, with pederastic interests who was sometimes bisexual. Hans Blüher accused Hirschfeld of falsifying the text of his 1912 work *The Wandervogel Movement as an Erotic Phenomenon.* This book, which was concerned with the German youth movement, stressed the role of male comradeship in mass organizations and public life.

Hirschfeld's disagreements with Friedlaender and Blüher stemmed in large measure from his attachment to the concept of the third sex. The notion that homosexuals constitute a third sex, intermediate between the poles of the heterosexual male and the heterosexual female, had already become popular towards the middle of the nineteenth century. It had early analogues in ancient Greece and Rome.

The German equivalent, *drittes Geschlecht,* was introduced by the homosexual reformer K. H. Ulrichs in 1864. At the turn of the century the notion seemed to fit well with the *Zwischenstufen* (intergrade) theories of Hirschfeld and his circle. Hirschfeld and his colleagues collected data that seemed to show that homosexual subjects tended to fall halfway between the normal man and the normal woman. Hirschfeld himself wrote a book on the gay subculture of Wilhelmine Berlin under the title *Berlins drittes Geschlecht*, and the committee prepared a propaganda pamphlet entitled *Was soll das Volk vom dritten Geschlecht wissen?* (*What Should the People Know about the Third Sex?*). However, a considerable number of homosexual men and women deviate from the norm for their gender solely in their sexual orientation, so that even sympathizers of Hirschfeld dismissed the label as untenable.

Hirschfeld's Legacy

Undoubtedly Hirschfeld was not a perfect person. The pressures to which an individual in his situation was subjected precluded that. Moreover, many of Hirschfeld's scientific findings were inevitably made obsolete by further advances in human knowledge.

Yet Hirschfeld has left behind an imperishable legacy in his clear distinction between scientific investigation and social advocacy. The motto of the committee was "Per scientiam ad justitiam" ("Through science to justice"). Hirschfeld held that political and social goals must never call the tune in matters of scientific and scholarly investigation. He was equally loyal both to knowledge and social reform.

References:

Herzer, Manfred. *Magnus Hirschfeld: Leben und Werk eines jüdischen, schwulen und sozialistischen Sexologen*. Frankfurt: Campus Verlag, 1992.

Hirschfeld, Magnus. *Von einst bis jetzt: Geschichte einer homosexuellen Bewegung*, edited by James Steakley. Berlin: Verlag Rosa Winkel, 1986.

Steakley, James D. *The Homosexual Emancipation Movement in Germany*. New York: Arno Press, 1975.

———. *The Writings of Dr. Magnus Hirschfeld: A Bibliography*. Toronto: Canadian Gay Archives, 1985.

Wolff, Charlotte. *Magnus Hirschfeld: A Portrait of a Pioneer in Sexology*. London: Quartet Books, 1986.

—Wayne R. Dynes

David Hockney

1937-

British artist

David Hockney is one of the best-known and most popular living artists in the world today. He has worked in a variety of traditional media—painting, sketching, and etching—and has been quick to take up new technological methods—the Polaroid camera, the colour photocopier, the digital paintbox, the fax. His set designs for opera are widely celebrated. Hockney combines great ability as a draughtsman and colourist with an endless pictorial curiosity and inventiveness. A vigorous defender of the human element in art, he is also aware of the challenges and opportunities created by Modernism. From his student days in London, he has incorporated gay images and concerns into his work, and has proved himself to be a staunch supporter of gay rights and an implacable opponent of censorship.

David Hockney, the fourth of five children, was born in the northern city of Bradford, England, on 9 July 1937. His father, Kenneth, who worked as an accountant's clerk, was a man of independent mind, a pacifist, and himself an amateur artist, whose painting of Laurel and Hardy always hangs on his son's studio wall; his mother, Laura, was a strict Methodist, a teetotaller, nonsmoker, and vegetarian. Hockney won a scholarship to Bradford City Grammar School and in 1953 entered Bradford School of Art. He first sold a painting, *Portrait of My Father*, for £10 in 1955. At art school, his sexual preference was not evident; he had become conscious of his orientation in his mid-teens, but in 1950s Britain, homosexual acts were still illegal and bore a strong social stigma.

From 1957 to 1959, Hockney, exempted from military service as a conscientious objector, worked in hospitals in Bradford and Hastings, and did little painting. In September of 1959, he became a postgraduate student at London's Royal College of Art. There, he began to tackle gay themes in his painting and to acknowledge his sexual preference more openly. The painting *Erection* (1959-60) was the first sign of his new openness, and he carried it further in *Doll Boy* (1960), the title of which referred to a recent record by the pop singer Cliff Richard, on whom Hockney had a crush. In his first autobiographical volume, *David Hockney by David Hockney* (1976), he says that some of his pictures at this time "were partly propaganda of something I felt hadn't been propagandized, especially among students, as a subject: homosexuality."

Hockney was impressed by the power of the male nudes in a London exhibition of Francis Bacon's paintings in the spring of 1960. In his second year at the Royal College of Art, he made friends with Mark Berger, an American fellow-student. Berger introduced him to gay places and people, and they discussed the poetry of Whitman and Cavafy. Hockney had read Whitman's complete poems in the summer of 1960, and Whitman's words started to figure significantly in his painting. *Adhesiveness* (1960) takes its title from Whitman's term for friendship between two men, while Whitman's *Leaves of Grass* provides both the title, and some lines which are incorporated into the actual painting, of *We Two Boys Together Clinging* (1961). This title is also, however, a joking reference to a newspaper headline about a climbing accident which could be taken to refer to a homoerotic idyll with Cliff Richard: "TWO BOYS CLING TO CLIFF ALL NIGHT LONG."

First Exhibition Sells Out

In 1961 Hockney made his first visit to the United States, to New York City, where he dyed his hair blond, thus creating a key feature of what was soon to be his public image as a star of "Swinging London." On his return from New York, he painted a large picture called *A Grand Procession of Dignitaries in the Semi-Egyptian Style*, inspired by Cavafy's poem "Waiting for the Barbarians." The sight of a friend juxtaposed with an Egyptian statue in an East Berlin museum sparked off a further important painting of this period—*The First Marriage* (1962). As well as painting, Hockney also produced, between 1961 and 1963, his first major series of etchings: *A Rake's Progress*, a witty and stylish modern version of

David Hockney

William Hogarth's pictorial warnings of the dangers of loose living. In September of 1963, he accepted a *Sunday Times* invitation to travel to Egypt to make drawings for its colour supplement, although these were not published as the Kennedy assassination took precedence.His most notable triumph in 1963 was his first solo exhibition at the London gallery of his dealer John Kasmin: all his paintings were sold.

Hockney was starting to dream of California. Early in 1963, he painted *Domestic Scene, Los Angeles,* working from his imagination and from photographs in the magazine *Physique Pictorial.* John Rechy's novel of Californian gay life, *City of Night* (1963), excited him. In December of 1963, he went to New York again, where he met artist Andy Warhol and Henry Geldzahler, a curator of twentieth-century art at the Metropolitan Museum, who was to become a friend and a subject of several paintings and drawings. He flew to California in January of 1964. In his book *David Hockney* (1987), Marco Livingstone quotes a *Listener* interview of 22 May 1975 in which Hockney recalls that in his first week on the West Coast, the sight of a freeway ramp rising into the air made him think: "My God, this place needs its Piranesi; Los Angeles could have a Piranesi, so here I am!"

Hockney rented a studio in Santa Monica and started to use acrylic paint. He taught at the University of Iowa in the summer and travelled extensively in the United States, through New Mexico, Oklahoma, and Kansas to Chicago, and by the Grand Canyon to New Orleans and then to New York. There his first one-man American exhibition was held, and, like his London exhibition the year before, it was a success. In December he returned to London but was back in the United States the following year, teaching at the University of Colorado in the summer, visiting Los Angeles and New York again, and producing the set of six lithographs called *A Hollywood Collection.* He returned to London in October for a further one-man exhibition at the Kasmin Gallery. By now, he had made a reputation in both Britain and the United States as a talented young artist and as an embodiment of what was seen as the vibrant, hedonistic "Swinging London" of the 1960s.

In January of 1966, Hockney travelled to Beirut and produced drawings for what was to become his *Illustrations for Fourteen Poems from C.P. Cavafy,* his first major series of etchings since *A Rake's Progress.* He then accepted a commission from London's Royal Court Theatre to design a production of Alfred Jarry's absurdist play *Ubu Roi.* After finishing these, he returned to California to teach painting for six weeks at the summer school of the University of California, Los Angeles. To Hockney's disappointment, his students were mainly housewives; there was, however, one deeply attractive young man, Peter Schlesinger. Hockney and Schlesinger were to become partners for six years, living together in both California and London. Schlesinger started to figure prominently in Hockney's work, for example in the paintings *Peter Getting Out of Nick's Pool* (1966) and *The Room, Tarzana* (1967). But Hockney's most memorable painting of this period was one in which the human figure was only implied: the quintessential Californian painting *A Bigger Splash* (1967) captures the immediate aftermath of a dive into a swimming pool in such a way as to transform an instant of hectic activity into an image of hypnotic stillness.

Photography, Portraiture, and Opera

Hockney's interest in photography increased from 1967; he started to mount his photographs in large albums, and he bought a 35mm Pentax camera. The following year, making some use of photographs, he painted *American Collectors: Fred and Marcia Wiseman,* the first of a number of double portraits which were to form a significant strand of his work: these included *Henry Geldzahler and Christopher Scott,* and *Christopher Isherwood and Don Bachardy,* both in 1968, and, in 1971, *Mr and Mrs Clark and Percy,* which was to become the most popular picture at London's Tate Gallery.

In 1970, at the age of 32, Hockney enjoyed the accolade of a large retrospective exhibition, first at London's Whitechapel Gallery and subsequently in Hanover, Rotterdam, and Belgrade. But his personal life was unhappy during this period. His relationship with Peter Schlesinger broke up in 1971, plunging him into deep depression. In 1972, he put in six months' work on another double portrait, that of the ballet dancer Wayne Sleep and his partner George Scott, but he was dissatisfied with it and would finally abandon it. The year 1972 also saw, however, an increase in his activity as a photographer. In preparation for the painting *Portrait of an Artist (Pool with Two Figures)* (1972), he took about 200 photographs, using a new Pentax camera with automatic exposure.

When Pablo Picasso died in 1973, a Berlin publisher commissioned a number of artists, including Hockney, to produce a print for a portfolio called *Homage to Picasso.* Hockney went to Paris to work on this etching with the master printer Aldo Crommelynck, who had been Picasso's close associate for 20 years. Crommelynck introduced Hockney to sugar lift and colour etching techniques, and Hockney, characteristically, became fascinated with this new medium. Another new field opened up to him in 1974, when he was asked to design the sets for a production of Stravinsky's *The Rake's*

Progress at Glyndebourne, the rural opera house in the English county of Sussex. Hockney had loved opera since his father had taken him to see Puccini's *La Boheme* in Bradford when he was about ten, and the design of operatic sets was to become a major aspect of his work. The year 1974 also saw the release of Jack Hazan's film *A Bigger Splash* and the start of Hockney's relationship with Gregory Evans.

Fighting for Figurative Art

In 1976, Hockney, at Henry Geldzahler's suggestion, read Wallace Stevens's long poem "The Man with the Blue Guitar," a meditation on the transformative power of art which alludes to Picasso's Blue Period painting *The Old Guitarist* (1903). The poem fascinated him, and he produced first a set of drawings, and then a series of coloured etchings using the technique that Crommelynck had developed for Picasso. These were published in the spring of 1977. By then, Hockney was embroiled in controversy about the relative merits of abstract and figurative art. The January/February issue of the London magazine *New Review* carried on its front cover a photograph of Hockney and his friend and fellow-artist R. B. Kitaj in the nude. In a conversation published inside the magazine, they affirmed the importance of figurative art and attacked what they saw as the sterility of abstraction. Hockney enjoyed pointing out later that the outraged reactions to the cover photograph proved the point about the importance of the human image.

Hockney started work in New York in mid-1977 on designing *The Magic Flute* for Glyndebourne, and worked extensively in gouache for the first time. In the same year, he also painted the restrained and moving double portrait *My Parents; Model with Unfinished Self-Portrait,* which shows Hockney himself drawing and Gregory Evans curled up asleep; and *Looking at Pictures on a Screen,* in which Henry Geldzahler is looking at paintings by Vermeer, Piero della Francesca, Van Gogh, and Degas. The following year, he completed, in six weeks, 29 pressed colour paper pulp pictures called *Paper Pools,* which explore his fascination with water and light.

On 4 March 1979, the British Sunday newspaper the *Observer* carried an interview with Hockney headed "No Joy at the Tate," which attacked the acquisitions policy of Norman Reid, then the director of London's Tate Gallery, for its emphasis on abstract art at the expense of modern figurative work. A major controversy ensued. Meanwhile, Hockney went on with his work in theatre design, producing, early in 1980, set and costume designs for a triple bill of Satie, Poulenc, and Ravel, which was staged the following year at the Metropolitan Opera in New York. In his painting, he was now concerned to escape from what he saw as the trap of naturalism and to explore further the possibilities opened up by Cubism. Over three weeks in November of 1980, he painted *Mulholland Drive,* which offers a montage of multiple views of the road that led down into Los Angeles from his Californian home.

From Photo-Joins to Very New Paintings

For two years from 1982, photography became Hockney's chief preoccupation. He produced over 140 montages of Polaroid pictures, a selection of which was exhibited in Paris, and many "photojoins," collages of 35mm prints intended to create multi-perspective images. Meanwhile, his work in theatre design was the subject of an exhibition called *Hockney Paints the Stage,* shown in a range of venues in the United States, and in Mexico and London. He started painting again in 1984; he also began to produce lithographs in 1984 and 1985, some of them in large formats, and these were exhibited at Kasmin's gallery in London in 1985. The December 1985 issue of *Vogue* magazine featured 41 pages of Hockney's photographs and drawings.

In 1986, his interest in the artistic potential of the colour photocopier resulted in the *Home Made Prints.* In his stage work, he took on the task of designing the sets for the Los Angeles Music Center Opera's production of Wagner's *Tristan und Isolde,* and in 1987 he also designed the Waltz Pavilion for Andre Heller's Luna-Luna Park in Hamburg. The year 1988 saw a major Hockney retrospective, first at the Los Angeles County Museum of Art, and then at New York's Metropolitan Museum and London's Tate Gallery. He bought a house next to the sea at Malibu, where he set up a studio, producing a set of small portraits and, in October, his first fax-machine works. These works were shown in 1989 at the Sao Paulo Biennale and a range of other venues. Towards the end of the year, he produced his first computer drawings.

In the 1990s, Hockney's energies show no sign of flagging. He has designed sets for Puccini's *Turandot* for the San Francisco Opera and Chicago Lyric Opera, and for Strauss's *Die Frau ohne Schatten* at London's Royal Opera House; he has drawn portraits and collages, and has done further work in gouache; he has made drawings on his Macintosh PC, such as *Beach House Inside* (1991); and, above all, he has painted the series of abstract *Very New* (or *V. N.*) *Paintings* (1992-93), which are remarkable for their exuberance of colour and their energy and grace of form. Most recently, he has exhibited inkjet prints of photographs exploring the relationship between photography, painting, and reality. In the London *Times* of 3 June 1996, he says that inkjet technology produces "the most beautiful printing of photography I have ever seen." Hockney is still a very active artist, and it is impossible, as yet, to attempt a conclusive assessment of his achievement. The chief criticism of his work has been that it fails to grapple with the darker side of life, and it is true that suffering—the anguish of AIDS, for example—finds no echo in his art. But he has amply demonstrated his capacity to provide rich and stimulating feasts of visual pleasure.

Current Address: 7508 Santa Monica Boulevard, West Hollywood, California 90046-6407.

References:

Alberge, Dalya. "Hockney's Camera Puts New Technology in Focus," in *The Times* (London), 3 June 1996: 3.

Friedman, Martin. *Hockney Paints the Stage.* London: Thames and Hudson, 1983.

Hockney, David. *David Hockney by David Hockney: My Early Years,* edited by Nikos Stangos. London: Thames and Hudson, 1976.

———. "No Joy at the Tate," interview with Miriam Gross, in *Observer,* 4 March 1979, review section: 1-2.

———. *Paper Pools,* edited by Nikos Stangos. London: Thames and Hudson, 1980.

———. "R. B. Kitaj and David Hockney Discuss the Case for a Return to the Figurative...," in *New Review,* vol. 3, no. 34, February 1977: 75-77.

———. *That's the Way I See It,* edited by Nikos Stangos. London: Thames and Hudson, 1993.

Livingstone, Marco. *David Hockney.* Rev. ed. London: Thames and Hudson, 1988.
Melia, Paul, and Ulrich Luckhardt. *David Hockney: Paintings.* Munich and New York: Prestel, 1994.
Melia, Paul, ed. *David Hockney.* Manchester and New York: Manchester University Press, 1995.
Webb, Peter. *Portrait of David Hockney.* London: Chatto and Windus, 1988.

—Nicolas Tredell

Rock Hudson

1925-1985

American actor

For three decades, Rock Hudson was a popular actor, whose handsomeness led many to underestimate his talents. Then, for three months, while dying of AIDS, he became—unintentionally—the world's most famous homosexual and a significant contributor to increased public awareness of AIDS, garnering increased sympathy for its predominantly gay victims.

Hudson was born in Winnetka, Illinois, on 17 November 1925, as Roy Harold Scherer, Jr., the son of Roy Scherer, an auto mechanic, and Katherine Wood Scherer, who later became a telephone operator. When Roy Jr. was four, his father lost his job and moved away, so Katherine divorced him and married Wallace Fitzgerald, who adopted Roy Jr.. Wallace proved an abusive stepfather, and Katherine eventually divorced him as well. After high school and undistinguished military service, Roy moved to California to pursue an acting career.

He obtained an agent, Henry Willson, who named him "Rock Hudson" and convinced Raoul Walsh to give him a tiny part in *Fighter Squadron* (1948). Hudson then became a contract player at Universal Studios, playing small roles in colorful adventure movies. After working his way up to star billing, Hudson's breakthrough performance came in *Magnificent Obsession* (1954), a melodrama with Jane Wyman that demonstrated his sensitivity as an actor. Similar films followed, most notably *Giant* (1956), where he held his own opposite Elizabeth Taylor and James Dean and earned his only Oscar nomination. Another film, *Pillow Talk* (1959) with Doris Day, displayed his talent for comedy and led to other comedies with Day, including *Lover Come Back* (1962) and *Send Me No Flowers* (1964).

The public never knew that Hudson was a confirmed, and active, homosexual. While he had long-term relationships with several men over the years, including Willson, business manager Tom Clark, and Marc Christian, he was always promiscuous, sometimes recklessly so. Twice, possible revelation of his homosexuality almost destroyed his career. In 1955, Willson learned that *Confidential* magazine was about to expose Hudson but managed to squelch the story. To quiet gossip, he arranged for Hudson to marry Willson's secretary, Phyllis Gates. Though some insist that Hudson truly loved her, they were divorced in 1958. In 1971, a bizarre rumor circulated that Hudson had secretly "married" Jim Nabors, another closeted homosexual; though Hudson's career was not affected, Nabors's was ruined. It was during this period that Hudson briefly considered "coming out" but decided that the time was not right.

Rock Hudson

In 1966, Hudson appeared in *Seconds,* a grim drama about an aging man transformed into a handsome youth who comes to despise his false new existence. Though it resonates with autobiographical implications and features Hudson's finest acting, the film failed, and a disheartened Hudson turned to routine action movies like *Ice Station Zebra* (1968). Hudson next starred in a successful television series, *Macmillan and Wife* (1971-76), and acted on the stage in productions of *I Do! I Do!, John Brown's Body, Camelot,* and *On the Twentieth Century.* During his last decade, he appeared in a few films, several mini-series, and an unsuccessful series, *The Devlin Connection* (1982).

By this time, years of heavy drinking and smoking had caused Hudson health problems—including two heart operations—and on 8 June 1984, he learned that he had AIDS, though he revealed that fact to only a few friends. Attempting to remain active, he interrupted secret treatments in Paris to appear in nine episodes of *Dynasty* (1984-85) and considered an offer to appear on Broadway in *La Cage aux Folles;* but he could not conceal his failing health, and when he attended a press conference with Day on 15 July 1985, his haggard appearance shocked everyone. After flying to Paris for more treatments, Hudson collapsed and was hospitalized. On 25 July, Hudson authorized a statement that confirmed he had contracted AIDS. While the news made headlines throughout the world, the dying Hudson quietly returned to Los Angeles. At an AIDS benefit on 19 September, his final public statement was read, which included these now famous words: "I am not happy that I have AIDS. But if that is helping others, I can, at least, know that my own misfortune has had some positive worth." He died at home on 2 October 1985.

Considerable controversy continues to surround Hudson's final months. While intimates insist that he agreed to the 25 July announcement and 19 September statement, some argue that he was far too ill to be involved in such decisions; there was also a notorious lawsuit filed by Christian, alleging that Hudson had not informed him of his condition, that was eventually settled out of court. Still, Hudson's courage in revealing his condition inspired many, and for a while, his impact on AIDS fund-raising and research, and public acceptance of homosexuality, seemed to outweigh his contributions as an actor—though his film performances, especially in *Giant* and *Seconds,* deserve continuing attention.

References:

Bego, Mark. *Rock Hudson: Public and Private.* New York: Signet Books, 1986.

Clark, Tom, with Dick Kleiner. *Rock Hudson, Friend of Mine.* New York: Pharos Books, 1989.

Friedman, Jeanette. *Rock Hudson: Death of a Giant.* Cresskill, New Jersey: Sharon Starbooks, 1985.

Gates, Phyllis. *My Husband, Rock Hudson.* Garden City, New York: Doubleday & Company, 1987.

Hadleigh, Boze. *Conversations with My Elders.* New York: St. Martin's Press, 1986: 175-207.

Hicks, Jimmie. "Rock Hudson: The Film Actor as Romantic Hero," in *Films in Review* (New York), May 1975: 267-89.

Hudson, Rock, and Sara Davidson. *Rock Hudson: His Story.* New York: William Morrow and Company, 1986.

Mercer, Jane. *Great Lovers of the Movies.* New York: Crescent Books, 1975: 137-45.

Oppenheimer, Jerry, and Jack Vitek. *Idol Rock Hudson: The True Story of an American Film Hero.* New York: Villard Books, 1986.

Parish, James Robert, and Don Stanke. *The All Americans.* New Rochelle, New Jersey: Arlington House, 1977: 197-249.

Parker, John. *Five for Hollywood.* London: Macmillan, 1989.

Royce, Brenda Scott. *Rock Hudson: A Bio-Bibliography.* Westport, Connecticut: Greenwood Press, 1995.

—Gary Westfahl

Holly Hughes

1955-

American performance artist

In the introduction to her collection of plays and performances, *Clit Notes: A Sapphic Sampler*, Holly Hughes encourages her audience to resist what she describes as "the epidemic of easy answers." She writes that "the truth is fine for some people, but a lot of us need more. We need a story." The complex, controversial and necessary stories that Hughes performs are rooted in questions without easy answers—questions like: What does it mean to speak of lesbian sexual desire? What language(s) can you use—create, borrow, or steal? What iconography? How does your family of origin influence/ disrupt/ resist/ encourage those desires? What kind of theater can accommodate them? How will public performance of such questions affect your reception and funding? This last question was met with some frightening answers in 1990, when the National Endowment of the Arts (NEA) canceled the grants awarded four controversial artists, including Hughes. Though the "NEA Four" sued the endowment and the denied grants were reinstated in 1993, the ugly, resonating "easy answer" was that some stories—especially the "obscene" stories of homosexual desire—were too threatening to be shared.

Born 10 March 1955 in the navy bean capital of the world—Saginaw, Michigan—Holly Hughes grew up in a Republican upper-middle-class family. Her mother was unhappy. Her father was often absent. She and her younger sister were raised with traditional values, but that did not mean she was doomed to lead a "normal life," meaning a life like her parents'. Only if she wanted to. And she did not. Perhaps without even meaning to, her parents encouraged the life of an escape artist. "It was my parents who taught me how to imagine a life different from theirs," says Hughes. "They gave me stories." As a child, Hughes imagined alternate stories, ones that "opened places for [her] to disappear, where no one could follow." The ability to create such places was a skill that she would use later, in her writing and performance, with a more extroverted purpose. Hughes attended Kalamazoo College, graduating in 1977. Soon after, she moved to New York City, a place where anything could happen, to take classes at the New York Feminist Art Institute. But her aspirations of becoming a painter were frustrated after the first few months of exposure to the overabundance of disappointing minimalist art in SoHo. Between shifts as a waitress, she searched for other outlets for her creativity. Such wanderings eventually led her to the East Village's WOW (Women's One World) Cafe, a collective performance space, run by a group of women who were, as Hughes puts it, primarily "refugees from lesbian feminism who had gone AWOL from other collectives." A butch/femme dynamic was at home with them. Sex was not enemy territory. Hughes' curiosity about the women and events at WOW seduced her into volunteering at the cafe. That was the beginning.

Wowing the WOW Cafe

In the encouraging environment of WOW, Hughes began making theater in 1983. As she writes in *Clit Notes*, "The kind of theater I make is generally and often pejoratively called performance art." And further, as she explained to Joe Brown and Kara Swisher of the *Washington Post* in a 1995 interview, "The term 'performance artist' exists primarily because mainstream theater is so conservative and married to naturalism and so uncomfortable with autobiography that they had to create this whole other category." Whatever the name for the kind of theater that she was creating, Hughes began using it as a vehicle to explore and articulate her desire for women. The audience at WOW was listening and watching. Her first evening of performance there, called *Shrimp in a Basket*, contained the first part of what was to become her first major play, *The Well of Horniness*.

Filled with allusive, campy, dyke sexiness, Hughes' first play used some of the same parodic strategies that were a feature of WOW productions. Mining the imagery of pulp novels, soap opera TV culture, and the butch-femme dynamics of lesbian subculture, *The Well of Horniness* introduces Garnet McClit, lady dick, a stock

Holly Hughes. ***Photograph by John Lovett.***

figure for Hughes of the tough, girl-clue-watching detective. Late in the play, Hughes offers this useful stage direction, which seems to speak as a prime directive for the production: "Feel free to go too far; it's the only way to go in this play." The play was performed several times in the East Village and in several different forms, including a production as a radio-show for WBAI in New York City. Hughes was on her way.

The Lady Dick (1985) reintroduces the she-dick Garnet McClit. In the headnote accompanying the piece in *Clit Notes*, Hughes offers a tribute to the pulp murder mystery novels that her mother used to read and that she also picked up—the stuff she found sexy, even though she was not supposed to. In *The Lady Dick* Hughes transforms the iconography of such novels and their attendant mystery into a different sort of mystery, one that can puzzle over questions of identification such as "I still don't get how you can be a dick and a lady at the same time," while challenging assumptions about what it means to be either.

Hughes Takes *Dress Suits* on the Road

Dress Suits to Hire, which Hughes wrote for Lois Weaver and Peggy Shaw of The Split Britches theater troupe, marked a turning point for her because it was written with the intention of being performed outside WOW, at the East Village's Performance Space 122—not primarily a lesbian space. After opening at P.S. 122 in May 1987, the play moved to midtown Manhattan's Women's Interart Center and then on tour to Milwaukee, Wisconsin, and to the University of Michigan. Several theater critics and scholars have addressed the complications and concerns of performing "lesbian theater" in a larger venue, questioning whether a more conventional theater setting and a heterosexual appropriation undermines its subversive methods and content. But Hughes, in an interview with Rebecca Schneider printed in the Spring 1989 issue of the *Drama Review,* insists that it is important to put the work out there in a larger context, even if that move can be scary. As for the issue of "heterosexual appropriation," Hughes resists the idea of some particular correct (lesbian) reading. She says, "People will approach my work in different ways....People have thought all sorts of things. And those things could be there! I really believe in art and I believe in allowing the audience to have their own personal subjective view."

In addition to stirring up scholarly conflict on the state(s) of lesbian theater, *Dress Suits* also earned Hughes authorship of her own genre, "Dyke Noir." In a review for the *Village Voice*, C. Carr uses this term to describe the world of Hughes' play—the tough talkers and "the shady, shifty operators" from hard-boiled fiction as well as the kind of gallows humor her work employs. *Dress Suits to Hire* begins with Deeluxe's strangling by her own right hand, which is inhabited by Little Peter. So there is a dead body and a mystery from the first scene. As the character Michigan questions and answers the authorities via a disconnected plastic phone, "did I discover it? Many years ago. I first discovered the body in the Hotel Universal in Salamanca." Has there been a crime? And, if so, who has committed it? As Carr puts it in her review, "the *characters* are the crime—women who drive each other to emotional extremes, who put their sexuality upfront where everyone has to acknowledge it." These are the kinds of crimes and mysteries and dicey territories that Hughes relishes exploring in her work.

After the success of *Dress Suits*, Hughes continued to write and perform and to garner attention. In 1988 at P.S. 122 she introduced a version of her next major work, *World without End,* which is in the form of a monologue. In it Hughes speaks from the point of view of the daughter who, after her mother's death, interrogates her own sexuality and the complex legacy of her mother. Hughes' own mother had died in 1987. The daughter asks those burning questions that remain after the body is gone, and in asking, tells a powerful story of origins.

The NEA Controversy and Its Aftermath

In the late 1980s, public funding of art became a battleground of ideologies. Work that addressed the body was especially vulnerable to attacks, particularly if that body was queer. Artists such as Hughes, who had received NEA funding for "out" work performed in spaces that were publicly funded, began to expect trouble in 1989 when Congress passed a restrictive language code which equated homosexuality with obscenity. Work that was deemed "obscene" would not receive public funding. In 1990 John Frohnmayer, then chairperson of the NEA, vetoed funding for Hughes, and three other performance artists, Tim Miller, Karen Finley, and John Fleck. The NEA Four, as they were called, were attacked in Congress by Jesse Helms and other conservatives, and in the press, often by people who had never even seen their work. Hughes and the other artists became symbols of the "art wars."

Though the artists sued the NEA, challenged the political grounds on which the defunding was made, and eventually won back their grants, an atmosphere of homophobia loomed large. The negative publicity also took a personal toll on the artists. In a June 1994 article for the *New York Times,* Hughes told William Harris that basically she lost two years of her life. She endured public humiliation, death threats, and pressure from the anti-censorship movement not to bring up the issue of homophobia because it would turn off straight people and threaten the success of the campaign. She was depressed and felt a hopelessness that kept her from writing. The public nature of the debate also affected her family of origin; a section of her performance *Clit Notes* addresses their hurtful response to her ordeal.

After several years of difficulties, including the illness and death of her father in the summer of 1993, Hughes, with the support of her friends and colleagues, began writing, performing, and teaching again, with a vengeance, in New York and across the country. Her solo work *Clit Notes* was commissioned by the New York Shakespeare Festival and opened at P.S. 122 in February 1994 and went on tour in 1994 and 1995, after having been performed in progress around the U.S. and England in the fall of 1993. In a March 1994 review for the *Village Voice* of the Hughes performance, Laurie Stone wrote the following: "Blistering and poignant, *Clit Notes* is an apologia, a kind of letter to her dead father, chronicling how she came to be a lesbian and how sex, the out life, and solo performance merged into a calling." The piece won a prestigious Obie Award, which honors the best Off-Broadway work in New York.

Clit Notes Hits the Shelves

In April 1996 Grove Press published *Clit Notes: A Sapphic Sampler*, Hughes' first collection of plays. The collection includes the major pieces discussed above and is a testament to her craft as a storyteller. Part of Hughes' introduction to the collection also exists in her current work in progress, tentatively titled *Cat O' Nine Tales*, which was performed in the winter of 1996 at P.S. 122. Laurie Stone's February 1996 review for the *Village Voice* includes Hughes' comments on the changing nature of her work: "The earlier work showed the escapades of an escape artist. Now I'm writing as an exile. There is no complete escape from the original family."

As Holly Hughes' work continues to grapple with difficult questions from many different vantage points, her audience continues to benefit from her astute observations and her resistance to the easy answers. Her stories are intimate and vital and human, the telling is magical.

References:

Brown, Joe and Kara Swisher. "Holly Hughes's Main Man," in *The Washington Post*, 18 March 1995: DO2.

Carr, C. "The Lady Is a Dick: The Dyke Noir Theater of Holly Hughes," in *Village Voice* (New York), 19 May 1987: 32.

Davy, Kate. "Reading Past the Heterosexual Imperative: *Dress Suits to Hire*," in *Drama Review* 33, spring 1989: 153-170.

Harris, William. "The NEA Four: Life After Symbolhood," in the *New York Times*, 5 June 1994.

Hughes, Holly. *Clit Notes: A Sapphic Sampler*. New York: Grove, 1996.

Jaques, Damien. "Holly Hughes' Annual Fall Gig is Still Engrossing," in *Milwaukee Journal Sentinel*, 28 September 1995: 8.

Nichols, John. "The Bete Noire of the Radical Right," in *Capital Times* (Madison, Wisconsin), 10 October 1994: 1C.

Schneider, Rebecca. "Holly Hughes: Polymorphous Perversity and the Lesbian Scientist," in *Drama Review* 33, Spring 1989: 171-183.

Stone, Laurie. "Holly Daze," in *Village Voice* (New York), 13 February 1996: 11.

———. "Holly Hughes: Her Heart Belongs to Daddy," in *Ms.* September/October 1994: 88.

———. "Mama Mia," in *Village Voice* (New York), 16 February 1993.

———. "Tongue Untied," in *Village Voice* (New York), 22 March 1994: 92, 96.

Welsh, Anne Marie. "Monologues Hold Audience Spellbound," in the *San Diego Union-Tribune*, 6 May 1995: E-6.

Wilmoth, Charles M. "The Archaeology of Muff Diving: An Interview with Holly Hughes," in *Drama Review* 35, Fall 1991: 216-220.

—Karen Helfrich

Langston Hughes

1902-1967

African-American author

One of the giants of American and African-American literature, Langston Hughes developed his craft inside the lesbian and gay communities of New York City, Mexico, Paris, the Soviet Union, and Africa.

Early Life

Born 1 February 1902 in Joplin, Missouri, Langston Hughes early faced one of many contradictions in his life. His mother and father had mixed and rich backgrounds, but they lived in a society that classified them as black and inferior. His father, James Nathaniel Hughes, a lawyer, worked with a mining company and his mother, Carrie Mercer Langston Hughes, wrote verse, acted, and taught school.

His father rejected the race barrier in the United States and took the family to Cuba and Mexico, but the mother soon returned to the United States. She and Langston lived with her mother Mary Langston, a widow of one of John Brown's soldiers killed in the attack on Harper's Ferry. She once appeared on the platform with Theodore Roosevelt to commemorate the famous rebellion. After his grandmother died and his mother had remarried, Langston shifted about until he went to high school in Cleveland.

In high school, Langston followed the path described in his short story "Blessed Assurance," about a young homosexual. Dilly "was good at marbles, once fair at baseball, and a real whiz at tennis. He could have made the track team had he not preferred the French Club, the Dramatic Club, and Glee Club." While he himself excelled in track, Hughes particularly enjoyed acting with his closest friend in the school's Dramatic Club. Taking Paul Dunbar and Walt Whitman for his models, Langston wrote poetry and short stories that the school paper published. Elected class poet, he graduated from Cleveland Central High School in 1920.

Mexican Connections

In the summers of 1919 and 1920, Langston Hughes lived with his father in Mexico City and nearby Toluca where James had prospered during the revolution (1910-20). Langston came to hate his father intensely but he loved Mexico for its different sexual, racial, and intellectual milieu. During the revolution, José Vasconcelos became minister of education and pushed the doctrine that Mexico represented a mix between strains of indigenous, European, and other groups who had created a new cosmic race. Under his direction in the department of education, a group of homosexuals assembled, who undertook to transform Mexican drama, poetry and literature. Hughes met the *Contemporaneos.* Carlos Pellicer (to whom Hughes inscribed his first book) dedicated a poem "Desires" to the well know gay poet Salvador Novo:

Tropics, why did you give me
these hands brimming with color?
Whatever I touch
turns over with sunlight.

When the celebrated bullfighter Sanchez Mejias (a lover of Lorca) appeared in Mexico, Langston in his autobiography described how his own hair stood on end and cold chills ran down his back "with the daring and beauty" of the athlete. After the fight, Hughes leaped into the ring and carried off "a pair of golden banderillas as a souvenir, with the warm blood still on them." (*Big Sea,* 70)

Gay Network

With funds from his father, Hughes entered Columbia University in the fall of 1921, where he faced discrimination in the dormitories but found another life in nearby Harlem. His poems had been published in the *Crisis* edited by W.E.B. Dubois of the NAACP. Hughes soon took up with Augustus Dill, a gay secretary to DuBois. Dill introduced him to the Harlem branch of the YMCA and a whole circle of gay or bisexual black writers: Countee Cullen, Wallace Thurman, Bruce Nugent, Alain Locke and others. Through them he met gay patrons such as Carl VanVetchen and Noel Sullivan.

When Harlem was in vogue, Hughes picked up the sounds of jazz bands and banter at such ambient parties as those of Aleia Walker. Harlem bars and rent parties offered gay and Lesbian performers like Gladys Bentley or Earl "Snakehips" Tucker, who ground his pelvis to rotate a long tassel on his sequined girdle. Hughes incorporated these rhythms in his first book *The Weary Blues* (1926). Mexican artist Miguel Covarrubias drew the cover and Hughes inscribed a copy for Carlos Pellacier. During his lifetime, Hughes sent fifteen books of poetry to press.

International Horizons

Hughes never liked to stay long in one place and found it hard to understand people who could not sleep in a strange bed. After a year at Columbia, Hughes took off as a crew member on a freighter bound for Africa in June 1923. Sexuality and homosexuality appeared everywhere the sailors went. In Africa the openness found in the ports stunned him; he may have visited male and female prostitutes there, but when the crew of his ship gang-banged two poor women, he did not join them.

The beauty of the black youth turned him on more than any women. In his autobiography he wrote admiringly of "a host of naked Africans," who joined the crew and when the missionaries complained of their nude bathing, "they turned their backs and hid their sex between their legs, evidently not realizing it then stuck out behind." Watching the youth load mahogany logs, Hughes felt the same excitement as watching Sanchez Mejias in Mexico: "It was beautiful and dangerous work, those black boys swimming there in the tossing waves among iron chains and the great rolling logs...."

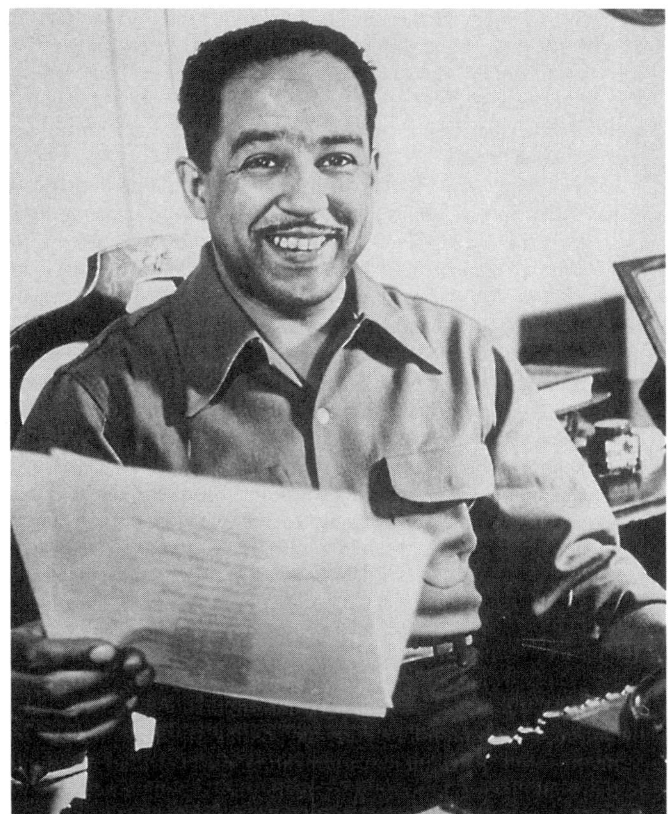

Langston Hughes

In 1924 he took a second freighter to Africa but jumped ship and made his way to Paris and eventually Italy. He worked lesbian, gay, and back alley clubs in Paris. Again he found a milieu in which racial and sexual lines followed very different directions than in the United States. A line from "Bird in Orbit" in *Ask Your Mama* salutes the negritude poets from the Paris twenties: "ALIOUNE AIME SEDAR SIPS HIS NEGRITUDE" celebrates Alioune Diop, Aimé Césaire and Léopold Sedar Senghor.

Radicalism

For many whites just the demand for citizenship for African-Americans smacked of communism. During the 1930s as the Great Depression struck blacks even harder than whites, many looked with fear and others with hope toward the downtrodden. Langston Hughes stood with the party of hope. He wrote *Scottsboro, Limited* (1932) and visited the young black men accused of sexually assaulting a white woman. He joined a group of blacks who attempted to make a movie in Russia on United States race relations. In 1937 he went to besieged Madrid and lived with the Republican Alianza Para Intellectuals, where he translated poems by Frederico Garcia Lorca, who had been assassinated by Falangists the previous year.

Good Morning Revolution: Uncollected Writings of Social Protest (1973) begins with his lines: "A world I dream where black or white,/ Whatever race you be,/ Will share the bounties of the earth/ And every man is free." Among his plays of protest *Mulatto* (1931),

Soul Gone Home (1937), *Little Ham* (1935), and *Tambourines to Glory* (1949) built up to his great work *Montage of a Dream Deferred* (1950) with the memorable:

What happens to a dream deferred?
Does it dry up
like a raisin in the sun? Or fester like a sore —
And then run?
Does it stink like rotten meat?
Or crust and sugar over—
like a syrupy sweet?
Maybe it just sags
like a heavy load.
Or does it explode?

As he became more successful and more radical, Hughes became a marked man. As early as 1934, when he stayed in Carmel, California, the local newspaper attacked him and rumors spread that he would be assassinated. In 1940 evangelical Christians picketed his engagement in Los Angeles. During the 1940s on the lecture circuit, Hughes found hecklers organized by protofascist Gerald L.K. Smith and in 1944 the FBI stepped up its surveillance of him. In 1949, *Life* magazine attacked him along with Albert Einstein, Paul Robeson, and Leonard Bernstein as "commie dupes." In 1953, Senator Joseph McCarthy subpoenaed him to account for his behavior.

Hughes approached radicalism as he approached sexuality: cautiously but nonetheless firmly and humorously. Within *Montage of a Dream Deferred* appeared his most explicitly gay poem "Café: 3 a.m.":

Detectives from the vice squad
with wary sadistic eyes
spotting fairies.
Degenerates,
some folks say.
But God, Nature,
or somebody
made them that way.
Police lady or Lesbian
over there? *Where?*

Hughes' Homosexuality

Biographers have approached Hughes' sexuality in various ways. Hardly any knowledgeable person has argued that he was primarily interested in women or even bisexual. The argument rests between those who claim he was homosexual and those who claim he was asexual. Faith Berry, in *Langston Hughes: Before and Beyond Harlem* (1983) asserts that while he struggled against it, by age thirty-one, Hughes "had lost his battle against homosexuality, but it was not easy for him to accept defeat." Arnold Rampersad's two volume *Life of Langston Hughes* (1986, 1988) presents the poet as essentially asexual and certainly not homosexual. In the acknowledgement to the first volume, he writes: "As for the increasingly fashionable tendency to assert, without convincing evidence, that Hughes was a homosexual, I will say at this point only that such a conclusion seems unfounded, and that the evidence suggests a more complicated sexual nature." Hughes series of simple stories, ironically poked fun at those trying to complicate things.

Commentators have had too narrow a view of homosexuality and some have weighed the particular burdens laid on black gay men in the United States. In Hughes' short story "Blessed Assurance," the father worries about his son being a homosexual and thinks he's "more disturbed about his son's transition than if they had been white. Negroes have enough crosses to bear." The father worried about effeminacy as well, praying "God, don't let him put an earring in his ear like some...." Arna Bontemps (perhaps Hughes closest friend) praised Langston with an ambiguous note: "Never betrayed the mincing or posturing offensive to the straight world." (Rampersad)

Hughes, of course, kept his sexual interests to himself, but one problem the biographers cannot understand that is all of Hughes' many relatively open (or at least well documented) homosexual friends all agree with one voice that they never had sex with Hughes. Countee Cullen and Alain Locke's letters contain stories of their unsuccessful efforts to get Hughes to bed. This seeming paradox can be resolved simply: Hughes did not care for educated men as sexual partners. Not that he had any aversions to gay men or to women, but Hughes did not want entanglements, marriage, or to have or be a lover to anyone.

Like Walt Whitman he preferred working-class men, but unlike Whitman he most enjoyed black men. Rampersad concludes that "Virile young men of very dark complexion fascinated him." In Africa Hughes had met many men who attracted him and he had felt great anxiety that his skin was too light.

While Hughes kept much to himself, he slyly crafted the first volume of his autobiography, *The Big Sea* (1940) to celebrate his love for George. George came from Kentucky and had previously worked as a valet for a traveling drag queen. Hughes discreetly describes George's sexual play: "talking and laughing and gaily waving his various appendages around." George and Langston shared their quarters with a Puerto Rican queen who liked George and silk stockings. After crossing the Atlantic, while the other sailors went for women and drink, George and Langston slipped off together. Langston bought him a bottle of cognac. They "walked up a hill to the top of the town to drink it. The sun was setting. The sea and the palm trees of Horta were aglow." Hughes doesn't say whether they had sex or not (does it really matter?) but the symbolism of their descent into the town is suggestive. "George smashed the cognac bottle against the wall of a blue house and said: 'I wants to holler.'" Langston didn't want to draw attention, but George said "This town's too small to holler in, but I got to holler, anyhow." He let out a great "Yee-hoo-oo-o!" A nearby policeman ignored them.

Hughes had a fascination for policemen in uniform. In 1950, he explored writing a biography of Samuel Jesse Battle, the first black police officer in New York City. That project fell through as publishers turned the book down. In November 1960, invited to Nigeria to witness the inauguration of Nnamdi Azikiwe, Langston caught the eye of a handsome young policeman, Sunday Osuya, and met him later in the art museum where they exchanged addresses; Osuya also gave him the names and addresses of other policemen. They exchanged letters. Osuya wrote, "I still remember, how we met and how you treated me from then and I have, till now, begin to think the type of person you are and the God who brought me your way." (Rampersad) In his will, Hughes "made generous financial provision for ... Sunday Osuya of Nigeria."

Gay Themes

Hughes became uncomfortable with what he saw as harshness in the work of Richard Wright, Leroi Jones (Amiri Baraka), and James Baldwin. He never relinquished the joy of laughing. His story

"Blessed Assurance" uses humor in telling the story of Delly the choirboy, his father and the choirmaster, who faints when overcome with the beauty of the boy's voice. Hughes later described what he said was his "first homosexual experience" in Tenerife: "'Won't it hurt you,' I said./ 'Not unless it's square,' he said. 'Are you square?"/ 'Could be,' I said./ 'Let's see,' he said..." (Rampersad).

A great number of Hughes poems can be read as either gay or straight: "Sailor," "Water-Front Streets," "Port Town," "Young Sailor," "Joy," or "Trumpet Player" all sustain homoerotic readings. "Cabaret" appeared in Weary Blues (1926):

> Does a jazz-band ever sob?
> They say a jazz-band's gay.
> Yet as the vulgar dancers whirled
> and the wan night wore away,
> One said she heard the jazz-band sob
> When the little dawn was grey.

In his *Life of Langston Hughes,* Arnold Rampersad suggests that Hughes held on to "a quality of ageless, sexless, inspired innocence, Peter Pan-like, which race and even sex brought down to earth without sullying."

References:

Berry, Faith. *Langston Hughes: Before and Beyond Harlem.* Westport, Connecticut, 1983.

Rampersad, Arnold. *The Life of Langston Hughes.* Volume I: *1902-1941: I Too Sing America.* New York: Oxford, 1986. Volume II: *1941-1967, I Dream A World.* New York: Oxford, 1988.

Wagner, Jean. *Black Poets of the United States from Paul Laurence Dunbar to Langston Hughes,* translated by Kenneth Douglas. Urbana: University of Illinois, 1973.

Watson, Steven. *The Harlem Renaissance, Hub of African-American Culture, 1920-1930.* New York: Pantheon, 1995.

Wood, Gregory. "Gay Re-Readings of the Harlem Renaissance Poets," in *Critical Essays: Gay and Lesbian Writers of Color,* edited by Emmanuel S. Nelson. Binghampton: Haworth, 1993.

—Charles Shively

Alberta Hunter

1895-1984

African-American singer and songwriter

Alberta Hunter's long life and marvelously varied career reads like a chronicle of twentieth-century blues and jazz. From Memphis to Chicago to New York—and then to London, Paris, and Copenhagen—Hunter was living proof that drive, determination, and a desire to sing "like a million dollars" can lift one up from poverty and discrimination to heights undreamed of, especially for a black woman in whose mind lesbianism tarnished the image of respectability she so desperately sought. Hunter sang with and composed for the likes of Louis Armstrong, Ethel Waters, Fats Waller, Bessie Smith, Josephine Baker, and Paul Robeson, and crossed paths with presidents, prime ministers and princes around the world. Yet, somehow she always maintained a down-home dignity and common sense, balanced by the sparkling wit and naughtiness of her lyrics. As her nephew Sam Sharpe told biographers Frank C. Taylor and Gerald Cook in, "going to see her was like going to an old-time faith healer."

Alberta Hunter was born on April Fool's Day in 1895 in Memphis, Tennessee. She was the second of two girls, and claimed her older sister, La Tosca, was always preferred by her mother because she was lighter-skinned and prettier. Her father, a Pullman porter, abandoned the family soon after Alberta's birth, although her mother insisted for years that he had died of pneumonia. After he left, Alberta's mother was forced to take a job as a maid in a white bordello. Starting when she was ten, Alberta was molested by both a family friend and her school principal, traumas she later realized instilled in her a resentment for most men.

Going Places

From early on, it was obvious Hunter was going places. Her strict mother taught her to respect herself, while her beloved Granny gave her "the sweets while Mama was slapping out the discipline," according to Taylor and Cook. Every time Granny would bathe Hunter, she would touch the three moles on the bottoms of her feet and say: "This child is going to be a wanderer." "She was right, too," Hunter said decades later after circling the globe many times. "I've been more places accidentally than most people have been on purpose."

Hunter showed no signs of being a musical prodigy. She was shrewd with money and "always jiving," she claimed. Stuck with Granny at church each and every Sunday "from the minute they opened the doors to the time they closed them," she and a friend would mug the kids at church for the pennies they had brought for the offering and sneak off to buy ice cream. Years later, she would surreptitiously slip tips intended for all the musicians in her cleavage (feigning an itch) and was even caught with her hand in the tip jar during club raids. Near the end of her life, she had numerous tax problems, claiming she could never understand why anyone like herself should have to pay more than $7000 a year.

What early musical education she did get came from Beale Street and the flashy blues bands that would parade up and down it. Between 1890 and 1900, the population in Memphis doubled, primarily because blacks from the South were drawn to job opportunities and the comparatively open sociability this new black capital of the mid-South evidenced. The reputed father of the blues, W.C. Handy, moved from Alabama to Memphis in 1905, and Hunter would run down to Beale Street the minute she heard the brassy Handy band. Years later, when Hunter was making a name for herself in Chicago, Handy would come and look *her* up.

When she was eleven, Hunter's mother remarried, and she got even less attention when her half-sister Josephine was born. In school, things were not much better. "I was never playful like a child," she told Taylor and Cook. "I was always like you'd expect a grown woman to be." Truth was, she was also avoiding any of the boys' sexual advances. She claimed every boyfriend she ever had was soon stolen by some other girl, and years later she waxed philosophical on this point when she exclaimed to Taylor and Cook: "Oh Lord, God is good! They got the marriage, and I got the fame."

At sixteen, Hunter made her way to Chicago, hoping to get a job singing like the daughter of a friend of her mother, who was making a whopping $10 a week. After spending some time as a cook in a boarding house and dutifully sending money home to her mother, she finally wore down the owners of Dago Frank's, one of the city's wilder whorehouses, and got a job there as a singer. She stayed on for two years, honing her performance skills and earning both admiration and good tips from the girls, pimps, and customers.

Over the next few years, she worked her way up through a succession of both black and white clubs and cabarets, earning respect as both a singer and a composer, and gained a following. Soon she was known as the "south-side's sweetheart," and songwriters were flocking to her to try and get exposure for their new blues material. When her step-father and mother separated, she moved her mother up to Chicago.

Hunter got her first taste of the big time with an extended engagement at Chicago's Dreamland Cafe in 1917. There she sang with Joe "King" Oliver's band and earned $17.59 week. Within a few years, she was making $35 a week and an unheard-of $400-$500 in tips. It was around this time that she also premiered her most famous composition, "Down-Hearted Blues," which was recorded and made a "signature" song by Bessie Smith in 1923. In six months, the record sold 800,000 copies, and Hunter never saw any royalty payments.

Alberta Hunter

Propriety and Lesbianism

In the 1920s and early 1930s, Hunter and Smith found themselves recording some of the same songs, "'Taint Nobody's Business If I Do," and "Aggravatin' Papa," among them. Yet, there was no animosity between them, and Hunter always said she admired Smith's singing, just as she did that of her other contemporaries, like Ethel Waters. She would never, of course, try to sing like them, but she also avoided them partly because of their sometimes-public problems with lovers, Smith with her men and Waters with her women. Hunter was always closeted about her lesbianism, concerned with propriety and the progression of her singing career. She simply never discussed it.

While singing at a club in Cincinnati in 1919, she set her sights on a handsome waiter named Willard Townsend. The two impulsively crossed the border into Kentucky and were married, partly to squelch the gossip that Hunter was a lesbian, according to Taylor and Cook, and partly because Willard represented the respectability Hunter longed for. The couple returned to Chicago, but Hunter could not bring herself to sacrifice her career for the marriage and would not even sleep with Townsend under her mother's roof. They stayed together only two months, though Hunter did not divorce him till four years later. "Lord, I treated him awful," she confessed years later.

The closest Hunter came to coming out of the closet was when she applied for a passport in 1920. She had moved to New York to further her career, and listed her address for the U.S. Department of Commerce as 109 West 139th Street, c/o Miss Lottie Tyler. Lottie, a maid to a touring white actress, had handed her card to Hunter after one of her performances in Chicago, whispering, according to Taylor and Cook: "If you ever come to New York, come and see me." She must have made an impression for, although one or both of them eventually changed their mind about the trip to Europe, they remained, according to Taylor and Cook, "friends and lovers for many years." Hunter's strong, independent will to travel and pursue her career no doubt accounted for the fact that they did not live together for long, though they did meet whenever their conflicting schedules permitted, and actually did travel to Europe a few years later.

The Pay-Off

Hunter's ambition was beginning to pay off. Traveling between New York and Chicago, she met and worked with Louis Armstrong, Sidney Bechet, Eubie Blake, Fletcher Henderson, and Fats Waller. Sophie Tucker even asked her to teach her how to sing "A Good Man Is Hard to Find," but Hunter wasn't about to give away any of her secrets. Besides, as she told Taylor and Cook, "nobody can learn my style because I don't even know it myself. It's always changing."

She started landing roles in various musicals both on and off Broadway. She also began recording under contract with the Gennett label, which was making a nice little profit with so-called "race" recordings. Ever the shrewd businesswoman, she also recorded for other labels under pseudonyms to maximize her own profits, using names like Mae Alix, Helen Roberts, Monette Moore, and (perhaps with a little vengeance in mind) that of her half-sister Josephine Beatty.

Feeling she had conquered the Big Apple, she set her sights on Europe, following in the footsteps of Josephine Baker. In 1927, she and Lottie headed for Paris, ostensibly on vacation but, at least in Hunter's mind, also to look for work. Two months after their arrival, Lottie returned to the States with another woman, but Hunter stayed on. "I tore the place up," she told Taylor and Clark. "I put my foot down and went to town," she recalled, as she moved both socially and professionally to the Riviera and finally to London in 1928. Oscar Hammerstein and Jerome Kern saw her there and offered her the part of Queenie opposite Paul Robeson in the London production of *Showboat* in 1928.

Between 1927 and 1937, Hunter worked chiefly in Europe, eventually traveling with her own musical company to enormous success in Stockholm, Copenhagen and even Alexandria, Egypt. She returned briefly to New York and Chicago during this decade, but was now labeled too sophisticated for a black entertainer in the ever-racist States. "They do not want refinement and finesse in a Negro performer," she later said. "All they want is niggerism, a whole lot of foot-stomping and shouting." Biographers Taylor and Cook righteously label this period in Hunter's life as her "commute between pride and prejudice." Alas, in 1938, while in Paris, she received a letter from the American Consulate advising her—like scores of other Americans—to return home. War loomed on the horizon, and even Hunter's courage was no match for Hitler's bellicose aims.

Where Is Home?

But home was both not what it used to be ... and ever the same. Spoiled by the more egalitarian Europeans, she found it painful and demeaning to step back onto America's racist shores. Moreover, the blues was being supplanted by the more romantic melodies of the burgeoning big-band era. With lucrative engagements scarce, she savvily softened both her look and style and signed on for a series of tours with the USO, traveling extensively to perform for the troops during World War II, and again in the early 1950s in Korea. She continued to perform sporadically both stateside and in London, but by 1954, she fell on increasingly hard times and retired from show business.

By now, Hunter was nearly 60 and had enjoyed a full and exciting career well beyond her wildest Memphis-girlhood dreams. Many would have been content to rest on such substantial laurels well into their old age, but not Hunter.

In 1954, she went back to school and studied to be a nurse. In 1957, she got a job at Goldwater Hospital in New York City, but only after she lied about her age, saying she was only fifty when she was already sixty-two. "I wanted to give something back to my fellow man," she said of this period in her life. "I learned more about compassion during this time than in my whole life previous." Twenty years later, after the hospital believed it had allowed her to work a full five years beyond mandatory retirement at sixty-five, she retired at the age of eighty-two.

Coming Back with All Her Teeth

In May of 1977, Hunter was persuaded to go to a party at jazz pianist Bobby Short's Manhattan apartment. Barney Josephson, the owner of New York's popular jazz club the Cookery, was amazed and delighted to learn she was still alive, and invited her to perform "provided she still had all her teeth and would not whistle into the microphone," according to Taylor and Cook. When she opened there in October of that same year, she was an instant success, even after twenty years of not singing. The *New York Times* said she was "as relaxed as a bag of bones," and the following spring, the *Toronto Globe* described her—with her husky, risque renditions of songs like "Handyman"—as "a contralto that wears boots."

Though she was now in her eighties, there was no slowing Hunter down. She had her audience back in her sure, delicately iron hand. Through the late 1970s and into the 1980s, she made numerous television appearances, appeared at Carnegie Hall, sang for President Jimmy and Roslynn Carter (wearing her coat in the reception line "just so he could see I had one"), wrote the title song and recorded the soundtrack for Alan Rudolph's film *Remember My Name,* and recorded two albums featuring her favorite hits, *Amtrak Blues* in 1980, and *Look for the Silver Lining* in 1983. She also received an award from the city of Memphis "for her immense contribution to the development of an important art form, the blues." In accepting it, Hunter wasted no time reminding city fathers that as a child, she wasn't even allowed to walk on the sidewalks because of her color.

In 1983, Hunter fell ill and required colon surgery; but ever the crowd-pleaser, she still managed to complete a scheduled concert in Brazil. In the summer of 1984, her health still failing, she cut short a concert in Denver and was rushed back to New York. She died at home soon after.

Power, Conviction, Compassion

In the end, the woman who was always stingy with money but generous in spirit and song had stipulated only $700 be spent on her funeral. So, though a prominent undertaker picked up her body, a cut-rate Staten Island company cremated it. According to Taylor and Cook, Hunter's thoughts on death mirrored those of her long-time English friend Lady Mendl as reported in an article Hunter had clipped and saved from the *Montreal Herald* in 1950. "No funeral, no flowers, please and above all no exhibition even from the most loving friends. I want their memories of me to be in their hearts. If I have been of any help to any living being, let them think of that the day they hear I am dead."

Hunter closed many a show with the following sentiment: "If you came in with a troubled mind or heart and I have erased some of it, then I feel that my living has not been in vain." It is for these sentiments of power, conviction, and compassion—this triad of strengths that fired her contralto voice and fueled her life—that Alberta Hunter is best remembered.

References:

Alberta Hunter: My Castle's Rockin' (film). New York: View Video, 1992.

Taylor, Frank C. and Gerald Cook. *Alberta Hunter: A Celebration in Blues.* New York: McGraw-Hill, 1987.

—Jerome Szymczak

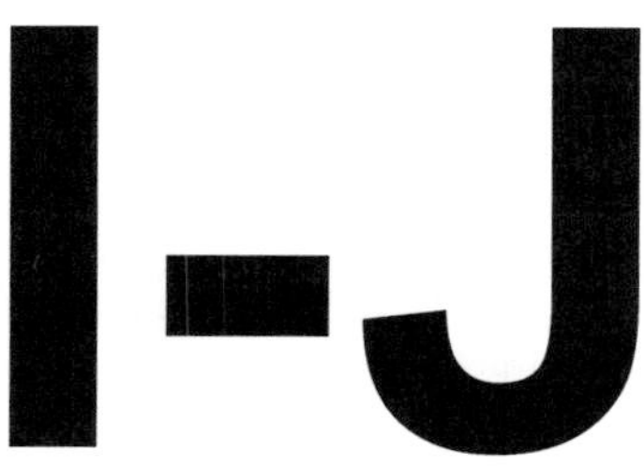

Christopher Isherwood

1904-1986

American novelist

By the time of his death from cancer on 4 January 1986, Christopher Isherwood had become a revered icon of contemporary Anglo-American gay culture, a courage-teacher who vigorously protested the "heterosexual dictatorship" and unashamedly expressed solidarity with his "kind." But he was more than merely a celebrity and role-model. He was also a masterful stylist, a subtle ironist and a witty and compassionate moralist. Indeed, he has a genuine claim to being considered the best British novelist of his generation.

He was born Christopher William Bradshaw Isherwood on 26 August 1904 in High Lane, Cheshire, the son of Kathleen Machell-Smith and Frank Bradshaw. An old and distinguished family of landed gentry, the Bradshaw-Isherwoods were among the principal landowners in Cheshire. In 1915, while a student at St. Edmund's preparatory school in Surrey, Isherwood learned that his father, a professional soldier, had been killed in action. In 1919, he entered Repton, a prestigious public school, where he formed a close friendship with future novelist Edward Upward, whom he joined at Corpus Christi College, Cambridge in 1923.

At Cambridge, Isherwood soon became disillusioned with the university's academic and social life and, by extension, with the social life of England. He and Upward collaborated on surrealistic fantasies that satirized the hypocrisy of English society. Unprepared for his examinations in 1925, Isherwood deliberately answered the questions facetiously and was asked to withdraw from the university. He took a job in London as secretary to a string quartet and began to write novels. At this time, he frankly acknowledged his homosexuality to himself and to his mother. In 1925, he also renewed his friendship with W. H. Auden, whom he had met during his last year at St. Edmund's. For over ten years, the two were to share an unromantic sexual relationship that gave their friendship an added dimension.

Auden cast Isherwood in the role of literary mentor and soon introduced him to a fellow Oxford undergraduate, Stephen Spender. The trio formed the nucleus of what would later be called "The Auden Gang," the angry young writers who dominated the English literary scene of the 1930s. Isherwood's early years are memorably captured in his first autobiographical work, *Lions and Shadows: An Education in the Twenties* (1938), which is in effect a portrait of the artist as a young man. In this book, the author observes with scientific detachment his earlier self as an exhibit "in the vast freak museum of our neurotic generation" and offers memorable depictions of Auden, Upward, and Spender.

Christopher Isherwood

Visits Berlin and Decides to Live There

Isherwood's first novel, *All the Conspirators*, was published in 1928. Studiedly experimental in its cinematic montages, abrupt shifts in point of view, and coded language and obscurity, the novel angrily indicts the family as the social agency most guilty of maiming an entire generation of young people, who themselves are exposed as co-conspirators against their own maturity. The book's poor sales did not encourage Isherwood's pursuit of a literary career, so he briefly attempted to study medicine at King's College, London. On 14 March 1929, however, Isherwood visited Berlin and decided to move there, abandoning his mother's dream of a medical career for him. In the German city, he felt liberated from the sexual and social inhibitions that stifled his development in England. Immersing himself in the bohemian world of male prostitutes, he lived almost anonymously in shabbily genteel and working-class areas of the city, where he revised his second novel, *The Memorial*, and translated his experience of the demimonde into what would eventually become the unsurpassed portrait of pre-Hitler Germany—the Berlin Stories.

In 1932, Isherwood fell in love with a German working class youth, Heinz. After Hitler's appointment as Chancellor in 1933, the couple resolved to leave Germany, a decision made urgent by Heinz's eligibility for military conscription. For the next four years, the lovers wandered restlessly from one European country to another searching for a place where they could settle together. The odyssey ended when Heinz had to return to Germany, where he was arrested and sentenced first to prison for homosexual activities with Isherwood and then to service in the German army.

Reputation Soars in the 1930s

During the 1930s, Isherwood rapidly gained a reputation as the most promising novelist of his generation. *The Memorial*, published in 1932, explores the continuing effects of World War I on English society, as crystallized in a complex portrait of a prominent country family. Described by Isherwood as "an epic disguised as a drawing room comedy," it is a novel of unusual depth and scope.

The publication of the Berlin Stories, comprised of *The Last of Mr. Norris* (1935) and *Goodbye to Berlin* (1938), made him famous. Portions of *Goodbye to Berlin*, including the novella-length section entitled "Sally Bowles," had been published earlier, attracting a great deal of attention to their author. In these works, Isherwood evokes a mythic city of sexual and political excitement only to expose the artificiality of myth in the harsh reality of loneliness and despair. He masters a unique voice, creates some of the most memorable characters in modern fiction, and movingly depicts a city in the process of internal decay. The brooding specter of Nazism hovers in the background of the Berlin Stories, finally to impinge even on characters as indifferent to politics as the landlady Fraulein Schroeder and the innocently naughty cabaret singer Sally Bowles.

In the 1930s, Isherwood became friends with his hero E. M. Forster, the only living writer whom he regarded as his master, and was hailed by Somerset Maugham and Virginia Woolf. By collaborating with Auden on three avant garde plays—*The Dog Beneath the Skin* (1935), *The Ascent of F6* (1936), and *On the Frontier* (1938)—and by supporting various left-wing causes, Isherwood gained a reputation for ideological commitment. However, partly because of his awareness of himself as a homosexual, he deeply distrusted communism and grew more and more disenchanted with left-wing rhetoric. In 1938, he and Auden traveled to China to report on the Sino-Japanese war. On their return, they stopped briefly in New York. The results of this trip were *Journey to a War* (1939), the only truly distinguished fruit of the Auden-Isherwood collaboration, and the fascination of both writers with America.

Emigrates to the United States and Converts to Vedantism

In January 1939, Isherwood and Auden emigrated to the United States, an action that reflected both their disenchantment with England and their loss of political faith. On board the ship bringing them to America, Isherwood realized that he was a pacifist, a conviction prompted by his fear that Heinz might be serving in the German army. When Auden and Isherwood arrived in New York, Auden almost immediately found the city stimulating and enjoyable, while Isherwood was overcome with despair. At the invitation of the English philosopher and expatriate Gerald Heard, he traveled to Southern California, where he was to settle for the rest of his life, working largely in the motion picture industry but occasionally accepting teaching appointments at area universities. He registered as a conscientious objector during World War II and became an American citizen in 1946.

Soon after his arrival in Los Angeles, Heard introduced Isherwood to Aldous Huxley and to Swami Prabhavananda, a Hindu monk of the Ramakrishna order who was head of the Vedanta Society of Southern California. Under the direction of Prabhavananda, Isherwood embraced Vedantism and seriously considered becoming a monk. His conversion after a long history of opposition to religion acknowledged a spiritual need that the narrowly moralistic Christianity of his youth could not satisfy. The importance of Isherwood's conversion can hardly be overstated, for all his later novels are influenced by Vedantism. In addition, he collaborated with Swami Prabhavananda on translations of several Hindu religious works, edited the journal *Vedanta and the West*, and wrote a biography of Ramakrishna (1965), as well as personal accounts of his religious experience, *An Approach to Vedanta* (1965) and *My Guru and His Disciple* (1980).

American Books, American Lovers

In 1945, Isherwood published *Prater Violet*, his first American novel, though it is set in London in the 1930s. At first glance, the brief novel appears to be a continuation of the Berlin Stories in a lighter vein and in a different place. Actually, however, the work's comic veneer conceals a deep seriousness and a new religious perspective. Also in 1945, Isherwood set up housekeeping with William Caskey, a handsome young photographer from Kentucky. In 1947, the couple made a six-month tour of South America, which resulted in the 1949 travel book, *The Condor and the Cows*, which was illustrated with Caskey's photographs. The Isherwood-Caskey relationship dissolved amicably in 1951, when Caskey embarked on a career as a merchant seaman.

In 1953, Isherwood fell in love with an eighteen-year-old college student, Don Bachardy, and in February 1954, the two began living together. Although the thirty-year discrepancy in their ages scandalized many of their friends, the union proved the most enduring and fulfilling of Isherwood's life. Bachardy has since achieved independent success as a portrait artist, and he and Isherwood collaborated on a number of motion picture and television scripts and on a dramatization of Isherwood's 1967 novel, *A Meeting by the River*. At the conclusion of his 1976 autobiography, *Christopher and His Kind*, Isherwood describes Bachardy as "the ideal companion to whom you can reveal yourself totally and yet be loved for what you are, not what you pretend to be."

Novel Hits Best-Seller List but Reputation Falls

Isherwood's reputation declined precipitously in the 1950s and 1960s, partly the result of the critical failure of *The World in the Evening* (1954), his first novel set in America. Although it achieved a wide popular audience, staying on the *New York Times* best-seller list for several months, it is generally regarded as the least successful of Isherwood's novels, marred as it is by wooden characterizations and sentimentality. Still, the book retains genuine interest, not least of all for its pioneering depiction of gay militancy and a famous definition of a gay aesthetic, "High and Low Camp." Indeed, Isherwood's increasingly frank depiction of homosexuality in the novels of the 1950s and 1960s probably contributed to the decline in his reputation. In addition, British critics may have harbored resentment over his expatriation, while his larger audience may have been unprepared for the new spiritual dimension of his later work.

The decline in Isherwood's reputation in the 1960s is particularly ironic, since the novels of the 1960s include some of his very best work. *Down There on a Visit* (1962) is a powerful exploration of the failure of commitment. Returning to the namesake narrator and loosely connected structural organization of *Goodbye to Berlin, Down There on a Visit* is the most insistently autobiographical of Isherwood's novels; as its separate sections cohere, it becomes a fascinating study of the changing self. Isherwood's eighth novel, *A Single Man* (1964), is his masterpiece. The novel traces one day in the life of George, a gay, middle-aged English professor grieving at the death of his lover of many years. Written in a style that alternates between poetic intensity and gentle irony, the book is at once a classic of gay literature and a profound meditation on death and decay and on the disparity between the body and the spirit. Isherwood's last novel, *A Meeting by the River* (1967), is set in a Hindu monastery on the banks of the Ganges and incorporates most directly the religious values that shaped his postwar fiction. The plot pivots on the unsuccessful attempt of a bisexual movie producer to dissuade his younger brother from taking final vows as a swami.

Gay Activism and Autobiographies

While Isherwood was always open about his homosexuality with friends and colleagues, he did not publicly declare his homosexuality until 1971 in *Kathleen and Frank*, a biography of his parents constructed from their diaries and letters. Pointing the direction of his growing interest in autobiography, the work is "chiefly about Christopher." As part of the promotional effort for the book, Isherwood appeared on several television interview programs in early 1972 and openly discussed his sexual orientation, explaining its centrality in his life. From that time onward, he became an active and open participant in the American gay liberation movement, frequently appearing on behalf of the equal rights struggle at political rallies and fund-raising events. His activism in the 1970s coincided with a revival of his critical reputation and a renewal of interest in his works. The 1966 musical and 1972 movie *Cabaret*, inspired by the Berlin Stories, brought new attention to the works of the 1930s, but the novels of the 1960s were also rediscovered in the 1970s and 1980s.

The autobiographical impulse that influenced nearly all his novels and that had already been explicitly expressed in *Lions and Shadows* and *Kathleen and Frank* found its most sustained expression later in the 1970s.

In this decade, Isherwood became even more preoccupied with the pattern of his life, and especially with the shaping influence of his homosexuality and his religious beliefs. This preoccupation led to the writing of two significant books, *Christopher and His Kind* (1976) and *My Guru and His Disciple* (1980). A revisionist reinterpretation of a legendary era, the 1930s, *Christopher and His Kind* is a sexual and political autobiography. In this beautifully written work, which is complexly structured like a novelistic saga of Christopher and Heinz, Isherwood makes clear that homosexuality was one of the central aspects of his life and that the homophobia of the West necessarily invested his sexuality with political significance. For Isherwood, homosexuality was not only his nature but also his way of protesting the "heterosexual dictatorship." The militancy of the author's commitment to gay liberation invigorates and humanizes the book.

Complementary to *Christopher and His Kind* is *My Guru and His Disciple*, Isherwood's spiritual autobiography. The latter book begins where the former concludes, with the arrival of Auden and Isherwood in New York near the end of January 1939. A "one-sided, highly subjective story" of Isherwood's relationship with Swami Prabhavananda, *My Guru and His Disciple* recounts its author's sometimes painful, frequently humorous, and finally liberating search for God. Isherwood offers this refreshingly non-dogmatic work to his fellow travelers on the journey through life "in the hope that it may somehow to some readers, reveal glimpses of inner truth which remain hidden from its author."

Isherwood died in 1986, but his work remains as an extraordinary record of a journey made—as Paul Piazza observed—"in the center, or on the border, of the dangers and difficulties, the terrible Tests of our time." He seemed always to be in the right place at the right time: England between the world wars, Berlin in the 1930s, Los Angeles in the 1960s. His reputation having fully recovered from the decline of the 1950s and 1960s, he died laden with numerous awards and honors. Hailed by Gore Vidal as "the best prose writer in English," he was also one of the twentieth century's most insightful observers of the human condition.

References:

Finney, Brian. *Christopher Isherwood: A Critical Biography.* New York: Oxford University Press, 1979.

Fryer, Jonathan. *Isherwood: A Biography of Christopher Isherwood.* London: New English Library, 1977.

Heilbrun, Carolyn C. *Christopher Isherwood.* Columbia Essays on Modern Literature 53. New York: Columbia University Press, 1970.

Hynes, Samuel L. *The Auden Generation: Literature and Politics in England in the 1930s.* London: Bodley Head, 1976.

King, Francis. *Christopher Isherwood.* Writers and Their Work 240. Harlow, Essex: Longman, 1979.

Lehmann, John. *Isherwood: A Personal Memoir.* New York: Holt, 1987.

Piazza, Paul. *Christopher Isherwood: Myth and Anti-Myth.* New York: Columbia University Press, 1978.

Schwerdt, Lisa M. *Isherwood's Fiction: The Self and Technique.* London: Macmillan, 1989.

Summers, Claude J. *Christopher Isherwood.* New York: Ungar, 1980.

———. *Gay Fictions: Wilde to Stonewall.* New York: Continuum, 1990.

Vidal, Gore. "Art, Sex and Isherwood," in *New York Review of Books,* 9 December 1976: 10-18.

Wilde, Alan. *Christopher Isherwood.* Twayne's United States Authors Series 173. New York: Twayne, 1971.

—Claude J. Summers

Henry James

1843-1916

American writer

Often called one of the greatest novelists in the English language, Henry James wrote fiction and criticism that altered the course of contemporary literature. His introduction of new themes led to the

Henry James

development of the "international novel"; his experiments with narration and point of view anticipated Woolf's and Joyce's stream of consciousness technique. His keen observation of life initiated the call for more realism in fiction and led critic Van Wyck Brooks to call him an "historian of his age."

Henry James, Jr., was born at 21 Washington Place, Greenwich Village, New York City, on 15 April 1843, the second of five children of Mary Robertson Walsh and Henry James, Sr., a lecturer and writer on religious, social and literary issues. His youngest sibling, Alice (1848-1892), an invalid spinster, kept a journal edited by Leon Edel, Henry's biographer, originally as *Alice James, Her brothers—Her journal* (1934), later as *The Diary of Alice James* (1964); it serves as a valuable source of information about the entire family. His elder brother William (1842-1910) gained international recognition as the foremost American philosopher of his time, famous for coining "pragmatism" and the concept of "stream of consciousness." The children viewed their mother Mary as "the keystone of our arch," as Henry wrote after her death (Edel, *A Life*). Seeking a broad education for his children, Henry, Sr., often relocated the family; home tutoring and a privileged, cosmopolitan life in London, Paris, Geneva, New York, Newport, Venice and Boston developed in young Henry an urbanity he never lost.

Unwitting Revelations

James's autobiographies *A Small Boy and Others* (1913) and *Notes of a Son and Brother* (1914) provide fascinating accounts of this early education, as well as unintentionally revealing details of his fierce rivalry and homoerotic attraction to William. He tells of suffering a "horrid even if an obscure hurt" of "an extraordinarily intimate" nature in a Newport stable fire, perhaps sufficient to prevent Civil War service. Never fully explained, but probably a back injury, the accident and James's single, celibate, sexually diffident life fueled speculation that he suffered castration. Shortly after, James spent a year at Harvard Law School and then traveled extensively on the Continent. Quite soon, his life assumed a pattern which Robert L. Gale describes as "travel, observation, writing, much solitude, decorous friendships with men and women of the arts, homesickness and mellow letters to loved ones." (*Dictionary of Literary Biography* vol. 12)

Phases of Career and Popularity

James's career is usually divided into three phases beginning in 1876 with his permanent relocation to London. During this phase he originated the "international novel" and masterfully portrayed the American character abroad in the more sophisticated European setting in works such as *Roderick Hudson* (1878), *The American* (1877), *The Europeans* (1878), and "Daisy Miller" (1878); much of his work was serialized in *Atlantic Monthly*. In the mid-1880s, James turned his attention to new themes, including social issues, such as the women's issues and lesbianism of *The Bostonians* (1886), and honed his narrative skills, especially in short stories. Work included "The Real Thing," "The Beast in the Jungle," *The Aspern Papers* (1888), and *The Princess Casamassima* (1886). The final phase began in 1897 when, after an unsuccessful period of writing drama, James refined his famous point of view narration by narrowing it to a single angle of vision. Important from this period are *The Spoils of Poynton* (1897), "What Maisie Knew (1897)," "The Turn of the Screw" (1898), *The Ambassadors* (1903), and *The Wings of the Dove* (1902).

In his later years, James garnered many honors. In 1911, Harvard University and the next year Oxford conferred honorary degrees upon him. On 28 July 1915, he became a British citizen and on New Year's Day 1916, George V conferred upon him The Order of Merit. He died of pneumonia and complications from several strokes on 28 February 1916. Sixty years later, his memorial stone was dedicated in Westminster Abbey's Poets' Corner.

Decoding the Texts

After his death, James's popularity declined, only to be revived in the 1940s and 1950s and again in the 1960s; critics such as Edel, F. O. Matthiessen and F. W. Dupee led readers to appreciate James's symbolism and subtle character development. More recently, new critical techniques occasion another resurgence. Theorists such as Richard Hall, Eve Sedgwick, and Kaja Silverman have analyzed James's life and encoded writings so that many now presume James's homosexuality while his contemporaries and earlier critics only surmised it; as Wendy Graham points out in "Henry James's Thwarted Love," James enthusiasts were "bedeviled" by charges of his effeminacy (*Genders*, 1994). In 1935, Stephen Spender wrote, "He was not interested in 'men of action' ... there was some conflict in James's mind on the subject of sex, which may explain much about him" (*The Destructive Element*). Two decades later, Rene Wellek wrote, "James held two views which he felt perfectly compatible: discontent with the timidity of the Anglo-Saxon conventions and embarrassment and even horror at the eroticism of the French novel" (*American Literature*, 1958). In *The Gay 100*, Russell reminds us that encoded texts are the result "of the tension between the need to survive in a homophobic world and the longing to express the inner truths that world forbids."

Encoded fiction notwithstanding, James's autobiographies and letters, especially those to his young men, provide a fuller portrait of his sensibilities. Thus, by 1984, while Edel acknowledges an "intimate affection" (*A Life*), Gore Vidal writes in the *New York Review of Books*: "At 60 James fell in love with a young man named Jocelyn Persee ... this 'love affair' (with The Master, quotes are always necessary because we lack what Edith Wharton would call the significant data) had a most rejuvenating effect on James." A decade later, Graham's *Genders* article confirms, "James's self-portraits (fictional, epistolary and autobiographical) are consistent with sexologists' constructions of homosexuality during his lifetime" and places James in the context of "the construction of homosexuality at the fin de siecle" when, she writes in "Henry James's Subterranean Blues," the "covert issues of *The Princess Casamassima* would have been legible to anyone who cared to read between the lines" (*Modern Fiction Studies*, 1994). She reads this novel's subtext in the light of British law and homosexuality as rebellion.

Additional re-readings challenge the received interpretation of other "brotherly" relationships in *Roderick Hudson* and *The American*. Helen Hoy analyzes "The Pupil" (1891), often described as a "family story." Her "Homotextual Duplicity in Henry James's 'The Pupil'" identifies a palimpsest where age displaces homosexuality in the story of the tutor Pemberton and his eleven-year-old pupil Morgan Moreen (*Henry James Review*, 1993). Additionally, in "Henry James, Charles Sanders Peirce, and the Fat Capon: Homoerotic Desire in *The American*" Cheryl B. Torsney concludes through her analysis of the participants' letters that Chapter 5 of *The American* is a fictionalized rendering of James's interlude with Peirce in Paris in November 1875. She argues that Benjamin Babcock, the Peirce character, flees from Christopher Newman in "homosexual panic" (*Henry James Review*, 1993).

In 1993, the Henry James Sesquicentennial Conference devoted two days to "Rethinking Gender and Sexual Politics: Henry James in the New Century." Leon Edel referred attendees to "The Thin Man," a tale filled with "vivid libidinal language" which thinly disguises Henry's homoerotic feelings for his brother William. Two years later at Modern Language Association Convention, the session "Henry James and Queer Theory" included discussion of *The Tragic Muse* and *The Bostonians*. These recent analyses may clarify some of the baffling ambiguities for which James's technique is so famous.

Aspects of James's life, however, may well remain forever an ambiguity as he burned some papers and photographs during the final year of his life; although a recent biography by Sheldon M. Novick, called *Henry James: The Young Master,* provides new insight into James's personal life, including evidence of an affair with Oliver Wendell Holmes, Jr. Those remaining are deposited mostly in the Houghton Library at Harvard, the Beinecke Library at Yale, and the Library of Congress.

References:

Edel, Leon. *Henry James: A Life*. New York: Harper & Row, 1985.

Gale, Robert L. "Henry James," in *Dictionary of Literary Biography. Vol. 12: American Realists and Naturalists.* Detroit: Gale Research, 1982: 305.

Graham, Wendy. "Henry James's Subterranean Blues: A Rereading of *The Princess Casamassima*," in *Modern Fiction Studies,* Spring 1994, no. 40: 54.

———. "Henry James's Thwarted Love," in *Genders,* Fall 1994, no. 20: 67.

Hoy, Helen. "Homotextual Duplicity in Henry James's 'The Pupil'," in *Henry James Review,* Winter 1993, no. 14: 37.

James, Henry. *The American* and *Roderick Hudson,* in *Henry James: Novels 1871-1880.* The Library of America, 1983.

Russell, Paul. *The Gay 100.* New York: Citadel Press, 1995.

Sedgwick, Eve Kosofsky. *Epistemology of the Closet.* Berkeley: University of California Press, 1990.

Spender, Stephen. *The Destructive Element: A Study of Modern Writers and Beliefs*. London, Jonathan Cape Ltd, 1935.

Torsney, Cheryl B. "Henry James, Charles Sanders Peirce, and the Fat Capon: Homoerotic Desire in *The American*," in *Henry James Review,* Spring 1993, no. 14: 166-178.

Vidal, Gore. "Return to 'The Golden Bowl'," in *New York Review of Books,* 19 January 1984: 8-12.

Wellek, Rene. "Henry James's Literary Theory and Criticism," in *American Literature*. Chapel Hill: Duke University Press, 1958.

—Judith C. Kohl

Derek Jarman

1942-1994

British filmmaker, writer, and artist

As an artist, poet, and founding father of the New Queer Cinema, Derek Jarman thrived on the notion of a twentieth-century gay renaissance in the arts. His considerable creative energies—painting, set-design, filmmaking, writing, even gardening—purposefully spilled over established artistic boundaries to reinforce and inform each other while at the same time inviting a greater audience involvement. As cited in the prologue to *Derek Jarman—A Portrait*, he observed after just over a year at art school in the early 1960s that "theater, ballet, and painting must be revived. This cannot be achieved separately. There must be intercommunication. The genuine participating audience has been lost. Lack of audience reaction has been made a virtue."

Jarman was born in Northwood, England at the outset of World War II. He spent his formative years on Royal Air Force military bases and in a variety of public schools, where he quickly developed a love for gardening, art, and English literature. By the time he was in his early teens, he was winning prizes for his garden designs, acting in school plays that he had likewise designed the sets for, and exhibiting and selling the drawings and artwork that already showed promise.

Yet he was also under the firm hand of his father, who insisted he earn a "practical degree" in English and Art History at King's College first. In true renaissance form, Jarman managed to do so while editing the student magazine, working as a designer with student drama groups, developing an interest in American beat poetry, and indulging his ongoing love for English landscape and architecture.

In 1960, Jarman was offered a place at London's popular Slade Art School. London in the 1960s was a hotbed of artistic and sexual freedom, and at college Jarman's imagination and creativity was given full rein alongside other openly gay artists like David Hockney and Patrick Procktor.

Jarman eschewed the "pop" styles of the period, and instead embraced early performance art—or what were then known as "happenings." "I like working on shared projects," he told interviewer Lynn Barber in 1991. "There is much greater aesthetic freedom ... I can employ imagery I would not dare or wish to use in my painting." Indeed, one of the reasons Jarman said he turned to film at all was the fear of being labeled a mere follower of Hockney.

Film for the Dispossessed

In 1970, Jarman acquired a Super 8 camera and, according to Lawrence Normand in *The Gay and Lesbian Literary Heritage*, he "began recording the details of his own life and discovered the autobiographical subject that was to become the driving force of all his subsequent films and books." He got his film career off the ground as art director for Ken Russell's *The Devils* (1971) and *Savage Messiah* (1972).

In 1975, Jarman released his own first feature film—*Sebastiane*—a shocking and surprise success not only for its use of Latin, but also for its lush, unapologetic homoeroticism. "When I made *Sebastiane*," Jarman told Barber, "there was no way of imagining yourself as a gay,... [it was] a message of solidarity to people who have been dispossessed." In 1978, he followed with *Jubilee*, an unrelentingly frank fable on the gloomy future of England where, among other punk scenarios, brutal police have sex with one another and then kill beautiful young men.

He revamped the works of Shakespeare in *The Tempest* (1979) and *The Angelic Conversation* (1985), and followed through with his poetic—and sometimes audience-challenging—tributes to historical homosexuals with *Carravagio* (1986) and *Edward II* (1991). What his specialized approach "sacrificed in popular appeal," wrote Raymond Murray in *Images in the Dark*, "they made up with a singularly impressive body of intellectual and moving films." Indeed, right up to his final film *Blue* (1993)—a meditative, blue-screened narrative of reminiscences completed as CMV retinitis was stealing his eyesight—Jarman yearned to both reach and tweak the consciousness of the disenfranchised via the disenfranchised medium of experimental film. The screen was blue, Jarman said, simply because you can't see the virus.

"The Haughty Groom"

Neither would Jarman's cross-disciplinary artistic vision allow him to be simply a filmmaker. From the mid-1960s on, he also pursued his painting and sculpture—exhibiting mostly abstract works in various mixed-medias in galleries and shows throughout the United Kingdom. His set, stage, and costume designs for a myriad of films, plays, and (later) rock videos likewise spanned the decades—and the realm of artistic possibilities. Even his writings—whether poetry, prose, journal entries, or mere philosophical musings—reflected the influence of Egyptology, Elizabethan and Jacobean drama, metaphysics, and even alchemy.

Indeed, Jarman's literary works alone are touted by critics as insightful, unparalleled glimpses into English culture over three decades as well as classic examples of writing to unearth self-knowledge. He began writing autobiographically in 1984 with *Dancing Ledge*, where he observed that "you don't know what you have to say until you've said it." In *Modern Nature* (1992) and *At Your Own Risk* (1992) he continued this thread of "writing in order to be" by recounting his life in London and Dungeness (his final cottage-home) and—perhaps partly because these followed his AIDS diagnosis—evoking the brutal aesthetic honesty that informed all his work. "I knew the joy of heaven was there," he wrote of an uncaring and corrupt establishment in *Modern Nature*, for example: "and I vowed to revenge my generations,... fuck the haughty Groom,... and gang-bang the Trinity on its throne of gold ... until this Christ repented and confessed his true love for St. John."

Anger and irreverence are only half the story, though. In the last few years of his life, Jarman returned (perhaps not surprisingly) to the love of his boyhood—gardening. His last "landscape of personal reflections" was written from his cottage in folkloric Dungeness. *Derek Jarman's Garden* (1995) is full of contemplations on the temporalities of plants, their mythical associations, and the fate of his frosted generation. "The gardener," he wrote, "digs in another time, without past or future, beginning or end. A time that does not cleave the day with rush hours, lunch breaks, the last bus home."

In his last few years, anger and urgency gave way to a measured vision of hope for the future, even as his own darkness was imminent. "As I leave you Queer lads," he wrote in *At Your Own Risk*, "let me leave you singing. Please read the cares of the world I have locked in these pages; and after, put this book aside and love. May you of a better future, love without a care and remember we loved too."

References:

Barber, Lynn. In *Independent on Sunday*, 4 August 1991.

Derek Jarman—A Portrait. London: Thames and Hudson, 1996.

Jarman, Derek. *At Your Own Risk—A Saint's Testament.* London: Hutchison Publishers, 1992.

———. *Derek Jarman's Garden.* London: Thames and Hudson, 1995.

———. *Modern Nature.* London: Century Publishers, 1991.

Murray, Raymond. *Images in the Dark—An Encyclopedia of Gay & Lesbian Film and Video.* Philadelphia: TLA Publications, 1995.

—Jerome Szymczak

Karla Jay

1947-

American educator, writer, editor, and activist

Karla Jay is a leading scholar in the field of gay and lesbian studies, dedicated specifically to promoting lesbian visibility in all of its "wonderful diversity." Most recently, Jay has devoted her scholarly pursuits to documenting the historical, material, erotic, and psychic vicissitudes of lesbian life. As the series editor of New York University Press's *The Cutting Edge: Lesbian Life and Literature*, the only lesbian studies series in the world published by a university press, she is responsible for selecting new scholarship and biography in lesbian studies as well for reprinting lost or never-published lesbian texts. She has written for numerous popular periodicals, including *Ms.* magazine, *New York Times Book Review*, and *Village Voice*, and is currently Professor of English and director of Women's Studies at Pace University in New York City.

The second of two children, Karla Jay was born on 22 February 1947, in Brooklyn, New York. Jay's parents placed a high value on education and, subsequently, she attended, from eighth-grade on, an all-girls academy which she credits with fostering her intellectual development. Excelling both in the classroom and on the playing field, she won a Regent's Scholarship which enabled her to attend Barnard College in New York City, where she majored in French.

According to her profile in Martin Duberman's cultural history *Stonewall*, Jay's social consciousness was awakened during her senior year at Barnard. At this time, she witnessed and participated in the student protest at Columbia University in April 1968, over the administration's insensitive policies toward its black neighbors, its involvement with government-sponsored weapons research, and its complicity with the Vietnam War. For Jay, the Columbia fracas marked the starting point of her political and feminist struggles.

With a sharpened political awareness resulting from the events at Columbia, Jay joined the Redstockings (a radical feminist and Marxist group) shortly after its founding in 1969. Other prominent members of this organization include Ellen Willis, Alix Kates Shulman and Rita Mae Brown. Jay spoke widely at this time on feminist consciousness-raising and participated in the second protest of the Miss America contest in Atlantic City. While not directly embroiled in the events at Stonewall in 1969, she enthusiastically joined the Gay Liberation Front (GLF), embracing its credo for substantive social change through political action. Jay spent the early 1970s committed to the feminist and gay and lesbian liberation movements, working between New York and California—the 1995 documentary *A Question of Equality* features her activist experiences and insights on the era. Awarded a teaching assistantship in the French department at New York University in the mid-1970s, Jay eventually settled on the East coast, earning a Master's degree in 1978 and a doctorate in 1984 in comparative literature.

A prolific scholar and full professor at Pace University since 1990, teaching courses ranging from "Introduction to Women's Studies" to "Modernism and Gender," Jay has also edited, written, or translated over nine volumes. She researches extensively on lesbian modernism and has produced the first in-depth, feminist biographical and literary study of Natalie Clifford Barney and Renée Vivien entitled *The Amazon and the Page* (1988). This work recovers Barney and Vivien, two lesbian expatriates living in Paris at the turn of the century, from literary obscurity and establishes for them a position in a continuing female tradition.

Jay's most recent endeavors clearly translate her activist principles into scholarship. As editor of *Dyke Life: From Growing Up to Growing Old: A Celebration of Lesbian Experience* (1995) and *Lesbian Erotics* (1995) and as co-editor with Joanne Glasgow of *Lesbian Texts and Contexts: Radical Revisions* (1990), Jay validates lesbian existence and literature as worthy areas of analysis. These volumes investigate the heterogeneity of lesbian communities, the history of lesbian eroticism, and the methodologies of lesbian interpretation. Covering topics such as lesbian parenting, femme sexualities, and lesbian narrative space, these anthologies fortify the richness of lesbian studies as an academic field.

The Lambda Literary Awards have recognized Jay's written work on three separate occasions. Most recently, *Dyke Life* was a Lambda Literary Awards finalist in the categories of anthologies and lesbian studies. Both *Lesbian Texts and Contexts* and *The Amazon and the Page* were finalists in the best anthology and best non-fiction categories respectively in 1991 and 1989.

Jay's dynamic publishing history is complemented by the active role she has taken in academia. Besides co-chairing the Lesbian and Gay Caucus of the Modern Language Association from 1993 to 1995, Jay serves on the editorial boards of the *Lesbian Studies Journal* and *The Lesbian Review of Books*. Her prolific publishing career, committed to representing the diversity of lesbian lives, places Karla Jay on the "cutting-edge" of gay and lesbian studies.

Current Address: 392 Central Park West 11M, New York, New York 10025.

References:

Duberman, Martin. *Stonewall*. New York: Dutton Books, 1993.

Jay, Karla. *The Amazon and the Page*. Bloomington: Indiana University Press, 1988.

Jay, Karla, ed. *Dyke Life: A Celebration of the Lesbian Experience*. New York: Basic Books, 1995.

———. *Lesbian Erotics*. New York: New York University Press, 1995.

Jay, Karla and JoAnne Glasgow, eds. *Lesbian Texts and Contexts: Radical Revisions*. New York: New York University Press, 1990.

—Annmarie Pinarski

JEB

1944-

American photographer and video producer

Joan E. Biren, who is perhaps better known as JEB, was the first, and the most expressive, lesbian to photograph lesbians of all races, creeds, and colors. Biren's art necessitated the locating of lesbians who were willing to be openly identified as such and have images of themselves published. Her efforts through still photography and as a video producer managed to bring popular visibility to an otherwise invisible, marginal population.

On 13 July 1944, Joan Elisabeth Biren was born in Washington, D.C. The first daughter of civil servants Jack M. and Simone D. Biren, Biren and her younger sister, Andrea (born in 1950), grew up in the "company town" of Washington, D.C. Throughout Biren's childhood, it was assumed that she would "go into politics" or work for the government in some other capacity as her parents had done. She was consequently very active in student government while attending high school, helping to achieve racial integration in the Maryland student government in the 1960s.

Photography, according to Biren, was present during her early years but not very influential. "I suppose I might have had a Brownie," she says, but if so, that camera left little or no impression. It would not be until the 1970s that Biren would begin to "play around" with photography. Meanwhile, she would continue to be politically active well into college when she planned to go to law school. But Biren never got to law school. After receiving her Bachelor of Arts in political science from Mt. Holyoke in 1966 and graduating with honors, she decided to go to England for a year. (She would eventually earn an M.A. in communication from The

JEB

American University.) Biren remained in England for three years, studying for her doctorate at Oxford University and working against the war in Vietnam.

It was during this period that sexuality became a major concern for Biren. "I knew I was a lesbian," she says, "I had all kinds of crushes in high school, [and] in grade school, for that matter. In pictures I always have my arm draped around my girlfriends." She had had two relationships in college when she came out at age 19. "By doing it," says Biren, "we weren't coming out to the world—this was still the mid-1960s. Nobody was out, even to each other." Because of societal roles and rules—Biren's first girlfriend was president of the student body while she was vice president—coming out wasn't an option before this. During her years at Mt. Holyoke, recalls Biren, she had felt that "there [was] no way to be a lesbian in [this] world." While in England she had tried to "go straight" but wasn't successful.

Biren returned home at age 26 to find a burgeoning women's liberation movement. But, according to Biren, "there was no lesbian component to the movement," so she found herself coming out all over again. Biren and her lover were the first in the Washington-area movement to come out. Together with a handful of other lesbian feminists, Biren founded the lesbian feminist collective, the Furies. The Furies published a newspaper and other literature through which they articulated "a lesbian separatist perspective" since, according to Biren, "progressive politics were dominated by men ... and the women's movement was fairly anti-lesbian."

Biren picked up a camera seriously at this time, "and just loved it." All of her education, she says, "was tainted by male supremacy." Not willing to trust anything that she had been taught, Biren sought a new "means of expression for her new vision." The camera, which was not "polluted," served that purpose. Biren also found that with the camera she could make the invisible visible. Her first photograph, a now-famous self-portrait, was taken at arms length of herself kissing her lover. It was the picture Biren had never seen, the picture she needed to see. She has been "creating the images" that she, and other lesbians, have needed to see ever since. Biren has managed to support herself with her photography and other related endeavors since 1975. She published her first book, *Eye to Eye: Portraits of Lesbians,* in 1979. When she began to tour to promote her book, she found herself touring with a lesbian photography slide show that profiled historical lesbian photographers, their photos, and other contemporary lesbian photographers and their work. One slide show led to another, and *Eye to Eye* led to a second collection of photos—*Making A Way: Lesbians Out Front.*

For more than a decade Biren has traveled with her slide shows and photography workshops introducing people everywhere to her work and offering lesbian images for sale in books, postcards, and note cards. But, lesbians are not her only subject; other major areas of focus for Biren are gay and lesbian history as well as feminism and the peace and anti-nuclear movements. Her work has appeared in dozens of books ranging from sociology and photography textbooks to books by, for, and about gays and lesbians and their history, including: *Out in America, Out in All Directions, The Question of Equality, Long Road to Freedom, Our Right to Love,* and *Nice Jewish Girls.* In addition to these, Biren's work has appeared in films, newspapers, magazines, and on album covers. She has also become something of an archivist since her photos document not only the history of a movement and its more notable celebrities, but the people behind the scenes as well.

For the last six years, Biren has devoted herself to video production. "I have no new still photography" as a result, she says. Her documentary of the 1987 March on Washington, *For Love and For Life,* was transferred to videotape and aired on public television. She signed on as the video producer of the 1993 March on Washington, and her video of that historical event, *A Simple Matter of Justice,* is considered the official March documentary.

Naturally, there have been professional and more intimate relationships that have had profound effects on Biren. For many years she has been involved with a group of Jewish lesbians she considers her "chosen" family. "We celebrate the holidays together," she says, but clarifies that she sees herself as a spiritual, rather than a religious person. Currently, one of her most treasured relationships is with Zoey, her two-year-old Maltese—a present from friends on her 50th birthday. "There was a time," she says, "when I took my camera everywhere with me. Now I take Zoey."

References:

Biren, Joan E. *Eye to Eye: Portraits of Lesbians.* N.p., 1979.

———. Interview with Andrea L.T. Peterson, July 1986.

—Andrea L.T. Peterson

Sarah Orne Jewett

1849-1909

American writer

The ongoing American fascination with rural utopias and simpler values has sustained and contemporized the work of Sarah Orne

Jewett down through the decades. However, as an early feminist, ecologist, and architectural preservationist, Jewett was also uniquely well-respected in her own time both as a novelist and a literary chronicler of bucolic New England before the headlong, post-Civil War rush to industrialization. In her impressive collection of stories—*Deephaven* (1877) and *The Country of the Pointed Firs* (1886) most famous among them—women's lives are central, with keen attention paid to their cross-generational bonding and loving relationships. Jewett herself enjoyed a rather open (for her time) series of (it is widely assumed) intimate relationships with women, the most central of which was a 30-year "Boston marriage" to essayist and socialite Annie Adams Fields.

Sarah Orne Jewett was born and died in a house built by her paternal grandfather—an adventurous seal-hunter and shipbuilder—in South Berwick, Maine, one of the oldest permanent settlements in America. It was here that she absorbed the inner peace of being surrounded by nature and the intellectual spark of being immersed in history. Her various aunts, uncles, and grandparents were her best playmates, and an early source of fascination for geography and American lore as she eavesdropped on their parlor conversations. Her lifelong battle with rheumatoid arthritis, and subsequent long absences from school, fostered a sense of isolation and contemplation that also fed her creativity. "There is a strong influence of place," she wrote in her collection of stories *Old Friends and New* (1879), "and the things which surround us indoors and out make us follow in our lives their own silent characteristics."

After a brief flirtation with following her beloved country-doctor father into medicine, the self-described "wild and shy" Jewett shadowed her older sister to Berwick Academy at the age of twelve. Her three years here (1861-1864) coincided with the Civil War, and Sarah found formal education dull, often choosing instead to accompany her father on his rounds, or delve in private—and usually outdoors—into the books both of her parents encouraged her to read. Her father introduced her to authors like Henry Fielding, Izaac Walton, and Cervantes; while her mother gave her an appreciation for Jane Austen, George Eliot, and Margaret Oliphant. "I remember a good deal more about the great view toward the mountains," biographer Elizabeth Silverthorne quotes Jewett as writing, "or down river, and the boys and girls themselves, or even the ground sparrows and the field strawberries that grew in the thin grass, than I do about learning my lessons." She said that Harriet Beecher Stowe was the inspiration for both her subject matter and her technique, just as Willa Cather later claimed Jewett as her mentor and model.

Sarah began keeping intermittent diaries of her experiences in 1867, often lamenting her "chronic laziness" and her seeming "unwillingness to grow up," which back then meant grooming oneself for a husband. She sustained her choice of spinsterhood with the companionship of friends in nearby Newport and Boston, and the mentorship of noted writers and their families—James Russell Lowell, James Fields, and Horace Scudder (editor of the newly formed *Atlantic Monthly*) among them. By her early twenties, it was clear that she was developing a heavy "dependency" on her female friends even as her writing was achieving some success via publication in literary journals like the *Monthly, Scribner's,* and *The Riverside Journal*. Her network of friendships was bolstered by frequent correspondence and long visits to more cosmopolitan Boston, as well as trips to Cleveland and Chicago.

Luckily, Jewett's "Wordsworthian eccentricity" and striving for decidedly "singular success" was blossoming at an appropriate time in history, and was thus largely accepted. Her family and their fortunes had been mostly unscathed by the Civil War, the male population across the country had been severely depleted, and the increased pace of development and industrialization following the war was to forever change peaceful New England and the country. This "grave new world" was to give rise to a more politicized generation of "new women" with an interest in temperance, feminism, and the abolition of slavery. Moreover, an expanding middle class offered more economic independence to women, and plunged Jewett into the midst of a "golden literary age" in company with the likes of Henry James and Oliver Wendell Holmes.

A Boston Marriage

With the emergence of the "new woman" came new living arrangements, cleverly called "Boston marriages". The term, popularized even at the time in Henry James' *The Bostonians,* was commonly used to describe a long-term relationship between two unmarried women. Such relationships, according to Neil Miller in *Out of the Past*, were "primarily an upper- and middle-class phenomenon," and "such women were usually feminists, most often financially independent because of inheritance or career, and frequently involved in the "social betterment" movements of the day."

It was in the Boston home of literary biographer and hostess Annie Adams Fields that Jewett met some of the literary giants of

Sarah Orne Jewett

her day. James T. Fields was publisher and editor of *The Atlantic Monthly* from 1861 to 1871 and, particularly after his death in 1881, Annie became a friend and confidant to many women writers. But she formed her closest alliance with Jewett who, by the time she moved in with Fields in 1882, had published a dozen short stories in magazines and her well-received collection of stories titled *Deephaven* (1877). Though Fields was fifteen years older than Jewett, both women were financially independent and what might be called "discreet but open" about the love they shared over the next thirty years. "Do you remember, darling," Jewett wrote in a poem to Annie in 1880, "A year ago today. When we gave ourselves to each other. Before you went away."

Such "evidence" notwithstanding, biographer Paula Blanchard warns against categorizing their relationship as "lesbian" by our "twentieth-century definition of the term." "Sarah Orne Jewett's love for other women was as passionate and absorbing as any heterosexual man's," Blanchard has written, "but from all available evidence it never led to direct sexual expression."

But surely we must not overlook the fact that nineteenth-century women, no matter how "liberated", were far from inclined to discuss their sex lives. And the numerous references in Jewett's writing to the importance of "mates", her disdain for marriage, and even the peacefulness, as Blanchard herself quoted Jewett, of "sharing a bed with a loved friend' beg the implication, even if Jewett and her contemporaries were not familiar with the term "lesbian". "Each" according to biographer Silverthorne, "was independent in her thinking and ambitious to pursue her own career, but each craved the emotional security of a significant person in their lives—a soulmate in whom they could confide and trust completely."

The Power of Devotion

By the turn of the century, the public attitude toward lesbianism, or even the implication of such, was beginning to harden. Fields and Jewett, however, continued to sustain each other emotionally and creatively. Fields published her insightful account of nineteenth-century literary life, *Authors and Friends*, in 1896, as well as biographies of Harriet Beecher Stowe and her late husband James T. Fields. Jewett went on to write a novel, *A Country Doctor* (1884), and even more vivid collections of short stories including *A White Heron* (1886) and *The Country of the Pointed Firs* (1896). In 1901, she even tried her hand at historical romance with *The Tory Lover*, a fictionalized account of her hometown during the American Revolution.

Beyond their literary accomplishments, though, both women continued to offer an authentication of loving partnerships between women, if only because of their steadfast devotion to each other. In 1905, author Willa Cather sought out Jewett for advice on her blossoming career as well as her love life. "She (Cather) was about to make a decision to live with her friend and *McClure's* colleague Edith Lewis," noted Blanchard, and "possibly she had never seen one that so perfectly enhanced the lives and careers of both friends."

Sarah Jewett died in the Summer of 1909—under the same roof in South Berwick where she had been born—from complications of a series of strokes she had suffered in the few years previous. Though the very act of writing had become increasingly painful for her, she continued to draft letters to friends and colleagues, persevering through her pain in much the same way she had as an arthritic young woman.

Annie Adams Fields outlived Sarah by six years, and spent most of that time compiling Jewett's letters and notes into a book. Published in 1911, it is obviously a labor of love, according to Silverthorne, right down to the "cropped and edited personal references and some of the nicknames and affectionate 'little language' Sarah used so freely." Perhaps the best tribute to Jewett lies between the lines of Fields' preface to the book, which she describes as "the portrait of a friend and the power that lies in friendship to sustain the giver as well as the receiver."

References:

Blanchard, Paula. *Sarah Orne Jewett—Her World and Her Work.* New York: Addison-Wesley, 1994.

Fields, Annie. *Letters of Sarah Orne Jewett.* Boston: Houghton, Mifflin and Company, 1911.

Miller, Neil. *Out of the Past—Gay and Lesbian History from 1869 to the Present.* New York: Vintage Books, 1995.

Silverthorne, Elizabeth. *Sarah Orne Jewett—A Writer's Life.* New York: The Overlook Press, 1993.

—Jerome Szymaczak

Elton John

1947-

British rock singer, songwriter, and pianist

In 1971, Elton John had four albums simultaneously in the top ten, making him the first artist since the Beatles to achieve that distinction. During the 1970s, John was without a doubt the most popular musical performer on the planet. In the short span of the decade he recorded five No. 1 songs, 15 Top 10 songs, 23 Top 40 singles, and 15 of his 16 albums went gold.

On 25 March 1947, Reginald Dwight was born in Middlesex, England to Stanley and Sheila Dwight. Although he found solace in the piano at a very early age, Reginald was 21 before his career in rock music, under the now universally recognized name of Elton John, took off.

Young Dwight was a relatively happy boy—with a life occupied by music at a very early age, and a father who traveled, making the relationship between father and son much more manageable for both. Among their major disagreements, and a constant source of contention between both parents, was whether this gifted boy who began piano lessons at the age of six, should be encouraged—or even permitted—to play rock 'n' roll. For Dwight, a rather chubby boy who never quite fit in, the piano was consolation for the loneliness of being an only child, and companionship when friends were scarce. By the time he was three, he was playing his first notes. By the age of 10 he was the "official school pianist," playing at school assemblies. Although he would, almost 40 years later, come out as homosexual, he had his first girlfriend by the age of four.

Rocky Road to Rock 'n' Roll

Dwight attended the Reddiford School, a private school where he shined as a musician, impressing his friends on the piano, but strik-

Elton John

ing out socially and athletically. In spite of his love for soccer, and his strong desire to earn his father's respect by excelling in the sport, it was his cousin Roy who played professionally, made a name for himself in soccer, and won the respect of the elder Dwight. When Dwight heard Elvis Presley's "Heartbreak Hotel" his life was truly changed. In spite of his parents resistance, he knew, even then, that "pop" would be his "whole life."

In 1957, the 10-year-old Dwight auditioned for and was accepted into the Royal Academy of Music—Britain's senior conservatory and one of the oldest institutions for the advancement of music education in the world—where he concentrated on Beethoven and Bach. Afraid that Dwight might quit the conservatory, his mother encouraged his excursions into pop music. This, of course, increased the conflict between Dwight's mother and father.

When Dwight was 15, his parents finally divorced. A local handyman, Fred Farebrother, soon came onto the scene and eventually became Dwight's stepfather. It was around this time that Dwight formed his first band, the Corvettes—with guitar player Stuart Brown—but the band didn't fare very well. Brown and Dwight then formed a second band. They added a sax and trumpet and the band, Bluesology, began to get regular work. Though the band was moderately successful, Dwight was interested in being a soloist and Brown wasn't forthcoming with the microphone.

As a result, when confronted with the opportunity to work at Mills Music as a messenger—which he saw as at least a foot in the industry—Dwight quit school even though he had not taken his A levels (the exams necessary for entrance into college or to obtain a white collar job in England). The British invasion had just hit the U.S., and Dwight, who had donned spectacles to emulate his hero Buddy Holly, became even more anxious for success.

At the age of 18 Dwight was still at Mills and still playing with Bluesology, now a professional band on weeknights. He had also gotten a regular gig playing piano at a local hotel's pub on weekends. In 1965, Dwight managed to get Mills to publish "Come Back Baby," one of his original songs.

Bluesology was also beginning to enjoy a minimal amount of fame. The band was asked to tour with Wilson Pickett—a gig that never panned out—and with a number of acts that did, from the American soul star Major Lance to Patti LaBelle to the Ink Spots. The band eventually signed with Marquee Artists and played numerous trendy clubs, but it was the professional alliance with Long John Baldry, who shared vocals with Rod Stewart in Steampacket, that offered Bluesology a professional break. Steampacket needed a backup band and Bluesology needed a change. But once again, this wasn't the opportunity that Dwight had hoped it would be to sing—no one thought he had much of a voice, and weighing in at over 200 pounds, no one felt he projected the right image.

Through his association with Baldry, Dwight gained entry to the gay community. At the apartment of then reporter-photographer Mike McGrath, himself rather blatant about his homosexuality, Dwight met many gay men as well as important people in the music industry, including his future manager, John Reid. Even though his own sexuality was becoming apparent, Dwight proposed to Linda Woodrow, a women with whom he was quite smitten—in spite of himself.

Becoming a Superstar

In 1967, disappointed with how staid Baldry and his band had become, a twenty-one-year-old Dwight decided it was time to move on. In spite of a dreadful audition with Liberty Records, his voice caught the talent scout's interest and Dwight was asked to do some demos. Seventeen-year-old Bernie Taupin also responded to the same advertisement placed by Liberty. In late 1967, Dwight and Taupin were signed as a songwriting team with Dick James Music (DJM), with Dwight writing music to accompany Taupin's lyrics.

It was at this time that Dwight's search for a new name began. He felt that "Elton Hercules John" gave him the originality and the sense of self-confidence that he was lacking. In spite of strong objections from his mother and disbelief among his peers, he legally changed his name in 1968 to Elton John. DJM saw the potential of the John/Taupin duo, but was greatly challenged by it. They could find no suitable singer for the duo's songs. By default, John ended up singing his and Taupin's songs.

In 1970, after many failed attempts to chart in the United Kingdom with a handful of original songs, John turned the music world upside down with his U.S. debut, "Your Song." John is essentially a derivative artist, gleaning the best from almost every genre of music ranging from gospel to rock. This led to a style that is distinctively his own. No composer or artist before or since even faintly resembles the performer who has topped the charts for more than 25 years.

On the heels of his U.S. debut, at John's insistence, James agreed to take John Reid on as John's manager. In spite of John's long term engagement to Woodrow, no one ever questioned the intimate relationship between John and Reid, but no one mentioned it either. It wasn't until 1976, in a *Rolling Stone* article, that John came out as bisexual. In keeping with this statement and with his stated desire to have children, he married Renate Blauel, a German-born recording engineer, in a London recording studio. The two were wed on Valentine's Day 1984. The marriage lasted for four-and-a-half years. Over ten years would pass before John would finally come out as gay.

John has consistently been involved in the fight against AIDS, organizing, participating in, and supporting fundraising events around the world. His tireless efforts have greatly increased the public's limited knowledge of AIDS and have raised considerable sums for a variety of AIDS research causes. In fact, the record collection he spent years collecting was auctioned at Sotheby's in London for a total of $272,000 for such charities. In addition, his clothes and often outrageous stage costumes have been auctioned, raising almost as much as his records.

Throughout his career John has enjoyed tremendous success, from his unparalleled triumphs in the 1970s to his graceful ascension to elder statesman of pop music in the late-1980s and 1990s. The induction of John in 1994 to the Rock and Roll Hall of Fame in Cleveland, Ohio solidified the place in musical history that he now holds and the influence he has had over the past three decades.

Current Address: c/o John Reid Enterprises Ltd., 32 Galena Rd., London W6 OLT, England.

References:

Crump, Susan and Patricia Burstein. *The Many Lives of Elton John.* New York: Carol Publishing Group, 1992.

Norman, Philip. *Elton John.* New York: Harmony Books, 1991.

—Andrea L.T. Peterson

Jasper Johns

1930-

American painter

Jasper Johns was a major figure in the Pop art movement of the 1960s; indeed, Pop art is generally agreed to have begun with a 1958 exhibition of Johns's work, which included representational paintings of mundane objects such as flags, numbers, and letters, in stark contrast to the prevailing Abstract Expressionist aesthetic of the period. Johns's work, like that of Marcel Duchamp earlier in the century, challenged basic assumptions about the nature of art and about the relationship of objects to their images on canvas, provoking controversy among critics and providing the theoretical groundwork for subsequent movements.

An Artist from the Start

Johns was born in Augusta, Georgia, the only son of Jasper Johns Sr., a farmer, and Jean (Riley) Johns. His parents divorced when he was very young, and Johns subsequently went to live with his grandfather, a stern Baptist. After his grandfather died, Johns, still in grade school, lived with a series of other relatives in South Carolina and spent several years with his father's sister in a tiny town called The Corner. When later asked why he didn't return to his father, Johns said simply, "He didn't invite me."

Johns displayed an interest in art very early in his life and began drawing and painting at the age of five. After studying briefly at the University of South Carolina, he moved to New York and enrolled in art school, but when he ran out of money he was forced to quit and take whatever jobs he could find. In 1950 he was drafted for service in the Korean War; while in the army he spent six months in Japan and developed a great appreciation for Japanese art, which would later manifest itself in his own work.

Upon his discharge, Johns returned to New York and began working at a bookstore, still unsure of how to launch his career as an artist. It was at this point that he met Robert Rauschenberg, who was already an artist of some note and who encouraged Johns's ambitions. Within a few years, Johns and Rauschenberg were renting loft space in the same building, having developed a friendship that provided inspiration for both artists. Rauschenberg was then working as a window designer for upscale stores; Johns eventually

Jasper Johns

quit his job at the bookstore to work with him. It was also through Rauschenberg that Johns became acquainted with the avant-garde composer John Cage and his companion, the choreographer Merce Cunningham; these friendships were also crucial to Johns personally and professionally.

Deciding that he needed a fresh start, Johns destroyed all of his work in 1954; he later noted that he wanted to create works that would bear no resemblance whatever to any others. He began working in the unusual encaustic medium, using a thick layer of beeswax on his canvases to give them added interest, and focusing on the everyday objects that would become his trademark.

The unique and aesthetically radical quality of Johns' work quickly drew attention. In 1957 his *Green Target* was exhibited at the Jewish Museum in New York, and the following year the noted gallery owner Leo Castelli mounted a solo exhibition of his work. The show was a huge success; critics immediately perceived that Johns was presenting the next stage in the developing exploration of the meaning of art, rejecting the rigidly non-representational aesthetic in order to depict objects that were transformed by the simple act of representation. Commentators also noted the subtle ironic humor in Johns's method of elevating a simple figure to the stature of art. Collectors, too, approved of Johns's approach; all the paintings in the exhibit were sold, and the Museum of Modern Art purchased four of his works. Deborah Solomon, in a 1988 appreciation in the *New York Times,* wrote: "No artist was ever catapaulted into fame more suddenly than Johns."

A Growing Influence

During the 1960s, Johns continued to explore the aesthetic presented in his first show, using mundane in a variety of ways and in both paintings and sculptures. He also began incorporating more real objects to his works, gluing them onto the canvas or incorporating them into bronze sculptures in an attempt to further literalize his art. At the same time, his inflence began to manifest itself in the work of other artists. Solomon has noted:

> When Frank Stella painted the austere black-striped canvases that heralded the beginning of Minimalism, he was improvising on the "you see what you see" literalness of Johns's flags and targets. When Andy Warhol painted a picture of a Campbell's soup can, when Claes Oldenburg made a sculpture of a hamburger, when Roy Lichtenstein elevated comic-book blondes to the realm of high art, they were all exploring the ideas set forth in Johns's (and Rauschenberg's) paintings of commonplace objects.

In 1964, only six years after his first solo exhibition, Johns' works were displayed in retrospectives at the Jewish Museum in New York and the Whitechapel Gallery in London, an exceedingly unusual event for an artist of Johns' relatively young age. In 1977, another retrospective, this time at the Whitney Museum in New York, drew 4100 visitors and subsequently travelled to San Francisco, Cologne, Paris, and Tokyo.

As his career progressed, Johns' work became more autobiographical, sometimes incorporating materials used in the studio in the canvases or displaying handprints left by the artist. This trend culminated in the large 1987 work *The Seasons,* which features a large shadowy silhouette of Johns and depicts the cycles of life.

Johns also designed sets and costumes for Cunningham's dance troupe—the inspiration for his painting *Dancers on the Plane.* In addition to set and costume designer, he was artistic adviser to the Merce Cunningham Dance Company in New York from 1967. He also collaborated with Cunningham and Cage on the ballet *Un Jour ou Deux* in 1973. One of Johns' most fruitful collaborations was with the renowned author Samuel Beckett; the 1977 volume *Foraides/Fizzles* features five stories by Beckett and 33 etchings by Johns, considered to be among his finest works in that medium.

Although his later works have not drawn the same level of praise and attention as his earlier ones, Johns remains a revered figure in American art. His works were selected to represent the United States in the 1988 Venice Biennale, and he has received a wide variety of honors and awards. His works also continue to be highly sought-after; in 1980, *Flag* was purchased by the Whitney for $1 million and was described by the museum's director as "a monument of twentieth-century art." In 1988 his *Diver* sold for $4.2 million, the highest sum ever paid for the work of a living artist.

Current Address: c/o Leo Castelli Gallery, 420 W. Broadway, New York, New York 10012-3764.

References:

Cerrito, Joann, ed. *Contemporary Artists.* Detroit: St. James Press, 1996.

Current Biography Yearbook. New York: H. W. Wilson, 1987.

Solomon, Deborah. "The Unflagging Artistry of Jasper Johns," in the *New York Times Magazine,* 19 June 1988: 20.

—Andrea L.T. Peterson

Bill T. Jones

1952-

African-American choreographer, dancer, and writer

Genius, iconoclast, romantic, post-modernist, preacher, hero, victim, and survivor are just a few nouns used to describe Bill T. Jones. Brilliant, fearless, arrogant, defensive, offensive, frightening, generous, humble—just a few adjectives. His work summons similar reaction. In addition to having choreographed over 50 works, Jones is artistic director of Bill T. Jones/Arnie Zane Dance Company and associate artistic director of the Lyon Opera Ballet, with works in the repertories of Alvin Ailey American Dance Theater, Boston Ballet, and Berlin Opera Ballet, among others. He has directed theater—for The Guthrie Theater in Minneapolis, Minnesota—and opera—for Glynbourne Festival Opera, New York City Opera, and the Houston Grand Opera. He is a 1994 recipient of the MacArthur Genius Fellowship, numerous NEA fellowships, two New York Dance and Performance (Bessie) Awards, and a *Dance Magazine* Award. He co-authored *Body Against Body* with his late partner and lover Arnie Zane and is the author of an autobiography, *Last Night on Earth.* He is also African-American and HIV-positive, which he discusses with zeal, eloquence, pathos, and violence, in performances that often move audiences to tears.

William Tass Jones was born in Bunnell, Florida, April 1952, the tenth of twelve children. His parents, Estella and Augustus Jones, were migrant farm workers who picked their way north or south depending on the season. In 1959, the family settled in Wayland in the Finger Lakes region of upstate New York, allowing the children continuity and the family a home base. There his parents variously harvested crops, managed a camp of migrating farm workers, and operated a restaurant/juke joint. In the shadow of the juke joint, the seeds for Jones's artistic imagination sprouted. He and his siblings, especially his sister Rhodessa, a performance artist, entertained themselves by singing while they harvested crops in the fields together. In school, Jones distinguished himself as an actor and athlete, graduating with the dubious self-congratulation of having not written a single paper.

Vision and Direction

At the State University of New York at Binghamton, in fall 1970, Jones discovered dance. Martha Graham had come to town, and seeing her company perform was a life-changing experience. In high school he had performed in theater and with a rock band called Wretched Souls, and so was no stranger to performance. But dance spoke to him in ways unexpected and deep, allowing him to see the potential of merging his athleticism with a more theatrical expression. Completely won over, he went immediately to dance class, where he encountered body-type prejudice. He realized the necessity of developing, defining, and articulating a movement vocabulary of his own, one which countenanced all body types—high buttocks and low, feet arched or flat, body corpulent or rail thin—and which didn't rely solely on the articulation of the pointed toe or turned-out foot, but on dancing itself as a partner to language. In addition to Graham (modern dance) and Jerome Robbins (*West Side Story*), his early influences were Percival Borde (African dance), George Balanchine (classical ballet), Yvonne Rainer (post-modern choreographer and filmmaker).

That same year Jones met Arnie Zane and had another life-changing experience. A small Jewish-Italian man, Zane caught Jones' eye at a campus pub in Binghamton. Sexually curious and very much a product of the 1960s, Jones desired to experience another man and made no secret of his sexual interest in Zane. The two went back to Jones' room in the Third World corridor of the university dorm and spent the night together. For the next seventeen years, they would be called *BillandArnie* or *ArnieandBill*. Or they were described by the media as "tall and black with an animal quality of movement" (Jones) and "short and white, with a nervous, pugnacious demeanor" (Zane). Together they would define a new audacious dance that was non-traditional, athletic, provocatively homoerotic, and often personal. Together they would become perhaps the most celebrated, if not the most notorious, *out* gay couple in America.

Less than a year after meeting, the two moved to Amsterdam. Before packing up and leaving, they hitchhiked to Wayland to visit Jones' parents. Estella Jones was more alarmed by the possibility that her son would be lost in Europe beyond her reach and protection than by the fact that he was having sex with a man. A deeply religious woman, she was first and foremost a mother and ruled her family with fiery love. Once gaining assurance that Zane would not leave Jones behind in Europe, she offered her blessings, and from that moment on, as long as her son was all right, she stayed clear of the relationship between the two men, neither discussing nor acknowledging it.

In Amsterdam the young lovers supported themselves with menial employment while indulging in the liberties of the city. Chatting over tea and opium, they visited with artists, composers, and designers, gathering ideas and observing life abroad as Bohemians. Though still very much driven by the 1960s' sexual ethos, Jones was quite taken by the casualness of sex, and became involved with a mutual friend of Zane's and nearly ruined his relationship. Neither accomplished much creatively during this time, though Zane, who was well on his way to establishing a career as a photographer, was actively taking pictures. Still, as exciting as it was, Amsterdam was not what they thought it would be, so the decision to leave was easily arrived at.

Learning the Language of Dance

On their return, Jones met Zane's parents, who owned a bakery in the Bronx. The occasion ended violently, and five years would pass before the couple would see Zane's parents again. Jones fell back into dance with fever and fervor. After the long months of physical and creative inactivity abroad, he was determined to make something artistically important. He re-enrolled at Binghamton, and soon after created with Zane their first duet. Called *Begin the Beguine* after a Benny Goodman record, the piece was a romping parody of 1930s-style dancing and earned them a bit of notoriety on campus. Afterward, Zane, who still mostly considered himself a photographer, began choreographing.

Jones felt he needed to learn more. In the dance department, under the mercilessly critical eye of Percival Borde, Jones determined that he was missing a more formal dance education, with which he would have the vocabulary to create his own movement language. Zane and Jones moved to Brockport, where Jones enrolled at the university as a dance major. The antecedents of his formal ideas about dance begin here. In a contact improvisation class taught by dancer/choreographer Richard Bull, Jones began to see dance as solving problems with movement. Jones and Zane explored the idea further when they met choreographer/contact improvisationist Lois Welk. Physical awareness was heightened with contact improvisation, and Jones, with comparatively pedestrian movements, was finding his voice and defining a vocabulary. This was a remarkably rich period, threatened only by his interest in the Krishna Consciousness Movement and missing his family.

In the summer of 1972, Lois Welk moved to San Francisco to revitalize the American Dance Asylum, a collective of former Brockport choreographers Welk had founded. Azel, Jones's closest brother, had moved to the Bay Area several years before and most of the east-coast family had since followed him there, including his sister Rhodessa. Without Welk, there was no reason to stay in New York, so Jones and Zane followed her, moving into Rhodessa Jones's home—Tomato—which she shared with her partner and their child. The experience of San Francisco underscored Jones's need for family more than it inspired creativity. The social climate, still very much tinged with the anti-materialism resistance of the 1960s, sneered at success of all kinds, and Jones, Zane, and Welk soon found themselves very frustrated. After a year and the tragic death of a niece, Jones, along with Zane and Welk, moved back to Binghamton, and the business of making art began.

Learning the Language of Art

The American Dance Asylum put roots in an old, dilapidated Elk's Club, with its members—the trio plus another dancer and a poet—living in contented poverty eating pancakes, peanut butter, and apples picked from a nearby tree. Each artist experimented with form and presentation, often showing works in their large, open home to an audience of just themselves or to a few intrepid people from the university. Shortly after his return, Jones began to have success. The work which put him on the map was called *Everybody Works/All Beasts Count*, an imaginative dance which he and sixteen other dancers dramatized with vocals. It earned him a 1976 Creative Artist Public Service Award (CAPS). Soon after he appeared at the Clark Center Dance Festival at CUNY Mall and received very encouraging reviews. *Everybody Works* was performed in Central Park, then at Dance Theater Workshop and the Kitchen.

The first reviews came in: *The New York Times* said Jones was a "performer worth watching." *The Soho News* said that he had "an engaging stage presence." The duets Jones and Zane did together grabbed attention and critical acclaim. Jones was on his way.

In 1980 Jones and Zane broke away from the American Dance Asylum. Their sights were set on New York City, but neither felt comfortable living in Manhattan; so they settled in Valley Cottage, New York, some forty-five minutes away. There they created their first major work. Inspired by non-narrative cinema and visual arts, *Blauvelt Mountain* is a seventy-minute long tour de force, involving a number of different activities, from *a capella* singing to talking to pedestrianisms like standing, sitting and walking, all arranged and rearranged for perceptual effect. It premiered at the Dance Theater Workshop in 1980 and toured Europe with The Kitchen Center for Dance, Music, and Video.

Social Intercourse: Pilgrim's Progress, Jones's next major work, appeared the following year at the American Dance Festival, with Jones billed as an "Emerging Choreographer" and Zane as Jones' administrator and artistic consultant. The work was a melange of oppositional ideas, traditional versus new wave, formal gestures versus informal. It included an improvised solo, in which Jones by turns told the audience, "I love women," then, "I hate women."

> I love white people. I hate white people. I'd like to kiss you. I'd like to tear your fucking heart out. Why didn't you leave us in Africa? I'm so thankful for the opportunity to be here.

The audience was shocked. This one performance tagged Jones with the reputation of being angry and unpredictable. Not surprisingly, another invitation from the American Dance Festival was not forthcoming—not for ten years.

At the 1982 New York premiere, at Downstairs at City Center, dance critic Arlene Croce was in the audience. "Bill T. Jones has marched the New Narcissism right into the fever swamp," she wrote in the *New Yorker*. Jones and Zane were offended. Previously she had taken exception to a prayerlike solo Jones had done in performance, dismissing it. When Jones was offered a commission for a new work by Alvin Ailey for his dance company, Jones named his new work "Fever Swamp." Ms. Croce was not amused and would later be at the center of a storm of controversy surrounding Jones.

Artistic success, though, had been brokered and Bill T. Jones/ Arnie Zane and Company, which officially incorporated in 1982, was in demand. In 1984 they created "Freedom of Information" for the Théâtre de Ville in Paris. The work was loosely based on an air crash in Washington D.C., and featured a man recounting the tragedy while dancers wildly and variously barked, crawled, tumbled and turned, and fell. The scandalous work was well-received and

Bill T. Jones

the company, through the United States Information Agency, was invited to tour Asia in 1986.

Success was not the only change in their lives. AIDS had settled among them. In 1984 Zane began to show signs of illness and in 1986 was diagnosed with lymphoma. A terrible two-year battle began of slow deterioration, with Zane fighting against it until he could not fight anymore. During Zane's illness he created "The Gift/No God Logic," and finished what would become their last collaboration, "A History of Collage." The company continued touring with Zane more often than not staying behind. Then touring stopped, art stopped. Zane was near death. Jones, himself diagnosed HIV positive but asymptomatic, stayed by his lover until Zane died 30 March 1988. Now alone, Jones was devastated.

Tragedy, Creativity and Survival

Almost immediately, a remarkable period of creativity supplanted the apathy of tragedy, and Jones rebounded, driven by both loss and fear of his own mortality, and in the midst of a management crisis. Since 1988 he has created over twenty new works, two of them full-evening in length. Both evening-length works—"Last Supper at Uncle Tom's Cabin/The Promised Land" and "Still/Here"—and two comparatively smaller ballets, "D-Man in the Water" and "Absence" are, by all standards, considered American masterpieces. Each fixates on an element of disorienting tragedy, and finds ground and centeredness in humanity. Each is the apotheosis of faith.

"Absence" (1989) was the first work Jones created after Zane's death. Using pantomime and the rituals of weddings, the ballet is an almost Zenlike study of death. While posing before the camera and dancing with his bride, the groom, without warning or cause, is chosen. Before the everyone's eyes, he is taken away. Devastated, the bride struggles with loss, but eventually is able to move away from her grief and live. Alone and lost, the groom struggles among the dead but eventually, like his widowed wife, is resigned.

"D-Man in the Waters" has roots in a daydream in which Jones envisioned living and dead friends trapped in a lake, futilely swimming against a current, many of them already drown. Remarkably, everyone tries to save everyone else. Inspired by and wedded to Felix Mendelssohn's *Octet in E-flat major*, the ballet is considered by many to be Jones's signature repertory work. The work garnered two Bessie Awards.

"Last Supper at Uncle Tom's Cabin/The Promised Land" (1990) is a virtuosic, albeit rambling, dissecting work on American racial violence, racial history, marginality, and commonality. Three and one-half hours long, the opus retells (via libretto by poet Ann T. Greene) the story of Harriet Beecher Stowe's famous slave tract, *Uncle Tom's Cabin*, with comically painful tableaux; segments the tragedy of slavery into parts corresponding to the terrifying ordeal of Stowe's runaway slave, Eliza; interrogates faith and Christianity by asking of a clergyman questions like, "Is Christianity a slave religion? Is AIDS God's punishment?"; and realizes humanity in its purest, most vulnerable state. From each community where the work was performed, fifty people, one-thousand in all, participated in this last section, "The Promised Land," standing naked, hand-in-hand, on stage. The work, denounced by the Vatican, was often unfairly criticized, but even so, was an enormous success. Julius Hemphill, the composer, was awarded a Bessie for his original score.

"Still/Here" (1994), Jones's most controversial work to date, is about survival with life-threatening illness. For theatrical fodder and movement inspiration, Jones conducted around the country what he called "Survival Workshops"—group interviews and movement exercises directed by him and set-designer Gretchen Bender with terminally-ill women and men, geriatrics and children, African-, Asian-, Latin-, and Caucasian-Americans. These sessions were videotaped and used as the visual background for the staged work, and shaped the libretto/compositions of Kenneth Frazelle and rock/musician Vernon Reid. "My intention has been to create a work, not as a rumination on death and decline, but on the resourcefulness and courage necessary to perform the act of living," said Jones of his drama.

Almost immediately the work was at the center of a storm of controversy. At its New York premiere, the work was attacked in *The New Yorker* by its dance critic, Arlene Croce, who refused to see the work on the grounds that victimization as art renders the work undiscussable by critics. Suddenly the work was grist for newspaper and radio debate, largely carried on by people who, like Croce, had not even seen the work. Controversy followed the project on its tour to London and Edinburgh, where an effort had been mounted to prevent the work from being shown. The attacks were in vain; the work's integrity and originality were unassailable, "its place among the landmarks of twentieth century dance [is] assured," proclaimed *Newsweek* Magazine.

True to form, Jones moved on to new projects, including: a collaboration with Nobel Laureate Toni Morrison and legendary drummer Max Roach, called "Dega," (1995), a world premiere with the Lyon Opera Ballet called "24 Frames Per Second," and a 1996 season of repertory works in New York. With his new companion, Bjorn Amelan, Jones lives a life unimaginable when Arnie Zane died in 1988. The last lines of his autobiography *Last Night on Earth* are "Tomorrow will come. It always has. It will be all right."

Current Address: Bill T. Jones/Arnie Zane & Co. Image Artists, 853 Broadway, Suite 1706, New York, New York 10019.

References:

Jones, Bill T. *Last Night on Earth.* New York: Pantheon Books, 1995.

Jones, Bill T. and Arnie Zane. *Body Against Body: The Dance and other Collaborations of Bill T. Jones & Arnie Zane.* New York: Station Hill Press, 1989.

Gates, Henry Louis, Jr. "The Body Politic," in *New Yorker*, 21 November 1994: 112-124.

Jowitt, Deborah. "Bill as Bill," in the *Village Voice* (New York), 20 October 1992.

Kaplan, Larry. "Delicate Dance," in *POZ Magazine*, June/July 1994: 40-44, 69.

Kaye, Elizabeth. "Bill T. Jones," in the *New York Times Magazine*, 6 March 1994: Section 6.

Shapiro, Laura. "Dancing in Death's House," in *Newsweek*, 7 November 1994: 66-68.

Stearns, David Patrick. "Dancing with Death," in *USA Today*, 31 October 1994.

—Shawn Stewart Ruff

Cleve Jones

1954-

American AIDS Quilt founder

A co-founder of the San Francisco AIDS Foundation in 1982 and originator of the NAMES Project AIDS Memorial Quilt, Cleve Jones is a long-term survivor of AIDS. Among his many accomplishments, Jones was an administrative assistant to California State Assemblyman Art Agnos (who eventually became Mayor of San Francisco), served three terms on the San Francisco County Democratic Central Committee, and lobbied for the Quaker-sponsored Friends Committee on Legislation.

Through the NAMES project, Jones conveyed the personal side of the AIDS pandemic: a dimension beyond statistics and scientific theories. At a time when AIDS was often perceived as a disease affecting mostly gays and intravenous drug users, Jones heightened the American consciousness about a virus that knows no bounds. Cleve Jones was born on 11 October 1954 in West Lafayette, Indiana, to Austin and Marion Jones. Both his parents are professors at Arizona State University. Jones moved to San Francisco in the early 1970s.

Following the 1978 assassination of Jones's friend, openly gay San Francisco Supervisor Harvey Milk, Jones participated in each annual candlelit march commemorating Milk. By November 1985, with the AIDS epidemic having taken more than 1,000 lives in San Francisco, Jones asked each of the march's participants to make placards showing the names of friends and family who had died of AIDS. Despite the death toll, Jones felt the subject of AIDS remained shrouded in confusion and denial. "We could all die without anyone really knowing," he said in the summer 1993 issue of *Critical Inquiry*.

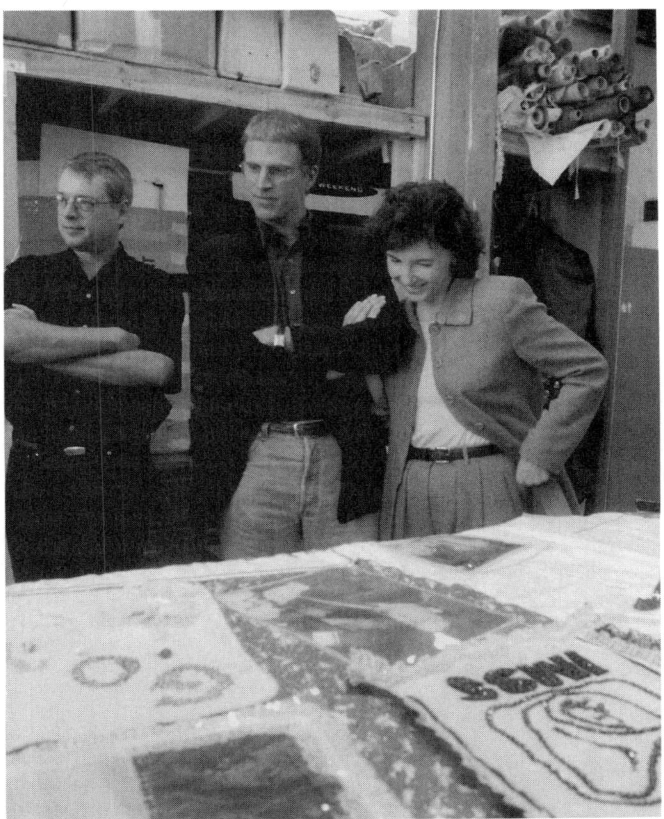

Cleve Jones (left) with (l-r) Ted Danson and Mary Steenburgen observing the AIDS Memorial Quilt.

After the march ended, Jones and many others taped the placards to the San Francisco Federal Building's facade. Jones compared the sight to that of a patchwork quilt passed down over many generations. "I thought of my grandmother, and my great-grandmother, and it was such a warm, middle-class, traditional values kind of feeling," Jones told the *Desert Sun*.

With this image in mind, Jones created the first panel for the NAMES Project Memorial Quilt in memory of his best friend Marvin Feldman. Completed in February 1987, the panel's abstract design consists of five stars of David—each dominated by a pink-red triangle—and Feldman's full name spray-painted on a white sheet. Four months later, the quilt's 2,000 panels were shown in Washington, D.C., an event which drew about 500,000 people.

By the mid 1990s, the AIDS Memorial Quilt comprised 32,000 panels from all 50 states and 28 countries and there were 38 NAMES Project chapters in the United States and 32 independent Quilt initiatives worldwide.

In the January 1989 issue of *Mother Jones*, Jones called the AIDS Quilt an internal and external strategy. "I needed to take care of myself, to make changes that would keep me strong and able to fight. And needed a strategy that would affect the outside world, which clearly is going to decide whether we're going to survive."

Unlike organizations such as ACT-UP, The AIDS Quilt relies on mainstream appeal. Jones said in *Mother Jones*, "Our posture just isn't going to be angry. We're not a political organization."

Jones further explained: "We're not lobbying or endorsing candidates. We want the grandmother from Iowa who hand-stitched her boy's flannel shirts together to be comfortable enough with us to come and see the panel. We don't use the rhetoric of the gay liberation movement or the Left or the 'New Age.' We don't allow ourselves to be defined in a way that will exclude anyone."

Jones has collected many awards. He was named "Person of the Week" by ABC News following the Quilt's inaugural display in Washington, D.C. in October, 1987. In 1993, he received Harvard AIDS Institute's second annual AIDS Leadership Award. In February 1996, he received a Steve Chase Humanitarian Award.

He has many admirers. "60 Minutes" aired a favorable story on him. Randy Shilts, who wrote the best-selling book *And The Band Played On*, once described his friend in a *Mother Jones* interview as "rare among political types, in that he doesn't take himself very seriously. He promotes himself, but he promotes a larger cause. He understands politics with a capital P: the point is to change people, not just to campaign or get elected."

In the 1990s, the AIDS Quilt has become a teaching tool for educating young adults. According to an article in *The San Francisco Chronicle* (3 December 1995), "Follow-up surveys at schools that display pieces of the quilt show that more than two-thirds thought more about their own chances of being infected after viewing it; nearly 90 percent said they would be more willing to take steps to avoid contracting the AIDS virus."

Jones sees another purpose for the AIDS Quilt: to encourage the federal government to increase its research endeavors and clinical trials programs. In an article in the *San Francisco Examiner* (30 November 1995), he wrote, "I am a long-term survivor of AIDS ... Ten years ago, I never imagined that I would be alive today." But he also acknowledged that only more research can save his life or any other infected with HIV.

Current Address: c/o The NAMES Project, 310 Townsend Street, Suite 310, San Francisco, CA 94117. Telephone: (415) 882-5500.

References:

"And Sew It Goes," in *Mother Jones*, no. 14, January 1989: 34-35.

Haberman, Douglas. "Humanitarian Award Honors 'activist side, Scientific Side'," in the *Desert Sun*, 17 February 1996: E-18.

Hawkins, Peter S. "Naming Names: The Art of Memory and the NAMES Project AIDS Quilt," in *Critical Inquiry*, no. 19, Summer 1993: 752-779.

Jones, Cleve. "AIDS Quilt: A Call for Research," in *San Francisco Examiner*, 30 November 1995: A-16.

—David Levine

Sor Juana Inés de la Cruz

c.1648-1695

Mexican poet, playwright, philosopher, and nun

Sor Juana Inés de la Cruz, or the "tenth muse" of Mexico, was renowned during her lifetime for her intellect, wit, and literary skill. In an age when few women could read, Juana's capacity to undermine the superiority of respected male scholars, to write poetry

Sor Juana Inés de la Cruz

and plays fit for royalty, and to have her works published in Spain, made her a celebrity. While Juana was frequently praised and admired, friends and enemies alike attempted to restrain her creativity and outspokenness.

Just as she elicited both praise and censure in the seventeenth century, Juana incites debate in the twentieth. Was she a Mexican poet, a Spanish one, or, as Mexican Nobel prize winner Octavio Paz asserts in *Sor Juana Inés de la Cruz; or, the Traps of Faith*, "a universal poet"? Does she deserve the title "First Feminist of the New World"? Finally, why did she eschew life among the elites of New Spanish society for that of a nun? Offering an explanation for this latter question, Dorothy Schons provides some sound advice in *Feminist Perspectives on Sor Juana Inés de la Cruz*: instead of examining Juana's life and motives with the "eyes of the present," we must view it "with the eyes of the past," and "study the social conditions of her time."

Sor Juana (Juana Ramírez de Asbaje) was born in San Miguel de Nepantla, New Spain, in November 1648 (some sources say 1651). Her parents were never married, and she grew up in the family home of her mother. There, as Paz explains, she witnessed the strength and relative independence of the women in her mother's family, and found a haven in her grandfather's library. Juana learned to read when she was just three years old, and to write by the time she was six; when she failed to progress in her Latin studies, she punished herself by cutting off her hair.

Juana was sent to Mexico City when she was ten years old, and she was later invited to live at the viceregal court. Although she was poor and illegitimate, the brilliant, beautiful young adolescent was a popular figure in high society, and she enjoyed the favor of powerful patrons. By the time Juana was fifteen, according to Schons, she "had already established a reputation as the most learned woman in Mexico."

In 1667, when she was just sixteen years old, Juana decided to leave the court and enter a convent (first that of the Discalced Carmelites and finally San Jeronimo). Rejecting alternative explanations for Juana's decision to become a nun, Schons demonstrates that Juana sought "the seclusion of a cloister" to indulge "her first love"—her books. According to Schons, as a young woman of New Spain, Juana's only options were to become a wife, a prostitute, or a nun—and the latter occupation was the only one which would afford her security *and* time to devote to her studies and writing.

When she was not performing her duties as a nun, Sor Juana spent much time in her convent room, which was filled with books and scientific instruments. While she wrote works for the New Spanish officials and socialites who often visited her, these were rooted in the Spanish literary tradition. As Gerard Flynn relates in *Sor Juana Inés de la Cruz*, she wrote "sacramental plays and ... comedies" in the "school of Calderón," poetry inspired by the "sonnets and *liras*" of the Spanish golden-age, and prose "concerned with the ecclesiastical society she lived in ... a mirror reflection of society in Spain."

Like some of the Spanish poets and playwrights she admired, Juana wrote the parts for both her male and female characters in the first person. As Ester Gimbernat de González argues in *Feminist Perspectives*, this allowed Juana to control "discourse through the man's voice," to assume "a certain superiority," and to exercise "a new power." In addition, as Georgina Sabat-Rivers explains in *Feminist Perspectives*, Juana "proclaimed her neuter status as a virgin, free from the domination of any man." Sabat-Rivers points out that, like Calderón, Juana also asserted the right of people to think and love regardless of gender; she wrote a poem (number 403) for her beloved benefactor, the Countess de Paredes, which Sabat-Rivers translates in part: "Neither being a woman nor being far away keeps me from loving you, for, as you know, souls are ignorant of distance and of gender."

The debate about Juana's feminism continues. In Paz's perspective, her "satire of men and her defense of women cease to be opinion" and become "moral, even visceral, reaction to lived experiences" when we consider the women and men she knew as a child. Sabat-Rivers, on the other hand, asserts that what "really mattered to [Juana] was to give to the feminine sex a literary and intellectual status equal to that of men, as can be seen explicitly or implicitly throughout her works." While Sabat-Rivers contributes a "feminist rereading" of Juana's "beloved" and most famous poem, *Sueño* (Dream), a more explicit example of Juana's independence of action and thought is found in her *Reply to Sor Filotea*. In this famous 1690 letter, Juana risked the notice of the Spanish Inquisition by challenging the wisdom and authority of an official who wanted her to spend less time thinking and writing and more time quietly at prayer.

Juana continued her work writing and preparing manuscripts for publication in Spain until 1693, when, according to Schons, floods, famine, and disease led Juana to believe her critics; she began to see her intellectual activity as sinful, part of the reason why disaster had descended upon Mexico. It was a that point that, as Asunción Lavrin remarks in *Feminist Perspectives*, the "'odel nun' overpowered the exceptional genius." Juana renounced her studies, sold all of her books, gave the money to the poor, and devoted herself to her prayers, duties, and nursing the sick. In the words of Paz, she "scourged her body, humbled her intelligence, and renounced the gift that was most her own: the word." Soon afterwards, on 17 April 1665, Sor Juana Inés de la Cruz fell ill during an epidemic and died.

References:

Flynn, Gerard. *Sor Juana Inés De La Cruz.* New York: Twayne, 1971.

González, Ester Gimbernat de. "Speaking Through the Voices of Love: Interpretation as Emancipation," in *Feminist Perspectives on Sor Juana Inés de la Cruz,* edited by Stephanie Merrim. Detroit: Wayne State University Press, 1991: 162-176.

Lavrin, Asunción. "Unlike Sor Juana?," in *Feminist Perspectives on Sor Juana Inés de la Cruz,* edited by Stephanie Merrim. Detroit: Wayne State University Press, 1991: 61-85.

Paz, Octavio. *Sor Juana: or, The Traps of Faith,* translated by Margaret Sayers Peden. Cambridge, Massachusetts: Belknap Press of Harvard University Press, 1988.

Sabat-Rivers, Georgina. "A Feminist Rereading of Sor Juana's *Dream,*" in *Feminist Perspectives on Sor Juana Inés de la Cruz,* edited by Stephanie Merrim. Detroit: Wayne State University Press, 1991: 142-161.

Schons, Dorothy, "Some Obscure Points in the Life of Sor Juana Inés de la Cruz," in *Feminist Perspectives on Sor Juana Inés de la Cruz,* edited by Stephanie Merrim. Detroit: Wayne State University Press, 1991: 38-60.

—Ronie Garcia-Johnson

Isaac Julien

1960-

British filmmaker

Isaac Julien is a black, gay, and decidedly independent British filmmaker who makes his race and sexual orientation an integral part of his work. Owing to such provocation, it was unavoidable that the press would eventually dub him Britain's "bad-boy" answer to Spike Lee, but it is a title he eschews. As is evidenced in the cooler, though nonetheless political, temperament of his work, Julien distances himself from what he sees as the "middle-class concerns" of current African-American filmmakers, opting instead for the more all-encompassing problems of the working-class from which he comes. As he told Gerard Raymond in a January, 1992 interview in *Premiere*, he is "uncomfortable" with what he calls Spike Lee's "romantic engagement with Black nationalism," and would rather focus on "dealing with identity in a pluralistic fashion." This is, perhaps, more understandable when we remind ourselves that the "black" community in England encompasses people from Asia, the Caribbean, India, and other far-flung colonies of the British Empire. "The Empire and sex," Julien told Raymond, smiling, "that's what I love to explore."

Julien was born in 1960 to West Indian parents and grew up in London's working-class East End. He studied visual arts and later film at St. Martin's School of Art. In 1983, he and four other film-school friends—black, feminist, and gay to varying degrees—founded Sankofa Film and Video, named for the mythical Ghanaian bird that looks into the past to prepare for the future. "We realized that there could be a lot of individual filmmakers, freelancers and auteurs, but there was no systematic way of them continuing their practice," Julien told Raymond.

Sankofa's very first production, *Territories* (1984) set the political tone for future projects, what Julien described to Raymond as "exploring questions of racial and sexual representations and issues of marginalization and hybridity." By 1986, Sankofa's *The Passion of Remembrance* (co-directed by Julien and Maureen Blackwood) was receiving rave reviews for its unflinching look at the black "experience" in Britain—both gay and straight—from the 1950s onward, and its examination of the diversity of the community through documentary footage and acted scenes of confrontation between older and younger blacks, gay and straight blacks, men and women, etc. "Why is it," one man in the film asks the audience, "that every time a black face appears on the screen ... it has to represent the whole race?"

Julien is perhaps best known in the United States for his lyrical, 45-minute, black-and-white film *Looking for Langston* (1989). This loving meditation on black poet Langston Hughes—set among the gay *demimonde* of the Harlem Renaissance of the 1920s—is still stunning not only because of its rarely-explored theme (black-on-black and black-on-white male love), but also for the sensual originality of its non-narrative style ("caressing" camera angles, the poetry of Essex Hemphill and Bruce Nugent, reenacted Cotton Club scenes, photography by Mapplethorpe). The film caused quite a stir at the 1990 New York Film Festival, and even prompted the Hughes estate to threaten legal action. All of which worked to serve up what some critics called simply one of the most visually satisfying and intellectually stimulating gay films made to date.

Julien's first feature film, *Young Soul Rebels* (1991), underscored his concerns for the pluralism of identity, but received little playtime in American cinemas. It is set in Britain in 1977, the anniversary of the Queen's Silver Jubilee ("Stuff the Jubilee" is an ongoing anthem), and tells the story of two black disc jockeys (one gay, one straight), a love affair between a black "soul boy" and a white "punk boy", a murder, and what Julien told Raymond in 1992 was "the relatively new phenomenon of dance clubs, where different groups—black, white, straight, and gay—were brought together into the same space because of the music." The film elicited some negative reaction from black audiences who objected to the explicit interracial love scene, but gay audiences wanted to see more—all of which serves to keep Julien grinning. "One of the underlying themes of *Young Soul Rebels*," Julien told Amy Taubin in an August, 1991 interview for *Sight & Sound*, "is that 'difference' *does* make a difference, but that doesn't necessarily mean that you have to enter into the tunnel vision of essentialism to provide answers." The film received the Critic's Award at Cannes in 1991.

Eight very queer minutes of total whimsy followed with Julien's *The Attendant* (1992), a story about a middle-aged museum guard who allows his wild S&M fantasies to breathe life into several 19th-century paintings after the galleries are closed. In 1993, Julien explored the advocacy of homophobic violence in hip-hop, gangsta' rap, and reggae music in his *A Darker Side of Black.* While the gay aspect of his outlook remains important, Julien here broadened his theme to examine the racism, slavery, and escalating gun culture that has fostered such hatred. According to Stephen Holden's review in the 6 January 1995 *New York Times*, "the film suggests that the vicious intolerance in a significant segment of black popular culture is a legacy of slavery itself. Oppression begets oppression."

Julien is also currently seeking the film rights to James Baldwin's *Giovanni's Room*, and is finishing a film about Sir Roger Casement—a "gay, Irish Lawrence of Arabia type who wrote against colonial violence and the atrocities that were happening in the early part of this century," he told Raymond. "It's a very complicated story," Julien told Amy Taubin. "Basically he ended up being executed by the British. They found diaries about his sexual activities. The person who put him on trial put Oscar Wilde on trial as well."

Isaac Julien's lens has always been keenly pointed toward the dilemma of pluralistic identity, but he is today likewise focusing on a more socio-political realm, claiming he is prompted to present Casement's story because of England's Section 25 and Section 28 bills which attack both basic civil rights and the "promotion" of homosexuality in education. He does not, however, like to speculate about commercial success—"a very American word to use," he told Laurence Jarvik in the August 1991 issue of *American Film*, "the kind of word, obviously, that British people feel uncomfortable with." It is all the new and heretofore unexplored themes in film that seem to excite Julien most. Casement's story represents his first non-black narrative and the first time he has directed a script written by someone else. I, for one, am looking forward to his handling of *Giovanni's Room*.

Current Address: c/o British Academy of Film and Television Arts, 195 Piccadilly, London W1V 9LG, England.

References:

Dyer, Richard. *Now You See It.* New York: Routledge Press, 1990.

Holden, Stephen. "Examining Gay Issues in Racial Settings," in *New York Times,* 6 January 1995: C-10.

Golden, Thelma. *Black Male.* New York: Harry N. Abrams, 1994.

Jarvik, Laurence. "British Bad Boy," in *American Film,* August 1991: 1-2.

Murray, Raymond. *Images in the Dark-An Encyclopedia of Gay and Lesbian Film and Video.* Philadelphia: TLA Publications, 1994.

Nolan, Abby McGanney. "Double Dare," in *Village Voice,* 10 January 1995: 50.

Raymond, Gerard. "Isaac Julien," in *Premiere,* January 1992: 45.

Ried-Pharr, Robert F. "Disseminating Heterotopia," in *African American Review,* Summer 1994: 347-357.

Taubin, Amy. "Soul to Soul," in *Sight & Sound,* August 1991: 14-19.

—Jerome Szymczak

Frank Kameny

1925-

American astronomer and activist

Frank Kameny's quiet scientific career abruptly ended in the late 1950s when he was fired for being a homosexual. He promptly challenged the federal government's ban on the employment of homosexuals and later took on federal policies on security clearances for homosexuals and the nation's perception of gays as sick people, among other battles. His 1968 slogan "Gay Is Good" helped change the gay movement's self-perception, paving the way for gay pride.

Franklin Edward Kameny was born on 21 May 1925 in Queens, New York. By the age of four, he had taught himself to read, and he aspired to be an astronomer at six years old. As a pre-teen he was aware of homosexual feelings, but he assumed they were temporary.

He entered Queens College at 16, but World War II interrupted his education. In 1945, he served in an armored infantry battalion in Germany, where he survived dangerous combat. After returning to the United States in 1946, he earned his B.S. degree in physics.

Kameny dutifully dated young women throughout high school and college, though his attractions to men never subsided. In 1954, while studying astronomy at the graduate level, Kameny acknowledged his homosexuality. In 1957, a year after earning his Ph.D. from Harvard, he landed a Civil Service job with the Army Map Service in Washington, D.C., where he received superior performance ratings. At the end of that year, however, he was discharged because of homosexuality. This moment, Kameny admits, catalyzed a shy astronomer into a full-time advocate for gay civil rights.

He contested the dismissal through every possible channel. His lawyer abandoned the fight after a few years, but Kameny personally petitioned the United States Supreme Court. By the time the high court refused to hear his case in 1961, his drive and intelligence had rendered him an amateur lawyer. With a few dedicated peers, he started the Mattachine Society of Washington (MSW), the nation's first "civil-liberties, social-action organization dedicated to improving the status of the homosexual citizen through a vigorous program of action," according to an MSW brochure. The group targeted employment discrimination in the government, and Kameny, recognized as the authority on security clearances for gay people, personally worked on hundreds of cases against the Civil Service Commission and the Pentagon during the next three decades.

Kameny also attacked the assumptions that pervaded society and damaged many gays. "We are the experts on our homosexuality," he declared in the early 1960s, refuting countless psychiatrists, ministers and others. This view became more influential after his article for *Psychiatric Opinion* (February 1971), in which he assailed the unscientific nature of psychiatric "sickness" claims that reinforced society's bigotry. He followed with protests of the American Psychiatric Association, calling for it to strike homosexuality from its list of pathologies (which it finally did in 1973).

Frank Kameny

Inspired by the "Black Is Beautiful" rallying cry in the late 1960s, Kameny coined the phrase "Gay Is Good," which became the slogan in 1968 for the North American Conference of Homophile Organizations. The phrase helped to augment the confidence that began after the 1969 Stonewall uprising, and thousands joined in fighting military discharges, employment discrimination, and sodomy laws.

In 1971, several friends persuaded Kameny to become the first self-declared gay man to run for congress. He campaigned against five other candidates for the District of Columbia's nonvoting post in the House of Representatives, championing personal freedom and gay rights in every appearance. Though he finished fourth, some of his rhetoric reads like a prophecy: "As homosexuals, we are fed up with a government that wages a relentless war against us and others of its citizens, instead of against the bigotry of our society. This is our country, our society, our government—for homosexuals quite as much as for heterosexuals.... You will be hearing much from us in the next thirty days—and long thereafter!" (*The Gay Crusaders*, p. 129)

His activist achievements include the reversal of the Civil Service Commission's anti-gay policy on 3 July 1975, and the repeal of D.C.'s sodomy law on 13 September 1993. The latter feat represents a three-decade battle for Kameny, who personally drafted the new law at the request of a city council member.

In a 1995 interview with the *Washington Blade* before his 70th birthday, Kameny said that he has not had many long-lasting committed relationships. "I'm emotionally independent," he said, "and I'm not looking for the love of my life."

After reflecting on a long career of activism, he told the *Blade* interviewer: "If I had to choose one particular thing I've done and put it at the pinnacle of all of which I'm proud, it would be 'Gay Is Good.' It encapsulates, in a way that has been taken up by others, everything that I stand for and have worked for."

References:

Fox, Sue. "At 70, Activist Frank Kameny Is Still Fighting," in *Washington Blade*, 19 May 1995.

Katz, Jonathan Ned. *Gay American History: Lesbians & Gay Men in the U.S.A.* New York: Penguin Books, 1992.

Shilts, Randy. *Conduct Unbecoming: Gays & Lesbians in the U.S. Military.* New York: St. Martin's Press, 1993.

Tobin, Kay and Randy Wicker. *The Gay Crusaders.* New York: Arno Press, 1975.

—Tom Musbach

Arnie Kantrowitz

1940-

American writer and activist

Responding to a questionnaire from the biographical series *Contemporary Authors* in 1977, Arnie Kantrowitz stated that the two primary subjects of his writing were "gay liberation and mysticism." This deceptively simple answer offers a window into the complex mind and spirit of one of the more widely read gay journalists of the twentieth century.

Born in Newark, New Jersey, on 26 November 1940, Kantrowitz developed an interest in literature and films early in his childhood. On completion of his secondary education, he landed a position as a promotion writer for New York television station WNEW, leaving in 1962 to accept a teaching job as instructor in English at the State University of New York College at Cortland. In 1965, he was appointed as assistant professor of English at the College of Staten Island, where he remains a faculty member.

Although aware of his attraction to persons of his own gender, Kantrowitz's early explorations of the heavily secretive homosexual world of Manhattan in the early 1960s both helped him define his sexual identity and provided first-hand information on the legal and

Arnie Kantrowitz. ***Photograph by Gene Bagnato.***

social situation of America's homosexual community, laying the foundation for his later activism. Following the Stonewall Riots of 28 June 1969, he joined the Gay Activists Alliance (GAA), the organization which would become the model for local gay civil rights organizations across the United States, being elected secretary in 1970 and vice president in 1971. He was a marshal for the first Gay Pride Parade in June 1970 and took part in many of the first public demonstrations held in New York City to improve the social condition of gay people. In his role as an officer of the GAA, and through life in one of the first gay men's communal houses, he established connections with a wide range of people who would eventually contribute to the redefinition of American homosexuality, including film historian Vito Russo and biologist Bruce Voeller.

Kantrowitz' activist sensibilities carried over into academic life as well, through his creation of an elective English course at Staten Island on "Homosexuals and Literature." This was one of the first such experimental classes in the United States and stands as a forerunner of the crystallization of gay and lesbian studies as a distinct field of study. Reflecting on the course and its implications in an essay done for the special 1974 issue of *College English* entitled "The Homosexual Imagination," Kantrowitz frankly addressed the tangled question of the relationship of education to gay liberation, stating that "consciousness-raising is not merely a political act; it is primarily an act of education, an act of communication on a human scale."

In addition to involvement in direct action and political activism, Kantrowitz brought his professional abilities as a writer and critic to the emerging field of gay journalism. Beginning as a book reviewer for the nationally circulated newspaper the *Advocate*, he became a familiar name and voice to thousands of readers through authoring feature articles and a regular column, "Christopher Street." His was a highly personal voice, speaking from inside an ongoing and often bewildering development as an intellectual examining his own life for the meaning of being an openly gay man. In 1977, this sharing of life experience in the public record culminated in the publication of his autobiography *Under the Rainbow: Growing Up Gay*. One of the few eyewitness accounts by an activist from the first years of the New York gay movement, its pages discuss the themes of personal responsibility for growth and the philosophical and political duties and definitions of community. Issues involved in reconciling the dual identities of being a homosexual and a Jew are also addressed, foreshadowing later similar literary explorations by the novelist Lev Raphael.

The impact of AIDS on the gay and lesbian community in one of the earliest American national epicenters was observed and chronicled by Kantrowitz throughout the early 1980s. By 1985, his activism and writing had taken on new direction through his work as a founding member of the Gay and Lesbian Alliance Against Defamation (GLAAD) and service as its secretary. Opposing journalistic homophobia at all levels (including participating in a demonstration against the virulently anti-gay *New York Post*), he also addressed the preservation of human dignity and courage in the face of both the pandemic and resurgent homophobia. His continuing philosophy of consistent (if wry) activism is perhaps best expressed in a 1975 essay for the *Advocate*, where he states that "when it comes time for singing or weeping or fighting to survive, I am part of my people, part of the human race and proud of it."

Current Address: Department of English, College of Staten Island, Staten Island, New York 10301.

References:

Hall, Richard. "Arnie Kantrowitz: Rainbows and Reality," in *Advocate*, no. 218, 29 June 1977: 30-31.

Kantrowitz, Arnie. "Friends Gone With the Wind," in *Advocate*, no. 454, 2 September 1986: 43-47, 108-109.

———. "Homosexuals and Literature," in *College English*, vol. 36, no. 3, November 1974: 321-330.

———. "I am Part of My People ... I am a Gay Jew," in *Advocate*, no. 165, 4 June 1975: 17.

———. *Under the Rainbow: Growing Up Gay*. New York: Morrow, 1977.

—Robert B. Marks Ridinger

Jonathan Ned Katz

1938-

American historian and activist

Called "the learned and constitutionally irreverent" by Gore Vidal, Jonathan Ned Katz has played a central and decisive role in creating the field of gay and lesbian history. Galvanized by the gay liberation movement that followed the Stonewall uprising of 1969, Katz, in his early work, captured the personal and collective shift in the sense of self, from the shamefully "homosexual" to the affirmatively "gay" and "lesbian." As an independent scholar, without academic affiliation or outside funding, Katz manifested his vision through his seminal *Gay American History*, published in 1976. From the start Katz's vision has been one of inclusive diversity among lesbians and gay men and ethnic groupings in America. While uncovering previously hidden gay and lesbian history, Katz realized that the "homosexual" and "heterosexual" categories were an historically recent development. First in *The Gay/Lesbian Almanac* (1983), and more substantially in *The Invention of Heterosexuality* (1995), Katz develops the idea of "heterosexuality" and "homosexuality" as social-historical constructions.

Jonathan Ned Katz was born in New York City on 2 February 1938, to Phyllis B. and Bernard Katz, and grew up in Greenwich Village. His mother supported his scholarly endeavors in both a professional manner (as an editor), and his father, according to Katz, taught him "to be outraged at social injustice, and about the need for united action toward radical change"—which his life's work bears out. Jonathan Katz changed his name in the public record to Jonathan *Ned* Katz in the mid 1980s, after another Jonathan Katz publicly advertised his conversion to heterosexuality through a cult philosophy. Katz has lived in a companionate relationship with David Barton Gibson in Manhattan since June 1976.

Katz "Comes Out" as a Gay Man

Katz grew up in the 1950s, a time of conformity, anxiety, and McCarthyism—Senator Joe McCarthy seemed to find "un-American" communists and homosexuals under every other bed—when homosexual was one of the worst things anyone could be. In *The Invention of Heterosexuality* Katz reports, "with a new and dawning horror, I had first consciously applied the word 'homosexual' to my feelings for men ... Even now, after all these years, I still recall the dread that the word 'homosexual' evoked on that conformist fifties morn."

He spent the next fifteen years in a state of isolation and shame, reading a great deal. He participated in marches against the war in Viet Nam and "applauded (from the sidelines) the black civil rights struggle and, later, the rise of the black power movement." Katz researched and wrote two radio scripts for WBAI-FM in New York City, "The Dispute Over the Ownership of Anthony Burns" (1968) about a fugitive slave case and "Resistance at Christiana" (1969) about a fugitive slave rebellion, and the script for two volumes of educational recordings, "Black Pioneers."

Although Katz was oblivious to the Stonewall uprising while it was taking place, virtually under his nose, its import reached him a year later when a friend in his therapy group gave him an article to read, "Homo/Hetero: The Struggle for Sexual Identity" by Joseph Epstein. "I experienced with new and stunning force the depth of antihomosexual hatred.... I understood: My homosexual feelings made me and others objects of 'prejudice'—subject to stigma, as a group, like black people, like women." In the winter of 1971 he began attending Gay Activist Alliance meetings. He found himself "exhausted and reeling from the intense, abrupt shift in understanding and emotion I was so quickly undergoing," an experience common to many middle-class homosexuals who had become adults before Stonewall.

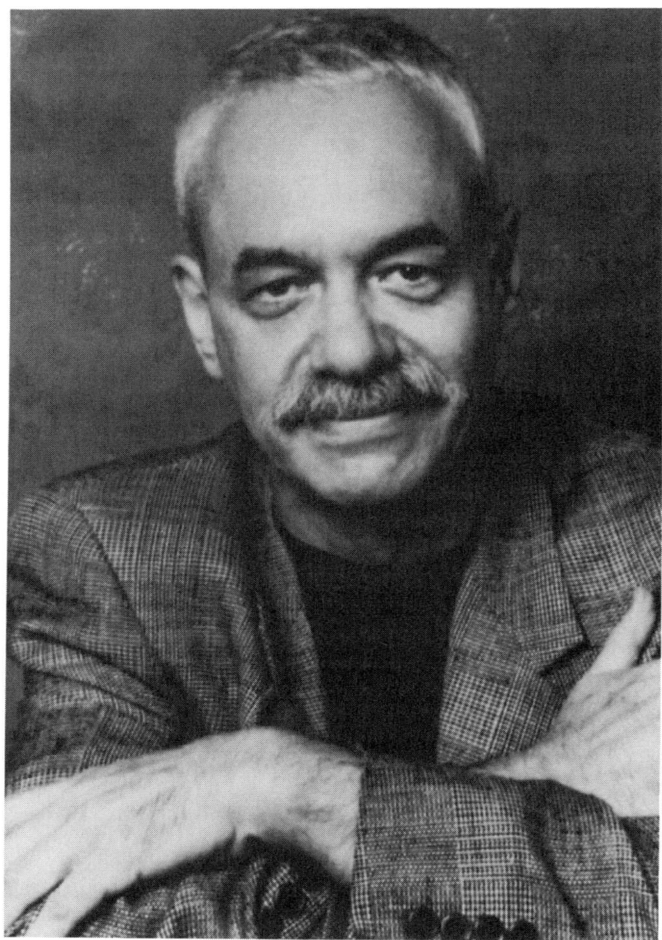

Jonathan Ned Katz

Coming Out!

In the early 1970s Katz read voraciously, and to gain insights into oppressed social groups—blacks, women, and gays. He turned one of his radio plays into a book, *Resistance at Christiana;* published a book for young people about a black pioneer woman; reviewed Dennis Altman's 1971 *Homosexual Oppression and Liberation* for the *Nation;* and participated in the founding of the Gay Academic Union in 1973. As a gay activist scholar he has played founding roles in numerous gay academic groups, and was on the founding committee of the organization now known as the National Writers Union.

Katz sought to capture the exuberance of "gay liberation" and to spread the word. Borrowing from the black, women's, and anti-war movements, he conceived an agit-prop documentary play. Katz envisioned *Coming Out!* as part historical, part literary, itself a document of the historic changing times. It is a two-act play with ten actors who speak many more voices of characters in situations of historic importance to the new movement. It premiered in June 1972.

"Coming Out! is intended to express," commented Katz in *Coming Out!*, "the sense of justified outrage at our oppression; a new militant determinism to subvert the heterosexual dictatorship by organized, united action; a new sense of ourselves as a social group with a history not only of persecution, but also of resistance." In her review of a 1973 performance on the SUNY/Albany campus, Nancy Miller observed that, "the value of *Coming Out!* is not ... primarily as a theatrical piece, but in its expression of the bitterness and resentment and the hopes and aspirations of homosexuals in the U.S." Identifying the gay liberationist strategy, Miller concludes, "the process of "Coming Out" as a force quite apart from the play is not only *not* ending, but, on the contrary, is just beginning."

Martin Duberman's comments on *Coming Out!*, on the front page of the *New York Times* Sunday drama section, brought Katz to prominence unexpectedly, and he accepted a publisher's small advance to write a book of documents on homosexual history; *Gay American History* would be published three years later. During this period Katz oversaw the Arno Press Series on Homosexuality, reprinting over fifty titles of mostly forgotten works (such as novels by Ann Bannon, the Daughters of Bilitis' the *Ladder*, Ford and Tyler's novel *The Young and Evil*) and a few new titles, notably James Steakley's *The Homosexual Emancipation Movement in Germany.*

Gay American History

Katz's vision took definite, if massive shape. The documents he unearthed revealed "evidence of a vast, subterranean world of same-sex relations, coexistent with the ordinary historical universe." Mainstream academic scholars of the day direly warned any would-be "gay" scholar against pursuing such activities as "professional suicide." Non-affiliation with academia ultimately gave Katz the intellectual freedom to pursue his ideas unhampered by professional politics. "The aim of my research," Katz asserted, "was intellectually quite modest—to simply recover and present a significantly large, wide-ranging collection of historical documents ... of Gay American history."

Gay American History: Lesbians and Gay Men in the U.S.A. was massive, but hardly exhaustive. Katz organized the documents into six categories: "Trouble"(legal persecution), "Treatment" (homosexuality as medical pathology), "Passing Women" (female cross-dressing, lesbians), "Native Americans/Gay Americans" (same-sex affection among indigenous peoples), "Resistance" (political action), and "Love." Katz reprinted some rare, original documents—some first-time translations (especially from the German), records from insane asylums, universities, churches, articles from psychiatric, psychological, and legal journals, court records, diaries, literary sources—most of which focused on "ordinary" gay and lesbians people and how they had lived their lives. Katz acknowledged that his book represented but one of many possible "authentic gay" views.

It seems impossible to overestimate the impact, direct or indirect, of Katz's *Gay American History.* Its publication triggered an explosion of research across academic disciplines (history, sociology, anthropology, literature), leading to new interdisciplinary work and competing theories, and a major boom in gay publishing, first in the small presses, and increasingly in the major houses. This boom has undergone several permutations in twenty years, but has yet to show signs of slowing down. Katz had started out to counter "the prevailing notion of homosexuality as a purely psychological phenomenon" which focused discussion and research "almost exclusively on three areas: the causation, character, and treatment of homosexuality as a psychosexual orientation disturbance" and to conceive the notion "as a historical, social, political, and economic phenomenon, as well."

In his introduction, Katz stated that he intended *Gay American History* as a catalyst for gay liberationist social change, "part of that national and worldwide organization and activity for radical social change in which each group, starting from a sense of its own particular oppression, is struggling for the democratic control of that society in which all work, live, and try to love." In 1977, Katz read Jeffrey Weeks' *Coming Out: Homosexual Politics in Britain, from the Nineteenth Century to the Present,* which confirmed the direction of Katz's own thinking. Immediately, he wrote to Weeks "eager to contact a like-minded gay historian of the left, pleased that a small international group of gay and lesbian conspirators was quietly starting homosexual history recovery work."

Discovering the Dialectical Embrace

Throughout the rest of the 1970s and into the early 1980s Katz continued assimilating new insights and adjusting his theories to accord with what he and others were discovering to be the unstable, shifting historical nature of sexual categorizing. He incorporated these ideas in the second volume of documents, published in 1983 as *Gay/Lesbian Almanac: A New Documentary.* Foremost was the idea that "heterosexuality" is a modern fabrication with a history of changing, contested meanings. In America since the late nineteenth century, "the heterosexual and homosexual have danced in close dialectical embrace," Katz wrote. Katz stressed again his own focus on eroticism and erotic feelings (including genital, erotic, and/or emotional intimacy), rather than social identities or persons, and cautioned against the false and ahistoric tendency in modern society to universalize "sexualities." Historical analysis, Katz concludes, reveals that the way we lust is not a "scientific" matter, and therefore does not have a "scientific" answer.

By the 1980s Katz had established himself as a public scholar, speaking, giving lectures at major universities, and receiving an occasional teaching appointment and small grants. Over a two-year period (1988-1990), Katz penned nineteen monthly "Katz on History" columns for the *Advocate.* In 1989 he scripted a theater piece on Walt Whitman, "Comrades and Lovers" (produced between 1989 and 1992), and in 1992 a committee sponsored by the Rockefeller Foundation invited Katz and others to help plan the 25th-anniversary exhibit commemorating Stonewall.

The Invention of Heterosexuality

Reading Mary P. Ryan's *Womanhood in American: From Colonial Times to the Present* and Lisa Duggan's work on women and American society in the 1920s spurred Katz to get to the bottom of "the social enforcement of heterosexuality." His initial inquiry into the history of heterosexuality as a social institution appeared in the January-March 1990 issue of *Socialist Review.* Five years later, Dutton published the book-length *Invention of Heterosexuality.* Katz's work has never wandered far from the feminist tenet that "the personal is political." *The Invention of Heterosexuality* is the first extended, explicit history of "heterosexuality" as a normalizing social institution. It is also, in part, an autobiography and an intellectual history of recent feminism.

In seven chapters, Katz roams from the personal to the collective, demonstrating the dialectical process of change. Starting from a personal account of his development as an activist scholar and historian, Katz returns to the late nineteenth century, when the sexologist Krafft-Ebing and his contemporaries made "sexuality" a scientific concern. From here, Katz summarizes and synthesizes several developments in the history of sexuality. The earliest, transitional "medical model" of sexuality distinguished between sexual acts as "perverted" because they "turned away from" procreation and "sex-love," as good and healthy, as long as it occurred within the context of "true love" and marriage.

Earlier, in the early nineteenth century, society drew distinctions not between different- and same-sex eroticism, but between true love and false love, and distinguished between sexual acts which maximized procreation or "sinfully" wasted human seed. When the middle class generally adopted contraception, non-reproductive intercourse was normalized as "heterosexual." "The making of the middle class and the invention of heterosexuality went hand in hand," observes Katz. Freud is presented by Katz as both the "major modern maker of heterosexuality's ahistorical medical model *and* as subversive theorist of heterosexuality's social construction—its historical invention." Freud, says Katz, would play an important role in transmuting sex from productive duty to acts of pleasurable consumption. But if non-reproductive sex was now "normal," the deviant could no longer be defined simply as the non-procreative. Homosexuals had to represent a neurotic failure of emotional development. The purpose of "the homosexual" in this was to validate the middle-class's assertion of being "normal" in contrast, and to naturalize and universalize the dominance of the middle class social order. Katz then connects Freud's (and others') idea of normative heterosexuality to the larger social project of normalizing and standardizing everything, from the gauge of railroad tracks to train schedules, time zones, and, even intelligence (the "IQ test"). Kinsey's six-point scale gave the bipolarity of sexual social identity a more nuanced range of differentiation.

Katz now reviews developments in modern feminist thought. In *The Feminine Mystique* (1963) Betty Friedan demonstrated how the personal and sexual are linked with power and politics. Ti-Grace Atkinson targeted heterosexual society as a culturally enforced, inequitable arrangement. Kate Millet introduced the concept of *Sexual Politics.* In "The Traffic in Women" (1975), Gayle Rubin theorized the "sex/gender system" (gender is the socially imposed division of the sexes). Katz notes the 1970 Radicalesbians' "zap" confronting feminists with their own fear of lesbians, and dominance of heterosexual assumptions. He also observes that the operation of a powerful taboo continues to keep heterosexuality outside of analysis to this day. Katz confesses to finding Michel Foucault's work rich with suggestion for his own understanding of the changing social-historical organization or eroticism and gender.

As Lisa Duggan says in her afterword, "In putting the arguments of historians of sexuality,that the categories heterosexual/homosexual are historical and changeable, into public discourse, Katz has done us a very significant service. If such arguments remain confined to the university classroom and academic conference, they won't push public debate and policy the way we need them to."

In 1995, Jonathan Ned Katz received the Publishing Triangle's Bill Whitehead Award for "Lifetime Achievement in Lesbian and Gay Literature." His papers are collected in the manuscript division of the Research Libraries of the New York Public Library.

Current Address: c/o Joan Raines, Raines & Raines, 475 Fifth Avenue, New York, New York 10017.

References:

Abelove, Henry, Michèle Aina Barale, and David M. Halperin, eds. *The Lesbian and Gay Studies Reader.* New York: Routledge, 1993.

Chauncey, George. *Gay New York: Gender, Urban Culture, and the Making of the Gay Male World, 1890-1940.* New York: Basic Books, 1994.

D'Emilio, John. *Making Trouble.* New York: Routledge, 1992.

Duberman, Martin, Martha Vicinus, and George Chauncey, Jr., eds. *Hidden from History: Reclaiming the Gay and Lesbian Past.* New York: Meridian, 1989.

Greenberg, David F. *The Construction of Homosexuality.* Chicago: University of Chicago Press, 1988.

Katz, Jonathan Ned. *Coming Out! A Documentary Play about Gay Life and Liberation in the U.S.A.* New York: Arno Press, 1975.

———. *Gay American History: Lesbians and Gay Men in the U.S.A.* New York: Crowell, 1976.

———. *Gay/Lesbian Almanac: A New Documentary.* New York: Harper and Row, 1983.

———. *The Invention of Heterosexuality.* New York: Plume, 1995.

Morton, Donald, ed. *The Material Queer: A LesBiGay Cultural Studies Reader.* Boulder, Colorado: Westview Press, 1996.

—Les K. Wright

John Maynard Keynes

1883-1946

British economist

The son of two unusual people imbued with a sense of duty and acute intelligence, John Maynard Keynes was born on 4 February 1883. He, along with younger brother Geoffrey, younger sister Margaret, and three servants, grew up in a nurturing middle-class Victorian household with parents so ideal that there was never a hint of rebellion even when the children were approaching adulthood. Between father and Maynard, as he was known to everyone but his mother, there was a closeness that could serve as a model for father-son relationships. They shared an avid passion for puns, stamp-collecting, playing golf, and any activity that lent itself to measurement. Maynard was not a pretty or handsome boy; at first sight, he was even found ugly, an impression that was soon dispelled by virtue of a pleasant voice, lively expressive eyes, and winsome ways. In short, he led a charmed and fulfilling existence as a child and adolescent, and, ultimately moved in elite company his entire life.

At fourteen, Keynes was admitted to Eaton, the most prestigious boys' school in England, where he was a model student. Because of his intelligence and quiet authoritative manner, he was soon looked on as the natural spokesman for his class and never received anything but the highest commendations from his teachers. His letters home are full of figures: classmates' heights and weights, times of trains, his own temperatures, and the number of hours he worked per day, a habit he took up from his father. Never bored, even at school, he wished a day had thirty-six hours and a week fourteen days.

Witty, conscientious, very quick, sometimes irreverent, Keynes was driven at school, and for the rest of his life, by a sense of public duty, by prolific energies, by far-ranging curiosity, and by a need to do many things well.

An understanding of John Maynard Keynes would be incomplete without some discussion of the elite group into which he was initiated at Cambridge. The Cambridge Conversazione Society, better known as the Society, or the Apostles, was founded in 1820. Its aim was to give a group of like-minded students the private and intimate forum they needed to work out a philosophy of life. It would be philosophy—with economics in second place—that provided the foundation of Keynes' life. From each successive class, new members would be recruited and bound together in secrecy and friendship. The Society's credo flowed from strong allegiance to love of truth and communion with friends. This, not service to God, inspired their conduct. Their secret meetings remained open to alumni for life. Keynes was interviewed for membership in his first year—a rarity—the interviewers being Lytton Strachey and Leonard Woolf, husband of Virginia. Satisfying the members with his cleverness and unworldliess, he was soon initiated. During his next six years, most of his private life unfolded within this group of apostles, who, along with their friends and family members, became the people Keynes would largely socialize with most of his life.

Keynes' early work included a civil service stint in the India Office and another in the British treasury, serving as its chief representative at the peace negotiations at Versailles in 1919. In the meantime, he had been appointed fellow in Kings College at Cambridge—he was an excellent lecturer—where he remained active for the rest of his life. He was catapulted to world fame with his publication of *The Economic Consequences of the Peace* (1919). His masterpiece, however, was *The General Theory of Employment, Interest, and Money*, which is still a classic today. Keynes biographer, Robert Skidelsky states:

> In its refusal to stale, the book reflects its author. Keynes was a magical figure, and it is fitting that he should have left a magical work. There has never been an economist like him: someone who combined so many qualities at such a high level, and allowed them all to fertilize his thought. He was an economist with an insatiably curious mind; a mathematician who could dazzle people with the most unmathematical of fancies; a logician who accepted the logic of art; a masterbuilder who left monuments in stone as well as words; a pure theorist, an applied theorist and a civil servant all in one; an academic intimate with the City. Even his sexual ambivalence played its part in sharpening his vision. He was, above all, a buoyant and generous spirit who refused to despair of his country and its traditions, and offered the world a new partnership between government and people to bring the good life within reach of all.

The book had profound influence upon the American scene, then in the throes of the century's worst depression. Keynes' theory, in fact, was an important component in Roosevelt's New Deal.

Most economists currently accept the main implications of Keynes' analysis. He rejected that part of economics which aims at preciseness—which he referred to as "specious precision"—asserting that it was impossible to be precise about what was inherently vague and complex.

Keynes put new emphasis on the function of money—on liquidity as a measure, not of purchasing power, but of mistrust of the future. His other chief contribution was to show that an economy had no natural tendency to full employment. Calling in the state to act carried risks, but these risks seemed small compared to the risk of doing nothing. His economic theories were followed world-wide for almost forty years, governments finally accepting responsibility for full employment. Only since 1973 have they ceased to be Keynesian in its fullest sense.

Keynes' great gift was grounded in extraordinary intuitive powers. While he had an obsession with numbers, he was always prepared to go beyond mere statistical interpretations. For him, numbers were springboards to truth that lay beyond mere theorems of classical economics. His imagination teemed with figures from legend and mythology, which he used, like Freud and Joseph Campbell, to suggest patterns and archetypes useful in explaining the mysterious workings of his world.

G. E. Moore's *Principia Ethica* was the most important book in Keynes' life. To understand Keynes, one must understand his loyalty to the ideas of this contemporary thinker, who gave new impetus and direction to philosophical discussion in England. Keynes was inspired by Moore's assertion that one's duty is to be committed to a line of action which produces the greatest possible amount of good—not just good for others but also good for oneself. Keynes did not ignore claims for personal happiness and a civilized life. "To be in love with one's friends, with beauty, with knowledge; these remained Maynard's lodestars." Keynes was preoccupied with the relationship between being rich and being good though never made much headway in resolving this preoccupation. Why support the existing system of creating wealth? Because, he concluded, its collapse would be worse than its success. A question of importance to Keynes was: what is a person to do with his life if he has the temperament and interests of the artist but does not have the talent to create works of art?

Keynes came to worship Bloomsbury figure Lytton Strachey who became the most important friend he ever had. Love of someone of their sex was, they believed, ethically better than love of the opposite sex. It gave neither of them the slightest sense of guilt. In fact, they felt that theirs was a superior calling and that later generations would regard them as pioneers. To this end, they preserved their correspondence for posthumous publication. But his friendship with Lytton Strachey was twice compromised by their competing for the same individual: the first, a stunningly handsome freshman by the name of Arthur L. Hobhouse, who was Keynes's first important love; the second, a talented young painter, Duncan Grant, who was first pursued by his cousin Lytton Strachey. Over the next seventeen years, Keynes was to have several love affairs with men along with a fair amount of casual sex. As for Duncan, the love of Keynes life, he ended up sharing his life with Virginia Woolf's sister, Vanessa, both of them benefitting from the generous settlement that Keynes made on Duncan in 1937, proof that his love for Duncan never faded.

Then came a Russian ballerina. It is difficult to explain Keynes' flip-flop from homo- to heterosexuality at almost forty years of age. Nothing in his emotional life prior to his falling in love with Lydia Lopokova indicated that he was bisexual. All his early experiences pointed toward an exclusive preference for men as sexual/emotional partners. For a while Keynes tried to balance his affair with her with one with Sebastian Sprott. Lydia soon demanded that he end his liaison with Sprott. The attraction of Lydia, as with Duncan Grant, was her original but completely untrained intelligence, which was entirely intuitive; what was lucky for Lydia was that Keynes sought not his likeness but an opposite. Like Keynes, she had curiosity about everything. They were also both gamblers which helped them undertake their improbable relationship. She admired the complexities inherent in Keynes' intellectual life. What smoothed the way was no doubt Lydia's acceptance of Keynes' past and her willingness to gamble on his closing the door on that past. Which is precisely what he did, and there is no indication that he ever opened it again.

John Maynard Keynes

The Bloomsbury group, to which Keynes had been a late-comer, proceeded to exclude Lydia, whom they considered little more than a chorus girl. This was the price Keynes had to pay for his change in lifestyle, not that Bloomsbury had anything against heterosexual marriage or bisexuality. Actually, Keynes and Lydia became a very successful combination in circles that extended far beyond Bloomsbury, he for his intelligence, she for her gaiety and charm. It is more than clear that they had an extremely happy and fulfilled marriage.

No economist has ever wielded such a style. Keynes wrote in short sentences and paragraphs in a style that was economical and direct, and he almost never had to revise. Though the greatest economist of this century—yet with no economic degree—he was at or near the center of British economic life during both world wars. The Keynesian Revolution was possible because the world had seen that ideals were too costly. It is not then the lack of ideals which raises Keynes' ire—it is the lack of competence. The world was to be saved by intelligence, not by morals—this was the conclusion of Wilson's failure at the Peace Conference.

"Many theorists have been more elegant; many economists have had higher ethical ideals; none have achieved so much practical good." Keynes' genius was to analyze economic disorder and call for state intervention as a way to stabilize the social order—but only as a last resort. His dazzling intellect and infectious buoyancy shone through in everything he did. He had a strong cult of living the good life, surrounded by beauty and civilized friends. He died of heart disease at Tilton, his home in Sussex, on 21 April 1946. His monument, if we may call it that, is the Arts Theatre he had built in Cambridge in 1935.

References:

Harrod, R. F. *The Life of John Maynard Keynes*. New York: Macmillan, 1951.

Skidelsky, Robert. *John Maynard Keynes, Hopes Betrayed, 1883-1920*. New York: Penguin Books, 1992.

———. *John Maynard Keynes, the Economist as Savior, 1920-1937*. New York: Penguin Books, 1992.

(All quotes are from the Skidelsky sources unless otherwise indicated.)

—Robert F. Jones

Willyce Kim

1946-

Asian-American writer

Though she started out as a poet in the 1970s, Willyce Kim is perhaps best known as the self-styled writer of a new genre she gave life to in the early 1980s—the highly comic, yet politically significant Korean-American lesbian Western. In both her poetry and prose, Kim strives to break free from sexualized and racialized notions of what it means to be female, Asian-American, and lesbian. While other lesbian writers strive to revise history, Kim sets out to celebrate the joy and power of being a lesbian right now, and calls attention to the injustice of being stereotyped and made "ornamental" and invisible in the lesbian as well as the larger, Westernized community.

Amazingly, she does it in a way that is decidedly fun. As writer Kitty Tsui notes in *Contemporary Lesbian Writers of the United States:* "Kim writes about love, sex, fun, friendship, and food. She can make the reader's mouth water with descriptions of buckwheat pancakes, spaghetti squash stuffed with mushrooms, onions and green peppers,... and vanilla bean ice cream.... [She] combines wit and deadpan humor with a thick plot, vibrant characters, and great visuals."

Kim was born in 1946 in Honolulu, a second-generation Korean-American from a devout Catholic family. "The church taught us that homosexuals were living in a state of mortal sin," she told Cathy Cade in *Lesbian Photo Album: The Lives of Seven Lesbian Families*. "There were a lot of butchy-looking women in Hawaii.... Everyone loves them. I still don't know if these women were gay or not. They were all devout Catholics."

In 1964, Kim widened her horizons by moving to the mainland, and in 1968 she got her bachelor's degree in English literature from San Francisco College for Women at Lone Mountain. She was soon caught up in the burgeoning women's liberation movement of the time, reading her poetry at bars and women's coffeehouses with the likes of Judy Grahn and Barbara Smith. In 1971, she was the first Asian-Pacific lesbian to self-publish her own collection of poetry—*Curtains of Light*—that was not part of an anthology. She "rode the wave" of affirming lesbian love in joyous poetry by publishing two more popular collections in the 1970s—the decidedly lusty *Eating Artichokes* (1972), and the romantically defiant *Under a Rolling Sky* (1976). "I splinter trees/with the roar/of my voice," she wrote in *Sky*.

Like their counterparts everywhere, Asian-American and Asian-Pacific lesbians have been writing and speaking of their experiences for decades. (Margaret Chinen's 1947 play *All, All Alone* is perhaps one of the earliest examples). Living at the crossroads of a predominantly heterosexual and male-dominated Asian community and that of the Western-dominated lesbian community, however, puts these women in the frustrating position of always having to "prove" the efficacy of their love. As writer Alice Hom notes in *The Gay and Lesbian Literary Heritage,* women who glance at her in a lesbian bar "are surprised to see me because Asian-Pacific stereotypes are so ingrained in the heterosexual context that Asian lesbians do not even come to mind."

Perhaps in a valiant effort to shatter these stereotypes and be truly "noticed," Kim embarked, in the 1980s, on two "women's-western-style" novels packed with colorful adventures and randy anti-heroines. In the first, *Dancer Hawkins and the California Kid* (1985), Dancer and The Kid have a fist-fight, find a common love in food, cavort with canine characters like "Killer Shep" and "Gypsy," rescue Dancer's girlfriend from a fiendish cult, and save the Napa Valley from total defoliation. In the sequel, *Dead Heat* (1988), our heroes seek solace with friends, food, and gambling in San Francisco, and The Kid falls in love with a woman jockey.

Throughout these works, Kim utilizes a new, comedic, action-packed style of short vignettes to punctuate this new genre of "lesbian neo-Western." Her characters are strong, outrageous, and brazen women who fight, swear, fuck, carry knives, smoke, and, as Kitty Tsui says: "Use their eyes to steer a path through a crowd or stop a mad dog in its tracks.... Women who battle addictions and phobias and triumph to emerge into sunlight."

In the end, Kim's poetry and prose is about friendship—its importance, its power, the necessity of it in our lives. The power of this friendship is tantamount to the power of sometimes-overrated "love." And always, there is in her work the joyful "noise" of affirmation for the lesbian "family"—in whatever size, skin-color, and/or configuration that family may take. As Kim writes in "Poem for Zahava": "We could:/roll five joints with either hand,/rescue ten women with smile,/and kick the shins out of any man."

References:

Cade, Cathy, ed. *Lesbian Photo Album: The Lives of Seven Lesbian Feminists*. Oakland, California: Waterwomen Books, 1987.

Kim, Willyce. *Curtains of Light*. Albany, California: self-published, 1970.

———. *Dancer Dawkins and the California Kid.* Boston: Alyson Publications, 1985.
———. *Dead Heat.* Boston: Alyson Publications, 1988.
———. *Eating Artichokes.* Oakland, California: Women's Press Collective, 1972.
———. *Under a Rolling Sky.* Oakland, California: Maud Gonne Press, 1976.
Pollack, Sandra and Denise D. Knight, eds. *Contemporary Lesbian Writers of the United States.* Westport, Connecticut: Greenwood Press, 1994.
Summers, Claude J., ed. *The Gay and Lesbian Literary Heritage.* New York: Henry Holt, 1995.

—Jerome Szymczak

Billie Jean King

1943-

American tennis player

An overview of Billie Jean King's remarkable tennis career yields a seemingly endless lists of firsts—the first woman to make more than $100,000 from tennis in a year (in 1971); the first woman to be named *Sports Illustrated*'s "Sportsperson of the Year" (in 1973); the first woman to win a record twenty titles at Wimbledon, six of them in singles; founder of the first women's professional tour in 1970; and the first woman player to publicly acknowledge having an affair with another woman.

Born in Long Beach, California, on 22 November 1943, Billie Jean Moffit enjoyed the loving support of a close-knit family. Religion was important to the Moffits, and Billie Jean originally wanted to become a missionary. However, when she discovered a talent for softball at an early age, sports soon replaced religion in her career goals. Quickly realizing that softball had no real prospects for a woman player, she switched to tennis—always sustained by a passionate belief that she could be the best in the world.

Her parents, Bill and Betty, encouraged her sporting achievements, as did her younger brother Randy, who was himself later to become a professional sportsman as pitcher for the San Francisco Giants. While the Moffits were not poor, in the 1950s tennis was very much an upper-middle-class pursuit, centered around the country clubs of the well-heeled—clubs to which the Moffits could not afford to send Billie Jean. Undeterred, the family saved nickels and dimes to buy King her first tennis racket for eight dollars, and she played whenever, wherever she could—she was later to suggest in her 1982 autobiography, that "being a little bit less advantaged in a middle-class world gave me a great drive."

King's physique was not that of the natural athlete: at five feet four-and-a-half inches, she was to experience constant difficulty in maintaining her optimum weight, and suffered knee problems necessitating countless operations. However, her talent and professionalism always outweighed these drawbacks, right from the beginning of her career. A fiercely competitive, aggressive, and volatile player, she took winning extremely seriously, finding the limitations placed on her as a woman at the outset of her career deeply frustrating.

King Travels to Australia to Develop Her Game

Her initial forays into tennis were hampered by the sporting climate of the time, in which men were given preferential treatment by the United States Lawn Tennis Association (USLTA) and outstanding women such as King were often given less attention than even mediocre male players. College athletic scholarships for women did not exist, nor did the professional tour for women which we now take for granted: women competed in what King referred to as the "shamateur" game, being paid "under the table" for their participation in sporting events. Despite this, King showed immediate promise, winning the Californian championships in 1958 and thus earning a trip to the National Tennis Championships in Ohio, where though she lost in the quarter-finals to Carol Hanks of St Louis, she was encouraged by the chance to meet the competition and found it "not at all intimidating," as she was later to recount in her autobiography.

On her return to California, Moffit began attending Los Angeles State University, where she met Larry King, whom she was to marry in 1965. For the next few years she, by her own account, "drifted," continuing with school and playing where possible, with considerable success. King took the Wimbledon doubles title in 1961, partnering Karen Hantze, and won again the following year, and reached the singles final for the first time in 1963, but in the absence of an organized touring circuit for female tennis players, she found it difficult to shape a professional career. The attitude of the USLTA towards female players, who received less money and less assistance than their male contemporaries, angered King and, she felt, slowed her progress.

A breakthrough came in 1964 when Bob Mitchell, a former benefactor of the legendary Margaret Court, gave her the opportunity to travel to Australia and be trained by Mervyn Rose, a former Davis Cup player and renowned coach. This was to be a turning point for King, as Rose helped her to completely reshape her game, altering her serve and forehand. While initially these changes led to a string of defeats by lesser players in Australia, in the longer term her game was stronger than ever, and it remained so for many years. It was said by Wimbledon historians Alan Little and Lance Tingay in their 1984 tribute to Wimbledon's great female champions, *Wimbledon Ladies: A Centenary Record 1884-1984—The Singles Champions,* that it was "impossible to find any aspect of her game that was less than strong"; a superbly quick volleyer, she was said to have gone through entire seasons without missing a single smash shot. She was a versatile player, always competitive in doubles where, she said, the mind was as important as the body in achieving success.

Her game thus restructured and much improved, King returned to the United States in 1965 to be runner-up in the Forest Hills championship, her first appearance in the final there. The following year she was to win her first Wimbledon singles title beating Maria Bueno in three sets. With this, her first Grand Slam victory, an outstanding career was now well under way.

King Sets Up Women's First Pro Tour

King continued to collect major titles through the late 1960s. Her dominance of Wimbledon, her favorite tournament, was established with her triumphs in the singles titles of 1967 and also 1968, the year she first reached the U.S. Open final. Her success was financial as well as sporting. In 1968, she signed a contract to join the previously men-only National Tennis League, along with her contemporaries Rosie Casals, Françoise Durr, and Ann Jones, and by

Billie Jean King

1970 she was earning up to $2,000 a week in "private," semi-official fees. The following year, she became the first female player to make more than $100,000 in a year.

Despite this, she was growing more discontented with the vast discrepancies in fees between men and women players, both in the U.S. and Europe. In 1970, when King won the Italian Championships, she was paid $600 to the male champion's $3,500: similarly, in that year's Pacific Southwest Championships, the men's purse was $12,500, the women's $1,500. Dissatisfied, King led calls for a boycott, but the USLTA resisted. Instead, King helped organize the first successful women's professional circuit, sponsored by Philip Morris, the tobacco company. By 1973, the Virginia Slims tour was established, covering 22 cities, with a total prize fund of $775,000 (in comparison to the men's circuit of 24 cities and $1,280,000).

King Has Affair with Marilyn Barnett

In 1972, King met and befriended hairdresser Marilyn Barnett. Under stress from the demands of the circuit, she found being with Barnett extremely relaxing and, as their relationship developed, King "realized that something was different, that I seemed to be falling in love with Marilyn." Their relationship became a physical one, intense and passionate.

King employed Barnett as a "Girl Friday" the following year, and they travelled together on the tour. Unfortunately, in 1974 the relationship deteriorated and King asked Barnett to leave her employ. King continued to rent Barnett a house in Malibu owned by the couple. While the women continued to spend time together on and off until 1979, in which year a financial settlement was made between the couple, the relationship, by King's decision, was effectively over. Until Barnett filed a palimony suit in 1982, their affair was not public knowledge.

Meanwhile, King's tennis career continued, with wins at the 1972 French Open and her cherished first U.S. Open title in 1974, where she beat Evonne Goolagong 3-6, 6-3, 7-5. She also won the Wimbledon ladies singles in 1972, 1973, and 1975, consolidating her dominance of the tournament. In 1973, partly as a result of King's lobbying and the success of the women's tour, the U.S. Open equalized the prize money for men and women at $25,000 each.

As well as playing, King, along with Martina Navratilova and Chris Evert, was trying to get a women's organization, the Women's Tennis Association (WTA), off the ground. Some of the top women were wary of antagonizing the national federations, but with the help of former National Tennis League colleagues Rosie Casals, Ann Jones, and Françoise Durr, King persuaded almost all the female players to lend the union their support and, like the men's Association of Tennis Professionals the year before, the WTA was formed that year.

King vs Riggs: "A Victory of Sorts for Feminism"

Also in 1973, the former Wimbledon men's champion Bobby Riggs, King's senior by 25 years, challenged her to a match at the Houston Astrodome. Riggs had previously challenged and beaten Margaret Court, and King had winced at the media ridicule of women's tennis that had resulted. Forty million TV watchers worldwide watched her despatch Riggs 6-4, 6-3, 6-4, her victory "mercilessly professional" according to journalist Rex Bellamy in *Love Thirty—Three Decades of Champions.* The publicity was enormous, and the game hailed as a triumph for women's tennis: though sports historian Allen Guttman referred to it in his book, *Women's Sports—A History,* as "a travesty of modern sport," he also conceded it as "a victory of sorts for feminism."

A year later, King formed the Women's Sport Foundation (with swimmer Donna de Varona), and a magazine, *womenSports.* By the mid-1970s, women's tennis was enjoying a surge of popularity, brought about by nobody so much as the tirelessly inventive King.

King's Affair Becomes Public

By 1975, however, King had begun trying to "wind-down" her career prior to retirement. Her knees, never strong, were causing her increasing trouble, and while she continued to win matches, professional tennis was taking its toll, physically and mentally. She was also beginning to lose her enthusiasm for the sport, but since she still enjoyed and excelled at doubles, she had not yet announced her full retirement.

Her singles career on the wane, King was in Florida participating in a 1981 tournament when she learned from the *Los Angeles Times* that her former lover, Marilyn Barnett, was about to sue her for the house she had been living in, and associated expenses. At the time, King was negotiating a lucrative endorsement contract with Wimbledon, who were bringing out a line of ladies' tennis clothes, and she was discussing with American broadcasting company NBC the possibility of becoming a regular commentator. Her personal concern for these deals was matched only by her worry that the constant media speculation about lesbians in sport would be fuelled by the inevitable publicity, and damage the sport she had worked so hard to promote.

In a state of shock, King immediately left Florida for her home in New York where, after a night spent thinking and conferring with her family and business associates, she made the decision to go public and acknowledge the affair at a Los Angeles press conference. Spurred on by a determination to be true to herself, King's brave and honest acknowledgement made her an important figure for gays and lesbians worldwide, and to this day she features in such community exhibits as the *Advocate*/GLAAD "Long Road to Freedom" travelling exhibit on lesbian and gay history. However, King was later to estimate that her disclosure cost her $1.5 million, as well as lost sponsorship on the women's tour, although her position with NBC as commentator was unaffected.

While always supportive of gay rights, King was reluctant to identify herself as a member of the gay community: this was based partly on a distaste for labels of any sort, and partly on her belief that in her relationship with Barnett, King "felt no differently than when I made love to a man." While King felt uncomfortable with what she referred to as "a typical heterosexual suburban lifestyle"—and certainly had with her husband an unconventional relationship for the times, choosing to travel the circuit alone while he remained in the United States—she also felt she had never lived as part of the gay community either. "Obviously I must be bisexual. I suspect many people are, only they're not aware of it," she said in her autobiography. "I couldn't have sustained the affair with Marilyn and not be bisexual.... Love is the same, whoever is involved, and it isn't the gender so much as the individuals." Throughout her career, King was consistently to reject the labels put on her by the media, whether of feminist, lesbian, leader, or symbol of women's achievement, preferring to be seen as an individual.

After Retirement: King Coaches Navratilova

Even after retirement from singles competition, King continued to participate in doubles, partnering with the 13-year-old American Jennifer Capriati in the Virginia Slims Florida tournament in 1990. She also became involved in top-seeded Martina Navratilova's efforts to win her ninth Wimbledon singles title, working alongside her coach Craig Karden. Navratilova, also the victim of a lawsuit from a former girlfriend, approached her for assistance in 1989, although King has always denied speculation that they were ever romantically involved.

King also continued to lobby for the women's game. In 1994, in a echo of her 1970 role in establishing the Virginia Slims tour, King spearheaded a proposed new circuit backed by sports management group IMG, a threat which the *Guardian* of 8th September 1994 suggested "has forced the Women's Tennis Council to look at ways of making the existing one more attractive to the top players." The same year, she agreed to form part of a Women's Legends Tour for 1995, with Chris Evert, Martina Navratilova, and ten other former champions including Briton Virginia Wade and her former doubles partner Rosie Casals.

Though there have been reports that King has developed the eating disorder bulimia, after a lifetime of battling with her weight, her enthusiasm for tennis seems not to have waned as she enters her fifth decade. In 1996 she captained a team of tennis legends such as Pam Shriver and Zina Garrison Jackson in the *Family Circle* magazine cup. Throughout her career as one of the world's greatest sportswomen, King has not only produced some brilliant tennis, but has done more than perhaps any other player to force the sporting establishment to reward and recognize women's sport. A natural leader who effervesced with promotional ideas, King popularized tennis for everyone, and just as importantly, showed the world that women-loving women could and did succeed and triumph, on and off the court.

Current Address: c/o World Team Tennis, 445 North Wells Street, Suite 404, Chicago, Illinois 60610-4512.

References:

Bellamy, Rex. *Love Thirty—Three Decades of Champions.* London: Simon & Schuster, 1990.

Guttman, Allen. *Women's Sports—A History.* New York: Columbia University Press, 1991.

Irvine, David. "Breakaway Threat Galvanises WTC," in *Guardian,* 8 September 1994.

King, Billie Jean, and Frank Deford. *The Autobiography of Billie Jean King.* London: Granada, 1982.

Little, Alan, and Lance Tingay. *Wimbledon Ladies: A Centenary Record 1884-1984—The Singles Champions.* London: Wimbledon Lawn Tennis Museum, 1984.

—Dianne Millen

Irena Klepfisz

1941-

American poet, essayist, and editor

When Irena Klepfisz self-published her first volume of poetry, *periods of stress,* in 1975, she opened a door and filled a void. She became the first poet in the United States to chronicle her experiences as a Jewish lesbian and child survivor of the Holocaust. From that time over 30 years ago until now, Klepfisz has published two more volumes of poetry, *Keeper of Accounts* (Persephone Press) and *A Few Words in the Mother Tongue, Poems Selected and New* (Eighth Mountain Press); an omnibus volume, *Different Enclosures: Poetry and Prose of Irena Klepfisz* (Onlywomen Press, London); and a volume of essays, *Dreams of an Insomniac, Jewish Feminist Essays, Speeches and Diatribes* (also Eighth Mountain). In addition, Klepfisz was a cofounder and editor of *Conditions,* the influential and radical journal of lesbian feminist literature, theory, and criticism; and with Melanie Kaye-Kantrowitz, edited *The Tribe of Dina: A Jewish Women's Anthology* (Beacon Press). Klepfisz is also the author of numerous critical reviews and articles, most recently, the introduction to *Found Treasures* (Second Story Press), the first anthology of Yiddish women's writing in translation. She is also the author of an extensive article called "*Di mames, dos loshn*/ The mothers, the language: Feminism, *Yidishkayt,* and the Politics of Memory," which appeared in *Bridges* in 1994. Today, Klepfisz serves as the editorial consultant for Yiddish language and culture to the Jewish feminist journal *Bridges* and is a member of a new collective, *Hemshekh*: Feminist Institute for Secular Jewish Cultural Continuity.

Escaped Warsaw Ghetto As Infant

Born in the Warsaw Ghetto in 1941 to Rose Percyzkow Klepfisz and Michal Klepfisz, Irena Klepfisz was smuggled out of the ghetto as an infant. Her mother, who was blond, blue-eyed, and fluent in Polish, also escaped by passing as a gentile. Her father, Michal Klepfisz, was killed by Nazi soldiers while resisting them during the Warsaw Ghetto Uprising.

Much of Klepfisz's work, including the riveting poems "Searching for My Father's Body," "The Widow and Daughter," and "*Bashert,*" all of which can be found in *A Few Words in the Mother Tongue,* explores the poet's complex relationship to these events.

After World War II, Klepfisz and her mother went to Sweden, and in 1949, when Klepfisz was eight years old, she and her mother emigrated to the United States. Klepfisz spoke Yiddish at home in Brooklyn, New York, and learned English in school. She attended City College of New York, where she majored in English, and attended graduate school at the University of Chicago, where she received her Ph.D. in English.

Klepfisz worked her way through both college and graduate school as a baby sitter, pianist, typist receptionist, library assistant, insurance claims adjuster, and medical transcriber. In 1969 she taught English, then, after being laid off, began to teach Yiddish, women's studies, and women's poetry workshops in order to support herself. More recently she has worked as a visiting professor in English, Women's Studies, and Judaic Studies at State University of New York, Albany; University of California, Santa Cruz; Wake Forest University; Barnard College; and Michigan State University.

Life into Art

Like most authors who choose to publish with independent presses and take a political stand on difficult issues, Klepfisz has always needed to supplement her writing income with other work. Poems such as "Work Sonnets with Notes and a Monologue about a Dialogue," "A Poem for Judy/beginning a new job," and the essay "The Distance Between Us: Feminism, Consciousness, and the Girls at the Office," confront the conflicts and realities present in this aspect of her life.

Klepfisz has also been outspoken in her poetry and her prose on the issues surrounding the conflicts between Palestinians and Israelis in the Middle East. Essays such as "*Yom Ha Shoa: Yom Yerushalaim*: A Meditation" and poems such as "East Jerusalem, 1987: *Bet Shalom* (House of Peace)" explore the poet's connection as an activist and an artist to events leading up to the Palestinian uprising or *Intifada.* At the beginning of the *Intifada,* Klepfisz became cofounder of the Jewish Women's Committee to End the Occupation of the West Bank, which for almost five years served as a link to the Israeli organization Women in Black. In 1990, Klepfisz became executive director of New Jewish Agenda, a multi-issue educational organization. She served in that capacity for two years, focusing on Middle East issues, anti-Semitism, and racism.

Finally, Klepfisz is a heartfelt advocate of Yiddish as a language, and Yiddish language writers. In her introduction to *Found Treasures: Stories by Yiddish Women Writers* entitled "Queens Contradiction," Klepfisz presents a comprehensive history of Yiddish, its particular place in Ashkenazi, or Eastern European Jewish women's lives; and a thorough survey of Yiddish women writers from the turn of this past century to the present. Much of her poetry uses some Yiddish, and the title of her volume of selected poems, *A Few Words in the Mother Tongue,* is a direct reference to Yiddish, known as *di mame-loshn,* literally translated, the mother tongue.

As Adrienne Rich states in her introduction to *A Few Words in the Mother Tongue,* "Born in 1941 in the Warsaw Ghetto, this poet is unequivocally rooted in the matrix of history. Beginning with almost total disintegrative loss—of family, community, culture, country and language—she has taken up the task of recreating herself as a Jew, woman, and writer...." In so doing, Klepfisz has made a clear path for other generations of Jewish lesbian writers to work and tell, to continue to create a culture.

References:

Forman, Raicus, Swartz, and Woolf, eds. *Found Treasures: Stories by Yiddish Women Writers,* introduction by Irena Klepfisz. Second Story Press, 1994.

Klepfisz, Irena. *Dreams of an Insomniac: Jewish Feminist Essays, Speeches and Diatribes,* introduction by Evelyn Torton Beck. Eighth Mountain Press, 1990.

———. *A Few Words in the Mother Tongue: Poems Selected and New,* introduction by Adrienne Rich. Eighth Mountain Press, 1990.

———. *periods of stress.* Out and Out Books, 1975.

—Judith Katz

David Kopay

1943-

American football player and activist

David Kopay was the first professional football player to come out publicly as a gay man. After completing a career that included ten years as a running back in the National Football League, Kopay in 1975 gave an interview to Lynn Rosellini of the Washington (D.C.) *Star* as part of her series on "Homosexuals in Sports." The articles shocked the sports world. And given the social climate of the time, it was not surprising that only one athlete was willing to be quoted by name: David Kopay.

Kopay was instantly thrust into the national spotlight. He was interviewed on talk shows, his life discussed on sports pages, his relatively quiet routine ended. He became the object of critical attacks by the sports establishment and, when he was not pointedly ignored, was condemned and ridiculed by sports writers and general commentators across the land.

Some straight journalists, and the then-fledgling gay press, however, rallied in support, though "gay liberation" activists were often unsure what to make of a representative from the seemingly brutal world of professional football.

In 1977, Kopay published his autobiography, *The David Kopay Story*, written with Perry Deane Young. In 1988, when a new version of the book was issued, the sportswriter Dick Schaap wrote in his foreword, "Now, more than a decade later, the most shocking thing about Kopay's [1975] statement is that no one has followed it up, not a single prominent male professional athlete has either professed or confessed his homosexuality."

Kopay was an important role model at a time, and in an arena, where, previously, there had been none.

A Traditional Upbringing

David Marquette Kopay was born on 28 June 1942 in Chicago to Anton and Marguerite (Hahn) Kopay. (The original Croatian family name was Kopaytich.) David was the second of four children in a strict Roman Catholic household. As a child his father had been forced to drop out of the sixth grade to work in the mines of Cherry, Illinois. Later as an ex-Marine, Anton Kopay supported the family by working in the Chicago stockyards and as a conductor on an open streetcar.

When David was in the fourth grade, the family moved to North Hollywood, California. His father found work in a desk factory and his mother took an office job. The Catholic Church still played a central role in the family's life, and at age fourteen, David enrolled in the nearby Claretian Junior Seminary, a boarding school for students preparing for the priesthood. Though he prospered there and appreciated the guidance of the prefect, Father Ernest Hyman, Kopay left the seminary after eighteen months. He had been encouraged at Claretian to excel in athletics (at fourteen, he was already six feet tall and weighed 175 pounds). Now he wanted to attend a school with a more prominent, organized football program.

Following his older brother Tony's lead, he enrolled at Notre Dame High School, run by the Brothers of the Holy Cross. He was named to the all-Catholic Conference football team, and suddenly the prospect of winning an athletic scholarship made college a possibility. Eventually, Kopay chose the University of Washington, where Tony was already on the football team.

There, under the Spartan regime of Coach Jim Owens, Kopay earned a reputation as a hard worker. He was tough and versatile, fighting through injuries and changing playing positions when he had to. He was blessed with good hands as a receiver, had adequate speed and, most impressively, was a ferocious blocker. His senior year he was named co-captain, leading his Pac-10 Champion team into the Rose Bowl game on New Year's Day. Before a huge crowd, including the Grand Marshall, Dwight D. Eisenhower, Kopay scored the only Washington touchdown in a 17-7 loss to the University of Illinois, which was led by All-American Dick Butkus. The *Los Angeles Times* of 2 January 1964 noted a "budding romance" between Kopay and Rose Queen, Nancy Kneeland, whom he had dated that week.

Ten Years in the Pros

Kopay was not picked in that year's National Football League college draft, but his Rose Bowl performance had drawn attention, and he signed as a free agent with the San Francisco '49ers. Again he proved himself, ending his first professional season as the team's leading rusher. He lost his starting job the next fall when an eight-year veteran was brought in, but Kopay performed well and was praised, as usual, for his intensity, dedication, and toughness.

A solid player, though not one of the few franchise-making stars, Kopay had to work hard to make the team in each of his ten years in the demanding and punishing world of professional football. At the end of his fourth year, he tore the cartilage in his knee and was out for five weeks. In 1968 he was traded to the Detroit Lions where he played alongside the great Alex Karras. More knee surgery followed, and in 1969 Kopay was traded to the Washington Redskins, where he played for legendary coach Vince Lombardi. Again, he was tough and tenacious. In the *Washington Daily News* column, "Sports Log" (26 November 1969), Earl Leubker wrote: "Kopay is Lombardi's type of football player. All-out is the only way he knows how to play."

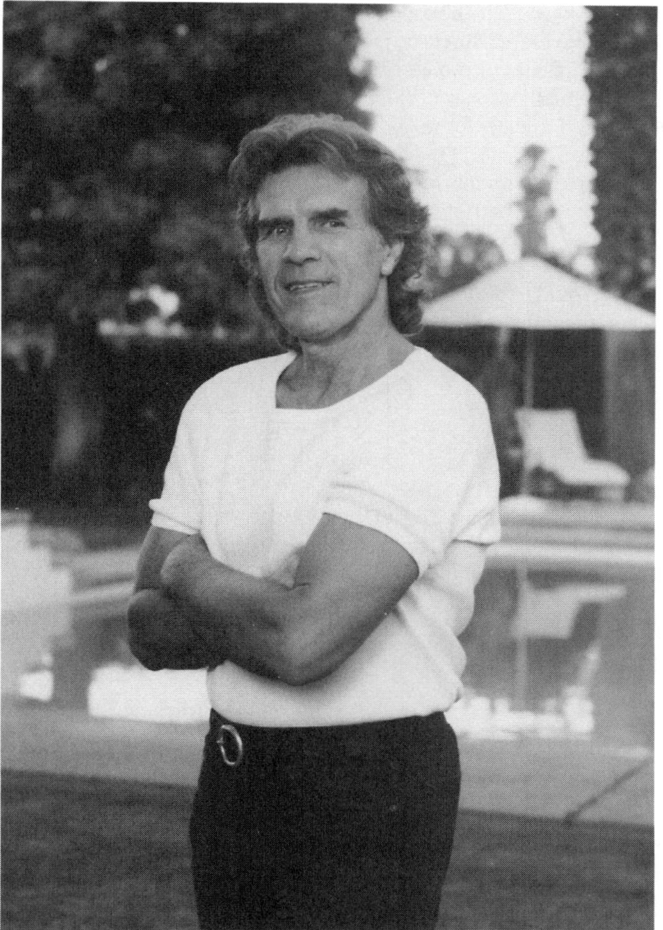

David Kopay

In 1972 Kopay was cut by the Redskins and signed with the New Orleans Saints, where his aggressiveness on special teams—the "suicide squad"—was appreciated. His final pro season was spent with the Green Bay Packers.

Throughout his professional career, Kopay was slowly coming to terms with his sexual orientation. He had had his first sexual experiences with men during his college years. Kopay even married briefly, in 1971, at the urging of a psychotherapist he had seen for help with a growing depression. The treatment, however, evolved into the therapist's using hypnosis in an attempt to "cure" Kopay of his homosexuality. In his autobiography, Kopay refers to his ex-wife by the pseudonym, "Mary Ann Riley." The long-distance marriage lasted through his 1971 season with the New Orleans Saints, but after that the two separated and later divorced.

Life after Football

His playing days over, Kopay was not able to find the coaching job he wanted, as a specialty coach on either the pro or major college level. His being openly gay was simply too controversial. After several different ventures, he joined his uncle's long-established business, Linoleum City, in Hollywood. There, his being gay was actually an asset, as he brought in important new customers: the set designers for major television, movie, and stage show companies.

Kopay continues to make appearances for gay causes, and still receives letters from people—especially young athletes struggling come to terms with their own homosexuality—who tell him what a difference his example has made in their lives.

"Would I speak out again if I had a choice?" Kopay asked in his autobiography. "Absolutely" was the answer. "It's the best thing I've ever done. I have no regrets."

References:

Kopay, David, and Perry Deane Young. *The David Kopay Story.* New York: Arbor House, 1977; new edition: New York: Primus, Donald I. Fine, Inc., 1988.

O'Connor, Michael E. "The David Kopay Story ... A Decade Later," in *Torso*, October 1989: 30-35, 82, 86.

—Michael E. O'Connor

Sharon Kowalski

American activist

Karen Thompson

American activist

In December of 1991, on the twelfth anniversary of a commitment ceremony in which they had exchanged rings and vowed to share the rest of their lives with each other, Sharon Kowalski and Karen Thompson were finally allowed to go home together. Kowalski, who is confined to a wheelchair and suffers from brain damage, didn't have the short-term memory to recall what had just transpired in court, but she did remember Thompson, did remember much of the past, and did remember that she was a lesbian.

From 1983 through 1991, Thompson and Kowalski were involved in one of the most protracted, nightmarish guardianship battles in U.S. history. Thompson's fight to keep Kowalski with her—a scenario Kowalski's parents, Donald and Delia, vehemently opposed—became the subject of hundreds of vigils and rallies across the country, and a landmark case in the fight for the equal rights of gays and lesbians with disabilities.

That it transpired in the midst of the AIDS epidemic augmented the importance of the case. Gay men in particular had found that, without durable power-of-attorney agreements, they had no rights when it came to medical decisions, estate settlement, burials, maintaining legally shared homes or apartments once partners die, or even visiting a sick lover's bedside while they were still alive. "The remarkable thing about this case," director of the American Civil Liberties Union's Gay Rights Project William Rubenstein told the *New York Times* in 1991, "is not that Karen Thompson finally won guardianship, but that it took her seven years to do so, when guardianship rights for a heterosexual married couple would be taken for granted."

Anger and Disbelief

The nightmare began on a cold November afternoon in northern Minnesota in 1983. Sharon was hit by a drunk driver while driving with her four-year-old niece and seven-year-old nephew. Her niece was killed, her nephew was injured, and Sharon, not initially expected to live, had severe brain stem injuries that left her nearly paralyzed, with short-term memory loss, and an impaired ability to speak.

Although the two women had recently exchanged rings after four years together and had bought a house together in St. Cloud, they had not made their relationship public for fear that their coming-out might jeopardize Kowalski's job as a high-school gym teacher. (Thompson was, and is still, a physical education and human relations professor at St. Cloud University). However, as it became evident some major decisions had to be made regarding the rest of Kowalski's life and care, Thompson told Kowalski's parents about their relationship. The parents reacted with anger and disbelief, and immediately took steps to end the relationship and take Kowalski home with them. To this day, despite repeated, consistent pleas by Kowalski to let her stay with Thompson, they deny she is really a lesbian.

Handicapism and Homophobia

After much squabbling, Kowalski's father obtained legal sole guardianship of his daughter in July of 1985, moved her to a nursing home some five hours from St. Cloud, and even went so far as to have Thompson barred from visiting her. Over the next three years, Thompson filed numerous appeals in local, state, and federal courts to have the guardianship revoked. Her argument was that Kowalski was being denied access to therapy that would advance her physical and mental capacity considerably. Both women were getting a quick, brutal education in handicapism as well as homophobia, learning how people's wishes and recovery are largely ignored when they are warehoused. "I didn't want Sharon in a nursing home," Thompson recalls in *Why Can't Sharon Kowalski Come Home?* "To me that implied a step down—that they had given up, that they believed she was never going to recover enough to leave."

In September of 1988, Judge Robert Campbell of the St. Louis County District Court ordered a comprehensive evaluation of Sharon Kowalski's condition. In his decision, he wrote that Thompson had "demonstrated commitment and devotion the welfare of Sharon Kowalski [and her] medical, material, and social needs." He even noted that Kowalski had, over the last two years, repeatedly expressed her desire to go home with Thompson to St. Cloud. Although there were ongoing doubts as to Sharon's competency, she had repeatedly typed the words "lovers" and "us" when asked by Thompson what it meant to be gay.

However, in another part of Campbell's ruling titled "outing," Campbell said that Thompson had violated Kowalski's privacy by disclosing her lesbianism to Kowalski's parents without Kowalski's consent. In addition, he cited as a consideration the fact that Thompson was now having "other domestic partnerships." After three and a half years of being separated from Kowalski, Thompson was admittedly leaving herself open to other relationships. "The system separated us," she told the *New York Times,* "and we became strangers. For Sharon, I will always be what I was years ago. She can never know me as I am today, but I will love her for the rest of my life."

In the end, Judge Campbell equated Kowalski's predicament to that of a child whose parents were fighting for custody, arguing that Kowalski herself could not express a preference for guardianship. Thomas B. Stoddard, executive director of the Lambda Legal Defense Fund in 1991, characterized Campbell's decision as deeply offensive not only to gay men and lesbians, but to any and all couples who chose to cohabit on their own terms. "The idea of neutrality does not apply in any other area of family law," Stoddard told the *Times.* "Sharon chose her family. But the judge doesn't agree, so he imposed his own vision on her." Kowalski was eventually moved to a Duluth nursing home where Thompson was allowed to visit.

Early in 1990, Donald Kowalski relinquished legal guardianship of his daughter, citing heart problems and a general weariness with the years of legal wrangling. In April of that same year, Judge Campbell awarded guardianship to a third party, Karen Tomberlin, who had been Kowalski's track and volleyball coach in high school. But Tomberlin was just a stand-in for Kowalski's parents, Thompson claimed, and Kowalski was quite visibly upset and shaken following the decision.

A Family of Affinity

Finally, in December of 1991, seven years after Thompson's legal battle began, and almost twelve years to the day after they had first officially committed to each other, a Minneapolis appeals court granted sole legal guardianship to Thompson. "All the medical testimony established that Sharon has the capacity reliably to express a preference in this case, and she has clearly chosen to return home with Thompson," the court said. Furthermore, the court concluded that Thompson and Kowalski's relationship amounted to a "family of affinity" that ought to be accorded the same respect as any other. And finally, it was duly noted that Thompson was the only person willing or able to care for Kowalski outside of an institution, and she had fully equipped their home in St. Cloud to be wheelchair accessible.

Since that decision, Kowalski's parents have decided never to see their daughter as long as she lives with Thompson. "The void is too deep," Tomberlin told the *Times,* avoiding the fact that they had initiated the split from the beginning.

The lesson to be learned from Sharon Kowalski and Karen Thompson's years of legal anguish is clear, not only for gay and lesbian couples, but for all unmarried couples, disabled people, and anyone who has not designated a guardian of his or her choice. Creating a durable power of attorney is critical for any unmarried couple's peace of mind, especially in this age of AIDS. A clear-cut delineation of each partner's rights, (forms for which are included in an appendix to *Why Can't Sharon Kowalski Come Home?*), helps define everything from life-and-death medical decisionmaking to who is allowed at the bedside—*before* the tragic fact.

References:

Brozan, Nadine. "2 Sides are Bypassed in Lesbian Case," in *New York Times,* 26 April 1991.

Lewin, Tamar. "Disabled Woman's Care Given to Lesbian Partner," in *New York Times,* 18 December 1991.

Thompson, Karen and Julie Andrzejewski. *Why Can't Sharon Kowalski Come Home?* San Francisco: Spinsters/Aunt Lute, 1988.

—Jerome Szymczak

Larry Kramer

1935-

American writer and activist

Larry Kramer is best known for his leadership in the gay community's fight against AIDS. Throughout the 1980s, as the disease spread from a few isolated cases into a plague that decimated the gay-male community, Kramer unrelentingly prodded gays—and all Americans—to action through his political and theatrical writings and speeches. He has often been called the angriest man in America.

Getting Started

Kramer was born 25 June 1935, in Bridgeport, Connecticut, to George L. and Rea W. (Wishengrad) Kramer. He attended Yale University, graduating with a B.A. in 1957. After a stint in the army and an attempt to find theater work, Kramer started working at the William Morris Agency, the training ground for many a show business career, in 1958. He was an assistant story editor at Columbia Pictures in New York from 1960 to 1961 and a production executive in London until 1965, when he became an assistant to the president of United Artists in New York. In 1967, he was the associate producer for the film Here *We Go Round the Mulberry Bush.*

His most significant contribution to film was 1969's *Women in Love*, which he adapted from D.H. Lawrence's novel and produced. It earned him Best Screenplay nominations in 1970 from both the Academy of Motion Picture Arts and Sciences and the British Film Academy. *Women in Love* represents Kramer's first attempt to address homosexuality in his work, and his efforts at interpreting Lawrence's thinly veiled portrayals of homosexual love were critically well-regarded.

La vie New York

After the success of *Women in Love*, Kramer went through a period of self-discovery as a gay man. He knew he was gay during the 1960s, but he spent that time concentrating on his career, not his sexuality. Now, as a thirtysomething gay man living in the midst of the burgeoning gay movement, Kramer wished to portray that aspect of his life further in his work.

Kramer started writing a novel in 1975. His life in the mid-1970s was typical of that of many upper-class Manhattan gay men at the time: discos, drugs, bathhouses, Fire Island weekends, and a new promiscuity engendered by the gay sexual revolution. Kramer dove into the gay scene but remained unfulfilled, seeking love but finding

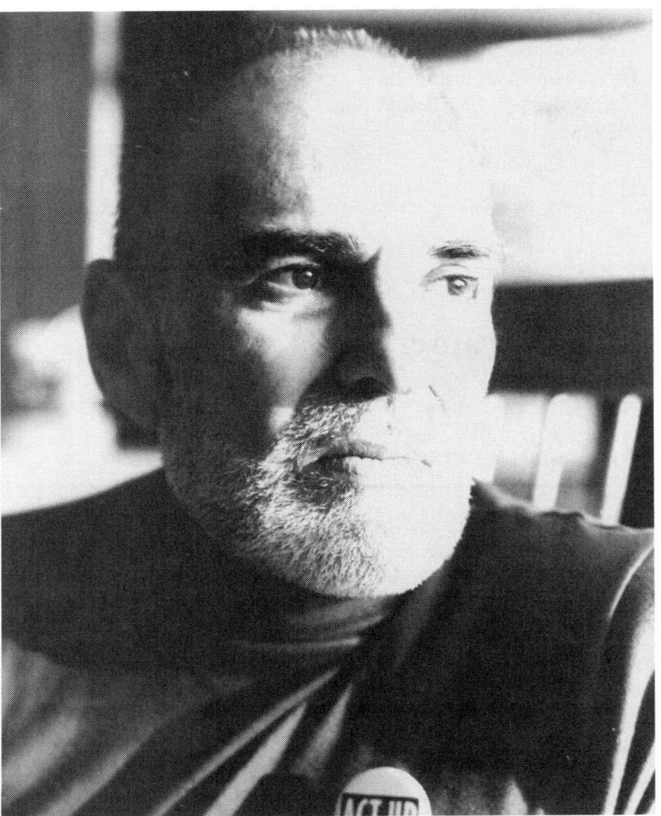

Larry Kramer

only sex. His disenchantment was all too evident when his autobiographical novel, *Faggots*, was published in 1978 at the apex of gay sexual freedom. The novel, which graphically depicts the lifestyle of Fire Island's gay male community, features Fred Lemish, a gay man who vainly searches for true love, family, and stability in a world bent on momentary sexual pleasure. Kramer was savaged by many gay critics, who accused him of sacrificing hard-won sexual liberation. Nevertheless, the book became a best seller, has remained in print for two decades, and is now considered a ground breaking portrayal of modern gay history.

A Public Figure Emerges

After *Faggots*, Kramer found himself in the gay public eye, where he has remained ever since. He reflects on the genesis of his public life in *Holocaust*: "I learned that if one is going to speak one's mind, best be prepared to get as good as you give. This was a lesson—violent, vocal, vociferous—I was to learn a thousand times over with the appearance of *Faggots*. I thought I'd written a satirical novel about the gay life I and most of my friends were living. I'd meant it to be funny…It never occurred to me that *Faggots* would be *controversial*. I was completely unprepared for its hostile reception in certain political quarters." It was a lesson that would be useful in the tumultuous decade to come.

The AIDS Years

In 1981, when a few dozen gay men in New York and San Francisco were found to be suffering from a rare form of cancer called Kaposi's sarcoma, it was not long before Larry Kramer was warning the gay community of the impending danger in the pages of the *New York Native*. Most gays were either indifferent or hostile. With memories of *Faggots* still fresh, critics accused him of inciting panic and of instilling gay homophobia and anti-eroticism.

By 1982, when it was clear to Kramer and some of his friends that gay men with AIDS could not rely on their local or national governments to provide the health care services they needed, let alone a cure, they formed Gay Men's Health Crisis. Kramer helped supervise the daily running of the organization. He recalls in *Holocaust*: "…it became a consuming passion—helping, urging, nurturing, watching this small group develop, at first falteringly, but then beginning to grow as increasing numbers of dedicated men and women came to join us. It was one of those rare moments in life when one felt completely utilized, useful, with a true reason to be alive."

In early 1983, the AIDS infection and death rates continued escalating, no answers were forthcoming from the medical and governmental establishments, and most gays still considered AIDS a temporary problem. A frustrated Kramer made one of his most fervent calls to action in his now-famous article "1,112 and Counting" in the 14-17 March 1983 *New York Native*. At that time there were 1,112 documented cases of AIDS, with 418 deaths, so he implored the gay community to fight:

> If this article doesn't scare the shit out of you, we're in real trouble. If this article doesn't rouse you to anger, fury, rage, and action, gay men may have no future on this earth. Our continued existence depends on just how angry you can get.…Unless we fight for our lives, we shall die. In all the history of homosexuality we have never before been so close to death and extinction. Many of us are dying or close to dead.

The article, which called for more money for AIDS research, better treatment of AIDS patients, better media coverage of AIDS, and better political representation, was reprinted by gay newspapers around the country. It caused the final break in Kramer's already-strained relationship with the Gay Men's Health Crisis board. He reluctantly resigned.

Suddenly having little to do, he wrote a play as an outlet for his activist voice. *The Normal Heart* opened in early 1985 to positive reviews and ran for more than a year. It has been restaged around the world. The play was a vehicle for Kramer's anger at the government, the medical establishment, and the media for not acting to combat AIDS.

By 1987, Kramer had been at the forefront of AIDS activism for six years but was still frustrated by the lack of progress in battling the epidemic. On 10 March 1987, he gave a speech at New York's Gay and Lesbian Community Center detailing the incredible difficulties doctors were experiencing in getting new AIDS drugs. He pleaded for his audience to take responsibility for themselves and to demand immediate action from the Food and Drug Administration (FDA) and other government agencies charged with AIDS research. The emotional speech inspired the formation of the AIDS Coalition to Unleash Power, or ACT UP. ACT UP used civil disobedience, protests, sit-ins, and other public demonstrations to convince the FDA to release experimental AIDS drugs. The organization proved remarkably effective in bringing AIDS to the forefront of America's consciousness. Soon, ACT UP chapters opened across the country, and the organization's motto, "Silence = Death," became a rallying cry for its young activists.

In 1988, Kramer himself discovered that he was HIV-positive and that he suffered from a liver disorder that threatened his life as much as AIDS. He was told he had two years to live, but he has remained healthy much longer than he or his doctors expected.

In 1992, *The Destiny of Me*, the sequel to *The Normal Heart*, opened in New York. In an 4 October 1992, *New York Times* essay about *Destiny*, Kramer said:

> I further complicated my task by determining to write a personal history: a journey to acceptance of one's own homosexuality...This journey, from discovery through guilt to momentary joy and toward AIDS, has been my longest, most important journey...Indeed, my homosexuality...has been the single most important defining characteristic of my life....I think the lives that many gay men have been forced to lead, with AIDS awaiting them after the decades-long journey from self-hate, is the stuff of tragedy.

As this was written in 1996, Kramer continued work on "a very long novel about the plague," tentatively titled *The American People*, and prepared to film *The Normal Heart*, directed by John Schlesinger, commencing fall 1996. He lives with his partner, David Webster, an architect and designer, in New York and Warren, Connecticut, where they are currently restoring a house.

Larry's Legacy

Kramer's contributions to the gay community are testament to the power of words. His endless diatribes in the form of essays, books, speeches, and plays served to galvanize gay men and lesbians as no individual ever has. As much as anything, his angry activism proves that, when faced with death and indifference, one individual can effect change. Kramer summed it up in the June 1994 Progressive: "There are very few voices as loud as mine. And I don't think I'm doing anything special. I'm fighting for my own life as well as everybody else's. I don't want to die."

References:

Drane, Janice E. "Kramer, Larry," in *Contemporary Authors*, vol. 126. Detroit: Gale, 1989: 239-241.

Kramer, Larry. *The Destiny of Me.* New York: Penguin Books, 1993.

———. Interview with Joseph E. DeMatio, 8 May 1996.

———. "A Man's Life, and the Path to Acceptance," in *New York Times*, 4 October 1992.

———. *The Normal Heart.* New York: New American Library, 1985.

———. *Reports from the Holocaust: the Making of an AIDS Activist.* New York: St. Martin's Press, 1989.

———. "When a Roaring Lion Learns to Purr," in *New York Times*, 12 January 1995.

Shnayerson, Michael. "Kramer vs. Kramer," in *Vanity Fair*, October 1992: 228-231, 293-297.

Winokur, L. A. "Larry Kramer," in *The Progressive*, June 1994: 32-35.

—Joseph E. DeMatio

Sheila James Kuehl

1941-

American politician and actress

On the wall of Sheila James Kuehl's home in Santa Monica, California, hang pictures of two of her heroes, James Dean and John F. Kennedy; and she has appropriately distinguished herself in both acting and politics. After earning some fame for youthful television performances, Kuehl launched a second career as a lawyer, law professor, openly lesbian activist for feminist causes, and, in 1995, member of the California State Assembly. Today, drawing upon a residue of public good will from her acting days, and developing a new reputation for her considerable intellect and political savvy, she seems well positioned for further political advancement.

Acting Career Began in Los Angeles

She was born Sheila Ann Kuehl on 9 February 1941 in Tulsa, Oklahoma, the daughter of Arthur Kuehl, a window dresser, and Lillian Kuehl, a factory worker. Because of her father's work, she moved with her family to Los Angeles, where she took dance and drama classes and landed a role in a radio series, using the name Sheila James, in 1949. A year later, she was cast in the television series *Trouble with Father,* also called *The Stu Erwin Show* (1950-55), playing Erwin's tomboy daughter Jackie. She also appeared in episodes of *My Little Margie* (1953), *Four Star Playhouse* (1953), and *General Electric Theater* (1954), and a few films—*Those Redheads from Seattle* (1953), *Seven Brides for Seven Brothers* (1954), and *Teenage Rebel* (1956). From 1957 to 1962, she attended the University of California at Los Angeles, earning a B.A. in English. In 1959, she guest-starred in the fourth episode of the series *The Many Loves of Dobie Gillis* (1959-63), playing Dobie's lab partner Zelda Gilroy, then was added to its regular cast.

Though it may seem like the least of her accomplishments, Kuehl's portrayal of Zelda represented a definite breakthrough of sorts. While infatuated with Dobie, Zelda made no effort to conceal the fact that she was more intelligent and more decisive than Dobie, and her assertiveness in dealing with the ineffectual Dobie and beatnik Maynard G. Krebs stood in sharp contrast to other television depictions of male-female relationships at the time. (And her youthful aptitude was not simply an act: in his autobiography, *Forever Dobie,* costar Dwayne Hickman recalled her as "very bright," with a "photographic memory.") While appearing in the series, Kuehl's sexual preference first affected her life: after love letters from a girlfriend were discovered, her UCLA sorority expelled her, and she feared that the producers of *Dobie Gillis* might find out that she was a lesbian. Then, during the series' third season, she starred in a pilot for a spinoff series, *Zelda,* but was told, as she related to David Dunlap of the *New York Times,* that "the president of CBS said no to the pilot and said you were just a little too butch." In the fourth and final season of *Dobie Gillis,* she made only four appearances, and she attributes the pilot's failure and her subsequently reduced status to homophobia.

While *Dobie Gillis* was on the air, Kuehl also acted in episodes of *The Millionaire* (1960), *National Velvet* (1961), and *The New Loretta Young Show* (1962); after the series was canceled, she appeared in episodes of *McHale's Navy* (1963), *The Donna Reed Show* (1964), *Bob Hope Chrysler Theater* (1964), and *Petticoat Junction* (1964)

Sheila James Kuehl

before being cast in another, short-lived series, *Broadside* (1964-65), a female version of *McHale's Navy* in which she played Machinist Mate Selma Kowalski. She continued to make occasional television appearances—in episodes of *The Adventures of Ozzie and Harriet* (1965), *The John Forsythe Show* (1966), *The Beverly Hillbillies* (1967), *Marcus Welby, M.D.* (1970), and *Love, American Style* (1972), along with a television movie, *The Feminist and the Fuzz* (1971)—but was dissatisfied with the few roles she was offered and, realizing her career was over and not really knowing what to do next, Kuehl briefly contemplated suicide before deciding to shift her attention to other work. Since 1972, she has had only two acting roles, both as Zelda, in an unsuccessful 1977 pilot, *Whatever Happened to Dobie Gillis?*, and a 1988 television movie, *Bring Me the Head of Dobie Gillis*.

Launched Career in Law

As her television credits dwindled, she took a position as assistant, then associate, dean of students at UCLA (1969-75), now using the name Sheila James Kuehl. In 1975, after advising a number of new student activist and feminist groups as part of her work, she decided to pursue a law degree at Harvard Law School, where she distinguished herself by becoming only the second woman to win the school's moot court competition; one of the moot court judges, Supreme Court Justice Thurgood Marshall, told her, "Lady, I like your style," as Warren reported. After earning her degree in 1978, she returned to Santa Monica, entered private practice (1978-85), worked as director of off-campus housing at UCLA (1980-84), and gradually revealed her sexual orientation to colleagues and family members.

Soon noted for her expertise in law and gender issues, Kuehl then became a law professor, teaching at California State University, Long Beach (1980-83), the University of Southern California (1982-83), Loyola Law School in Los Angeles (1985-89), and UCLA (1990-91). She served as chairwoman of the Sojourn Center for Battered Women in Santa Monica (1979-95) and president of the Women Lawyers' Association of Los Angeles (1986-87). In 1989, she took a one-year leave of absence from teaching to cofound the Southern California Women's Law Center, an institution devoted to policy development and technical assistance to prosecutors, judges, and women's advocates on issues such as domestic violence and sex discrimination. In her personal life, she met a UCLA student named Torie Osborn in 1982, and the women began what Osborn later called, according to Dunlap, a "nine-year marriage." After their relationship ended amicably in 1991, they remained close friends. Kuehl now describes herself as "unattached."

Successful in Politics

In 1994, when the Democratic Assemblyman for her West Los Angeles and San Fernando Valley district declined to seek re-election, Kuehl decided to run for his seat; one factor in her decision was a poll showing that 76 percent of the voters still remembered *Dobie Gillis*, and she credits part of her success as a lesbian politician to fond memories of her Zelda character—it "jams the homophobic radar," as she told Warren. She won decisive victories in both the Democratic primary and general election. During her campaign, she was briefly involved in the controversial O. J. Simpson case when she publicly revealed that Nicole Simpson had phoned the Sojourn Center for help, and she was criticized for a campaign mailer on domestic violence featuring a photograph of the battered Nicole Simpson.

In 1995, she joined the California State Assembly and quickly earned the respect and admiration of her colleagues. As reported in Warren's article, even conservative Republicans praised her, calling her "one of the most charming ladies I've ever met ... a winner" and "just about my favorite person on [the Democrats'] side of the aisle"; while the Democratic Speaker of the Assembly, master politician Willie Brown, said that "Sheila Kuehl reminds me more of myself than anyone I've seen in politics. Ever." Some predict that she will eventually lead the assembly or successfully run for higher office. As one of the most prominent openly gay officials in the nation, she has also become a popular spokesperson for feminist and gay causes; as one gay activist, Eric Baumann, declared, Kuehl is "like a beacon for gay and lesbian people."

Current Address: Southern California Women's Law Center, 11852 Santa Monica Blvd., Suite 5, Los Angeles, California 90025.

References:

Diliberto, G. "Sheila Kuehl, the Brainy Bird on *Dobie Gillis*, Likes to Lay Down the Law as a Professor," in *People Weekly*, no. 24, 2 December 1985: 14+.

Dunlap, David W. "Zelda's Unwavering Love Is No Longer Unrequited," in *New York Times Biographical Service,* no. 25, November 1994: 1794-95.

Hickman, Dwayne, and Joan Roberts Hickman. *Forever Dobie: The Many Lives of Dwayne Hickman.* Secaucus, New Jersey: Carol Publishing Group, 1994.

Hill-Holtzman, Nancy. "Kuehl Blasted for Mailer Showing Nicole Simpson," in *Los Angeles Times,* 3 November 1994: B1, 3.

———. "Running for a New Role," in *Los Angeles Times,* 25 October 1994: B3.

Kuehl, Sheila James. "Neutral Treatment Only Works for Neuters." Review of *The Female Body and the Law,* by Zillah R. Eisenstein, in *Los Angeles Times,* 4 June 1989: Sunday Book Review Section, 21.

———. *Using the Law to Empower Immigrant Women: Information and Resources for Service Providers to Immigrant Women in California.* Los Angeles: Southern California Women's Law Center, 1990.

Min, Janice, and Mark Morrison. "Zelda's Choice," in *People Weekly,* no. 41, 16 May 1994: 93-94.

Ness, Carol. "Lesbian Lawmaker's Counter-Revolution: Liberal Kuehl Gives GOP-Led Assembly a Lesson in Tolerance," in *San Francisco Chronicle,* 4 February 1996: C1, 5.

———. "Lesbian, Leftist, and Electable: 'Dobie Gillis' Star May Be First Open Gay in Legislature," in *San Francisco Chronicle,* 18 September 1994: A1, 6.

Scott, Steve. "Profile: Sheila James Kuehl," in *California Journal Weekly,* 5 December 1994: 4.

Warren, Jennifer. "Kuehl's Work and Wit Break Barriers in Assembly," in *Los Angeles Times,* 12 September 1995: A1, 16.

—Gary Westfahl

L

k. d. lang

1961-

Canadian singer

k. d. lang is a vocalist, an avant-garde performance artist, and a songwriter who has made valid contributions in the areas of western music, pop, or is it jazz? Maybe alternative would be a better word to describe her musical style. She certainly gives a listener plenty of choices. Her earliest performances could be classed most clearly as "alternative," but she quickly began to evidence a more traditionally western music style, clearly influenced by Patsy Cline. Her performances, however, remained more energetic and fantastic than is usual on a western stage. In other words, she entertains her audiences. lang has said that her vocal style is dictated by her voice. Just as one does not play Gregorian chants on a piccolo, she cannot sing truly alternative music with her "instrument."

Kathy Dawn Lang was born in Edmonton, Alberta, Canada on 2 November 1961, the fourth and last child of Audrey and Adam Lang. Her brother John is eleven years her senior, her sister Jo Ann is six years older, and her sister Keltie was only three at the time of her birth. Her ancestry is Icelandic, Dutch, Irish, Scottish, English, and German Jewish; she has been known to claim Sioux as well. In other words, she is a typical mixture of the many people who came to settle in North America. In 1962, the family moved to Consort, Alberta where lang grew up.

Consort is a small town, with a population of fewer than 1,000 people. The area is farm and ranch country with wheat as the major crop, and cattle as the most popular range animal. Despite her reputed comment that, "It was the kind of place where you knew everyone from the day you were born until the day you could get yourself out of there," she was able to gain from her childhood the kind of knowledge and experience which was important to her development as a performer.

Her mother, Audrey Lang, bought the family a used piano and saw to it that her children had music lessons. Once a week for many years Audrey Lang drove the children to their lessons held in a convent in Castor, Alberta, fifty-two miles west of Consort. At the age of seven, lang was being instructed in the mysteries of the piano by a nun. Sister Xavier taught the little girl music basics and soon had her singing, encouraging her to compete in a number of talent contests during her childhood. At the age of ten, lang picked up her brother's guitar and taught herself to play. When she was twelve her parents divorced and her father moved away. Her mother continued with her teaching job, and took over the running of the family business, a local drug store.

Lang joined the Consort High School volleyball team at fourteen and tackled that sport with the determination that later lead her to a successful music career. An interest in music wasn't all that unusual in her hometown but she often took her guitar, as well as her gym bag, when the volleyball team played out of town. She graduated from the local high school in 1979, having won the Athlete of the Year award in 10th, 11th, and 12th grades, an unusual honor. She was popular, well-liked by her classmates, and her friends were spread among both sexes.

k. d. lang

Lang Comes Out

From her 1992 interview with the *Advocate,* where she stated that she was a lesbian, to the current time, she has been publicly matter-of-fact about her sexuality. She keeps her private life quiet, anticipating and receiving respect. Lang expects that same respect in return in a style that has since become famous. That acceptance hasn't been achieved with any more ease than most people experience, but the point is that it has been achieved.

Not that she doesn't have a sense of humor about all the furor. She appeared on a *Vanity Fair* cover wearing a men's suit, sitting in a barber's chair, and pretending to be shaved by barely clothed super-model Cindy Crawford. A good-humored appearance on the

Tonight Show with host Jay Leno and a little green puppet, Kermit the Muppet, gave further evidence of her sense of humor. When the talking frog seemed about to descend into the swamp of sexism, lang warned him that he "didn't want to go there." A warning which caused him, apparently, to gulp. In a publicity announcement for a cosmetic company, during the spring of 1996 she and drag-queen RuPaul appeared to have great fun as the spokespersons. For lang, good humor makes for good promotions, both for cosmetic companies and singing careers.

Country and Western, Torch, and Twang

She and her band, The Reclines, first appeared on the album scene back in 1984 with, *A Truly Western Experience* (Homestead). It was independently released 8-track recording made with $2,000 borrowed from her mother. After being on the road, paying their dues one night at a time, and building a back-log of fans, lang and the band was ready for bigger and better experiences. The album was released at the same time lang and The Reclines had achieved a coveted spot at the Edmonton Folk Festival, an important event in the Canadian western music world.

From there they took their music, and lang's high energy, vocally superb performances to more professional venues. Her manager, Larry Wanagas and Richard Flohil, a publicist and concert promoter from Toronto, booked "k.d. lang and the reclines" into a Toronto blues bar called Albert's Hall for the end of October of 1984. It was their East Coast debut. From there she became a celebrity.

By the time her second album, *Angel With a Lariat* (Sire, 1987), was released lang had gone international, wooing the American audience. The audience was more appreciative than the male establishment of the country and western music hierarchy. However, many performers were more interested in her talent than her lesbianism as evidenced by the number of collaborations of which she has been part. It was difficult getting air-time during this period. This marriage of lang and country and western music couldn't last forever.

Le Jazz Hot

Ready to experiment with different styles of music, and looking, perhaps, for some room to stretch her talent, lang broke away from country music with her fifth album, *Ingenue* (Sire, 1992). Reinventing her career? Not really, her popularity depends more upon her enduring talent than upon a style of music. Just as it was when she announced her homosexuality, nobody was all that surprised.

Now, more than thirteen years after making a start with a little band, and hoping for success, lang is an established star in the business of music. She has also established a place in the public eye for the straight-forward acceptance of gay performers. Those are about the only certain things in her career, because she has a talent for re-inventing herself.

Current Address: c/o Sire Records, 75 Rockefeller Plaza, New York, New York 10019.

References:

Ali, Lorraine. "k. d. lang," in *The Rolling Stone*, 30 November 1994.

Gillmor, Don. "Torch and Twang: Country Music's k.d. lang," in *Reader's Digest* (Canadian), October 1990.

Gore, Lesley. "Lesley Gore on k. d. lang ... and vice versa," in *Ms.*, July-August 1990.

Johnson, Brian D. "A Lighter Side of Lang," in *Maclean's*, 6 November 1995.

k. d. lang Background Info, in *Obvious Gossip*. World Wide Web, 1996.

Leblanc, Larry, and Richard Flohil. "Best of the 80's," in *The Canadian Composer*, winter 1991.

Leland, John. "Escape from Nashville," in *Newsweek*, 27 April 1992.

The New Rolling Stone Encyclopedia of Rock and Roll, edited by Patricia Romanowski and Holly George-Warren. New York: Rolling Stone Press, 1995.

Scott, Jay. "Yippee-i-o k. d.," in *Chatelaine*, January 1988.

Starr, Victoria. *k.d. lang: all you get is me*. New York: St. Martin's Press, 1994.

Stolder, Steven. "Q and A with k. d. lang," in *San Francisco Chronicle*, Datebook, 15-24 February 1996.

—Sandra Brandenburg

Eva Le Gallienne

1899-1991

American actor, director, and producer

Le Gallienne was for several decades one of the premier figures in American theater. An accomplished and highly regarded performer, she also translated the works of Ibsen, Chekhov, and others, produced and directed a number of plays, and throughout her life struggled to ensure that classic dramas appeared on the American stage. "I would rather play Ibsen than eat," she once wrote, "and that's often just what it amounts to."

The Theater in Her Blood

Born on 11 January 1899 in London, Le Gallienne was the daughter of the English poet Richard Le Gallienne and his second wife, the Danish journalist Julie Norregaard. She spent her early years in London with her parents and older half-sister, Hesper. However, in 1903 her parents were divorced and Le Gallienne and her mother moved to Paris.

A bright and talented child, Le Gallienne showed an interest in theater at a very early age. She later noted that after seeing Sarah Bernhardt play the role of Prince Charming in *Sleeping Beauty*, she decided she would become an actress. A few years later, Le Gallienne and her mother returned to England, where they lived with the actor Will Faversham and his family at the Le Gallienne's large manor house. There young Eva's ambitions were nurtured, and she came into contact with a number of prominent figures in the London theater. She made her stage debut at the age of fifteen, playing the role of a page in Maurice Maeterlinck's *Monna Vanna*, and, after studying briefly at the Tree Academy (later the Royal Academy of Dramatic Art), she accepted the role of a poor cockney girl in *The Laughter of Fools* at the Prince of Wales Theater. Her performance was a great success, and at the age of sixteen her career in the theater was launched.

American Trials

Soon afterward, Le Gallienne and her mother decided to move to the United States, where Le Gallienne spent five difficult years seeking recognition, performing in undistinguished roles, and often unable to find any work at all. However, in 1920 she accepted a role in Arthur Richman's *Not So Long Ago,* which became a great success and brought Le Gallienne critical recognition. A year later, in April of 1921, her career was firmly established with the role of Julie in Ferenc Molnar's *Liliom.* Thereafter, she was one of the most sought-after actresses on the American stage.

During her early years as a performer, Le Gallienne began to envision a better way of presenting dramas, a repertory style of theater that would allow artists more freedom and variety while offering reasonably priced entertainment for audiences. She lamented the fact that, as she later put it, "the theater has fallen into the hands of real estate men and syndicates and those who have no love or interest in the stage." In order to realize her vision she founded, in 1926, the Civic Repertory Theater in New York City, where she produced, directed, and acted in a number of plays. The theater provided Le Gallienne with an opportunity to stage the classic dramas she loved, most notably the works of Ibsen, Chekhov, and Shakespeare. On occasion she served as translator for such plays when no adequate translations were available. The theater also provided free classes for aspiring actors. Although popular with audiences, the company required subsidies from wealthy backers to survive, and when such backing became unavailable during the Great Depression, the Civic Repertory Theater was forced to close.

After the closure of her theater, Le Gallienne continued to perform in, produce, and direct plays. She also published translations of the works of Chekhov and Ibsen, as well as two autobiographical works, *At 33* (1934) and *With a Quiet Heart* (1953), a biography of the noted actress Eleanora Duse, and stories for children. In 1946 she once again attempted to establish a repertory theater, but the company lasted only one season. Although she continued performing to the end of her life, in later years she spent much of her time at her Connecticut home with her companion, Marion Evensen. In 1964 she was awarded a special Tony for her production of Chekhov's *Seagull,* and in 1978 the American National Theater and Academy presented her with the National Artist Award. At the age of 82, she received an Academy Award nomination for her performance in the film *Resurrection.* Her last role was that of the White Queen in a revival of her production of *Alice in Wonderland* in 1982.

Friends and Lovers

Recent biographers have argued that Le Gallienne's reputation in the theater was damaged by her frank lesbianism. Robert A. Schanke, in his *Shattered Applause: The Lives of Eva Le Gallienne,* compares her stature with that of Lynn Fontane and Katharine Cornell, both of whom kept their lesbianism secret and so enjoyed greater renown than did Le Gallienne. The list of women with whom Le Gallienne's life was entangled—some of whom she loved—is not a short one. Included are the Russian actress, Alla Nazimova; another actress, Mary "Mimsey" Duggett Benson; the exotic looking Mercedes de Acosta; a pioneer in the male-dominated field of set design, Gladys Calthrop; the ambitious actor and wife of Alexander Graham Bell's nephew Robert Bell, Josephine Hutchinson; and the heiress Alice De Lamar whose friendship, encouragement, support, and love Le Gallienne accepted but did not return. Indeed, Barbara Gelb, in a review of *Shattered Applause,* maintained that Le Gallienne was "predatory, promiscuous, fickle, faithless, selfish, and mean to most of the women she loved." It was in 1930, when Hutchinson's husband filed for divorce and implicated Le Gallienne in a love triangle, that Le Gallienne's private life became front page news. If in fact her career was hampered by her overt homosexuality, it would be fascinating to see just what this stellar presence in American theater would have accomplished had it not been.

Eva Le Gallienne

References:

Gelb, Barbara. "The Actress Who Wouldn't Pretend," in the *New York Times Book Review,* 27 December 1992: 10.

Madsen, Axel. *The Sewing Circle.* New York: Birch Lane Press, 1995.

Schanke, Robert A. *The Lives of Eva Le Gallienne: Shattered Applause.* Carbondale: Southern Illinois University Press, 1992.

Sheehy, Helen. *Eva Le Gallienne: A Biography.* New York: Knopf, 1996.

—Andrea L.T. Peterson

W. Dorr Legg

1904-1994

American activist and scholar

William Dorr Legg was perhaps the most stalwart of the major leaders of the homosexual movement who emerged before the Stonewall riots of 1959. He was long identified with the social programs and research activities of ONE, Inc. in Los Angeles, which he guided through several difficult crises.

Legg was born in Ann Arbor, Michigan, on 15 December 1904. He obtained a Master of Landscape Design degree from the University of Michigan, then spent several years in architectural practice in New York City. He taught for many years as professor of landscape architecture at Oregon State College. Settling in Los Angeles in 1949, Legg quickly became involved in the burgeoning gay movement. After participating in several other groups, he gravitated to ONE, for which he was the mainstay for 42 years. Legg died on 26 July 1994, in Los Angeles.

With Merton Bird, a young African-American accountant, Legg cofounded an interracial, cosexual self-help organization for homosexuals. The group was purposely given an ambiguous name, The Knights of the Clocks, and was active for several years beginning in 1950.

In 1951 Legg joined the Mattachine Society, whose birth and spectacular rise in Los Angeles was already attracting international attention to the "homosexual question." The following year he became one seven founders of still another organization focusing upon such concerns, ONE, Inc. Absorbed in the demands of three such projects, he elected to give up the relative comforts of a successful professional career to become the first full-time employee in a cause that was just beginning to define itself.

In 1956 ONE's Institute of Homophile Studies was established, a then-unique facility dedicated to the proposition that such studies constituted a new and essentially unexplored field long ignored by academia. Writing under the name of Marvin Cuttler, Legg edited the first American survey of the homophile movement, as it was then called, *Homosexuals Today: A Handbook of Organizations and Publications* (1956). As ONE officer Dorr courageously fended off unwarranted snooping by agents of the Federal Bureau of Investigation. A landmark achievement was a 1958 U.S. Supreme Court decision that reversed the refusal of the Los Angeles postmaster to allow *ONE Magazine* to be mailed.

In 1981, when the state of California authorized ONE Institute the power to grant M.A. and Ph.D. degrees, Legg was director, then becoming dean. In that capacity he developed a course sequences on the history and sociology of homosexuality, lecturing on these topics for university and other audiences across the United States and in Europe. During the course of his career, he wrote many articles for ONE's publications and other periodicals,and coedited the two-volume *Annotated Bibliography of Homosexuality* (1976). He wrote and edited with David G. Cameron and Walter L. Williams *Homosexual Studies in Theory and Practice: A Survey*, published by One Institute Press in 1994. The last volume is invaluable for the documentation of almost three decades of scholarly and educational work achieved under the auspices of ONE.

For many years Legg faithfully presided in ONE's Los Angeles headquarters located in a somewhat rundown building on Venice Boulevard in an inner-city district of Los Angeles. Students and researchers were always free to drop in, and Dorr would suggest ways of advancing their work. Not infrequently, this involved recourse to the books and periodicals of the Blanche M. Baker Library, which contained many items not then available in public or university collections. His own approach to research was holistic. "Homophile studies calls for nothing less than a field theory which will cut across the whole range of scholarly investigations, revealing their mutual actions and interactions," he argued. "Departmentalized disciplines cannot possibly provide comprehensive understanding of a worldwide population of men and women known to have existed for thousands of years and in innumerable cultures." The participation of donors was encouraged through a parallel organization, the Institute for the Study of Human Resources.

In the early 1980s, thanks to the help of a wealthy, but eccentric supporter, ONE was able to move into luxurious quarters in a historic mansion on Country Club Drive. Unfortunately, the donor capriciously withdrew his support, and a lengthy court battle ensued, yielding a split decision. Even at his advanced age, Legg never wavered in this battle. Immediately after his death, it was announced that the legacy of W. Dorr Legg would be secured by the permanent attachment of ONE to the University of Southern California. Legg was survived by John Nojima, his partner of thirty years, who was also a supporter of ONE.

Legg's record of continuous, tenacious effort was unsurpassed by any other American movement leader of his generation. He always recognized that activism and education are inseparable. His quiet, though genial personality touched thousands, always offering assurance of the rightness of the task which he has served so valiantly.

—Wayne R. Dynes

Leonardo da Vinci

1452-1519

Italian artist, scientist, and inventor

A leading painter of the high Renaissance, Leonardo da Vinci created what is arguably the most famous painting in the world, the *Mona Lisa,* as well as one of the most moving, the fresco of the Last Supper. In addition, Leonardo was outstandingly active as a scientific observer and an inventor of machinery. Deprived of the highly sophisticated Humanist education prevalent in his time, Leonardo more than made up for his handicap by his empirical approach: the direct observation of natural phenomena. His curiosity was unquenchable, so much so that he oftentimes allowed himself to be distracted from one project in order to start another. Attentive as he was about the world around him, Leonardo did not encourage such curiosity about himself. His "mirror writing" (from right to left) was intended to discourage any casual snooping into his records. Combined with his achievements, which are of a high order, the enigmas that surround Leonardo have produced a rich harvest of ever-changing interpretations.

A Varied Life

Leonardo was born in Vinci, a town in the hills west of Florence, on 15 April 1452. He was the illegitimate son of a peasant woman,

Caterina, and a notary, Ser Piero di Antonio. His mother soon married another man, and Leonardo was raised in his father's household.

In his mid-teens, about 1467, he was apprenticed in the workshop of Andrea del Verrocchio, a sculptor and painter prominent in Florence. An early account reports that he eventually surpassed his master, to the point that Verrocchio is supposed to have given up painting in disgust (though he continued to practice sculpture). In 1476, while still living in Verrocchio's house, an anonymous accusation of sodomy was lodged against him. He was said to have had, along with three others (one a Medici), active homosexual relations with a seventeen-year-old male model. Eventually the prosecution was dropped, but not until after the accused had become frightened. It is not surprising that the young Leonardo should be drawn into the lively gay subculture of the Florence of his day. Homosexuality particularly flourished among artists, as the careers of Donatello, Sandro Botticelli, Michelangelo Buonarroti, Benvenuto Cellini, and others attest. In addition to the temptations of models and shop assistants in the ateliers, street prostitution among young males, as recent research has shown, was ubiquitous. However, the stress of being denounced for such behavior seems to have induced in Leonardo a lifelong sense of caution and a wish to preserve his personal privacy. The artist never married and no heterosexual affairs are known.

A portrait of his early years, the radiant *Ginevra de' Benci* shows his mastery of the presentation of nature and his careful control of light and shade, which became hallmarks of his style. At this time he also began to make studies of deformed people. Leonardo's attraction to the opposite poles of beauty and ugliness typifies his complex personality. The major work of these years, the panoramic Adoration of the Magi, remained unfinished. The twin problems of procrastination and easy distractibility were to dog him for the rest of his life.

In late 1481 or 1482 Leonardo left Florence for the prosperous city of Milan. He rightly calculated that his proficiency in machinery, and especially in military engineering, would make him attractive to the court of Duke Lodovico il Moro. Leonardo's contributions of machinery and engineering have sometimes been discounted as impractical. However, his emphasis was on innovation itself. He probably did not care whether his far-seeing design for a bicycle was workable or not—though it was. The important thing was to achieve in visual form, through drawings, the concept.

His first major task in Milan, however, was the preparation of a monumental equestrian portrait of the duke's father, Francesco Sforza. This sculpture was never completed, though in this case not through Leonardo's fault, for the clay model was destroyed by shelling. He painted two versions of the haunting *Virgin of the Rocks,* showing his remarkable mastery of detail. The reasons for the duplication, as well as the dating, are disputed.

His greatest accomplishment in Milan is the celebrated mural of the *Last Supper* (1495-98) in the refectory of Santa Maria delle Grazie, which culminated the efforts of generations of Italian artists to come to terms with this complex problem in composition, psychology, and religious content. Unfortunately, Leonardo executed the work in an experimental fresco technique, and it was already said to be ruined in the middle years of the following century. Only a wraith of its former self, enough has remained to retain the passionate interest not only of art historians and intellectuals but of common people throughout the world.

The French invasion of 1499 drove Leonardo out of Milan, to begin a period of wanderings that lasted until the end of his life. He first returned to Florence, where he found work as a military engineer for Cesare Borgia. He also took great interest in dissection and anatomy, attending (among other things) to the mechanisms of human copulation and reproduction. His major fresco project of this period, a state commission to commemorate a battle which pitted him against the young Michelangelo, was never completed—again because he insisted on using an experimental medium that could not be continued beyond the central group (1503-05). The dramatic brilliance of the group is nonetheless indicated by drawings and partial copies. Leonardo also grappled with the compositional problem of the Madonna and child with Saint Anne, which resulted in several works, notably the cartoon in the National Gallery in London.

Leonardo da Vinci

One of his few finished works of this period is his portrait of the wife of Francesco del Giocondo, the *Mona Lisa,* now in the Louvre in Paris. In addition to the mysterious smile this painting its enduring fascination in large measure to Leonardo's mastery of the sfumato technique, permitting him to envelop sitter and background in an air of impenetrable mystery.

In 1507 Leonardo entered the service of the French King Louis XII—at first in Milan and in Rome, and then in France itself. He spent much of this last period of his life in scientific pursuits and architectural schemes. Unfortunately, none of the buildings he designed was executed. He also extended his voluminous writings—8,000 manuscript pages have survived—including a treatise on painting, which was only published in 1651.

His last significant painting was the androgynous *St. John the Baptist.* The ambiguous stance of this figure has disturbed some, but in 1904 the French gay writer and occultist Josephin Péladan acclaimed it "the greatest painting in the world."

The legend that Leonardo died in the arms of the French King Francis I is impossible, for the king was far away at the time. Nonetheless, the story has a poetic truth, completing the career of an illegitimate child—and homosexual—who gained the admiration of the highest circles of society.

Changing Perceptions of Leonardo's Genius

Over the centuries Leonardo has attracted a variety of interpreters. Giorgio Vasari, himself an artist, ranks as the first major art historian; his vast work, the *Lives of the Painters, Sculptors, and Architects,* was first published in 1550. Born in Arezzo in 1511, Vasari did not know Leonardo personally. However, his biography of the artist is so vivid and laudatory that it ranks immediately after the works of Leonardo himself as a guarantee of his continuing fame. His genius was "the gift of God." The artist's "personal beauty could not be exaggerated" and "his every movement was grace itself." With regard to the *Last Supper,* Vasari stressed that the artist had seized the moment when the disciples sought, anxiously and urgently, to know who among them would betray their master. Vasari conceived the history of Italian art as having three periods of which the last was the culmination or zenith. The Leonardo biography is the first of the sequence belonging to the third period. This positioning was not an accident, for in Vasari's view it was Leonardo's singular honor to usher in this great epoch.

During the seventeenth century academic artists admired him for his combination of careful observation of nature and ideal beauty, and this conception long remained in force. Unfortunately, the idea that Leonardo constituted some sort of norm was an impediment to the understanding of his own unique qualities.

At the beginning of the nineteenth century scholars began to emphasize Leonardo's gifts as an interpreter of the human emotions.

The pioneer of this view was the Milanese writer Giuseppe Bossi (1777-1815). After long reflecting on the *Last Supper* (of which he made a meticulous, full-scale copy), Bossi concluded that the most important point was the expressivity of the individual Apostles. Bossi's approach was the basis for an eloquent essay (1817) by Johann Wolfgang von Goethe. The great German writer treated the Leonardo of the *Last Supper* as a kind of dramatist, who contrasted the individual roles of the Apostles to the maximum extent. In this interpretation Goethe ignored the underlying religious motivation of the work, which is after all placed in a monastic refectory and refers to the institution of the sacrament of the eucharist. This was the beginning of a new view of Leonardo as an artist who addressed primarily secular and worldly concerns, though in a profound way.

This secularization of Leonardo was taken a step further by French romantic writers, such as Théophile Gautier and Charles Baudelaire, who interpreted him as a nonconformist and precursor of the skeptical modern view of the world.

In its turn, this concept acquired a special inflection by the *Mona Lisa* essay of the homoerotic English writer Walter Pater. In the splendid prose of his *Studies in the History of the Renaissance* (1873), Pater attributed to the sitter "a beauty wrought out from within upon the flesh, the deposit, little cell by little cell, of strange thoughts and fantastic reveries and exquisite passions." In Pater's view Mona Lisa has the sinister fascination of a timeless creature, almost a vampire.

Pater, who led a quiet life as a closeted professor in Victorian Oxford, did not dare openly to address the homosexual side of Leonardo. That was left to a Viennese heterosexual. In a controversial study of 1910 Sigmund Freud, the founder of psychoanalysis, drew attention to a recollection of childhood in which Leonardo imagined that his open mouth was invaded by the wings of a bird. Presumably, this memory is related to fellatio. Deceived by a translation error, Freud believed the bird to have been a vulture, rather than the kite (*nibbio*) of Leonardo's description. Freud also thought that the composition of the *Madonna, St. Anne and the Child* was an innovation, reflecting Leonardo's troubled upbringing. In fact the theme was quite common during the period.

Freud's ideas rest upon psychoanalytic assumptions that one's psychosexual constitution is formed decisively in early childhood and, moreover, that a homosexual outcome reflects a conflicted relationship with the mother. These views may be true on other grounds—though many doubt them. But at all events the meager and uncertain facts Freud adduced about Leonardo do not suffice to prove his case. Still, despite the failure of his essay, Freud deserves credit for confronting an issue that too many distinguished scholars, before and since, have chosen to ignore.

After Freud's time interest began to focus increasingly on Leonardo's scientific pursuits, so massively documented, both pictorially and verbally, in the surviving corpus of manuscript sheets. Given the circumstances of his time, concern with anatomy is understandable, because artists were trying to improve their knowledge of the human body through the dissection of cadavers. Leonardo showed a special interest in human organs of reproduction, an interest surely connected with his inquisitiveness about his own sexuality. Moreover, although Leonardo was fascinated by clouds, water, and the geological formation of rocks, these investigations also contributed to the success of his art. Even his studies of military machinery and defense installations reflect an older tradition—found mainly in northern Europe—in which court artists were expected to participate in the creation of machinery. Despite all these parallels, Leonardo's preoccupation with these, to our view, nonartistic matters far surpasses that of any contemporary artist. The investment in time and energy must be regarded as reflective of his most outstanding characteristic: his boundless curiosity.

Leonardo, Enigmatic Yet Indestructible

Since Leonardo sought to cover the traces of his sexuality, it has been easy for those who do not wish to discuss the issue to downplay it. Although Leonardo was devoted to a scamp-like assistant, Salai, and later to a young aristocrat, Francesco Melzi, whom he adopted, not much is known about his emotional life.

In an age in which artists—and many others—were relatively forthright about their sexual tastes, Leonardo felt an instinctive need to guard his privacy. Grounded in his illegitimacy, as it surely is, this reclusiveness has other well-springs that cannot now be gauged. In this realm, as in others, Leonardo transcended his own age, producing endless food for thought and study on the part of each generation of scholars.

Two paintings, the *Mona Lisa* and the *St. John the Baptist,* have fascinated many observers through their androgynous quality. The modern artist Marcel Duchamp drew attention to this characteristic in the former work by "doctoring" a reproduction so as to give the lady a moustache. (Although Duchamp was not gay, he sometimes cross-dressed.) Still, unlike the achievements of such contemporaries as Botticelli and Michelangelo, the work of Leonardo has not appealed broadly to the modern gay sensibility. The artist attracts gay and lesbian people for much the same set of reasons as he does the general public, through his inquiring mind, his special excellences as an artist and a scientist, and through the potency of certain images, which have become inseparable parts of the cultural heritage of humanity.

References:

Clark, Lord Kenneth. *Leonardo da Vinci.* New edition, New York: Penguin Books, 1989.

Freud, Sigmund. *Leonardo da Vinci and a Memory of His Childhood* [1910]. Translated by Alan Tyson with an introduction by Brian Farrell, London: Penguin Books, 1962.

Kemp, Martin. *Leonardo da Vinci: The Marvelous Works of Nature and Man.* Cambridge, Massachusetts: Harvard University Press, 1981.

Pater, Walter. *Studies in the History of the Renaissance.* N.p., 1873.

Pedretti, Carlo. *Leonardo da Vinci: A Study in Chronology and Style.* Berkeley: University of California Press, 1973.

Reti, Ladislao, editor. *The Unknown Leonardo.* New York: McGraw-Hill, 1974.

Turner, A. Richard. *Inventing Leonardo.* Berkeley: University of California Press, 1992.

Vasari, Giorgio. *Lives of the Painters, Sculptors, and Architects.* N.p., 1550.

—Wayne R. Dynes

Edmonia Lewis

1843-c.1911

African-American sculptor

As she followed her course in life, Mary Edmonia Lewis remained steadfastly at the helm, covering vast distances both geographic and economic. She achieved a high level of success and fame in the arts that was unusual for a woman, particularly Black women, of the Victorian era. Her mother was a Chippewa Indian and her father an African American who immigrated from the West Indies. Lewis's Indian name was Wildfire.

Lewis and her marble sculpture first came to the attention of the world with the debut of her work *Cleopatra* at the 1876 Philadelphia Centennial Exhibition. Although *Cleopatra* was recognized as a significant achievement in Neo-Classical sculpture, it was Lewis's ethnicity, following the Civil War and the recent achievements of the Abolitionist Movement, that excited the Victorian imagination. As a whole, Lewis's marble sculptures celebrated both her Native and African American heritages, while reflecting feminist ideals.

Cosmopolitan Youth and Scandal At Oberlin College

Lewis was orphaned around the age of five, and continued to live with her mother's Ojibwa nomadic tribe, with periodic contacts with local European American settlements for what was deemed more traditional education, or "schooling." When her older half brother, Samuel Lewis, moved west to seek his fortune prospecting for gold, he arranged for Lewis to board with a Capt. S. R. Mills, in the North Ward of Newark, New Jersey. Samuel Lewis found success, and began financing his sister's education, and continued to support her well into her artistic career. Lewis's early life, and that of her brother, suggest a relatively cosmopolitan experience that encouraged and enabled Lewis to claim her place in the world of art and ideas that lay beyond the reach of many, but not all, Black women of the Victorian era.

In 1859, Lewis entered the preparatory department of Oberlin College, a liberal institution dedicated to the cause of abolishing slavery while realizing racial equality through education. Initially, Lewis was judged as being "too wild for much book learning," although her intelligence and bright, winning personality were recognized. She completed three years of satisfactory course work.

In the winter of 1862, a scandal erupted at Oberlin College, centered on Lewis, that aggravated racial tensions between the more conservative residents of Oberlin and the insular, liberal community at the college. Lewis had been accused of attempting to poison two of her white, female friends with the aphrodisiac Spanish Fly. Before her trial could begin, Lewis was captured one night by an angry mob of white townspeople and viciously beaten. She was found in a field near campus, unconscious and bleeding. Her trial was postponed for a few months to give her time to recover. She was defended in court that spring by the first African American lawyer in America, John Mercer Langston, who portrayed the incident as a school girl prank that got out of hand. Lewis was found innocent. Nevertheless, the furor over her case made it impossible for her to continue her academic career at Oberlin.

Lewis Finds Sculpture

After leaving Oberlin, Lewis first considered returning to her mother's Ojibwa tribe. Changing her mind, she traveled instead to Boston, having acquaintances in the Abolitionist Movement there who would support her. One afternoon while walking around the city, she happened to see a bust of Benjamin Franklin by the internationally famous Neo-Classical sculptor William Storey in a shop window. The work amazed and delighted Lewis. She became passionately interested in sculpture, and resolved to learn how to make one of her own as fine as what she had seen in the shop window.

Lewis contacted Rev. Highland Brown, a friend and admirer of John Brown, and asked for financial backing to study sculpture in Rome. In the mid 19th century, Rome was recognized internationally as the seat of the Neo-Classical sensibility and patronage, as well as the place to go in order to finish one's training as a sculptor. Unfortunately, Rev. Brown's congregation was too poor to send Lewis abroad and they declined her request. Next, Lewis contacted the abolitionist William Lloyd Garrison, who gave her instead a letter of introduction to the sculptor Edward Brackett in Boston. Accepted by Brackett, Lewis worked in his studio, apprenticing for three years. In 1865 she created a bust of Col. Robert Gould

Edmonia Lewis

Shaw, a Boston Brahmin and Civil War general who died while leading the African American 54th Massachusetts Infantry in battle. The sculpture was a great success, selling 100 copies, and its sales financed Lewis's relocation to Rome. At the age of 22, Lewis embarked on her professional career in art.

The American Colony, Success, and Fortune

In a *New York Times* interview, dated December, 1878, Lewis said: "I was practically driven to Rome in order to obtain the opportunities for art culture, and to find a social atmosphere where I was not constantly reminded of my color. The land of liberty [America] had no room for a colored sculptor."

Lewis was introduced to members of the American colony in Rome by the Abolitionist Lydia Marie Child. Child risked her reputation for the cause of abolition and was deeply involved in the plight of African Americans. She also provided significant financial support for Lewis during her early years in Rome. The American colony was an informal group of actors, artists, writers, and expatriate socialites, that included a coterie of women sculptors. Of these was the sculptor Harriet Hosmer: a longtime friend of the Child family. Hosmer, variously described as impudent and as dressing and behaving like nobody else, befriended Lewis almost immediately upon her arrival in Rome. In a letter to Mrs. Child, Lewis recounted her first meeting with Hosmer, "A Boston lady took me to Miss Hosmer's studio. It would have done your heart good to see what a welcome I received. She took my hand cordially, and said, 'Oh Miss Lewis I'm glad to see you here!' and then, while she still held my hand, there flowed such a neat little speech from her true lips." Lewis added, "Miss Hosmer had since called on me, and we often meet." Photographs of Lewis from that time show her dressed in a bohemian style similar to Hosmer's—the tailored white shirt and neck tie fastened with a brooch—that could be considered either standard period attire for an emancipated woman, or Lewis's desire to emulate her friend.

Through Hosmer, Lewis became acquainted with the actress Charlotte Cushman, who extended her financial support to the young artist as well. In Cushman's biography, *Bright and Particular Star*, she described Lewis as a "poor little soul, who has more than anybody else to fight." Cushman was impressed deeply by one of the first sculptures Lewis made in Rome, "Hiawatha's Wooing," and with friends, bought the work and presented it to the Boston YMCA.

Although Lewis was an associate of the American colony in Rome, and well acquainted with its adjunct clique of women actors, artists, and writers that Henry James termed "that Great Mamarian Flock"—representing the circumspect lesbian world of Victorian Europe—Lewis's personal life remains obscure. She never married. However, her current biographer, Dr. Marilyn Richardson, maintains that Lewis is rather of a mysterious figure, and that extensive research into Lewis's life has not yet revealed any concrete information about her romantic involvement with anyone, male or female.

Subtle Pioneer In Sculpture

Lewis created over 60 marble sculptures during the course of a career in art that spanned five decades. Her sculptural style fell solidly into the category of Neo-Classicism, and was termed "ideal work" as her imagery was largely based on narrative from literature, mythology, and the Bible. Much of her early sculpture focused on themes related to the abolition of slavery in the United States, and to the precarious social position of newly freed Blacks. Later sculptures illustrated episodes from Henry Wadsworth Longfellow's *The Song of Hiawatha* which was at that time a popular motif in decorative art. Despite the commercial nature of much of her sculpture, Lewis managed to challenge and elevate Victorian ideas of Native and African American peoples.

Lewis's major works include, *Forever Free,* done in 1867, the title inspired by a line of text from the Emancipation Proclamation. An African American man stands next to a kneeling woman, who were just freed from the bonds of slavery. In her 1868 bust of *Minnehaha,* Lewis sculpted the princess with perceptible Native American facial features. In the *Old Arrow Maker and His Daughter* of 1872, the girl's nose is straight, while her father's is not, and his cheekbones are high and prominent. The narrative behind Lewis's 1875 work, *Hagar in the Wilderness,* came from the Bible, and became an allegorical statement about the abuses suffered by Black women when a Black patriarchy was not in place to protect them. Speaking in reference to an earlier version of *Hagar* which is now lost, Lewis is widely quoted as having said, "I have a strong sympathy for all women who have suffered."

Her best known work, *Cleopatra,* was a deliberately exalted image of ethnic identity. In the late 19th century, Egypt was a code that meant Black Africa to Victorian culture, and Lewis's contemporaries used the Egyptian queen to illustrate themes of lust, greed, violence, and decadence. Lewis countered these Western fantasies by depicting her Cleopatra as a noble, dying queen. Thus she restored the historical reality of a remarkable woman, and to some extent, the African people as a whole.

Cleopatra disappeared around the turn of the century, and recently turned up thanks to the research effort of Dr. Richardson. After the Philadelphia Centennial exhibition, the statue was moved to Forest Park, Illinois where it marked the grave of a horse named Cleopatra. Here it remained as the track was converted into a golf course, then a torpedo factory, a bulk-mail center, and finally a shopping mall. The sculpture was placed in storage at the mall. In 1985, *Cleopatra* was rediscovered by a fire inspector in a pile of junk. He had some boy scouts dig it out and coat it with latex paint to cover graffiti, with the intent of displaying the sculpture in the mall. Instead, *Cleopatra* went back into storage where Dr. Richardson found it a few years later. Since that time, Dr. Richardson prevailed in having *Cleopatra* donated to the Smithsonian Institution.

In modern times, Lewis's sculptures have been criticized or dismissed for depicting ethnic subjects with caucasian faces. Lewis based her figures on the examples of Greek and Roman sculpture she saw at the Vatican Museums, and in other great art collections of Rome. The men she sculpted looked more specifically ethnic. Black men were given curly hair and thickish lips, while Native American men had high cheekbones and pronounced bumps on the bridge of their noses. Lewis's women, on the other hand, do appear caucasian while bearing the trappings of their ethnicity. The Black women wear chains, manacles, iron balls, and the Native women wear animal skins, beads, and feathers. However, what is more significant is what Lewis chose not to sculpt: half naked indian or black women representing the erotic exploitation of the non-white female body as the "exotic other."

In the late 19th century, Lewis walked a fine line. Her content is an assertion of ethnic truth within the bounds of what white patrons would allow. The Western-European faces of her women conformed to fashionable Victorian prescriptives that defined the cult of True Womanhood, found throughout the literature of the period. In the context of Victorian society, she took her intent a necessary step further, and eliminated ethnic identity as a strategy to eliminate the stereotype. By mediating the experience of her racial heritages through sympathetic models sanctioned by the dominant culture, Lewis recreated the image of African and Native American women in European discourse. This is the work of a quiet revolutionary. Her intent might be difficult to understand or even believe in the context of present day—positive and strong ethnic identification of racial groups. Her approach also seems naive.

Lewis Remained In Rome

Although Lewis returned to the United States from time to time because of her work, she preferred living in Rome and stayed there until her death. In the *New York Times* article of 1878, Lewis said: "They treat me very kindly here [New York], but it's with a kind of reservation. I like to see the opera, and I don't like to be pointed out as a negress." In her later years, Lewis's finances declined, and her exact year of death is not known. The last recorded account of Lewis—20 years before her death—came from Frederick Douglass, who visited the artist in 1887 while on his honeymoon in Rome with his second wife. Douglass wrote in his diary that they "found [Lewis] in a large building, near the top in a very pleasant room with a commanding view, No.4 via XX Settembre, Roma. Here she lives, and here she plies her fingers in her art as a sculptress. She seems very cheerful and happy and successful."

References:

Blodgett, Dr. Geoffrey. "John Mercer Langston and the Case Of Edmonia Lewis: Oberlin, 1862" in *The Journal of Negro History* (Washington, D.C.), Vol. 53, July 1968: 201-218.

Brown, Dr. Wm. Wells. *The Rising Son; The Antecedents And Advancement of the Colored Race.* Boston, 1876: 463-468.

Buick, Kirsten P. "The Ideal Works of Edmonia Lewis" in *American Art*, summer, 1995: 5-19.

Douglass, Frederick. Diary. Washington, D.C., Library of Congress, microfilm. Diary entry date, 26 January 1887.

Leach, Joseph. *Bright and Particular Star: The Life and Times Of Charlotte Cushman.* New Haven: Yale University Press, 1970.

Nesbitt, Lois. "Cleopatra at the Mall" in *ARTnews* (New York) Vol. 87, No. 8, October 1988: 19-20.

"Seeking Equality Abroad" in *The New York Times*, 29 December 1878: 5.

Richardson, Dr. Marilyn. "Edmonia Lewis and the Death of Cleopatra" in *The International Review of African American Art* (Hampton, Virginia) Vol. 12, no. 2, 1955: 36-52.

———. Conversation with Dr. Richardson, February 1996.

Sherwood, Dolly. *Harriet Hosmer, American Sculptor.* University of Missouri Press, 1991.

—Laurie Fitzpatrick

Liberace

1919-1987

American musician

Born 16 May 1919, the man known to millions of fans as Liberace originally had first and middle names, but wisely realized the public probably would not be able to pronounce Wladziu and Valentino was yesterday's news. Liberace's mother was Polish and his father was an Italian orchestra musician. He had two brothers and one sister; his brother George was also a musician, his sister Angelina assisted him in the writing of his 1973 autobiography.

The Liberace children began musical instruction when they turned four. Liberace studied at the Wisconsin College of Music on scholarship. At fourteen he began playing the piano at Little Nick's bar in Milwaukee. From there he moved up to roadhouses, local orchestras, and performances. When he graduated from high school he was invited to play with the Chicago symphony. He performed under the name Walter Buster Keys for about six months.

Liberace's first performance with the Chicago symphony was on 14 January 1940. In 1941, he went to New Jersey to play at a resort and made frequent trips to New York City. It was here that he first admitted his homosexuality and entered a gay social milieu. But Liberace could not seem to break into the artistic world of New York except for a few disappointing bookings, and headed out to California. A friend named Clarence Goodwin became his first manager. With Goodwin's help over a year's time Liberace's act was perfected. Liberace opened at The Plaza in New York City with great success. From there he went on to play all over the country, and became a popular regular in Las Vegas.

Liberace

Established Career in Movies, Radio, and Television

In 1945 his brother George left the U.S. Navy and became Liberace's second manager (he was booked by MCA). Liberace appeared in his first film, *South Sea Sinner,* in 1950. This film was generally considered to be a pretty bad film, and only Liberace, as the piano player in an island establishment, got good reviews. Liberace went on to radio and eventually, in 1953, premiered in a television show, and achieved his first sold-out concert at Carnegie Hall. The media had begun their hate campaign of Liberace, and savaged him whenever they had the opportunity. However, as with many rock stars, Liberace's public ignored the criticism. By 1954 the Liberace television show played on 184 channels.

Liberace was aware that the taint of homosexuality could destroy a career in the straight-laced 1950s. He claimed to have been engaged three times, and told interviewers that he was waiting for the perfect bride to come into his life. His first public engagement was with a dancer named Joanne Rio. Now known as Lee in Hollywood, Liberace announced before leaving for a five-month tour of Europe that he and Joanne would be married in a year, if she was willing to wait for him to finish his tour. But her father, Eddie Rio, knew Liberace was gay, and convinced his daughter to end the engagement. Twenty years later, Rio sued Liberace for libel. The case was settled out of court.

In 1955, Liberace signed to star in a remake of *The Man Who Played God,* for Warner Bros. The remake, entitled *Sincerely Yours,* was expected to do phenomenally well, and even got good critical reviews, but Liberace's fans rejected it—they were not willing to pay to see someone they watched for free on television every week.

Denied Homosexuality and Sued Periodicals

Liberace continued to deny his homosexuality, but he was now rich and famous enough to indulge his tastes. Details about his life published in an article in *Confidential* spawned a lawsuit, and Liberace testified against the magazine at a grand jury hearing. He settled his suit for $40,000, which went to charity. Liberace denied under oath that he was gay or that he had ever engaged in homosexual sex. He won a second lawsuit against the *Daily Mirror* in England, again for imputing his homosexuality.

But Liberace had been flamboyantly outrageous long before Elton John or David Bowie were ever appeared on the music scene. The late 1950s were a trying time for Liberace, both professionally and personally. His mother was attacked and beaten at his house in Beverly Hills, by two men who were never found. Liberace had an argument with his brother over the gay parties George held at a house Liberace bought in Palm Springs. As a result, George resigned as his orchestra conductor. And by 1957 he was losing his audience—what should have been a four-week run at The Palace in New York City was cut short due to low ticket sales after the second weekend. Liberace's new television series, aired during the day, was a failure, and was canceled after six months.

With the help of former manager, Sam Lutz, Liberace worked hard to get his career got back on-track. He changed his act, adding rock numbers and making his costumes more and more ostentatious. In 1965, he turned 46, and announced he was celebrating his 25th anniversary as an entertainer. He was earning $800 thousand a year. He also opened an interior decorating shop called Liberace Interiors and Objets d'Art, on La Cienega Blvd. It was short-lived—a lot of people came to look, but few bought.

In 1968, he went to England and filmed ten television specials to be summer replacements for *The Red Skelton Show.* On 16 May 1969 he turned 50, Liberace was one of the richest and most popular entertainers on the planet. He appeared as one of the villains (Fingers) on the *Batman* television show, and published a cookbook in 1971. In 1973, Putnam published his autobiography. In the book Liberace still maintained his heterosexuality, though it was well known by this time how many young men he'd supported. He opened the Liberace Museum in Las Vegas, consigning many of his treasures to it—the term "conspicuous consumption" could have been invented to describe Liberace. This was followed by the opening of Liberace's restaurant, Tivoli Gardens. In 1976, he published his third book, *The Things I Love.*

When he was in his 60s, Liberace embarked on an affair with an eighteen year-old named Scott Thorson. Thorson worked for an animal trainer, and met Liberace at one of his Las Vegas shows. Thorson went to live with Liberace after knowing him for only a couple of days, and became his chauffeur. He accompanied Liberace to interviews, dined with him at restaurants, and accompanied him to parties. This was the longest-lasting of any of his liaisons, but when Thorson began to drink and take drugs regularly and heavily, Liberace ended the relationship. Six months later, Thorson sued him for palimony. Although Thorson lost the suit, Liberace finally paid him off in December of 1986 to stop him from filing more suits. Brother George had died in 1985, of leukemia and heart disease.

Liberace embarked on a new affair with one of his backup singers, nineteen-year old Cary James. In 1986, his fourth and last book, *The Wonderful Private Life of Liberace* was published. Scott Thorson wasn't mentioned. He published his own tell-all book, *Behind The Candelabra,* in 1988.

Liberace's final performance was at Radio City Music Hall on 3 November 1986. He gave his final lavish party that Christmas in Malibu. Liberace died of AIDS in 1987, though his death certificate was read that he died of heart disease.

References:

Liberace. *Liberace: An Autobiography.* New York: G. P. Putnam's Sons, 1973.

———. *The Things I Love.* New York: Grosset & Dunlap, 1976.

———. *The Wonderful Private World of Liberace.* New York: Harper & Row, 1986.

Thomas, Bob. *Liberace.* New York: St. Martins' Press, 1987.

Thorson, Scott, with Alex Thorleifson. *Behind the Candelabra: My Life With Liberace.* New York: E. P. Dutton, 1988.

—Debora Hill

Lisa Ben

American editor, activist, songwriter, and performer

The woman who uses the pseudonym Lisa Ben (an anagram for Lesbian) was, in the late 1940s, a Los Angeles secretary who published a journal for lesbians entitled *Vice Versa: America's Gayest Magazine.* She is today celebrated for her courage in doing so. Those were pre-Stonewall days. Lesbian and gay culture were of necessity underground phenomena, and the publication of such materials was strictly prohibited.

In June 1947, Lisa sought to further awareness of gay issues by starting her own publication. Feeling isolated in the rigorously heterosexual world of the late 1940s, she also hoped to establish through the magazine a network of personal acquaintances. Ben put the magazine together singlehandedly during slow periods at work, using carbon paper and a typewriter to create the copies. Nine issues of the monthly publication were created and distributed in Los Angeles between June 1947 and February 1948, featuring play, film, and book reviews, poetry, short stories, editorials, and an annotated bibliography of novels about lesbianism. Ben's criteria, however, were not limited to the sexual orientation of her material. An editorial in the first issue admonished:

> If *Vice Versa* should be subjected to the glance of unsympathetic eyes, let us at least show that our magazine can be just as interesting and entertaining on as high a level as the average magazines available to the general public.

Ben stopped producing *Vice Versa* when the company for which she worked closed and she was forced to find a new job. Nevertheless, the first small battle in the war on homophobia had successfully been waged, and *Vice Versa* did bring an awareness of lesbian issues to its readers.

Moreover, Ben herself continued to be active in the gay community. Partly as a tonic to the self-deprecating antics of female impersonators, Lisa started writing gay parodies of popular tunes in 1948. Ben later commented:

> I was absolutely appalled at the gay male entertainers who would, on stage, make derogatory remarks and dirty jokes about themselves to entertain non-gay people.... No wonder society had such a bad opinion of us.

Ben performed her parodies at bars and small gatherings, and they soon became widely known and popular among gays.

Lisa's artistic talents facilitated her developing an ever-widening circle of friends. Among the women she met were members of the pioneering lesbian organization, the Daughters of Bilitis (DOB), which she eventually joined.

She remains active in the gay community of southern California, where she lives with her cats.

References:

Brandt, Kate. "Lisa Ben: A Lesbian Pioneer," in *Visibilities: The On-Line Lesbian Magazine,* http://www.qworld.org/Visi.

—Sarah Watstein

Anne Lister

1791-1840

British diarist, heiress, and landowner

Anne Lister was an upper class woman from Yorkshire, England. Her diaries, which she kept for most of her life, chronicle everyday events and her romantic and sexual relationships with women. Lister fully accepted her lesbian sexuality, stating in her diary entry for 29 January 1821; "I love, & only love, the fairer sex & thus beloved by them in turn, my heart revolts from any other love than theirs."

Anne Lister was born 3 April 1791 in Yorkshire, where her family owned land. Her father, Captain Jeremy Lister, a veteran of the American War of Independence, had resigned his commission to settle with his wife Rebecca Lister (nee Battle) on a small estate at Market Weighton. They had four boys and two girls, but only Lister and her younger sister Marian survived, the girls becoming heirs to the family estates.

Lister began exploring her sexuality at the age of about 14 while at boarding school. Her first lover was her roommate Eliza Raine, who was intensely jealous of Lister's tendency to flirt with other girls. Medical experts at the time took Raine's emotional state as an indication of insanity and by 1814 Raine was declared incurably insane and spent the rest of her life in medical care.

Through Raine's guardians, Mr. and Mrs. Duffin, Lister widened her social circle and became friendly with the Norcliffes of Langton Hall, situated in between York and Scarborough. Lister developed a sexual relationship with the Norcliffes' eldest daughter, Isabella, whom she met in 1810. Isabella wanted to become Lister's lifelong partner, but Lister grew to dislike Isabella's temper and, in later life, her drinking. Isabella introduced Lister to Marianna Belcombe, the daughter of a York doctor. Lister quickly developed a sexual passion for Marianna, which Marianna reciprocated in 1814.

Lister's relationship with Marianna lasted for many years, but they were unable to realize their dream of living together because, initially, neither had sufficient income. Marianna made an unhappy marriage to an older man, Charles Lawton, for financial security. The two women hoped to be united when Charles died, but this was not to be.

In May 1815 Lister began living at Shibden Hall with her unmarried aunt and uncle, James and Lister. She was to inherit Shibden Hall on her uncle's death and needed experience of running the estate. Lister's aunt and uncle allowed her plenty of freedom and seem to have understood her intention to search for a lifelong female companion instead of a husband.

Lister and Marianna continued their sexual relationship when they had the opportunity, but exercised extreme secrecy in fear of York society discovering their relationship. They used a code when writing to each other, which Lister also used for her more explicit journal entries.

Lister enjoyed walking, horse riding, shooting and flute playing and embarked on courses of studying, partly to keep her mind from her unhappiness at her separation from Marianna. She used her journal to unburden herself of her worries, recording such details as her discovery in 1821 that she had caught a venereal disease from Marianna, later passing it to Isabella.

In 1823 Marianna and Lister's relationship suffered another setback when Marianna told Lister that she was ashamed to be seen with her because of her masculine appearance and unfashionable dress sense. Lister was normally proud of her "masculine beauty" and felt hurt at Marianna's comments.

Although Lister considered that she had a commitment to Marianna, she nevertheless flirted widely and had several affairs. She travelled to Paris in 1824, partly in search of a cure for her venereal complaint, where she had an intense liaison with an older widow called Maria Barlow. Lister's longing was always for a lifelong partner and she considered that Mrs. Barlow might fill that role but when she returned to England the relationship dwindled. Lister and Marianna spent some time together in the summer of 1825 and managed to rekindled their love. Lister decided to consider Marianna as her wife and Mrs. Barlow as her mistress.

In January 1826 James Lister died suddenly of an aneurism of a blood vessel. In his will he bequeathed "all his real and personal estates to his niece, Anne Lister." Lister managed the estate competently, generating enough income for her plans for foreign travel.

Lister visited Paris again later that year, first with her aunt and Marianna although Marianna returned to England with her husband in the autumn. In 1827 Lister, Mrs. Barlow, and Mrs. Barlow's daughter toured Switzerland. In the winter of 1827-28 Lister began an affair with Mrs. Rosny, a Parisian widow of high social standing. She enjoyed sophisticated Parisian society and realized that she and Marianna had grown apart.

Lister eventually found a suitable life partner with adequate independent means. Ann Walker, heiress to an estate near Shibden, came to live at Shibden Hall in 1834. In 1839, the two women set off to realize Lister's dreams of travelling to Russia, Persia, and Turkey. They had reached Georgia, Russia in the foothills of the Caucasus Mountains by September 1840 where Lister caught a fever from which she did not recover. Her companion brought her body back to England for burial.

Lister's diaries are valuable as a chronicle of English life in the 1800s and for their explicit portrayal of a lesbian at that time. More than anything, however, they allow an insight into the fascinating and highly individual character of Lister.

References:

A Skirt through History. BBC Television.

Whitbread, Helena, editor. *I know my own heart: The Diaries of Anne Lister 1791-1840.* London: Virago Press, 1988.

———, editor. *No Priest But Love: The Journals of Anne Lister from 1824-1826.* London: Smith Settle Ltd., 1992.

—Lucya Szachnowski

Ladies of Llangollen

Lady Eleanor Butler

1739-1829

Irish writer

Sarah Ponsonby

1755-1831

Irish writer

The Irish noblewomen Sarah Ponsonby and Lady Eleanor Butler—known as the "Ladies of Llangollen" for the Welsh village near where they lived in "delicious retirement"—enjoyed a relationship that lasted over half a decade. That their highly romantic friendship was indeed sexual would hardly seem debatable today. But for the era and society they lived in, particular and passionate friendships like theirs were easily tolerated, and they gained respect and notoriety for their romantic devotion to each other largely because no one dared dream they might also prefer each other sexually. Add to this their upper-class status, their attachment to rural life (as opposed to the more theatrical antics of possible homosexuals in the cities), and the courage they exemplified in eschewing marriage and "eloping" together (the word did not have any sexual connotation then) and the respectability that rendered them relatively immune from scandal becomes apparent.

According to writer Susan Lanser in *The Gay and Lesbian Literary Heritage,* the "women shared bed, board, books, income, and daily walks; dressed similarly in men's waistcoats and women's skirts; signed their correspondence jointly; named one of their dogs Sappho; and refused to spend even one night away from home." In their diaries as well, they readily referred to each other as "my beloved" and "my sweet love." But, as writer Paul Russell notes in *The Gay 100,* historian Lillian Faderman observed that "one reason (their relationship) was so revered was that it was thought to be nongenital.... Their society was happy to see them as the embodiment of the highest ideals of spiritual love and the purest dreams of romantic friendship."

Once together and ensconced in the country, they set themselves a lifelong program for living—their "system" they called it—that included: voracious reading (often aloud to each other) in languages, literature, and geography; astute attention to the "cult of nature" as evidenced in the meticulous management of their farm; journal entries that chronicled their lives and times; and reams of correspondence with friends and other literary figures. William Wordsworth, Robert Southey, Edmund Burke, Anna Seward, and Stephanie de Genlis (who, according to Lanser, coyly termed the women "imprudent victims of an excessive sensibility") all spent time writing under their roof.

No Interest in Marriage

Lady Eleanor Butler was born into a noble Irish Catholic family and was educated at a convent in France. After her schooling, she returned to Kilkenny, where she showed no interest in the marriage prospects her family had arranged, and instead immersed herself in books. Sarah Ponsonby, sixteen years younger than Butler, lost both of her parents in childhood and her stepmother when she was thirteen—the same year she first met Butler.

Ponsonby had been sent to Miss Parke's boarding school in Kilkenny. She was considered sensitive and shy, but likewise eager to learn—the perfect counterpart to Butler's sharp-tongued and more bitter—yet no less sensitive—personality. Despite their difference in age, their romantic pupil-teacher relationship was considered quite common and even desirable at the time. As biographer Elizabeth Mavor observes in *The Ladies of Llangollen: A Study in Romantic Friendship,* "their friendship most likely began, as so many before and since, with books ... [and] passed on to discuss the world as it was, as it might be ... slowly discovering over the five years of growing intimacy that they both ... had a longing for the simple life."

In 1773, Ponsonby, now eighteen, left Miss Parke's school and went to live with Sir William and Lady Betty Fownes at Woodstock in Ireland. Here, she was truly able to indulge her growing passion for peace and quiet—working in the garden, galloping around the grounds with the Fownes' son on her shoulders, and generally devoting herself to Lady Fownes as the "substitute daughter" she had become.

Ponsonby did not, however, approve of Sir William, who was eyeing her with a shady plan of future marriage. It was a notion Lady Betty also seemed to condone, for her health was deteriorating and she had never produced for him a male heir. Thus began the long, anguished, and secret correspondence between Ponsonby and Butler that was to lead to their first attempt at elopement.

Back to the Convent

Bulter's sorrow sprang from the fact that her mother was considering sending her back to the convent to become a nun. In 1778, Bulter was 39, and her prospects for a "good" marriage—which her family still held as the ultimate goal for a woman of her class—were unlikely. Besides, the family felt that Butler's embrace of "the faith" might balance-out the fact that her brother had recently converted to the Church of England, and it would mean that her portion of the family fortune might be "redeployed" for other purposes. "Something now drove (Butler) to open her heart secretly to the only friend (Ponsonby) that she could trust," says Mavor. "It was a correspondence of mutual complaint."

Not surprisingly, the two women soon hatched their own plans. What had begun years ago as a fantasy of the perfect life together now seemed altogether possible—indeed, necessary—as they shared the details of their growing misery and feelings of entrapment. Their idea of hiding from society was bolstered by the prevailing fashion for French romantics who had done the same, and the notion of retiring to a small cottage somewhere in the country was also one of the few feasible financial options.

Both were passionate about the writings of French romantic Jean-Jacques Rousseau. Rousseau had written a novel, *La Nouvelle Heloise,* that certainly inspired the women with its tale of lovers' trials, passion for books, and the strains of living according to society's strictures. They may also have had some encouragement from the fictional example of two women living together as outlined in the novel about a feminine utopia titled *Millennium Hall,* published anonymously but already popular and in a fourth edition by the 1770s.

In April of 1778, the two women donned men's clothes and, with Ponsonby literally leaping out of her bedroom window, they eloped together. Their prearranged rendezvous was Waterford, twenty-five miles away and an embarkation point for England. The Fownes suspected immediately that Ponsonby had run off with Butler, while Lord Butler at first thought his daughter had run off with some man. When, in the next breath, he was unable to think of who that might be, he also detected the truth.

Ironically, the two fugitives were caught the very next day just as they were about to board the boat for England. Ponsonby had a terrible cold from sleeping in a barn the night before, and Butler nearly fainted when she was told she would not be going back to Woodstock with Ponsonby and Lady Betty. Over the next few months, Ponsonby became even more ill, Bulter's parents were even more determined to send her to the convent in France, and the correspondence between the two women and various family members continued in anguished tones that begged for temperance on all sides. At one point, Ponsonby even promised to give up any idea of running away if only the Butlers would spare their daughter the hell of convent life. "I would do anything," Mavor cites Ponsonby as writing to the family, "to save Miss Butler from ... a Convent."

The Secret

A few months later, when it became obvious that no amount of pleading or cajoling was going to sway the Butlers from their course, Ponsonby and Butler eloped again, this time making it to the "horridly beautiful" mountains in Wales. They found a small cottage near Llangollen and set about their rigorous system of independent self-improvement. They rose at eight nearly every morning, read to each other, and went for long, serious walks in the surrounding countryside, often covering ten miles or more in a single afternoon. Though their "system" for a bucolic life was never written down, their journals, according to Mavor, suggest that they were determined never to leave home and strived "to devote hearts and minds to self-improvement; to eschew the vanity of society; to beautify their surroundings and to better, in so far as they could, the lot of the poor and unfortunate."

They avoided contact with family and friends for several years, opting instead for obscurity and the growing, if wary, friendship (and credit) of local farmers and shopkeepers who referred to them simply as "the ladies." Soon, however, their pastoral retreat was drawing both the curious and the likewise romantic. Wordsworth visited and composed a poem ("Sonnet Composed at Plas Newydd") to them, as Russell notes, calling them "Sisters in love, a love allowed to climb / E'vn on this earth, above the reach of time." Likewise, the poet Anne Seward stayed with them and termed their relationship biblically "Davidean" in her poem "Llangollen Vale."

In short, there was a movement of its own beginning to surround the women, a cult of romance bred on the idea of true choice in passionate friendships (but no sex, please). If Ponsonby and Butler had chosen to speak of sex, society would no doubt have knocked them violently from the idealized pedestal they were being placed upon. Indeed, they never did speak or write of sex overtly, unless one is inclined to read some contemporary code into their journals. Whether they didn't speak of their lesbianism for "romantic" reasons, out of shame and fear of certain oppression, or if they were indeed celibate—the nature of their sexual relationship is a secret that went with both of them to the grave.

And such secrets are surely all part of the mystique surrounding the Ladies of Llangollen to this day. One visitor to Llangollen in 1822 named Anne Lister, who according to writer Lanser recorded her own homosexual activities in coded diaries, wrote: "I cannot help thinking that surely it was not Platonic. Heaven forgive me, but I look within myself and doubt."

Country Butch & Femme

Despite this intrigue, and however hard they tried for obscurity, Ponsonby and Butler became extraordinarily well-known. Over time, they surrendered to their notoriety, receiving notable visitors and carrying on voluminous correspondence with others. The Duke of Wellington, Sir Walter Scott, Edmund Burke, and Lady Caroline Lamb were among the "pilgrims" who made it to Llangollen. In 1788, the King of England even granted Ponsonby a pension to supplement the small stipend each of them were, by then, receiving from their families. After a time, visitors were so common, the two began to crave their solitary life again. "When shall we be quite alone," Mavor has Butler noting in her journal on 25 October 1785.

Despite their lifetime together, arguments between them were rare. Perhaps the greatest source of pain and upset occurred when an article in England's *General Evening Post* appeared in 1790 titled "Extraordinary Female Affection." The article, as cited by Russell, proceeded to describe the pair in terms we might today characterize as "butch" and "femme," but it was a classification neither of them were fond of at the time. "Miss Butler," it said, "is tall and masculine, she wears always a riding habit, hangs her hat with the air of a sportsman in the hall, and appears in all respects as a young man, if we except the petticoats which she still retains. Miss Ponsonby, on the contrary, is polite and effeminate, fair and beautiful." Whether the article offended them because they felt they'd been "found out," we'll never know. When they asked their friend Edmund Burke whether they should sue the newspaper, he wisely talked them out of it.

"Supernatural" Resonance

Butler died at their beloved cottage in 1829, at the age of 90. The funeral was almost royal, and Ponsonby was so grief-stricken that she could not even attend. In the ensuing two years before Ponsonby followed Butler into death, at the age of 76, Mavor notes some bizarre "supernatural" events taking place. First, a stray dog showed up at the cottage on the day of Butler's funeral. Ponsonby proceeded to call it "Chance." A few weeks later, when Ponsonby was taking down a book of verse to give to visiting friends as a keepsake, the dog looked at her and began to howl inconsolably. It was as if, according to one of the visitors, the creature was "reproaching her for giving away the book ... its anger could not be appeased and Miss P wrote the following day to beg the friend (to) exchange that book for another." Also, that same year, all their cows gave birth to black calves, a rarity Ponsonby took as evidence of Butler's departed spirit.

The obituary written in the *General Evening Post* following Butler's death was certainly no comfort. Not only did it outline and malign their lives verbatim from the offensive copy of 1790, but it added the erroneous information that Lady Butler had declined five offers of marriage to run away with Ponsonby. But Ponsonby was without vindictiveness, and lived out her remaining years in the same loving simplicity that had served the two women so well for so long. "I hope it will be in my power," Mavor cites Ponsonby as writing in 1829, "to pass the remainder of My Days under this little Roof without lessening the number of my present and faithful establishment."

In the end, whether Ponsonby and Butler were lovers in the physical sense is beyond the point. Words like "passion" and "love" were not terms they were shy of when describing their relationship. As Evelyn Gettone notes in the *Encyclopedia of Homosexuality,* "before the medically inspired 'morbidification' of romantic friendship between women, theirs was a true marriage of the mind, spirit, and affections." They had a bond that earned them respect not only for their devotion to each other, but also for their adherence to an ideal of "natural living" that still serves as a model.

The Ladies of Llangollen had a relationship that fired not only the imaginations of other romantics of their time, but resonates even today. One of France's most beloved lesbian authors, Colette, wrote about them in *The Pure and the Impure* (1928), and contemporary authors continue to write loosely fictionalized histories of their love, most notably Doris Grumbach's *The Ladies* (1984) and Morgan Graham's *These Lovers Fled Away* (1988).

References:

Dynes, Wayne R., ed. *Encyclopedia of Homosexuality.* New York: Garland Publishing, 1990.

Mavor, Elizabeth. *The Ladies of Llangollen.* Middlesex, England: Penguin Books, 1973.

Russell, Paul. *The Gay 100: A Ranking of the Most Influential Gay Men and Lesbians, Past and Present.* Secaucus, New Jersey: Citadel Press, 1995.

Summers, Claude J., ed. *The Gay and Lesbian Literary Heritage.* New York: Henry Holt, 1995.

—Jerome Szymczak

Audre Lorde

1934-1992

African-American writer and activist

An international political and social activist, Audre Lorde used transforming incidents in her life to craft her essays and poetry and, in turn, to recreate herself; hence, the truth of her often quoted, "I cannot be categorized." Nonetheless, recognizing through experience the reality of world wide societal categorizations which marginalized, Lorde's confrontation of racism, sexism, and homophobia empowered those many women experiencing personal violence or battling cancer and especially, black women, women of color, and lesbians. A "sister/outsider" as a black lesbian, Lorde's dialogue insisted on inclusion and breaking silences; she contributed generously to build a global women's collective. In 1991 after receiving the Walt Whitman Citation of Merit in Albany, Lorde, speaking as state poet for the State of New York, raised her familiar question "What does it mean for a black, lesbian, feminist, warrior, poet, mother to live in a world full of the most intense contradictions?" The documentary *A Litany for Survival* filmed from 1986 to 1992 conceived by Ada Gay Griffin and directed by Michelle Parkerson records Audre Lorde's own life and work as an answer.

Words Get Her High

Born 18 February 1934, in New York City, Audre Geraldine Lorde was the third daughter born to Linda Balmar and policeman and real estate owner Frederic Byron Lorde, West Indians who emigrated from Grenada to Harlem where, Robert Ridinger asserts in *The Gay & Lesbian Literary Companion*, the young Audre was raised "to fit the mold of many young woman maturing in that metropolitan area." Lorde's upbringing included Catholic schools, where she says, "being smart was sometimes not as important as being good, and I was really bad" (*Litany*). Nevertheless, Lorde, whose near blindness until fitted with glasses at age three or four forced her to observe the world at close range, early on discovered a love of language, especially of poetry. "Words would get me high"; she especially liked the love poems of Edna St. Vincent Millay and would often quote lines of memorized poetry in response to others' questions.

Lorde began writing poetry at twelve or thirteen "because I had a need inside of me to create something that was not here" (*Litany*). At Hunter High School, one poem was considered "much too romantic" for inclusion in the school paper. She triumphed when the poem was published in *Seventeen* (April 1951).

Two weeks after high school graduation, Lorde moved to her own apartment on the Lower East Side; she started classes at Hunter College, had a brief affair which resulted in a terminated pregnancy, and tried various jobs, including factory worker, nurse's aide and domestic cleaner. In 1954, Lorde abandoned the very white "gay girl" scene in Greenwich Village to study at the National University of Mexico where for the first time she was surrounded by brown-skinned people and, most important for her poetry, discovered that words could re-create rather than create her emotional world. Returning to New York, Lorde published "La Llorono" in *Venture* under the pseudonym Rey Domini (Audre Lorde in Latin). The mythical story captures the complex relationship with her mother which is also evident in "Black Mother Woman" in *From a Land Where Other People Live* (1973). With *Zami: A New Spelling of My Name; A Biomythography* (1982), Lorde acknowledges the strong influence of her mother's recounts of her island life ("Zami" is "a Carriacou name for women who work together as friends and lovers," Lorde writes) and stresses the importance of learning from the continuity of historical roots, particularly from other cultures. In this autobiographical novel infused with myth, Lorde traces her adolescence and growing self-awareness and with her lyrical, vivid descriptions breaks the silence about lesbian lovemaking. In *Contemporary Lesbian Writers of the United States*, Elaine Upton identifies "Martha" in *Cables to Rage* (1970) as "an early overtly lesbian poem" (318). In 1972, Lorde read "Love Poem" in an Upper West Side coffeehouse no longer worrying who knew that she had always loved women, as she told Adrienne Rich in "An Interview" first published in *Signs* (1981); after the poem's publication in *Ms*, she posted it on the English Department bulletin board at John Jay College of Criminal Justice, where she was teaching. But Lorde was not always overtly a lesbian.

By 1959, Lorde had earned a B.A. in literature and philosophy from Hunter College where she edited the student magazine *Echo* and met a lifelong friend, historian Blanche Wiesen Cook. By the late 1960s, Cook and her partner Clare Coss formed part of Lorde's women's support network joining her in numerous political and personal activities. After earning a M.L.S. at Columbia University, Lorde served as a librarian at the Mount Vernon [N.Y.] Public Library and the Town School Library in New York City.

"Learning from the 1960s"

Lorde's marriage in 1962 to attorney Edwin Ashley Rollins shocked the women who loved her. But as Cook suggests in *Litany*, women, especially lesbians, married at that time. As Lorde says, "to be a Black woman poet in the 1960s was to be invisible, really invisible ... triple invisible as Black, lesbian and feminist" ("Litany"). Before the interracial couple divorced in 1970, two children, Elizabeth and Jonathan, added "lesbian mother" to Lorde's many dimensions. She raised her children "as warriors, not cannon fodder," Jonathan attests, "she never let us get away with not fighting" (*Litany*). Lorde's essay "Man Child: A Black Lesbian Feminist's Response" collected in *Sister Outsider: Essays and Speeches* (1984) offered understanding to other lesbian mothers facing their sons' manhood. In "Turning the Beat Around: Lesbian Parenting 1986" (*A Burst of Light*), she reflects on learning to control her Black woman's pent up anger and guide her children towards self definition. The dialogue continued in the 1993 *Ms* article "Raising Sons."

Earlier, however, in 1968, amidst her collapsing marriage, Lorde began to achieve some recognition: she won a NEA grant and her first book of poetry, *The First Cities* (1968) was published just after she spent six weeks as poet-in-residence at Tougaloo College, a Black college in Mississippi. Despite her fears, Tougaloo's nurturing environment provided Lorde with her first opportunity to work with Black people. She identified their need for "strong Black people" under their own definitions and offered them her strength and honesty. Most of the poems in *Cables to Rage* were written at Tougaloo. When Lorde left Tougaloo she knew that being a librarian was not enough—she had to teach. She also knew that Frances Clayton, whom she met there, would be a permanent part of her life. For nineteen years, Clayton shared Lorde's house on Staten Island as lover and co-mother to Lorde's children. Martin Luther King's assassination, announced while she listened to her former

Tougaloo students in a concert at Lincoln Center, galvanized her resolve to become more involved.

The publication of her first poetry collection *The First Cities* precipitated another important decision: Lorde began teaching, at first holding several part time positions. She accepted Mina Shaughnessy's invitation to teach in the pre-baccalaureate SEEK writing program at City College. Again terrified, Lorde taught her students as well as herself; with them, she learned prose writing. Teaching "Race and the Urban Situation" in the Education Department at mostly white Herbert H. Lehman College of the City University of New York helped Lorde clarify her responsibility to black students, especially to black women.

Next, she successfully petitioned John Jay College to offer a course on racism as well as a remedial writing course using creative writing. At John Jay, as an open lesbian in the Black community, Lorde again used honesty and openness in heading off her critics. In "Learning from the 60s" (*Sister Outsider)* and again in *Litany*, Lorde stresses that differences must be respected and used for change, a directive she followed in and out of the classroom. With her induction into the Hunter College Hall of Fame in 1980 Lorde capped a distinguished teaching career within the City University of New York. After a decade at John Jay, she moved to Hunter College and subsequently held the Thomas Hunter Professorship; in 1985 students and friends dedicated the Audre Lorde Women's Center on her alma mater's campus.

Teaching a New Generation

Over the next decade Lorde's work as teacher, contributor to journals and poetry editor of *Chrysalis* and *Amazon Quarterly* placed her in the forefront of feminist voices within the academy. In 1972 and again in 1976, she won Creative Artists Public Service Grants. The first supported preparation of *From A Land Where Other People Live*, nominated for the National Book Award along with work by Alice Walker and Adrienne Rich. When Rich received the award she accepted for all three "in the name of all women whose voices have gone and still go unheard in a patriarchal world" (Russell 202). In 1975 Lorde won the Broadside Press Poet's Award and Staten Island Community College named her Woman of the Year. Continuing to teach at John Jay College, Lorde published additional volumes of poetry and essays, including the political poetry in *New York Head Shop and Museum* (1974), *Between Ourselves* (1976), *Coal* (1976), and *The Black Unicorn* (1978). She delivered papers, such as "The Transformation of Silence Into Language and Action" at the Modern Language Association's "Lesbian and Literature" panel in 1977. The Out and Out pamphlet *Uses of the Erotic: The Erotic as Power*, first delivered at the Fourth Berkshire Conference on the History of Women at Mount Holyoke in 1978, asserts the erotic as "the nurturer or nursemaid of all our deepest knowledge" (*Sister Outsider*, 56). In the late 1970s, Lorde and Barbara Smith co-founded Kitchen Table: Women of Color Press in a fusion of politics and art to further women of color's liberation.

Lorde kept personal journals; they provided "seeds" for poems, such as "Harriet," "Suckle," and "The Litany for Survival" all found in *Black Unicorn*. Considered Lorde's most mature poetry the volume has as central motifs the ancient women of Dahomey and repression as a means of control. "Notes from a Trip to Russia" records her observations from the 1976 Africa-Asian Writers Conference in Moscow. This and others of her essays and addresses from 1976 to 1983 are collected in *Sister Outsider: Essays and Speeches* (1984). The book is a classic in women's studies courses and takes its name from a poem in *Black Unicorn* "Sister Outsider" which, as Barbara Christian notes in *The Women's Review of Books* (1984), is a compression of most of Lorde's concerns.

Breaks Another Taboo

The journal entries also proved the source for another book. In 1978, Lorde was diagnosed with breast cancer and, thus, began a fourteen year battle. *The Cancer Journals* (1980), even with its title, meets the disease and the medical profession head on. Lorde documents her mastectomy and subsequent decision not to implant a prosthesis. By now, the formerly "tongue-tied" Lorde could skillfully use language to record the roller coaster ride of her emotions and her outrage at medical assumptions and women's lack of choices. The book won Book of the Year for 1981 from the American Library Association's Gay Task Force. Again Lorde's honest voice led the way in writing about taboo subjects. Her courage and forthrightness about cancer empowered other women to do the same. Paul Russell accurately notes, "Lorde was a fierce truth speaker who influenced a whole generation to see with new eyes" (*Gay 100* 202).

As one expects, cancer did not slow Audre Lorde. If anything, as Jonathan Rollins says of his mother, her "life took on a kind of immediacy; there was a change in the tone of her writing" (*Litany*). On her fiftieth birthday, she wrote in her journal essay "A Burst of Light: Living with Cancer": "Cheers to the years! Doing what I like to do best" (*A Burst of Light* 53); she was at the University of Ohio addressing the Black students. With Gloria I. Joseph, Lorde comothered Sisters in Support of Sisters in South Africa (SISA). By March 1984, however, doctors were urging a liver biopsy; she refused the invasive surgery.

In "Living on the Line," Gloria T. Hull observes that "Place is central in Lorde's work." Indeed, Audre cared deeply about people and the global environment. She traveled to reach across differences, especially internationally. May and June 1984 found her in Berlin teaching a course on black American women poets and leading a workshop in English. She introduced German women of the Diaspora to the word "Afro-German" and encouraged them to organize. Eventually they published *Farabe Bekennen* (*Showing Our Colors*). She read her poetry in Switzerland. While in Berlin she sought advice and treatment from an anthroposophic doctor which continued yearly until shortly before her death. In 1984, Lorde was awarded the Borough of Manhattan President's Award for Literary Excellence. Indefatigable, she visited women writers in Cuba and in August 1985, delivered "The Language of Difference" as the keynote address at a Woman's Writing Conference in Melbourne, Australia, incorporated in the journal essay "A Burst of Light" from *A Burst of Light* (1989) which won the American Book Award.

By November 1985, however, a second anthroposophic doctor recommended Lorde seek treatment at the Lukas Klinik in Arlesheim, Switzerland, where, accompanied by Frances Clayton, Lorde accepted the diagnosis and challenge of living with metastasized cancer. As she said: "Battling cancer is very, very much to me like battling racism, like battling sexism. I often visualize it in very political terms ... [I visualize] cancer cells as white South African policemen" (*Litany*).

In 1986 in St. Croix, Lorde participated in "The Ties that Bind," a conference on Caribbean women and in Bonnieux, France, met with the Zamani Soweto Sisters from South Africa as part of her ongoing work with SISA. As guest professor at the University of Berlin in 1989, Lorde continued her work with Afro-German women.

In 1990 Lorde's life and work were honored and celebrated when over a thousand women from twenty three countries gathered for the "I Am Your Sister" conference in Boston. Nnosing Ellen Kuzwayo, a member of the South African Parliament, addressed Audre, "You have sent your message just through your love, your warmth and everything a human being in the leadership should have" (*Litany*). Other accolades included The Walt Whitman Citation of Merit in 1991 and appointment as the Poet Laureate of New York State by then-Governor, Mario Cuomo. In St. Croix, The Pan African Support Group organized the ceremony at which Lorde received the name Gamba Adisa meaning "warrior, one who give meaning to her words." She continued to write poetry, many collected in *The Marvelous Arithmetics of Distance: Poems 1987-1992* (1993), for as she wrote to women: "Poetry is not a luxury. It is a vital necessity of our experience" (*Sister Outsider*, 37).

She danced until the end; the final poem in the collection is "The Electric Slide Boogie" dated 3 January 1992.

Lorde died on 17 November 1992, in St. Croix where she lived with her companion Dr. Gloria I. Joseph. Since then, the documentary "A Litany for Survival" has been released and in the summer of 1994, the Caribbean Cultural Center African Diaspora Institute saluted her with the exhibit "Transcending Silence: The Life and Poetic Legacy of Audre Lorde." The political legacy of Audre Lorde, as friend Blanche Wiesen Cook reminded at the memorial service held at The Cathedral of St. John the Divine on 18 January 1993, is for "each of us to dedicate our lives to activism ... so that we may reclaim and re-vision the world" (*Transcending Silence* 8).

References:

Christian, Barbara. "Dynamics of Difference" in *The Women's Review of Books I*, August 1984. Excerpted in *Contemporary Literary Criticism*, Volume 71. Detroit: Gale, 1992.

Cook, Blanche Wiesen. "Audre Lorde: Friend of Friends" in *Transcending Silences: The Life and Poetic Legacy of Audre Lorde.* Edited by Gayle Louison and Mora J. Byrd. New York: The Franklin H. Williams Caribbean Cultural Center African Diaspora Institute, 1994. First printed in the Program of Audre Lorde Memorial Service. Cathedral of St. John the Divine, 18 January 1993.

Dictionary of Literary Biography, Volume 41: *Afro-American Poets Since 1955.* Detroit: Gale Research, 1985.

Griffin, Ada Gay, creator, and Michelle Parkerson, director. *A Litany for Survival: The Life and Work of Audre Lorde.* Third World Newsreel, 1995. Referred to as *Litany* in essay.

Hull, Gloria T. "Living on The Line: Audre Lorde and 'Our Dead Behind Us'" in *Changing Our Own Words: Essays on Criticism, Theory and Writing by Black Women.* Edited by Cheryl A. Wall. New Brunswick, New Jersey: Rutgers, 1989. Excerpted in *Contemporary Literary Criticism,* Volume 71. Detroit: Gale, 1992.

"An Interview: Audre Lorde and Adrienne Rich." *Signs* 6, summer 1981. Reprinted in Audre Lorde, *Sister Outsider.* Trumansburg, New York: The Crossing Press, 1984.

Lorde, Audre. *A Burst of Light.* Ithaca, New York: Firebrand Books, 1988.

———. *The Marvelous Arithmetics of Distance: Poems 1987-1992.* New York: Norton, 1993.

———. *Sister Outsider.* Trumansburg, New York: The Crossing Press, 1984.

———. *Uses of the Erotic: The Erotic as Power.* Out and Out Books, 1978 (available through The Crossing Press). Reprinted in *Sister Outsider.*

———. *Zami: A New Spelling of My Name: A Biomythography.* Trumansburg, New York: The Crossing Press, 1982.

Ridinger, Robert. "Audre Lorde" in *The Gay and Lesbian Literary Companion.* Edited by Sharon Malinowski and Christa Brelin. Detroit: Visible Ink Press, 1995.

Russell, Paul. *The Gay 100.* New York: Citadel Press, 1995.

Upton, Elaine. "Audre Lorde" in *Contemporary Lesbian Writers of the United States: A Biobibliographical Critical Sourcebook.* Editor by Sandra Pollack and Denise D. Knight. Westport, Connecticut: Greenwood Press, 1993.

—Judith C. Kohl

Greg Louganis

1960-

American athlete

Greg Louganis is considered by sportswriters, fellow athletes, and fans to be the greatest diver in world history. For over a decade he was unbeatable in diving competitions. He found comfort in the natural athletic finesse of acrobatics and the springboard. The pool was a sanctuary where he could be himself and do what he most enjoyed.

Gregory Efthimios Louganis was born on 29 January 1960, in San Diego, California. His biological parents of Samoan and Northern European ancestry were 15 at the time of Louganis' birth and placed him up for adoption. He was adopted by Peter and Frances Louganis of El Cajon, California. His father, Peter, was a controller for the American Tuna Boat Association in San Diego. Reared in a middle class neighborhood Louganis had a difficult childhood. Because of dyslexia and his dark Samoan complexion he was often ridiculed as a child. Adolescence was a time of confused sexuality, and being adopted he was unsure of parental affection.

Louganis and adopted sister, Despina, took dance lessons as young children. During the dance lessons he was taught to visualize and think through complex routines which would later assist him in performing highly technical dives in competition.

Great Talent Evident Early

Dr. Sammy Lee, a two-time Olympic diving gold medalist, watched Greg Louganis' 1971 AAU Junior Olympics performance at Colorado Springs, Colorado. Afterward Lee stated: "His spring was so much higher than that of any child his age.... He was years ahead of his group." Coached by Dr. Lee in the 1976 Olympics in Montreal, Canada, Louganis captured the silver medal in the platform diving finals and finished sixth in springboard diving.

In 1978, Louganis emerged as a preeminent diver, winning the platform championship at the World Aquatic Championship and the U.S. Diving indoor 1-meter and 10-meter titles. He entered Florida's University of Miami the same year. While attending the university, Louganis captured numerous titles. Since the NCAA

Greg Louganis

had no platform diving event Louganis was restricted to springboard diving, forcing him to concentrate and improve his technique in this area.

The following year Louganis won gold medals in the springboard and platform events at the Pan American Games. He was favored to win both competitions at the 1980 Olympic Games in Moscow, but was prevented from participating by the United States boycott of the games. Louganis transferred to the University of California at Irvine in 1981 to train under coach Ron O'Brien, of the Mission Viejo Nadadores Diving Club.

Under O'Brien's direction Louganis repeated winning both springboard and platform titles in the 1982 World Championships. At the meet he became the first diver in international competition to be awarded scores of a perfect 10 from all seven judges, performing an inward one-and-one-half pike. His front three-and-one-half pike received, 92.07 points, the highest score ever awarded a single dive.

Awarded for Achievements

At the 1984 Olympic Games in Los Angeles Louganis captured gold medals in both the platform and springboard diving events; the first time since 1928 that a male diver captured the title in both events. His score of 710.91 points in the platform diving event made him the first diver to break the 700 point barrier in championship competition. This same year Louganis was given the Sullivan Award naming him the country's amateur athlete of the year. He graduated from the University of California at Irvine in 1983 with a Bachelor of Arts degree in drama. In 1986, he was awarded the Jesse Owens International Trophy and in the following year was named the 1987 USCO Sportsman of the Year.

Louganis held an undefeated string of 3-meter springboard titles from 1981 to 1987 until he took second place at the U.S. Diving Indoor Championships. Louganis won the springboard and platform diving events six years straight at the U.S. Olympic Festival from 1982 through 1987. He repeated as double gold medal winner in both platform and springboard diving at the 1986 Worlds and the 1987 Pan American Games. By August 1988 Louganis had garnered an impressive record of diving victories. He had won 47 of 67 indoor or outdoor U.S. Diving National Championships, went undefeated in Olympic Trials from 1976-88, and won Pan American gold medals a record ten times from 1979-87.

O'Brien trained Greg Louganis for the 1988 Olympic Games in Seoul, South Korea. O'Brien like Dr. Lee, believed that Louganis was the best diver in the history of the sport. Louganis had the rare talent to combine strength, power, and grace in a unique blend that was his trademark. He captured gold medals in both the springboard and platform events for a second consecutive time. In order to capture the gold in platform diving Louganis had to successfully complete a reverse 3½ somersault in the tuck position, the "dive of death." The dive had a degree of difficulty of 3.4, compounded by the fact a Russian diver had died striking his head on the platform, while attempting the dive at the World University Games in Edmonton, Canada. Louganis skillfully hit the dive and won the gold medal.

But the Seoul Olympics would not be one without controversy for Louganis. Early in 1988 he tested HIV-positive and Coach O'Brien was the only person at the games who knew of his HIV status. On the ninth of his eleven qualifying springboard dives Louganis struck his head on the diving board, leaving an open wound. While the risk of HIV transmission was extremely negligible, the attending physician Dr. Puffer was not informed of his status and stitched Louganis' head wound without gloves or adequate precautions.

Following the 1988 Olympic Games, Louganis "lost the water" in diver's terminology. His personal life had been marred by an abusive relationship in the mid 1980s. His manager quickly took over managing Louganis' career and their life, at the same time embezzling most of his money. While Louganis' homosexuality was an open secret in diving circles and his HIV status a guarded secret, it wasn't until the 1994 Gay Games IV in New York that he came out publicly.

Autobiography Proved Cathartic

In 1994, Louganis met author Eric Marcus. He collaborated with Marcus on his autobiography, *Breaking the Surface*, which was a cathartic event for Louganis. In over seventy hours of taped interviews Louganis revealed his bouts of depression, attempted suicide, drug abuse, rape at knife point by a lover, abusive relationships, loss of a loved one to AIDS, and the revelation of his own HIV status. His autobiography showed how he overcame these obstacles with the same grace, prowess, and beauty that signified his diving career. The book soon appeared on the *New York Times* bestseller list and negotiations were underway for a television movie based on the book. Louganis then went on to star in the 1995 Off

Broadway one man show, *The Only Thing Worse You Could Have Told Me.* He also appeared as Darius in the New York production of *Jeffrey,* a play about gay dating and HIV in the 1990s. Delivering the most poignant line in the play Darius states to Jeffrey, "Hate AIDS Jeffrey, not life."

Louganis has set the mark in athletic competition which few other athletes have achieved. He has overcome adversity in his personal life with the same skill and finesse that was the trademark of his diving career. And he has lead the way for a greater understanding of the personal side of AIDS.

Current Address: P.O. Box 4130, Malibu, California 90265-1430.

References:

Biographical Dictionary of American Sports: Basketball and Other Indoor Sports. New York: Greenwood Press, 1989.

Cray, Dan. "Heart of the Diver," in *Time,* 6 March 1995.

Galvin, Peter. "Below the Surface," in *Advocate,* 4 April 1995.

Goff, Michael. "Depth of a Diver," in *Out,* April 1995.

Hickok, Ralph. *Who's Who of Sports Champions: Their Stories and Records.* Boston: Houghton Mifflin Company, 1995.

Louganis, Greg. *Breaking the Surface.* New York: Random House, 1995.

Mallon, Bill. *Quest for Gold: The Encyclopedia of American Olympians.* New York: Leisure Press, 1984.

Polly, John. "Greg Louganis' Wild Ride," in *Genre,* December-January 1996.

Quintanilla, Michael. "The Truth Shall Set You Free," in *Los Angeles Times,* 28 February 1995.

—Michael A. Lutes

JoAnn Loulan

1948-

American psychotherapist and author

JoAnn Loulan is a woman of many hats. She is the author of three books on lesbian sexuality that speak with the candor and humour that have been lacking in the area of lesbian sexual literature. In addition to writing, Loulan is a psychotherapist and travels around the continent, speaking to audiences on issues such as sexuality, women's health care, and the joys of motherhood. She currently resides in the San Francisco area.

JoAnn Loulan was born on 31 July 1948, in the small midwestern town of Bath, Ohio. Her father, James (1919-1985), was a chemist and manager of Goodyear Tire and Rubber. Her mother, Billie (1921-1975), was a registered nurse. Loulan has one sibling, John, who is two years her senior.

Loulan embarked upon her post-secondary education at Northwestern University in Evanston, Illinois, with the intention of pursuing a degree in Theater. However, the climate of the "socially-conscious" 1960s lead Loulan to choose a more practical path. She explains that "theatre was seen as something frivolous when everyone was trying to change the world." In 1975, Loulan received her degree in political science, with minors in history and sociology. She then moved to California and opened up her own clothing shop.

It was at this time in her life that Loulan found herself in therapy. She had come from an alcoholic family. She was not the only one benefiting from therapy in California. "Truman Capote has a great quote about California," Loulan says. "'In California, everybody is a therapist, has a therapist, or is a therapist that has a therapist.'" Through her own personal benefits from therapy, Loulan decided to head back to school. She went to study clinical psychology at Lone Mountain College. ("A Catholic's girl's school," she says with a smile. "My grandmother would have been so happy.")

It was while taking human sexuality that Loulan began to understand her own sexuality and officially came out as a lesbian. Her previous theatrical training made her a natural when it came to speaking before large groups, and not long afterwards, Loulan became a part of the core staff teaching in the Human Sexuality Department at the University of California Medical School at San Francisco.

During this time, Loulan co-authored a successful book for premenstrual girls entitled *Period* (Volcano Press, 1979), along with two of her colleagues—Marcia Quackenbush and Bonnie Sankey. Shortly thereafter, Loulan began to focus her energies on lesbian culture, and realized the immense need for sexual literature in the lesbian community.

Loulan left her position at the university, and began orchestrating weekend lesbian sex courses. Through the success of the workshops and the encouragement of the women who attended them, Loulan completed her first independent book, *Lesbian Sex* (Spinster's Ink, 1984).

In order to promote the book, Loulan traveled to various cities across the country for signings and lectures. Relatively unknown at the time, Loulan recalls her amazement when encountering up to five hundred women in attendance. "All of us were so starved for information regarding lesbian sexuality," she says. "By the time I had written my three books, I often joke that I had written one third of the literature on lesbian sexuality." Those three books include *Lesbian Sex*, *Lesbian Passion* (Spinster's Ink, 1987), and *The Lesbian Erotic Dance* (Spinster's Ink, 1991).

Twelve years have passed since the publication of *Lesbian Sex* and Loulan continues to speak with enthusiastic lesbian audiences on issues of sexuality and self. However, she tries to keep her travels limited to weekends, preferring to stay home during the week and share most of her time with her fourteen year old son.

At age forty-eight in 1996, Loulan had entered what she calls a "new phase" in her life. Three years previous, Loulan was diagnosed with breast cancer. Since that diagnosis, Loulan's lectures and discussions with her audience include an important focus on women's health. It is an area that Loulan feels has been ignored for far too long. "For centuries, women's bodies and sexuality have been used against us," she says. "Sex has been such a weapon against us that celebrating and taking pride in our bodies is seen as a negative thing. I want to change that perception for all women."

In addition, in 1996, Loulan was working on two new books. The first offers a personalized account of her battle with cancer. The second is a collection of humorous memoirs and fond recollections of her life and those who have shared it with her. There is little doubt that these new books will speak with the candid, humorous and warm voice that so distinctively belongs to JoAnn Loulan.

—Brian Francis

Susan M. Love

1948-

American surgeon, oncologist, and social activist

"The most frightening thing about breast problems isn't the possibility of cancer," writes Susan M. Love in *Dr. Susan Love's Breast Book.* "The most frightening thing is not knowing, not understanding what's happening to one's own body. Even the most life threatening situations are less terrifying when people understand what they are facing. Knowledge is power, and most women have been denied real knowledge about their own breasts." Susan Love, one of the country's leading breast surgeons, has made it her mission to give women this knowledge. Her efforts have earned her a reputation for being a controversial critic of the medical establishment's treatment of women, a tireless activist for increased funding for breast cancer research, and have made her, arguably, the best-known lesbian physician in the country.

Born in Long Branch, New Jersey, on 9 February 1948, Susan Margaret Love was the oldest of Peggy and James Love's five children. James Love worked as a salesman for Eaton machinery, and due to company transfers, Love spent her teenage years first in Puerto Rico and then in Mexico City, where she received her high school diploma.

Love began her pre-med studies at the College of Notre Dame of Maryland, in Baltimore. After completing her sophomore year, Love had second thoughts about becoming a doctor and explored the possibility of becoming a nun by entering the School Sisters of Notre Dame convent in New York City. But Love's desire to become a nun proved short-lived, and she left the convent six months later to attend Fordham University in New York City. "I wanted to save the world," Love explained to Molly O'Neill in the 29 June 1994 *New York Times,* "but they wanted to save their own souls."

In 1970, Love entered medical school at the State University of New York, Downstate Medical Center, in Brooklyn. At the time, most medical schools admitted only one woman for every nine men into each incoming class, a fact Love accepted. "I wasn't political; I was a nerd," she told O'Neill. "I've always been mainstream, pretty conservative."

A Career Becomes a Mission

Love received her M.D. in 1974, graduating *cum laude* and fourth in her class. She completed her medical training in the surgical residency program at Beth Israel Hospital in Boston, and in 1980 she opened her private practice. During those six years Love became increasingly aware that, as a woman, she brought a unique perspective to the male-dominated field of surgery in general and to breast cancer treatment in particular. "I was sent women patients with breast cancer, and I realized they were not being given all their options," Love explained to Kathleen Neumeyer in the April 1995 *Los Angeles Magazine.* "Doctors weren't taking the time to explain things to them. They were scared, and they were not being well-handled. I began to see this was an area where I could make a difference. What started out as a career became a mission."

After a year in private practice, Love was hired as the breast surgeon for the Breast Evaluation Clinic of the Dana Farber Cancer Institute, in Boston. Shortly thereafter, she began to attract attention both inside and outside the medical establishment for her controversial views. As lead author of "Fibrocystic 'Disease' of the Breast: A Nondisease?" (*New England Journal of Medicine,* October 1982), she disputed the link between "fibrocystic disease" and breast cancer and clearly demonstrated that "fibrocystic disease" was not, in fact, a disease at all. And at conferences and in the media, she began to publicly criticize the widespread use of radical mastectomies to treat breast cancer. An advocate of less invasive surgeries, Love argued that surgeons often performed mastectomies because these were the operations they had been trained to do, not because they were needed.

Love's critique of the medical establishment benefitted women's health care, but Love's criticisms disturbed many of the physicians in her field. "Dr. Love constantly challenges dogma," Dr. Jay Harris, a radiation oncologist and professor at Harvard University who has known Dr. Love for more than 15 years, told O'Neill. "Surgeons aren't supposed to do that. Susan makes many surgeons uncomfortable."

Harvard Medical School appointed Love an assistant professor of surgery in 1987, and the following year she founded the Faulkner Breast Centre, a surgical practice affiliated with Faulkner Hospital and the Dana Farber Cancer Institute in Boston. Shortly thereafter, in 1992, Love was offered the coveted position of director of the Revlon-UCLA Breast Center at the University of California at Los Angeles. Along with her work as a surgeon and activist, Love teaches medical students, lectures to women's groups and health care professionals throughout the country, and frequently appears on television and radio shows. In all the work that she does, she is open about her sexual orientation. "I feel an obligation to be out," she told Elizabeth Gleick in the 25 July 1994 *People Weekly.* "It helps others. I like to change the world and fix it."

First Book Becomes Best-Selling "Bible"

Love's reputation grew widely with the publication, in 1990, of *Dr. Susan Love's Breast Book.* The first book that clearly explained common breast problems and the diagnosis and treatment of breast cancer to a lay audience, it was highly praised in the medical and mainstream press. *Dr. Susan Love's Breast Book* quickly became a bestseller and is often referred to as "the bible of women with breast cancer."

The publication of Love's book coincided with the advent of the breast cancer movement. In the late 1980s, motivated by the statistic that one in eight women would be diagnosed with breast cancer in their lifetime as well as by the work of AIDS activists, women had begun organizing support and advocacy groups for women with breast cancer. In 1991, Love cofounded the Washington, D.C.-based National Breast Cancer Coalition (NBCC), an umbrella organization formed to unite the activities of these cancer projects and to help start new groups throughout the country. By 1995, more than 250 grassroots feminist and lesbian cancer projects existed nationwide.

Susan Love

"Many of the women in the coalition have never been involved in political action before," Love wrote in *Dr. Susan Love's Breast Book,* "and they're finding themselves working side by side with baby boomers who marched in the 1960s and learned the value of political protest—and now are confronting breast cancer, and realizing that like civil rights and war resistance and the early women's movement issues, breast cancer research needs to be fought for." And their fight has been successful. The national budget for breast cancer research and prevention has increased nearly fivefold, from $90 million in 1990 to $420 million in 1994.

Love believed that when she completed medical school she would then begin her search for a husband. But when the time came, she told Gleick: "It occurred to me that I really wasn't interested in a man. They're perfectly fine for sleeping with, I just didn't want to spend the rest of my life with one."

In 1982, a few years after this realization, Love remet a lesbian friend from medical school, Dr. Helen Cooksey. That September, Cooksey invited Love to spend a weekend with her at a cabin in New Hampshire, and they have been together since. In 1988, Love gave birth to the couple's daughter, Katie, who was conceived through sperm donated by Cooksey's first cousin. In 1993, after a four-year battle to have both women legally recognized as Katie's parents, Massachusetts' highest court, in a precedent-setting decision, granted Love and Cooksey joint adoption rights to their daughter. At the time, only three other states had permitted similar adoptions.

The second edition of *Dr. Susan Love's Breast Book* was published in 1995, and her second book, *Dr. Susan Love's Hormone Book,* for women approaching menopause, is scheduled for publication in 1997. Additional writings include 19 journal articles and chapters in seven books. She is active in many national organizations and committees, including the Lesbian Health Foundation, the Journal of the American Medical Women's Association, and the National Institutes of Health Women's Health Initiative Program Advisory Committee. Love has received three honorary doctoral degrees and numerous awards for her activism on behalf of women with breast cancer from groups ranging from the Canadian Women's Breast Cancer Foundation and the American Medical Writer's Association to two prominent national gay and lesbian organizations, the Human Rights Campaign and the Gay and Lesbian Medical Association.

By combining the seemingly disparate lives of a doctor and an activist, Love has had a tremendous impact on the public's knowledge of breast cancer. And she will undoubtedly be at the forefront of the breast cancer movement until there is a cure. "The way things have changed in breast cancer treatment has not been because the medical profession thought it was a good idea," Love told Laura Briggs in the 3 June 1990 *Gay Community News.* "Things have changed because women have wanted them to change. We just have to keep it up."

References:

Briggs, Laura. "Organizing for Women's Health," in *Gay Community News,* 3 June 1990: 1.

Gleick, Elizabeth. "Susan Love: A Surgeon Crusades Against Breast Cancer," in *People Weekly,* 25 July 1994: 147.

Graham, Judith, ed. *Current Biography Yearbook.* New York: H. W. Wilson Company, 1994.

Love, Susan M., with Karen Lindsey. *Dr. Susan Love's Breast Book.* 2nd ed. Massachusetts: Addison-Wesley, 1995.

O'Neill, Molly. "A Surgeon's War on Breast Cancer," in *New York Times,* 29 June 1994: C1, C12.

Neumeyer, Kathleen. "LA Hope," in *Los Angeles Magazine,* April 1995: 58.

—Susan Rochman

Amy Lowell

1874-1925

American poet

At the time of her death in 1925, Amy Lowell was a formidable figure in American and British literary circles. Twenty years later she had been largely forgotten, a handful of her poems (primarily "Patterns" and "Lilacs") appearing in the occasional anthology of American verse. Since the mid-1970s, however, several critical and biographical studies have re-appraised Lowell in the context of her preeminent place in the influential imagist movement. More re-

Amy Lowell

cently, Lowell's poetry has been celebrated as an eloquent example of what Lillian Faderman terms in the anthology *Chloe Plus Olivia* "the literature of lesbian encoding."

Amy Lowell was born on 9 February 1874 in Brookline, Massachusetts, the daughter of Augustus and Katherine Lawrence Lowell. Her education and upbringing were that of the privileged daughter of a socially prominent, affluent Boston family. Although Lowell's formal schooling ended at the age of seventeen, she continued to read voraciously from the 7,000-book library of Sevenels, the ten-acre estate she was to occupy all her life. By her late twenties, Lowell had embarked on a literary career as poet and critic.

Lowell and the Imagists

The year 1912 was pivotal for Lowell. Shortly after completing the manuscript for her first published book of poems, *A Dome of Many-Colored Glass*, Lowell became acquainted with the work of the French symbolists and, most significantly, with the poetry of T. E. Hulme and Ezra Pound and the so-called imagist movement. Lowell became a fervent spokesperson for this "new poetry." Although she and Pound later quarrelled, her poems continued to reflect a break with Victorian sentimentality in their use of free verse, common speech, and clear and precise word pictures, all characteristics of the imagist school.

It was also in 1912 that Lowell met Ada Dwyer Russell, a successful actress 11 years her senior. Variously described in accounts of the time as Lowell's travelling companion, helpmate, secretary, and friend, Russell was without question the most important person in her life. Her relationship with Russell inspired much of Lowell's later poetry and formed a basis for Lillian Faderman's studies as well as Cheryl Walker's perceptive chapter on Lowell ("Amy Lowell and the Androgynous Persona") in her book *Masks Outrageous and Austere*.

In Her Prime

From 1912 to 1925, Lowell occupied a central role in American and English literary life, lecturing, editing, mentoring younger writers, and publishing several volumes of criticism as well as a massive biography of Keats. In addition to Pound, she formed long-standing friendships with D. H. Lawrence, Thomas Hardy, and Robert Frost. Above all, she was a prolific and popular poet, the volumes *Sword Blades and Poppy Seed*, *Pictures of the Floating World*, and *What's O'Clock* (for which she received the Pulitzer Prize in 1926) being notable examples of her mature work.

Lowell's celebrity during these years was doubtless enhanced by her public persona. She dressed in severely tailored coats, smoked small Manila cigars, wore a pince-nez, and affected a certain *noblesse oblige*. She was aggressive and tireless in promoting her literary causes and did not suffer kindly those who opposed her. Lowell's industry and tenacity are the more remarkable considering the ill-health that marked her later years.

Lowell died of a stroke in 1925 at the age of 51. Russell, to whom she left her home and fortune in trust, served as literary executor for three books of poems published posthumously. Russell died in 1952.

Poems That Celebrate Love

The "Two Speak Together" section of *Pictures of the Floating World* reveals in a series of love poems the range of Lowell's feelings towards her beloved. Although Russell is never named, there is little doubt it is she to whom Lowell is speaking. In her study *Surpassing the Love of Men*, Lillian Faderman recounts a letter sent by Lowell to her friend John Livingston Lowes, who had admired the depiction of Russell: "I am very glad indeed that you liked 'Madonna of the Evening Flowers,' " writes Lowell. "How could so exact a portrait remain unrecognized?"

Although "Madonna" is perhaps the best-known of these lyrics, others depict a wide range of emotion, from the passion of "Opal" ("You are ice and fire,/ The touch of you burns my hands like snow ") to the melancholy harmony of "Penumbra":

And my love will go on speaking to you
Through the chairs and the tables and the pictures,
As it does now through my voice,
And the quick, necessary touch of my hand.

Relegated to relative obscurity soon after her death, Lowell has emerged as a significant and influential figure in the canon of twentieth century lesbian literature. As Cheryl Walker writes in *Masks Outrageous and Austere*, "At her best, Lowell's poems have psychological resonance, lyric beauty and a courageous, recognizable voice."

References:

Benvenuto, Richard. *Amy Lowell.* Boston: Twayne Publishers, 1985.
Damon, S. Foster. *Amy Lowell: A Chronicle.* Boston: Houghton Mifflin, 1935.

Faderman, Lillian. *Chloe Plus Olivia: An Anthology of Lesbian Literature from the Seventeenth Century to the Present.* New York: Viking, 1994.

Faderman, Lillian. *Surpassing the Love of Men: Romantic Friendship and Love between Women from the Renaissance to the Present.* New York: William Morrow, 1981.

Gould, Jean. Amy: *The World of Amy Lowell and the Imagist Movement.* New York: Dodd, Mead & Company, 1975.

Lowell, Amy. *The Complete Poetical Works.* Boston: Houghton Mifflin, 1955.

Ruihley, Glenn Richard. *The Thorn of a Rose: Amy Lowell Reconsidered.* Hamden, Ct.: Archon Books, 1975.

Walker, Cheryl. *Masks Outrageous and Austere: Culture, Psyche, and Personal in Modern Woman Poets.* Bloomington: Indiana University Press, 1991.

—David Garnes

Charles Ludlam

1943-1987

American playwright, performer, and producer

Charles Ludlam was one of the most influential gay theater artists of the twentieth century. A favorite of the gay subculture which thrived in Greenwich Village during the 1970s and 1980s, he provided a venue where gay audiences could laugh at themselves and revel in the outrageousness of their own community. As co-founder and director of the Ridiculous Theatrical Company, he created the first openly gay aesthetic: one which combines burlesque, vaudeville, outrageous campy humor, and cross-dressing to parody major artistic genres.

Charles Ludlam was born in Floral Park, New York on 12 April 1943, the middle son of Joseph William Ludlam and Marjorie Braun. He grew up on Long Island, where he frequented the movie houses and developed an interest in classic films. Ludlam also developed an early love for theatricality and became fond of secretly dressing up in his mother's clothes, a practice which would serve him well later when he would become one of the most skilled drag performers of the time. The close proximity of New York City provided an opportunity for Ludlam to occasionally attend avant-garde theater performances which also helped to shape his unique artistic vision.

In 1958 Ludlam learned more about the behind-the-scenes workings of theater during a brief apprenticeship with a local summer stock company. He was fascinated by the communication opportunities theater provided and decided to make his career in the field. Fortunately, Ludlam not only had the interest but also the talent and was able to earn an acting scholarship to Hofstra University, which he entered in 1961. During his years at Hofstra he began to develop his own outrageous campy acting style—much to the chagrin of his professors. It was also during his college years that Ludlam realized he was homosexual and after graduation moved to New York City and became immersed in the gay subculture which thrived in Greenwich Village.

In 1966 playwright Ronald Tavel and director John Vaccaro founded the Play-House of the Ridiculous, and Ludlam made his first New York stage appearance as Peeping Tom in the company's premiere production, *The Life of Lady Godiva.* Ludlam's second production with the company, *Screen Test,* gave him the opportunity to give his first public drag performance. Soon after *Screen Test*, Tavel and Vaccaro decided to go their separate ways, so Vaccaro began to look for new playwrights. He turned to Ludlam who was working on a play entitled *Big Hotel.* Vaccaro planned on staging the piece with Ludlam as the lead, but this was not to be. Unable to control Ludlam's penchant for flamboyant improvisation, Vaccaro fired him in the middle of rehearsals. Half of the cast walked out with him and convinced Ludlam to stage the play himself. They also elected him leader of their newly formed troupe and thus, the Ridiculous Theatrical Company was born.

Bluebeard Garners Critical Success

At first, the Ridiculous Theatrical Company was little more than a vagabond troupe, moving from venue to venue, staging their brand of flamboyant, avant-garde comedy. With their production of *Bluebeard* in 1970, however, they gained critical and financial success. The play was originally presented at Christopher's End bar in New York City, but the production's popularity subsequently lead to an acclaimed European tour and the troupe's first support from the New York State Arts Council and the National Endowment for the Arts. *Bluebeard* also earned a Guggenheim playwrighting fellowship for Ludlam.

Charles Ludlam

In 1973 Ludlam performed a role which would become his signature piece: the title role in his own version of *Camille*. Over the next seven years he would perform the role over 500 times, taking audiences from laughter to tears with his sensitive drag portrayal of the courtesan who dies of tuberculosis. It solidified Ludlam's reputation as a drag performer of brilliant stature. His performance was so polished that many forgot they were watching a man portraying a woman, even though he performed the role with his hairy chest showing out from under his low-cut dress.

Throughout the 1970s Ludlam continued to develop his performance and playwrighting skills, staging productions which reflected his passion for the gay subculture through the use of campy humor and gender-bending. In 1975 Ludlam met Everett Quinton, the man who would become his life-long companion. Quinton joined the company the following year and worked side-by-side with Ludlam to help foster his vision of theater. The Ridiculous Theatrical Company still struggled financially, however, until 1978 when Ludlam produced the popular *The Ventriloquist's Wife*. This production toured successfully throughout the United States and provided the means for the Ridiculous to gain a permanent home at the Sheridan Square Theater.

In 1984 Ludlam presented the play for which he would become most well-known: *The Mystery of Irma Vep*. The play is a spoof of gothic horror films which requires lightning-fast costume changes, as two performers play all of the characters which people the mysterious Hillcrest mansion. Ludlam and Quinton starred in the premiere production which became an instant hit. *Irma Vep* was subsequently produced by many regional theaters throughout the United States and became Ludlam's most widely produced play both nationally and internationally. Throughout the following years Ludlam continued to develop the repertory of the Ridiculous Theatrical Company, writing and producing plays which were often adaptations of classic literature or spoofs of classic genres such as: *Medea*, *Salammbô* (an adaptation of Gustav Flaubert's novel), and *The Artificial Jungle* (a suspense thriller). He also expanded his own artistic influence through teaching, working with numerous other theater companies, and working in television and film. In early 1987 he completed a major role in the motion picture *The Big Easy*.

Ludlam's Legacy Lives On

On 28 May 1987 Ludlam died of AIDS-related pneumonia at the age of 44. He had learned of his illness only a few months earlier. Right up to the time of his death he continued to work on his many projects, the latest of which was a new play about the life of Harry Houdini entitled *Houdini, A Piece of Pure Escapism*. During his brief life, Ludlam wrote twenty-nine plays, received numerous awards, and became one of the most influential gay theater artists of his time. Over one thousand people attended a memorial service in his honor. Ludlam's legacy lives on in the work of the Ridiculous Theatrical Company which continues to produce campy "Ludlamesque" comedies under the direction of Everett Quinton. In his own manifesto of "Ridiculous Theater" Ludlam states: "You are a living mockery of your own ideals. If not, you have set your ideals too low." This was never a problem for Ludlam. He was able to recognize the absurdity of the human condition, to laugh at himself, and to share that laughter with his community. He forged a new gay aesthetic which has been passed on to the theater artists of today.

In the forward to John Clum's anthology *Staging Gay Lives: An Anthology of Contemporary Gay Theater*, Tony Kushner honors Ludlam as being the "great antecedent" of gay theater artists and praises him as being "the funniest man who ever lived."

References:

Bartlett, Neil. "Just Ridiculous" in *American Theater*, April 1990: 50-51.

Davy, Kate. "Fe/male Impersonation: The Discourse of Camp" in *Critical Theory and Performance.* Edited by Janelle G. Reinelt and Joseph R. Roach. Ann Arbor: University of Michigan Press, 1992.

Gerard, Jeremy. "Charles Ludlam is Eulogized By Friends from the Theater" in *New York Times*, 14 July 1987: D:27.

Gerard, Jeremy. "Charles Ludlam, 44, Avant-Garde Artist of the Theater is Dead" in *New York Times*, 29 May 1987: A1.

Kushner, Tony. "Foreword: Notes Toward a Theater of the Fabulous" in *Staging Gay Lives: An Anthology of Contemporary Gay Theater.* Edited by John M. Clum. Boulder, Colorado: Westview Press, 1996.

Ludlam, Charles. *The Complete Plays of Charles Ludlam.* Edited by Steven Samuels and Everett Quinton. New York: Harper and Row, 1989.

———. "Manifesto: Ridiculous Theater, Scourge of Human Folly" in *Ridiculous Theater: Scourge of Human Folly, the Essays and Opinions of Charles Ludlam.* Edited by Steven Samuels. New York: Theater Communications Group, 1982; reprinted in *The Complete Plays of Charles Ludlam.*

———. *Ridiculous Theater: Scourge of Human Folly, the Essays and Opinions of Charles Ludlam.* Edited by Steven Samuels. New York: Theater Communications Group, 1992.

Rothstein, Mervyn. "Everett Quinton's Life After Ludlam" in *New York Times*, 20 January 1989: C3.

Shewey, Don. "Gay Theater Grows Up" in *American Theater*, May 1988: 11-17+.

—Beth A. Kattelman

Phyllis Ann Lyon

1924-

American writer and activist

Del Martin

1921-

American writer and activist

For well over forty years, two American women have stood for much that is insightful, brave, pioneering, and progressive in the development of a successful lesbian community in the United States: Phyllis Lyon and Del Martin of San Francisco.

Though born in Tulsa, Oklahoma, Lyon was raised and educated primarily in the San Francisco area. Martin is a San Francisco native. Both concentrated on journalism as a career, with courses and newspaper posts at both San Francisco State and the University of California at Berkeley. At both institutions, they held editorial positions at the campus newspapers. There followed work on trade publications in architecture and building in both Seattle and San Francisco. Additionally, Lyon attained a Doctor of Education degree in human sexuality at Berkeley.

When she was just 19, Martin married James Martin. They had one daughter and were subsequently divorced. Lyon has never married. From the time when they really formed their lesbian partnership, on 14 February 1953, Lyon and Martin have been unceasing in their activities to change the self-understanding of lesbians from the perverted, guilt-ridden, oppressed persona that most homosexual women of that time maintained to that of the healthful, proud, assertive, lesbians of today. In the process of their own self-revision, Lyon and Martin led other women out of the closet, gradually eliminating the stigma stamped on them by a homophobic society and replacing it with a new identity of pride and social validity.

Organized the Daughters of Bilitis

It must be remembered, however, that the beginning of the change was small, informal, and even somewhat furtive. In the early 1950s, when the scourge of McCarthyism was rampant in the nation, exposure of any gay person's homosexuality was as sought after as a revelation of association with communism. Gay groups such as the early Mattachine often felt only marginally safe even behind drawn shades in supposedly private homes. In this atmosphere, the beginning of a secret society of lesbians was a little party of eight women meeting in Lyon and Martin's apartment in a Castro neighborhood that was still far from being an internationally famous gay enclave.

By the fourth meeting, a name for the group was seen as necessary, and one member suggested Daughters of Bilitis. Bilitis was identified from a long love poem by the French writer Piere Louys (1870-1925). She was supposed to have lived on the island of Lesbos at the time of lesbian poet Sappho (600 B.C.). The name had an appropriateness for the group and could also be thought a sly screen because it sounded as innocuous as any other "ladies' lodge." The organization became familiarly known as DOB.

After a first year of working out rules and regulations, the DOB brought out the first issue of the *Ladder,* a twelve-page mimeographed magazine, with Lyon as editor. This publication asserted the DOB's purpose: to help lesbians discover their potential and place in society. Specifically, it would assist the lesbian in her search for her personal, interpersonal, social, economic, and vocational identity.

The fame of the *Ladder* and the DOB spread. At the crest of its fame and influence, there were chapters of the DOB in Chicago, Boston, New Orleans, Reno, Portland, San Diego, Cleveland, Denver, Detroit, Philadelphia, and even Melbourne, Australia. In the early 1960s, the DOB gained greater notice throughout the country, beginning with its first national convention in San Francisco in 1960.

In the immediately following years, the DOB was active everywhere in encouraging lesbians to come out and in preparing for legal changes, enlisting support from such politicos as Philip Burton, at that time a member of the California Legislature. Lyon and Martin today believe that the first convention and the later founding of the Council on Religion and the Homosexual are among the highest points in their careers in the advancement of lesbian status.

The protest of the CRH against the police conduct at the New Year's Ball on 1 January 1965, where such tactics as the photographing of all entering and other acts of intimidation were utilized, marked a powerful first in organized condemnation of the harassment of gay and lesbian people. The spectacle of organized religion rebuking the police was an astonishing development.

Episcopal Bishop James A. Pike named Martin and Don Lucas of the Mattachine Society to a Joint Committee on Homosexuality from the Diocesan Departments of Ministry and Social Relations. A major result was an endorsement of homosexual law reform, along with a denouncement of entrapment procedures and an assertion of the need for a broad sex education program for clergy and laity alike. Another important consequence was support from the Northern California Council of Churches for the elimination of the anti-sodomy law.

Clashes with Gay and Feminist Movements

A recurring irritant to active lesbians during the 1960s and 1970s was the tendency of gay male groups to marginalize lesbians. Such groups as the DOB were ignored, their achievements disregarded. Martin points out that even such reputable figures as the historian Martin Duberman gave next to no attention to such events as the first DOB convention. Finally, in some disgust, Martin published an article called "Goodbye, My Alienated Brothers" in an autumn 1970 *Advocate* (the national gay news magazine). The following statement was typical: "Goodbye the male chauvinists of the homophile movement who are so wrapped up in the 'cause' they represent that they have lost sight of the people for whom the cause came into being."

Today, Martin feels that the piece was quite true at the time of publication and is, even now, not without relevance, though relations between the gay sexes have improved. "The situation now," she stated in interview, "is that in times of crisis, the two sexes unite in effort. And since 1980, the accepted practice of using the phrase 'gay and lesbian' has diminished the assumption that 'gay' is all inclusive."

Lyon and Martin have also seen through difficult relations between lesbians and the National Organization for Women. DOB's leaders did not find an immediate response for the women's movement even from lesbians themselves. Lyon and Martin point out that many members of the homophile movement and the women's movement found themselves torn between the two, citing Barbara Gittings and Kay Tobin especially. But the most adamant single opponent to lesbians in the women's movement was NOW's original leader and longtime reigning high priestess, Betty Friedan. When in 1969 Martin wrote to Friedan suggesting that NOW take a definite stand on the lesbian issue in its March national conference, Friedan did not reply.

Lyon and Martin point out that this reticence was, in a way, to be expected, given the long history of male rejection of NOW or any other effort of women to achieve equality by simply calling such women "dykes." But gradually, the women of NOW came to realize that many of the members, including some in leadership positions, were lesbians.

Resolution of the conflict came when some 750 delegates to the 1971 conference of the National Organization for Women in Los Angeles voted overwhelmingly that "a woman's right to her own

Del Martin and Phyllis Lyon (l-r)

person includes the right to define and express her own sexuality and to choose her own life style" and that "the oppression of Lesbians is a legitimate concern of feminism."

Expanding Public Understanding of Lesbian Issues

Such statements reflect the change that swept the gay movement for both men and women in the post-Stonewall period. From the drive for rights and decent tolerance, the more militant activists of both sexes demanded liberation. This difference is strong in Lyon and Martin's 1973 book, *Lesbian Love and Liberation.* They state now that this volume should be thought of as "The Yes Book on Sex." Also, the inclusion of pictures was an advancement.

Other developments demonstrated that Lyon and Martin were involved in a wider variety of feminist issues. Martin's 1976 book *Battered Wives* asserts that liberation of women must include recognition of injustice against spouses, including those in both heterosexual and gay unions.

But the work which is their greatest contribution to lesbianism is still *Lesbian/Woman,* which first appeared in 1972 and was re-published with updates in a special Twentieth Anniversary Edition in 1992. In the introduction, Lyon and Martin are emphatic that while there can probably never be a definitive or a truly objective book on the Lesbian, they believe that a representation of the experiences of lesbian life, expressed in lesbians' own terms and in the context of lesbians' own self awareness, is the best single means for bringing understanding of lesbian nature to all who need to know it.

They set about accomplishing this goal by first differentiating between myth and reality through describing their own discoveries and then showing how diverse lesbians can be in our own society and other cultures of the world, correcting stereotypes and misinterpretations enroute.

Similarly, descriptions of the development of self-image in Martin's own experience, compared with those of other lesbian observations, demonstrates how the growth of a lesbian's psychological self is little different from that of heterosexuals. But here too those influences which distort and therefore warp the psyche are excoriated. The authors conclude this chapter on the lesbian's evolution of her own identity with this observation, "she must find her own destiny out of her own guts."

"What do lesbians do sexually?" With that arresting question, the authors open their chapter on sexuality and sex roles. Their multi-faceted answer is candid and helpful, including a blunt warning against such chauvinist distortions as those of Dr. David Reuben in his *Everything You Always Wanted to Know About Sex but Were Afraid to Ask.* As for social stereotypes of "butch" and "femme," Lyon and Martin's familiarity with many different lesbians in a wide variety of situations, including therapeutic ones, affirm that such role playing is followed in only a minority of pairings.

The chapter "Life Styles" explores the relationships of major life components, such as matings, vocations, families, races, and scenes for socialization. After a review of all influential aspects, Lyon and Martin conclude that "Lesbians are pretty much the same around the world." But the reader is well prepared for that statement by a thorough and often vivid depiction of individual cases. The next chapter extends the life styles consideration to include the role of mothering.

In "Growing Up Gay," Lyon and Martin delineate the needs and problems of girls realizing their lesbianism and trying to act on it in a fulfilling way. The most difficult hurdles facing emerging lesbian young women involve their family relationships. Much of this chapter is straightforward advice to both the girls and their parents. A major warning for parents is to not immediately run to a psychiatrist, especially since many of these therapists are ill-informed and ill-suited to be truly therapeutic to such troubled young women.

In "Lesbian Paranoia—Real and Imagined" Lyon and Martin explore the differences between the two states of mind, carefully advising the use of a positive self image coupled with a growing understanding of how the individual can change. The concluding advice is to be "honest about yourself" and make decisions on that basis.

One of the main advantages for lesbians today, Lyon and Martin affirm, is that there are organizations which provide a social-psychological context which gives strength to a developing identity. While they hold to civilized processes vital to a democratic society, they certainly do not devalue the defiant militancy that appeared after Stonewall, citing the example of an eastern U.S. group called the Lesbian Avengers, who marshalled gay power to defeat a statewide anti-gay initiative in Idaho.

For the twentieth anniversary edition of *Lesbian Woman,* Lyon and Martin have wisely added an update which combines carefully selected anecdotal pieces and mini-histories of developments showing the presence of lesbian influence in many fields of endeavor. Typical is the story of Miriam Ben-Shalom, who made blazingly clear her self identity as a "radical Lesbian feminist" in the U.S. Army Reserve and fought court battles to stay in the service as a constitutional right. Similarly, the growth of lesbian influence in the arts of comedy, music, theater, film, and video is well-documented. Health matters, such as a discussion of Chronic Fatigue Syndrome and cancer, the latter as a "silent crisis," are also reviewed. Most important to both lesbians and gay men, the AIDS epidemic and its consequences are discussed.

Gay and lesbian events that have become international institutions are traced in genesis, development, and preservation. The Gay Olympics is a prime example, with the authors recapitulating how the games originated in the vision and drive of Dr. Tom Waddell, were extended in four-year intervals, and had to suffer the ignominy of being refused the use of the term "Olympic" by U.S. court order because Congress had made the term the property of the Oympic Committee. Nevertheless, the Gay Games go on in much the same spirit as the original. The authors captured this spirit when they described the feelings of the spectators when the participants were formed on the field of Kezar Stadium at the 1982 games, "everyone at the ceremonies was moved emotionally by the pride of belonging to a Lesbian/Gay extended family that encompasses the planet."

Concluding their update, Lyon and Martin outline a "Lesbian Agenda for the 1990s." Applauding the growing movement to come out, the authors see the appearance of new leaders among many groups, ethnic and youth organizations especially, as a great harbinger, advising followers and supporters to "develop and treasure our new leaders."

Far from diminishing their activities, Lyon and Martin remain busy as ever in the mid-1990s. They have their own company, LyMar Associates, an agency for consultation, writing, and lecture sponsorship. Reflecting their own age, but also pioneering for the lesbian movement as a whole, they now are deeply involved in "old lesbians organizing for change," as they put it.

Current Address: 651 Duncan St., San Francisco, California 94131; telephone: (415) 824-2790.

References:

D'Emilio, John. *Sexual Politics, Sexual Communities.* Chicago: University of Chicago Press, 1983.

Lyon, Phyllis and Del Martin. Interview with Marvin S. Shaw, 17 October 1996.

———. *Lesbian/Woman* (Twentieth Anniversary Edition). Volcano, California: Volcano Press, 1991.

Sue, Eleanor and Pam Walton. *Forty Years of Women's Herstory* (video). Sue Walton Productions, 1996.

—Marvin S. Shaw

Robert Mapplethorpe

1946-1989

American photographer

It is unfortunate that Robert Mapplethorpe is probably remembered more for the controversy that surrounded his photographs than he is for the work itself. The photos with a theme of homosexual sadomasochism, which are unflinching in their stark reality and at the same time tempered by their classical arrangement, sparked a national debate over censorship and public funding of the arts. There was also debate among critics, some of whom felt Mapplethorpe's popularity was due to his notoriety rather than a technical or artistic complexity. Those photographs represent only a small portion of the work he produced, however, and his photos of flowers and celebrities are often quite beautiful in their straightforward simplicity.

One of six children, Robert Mapplethorpe was born in Floral Park, New York, to Harry and Joan Mapplethorpe on 4 November 1946. He had a rather strict Catholic upbringing that, according to the photographer, accounted for the symmetry that appeared in the arrangement of so many of his photos. Wanting to be free of his parents' judgement, Mapplethorpe left home at the age of 16 to begin studying drawing, painting, and sculpture at Brooklyn's Pratt Institute.

It was while he was a student that Mapplethorpe met Patti Smith, who was accidentally given directions to his apartment when looking for another Pratt student. It was the beginning of a long and strangely symbiotic relationship. Smith's androgynous looks appealed to Mapplethorpe, who had already begun struggling with his sexuality. After a second chance meeting, Smith moved into Mapplethorpe's apartment, and eventually the pair found a place together in Brooklyn.

Smith: Mapplethorpe's Missing Half

Although their relationship was unrewarding sexually, Mapplethorpe and Smith helped to fuel each other's creativity. When Mapplethorpe declared that working at the F. A. O. Schwarz toy store was leaving him too drained to work on his art projects, Smith took on the responsibility of supporting them both with her job at the Scribner's bookstore. For his part, Mapplethorpe thought Smith was a genius, and his admiration infused her with confidence.

Smith had begun to see another man, informing Mapplethorpe that she was moving out. There was now nothing to keep him from pursuing the homosexual liaisons that he craved, and friends were surprised at the rapidity with which he embraced a gay lifestyle. When Smith's relationship fell apart, however, the pair moved back in together, although they continued to lead separate sex lives.

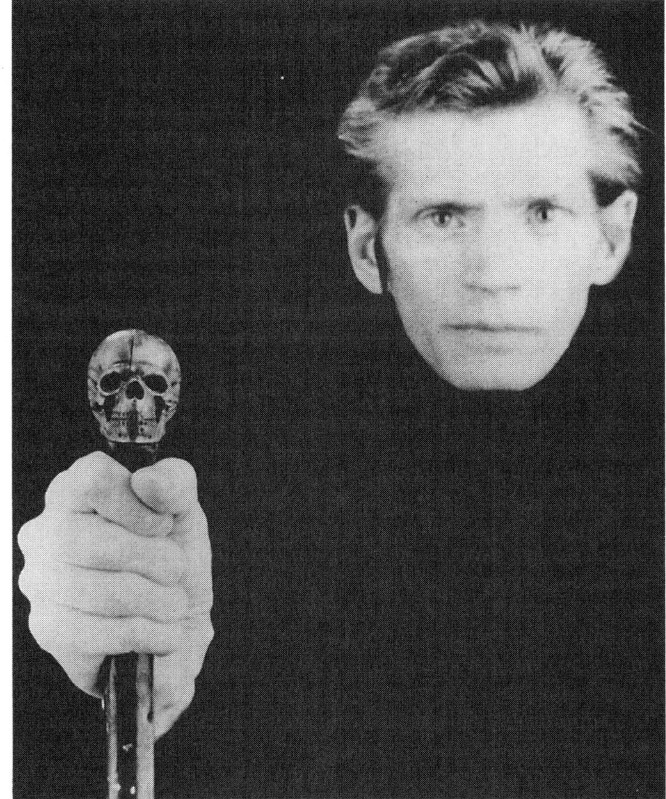

Robert Mapplethorpe

Mapplethorpe did not begin taking traditional photographs until later in his career. Instead, he initially incorporated images from magazines into collages that were influenced by the work of such artists as Andy Warhol and Marcel Duchamp as well as the photographer Man Ray. Mapplethorpe became impatient, however, with the length of time it took to produce one of his pieces and began to think of taking his own photos.

Mapplethorpe and Smith met the filmmaker Sandy Daley at the Chelsea Hotel, to which the pair fled when they were unable to pay their rent, knowing that it was a place hospitable to the poor, arty set. Daley, who later made a film about Mapplethorpe titled *Robert Having His Nipple Pierced* for which Smith served as narrator, was responsible for encouraging Mapplethorpe to use her Polaroid camera to take his initial photographs.

Traditional Photography, Non-Traditional Subjects

On his birthday in 1970 Mapplethorpe had his first solo show, which was held at the Stanley Amos gallery in the Chelsea Hotel and focused on his collage work. At that time he was seeing a model and illustrator, David Croland, who was acquainted with Maxime de La Falaise and her husband John McKendry, the curator of photographs and prints at the Metropolitan Museum of Art. Croland introduced Mapplethorpe to the couple, and he and McKendry, who was bisexual, began having an affair. It was McKendry who gave Mapplethorpe a Polaroid camera of his own to work with.

In 1972 Mapplethorpe met Sam Wagstaff, a collector and former museum curator who became his patron and lover, though their relationship eventually turned to friendship. Wagstaff bought Mapplethorpe a loft near his own and used his connections in the art world to promote the budding photographer.

Smith and her four-piece band recorded her first album, *Horses,* in 1975, and she asked Mapplethorpe to take the photos for the cover. As part of her contract Smith had been given artistic control over her albums, so despite the record company's negative reaction to the black-and-white, androgynous photos, they remained. While Mapplethorpe often used Smith as the subject of his photographs, including the series *Patti Smith (Don't Touch Here),* he had also begun to explore homosexual themes in his work, including those that touched on the world of S&M in which he had become involved.

In 1976 the Light Gallery showed some of Mapplethorpe's Polaroids, marking the first time he'd shown in this medium, and the show's opening garnered an impressive turnout. Having been introduced to the New York social set by first McKendry, then Wagstaff, Mapplethorpe also started doing portrait work for the wealthy socialites and began using a large-format camera, eventually turning to a Hasselblad. The following year Mapplethorpe was invited to show his work at the Holly Solomon Gallery in SoHo. Sensing that Solomon was uncomfortable exhibiting the S&M photos, arrangements were made for a simultaneous show of these photographs, "Erotic Pictures" at the Kitchen, and "Portraits" and "Flowers" at Solomon's space. Both shows were successful and Mapplethorpe and his work became the latest New York craze.

Work Moves in a New Direction

Although sex and sexuality were still very important themes for Mapplethorpe, the 1980s found him beginning to focus more often on portraits and still lifes. He published several books during this time, including *Robert Mapplethorpe: Black Males* in 1980; *Lady: Lisa Lyon,* a collection of photographs of the female bodybuilder, in 1983; and *Certain People* in 1985. In addition, he started to experiment with many different printing techniques as well as elaborate matting and framing. Two other books were published after his death: *Some Women* in 1989 and *Flowers* in 1990.

Mapplethorpe found out he had AIDS in late 1986, shortly before Wagstaff died of the disease, leaving the majority of his estate, estimated at $7 million, to Mapplethorpe. His health deteriorated quickly, but he managed to become involved in the AIDS awareness movement and establish the Robert Mapplethorpe Foundation, which provided funding for AIDS research as well as the visual arts. One of Mapplethorpe's most haunting images is a self-portrait he took after becoming ill. His gaunt face seems to float against the black ground, while his fist thrusts a skull-topped cane toward the viewer.

The first major retrospective of Mapplethorpe's work was held in 1988 at the Whitney Museum and included 110 photos. The photographer managed to attend the opening, although he was confined to a wheelchair. A somewhat larger retrospective opened later the same year at the University of Pennsylvania's Institute of Contemporary Art in Philadelphia. Titled *Robert Mapplethorpe: The Perfect Moment,* the exhibition traveled to Chicago, Boston, and Washington, D.C. It was here that the museum's director succumbed to political pressure and canceled the show after the public outcry of a few conservative congressmen who were angry that public tax dollars (just $40,000) from the National Endowment for the Arts had helped to support the show. This set the stage for the legal action taken in Cincinnati against the Contemporary Arts Center and its director after the exhibition appeared there. The case went to trial, but the prosecution failed to provide witnesses that could adequately counter the defense witnesses, who intelligently and plainly explained why the photographs should be considered art and not pornography. Sadly, Robert Mapplethorpe died on 9 March 1989, before learning that the jury in Cincinnati had decided his work was most definitely art.

References:

Annual Obituary, 1989. Chicago: St. James Press, 1990: 185-88.

Cembalest, Robin. "The Obscenity Trial," *ARTnews,* December 1990: 136-41.

Current Biography Yearbook, 1989. New York: H. W. Wilson, 1990: 369-74.

Morrisroe, Patricia. "The Demon Romantics," in *Vanity Fair,* July 1995: 114-24.

Scully, Julia. "Seeing Pictures," in *Modern Photography,* April 1989: 26-27.

Sischy, Ingrid. "White and Black," in *New Yorker,* 13 November 1989: 124, 129-46.

—Nicolet V. Elert

Christopher Marlowe

1564-1593

British playwright and poet

Probably the most gifted Elizabethan dramatist after Shakespeare, Christopher Marlowe's writings cast exciting subjects into a formal dress of great intensity—"his mighty line." His tempestuous life matched his writings perfectly. Marlowe's life and work distill the quicksilver brilliance that is one of the leading characteristics of the English Renaissance.

The son of a shoemaker, Christopher Marlowe was born in Canterbury in 1564, in the same year as Shakespeare. He attended the King's School in Canterbury as a scholarship student. At the age of 20 he received his B.A. at Corpus Christi College, Cambridge, going on to take the M.A. One month before his commencement in 1587, the university authorities, disturbed by rumors of his conversion to Roman Catholicism and a possible flight to France, received an official letter from the Privy Council in London assuring them of

Christopher Marlowe

his loyal service to the Queen. This letter has fueled speculations that he may have been working as a government spy.

Marlowe spent the last six years of his short life in London, where he circulated in street society, "feasting with panthers," to use Oscar Wilde's expression for this dangerous lifestyle. Inevitably, the playwright got into scrapes with the law, earning at least one prison sentence. On 30 May 1593, Marlowe was killed, perhaps murdered, by a knife wound to the head in a Deptford inn.

Shortly before his death, Marlowe had been arrested on charges of atheism, reflecting his general notoriety and more particularly responding to an allegation of fellow dramatist Thomas Kyd. Kyd's accusation rested on documents seized during a search of the rooms both men shared as their study. Such scandals, seemingly fostered by the poet himself, accompanied Marlowe throughout his adult life.

After his death, even more shocking assertions were voiced. At the inquest, a government informer named Richard Baines reported that the dramatist had insisted that "all they that love not tobacco and boys were fools." In keeping with his religious iconoclasm, Marlowe pronounced that Christ and St. John were homosexual lovers. In 1598, Francis Meres wrote that the playwright "was stabbed to death by a bawdy serving man, a rival of his in his lewd love." Together with the explicit treatment of the matter in *Edward II*, these comments establish Marlowe's homosexuality.

During his London years, Marlowe produced his slender but highly important body of plays. *Dido Queen of Carthage* (1586) deals with a classical subject. The two parts of *Tamburlaine* (1597) are the extravagant chronicle of a Central Asian tyrant. *The Jew of Malta* (1589) centers on a wily, persecuted outsider, with whom an English homosexual of the time might easily identify. *The Massacre at Paris* (1590) concerns contemporary French history. *Doctor Faustus* (1592), the first major drama on this subject, is about the hubris of intellectuals.

His only play featuring a homosexual hero is the powerful historical drama *Edward II* (1591). In an effort to toughen up his effeminate offspring, at the age of 14 Edward's royal father gave him as a companion the orphaned son of a Gascon knight. The king hoped that the example of the dashing and virile 16-year-old Piers Gaveston could "save" his son. The reverse occurred: Edward fell passionately in love, and the king was obliged to banish Gaveston in 1307. The action of Marlowe's play starts shortly after this point. Edward, who had taken the throne upon his father's death, wastes no time in regaling the court with his love. The infuriated barons demand Gaveston's permanent banishment. But Edward, his love eclipsing his rulership, rejects this out of hand. He even shares his throne with Gaveston, who is eventually seized and beheaded. Plunged into despair by his grief, Edward is embroiled in a bloody civil war. He takes another lover, young Spenser, who also falls victim to the barons. Finally, Edward himself is seized and forced to abdicate. In 1327 he is murdered by having a heated poker forced into his anus, "intended as just retribution for his sins."

An exceptional work in his oeuvre is Marlowe's narrative poem *Hero and Leander*, which is unfinished. The poem deals directly with the passion of Jupiter, the king of the gods, for the youth Ganymede, a story which had also been mentioned in *Dido*.

The central theme of Marlowe's plays recalls that of his Greek predecessor Euripides: the conflict of a passionate, headstrong individual with the conventional norms of his or her society. *Edward II* fits this pattern. In this play, the first landmark in gay theater in English, Marlowe sets a high standard that has rarely been equaled with his sensitive portrayal of a stormy relationship between two men caught up in a repressive homophobic society.

References:

Kocher, Paul H. *Christopher Marlowe: A Study of His Thought, Learning, and Character*. Durham: University of North Carolina Press, 1946.

—Wayne R. Dynes

Johnny Mathis

1935-

African-American singer

A balladeer from the Golden Age of Rock and Roll, Johnny Mathis still entertains full houses in Atlantic City and Las Vegas singing the songs he made into hits during his 40 year career. He is one of the most enduring performers in America, and the nostalgic power of his music is as strong as ever. Mathis's life is a classic American rags to riches tale. At the age of 19, he rocketed to wealth and stardom with his first pop hit, "Wonderful, Wonderful." By

Johnny Mathis

1962, he had become one of wealthiest African-Americans in the country, and has to date sold over 100 million albums.

John Royce Mathis was born on 30 September 1935, in Gillmore, Texas. The fourth of seven children, he was raised in San Francisco, California. His mother, Mildred, was a domestic worker, and his father, Clem, made a living as a limo driver, although he had enjoyed a bit of a vaudeville career when the family lived in Texas. Both parents nurtured Mathis's talent, however Clem was the guiding force behind his son's early development as a singer. Clem bought a secondhand piano and taught his son vaudeville routines for performance within the family, and played records for Mathis by singers like Peggy Lee, Lena Horne, and Ella Fitzgerald. In *People* magazine, Mathis described his father as, "my biggest hero, the reason I started to sing."

Known as "the kid who sings," Mathis sang in his church, in children's performances of the San Francisco Opera, and at women's club competitions. At the age of 13, his singing caught the attention of voice teacher Connie Cox, who offered Mathis free voice lessons. In a *New York Times* interview, Mathis described Cox's influence on his vocal technique: "She taught me to sing soft, high notes. For example, Nat King Cole and Billy Eckstine had these big, booming voices, but my voice was quite different than that."

Breaking into Superstardom

While attending San Francisco State College, Mathis became interested in jazz, and began performing in local nightclubs. He met Virgil Gonsalves, a baritone saxophonist, and sang with his sextet at a the Black Hawk nightclub, then co-owned by Helen Noga. When Noga heard Mathis sing, she immediately assumed the job of managing his career. She helped him obtain more bookings, including the fateful 1955 gig at the 440 Club in San Francisco—a gay bar that featured female impersonators—where Mathis's act was seen by Columbia record producer, George Avakian. Although Mathis caught Avakian's attention, the New York producer felt the singer needed time to mature. Returning to San Francisco a year later, Avakian heard Mathis sing at the nightclub, Ann Dee's. Avakian quickly signed Mathis to produce an album for Columbia, *Johnny Mathis, A New Sound in Popular Song.*

Mathis's first album had a decidedly jazz flavor, and was not a great success. Avakian then brought Mathis to New York, where he enjoyed modest success singing jazz at the Blue Angel, the Apollo, and other top clubs and concert halls. Avakian was convinced that Mathis had the talent to become a big star, and sent him to work with Mitch Miller, who was the first to steer Mathis from jazz singing to a soft ballad style.

Mathis's first pop ballads, "Wonderful, Wonderful," and "It's Not For Me to Say," were recorded and released in 1957. He became famous overnight. Having discovered a tremendously successful formula, Mathis quickly followed these hits with "Chances Are," "The 12th of Never," "Misty," and "A Certain Smile." His 1958 album, *Johnny's Greatest Hits* went to number one on *Billboard*'s pop chart, held that place for three weeks, and remained on the chart for another 490 consecutive weeks—a little over 10 years. Throughout the 1960s, Mathis continued to record three to four albums per year.

Despite Mathis's superstar status and frequent public appearances, he was at first a painfully shy performer. Early critics incessantly pointed out his discomfort in front of audiences. In a 1978 *Philadelphia Inquirer* interview, Mathis explained: "I worked on it, though. I would stand in front of a mirror and perform and try to cut out anything that made me feel ill at ease." Mathis went further by mimicking other stars, such as Billy Eckstine, Sara Vaughn, and especially Lena Horne, whose signature phrasing and mannerisms began taking over his act. In a *New York Times* interview, Mathis said: "My appearances were godawful. I was up there doing Lena. I wanted to be her."

In the early 1960s, Mathis suffered a drug problem brought on by overwork—he recalls doing 101 one-night shows in a row—and a subsequent addiction to sleeping pills. Mathis was hospitalized after collapsing on stage at a Denver concert. In the *Inquirer* article, Mathis reflected on that time, "The doctor who prescribed [the pills] meant well ... I was never on hard drugs, but I needed pills to work, then I needed more to sleep." He informed the interviewer: "I've been off pills about ten years now. I don't even take aspirin."

In 1964, Mathis split from his long time manager, Helen Noga, feeling that he wanted to take care of his own career and move in different directions. His first enterprise was the founding of his company, Rojon Productions, through which he became his own manager and also produced new talent. Initially, the separation between Mathis and Noga was bitter. However, in a 1981 interview in *Jet* magazine, Mathis said of he and Noga: "[We are] very close friends. We talk on the telephone all the time. I go to her house and visit her grandchildren, and we're very close because she's a very special person in my life."

Through the late 1960s and 1970s, Mathis remained a popular entertainer in larger venues and on television. His albums had a tendency to recycle the material of his contemporaries, with titles such as "The Long and Winding Road" (1970), "The First Time

Ever I Saw Your Face" (1972), "Killing Me Softly With Her Song" (1973), "Me And Mrs. Jones" (1973), "Song Sung Blue" (1974), and "You Light Up My Life, (1978). Stylistically, he embraced Latin, soft rock, and disco, sold millions of albums, but success on the pop charts eluded him. Then, in 1978, he hit upon a new formula. His duet with Deniece Williams, "Too Much, Too Little, Too Late," became a number one hit, rivaling his successes of the late 1950s. As a bonus, Williams's had a large following in the African-American community, and Mathis became popular with Black audiences for the first time. Throughout the 1980s, Mathis teamed up to record more pop tunes with Gladys Knight, Dionne Warwick, Natalie Cole, and Barbra Streisand, among many others.

A Pioneer in Being "Outed"

In 30 years of interviews, Mathis was questioned often about his bachelor status. The 1981 *Jet* article features two obligatory photographs of Mathis in classic Hollywood romantic couplings with beautiful black women, in this case he's paired with model Beverly Gillohm, then with actress Mimi Dillard. When asked about marriage in the same interview, Mathis glibly replied: "I've come awfully close to becoming involved with matrimony. But, so far, I've avoided it because I'm so set in my ways, my wife would probably be a golf widow, because I play golf every day." A scant four years later, when asked about his romantic life in an *Us* magazine interview, Mathis discussed his first love at 16 with the "best baritone sax player in the world." He later said, "homosexuality is a way of life that I've grown accustomed to." These revelations barely caused a ripple because few people had doubted Mathis's sexuality to begin with, or even cared. However, Mathis maintained in the 1993 *New York Times* interview that what he disclosed in *Us* had been quoted off the record. He has since barred all questions about his sexuality. In 1992, when gay activists tried to "out" Mathis, they were embarrassed to learn that *Us* magazine had beaten them to it.

Mathis is the third most successful recording artist in the world, behind Frank Sinatra and Elvis Presley. Despite his success, he keeps a low profile and indulges in his hobbies, such as golf and cooking. In a *Philadelphia Inquirer* interview from 1970, Mathis said, "You have to remember that when I first came along—that same week as a matter of fact—there was another young fellow just starting out named Elvis Presley." A legend in his own right, in the *Jet* article, Mathis maintains that, "I still feel like the kid that was tagging along behind my father, when we were going out looking for somebody to listen to me sing."

Current Address: c/o Rojon Productions Inc., P.O. Box 2066, Burbank, California 91507.

References:

Gavin, James. "A Timeless Reminder of Back Seats in '57 Buicks," in *New York Times,* 19 December 1993.

Haile, Mark. "Out of Fashanu," in *BLK,* October, 1992.

Hunter, Norman. "Johnny Mathis Celebrates 25 Years In Show Business," in *Jet,* 29 January 1981.

"Johnny Mathis," in *Guinness Encyclopedia of Popular Music.* Guinness Publishing Ltd., 1992.

"Johnny Mathis," in *Time* (New York), 30 November 1962.

Lloyd, Jack. "An Interview with Johnny Mathis," in *Philadelphia Inquirer,* 4 February 1970.

Nazzaro, William J. "Johnny Mathis Wins Over Shyness, Pills," in *Philadelphia Inquirer,* 29 July 1973.

Petrucelli, Alan W. "Celebrity Q & A," in *Us,* 22 June 1982.

Thomas, Elizabeth. "Johnny Mathis," in *Contemporary Musicians.* Detroit: Gale Research, Inc., 1990.

Windeler, Robert. "Happy," in *People,* 23 October 1978.

—Laurie Fitzpatrick

Leonard P. Matlovich, Jr.

1943-1988

American Air Force technical sergeant and activist

"I Am a Homosexual," shouted the 8 September 1975 cover of *Time,* directly below the face of Air Force Technical Sergeant Leonard P. Matlovich, Jr. Matlovich had provided almost 12 years of unblemished service to the Air Force, volunteering for three tours of duty in Vietnam and earning four medals, when he became a national celebrity by launching a battle against the military's anti-gay policy with a letter to his superior declaring both his homosexuality and his intent to continue serving in the Air Force.

An "Air Force brat" born 6 July 1943 in Savannah, Georgia, to Vera and Air Force Sergeant Matlovich, Sr., young Matlovich grew up on military bases mostly in the South. A conservative, religious, and, as he told Lesley Oelsner of the *New York Times,* "white-racist..., flag-waving patriot" who used words like "nigger" and who believed that the sexual inclinations he'd had since the age of 12 were wrong. Matlovich prayed that God would make him normal. But, according to Randy Shilts in *Conduct Unbecoming: Gays & Lesbians in the U.S. Military,* "the harder he prayed, the queerer he got."

After graduating from high school, Matlovich joined the Air Force in 1963, hoping to make a career and overcome his homosexuality. He won the Bronze Star, a Commendation Medal, and the Purple Heart in Vietnam—and he remained gay. And, slowly, his attitude about being a homosexual changed.

They Were Wrong Once ...

Forced to serve with "niggers," Matlovich realized that the things he'd been taught about blacks were wrong. Stationed in Florida, he enrolled in a race relations course and later became an instructor, where he received high ratings from his 1500 students and where his outstanding performance earned him yet another medal. He started to believe that if society had been wrong about blacks, it might also be wrong about homosexuals; his work also taught him to firmly believe in equal opportunity.

At the age of 30, Matlovich's first visit to a gay bar finally led him to admit his homosexuality, to himself and his friends. Two years later he decided that he also had a Constitutional duty to fight for equal rights. With the help of American Civil Liberties Union lawyer David Addlestone, who had been looking for a gay soldier with Matlovich's qualifications—a perfect record so that nothing

Leonard P. Matlovich, Jr.

would be at issue except sexual orientation, and a willingness to risk his career for civil rights—Matlovich drafted the letter that signaled his coming out to the Air Force and that launched his battle against the military's anti-gay policy. What follows is a timeline of Matlovich's case:

8 March 1975: Sgt. Matlovich handed his letter to his superior officer at Langley Air Force Base; when asked what the letter meant, Matlovich is quoted in *Time* as asserting: "It means *Brown vs. the Board of Education*"—Matlovich intended to do for gay rights what that landmark 1954 school integration case had done for Civil Rights.

19 September 1975: A three-member Air Force panel recommended a general discharge.

22 October 1975: Matlovich received an honorable discharge; his base commander had ordered the change from the recommended general discharge.

16 July 1976: Federal District Judge Gerhard Gesell upheld the discharge in civilian court.

6 December 1978: The U.S. Court of Appeals in Washington, D.C. ruled that the Air Force had discharged Matlovich unfairly since its policy on homosexuals was too ambiguous.

9 November 1980: Judge Gesell ordered Matlovich reinstated with $62,000 in back pay.

24 November 1980: Upon advice from his lawyers that he would lose and set gay rights backward in the Air Force's appeal of his reinstatement, Matlovich dropped his case for a $160,000 tax-free settlement.

A National Crusader

During his five-year struggle for reinstatement, Matlovich became a national crusader for gay rights, speaking out on television and radio, at rallies, parades, and in specific battles, such as the losing 1977 Miami fight against celebrity Anita Bryant and the repeal of homosexual anti-discrimination legislation. In 1978, NBC aired *Sgt. Matlovich vs. the Air Force,* the first nonfiction gay rights story ever sponsored by network television. Matlovich attempted to enter politics in 1979 as the Republican candidate for the San Francisco Board of Supervisors. And, in 1980, he ended his battle with the military with, as he told the *New York Times,* "a great victory. The fact that they are willing to pay $160,000 shows they feel they did discriminate."

After the settlement, Matlovich started a business (which folded in 1983) and again became involved in Republican politics. Elected to the Russian River Chamber of Commerce Board of Directors, he helped new gay businesses.

Diagnosed with AIDS in 1986, Matlovich continued his crusade. "If I can spend three years fighting for democracy in Vietnam, I can spend an hour in jail fighting for our lives," Matlovich is quoted as saying in the 1987 *Facts on File* for 12 June when arrested at the White House for protesting the Reagan administration's AIDS policies. He brought news cameras to Northwest Airlines, forcing it to reverse its policy of denying AIDS patients passage. With hundreds of thousands of others, he participated in the October 1987 March on Washington for Lesbian & Gay Rights, and he directed the ceremony dedicating a gay memorial in the Congressional Cemetery. At a gay march in Sacramento, Matlovich made his final public appearance.

Then, on 22 June 1988, Leonard P. Matlovich, Jr. died from AIDS. At the Congressional Cemetery in Washington, D.C., with full military honors and a 21-gun salute, Matlovich was buried at a monument he'd erected at the grave before his death, a monument signifying his struggle for gay rights with the words:

> *When I was in the military they gave me a medal for killing two men and a discharge for loving one.*

References:

Facts on File, Yearbook 1987. New York: Facts on File Publications, vol. XLVII, 1988: 426.

Hippler, Mike. *Matlovich.* Boston, Massachusetts: Alyson Publications, 1989.

Oelsner, Lesley. "Homosexual Is Fighting Military Ouster," in *New York Times,* 26 May 1975: 24.

"The Sergeant v. The Air Force," in *Time* (New York), 8 September 1975: 34.

Shilts, Randy. *Conduct Unbecoming: Gays & Lesbians in the U.S. Military.* New York: St. Martin's Press, 1993: 76.

"U.S. to Pay $160,000 In Homosexual's Suit On Air Force Ousting," in *New York Times,* 25 November 1980.

—Tracy White

Carson McCullers

1917-1967

American writer

One of the most accomplished modern writers, Carson McCullers is noted for her keen psychological perception and insights, exploring in her novels the darker, more fragile side of human nature. A chronicler of the grotesque, she emphasizes the humanity of her misfit characters. Loneliness and the pursuit of love lie at the heart of her work, and echo an unremitting personal quest which involved acceptance and assertion of her own bisexual identity.

Born on 17 February 1917 in Columbus, Georgia, as Lula Carson Smith, McCullers was the eldest child of Lamar and Marguerite Waters Smith. Raised in a loving family environment, she was constantly assured of her genius, a feeling she retained all her life. This awareness was balanced by an acute self-consciousness; gangling and awkward, McCullers was regarded as an eccentric by classmates and neighbors. Herself an outsider, she became fascinated by the circus freaks she encountered at the Chattahoochie Valley Fair, feeling a strange kinship with them. She also identified with the plight of neighboring blacks, and later expressed her outrage at their unjust treatment. Never physically strong, she was often ill, but bouts of sickness alternated with spells of violent exertion.

McCullers originally aimed to be a concert pianist, and in 1930 took lessons with Mrs. Mary Tucker, whom she came to regard as a close friend. When the Tuckers left the area she was devastated, and decided against a musical career, devoting herself to writing. Graduating from Columbus High in 1933, she completed an unpublished novel *A Reed of Pan* and her first short story "Sucker."

The Writer Moves to New York

McCullers arrived in New York in 1935, intending to study at Juilliard, but lost her tuition money on the subway on her second day. She enrolled briefly at Columbia University, and at New York University joined the writing class of Sylvia Chatfield Bates, who encouraged her to submit stories for publication. She later met James Reeves McCullers, her future partner in two stormy marriages. Her stories "Wunderkind" and "Like That" were accepted by *Story* magazine, and launched her career as an author.

Carson McCullers

In 1937 Reeves McCullers and Carson Smith were married. They spent eight happy months in Charlotte, North Carolina, but on moving to Fayetteville their marriage came under strain. With their money problems, McCullers' earnings assumed great importance, and she took to writing with a ruthless single-mindedness resented by Reeves, whose own efforts had failed dismally. McCullers' novel, *The Heart Is a Lonely Hunter* (1940), established her as a leading modern writer at the age of 23. *The Heart Is a Lonely Hunter* deals with the loneliness and vain search for love by a group of misfits in a Southern town. Singer, the saintly deaf-mute, serves as a focus for the dreams and desires of the rest—tomboy teenager Mick Kelly, Copeland the black local doctor, and socialist reformer Jake Blount. Yet Singer's own love is directed at the dissolute Antonopoulos, whose death drives Singer to suicide and the rest to defeat and disillusion. Her most famous novel, *Heart* combines sensitivity and violence, and presents a view of several troubled inner lives. Soon afterwards McCullers began work on *Reflections in a Golden Eye* (1941). Set on an Army post, it describes a fraught tangle of relationships, and includes some macabre scenes. McCullers thought them amusing, but they are very much gallows humor. *Reflections* had a mixed reception, but few now doubted the author's ability.

Marital Strain and Sexual Orientation

Relations with Reeves were strained, and she returned to New York, where she met the young Swiss writer Annemarie Clarac-Schwarzenbach. The two women entered into an intense personal relationship, McCullers acknowledging her physical attraction to her own sex, and in December of 1940 she and Reeves separated. Sadly, her time with Annemarie was brief, and the Swiss girl's tragic death in 1942 left McCullers devastated. McCullers enjoyed a more platonic friendship with Gypsy Rose Lee, and both shared a Greenwich Village apartment with poet W. H. Auden.

At the end of 1940 McCullers fell ill, and in February 1941 suffered a severe attack that left her briefly with impaired vision. She and Reeves were reconciled, and for a while formed an unusual ménage-à-trois with composer David Diamond. McCullers attended the Yaddo Artists Colony at Saratoga Springs, and there declared her (unrequited) love to an embarrassed Katherine Anne Porter. At home the marriage worsened, and she considered divorce while Reeves, realizing his own bisexual nature, moved in with Diamond. McCullers secured a Guggenheim Fellowship in 1942, and in 1943 sold her novella *The Ballad of the Sad Café* (1951) to *Harper's Bazaar*. *Ballad* re-examines her familiar themes in masterly fashion through an unusual love triangle. Divorced from Reeves, McCullers suffered bouts of illness; Reeves, meantime, saw combat in France and Germany with a Ranger unit. He returned a decorated hero, and the couple remarried in 1945. McCullers completed *A Member of the Wedding* (1946), which with *Heart* and *Ballad* ranks as her finest work, and established a deep and lasting friendship with playwright Tennessee Williams. Reunited, she and Reeves set up home in Paris.

Disaster struck in 1947 with a crippling stroke that left McCullers paralysed down her left side. Reeves, whose new-found identity as a war hero was threatened by her fame, was drinking heavily, and both were flown home ill in December. Separation followed and McCullers, at a low ebb, attempted suicide. Recovering, she was again reconciled with Reeves, and completed her dramatic version of *A Member of the Wedding,* which opened to critical acclaim on Broadway in January 1950. It won the New York Drama Critics Circle and Donaldson awards. Another separation from Reeves was followed by friendship with British poetess Dame Edith Sitwell. Reeves returned, and in 1953 they settled at Bachvillers in France, but McCullers' marriage was almost over. In despair, Reeves suggested a suicide pact, and McCullers fled in terror. Reeves killed himself on 19 November.

In her last years McCullers battled constant pain, severe illness, and her own heavy drinking. Her play *The Square Root of Wonderful* (1958) was badly received, and she suffered depression, but with the help of psychologist Mary Mercer returned to writing again. Her last novel *Clock without Hands* (1961) indicted Southern racism, while *Reflections* and *Heart* were both filmed in the 1960s. The death of her mother in 1955 was a terrible blow, but she enjoyed secure friendships with Mary Mercer, her old teacher Mary Tucker, and at a more intimate level with French artist Marielle Bancou. After escalating illness, McCullers suffered a final stroke in August 1967. She died on 29 September at Nyack Hospital, and was buried at Oak Hill Cemetery on 3 October.

Carson McCullers was given to extremes, and provoked extreme reactions, being loved or loathed by those who knew her. What cannot be doubted is her skill as a writer, and her indomitable courage in the face of illness and trauma. Her novels and stories confirm her genius, and her continuing search for love.

References:

Carr, Virginia Spencer. *The Lonely Hunter: A Biography of Carson McCullers.* London: Peter Owen, 1975.

Current Biography. New York: H. W. Wilson, 1940.

Kunitz, Stanley J. and Howard Haycraft, eds. *Twentieth Century Authors: A Biographical Dictionary of Modern Literature.* New York: H. W. Wilson, 1942.

McCullers, Carson. *The Mortgaged Heart: Stories,* introduction by Margarita G. Smith. Harmondsworth, Middlesex: Penguin, 1975.

—Geoff Sadler

Sir Ian McKellen

1939-

British actor, writer, and activist

Ian McKellen has long been considered one of the theatre's finest classical actors, particularly for his roles in a variety of Shakespeare productions. Apart from his acting career, however, McKellen has also worked as an activist. Because of his distinction of being the first openly gay British actor to have been recognized by his country's government, McKellen has succeeded in gaining considerable public attention for the cause of gay rights.

Ian Murray McKellen was born in Burnley, England, on 25 May 1939. He attended Wigan Grammar School and the Bolton School. By the age of 12 he was acting regularly in productions at Bolton. But, while he was aware of his attraction to men long before adolescence, his life, even as a young teen, was focused on his acting, not on his libido. McKellen later attended St. Catharine's College, Cambridge, where he earned his Bachelor of Arts degree in 1962.

Sir Ian McKellen

During his time at Cambridge—nine terms in all—McKellen began his acting career, playing 21 parts over the years. He made his stage debut in 1961 in *A Man for All Seasons* at the Belgrade Theater, Coventry. McKellen's London debut came in 1964 in the role of Godfrey in *A Scent of Flowers,* for which he won a Clarence Derwent Award. His performance was sufficiently impressive and, as a result, landed him a season with the National Theatre, thereby beginning to cultivate a professional reputation. In 1967, McKellen made his New York debut. He performed in *The Promise,* and in 1968 his performances in *White Liars* and *Black Comedy* earned him rave reviews. By 1970, McKellen had established himself as one of the contemporary theatre's finest performers with title roles in *Richard II* and *Edward II.*

In addition to his acting, McKellen has helped to found and establish his own theater companies. Most notable of these was the Actor's Company, founded in 1972. In the Actor's Company all of the performers were equal, sharing in choosing plays, receiving equal pay, billing, and in playing lead roles. In 1974 McKellen joined the Royal Shakespeare Company where he performed in a number of acclaimed productions over a four-year period. McKellen left the Royal Shakespeare Company in 1978 when he accepted a role in *Bent,* a drama about gays in Nazi concentration camps for which he was given the Laurence Olivier Award for Best Actor. Around this time he began touring with his extremely popular one-man show, *Acting Shakespeare,* which also garnered several awards, including the Edinburgh Festival's: Drama Desk, Elliot Norton, and Antionette Perry Awards.

In 1988, McKellen decided to come out and thus became the first major actor in England to do so. At that time, Great Britain—or rather, Margaret Thatcher's conservative party—was considering an anti-gay measure known as Clause 28. Clause 28 would have once again made gay behavior between consenting adults illegal in addition to, according to Ephraim Katz, forbidding the government "from allocating monies that would in any way 'promote' homosexuality." Because of this, McKellen received much criticism in 1991 for accepting knighthood from Thatcher, especially from the now-deceased Derek Jarman who saw Thatcher as an enemy of the gay and lesbian community. McKellen didn't see these incidents in the same way. As England's pre-eminent interpreter of Shakespeare, and the first actor of his generation to be knighted, McKellen believes that he, as part of the establishment, is in a strategic position to "dismantle it."

Others, arguing in favor of McKellen's knighthood, saw it as the recognition and acceptance of an openly gay actor by the government and the beginning of the end of the need for public figures to keep their sexual preference secret. McKellen, they argued, made no secret of his contempt for the government's policies concerning gays. As a gay man who has been successfully functioning in straight society for more than 30 years, McKellen considers himself a "gay communicator with the straight population." Since coming out, McKellen has become a vocal spokesperson for gay rights, and a regular visitor to Prime Minister John Major's residence at 10 Downing Street to lobby for lesbian and gay rights. McKellen regrets that so many gays and lesbians live in what they believe is the safety of the closet. Many, he says, do as he did when he was their age; but, out and out lying about their sexuality, pretending to wait for the right woman or man, or entering into sham marriages is not anything he encourages. "In my own defense," he says, "I never lied."

Although McKellen speaks of two committed relationships, each eight years long, the theater is the one place where he has consistently devoted himself and where he feels he is most at home and in control of himself. When judged solely on his success in that medium, it would seem that he is correct.

Current Address: c/o James Sharkey, 21 Golden Square, London W1R 3PA, England.

References:

Gibson, Melissa. "Ian McKellen," in *International Directory of Theatre, volume 3: Actors, Directors and Designers,* edited by David Pickering. Detroit: St. James Press, 1996: 503-506.

Katz, Ephraim. *The Film Encyclopedia.* New York: HarperCollins, 1994: 872.

—Andrea L.T. Peterson

Herman Melville

1819-1891

American writer

The literary genius of Herman Melville was not widely recognized and evaluated until after the 1930s, and his acceptance as an

Herman Melville

important early contributor to the gay canon began only in 1975 with the publication of Edward Haviland Miller's Freudian psychobiography. Since then half-a-dozen major works by gay critics have confirmed Miller's assessment.

Herman Melville was born in New York City on 1 August 1819, the third child of Allan and Maria (Gansevoort) Melvill (as they spelled their name). Melville's father failed in business and became frighteningly deranged before his death in 1832. To his 12-year-old son, who seems to have spent the whole of his life looking for a surrogate father, Allan Melvill was the supreme symbol of Apollonian grace. The young writer was overshadowed by his glamorous older brother Gansevoort and always saw himself as lumpish and unattractive, despite appearances very much to the contrary.

At the age of 19, with no hope of attending college, Melville signed up as a cabin boy on a merchant ship crossing to Liverpool—a voyage he would recreate in *Redburn.* Two years later he signed on with a whaling ship bound for the South Seas, but life was so intolerable that he and a companion jumped ship in the Marquesas and lived for a month with the allegedly cannibalistic Typees. After being rescued by an Australian whaler, Melville spent time in Tahiti and other Pacific islands before coming home in 1844.

Then, simply because he needed an occupation and had a great deal of material to write about, Melville took up writing. His early novels: *Typee: A Peep at Polynesian Life* (1846), *Omoo: A Narrative of Adventures in the South Seas* (1847), and *Redburn* (1849) were extremely popular, and all were casually homoerotic. In *Typee* he described the gentle, hospitable South Sea Islanders as "lovers of human flesh," savoring the double meaning beyond its literal implication of cannibalism. *Omoo* means "rover," which was slang in Melville's time for "sexual outlaw," implying that sailors were beyond the land-locked pale of heterosexual routine. And Harry Bolton in *Redburn* is glowingly described as "one of those small but perfectly formed beings, with curling hair and silken muscles." The psychological depth that would be most evident in his masterpiece, *Moby-Dick* began to emerge in *Mardi: and a Voyage Thither* (1849) and *White-Jacket; or, The World in a Man-of-War* (1851).

Moby-Dick (1851), the allegorical adventure of Captain Ahab and the white whale which Melville dedicated to Nathaniel Hawthorne, is now regarded as one of the great masterpieces of world literature. But *Moby-Dick* proved too difficult for critics and the public alike when first published, as did *Pierre; Or, The Ambiguities* (1852), which was repellent in its psychological complexity and elaborate prose with hints of incest and anti-Christian tirades.

In 1847, Melville married Elizabeth Shaw, daughter of Massachusetts Supreme Court Chief Justice Lemuel Shaw. The marriage produced four children. Melville's commitment to marriage and parenthood may have been less than total, and both of his two sons came to grief. Malcolm committed suicide at the age of 18, and Stanwix, a pathetic drifter, died of tuberculosis in a San Francisco hospital at 35.

Melville-Hawthorne Friendship

Melville purchased "Arrowhead" near Pittsfield, Massachusetts in 1850. It was here that he became friendly with Nathaniel Hawthorne, 15 years his senior. In an enthusiastic review of Hawthorne's *Mosses from an Old Manse* Melville wrote that the older man "dropped germinous seeds in my soul ... and shoots his strong New England roots into the hot soil of my Southern soul." Melville seems to have pressed too eagerly, and Hawthorne soon withdrew, causing Melville no end of grief. Miller, a biographer of both Melville and Hawthorne, actually pinpoints the time (mid-September 1851) and the occasion ("advances" made to Hawthorne as the two strolled in the woods near Stockbridge Bowl) that ended the friendship.

In 1876, Melville published the long poem *Clarel,* whose 150 cantos explore a failed friendship, probably inspired by Hawthorne. Clarel, a young theology student who goes to the Holy Land to stimulate his faith, is drawn to an older man named Vine. When his "advances" are "unreturned," Clarel accepts the rejection but persists in his belief that Vine harbors a secret to which Clarel can never find "the key."

Billy Budd Is Posthumously Published Masterpiece

Of all Melville's work, it is *Billy Budd,* published more than three decades (1924) after the author's death, that has given heterosexual critics the most pause. Based in part upon an actual mutiny at sea, it is the tragedy of a beautiful and lovable but naive sailor who is accused of conspiracy by the master-at-arms, Claggart, who is fascinated by the beautiful Billy and "but for fate and ban" could even have loved him. When the wrongfully accused Billy impulsively strikes and kills Claggart, he is condemned to death by hanging, a punishment Melville supports because the larger issue of what is best for society must take precedence.

Melville died at a time (1891) when the concept or construct of homosexuality was just appearing in Western society, so it is difficult, if not impossible, to orient Melville vis-à-vis the modern term. In *White Jacket* he strongly condemns the frequency of maritime sodomy, yet he appears comfortable with mutual masturbation, which is evident in the richly erotic chapter (94) of *Moby-Dick* called, "A Squeeze of the Hand." Here Ishmael and shipmates work to get the lumps out of a dead whale's spermaceti by squeezing it. Drenched in the milky fluid, hands begin to touch other hands, and an abiding camaraderie engulfs the men. The following chapter (95) called "The Cassock" is also unabashedly phallic as well as anti-Christian. The cassock turns out to be none other than the foreskin of the dead whale, and the mincer who dries the unusual pelt dons it as a garment and thus arrayed in decent black is suited for an "archbishoprick."

Melville's death on 28 September 1891 went virtually unnoticed. He was buried in Woodlawn Cemetery, in the northern part of the Bronx, near Yonkers. His obituaries alleged that his literary popularity had begun waning about 1852 and it would take at least another generation after his death for his literary reputation to be rehabilitated.

References:

Arvin, Newton. *Herman Melville: A Critical Biography.* New York: Sloane, 1950.

Creech, James. *Closet Writing/Gay Reading: The Case of Melville's Pierre.* Chicago: University of Chicago, 1993.

Fone, Byrne R. S. *A Road to Stonewall 1750-1969: Male Homosexuality and Homophobia in English and American Literature.* New York: Twayne Publishers, 1995.

Laskin, David. *A Common Life: Four Generations of American Literary Friendship and Influence.* New York: Simon and Schuster, 1994.

Martin, Robert K. *Hero, Captain and Stranger: Male Friendship, Social Critique and Literary Form in the Sea Novels of Herman Melville.* Chapel Hill: University of North Carolina Press, 1986.

Miller, Edward Haviland. *Melville.* New York: Braziller, 1975.

———. *Salem is My Dwelling Place: A Life of Nathaniel Hawthorne.* Iowa City: University of Iowa Press, 1991.

Rogin, Michael Paul. *Subversive Genealogy: The Politics and Art of Herman Melville.* New York: Alfred A. Knopf, 1983.

Sarotte, Georges-Michel. *Like a Brother, Like a Lover: Male Homosexuality in the American Novel and Theatre from Herman Melville to James Baldwin,* translated by Richard Miller. Garden City, New York: Anchor Press/Doubleday, 1978.

Sedgwick, Eve Kosofsky. *Epistemology of the Closet.* Berkeley: University of California Press, 1990.

—Jack Shreve

Gian Carlo Menotti

1911-

American composer

Gian Carlo Menotti has earned the distinction of being one of the most popular composers of the 20th Century. His operas, particularly his early ones, have not only won the highest critical acclaim, but also have won over to the joys of opera many who might otherwise have found the genre inaccessible to them. Menotti's most successful works skillfully combine musical and theatrical elements to express his own unique insights, be they humorous or tragic, into what constitutes the human experience.

Gian Carlo Menotti was born to a prosperous merchant family in the Italian country town of Cadegliano on Lake Lugano in 1911, the sixth of ten children. His father Alfonso was in the import-export business, and his mother Ines was a talented amateur musician. She communicated her love of music to her children, and the house was the scene of many family musical performances. Menotti's mother herself began giving Gian Carlo piano lessons when he was four years old. By the age of six he had already composed melodies, and by the age of 11 had written his first of two childhood operas, *The Death of Pierrot.*

Menotti's early years in the family's pink stucco villa were happy ones. In an interview with John Ardoin in the Spring 1989 issue of *Opera Quarterly*, Menotti fondly recalls his bedroom, its ceiling painted with swallows, and the sound of ringing church bells which still, he says, echoes in his music.

When Menotti was 13, his father became too ill to spend the winter in the country, so the family took an apartment in Milan. There he attended high school and studied at the Verdi Conservatory. Menotti was an attractive, precocious youth, and became the pet of the salons in Milan, to the extent that he neglected his studies. When his father died, his mother sought advice from Arturo Toscanini as to what was the best course for her talented son to

Gian Carlo Menotti

take. Toscanini recommended that the young man pursue his studies in the United States, far away from the hot-house atmosphere of the salons. She followed the great conductor's advice, and 1927 found Menotti and his mother arriving in New York.

A Life-Long Friendship Begins

Menotti was granted a scholarship to the Curtis Institute in Philadelphia on the condition that he reapply himself to his neglected studies. His mother's return to Europe left Menotti all alone in a strange country, unable to speak a word of English. In his interview with Ardoin, Menotti recalls the loneliness of his rented room and the foreignness of Philadelphia: "The city seemed so strange to me. In Italy everyone walks; the streets are full. But in Philadelphia there were only cars, especially in the evening when the stores are all closed."

Samuel Barber was also a student at the Curtis Institute with Menotti. He knew a smattering of Italian and a good deal of French, and their opportune meeting led to a close and lengthy friendship. Barber's family and friends in West Chester, Pennsylvania welcomed Menotti and provided him with what he came to regard as a second home.

After graduating from the Curtis Institute in 1933, Menotti and Barber spent the winter in Vienna. It was there that Menotti found, in the form of their landlady's huge and highly ornamented dressing table, the inspiration for his first adult opera. This elaborate piece of furniture, along with its rather eccentric owner, the Baroness von Montechivsky, reminded Menotti of the salons of his youth with their gossip, intrigues, and frivolities. The result of this inspiration was the delightful one-act *opera buffa*, or comic opera, *Amelia Goes to the Ball*. The opera was immediately successful; it premiered in Philadelphia in 1937, and was performed at the Metropolitan Opera in New York the following year.

Commissions for more operas swiftly followed. *The Old Maid and the Thief* was commissioned by NBC, and was performed on the radio network in 1939. This comedic opera featured caricatures of West Chester locals whom Menotti had met during his stays with the Barbers. Menotti abandoned comedy for tragedy in response to a commission from the Metropolitan Opera. *The Island God*, produced in 1942, was a tragic opera in every sense of the word. It enjoyed only four performances at the Met before being withdrawn from the repertoire. Yet the opera was not a total loss, for Menotti came to realize that, in his own words, "My vein was not heroic. *The Island God* taught me that I was no Wagner."

Menotti abandoned opera for concert music for the next few years, composing a piano concerto and the score for the ballet *Sebastian*. He and Barber had bought a country home together in Mount Kisco, New York, and it was there that Menotti sought solace after the *Island God* debacle. Menotti described the house, "Capricorn," to Ardoin as "not a particularly beautiful house; in fact, it was a rather strange house," with a "strong atmosphere." Menotti recalls that he and Barber played host to many famous artists during their nearly 30 years in Mount Kisco, among them Vladimir Horowitz, Laurence Olivier, Vivien Leigh, and Jerome Robbins.

The Medium, completed in 1946, marked Menotti's return to opera. It was a complete departure from his earlier comedic works and demonstrated his ability to produce an opera in the naturalistic style associated with Puccini. *The Medium* was a great success. It ran for seven months on Broadway, paired with a delightfully witty one-act *opera buffa*, *The Telephone*.

Wins Highest Critical Acclaim

This triumph was followed in 1950 by an even greater one, *The Consul*, which was not only a box-office hit on Broadway, but also won both the Pulitzer Prize and the New York Drama Critics Circle Award. The following year saw the production of what is perhaps Menotti's best loved work, *Amahl and the Night Visitors*, which was first televised in 1951 and remained an NBC Christmas favorite for many years.

Menotti's next opera also had a religious theme. *The Saint of Bleecker Street* tells the tragic story of a young mystic, who receives the stigmata, and her delinquent brother. It was awarded the Pulitzer Prize in music, the Music Critics Circle Award, and the Drama Critics Award.

The 1940s and 1950s marked the height of Menotti's popular and critical acclaim. He has continued to write operas and concert music, and his works continue to be performed all over the world. He collaborated with Barber, writing the libretti for Barber's operas *Vanessa* and *A Hand of Bridge*. In 1958 he founded the Festival of Two Worlds in Spoleto, Italy, and, in 1977, the Spoleto Festival USA in Charleston, South Carolina. He has been generous in bestowing both talent and funds in support of the arts and individual artists.

In his 4 May 1963 *New Yorker* profile of Menotti, Winthrop Sargeant describes the composer as being "rather buoyant and whimsical" yet preoccupied with ideas of "imperfection, sin, and the hope of redemption and holiness." The writer also notes that Menotti is "insatiably curious about other people, and is more apt to lose himself in contemplation of somebody else's private life than to exhibit his own." Indeed, Menotti's fascination with other people's lives is obvious from the frequency with which the characters and situations in his operas are drawn from real life and real people. He claims, in his interview with Sargeant, that the dominance of women in his operas is due to the fact that he has a better understanding of women than of men, and that he himself is reflected in the "halt, lame and blind" male characters he has created.

In an article written by the composer for the *New York Times*, 10 June 1989, Menotti bemoans the current fashion of trying "to understand artists by delving into their private lives rather than into their works." He himself believes that art "is no easy hobby only requiring genius, but, rather, a whole way of living."

References:

Ardoin, John. "Gian Carlo Menotti: Dialogue V," in *The Opera Quarterly*, Spring 1989: 39-47.

Ewen, David. *American Composers: A Biographical Dictionary.* New York: G. P. Putnam's Sons, 1982.

Ewen, David, ed. *Composers Since 1900: A Biographical and Critical Guide.* New York: H. W. Wilson Company, 1969.

Harewood, The Earl of, ed. *The Definitive Kobbe's Opera Book.* New York: G. P. Putnam's Sons, 1987.

Menotti, Gian Carlo. "I Forgive Goethe, Tolstoy, and, Above All, Mozart," in the *New York Times*, 10 June 1989: I, 27:1.

Morton, Brian, and Pamela Collins, eds. *Contemporary Composers.* Chicago: St. James Press, 1992.

Sadie, Stanley, ed. *The New Grove Dictionary of Music and Musicians.* Vol. 12.

Sargeant, Winthrop. "Orlando in Mount Kisco," in *New Yorker,* 4 May 1962: 49-89.

—Jean Edmunds

Ismail Merchant

1936-

Indian filmmaker

James Ivory

1928-

American filmmaker

Producer Ismail Merchant and director James Ivory have worked and lived together for over 30 years, forming one of the longest-standing, most highly respected, and most popular creative partnerships in cinema history. "Some people meet and part ways," Merchant told interviewer John Stark in *People Weekly* about living with Ivory, "others bond together on a lifelong stream. I guess you could call our relationship destiny."

With German-born screenwriter Ruth Prawer Jhabvala completing the "creative trident" on most of their more than two dozen films to date, their collaboration is more than just a meeting of mind and spirit. "We're like one of those Hindu deities," Prawer told author Raymond Murray in *Images in the Dark,* "with three heads and six arms and six heads. We're one person—a Jew, a Catholic and a Moslem—embodying good and evil." It's "a partnership," Merchant told *60 Minutes* in 1992, "that is not in business but in life."

Ivory is admittedly the more reticent of the two, the more private man, and the perfectionist. Merchant is the gregarious money-raiser, the cook and cookbook publisher, and the one to whom both Ivory and Jhabvala must first "sell" their idea for a film. Merchant claims to have inherited this "spirit of gambling" from his father, a middle-class East Indian textile merchant with concurrent interests in fast cars and racehorses.

Given this time-tested but dichotomous partnership, it is perhaps not surprising that their films are mostly leisurely paced (some say slow) period pieces reflecting intercultural conflict, sexual repression, and/or the opportunities afforded a "stranger in a strange land" to break free of convention. Masterpiece Theater with a headier sub-text.

"Shy" of Labels

While their adaptation of E. M. Forster's *A Room with a View* was receiving rave reviews and eight Academy Award nominations in 1985, few moviegoers realized that the Merchant and Ivory had already been struggling together for 25 years, and had already independently released over 15 films. With the success of *Maurice* two years later—a classic gay love story also written by Forster in 1914 that was not published (at his request) until after his death in

Ismail Merchant

1970—their popular fame with a gay audience was sealed, even though some had warned that they were foolish to attempt such a lush tribute to gay passion in the middle of the AIDS crisis.

Their other films—with the exception of Vanessa Redgrave's repressed lesbian character in *The Bostonians* (1984)—are as "shy" of being labeled "gay" as they seem. "Homo- hetero-, or bisexual," Merchant told Murray, "the story is what is attractive to me." In commenting about *Maurice* in *People Weekly,* Ivory added that he felt "no more obligation on this film than any other to answer questions about our relationship." Yet, he underscored some "personal meaning" for them by adding that of course "our films reflect our lives—where we've lived—what we've done, whom we know—and our interests. Where else could they come from?"

A Belief in "Kismet" ...

James Ivory was born in 1928 in Berkeley, California, but soon moved with his family to Klamath Falls, Oregon where his father ran a sawmill. He remembers his mother, he told the London *Observer* in 1978, as "a Southern woman with lots of memories of Louisiana and a strong desire to go back there and escape from the cold. [She] hated the wind whistling round the corners of the house and the long winters and the strange plants that barely put out a blossom before they shriveled up." This scenario of longing bred in him an interest in set design and later film—which he pursued at the

University of Southern California—and is probably the bedrock for those long, lingering shots and lush emotional undercurrents typical of Merchant-Ivory productions.

For his master's thesis at USC, Ivory made a 24-minute documentary on Venice, Italy, designed as a portrait of the city using paintings to get a sense of its past social life. In 1957, it made the *New York Time*'s list of ten best documentaries. "The reason I chose Venice," he told the *Observer*, "is simply that I was attracted to the place, and making the film was an excuse to go there.... I think this is typical of my whole career, in a way."

This belief in "kismet" also finds its way into Merchant-Ivory films in the form of parlor-room romanticism (furtive glances across the long, silent dinner table), and happy endings that illustrate triumphs over class and social repression, and, in the case of *Maurice*, sexual strictures. Chance research for his Venice film, for example, led Ivory to a shop in San Francisco displaying vividly-colored, exquisitely detailed miniatures depicting the lives of Indian royalty in their "golden age." This became the subject of his next film, *The Sword and the Flute* (1959), which in turn so impressed the Asia Society of New York that they commissioned him to make a documentary about Delhi (released as *The Delhi Way* in 1964). As fate would have it, Ivory first met Merchant during a screening of *The Sword and the Flute* in New York in 1961, and their partnership was born.

Ismail Merchant had been en route to Cannes for a showing of his own highly acclaimed first film *The Creation of Woman* (1960), made in one weekend with money he received from backers he had met via his advertising job in New York. "During our conversation, that first evening," Merchant told author Robert Emmet Long in *The Films of Merchant Ivory* (1992), "I realized that he knew about India not in a dry academic way but with understanding—something I have never encountered in an American either before or since."

... and Just Plain Tireless Work

If it seems ironic that the California born-and-bred Ivory understood so much about India, the Bombay born-and-educated Merchant balanced it with a savvy for raising film money in America. While skipping graduate classes in business administration at New York University in the late 1950s, Merchant had discovered the films of the legendary Satyajit Ray. "Snap, like that," he told Long, "European films became a passion—Ray, De Sica, Bergman, Fellini." While working as a messenger for the Indian delegation to the United Nations, Merchant made the business contacts that led to his job in advertising and his first backers. With the critical success of *Woman*, he set out for Hollywood, paving his way with a fake press release announcing the arrival of a "famous" Indian producer. "I had discovered that you didn't need money to achieve something," he told Long. "I had done nothing, but I was confident that I *would* do all the things that I said I had done."

Such cunning was also coupled with persistent "networking" and just plain tireless work. In Hollywood, Merchant was forced to take a night job at the *Los Angeles Times* and a day job selling men's clothing. When he learned that a film was required to play at least three days in a commercial venue in order to be considered for an Academy Award, he cajoled the owner of the Fine Arts Cinema in Los Angeles to show *Woman*. As a result, it was seen by enough Academy members to earn a nomination. "I never take no for an answer," Merchant told interviewer Gerald Clark in *Time* in 1987. "It simply does not exist as an option."

Most of the early films of Merchant and Ivory were shot in India, and were geared toward a Western audience. They did not achieve critical world success, however, until they released Jhabvala's adaptation of Henry James's novel *The Europeans* (1979). They followed in 1982 with Jhabvala's screenplay of her own novel, *Heat and Dust*—a story of two English women discovering India—and in 1984 with Henry James's *The Bostonians*. Vanessa Redgrave won an Oscar nomination for her portrayal of a closeted, 19th-century lesbian in *Bostonians*, battling for the love and idealism of a young Madeline Potter against actor Christopher Reeve (he wins).

Timelessness and Fidelity

With the world now watching, Merchant and Ivory were poised for a few "blockbusters." Their first was *A Room with a View* (1986), which opened to astounding commercial, critical, and popular success. It grossed over 60 million dollars worldwide, unheard of for an art film produced on a three million dollar budget!

With *Maurice* (1986)—which Jhabvala backed out of because she felt the story was flawed—the two men obviously felt their better-late-than-never notoriety allowed them to follow their hearts and remain true to author Forster's desire that his two early-twentieth-century lovers remain happy, together, and (after much tribulation and persecution) content with their sexuality and each other at the end. "The laws may have changed regarding homosexuality," Merchant told *People Weekly*, "but people's feelings—the dismay, panic and compromises—they endure." "Gay characters have worked best on the screen when filmmakers have had the rare courage to make no big deal out of them," wrote critic Vito Russo in the *Nation* in 1987. "*Maurice* goes one step further. It is a film about homophobia, repression, and personal courage that takes the sexuality of its characters for granted, even though it depicts a world in which people do not."

Timeless filmmaking has thus become the Merchant-Ivory calling-card. Their style is always sumptuous and emotionally opulent, defying their modest budgets and offering a fidelity to the literary form of whatever adaptation is being brought to the screen—Evan Connell's *Mr. and Mrs. Bridge* (1990), Forster's *Howards End* (1992), and Kazuo Ishigura's *Remains of the Day* (1993) among the most recent. With a few misses—*Slaves of New York* (1989) and *Jefferson in Paris* (1995) among them—their films continue to transport the moviegoer into a realm that surpasses nostalgia and aims for a deeper satisfaction.

Although they obtained dedicated funding by signing a multi-picture deal with a subsidiary of Disney films in 1993, "we don't want to become the flavor of the month," Merchant told Long. "We haven't done everything we wanted to," he also told the *Manchester Guardian* in 1992, "but we wanted everything we've done."

Current Address: Ismail Merchant: 400 East 52nd Street, New York, New York 10022; Garden View, Sutter Street, Bombay, India. James Ivory: P.O. Box 93, Claverack, New York 12513.

References:

Clark, Gerald. In *Time* (New York), 12 January 1987.
London Observer, 9 July 1978.

Long, Robert Emmet. *The Films of Merchant Ivory.* New York: Harry N. Abrams, 1991.
Manchester Guardian, 31 May 1992.
Murray, Raymond. *Images in the Dark: An Encyclopedia of Gay and Lesbian Film and Video.* Philadelphia: TLA Publications, 1994.
Russo, Vito. In *The Nation,* 31 October 1987.
Stark, John. In *People Weekly* (New York), 11 November 1986.

—Jerome Szymczak

Michelangelo Buonarroti

1475-1564

Italian painter, sculptor, poet, and architect

As a genius who excelled in painting, sculpture, poetry, and architecture Michelangelo Buonarroti is the very embodiment of the Renaissance man and one of the greatest artists of all time. Moreover, his love poetry to males constitutes the first large body of such writings in any modern European language and is more extensive than any corpus of pederastic verse that has come down to us from classical antiquity.

We know a great deal about Michelangelo's life. Five volumes of his letters survive, as well as two contemporary biographies. Giorgio Vasari published his in 1550 and expanded it in 1568 after Michelangelo's death. Ascanio Condivi's biography appeared in 1553. To what extent Michelangelo dictated the content of the Condivi text, however, remains unclear.

Michelangelo Buonarroti was born on 6 March 1475 when, Vasari tells us, Mercury and Venus were in the house of Jupiter. Astrologers held that such a configuration would incline the child to the love of men. Both Vasari and Condivi note that Michelangelo considered this tradition to be significant. The second of the five sons of Ludovico Buonarroti Simoni, Michelangelo grew up on the family estate at Settignano, near Arezzo. A stone cutter's wife nursed him. "What good I have comes from the pure air of Arezzo, and also because I sucked in chisels and hammers with my nurse's milk," he told Vasari.

Michelangelo's long career reflects certain aspects of the evolution in taste and temperament that occurred over his lifetime. His first masterpiece, the statue of David completed in 1502 for the city of Florence, captures the Renaissance enthusiasm for the perfection of the male body. The two unfinished Pietàs of his later years possess a rather abstract quality and a pronounced spirituality consistent with the introspection of an old man; yet they also remind us that the artist lived into the period of the Counter-Reformation. The catalog of his intervening accomplishments is remarkable for the monumentality of the work—the nine panels of the Sistine Chapel (1508-1512) to which he later added the "Last Judgment" (1534-1541)—as well as for the range of talents exhibited. In 1547 Michelangelo became chief architect of St. Peter's in Rome. The original architect had died before the projected dome could be built, and those who had attempted to achieve a satisfactory design for the structure had all failed. Michelangelo succeeded.

Michelangelo's Sexuality ...

While documented evidence that Michelangelo had sexual contact with other males is lacking, many contemporary writings hint at the possibility. In a letter dated 1545 which has the stench of blackmail about it, Aretino writes that if Michelangelo will send him a painting, he will quiet the gossips who say that only handsome youths receive the artist's gifts. Benvenuto Cellini relates how Michelangelo supposedly chased after Luigi Pulchi, a young Florentine street performer, who had contracted syphilis from a French bishop. Cellini laments that the artist's "bestial vice" will be his downfall. In another revealing passage from Cellini's autobiography, we learn that at an artist's ball Michelangelo kissed and fawned over a youth in full drag.

To posit that Michelangelo loved and made love to young men does not betray the facts about life in fifteenth-century Florence as we are coming to understand them. Michael Rocke's study of contemporary records reveals that between 1432 and 1502 some 17,000 men were investigated for sodomy or, more precisely, for penetrating teenage males. In addition, within the world of artists, the practice of apprenticing young boys to master artists was widely accepted and created situations in which pederasty might flourish. In a surviving letter Michelangelo tells how a father once offered his son, not only as an apprentice, but also as a bedfellow.

The passion in Michelangelo that Cellini and others allude to surfaces no less in the artist's own writings. He penned 48 quatrains upon the death of Cecchio de' Bracci, who died when only 15. In his study *The Poetry of Michelangelo,* Robert Clements has

Michelangelo Buonarroti

concluded from these verses that the two had sex. To a certain Gherardo Perini of unknown age Michelangelo composed ardent verses and made several gifts. However, according to Vasari, "Immeasurably more than all the rest he loved Tommaso dei Cavalieri," a young nobleman whom Michelangelo met in 1532 when he was 57 and Cavalieri, 23. His relationship with the youth lasted the rest of his life, and Cavalieri was at his bedside when he died. Michelangelo's sonnets to Cavalieri rank among his most powerful and beautiful poetic works.

Although neither his sonnets nor his letters to Cavalieri prove that they shared a sexual bond, it is intriguing to note that Michelangelo gave Cavalieri a drawing depicting the rape of Ganymede. In his *Ganymede in the Renaissance,* James Saslow observes that Michelangelo's Ganymede departs in several respects from earlier treatments. Whereas Ganymede had usually appeared clothed, Michelangelo's version depicts a naked pose "that for the first time exposes Ganymede's genitals." Another innovation is the front-to-back positioning of boy and eagle, which suggests to Robert Liebert "the ecstasy of passive yielding to anal eroticism in the embrace of a more powerful being."

... and the Confusion Surrounding It

Despite the existence of such documents and artifacts, or perhaps because of them, an effort to deny the suggestion of Michelangelo's homosexuality surfaces as early as 1623. In that year his grand nephew published Michelangelo's sonnets for the first time and bowdlerized them, repeatedly replacing the masculine pronoun with a feminine equivalent and in one sonnet excising a pun on Cavalieri's name. He justified his actions on the grounds that if he left the text unchanged it would give ignorant men occasion to murmur. Michelangelo's sexuality became so confused that one scholar, as John A. Symonds notes, asserted that Michelangelo and the writer Vittoria Colonna were lovers. Another concluded that one passionate letter to Cavalieri must have been intended for Colonna with Cavalieri serving as an intermediary.

Symonds was the first person to break with the then centuries-long desire of biographers and histories to whitewash Michelangelo's sexuality. To produce his two-volume biography, *The Life of Michelangelo Buonarroti* (1893), Symonds read all of Michelangelo's letters and poetry and returned consideration of the artist to the reality of the documents that he left us. Nevertheless, even today, considerable disagreement exists over Michelangelo's sexual life. As we have seen, Clements believes that Michelangelo and Bracci were sexually intimate. Liebert and Saslow do not deny that the artist was attracted to males but conclude that he sublimated his homosexual desires. For this divergence of opinions Michelangelo himself bears some responsibility.

On the one hand, he could tell a friend: "Whenever I behold someone who possesses any talent or displays any dexterity of mind, who can do or say something more appropriately than the rest of the world, I am compelled to fall in love with him." On the other, and both of his biographers agree on this point, Michelangelo was a great admirer of Savonarola. In the same year that Michelangelo entered the Medici household, Lorenzo recalled Girolamo Savonarola to Florence. Savonarola harshly criticized sodomy and won over many of Florence's artists to his position. Under his influence, Botticelli returned to the Church; Pico burned five volumes of love poetry. In Michelangelo's case, concern about sin and damnation pervade his later poetry, and his "Last Judgment" makes his fears explicit. We do not know whether sodomy figured among the sins that tormented him, but Symonds, who, it will be recalled, poured over Michelangelo's letters and poetry, concluded that "the tragic accent discernible throughout Michelangelo's love poetry may be due to his sense of discrepancy between his own deepest emotions and the customs of Christian society." Condivi stated flatly in his biography that Michelangelo was sexually continent.

No doubt the debates over Michelangelo's sexuality will continue. However, two indisputable facts remain: Michelangelo produced artistic masterpieces that the passage of time has not diminished, and males inspired much of the finest work he achieved in poetry, sculpture, and painting. The precise nature of Michelangelo's involvement with those males may escape us, but its effect is radiant and enduring.

References:

Cellini, Benvenuto. *Autobiography of Benvenuto Cellini,* translated by J. A. Symonds. New York: Dolphin Books, 1961.

Clements, Robert J. *The Poetry of Michelangelo.* New York: New York University Press, 1965.

Condivi, Ascanio. *The Life of Michelangelo,* translated by Alice Sedgewick Wohl. Baton Rouge: Louisiana State University Press, 1976.

Dynes, Wayne. *Encyclopedia of Homosexuality.* New York: Garland Press, 1990.

———. *Homosexuality: A Research Guide.* New York: Garland Press, 1987.

Liebert, Robert S. *Michelangelo: A Psychoanalytic Study of His Life and Images.* New Haven, Connecticut: Yale University Press, 1983.

Rocke, Michael. *Forbidden Friendships: Homosexuality and Male in Renaissance Florence.* New York: Oxford University Press, 1996.

Saslow, James M. *Ganymede in the Renaissance.* New Haven: Yale University Press, 1986.

———. *The Poetry of Michelangelo.* New Haven, Connecticut: Yale University Press, 1991.

Symonds, John A. *The Life of Michelangelo Buonarroti.* New York: Modern Library, 1928.

Vasari, Giorgio. *Lives of the Most Eminent Painters, Sculptors, and Architects.* London: H. G. Bohn, 1850.

—William Armstrong Percy III

Harvey Milk

1930-1978

American politician and activist

Harvey Milk was a caring, hard working man, devoted to the people he represented. He symbolized the strength of the gay and lesbian community in the face of political opposition. His greatest message was one of hope for the gay community in the face of adversity. While he made many contributions and impetus to the gay rights movement in the 1970s, his life was tragically ended by an assassin. As Milk prophetically stated, "If a bullet should enter my brain, let that bullet destroy every closet door."

Harvey Milk was born in the village of Woodmere, New York, on 22 May 1930. The second son of Russian-Jewish immigrants he grew up in the city of New York. He graduated from the Albany Teachers College in 1951. During the Korean War he served as a Navy deep sea officer in the Pacific. Two years later the Navy discovered his homosexuality and he was dishonorably discharged. As a New York Jew born before World War II he carried memories of the Holocaust, and as a gay man who came of age during the 1950s he vividly remembered being arrested with other gay men for sitting in Central Park without a shirt.

The military's dishonorable discharge stopped Milk from pursuing his teaching career. During the 1950s and 1960s he lived in New York as did many gay men of his generation. He worked for insurance and brokerage firms in the city. He became a prosperous Wall Street financial analyst, living with a male spouse, but remained in the closet except to those nearest to him. He campaigned for Barry Goldwater during the 1964 presidential election. He invested in the musical *Hair* and helped produce several other Broadway plays and musicals. Milk's work in the theater began to dissolve his social and political conservatism. In 1969 he moved to San Francisco and became a securities analyst with a large city firm.

San Francisco Politics

Moving to San Francisco altered Milk's outlook dramatically. After he opened a camera shop on Castro street his fame grew alongside that of the neighborhood. He was the center of attention and helped shape activities in the Castro. Milk soon proceeded to shake up the status quo of the city's gay establishment.

Milk first campaigned for the San Francisco Board of Supervisors in 1973, a decision he felt was precipitated by anger at the Senate Watergate hearings. Standing before the voters with a long ponytail and moustache Milk stated, "I stand for all those who feel that the government no longer understands the individual and no longer respects individual rights." He came out to his constituency at the start of the campaign but only garnered a small number of votes.

He again ran unsuccessfully for supervisor in 1975, on a platform which would return city government to the residents of San Francisco. The next year Milk ran for a seat on the California State Assembly. Many gay leaders supported his heterosexual opponent, Art Agnos. After he decided to run for the Assemblyman seat, Milk was fired from his appointment on the city Board of Permit Appeals by Mayor George Moscone. He went on to lose the campaign to Agnos.

Two years later Milk campaigned again for a seat on the Board of Supervisors. While he had gone relatively unnoticed in the two previous elections, his run for office in 1977 brought him into the national media spotlight as an openly gay politician. People were hired off the street to work his political campaign; sometimes because of their good looks and others on political savvy. Milk proved to know the political game well and how to work the system effectively. He intimately sensed the mood, feelings, and desires of the gay community. He successfully developed a rapport with non-gays, political associates, the media, and the public at large. Milk parlayed an alliance of gay, blue collar, and ethnic voters into a powerful voting bloc. He also made room for the politically disenfranchised: drag queens, dykes on bikes, and boho exiles. Milk, a

Harvey Milk

liberal democrat, campaigned on a "big tent" platform which included expanded child care facilities and programs, free municipal transportation, subsidized housing, and development of a civilian police-review board. His grasp of constituency desires went beyond the confines of the Castro neighborhood.

In the election Milk defeated 16 other candidates with 30 percent of the vote. His victory was part of a populist sweep of city government when the supervisors ran in districts rather than city-wide races. The shakeup in government brought in not only gays, but also, Hispanics, African-Americans, and Asians to city hall.

Following the election victory Milk triumphantly declared to the city and media, "I understand the responsibility of being gay.... I was elected by the people of this district, but I also have a responsibility to gays—not just in this city, but elsewhere." At his supervisor swearing-in ceremony, after other officials had introduced their wives, he presented Jack Lira as "my lover—my partner in life." He was thrust into the political spotlight not only as the city's first openly gay official, but the highest gay government official in the United States. Many believed he had aspirations for higher office.

Working for Change

As San Francisco's first openly gay supervisor, Milk became a symbol of the gay community's will to be included in the functioning of city government. His presence at City Hall forced residents of San Francisco to acknowledge the role gay men and lesbians played in the life of the city.

While Milk was a self described liberal Democrat, many portrayed him as a radical leftist. A careful study of his political career reveals that he retained many of the earlier elements of a conservative upbringing. He believed in the Jeffersonian ideal of the autonomy of small neighborhoods, which prospered through small businesses, local concern for community problems, and grass roots activism. The Castro district was his proving ground. He also held strong belief in the power of the ballot box which many radicals denied. He was a shrewd power broker who knew how to bend and blend with the system. Milk was at home on Castro Street and Polk Street with his gay and lesbian community. He was also just at home in San Francisco's centers of political power whether at City Hall or the state capitol in Sacramento.

Milk often led and managed the direction of the newly elected majority on the board of supervisors. He and his colleagues openly challenged the corporate vision for San Francisco. He vigorously fought for laws that would slow corporate land speculation. He proposed commuter taxes for those working and driving into the city and the legalization of gambling. His crowning achievement during the first term was the approval of a landmark citywide gay-rights ordinance which he submitted and marshalled through the Board of Supervisors. The ordinance forbid antigay discrimination in employment, housing, or public accommodations. The only supervisor to cast a dissenting vote on the ordinance was Dan White. Milk took his message of inspiration and dedication to lesbian and gay organizations around the country.

There was also sex and romance in Milk's life and he knew how to use it effectively as a lethal weapon towards puritanical leaders. Such was the case when he squared off against State Senator John Briggs in a televised debate prior to California's vote on Proposition Six in 1978. The proposition would have prohibited anyone who even advocated homosexuality from teaching in California's public school system. The proposal was Briggs attempt to bring a halt to gay rights in the state. During the debate when Briggs declared that a quarter of all gay men had over 500 sexual encounters, Milk focused upon the camera and said, "I wish." He brilliantly challenged Briggs on his own turf and won hands down. In the fall election Proposition Six went down to defeat.

In a strange twist of fate both Mayor Moscone and Milk were strongly opposed to capital punishment measures. They unsuccessfully fought another November California ballot initiative which expanded the coverage of the death penalty in the state to include among other categories, the murder of a public official in pursuit of duties.

Political Rival Turns Assassin

Milk experienced the dark side of life also. In the fall of 1978 he returned home to discover the lifeless body of his lover Jack Lira, taken by suicide. He kept the grief to himself and maintained the day to day activities of his public office. He allowed the event only minimal attention and focused upon the needs of his constituency.

Milk's vote to place a psychiatric treatment center in the district headed by Supervisor Dan White placed him at further odds with his colleague. In the following months, White resigned from the Board of Supervisors claiming the $9,600 half-time salary was not enough to support his family. Milk urged Mayor Moscone not to reappoint White three weeks later when he requested the supervisor seat be returned to him. After learning his attempt to be reappointed was thwarted, White decided to shoot Mayor Moscone and get even with Milk.

Harvey Milk's first year in public office was tragically cut short by the assassin's bullets on 27 November 1978. Former supervisor White, a political conservative and nemesis of Milk, gunned down both Milk and Mayor Moscone in their City Hall offices. Police alleged that after shooting the Mayor, White hurried past Supervisor Dianne Feinstein's office and approached Milk, asking him if he could talk to him for a moment. After stepping into the office cubicle, five shots rang out. Milk was found with a bullet hole in his back, two body wounds, and two fatal shots to the head. White scrambled out of City Hall undetected by the incoming police units. Later that day, White turned himself in at the Northern Police Station, and confessed to the double murders.

The act of political revenge stunned the city of San Francisco. That evening a crowd of 25,000 mourners held a candle light vigil on the steps of City Hall. Saddened reactions to the murders came from friends, colleagues, and political admirers locally and nationally. They were remembered as politicians who listened to the needs of their constituencies, with concern and compassion. Acting Mayor Dianne Feinstein said of Milk following the tragedy, "The fact of homosexuality gave him an insight into the scars which all oppressed people wear."

Moscone and Milk lay in state in San Francisco's City Hall for two days while thousands of mourners passed by the caskets. Throughout the ensuing week memorial services held throughout the city honored the two slain city officials.

Milk's funerals services were reminiscent of his theatrical background. Mourners arriving aboard ship for the scattering of ashes at sea were greeted by a curious shrine—a dictionary sized box wrapped in Doonesbury comics and on top a single crimson rose. R.I.P was spelled out in rhinestones on the box. Surrounding the container an assortment of grape Kool-Aid packs and a bottle of bubble bath. At sea the crematory box was emptied into the Pacific along with the Kool-Aid and bubble bath. Harvey was gone in a patch of bubbling lavender sea foam into the hereafter.

Death Creates a Political Icon

Milk had a premonition of an early violent death before the age of 50. He deposited at his lawyer's office a last will in the form of three tapes, which were to be played following the occurrence of his death. In the tapes he asked supporters to channel anger in constructive means, to come out and not conceal their identities. Milk said, "I cannot prevent anybody from getting angry, or mad, or frustrated.... I can only hope they turn that anger and frustration and madness into something positive ... and hundreds will step forward, so that gay doctors come out, the gay lawyers, gay judges, gay bankers, gay architects. I hope that every professional gay would just say 'Enough'."

In White's trial defense lawyers mounted the infamous "twinky defense," claiming their client consumed so much junk food that it impaired his judgement. In May of the year following the murders White was found guilty of a lesser charge of voluntary manslaughter and was sentenced by the judge to serve seven years, eight months in the California prison system.

The sentence triggered the White Night Riots in San Francisco. The city's gay and lesbian community erupted in rage at the verdict. Three thousand angry protestors converged on City Hall causing an estimated one million dollars in damage. Addressing the crowd the next day Professor Sally Gearhart declared, "There is no way I will apologize for what happened last night.... Until we display our ungovernable rage at injustices, we won't get heard." After White's release from prison in 1984, he took his own life one year later.

The murder of Harvey Milk ended the rising political career of an openly gay man who may have become a national political figure. In San Francisco politics he mastered the art of building a "rainbow coalition" of disenfranchised voters. Because of his political savvy Milk made it work more successfully for gay and lesbian politics than any other individual before or after. Milk was a man of integrity, courage, idealism, and determination; who has become a political icon. He has left a legacy of gay activism for his followers to strive for. The deep sense of loss experienced by many following his death was a commentary on Milk's life and how he had affected and reached many people.

References:

"Another Day of Death," in *Time,* 11 December 1978: 24-26.

Boyd, Malcolm. "Harvey Milk: A Tribute on the Occasion of Gay Pride Month 1979," in *Blueboy*, July 1979: 8.

"Day of the Assassin," in *Newsweek*, 11 December 1978: 26-28.

Encyclopedia of Homosexuality. New York: Garland Publications, 1990.

Goldstein, Richard. "What He Did for Love," in *Village Voice*, 23 March 1982: 40-41.

Hinkle, Warren. *Gayslayer!: The Story of How Dan White Killed Harvey Milk and George Moscone and Got Away With Murder.* Virginia City, Nevada: Silver Dollar Books, 1985.

Long Road to Freedom: The Advocate History of the Gay and Lesbian Liberation Movement. New York: St. Martin's Press, 1994.

Shilts, Randy. *Mayor of Castro Street: The Life and Times of Harvey Milk.* New York: St. Martin's Press, 1982.

Smenyak, Joe. "Legacy: Pride and Hope," in *Mandate*, July 1982: 10-11, 18-20.

Turner, Wallace. "San Francisco Mayor is Slain; City Supervisor Also Killed; Ex-Official Gives Up to Police," in *New York Times*, 28 November 1978: A1, B12.

Witt, Lynn. *Out in All Directions: The Almanac of Gay and Lesbian America.* New York: Warner Books, 1995.

—Michael A. Lutes

Edna St. Vincent Millay

1892-1950

American poet

Edna St. Vincent Millay was acknowledged as the preeminent woman poet of her time. She won various awards, the most outstanding of those being the Pulitzer Prize for poetry in 1923. Her writing career began early; her first published poem, *Forest Trees*, appeared in *St. Nicholas* magazine when she was 14. *St. Nicholas* was a popular children's periodical that published a number of her juvenile works. Indeed, her letters suggest that she only stopped submitting to them because she passed the age of 18 and was ineligible for publication by their rules.

She was born to Cora Buzzelle Millay and Henry Tolman Millay on 22 February 1892 in Rockland, Maine. She was the eldest of their three daughters, and the only one old enough, at seven years of age, to have some sense of what was happening when her parents separated. They divorced in 1900, and Cora moved herself and her daughters to Camden, Maine, where she brought them up. Despite their disagreements, Cora and Henry Millay seemed to have kept in contact concerning the children. Reputedly, it was his propensity for gambling that broke apart their marriage, but he communicated with his daughters, and occasionally sent money to help with their support. As a young woman, Edna visited him when he was ill. Her letters to him show that she got on well with him, respecting his stable career as an educator, and delighting in his popularity as a person.

Her childhood did not follow the accepted path for a young lady of the time. Her mother certainly believed in education, but she also embraced ideals about personal freedom, and a few notions about how to raise a genius. Obviously, she knew what she was about. Survival, in a financial sense, was often difficult, and Cora Millay worked as a district nurse to support them all. In the early years she stayed near her home, where she could keep a close eye on her girls, but as they grew up she was able to take positions that kept her away from home for days and later even weeks. By dint of all this hard work Cora Millay was able to provide not only the staples, but some "advantages" as well, in the form of music and the materials needed to learn. By the time Edna 12 years old, she was directing her sisters', and her own, study schedules. She wrote elaborate lists, allotting time for music studies, reading, drama, and art. Not too much emphasis on math or science here, but it was an ambitious program of study nonetheless. The three girls had great respect for their mother's work, and her efforts to support them, and it is clear that they loved her and she, them.

Millay was not only published in *St. Nicholas*, but wrote for, and finally became editor of, the Camden High School magazine. She recited an original poem at her graduation in 1909. This foreshadowed her later reading tours. These tours were one way for the dramatically talented Millay to keep the money rolling in. Her voice on the radio, and in personal appearances in the drawing rooms of America, paid for the lifestyle that supported her art. Of course, making a living as a poet, even a well received and frequently published one, can be problematic.

"Renascence," The Beginning

In 1912, at the age of 20, Millay submitted a 214-line poem to Ferdinand Earle, editor of the *Lyric Year*. He was one of three judges in the national poetry contest that was expected to result in an anthology of the 100 best poems in America. She submitted as E. Vincent Millay, and when the editor responded, delighted with her work, he addressed her as 'Dear Sir.' Her letters on this subject suggest that this greatly amused her. Her poem, "Renascence," received fourth prize, despite Earle's emphatic endorsement. When the *Lyric Year* came out, her fourth prize placement created a minor scandal. Orrick Johns, who had been awarded first prize, said, "The outstanding poem in that book was 'Renascence' by Edna St. Vincent Millay, immediately acknowledged by every authoritative critic as such. The award was as much an embarrassment to me as a triumph."

"Renascence" was an amazing accomplishment for a young writer. It begins with great simplicity:

All I could see from where I stood
Was three long mountains and a wood.

Edna St. Vincent Millay

She then progresses through the great mysteries, creation, the creator, and death, in a whirl of language that pulls the reader into the maelstrom, culminating in rebirth:

> The soul can split the sky in two,
> And let the face of God shine through.

When she read the poem publicly she attracted the attention of Caroline Dow of the National Training School of the YWCA, who became her benefactor. Dow helped Millay to shore up the weaknesses in her education so that she could pass the entrance exams to Vassar. Millay had some difficulty in following the rules at Vassar. After all, she was already 21 and used to her freedom, and the college was very restrictive in their attitudes towards young women, as colleges continued to be for another 50 years or so. Vassar College President Henry MacCracken refused all bids to expel her, saying, "I know all about poets at college and I don't want a banished Shelley on my doorstep." She graduated with honors.

Bohemian Youth

Millay lived in New York after her graduation and engaged in a lifestyle that was characterized as bohemian. While maintaining her close ties with her family, for they supported her in most things, she loved often and well. Her letters and poetry speak clearly of her love for both women and men. One or two more amusing poems wonder at discarded loves who expect remembrance and constancy.

Her second volume of poems, *A Few Figs from Thistles*, published in 1920, contains the quatrain that seemed to capture the imagination of a country worried about its flaming youth. She does not, perhaps, deserve to be remembered for such a slight poem, when she has contributed so much greatness.

> My candle burns at both ends;
> It will not last the night;
> But, ah, my foes, and, oh, my friends—
> It gives a lovely light!

Millay's poetry is romantic and conservative in style. Not for her were the wild forms of "modern poetry" that swept the country during her time. She wrote personal lyric poetry, and paved new ground in content, not in form. Conventional subject matter for women included nature, religion, and marriage, and she would not be confined. Millay wrote about her life as she lived it, and about her fears of death and other mystical experiences as they came to her. She displayed the depth, range, and mastery of the feminine character for all the world to read. She did not, however, eschew nature in her poetry. Birds, rabbits, and even the occasional snake all make their appearances. She kept a battered copy of a book on birds that contained many jotted notes on sightings.

Millay went on to write 15 volumes of original poetry, several translations, five verse plays, short fiction, dialogues, and essays. She was prolific because she worked hard at her craft. In 1923 she married Eugen Jan Boissevan, a Dutch-born widower then living in New York. He devoted himself to her care and she, having always been delicate and often in fragile health, rewarded his support with her accomplishments. In 1949 he died, and she followed him in death at their home in Austerlitz, New York on 19 October 1950.

References:

Brittin, Norman A. *Edna St. Vincent Millay.* New York: Twayne Publishers, 1967.

Burko, Miriam. *Restless Spirit.* New York: Crowell, 1962.

Cheney, Anne. *Millay in Greenwich Village.* University of Alabama Press, 1975.

Daffron, Carolyn. *Edna St. Vincent Millay.* New York: Chelsea House Publishers, 1989.

Dash, Joan. *A Life of One's Own: Three Gifted Women and the Men They Married.* New York: Harper and Row, 1973.

Sheean, Vincent. *The Indigo Bunting.* New York: Harper, 1951.

—Sandra Brandenburg

June Millington

1949-

Asian-American musician

June Millington was the leader of Fanny, one of the first and most successful female rock bands in the United States. She subsequently left the rock scene to concentrate on creating women's music, and her achievements in both areas have made her a feminist hero.

When Millington and her sister Jean arrived in California in 1961 from their native Philippines, they received the cold shoulder most newcomers get in American high schools. Sacramento was no different from other American cities where rites of passage included proving yourself to your peers. Like millions of other teenagers in the 1960s, the Millington sisters solved their dilemma with music, trading the ukeleles they had played in the islands for electric guitars. As soon as they started to play music, they made friends. Rock and roll proved to be their lifeline.

Millington and her sister formed several bands before assembling the members of Fanny. They released their first album in 1970 and were an immediate hit. The group recorded and toured for three years, and were particularly successful in England. Their fourth album, *Mothers Pride,* was produced by the renowned Todd Rundgren.

When June and Jean started out in the 1960s, there were few models of strong, successful women in the rock and roll arena. As Fanny's lead guitarist, June found herself in the spotlight, the subject of adulation and admiration. Fame and fortune charged a heavy toll. The pressure led to a nervous breakdown and June's withdrawal from the band in 1973.

She was later initiated into the budding women's music genre through touring with singer-songwriter Cris Williamson, and playing on Williamson's seminal LP, *The Changer and the Changed.* Millington involved herself in the women's music circuit, aghast at the qualitative differences in both the kind of music and the accompanying atmosphere in which it was supported. Millington traded fame and fortune for nurturing, networking, and growth-oriented ideology. She traded the worldly for a more spiritual life. She exchanged the raucous life of the rock and roll road tour for a more peaceful existence, staying in private homes while on the road. Millington changed from a rocker without a cause to a feminist. Finding strength in sisterhood, she appears to have renewed her artistic faith through the women's music movement.

Millington's response was to move toward the positive, to develop a vehicle for teaching the unwary how to make their way in the wilds of the business. In 1987 she founded the Institute for Musical Arts, a North Coast nonprofit center dedicated to furthering the aims of talented women musicians through classes, workshops, lectures and performances. Millington was able to apply knowledge gained from producing solo albums on her own Fabulous Records label to the institute's multi-track Bodega recording studios. Although a fledgling organization based as much on goodwill contributions as on any organized funding drives, the institute put out three albums in 1992.

—Sarah Watstein

Yukio Mishima

1925-1970

Japanese writer

Yukio Mishima was the pen-name of Kimitake Hiraoka. He was born in Tokyo on 14 January 1925, the eldest son of Azusa and Shizue Kiraoka, who were respectively a bureaucrat and the daughter of a school principal. In his relatively short life he rose to become one of Japan's most distinguished and prolific novelists, as well as the author of many plays, short stories and essays.

In his often closely autobiographical first novel *Confessions of a Mask* (1949), Mishima gives an account of his childhood and adolescence. He was taken from his mother almost at birth and for the first 12 years of his life was raised by his domineering and embittered grandmother. In the novel he speculates that her bitterness might have been the result of contracting syphilis from her husband. His first sexual experience was that of masturbating in front of a reproduction of Guido Reni's painting of the "Martyrdom of St. Sebastian." He writes, "The arrows have eaten into the tense, fragrant, youthful flesh and are about to consume his body from within with flames of supreme agony and ecstasy." Here for the first time the erotic connections between male beauty and youth on the one hand and violence and death on the other that mark all his work and culminate in his horrifying death by *seppuku* are clearly established.

In another crucial incident which took place when the author was four, he used to gaze with intense admiration at a picture of a beautiful knight in armor brandishing a sword and confronting "either Death or, at the very least, some hurtling object full of evil power." One day his nurse revealed to him that the figure was actually Joan of Arc dressed as a man and the narrator observes, "I felt as though I had been knocked flat. The person I had thought a *he*

Yukio Mishima

was a *she*. If this beautiful knight was a woman and not a man, what was there left? (Even today I feel a repugnance, deep rooted and hard to explain, toward women in male attire.) This was the first 'revenge by reality' that I had met in life." The novel also documents Mishima's being forced to play only with girls, his frail physique, his falling in love with an older boy, and the deception he practiced on an examining doctor in order to avoid being drafted near the end of the war.

Mishima had a brilliant school career and was accepted into print with a long story "The Forest in Full Bloom" when he was only 16. He graduated at the top of his class from the elite Gakushuin, or Peers School, receiving a silver watch personally from the Emperor, and followed his father's wishes dutifully if reluctantly by studying law at Tokyo University. He worked briefly for the Ministry of Finance before abandoning his position to write full time. He was very quickly successful, following up *Confessions of a Mask* with one of his most subtle and psychologically perceptive novels, *Thirst for Love* (1950), the story of a widow who murders the beautiful, inarticulate peasant with whom she falls in love.

Throughout the 1950s Mishima continued to publish prolifically and sell in large numbers, also producing regular pot-boilers to subsidize the writing of his "real" books. Among his best-known works from this period are *Forbidden Colors* (1951, 1953), one of his few explicitly homosexual works, *The Sound of Waves* and the play *The Nest of the White Ants* (both 1954), *The Temple of the Golden Pavilion* (1956) and the play *Rokumeikan* from the same year. He frequented saunas and bars in the fashionable Ginza district of Tokyo, making friends with various kabuki players, and from 1955 began intensive and widely publicized courses in body building. In 1958, he followed his father's wish and married 21-year-old Yoko Sugiyama, the daughter of a well-known painter. The marriage was organized by Mishima's friend Yasunari Kawabata, who was to win the Nobel Prize for Literature in 1968 that Mishima himself had been widely tipped for. Their daughter Noriko was born in 1959 and son Ichiro two years later.

Mishima's literary reputation began to decline slightly in the 1960s though in 1963 he published one of his best novels, *The Sailor Who Fell from Grace with the Sea.* At the same time, beginning with the U.S.-Japan Security Treaty of 1960 and the resultant riots, he began to grow more politically active and concerned with military things, as if to compensate for his earlier evasion of service. In a brilliant short story, "Patriotism" (1960) he predicts his own death with extraordinary prescience and detail. The story concerns a handsome young officer and his beautiful wife. When the lieutenant's colleagues rise up in 1936 in defence of the Emperor but fail to include him, perhaps out of consideration for his recent marriage, he is called upon to fight against them but cannot do it in honor. He decides to kill himself by *seppuku,* or ritual disembowelment and his devoted wife demands that she be permitted to join him. The story describes their agonizing deaths in excruciating detail. Mishima made a film of it five years later, taking the main role himself.

In much the same way, Mishima began to prepare quite early for his own death. Throughout the last decade of his life he continued to write prolifically, while at the same time attempting to organize a private army, appear in and direct films, and work hard in the theater. He divided his life methodically into four Rivers: Writing, Theater, Body, and Action.

During the final years of his life, writing in enormous haste, he produced the four novels: *Spring Snow, Runaway Horses, The Temple of Dawn,* and *The Decay of the Angel,* of the tetralogy known collectively as *The Sea of Fertility.* In it he sets out, in a fairly lengthy and tedious form, many of his ideas on what he sees as the progressive corruption of Japan in the twentieth century, its secularization and sacrifice of principle and spirituality for material affluence.

On 25 November 1970 Mishima went with his lover, the 24-year-old Masakatsu Morita, and three other followers to the national army headquarters in Ichigaya, central Tokyo. In a series of moves which had clearly been planned with careful precision they captured the commander of the base and demanded the right for Mishima to address the soldiers in return for the general's life. When the troops jeered and refused to listen to his speech Mishima gave up in resigned despair and disembowelled himself, then leaned forward for Morita to behead him. The terrified young man swung wildly, twice missing his head and cutting open his shoulders and back, before another of the disciples more skilled in sword-play took the sword and completed the job successfully. Morita then cut open his own belly and was beheaded.

Mishima presented his carefully planned death as a political act aimed at resurrecting Japanese militarism and returning power to the Emperor but its aesthetic and erotic sources are transparently clear in both his life and work. Only Morita's fear prevented the beautiful and heroic death of which Mishima had long dreamed.

References:

Mishima, Yukio. *Confession of a Mask.* New York: New Directions, 1958.

Nathan, John. *Mishima: A Biography.* Boston: Little, Brown, 1974.

Stokes, Henry Scott. *Life and Death of Yukio Mishima.* New York: Farrar, Straus, 1974.

—Laurie Clancy

Agnes Moorehead

1906-1974

American actress

While she is perhaps best known as Elizabeth Montgomery's manipulative, witchy mother in the 1960s television series, *Bewitched,* actress Agnes Moorehead became famous when she created the role of the bedridden eavesdropper in the radio play, *Sorry Wrong Number.* Moorehead had parts in nearly 60 Hollywood films; and was nominated for best supporting actress Oscars in the films *The Magnificent Ambersons* (1942), *Mrs. Parkington* (1944), *Johnny Belinda* (1948), and *Hush, Hush Sweet Charlotte* (1964). Toward the end of her career, Moorehead was relegated primarily to B movies, where she continued to play the parts of unpleasant, bossy women, including roles in *The Singing Nun* (1965), *What's The Matter With Helen* (1971), and her only starring role in the horror flick *Dear, Dead Delilah* (1971).

Born in Clinton, Massachusetts in 1906, Agnes Robertson Moorehead worked in vaudeville, radio, and stage before making her first movie in 1941. Moorehead married and divorced twice, first Jack G. Lee, and then the much younger Robert Gist.

Agnes Moorehead as she appeared in the television show *Bewitched*.

Moorehead became a member of Orson Welles' innovative Mercury Theatre Company in the 1940s. When Welles made his historic film, *Citizen Kane,* he cast Moorehead as Charles Foster Kane's cold hearted mother. This small role marked the beginning of a long, serious screen life for Moorehead that would consist mainly of playing manipulative, unpleasant, and neurotic women.

Moorehead made Booth Tarkington's *The Magnificent Ambersons* with Welles in 1942, and her role as the frustrated, embittered Aunt Fanny, won her an Academy Award nomination for best supporting actress that year. She worked with Welles again in a small part as a quirky, sullen French woman in *Journey Into Fear* (1942), and in 1943, she played a part similar to Aunt Fanny when she took on the role of the remorseless Mrs. Reed in Welles' production of Robert Stevenson's *Jane Eyre.*

Welles had planned to cast Moorehead in the role of the war crimes commissioner in his 1945 film, *The Stranger,* but executives at RKO studios wanted to cast Edward G. Robinson in the role, and Welles went along with their decision.

Moorehead continued to be cast as repressed women with hidden agendas, frequently to critical acclaim. She was nominated for best supporting actress for her roles in *Mrs. Parkington* (1944), *Johnny Belinda* (1948), and *Hush, Hush Sweet Charlotte* (1964). Long before she was making trouble for the henpecked husband on television's *Bewitched,* Moorehead was mixing it up on screen with Hollywood heavy weights like Joseph Cotton, Walter Pidgeon, and Humphry Bogart. In the 1947 *film noir, Dark Passage,* Moorehead co-stars with Bogart and Lauren Bacall as their bizarre nemesis, and makes a spectacular exit through a plate glass window.

Although she was married twice (her second husband, Robert Gist was twenty years younger than she and the marriage lasted less than a year) and her friend Elsa Lanchester called her the soul of discretion, character actor and comedian Paul Lynde named her "one of the all time Hollywood dykes" in Axel Madsen's exposé, *The Sewing Circle.* "She had a succession of intimate lady friends she'd often go out with," Madsen quotes Lynde. "When one of her husbands was caught cheating, so the story goes, Moorehead screamed at him that if he could have a mistress, so could she!"

Moorehead played opposite Paul Lynde in the television situation comedy, *Bewitched* from 1964-69. She played Elizabeth Montgomery's upper-middle-class witch mother and he played Montgomery's warlock uncle. Moorehead's last performed as a farm animal voice in the animated version of *Charlotte's Web* (1973).

She died of lung cancer in St. Mary's Hospital, Rochester, Minnesota on 30 April 1974. It is a tribute to her acting abilities and her tenacity that Moorehead, like her contemporaries, Barbara Stanwyck, Judith Anderson, and Elsa Lanchester, worked right up to the end of her life, and continued to create hawklike, eerie, and dangerous women for the screen.

References:

Bawden, Liz-Anne, ed. *The Oxford Companion to Film.* Oxford: Oxford University Press, 1976

Halliwell, Leslie. *The Filmgoer's Companion.* New York: Avon, 1971.

Higham, Charles. *The Films of Orson Welles.* University of California Press, 1970

Madsen, Axel, *The Sewing Circle.* Birch Lane Press, 1995

Truitt, Evelyn Mack, ed. *Who Was Who On Screen.* New York: R. R. Bowker, 1983.

—Judith Katz

Cherrie Moraga

1952-

Hispanic-American writer and activist

As a playwright, poet, and essayist who gained mainstream acclaim in the late 1970s and 1980s, Cherrie Moraga was among the first to break through the suffocating boundaries of Chicana/lesbian/feminist writing. Her work not only embodies and speaks to the Chicana experience in general—domestic violence, immigrant rights, male and Catholic domination—but throws open the closet door for lesbian Chicanas to embrace their unique status as newly radicalized voices for their own culture within a culture. "My lesbianism is the avenue through which I have learned the most about silence and oppression," she told interviewer Skye Ward in 1991, "and it continues to be the most tactile reminder to me that we are not free human beings."

Cherrie Moraga was born on 25 September 1952 in Whittier, California to a Chicana mother and an Anglo father of British-

Canadian descent. Her childhood was thus defined by a dichotomy of cultures; she was surrounded by the Spanish language and Mexican traditions of her mother's family, yet she avoided alienation by being able to easily blend in with her white schoolmates. Her mother and aunts were passionate storytellers, and her paternal grandmother was a vaudeville actress who also instilled in her a love for theater. Countless childhood hours were spent in the family kitchen listening to stories, giving Moraga an early appreciation for writing and drama. "The oppositions of race collide inside of me," she told Ward, "[and] my writing is always an attempt at reconciliation."

"Writing to Save My Life"

In 1974, Moraga received a Bachelors degree in art from a private college in Hollywood, becoming one of the few college-educated people in her family. She then taught English at a private high school in Los Angeles for two years, a period she credits with solidifying her need to write. After enrolling in a creative writing class at the Women's Building, she began the tentative process of coming out both as a Chicana and as a lesbian, spurred by the dual injustice of heterosexism and the fact that lesbian literature at the time largely reflected the experiences of white women. "Fundamentally," she told *Art in America* in 1990, "I started writing to save my life. Yes, my own life first."

Her first works were lesbian love poems, and Moraga cites her discovery of Judy Grahn's poem "A Woman Is Talking to Death" as instrumental in cementing her need to write not only as a lesbian, but as a Chicana as well. In 1977, she left the comfort of her teaching position and her extended family in Los Angeles to move to San Francisco, where she pursued an education in feminist/lesbian/Chicana literature at San Francisco State, in coffeehouses, and among a rich variety of like-minded women.

In 1979, Moraga met writer Gloria Anzaldua, and together they edited the groundbreaking anthology *This Bridge Called My Back: Writings by Radical Women of Color* (1981). The collection was precedent-setting because it gave voice to women of color, and expressed their rage at racism and oppression not only in general society, but in the women's movement as well. *Bridge* was a testament to Moraga's drive and vision. After being rejected by dozens of squeamish publishers, Moraga, African-American lesbian activist Barbara Smith, and writer/poet Audre Lorde co-founded Kitchen Table/Women of Color Press to publish it. The book went on to win the American Book Award from the Before Columbus Foundation and is widely used in women's studies courses around the country.

In the preface to *Bridge*, Moraga politicized her literary stance by identifying these women as "the revolutionary forces who bridge the divisions within society." Moraga's own contributions, an essay titled "La Guera" and two poems called "The Welder" and "For the Color of My Mother," launched her work into a political orbit with pressures of its own. "After *Bridge*," she told Ward, "I felt my communities were standing over my shoulders whenever I tried to write.... When one has to represent a community, you can lose the integrity and freedom of your own individual perspective."

"The Woman I Was Raised to Be"

Loving in the War Years (1983) followed soon after, revolutionary as well because it was the first collection of celebratory, passionate poems and journal entries written by a Chicana lesbian, and written in Spanish and English. But in *Loving,* Moraga also includes two essays that take Chicano culture to task for its verbal and sexual silencing of Chicanas. "I am a Chicana lesbian," she writes. "My own particular relationship to being a sexual person, and a radical, stands in direct contradiction to, and violation of, the woman I was raised to be." The seed of Moraga's yearning to speak to her larger community was planted.

In 1983, Moraga co-edited and contributed to *Cuentos: Stories by Latinos,* also published by Kitchen Table-Women of Color Press and, like *Bridge,* a standard text in women's studies courses across the country. In her review of *Cuentos* for the magazine *Third Woman*, Ana Castillo summed up the sentiments of many Chicanas when she said that "the book resounds with the exhilarated breath of the degagged."

In 1984, Moraga presented her first play, *Giving Up the Ghost,* at the Minneapolis women's theater, Foot of the Mountain. In moving monologues, her three main characters explode myths of sexual isolation, challenge claims that defiant Chicanas are traitors to their race, and underscore the complexities of women's relationships in Chicana culture. According to Ward, *Ghost* points out "the salvation and liberation of Chicanas [as] realized through Chicana sisterhood—women loving women as sisters, mothers, daughters, and lovers."

Perhaps one of Moraga's most moving tributes to Chicano, Indian, homosexual, and half-breed culture in general is *The Last Generation,* a collection of her poems and essays dedicated to Audre Lorde and Cesar Chavez which was published in 1986. There she describes her work as "a prayer at a time when I no longer remember how to pray ... [a recognition of] the violent collision between the European and the Indigenous, the birth of a colonization that would give birth to me."

Reunion and Recuperation

Moraga herself describes her shift to playwrighting as a reunion with her people. "It was a great revelation," she told *Art in America* in 1990, "that a much larger community of people could inhabit me and speak through me." Her second play, *Shadow of a Man* (1990), examines the relationship between a mother straightjacketed by tradition and a daughter bent on making her own rules. Generational struggles within the Chicano family are made analogous to those between Chicanos and the dominant Anglo culture. After cavalierly losing her virginity, the daughter exclaims: "I wanted it to be worthless, Mama ... not for me to be worthless, but to know that my worth had nothing to do with it."

Moraga's third play, *Heroes and Saints,* also dramatizes a Chicana woman's struggle for freedom and individuation, but from a more mythic perspective. Here, the main character, Cerezita, is a head without a body, confined to a wheelchair because of her mother's pesticide exposure in the fields, who dreams of liberation for herself and her people.

"Just as we have been radicalized in the process of writing this book," Moraga and Anzaldua wrote in the preface to *Bridge,* "we hope it will radicalize others into action." And just as Moraga has found a recuperative voice within her own struggle for identity, she imparts a wish for that same sense of recuperation and reunion among her readers. "If in the long run," she writes in her poem *If,* "we weep together, hold each other, wipe the other's mouth, dry the kiss pressed there, to seal the touch, of spirits separated, by something as necessary, as time, we will have done enough."

Current Address: c/o Chicano Studies Department, University of California, 3404 Dwinelle Hall, Berkeley, California 94720.

References:

Anzaldua, Gloria and Cherrie Moraga, eds. *This Bridge Called My Back: Writings by Radical Women of Color.* Watertown, Massavhusetts: Persephone Press, 1981.
Castillo, Ana. Review in *Third Woman,* 1986: 135.
Moraga, Cherrie. *Loving in the War Years.* Boston: South End Press, 1983.
Pollack, Sandra and Denise D. Knight, eds. *Contemporary Lesbian Writers of the United States.* Westport, Connecticut: Greenwood Press, 1993.

—Jerome Szymczak

Dee Mosbacher

1949-

American filmmaker and psychiatrist

Dee Mosbacher's career as a psychiatrist, filmmaker, and a lesbian with a politically famous family have earned her support and acclaim in the gay and straight communities in the United States.

Emil Mosbacher, Dee's paternal grandfather, was a millionaire by the age of 21 and her uncle Emil Mosbacher Jr. was Richard Nixon's first Chief of Protocol. Her father, Robert Mosbacher, is a businessman. He was National Finance Chairman for George Bush during his 1988 presidential campaign and Bush's Secretary of Commerce during his presidential term. Her father, although politically conservative, is supportive of his daughter and her coming out. Her mother died in 1970 when Dee was 21. Her father's second wife, Georgette, is the owner of La Prairie Cosmetic company. She has two sisters and a brother.

In high school in Houston, Mosbacher was active in sports. She graduated from Pitzer College, attended Houston's Baylor College of Medicine, did her residency in psychiatry at Harvard University and received a Ph.D. in Social Psychology from Cincinnati's Union Graduate School. Her career includes work as Medical Chief for San Mateo County California's Health Department, and a private psychiatric practice in San Francisco. She serves on several boards including the Lyon-Martin Clinic in San Francisco which serves the needs of poor women in that area. Although the clinic began as a center for lesbian health services, it now serves women who could not otherwise afford private services.

It was when she moved to Washington D.C. that Mosbacher came out to herself. While living there she became involved in several radical political movements including the abortion rights movement, the women's movement, the Young Socialist Alliance, and the anti-war movement.

Mosbacher sees coming out as a powerful political strategy in which to help influence those who create public policy. In an interview with Robert Julian she said, "I'm a strong advocate of coming out. As a physician and psychiatrist I really do believe that our mental health suffers more than we'll ever know by maintaining that kind of secrecy. It just chips away at us." Her own coming out received much public attention, but the outcome was mostly support.

In 1991, Mosbacher created *Lesbian Physicians on Practice, Patients and Power*, a 30-minute-video which includes interviews from the Seventh Annual Lesbian Physicians Conference held in Provincetown, Massachusetts.

Her film, *Straight from the Heart*, was nominated in 1995 for an Oscar in the Best Documentary Short Subject Category. This film written, co-directed and co-produced with Frances Reid, is a documentary in which conservative parents speak about homophobia and dealing with their gay children's sexuality. A minister delivers narration to connect Mosbacher's interviews which include a Mormon family whose son died from AIDS related complications, Conservative Christians, an African-American mother of two lesbians, and a police chief. Because the film includes interviews with Christian families of gay children, it has been helpful to other gay and lesbian children of Christian parents. The video has been targeted to churches and legislators as an educational tool to combat the homophobic efforts of the Radical Right.

Another of her films, *Out for a Change: Addressing Homophobia in Women's Sports*, is a 29-minute-documentary video about lesbians in sports. It features tennis star Martina Navratilova, Helen Carrol, Athletic Director at Mills College and professional basketball player, Mariah Burton Nelson. This film addresses the way in which homophobia operates in women's sports. The assumption that women coaches and sports players are lesbians creates discrimination for all women athletes. Included with the video is a curriculum guide written by Pat Griffin.

As well as her work as a psychiatrist and videographer, Mosbacher has published in *The Journal Of Gay and Lesbian Psychotherapy* and conducted an interview of John Schafly, the gay son of Phyllis Schafly for *10 percent*.

References:

Julian, Robert. "Tales of a Republican Scion," in *The Advocate,* 22 October 1991: 56-58.
Kort, Michele. "Real Life," in *The Advocate,* 4 April 1995: 48-52.
Mosbacher, Dee. "Alcohol and Other Drug Use in Female Medical Students: A Comparison of Lesbians and Heterosexual," in *The Journal of Gay and Lesbian Psycotherapy,* 1993, vol. 2, no. 1: 37-48.
———. "Right. Dee Mosbacher Interviews John Schafly," in *10 percent,* Spring 1993, vol. 1, no. 2: 32-35.
Mosbacher, Dee, dir. *Lesbian Physicians on Practice, Patients and Power*, 1991.
———, dir. *Out for a Change.* Berkeley: Woman Vision Productions and the University of California Extension Center for Media and Independent Learning, 1994.
Mosbacher, Dee and Frances Reid, dirs. *Straight from the Heart.* New York: Cinema Guild, 1994.

—Danielle M. DeMuth

N-O

Martina Navratilova

1956-

American tennis player and activist

From 1970's apolitical athlete to 1990's lesbian and gay activist/spokesperson, Martina Navratilova has held steadfast to the often-brutal roller-coaster ride of fame. From the tennis court to the palimony court, from the painful decision to defect from Czechoslovakia for her beloved America to an outright rejection by a homophobic tabloid and sports press, Navratilova has courageously held out for true acceptance—not mere tolerance—on *her* terms. "What our movement needs most," she told a crowd of hundreds of thousands at the Gay and Lesbian March on Washington in 1993, "is for us to come out of the closet."

"I don't like labels," she wrote in her 1985 autobiography *Martina*. "Just call me Martina." Now retired from tennis at 40, Navratilova is devoting her considerable energy to the fight for gay and lesbian rights—working for the National Gay and Lesbian Task Force and the American Civil Liberties Union, among others. When a reporter at the March on Washington asked her why she was doing all this, she simply, profoundly said that it felt right.

Navratilova has always led with her heart it seems, both on the court and off—a stance that has cost her considerably in both prestige and endorsements (albeit rarely among her gay, lesbian, and straight-but-sensitive admirers). The fact that she and Greg Louganis are still the only two major athletes out of the closet is a testament to the ingrained homophobia still prevalent in the world of sports. "Because she is comfortable in her own skin," author Neil Miller quotes Navratilova's mentor Billie Jean King as saying, "she helps all of us be more comfortable in ours."

"Too Small" to Compete

Navratilova was born to play tennis. Her grandmother was a highly ranked player in Czechoslovakia in the 1940s, both her parents served as tennis coaches for the government, and her sister Jana was also something of an amateur champion in Eastern Europe. All of which is more remarkable given that the Communist-controlled Czechoslovakian Tennis Federation (CTF) discouraged sports over education—"frivolity" over political indoctrination—throughout most of Navratilova's young life.

She grew up skiing in the Krkonose Mountains, and when her family moved to a suburb of Prague in 1961, she spent her summers watching her parents play in one amateur tennis tournament after another. "They took me with them every day," Navratilova recalled in an interview for *Sports Illustrated* in 1975. "I had an old racket my father cut down and I hit a ball against a wall. I could do it for hours. They would make me stop and sit me in a chair, but whenever they didn't watch me I would go to the wall again." Recognizing her dedication, her father started coaching her, and did so until she turned professional in 1973.

By the time she was 14, Navratilova had captured her first national title, despite the fact that Czech officials said she was 'too small' to compete. In an effort to strengthen her legs and arms, she took up ice hockey, swimming, and soccer off the courts. By the age of 16, inspired by her idols Margaret Court and Billie Jean King, she had won two more national women's championships and a junior title to become Czechoslovakia's ranking female player. Thumbing her nose at official pressure and finding less and less time to study anyway, she nonetheless excelled academically. "I never studied" she told *Sports Illustrated*, "but I loved geography, and I imagined myself in places like Chicago and New York."

"Play Like a Boy"

In 1973, the CTF allowed her to play in an eight-week circuit sponsored by the United States Lawn Tennis Association. She

Martina Navratilova

failed to win any of the tournaments—thanks to champion Chris Evert—but played well enough to earn a standing in regular tournament draws. Despite her promise, all the media could focus on was her weight gain and addiction to junk food. In true Western fashion, she admittedly devoured Big Macs, pizzas, and pancakes like they were going out of style. "I was really fat and really slow," she told the *New York Times* years later with some amusement, "but I didn't know it."

Back in Europe the following year, Navratilova lost the weight and fought her way to the doubles finals in Italy and Germany, won the Junior Girls' Championship at Wimbledon, trounced expert clay player Nancy Gunter in the French Open and won a spot on the lucrative U.S. Virginia Slims tour. The former "fatty" astounded the cynical American press with astounding victories in 13 out of 22 matches against some of the toughest competition in the world. By the end of the circuit, she was the tenth-leading money winner in the world, and ranked as Rookie of the Year for *Tennis* magazine.

She was undoubtedly the strongest woman athlete in the game, and often displayed a force and determination on the court that rivaled that of the men. "My father taught me to play aggressively," she said in her autobiography *Martina*, "like a boy. Rush the net. Put it past them. Take a chance. Invent shots." By the summer of 1975, she had made it to the singles finals of seven major international tournaments, captured four doubles championships with partner Evert, and led the Czechs to their first international women's cup victory since 1963. Her winnings totaled over $200,000, second only to Evert's.

Psychological Freedom to Play

Even as her career continued to skyrocket, the CTF watched with trepidation, claiming she was "getting too Americanized." After she "snubbed" Czech officials during the 1975 playoffs at Wimbledon, and extended her stays in America as long as she dared, they clamped down on her commercial endorsements and refused to approve her request to sign up for World Team Tennis. At one point, they actually asked her to quit tennis and finish school. "That's when I realized I would never have the psychological freedom to play the best tennis as long as I was under their control," she said in a 1976 interview for *Sport* magazine.

In September of 1975, she asked the U.S. Naturalization and Immigration Service for asylum, claiming she had no interest in politics but simply wanted to play tennis wherever and whenever she wanted. Two weeks later she asserted her new-found independence by signing a $300,000 three-year contract as a World Team player with the Cleveland Nets, and agreeing to endorse tennis products for another $100,000 a year. "This country was waiting for me," she said in *Martina*. "It would give me the friends and the space and the freedom and the courts and the sneakers and the weight machines and the right food to let me become a tennis champion, to play the best tennis any woman ever played."

All the same, Navratilova recalls this period as the most lonely in her life. Here was a 20-year-old world champion thrust into the unrelenting media spotlight, unable to share her success with the parents so supportive of and instrumental to her earlier achievements. "I wanted them up there in the stand," author Trent Frayne quotes her as saying after her Wimbledon win in 1976. "It's practically impossible for me to go back. The only way I can see them again is if they leave." She did not become a naturalized citizen until 1981, and therefore lived those six years under constant fear of some retaliation against her family. When it was necessary to fly over Communist airspace, she would even make appeals to pilots to alter the flight-path for fear that some mechanical breakdown would force them to land and trap her back behind the Iron Curtain.

This life-wrenching decision was unfortunately not without its consequences on the court. The next two years found her generally floundering, impatient, and out-of-control, even sometimes breaking into tears following a loss or a difficult call by the line-judge. What saved her was her friendship with retired golf champion Sandra Haynie, who represented professional athletes in business. "I tried to assure her she was in the sort of a slump that overtakes everybody," Haynie told Frayne. "When she couldn't understand her bad year, I kept telling her it was normal."

The huge ranch house in Dallas, Texas, that Navratilova shared with Haynie soon became her refuge—the "power-spot" from which she gathered her wits and bounced back as competent on the courts as ever. Haynie encouraged Navratilova to regain control of her weight and her temper. The slightest gesture from Haynie on the sidelines would calm the volatile star, but if the two women were ever more than just good friends, it was never publicly acknowledged.

Romance with Rita Mae Brown

Not that Navratilova had ever been coy about her sexuality, but her new-found American freedom and confidence on the court enabled her to fully explore her lesbianism. But given the high profile of women's tennis in the late 1970s and early 1980s, the rabid pursuit of a now-global tabloid press, and the fact that her family's livelihood back in Czechoslovakia was largely dependent on her notoriety, Navratilova cultivated a low profile. "Looking back to when I was 16 or 17," she wrote in *Martina*, "I can see I had some crushes on women players and didn't really know it. I just liked being with them. By the time I was 18 I knew I always had these feelings." But a political Navratilova was yet to be born. She did not want, according to author Neil Miller, "the sport to be tarred with the brush of lesbianism [any more than it was already]."

Back on top of her game and temperament, Navratilova won seven straight Virginia Slims tournaments beginning in 1978, setting a record by winning 37 consecutive matches and losing only six sets. As her game improved, her confidence swelled, and she overtook close friends Chris Evert and Billie Jean King both on the court and as the media darling. Between 1979 and 1982, her romance with author Rita Mae Brown was as hot a tabloid topic as her burning left serve. The couple bought a house together in Charlottesville, Virginia, and even a Rolls-Royce Silver Cloud II with, according to author Neil Miller, a quote from Virgil—*Amor Vincet Omnia* (Love conquers all)—written on the side. Navratilova found it refreshing to finally be involved with someone who did not really care about her tennis game—someone who in fact did not think much of sports altogether. By Navratilova's own admission, Brown was simply the most interesting, literary person the 23-year-old had ever met. And Brown was obviously smitten beyond the mere research for a Czech character in an upcoming novel that originally brought them together.

According to Miller, it was Navratilova who broke off the relationship in the early 1980s, just as her career began to founder, suggesting that tennis still took precedence in her life. Indeed, as a result of her openness, Navratilova was forced to resign as head of the Women's Tennis Association. Brown got her revenge, Miller notes, by portraying Navratilova "as a temperamental Argentine tennis player in her satirical novel about the women's tennis circuit,

Sudden Death." Nonetheless, the spilt was amicable, the Rolls-Royce was sold, and both women remain friends.

Palimony and Southern "Divorce"

Back on the clay court, Navratilova continued to thrive, capturing nine Wimbledon singles titles and four U.S. Open championships between 1978-1990. Yet now that her sexuality was public knowledge, a cowardly press and squeamish advertisers cost her millions in commercial endorsements. Tennis fans were even sometimes heard yelling "dyke" and "Martina is really a man" from the stands.

In 1984, she embarked on a relationship with Judy Nelson, a former Southern model and "Cotton Maid" queen who actually left her husband and two children to move in with Navratilova. In love, but cautious and aware of the pitfalls of fame and fortune, Navratilova and Nelson videotaped a financial agreement in Texas in 1986, essentially promising Nelson half of everything Navratilova was to earn during the run of the "marriage" should they eventually split up.

In 1992, when they broke up and Nelson sued, Navratilova was livid over what she saw as Nelson's betrayal and what she characterized to the press as a premeditated attempt to line her pockets with "Martina's millions." "I thought I was paying Judy a certain amount of money for every year we were together," Navratilova told Barbara Walters in an interview that year. "But certainly not if I go out and win a tournament and make $100,000 that $50,000 of that should go to Judy."

Obviously Nelson thought otherwise, and a rather healthy palimony settlement (rumored to be nearly $2,000,000) was finally reached out of court. "I did everything for Martina but hit the tennis ball," Nelson was known to remark. But from Navratilova's viewpoint, her only crime was that she did not love Nelson anymore. "Should you have to pay for that?" author Sandra Faulkner quotes her as asking.

In an ironic turn of events, former lover Rita Mae Brown was asked to comment on the breakup in the introduction to Sandra Faulkner's book *Love Match—Nelson vs. Navratilova.* There were even rumors that Nelson and Brown had since become lovers. "Martina hasn't been trained to feel responsible for a partner once the bloom is off the rose," wrote Brown. "As far as I know, no woman has ever been inculcated into this way of thinking toward another woman." In the end, Navratilova was generally and unfairly miscast by the press as the predatory lesbian who had led Nelson astray.

Celebratory Love

"Martina wears her heart on her sleeve," notes Faulkner, "but once it has been broken, she conceals the pain quickly." Such is the perhaps understandable behavior of a champion who has faced off squarely and resolutely with adversity all her life—hiding from Russian tanks as a young girl in Prague, facing continual harassment by Czech secret police, making an emotionally wrenching decision to abandon her family for her treasured America, and then facing rejection and homophobia in her adopted homeland by many of the same people who cheered her lightening performances on the tennis court. "Only life itself is extraordinary enough to tolerate the story of Martina Navratilova," notes author Trent Frayne. "Put it on the silver screen and audiences would figure the [unlikely] plot an insult."

No doubt it is the very circumnavigation of this sometimes-thorny path that has led Navratilova to feel comfortable in the public spotlight of gay activism. In 1996 at the age of 40, she is learning to apply the same stamina that distinguished her on the tennis court to the fight for gay and lesbian rights and the endorsement of gay and lesbian-owned businesses.

Finally, as she told the *International Herald Tribune* in the Summer of 1996, she is in love "in a way I haven't loved before" with L'Oreal model (and niece of U.S. Attorney General Janet Reno) Hunter Reno. It is Navratilova's lifelong outspokenness and determination to be accepted on her own terms that has elevated such a pubic declaration of love above the merely tolerable and into the realm of the celebratory. Such stands make declarations of love and pleas for full acceptance all the more possible for all the rest of us. "Don't worry," she remembers her father telling her as a young girl. "You're a late bloomer."

Current Address: c/o International Management Group, 1 Erieview Plaza, Cleveland, Ohio 44114.

References:

Faulkner, Sandra and Judy Nelson. *Love Match—Nelson vs. Navratilova.* Birch Lane Press.

Frayne, Trent. *Famous Women Tennis Players.* New York: Dodd, Mead & Company.

International Herald Tribune, 18 July 1996.

Jaref, J. "Love Conquers All," in *Sports Illustrated,* 14 April 1975.

Miller, Neil. *Out of the Past—Gay and Lesbian History from 1869 to the Present.* New York: Vintage Books, 1995.

Navratilova, Martina and George Vecsey. *Martina.* New York: Alfred A. Knopf, 1985.

New York Times, 28 August 1976.

Sport, 1976.

—Jerome Szymczak

Holly Near

1949-

American singer, songwriter, actress, and activist

In 1991 Holly Near won *Hot Wire*'s Reader's Choice Award for "her unflinching positivity and ongoing commitment to women and our movement." She has been touted as "an international musical troubadour-ambassador" (Armstrong) as well as "a spy of the heart .. . [who] makes sense to everyone in the neighborhood" (Fissinger). With such widespread acclaim, it is no wonder that she has made cultural bridge building through music her life's work.

Holly Near was born on 4 June 1949 in Ukiah, California, growing up on a ranch in Potter Valley with two sisters and one brother.

Her parents, Anne and Russell Near, raised their children in an atmosphere endowed with both a political leaning for justice and a sky's-the-limit attitude toward ambitions. In her autobiography, *Fire in the Rain ... Singer in the Storm* (1990), Near comments that while they were not "red-diaper babies,... a red shirt had accidentally gotten thrown in the wash with the whites." Near's parents encouraged the developing talent they saw in their daughter. Her father's response to a young Near's request to fly like Peter Pan in a local talent show was, "Every kid deserves to be Peter Pan, isn't that what revolution is for?"

Developing a Talent

Near's early participation in talent shows may not have resulted in the first prize she craved, but it did land her Johnny Mathis's singing coach with whom she trained for nine years. That Near's life was going to be spent singing and performing was clear from an early age. Exactly how that desire was to be realized was yet to be seen. Her earliest dream was to be in Broadway musicals, and in 1969 she was cast in the original Broadway production of *Hair*. From 1968 to 1973, she pursued her acting career, appearing in such films as *Minnie & Moskowitz* and *Slaughterhouse Five* and such TV shows as *All in the Family*, *The Mod Squad*, *Room 222*, *The Bold Ones*, and even *The Partridge Family*. She has since returned to both these mediums: her 1992 play *Fire in the Rain*—based on her autobiography and directed by her sister, Timothy—played in San Jose, San Francisco, Los Angeles, and off-broadway in New York City. In 1992 she played a woman who sued her doctor after surgery on *L.A. Law* and did a small part in Nancy Sevoca's film *Dog Fight*. Her dreams were not limited to singing and acting. With the help of first her parents then many friends, she founded her own record company, Redwood Records, to help both herself and other artists record their music at lower costs.

In 1971 Near was asked to join an antiwar show, *FTA* (*Free the Army*), produced by Jane Fonda, Donald Sutherland, and Francine Parker. The show, although not allowed on military bases, "made soldiers laugh and cry at material that objected to war, racism, and sexism rather than perpetuating them" (Near). This was the first time Near was to touch people by mixing art with politics in a live performance, and it became her medium of choice. For the first time in her life, Near would wake in the middle of the night with such burning questions as "why is it that so many of the soldiers stationed in Viet Nam are Black or Latin" (Near), questions that she could only attempt to answer through songwriting and which led to her first LP, *Hang in There* in 1973. This experience was the catalyst for her singing career in which she performed solo with such accompaniment as Jeff Langley on piano or in collaboration with such artists as Meg Christian, Ronnie Gilbert, and the Chilean group Inti-Illimani.

Clashing Politics/Building Coalition

Near's first political endeavor may have been the peace movement but it certainly was not her last. One of the few strong woman singers who sang with political content, Near was asked to perform at the fund-raiser for the L.A. Women's Building in 1975, the National Women's Music Festival in Champaign-Urbana in 1976, and the first Michigan Women's Music Festival in the summer of 1976. Her role was immediately one of coalition building. She was known to attract a broader audience, including the straight press and members of the peace movement. Friendships with such women as Meg Christian, Margie Adam, Chris Williamson, and Lily Tomlin soon introduced Near to a further political endeavor—feminism. Her growing love for Meg then put her heterosexual tokenism on shaky ground and she was introduced to yet another political endeavor: lesbianism.

But she was never to leave one cause behind for another. Near's most important contribution to both politics and music is her ability to weave together different political tacks and to build harmony through different, potentially opposing, voices.

Near's greatest asset, however, has also brought her the most criticism. First, she is criticized for mixing politics and art. One reviewer of her 1990 *Singer in the Storm* LP comments, "There are times when Near's political rallying cries sound too much like rhetorical cliches" (Nash). Second, she is criticized by her peace movement followers for singing too much about women, often, in the early phases of feminism, being accused of "reverse discrimination." During this time, one group of men who supported women's rights came back stage to voice their disappointment in Near's performance saying she had criticized men throughout her set. Near pointed out she had not been critical of men—in fact had not mentioned men at all—suggesting "they were hurt not because they felt criticized but rather because they had been completely ignored. I asked if they thought they could celebrate women without being the center of attention" (Near). After working on the question, the men sent Near a letter of appreciation and understanding. Finally, she is criticized by women for singing about other political causes that are not central to women's music. Feminists often asked, "Why are you working with all these macho men?" (Near). A reviewer of her 1982 LP *Speed of Light* reminds us how "she's caught hell for not penning more expressly lesbian lyrics" (Walter).

Despite such criticism, Near has kept coalition building at the center of her music and life. She loves "being a weaver, a quiltmaker ... a student of the art of diversity," commenting, "We can take our differences to war or turn them into song, not a song that sounds like either of us alone, but a new song that is a coming together without either of us losing who we are" (Near). Additionally, she challenges those who are not weavers of diversity. During one concert with the Chilean group Inti-Illimani, Near noticed they were not singing on the verse "We are gay and straight together" from "Singing for Our Lives." After the concert, she confronted them, as told in *Fire in the Rain:*

> I am putting my whole organization into strain mode for this peace tour. It is our understanding that this is a collaboration, a coalition, not a service that we are providing.... What do you think is your part in this coalition? In press conferences and from stage, I speak of Chile. But you never mention the women's movement or the condition of women in Chile or the complex effects of exile on women and their children. Do you mention Redwood even once for every ten times I mention Inti? Do you speak of gay rights? (Near 198-99)

The group took Near's words to heart.

Clearly, coalition building is central to Near's project, and she is dedicated to making bridges not only across racial and sexual barriers but also across any barrier that might potentially separate humans. She was one of the first singers to have her concerts signed for the hearing impaired.

Holly Near. ***Photograph by Susan Wilson.***

A Reason to Make the Music Soar

Near's mix of politics can best be seen in the lyrics of her songs. Her output is inspiring—she recorded 16 albums between 1973 and 1993: *Hang in There* (1973); *A Live Album* (1975); *You Can Know All I Am* (1976); *Imagine My Surprise* (1978); *Fire in the Rain* (1981); *Speed of Light* (1982); *Journeys* (1983); *Lifeline* (with Ronnie Gilbert, 1984); *Watch Out!* (1984); *Sing to Me the Dream* (with Inti-Illimani, 1984); *Harp* (with Arlo Guthrie, Gilbert, and Pete Seeger, 1985); *Singing with You* (with Gilbert, 1986); *Don't Hold Back* (1987); *Sky Dances* (1989); *Singer in the Storm* (1990); and *Holly Near: Musical Highlights From The Play Fire in The Rain* (1993).

Some have suggested that Near could do more for the lesbian community by writing more songs that more obviously support lesbianism. Near, however, keeps all of her audiences in mind. She has even commented on the difficulty of writing genderless lyrics but feels politically committed to doing so. This leaning, however, does not mean that she has not written many songs with obviously lesbian content. For example, "Perfect Night" from *Lifeline* contains the satisfying lines: A gentleman asks, "'Are you ladies alone'/ They smile and say, 'No, we're together.'"

Moreover, Near does not shy away from singing such songs to all of her audiences, trying to build bridges even in the face of homophobia. Remembering one predominantly heterosexual folk festival where she felt particularly upset, Near explains:

> I realized I was scared. This is 1988! Can you imagine how huge is the oppression if I, who have been singing and talking about lesbianism and gay rights, I who have been out all over the world for more than a decade, still from time to time am filled with terror?... I stood before the audience as they sat in the silence, waiting for me to do my next song, but the voices inside me were talking loud and deep and the faces of the few gay men and lesbians who had ventured into this family scene burned into my eyes.

Near sang "Simply Love," whose first lines ask "Why does my love make you shift restless in your chair/ And leave you in despair/ It's simply love, my love for a woman." She probes further into the senselessness of homophobia by stating:

> It's the bombs across the border
> That should make you tear your hair
> And yet it's my love leaves you
> Screaming out your nightmare.

She ends the song enigmatically with the suggestion that there may indeed be something to fear: the hatred behind a view that celebrates one type of love while making another disappear. But she does so by switching the hierarchy to ostracize heterosexuality, saying, "Perhaps there's something you know you should fear/ If my love makes me strong and makes you disappear." Of course, there is also the almost pleading suggestion in these lines that the power of love must ultimately overcome that of hate.

Near also celebrates the essence of lesbianism in many of her songs, an essence that she sees breaking the boundaries of sexual expression. This celebration is most clear in her song "She" from *Watch Out!* The lesbian commitment to freedom is seen in the verbs used to describe her actions, "danced" and "soared," and in her lineage: "For she is Freedom's daughter and Mother Nature's child." She is also committed to struggle despite the personal cost as "she found another mountain to be climbed" despite the fact that she "stumbled once in the freezing sand" and "swam" with "her muscles straining strong." She stands for "love and dignity" and "the power of people singing songs/ That celebrated living." And "She is" ongoing peaceful revolution in the face of injustice:

> The killer saw her power, the tyrant saw her skill
> The women saw themselves in her and the people saw her will
> Divided by their colors, betrayed by fear's decree
> But no matter how the future goes, She has been and
> She will always be.

These are just a few of her songs that show how, even in her lyrics, Near constantly brings together her commitment to peace, feminism, lesbianism, and coalition building. It is no surprise that she also has songs celebrating Harriet Tubman, telling of the need to listen to the men and women in prison in Turkey, in El Salvador, in Mississippi, and naming the women missing in Chile. It is no surprise that the song she was asked to write for the students killed at Kent State by the National Guard in 1970 begins, "It could have been me but instead it was you/ So I'll keep doing the work you were doing as if I were two." It is no surprise that thousands of voices have joined to sing her best known song, "Singing for Our Lives," weaving together such verses as

> We are Gay and Straight together ...
> We are an anti-nuclear people ...

We are old and young together ...
We are a gentle loving people
And we are singing, singing for our lives.

Is She or Isn't She

There can be no question that Near's lyrics have helped many lesbians come out and have healed many of the wounds of being in the closet. In addition, Near's willingness to be out on stage at a critical time in our history has done much for the movement. At times, her name has even been used as a code word to help lesbians identify each other (Near). However, since the late 1980s, Near is just as apt to be criticized as praised by the community she has done so much for. Her crime? Sleeping with men.

It should be noted that not all lesbians had trouble with Near's changes—only the loudest ones. The rift was caused as much by those who criticize Near's definition of "lesbian" as by those who, understandably, felt betrayed by a role model. At the time she wrote her autobiography, Near continued to choose to self-define as lesbian. She claimed, "I didn't feel like a bisexual. I felt like a lesbian when I was with a woman and a lesbian making love to a man when I was with a man." Her definition of "lesbian" is reminiscent of Adrienne Rich's "lesbian continuum" by which Rich means "to include a range—through each woman's life and throughout history—of women—identified experience; not simply the fact that a woman has had or consciously desires genital sexual experience with another woman." Rich asks us to expand *lesbian* "to embrace many more forms of primary intensity between and among women, including the sharing of a rich inner life, the bonding against male tyranny, the giving and receiving of practical and political support." Near states, "My lesbianism is not linked to sexual preference. For me, it is part of my world view, part of my passion for women and central in my objection to male domination."

Near's definition of "lesbian" continues in a vein which prefigured Judith Butler: "And due to the nature of my world view, I find I'm not good in narrow spaces. Life doesn't fit neatly into simple categories for me." Butler argues, "[I]dentity categories tend to be instruments of regulatory regimes, whether as the normalizing categories of oppressive structures or as the rallying points for a liberatory contestation of that very oppression. This is not to say that I will not appear at political occasions under the sign of lesbian, but that I would like to have it permanently unclear what precisely that sign signifies."

Holly Near has clearly served as another voice in the debate of the definition of "lesbian" which is at the heart of much of lesbian culture. A quote from a letter dated 22 April 1996 allows an understanding of where Near is today:

> I am in a relationship with a man, have been for almost two years. Before, when I was just having "affairs" I could say I felt like a lesbian sleeping with a man. Now, I can not say that I am a lesbian sleeping with a man. I am a woman in relationship with a man. I am monogamous. I am active in honoring and celebrating lesbian rights and culture just as I am a part of the world peace movement. I sing lesbian songs as well as gender free songs from the stage. I do not know where I go next. This is where I am now.

Ultimately, those who know Near's music must remember what it means to us, those who do not should listen to it and decide for themselves. Hearing Holly Near sing at the 20th Michigan Women's Music Festival in 1995, I remembered the first time I had heard her and again revelled in the impact one female voice can make on one woman's life. I still don't know if it was the strength of her voice or the words she sang, but listening to her, I felt a paradigm shift happen deep within me that stilled the storm. Imagine my surprise!

Current Address: c/o Jo-Lynne Worley, P.O. Box 10408, Oakland, California 94610.

References:

Armstrong, Toni Jr. "Holly Near's Autobiographical Musical Docudrama: Fire in the Rain ... Singer in the Storm," in *Hot Wire,* May 1992, vol. 8, no. 2: 50-51, 54.

Butler, Judith. "Imitation and Gender Insubordination," in *The Lesbian and Gay Studies Reader,* edited by Henry Abelove, Michele Aina Barale, and David M. Halperin. New York: Routledge, 1993: 307-320.

Fissinger, Laura. "Fire in the Rain: Holly Near," in *Rolling Stone,* 25 June 1981, no. 346: 56.

Nash, Alanna. "Holly Near," in *Stereo Review,* January 1991, vol. 56, no. 1: 122.

Near, Holly. *Fire in the Rain ... Singer in the Storm: An Autobiography,* with Derk Richardson. New York: William Morrow and Company, Inc., 1990: 58, 71, 134, 161, 197-99, 205, 275.

Rich, Adrienne. "Compulsory Heterosexuality and Lesbian Existence," in *The Signs Reader: Women, Gender, and Scholarship,* edited by Elizabeth Abel and Emily Abel. Chicago: University of Chicago Press, 1983: 139-68.

"The Sixth Annual Reader's Choice Awards," in *Hot Wire,* September 1991, vol. 7, no. 3: 40.

Walter, Kate. "Something About These Women," in *Village Voice,* 26 April 1983, vol. 28, no. 17: 68-69.

—Liz Cannon

Joan Nestle

1940-

American archivist and writer

For Joan Nestle, history and literature are inextricably connected. For over thirty years, she has written political essays, poetry, and erotic short stories designed to address common assumptions and misconceptions surrounding lesbian sexuality, butch-femme relationships, pornography, censorship, and the often-shaky camaraderie among lesbians as that community continues to flex its diversity. She has published her work in dozens of wide-ranging women's periodicals and anthologies, edited several more on female sexuality and femme-butch desire, explored the rich relationships between gay brothers and sisters, and lectured at hundreds of university campuses and forums on the importance of not marginalizing "traditional," pre-Stonewall gays and lesbians and consequently "losing" them in the current politically-correct shuffle.

As a result of her outspokenness, Nestle has tackled issues of prejudice and what she terms "sexual bigotry" not only from heterosexuals, but from within lesbian/feminist communities as well. Only the most unflinching look at the diverse history of lesbian life is valid, she asserts, even if such rebel sexuality as butch-femme identification—not mere role-playing—is now considered taboo. Members of Women Against Pornography (WAP) have even called for censorship of what they feel are Nestle's pornographic depictions of lesbian sex—but Nestle holds fast. "I wanted people," she told *Advocate* interviewer Victoria A. Brownworth in 1992, "especially lesbians, to see that the butch-femme relationship isn't just some negative heterosexual aping." "If I wrote about flowers," she told writer Holly Metz in *The Progressive* in 1989, "if I used metaphors, it would be okay. But I couldn't."

Pre-Stonewall Pioneers

Joan Nestle was born on 12 May 1940 in New York City. Her father died before her birth, so she was raised by her mother Regina who, according to Nestle in her own collection of writings titled *A Restricted Country,* "left her with two satchels of scribbled writings" and a "belief in a woman's undeniable right to enjoy sex" (see "My Mother Liked to Fuck").

In 1957, Nestle graduated from Martin Van Buren High School in Queens. In 1963, she got her B.A. in English from Queens College in Flushing, New York, where she still teaches English and Creative Writing. In 1968, she got her M.A. in English from New York University, and spent the next two years as a doctoral candidate in English, where she completed all her doctoral work except for her thesis.

Nestle's academic education was augmented by her visits to the gay and lesbian bars in Greenwich Village during the late 1950s and throughout the 1960s. From adolescence on, Nestle was aware of her attraction to women. She readily identified her teenage self as a "femme" and soaked-up the edgy, furtive experiences—the sharply delineated and courageous butch/femme characters, frequent raids by the vice squad—that defined Village lesbian bar-life in mid-century America.

These were women with pre-Stonewall fearlessness, struggling for acceptance and social connectedness in a time when their lifestyles were considered criminal. They were pioneers whose struggles Nestle determined should never be forgotten. In short, it was an era that has animated Nestle's political work and writing ever since. "My writing life began in the smoky backroom bars of the 1950s," she told Deborah A. Stanley in *Gay & Lesbian Literature,* "where as a young femme I witnessed both the glory of individual courage and the terror of institutionalized oppression. The work I do is in memory of their courage."

Herstory is Born

At the same time, however, Nestle's beliefs in equal rights overall were broadening. A life "in the shadows" was to prove inadequate for the challenges she saw looming ahead. Her political passion was formalized when she joined in the civil rights march from Selma to Montgomery, Alabama in 1965. In the mid-1960s, she also became involved with the Congress of Racial Equality (CORE) and went South to assist in voter registration drives. In 1971, she became officially active in the feminist movement by joining the Lesbian Liberation Committee. And in 1972, she helped establish the Gay Academic Union (GAU) to speak to and for lesbians and gays on college campuses across the country. Even in post-Stonewall times, Nestle contends, butch-femme lesbians shoulder a growing contempt for who they are; and now it also comes from their own sisters and brothers who want them to assimilate for the "political progress" of the cause.

In 1973, Nestle and a group of lesbians she had met via the GAU decided to chronicle and document the lesbian experience in the United States prior to the feminist movement. The result was the Lesbian Herstory Archives, first housed in a room in Nestle's apartment and, by 1992, large enough to fill a three-story house in Park Slope, Brooklyn, which is still their permanent home. "To live without history is to live like an infant," Nestle wrote in *A Restricted Country,* "constantly amazed and challenged by a strange and unnamed world."

The thousands of books, letters, photographs, and private journal entries that comprise the still-growing archives are an effort to define the lesbian experience on both an individual and a communal level. "I see literature," Nestle told writer Susan Rochman in *Contemporary Lesbian Writers of the United States,* "as the expression of history and history as a form of literature." According to Nestle, history allows us to examine what went wrong and what went right, and documenting it allows us to experience the changes we observe both as individuals and as a community. What results is a certain "complication of issues" that defy simplistic analysis—an unwillingness on the part of the young to believe some stories of oppression are even real. "My roots lie in the history of a people who were called freaks," Nestle says in *A Restricted Country.* "I need to keep alive the memory that in the 1940s doctors measured the clitorises and nipples of lesbians to prove our strangeness ... [and that] transvestites and transsexuals [were routinely] beaten by the police."

Even in the so-called "progressive" 1980s, Nestle recalls an article appearing in the *Journal of Homosexuality* in 1981—provocatively titled "Sexual Preference or Personal Style: Why Are Lesbians Disliked?"—which recommended that queer women "tone-down" their butch/femme personalities for a more placating androgynous one in order to find "greater homosexual acceptance." Such respectability and safety is not, according to Nestle, worth the price of separating ourselves from what she calls in *A Restricted Country* "the easily recognizable other."

"Deviant, Outcast, Other"

Overall, Nestle strives to speak for all "lesbian rebels" in the same way she has always proudly presented all of who she is in her writings. What is or is not permissible, the testing of boundaries, the stigma and strength of being an outsider—all of these are intertwining themes in her work. Just as she proudly presents all of herself—feminist, lesbian, Jewish, femme—she also describes, according to Rochman, "how her body—strong, defiant, and sexual—provided her with the ability to take part in and define history, and how it became a living marker for others' definitions: deviant, outcast, other.

What results, particularly in *A Restricted Country* and essays like "The Fem Question," is a challenge to the oppressors and "mainstreamed lesbians" alike. Individual memory is elevated above that of mere autobiography and into the realm of collective history which, in Nestle's focus, becomes a history of lesbian passion, discrimination, and (sometimes) censorship and criticism from within her own community. "History will betray us if we betray it," she writes in *A Restricted Country.* "I write [erotica] to celebrate the fineness and richness of sexuality, the complexity of women's desire, because it is at the center of our history as it is at the center of our oppression as gay people."

One of Nestle's most notorious works—*Esther's Story*—is often held up as a prime example of her "pornographic" bent. It's about a one-night stand Nestle had with a woman passing as a man in the straight world. Feminists on all sides have attacked it and other stories (including her account of her mother's free spirit in *Country*) as "offensive." Others have praised these as revelatory and revolutionary for breaking long-held silences on women's sexuality in general.

"I listen very quietly to their expressions of pain, fear, or anger," Nestle told Metz, "and I have to pay it respect if I'm going to have any kind of dialogue at all." In her defense, however, Nestle notes that women have long enjoyed a variety of ways to be sexual that is beyond the label of victimization. Anti-pornographers must be willing to recognize that women have varied sexual experiences—both celebratory and "dangerous"—of their own free will. "Politically," Nestle told Metz, "the [anti-pornography] setting is one that will NOT save women, and in fact will do terrible damage to sexual minorities." In the end, Nestle sides with those who believe sexual experimentation and independence should never be regulated or silenced. New sexual territories should always—indeed, HAVE always—been open to and explored by women, as her unflinching look at lesbian history proves.

Women on Women

In 1990, Nestle joined with Naomi Holoch to co-edit an anthology of American lesbian short stories called *Women on Women.* By 1996, Holoch and Nestle were publishing a popular third edition designed to overturn the notion that lesbian writing is somehow a homogeneous, predictable genre. Their goal was to provide lesbians with an outlet "to see their lives in a different way," as they note in the introduction.

But beyond this, the collections stand out because they capture the magic of women's similarities and differences with one another in socioeconomic, historical, and familial terms—areas of distinction and difference too long ignored and unspoken. Contributions by Barbara Smith, Sheila Ortiz, Taylor, Frankie Hucklenbroich, and Lu Vicker, for example, attest to the vastly different ethnic and intergenerational experiences among American lesbians who were "coming of age." "Most of my friends have such passionate, complicated relationships with their mothers," writes Smith, for example, in her contribution to *Women on Women 3* titled "Home Story." "Since they don't get married and dragged off into other families, they don't have to automatically cut off their ties, be grown-up heterosexuals. I think their mothers help them to be lesbians.... I still want what they have, what they have taken for granted."

Can We Talk?

In 1994, Nestle and fellow editor John Preston set out to explore gay and lesbian sibling similarities and differences in a collection of 33 stories titled *Sister & Brother: Lesbians and Gay Men Write About Their Lives.* What may at first have seemed a departure for Nestle was, in reality, not one at all. Here she was setting-out to expose another intricate and complicated, heretofore unexplored history and culture—only this time of the kind brothers and sisters share when they both realize they are gay ... are both alone and not alone in the family.

When contributor Joyce Zonana writes, for example, of her relationship with her gay brother, she seems to reflect what Nestle has strived to do for decades with her own political essays on butch-femme marginalization. "Suddenly," Zonana says, "I knew that he was one kind of child, that he was another.... He was at the center; I was at the margin. [Now] Victor's still the one with the penis, I'm still the one in the dress. But we're also both the ones who are queer.... We've left behind the roles assigned to us ... having found places to stand where we are equally at the center or at the margin, each simultaneously speaking or silent, each simultaneously nurturing or nurtured."

Nestle no doubt appreciates the sentiment, the re-examination of different ways of "being" lesbian, and the re-establishment of a certain erotic responsibility for who we are. "If the personal is political [as the women's movement taught us]," she says in *A Restricted Country,* "the more personal is historical. [It] demands attention be paid to how we fill our days and nights in any given economic system, how our flesh survives under different political systems, how we humanize gender tyranny, how we experience womanness and maleness in all the superstructures of class and race."

Current Address: 215 West 92nd Street, New York, New York 10025.

References:

Brownworth, Victoria A. "Joan Nestle: The Politics of *The Persistent Desire,*" in *Advocate* (New York), 2 June 1992: 39.

Metz, Holly. In *The Progressive* (Madison, Wisconsin), August 1989: 16-17.

Nestle, Joan. *A Restricted Country.* Ithaca, New York: Firebrand Books, 1987.

Nestle, Joan and John Preston, eds. *Sister & Brother: Lesbians and Gay Men Write About Their Lives Together.* San Francisco: Harper, 1994.

Nestle, Joan and Naomi Holoch, eds. *Women on Women 3: A New Anthology of American Lesbian Short Fiction.* New York: Plume, 1996.

Rochman, Susan. In *Contemporary Lesbian Writers of the United States,* edited by Sandra Pollack and Denise D. Knight. Westport, Connecticut: Greenwood Press, 1994.

Stanely, Deborah A. In *Gay & Lesbian Literature.* Detroit, Michigan: St. James Press, 1994: 279-280.

Summers, Claude J., ed. *The Gay and Lesbian Literary Heritage.* New York: Henry Holt, 1995.

—Jerome Szymczak

Florence Nightingale

1820-1910

British nurse, medical reformer, and diarist

Florence Nightingale is best remembered as the founder of modern nursing. But she was also an astounding woman of letters, who left behind over 10,000 diary entries and manuscripts calling for hospital reforms, extolling the virtues of preventive medicine throughout the British Empire, and calling attention to the "Cassandra" plight of Victorian women. Any strong-willed woman of her time was expected to sacrifice her "natural state" if she did not marry (Florence chose God and her vocation over matrimony), and was reduced to suffering and illness in order to maintain any control over her life (she was an enervated, yet powerful and influential invalid for the last 50 years of her life following her famous work on the battlefields during the Crimean War).

It is this mix of independent action and strategic sickness in Nightingale's two-act life that makes it so fascinating—and so contradictory. Although she struggled throughout her life against the constraints placed on women, she nonetheless praised the virtues of female modesty and anonymous service. She looked to female friends for emotional support, and to male colleagues for respect and assistance. The nursing reforms she pioneered are best remembered because they were appropriately female for her time, while her other major contributions as a sanitarian and political advisor are overlooked because of their male nature.

Rebel Daughter

Florence Nightingale was born in Florence, Italy on 12 May 1820 to Fanny and William Edward Nightingale. She was the second of two daughters christened by their mother in honor of European cities—what was then a novel approach. (Her older sister was named Frances Parthenope after Fanny's Greek birthplace.) By the mid-1800s, thousands of girls around the world would be named Florence in honor of this remarkable woman.

Both "Pop" and "Flo" (as they were called) grew up with all the affection and security, intellectual challenges, opportunities, and comforts that a fairly well-to-do nineteenth-century family could offer. Both girls were rigorously schooled by their liberal father in Greek, Latin, German, French, Italian, history, grammar, and philosophy. The more gregarious Fanny insisted on a governess to instruct them in music and art, and a certain rivalry between the sisters soon flourished. Flo rose to the challenges presented by her father and shared his passion for both accuracy and humanitarianism. Pop, on the other hand, excelled in writing and art and, as a result, evolved as the prettier and more popular favorite among her mother's set of wealthy socialites.

Nightingale thus became the introvert—the rebel daughter—variously described as strange, passionate, obstinate, and wrong-headed by her parents. As a young woman in her teens, she wrote in great length in her diaries of her retreat into dreams, her feelings of being called by God into a greater service than embroidery, walks in the garden, and planning parties, and her passionate attachments to her governess, her spinster aunt, and a beautiful older cousin. She never married, professing that "some [women] have every reason for not marrying,... it is much better to educate the children who are already in the world and can't be got out of it, than to bring more into it."

Her growing social consciousness was legitimized by four separate experiences in her life where she claims to have heard voices from God—the first when she was just 16—calling her to a life of toil to benefit the sick and poor. In this way her religious and vocational fervor has been likened to that of Joan of Arc.

When in her mid-twenties she announced her plans to become a nurse, her mother and sister were both horrified and hysterical, and her father, wary of family tensions, wrestled with ambivalence. His lack of outright approval sealed her resentment for him and drove her to the self-destructive fervor that characterized her work.

Florence Nightingale

"The Hey-Day of My Power"

Several more years of "Victorian respectability" were to stand between Nightingale and her dreams, however. Because she resisted the notion of marriage, she travelled extensively across Europe with friends, witnessing the plight of the poor and sick in Italy and Greece, and writing vociferously in her diaries, according to author Nancy Boyd, about the need to "play down biological mothering in favor of 'social mothering.'"

In 1851, Nightingale attended Kaiserwerth Hospital in London to learn the skills of nursing. She thrived on the demanding schedule and, as she wrote to her mother, seemed to come to life in contact with patients and co-workers. "The world here fills my life with interest and strengthens the body and mind," she wrote in 1851.

By 1853, Nightingale had secured a job as superintendent at an Establishment for Gentlewomen during Illness in Harley Street. It was soon apparent that her skills were best applied in administration. Much of her work and recommendations to committees of medical men had to be carried out with what she termed "intrigue"—which simply meant hiding the fact that suggestions for improvement were coming from a woman. "I am now in the hey-dey of my power," she wrote to her father of her time there.

England declared war on Russia in 1854, and in the resulting two-year Crimean War, vast numbers of British soldiers were dying due to a lack of medical provisions and proper nursing care. Nightingale recruited a staff of 14 nurses and headed for the battlefields. Working outside the constraints of bureaucratic strictures, she enraged doctors and incompetent politicians by simply acting as she saw fit. "She had powerful weapons at her command," wrote Boyd. "An able mind, a strong will, access to Cabinet officials, a sympathetic press waiting to publish words from her articulate tongue and pen, and—perhaps most important of all—money."

Lady of the Lamp

Here was born the legendary "Nightingale power" that became the archetype of heroic Victorian womanhood and brought hope to middle-class Victorian women for breaking out of their traditionally idle roles. She was celebrated in both picture and verse as "The Lady of the Lamp"—the tireless incarnation of Queen Victoria on the battlefield ministering to the sick, persevering in a setting of danger and excitement, making important decisions, and taking on critical responsibilities. In addition to her endless nursing and administrative duties, she surveyed grounds for a cemetery; handed out 50,000 shirts; planned, built, and paid for a hospital to accommodate over 800 patients; and wrote hundreds of letters describing the final hours of dying soldiers for their grieving relatives. "Without disturbing the underlying assumptions in the male-female relationship," notes Boyd, "[she] showed, perhaps, that you could have your cake without eating it; [providing] a halfway house between dependence and independence,... the best of two worlds, change without revolution, progress with security."

By August of 1856, the saint had become a not-altogether-unwilling martyr. In peace as in war, she had the ear of the press and the backing of England's leaders, a status she was to enjoy for the rest of her life. She had contracted a mysterious fever whose manifestations came and went over the next 54 years, leaving her severely debilitated and bed-ridden throughout most of it. There was little doubt on the part of doctors that her illness was physical, but she sometimes wrote that she believed it's cause was emotional, stemming from her troubled childhood. It put her in complete charge of her notoriety. People came to her only when she was fit to receive them, and she could finally avoid her family if and when she chose.

Her illness also gave her the upper hand over her fellow workers. How could able-bodied doctors and nurses strive for less than this woman who had been irreparably damaged in service to her country? "By appealing to the pride and the guilt of Cabinet members, Viceroys of India, generals, and prime ministers," wrote Boyd, "she spurred them to emulate the implacably high standards of devotion-unto-death set by The Lady of the Lamp."

Even as an invalid she continued to fight for medical reforms throughout the British Empire by championing the then-novel notion of preventive medicine in villages in India and hospitals in Australia. She also pioneered the use of statistical analysis to understand better the nature and genesis of disease, and she pursued her advocacy for better medical treatment for the poor.

Toward the end of her life, she more openly praised the efficacy of women tackling traditional male roles. "Why cannot a woman follow abstractions like a man? Has she less imagination, less intellect, less self-devotion, less religion than a man? I think not," she wrote to her father in 1846. With maturity and fame, she became less candid, writing late in life: "I have lived and slept in the same bed with English countesses and Prussian farm women ... no woman has excited passions among women more than I have."

References:

The Alyson Almanac. Boston: Alyson Publications, 1994-95.

Boyd, Nancy. *Three Victorian Women Who Changed the World.* New York: Oxford University Press, 1982.

Showalter, Elaine. *The Female Malady—Women, Madness, and English Culture, 1830-1980.* New York: Pantheon Books, 1985.

Vicinus, Martha and Bea Nergaard, eds. *Ever Yours, Florence Nightingale—Selected Letters.* Cambridge, Massachusetts: Harvard University Press, 1990.

—Jerome Szymczak

Simon Nkoli

1957-

South African activist and AIDS educator

Simon Nkoli is the first black South African to have gained national and international attention for coming out as a gay man. Nkoli's arrest and trial as a member of the anti-apartheid movement—combined with the efforts of like-minded gay and lesbian nonracialists—forced South African white gay men and lesbians to take positions about apartheid, propelled the anti-apartheid movement to include gay and lesbian rights within its vision of a more just society, and contributed strategically to a worldwide discussion of the place of sexual liberation within the politics of social justice.

Tseko Simon Nkoli (last name pronounced Ni-ko-dy) was born in the South African township of Phiri, in Soweto, the area which the apartheid-era Group Areas Act designated for African and mixed-race residence outside of Johannesburg, which was reserved by law for those of European descent. His parents separated while he was young and at age two he was sent to live with his grandparents, tenants on the property of a white farmer in the rural Orange Free State. Nkoli walked 14 kilometers a day for schooling and worked on the farm as required by the landowner.

In an interview published in the anthology *The Invisible Ghetto*, Nkoli recalls, "I would leave the work and run to school, and then I would quickly return to the farm at playtime.... I used to reap the mealies, which was quite a heavy thing for a child.... Once a child had completed 10 bags, it would get 10 cents.... And if you hadn't done anything by a certain time,... [the farmer would] chase us on his horse, and then we would get flogged with his whip."

At age 13, Nkoli ran away from the farm because his grandparents and the farmer agreed that his schooling should end. Traveling by foot and train and by hitchhiking, Nkoli managed to make his way back to the Johannesburg township of Bophelong where his mother, stepfather, and two younger half-sisters lived. Nkoli's mother, Elizabeth, worked as a domestic, later as a sales clerk; his stepfather, Elias, was a hotel chef.

Fighting Apartheid and Coming Out

While a high school student, Nkoli became a member of the United Democratic Front (UDF), the leading legally permitted anti-apartheid group. Nkoli's position as a student leader during the Soweto uprising of 1976 led to his imprisonment for three months. By 1981, Nkoli earned the position of Secretary of the Johannesburg regional branch of the Congress of South African Students.

Like many gay men, Nkoli became aware of his homosexuality during his teen years. His first gay relationship began at the age of 19 with Andre Van Zyl, a 22-year-old white bus driver who had placed an ad in *Hit Magazine* for teens, requesting black pen pals. At Nkoli's 20th birthday party, he came out to his parents who reacted with anger and bewilderment. Though they eventually accepted his homosexuality, they first took Nkoli to all manner of "healers," including traditional African *sangomas*, their parish priest, and finally a psychiatrist. Ironically, the psychiatrist turned out to be gay himself and gave the lovers the idea of living together under the pretense that Nkoli was his lover's domestic servant.

In an interview published in the *Advocate*, Nkoli talked about this relationship, "It was not a comfortable relationship because of the political climate of the time. We didn't live together until we both decided to go to college.... The problem was with our parents. His family accepted his being gay, but not the fact that he was having a relationship with a black." From his political associates at the time, Nkoli experienced mixed reactions. He told the *Advocate*, "Some people did not believe that I was gay, and some people did reject me. There were those who were actually afraid to walk down the street with me. But I was lucky because the majority of people I was working with did not shun me."

Nkoli joined GASA (the Gay Association of South Africa) in 1980, but quickly became frustrated by its lack of black members and lack of attention to political issues. Nkoli told the *Advocate*, "I tried to go to GASA functions, but I couldn't attend those in the evening because of the Group Areas Act. I then tried to go to some gay nightclubs but was chased out or told they were for members only. I'd write letter to gay newspapers, telling them I was discriminated against and that GASA didn't seem interested in taking up political issues." In 1983, Nkoli began organizing an explicitly nonracial subgroup of GASA. "I decided to reach out to the black community. I wrote an article in the *City Press*, [a major black newspaper] calling on gay black people, if there were any, to contact me. I gave my address even though I could have been bashed. I got lots of responses, not only from Johannesburg, but from all around South Africa," Nkoli recalled for the *Advocate*. This led to the formation of The Saturday Group, the first predominantly black gay organization in South Africa.

Imprisoned for Treason

Soon after the formation of the Saturday Group in 1984, Nkoli was arrested with 21 other prominent leaders of the UDF and charged with treason and murder for deaths following a protest march against rent hikes in the townships. The Delmas Treason Trial became the most important rallying point for the liberation movement since Nelson Mandela's treason trial in 1962. Nkoli spent three years in jail, was released on bail 30 June 1987 and finally acquitted on 17 November 1987.

Gay and lesbian activists in South Africa and in the international anti-apartheid movement focused great attention on Nkoli's confinement and trial. In an interview published in the anthology *Defiant Desire*, Nkoli credited this worldwide support with helping to sway his codefendants to accepting him as a gay man: "What helped me most was that I received so many letters. I was the focus of attention in the trial, especially because of my homosexuality.... And so I would say to the others, 'Look people won't be against us [because of my homosexuality]. Look how much support I'm getting.'"

GASA's lack of effort on Nkoli's behalf resulted in its expulsion from ILGA (the International Lesbian and Gay Association) and to the formation of more politically involved gay/lesbian organizations in South Africa, including Lesbians and Gays Against Oppression and Organization of Lesbian and Gay Activists (OLGA) in Cape Town. Soon after his release from prison, Nkoli co-founded GLOW (Gay and Lesbian Organization of Witwatersrand [the Johannesburg area]), a predominantly black group which became the leading gay activist group in the region. He also made a 26-city tour of Europe and North America speaking about his experiences during the trial and solidifying the bridge between anti-apartheid activists and gay men and lesbians.

The New South Africa

The formation of GLOW marked a watershed in the gay/lesbian movement in South Africa, from a white middle-class male leadership and constituency aligned with the apartheid system to a predominantly black, working-class male and female leadership and mixed constituency aligned with the liberation movement. In 1990, GLOW recognized the dawning of the new South Africa—signaled by the release that year of Nelson Mandela from prison—by organizing the first annual Lesbian and Gay Pride March in Johannesburg. GLOW and OLGA consistently called on the liberation movement to embrace the cause of gay/lesbian rights and in 1993 the ANC endorsed such a platform in their draft constitution.

Realizing the dearth of AIDS information reaching the townships, GLOW initiated the Township AIDS Project (TAP), employing Nkoli in its efforts to reach black gay men and lesbians. Nkoli told the *Progressive*, "When we go to the townships and try to explain to the people what AIDS is all about, black people are not convinced that they can get it, because they have never heard of AIDS.... I believe there are many unreported cases [among township residents]. There are 4.5 million people living in Soweto and only about 600,000 in Johannesburg. Maybe 70 white people have died of AIDS in Johannesburg. But there are no statistics about us." In 1996 TAP will sponsor its fourth annual conference in Soweto on AIDS. In contrast to more affluent white South Africans, the African community continues to lack basic infrastructure to support people living with AIDS. TAP is working to address this lack.

Also in 1996, Nkoli has come out as HIV-positive in articles in the *Sowetan* and the *Sunday Independent*. He has known his antibody status since 1985 while he was imprisoned. Fortunately, his most serious infection—tuberculous—was successfully treated in 1992. Nkoli is grateful to have a supportive work environment where he has been able to work part-time in order to conserve his strength, as well as the support of key friends and lovers including Rod Sharp in South Africa, Roy Trevelion in England, and Chuck Goldfarb and Matt Brosius in Washington, D.C., Nkoli remains committed to the struggle for justice. He told this writer, "While life is still there, there is lots of work to be done."

Nkoli's lifetime has spanned a remarkable four decades in the life of his country and the history of the international movements for gay and lesbian liberation—from the earliest signs of progress to the defeat of apartheid and the worldwide acknowledgment that gay men and lesbians exist and will not quietly accept second class status. Unfortunately our lifetimes will remain a time of struggle, as the battles for liberation are fought on increasingly intimate and systemic levels. To progressive gay men and lesbians around the world, Tseko Simon Nkoli remains an icon, setting an example for all people to be who they are with dignity and power.

References:

Gevisser, Mark and Edwin Cameron. *Defiant Desire: Gay and Lesbian Lives in South Africa.* New York: Routledge, 1995.

Krouse, Matthew and Kim Berman. *The Invisible Ghetto: Lesbian and Gay Writing from South Africa.* London: The Gay Men's Press, 1995.

Patron, Eugene J. "Out in Africa," in *Advocate*, 17 November 1992: 45-47.

Shenitz, Bruce. "Coming Out in South Africa," in *Progressive*, March 1990: 14.

—Loie Hayes

Elaine Noble

1944-

American politician and activist

Elaine Noble is a woman defined by adjectives. It is hard to read anything about her without the qualifier "the first openly lesbian state representative in U.S. history" somewhere in the same sentence. After her political career ended, "controversial" was added to the appellation.

Noble was born in New Kensington, Pennsylvania, on 22 January 1944. A graduate of Boston University with a BSA degree, she also holds graduate degrees in speech and education from Emerson College and Harvard University. However, it is mostly as a political pioneer that Noble is remembered. While not the first open lesbian voted into office (Kathy Kozachenko won a seat on the Ann Arbor, Michigan, city council in early 1994), Noble was the first openly gay person to win election to a state legislature. In November of 1974 she ran for the Massachusetts House of Representatives from Boston's Back Bay; she won with 59 percent of the vote. Yet, winning and being a pioneer had its price.

She was confronted with homophobic slurs from heterosexuals and often chided by gays and lesbians for not fulfilling all of their expectations. In a massive redistricting plan, her district merged with Beacon Hill, and she decided not to stand for reelection, allowing (now Congressman) Barney Frank to run for (and win) the new seat in 1978. In an interview with Sasha Gregory-Lewis, found in Mark Thompson's *Long Road to Freedom,* Noble explained why she would not run again: "The gay community expected me to be on call 24 hours a day. It was like they felt they owned me ... I think the level of self-hate now among gay people is so damn high ... They can't hit the straight world, they can't swing at the straight world, so they swing at the person who's nearest to them." She spoke about the burden of being the first and only openly gay member of the state legislature: "I'm not sure that I want to run for public office if I have to carry the heavy burden that I've had to carry from the gay community. One of the things that's got to happen is that there's got to be more gay people who are going to take on part of that burden, or at least help."

But Noble did run again. She ran unsuccessfully for the U.S. Senate in 1980, losing in the primary to Paul Tsongas. She ran twice for a seat on the Cambridge city council (1991 and 1993) and lost both times. But by that time the new adjective "controversial" began to overshadow her pioneer status. After leaving elected office, she landed a job in the intergovernmental affairs office of Boston Mayor Kevin White. It was during this time that she became tangled up in an FBI sting of the White administration. The confusing episode reads like a breathless Lillian Hellman memoir: it involved another city official named Williams and his attempt to extort money from a real estate developer known as Kelly (who was actually an FBI agent named D'Alesandro). Kelly told Noble he was gay and offered to help her find a house in return for her assistance with a proposal for the development of a piece of property. The proposal was not going well however, and Noble claimed that Kelly took out a gun at one point and told her of a pay-out to Williams. During the ensuing publicity, she made the headline-grabbing statement: "Why do business with princes when you can deal with kings?"

She testified for 19 hours before a federal grand jury. Noble herself was not accused of anything, but the matter did put an effective end to her political career. In an interview with the *Boston*

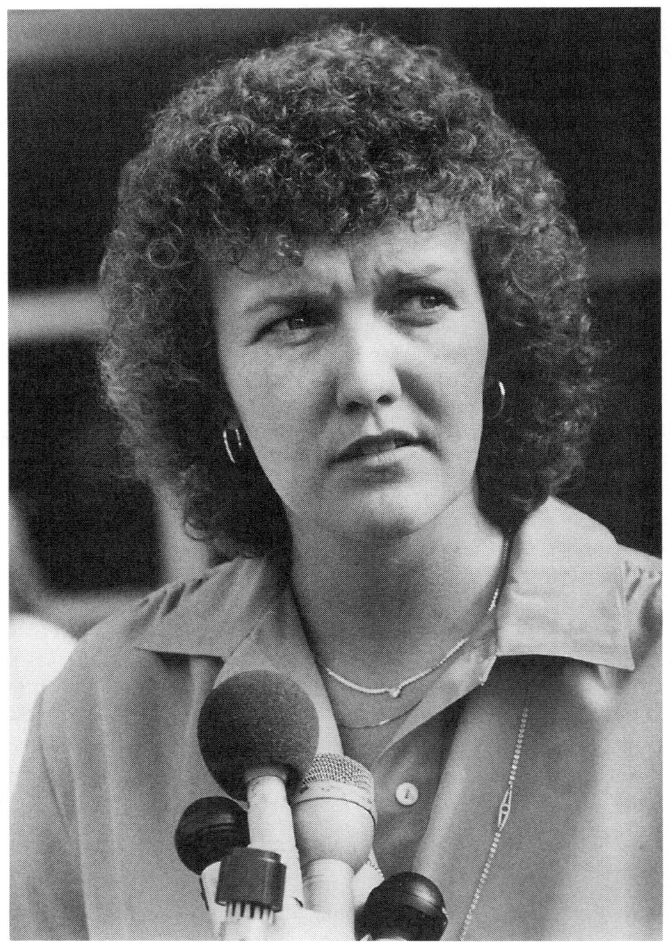

Elaine Noble

Globe Noble recalled: "I chose not to take the fifth ... Now I would take the fifth if they asked me what I wanted for breakfast. I thought I did nothing wrong. I would tell the truth. I practically went through menopause in that place."

She left the White administration and set up a health care consulting business—Noble Associates. She, along with Ellen Ratner, founded the Pride Institute in Minneapolis, a gay and lesbian alcohol and drug treatment center. Noble tried to establish a similar facility in Boston, but was twice rebuffed (first in Waltham and then in Cambridge). It was this setback in East Cambridge that caused her to run again for public office. In November of 1994 Middlesex County Hospital hired her as their top administrator. This appeared to be a last-ditch effort to save a failing institution. Noble was unable to turn things around and stepped down, under pressure, six months later.

Despite professional and personal setbacks, Elaine Noble has always managed to keep a sense of who she is and deliver any message with acerbic wit. During her 1993 campaign for the Cambridge city council, a supporter discovered a Noble campaign sign torn from her lawn and the letters d-i-k-e scratched into her car. Commented Noble to the *Boston Globe:* "What offended us most is that they misspelled dyke."

References:

Black, Chris. "Older, Wiser Noble On Hustings Again," in *Boston Globe,* 24 October 1991.

Connolly, Richard J. "Why Do Business With Princes When You Can Deal With Kings?," in *Boston Globe,* 5 March 1982.

"County Hospital Is Up For Sale," in *Boston Globe,* 13 September 1996.

Hanafin, Teresa M. "Gay Political Pioneer Elaine Noble Will Seek Cambridge Council Seat," in *Boston Globe,* 31 July 1991.

Lupo, Alan. "Where Stupidity Works Both Sides of Center," in *Boston Globe,* 10 October 1993.

Radin, Charles A. "City Official Explains Role in Extortion Probe; Says the Developer Told Her of Bribe," in *Boston Globe,* 21 November 1981.

Rutledge, Leigh W. *The Gay Decades.* New York: Plume, 1992.

Thompson, Mark. *Long Road to Freedom: The Advocate History of the Gay and Lesbian Movement.* New York: St. Martin's Press, 1994.

Witt, Lynn, et al., eds. *Out in All Directions: The Almanac of Gay and Lesbian America.* New York: Warner Books, 1995.

Wong, Doris S. "Elaine Noble Wins Reversal of Judgment," in *Boston Globe,* 14 August 1993.

—Lee Arnold

Rudolf Nureyev

1938-1993

Russian dancer

Everything about Rudolf Nureyev, who defected to the West from the Soviet Union in 1961, seems larger than life. While his legend was nourished by the media—Nureyev became instantly newsworthy—the fact is that his life and art defy understanding. In an age of television, jet travel, and mass adulation, Nureyev, a tireless performer and world traveler, stimulated an interest in ballet that was without precedent. For a long period, he gave close to 200 performances per year, while also working as a choreographer. He displayed a unique range of abilities, including extraordinary athleticism, superb musicality, unusual intelligence, and above all a commanding, indeed charismatic stage presence. It is no exaggeration to say that he reinstated the male dancer as a central figure. After the death of Diaghilev in 1929, this centrality had largely been lost. Balanchine's remark, that "ballet is woman" held sway. Nureyev changed that, bringing to the male role a prominence, visibility, and electrifying erotic charge that it had either lost or never possessed. His longstanding partnership with the English ballerina Margot Fonteyn was uniquely beautiful and exciting to a wider audience than had ever before seen ballet. The tenacity of will that brought Nureyev from desperate poverty to extraordinary riches and world renown was never more in evidence than in his long, courageous fight against AIDS, of which he died 6 January 1993.

Childhood in Stalin's USSR

Rudolf Hametovich Nureyev was born near Irkutsk, by Lake Baikal, 17 March 1938, on a train on the Trans-Siberian railroad going from Moscow to Vladivostock. His mother Farida and his three sisters had undertaken this perilous, 12-day journey to meet up with his father, Hamnet, a soldier stationed in Manchuria. Both his parents were Tatars of Muslim origin. After some years of moving about, the family settled in Ufa, some two thousand miles from Leningrad and the Kirov Ballet, but near to where Nureyev's father had been born. The father remained on active service as a political instructor with the army, and did not come home for good until Rudolf was eight. The family lived in extreme poverty in a one-room shack, often going hungry, barely surviving. His mother would barter what remaining civilian clothes she had belonging to her husband for food.

In the midst of this grinding poverty, Nureyev was loved by his mother and very close to his sister Rosa, but there could be no bond between father and son. The father, a decorated war hero, fond of hunting, wanted his son to become an engineer or doctor, and join the Communist Party. He could not abide the idea that his son wanted to become a dancer, and tried by all means possible to prevent it. Nureyev had joined a local Bashkir folk dance group, but when his mother was able to smuggle all her children into the ballet *The Song of the Cranes,* at the Ufa Opera with just one ticket, the magic of the theater hardened his resolve to become a ballet dancer. Nureyev felt possessed from the age of eight by the single passion to dance ballet.

At the age of 11 Nureyev met in his hometown Mme. Udeltsova, a woman who had once danced with Diaghilev. She helped him as best she could, then introduced him to her friend Mme. Vaitovich, who had been a soloist with the Kirov. For several years, Vaitovich gave him lessons, while recognizing that he really needed to be with the Kirov. When he was 17, on a trip to Moscow with the Ufa Opera to appear with Bashkir Republic artists, he summoned up the courage to audition for the Bolshoi and was accepted into the school. But he turned down the invitation, and with money owed to him by the Ufa Opera, he bought a one-way train ticket to Leningrad. He was able to obtain an audition at the Kirov and was accepted into the Kirov school, where he started in August 1955. His success in being admitted is astonishing, given that he was not young, and had relatively little training. Years later, the dancer Peter Martins would comment on how unpolished Nureyev was. But at the Kirov, they saw his passion and potential for greatness.

Life at the Kirov: Student and Star

Brash as ever, Nureyev was unhappy with his first teacher and at being placed in a lower-level class. He asked to be moved up and, in a stroke of unusual good fortune, was placed in the class of Alexander Pushkin. Pushkin, teacher to Nureyev, Valery Panov, and Mikhail Baryshnikov, each very different from the others, has become a legend as a teacher, bringing out the best in his dancers without forcing them into one regimented style. Nureyev spent three years as a student at the Kirov. He was allowed—or took—liberties that no other had ever dared to take. But his brilliance was recognized. As a student in his final year, when much of the company was on tour, he danced the male lead in such standards as *Le Corsaire* and *Swan Lake,* and many others, an unprecedented honor. By the time of his graduation in the summer of 1958, he had made many enemies, including, especially, the director of the school, Chelkov. But his growing national reputation was confirmed at the end of his last year in school with his performances in a national competition in Moscow, and his graduation performance of the *Corsaire* pas de deux with Alla Sizova. He was offered contracts with the Bolshoi, and with the Stanislavsky, the other leading Moscow company, as well as the Kirov. He chose the Kirov. In a signal honor, Dudinskaya, the prima ballerina of the Kirov and wife of its director, Sergeyev, intimated that she wished to have Nureyev as her partner.

In November 1958, Nureyev danced his first official role at the Kirov, opposite Dudinskaya, in *Laurencia.* The performance was a stunning success, and over the next three years with the Kirov, Nureyev became a cult figure in the USSR, recognized as the most brilliant dancer of his generation, given the male lead in both experimental ballets and standard classics such as *Don Quixote, Swan Lake, La Bayadère, The Sleeping Beauty,* and *Giselle* with the Kirov's finest ballerinas, almost all much older than he, and allowed to change the choreography to suit his own abilities. On the other hand his flouting of the rules, independent spirit, and uncompromising arrogance, as well as the secrecy of his private life, caused him to be viewed with distrust. Stalin had declared homosexuality a crime, and, of necessity, Nureyev had to keep his private life to himself. He was given very little opportunity to dance outside Leningrad, or to meet with foreigners visiting the city.

Nureyev was a last-minute addition to the Kirov troupe invited to perform in Paris and London in May and June of 1961. He did not dance until the fifth evening of their booking at the Paris Opéra. If the Kirov at large was dazzling, Nureyev in particular proved to be a sensation. When he was not performing, he refused to be herded around with the other members of the company, but went his own way, making friends in Paris, trailed by two KGB agents.

Escape to the West

Nureyev's decision to go over to the West can be interpreted in many ways. Given that his family remained behind under a tyrannical regime, subject to reprisals, Nureyev never spoke out against conditions in the Soviet Union. But it seems clear that he found in the West a level of personal and professional freedom undreamed of at home. Certainly the actual decision does appear to have been rather spontaneous, although he had more than likely anticipated that it would happen some time. On 16 June, while the company was waiting at Le Bourget airport to take a flight to London, Nureyev was told that he would not be going to London but instead, as a special honor, to Moscow, to dance at a function at the Kremlin. He was told that he would be able to join up with the Kirov in London. He understood immediately that this was a ploy to return him to the Soviet Union as a virtual prisoner. Nureyev informed a friend of his wish to seek asylum, and the friend in turn informed the French police. After a scuffle, and over the objections of KGB agents, he was able to stay.

Nureyev had always been willing to take risks, and generally his daring had been rewarded. In choosing to cross to the West, he took the greatest risk of his career, giving up the security of the Soviet system for a leap into an uncertain future. The Soviet authorities persisted in trying to bring him back, and he received pleading telephone calls and letters from his mother and father, and his favorite sister Rosa, as well as from his teacher Pushkin and his wife. The pleas and promises did not let up, but Nureyev, distrustful, preferred exile to return. Again, Nureyev's daring was to be rewarded.

He received an offer almost immediately. On 23 June, he made his debut with the Marquis de Cuevas ballet, as the prince and the Bluebird in a new production of *The Sleeping Beauty,* alongside the great French ballerina Nina Vyroubova. Many in the audience at the Théâtre des Champs-Elysées, Soviet sympathizers, jeered him, calling him a traitor. The Cuevas offered Nureyev a six-year contract, but he refused a long-term commitment, since he wished to study in Copenhagen with Russian expatriate Vera Volkova, balletmistress of the Royal Danish Ballet, and Erik Bruhn, the premier male dancer of the period. Nureyev went to Copenhagen at the end of the summer. Bruhn and Nureyev fell in love, and their passionate friendship was to continue through much of the 1960s.

From Closed to (Partially) Open Society: Homosexuality

Inevitably, Nureyev's background of poverty and deprivation marked him deeply. In the West, he acquired sybaritic tastes, a vast personal fortune, and seven homes in various parts of the world, including an Italian island that once belonged to Massine. Related to this restless acquisitiveness was a compulsive sexuality, a constant in his life.

At the Kirov, the authorities resented his need for secrecy, and suspected him of being a homosexual. Consensual sex between two adult males was a crime, severely punished. Of necessity, therefore, Nureyev's homosexuality could only be expressed within a private club or in a friend's apartment, with the risk of arrest by the KGB. Nureyev enjoyed greater freedom than any student before him, but even for him there were limits to what would be tolerated.

In the 1960s and 1970s, the contrast between the closed lifestyle of Leningrad and, say, Paris, London, or New York was enormous. In these Western cities and others, Nureyev became part of local gay legend. He was remembered for his prodigious sexual appetites in the bath houses, his picking up of "butch boys" (boy prostitutes), his alleged sexual encounter with Mick Jagger, and even (in Melbourne, Australia) for rushing out of the theater during intermission to have sex, only to be caught by the vice squad and let go to return and dance his final act.

But for all the flamboyance and all the stories that grew up around him, Nureyev never lost his need for privacy and secrecy. Coming from the Soviet Union, he never learned to accept the

Rudolf Nureyev

profligate intrusion of the Western press into his private life, though he was a master at manipulating that same press.

There will always be conjecture about the true nature of his private relationship with Margot Fonteyn, and it is clear that in their way each loved the other, There has been speculation that she had a miscarriage while carrying his child. He was deeply affected by her death from cancer in 1991. While quite misogynistic, and unambiguously homosexual, he was involved sexually with many women, including no doubt Mme. Pushkin of the Kirov (as well as with her husband), and the dancer Maria Tallchief in his first months in Paris.

Alongside the numberless brief encounters that marked Nureyev's passage from city to city, there were lasting relationships of real love. The first and greatest was that shared with Bruhn in the 1960s. In many respects, Bruhn, an elegant, smooth, and flawless dancer, was Nureyev's polar opposite. Nureyev admired him greatly. Until Nureyev's arrival, Bruhn was the premier male dancer in Europe, and he came to suffer greatly, though without temperament, from the inevitable comparisons with his friend. Later, Nureyev would have two long-term relationships. The first, with Wallace Potts, a young American Southerner, lasted through the late 1960s and early 1970s, though Potts remained a loyal friend until the end. The other, with Robert Tracy, a young dancer whom Nureyev met in 1979, was long-lasting but ended in acrimony.

Although Nureyev never declared his homosexuality candidly, it was hardly a secret. Quite apart from the specifics of his sexual orientation, his sheer sexuality was readily apparent—literally as well as figuratively, given his choice of revealing costumes—in his diverse roles, from *Le Corsaire* to his resurrection of Nijinsky's faun in *L'Après-midi d'un faune,* to Martha Graham's *Lucifer,* to many others. With Fonteyn, that sexuality would capture the attention of the world.

A Stellar Partnership: Nureyev and Margot Fonteyn

It was while he was in Denmark, with Volkova, that Nureyev received a call from Margot Fonteyn, inviting him to dance at the annual gala for the British Royal Academy of Dance in London in November 1962. He danced the solo *Poème tragique,* to music by Scriabin, choreographed especially for him by Frederick Ashton, and the Black Swan pas de deux from *Swan Lake,* with Rosella Hightower. Fonteyn was not at first eager to dance with him. The frenzy unleashed by Nureyev had no precedent in the annals of British ballet. Most members of the audience—and this would continue to be true for a long time to come—simply suspended critical judgment and were caught up in the sheer excitement of the spectacle.

From the beginning, Ninette de Valois, founder of London's Royal Ballet, championed Nureyev, and encouraged Fonteyn, its prima ballerina, to dance with him. Although Nureyev would always be just a guest artist at the Royal—he was not British—for many years, he was closely connected to it. After some hesitation, she joined him in a performance of *Giselle* at Covent Garden in February 1962. In every respect this was a major balletic event: a captivating performance in itself by both dancers, it was also the beginning of a partnership that is without equal in the history of ballet. Shortly before, Fonteyn, almost 20 years Nureyev's senior, was about to retire. Now, infused with a new vitality and radiance, she traveled extensively with him, often taking on very demanding roles. In just the first two years of their collaboration, they put on close to 200 performances. They helped spark a new interest in ballet in many parts of the world, playing to sold-out houses, both with the classics and with such new productions as *Marguerite and Armand,* created for them by Frederick Ashton, and Kenneth MacMillan's *Romeo and Juliet,* which, after Nureyev and Fonteyn danced it, became in effect the Royal Ballet's standard *Romeo.*

From early on, Nureyev evinced an interest in the choreography of Balanchine and Martha Graham, and other masters of modern dance. Balanchine discouraged this interest when they first met in 1962. No one understood better than he that modern dance would require an unlearning of much of the splendid classical ballet training of the Kirov. But Nureyev did eventually achieve considerable success dancing in modern works by Paul Taylor, Maurice Béjart, Glen Tetley, and many others. His ten-year association with Martha Graham, beginning with her *Lucifer* in 1975, which she created for him and Fonteyn, provided a new source of inspiration. His ongoing fascination with Balanchine was crowned with success when Balanchine asked him to dance with Patricia McBride in an adaptation of Molière's *Bourgeois Gentilhomme* (1979), from which he learned, belatedly, to be a modernist in modesty and simplicity.

The Paris Opéra

From 1983 to 1989, Nureyev assumed a new role as artistic director of the Paris Opéra Ballet, a notoriously difficult assignment, complicated by his increasingly ill health, the first signs of what would later be recognized as AIDS. Three ballet directors had come and gone in the decade before. In spite of the many obstacles, through sheer force of will, Nureyev imposed a personal vision on the Opéra that shook it out of its lethargy and transformed its lackluster company. He overthrew the hierarchy which stifled young talent, changed the repertory, adding many new ballets, a good number of which, including *Swan Lake,* he choreographed himself, and fought the unions over their impossible demands. In his years as director, his own strength was failing, and, defying reason, he continued to insist on dancing a full schedule. But now the achievement was not the personal one of Rudolf Nureyev, but that of the Paris Opéra Ballet, which could hold its head high anywhere in the world. In 1986, on its first visit to the United States in close to 40 years, it enjoyed huge success in a three-week engagement at the Metropolitan Opera House.

Fittingly, Nureyev made his last public appearance where his career in the West had begun, at the Paris Opéra. It was the premiere, 8 October 1992, of his production of *La Bayadare.* Dressed in red satin, he watched from a couch in a box. He died two months later, after losing a heroic, 12-year fight against AIDS.

Nureyev's influence has proved long-lasting, not just in Paris, but in many parts of the world. He breathed new life into ballet, conquered a vast new public for it, and restored the male dancer to a position of prominence.

References:

Andersen, Christopher. *Jagger Unauthorized.* New York: Dell, 1993.
Barnes, Clive. *Nureyev.* New York: Helen Obolensky, 1982.
Buckle, Richard. *Nijinsky.* New York: Simon & Schuster, 1971.
Fonteyn, Margot. *Autobiography.* London: W.H. Allen, 1975.
Martins, Peter. *Far From Denmark.* Boston: Little, Brown, 1982.
Stuart, Otis. *Perpetual Motion. The Public and Private Lives of Rudolf Nureyev.* New York: Simon & Schuster, 1995.

—James P. McNab

Jean O'Leary

1948-

American activist

A former nun, Jean O'Leary is now an outspoken and highly successful advocate for gay rights.

Jean O'Leary was born in Cleveland, Ohio, and attended Catholic schools there. In her graduation speech at Magnificat High School, she announced that she would be entering a convent, a decision that surprised many of her friends, who had known her as an irreverent rock-and-roller. True to her word, in 1966 O'Leary entered the convent of the Sisters of the Holy Humanity of Mary, a teaching and nursing order. In the 1984 anthology, "Lesbian Nuns: Breaking the Silence," O'Leary explained her reasons for joining a religious order: "There was no anti-war movement, no women's movement, no gay movement in Ohio in 1966. I wanted to do something special, to have an impact on my world." During her years as a nun, O'Leary studied psychology at Youngstown University and subsequently received her diploma from Cleveland State University.

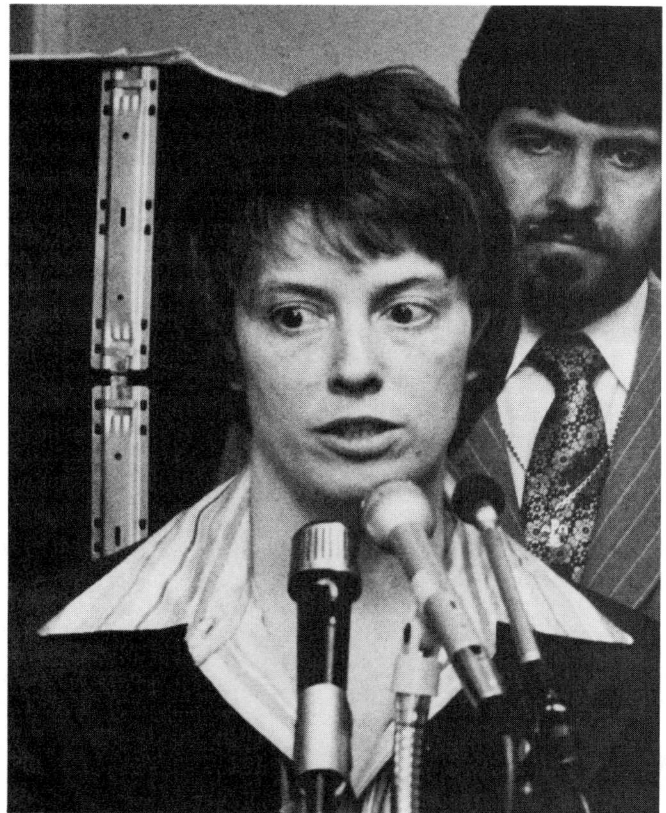

Jean O'Leary

Unable or unwilling to suppress her romantic attractions for other women, she was forced to leave her order after four years.

Having read in a *Cosmopolitan* magazine article that homosexuals congregated in Greenwich Village, O'Leary settled there in 1971, enrolling in the doctoral program in organizational development at Yeshiva University. She quickly became embroiled in radical gay and lesbian politics, joining the Gay Activists Alliance and establishing the Lesbian Liberation Committee to offset what she regarded as male domination of the GAA. Soon, she was driving up to Albany once a week to lobby the legislature on gay rights issues. During this period she also worked on gay and lesbian research for the American Psychiatric Association.

In 1977 O'Leary organized meetings between representatives of the gay community and the federal government. The gatherings brought gay issues to national attention and led to a series of talks between the gay representatives and key federal agencies, including the State and Justice departments. In 1979 she moved to Los Angeles to serve on the board of directors of National Gay Rights Advocates, a nonprofit law firm devoted to the protection and promotion of gay rights. In 1981, she assumed the post of executive director. Aggressive defenders of the rights of AIDS patients, the NGRA includes among its achievements a major lawsuit against several federal agencies, including the Food and Drug Administration, calling for fair and speedy access to drugs for HIV treatment.

O'Leary's accomplishments have been many and varied. She was the first openly gay person to be appointed to a presidential commission. She is credited with persuading women's groups to acknowledge the needs and rights of lesbians as a concern. In 1988, she was appointed to the National Democratic Committee, giving her the power to push for reforms from within. Additionally, she guided the NGRA organization to legal victories in such areas as fairness for AIDS patients and protection of gay rights in the workplace.

—Sarah Watstein

Pat Parker

1944-1989

African-American poet

When Pat Parker's poetry was first being published in 1972 gay African-Americans were just beginning to find their collective voice. Parker would eventually become one of the women who would help contribute to the creation of a literary identity for African-American lesbians. But, Parker's poetry has the ability to transcend such a label since, as Robert B. Marks Ridinger writes, she "was distinctive for her willingness to engage problematic topics such as alcoholism and freedom of speech within her verse."

Pat Parker was born on 20 January 1944 in Houston, Texas, to Marie Louise Anderson, a domestic worker, and Earnest Nathaniel Cooks, a tire retreader. She was the youngest of four sisters when she was born two months premature and, as a result, caught pneumonia and had to remain in the hospital for another three months. This was a hardship for the working-poor Cooks family, but they survived it and Parker grew strong, talented, and intelligent despite the racism, sexism, poverty, classism, and Jim Crow segregation that pressed against her each day of her life.

After graduating from high school in 1962, Parker moved to California. She then went on to earn undergraduate and graduate degrees while attending Los Angeles City College and San Francisco State College. In 1962 she married Ed Bullins and in 1966 she divorced him and married Robert F. Parker. After her divorce from Parker, she worked as a feminist medical administrator to support her two daughters in addition to writing and publishing poetry.

When Parker moved to California in the early 1960s the gay liberation movement was still in its infancy. But, by the time of the Stonewall Riots in 1969, Parker had created "a place for herself among the women who would later form the Lesbian Tide Collective," according to Ridinger. It was also during this time that Parker first met Judy Grahn, whom she would collaborate with on a number of projects.

It was around this time that Parker began writing poetry. Her first book of poems, *Child of Myself*, was published in 1972. As the title suggests, the collection is a declaration of Parker's selfhood and personal authority over her own life. The opening poem responds to and contradicts the general patriarchal assumption that woman is forever second to man. Since patriarchy is supported and maintained through religious institutions, Parker does this by using Genesis 1:23 of the King James Bible as an epigraph to her poem, and then writes against the ancient myth and present assumption that women are the Second Sex: "to think second/to believe first/a mistake/erased by the motion of years./i, woman, i/can no longer claim/a mother of flesh/a father of marrow/I Woman must be/the child of myself."

Parker's second collection of poems, *Pit Stop: Words,* was published in c.1973. This collection explores the pain that can lead to despair and manifest itself in alcoholism and other means of self destruction. In c.1975 Parker and Grahn recorded their poetry on an album for Olivia Records, including selections from *Pit Stop* and *Child of Myself.* According to Grahn, in the introduction to *Movement in Black,* they "called it, in honor of ourselves as well as other women, 'Where Would I Be Without You.'"

In 1978, Parker's third collection, *WomanSlaughter,* was published. In it Parker confronts the *manslaughter* of women, the law's inadequacy or unwillingness to protect women from domestic abuse, and its reluctance to prosecute their perpetrators to the full extent of the law. In the title poem Parker exposes the intolerable circumstances of her sister's murder by her "quiet" ex-husband: "Hello, Hello Police/I am a woman alone/& I am afraid./My husband means to kill me.... Lady, there's nothing we can do/until he tries to hurt you./It was too late,/when he was caught./One day a quiet man/shot his quiet wife/three times in the back." *Movement In Black,* a collection of Parker's poetry, was published in 1978. *Jonestown, and Other Madness,* published in 1985, directly confronts and addresses the social conditions of racism and the toll it takes on black psyches and lives. It challenges the concepts of madness, justice, and gratitude by forcing the reader to reconsider and question the concept and act of suicide in the context of the Jonestown, Guyana, massacre. Parker writes in the title poem: "November 18, 1978/more than 900 people/most of them black/died in a man-made town/called Jonestown.... The Black people/in Jonestown/did not commit suicide/they were murdered/they were murdered in/small southern towns/they were murdered in/big northern cities/they were murdered." Though the realities of the world's madness are harsh, Parker completes this collection on a positive note in the poem "legacy for Anastasia Jean," her daughter: "but I give you/a legacy/of doers/of people who take risks/to chisel the crack wider. Take strength that you may/wage a long battle./Take the pride that you can/never stand small./Take the rage that you can/never settle for less."

Parker lived her adult life in California, with her last place of residence being Pleasant Hill, California. She also served as director of the Feminist Women's Health Center in Oakland, California from 1978 until illness prevented her from continuing in that capacity. In 1980 she founded the Black Women's Revolutionary Council. Suffering from breast cancer, Parker died on 4 June 1989 at the age of 45. She was a revolutionary and a woman of courage whose work is political and bears the mark of a woman who was a warrior. Parker was a risk taker and dedicated her life to breaking silences, and as Adrian Oktenberg writes, she was "the poet laureate of the Black and Lesbian peoples."

References:

Blain, Virginia, Patricia Clements, and Isobel Grundy. *The Feminist Companion to Literature in English: Women Writers from the Middle Ages to the Present.* New Haven, Connecticut: Yale University Press, 1990: 833.

Oktenberg, Adrian. In *Women's Review of Books* (Wellesley, Massachusetts), April 1986: 17-19.

Parker, Pat. *Child of Myself.* Oakland, California: Women's Press Collective, 1972.

———. *Jonestown, and Other Madness.* New York: Firebrand Books, 1985: 56, 63-64, 74-75.

———. *Movement in Black: The Collected Poetry of Pat Parker, 1961-1978.* Oakland, California: Diana Press, 1978: 10-11, 157.

———. *WomanSlaughter.* Oakland, California: Diana Press, 1978: 53-54.

Ridinger, Robert B. Marks. "Pat Parker," in *Gay & Lesbian Literature.* Detroit, Michigan: St. James Press, 1994: 289-290.

—Ekua Omosupe

Michelle Parkerson

1953-

African-American writer, filmmaker, and teacher

Since the late 1970s, writer and independent filmmaker Michelle Parkerson has produced four public television specials, co-directed a full-length documentary movie, and written and directed a science fiction short film. Her body of work celebrates the less traditional and more diverse aspects of the African-American experience, including that of black lesbians and gays. In an early interview for *Essence,* Parkerson described her filmmaking in general: "We're forging a new frontier for Blacks in the arts, using a medium that was formerly used against us. Before, our customs and culture were passed on through music, textiles, sculpture, and other art forms. Now it's also done through film." In 1987, Parkerson was contacted by producer/director Ada Gay Griffith, and they soon began filming *A Litany for Survival: The Life and Work of Audre Lorde.* After many years of financial struggle, the 90-minute documentary about Lorde—describing herself in the film as a "Black, lesbian, feminist, warrior, poet,"—premiered at the 1995 Sundance Festival, and has since been shown worldwide.

Michelle Parkerson was born in 1953, in Washington, D.C., to William and Marie Parkerson. She studied filmmaking at Temple University, Philadelphia, earning her B.A. in Communication in 1974. While an undergraduate at Temple, Parkerson won a "Student Oscar" from the Academy of Motion Picture Arts & Sciences for her movie *Sojourn.* This recognition affirmed her artistic vision, and she grew stronger in her resolve. In a recent Time/Life publication, *African Americans: Voices of Triumph,* Parkerson relates how the award enabled her to tell herself, "You can do this. You can make your own version of a history that has been manipulated and mutilated and stereotyped since films began."

After graduating from Temple, Parkerson's next filmmaking success came through writing, directing, and producing documentaries that were shown on public television. Her major filmography began in 1980 with *But Then, She's Betty Carter,* a portrait of the jazz vocalist. Next came *Gotta Make This Journey,* the 1983 documentary showcasing the talent and group harmony of the black women's *a cappella* ensemble, Sweet Honey in The Rock. Her next film, *Urban Odyssey,* followed a black biker's trek through urban life. In 1987, Parkerson for the first time combined themes of race, gender, and homosexuality in *Stormé, The Lady of the Jewel Box.* Exploring the life of an African-American male impersonator, Parkerson began to challenge existing stereotypes about gay African Americans.

In her essay published in the *Advocate,* Parkerson wrote, "The litany of black gay and lesbian characters in Hollywood film and network television reads like its own form of black face." In the same essay, Parkerson maintains that "Historically, [blacks] have been locked out of the Hollywood and television industries. But such challenge inspires me to make movies that *Desert Hearts* and *She Must Be Seeing Things* are not: lesbian specific and, just as important, race conscious." Parkerson's growing interest in depicting lesbian and gay subjects remained consistent with her earlier ambition to transform the image of blacks in film. Many of her subsequent creative efforts continued to focus upon achieving a fusion of these themes.

Parkerson's documentation of the life of Audre Lorde, a black lesbian poet whose work is regarded by many as seminal, began in 1987. Ada Gay Griffin, a fellow African-American media activist involved in filmmaking, learned that Lorde's cancer was again threatening her life. In Griffin's discussions with Lorde, they decided that Parkerson, then known for her documentaries *Stormé* and *Gotta Make This Journey,* should direct the film. Griffin particularly admired Parkerson's documentary style that portrayed her subjects as real people rather than rare, precious, artistic giants. When approached, Parkerson immediately agreed to do the project, and it garnered modest financial support from individuals and feminist foundations, including the Chicago Resource Center, the Open Meadows Fund, and the Astraea Fund. Unfortunately, funding remained a persistent obstacle that slowed production of the film. After eight years, *A Litany for Survival: The Life and Work of Audre Lorde* was finally released. Through Lorde, Griffin and Parkerson had succeeded in creating a unique film that linked black, gay, and women's rights.

The film enjoyed an enthusiastic reception at the 1995 Sundance Film festival, then was warmly received at the 45th Annual Berlin Film Festival. The greatest achievement of *A Litany for Survival* is its illustration of the formulation of a complex modern identity. The film focused upon Lorde's successful, albeit difficult, combination of the many contradictory roles she filled throughout her life: wife, mother, accomplished poet, militant warrior against racism, outspoken lesbian, and cancer survivor. Griffith and Parkerson transformed Lorde's life story into a paradigm for others in American society who live with multiple social identities, and employ varied survival strategies.

Parkerson's newest video, *Odds and Ends,* is a science fiction short about black Amazon warriors fighting racial and gender annihilation in the year 2096. Both *Litany* and *Odds and Ends* are distributed through Third World Newsreel, in New York City. Aside from making films, Parkerson, currently teaching at Temple University, has served on the faculties of the University of Delaware, Howard University, and Northwestern University. She was awarded a Rockefeller Foundation Film/Video Fellowship in 1992 and is a member of the American Film Institute's Directing Workshop for Women.

Current Address: 1716 Florida Avenue N.W., No. 2, Washington, D.C., 20009.

References:

African Americans: Voices of Triumph. New York: Time-Life Inc., vol. 3, 1994: 62, 65.

Brown, Dwight. "Black Filmmakers: The Trials and Triumphs of Bringing Our Culture into Focus," in *Essence* (New York), April 1986: 54.

Burdette, K. "Remembering Audre Lorde," in *Washington Blade,* 7 April 1995: 53.

Gallagher, Stephen. "Poet Warriors," in *Filmmaker Magazine,* Winter 1995: 45.

Griffin, Ada Gay. "A Litany For Survival: The Life and Work of Audre Lorde," in *Transcending Silence: The Life and Poetic Legacy of Audre Lorde.* New York: Caribbean Cultural Center, 1993.

Levy, Emanuel. "A Litany for Survival: The Life and Work of Audre Lorde," in *Variety* (New York), 30 January-5 February 1995.

Parkerson, Michelle. "Gay Voices, Black America," in *Advocate,* 12 February 1991: 32.

Interview with Laurie Fitzpatrick, February 1996.

—Laurie Fitzpatrick

Pratibha Parmar

Indian filmmaker and critic

When Pratibha Parmar's family immigrated to England from India, the young schoolgirl experienced firsthand the rampant racism of the mid-1960s. As a South Asian, Parmar and her family, along with immigrants from the Caribbean and Africa, were labelled "black," and as such, as Parmar describes in the article "That Moment of Emergence" which appears in the book *Queer Looks: Perspectives on Lesbian and Gay Film and Video,* were "perceived as 'marginal,' 'peripheral,' and 'other.'" In her films and videos, Parmar attempts to reflect the struggle of those perceived by others as being "marginal" to confront and challenge prejudice, be it based on race, gender, or sexual orientation.

The Beginnings of Activism

Parmar describes one of her first excursions into activism in the article "Other Kinds of Dreams" in *Feminist Review.* She was a coauthor of an article, concerning the failure of the women's movement in Britain to address racial issues of importance to black women, which was to be discussed at the Socialist-Feminist conference held in 1978. Acting on a suggestion from women who had participated in the discussion, the authors sent the article to the feminist publication *Spare Rib.* The resulting three-page letter of rejection made Parmar feel that black women were regarded by white feminists as being outsiders and that the opinions and concerns of black women were not central to the "white" women's movement.

While a postgraduate student at the Centre for Contemporary Cultural Studies at the University of Birmingham in 1982, Parmar was one of a group of students involved in writing and publishing the book *The Empire Strikes Back: Race and Racism in 70s Britain.* In the article "That Moment of Emergence," Parmar describes herself and her fellow contributors to this project as "the new generation that saw ourselves as both black and British...." *The Empire Strikes Back,* she continues, "examines the everyday lived experiences of black British people as culture," and presents critical analyses of such topics as race relations, white feminism, and sexual identity.

In the July 1984 issue of *Feminist Review,* a special issue on the subject of black women in Britain of which Parmar was one of the guest editors, she and three other black lesbians "came out" in a very public way in the article "Becoming Visible: Black Lesbian Discussions." The four women expressed their doubts and fears about the wisdom of coming out in print, and Parmar herself revealed that her "greatest fear [was] total rejection from my family, who I am really close to." She makes the point that losing family as a support group would be far more devastating for a black than for a white lesbian, since the family represents the security and support not otherwise readily available to black women living in a racist society. Parmar's fear of being identified as a lesbian, however, is counterbalanced by her conviction that "the more of us that come out the stronger we are going to be, and the more other women are going to feel they are able to come out, because we are creating that kind of a situation where it is possible."

In the same article, Parmar reveals a situation in her life that had made a lasting impression on her and helped her form her own identity as a black lesbian. In 1981, Parmar attended the OWAAD (Organisation of Women of African and Asian Descent) conference. The dissention among the women at the conference over whether or not black lesbians should have the right to hold their own independent workshop resulted in feelings of anger and alienation among homosexual and heterosexual women alike. In spite of the uproar, about 40 black lesbians, including Parmar, did meet. Parmar credits the "horrible things" that happened at the OWAAD conference with the birth of the Black Lesbian Group (BLG). This was the first group for black lesbians in Britain, and Parmar states that it "gave me the confidence and support of other lesbians to be able to come out in ways that I'd not been able to before and be much stronger in myself about my own lesbianism."

Also in that same issue of *Feminist Review,* Parmar coauthored with Valerie Amos the article "Challenging Imperial Feminism." In it, the authors set out "to show that white, mainstream feminist theory ... does not speak to the experiences of Black women and where it attempts to do so it is often from a racist perspective and reasoning." The article offers a critique of white feminist literature and scholarship, and the "white feminists' failure to acknowledge the differences between themselves and Black and Third World women." The authors discuss the effects of imperialism on white feminist attitudes towards family, sexuality, and the women's peace movement. In the area of sexuality, for example, Parmar and Amos point out that the feminist debates concerning gender roles, rape, pornography, homo- and heterosexuality, etc., are simply not as central to the black experience in a racist society as are other, more survival-oriented issues. As black women become more confident, the area of sexuality will become a more important topic of discussion. The authors also mention the difficulties black lesbians face in expressing their sexual identities, as they must endure the homophobic reactions not only of the white community, but of the black community as well.

Parmar and Amos conclude the article with a statement of rejection of the "white" women's liberation movement's theories and practices on the grounds that white feminists have not come to grips with the problems of imperialism and racism. They state that it is necessary for black feminists to treat "the totality of our oppression.... Only a synthesis of class, race, gender and sexuality can lead us forward, as these form the matrix of Black women's lives."

Expressing Herself through Film

In the mid-1980s Parmar began making films and videos, commencing this career without having art or film school training. In the article "Filling the Lack in Everyone Is Quite Hard Work, Really...," which appears in *Queer Looks,* she relates that she did interview with the head of documentary at the National Film School, but the two did not see eye-to-eye on theories of documentary filmmaking, and "a very heated discussion" ensued. Without any training, then, Parmar found herself learning "on the job," a process that she describes in the article as "frightening and scary." "It's scary because you're judged on what the audience sees," she said. "They don't know that you had to do the camera at one point, or you had to do the production managing and the off-line editing and everything else that you did on your own. And it's the first time you've ever done it, and you've had to learn it as you go along."

Parmar's early documentaries have themes that are reflective of her activities as a black feminist activist. The 1986 video *Emergence* examines the problems of alienation and loss of identity facing black and Third World women artists. Among those featured are Audre Lorde, a feminist poet, and Mona Hatoum, a Palestinian performance artist. *Sari Red,* Parmar's second documentary, addresses the threats of racism and violence faced by South Asian women. It was made in memory of Kalbinder Kaue Hayre, who was the victim of a racially motivated attack in Britain in 1985.

The homophobic tone of Britain's AIDS-awareness campaigns inspired *A Plague on You,* which was produced by London's Lesbian and Gay Media Group and appeared on British television in 1987. Parmar continued her exploration of AIDS and its effect on the gay community in 1988. *ReFraming AIDS* features interviews with AIDS-stricken gays and lesbians of different races, and shows how the lesbian and gay community has been affected not only by the disease itself, but by the myths surrounding it and the resulting anti-gay backlash. One of the topics covered was how AIDS was being used as a reason for restricting black immigration to Britain.

Parmar was criticized for including black and white gay men in *ReFraming AIDS,* and not limiting herself to black lesbians. This attitude, Parmar claims in "That Moment of Emergence," "reinforced my criticism of an essentialist identity politics as being divisive, exclusionary, and retrogressive. I would assert that our territories should be as broad as we choose."

Parmar continued the exploration of this broader territory in her next three works, examining, as she states in the above-mentioned article, "our histories of diaspora, the memories of migration and upheaval, the search for an integration of our many selves, and the celebration of 'us,' our differences, and our eroticisms." The 1989 video *Memory Pictures* treats the effects of racism and sexual identity on the life of gay Indian-born photographer Sunil Gupta. *Flesh and Paper,* a documentary made for British television in 1990, has as its subject the Indian-born lesbian poet and writer Suniti Namjoshi, author of "Feminist Fables" and "Conversations with a Cow." Parmar, in "Filling the Lack...," tells of her satisfaction in presenting for the first time on British television, for nearly a million viewers, "an Indian woman in a sari talking about being a lesbian and Indian in a way which was not apologetic or explanatory." The half-hour film was made for Channel Four's gay and lesbian series *Out on Tuesday.*

The title of Parmar's 1991 film *Khush* is the Urdu word meaning "ecstatic pleasure." This film explores the difficulties, as well as the joys, of South Asian gays and lesbians living in India, Britain, and North America, and documents their "coming out." *Khush* originally was made for *Out on Tuesday,* and also has been shown at various lesbian and gay film festivals. It won an award for Best Documentary Short at the Frameline Festival in San Francisco. Parmar recalls in "Filling the Lack ..." the thrill of that evening: "It was a very special moment. To get that kind of validation from your own peer group mattered much more than getting a great review from a critic. That kind of nurturing is very important. It's what's kept me going." *Double the Trouble, Twice the Fun,* also made for *Out on Tuesday,* is a docudrama featuring the gay writer Firdaus Kanga. It deals in a positive way with the challenges faced by disabled lesbians and gays.

As her films illustrate, Parmar has found inspiration in the writings and achievements of black American feminists. In the 1991 documentary *A Place of Rage,* she interviews black activist Angela Davis, poet June Jordon, and writer Alice Walker. Parmar went on to collaborate with the Pulitzer prize-winning Walker in the creation of the film *Warrior Marks,* a 1993 documentary which treats the subject of female circumcision. This "initiation ritual," which involves the excising of all or part of the exterior female genitalia, is often performed under unsanitary conditions using the crudest of instruments and often ends in death. The filming required travel to the Gambia, Senegal, Burkina Faso, Britain, and the United States. The documentary features interviews with those who defend as well as those who condemn the practice, and also includes interviews with children who have themselves endured the procedure. Parmar and Walker also have collaborated on a book, *Warrior Marks: Female Genital Mutilation and the Sexual Blinding of Women,* which chronicles the making of the film.

The Future of "Queer Cinema"

In the article "Queer Questions" Parmar gives her views on the current state of "queer cinema." She points out that queer cinema is not just white, gay cinema, and expresses her dismay that it is still difficult for lesbian filmmakers to get funding. She emphasizes the positive benefits of gay and lesbian film festivals. Although these festivals do tend to be organized by white gays and lesbians, and white films predominate, they still often represent the only opportunity available to gay and lesbian filmmakers to get their works before the public.

There may be a hint of the future direction of Parmar's films given in the roundtable discussion which took place at her home in North London, and which is chronicled in the article "Filling the Lack...." In the article, Parmar and her fellow filmmakers discuss the differences between fictional works and documentaries. Parmar expresses her occasional frustration with the documentary film, in that it limits the filmmaker's artistic freedom. She explains, "As a fiction filmmaker, you can say what you want to say through your characters, whereas with documentary you've got the subject matter but you've also got the subjects, and you can't put words in their mouths." Parmar has already introduced dramatic elements into her films. In *Khush,* for example, she describes using "dramatic scenarios, performance, dance, and archive footage, used not as wallpaper but in and for themselves, as different kinds of voices and different modes of telling." In whatever direction Parmar's creativity takes her, it is certain that her dedication to fighting racism, sexism, and homophobia will continue to provide the heart of her work.

References:

______, Carmen, ______, Gail, ______, Shaila, and ______, Pratibha. "Becoming Visible: Black Lesbian Discussions," in *Feminist Review* (London), July 1984: 53-72.

Amos, Valerie, and Pratibha Parmar. "Challenging Imperial Feminism," in *Feminist Review* (London), July 1984: 3-19.

Blackman, Inge, Mary McIntosh, Sue O'Sullivan, Pratibha Parmar, and Alison Read. "Perverse Politics," in *Feminist Review* (London), Spring 1990: 1-3.

Chamberlain, Joy, Isaac Julien, Stuart Marshall, and Pratibha Parmar. "Filling the Lack in Everybody Is Quite Hard Work, Really...," in *Queer Looks: Perspectives on Lesbian and Gay Film and Video.* Toronto: Between The Lines, 1993: 41-60.

Gever, Martha, John Greyson, and Pratibha Parmar. "On a Queer Day You Can See Forever," in *Queer Looks: Perspectives on Lesbian and Gay Film and Video.* Toronto: Between The Lines, 1993: xiii-xv.

Kuhn, Annette, ed., with Susannah Radstone. *The Women's Companion to International Film.* London: Virago Press Ltd., 1990.

Murray, Raymond. *Images in the Dark: An Encyclopedia of Gay and Lesbian Film and Video.* Philadelphia: TLA Publications, 1994.

Parmar, Pratibha. "Other Kinds of Dreams," in *Feminist Review* (London), Spring 1989: 55-65.

———. "That Moment of Emergence," in *Queer Looks: Perspectives on Lesbian and Gay Film and Video.* Toronto: Between The Lines, 1993: 3-11.

Parmar, Pratibha, et al. "Queer Questions," in *Sight and Sound* (London), September 1992.

—Jean Edmunds

Walter Pater

1839-1894

British writer

Although he produced only a relatively small body of published work during a writing career of 30 years, Walter Pater was a highly influential intellectual historian and literary and art critic whose essays on art were major statements of the British aesthetic movement. His studies, marked by an elaborate and complex sentence structure but often very impressionistic by today's academic standards, encouraged readers to respond to art on a personal level and to consider style as the most convincing indicator of an artist's greatness. His two outstanding collections of short essays are *Studies in the History of the Renaissance* (1873) and *Appreciations, with an Essay on Style* (1889). The hand of the essayist is also visible in his two relatively plotless historical novels, *Marius the Epicurean: His Sensations and Ideas* (1885), the incomplete *Gaston de Latour* (1888), and his eight short stories, four of which were issued as *Imaginary Portraits* in 1887.

Although it would be anachronistic to label Pater as gay or even to say that he writes directly about homosexuality, in his key works, Pater discusses or suggests desire between men in provocative ways. Some of his subtexts may be missed by the general reading public, for Pater did not want to forsake his role as a Victorian cultural spokesman. However, even before the advent of Oscar Wilde, he lived his life with style, and the idea of style cleared a space in which young gay men could live out their homosexuality more openly.

Rooted in the intellectual life of the academic middle class, Walter Horatio Pater's life was, on the surface, relatively uneventful. He was born on 4 August 1839, the second son of Richard Glode Pater, a physician, and Maria Hill. The third of four children—he had two sisters and a brother—he lost both of his parents before his enrollment at Queen's College, Oxford in 1858. In 1862 he graduated with second-class honors in Literae Humaniores, and in 1864 became a probationary fellow of Brasenose College, Oxford, where he was named a lecturer in 1867. His earliest published essays in the *Westminster Review* contain the essence of his thought: "Coleridge's Writings" (January 1866), "Winckelmann" (January 1867), and "Poems by William Morris" (November 1869). A student of contemporary German philosophy, the Italian Renaissance, and French literature, Pater expanded his horizons with travel to Germany in 1858, Italy in 1865, the Continent in 1868, and Italy again in 1882. In 1869 he established a household with his two sisters in Bradmore Road, Oxford. In 1885, two years after resigning his tutorship (but not his fellowship) at Brasenose, he set up a London residence with his sisters at 12 Earl's Terrace, Kensington. In 1893, they reestablished themselves at Oxford. Pater died a year later, at home, of a heart attack, on 30 July 1894.

Personal Struggles

Pater's life was marked by significant personal disappointments. How deeply these affected Pater is hard to say. It is not easy to take the pulse of Pater's emotional life, as he was a lifelong bachelor surrounded by the sisters who outlived him and guarded his reputation. In addition, the standard edition of his correspondence contains fewer than three hundred letters, and these reveal little of his interior life. Only through recent research by scholars such as Billie Andrew Inman has it become clear that it was primarily due to a same sex-attachment that Pater lost an important anticipated University Proctorship at Oxford in 1874. He had a romantic, emotional attachment to the undergraduate William Money Hardinge, and Hardinge was sent down from college temporarily for being too blatant about his own sexual orientation. Letters from Hardinge to Pater were brought to the attention of Benjamin Jowett, with whom Pater had studied classics. The formidable Jowett, Master of Balliol (1870), and translator of Plato's *Dialogues,* used his influence against Pater. The pain caused by this affair seems, unfortunately but un-

Walter Pater

derstandably, to have curbed Pater from approaching same-sex relationships in a more direct manner in his later work.

Another setback for Pater in terms of university advancement came when he was satirized as the effeminate Hellenizing aesthete Mr. Rose in W. H. Mallock's serialized novel, the *New Republic,* in 1876. A year later Pater issued a second edition of his book on the Renaissance, this time entitled *The Renaissance: Studies in Art and Poetry.* The "Conclusion" was omitted in this edition but was restored in the third, where Pater noted that he had left it out in 1877 because "I conceived it might mislead some of those young men into whose hands it might fall."

Refraining from collecting new essays, including two on Greek sculpture, "The Beginnings of Greek Sculpture" (1880) and "The Marbles of Aegina" (1880), Pater published his second long work, a novel, *Marius the Epicurean: His Sensations and Ideas,* in 1885. In his next two books, *Imaginary Portraits* (1887) and *Appreciations, with an Essay on Style* (1889), same-sex themes are of less importance than even in *Marius*, where they are woven into discussions of large aesthetic and religious issues. In his review of Oscar Wilde's *The Portrait of Dorian Gray* (1891), Pater is only half-hearted in his praise of the book and avoids commenting on some of the sexual themes raised by the novel. In his last work, *Plato and Platonism* (1893), although one can sense the same-sex attraction informing his respect for Plato, there is no extensive discussion of Plato's views on love.

Pater's name came up at Oscar Wilde's 1895 trials, although he was no longer alive to hear it mentioned. Consequently, under the watchful eye of his sisters, early writers of studies on Pater, Arthur C. Benson (1906) and Thomas Wright (1907), had to avoid close investigations of their subject's personal life. To this day no monumental, definitive biography of Pater has been written. Surviving unpublished material, such as incomplete imaginary portraits ("Gaudioso, the Second" and "Tibalt the Albigense"), can be found in the Harvard University libraries collections, and reports of new research are available in the twice-yearly *Pater Newsletter.*

Influence at Oxford

The first years of Pater's career at Oxford fall into what Linda Dowling in her book, *Hellenism and Homosexuality in Victorian Oxford,* has called the "unique moment of Oxford masculine comradeship, a window or halcyon interval of particularly intense male homosociality which flourished between the first two waves of university reform." This period at Oxford is marked on the opening end by the 1854 reforms, which expanded the number of nonclerical fellows, and, on the closing end, by the 1884 reforms, which by removing the celibacy requirement for fellows, brought to a close the age of the entirely male residential society.

Pater's Oxford had been nudged toward an acceptance of male same-sex relationships in the classical Greek world because Plato had become a significant author in the lives of undergraduates there, partially due to Benjamin Jowett's sponsorship of Plato as a classical author who offered a viable alternative to the rigidity of British religious thought, Anglican and Catholic. Young scholars, such as Pater and John Addington Symonds, both of whom were members of the Oxford essay society, Old Mortality, tried to further extend the influence of Plato through the adaptation of a Platonic/Socratic model of education to the all-male Oxford ethos. Dowling explains in her book that tutorials and essay society meetings were places where an older man, inspired by the good looks and intellectual promise of a younger man, could undertake his education in culture and virtue.

Pater's strong attraction for Hardinge in 1874 threatened this system internally, for if the tutor's and student's feelings were to become so intense that a physical relationship were to develop, the tutorials themselves could be put in jeopardy. Thus Pater's failure to move up through the university hierarchy reflects Oxford's determination to police the boundary between the acceptable homosocial world and the unacceptable homosexual lifestyle.

Pater's influence, despite his personal setback, lived on through his personal interactions, giving young men exacting intellectual training in tutorials at his primrose-painted college apartment. Wilde, one of many Oxford undergraduates who felt he was much indebted to Pater (although not a student of his, he met him in 1877), passed on Pater's ethic in his famous defense of same-sex intergenerational love at his trial and in his intensely moving confessional prison letter to Lord Alfred Douglas, *De Profundis.*

Among the recipients of Pater's letters are several whose lives were at least in part sexually non-conformist. These include Oscar Browning (1837-1923), who was dismissed from a mastership at Eton in 1875 under the cloud of a paederasty charge; and Violet Paget ("Vernon Lee," 1856-1935) some of whose short stories reflect the influence of Pater's *Imaginary Portraits.* Charles Lancelot Shadwell (1840-1919), fellow of Oriel College, Oxford, presumably the closest friend of Pater's adult life, received unfortunately unrevealing letters. Pater dedicated *Studies in the History of the Renaissance* to "C. L. S.," who had accompanied him on the 1865 trip to Italy. Shadwell became Pater's literary executor, writing prefaces for the posthumous editions of *Greek Studies, Miscellaneous Studies,* and *Gaston de Latour.* However, since these pieces are so perfunctory, it is possible that even he was not that close to Pater at the time of his death.

Pater may also have been completely or partially estranged from other friends and acquaintances after 1891. In this year his correspondence with poet Arthur Symons tails off almost totally. Furthermore, there are no surviving letters of Pater to Wilde after 1891, and Pater may have stopped seeing Wilde after Wilde introduced him to Lord Alfred Douglas. It is conceivable that Pater wanted to disassociate himself from the decadence and eroticism apparent in these writers of the 1890s, who, nevertheless, had been inspired by his work.

Writings on Same-Sex Themes

The most important essays by Pater for an understanding of homosexuality in the Victorian era are the early lecture/essay, "Diaphaneitè" (published posthumously in *Miscellaneous Studies*); "Two Early French Stories," "Leonardo da Vinci," and "Winckelmann" from *Studies in the History of the Renaissance*; "Lacedæmon" from *Plato and Platonism,* and "The Age of Athletic Prizemen" from *Greek Studies.* In addition, friendship between men is a feature of both novels, as well as the imaginary portrait "Emerald Uthwart," collected in *Miscellaneous Studies.* The mythology-based stories, "Denys l'Auxerrois" (1886), "Hippolytus Veiled" (1889), and "Apollo in Picardy" (1893), are more indirect in their treatment of same-sex desire.

Pater's major fictional representations of homosexuality are ones in which men are parted or in which feelings of same-sex attraction remain unfulfilled. In *Marius the Epicurean,* set in the time of Marcus Aurelius, the eponymous hero is much affected by the death of his best friend, Flavian, early in the novel. Flavian dies, asking whether it will be a comfort that he will come to Marius from beyond death to weep over him. Marius responds, "Not unless I be aware, and hear you weeping!" At the close of the novel Marius dies after helping enable his friend Cornelius, a soldier, to escape from captivity.

Gaston de Latour, set during the period of the French religious wars of the reigns of Charles IX and Henry III, includes a long reflection on Montaigne's deep friendship for Etienne de la Boétie. A discussion of the philosophy of the heretic Giordano Bruno leads Pater to a reflection of love as presented by Plato. Henry III's court with its male favorites prompts a digression on the court of the Emperor Elagabulus. More directly related to the thin plot line is a description of the unrequited, disturbing love of the servant Raoul for his master Jasmin.

"Emerald Uthwart" set in nineteenth-century England, tells of two friends, the older James Stokes and the younger Emerald Uthwart, who are tried in war for dereliction of duty. Stokes was shot by a firing squad and Uthwart discharged. Neither in this story nor in the novels does the plot line allow for a "happy ending" for the friends, and physical expressions of affection are avoided by Pater.

Pater's essays make more optimistic reading. In "Diaphaneitè" (*The Works,* 1910) homosexuality is not mentioned, but the appeal for an uncloseted existence can be read through the ideal of the transparent life open to the world: "The artist and he who has treated life in the spirit of art desires only to be shown to the world as he really is; as he comes nearer and nearer to perfection, the veil of an outer life not simply expressive of the inward becomes thinner and thinner." In "Two Early French Stories" Pater praises the thirteenth-century romance *Li Amitiez de Ami et Amile*, in which "a friendship pure and generous" is "pushed to a sort of passionate exaltation." The essay on Leonardo, in addition to its famous purple passage on the sexually ambiguous *Mona Lisa* hints at Leonardo's same-sex orientation through reference to a likeness sketched of the head of one "Andrea Salaino." However, here Pater has conflated two figures in Leonardo's life, and thus fails to make the appropriate biographical point. The most stirring of the essays is "Winckelmann," which champions the 18th century German aesthetician and his love for naked male forms in art and life.

Among the later essays, "The Age of Athletic Prizemen" (1894) discusses the beauty of Greek sculptures of men, including the *Discobulus.* "Lacedæmon" acknowledges the fighters of Sparta: "Lovers of youth they remained, those enstarred types of it, arrested thus at that moment of miraculous good fortune as a consecration of the clean, youthful friendship, 'passing even the love of woman,' which, by system, and under the sanction of their founder's name, elaborated into a kind of art, became an elementary part of education." This is one of the passages in which the connection between same-sex Greek love and an educational ideal for men is made most clear. Here Pater remains true to the spirit of Winckelmann in his assessment of a Greek ideal of physical beauty and emotional health, even though the social circumstances of his life prohibited him from achieving the degree of "diaphaneitè" that he had promoted 30 years earlier.

References:

Benson, Arthur C. *Walter Pater.* London: Macmillan, 1906.

Buckler, William E., editor. *Walter Pater, Three Major Texts: The Renaissance, Appreciations, and Imaginary Portraits.* New York: New York University Press, 1986.

Court, Franklin E. *Walter Pater: An Annotated Bibliography of Writings about Him.* DeKalb: Northern Illinois University Press, 1977.

Dellamora, Richard. *Masculine Desire: The Sexual Politics of Victorian Aestheticism.* Chapel Hill: University of North Carolina Press, 1990.

d'Hangest, Germain. *Walter Pater; l'homme et l'oeuvre.* Paris: Didier, 1961.

Dowling, Linda. *Hellenism and Homosexuality in Victorian Oxford.* Ithaca: Cornell University Press, 1994.

Evans, Lawrence, editor. *Letters of Walter Pater.* Oxford: Clarendon Press, 1970.

Fletcher, Ian. *Walter Pater.* London: Longmans, Green, 1971.

Hardinge, William Money. "Some Personal Recollections of the Master of Balliol," in *Temple Bar,* October, 1894.

Inman, Billie Andrew. "Estrangement and Connection: Walter Pater, Benjamin Jowett, and William M. Hardinge," in *Pater in the 1990s,* edited by Laurel Brake and Ian Small. Greensboro, North Carolina: English Literature in Transition Press, 1991.

Levey, Michael. *The Case of Walter Pater.* London: Thames and Hudson, 1978.

Monsman, Gerald. *Pater's Portraits: Mythic Patterns in the Fiction of Walter Pater.* Baltimore: Johns Hopkins University Press, 1967.

Ottley, May. "Introduction: Imaginary Portraits, An English Poet," in *Fortnightly Review,* April, 1931.

Pater, Walter. *Gaston de Latour: The Revised Text; Based on the Definitive Manuscripts and Enlarged to Incorporate All Known Fragments,* edited by Gerald Monsman. Greensboro, North Carolina: English Literature in Transition Press, 1995.

———. *The Renaissance: Studies in Art and Poetry: The 1893 Text,* edited by Donald L. Hill. Berkeley: University of California Press, 1980.

———. *Uncollected Essays,* edited by Thomas Bird Mosher. New York: AMS, 1978.

———. *The Works,* 10 volumes. London: Macmillan, 1910.

Rosenberg, John D. Review in *The Pater Newsletter,* Winter 1995.

Ward, Hayden. "Walter Pater," in *Dictionary of Literary Biography,* Volume 57. Detroit: Gale, 1987.

Wright, Samuel. *A Bibliography of the Writings of Walter H. Pater.* New York: Garland, 1975.

Wright, Thomas. *The Life of Walter Pater.* London: Everett, 1907, and New York: Haskell, 1969.

—Peter Christensen

Reverend Troy D. Perry

1940-

American religious leader and activist

Reverend Troy D. Perry

The Reverend Troy D. Perry founded the Universal Fellowship of Metropolitan Community Churches, the largest Christian church for lesbians and gay men, in 1968. Besides his work as a minister, he is also a prominent gay rights activist and author.

Perry was born in Tallahassee, Florida on 27 July 1940, the eldest of five sons of Troy D. Perry, Sr. and Edith Allen Perry. Troy Sr. owned a gasoline station and a farm, but derived most of his income from bootlegging in "dry" Leon County, Florida. When Troy Jr. was only a boy, his father was killed when his automobile crashed while being chased by police. Edith Perry, a homemaker with no job skills, soon remarried, but the marriage was short-lived. Her new husband, an abusive alcoholic, dissipated his wife's estate after moving the family to Daytona Beach, Florida. When Perry was 13, one of his stepfather's acquaintances sexually molested him. The next day Perry ran away to live with relatives in Georgia and Texas, and returned to his family only after his mother left his stepfather.

The fundamentalist Christianity that Perry's extended family practiced provided him with a variety of opportunities during his teenage years. Licensed to preach at the age of 15, he dropped out of high school after the eleventh grade to become an evangelist. He married a minister's daughter at the age of 18 and they had two sons. After five years of marriage, Perry and his wife split up because of his homosexuality. He has already been excommunicated from two denominations, the last one occurring while he was pastor of a church in Santa Ana, California.

With the exception of his U.S. Army service from 1965-1967, Perry has lived in the Los Angeles area since the early 1960s. For a period both before and after his military service, he worked for Sears, Roebuck and Company and shared a Huntington Park house with another gay man, Willie Smith. During this period Perry was often deeply troubled and attempted suicide after a failed love affair.

On 6 October 1968, a 12-person congregation met in the Perry-Smith living room for the first Metropolitan Community Church service. Perry officiated as minister, while Smith led the singing of hymns. Perry envisioned a Christian church to provide salvation, community and social action for Los Angeles homosexuals. To promote attendance at his weekly services, he placed advertisements in a local gay newspaper, the *Advocate*, which subsequently provided favorable reports on his endeavors. Perry, who appointed the church's first board of directors and deacons, organized a range of social services and religious programs to serve the homosexual community. Quickly outgrowing the Perry-Smith living room, the congregation worshipped next in a local civic hall and then in the Encore Theater, where Smith worked.

Perry dedicated the congregation's first permanent site in Los Angeles, the Mother Church, on 7 March 1971. During the next 25 years, he frequently traveled around the world to promote the church, which adopted the name of the Universal Fellowship of Metropolitan Community Churches (UFMCC).

Gay rights activism, one of the early hallmarks of the church, helped to swell its membership throughout the United States. In 1969 Perry and some followers joined a San Francisco picket line to protest the firing of a gay employee of the State Steamship Lines. He also helped to organize the first Los Angeles gay pride parade on Hollywood Boulevard in June, 1970. After the parade he was arrested as he began a prayer vigil and fast to protest California's anti-homosexual laws. Following a night in jail, he continued his ten-day fast amidst considerable press coverage. Perry's role as a California gay leader was strengthened further when he became allied with liberal California politicians such Assemblyman Willie Brown.

Although UFMCC membership multiplied throughout the United States and abroad in its early years, it faced many hurdles. Many of its worship sites, including the original Mother Church, were destroyed by arson. Perry's leadership, especially his emphasis on political and social action, was challenged on several occasions. Furthermore, in 1983 the National Council of Churches indefinitely tabled UFMCC's membership application and rejected its 1993 bid for observer status.

Although Perry's theology has usually been termed conservative, his social and political views are decidedly progressive. He performed holy union ceremonies for same-sex couples as early as 1970 and accepted the ordination of women ministers in UFMCC in 1972. In 1984 a majority of the UFMCC board of directors, as well as many of its ministers, were women.

Perry worked hard in 1977 to defeat Anita Bryant's successful Save Our Children crusade in Dade County, Florida. He was also a leading opponent of John Brigg's anti-gay ballot measure, Proposition 6, which was defeated in California in 1978. He served on the boards of the National Gay Task Force and the Gay Rights National Lobby and was a principal organizer of both the 1979 and 1987 national gay rights marches in Washington, D.C.

Perry's two autobiographical books, *The Lord Is My Shepherd and He Knows I'm Gay: The Autobiography of the Reverend Troy D. Perry* (1972) and *Don't Be Afraid Anymore: The Story of Reverend Troy Perry and the Metropolitan Community Churches* (1990) testified to the powerful combination of religion and gay liberation in his life.

The Reverend Troy D. Perry continues to lead the UFMCC in the 1990s. By 1996 the church had over 39,000 members and 301 congregations in 19 countries, and owned a five-story office building in Los Angeles that serves as UFMCC Global Headquarters.

Current Address: c/o Universal Fellowship Metropolitan Community Churches, 5300 Santa Monica Blvd., #304, Los Angeles, California 90029-1196.

References:

Contemporary Authors. Vol. 109. Detroit: Gale Research, 1983.

Dynes, Wayne R., ed. *The Encyclopedia of Homosexuality,* 2 vols. New York: Garland, 1990.

Enroth, Ronald M., and Gerald E. Jamison. *The Gay Church.* Grand Rapids, Michigan: Eerdmans, 1974.

Melton, J. Gordon, ed., *The Encyclopedia of American Religions.* Third ed. Detroit: Gale Research, 1989.

"NCC Rejects Ties With Gay Church" in *Christian Century.* December 1992, vol. 109, no. 2: 1097.

Perry, Troy D., with Thomas L.P. Swicegood. *Don't Be Afraid Anymore: The Story of Reverend Troy Perry and the Metropolitan Community Churches.* New York: St. Martin's, 1990.

———, as told to Charles L. Lucas. *The Lord Is My Shepherd and He Knows I'm Gay: The Autobiography of The Reverend Troy D. Perry.* Los Angeles: Nash, 1972.

Who's Who in America, 1996, vol. 2. New Providence, New Jersey: Marquis, 1995.

—Joseph M. Eagan

Charles Pierce

1926-

American female impersonator and actor

A legendary female impersonator for more than four decades, Charles Pierce's repertoire of larger-than-life, mostly deceased luminaries ranges from the beloved to the bitchiest to the many in between: Bette Davis, Joan Crawford, Barbara Stanwyck, Joan Collins, Katherine Hepburn, Tallulah Bankhead, Mae West, Gloria Swanson, Eva Peron, Maria Montez, Marlene Dietrich, Eleanor Roosevelt, Jeannette MacDonald, Carol Channing, and Lucille Ball. Some of Pierce's creations are fictional characters, for example, Doris Day's sister "Doo-Dah Day" and Tallulah Bankhead's grandmother "Pocahontas Bankhead." Now mostly retired, Pierce allows his fabulous females to emerge on special occasions, including his Christmas 1993 appearance with the Los Angeles Gay Men's Chorus and his May 1994 special appearance at the 20th Anniversary of San Francisco's popular show "Beach Blanket Babylon."

Mostly known for his nightclub appearances, Pierce also contributed solid acting performances to some movies in the 1980s. In his most famous role, his drag queen Bertha Venation lasciviously brushed up against Matthew Broderick in *Torch Song Trilogy*; he had a cameo role as the Queen of England in *Rabbit Test* (directed by Joan Rivers); in *Nerds of a Feather*, Pierce played Granny, a Russian fortune-teller. Occasionally, Pierce has appeared on television sitcoms, too. For example, he was a cruise director on *Designing Women*, and an assassin on *Laverne and Shirley*.

Born in Watertown, New York, in 1926, Pierce did his first drag performance at the age of nine when he borrowed one of his grandmother's dresses to entertain in a school Halloween show. During his teenage years, Pierce worked at a local radio station and saved enough money to attend the Pasadena Playhouse.

Charles Pierce

A few years later, Charles Laughton—the great, closeted English actor—suggested that Pierce put together a one-man show. Pierce took the advice, using a church auditorium to recite such classic works as "Casey at the Bat" and "The Highwayman." Pierce quickly realized that this was not his niche.

He did some summer stock but discovered his passion for the female impersonation at the Chi Chi Club in San Francisco. At the club, he met the impressionist Arthur Blake, who impressed him enormously. Money troubles characterized Pierce's early years, when he did his female impersonations and often passed around a hat for contributions. At one point, he was living in Manhattan Beach, California, and his savings were reduced to ten cents. His problems transcended money. Since full drag was illegal until the 1960s, Pierce often wore dresses over his pants.

According an article in the *Advocate* in 1989, Pierce did not have much difficulty coming to terms with his homosexuality. "I was always 'out,'" he says. "It was no problem. It was a slide right into it. I had to become aware—coming from a small town, growing up in the 1930s—of what was going on. My friends helped me there."

In interviews, Pierce often makes reference to one particular day as the turning point of his career. In an *Advocate* interview with Kim Garfield, he remembered, "On 28 September 1954, I opened [at] a small club in L.A., and I've been working ever since." The small club was called Club La Vie, and according to Pierce, it was the first place to have gay entertainment. When Pierce first performed there, they paid him five dollars for an afternoon's work.

Many of Pierce's one-liners are as memorable now as they were decades ago. Joan Collins: "Men are like diamonds—they're never too big or too hard." Joan Crawford: "Come and have your bath, Christina—I've been boiling the water for two weeks."

Pierce, however, does not consider himself a drag queen. As he told Ken Dickmann, "Apparently today, everyone's talking about drag queens rather than female impersonators. Way back when, female impersonators were entertainers whether they did impressions, dance or sang in their own voice or did some kind of novelty act. We called others drag queens. Drag queens went to balls where people dressed up and went out on the street and went to parties." In the January 1989 *Advocate* article, Pierce described most of the women he imitates as "campy, glamorous, and dressed up. They are not to be seen at a supermarket. These women are from a certain era, and they're imitable. Who are you going to imitate today—Molly Ringwald? And how do you imitate a Meryl Streep?"

Despite Pierce's commercial and critical success, one of his ambitions has gone unrealized: to bring his act to Broadway. He did get occasional offers, but none have come to fruition. Yet, he seems far from bitter. In interviews, he accentuates the positive events in his life, takes enormous pride in his Los Angeles home laden with Hollywood paraphernalia (e.g., Chita Rivera's jazz shoes from *West Side Story*; Margot Fonteyn's pink ballet slippers; sculptures of Bette Davis and Joan Crawford), and seldom speaks ill of anyone, least of all his fans. "God, they have been loyal," he told Garfield.

References:

Bean, Joseph W. "Famous People and How They Came Out," in *Advocate,* 10 October 1989: 34-38.

"Being Joan Is Often a Drag," in *Newsweek,* 24 October 1988: 62.

Garfield, Kim. "Charles Pierce. A Legend from Stage to Screen," in *Advocate,* 31 January 1989: 49-51.

Hammond, John. "So Many Women, So Little Time," in *New York Native,* 17 October 1988: 28-30.

"Wanna Buy An Illusion: Ken Dickmann Talks with Charles Pierce," in *Dragazine,* 1994, no. 7: 12-17.

—David Levine

Plato

427 B.C.-347 B.C.

Greek philosopher

A writer and thinker of enormous gifts, Plato occupies a pivotal position in the most brilliant phase of ancient Greek philosophy. Refining the ideas of his teacher Socrates, he in turn molded his successor Aristotle. Since his time Platonism, the transmission and creative reformulation of his distinctive doctrines has ranked as a major component of the European tradition. Plato's central insight lay in the sharp contrast that he drew between the imperfect observable world in which we live and another world that cannot be directly accessed. The latter, whose existence and characteristics can be demonstrated through argument, is the realm of "forms," which are eternal, changeless, and incorporeal. This dichotomy of the real and the ideal, and the privileging of the latter, represents the core of Platonism. Plato discussed many matters—including mathematics, politics, ethics, and aesthetics—but always in this perspective of idealism. Unfortunately, many of his admirers have glossed over the fact that he also placed in this context important observations about the special form of homosexuality known to the Greeks as *paiderasteia* or pederasty.

Plato deployed the resources of his literary art with superb skill, not hesitating to use such potentially misleading devices as irony and allegory, so that following his train of exposition is not always easy. Moreover, his dialogues present his ideas through several mouthpieces, of whom Socrates is the most important. Some views he expounds through this dramatic device seem close to or identical with his own; others are not. For his numerous interpreters these qualities have given rise to disagreements—as well as to the neglect or obscuring of concepts that the commentator finds unpleasant. Even the fairest of heterosexual Plato scholars find it hard to resist glossing over some aspects of Plato's profound affinity with homoeroticism. Finally there is a question for which no satisfactory answer is available. What are the underlying personal motives—perhaps unconscious ones—that Plato does not set forth in words? While it is important to understand his thinking against the backdrop of his society, with its customs, prejudices, and conventional wisdom, this approach does not suffice to explain Plato the person. And it is the dynamic relationship of the person with the ideas, in so far as we can hope to grasp this interaction, that offers the supreme challenge.

Plato was born into an aristocratic Athenian family prominent in politics. It seemed that Plato was destined to follow in this career path. However, his apprenticeship with Socrates caused him to shift his focus towards philosophy. This shift was encouraged by Plato's disgust with the course of contemporary politics, which led to the execution of Socrates for impiety in 399 B.C. While Plato lived mainly in Athens, on two occasions he traveled to Sicily, where he was influenced by the mathematical interests of the philosopher Pythagoras. While in Sicily he sought, in vain, to influence king Dionysius II to adopt his ideals so as to become the model "philosopher-king." About 387 B.C. he began teaching near the grove of Academus just outside the walls of Athens. This arrangement, a kind of fraternity of scholars with Plato at is head, has contributed the term "academy."

Over a period of 50 years Plato composed his philosophical dialogues. Modern scholars divide these into three periods. During the first, when he was most strongly under the influence of Socrates, Plato addressed basic questions of knowledge and methodology. His mature theory of forms appeared during his second period. The final period revised the doctrines elaborated during the second.

The Lyrical Advocate of Spiritual Pederasty

Plato's interest in homoeroticism centered on the venerable Greek custom of pederasty, the erotic attachment of an adult male for an adolescent boy. Although he did not deny the value of heterosexual marriage, it is significant that when he evokes the power of erotic desire the context is invariably homoerotic. The dialogues in which he treats the matter most fully are the *Phaedrus*, the *Symposium*, and the *Republic*, which belong to his middle period, and the *Laws*, composed at the end of his life.

In the *Phaedrus* Socrates combats the arguments of the sophist Lysias, who claimed that opportunistic love is better than devoted love. Socrates concedes that, by virtue of its often excruciating intensity, real love is a species of madness. However, the important thing is to utilize the madness to bring forth good. To explain how this is done, he introduces the allegory of the two horses, one noble and one base, controlled by a charioteer. The noble horse tends always to restraint, while the base one seeks immediate gratification. By preferring the noble horse, the lover disdains the opportunistic strategy of "nailing" the boy, getting sex from him as quickly as one can. Instead, he patiently builds up the boy's confidence. Understanding the nobility of the lover's motives, the boy is able to reciprocate his love, rather than merely reluctantly acquiescing for the sake of some material boon. Sexual union may occur, and is not dishonorable, but Plato thinks that a truly philosophical couple will abstain from sex in hopes of gaining a spiritual crown.

The *Symposium* is the only work of Plato that is concerned solely with love. It is somewhat surprising, then, that in this dialogue Plato introduced a non-Greek conception of the origin of sexual attraction. All human beings, Plato's character Aristophanes claims, represent the sundered halves of more complex creatures who had two heads, four arms, four legs, and two sets of genitalia. People of those early days fell into three genders: male-male, male-female, and female-female. Displeased with their insolence, Zeus, the ruler of the gods, punished them by dividing them in half. The halves developed from the separation of the male-male type are homosexual men, those stemming from the division of the male-female type are heterosexuals, and the ones tracing their existence back to the female-female types are lesbians. (Although this terminology is modern, it faithfully reflects Plato's thinking.) The sexual drive humans experience represents the unconscious but powerful longing of the halves of the original dual beings to reunite. By means of this myth Plato touches on a basic psychological truth: the universal desire, whatever one's orientation, to achieve wholeness through love.

Plato

The myth of lost wholeness, which is probably of Middle Eastern origin, has the merit of clearly distinguishing male homosexuality and lesbianism both from heterosexuality and from each other. Plato's concept shows that the ability to think of same-sex behavior as a distinct type (or types) is by no means a creation of the nineteenth century, as some recent advocates of the theory known as Social Construction claim, but is much earlier. Revealingly, a common saying used today to refer to one's spouse, "my better half," refers today to only *one* of Plato's three ideal ancestors, the one that determines heterosexuality. Similarly, Platonic love, originally a homoerotic concept, is currently understood as the love between a man and a woman that is not consummated.

In addition, the *Symposium* distinguishes two forms of love. The vulgar one, Aphrodite Pandemos, can be experienced by a male in relation to either women or boys. By contrast, the heavenly one, Aphrodite Uranios, focuses solely on males, rising above the desire for physical gratification. In this state of spiritual exaltation, the lover cherishes the vitality, intelligence, and potential of the beloved youth. For the elect, however, this love of beauty in a single youth is only the beginning of a spiritual journey which leads the individual to a contemplation of the highest forms of truth. In this way Plato sets forth an ideal of sublimation, not in the Freudian sense, but with the aim of returning to the primordial bliss of pure knowledge. Expanding on ideas adumbrated in the *Phaedrus*, the *Symposium* assumes that in the truly philosophical couple continence will reign, since this policy avoids the danger of admixture of base elements, while both individuals can devote themselves exclusively to the contemplation of philosophical truths. Even in this context, however, Plato takes it for granted that spiritual ascent can only begin with the love of a beautiful boy; attraction to a woman cannot have this supremely salubrious effect.

In the great treatise on the ideal society known as the *Republic* Plato's attitude toward active pederasty reinforces the negative shading that stems from the ideal of sublimation. He finds that males who have sexual relations with other males, even in the age-asymmetrical pairs prescribed by Hellenic tradition, show "vulgarity and lack of taste." The ideal of chastity joins with the notion that love of the soul should replace that of the body. This conclusion forms a bridge to Plato's last thoughts on the matter, which are decidedly disapproving.

The Curmudgeon

It is not clear why Plato, in contrast to the conventional wisdom of the Greeks, formulated his ideals of continence. In the thinking of his middle period, however, he still recognized homosexual behavior as permissible, while increasingly viewing it as a lesser option. In his final period he moved towards absolute prohibition.

Plato's last years were blighted by increasing disappointment. He was disgusted by the excesses that had marred the course of Athenian democracy. The *Laws*, written when Plato was in his 70s, reflects a sense that the blueprint for a perfect society espoused in the *Republic* is unrealizable. Settling for a second-best solution, he constructs a dense network of social controls foreshadowing modern totalitarian states. He also showed a kind of old-fogy attitude towards developments in culture. In painting, for example, he condemned the illusionism increasingly common in his time, commending a return to the rigidity of Egyptian art.

This bitter and reactionary mood also colors Plato's final thoughts about homosexual behavior. In the *Laws* Plato condemned pederasty and lesbianism as "contrary to nature." Although the accents are different, this notion of homosexual behavior passed into Christianity in the condemnation asserted by the apostle Paul in the Epistle to the Romans (1:26-27). After first idealizing homosexual response, Plato had the dubious distinction of inventing one of the most pernicious slogans attacking it.

The aged Plato even thought that it might be possible to drive homoerotic impulses underground by a policy of social defamation that would place it on the level of incestuous. He supported this proposal with the feeble claim that one cannot know in advance how young people will turn out, and hence the efforts of the pederast to educate his beloved boy are useless.

One aspect of homosexual behavior Plato never soured—because he never admired it in the first place. He dealt only fleetingly with the *kinaidos*, the passive-effeminate male who accepts the role of bottom, seeking to be sexually possessed by other men, and so behaves like a woman. His dislike of this aspect almost reaches the level of taboo. The example of the kinaidos proves that pleasure does not equal goodness. Here Plato was not in disagreement with his society, which distinguished, as we do not, the acceptable passive role in the youth from its unacceptable counterpart in the adult.

Platonic Aftermath

The influence of Plato's teachings has been as variable as it has been vast; no simple formula can encompass it. The enemies of homosexuality have raided Plato's arguments for their own purposes, neglecting the more positive ideas that occur in his early and middle periods. Despite the pronounced originality, and even waywardness of Plato's thinking, homophobes have even tried to depict the more negative views as typical of the whole of ancient Greek society—a manifest absurdity. Others have preferred to believe that Plato simply did not address homosexuality at all. This ostrich approach appears in the bowdlerized translations of his work that appeared in Victorian times, and in the modern, heterosexualized senses of the expressions "better half" and "Platonic love."

Over the centuries gay people have looked to the *Symposium* as ennobling sexual liaisons between males and even exalting them above heterosexual ones in their value to society. At times these enthusiasts have overlooked what was for Plato the crucial point—that these are age-asymmetrical relationships with an educational purpose. Others may have taken a harsher lesson from Plato. For the personal lives of a few gay people may have been stunted, by acquiescing in a celibacy that was not good for them on the seemingly Platonic grounds that continence is the noblest path to take.

Because of his importance in the history of philosophy and his mastery of the arts of literary exposition, Plato has been read, studied, and translated for more than two millennia. This attention will certainly continue in the age of electronic information.

Yet with our increasing knowledge about sexual behavior, the primary significance of his ambivalent legacy in this area is receding. Not only did he take his starting point from Greek concepts which are not necessarily ours, but his personal psychology seemed to have impelled him towards a denial of the sexual urge, precisely in the area where he conceded its appeal to be greatest, the homoerotic. Why he should commend this frustrating path remains a riddle, for unlike a few tormented modern gay people who internalize homophobia and thus become self-hating, he did not confront social pressures that might lead him to deny his own nature.

A clue may lie in Plato's capacity—which the more down-to-earth Socrates did not share—for ecstatic, piercing emotion. This capacity undergirds his aesthetic sensibility, and surely was part and parcel of his appreciation of the beauty of boys. It is almost as if he could not stand the intensity of this experience, and to cushion its full effects worked out an elaborate rationale of staying pure in order to ascend the ladder of being.

This riddle aside, Plato's eloquent discourses on love will always stand as the fascinating record of an effort by one supremely intelligent thinker to understand the sexual mores of his society and to reshape them in accordance with the basic principles of his own thought.

References:

Dover, Kenneth J. *Greek Homosexuality.* Cambridge: Harvard University Press, 1978.

Halperin, David. "Platonic Eros and What Men Call Love," in *Ancient Philosophy,* 1985, no. 5: 161-204.

———. "Plato and Erotic Reciprocity," in *Classical Antiquity,* 1986, no. 5: 60-80.

Kraut, Richard, ed. *The Cambridge Companion to Plato.* New York: Cambridge University Press, 1992.

Price, Anthony W. *Love and Friendship in Plato and Aristotle.* Oxford: Clarendon Press, 1989.

Vlastos, Gregory. *Platonic Studies.* Princeton: Princeton University Press, 1981.

—Wayne R. Dynes

Deb Price

1958-

American journalist

Journalist Deb Price writes the first nationally syndicated lesbian and gay column published by the mainstream press.

Deborah Jane Price was born in Lubbock, Texas on 27 February 1958 and grew up in Colorado. Her father, Allen Price, then an Episcopal priest, is now a psychologist. Her mother, Jane Price, is a receptionist in a law firm. "As a child, I was always 'different' in the way that gay adults often describe looking back. I hated dolls, dresses and pretty much anything that girls were supposed to crave. I loved to play and often found myself in play rescuing women! As I grew older, I had major crushes on women teachers and other girls," Price reflects.

When her parents divorced in 1973, Price, her brother Steve, and their mother moved to the East Coast. Price maintains a close relationship with her mother, asserting, "My mother has always been enormously supportive of me. She has always encouraged me, loved me and been a close friend as well as my mother. She has been remarkable since the column came out and outed her to her work colleagues and friends. She has marched in gay pride parades and is a tremendous source of strength for me. I never doubt her complete love for me. And that is something I have always drawn on to make it through the rough times."

Price had her first "romantic relationship" at the National Cathedral School for Girls in Washington, D.C. but did not really deal with being gay until she went to college. "I fully accepted myself in that I knew for certain I was a lesbian. But I was terrified of how other people might use that to hurt me. As a result, I dated men occasionally and was closeted even to gay friends," Price recollects.

Earning a B.A. and M.A. in literature at Stanford University, Price discovered a scarcity of academic positions and chose a career in journalism. She credits author Charles Dickens with influencing her choice: "In addition to being a novelist, he spoke out through the news periodicals against the horrible injustices of his day and he used his novels as well to educate readers about these terrible injustices. In hindsight, I am grateful that my path led me to where I am today. I feel tremendous gratitude that I was given the opportunity on a weekly basis to do something similar to what Charles Dickens did. Journalism combines a lot of my passions—writing, reading, thinking, debating, learning, exploring, talking, listening, caring, reaching out, growing."

Beginning her career at the *Northern Virginia Sun* in 1982, Price later moved to the States News Service, a Washington-based wire service covering Capitol Hill. In 1985, she became the news editor at *The Washington Post,* where she met her current "lovemate," Joyce Murdoch. Price asserts, "I wasn't able to put it completely all together—be who I am and be truthful about it to everyone—until I met Joyce who was totally at ease with being gay. She was just getting ready to start a process of coming out professionally. But she had the personal acceptance down perfectly! And that was the kind of role model and friend I had desperately needed my whole life. We've really helped one another get to the place where we are today—totally out and trying to help other gay people. We work as a team. And we always have."

In 1989, Price became Deputy Washington Bureau Chief for *The Detroit News.* While working for the *News,* she successfully pitched the idea of writing a column on gay and lesbian issues and on 8 May 1992 her column made its debut. Syndicated today in over 100 newspapers throughout the country, Price's columns add a human dimension to current gay and lesbian issues because she discusses them within the context of peoples' lives, often her own and Murdoch's. In a friendly, humorous manner, Price deftly educates her readers about commonly held misconceptions about gays and lesbians. Reflecting on the column's success, Price says, "Without a doubt, we both feel the most important thing we have accomplished professionally has been all the good that has come about through the column. We most love hearing from readers that the column helped bring their family back together. Sometimes, it's a letter from a parent; sometimes, it's from an adult child. But nothing gives us more joy than having been part of the process of healing in a family. We also love hearing from readers who find the column helpful in their journey of coming out."

Deb Price (right) with Joyce Murdoch. ***Photograph by Mary Lou Foy.***

Price and Murdoch have also collaborated on a book, *And Say Hi to Joyce,* the title of which derives from a concluding remark often found in Price's fanmail. Dedicated to "all the gay readers who've put twenty-five cents in a newspaper and found nothing reflecting their own lives inside," the book juxtaposes the first 18 months of Price's columns against Murdoch's commentary on their impact. Comments Price, "We've been most pleased that the book makes people happy, that it makes people feel good about themselves and about other people. We like tapping into the good in ourselves and in others. And we like sharing the joy we've experienced through the column."

Current Address: c/o *Detroit News,* 1148 National Press Building, Washington, D.C., 20045; phone: (301) 270-1594.

References:

Price, Deb. E-mail interview with R. Ellen Greenblatt, 1996.
Price, Deb and Joyce Murdoch. *And Say Hi to Joyce: America's First Gay Column Comes Out.* New York: Doubleday, 1995.

—R. Ellen Greenblatt

Marcel Proust

1871-1922

French novelist

With *A la recherche du temps perdu,* (literally *In search of time lost* or *gone by,* translated by C. K. Scott Moncrieff as *Remembrance of Things Past*), Marcel Proust left his mark on modern literature. Both highly biographical and intensely personal, the novel is at the same time a great work of imaginative fiction where the lines between the real and the imagined are successfully blurred. His vaunted technique of using everyday objects to summon up long-lost memories helped change our concepts of time in narrative structure. His attempt to heterosexualize his observed world led him to portray homosexual characters and relationships in a most negative manner. Nonetheless, there is no denying that this *magnum opus* of 15 volumes remains one of the most interesting and powerful works of twentieth-century literature.

Born 10 July 1871, son of professor of medicine Adrien Proust and his highly educated Jewish wife, Jeanne Weil, Marcel Proust led a privileged and sheltered life. In 1873 his brother, Robert, was born. The two boys grew up in the Paris region, but spent a good bit of vacation time at the home of their paternal aunt in Illiers, a town on the Loire southwest of Chartres. It is Illiers that Proust memorialized as Combray, the setting for the opening of his novel. In 1882, Proust entered the Lycée Condorcet where he was a good student, eventually winning the honors prize for philosophy. He also wrote for the student paper, the *Revue Lilas,* and left behind a great deal of written correspondence with his school friends.

In 1889, Proust took advantage of a special enlistment promotion and joined the military. Young men at that time could buy their way into the officer's corps, and Proust apparently liked being seen in the rather chic uniform of the day. He was posted to the 76th infantry regiment near Orléans, and spent every Sunday on leave in Paris visiting friends. This type of enlistment lasted just a year, and soon Proust was back in Paris and in school. He attended classes at the École des sciences politiques and at the Sorbonne, and received his degree in 1892. Thereafter he spent less and less time at Illiers and vacationed more frequently on the Normandy coast.

Proust wrote many articles during the next few years which were published in numerous magazines. Coming from a wealthy family, he was able to live comfortably without holding down any kind of regular job. He was regularly invited to the homes of Parisian high society, and later was to use these occasions as grist for his highly productive literary mill.

The Writer as Voyeur

Jewish on his mother's side, asthmatic, and homosexual, Proust found himself on the outside looking in. He became a keen observer of his contemporaries, and ultimately translated the world he saw into one of the greatest literary works of the twentieth century. In 1896, his first published work appeared under the title *Les Plaisirs et les Jours* (Pleasures and Days). This book, with a chapter titled "Personnages de la Comédie Mondaine" (Characters of the Worldly Comedy), drew from his experiences among the upper crust, and the author certainly felt a connection with his literary predecessors, most notably Dante with the *Divine Comedy* and Balzac with the *Human Comedy.* Arnold Hauser, in his *Social History of Art,* traces the development of the novel in western literature from the chivalric epics of the middle ages. He devotes a great deal of thought to such literary geniuses as Balzac, Flaubert and Proust. Where Balzac was concerned with the sociology of 19th Century France, and his characters were more sociological types, Proust was concerned with the inner life—with consciousness. Furthermore, Balzac portrayed a wide variety of French life, indeed the *Comédie humaine* portrays virtually all levels of French society. Proust showed only the upper classes. The only working people in his *comédie mondaine* are domestic servants. Curiously in Proust's private life, while he knew a great many men in the upper classes, his romantic liaisons were mostly with his social inferiors. One of his lovers was his chauffeur, Alfred Agostinelli.

A final comparison between these two great exemplars of the French novel: Balzac's oeuvre is made up of a number of individual novels, often with recurring characters showing up in several different works, but each novel can and does stand on its own. In the case of Proust, *A la recherche du temps perdu* is a single novel, tied together from beginning to end, even though it has been printed as three, seven, and even 15 volumes at various times in its history.

"To Be Separated from Mama"

As a child Proust had been devoted to his mother (and apparently she to him). Indeed, as his asthma grew worse and his health ever more fragile, his mother tended to spoil him. A popular game among young people of the day was to answer a questionnaire concerning their likes, dislikes, and philosophical thoughts. This type of questionnaire has been revised and can now be found each month at the back of *Vanity Fair* magazine where it is called the "Proust Questionnaire." At the age of 13, Proust answered one of these questionnaires, and in response to the question "What would be the worst thing you could endure?" he replied, "To be separated from mama."

Between the closeness of his family ties, the closeted nature of his own homosexuality, and the autobiographical elements that family and friends could not possibly miss in *A la recherche du temps perdu,* he apparently did not feel comfortable writing his novel until after the death of his parents in 1903 and 1905. Before their deaths, Proust wrote the manuscript of a three-volume novel, *Jean Santeuil.* This novel was set aside, and many of its themes were later incorporated into *A la recherche du temps perdu.* Long after Proust's own death, a niece found the manuscript and the novel was

Marcel Proust

published in 1952. Comparing the early manuscript with *A la recherche*, one notes a lack of candor in the former, possibly caused by the fear of hurting the author's parents.

After the death of his parents, Proust set to the task of composing his masterpiece. As his health continued to deteriorate, the question arose whether he would be able to finish the work. Moving to the Boulevard Hausmann in the center of Paris, he worked feverishly to complete his text, this time leaving nothing out, but as we shall see, twisting the truth so as to make the work more palatable for mainstream audiences.

Writing Them Back into the Closet

Homosexual himself, Proust wrote himself into a corner describing homosexual relationships. There has been much speculation about what kind of novel *A la recherche* would have been had Proust felt free to keep actual gender references true to their inspirations—had Albertine been Albert, for instance. This kind of speculation is pointless, however, since neither the times nor Proust's own conservatism would have allowed that measure of truth. Unfortunately, since the main relationships were transformed into heterosexual ones, and since Proust was unable to keep homosexuality out of his novel, the homosexual characters and relationships are shown in contrast to their heterosexual counterparts and come off much the worse for the comparison. André Gide was most concerned about this, and frowned on Proust's negative stereotypes of gay people. He apparently did not want to be seen in the same light as the Baron Charlus. As Gregory Woods writes in his excellent essay on Proust:

> As André Gide noticed, the major problem with Proust's representations of homosexuality is that he used his own most abiding and precious memories of love to flesh out the novel's picture of heterosexual relations and was inadvertently left, in the case of homosexuality, with predominantly negative themes and events.... By the time Proust was aware of the consequences of his initial decision to heterosexualize his narrator, it was too late to adjust the disproportionately negative view the book conveys of its homosexual characters and the relationships they form.

Gide found many problems with Proust's novel, and as editor of the Nouvelle Revue Française (NRF) he refused to publish the novel when it was first presented to him. He was not alone in this refusal. While Proust may not have invented the style, his "stream of consciousness" writing frightened off the publishers of his day. Every major publishing house in France rejected the first volume, *Du Côté de chez Swann* (Moncreiff's *Swann's Way*), when he submitted it for publication in 1913. In fact, when Bernard Grasset did publish *Du Côté de chez Swann,* the publishing house was acting in today's terms as a vanity press, the work having been paid for by the author.

Met with initial indifference, during the war years the novel did begin to garner attention and by the time the second volume appeared in 1919, Proust was under contract with Gallimard (the *Nouvelle Revue française*). The work itself, *A l'ombre des Jeunes Filles en fleurs* (Moncrieff's *Within a Budding Grove*), was awarded the Prix Goncourt, France's highest literary honor. With regard to Proust's style, Sharon Spencer has noted:

> In the first decades of the century, however, a very great transformation in the orientation of the novel to the concept of time was achieved by the "stream of consciousness" and its relation to the ideas articulated by Henri Bergson. These were reflected in Dorothy Richardson's *Pilgrimage*, in James Joyce's *Ulysses*, in Marcel Proust's *A la recherche du temps perdu*, in Virginia Woolf's novels, and in hordes of lesser works that embody "subjective" time schemes: the notion that time is "something having no existence apart from an observer and present only in experience."

In this context it is worth noting that Henri Bergson was one of Proust's professors at the Sorbonne.

Writing to Beat Death

Between the first volume, which appeared in 1913, and the second, which was published in 1919, France underwent the cataclysm of World War I. Proust used this time to write continuously and the Armistice found him happy with the end of the war, but concerned over his turbulent personal life. The Boulevard Hausmann apartment had been sold and he was forced to move into "temporary" lodgings at 44, rue Hamelin. Feeling ever more pressed to complete his work, Proust gave up all outside distractions. *Le Côté de Guermantes I* appeared in 1920 while 1921 saw *Le Côté de Guermantes II* and *Sodome et Gomorrhe I. Sodome et Gomorrhe II* was published in 1922. Moncrieff translates these titles as *The Guermantes Way* and *Cities of the Plain.* The remaining volumes of the book were not published until 1927, over four years after Proust's death. These volumes were titled *La Prisonnière*, *La Fugitive* (originally *Albertine disparue*), and *Le Temps retrouvé* (Moncrieff's *The Captive, The Sweet Cheat Gone,* and *The Past Recaptured*). I should note that while Moncrieff undoubtedly felt that he was complimenting Proust by using a line from Shakespeare's Sonnet XXX, "When to the sessions of sweet silent thought/I summon up remembrance of things past," Proust himself did not like the English title since it carried no indication of the quest or search inherent in the French title.

During the last few years of his life, Proust lived a veritable hermit, closed in his bedroom writing and editing his manuscript. He did, however, leave home to view the Ver Meer exhibit at the Jeu de Paume museum, one June day in 1921. While on this excursion of no more than a mile (the rue Hamelin is just past the Arc de Triomphe at the West end of the Champs Elysées and the Jeu de Paume in the Tuileries Gardens at the East end of that same great avenue), Proust had a severe attack—which he put to good use in describing the death of Bergotte. He lived another year, however, and died of severe bronchitis on 18 November 1922.

So Why Read Proust?

So what is the importance of Proust to the gay reader of the 1990s? In the first place, the work is undoubtedly a masterpiece. It is one of those defining moments in literature where the paradigm shifts. Furthermore, it is a portrait of a gay world at one important point in time, a portrait drawn by a homosexual (if not "gay") artist. If the artist disguised his own attractions by straightening them out, and left us with only negatives for our own role models, then we, as informed readers can approach the text with a clearer understanding. George Stambolian interviewed Eric Bentley on the question of homosexual imagination. Their conversation in time turned to Proust. Bentley, while admitting that he is an "unashamed Proust freak, maniac" states unequivocally that a modern gay reader would find *A la recherche du temps perdu* gloomy.

I disagree with Roger Shattuck about him and agree with an opinion of Edmund Wilson's which Shattuck derides: that *Remembrance* is "one of the gloomiest books ever written." And this, as I see it, is because Proust repudiates Eros. Finds him a cheat. Now the erotic experience that drove Marcel—the real-life Marcel—was all homoerotic. Which makes his work doubly sad for the homosexual reader. Writing in the same anthology, J.E. Rivers notes:

> What interests Proust about homosexuality is the paradox by which, in homosexual love, that which is natural and that which is against nature constantly reflect each other ... In Proust's realization the homosexual is the nexus, at once repugnant and fascinating, hideous and beautiful, grotesque and harmoniously conceived, of all the unnamed and dimly imagined potentialities of nature.

There you have it. Suffice it to say that Proust and *A la recherche du temps perdu* is not for everyone. Some readers will undoubtedly agree with the editor who rejected the manuscript because he did not want to read 30 pages about someone tossing and turning in bed. Others have, and will continue to, idolize the author and worship the book. There is even a site on the World Wide Web devoted to Proust and his work. The reader may wish to join the Proust Support Group, or may be content to spend the summer (or the next year or two) curled in front of the fire, or better yet lying in bed, reading the book from beginning to end.

References:

Bentley, Eric. "We Are in History," interview by George Stambolian in *Homosexualities and French Literature,* George Stambolian and Elaine Marks, eds. Ithaca: Cornell University Press, 1979: 138.

Brée, Germaine and Carlos Lynes, Jr. "Introduction," in *Combray.* New York: Appleton-Century-Crofts, Inc., 1952.

Hauser, Arnold. *The Social History of Art,* volume 4, Stanley Godman, translator. New York: Vintage Books, n.d.

Rivers, J. E. "The Myth and Science of Homosexuality," in *Homosexualities and French Literature,* George Stambolian and Elaine Marks, eds. Ithaca: Cornell University Press, 1979: 276.

Spencer, Sharon. *Space, Time and Structure in the Modern Novel.* New York: New York University Press, 1971: xix.

Woods, Gregory. "Marcel Proust," in *The Gay and Lesbian Literary Heritage,* Claude J. Summers, ed. New York: Henry Holt & Company, 1995: 570.

—Bryan D. Spellman

Manuel Puig

1932-1990

Argentinian novelist and playwright

Manuel Puig wrote eight novels now translated from Spanish into many other languages. His early work found enthusiastic readers, but *El beso de la mujer araña* (1976, *Kiss of the Spider Woman*) made him an international celebrity after the Hollywood version became a hit. Puig crossed over twice: first from Latin American and then from gay male literature into the mainstream.

Born 28 December 1932 in the small town of General Villegas in the Argentine Pampa, Manuel Puig, like Greta Garbo in MGM's *The Temptress* (1926), found the terrain tedious. His father Baldomero Puig was a businessman and his mother María Elena Delledonne de Puig a chemist. Puig described his hometown as "a place that had nothing, far away, very far away from the sea and the mountains and from Buenos Aires." But, Puig eventually found an escape: "when my mother took me to the cinema for the first time—I was four—I thought that was where life was, it all seemed so real to me." Puig went to the cinema five times a week and later moved to Buenos Aires for boarding school and in 1950 the University, where he studied philosophy and architecture; in 1953, he served in the Argentine Air Force as a translator.

Puig soon became a vagabond in pursuit of the gay life and a career in cinema. In 1955, he received a scholarship to study film in Rome, taught Spanish and Italian in London (1956-57), worked as an assistant film director in Rome and Paris (1957-58), as a dishwasher in Stockholm (1959), as a film director in Buenos Aires (1960), as a subtitler for foreign films in Rome (1961-62), and as a clerk for Air France in New York (1963-67), where he once served Greta Garbo.

His first breakthrough came with *La traición de Rita Hayworth* (1968, *Betrayed by Rita Hayworth*). The novel appeared in Buenos

Manuel Puig

Aires but mostly aroused suspicion because Toto the chief protagonist appears so swishy. Puig fled to Paris where Gallimard translated the work in 1969. *Le Mond* declared it one of the best novels of the year and in 1971 E. P. Dutton published an English version.

International success brought Puig recognition in Buenos Aires where his next two novels appeared. *Boquitas pintadas: Folletin* (1969, *Heartbreak Tango: A Serial*) and *The Buenos Aires Affair: Novelia policial* (1973, *The Buenos Aires Affair: A Detective Novel*) used pulp fiction and detective novel formats to probe bathos and misery. The author himself once defined "camp" as "ridiculing and trying to destroy something one loves in order to prove that it is indestructible."

As Argentine political conditions worsened, Puig's books could no longer be printed there. Seix Barral, a Barcelona publisher with several gay titles, published *El beso de la mujer araña* (1976, *Kiss of the Spider Woman*). "Footnotes" in *Spider Woman* provide a running commentary (perhaps gimmick or comic) discussing sexual repression and authoritarianism. Two protagonists—Molina the queen and Valentín the Marxist—share a cell where Molina seduces and ultimately absorbs Valetín through the narration of film plots.

In 1985 Hector Babenco made the novel into a movie and William Hurt who played Molina won an Academy Award for Best Actor. Terrence McNally adapted the book into a musical that brought John Cander and Fred Ebb a Tony Award in 1993. *Spider Woman* has changed as she has travelled from South America. In the original, Puig attempted to synthesize the Marxist, butch position with the popular, gay sensibility. Molina becomes a synthesis as he moves into Buenos Aires to carry on the revolution. Moreover, the Spanish version plays against the well-known events of post-Peron Argentina.

Before Puig became an international celebrity, he published three memorable novels: *Pubis angelical* (1979), *Maldición eterna a quien lea estas páginas* (1980, *Eternal Curse on the Reader of These Pages*), and *Sangre de amor correspondido* (1982, *Blood of Requited Love*). Each work surprised readers and critics as Puig developed new and unexpected material. *Blood of Requited Love,* like his last novella *Cae la noche tropical* (1988, *Tropical Night Falling*), incorporates stories from Brazil, where Puig lived during the 1980s.

In his final months Puig lived in the Mexican city of eternal spring, Cuenavaca, where Montezuma had a summer palace. Puig planted his garden with hundreds of gardenias, the favored flower of Billy Holiday. He died there, on 22 July 1990, of heart failure (a complication of AIDS).

References:

Bacarisse, Pamela. *The Necessary Dream: A Study Of The Novels of Manuel Puig.* Cardiff: University of Wales Press, 1988.

Kerr, Lucille. *Suspended Fictions: Reading Novels By Manuel Puig.* Urbana: University of Illinois Press, 1987.

Lavers, Norman. *Pop Culture Into Art: The Novels Of Manuel Puig.* Columbia: University of Missouri Press, 1988.

Manrique, Jaime. "Manuel Puig: The Writer as Diva," in *Christopher Street,* July 1993: 14-27.

Tittler, Jonathan. *Manuel Puig.* New York: Twayne Publishers, 1993.

—Charles Shively

Gertrude "Ma" Rainey

1886-1939

African-American blues singer

Nowadays revered as Mother of the Blues, Gertrude "Ma" Rainey was the first of the great female blues singers, bringing the music from its roots in African-American folksong to the recording studio, and marking the transition to a modern urban blues style. Equally important was her example as a role model, as a black woman achieving fame and respect in a white, male-dominated world.

Gertrude Pridgett was born 26 April 1886 in Columbus, Georgia, one of five children of Thomas Pridgett, Sr. and Ella Allen. Both her parents were entertainers, and Gertrude entered show business at an early age. She made her first appearance in the local show A Bunch of Blackberries at the Springer Opera House in Columbus around 1900, when barely 14 years old.

Rainey and Rainey Hit the Road

Gertrude married Will "Pa" Rainey, a singing comedian with the Rabbit Foot Minstrels, on 2 February 1904, and soon afterwards the couple set out as a song and dance act to tour the Southern tent shows. It was the start of a phenomenal career of live performances that were to occupy her through to 1920, and established her as a star with both black and white Southern audiences.

Rainey was a short, stout woman whose broad features and protruding teeth gave her a homely look. Some thought her ugly, but more were captivated by her kind, generous nature and her undeniable charisma.

By 1910, Rainey was a big attraction on the Southern touring circuit, and it was about this time that she and her husband met the young, unknown Bessie Smith in Chattanooga, Tennessee. Smith appeared with the Raineys in the Moses Stokes show at the Ivory Theater, Chattanooga, in 1912, and toured with them on Fat Chappelle's tent shows through the South in 1915. Her stay with them was brief, and her relationship with Rainey is still debated, but Smith's early singing owes something to Rainey's influence.

Rainey toured successfully with several live shows, notably the Rabbit Foot Minstrels and Tolliver's Circus and Musical Extravaganza, where she and her husband appeared as "Rainey and Rainey, Assassinators of the Blues." In 1917 she toured under her own name for the first time, when, as Madame Gertrude Rainey and her Georgia Smart Set, she performed to great acclaim at a number of Southern theaters. She was by now a leading figure on the live Southern circuit.

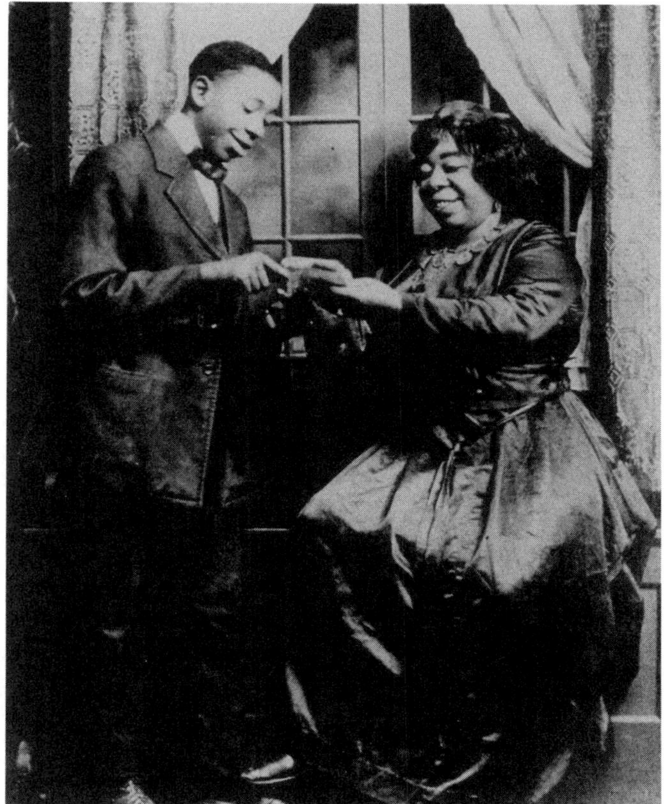

"Ma" Rainey with an actor from the "Rabbit Foot Minstrels" company

Records for Paramount

After brief retirement in Mexico in 1921, Rainey returned in a big way, making her first recordings for Paramount with Lovie Austin's Serenaders in December 1923. These magnificent early blues sides, featuring trumpeter Tommy Ladnier, included her best-known numbers "Moonshine Blues" and "Bo Weavil Blues," which proved so popular that she made new versions of them both in 1927. Other outstanding recordings included "See See Rider," with Louis Armstrong (1924), "Jelly Bean Blues" and "Countin' the Blues." With these sides, she became one of the great female blues recording stars, a position she was to hold to the end of the decade.

As an art form, the classic blues is unusual in presenting a female viewpoint to love, sex, and betrayal. Blues writer Paul Oliver commented in his *Blackwell Guide to Blues Records* (1989): "Perhaps the most overlooked aspect of the early 1920s blues era was its concentration on a woman's perspective regarding the central blues themes." Rainey, who wrote many of her own songs, deserves credit as the first great exponent of this style, which has become a milestone in 20th century music.

The careers of Rainey and Bessie Smith are closely interwoven. Both had strong contralto voices and sang with great feeling and sincerity, but Rainey's links were with the folk tradition of the tent show and the down-home blues of the country guitarists and minstrels. She impressed with the raw power and authority of her singing, while Smith scored with a majestic, skilled professionalism that looked ahead to the studios and the concert stage. While Smith's was the superior voice, most regarded Rainey as the greater live performer. Though rivals, they remained close friends, and perhaps something more. Both shared a bisexual lifestyle, and at least one sideman was convinced that they were lovers. Rainey's sexual preferences were open and direct. She liked young male musicians in her bands and propositioned several of them, while an intimate all-female party with her chorus girls led to her being arrested in 1925. "Prove It On Me Blues," which she wrote herself, gives clear expression to her lesbian desires which she "wants the world to know." Tommy Ladnier and Oran "Hot Lips" Page were among her favorite musicians, as were bluesmen Thomas Dorsey ("Georgia Tom") and Hudson Whittaker ("Tampa Red").

The tremendous success of Rainey's recordings led to further tours with her Georgia Wild Cats and others, on the newly formed T.O.B.A. circuit. She made the rounds of theaters in the Midwest and South to appreciative audiences from 1924 onwards. In 1927 she co-starred with Dan James in the Louisiana Blackbirds revue, a 1500 seater show which stayed a week at each venue, through the Southern theaters, before returning to Chicago to record more records for Paramount with increasingly down-home accompaniment from Georgia Tom and the Tub Jug Washboard Band.

Rainey wowed her audiences with a sensational stage act, decked out in a diamond tiara, twenty-dollar piece necklace, and sequin-covered gown. Mainly a blues performer, her routine also included vaudeville and show numbers, some of them risque material. "Sissy Blues," with its theme of gay love and the obvious double entendre in the title, and lyrics of her showstopper "Ma Rainey's Black Bottom" (1928), are two examples of many.

Last Years

Abruptly, disaster struck. The Wall Street Crash of 1929 coincided with a waning of interest in the blues. After 1929, Rainey made no further recordings, and found herself regarded as a fading star. She made two theater tours of the South in 1930, but her last appearances of 1933-35 were made with a carnival show, in venues under canvas, similar to those where she had begun her career twenty years before. Following the sudden deaths of her mother and sister, Rainey retired from the business in 1935 and settled in her home town of Columbus. There she divided her time between local church work and ownership of two theaters in Columbus and Rome, Georgia, until her death on 22 December 1939 at age 53.

Ma Rainey's achievement is hard to overestimate. She, more than anyone else, brought the raw strength of country blues out of the backwoods to the studio and gave it classic expression. Better yet, hers was the triumph of a plain black woman who despite sexism and racial prejudice made it all the way to the top by her own efforts and talent. Loved by her audiences, she was also fondly remembered by those who worked with her. Truly the Mother of the Blues, she remains a mighty figure in the landscape of modern music. Georgia Tom summed it up when, in an interview with *Living Blues* magazine in March 1975 he remarked: "Well maybe I'm partial, but far as I'm concerned, Ma was the greatest of blues singers."

References:

Carr, Ian, with Digby Fairweather and Brian Priestley. *Jazz, the Essential Companion.* London, Grafton, 1987.

Feather, Leonard. *The New Edition of the Encyclopedia of Jazz.* London, Arthur Barker, 1961.

Harris, Sheldon. *Blues Who's Who.* New Rochelle, New York, Arlington House, c.1979; New York, Da Capo, 1979.

Lieb, Sandra. *Mother of the Blues.* Boston, University of Massachusetts Press, 1981.

Oliver, Paul. *Blackwell Guide to Blues on Record.* Oxford, and Cambridge, Mass., Blackwell, 1989.

———. *Blues Off the Record.* London, Baton Press, 1984.

Oliver, Paul, with Max Harrison and William Bolcom. *The New Grove Gospel, Blues and Jazz with Spirituals and Ragtime.* London and Basingstoke, Macmillan, and New York, W. H. Norton & Co., 1986.

—Geoff Sadler

Toshi Reagon

1964-

African-American musician

Toshi Reagon's bluesy, gospel, reggae-like blend of music has made her influential in the New York music scene for nearly ten years. She has maintained this involvement not only by releasing her own albums, but by furthering the careers of other local artists via producing and guest performances. Reagon has also maintained a healthy activist-like presence, though she is quick to point out that fighting big issues is not what she is about.

On 27 January 1964, Bernice Johnson Reagon gave birth to her first child, Toshi. Bernice and husband Cordell Hull Reagon had another child, a son, but the couple were soon divorced. When Toshi was seven, she, her mother, and her younger brother moved to Washington, D.C. where Reagon attended private and public schools before graduating and leaving for New York. "New York, took me to New York," says the 32-year-old musician who relocated to Brooklyn in the late 1980s. In New York, she felt, "you could do everything at the same time." Reagon wanted to go to school and to be a musician. Though she frequently travels, New York is still her home.

Like many gays and lesbians her age, Reagon does not have much to say about "being out." According to Reagon, she has been out her "entire adult life" and does not really give it the kind of thought that those who came out into a more openly hostile climate do. Instead, her focus has always been on her music. She has been traveling nationally, and performing since she was 17. Reagon considers every step along the way in her music career a success. Though she

Toshi Reagon

already had two recordings—*Demonstrations* (1985) and *Justice* (Flying Fish Records, 1990)—her first really big break came when she opened for Lenny Kravitz's world tour in 1990. Her third album, *The Rejected Stone,* was released in 1994 on her own label, Pro Momma. Reagon hopes to have her fourth album, *Kindness,* released on the Folkways label in early 1997.

Reagon's activity is centered in some way around music. Although she is an accomplished performer, Reagon does much more than sing, she also writes songs. About 60 percent of what she performs are her own compositions, but she does a good bit of writing for others as well. "Everything I do," she says, "is something about music." If she is not singing, recording, or traveling so she can be doing one or the other, she is producing the work of other musicians. Reagon has co-produced several Sweet Honey in the Rock albums with her mother, including *Still on the Journey,* the group's 20th anniversary album in 1994. (In 1973, Reagon's mother was a founding member of Sweet Honey in the Rock, an a capella group that has enjoyed considerable success over the last two decades.) Reagon has also produced music by the duo Casselberry-DuPree and others. She has collaborated with the internationally renown dance troupe Urban Bush Women on their evening-length production "Bones and Ash" for several years as music director and composer, and in her spare time, she plays bass with the New York-based reggae band, JUCA. Reagon performed on *Roots of Rhythm: A Tribute to the Robert Johnson Era,* and was nominated for a grammy for her work with *Friends of Robert Johnson.*

Often referred to as a hybrid of an assortment of musical genres and styles, Reagon describes her music as a blend of "traditional musical formats, especially African American blues, gospel, spirituals, a capella." Having grown up in the 1970s, Reagon labels herself "a big rock 'n' roll fanatic," which means that Hendrix and groups like The Police and Led Zeppelin have left their mark on her, and in turn, her music.

Aside from commitments to music per se, Reagon is often asked to perform benefits for a variety of causes. She frequently agrees, but her primary goal, she maintains, is not to address major causes or fight for big issues but rather to "strengthen and work out of where I live on a daily basis, trying to live in a good way within my community, communicating with the people next door." Her hope is that through this one-to-one communicating, "the world will eventually be a better place." In terms of a vision for the future, she really just wants to keep doing what she is doing, happy to be able to do it full time. If Reagon does have an effect on people's lives, as some have told her, she asks, "What more can I ask for?"

References:

Publicity material. Flying Fish Records, 1996.

Reagon, Toshi. Interview with Andrea L.T. Peterson, 14 August 1996.

—Andrea L.T. Peterson

Mary Renault

1905-1983

British novelist

Mary Renault (pen name of Eileen Mary Challans) is best known for her novels set in ancient Greece. In evoking a society in which same-sex or bisexual love was common and often honorable, she influenced many straight and homosexual readers. Rigorous scholarship, appealing characters, and gripping plotlines helped make varied love understandable and natural.

Born in London, England on 4 September 1905, to Clementine Mary (Baxter) and Dr. Frank Challans, she took a B.A. in English at St. Hugh's College, Oxford, in 1928. She wrote an unpublished novel and then qualified as a nurse in 1937, where she met her lifelong partner, Julie Mullard.

Renault used hospital settings for her first three unexceptional novels. *Purposes of Love* (1939, in the United States, *Promise of Love*), has a brother and sister who love the same man; the brother's rather arbitrary death resolves the triangle. *Kind are her Answers* (1940) has conventionally straight characters, with lesbianism used to remove an unpleasant wife so that an adulterous heterosexual love may triumph. *The Friendly Young Ladies* (1944, in the United States, *The Middle Mist*, 1945) hints more strongly at lesbianism.

Return to Night (1947), which won a lavish MGM prize and enabled Renault and Mullard to move to South Africa, begins to use Hellenistic themes like the myth of Demeter. *North Face* (1948) is less successful, but her final contemporary work, *The Charioteer* (1953) develops ancient Greek imagery and for the first time deals openly with homosexuality.

With *The Last of the Wine* (1956), Renault began to match talent and material. The story of Alexis and his friend and lover, Lysis, relates their experiences during the last days of Athenian splendor, of war with the Spartans, of philosophy and political theory, of Alkibiades and Plato and Socrates.

After this novel, Renault seldom focussed on women. As she said, "Men have more fun," which was certainly true of Greece in that period. Julie remarked that "If people talked about lesbians, we used to draw our skirts away." Renault's friends increasingly were gay men and she adored the camp humor of actors. Although Julie experimented with heterosexuality early in their relationship, Renault was monogamous. Through her presentation of Hellenistic sexuality shines a conviction that it is most realized when based on loving commitment—and when society allows it to be an accepted part of life.

The King Must Die (1958) and *The Bull from the Sea* (1962) compellingly retell the Theseus legend, showing Renault's distaste for negative aspects of the mother-goddess archetype. Hippolyta, queen of the Amazons and the great love of Theseus' life, is a slender, athletic boy-woman who suffers from the Goddess as much as men. In *The Mask of Apollo* (1966), set in the generation following *The Last of the Wine*, Renault draws on the theater and thespians, and on her sound research into Greek drama. Her protagonist Niko, a prize-winning actor, is fully homosexual, and Renault makes us believe in a tolerant society in which gay men were able to work out their own truth.

Fire from Heaven (1970) and *The Persian Boy* (1972), novels about Alexander the Great, were followed by a biography, *The Nature of Alexander* (1975). Although overlong and turgid with detail, they splendidly resurrect a unique period. In *The Persian Boy*, Renault's amused detachment finds expression in the personality of the eunuch Bagoas, the product of a decadent empire: the contrast between him and Alexander's uncivilized Macedonian followers is often hilarious.

The heterosexual Simonides, the protagonist of *The Praise Singer* (1978), is an itinerant poet and singer in Greece of the 6th century B.C. For the first time since Hippolyta in *The Bull from the Sea*, Renault creates a fully-fledged female character. Simonides has an enduring relationships with Lyra, an hetaira—a prostitute but one whose wit, accomplishments, intelligence, and knowledge are valued as much as sex. Renault summons a world where such a remarkable woman's function is so normal that the reader passes no moral judgement.

Renault's final book, *Funeral Games* (1981), traces the disintegration that followed the death of Alexander. It is a book of the horrors that humanity can self-inflict, of intrigues, betrayals, tortures, and atrocities. When Renault died she was at work on a book about the Arthurian legends. True to her wishes, Julie Mullard destroyed the unfinished manuscript.

Mary Renault was never interested in movements and ideologies, though she was president of International PEN in Capetown and worked against apartheid. But she showed imaginatively how society could be different. Her convincing versions of ancient Greece return us to our own times altered, and with a clearer vision of how our world might be changed.

Mary Renault

References:

Buck, Claire, ed. *Bloomsbury Guide to Women's Literature.* London: Bloomsbury, 1992.

Sweetman, David. *Mary Renault: A Biography.* New York: Harcourt Brace, 1993.

Yaakov, Juliette and John Greenfieldt, ed. *Fiction Catalog.* New York, H. W. Wilson, 1991.

—Fraser Sutherland

Adrienne Rich

1929-

American poet, essayist, and educator

Over the past three decades the writings of Adrienne Rich have helped to transform the current understanding of women's experiences of such facets of identity as motherhood, lesbianism, and ethnicity. Rich's highly-acclaimed poetry which offers illuminating meditations on her personal experiences of womanhood has contributed to the critical acceptance of the politicization of poetry. A self-identified lesbian-feminist, Rich is a prolific writer of influential essays on the position of women. Her work has helped to give a language to aspects of women's experiences which have been previously considered "unspeakable" and also to shape the practice of feminist cultural studies today.

Rich was born in Baltimore, Maryland in 1929, to southern protestant Helen Jones and Dr. Arnold Rich, an assimilated Jew. As Rich explains in her essay *Split at the Root: An Essay on Jewish Identity,* Helen Rich was a composer and pianist who had sacrificed her artistic career to her domestic role as wife and mother according to the ideal of white, heterosexual femininity. It was by this ideal that she was to raise her daughter. Arnold Rich, who became a professor in the department of pathology at Johns Hopkins Medical School, was brought up to aspire to acceptance by the white American professional class. As he guided his daughter's education through her childhood and adolescence, Arnold Rich tacitly communicated the importance of acceptance by this class to her.

Rich was educated at home by her mother until the fourth grade. She first began writing poetry as a child under the supervision of her father who, she recalled in *Split at the Root,* "made me feel, at a very young age, the power of language and that I could share it." Her first, childhood publications were plays: *Ariadne: A Play in Three Acts and Poems* (1939) and *Not I, But Death, a Play in One Act* (1941). As Rich notes in *Split at the Root,* the world in which she grew up was one of "white social christianity": she attended the Episcopal church for five years and there were Episcopal hymns and prayers in her school every morning.

In 1947 Rich left Baltimore to attend Radcliffe College. As she recalls in *Split at the Root,* there she met young Jewish women amongst whom she "was doing something that *is* dangerous: I was flirting with identity." She graduated from Radcliffe in 1951 and in the same year her collection of poems, *A Change of World,* was chosen for the Yale Series of Younger Poets award by W. H. Auden. In her essay, *When We Dead Awaken: Writing As Re-Vision* (1971), Rich observes that her "style was formed first by male poets: by the men that I was reading as an undergraduate—Frost, Dylan Thomas, Donne, Auden, MacNiece, Yeats." She explains that looking back at the poems she wrote before she was twenty-one, she saw revealed beneath the carefully-crafted style "the split I even then experienced between the girl who wrote the poems, who defined herself in writing poems and the girl who was to define herself by her relationships with men." She had not yet consciously recognized "the suppressed lesbian" whom, as she explains in *Split at the Root,* she had been "carrying in [her] since adolescence." The following year Rich was awarded a Guggenheim fellowship which enabled her to travel in Europe and England. In the same year, the onset of rheumatoid arthritis began, for which Rich has continued to undergo surgery periodically throughout her life.

Of Woman Born: A Poet Becomes Radicalized

In 1953, Rich married the economist Alfred H. Conrad and for the next thirteen years they lived in what Rich has described in *Split at the Root* as "the predominantly gentile Yankee academic world of Cambridge, Massachusetts." In the same essay, Rich reflects: "Like many women I knew in the fifties living under a then-unquestioned heterosexual imperative, I married in part because I knew no better way to disconnect myself from my first family." Her parents refused to attend the wedding because she had connected herself to an orthodox Jewish husband and family of eastern European origin. Rich did not see her parents for several years after her marriage. By the time she was thirty, she and Conrad had three sons, David, Paul, and Jacob. During these years of undergoing difficult pregnancies and taking care of three small sons, she was struggling to conform with the "feminine mystique" of the 1950s, trying to be a "good" mother and the ideal faculty wife and hostess. This was compounded by her relation to her husband's family, whom she sought to please by conforming with the role expected of a Jewish wife and mother. She had little time or energy for writing during this time, publishing only *The Diamond Cutters and Other Poems* in 1955. Another eight years was to pass before she published another book. During these years, Rich was torn by the conflict between writing and motherhood which she experienced as a failure of love in herself. Retrospectively, she came to understand this conflict as social, not simply personal. "The experience of motherhood," she observes in *Split at the Root,* "was eventually to radicalize me."

It was during the 1960s that Rich's "radicalization" gathered impetus. In 1966, she separated from her husband, left Cambridge and moved to New York. From the late 1950s she had supported the Civil Rights Movement and yet she was still at this time "very politically ignorant," as she later explained to David Montenegro in an interview published in *American Poetry Review* in 1991. In New York, however, she became increasingly active in radical politics, especially in protests against the war in Vietnam. As she told David Montenegro, she was also persistently questioning "something that wasn't being talked about at the time very much. I was thinking about where sexuality belonged in all this." The relation between the personal and the political was further underscored for Rich in 1968, at a time when she was involved with work on racial issues, teaching in the SEEK and Open Admissions programs at City College of the City University of New York. The year saw for her not only momentous events on the larger political scene, but also the death of her father after a long illness. Following Conrad's suicide two years later, Rich was to spend years disentangling her relations with the two men.

Rich's poetry of the 1960s is also marked by an awareness of the political dimension of personal experience. She had first discovered a dialogue between art and politics in the work of W. B. Yeats which she read as an undergraduate at Radcliffe. Rich's *Snapshots of a Daughter-in-Law: Poems, 1954-62,* published in 1963, marks a shift from the detached formal elegance of her earlier work to a poetry informed by a conscious sexual politics whose voice is personal and immediate. The next four collections which Rich published between 1966 and 1971 show her involvement in black Civil Rights and anti-war protest and her increasing identification with women's experiences.

Rich Gives A Voice to Silenced Women

In her interview with David Montenegro, Rich commented that "where connections are being made always feels to me like the point of interest life" and that for her "the point of interest life is where I write poetry." Another important connection for her, she comments, was when the women's movement began to emerge out of the Left and the Civil Rights Movement at the end of the 1960s. From this time, Rich increasingly dedicated herself to feminism, whose aim as she understands it, is "the creation of a society without domination," as she explained in a 1984 speech, *Notes Toward a Politics of Location.* Politics, for Rich, has always involved a regeneration of the self as well as a revolution of society. Her work attends particularly to women's sense of self as this is experienced through a female body whose meaning is culturally determined and circumscribed. In her poetry, Rich seeks to create a language which

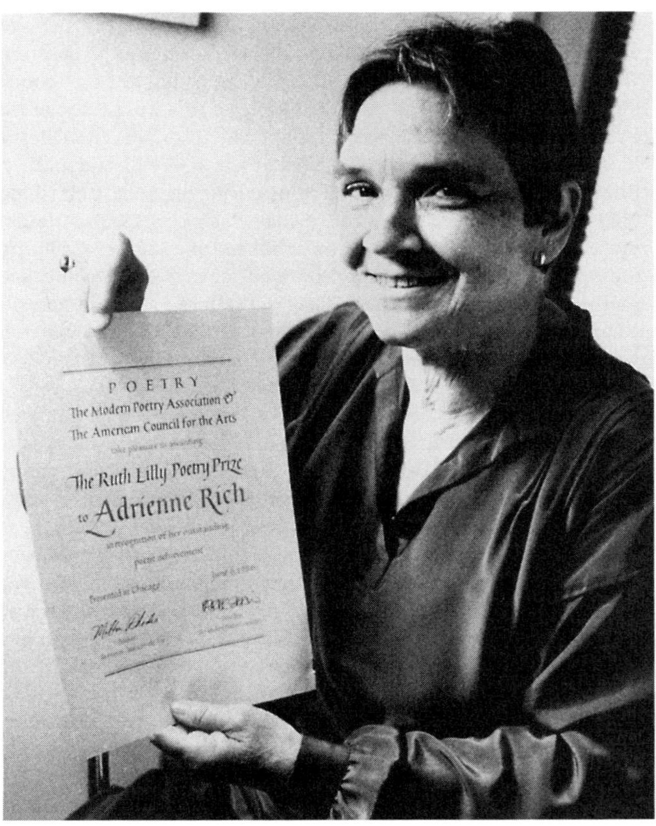

Adrienne Rich

will achieve a synthesis between the traditionally separated realms of art and politics, the self and the world. This is exemplified by *Diving into the Wreck* which expresses personal anger and political principal relating to Rich's experience of womanhood. The book was awarded the National Book Award in 1974, which Rich accepted on behalf of women with Audre Lorde and Alice Walker.

As she became increasingly more involved with politics, Rich also began to write more prose. From the 1960s, she had been writing essays about the ways in which women's experiences have been made invisible, omitted from history and misrepresented in literature. In her influential 1971 essay, *When We Dead Awaken: Writing as Re-vision,* she argues that women must look back "with fresh eyes" at representations of themselves by male writers in order to understand how they have been placed in male-dominated society. Such an act of re-vision is, for women, "an act of survival." Rich's exploration of women's experiences in male-dominated cultures was extended in her 1976 book *Of Woman Born: Motherhood as Experience and Institution,* a composite of autobiography, history, and anthropology. Here, Rich showed how the experience of motherhood, seemingly a natural condition, is in fact created by myths which are fostered by medical, social, religious, and political institutions. One of the main questions Rich asked in this book was why, "if heterosexuality was so natural," was it necessary for various cultures to control women through their prescriptive ideas about femininity and motherhood?

Rich asked the question again in a 1976 speech, *It Is the Lesbian in Us ...* where she recalled how her first love for women had been suppressed. This silencing, she discovered, had also taken place in literature, where lesbian identity was scarcely represented. Moreover, Rich argued, "it is the lesbian in us" who is creative: the woman who is submissive to male authority will always be a "hack." Rich's best-known contribution to thought about lesbian identity is her 1980 essay, *Compulsory Heterosexuality and the Lesbian Existence.* Here she sought to bridge the gap which she perceived between "lesbian" and "feminist" and was at pains to provide a new category and language through which to discuss lesbians. To this end, she coined the phrases "lesbian continuum" and "lesbian existence." By "lesbian existence" she designated the presence of lesbians in history and the way lesbians continue to "create the meaning of that existence." By "lesbian continuum," she drew attention to the importance and "primary intensity" of "woman-identified experience" in all women's lives. Through this specifically female experience, she argued, all women can be located at a point on the spectrum of lesbian identity, whether or not they choose to identify themselves as lesbians. Rich's argument has provoked controversy amongst lesbian critics, some of whom argue that the concept of a "lesbian continuum" negates the uniqueness of lesbian existence in which women relate to women sexually and form communities around this choice. For Rich, lesbian identity continues to embrace the woman who frees herself from the constraints of male images of women to become one who "has a sense of desiring oneself; above all, of choosing oneself." Through her writing about lesbian identity, Rich seeks to create a way of seeing which no longer needs men and heterosexuality at the centre of all women's relationships and activities.

In 1976, Rich began her life with Michelle Cliff, the Jamaican-American novelist and poet, Rich published *Twenty-One Love Poems,* where she expressed her lesbian sensibility through such lines as "I choose to love this time for once/with all my intelligence" in "Splitting." Her 1981 collection, *A Wild Patience Has Taken Me This Far: Poems 1978-1981,* in which she continues to represent silenced women, was awarded the National Gay Task Force Fund for Human Dignity Award. From 1981 to 1983, she edited, with Cliff, the influential lesbian/feminist journal *Sinister Wisdom.*

Rich Makes New Contribution to Identity Politics

Throughout the 1980s and into the 1990s, Rich continued to reflect on the position of women and the social factors which determine women's experiences, both in general terms and with reference to her own life. In two companion pieces, the 1983 poem sequence, *Sources,* and her essay *Split at the Root,* Rich began to disentangle her complicated relations with her Jewish father and husband, in this way addressing her own ethnicity and trying to "become free of all the ghosts and shadows of my childhood, named and unnamed." Remaining committed to her exploration of the question, "What did it mean to be a Jewish lesbian?," in 1990 Rich became a member of the founding editorial group *Bridges: A Journal for Jewish Feminists and our Friends.* Rich's involvement with the feminist debates over race since the 1980s has led her to examine her own position as a white woman through her poetry and prose.

Throughout the 1980s and 1990s, Rich has continued to teach in universities across America and has been awarded honorary doctorates by several universities in recognition of her work. Her ongoing attention to the need to highlight the importance of gender, race, class, nationality, and sexual orientation in the development of new ideas and knowledge continues to contribute to the directions taken by feminists working in the field today.

Current Address: c/o W. W. Norton Co., 500 Fifth Avenue, New York, New York 10110-0002.

References:

Blain, Virginia and others, eds. *The Feminist Guide to Literature in English.* London: Batsford, 1990.

Farwell, Marilyn R. "Toward a Definition of the Lesbian Literary Imagination," in *Sexual Practice, Textual Theory: Lesbian Cultural Criticism.* Cambridge: Blackwell, 1993.

Gelpi, Barbara Charlesworth and Albert Gelpi, eds. *Adrienne Rich's Poetry and Prose.* New York: Norton, 1993.

Rich, Adrienne. "Compulsory Heterosexuality and Lesbian Existence," in *Adrienne Rich's Poetry and Prose.* New York: Norton, 1993.

———. "An Interview with David Montenegro," in *American Poetry Review,* January-February, 1991.

———. "It Is the Lesbian in Us...," in *On Lies, Secrets and Silence: Selected Prose 1966-1978.* London: Virago, 1980.

———. "Notes Toward a Politics of Location," in *Women, Feminist Identity and Society in the 1980s.* Amsterdam: John Benjamins, 1985.

———. *Of Woman Born: Motherhood as Experience and Institution.* New York: Norton, 1986.

———. "Split at the Root: An Essay on Jewish Identity," in *Adrienne Rich's Poetry and Prose.* New York: Norton, 1993.

———. "When We Dead Awaken: Writing as Re-Vision," in *On Lies, Secrets and Silence: Selected Prose 1966-1978.* London: Virago, 1980.

West-Burnham, J. "Adrienne Rich," in *The A-Z Guide to Modern Literary and Cultural Theorists.* London: Prentice Hall/Harvester Wheatsheaf, 1995.

—Joanna Price

Marlon Riggs

1957-1994

African-American filmmaker

Brilliant, articulate, fearless, a consummate artist, a bright flame in the world of documentary film—all of these accolades and more have been used to describe the mere handful of documentaries Marlon Riggs made in his too-short life. From his scathing chronicling of black stereotypes throughout our culture and on our televisions, to his unflinchingly homoerotic "riff" on black gay men in our society, Riggs always challenged his audience with his clear, passionate voice—a voice that demanded full inclusion. "I loathe what has been routine in our culture," he told journalist Barry Walters in 1993, "that level of disclosure that is really narcissism. There's often no acknowledgment that one's struggle is part of a historical, social struggle. So I tend to go overboard to compensate."

Even as a child, Texas-born Riggs was a fighter, a leader—well ahead of the pack. In an article for the *San Francisco Chronicle* shortly after Riggs' death from AIDS complications in April 1994, longtime friend and co-producer of *Color Adjustment,* Vivian Kleiman recalls that "he was something of a child preacher. When he was a kid at church he would often be asked to get up and discuss the scripture, and I think that the sense of leadership and speaking to large groups was something he was comfortable with, and film is a logical extension of that." Riggs' mother Jean adds that, from early on, "he was very much an intellectual ... he did all the things that other kids do, but he talked very early, walked very early, and read very early. He seemed always to be very wise." Finally, in an interview for the *San Francisco Examiner* in 1992, Riggs himself offered that he had "always been more cerebral and got teased tremendously about it as a kid...."

Although best known for his films, Riggs was also a powerful writer and a natural teacher. In 1991, for example, he astonished participants at an Oakland poetry reading by getting up and reciting a fierce sexual fantasia about a black man's encounter with a white, racist skinhead. In the broadest sense then, all his work struggles to bridge the social and cultural chasms he experienced throughout his life—gay vs straight, black vs white, the poetic vs the professorial—not to mention the more complex interweaving of "priorities" (that) multi-cultural identification "affords." "Are we *black* gay men, or *gay* black men?" he once asked fellow black, gay and British filmmaker Isaac Julien, a question further complicated by the fact that both men had white lovers at the time.

Riggs received his Master's Degree from Harvard in the early 1980s and taught documentary filmmaking at the University of California at Berkeley in the final few years before his death. In addition to his films, he edited and contributed to the book *Brother to Brother: New Writings of Black Gay Men* and added his insights on living with HIV to a number of publications. "There was his academic side and his wild side," film editor and collaborator Deborah Hoffmann said in 1994, "and both sides were there every day. One minute he was this dry academic using billion dollar words and the next he was dancing down the hallway." "He was multi-voiced," said Essex Hemphill, a Philadelphia poet who figured prominently in Riggs' *Tongues Untied.* "Marlon's gift was his ability to weave together so many disparate elements and aspects of himself into his work."

Riggs' first important work was *Ethnic Notions* (1987), a documentary surveying 150 years of racial stereotyping in popular American culture—a look at "Negro-bilia" from Aunt Jemima dolls to cartoon "darkies." But his most controversial and autobiographical work—the first in which he appears himself—followed in 1988 (*Tongues Untied*). *Tongues* was lauded by critics as the first unflinching look at the black gay male sexuality in America in all its complexity. For once, the juxtaposition of black and male was not equated with rampant, predatory heterosexuality, but rather with a lyrical, randy, soulful reaching-out of brother-to-brother. The process of making the film was completely cathartic, Riggs told author Andrea Vaucher in 1993:

> So much of my life had been about effacement, self-effacement, pretense, masquerading, concealment, and indirection. When you are seeking empowerment and enfranchisement in the society, it requires that you negotiate with dominant cultures, whether straight, or mainstream African-American ... That is why the documentary is called *Tongues Untied.* It was almost earth-shattering in what it taught me psychically about the power of speech ... of self-affirmation ... of an articulated self-identity.

Not surprisingly, *Tongues* was lambasted by the political right, most notably in 1992 when presidential candidate Patrick Buchanan shuffled clips from the film and inserted them into TV spots accusing the Bush administration and the National Endowment for the Arts (NEA) of abusing government funds. (Never mind that the film received a meager $5,000 from the NEA).

Riggs was quick to fire back, charging Buchanan with copyright infringement and tearing into him in a *New York Times* op-ed piece "because my film affirms the lives and dignity of black gay men... presidential politics have thus been injected with a new poison: the persecution of racial and sexual difference...." A year later, Riggs provided a more academic but nonetheless burning insight into the controversy when he was interviewed by the *Examiner*.

> Our culture has reached the point where we can have some level of intelligent discourse on the subject of race without forcing one to be labeled as an extremist or polemic or militant or subversive. However, anyone who attempts to look at our sexualities, and simply doesn't privilege heterosexuality as the only model to which we should all aspire, gets labeled and discredited.

Riggs' *Color Adjustment* (1992)—which received the prestigious George Foster Peabody award—complemented *Ethnic Notions* with a look at the way African-Americans have been depicted on television, juxtaposing sit-com life with harsh realities outside the tube. Even as *The Cosby Show* grew in popularity, Riggs showed in *Color Adjustment*, crack cocaine was decimating an entire generation of young black men.

In 1990, Riggs released his 9-minute film *Anthem*, a poetic rap exploration of gay African-American love and desire. In 1991, he appeared in Peter Adair's film *Absolutely Positive*, a moving documentary about people living with HIV.

In 1992, Riggs released *No, Je Ne Regrette Rien* (*No Regrets*), a video that explores the impact of AIDS on the African-American male by mixing the testimony of five very different men with music and poetry. The visual metaphor for coming out of the AIDS closet is powerful, as critic Edward Guthmann noted in a *San Francisco Chronicle* review. "At first, we see them in isolated body fragments as they speak," he wrote. "One man's mouth, another's eyes, another's hands. Gradually they emerge in whole ... their tales of survival are told, each is identified by name."

Riggs worked right up to the time of his death from AIDS complications in the spring of 1994, filming but not completing a searing look into contemporary notions of "authentic blackness" entitled *Black Is ... Black Ain't*. Seven months later the film was completed by colleagues Christiane Badgley, Bob Paris, and Nicole Atkinson. The result is a highly personal, even playful, "deathbed confession" on Riggs' part about what it means to be called black, Negro, colored, African-American, whatever, in this culture. "Even while he was dying," one critic wrote in the *Nation*, "Riggs apparently could look into the mirror of his American self and see the beginnings of a good party gathering. The man had his eyes open."

Toward the end, Riggs described his too-short body of work to author Thomas Avena as an epiphany, a series of "lights" along the path toward "our own personal novas." "In the illumination of my own struggle around being black and gay and now HIV-positive," he told author Vaucher in late 1993, "I wanted to connect to the communal struggle and to an historic struggle so that my story was not simply my story, but our story... for liberation, and redemption, and self-love." Perhaps this is why, as fellow filmmaker Michele Wallace wrote soon after Marlon's death, "his flame was high and his art was not cool. He was burning up."

References:

Avena, Thomas. *Life Sentences: Writers, Artists, and Aids*. Mercury House: San Francisco, 1994.

Guthmann, Edward. "Marlon Riggs-A Voice Stilled," in *The San Francisco Chronicle*, 27 April 1994: E-1.

Hafferty, Bill. "Film Maker Reacts to Buchanan Commercial," in *The San Francisco Chronicle*, 28 February 1992: C-4.

Julien, Isaac. "Long Live the Queen," in the *Village Voice*, 26 April 1994: 60.

Murray, Raymond. *Images in the Dark: An Encyclopedia of Gay and Lesbian Film and Video*. Philadelphia: TLA Publications, 1994.

Vaucher, Andrea R. *Muses from Chaos and Ash: Aids, Artists, and Art*. New York: Grove Press, 1993.

Walters, Barry. "Filmmaker's Social Views Untied," in the *San Francisco Examiner*, 14 June 1993: E-5.

—Jerome Szymczak

Arthur Rimbaud

1854-1891

French poet

Paul Verlaine

1844-1896

French poet

Rimbaud and Verlaine, men linked not only by a common art but by a tempestuous relationship that sent Verlaine to prison and hastened Rimbaud's rejection of poetry, were at the center of a poetic revolution, the influence of which is still felt today.

Born in the border town of Metz, France in 1854, Paul Verlaine came from a bourgeois family, dominated by his mother. Verlaine's intelligence and creativity shone at an early age, though his family discouraged his interest in poetry. Nevertheless, at the age of fourteen, he sent his first poem to his idol, Victor Hugo. Verlaine went on to complete his high school education in Paris at the Lycée Bonaparte and soon began a career as a civil servant at City Hall. His nights were spent in the literary cafés where he became friends with other aspiring writers like Stéphane Mallarmé and Anatole France. Verlaine's poetic gifts soon began to flourish. By the age of twenty-one, he had published several poems as well as reviews of Barbey d'Aurevilley and Baudelaire in the journal, *L'Art*.

His first collection, *Saturnine Poems* (1866), demonstrated his originality not only in style but in theme. The works were characterized by a heightened interest in the musicality of the verses, a certain uneasiness of spirit, and a marked sensuality. Verlaine's life played out the same drama. The "saturnine poet" found himself caught between tendencies towards drink, violence, and debauchery and the lure of the conventional life of the Catholic bourgeoisie.

As Verlaine's reputation as a poet grew, so did his dependency on absinthe and his episodes of violence, so much so that he attacked his mother in 1869. That same year he met Mathilde Mauté, a sixteen year old girl, with whom he fell in love. Verlaine seemed to seek in Mathilde the innocence he had long lost and hoped that she would be both his muse and his source of strength to conquer his private demons. His *Good Song*, published in 1870, celebrates this love and the hope it symbolized for Verlaine. Their idyllic marriage was interrupted by the Franco-Prussian War and soon for a short period their lives would become enmeshed with that of Rimbaud.

Born in 1864 in Charleville, Arthur Rimbaud, like Verlaine was raised by a strict mother. As a child, he revolted against any type of control, especially that dictated by the norms of bourgeois society. At school Rimbaud proved to be a brilliant, albeit unruly, student. His gift for poetry revealed itself quite soon. In 1870, encouraged by his rhetoric instructor, Rimbaud began to hone his talents and wrote a series of highly original works.

But the chaos of the Franco-Prussian War changed Rimbaud's life. He quit school and fled to Paris in July of 1870; from there he traveled the French and Belgian countryside, avoiding the battles. He continued to write poetry but soon found that his irregular lifestyle caught the attention of the authorities who sent him back home. His rebellious spirit undaunted, Rimbaud again ran away, made his way to Paris, and then returned home once more.

These wanderings through war-torn France had a lasting effect on Rimbaud and led him to plunge more profoundly into his revolt. He passed his days drinking in cafés refusing to work, and began to study alchemy and the occult. During this period Rimbaud developed his theory of the poet as seer. In August of 1871, he sent some of his poems to the then-famous Verlaine, whom he thought to be a kindred spirit. The works so impressed Verlaine that he invited Rimbaud to Paris to stay with him and his family.

Rimbaud proved a highly disruptive force in the Verlaine household. Verlaine was fascinated and impressed by Rimbaud's undisciplined behavior while Mathilde, Verlaine's mother, and most of the Parisian literary establishment found it scandalous. Yet it is clear that Verlaine's admiration was grounded not simply on Rimbaud's rebelliousness but also on his unmistakable talent. Verlaine was again faced with the familiar conflict between his darker side—expressed by his growing passion for Rimbaud—and his desire for stability and normalcy through his marriage.

Absinthe, hashish, and poetry provided the mainstays of the turbulent relationship with Rimbaud. The younger poet persuaded Verlaine to leave his wife and the two set off for England and Belgium in 1872. A drunken quarrel in Brussels nearly two years later ended with Verlaine shooting Rimbaud in the wrist. The police were called and Verlaine found himself condemned to two years in prison. He and Rimbaud would meet only once more, in 1875 after his release.

Verlaine first experienced a spiritual revival, aided by the enforced abstinence from both drugs and sex during his confinement. Abandoned by both Rimbaud and his wife, he moved to England where he taught French and then returned to France. Although he continued to publish and enhance his reputation as a poet, he soon fell back into his dissipated way of life. Hailed as the prince of poets, yet as often penniless as not for most of his final years, Verlaine's final tribute to Rimbaud was the publication of the *Illuminations* in the year of Rimbaud's death. At his own death in 1896, Verlaine's funeral was attended by throngs of admirers, a posthumous compensation for his dying in poverty.

The term of Verlaine's imprisonment marked, in a sense, the apogee of Rimbaud's literary career. He completed the extraordinary prose chronicle of his experiences, *A Season in Hell*, which recounts not only the disillusionment of his relationship with Verlaine but also his poetic and spiritual crisis. The crisis engenders Rimbaud's final works, *Illuminations*. These texts fully reveal the perfection of his development as a poet and are among the first and finest examples of free verse.

And then, silence.

Not yet twenty-one, Rimbaud stopped writing and set out once more on the path of adventure. His experiences during these vagabond days could well serve as the basis for a B-movie. He roamed first through Europe and then Africa. He served in the Dutch army, trekked across the Alps, worked in a German circus, became a laborer in Cyprus, visited Egypt, and finally settled in Ethiopia where he lived with a "native woman" and earned his money as a slave trader. He remained there until 1891 when, seriously ill, he made his way to Marseilles, France where, attended by his sister, he died after the amputation of a leg.

The legend of Rimbaud, *enfant maudit*, persists today, often overshadowing both his originality as a writer and that of Verlaine. Yet it is fair to say that together they forged a poetic language that would not have been possible had they never spent their "season in hell."

References:

Adam, Antoine. *The Art of Paul Verlaine,* translated by Carl Morse. New York: New York University Press, 1963.

Aerde, Rogier van. *The Poor Wedding Guest: The Passionate Life of Paul Verlaine,* translated by Elfriede Zaeyen. London: Heinemann, 1960.

Ahearn, Edward J. *Rimbaud, Visions and Habitations.* Berkeley: University of California Press, 1963.

Carter, Alfred Edward. *Verlaine, a Study in Parallels.* Toronto: Toronto University Press, 1969.

Fowlie, Wallace. *Rimbaud.* Chicago: Chicago University Press, 1965.

Starkie, Enid. *Arthur Rimbaud.* London: Faber and Faber, 1961.

—Edith J. Benkov

Eleanor Roosevelt

1884-1962

American diplomat, humanitarian, and writer

Eleanor Roosevelt is often cited as the most influential woman of the twentieth century. The wife of President Franklin D. Roosevelt, she worked tirelessly to promote the causes of justice, humanitarianism, and tolerance, and biographers maintain that she exerted a liberalizing influence on the many policies enacted during her husband's dramatic twelve-year tenure. Her renowned humility, exemplary conduct, and passionate commitment made her a most compelling representative, and while her strident views often provoked opposition, she also earned the respect and affection of much of the world.

Troubled Child to Compassionate Woman

Roosevelt was born in New York City, the daughter of one of the country's most elite families and the niece of President Theodore Roosevelt. Despite this privileged background, Roosevelt's childhood was not a pleasant one; she was an extremely serious and shy child, painfully aware of her own shortcomings. Moreover, she suffered insults from her mother, an emotionally unstable woman who frankly admitted to finding her daughter ugly, and while she enjoyed a close relationship with her father, his severe alcoholism rendered him unreliable as a parent and occasionally abusive. By the age of ten Roosevelt was an orphan and had seen the death of one of her two younger brothers.

Following the deaths of her parents, Roosevelt and her surviving brother were sent to live with their grandmother. Roosevelt attended a prestigious private school in New York and an equally prestigious finishing school in England, where she excelled in her academic work and overcame to some extent her natural shyness, although she remained unsure of herself and particularly uncomfortable with public speaking throughout her life. Returning to New York at the age of seventeen, she reluctantly participated in the traditional debutante "coming out" activities. She much preferred to perform charitable work, including visits to slum children and investigation into the condition of exploited laborers.

A Developing Humanitarian

In 1905, Eleanor married her fifth cousin, Franklin Roosevelt, and for the next decade was primarily occupied with the care of the couple's six children while her husband finished his studies and practiced law. However, as Franklin's career progressed from lawyer to state representative in 1910 and to Secretary of the Navy in 1913, Eleanor's activities in politics and charitable causes increased. During the First World War, she worked with the Red Cross to coordinate activities in Washington D.C., where she and her family had taken up residence, and after the war she worked to improve conditions for wounded veterans. She later joined the League of Women Voters in an effort to promote women's rights, and the Women's Trade Union League, demonstrating her compassion for those who were being excluded from the economic gains of the 1920s.

Biographers suggest that Eleanor's increasing willingness to assert herself in the 1920s was triggered by a pivotal event which took place in 1918. In September of that year, Eleanor discovered that her husband had been engaging in a love affair with her trusted friend and secretary, Lucy Page Mercer. Devastated by this betrayal, Eleanor offered her husband a divorce, but the couple decided to stay together for a variety of reasons, including Franklin's political aspirations, his mother's disapproval, and the well-being of their children. In the words of David M. Kennedy, "thereafter, they were partners in politics but not companions of the heart," and Eleanor increasingly pursued her own interests. Both partners also sought emotional fulfillment elsewhere, Franklin with a series of mistresses and Eleanor with a group of close female friends, many of whom were lesbians. The nature of Eleanor's relations with her lesbian friends is not known with certainty, but one recent biographer, Blanche Wiesen Cook, argues compellingly that correspondence between Eleanor and her close friend Lorena Hickock indicates some degree of physical intimacy.

In 1920, Democratic presidential candidate James M. Cox chose Franklin Roosevelt as his vice-presidential running mate, but the Democrats were defeated that year by Republican Warren G. Harding. Following the election the Roosevelts returned to New York, and Franklin prepared to resume his law career. However, in the summer of 1921, he contracted polio and was seriously ill for several months; a lengthy and painful period of recovery ensued. Despite their emotional estrangement, Eleanor nursed her husband through his illness and encouraged him not to abandon hope of resuming his political career. Biographers note that Eleanor's support during this period was as crucial as it was remarkable: struggling with a disabling illness, Franklin might easily have surrendered hope of a career, as his dominating mother wished, to live the life of a wealthy invalid.

Beginning in 1926, with Franklin's health much improved, Eleanor made her primary residence a house she had built for herself near the Roosevelt's mansion at Hyde Park, which she shared with two of her close lesbian friends, Nancy Cook and Marion Dickerman. Shortly afterward, she and Dickerman bought a private school in New York City; Eleanor served as vice-principal and later taught history, sociology, economics, and government, continuing her active participation in the school until 1938. Roosevelt, Cook, and Dickerman also managed a small furniture factory that provided jobs for unemployed farm laborers, and they worked for the Democratic Party, Roosevelt serving as chair of the women's division during the 1928 elections that resulted in her husband winning the New York State governorship.

Still providing guidance and support for her husband, who never completely recovered his strength after his bout with polio, Eleanor rapidly became a respected figure. She accompanied Franklin on his various official visits as governor while promoting her own humanitarian and democratic causes at every opportunity. After Franklin became president in 1932, Eleanor refused to be relegated to the role of smiling spouse and White House hostess. She traveled extensively, renowned for her willingness to go wherever she thought she might be of use or uncover an unexposed injustice. She also began holding weekly press conferences, and in 1936 she began writing a daily syndicated column entitled "My Day," which initially focused on the domestic concerns of women but rapidly evolved to include commentary on a wide variety of social and political issues.

An Activist First Lady

As First Lady, Roosevelt continued to serve as an advocate for groups she believed were not being treated fairly or represented adequately, including Appalachian miners, southern sharecroppers, and urban garment workers. She stridently lobbied for legislative redresses, and commentators often view Eleanor as the moral conscience of the Roosevelt administration, noting that she urged her husband and his advisors not to make political compromises. She was particularly concerned about the plight of African Americans; Justus D. Doenecke has written that "few New Dealers did as much to advance the status of blacks." Roosevelt advocated racial equality in New Deal relief programs and urged her husband to support legislation designating lynching as a federal crime. The

Eleanor Roosevelt

most compelling evidence of her views is the renowned incident of 1939, when she resigned her membership in the elite Daughters of the American Revolution because they refused to allow the African-American singer Marian Anderson to perform at Constitution Hall. Roosevelt subsequently helped to arrange the alternative open-air concert which Anderson gave at the Lincoln Memorial for an audience of 75,000.

Consistent with her strong humanitarian views, Roosevelt advocated pacifism for much of her life. However, as Adolf Hitler's Third Reich grew more and more aggressive during the 1930s, she began to agree with the president's efforts to rally American support for intervention. In 1938 she wrote:

> I have never believed that war settled anything satisfactorily, but I am not entirely sure that some times there are certain situations in the world such as we have in actuality when a country is worse off when it does not go to war for its principles.

By the time war was declared in 1941, Eleanor Roosevelt, like the rest of the country, was fully convinced of the necessity of stopping German and Japanese aggression. She was particularly concerned about the fate of European Jews, and presciently urged her husband to do more to help them escape. At the same time, according to David M. Kennedy, she "tried to preserve New Deal liberalism amid the urgent crises of the war, " and was concerned about the necessity of making concessions to the industrial leaders whose good will was essential to the war effort but who had previously opposed the Roosevelt administration's commerce and labor reforms. Demonstrating great leadership in domestic war efforts, Roosevelt also showed a characteristic concern for the welfare of the American troops, and in 1943 she made a 23,000-mile tour of battle sites in Australia and the South Pacific.

Franklin Roosevelt died at his retreat at Warm Springs, Georgia, on April 12, 1945, in the company of Lucy Mercer. Eleanor, who had with her husband played a crucial role in leading the country during two of its most dramatic crises, the Great Depression and the Second World War, now led the country in mourning the loss of the much-revered leader.

Working for International Humanitarianism

In December of 1945, President Truman named Roosevelt one of the five United States delegates to the newly formed United Nations, and she was subsequently appointed chair of the U.N. Human Rights Commission. With the memory of her visits to soldiers in battle as well as the pitiful example of Hitler's extermination camps fresh in her mind, Eleanor worked hard to secure the passage of an international guarantee that human beings would never again be subjected to certain forms of brutality and torture. The campaign was not an easy one, and it required all of Eleanor's prodigious diplomatic skill, but on 10 December 1948 the United Nations formally adopted the Universal Declaration of Human Rights.

When Dwight D. Eisenhower assumed the presidency in 1953, he named another representative to take Roosevelt's place at the United Nations, yet Roosevelt continued to be one of the world's most renowned proponents of humanitarianism and tolerance. During the McCarthy era she voiced her strident opposition to the anti-communist hysteria that had taken hold of the country, and she eloquently argued against increasing hostility toward the Soviet Union. She continued to work for justice for the poor, women, and African Americans, and travelled extensively to lecture and to view firsthand the unsuitable conditions she strove to amend. She also remained active in Democratic politics, supporting in particular the presidential aspirations of Adlai Stevenson. Despite her dislike for the wealthy, controversial Joseph P. Kennedy, Roosevelt ultimately endorsed the presidential candidacy of his son, John F. Kennedy; after he assumed office in 1961, Kennedy appointed her to a special session of the United Nations General Assembly and asked her to lead his Commission on the Status of Women. She also served the Kennedy administration in its delicate negotiations with Cuba following the Bay of Pigs affair. Roosevelt remained active until her death from a rare bone-marrow disease in November of 1962.

A Legacy of Justice

Roosevelt's outspokenness and advocacy of the rights of women, African Americans, and other groups caused controversy and earned her a number of enemies during her lifetime. F.B.I. director J. Edgar Hoover was particularly suspicious of her activites and compiled a massive file on her beginning in 1924 and continuing until her death. During the 1940 presidential campaign in which conservative forces tried to regain control of the White House, criticism of both Roosevelt and her husband was particularly venomous. Eleanor, however, was undeterred. Believing strongly that those in power had a moral obligation to see that all people were treated equally and fairly, she worked vigorously to bring about that aim regardless of the personal consequences or costs. The result is a legacy of reforms that helped further the most laudable attitudes of the modern era.

References:

Cook, Blanche Wiesen. *Eleanor Roosevelt: Volume One, 1884-1933.* New York, Viking, 1992.

———. "Eleanor: Loves of a First Lady," in *Nation,* 5 July 1993: 24-25.

———. "An Ever-Changing Partnership," in *Los Angeles Times Book Review,* 9 October 1994: 2, 13.

Doenecke, Justus D., "Eleanor Roosevelt," in *Historic World Leaders,* vol. 5. Detroit: Gale Research, 1994.

Kennedy, David M. "Up from Hyde Park," in *New York Times Book Review,* 19 April 1992: 1ff.

———. "Affairs Both Foreign and Domestic," in *New York Times Book Review,* 11 September 1994: 9, 11.

Morris, Celia. "On *Eleanor Roosevelt,*" in *Los Angeles Times Book Review,* 8 November 1992: 8.

—Joann Cerrito

Gayle Rubin

1949-

American activist, scholar, and researcher

As an activist, Gayle Rubin has had immeasurable influence in the realms of pornography and sexuality; as an author, her writings on Feminist Theory, Sexual Diversity, Lesbian and Gay issues, and systems of social and ideological stratification are used in Women's studies programs in colleges and universities around the country, thereby illustrating the effect of her opinions and ideas.

In late June of 1949, Gayle Rubin was born in the Midwest. The youngest of two children, Rubin grew up in South Carolina, where she remained until she entered the University of Michigan in Ann Arbor in 1966. She received her undergraduate degree in 1972, a B.A. in Women's Studies from Michigan where she was the first person to graduate in Women's Studies. She later received her M.A. and her Ph.D., both in Anthropology, from the University of Michigan in 1974 and 1994, respectively.

During her time at the University of Michigan, Rubin became heavily involved in student and feminist activism. In 1967 she was instrumental in a successful effort to repeal rules imposing curfews on female students, as well as dress codes which required women in undergraduate dormitories to wear dresses or skirts for Sunday meals. In the late 1960s Rubin began to participate in the Thursday Night Group, Ann Arbor's first "ongoing local women's liberation discussion and activist organization." According to Rubin, "The Thursday Night Group was important in establishing a feminist presence at [the University of Michigan] by disseminating feminist literature, helping to organize a protest of the local Miss Ann Arbor beauty pageant, and holding the first Teach In on Women at the University." In 1969 she wrote her first feminist essay for the *Ann Arbor Argus,* a local underground newspaper.

Rubin came out as a lesbian in 1970 and was one of the founders of the Ann Arbor Radical Lesbians. In the early 1970s, she helped launch the Women's Studies Program at the University of Michigan. She lectured in the program's first course, taught feminist theory in 1974, and taught the program's first course on lesbian literature and history in 1975. Rubin also served on the Women's Studies Program Steering Committee from its inception until she left Ann Arbor in 1978.

In 1978, when she moved to Berkeley to teach at the University of California, Rubin became involved in the initial phases of what would later be dubbed "the feminist sex wars." She was an early and vocal critic of the feminist anti-pornography movement, and a founding member of Samois, the first lesbian sadomasochism support group. She also joined and became actively involved in San Francisco's Lesbian and Gay History project. Rubin moved to San Francisco in 1979 and, in 1984 helped found the Outcasts, which succeeded Samois as the main San Francisco organization for "woman to woman sadomasochism."

Because of her positions on pornography, sadomasochism, and other issues of sexuality, Rubin has been a controversial figure in the sex debates which have been ongoing over the last two decades in the lesbian and feminist communities. In 1982 she spoke at "Towards a Politics of Sexuality," the IX Scholar and Feminist Conference at Barnard College in New York, where she was one of several participants who were attacked for their views by a feminist anti-porn group.

Although her activist activities are plentiful, Rubin is perhaps best known as an essayist. Among her many writings are: "The Traffic of Women" in *Toward an Anthropology of Women* (Monthly Review, 1975) in which she introduced the concept of a "sex/gender system;" her biographical "Introduction" to Renee Vivien's *A Woman Appeared to Me* (Naiad, 1976); "The Leather Menace" in *Coming to Power* (Alyson, 1982); "Thinking Sex" in *Pleasure and Danger* (Routledge, 1984); "The Catacombs: A Temple of Butthole" in *Leatherfolk* (Alyson, 1991); "Of Catamites and Kings: Reflections on Butch, Gender, and Boundaries" in *The Persistent Desire* (Alyson, 1992); and "Misguided, Dangerous, and Wrong: an Analysis of Anti-pornography Politics" in *Bad Girls and Dirty Pictures* (Pluto, 1993).

Over the past thirty years Rubin has been named Woman of the Year by the National Leather Association in 1988, been given a Community Award by the Gay & Lesbian Historical Society of Northern California in 1991, and a Forebearer Award by the Pantheon of Leather in 1992.

In 1993, Rubin was a Visiting Fellow at the Humanities Research Centre at the Australian National University; in 1995 she was the Visiting Scholar at the University of Missouri-St. Louis's Institute for Women's and Gender Studies; and, in 1996, she was a Chancellor's Distinguished Lecturer at the University of California-Irvine. A collection of Rubin's essays can be expected in the near future. In addition, she is completing a study of the gay male leather community in San Francisco. Rubin currently lives with her partner of six years, and teaches Women's Studies at the University of California-Santa Cruz.

Current Address: University of California-Santa Cruz, Santa Cruz, California 95064.

References:

Rubin, Gayle. E-mail interview with Andrea L.T. Peterson, 15 August 1996.

—Andrea L.T. Peterson

Muriel Rukeyser

1913-1980

American poet

Muriel Rukeyser's poetry and prose integrates the politics of much of the twentieth century with a personal aesthetic. Indeed, she broke new ground as a "political poet/journalist" because so much of her work was inspired by the conflicts and abuses of power she witnessed around the globe. She was among the first to break through the conventional wall that separates public and private spheres in poetic tradition. In this sense, her work also speaks to both feminist and lesbian readers in that it "breaks silence" (a favorite theme of hers) around female experiences of sex, aging, mother-daughter relationships, menstruation, etc. "What would happen if one woman told the truth about her life?," she wrote in a tribute to German artist Käthe Kollwitz. "The world would split open."

Rukeyser spent a childhood in silence—sheltered amongst chauffeurs and servants and "protected" by parents who did not want her to play with other children. No doubt this helps explain her lifelong drive to both communicate her vision and foster the need for communication—for translation—amongst all of us. She wrote eighteen books of poetry, four of prose, a handful of children's books, and numerous translations—all in addition to her activities at anti-war and political rallies well into the 1970s. As she wrote in 1978 in the preface to the first complete edition of her collected poems: "Might it not be that poetry and indeed all speech are a translation? This translation, this music, speaks to our silence. It in my childhood did, and ever since. I hope these may speak to yours, as my silence goes on speaking."

Almost a Golfer!

Muriel Rukeyser was born in New York City in 1913, the daughter of an upper-middle-class construction engineer and a homemaker/bookkeeper. Although she attended Jewish religious schools as a young girl, and accompanied her mother to temple every Saturday, there were few Jewish rituals observed by her family. Rukeyser had a comfortable childhood amongst servants and maids, but was frustrated by the lack of books in her home and the eventual expectations placed on her by her upwardly-mobile parents. "I was expected to grow up and become a golfer," she recalled in Janet Sternberg's biography *The Writer and Her Work.* "There was no idea at that point of a girl growing up to write poems."

Nevertheless, Rukeyser was writing poems seriously by the time she was in high school, and was determined to learn more about life with other youngsters on the streets in her neighborhood. Though her strict parents did not even allow her to cross the street to play, she was soon cavorting with other gangs of kids in tunnels and basements beneath nearby apartment buildings, a form of rebellion that initiated a lifelong separation from her parent's values and an unflinching observance of what she termed in Sternberg's book "the terrible, murderous differences between the ways people lived." She would ultimately be disinherited by her father for her steadfast leftist views.

Rukeyser attended the Ethical Culture School in New York, and then spent two years at Vassar College until her father went bankrupt. It was at college that she remembered "everything intensifying." When her mother threatened to make her return home when she realized they did not "lock the gates" at Vassar, Rukeyser devoted herself more intensely to her poetry as a way of affirming her independence. A crowning glory came when she was appointed literary editor for Vassar's leftist *Student Review.*

In 1933, Rukeyser went to Alabama to cover the infamous trial of the Scottsboro Boys, nine African-Americans who had been accused of raping two white girls. (Their various death and life-imprisonment sentences were eventually overturned by the U.S. Supreme Court, although some of them did not get paroled until ten and twenty years later.) Rukeyser was among the few white journalists brave enough to speak out against the injustice of the sentences, (one of the victims recanted her testimony in 1937), and was promptly thrown in jail for simply talking with the African-American journalists who were also covering the story. During her short prison stay, she not only contracted typhoid fever, but cemented a lifelong commitment to social justice that is evident in her more political poetry. In her poem "The Trial," for example, she captures the tension of the time when she writes: "A blinded statue attends before the courthouse, bronze and black men lie on the grass, waiting, the khaki dapper National Guard leans on its bayonets. But the air is populous beyond our vision: all the people's anger finds its vortex here as the mythic lips of justice open, and speak."

Power to Change the World

In 1935, Rukeyser published her first book of poems titled *Theory of Flight,* for which she won the Yale Younger Poets Award. In *Flight,* she evidenced an interest in science, technology, and even film-editing, proving that collections of poetry could do more than recall some ethereal fantasy—they could also address contemporary concerns. She believed, according to Eloise Klein Healy in *Contemporary Lesbian Writers of the United States,* that "like Whitman,... the voice of the poet is an oracular one. She maintained, like T. S. Eliot and his followers, that poetry represented "the individual's power to change the world."

In 1936, Rukeyser found herself in Spain when the civil war broke out. A man she was in love with, Otto Bach, was killed in the fighting and Rukeyser was evacuated to England. In 1937, she traveled to West Virginia to investigate the deaths of miners working on a hydroelectric plant. Her 1938 collection of works titled *U.S. 1* ironically chronicled the powerlessness of these workers as they died trying to harness power. Rukeyser took a job at the Office of War Information as an artist in 1943, but she and other "lefties" were soon dismissed because of their political ideas. In 1945, she moved to San Francisco to teach at the California Labor School, and here met her husband Glynn Collins, a painter. Their marriage was annulled after a few months and, in 1947, Rukeyser had a son, out of wedlock, fathered by another man. That same year, she received notice of a yearly stipend available to her from an anonymous benefactor, but eventually gave this up to teach at Sarah Lawrence College in 1954. Her collection of poems *The Gates* (1978) documents her experience as a single mother in the straighter-laced 1950s. As Alice Walker noted in an essay titled "A Talk: Convocation 1972" published in *In Search of Our Mother's Gardens,* "another great teacher was Muriel Rukeyser, who could link up ... poetry to potty training."

Rukeyser also wrote three biographies: one about scientist *Willard Gibbs* (1942); *One Life* (1957), about Wendell Wilkie; and *The Traces of Thomas Hariot* (1971). Each of these individuals were,

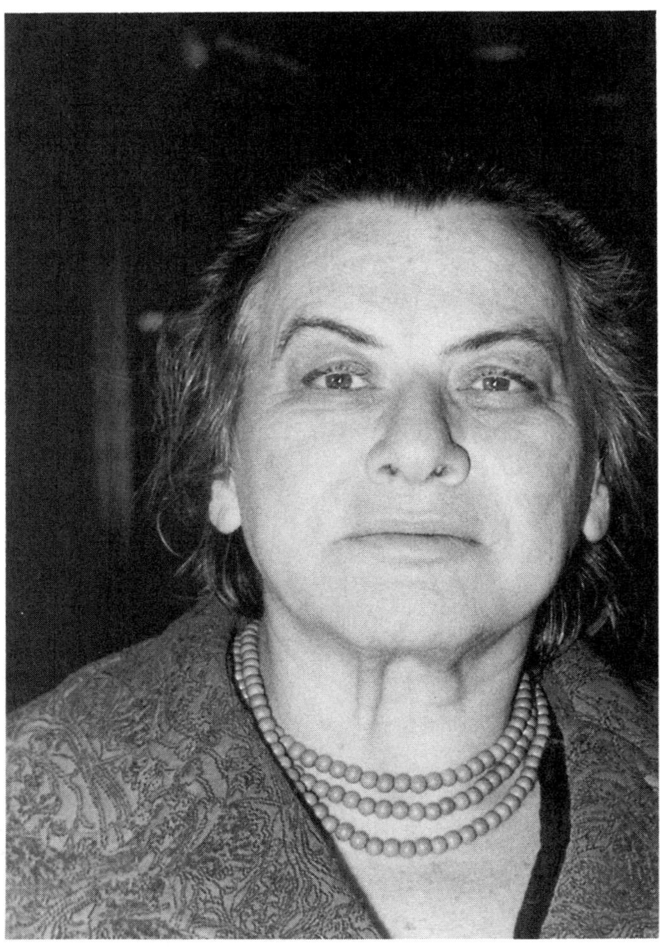

Muriel Rukeyser

like herself, independent thinkers with social consciences that filtered through to their work. According to Healy, Rukeyser's intention in each of these works was "to incorporate a mythic dimension" by using techniques from her poetry in describing their lives. Her examination of the academic, "Yale-ensconced" Gibbs, for example, begins by describing the experiences of African-Americans aboard a Spanish slave ship. In the end, Rukeyser makes profound connections between the two, illustrating her lifelong belief that everything is related to everything else in a deep "language of process," and indulging her notion that both scientists and poets are "hunters of the improbable." Not surprisingly, she also helped establish the interactive science-and-technology Exploratorium Museum in San Francisco.

In 1964, Rukeyser suffered a stroke, but was nonetheless able to bounce back as poetically-prolific and politically-active as ever. She was active in protests against the war in Vietnam throughout the 1970s, even going so far as to travel to Hanoi. (According to Healy, she termed the war "a failure of human imagination.") She also vociferously protested the threatened execution of Korean poet Kim Chi-Ha, and traveled to Seoul to seek his release.

Though Rukeyser never wrote or spoke publicly about her sexual identity, her later work especially became more women-identified (see *The Speed of Darkness* published in 1968). In 1978, she accepted an invitation to speak on a Lesbian Poetry Reading panel as part of the Modern Language Association Program—a move many heralded as her better-late-than-never coming out. Indeed, so much of her work had alluded to "secrets well-kept" and "exiles from the self" over the years, that the assumption of a long-repressed lesbian identity was well-founded. In her poem "The Transgress," for example, she speaks coyly of "thundering on tabu" and the "bed of forbidden things finally known." Alas, she suffered another stroke just prior to the event and could not attend. Never quite recovering from this one, she died two years later in New York.

There are so many ways to seek, Rukeyser seems to have been saying in so much her work—so many "ways in which one loves the people from whom one can learn," as she wrote in "The Education of a Poet" in *A Muriel Rukeyser Reader*. It is a passion so deep, it cannot simply end with life. One must believe that it lasts forever, as she says in her poem "Then": "When I am dead, even then, I will still love you, I will wait in these poems,... silence will be falling into that silence, it is building music."

References:

Levi, Jan Heller, ed. *A Muriel Rukeyser Reader.* New York: W. W. Norton, 1994.

Pollack, Sandra and Denise D. Knight, eds. *Contemporary Lesbian Writers of the United States.* Westport, Connecticut: Greenwood Press, 1994.

Rukeyser, Muriel. *The Collected Poems of Muriel Rukeyser.* New York: McGraw-Hill, 1978.

Sternberg, Janet, ed. *The Writer and Her Work.* New York: W. W. Norton, 1992.

Summers, Claude J., ed. *The Gay and Lesbian Literary Heritage.* New York: Henry Holt, 1995.

—Jerome Szymczak

Jane Rule

1931-

Canadian writer and educator

Jane Rule is a prominent lesbian writer and one of Canada's leading authors. In addition to her first and best known work, *Desert of the Heart* (1964), Rule has published six other novels, as well as a pioneering book of lesbian criticism, *Lesbian Images* (1975), and numerous short stories and essays. Rule considers herself a realist writer; she is committed to conveying truths about a world that she defines as "whole," "real," and "mixed." Perhaps for this reason, lesbian and gay concerns are at times central, at other times peripheral to her work's sustained exploration of individual development, especially in relation to community and landscape. Rule has received a number of awards, including the Canadian Authors' Association Award for Best Novel (1978), the Benson and Hedges Award for Best Short Stories (1978), the Literary Award for Gay Academic Union (1978), and the Fund for Human Dignity's Award of Merit (1983). In 1994 the University of British Columbia presented her with an honorary doctorate.

The daughter of Arthur Richards and Carlotta Jane Rule, Jane Vance Rule was born in Plainfield, New Jersey 28 March 1931 and grew up in the midwest and California, where she attended segregated and integrated schools respectively. Rule attributes her self-described independence from convention to these early experiences, which granted her insight into how communities can restrict or further interaction among their members. In 1952, Rule graduated with a B.A. in English from Mills College and spent the subsequent year in London where she studied at University College. In 1954 she began teaching at Concord Academy in Massachusetts. There she met her life partner, Helen Sonthoff. The couple moved to Vancouver, British Columbia in 1956, where Sonthoff accepted a teaching post with the University's English Department and Rule devoted herself to writing and teaching. In 1976 they moved to Galiano Island, British Columbia.

Rule's first two published novels are coming out narratives that play with and subvert the Christian paradigms and themes that have shaped the Anglo-American realist tradition. As in the work of lesbian and gay writers such as Radclyffe Hall, James Baldwin, and, most recently, Jeanette Winterson, the religious motifs in Rule's fiction serve a double purpose. On the one hand, by framing narratives of sexual awakening as spiritual quests, Rule underscores the serious moral purpose behind her writing. On the other hand, by making use of a literary tradition whose Christian themes are historically implicated in the oppression of same-sex love, Rule's "revisions" ironically disclose the immorality of adherence to religious conventions solely for convention's sake. In effect, Rule extends the community of realism to include and welcome lesbian and gay characters.

From this perspective, Rule's first published novel, *Desert of the Heart*, remains a landmark contribution to lesbian literature. One of the few positive portrayals of lesbianism in pre-Stonewall fiction, the novel draws on and critiques such canonical texts as the Bible, Dante's *Divine Comedy*, and Bunyan's *Pilgrim's Progress* in order to tell its tale of lesbian romance. With Reno, Nevada, complete with casinos and desert, serving as a biblically-charged backdrop, *Desert* recounts the love story of English professor Evelyn Hall and cartoonist Ann Childs, whose mutual vocation is arguably cultural critique. Director Donna Deitch's 1985 lesbian film *Desert Hearts* is loosely based on Rule's novel.

In contrast to *Desert of the Heart*, *This is Not for You* (1970) might be termed an anti-love story, which invites comparison with James Baldwin's *Giovanni's Room*. Written in the first person, Rule's novel takes the form of a letter not sent, of a confession whose penitent refuses absolution. So narrator-protagonist Kate admits to herself, more particularly to the mental image of her beloved Esther, but importantly not to Esther herself, "I've made a virtue of loving you badly.... This is not for you." Much like David, the self-loathing character of Baldwin's narrative, Kate can only express her commitment to Esther by continually disavowing it. (Indeed, both David and Kate only tell their stories once they have effectually lost their "lovers.") Implicated in this betrayal is Kate's training within the Episcopal church; her conventional morality proves the vehicle for her immoral betrayal of love.

In the 1994 documentary *Fiction and Other Truths: A Film About Jane Rule*, Rule observes that *This is Not for You* marked a turning point in her artistic vision. Subsequent works, focussing on several rather than on one or two principal characters, are committed to the exploration of communities and the possibilities of communal living. Such emphases direct *Against the Season* (1971), *The Young in One Another's Arms* (1977), and *Contract with the World* (1980), as well her two novels, *Memory Board* (1987) and *After the Fire* (1989). These novels map out communities that consist of patterns of differences, social as well as geographic. Characters unite across such conventional divides as orientation, ethnicity, race, age, and health. The various borders in Rule's fiction are psychological and social, but also geographical and topographical: characters move between country and city, rainforest and desert, water and land. Jane Rule's work is inclusive, transformative.

Aside from her seven novels, Jane Rule has published two short story collections, *Theme for Diverse Instruments* (1975) and *Inland Passage and Other Stories* (1985), and two essay collections, *Lesbian Images* (1975) and *A Hot-Eyed Moderate* (1985), as well as a collection of both short stories and essays, *Outlander* (1981). Like the novels, these works validate diverse models for human companionship that are not overtly ideologically driven. They portray "real" rather than "utopian" worlds. Rule's insistence on writing as a truth-telling medium, together with her reluctance to define her art as wholly "lesbian" or "feminist," has sparked the concern that her aesthetic position is theoretically naive. Language is, after all, inherently ideological; it structures one's thoughts and so determines which truths may be thought and which remain unthinkable. Yet, to fault Rule on this ground is to overlook her actual, crucial contribution to lesbian fiction: as a realist writer she tells truths traditionally left untold.

Rule has also actively fought government censorship of gay and lesbian work. When the Toronto-based gay liberation journal *The Body Politic* was tried for its 1977 publication of "Men Loving Boys Loving Men," Rule agreed to write a series of protest articles for the journal until the case was resolved; the trial lasted five years. Again, in 1992 when the Vancouver bookstore Little Sisters took Canada Customs to court for seizing its books at the border, Rule decided to testify on the bookstore's behalf. A champion of gay and lesbian concerns, Rule is no longer physically able to write because of arthritis. She continues to live on Galiano Island.

Current Address: Route 1, Station 19 C17, Galiano, BC V0N 1P0, Canada.

References:

Breen, Margaret Soenser. "Narrative Inversion: The Biblical Heritage of *The Well of Loneliness* and *Desert of the Heart*," in *Journal of Homosexuality*, no. 33: 3-4.

Fernie, Lynne and Aerlyn Weissman, dir. *Fiction and Other Truths: A Film About Jane Rule*. A Great Jane Production, 1994.

Hancock, Geoffrey, "An Interview with Jane Rule," in *Canadian Fiction Magazine*, Autumn 1976, no. 23: 57-112.

Schuster, Marilyn R. "Strategies for Survival: The Subtle Subversion of Jane Rule," in *Feminist Studies*, Fall 1991, vo. 7, no. 3: 431-450.

Sonthoff, Helen. "A Bibliography," in *Canadian Fiction Magazine*, Autumn 1976, no. 23: 133-138.

———. "Celebration: Jane Rule's Fiction," in *Canadian Fiction Magazine*, Autumn 1976, no. 23: 121-132.

Spraggs, Gillian. "Hell and the Mirror: A Reading of *Desert of the Heart*," in *New Lesbian Criticism: Literary and Cultural Readings*, edited by Sally Munt. New York: Columbia University Press, 1992: 115-131.

—Margaret Soenser Breen

RuPaul

1960-

African-American female impersonator and singer

RuPaul Andre Charles was born in 1960, the only son in a family of mostly women. It is to the strong women in his life that RuPaul dedicates his love of the feminine principle. He grew up in San Diego and developed a fascination with the theatre early in life. His introduction to drag occurred when a girlfriend took him to see *The Rocky Horror Picture Show* and when, in 1978, he met his first drag queens.

After dropping out of high school in the eleventh grade RuPaul sold cars for his brother-in-law and travelled around the country. In 1981 he saw a cable comedy show called *The American Music Show* and wrote to the producer, telling him how much he would like to appear on the show. When he did, it was with some female friends in an impromptu band called RuPaul and the U-Hauls. He became a regular on the show, but did not appear in drag until there was an on-air drag wedding.

From the U-Hauls he went on to an all-male band called Wee Wee Pole and played with them for about a year. In the mid-1970s RuPaul appeared in a series of underground films directed by John Witherspoon, the first three being *Trilogy of Terror*. He also published a series of pamphlets which were mostly photographs of himself. In 1984 RuPaul found himself broke and evicted from his apartment.

RuPaul then took off for New York with three other fledgling drag queens and put together a revue at The Pyramid in Greenwich Village. Being homeless in New York was a little rougher than in Atlanta, but RuPaul and his gang managed to stay alive and relatively unscathed. He returned to Atlanta for Christmas and recorded his first album, *Sex Freak*, for Funtone Records. The following summer he played Riff Raff in *The Rocky Horror Picture Show*.

In January 1986 RuPaul created a new persona for himself called Starrbooty. This led to another trilogy of underground films of the same name. He then went back to New York to promote the album at The New Music Seminar. After that he starred in *Mahogany II* (playing Diana Ross in drag), *American Porn Star, Psycho Bitch,* and *Voyeur*. He returned to New York, and by the beginning of 1987 was working as a coat check boy at the Amazon Hotel. In 1988, he went to Los Angeles and landed a spot on *The Gong Show*—he lost to an Elvis impersonator. When he turned 28 and found himself homeless again, he returned to Atlanta to live with his mother.

Upon returning to New York in 1989, RuPaul found that the drag scene had changed—it now demanded realism over style. RuPaul managed the transformation, and became a regular at a club called The Love Machine. It was there that he developed his signature perfume, Whore. This was the springboard of his career, and later that year he appeared in the B-52's "Love Shack" video.

In January 1990 he was crowned "Queen of Manhattan" and appeared on *Geraldo*. But RuPaul was also on his way to becoming a serious alcoholic. When he was fired from a video shoot for being inebriated, he decided it was time to rethink his life. After kicking his habits (in addition to alcohol he was far too fond of drugs, mostly pills), RuPaul made his album, *Supermodel of the World,* and performed the album's single for the first time at Wigstock in 1992. This was followed by the Supermodel tour, which lasted until January 1994 when he opened for Duran Duran in Hartford, Connecticut. The video was nominated for best dance video at the MTV Video Music Awards that year. He also toured Europe, and performed at the Cannes film festival. From there he hit Hollywood, appearing on *Arsenio Hall,* and was an award presenter at the Video Music Awards.

RuPaul

The straight media discovered RuPaul in 1995. Everybody wanted to interview him, review him, and get his advice on life. He sang a duet with Elton John—a remake of "Don't Go Breaking My Heart"—and filmed a video to go with it. He appeared in *Crooklyn, The Brady Bunch Movie,* and *Too Wong Foo, Thanks For Everything Julie Newmar*. He became the spokesmodel for MAC cosmetics, and in February 1996 was interviewed for *Harper's Bazaar* as the only male on a panel of supermodels, effectively announcing the impact RuPaul has had on the worlds of fashion, music, and movies.

Current Address: c/o World of Wonder, 1157 North Highland Ave., 1st Floor, Los Angeles, California 90038.

References:

De Jonge, Peter. "My Dinner with Kirsty," in *Harper's Bazaar* (New York), February, 1996.

"Forecasts," in *Publisher's Weekly* (New York), 24 April 1995.

Review of *Blue in the Face,* in *Rolling Stone* (New York), 5 October 1995.

Review of *Lettin' It All Hang Out,* in *Booklist* (Chicago, Illinois), 15 May 1995.
Review of *Lettin' It All Hang Out,* in *Library Journal* (New York), 15 May 1995.
Review of *Wigstock,* in *People Weekly* (New York), 12 June 1995.
RuPaul. *Lettin' It All Hang Out.* Westport, Connecticut: Hyperion Books, 1995.
Tresniowski, Alex. "Talking With RuPaul," in *People Weekly* (New York), 10 July 1995.

—Debora Hill

Vito Russo

1946-1990

American film historian and activist

Vito Russo's life reads like a Hollywood script itself, albeit in the vein of the new, more enlightened Hollywood he hoped his research into the homophobic history of movies would engender. He was a tireless gay-rights activist and film historian/critic from the early 1970s until his death in 1990, contributing to periodicals like *Esquire*, *The Village Voice*, *New York Magazine*, *Rolling Stone*, and *The Advocate*. He wrote and produced a WNYC television program titled *Our Time* (1985) which dealt with lesbian and gay issues, and was the national publicity director for the 1985 Academy Award winning documentary *The Times of Harvey Milk.*

He was among the first "gay liberationists" to protest against injustice with the Gay Activists Alliance and the Gay Liberation Movement in the early 1970s, and was a founding member of ACT-UP New York in the mid-1980s.

But Russo is no doubt best known for his book *The Celluloid Closet* (1981), and the series of lectures and film-clip presentations presented both before and after its publication that he took to over 200 colleges, museums, and film festivals around the world. Through his work, he hoped to shed some long-overdue light on the anti-gay history of Hollywood as evidenced in the movies that have so virulently tainted mainstream perception of gay and lesbian lives over the decades. "The history of the portrayal of lesbians and gay men in mainstream cinema is politically indefensible and aesthetically revolting," he wrote. "Gay visibility has never really been an issue in the movies. It's *how* they have been visible that has remained offensive for almost a century."

In 1996, *The Celluloid Closet* was made into a full-length feature, bringing Russo's inspired work to where it belonged all along—on celluloid—and to the very mainstream hearts he had always wanted to touch. Producers Rob Epstein and Jeffrey Friedman enlisted people like Gore Vidal and Lily Tomlin in a documentary-style series of interviews and clips that fully fleshed out not only Hollywood's often-distorted reflection of gay and lesbian lives, but also its very real—and historically tragic—influence on how those lives had been (and continue to be) distorted and stereotyped for mainstream consumption. Surely lesbians and gay men deserve better than to be portrayed as self-hating, suicidal or, at best (according to one critic in *The Nation*), "tragedy queens and vampires ... and friends who live down the hall."

Militancy Ready to Flare

Vito Russo was born and raised in New York's East Harlem, the son of a laborer and a homemaker. His classic working-class roots no doubt contributed both to his tenacity as an activist and to his perseverance in getting *The Celluloid Closet* published (while Russo continued to work as a waiter in the late 1970s, it was rejected by eighteen publishers).

Russo was both aware of gays and disdainful of stereotypes from a young age. "Even with all my Catholic religious education," he told author Eric Marcus in *Making History*, "and with all the stuff in the movies telling me that homosexuality was wrong, for some reason I instinctively knew they were full of shit." By the time he was in high school, he was sneaking off to parties hosted by some "loud, very out-front queens" and running off to Fire Island on the weekends.

Coming out publicly and politically, though, was another matter—one that Russo approached as painstakingly as his research. He told Marcus that he knew his only real choice was whether to express his homosexuality openly, but also claimed he had to keep his mouth shut with most of his peers through high school for fear of being beaten up. By the time he reached Fairleigh Dickinson University in Rutherford, New Jersey in the mid 1960s, a smoldering militancy was ready to flare—and the Stonewall riot was just the fuel required.

The gay New Yorkers who were there in June of 1968 invariably connect the night of the Stonewall riot with the day of Judy Garland's funeral. An afternoon that had witnessed thousands of despondent mourners lining up to view her body led, not so indirectly, to a night of rage on the part of Stonewall patrons unwilling to go along peacefully following yet another unwarranted raid. Russo was there, literally up in a tree across the street, unsure whether he should get involved, and unaware that an activist movement which would soon very much involve him was being born.

It was not until nearly a year later—following a raid on another bar called the Snake Pit during which a young Argentinean national jumped to his death from a second-floor window to avoid capture by the police—that Russo woke up. "He was pushed from that window," Russo told Marcus, "pushed by society ... for the first time, the organized response reached me on a gut level." Russo rallied his East Harlem fighting spirit and became avidly involved in demonstrations and zaps with both the emerging Gay Activists Alliance and the more radical Gay Liberation Front.

Synthesizing Politics and Work

At the same time, he was earning his Master's Degree in film at New York University, organizing movie and film discussion nights at a Gay Community Center, and working in the film department at New York's Museum of Modern Art. The combination of his being more comfortably, actively out coupled with the support of what he termed "interesting, intelligent, dynamic people who loved movies and didn't care if you were gay," led to a synthesis of his politics and work. In 1973, he began research on what was to become *The Celluloid Closet.* "Our negative image was at the root of homophobia," he told Marcus, "and (people) were being taught these things by the mass media, by movies. If I could address this issue, I felt that would be my contribution to the gay rights movement." Research was an uphill battle. People in Hollywood—actors particularly—were either too busy, too closeted, too homophobic, or only interested in what was in it for them. But

Russo persevered, and a handful of people, mostly screenwriters and directors, did speak out finally about homophobia in Hollywood over the years. In 1981, Harper & Row published *The Celluloid Closet* to mostly rave reviews. Few could believe the subject had been ignored for so long.

Russo's general battle plan for the book as well as the lecture series is evidenced in the "art-or-politics" criteria he used to select the "best" and "worst" gay films of the last few decades. He eschewed political-correctness. "As a rule," he told *The Alyson Almanac*, "I have chosen to list those films I think have illuminated diverse aspects of gay and lesbian experience in an exciting, personal, or unusual way. In doing so,... those listed among the best were generally good films and those listed on the worst list were usually not." Among Russo's best are: *Maurice* (1987), *My Beautiful Launderette* (1986), and *Victim* (1961). His worst list includes: *Partners* (1982), *Cruising* (1980), and *The Sergeant* (1968).

"Zaps" and Other Factors

While Russo's observations were enlightening and politicizing gay and straight film students, teachers, and even plain moviegoers across the country, he was humble about the book's impact on Hollywood films overall. "[I] may have raised the consciousness of the community as a whole about the issue," he told Marcus, "but I think there were other factors."

First, according to Russo, there were the demonstrations and zaps organized in New York against the movie *Cruising* (1979). Not since the weak protests that followed the release of *The Boys in the Band* (1970)—also directed by William Friedkin—had gay men organized to decry the depiction of themselves as self-loathing and/or inherently sadomasochistic. "I advise gay people to tell him (Friedkin) to fuck off and not allow him to film," wrote Arthur Bell in *The Village Voice* when Friedkin was filming in New York during the Summer of 1979. For the entire two months of shooting a series of disorganized-but-nonetheless-driven guerrilla warfare was carried out. Cables were cut, whistles were blown during filming, and producers were hit where it hurt the most—in the pocketbook.

In the end—in spite of the ideological split within the gay community itself as to whether films like *Cruising* should be made—filmmakers were forced to be more sensitive to gay and lesbian portrayals on the screen. "It was the first time," Russo told Marcus, "that an organized protest had an effect on the powers in Hollywood...."

Another significant event that dovetailed with the success of Russo's book was the release of *Making Love* (1982), the first film where, according to Russo, "a gay couple was permitted a happy ending." Finally two handsome leading men (Michael Ontkean and Harry Hamlin) went to bed together and dealt with the ramifications of falling in love without excessive, suicidal drama. "Now *that* (was) a great step forward," Russo told Marcus. "The young gay male population could se this movie and say, 'At the very least I'm not sick and I don't have to kill myself.'"

AIDS—Detour and Catalyst

Russo's final few years of life, work, and activism were shrouded by AIDS: he was diagnosed HIV-positive in 1986. AIDS is what finally detoured any forward progress in Hollywood, according to Russo. "Never before in the history of movies," he lamented to Marcus, "even in the worst periods of film history, have screenwriters felt so comfortable being antigay." As a test, he suggested counting how many times the word "faggot" is bandied about even in the supposedly enlightened new breed of socially-conscious, brat-pack films.

Yet, to the end of his life in the winter of 1990, Russo maintained that AIDS should also be seen as a catalyst—a cosmic call for gay rights activists to work even harder to put themselves out of business, to bring about "an end to this disease so we can all go home," as he told Marcus. "My whole life," he added, "(has been) to leave my book and the other things I've written behind me. I know that after I'm dead my book is going to be on a shelf someplace and that some sixteen-year-old kid who's going to be a gay activist will read my work and carry the ball from there ... they'll be fighting (the) battles long after you and I are gone."

References:

The Alyson Almanac. Boston: Alyson Publications, 1994-95.
Contemporary Authors, vol. 107. Detroit: Gale Research, 1983.
Marcus, Eric. *Making History: The Struggle for Gay and Lesbian Equal Rights, 1945-1990.* New York: HarperCollins, 1990.
The Nation, 1 April 1996.

—Jerome Szymczak

Bayard Rustin

1910-1987

African-American political strategist and activist

Though often called "Mr. March" for his prime organizational role in one of the most important nonviolent protests in American history—the 1963 March on Washington—Bayard Rustin is still something of an unsung hero in the history of the American Civil Rights Movement. The ongoing specter of homophobia and fear of "red menace" Communism that shadowed his career of over five decades reached a zenith in the middle part of this century and forced him to step behind the scenes at the height of his political power. Still, once his accomplishments are noted, Rustin is easily categorized as one of the most influential political, nonviolent strategists who fought not only for the rights of African-Americans, but for the dignity of all oppressed minorities. From his early labor union years to his "senior statesman" lectures at colleges and gay organizations around the country, Rustin held fast to the belief that the rights of African-Americans were best secured and maintained in the long run as an integral part of deeper social reforms for everyone.

In the 1930s and 1940s, a youthful, radicalized Bayard Rustin worked with and recruited for the Communist Party, the War Resisters League, and various labor unions. He teamed with Martin Luther King in the 1950s and was a confidant, advisor, and speech writer until King's tragic death in the spring of 1968. He helped create both the Congress of Racial Equality (CORE) and the Southern Christian Leadership Conference (SCLC). In the 1980s, he urged gays and lesbians to follow his example and embrace their role in furthering social equity for *all* minorities. It was this wholistic focus on broader social objectives that spotlight Rustin as unique among twentieth-century social activists, black or white, gay or straight. "I reject the idea of working for the Negro as being impractical as well as immoral, if one does that alone," he said in a 1965 interview. To the end of his life, Rustin maintained this world view—the political was ever the personal, and vice versa.

"Fated" Activism

Bayard Rustin grew up in a poor section of West Chester, Pennsylvania, one of nine children supported by parents in the catering business. At the age of eleven, he was told that the woman he thought was his sister was actually his mother, and that his "parents" were actually his grandparents. His father was a West Indian man whom his mother had never married and Rustin's grandmother was a devout Quaker. It was this combination of hard work, extended familial responsibility, and a commitment to social justice that formed the heart of Rustin's lifelong moral/activist code.

West Chester had been an important stop on the underground railroad, a fact which Rustin, in retrospect, felt fated his future as an activist. As he noted in his 1976 *Strategies for Freedom*, "The antislavery sentiment of the inhabitants was revealed in the town's architecture, for beneath its aging, Colonial homes ran hidden passageways which had concealed runaway slaves from (their) southern plantation owners...."

As gifted as he was, the beginning of Rustin's college career coincided with the onset of the Great Depression, so Rustin was forced to drop out. In 1931, he moved in with a relative in Greenwich Village and put himself through classes at New York City College by occasionally singing at local clubs with singers like Josh White and Leadbelly. Strictly enforced segregation in places of public entertainment was still the norm for most of New York, except in those integrated clubs operated by Communist organizers. It was during this time that Rustin, like many black intellectuals of his day, embraced the Communist promise of racial equality and a cure for economic ills. He was soon travelling to colleges and union halls throughout the United States speaking out against segregation and social injustice. With the outbreak of World War II and the subsequent shift by the Party away from domestic reforms, Rustin was asked to stop his anti-segregation work. He quickly resigned.

A Most Beloved Mentor

By the mid-1940s, an undaunted Rustin was principal aide to labor leader A. Philip Randolph, an originator of the 1941 March on Washington. One of Rustin's first tasks was to target racial discrimination in the defense industry. It was Randolph who had been instrumental in pressuring Franklin Delano Roosevelt into creating the Fair Employment Practices Commission, and it was Randolph who, according to Rustin in his *Strategies for Freedom*, used "careful daring, (and a) sense of timing and strategy" to get Truman to sign an executive order in 1948 that finally ended racial discrimination in the military.

Randolph was Rustin's most beloved mentor. Shortly after Randolph's death in 1979, Rustin wrote that Randolph had unearthed for him the critical *economic* roots of racism, and had taught him above all "that the struggle for the freedom of black people is intertwined with the struggle to free all mankind."

In 1942, Rustin was hired by radical reformer A. J. Muste, founder of the international pacifist organization Fellowship for Reconciliation (FOR), to spearhead a Department of Race Relations. From this committee emerged the interracial Congress of Racial Equality (CORE), whose philosophy was patterned after the nonviolent direct action as exercised by Indian leader Mohandas Gandhi, and whose focus was on challenging racial discrimination in public accommodation and transportation through nonviolent mass protest. Here, Rustin found the heart of lasting, truly forward moving success for the civil rights movement. CORE strategies satisfied his progressive agenda, utilized the energy and talents of both blacks and sympathetic whites, and salved his Quaker-bred sensibilities for nonviolence.

Bayard Rustin

Ironically, it was in the years during and immediately following the war that Rustin faced the most grueling mental and physical challenges to these ideologies. His life's work became a roller coaster ride of peaks and valleys. In 1942, he worked in California on behalf of the interned Japanese and, as a conscientious objector in 1943, served three years in the Lewisburg Penitentiary rather than perform hospital duties. On his release in 1946, he resumed his CORE duties and traveled to India as chairman of the Free India Committee and a guest of Ghandi's Congress Party. In 1947, he served 22 days on a North Carolina chain gang (just one of dozens of beatings and arrests he was to suffer in his life) for joining one of the first Freedom Rides through the South—dubbed the "Journey of Reconciliation"—designed to test the U.S. Supreme Court prohibition against segregation in interstate travel.

Career-Crippling Homophobia

In the early 1950s, Rustin fought for self rule in West Africa, assumed a leading role in the Aldermason Peace March in England, and joined the All African People's Conference in Addis Ababa. Yet despite his growing worldwide success, Rustin now faced the ongoing, career crippling isolation of homophobia, despite the "all encompassing" rhetoric of the political organizations he worked for. He had long been nonchalant and open about his homosexuality in private, and always discreet professionally. Yet, given the political/sexual hysteria and hypocrisy of the 1950s, he was now considered a potential liability by many of his colleagues.

According to *Contemporary Black Biography* (1993), "when Rustin began to run into trouble with laws against homosexual activity, FOR chairman Muste warned him that any such further actions would cause his dismissal." When he was arrested and sentenced to 30 days in jail on a morals charge in Pasadena, California in early 1953, a dispirited Rustin was forced to resign from FOR. It was a tragically humbling step behind the scenes that was to shadow his life and career to the end.

In December of 1955, the civil rights struggle in America reached a watershed when Rosa Parks refused to move to the back of the bus in segregated Montgomery, Alabama. The resulting bus boycott received nationwide attention and was viewed by Rustin as an opportunity to rejoin the fight and regain some lost political influence. He traveled to Montgomery, but was soon reproached by several black political leaders who feared that his personal life and past Communist connections would prove a liability to the cause. Led by A. P. Randolph, they convinced him to leave Montgomery.

Rustin had come too far to simply withdraw, however. As he wrote in his diary in 1956, "I had a feeling that no force on earth (could) stop this movement. I has all the elements to touch the hearts of men." Martin Luther King, Jr., then head of the Montgomery movement, was quick to recognize Rustin's talents, and thus initiated a lifelong professional liaison. Rustin became ghostwriter, confidant, and tireless promoter of the "cult of personality" that was growing around King. Recognizing the movement's need for a charismatic, younger leader (by now, Rustin was twenty years King's senior) and reluctantly acquiescent to his personal "liabilities," Rustin helped the emerging leader behind the scenes by briefing him for meetings, drafting speeches and press releases, and introducing him to wealthy civil rights supporters.

Marches and Morals

With the arrival of desegregation orders from the Supreme Court in December 1956, the Montgomery boycott ended. Strategies for expanding the campaign throughout the South were just beginning though, as was Rustin's role as senior statesman. But once again, the potential for scandal loomed large. In 1960, the powerful black congressman Adam Clayton Powell threatened to expose Rustin's personal and political past, which precipitated Rustin's resignation from the SCLC. He was forced to forfeit his role as official head of the 1963 March on Washington. However, his long association with King nonetheless assured his central role as a behind the curtain organizer of one of the most important nonviolent protests in American history, best remembered as the march at which King delivered his riveting "I Have A Dream" speech.

It is important to note the fear that political segregationists wielded at the time. Right down to the eve of the march, Rustin's most stalwart supporters were afraid that conservative and liberals alike would exploit Rustin's homosexuality and former Communist ties to "taint and dilute" the purpose of the protest—which was, for the first time in history, designed to draw attention to the *economic* roots of racism in America. But 73 year-old Randolph, considered the most politically safe figurehead to lead the march, was by then vesting responsibility for the day-to-day planning and logistics almost completely to Rustin. In the end, thanks largely to King's intervention, Randolph appointed Rustin as his official march deputy and he was back on board.

In a last ditch effort to derail the march, Senator Strom Thurmond told the press about Rustin's 1953 morals arrest and denounced him on the floor of the Senate as a draft dodger and Communist. The sabotage backfired and the attack served to rally black leaders around Rustin all the more. Throughout, Rustin kept a cool head, answering Thurmond's charges with prideful proof that he knew quite a bit more about morals and decency than the cagey Senator. "With regard to Senator Thurmond's attack on my morality," he wrote just prior to the march in 1963, "I have no comment. By religious training and fundamental philosophy, I am disinclined to put myself in the position of having to defend my own moral character. Questions in this area should properly be directed to those who have entrusted me with my present responsibilities."

Radicals "of All Stripes" Needed

By 1964, Rustin had grown disillusioned with nonviolent action as means of change. He turned his focus to the political arena, and from 1965 to 1979, he headed the A.P. Randolph Institute, a liberal think-tank sponsored by the AFL-CIO and designed to address social and economic ills. In 1975, he founded the Organization for Black Americans to Support Israel, a group that continues to this day.

From his "senior statesman" vantage point later in life, Rustin witnessed the violence, factionalism, and frustration that characterized the movement for racial equality well into the 1980s. His allegiance to radical reforms—total restructuring of political, economic, and social institutions—remained intact, and he continued to stress the importance of strong labor unions, coalition politics, and the vote. To those who advocated racial separatism, he answered that without equality for all, there simply is no equality for the few—no political base or ideology from which to take a stand. "The real radical," he wrote in a speech to black students in 1970, "is that person who has a vision of equality and is willing to do those things that will bring reality closer to that vision. And by equality I do not mean 'separate but equal', a phrase created by segregationists in order to prevent the attainment of equality. I mean equality based upon an integrated social order ..."

Toward the end of his life, Rustin often spoke to gay organizations, emphasizing the importance of including gays and lesbians of all colors and backgrounds in the ongoing struggle for racial equality. Integration and crossover radicalism were the keys to true progress, he would argue, one group's gain against oppression is a step forward for all. Radicals "of all stripes" were needed.

Another common theme when he spoke to lesbian and gay groups was the importance of coming out. "Although its going to make problems," the *Alyson Almanac* quotes him as saying, "those problems are not so dangerous as the problems of lying to yourself, to your friends, and missing many opportunities."

Bayard Rustin held fast to his dreams and his truths all his life, and consequently, never missed an opportunity to throw himself into the thick of this century's social struggle for equality.

References:

The Alyson Almanac. Boston: Alyson Publications, 1994-95: 185-186.

Contemporary Black Biography vol. 4. Detroit: Gale Research, 1993: 210-213.

Rustin, Bayard. *Down the Line—The Collected Writings of Bayard Rustin.* Chicago: Quadrangle Books, 1971.

———. *Strategies for Freedom—The Changing Patterns of Black Protest.* New York: Columbia University Press, 1976.

Williams, Julian. *Eyes on the Prize—America's Civil Rights Years, 1954-1965.* New York: Viking Penguin Books, 1987.

—Jerome Szymczak

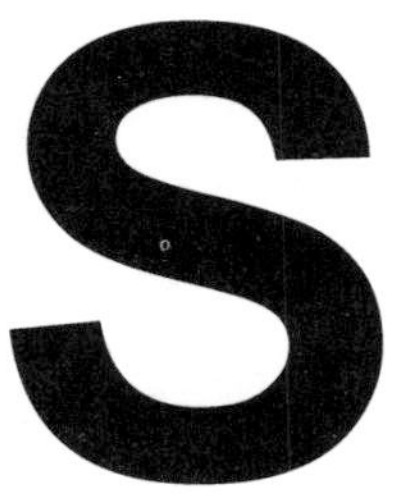

Vita Sackville-West

1892-1962

British author

Known today mostly for her relationship with Virginia Woolf and the magnificent gardens she created at Sissinghurst, Vita Sackville-West was also an extremely successful poet, novelist, biographer, broadcaster, and lecturer.

Victoria Mary Sackville-West was born 9 March 1892 at Knole Castle, Kent. Called Vita because her mother was also named Victoria, Sackville-West was the granddaughter of a Spanish gypsy, Pepita, and Lionel, the second Baron Sackville. Sackville-West's mother had married her cousin, Lionel, the third Baron Sackville. She was their only child; the marriage was not happy. All commentators on Vita Sackville-West's life make note of her troubled relationship with her difficult, flamboyant mother; as well, most note the fact that Sackville-West conceptualized her "nature" in terms of an internal duality which she traced back to the seemingly disparate union between her gypsy and noble maternal grandparents.

Educated at home by governesses until the age of 13, when she attended Miss Woolff's school for girls as a day student, Sackville-West began writing early; these early works remain unpublished. A solitary child for the most part, her childhood was made difficult by her mother's desire for a beautiful, feminine daughter, rather than the tomboy Sackville-West was. Her paternal grandfather, however, proved a steady, though reserved, source of affection. Her teen years were marked by family troubles about the Knole inheritance; these troubles culminated, in 1910, with a spectacular trial in which Sackville-West's maternal uncle unsuccessfully challenged the line of succession to Knole. The estate was entailed upon the oldest legitimate male, at this time Sackville-West's father, Lionel. When he died early in 1928, Sackville-West lost the estate, widely considered to be her first and most enduring passion.

Sackville-West was married in 1913 to a diplomat, Harold Nicolson, who worked in Constantinople and Teheran (as well as in Europe). Nicolson later did editorial duties on the *Evening Standard* and *Action,* and from 1935 to 1945 was the National Labour M.P. for West Leicester. Sackville-West and Nicolson had two sons, Benedict (born 1914) and Nigel (born 1917). Sackville-West also had a pregnancy which ended in a stillbirth in 1915.

Sackville-West's and Nicolson's relationship was unconventional, as both engaged in passionate homosexual partnerships outside of the marriage while maintaining a successful, even happy, marriage. The long-distance nature of their early marriage (Nicolson held various diplomatic positions with the Foreign Office until 1929) may have helped strengthen their relationship. In part, this union was a necessity of the times, which dictated that childbearing happened within marriage and that homosexual relationships could be legally punished. The union also owed something to Sackville-West's internalization of contemporary theories of the "invert," mixed with her desire for the privileges denied women at the time. Inversion theories, proposed originally by Karl Ulrichs and taken up and made popular during Sackville-West's lifetime by Havelock Ellis and Sigmund Freud, suggested that lesbians were male souls trapped in female bodies. Like many lesbians of the time, Sackville-West took delight in cross-dressing, wearing breeches, and calling her costumed self Julian and David. Her son Nigel speaks of "her masculinity, her enduring regret that she was not born a boy ... a boy who would have been sent to schools and a University, who would have learned Greek and Latin, and of whom it would have been assumed throughout his life that he could do things which girls could not do." As Victoria Glendinning (Sackville-West's biographer) states, however, scandal "frightened Vita" so that she was "never in the least tempted to become publicly known as a lesbian. Not only did she have a traditional care for her 'reputation'—and for Harold's—but the secrecy of her affairs added, for her, the element of adventure that she needed."

Sackville-West was a prolific author. Her fiction includes two *Wuthering Heights*-like tales, *Heritage* (1919) and *Grey Wethers* (1923). She wrote several book-length poems, the best known of which is *The Land.* Drafted originally in England in 1925, the poem was revised during Sackville-West's trip to Persia (now Iran), and published in 1926 by Heinemann. *The Land* is a feudal-pastoral overview of Kentish cultivation and agricultural labour history told with a definite nostalgic bent towards the "old" ways. "Poetry in gumboots," Glendinning calls it.

In 1924, Sackville-West began working with the Hogarth Press, owned and run by Virginia and Leonard Woolf. Hogarth published her works (until 1940) to wide popular and critical acclaim. Her first work for them, *Seducers in Ecuador* (1924), is her only experimental work. It is a rather disturbing little novella in which the principle character's ability to distinguish between "reality" and an instinctual, passionate, and imaginative response to life disintegrates. According to Howard Woolmer, *The Edwardians* (1930) which, along with *Family History* (1932), figures characters recognizably based on Leonard and Virginia Woolf, sold nearly 22,000 copies of the expensive version (at 7s6d) within three months. The cheap edition published in 1932 at 3s6d was a "best seller." Sackville-West, who travelled extensively throughout her life, also wrote extremely successful travel books: *Passenger to Teheran* (1926) and *Twelve Days: An account of a journey across the Bakhtiari Mountains in South-Western Persia* (1928). Her biography of her grandmother and mother, *Pepita* (1937), is a moving, entertaining tribute to those flamboyant characters. Along with other biographies (most notably of female saints and Aphra Behn), Sackville-West produced gardening books, a translation of Rilke, collections of *New Statesman* articles, and short stories.

Of particular importance to her lesbian identity are the *roman a clef, Challenge* (1923), and an autobiographical fragment written in

Vita Sackville-West

1920 but published posthumously in Nigel Nicolson's *Portrait of a Marriage* (1973). Both works deal with Sackville-West's overwhelmingly passionate relationship with Violet (Keppel) Trefusis, with whom she briefly eloped to France in 1920. The novel was withdrawn from publication in Britain because of family reaction to its recognizable characters and coded lesbian nature. Sackville-West's relationships with women were intense and enduring; she maintained friendships with women after the passion had died down. Her partners included Rosamund Grosvenor, Dorothy Wellesley, Mary Campbell, and Hilda Matheson. Sackville-West's *King's Daughter* (1929) contains love poems written to her female partners. She met Virginia Woolf in 1922, and began a sexual relationship with her in 1925. Their friendship was most important to both women until Woolf's death in 1941. Out of this relationship, Woolf produced the coded, fantastic "biography," *Orlando*, made into a popular movie, based on Sackville-West's ancestry and personality.

Sackville-West reviewed for the *Nation* beginning in 1924. She did radio broadcasts on both gardening and the "woman question" for the BBC. Her books sold briskly, and she received the Hawthornden Prize for *The Land* in 1927 and the Heinemann Prize for *The Garden* in 1946. She was made a Companion of Honour in 1948, and, as Glendinning notes, the National Book League's 1946 "exhibition of the 100 best books by 'representative authors' since 1920" included *The Land* (along with Nicolson's *Some People*) in its display.

Sackville-West died at home of cancer on the 2nd of June, 1962. Sackville-West's spectacular gardens at Sissinghurst (which she and Nicolson bought as a ruin in 1930 and subsequently developed) are open to the public through the National Trust.

References:

Glendinning, Victoria. *Vita: The Life of Vita Sackville-West.* New York: Penguin, 1983.

Nicolson, Nigel. *Harold Nicolson's Diaries and Letters 1930-39.* Bungay, Suffolk: Fontana, 1969.

Woolmer, Howard. *A Checklist of the Hogarth Press: 1917-1946.* Revere, Pennsylvania: Woolmer/Brotherson, 1986.

—Catherine Nelson-McDermott

Assotto Saint

1957-1994

African-American writer and performer

A man of diverse talents, Assotto Saint was a dancer, choreographer, writer, editor, publisher, and outspoken representative for victims of AIDS. After his premature death from the disease, his friend Franklin Abbott remembered him as "an intense character and fine performer." Abbott continued, "he was quite a beautiful human being. Losing him is just one of our tragedies."

Born Yves Francois Lubin on 2 October 1957 in Haiti, Saint was raised by his mother and never met his father until many years after his birth. "I must have been seven when I realized my attraction to men," wrote Saint in his autobiographical essay "Haiti: A Memory Journey." But knowing he was gay and being gay in his native Haiti were not easy. It wasn't until 1970, on the heels of Stonewall, when he came to New York to visit—then to stay permanently—with his mother that Saint saw there was such a thing as a gay world.

Saint attended college, pursuing a pre-med course of study before being seduced into the world of dance. In the early 1970s he secured a place as a dancer with the Martha Graham Dance Company, but his involvement in the performing arts quickly broadened and he began to write for the stage as well. He subsequently founded the Metamorphosis Theater in New York, where he also served as artistic director. Saint collaborated with his life partner, Jan Holmgren, on several theatrical works that dealt with the lives of black gay men: *Risin' to the Love We Need, New Love Song, Black Fag,* and *Nuclear Lovers.*

During this period Saint was also writing poetry, and his works were widely anthologized during the 1980s. His work was included in *In the Life: A Black Gay Anthology* (Alyson Publications, 1986), *New Men, New Minds* (Crossing Press, 1987); *Gay & Lesbian Poetry in Our Time* (St. Martin's Press, 1988); *Sojourner: Black Gay Voices in the Age of AIDS* (Other Countries Press, 1993); and *Jugular Defenses* (Oscars Press). In addition, he served as poetry editor of the anthology *Other Countries: Black Gay Voices.* Perceiving the need for wider dissemination of black gay literature, Saint also founded the Galiens Press, which published, among other things, two seminal anthologies of black gay poetry. One Galiens publication, *Here to Dare: A Collection of 10 Gay Black Poets,* was nominated for a Lambda Literary Award. "Galiens" is derived from the two words "gay" and "aliens."

Collections of Saint's own work include a chapbook, *Triple Trouble* (published in *Tongues Untied;* GMP; London; 1987) and two collections of poetry: *Stations* (Galiens Press, 1989) and the posthumously published *Wishing for Wings.* His manuscripts and personal papers are archived at the the New York Public Library's Schomberg Museum in the Bronx.

Saint made his voice and presence heard not only in his written and performed work, but also in his activism. He was an impassioned spokesman and one of a growing number of advocates for gay artists suffering from AIDS. According to his friend, Walter Holland, "Assotto was determined to appear as an out HIV-positive artist. He was most concerned about the fact that many black artists went to their deaths in complete secrecy." Holland says that Saint was "fierce in his politics. He told it like it was and he was very astute." He also fiercely advocated the need for black gay writers to be nurtured and for poetry in general to be supported and encouraged. However, he was not ethnocentric in his advocacy, and he fiercely defended his involvement with Holmgren, a Caucasian. Holland has tried to write about Saint in the novel *The March* (Masquerade Books, 1996), but Saint was as complex as he was intense and fascinating, and capturing his essence is no easy task.

Exactly why Saint took on a new name is not clear. However, according to a close friend the name Assotto Saint is far from randomly selected. "Assotto" is derived from a type of African ceremonial drum which presumably has a ritualistic connection as well as a practical function as a form of communication. The name "Saint" is believed to have been taken from the Haitian general and liberator Toussaint L'Ouverture (aka Pierre Dominique). Toussaint is a great symbol of liberation in Haiti and it is thought that it tied Saint to his roots while at the same time being reminiscent of his own rebellious nature and his commitment to civil disobedience and civil insurrection.

In the mid 1980s, Saint returned to Haiti to meet the father he "never met, never saw pictures of, never heard mention of and accepted as a non-entity in my life." The meeting was not particularly successful—his father was unable to accept his son's homosexuality and Saint was greatly frustrated over his father's rude and abrupt manner. The two parted with a handshake. Saint decided to phone his father one last time before leaving Haiti. His half-brother claimed that his father was not in. While Saint and Holmgren ate breakfast, a handwritten note was delivered to him. In the note, his father maintained that it was good that they finally met. He wished his son "good luck," a safe journey, and good health. "I crushed that note in my hand," says Saint in "Haiti: A Memory Journey," "and imagined it was his heart." No great reunion between son and long lost father would take place, and dreams of having at last a loving father were shattered. Saint returned home to live the final and most productive decade of his young life.

References:

Saint, Assotto. "Haiti: A Memory Journey," in *New Men, New Minds,* edited by Franklin Abbott. New York: Crossing Press, 1987.

Conversations with Michelle Karlsberg, Franklin Abbott, and Walter Holfrey.

—Andrea L.T. Peterson

George Santayana

1863-1952

American philosopher and writer

George Santayana is the most polished stylist among American philosophers and is the author of eighteen substantial works on philosophy, a three-volume autobiography, a best-selling novel (*The Last Puritan*, 1936), a play in verse, five volumes of literary and cultural commentary, and two volumes of poetry. Santayana's poetry is often similar to that of A.E. Housman, with whom Santayana compared himself sexually as well. His love poems, usually veiled in Christian imagery and allusion or disguised by ambiguous diction, have been acknowledged by most of his critics as homoerotic.

George Santayana was born Jorge Agustín Nicolás de Santayana y Borrás on 16 December 1863 in Madrid, Spain, the son of Agustín Ruíz de Santayana, a lawyer, and Josefina Borrás y Carbonell, widow of George Sturgis of Boston and mother by him of three older children. His parents had met in the Philippines, where his father and maternal grandfather were in the Spanish civil service.

Santayana's independent-minded mother returned to Boston with her older children while George and his father remained in Spain. When George joined her at the age of nine in 1872, he was still young enough to attend school and master English perfectly. All his life, however, he felt like a misfit, too Spanish for New England, and too Anglo for Spain. This dual nature produced an ironic de-

George Santayana

tachment which allowed him to isolate and identify dispassionately the qualities he found offensive in American life.

In 1882 Santayana entered Harvard University as a student and soon became an instructor there. When in 1898, his departmental colleagues proposed his advancement to assistant professor, homophobic President Charles Eliot jeopardized the promotion by applying such words as "abnormal" and "unnatural" to the young philosopher, probably in reference to his penchant for the company of young men.

In 1893 Santayana's "last real friend," Warwick Potter died of cholera, and he produced a remarkable set of four elegiac sonnets for him. Here the poet claims he is richer for the dead man's gifts to him but confesses, "I scarce know which part may greater be,— / What I keep of you, or you rob from me." Potter comes across as an "idealized figure of male beauty who by dying in his youth is protected from the ravages of time and, being dead, can offer no carnal temptation to the poet."

Because of the silent disapproval of "various people" and despite his popularity as a teacher, Santayana abandoned Harvard to travel around Europe in 1912 when he received his mother's inheritance. His Boston relatives managed his inheritance for him and until the advent of World War II when he moved into a convent in Rome run by an order of English nuns, he was comparatively affluent. He died in the convent on 26 September 1952 of stomach cancer.

Philosophically Santayana was a skeptic, a critical realist and an Aristotlean materialist more concerned with poetic power and qualities of experience and language than with logical and practical approaches to existence and discourse. Although he had faith in man's ability to evolve intellectually, he advocated skepticism as a means to free the mind from prejudice. This skepticism gave rise to his political conservatism; he favored government by honorable men (Plato's timocracy) who were optimally trained, personally disinterested and dedicated.

Although raised a Catholic, he was not a communicant and believed that religious dogma is created by the imagination as poetry and retained for its powers to console. Protestantism, which he felt was sanctimonious and often disingenuous, was alien to his temperament.

Santayana's accomplished style, combined with the brilliance of his ideas, won for him a unique place in American letters. He also created a wealth of memorable aphorisms, such as "Those who cannot remember the past are condemned to repeat it;" "There is no cure for birth and death save to enjoy the interval;" and "The young man who has not wept is a savage, and the old man who will not laugh is a fool." His scholarly reputation waned immediately after his death but revived considerably during the final two decades of the twentieth century.

References:

Cory, Daniel. *Santayana: The Later Years. A Portrait in Letters.* New York: George Braziller, 1963.

Holzberger, William G. *The Complete Poems of George Santayana: A Critical Edition.* Lewisburg, Pennsylvania: Bucknell University Press, 1979.

McCormick, John E. *George Santayana: A Biography.* New York: Alfred E. Knopf, 1987.

Martin, Robert K. *The Homosexual Tradition in American Poetry.* Austin: University of Texas Press, 1979: 110.

Woodward, Anthony. *Living in the Eternal: A Study of George Santayana.* Nashville: Vanderbilt University Press, 1988.

—Jack Shreve

Sappho

c.7th and 6th centuries B.C.

Greek poet

Many critics consider Sappho the greatest female poet of the classical world and the most accomplished and influential of a group of lyric poets who were active in Greece between 650 B.C. and 450 B.C.—a period often designated the Lyric Age of Greece. Although only a minute part of her work remains, Sappho's poetry has been respected and admired since antiquity for its characteristic emotional intensity, directness, simplicity, and revealing use of personal tone. It has also, however, been the subject of much critical controversy, with various scholars debating the precise nature of the eroticism typical of Sappho's verses. Throughout the centuries, she has remained a fascinating subject for poets, novelists, playwrights, and biographers; and, as David M. Robinson has written "nearly every thought in her fragments ... has been borrowed or adapted by some ancient Greek or Roman poet or some modern poet in English, Italian, French, German, or modern Greek."

Classicists point out that very few details of Sappho's biography survive, and that even fewer can be viewed as trustworthy because accounts of her life have become thoroughly interwoven with legend, myth, and rumor. The only standard—but unreliable—source of information about Sappho's life is the *Suidas,* a Greek lexicon compiled about the end of the tenth century. Based on earlier lexicons, scholarly commentaries, and excerpts from the works of historians, grammarians, and biographers, the *Suidas* records that Sappho was a native of Lesbos, an island in Asia Minor, and that she was probably born in either Eresus or Mytilene. Her father's name is given as Scamandronymus, and her mother's as Cleis. Evidence also suggests that Sappho had three brothers, and that her family belonged to the upper class. According to tradition, she lived briefly in Sicily around 600 B.C., when political strife on Lesbos forced her into exile. After returning, she probably married a wealthy man named Cercylas, had a daughter named Cleis, and apparently spent the rest of her life in the city of Mytilene.

Most of Sappho's time in Mytilene was occupied in organizing and running a *thiasos,* or academy for unmarried young women. As was the custom of the age, wealthy families from Lesbos and from the neighboring states would send their daughters to live for a period of time in these informal institutions, in order to be instructed in the proper social graces, as well as in composition, singing, and the recitation of poetry. Intended as a transition between their parental homes and the homes of their future husbands, Sappho's *thiasos* was also a religious community devoted to the cult of the Muses, Aphrodite, and Eros, where beauty and grace were taught as the highest values. Ancient commentary attests to the fact that Sappho's *thiasos* ranked as one of the best and most prestigious in that part of Greece, and as its dedicated teacher and spiritual leader, she enjoyed great renown for having educated generations of young women for fulfilling their social and marital responsibilities. Some legends of Sappho's life indicate that she lived to old age, but others relate that she fell hopelessly in love with a young boatman, Phaon, and, disappointed by their failed love affair, leaped to her death from a high cliff—a story made famous by the Roman poet Ovid in his *Heroides,* but one which has been largely discredited by modern scholars.

Elements of Poetry

The textual history of Sappho's poetry remains as sketchy as her biography. According to the *Suidas,* her substantial body of work was collected into a standard nine-volume edition in the third century B.C.; the arrangement of these volumes was based on the type of meter she used—Sapphic, choriambic, Alcaic, and others—with a whole volume devoted to epithalamia, or marriage songs. Nothing is known about the way Sappho's poetry was transmitted or recorded from her lifetime until the printing of the uniform edition in the third century B.C. Up until the nineteenth century, the only known texts of her poetry were miscellaneous fragments, quoted in the works of several Alexandrian grammarians to illustrate the Lesbian-Aeolic dialect (which was Sappho's native Greek variant), and two poems: the ode to Aphrodite, reprinted by Dionysius of Halicarnassus in his treatise on style, and the poem which begins "Peer of the gods he seems to me," presented by Longinus in *On the Sublime* as an example of polished style. Though composed in approximately the first century B.C., the two treatises, and the two poems by Sappho, were not discovered until the Renaissance, when they came to the attention of Italian scholars. The chief importance of the two poems lay in the fact that they were believed to be preserved in their entirety and therefore constituted the most substantial remains of Sappho to date. In 1898, knowledge of Sappho's works increased even more dramatically when scholars found third-century B.C. papyri containing additional verse fragments. Then, in 1914, archaeologists excavating cemeteries in Oxyrhynchus, Egypt, unearthed coffins made from papier-mâché composed of scraps of paper containing fragments of literary writings, including some by Sappho. These discoveries sparked renewed interest in Sappho and her poetry, inspiring new critical studies of the texts.

Sappho wrote poetry at a time when Greek literature was dominated by the influence of Homer and the epic narrative. Yet the tradition of lyric poetry was even older and had played an important part in Greek history. During Sappho's time, lyric poetry again became extremely popular, enjoying a successful revival. Besides Homer, Sappho seems to have been familiar with the poets Terpander and Alcaeus, both from Mytilene, and Archilochus, a poet from the nearby island of Paros. In turn, her poetry inspired such younger lyric poets as Anacreon, Ibycus, and Theocritus. Typical of Greek lyric poetry in general, Sappho's verses were first and foremost personal, conveying deeply felt emotion in a simple, translucent style, and often driven by a logic of emotion rather than of reason. Music, too, as in all early Greek lyric poetry, served an important function in her works: most of Sappho's poems are monodies, songs composed for the single voice, and intended to be sung to the accompaniment of the lyre. Even though the music of Sappho's

Sappho

lyrics has not survived, many critics have noted and praised the melody and cadence of her poetry. In terms of content, much of Sappho's poetry was occasional, usually meant to commemorate some event taking place in her *thiasos,* but she also composed narrative poetry, religious hymns, and epithalamia. Sources from antiquity have recorded that Sappho was especially famous for the latter, and that she was a frequent, sought-after guest at weddings where she would sing a marriage song composed especially for the couple; scholars believe that Sappho's epithalamia raised this ancient folk tradition to a new level of artistic excellence.

Poetry Has a Profound Influence

Despite the fact that only a miniscule portion of Sappho's total poetic output remains, her verses—or, rather, fragments of her verses—continue to have a powerful effect on readers and critics alike. One of Sappho's most noted translators, Guy Davenport, has written, "many of the fragments are mere words and phrases, but they were once a poem and, like broken statuary, are strangely articulate in their ruin." Indeed, her eloquent expressiveness, the individual voice revealing itself and communicating with the reader, is the trait most frequently singled out as the hallmark of Sappho's style. The speaker in the poems (generally assumed to be Sappho herself) spontaneously exhibits an unusually wide range of emotion, from tender protectiveness and friendship, to erotic longing and jealousy; from playful chiding of her pupils, to extreme anger toward those who have proven disloyal, and outright vilification of the headmistress of a rival *thiasos.* Scholars point out, as well, Sappho's unusual ability to analyze her feelings even as she is enacting them, sacrificing none of the immediacy and intensity of the moment, but simultaneously demonstrating remarkable insight into her own situation. Her sense of humor and proportion remains intact even in times of extreme mental anguish. C. A. Trypanis, among others, cites this combination of restraint and passion as conclusive evidence of Sappho's uniqueness among the Greek poets. Commentators also emphasize, however, that the spontaneous tone of Sappho's poetry is probably deliberate rather than accidental. They point out that her use of vernacular vocabulary instead of the more formal Homeric literary language helped to create the perception of natural speech in her poems. Yet, though she used a less refined language, her poetry exhibits an innate verbal elegance, partially the result of her writing in the melodic Aeolic dialect, and partially because of her use of the graceful Sapphic meter. Consisting of four lines, the Sapphic verse form calls for three lines of eleven syllables each, and a fourth line of five syllables, its meter necessitates the use of three spondees in each line, with variations allowed in the fourth and eleventh syllables of the first three lines, and in the final syllable of the fourth line. It is not known whether she invented the meter that today bears her name, but she must have perfected it and popularized it because it clearly came to be connected with her. Along with mellifluousness, Sappho's poetry exhibits a trademark directness whether she is writing about nature, the gods, or the voluptuous physique of one of her pupils. Willis Barnstone, another eminent translator of her works, concludes, "there is no veil between poet and reader ... Sappho makes the lyric poem a refined and precise instrument for revealing her personal and intense experience of life." The reader is made to constantly focus on Sappho's feelings and perspective, no matter what the subject of the poem.

Reputation Is Slandered, then Recaptured

Sappho's works have been admired for their stylistic merit from her own time onward. In a famous epigram, Plato remarked, "some say the Muses are nine, but how carelessly! Look at the tenth, Sappho from Lesbos." However, while her literary reputation has remained high, Sappho's personal reputation has been controversial, sometimes even to the point of overshadowing her status as a poet. The dispute over her reputation seems to have begun two or three centuries after her death, when the bawdy, irreverent writers of Athenian Middle and New Comedy used Sappho as an easy target for jokes about lesbianism and promiscuity. Rumors flourished, and further accusations—many now considered unfounded—were made: that Sappho was immoral, that she was the lover of Alcaeus, that she instructed her pupils in homosexual practices, and that she seduced Phaon in her old age. The ancient Romans, though they continued the tradition of "passionate Sappho," also paid tribute to her artistry, with Catullus and Horace openly imitating her style. Because of her sinful image, her works were burned in 380 by Bishop Gregory Nazienzen of Constantinople, and later, in 1073, by Pope Gregory VII. By the eleventh century, Sappho's poetry was known only in quotations cited by Alexandrian grammarians and critics, for no manuscript or edition of her work survived the two purges. She was thus virtually unknown in medieval times, except for brief mentions in the works of Giovanni Boccaccio and Francesco Petrarch. When Ovid's *Heroides* was discovered during the Renaissance, the story of Sappho's seduction of Phaon again came to light, but only to confirm her licentious reputation. Despite, or perhaps because of this air of scandal about her, Sappho again became a favorite subject for many prominent authors, and there followed numerous novels, plays, and poems based on her life. Anne Le Fevre published in 1681 in defense of her poetry and her reputation, *Le Poesies d'Anacreon et de Sapho,* but it accomplished little in changing the accepted view of Sappho.

In the nineteenth century, the reputation of Sappho and her works improved. For the European Romantics, she emerged as the symbol of passion. In 1816, the German classicist Friedrich Gottlieb Welcker published "Sappho von einem herrschenden Vorurtheil befreit," a seminal essay that proved pivotal in laying to rest the issue of Sappho's personal life and redirecting the focus of critics to her poetry. During the last two centuries, scholars have indeed concentrated on analyzing the elements of Sappho's style, and studies by such critics as John Addington Symonds, C. M. Bowra, and Hilda Doolittle, among others, have followed in the footsteps of Dionysius of Halicarnassus, Plutarch, and Longinus, who early on saw the extraordinary qualities in Sappho's poetry. Yet, all assessments of her work are intrinsically inconclusive because so little of her work remains.

Though most twentieth-century critics emphasize Sappho's poetic achievement, exploring her themes and imagery, the controversy surrounding her school and her sexual preference has not altogether abated. The true purpose of her *thiasos* still remains something of a mystery: was it mainly a religious association dedicated to the worship of Aphrodite, where young women were taught the fine arts; was it primarily a sort of finishing school intended to prepare young women for marriage; or was it a female retreat where women were instructed in lesbian practices? So entrenched was the opinion that Sappho was sexually deviant that her origin—Lesbian—came to denote female homosexuality, providing the basis for the modern term "lesbian." Modern scholars have grouped themselves around three views of Sappho's sexuality. Some, including

Ulrich von Wilamowitz-Moellendorff (as argued in his *Sappho und Simonides,* 1913) and Edwin Arnold, vehemently subscribed to the theory that Sappho's school was simply an institution of learning for chaste young ladies, and that her imagery, since it is figurative, does not imply that she was a lesbian. Others, D. L. Page, C. M. Bowra, and Werner Jaeger among them, do acknowledge that an element of homosexual love must have existed at Sappho's *thiasos* as well as in her poetry; yet, they point out the importance of not judging Sappho's relationships and emotions by today's standards, for norms of behavior and acceptable expressions of friendship in ancient Greece varied considerably from modern ones. Such critics as Judith P. Hallett, Eva Stehle, and Judy Grahn also emphasize the need for a better understanding of Sappho's historical and social context, and particularly of the position of women in antiquity. Still other commentators unequivocally claim that Sappho was a lesbian, discerning in her poetry the same emotions, concerns, and subtexts found in modern lesbian literature.

References:

Barnard, Mary, trans. *Sappho: A New Translation.* 1958.
Barnstone, Willis, trans. *Sappho: Lyrics in the Original Greek with Translations.* 1965.
Carman, Bliss, trans. *Sappho: One Hundred Lyrics.* 1907.
Cox, Edwin Marion, trans. *The Poems of Sappho.* 1924.
Davenport, Guy, trans. "Sappho," in *Archilochos, Sappho, Alkman: Three Lyric Poets of the Late Greek Bronze Age.* 1980.
———, trans. *Sappho: Poems and Fragments.* 1965.
Groden, Suzy Q., trans. *The Poems of Sappho.* 1967.
Haines, C. R., trans. *Sappho: The Poems and Fragments.* 1926.
Lobel, Edgar, and Denys Page, trans. *Poetarum Lesbiorum Fragmenta.* 1955.
Miller, Marion Mills, and David M. Robinson, trans. *The Songs of Sappho.* 1925.
Roche, Paul, trans. *Sappho: Love Songs.* 1966.
Rossetti, Dante Gabriel, trans. "Sapphic Fragments," in *Poems.* 1870.
Wharton, Henry Thornton, trans. *Sappho: Selected Renderings and a Literal Translation.* 1885.

—Jelena Krstović

José Sarria

Hispanic-American activist and female impersonator

One of the most colorful and outspoken pre-Stonewall political activists is actually a pioneer in gay political theater. Native San Franciscan José Sarria—legendary drag entertainer, self-confessed, tongue-in-cheek "widow" of San Francisco's infamous Emperor Norton, and first out gay person to run for public office—emerged in all his finery from the maelstrom of gay purges and persecutions that were standard operating procedure throughout mid-century America. Urging closeted "nelly queens" to stand up and be counted, stand out and take their prideful place in society, Sarria sounded the rallying cry for acting-up/out brothers and sisters to follow. He did it all, and continues to do it all, in song and high heels. Even today, "on the sunny side of seventy," he remains active as a nationwide AIDS fundraiser with the Imperial Court system he helped found in the 1965.

José Sarria as the Widow Norton. ***Photograph by Rick Gerharter.***

In the late 1940s, José and his sister, Maria, hung out with the bohemian likes of Allen Ginsberg, William Saroyan and even John Steinbeck at the Black Cat in San Francisco's North Beach. In no time at all, Sarria was drawing a Sunday afternoon crowd of hundreds with campy, high-heeled arias from *Carmen* and *Tosca.* Homosexuals soon packed the bar but, according to Sarria in Randy Shilts' *The Mayor of Castro Street,* they were "a dispirited bunch." "He'd be damned if he was going to see far more conventional men (than himself) wallow in self-contempt while he was having a good time," says Shilts. That is when Sarria claims the "preaching began." He turned the traditional form of gay self-deprecation—drag—on its heels and pioneered political theater, blazing a trail for all gay agitprop to follow.

For those precious few hours when Sarria was center-stage, gays in the sterile, oppressive early 1950s could actually be proud of who they were. Hundreds of men were being arrested every month on vice charges, and pleading guilty to anything in an often unsuccessful attempt to maintain their anonymity. Sarria's weekly drag shows were thus both bawdy revivals and the city's first gay news wire. "A blue fungus has hit the parks," Shilts quotes Sarria as telling his fans during a heavy crackdown on sex in the local parks. "It does not appear until about 2 am (and) twinkles like a star," he would add in direct allusion to some of San Francisco's police force.

This does not seem overly political by today's standards—until you note that, at the end of each performance, Sarria would invariably rouse the usually self-deprecating crowd to tearful defiance and pride sans satire. "Jose would make these political comments about our rights as homosexuals," pre-Stonewall activist George Mendenhall told John D'Emilio in *Making Trouble—Essays in Gay History, Politics, and the University*, "and at the end ... he would have everybody in the room stand, and we would put our arms around each other and sing 'God Save Us Nelly Queens' (sometimes stepping outside to be within earshot of police and gay men in jail right across the street). It sounds silly, but if you lived at that time ... to be able to put your arms around other gay men and sing.... We were not really saying 'God Save Us Nelly Queens.' We were saying 'We Have Rights Too.'"

Naturally enough, and in spite of the crackdowns and arrests, gays were already claiming Halloween as their high holy day—and here again Sarria took the lead. On this one evening a year, the infamous San Francisco "Lilly Law" would turn a blind eye to homosexual antics, even going so far as to have the chief of police escort the elegantly gowned Sarria to the center of North Beach, if only for a brief Cinderella star-turn that was to last only until the wee hours of November 1. It was Sarria's one-person campaign that was largely responsible for this one traditional night of "drag-rule."

By 1961, Sarria's politics took tangible form in a run for San Francisco city supervisor. He was the first openly gay person in the United States to run for public office. He knew he had no chance of winning, as he told D'Emilio, but "was trying to prove to my gay audience that I had the right, being as notorious and gay as I was, to run for public office, because people in those days didn't believe you had rights." In the end, he got glowing endorsements and collected well over 6,000 votes—particularly impressive considering that he did no campaigning, simply garnering votes via word-of-mouth. In the process, he forced a traditionally docile gay population to look at their lives in more political terms. As Shilts notes, Sarria's candidacy "stirred the imaginations of the handful of activists who then dared consider political action as a future option.... so few had bothered to consider that no matter what police or judges could deprive them of, they could still vote." As author Richard Dyer notes, the mere act of running "gave a politically explicit edge to the potential for defiance that he found in drag"—one that set a precedent for gay and lesbian political action to follow.

Today, Sarria travels the country as a founder of the Imperial Court system, raising hundreds of thousands of dollars yearly for a variety of AIDS causes—Operation Concern, Open Hand, and AIDS pediatric wards among them. There are over 67 Courts in as many cities raising money through fundraisers and local elections of worthy "Queens and Kings." The San Diego Court even extends its mission across the border to men and women in Tijuana in need of medical supplies and the like.

References:

The Alyson Almanac. Boston: Alyson Publications, 1994-95.

D'Emilio, John. "Gay Politics and Community in San Francisco Since World War II" in *Socialist Review,* February 1981, 22-25.

D'Emilio, John. *Making Trouble—Essays on Gay History, Politics, and the University.* New York: Routledge Press, 1992.

Dyer, Richard. *Now You See It.* New York: Routledge Press, 1990.

Miller, Neil. *Out of the Past—Gay and Lesbian History from 1869 to the Present.* New York: Vintage Books, 1994.

Shilts, Randy. *The Mayor of Castro Street—The Life and Times of Harvey Milk.* New York: St. Martin's Press, 1988.

—Jerome Szymczak

May Sarton

1912-1995

American writer

I do not have to love you
As I loved her,
To be devastated, but,
Angel and surgeon of the psyche,
I am free to love you now
Outside all the myths,
The confused dreams,
Beyond all the barriers,
In the warm natural light
Of simple day.
I am allowed to give you
Unstrained, flowing
Wise-infant
To wise-mother love.

—From *A Durable Fire*

In her first biography, *I Knew a Phoenix*, May Sarton recalled returning as a young girl to Wondelgem, her birthplace and the Belgian town she and her family had been forced to leave after the invasion by the Wehrmacht in 1915. Her family wandered disconsolately about the overgrown garden and the unnaturally solemn house where the rubbish was now knee-deep. Sarton recounts how her mother lifted from the ruins a single piece of Venetian glass that had stayed miraculously intact. Sarton kept this her whole life as "visible proof that it is sometimes the most fragile things that have the power to endure." This is an apt and eloquent description of Sarton herself, the solitary poet who lived out her days in a weathered clapboard house by the sea, writing, communing with friends and nature, following the feminine muse.

Sarton's father was Belgian, an historian of science who eventually taught at Harvard. Her mother, an English artist and designer, was uprooted a second time when the family left Cambridge, England where they had been staying during the war, and relocated to America. Sarton was just four years old when she and her parents moved to Boston. She was educated for eight years at the Shady Hill School in Cambridge, one of the country's earliest progressive schools. By the time she had graduated from Cambridge Public High School, Sarton had decided on a career as an actress.

In spite of her parents' reservations and her own untested talent, Sarton left for New York in 1929 at the age of 17. There she joined New York's Civic Repertory under Eve Le Gallienne, first as an apprentice and eventually as a member. Later, she would form a repertory theater herself, dubbed the Associated Actors Theater,

Inc., a venture which ultimately failed. After six years, Sarton left behind her dream of acting, and embarked on a career in writing.

In 1936, she journeyed to Europe, spending April through August in England, a sojourn she would repeat over the next several years. There Sarton met some of the most prominent English writers of the period, including Julian Huxley and Virginia Woolf.

In 1945, while vacationing in Santa Fe, Sarton met Judy Matlack, a professor of English at Simmons College. In *Honey in the Hive*, Sarton's lovely tribute to Matlack, she wrote: "It was not her looks that impressed me that first afternoon but the eager and attentive way she asked questions.... During the 10 days when we were alone, friendship became intimacy and I knew I was in love. And Judy? As things got more intense and we began to talk about possibly sharing an apartment in Cambridge, Judy began to have doubts ... Did we have what it takes for a lasting bond?... I was 33 and she was 47, and had never been loved as I loved her."

Sarton and Matlack lived together for 13 years. But in the late 1950s, shortly after the death of her father (her mother had died of cancer in 1950), Sarton moved to Nelson, New Hampshire, due in part to a crisis of faith, believing she had failed as a writer. Matlack stayed behind in Cambridge, and the two remained close friends throughout their life. Later, Sarton resettled in York, Maine, where she resided for the last 20 years of her life.

There were other romantic attachments, including infatuations with the writers Elizabeth Bowen and Louise Bogan. These relationships were intimate, if occasionally emotionally lopsided. It is uncertain whether they were erotic in nature. In interviews Sarton has referred to herself occasionally as bisexual and claims to have had a long affair with a man when she was 26. She continued to have love affairs into her 60s. Of these affairs, she once wrote, "They have been spiritual rather than physical adventures, in essence, and by them I have grown."

Although Sarton has often been characterized as a solitary writer, her personal diaries recount just how social and popular a person she was. A gracious host, she was nevertheless frustrated by these distractions from writing. For Sarton, work was a way of bringing order to chaos; it kept her grounded and at ease.

Sarton had professional frustrations of another kind as well. During the first third of her career, she had received a fair amount of critical acclaim. But the latter portion of her career was often marred by ambivalent, even harsh reviews of her work. *Simplistic*, *sentimental*, *genteel*, and *privileged*, were some of the adjectives applied to her novels and poetry. Her popularity among the reading public, however, continued to grow.

Like Virginia Woolf, Sarton wrote for the common reader, and when writing, behaved as if the critics did not exist. However, it is clear from her journals that she suffered moments of great self-doubt and was often quite hurt by negative reviews, or worse, by simply being ignored. She had bouts with depression throughout her life, and on one occasion felt so beleaguered that she almost stopped writing entirely. Sarton's reputation developed primarily through word of mouth. She received many letters from readers, especially women, who responded warmly to the courageous, poignantly independent women of her novels. She also received tribute and support from other writers. Her files contain letters from Marianne Moore, Archibald MacLeish, Leonard Woolf, among others.

At 45, with both parents now dead, Sarton discovered a new measure of freedom as a writer. She believed that without this new freedom she could never have written what was to be her most famous and controversial novel, *Mrs. Stevens Hears the Mermaids Singing*. In this novel, Sarton tacitly disclosed her homosexuality to the reading public, a terribly risky thing to do in 1968 when it was published. Sarton lost at least one job because of this, including a teaching position. When asked in an interview what the greatest risk in writing was, she said:

May Sarton

> Giving yourself away ... for me the risk was coming out as a homosexual, which I did in *Mrs. Stevens*.... I came out long before most people did and it cost me jobs, but I was very relieved when I had done it. I think the work has gotten steadily better as a result, although the lesbian theme doesn't necessarily come into the books. It's there somewhat, but I haven't written a lesbian novel—nor shall I.

In today's present climate of disclosure and indiscretion, Sarton's novels and poetry seem almost old-fashioned. Sarton never dealt with homosexuality in an explicit way in her fiction, and she is noticeably reticent about the subject in her letters and journals. But this was chiefly a matter of taste, for Sarton neither denied nor avoided her homosexuality. There were simply other, more universal themes that she wished to address. She was an essential humanist, with a great appreciation for mystery and the varieties of human experience. She often addressed the theme of "artists in life"—the conflict between artistry and living, and emphasized the importance of love that goes beyond eroticism. In one of her more recent novels, *The Magnificent Spinster*, Sarton stressed again relationships of permanence rather than passion, explored with great insight the various stages of grief, and continued to validate and elucidate the lives of older women.

"It is my hope," Sarton commented in a recent critical review of her work, "that all the novels, the books of poems, and the autobiographical works may come to be seen as a whole, the communication of a vision of life that is unsentimental, humorous, passionate, and, in the end, timeless."

In July 1995, Sarton died of breast cancer at the age of 83.

References:

Contemporary Novelists. Vol. 3, Detroit: St. James, 1996.

Daziel, Bradford Dudley, ed. *May Sarton: An Anthology of the Journals, Novels, and Poems of May Sarton.* New York: W. W. Norton & Company, Inc., 1991.

Evans, Elizabeth. *May Sarton Revisited.* (Twayne's United States Authors Series) Boston: Twayne Publishers, 1989.

Gussow, Mel. "May Sarton, Poet, Novelist and Individualist, Dies at 83" in *New York Times*, 18 July 1995, p. B12.

Hammon, Karla. 1978. "To Be Reborn: An Interview with May Sarton" in *May Sarton: Woman and Poet,* edited by Constance Hunting. Orono: The National Poetry Foundation, University of Maine, 1982.

Oliver, Myrna. "May Sarton: Prolific Poet and Novelist" in *Los Angeles Times*, 22 July 1995, p. A.22

Sarton, May. *At Seventy: A Journal.* New York: W. W. Norton & Company, Inc., 1984.

———. *A Durable Fire.* New York: W. W. Norton & Company, Inc., 1972.

———. *Encore: A Journal of the Eightieth Year.* New York: W. W. Norton & Company, Inc. 1993.

———. *Honey in the Hive: Judith Matlack, 1898–1982.* Boston: Warren Publishing Company, 1988.

———. *I Knew a Phoenix: Sketches for an Autobiography.* Toronto: Rinehart & Company, Inc., 1959.

———. *A World of Light: Portraits and Celebrations.* New York: W. W. Norton & Company, Inc., 1976.

Shelley, Dolores. "A Conversation with May Sarton" in *May Sarton: Woman and Poet,* edited by Constance Hunting. Orono: National Poetry Foundation, University of Maine, 1982.

Sherman, Susan, ed. *May Sarton Among the Usual Days: A Portrait.* New York: W.W. Norton & Company, Inc., 1993

Simpson, Marita and Martha Wheelock, eds. *May Sarton: A Self-Portrait.* New York: W.W. Norton & Company, Inc., 1982.

—Lynda Schrecengost

Sarah Schulman

1958-

American writer

Sarah Schulman has written several highly acclaimed novels, plays, and innumerable pieces of journalism. Her fiction and theater is peopled with New York lesbian protagonists and their friends and lovers. These characters are keen-sighted, making astute, often darkly humorous observations about the world in which they live. Their immediate world is Manhattan's tough Lower East Side, where they struggle to make a living and to maintain a sense of dignity and integrity, often in the face of tremendous odds: betrayal, personal loss, poverty, family rejection, AIDS, and homophobia. Schulman's characters are witnesses to their time, as Schulman is to hers. They are chroniclers in an era of forgetting. Critics have praised Schulman's handling of political themes in her fiction; she does not, however, subscribe to the idea that art or personal success is a substitute for political action. In her view, organizing and participating in direct action politics are the necessary means for building political power and creating positive change.

Schulman is an activist and analyst, as well as a writer. She has been involved in feminist organizations, the peace movement, the reproductive rights movement, gay liberation, AIDS Coalition To Unleash Power (ACT UP), and was one of the founding members of the Lesbian Avengers, a direct action lesbian rights organization. Her fiction and nonfiction writings record, interrogate, and contribute to the political and intellectual life of this country. So do her actions.

Born 28 July 1958, Sarah Miriam Schulman was raised in a Jewish household in New York City by her parents, David Schulman and Gloria Yevish Schulman. She has a sister and a brother, both younger. As she describes her early life in her preface to *My American History*: "From childhood I was emotionally a social realist." This outlook was partly influenced by her mother's career as a social worker—a career that also meant involvement in political life and raising children who were socially conscious. Her father was a doctor. Both parents read to their children before bed and gave books as rewards; one of the first books Schulman remembers receiving was *The Diary of Anne Frank*, particularly important to her for its example that Jewish girls could be writers. Her grandmother, Dora Yevish, was also a loving and supportive influence. Schulman wrote throughout her childhood, mostly histories and historical plays. She was a young intellectual and took herself seriously.

As a teenager Schulman faced family humiliation after her father caught her in a romantic embrace with a high school girlfriend, a lover. As she describes the incident in the preface to *My American History*, she was "emotionally rejected from [her] family and never allowed back in." Later, she went to college for a while, worked several jobs, and become involved in activism. She ended up in Cook County jail for a night for participating in a demonstration. She dropped out of college.

Back in New York City in the early 1980s Schulman was writing journalism for feminist and alternative publications, such as *Womanews* and *off our backs*. As she became more involved in the reproductive rights movement, she met Maxine Wolfe, an activist and environmental psychology professor, who became her mentor and friend. Schulman writes in *My American History* that much of what she has learned about political organizing she learned from Wolfe. Schulman also joined a theater company, collaborating with Robin Epstein on plays that were performed at University of the Streets in New York, and, later, writing and co-producing others that premiered at Women's One World (WOW) Cafe.

Schulman Publishes Her First Novel

Schulman was also working on her first novel, *The Sophie Horowitz Story*, which was rejected by several publishers before it was accepted and published in 1984 by Naiad Press, a feminist press based in Florida. The protagonist, Sophie Horowitz, is a journalist whose search for a story gets her caught up in the investigation of a crime. In a scholarly article published in *New Lesbian Criticism: Literary and Cultural Readings*, Sally Munt describes Schulman's first novel as part of the genre of lesbian crime fiction, but at the same time distanced from this genre through "the employment of a postmodern perspective," which uses such techniques as parody, excess, fragmentation, and self-reflexiveness. As Munt points out, this strategy is not political realism, like much lesbian crime writing. Roles and identities are not fixed, but are constantly reconstructed and undermined. Towards the end of the novel, Sophie's description of working on the story is self-conscious in its literariness—it can refer back to its own construction, to the writing of the novel: "The story was almost over. Soon I'd have to sit down and write it. There's a certain relief when that moment comes."

Girls, Visions, and Everything, Schulman's second novel, was published by Seal Press in 1986. Lila Futuransky, like Sophie Horowitz, is also a writer. Lila writes fiction that does not seem to get published. She and her friends are dykes about town in New York's East Village, who perform and hang out at a place called the Kitsch-In. They critique what they call "fake social realism" and in their Worst Performance Festival, they parody the liberal avant-garde art scene and the critics who applaud self-indulgent, socially irrelevant work. Poor, and stuck in New York's summer heat, Lila begins a romance with Emily, who works in the theater. Lila keeps looking to the Beats for a model of adventure and romance (and a good marketing strategy for lesbians); in particular, Lila repeatedly thumbs through Jack Kerouac's *On the Road*. Isabel, who has borrowed Lila's copy of the book, observes, "I guess the road is the only image of freedom that an American can understand." And in the end Lila is torn between that pull and committing to her relationship with Emily.

Though *Girls, Visions and Everything* received favorable reviews, and Schulman was earning respect as a writer, she was still relatively low-profile outside the gay and lesbian community. And she was still working as a waitress to support herself. While working on her third novel, Schulman went to the MacDowell Artists' Colony for a two-week residency, where she met other artists. This stay had a major impact on her views of herself as an artist and it fed her interests in theater, dance, performance art and experimental film. Not long after, she and Jim Hubbard co-founded the Lesbian and Gay Experimental Film Festival.

Dutton Takes *After Delores*

At the suggestion of a stranger, Schulman sent *After Delores*, her third novel, to Carole DeSanti, an editor at Dutton, a mainstream press. DeSanti, who would become Schulman's editor at Dutton for the next several years and three novels, was interested in *After Delores*, which Dutton published in 1988. The novel won the American Library Association Gay/Lesbian Book Award and was a finalist in the Lambda Literary Book Awards. In the novel, Schulman permits the unnamed narrator, who is seeking revenge for the pain caused by Delores' rejection of her, a wide range of emotional responses—some of them ugly. Operating on an alternative sense of justice, the narrator eventually avenges the murder of an acquaintance by killing the murderer. But this act does not resolve her personal feelings of injustice. She is still hurt. She still misses Delores.

Since *People in Trouble*, winner of the 1990 Words Project for AIDS Award and a Lambda Book Report bestseller, Schulman's novels have consistently addressed and reflected the gay and lesbian community's organization around AIDS. Schulman calls *People in Trouble* a "social realist" novel about AIDS and it is the first novel about AIDS activism. It also calls into question the role of art in effecting political change. Kate, an artist, insists that "artwork is very political. It teaches people to see things in a new way. My artwork is my political work. Form is content. New forms are revolutionary." Molly, her younger lover, responds, "I don't think you would be satisfied with that answer if it was happening to you." Kate, through her involvement in Justice, an AIDS activist group, begins to change her views. Her installation piece titled "People in Trouble" becomes instead a political action when she sets it on fire, accidentally killing the real estate giant who was evicting people with AIDS from their apartments in the process.

Schulman told Milyoung Cho in a 1993 interview for *BOMB* magazine that the original title for her fifth novel, *Empathy*, included the modifier "The Cheapest of Emotions." It referred to being liberal. But she changed it, because "even something as banal as empathy doesn't exist in the way America views gay people." The families of the gay characters are implicated in this lack, a subject that Schulman later takes on with even more force in her novel *Rat Bohemia*. The reality of AIDS' death toll is also omnipresent as Anna flips to the obituary pages of the newspaper help her to "keep up with her friends." *Empathy* received great critical attention and secured Schulman's place as a talented writer who keeps important issues alive in her work.

Collected Journalism Reaches Wider Audience

My American History: Lesbian and Gay Life During the Reagan/Bush Years, a collection of Schulman's essays, speeches, and news articles written from 1981 to 1994, mainly for gay and lesbian and alternative presses, was published by Routlege in 1994. In the foreword to the book, Urvashi Vaid describes Schulman as "an original and rigorous political analyst" who has "created a record, a history, that is invaluable." The pieces collected here tell about events, personal and political struggles, that were by and large ignored by the mainstream press. Schulman, as both witness and participant, fills in many of the gaps and erasures of this country's "official history" over the past fifteen years. On a national book tour, she also shared many of these stories and forgotten names with audiences who might otherwise have never heard them.

Rat Bohemia, Schulman's most recent novel, may be her most successful yet. Edmund White, in the 28 January 1996 *New York Times Book Review*, pays tribute to her writing about AIDS without sentimentality here, in a book "that refuses to find transcendence in the act of dying." The characters, buffeted by loss, cannot fully mourn. Funerals are part of their daily lives. So is their alienation and emotional abuse at the hands of their family members. As Schulman told Cynthia White in an December 1995 interview for *Outlines* during her book tour for the novel, "Being treated poorly by your family because you're gay, is probably the only thing that all gay people have in common besides coming out. Yet, it's not part of the political discourse." What Schulman recommends in an interview with Kore Alexis for the New York Weekly, *HOMO XTRA*, is that "we have to elevate it out of the family fight, into the arena of cultural crisis, which is what it is."

Another painful reality acknowledged by the characters of *Rat Bohemia* is the function of the closet in the mainstream success of gay and lesbian writers. Rita confronts the novelist Muriel Kay Starr, a lesbian who is not even out in her book's author bio. *Rat Bohemia*'s "appendix" contains the fictional first four chapters of Starr's novel *Good and Bad*, which recast in "straight" versions some of *Rat Bohemia*'s painful stories. In a review of the novel for *LA Weekly*, Marina Rosenfeld says the "'sanitized' pseudo-novel" within the novel "demonstrates the ultimate act of erasure: the sin is not indifference, but active war on gay people's right to live."

Sarah Schulman, in her writing and political activism, continues to challenge this kind of erasure. The quality of her work, which has never denied openly lesbian content, commands that it be taken seriously as part of our national literature.

Current Address: 406 East 9th Street, New York, New York 10009.

References:

Alexis, Kore. "Book Talk" in *HOMO XTRA*, 6 January 1996.

Bronski, Michael. "Cross-over Dreams: Sarah Schulman Says Her Books Are for Everyone" in *Boston Phoenix*, 3 November 1995.

Cho, Milyoung. "Sarah Schulman" in *BOMB*, Winter 1993: 12-13.

Contemporary Authors, Vol. 118. Detroit, Gale Research, 1986.

Graham, Renee. "Scraping Out Life on Society's Edge" in *Boston Globe*, 14 November 1995, 79.

Metz, Holly. "Sarah Schulman; Author, Lesbian Activist; Interview" in *Progressive* 58, October 1994: 37.

Munt, Sally. "'Somewhere over the Rainbow ...': Postmodernism and the Fiction of Sarah Schulman" in *New Lesbian Criticism: Literary and Cultural Readings*. New York, Columbia University Press, 1990: 33-50.

Rosenfeld, Marina. "Love in the Rat Zone: Tales from an Exile Culture" in *LA Weekly*, 10-16 November 1995, 29.

Schulman, Sarah. *My American History: Lesbian and Gay Life During the Reagan/Bush Years*. New York, Routledge, 1994.

Vaid, Urvashi. Foreword to *My American History: Lesbian and Gay Life During the Reagan/Bush Years*.

White, Cynthia. "Sarah Schulman: New York to the Apple's Core" in *Outlines*, December 1995.

White, Edmund. "A Witness to Her Time" in *New York Times Book Review*, 28 January 1996, 31.

—Karen Helfrich

Carol Seajay

American publisher, activist, and writer

Carol Seajay

Carol Seajay's work as a publisher and writer is informed by a sense of activism which has created a powerful network of women and information for the past 20 years. In 1976, she co-founded the feminist bookstore Old Wives Tales; she is also the publisher and editor of *Feminist Bookstore News* and she has contributed to *Ms.* magazine on the topic of feminist books and bookstores.

The women-in-print movement is both a social and political part of the feminist movement which recognizes that women need to control the entire means of production in order to get the truth of women's lives into print. Seajay describes the drive of the movement as "a vision that if you gathered this information and put it in women's hands, the whole world would change."

This movement grew out of the necessity to gather and print the truth about women's lives and to connect women through print. As Seajay explains in an interview with Kate Brandt, "Fifteen, twenty years ago, there was such a clear sense that women were *not* in print. Women existed in print in the male image only—which is hard to imagine at this point in time, that there really were not lesbian novels with happy endings."

While working for the feminist bookstore A Woman's Place in Oakland, California, Seajay attended the first annual Women in Print Conference. When the women attending the conference realized that they could benefit from the regular communication of a newsletter, Seajay volunteered to help. Since 1976, she has published and edited *Feminist Bookstore News,* a bimonthly magazine based in San Francisco. It represents over 100 bookstores and is distributed to presses and booksellers around the world.

To begin with, the five largest bookstores each put in 100 dollars. As Seajay said in her interview with Kate Brandt, "There was always an understanding that those stores that could afford to, put in more, and the stores that are tiny and [staffed by] volunteers, or are just surviving, put in less." The newsletter is funded in such a way that both large and small bookstores can participate.

Seajay runs *Feminist Bookstore News* full time. The newsletter has grown to include book reviews, discussions, debates, searches for out of print books, announcements, profiles of feminist bookstores, tips on new product lines, conferences and related trends.

Seajay is a writer as well as editor and publisher of *Feminist Bookstore News*. Her contributions to *Ms.* magazine include "20 Years of Feminist Bookstores" an essay describing the growth of feminist bookstores and the relationship of bookstores to the women's movement. In this essay she says of the women who enter these bookstores, "Once they made it through the doorway, they took what they found and changed their lives—left abusive relationships, found new self-images, came out, found sisterhood and a community."

In a more recent essay, "Feminist Bookstores Fight Back," Seajay describes the changing market for feminist bookstores as large chain bookstores have begun to target feminist book buyers and have tried to edge smaller bookstores out of the market. The Feminist Bookstore Network held a Strategic Planning Conference to discuss the future of feminist bookstores and created a strategy to combat the large book chains which includes National Feminist Bookstore Week, Feminist Book Awards, and developing a catalogue of feminist books which also includes a list of feminist bookstores in the United States and Canada.

Seajay's short story, "As Important as a Lamp," is included in *Dykescapes*, a collection of lesbian short stores edited by Tina Portillo. The story is told from the perspective of Jean, a woman involved in a relationship with an abusive lesbian partner. During a violent attack by her partner, Jean processes the messages of survival that she has gotten from women at a battered women's shelter. The story ends as Jean walks away from the house and the abusive partner.

Seajay's involvement in the vision of the women in print movement is reflected in the many ways that she herself is involved with women's words. Through her bookstore, the Feminist Bookstore Network, her essays and her fiction she creates and promotes positive images for all women.

Current Address: c/o *The Feminist Bookstore News*, P.O. Box 882554, San Francisco, California 94188.

References:

Brandt, Kate. "Carol Seajay Spreading the Word: Keeping Connected with *Feminist Bookstore News*," in *Happy Endings: Lesbian Writers Talk about Their Lives and Work.* Tallahassee, Florida: Naiad Press, 1993: 141-150.

Findlen, Barbara. "Bold Types," in *Ms.* January/February 1991: 65.

Seajay, Carol. "As Important as a Lamp," in *Dykescapes*, edited by Tina Portillo. Boston: Alyson Publications, 1991.

———. "Books: 20 Years of Feminist Bookstores," in *Ms.* July/August 1992: 60-63.

———. "Feminist Bookstores Fight Back," in *Ms.* May/June 1995: 68-71.

—Danielle M. DeMuth

Randy Shilts

1951-1994

American journalist

Randy Shilts, an openly gay television and print journalist, wrote three acclaimed books that chronicled contemporary gay and lesbian political, health and social issues. He was one of the first journalists to recognize AIDS as a critical health issue, and his second book, *And the Band Played On: Politics, People, and the AIDS Epidemic* (St. Martin's, 1987), is the definitive study of the spread of the epidemic in the early 1980s.

Born on 8 August 1951, in Davenport, Iowa, Randy Martin Shilts grew up in the Chicago suburb of Aurora, Illinois. His father, Bud Shilts, was a salesman, and his mother, Norma Shilts, was a homemaker. Both were Methodists and political conservatives.

At age twenty, Shilts announced that he was gay to his family and friends while attending Portland Community College in Portland, Oregon. He completed his education at the University of Oregon in Eugene, majoring first in English and later in journalism. He was the managing editor of the campus newspaper and became the head of the Eugene Gay People's Alliance.

After receiving his B.S. degree in 1975, Shilts became the Northwest correspondent for the *Advocate*, a gay publication. He moved to San Francisco shortly thereafter, where, as a staff writer with good research and writing skills, he reinvigorated the *Advocate*'s news coverage. In retrospect, among his most important articles were several detailing the alarming spread of sexually transmitted diseases among gay men amidst the indifference of government, medical and gay leaders. He resigned from the *Advocate* in 1978, partly because of editorial differences with its owner and publisher, David Goodstein.

Shilts, meanwhile, contributed freelance reports about San Francisco's burgeoning homosexual community and about local politics to the city's public television station, KQED, from 1977 to 1980, and to Oakland's independent station, KTVU, from 1979 to 1980. The income from these reports enabled him to commence an extensive career as a freelance writer on gay and lesbian issues for several major American newspapers and magazines. His first book, *The Mayor of Castro Street: The Life and Times of Harvey Milk* (St. Martin's, 1982), intertwined the story of the slain gay leader with the emergence of gay political power in San Francisco in the 1970s. Shilts received national attention as his book was critically acclaimed by both mainstream and gay publications.

The San Francisco Chronicle hired Shilts as a staff reporter in 1981, making him the first openly gay journalist to write for a major daily newspaper. Initially assigned to cover the gay community, his articles about an alarming new disease striking gay men were among the first reports on AIDS in the mainstream press. He eventually exposed the indifference of the Reagan administration and the slow response of the medical and scientific communities to AIDS. But, he also faulted anonymous sex commonly practiced in gay bathhouses for the spread of the disease, and criticized some gay leaders for viewing AIDS primarily as a public relations problem rather than as a medical crisis. Shilts was detested by many homosexuals for his early advocacy of lifestyle changes and safe sex practices, which many gay men initially saw as infringements on their hard-won cultural and sexual freedoms.

Randy Shilts

Based on Shilts' years of investigative journalism, *And the Band Played On: Politics, People, and the AIDS Epidemic*, documented the spread of AIDS from its possible origins to its global impact. Widely praised in the mainstream press, it was a finalist for the National Book Award in the nonfiction category, and won its author the American Society of Journalists and Authors Outstanding Author Award of 1988. It was adapted for a movie that was initially aired by the Home Box Office cable network in September 1993. Despite its commercial success, Shilts remained disappointed that his book failed to reverse government policies and personal lifestyle changes that would curtail the epidemic. In 1986 he himself had tested positive for antibodies to HIV, the virus that causes AIDS.

Shilts' final book, *Conduct Unbecoming: Lesbians and Gays in the U.S. Military, Vietnam to the Persian Gulf* (St. Martin's, 1993), was an exhaustive history of an explosive public issue at the time of its publication. It exposed the military's homophobia and hypocrisy, documenting its selective enforcement of its ban on homosexuals in its ranks. The book was favorably reviewed by the mainstream and gay press and was on the *New York Times* bestsellers list for six weeks. However, its author was lambasted by some lesbians and gays for his refusal to identify—to "out"—his sources in the military who were closeted homosexuals.

Researching and writing *Conduct Unbecoming*, coupled with his extensive writing for the *Chronicle* and other publications, hastened the decline in Shilts' health. He developed full-blown AIDS in 1992. On Memorial Day 1993, he participated in a commitment ceremony with his lover, Barry Barbieri, a film student.

Randy Shilts died from AIDS on 17 February 1994, at his ten-acre ranch along the Russian River in Guerneville, California. His life and work were commemorated in numerous articles in both the mainstream and gay press. His papers are held by the James C. Hormel Gay and Lesbian Center at the San Francisco Public Library.

References:

Contemporary Authors, vol. 127. Detroit: Gale Research, 1989.

Current Biography Yearbook, 1993. New York: H. W. Wilson, 1993.

Dutka, Elaine. "The Shilts Legacy Lives On," in *Los Angeles Times*, 22 February 1994: F1, 8.

Grimes, William. "Randy Shilts, Author, Dies at 42; One of the First to Write About AIDS," in *New York Times*, 18 February 1994: D17.

Malinowski, Sharon, ed. *Gay and Lesbian Literature.* Detroit: Gale Research, 1994.

Newsmakers. 1993 Cumulation. Detroit: Gale Research, 1993.

Steitmatter, Rodger. *Unspeakable: The Rise of the Gay and Lesbian Press in America.* Boston: Faber and Faber, 1995.

—Joseph M. Eagan

Charles Shively

1937-

American educator and activist

A gay scholar, poet, activist, and teacher, Charles Shively is among the most outrageous figures in the gay liberation movement—at least as far as people like Pat Buchanan and Peter LaBarbera are concerned. Buchanan calls Shively a heretic and regards him as a leader in the attack on family values. LaBarbera attacks Shively's books about Walt Whitman, *Drum Beats* and *Calamus Lovers*, in *Lambda Report*, a radical right publication whose goal is to "monitor" homosexual activity in American universities. Shively sees criticisms from such figures as clear signals that his work is having exactly the effect he intends.

Charles Shively was born in Stonelick Township, Ohio, near Cincinnati on 8 December 1937 to Florence Lillian Potrafke and Mearl Carlton Shively. Both of his parents were born in 1916. His mother was born in Cincinnati, Ohio and raised on a farm near Williamsburg, Ohio. She attended a one-room school and received a seventh grade education. Shively's paternal grandmother was divorced and worked in a shoe factory to support her family. Due to an injury, she was laid off and Shively's father, the eldest of three children, was forced to quit school and take a job in the shoe factory to help support his family. As a result, Shively was the first in his family to graduate from high school. After high school he went on to earn an A.B. from Harvard, an M.S. from the University of Wisconsin, and a Ph.D. from Harvard.

Now, as a professor of American Studies at the University of Massachusetts, Shively has dedicated his life to removing the social and cultural "filters" through which history, particularly gay and lesbian history, is read. He believes that those filters—religion, assumptions about race and class, the myth of objectivity, etc.—

suppress whole bodies of important knowledge by hindering our ability to acknowledge and celebrate our sexuality. Specifically, his work has focused on an attempt to liberate Whitman from the closet in which filtered history has placed him. Shively says that his primary effort has been to provide an anarchist theory of sexual action. His essays accomplish that goal by combining "high" social theory with discussions of the political implications of oral sex and sexual fantasy.

Shively has been active in the Gay Liberation Front in Boston since 1970, working to organize the publication committee that has produced *Fag Rag* since June of 1971. Besides *Drum Beats* and *Calamus Lovers*, which document Whitman's homosexuality and claim that both Abraham Lincoln and George Washington had homosexual affairs, Shively has published *A History of the Conception of Death in America, 1650-1860* and edited *The Collected Works of Lysander Spooner* and *Love, Marriage and Divorce and the Sovereignty of the Individual.* His articles include "Phantasy Revolution" (in *Lavender Culture*), "Cosmetics as an Act of Revolution" and "Old and Gay" (in *Pink Triangles, Radical Perspectives on Gay Liberation*), and "Beyond the Binary: Race and Sex" (in *Black Men/ White Men, A Gay Anthology*). In general, these works all reveal Shively's dedication to telling the truth as he sees and reads it. Shively says that people go out of their way to avoid noticing truth, particularly truth about class and sexuality; he uses as an example the inadequate discussion of gay issues in David Reynolds' recent biography of Whitman. However, Shively's truth telling is not confined to pointing out straight resistances to gay and lesbian reality; he has also made a point of dealing as honestly as he can with issues that the mainstream gay and lesbian movements sometimes neglect: class, race, and sexual practice, for example.

Shively says that he believes that working class sexuality is "different," more direct and having an earlier onset, than middle class sexuality. He remarks that he was surprised by what seemed to him to be the sexual immaturity of Harvard men when he first arrived there, joking that as he understood it Harvard men masturbated while they were undergraduates, then moved into sexual activity with others in graduate school. (He adds, though, that he hears that sexual maturity among Harvard men comes earlier today.) While these remarks are clearly entertaining, they also exemplify Shively's understanding of the relationship between the personal and the political. He acknowledges how his race, class, gender, and sexual perspectives clarify and limit his vision, then uses them to read the world and to challenge received ideology.

Shively's work as an academic and as an activist challenges us to speak openly about sex and sexuality and to embrace them as important sources of knowledge. He helped organized the Committee of Lesbian and Gay Historians at the American Historical Convention in 1972 and continues to introduce lesbian and gay history courses at the University of Massachusetts. He looks upon his academic work as essential to his activism because it helps him bring an awareness of lesbian and gay issues to groups—students and academics—that might otherwise be inclined to see those issues as divorced from their work.

Current Address: 2 Broadway Terrace, Cambridge, Massachusetts 02139.

Charles Shively. *Photograph by Timothy Mcmanus.*

References:

LaBarbera, Peter. "L.A. Educator Asserts Lincoln Had Homosexual Affairs," in *Lambda Report*, April-June 1995: 1-2.

———. "Prof. Shively's 'Censored' Lincoln," in *Lambda Report*, April-June 1995: 2.

Shively, Charles. *Calamus Lovers: Walt Whitman's Working-Class Camerados.* San Francisco: Gay Sunshine Press, 1987.

———. *Drum Beats: Walt Whitman's Civil War Boy Lovers.* San Francisco: Gay Sunshine Press, 1989.

———. *A History of the Conception of Death in America, 1650-1860.* New York: Garland, 1988.

———. Interview with Michelle Gibson, 25 March 1996.

———. *Nuestra Señora de los Dolores: The San Francisco Experience.* Boston: Good Gay Poets, 1975.

—Michelle Gibson

Michelangelo Signorile

1960-

American journalist

As a columnist for the now-defunct gay weekly *Outweek*, Michelangelo Signorile came to national attention on the back of a

Michelangelo Signorile

phenomenon that came to be known as "outing"—the exposing of public figures as gay. The controversy, both inside and outside of the gay community, over the tactic and the passion (critics would say "stridency") of Signorile's denunciations of those closeted gays he felt most harmed the gay community, helped position Signorile in the eye of the storm. As the preeminent practitioner of outing, and its most outspoken apologist, from 1990 through early 1994, Signorile become as hot a topic as outing itself.

Since those heady years, a kinder, gentler Signorile has emerged, as a contributing writer to *Out* magazine and most apparently in his second book, *Outing Yourself: How to Come Out as Lesbian or Gay to Your Family, Your Friends, and Your Coworkers* (Random House, 1995), a low-key self-help manual about the coming-out process.

Signorile grew up in close-knit Italian-American family in Brooklyn, New York. In his book *Queer in America: Sex, the Media, and the Closets of Power* (Random House, 1993), Signorile remembers his father calling him a "sissy" for wanting to play with dolls. Signorile was five at the time and was not sure what a sissy was exactly, but he pinpoints it as the first in a long series of painful slights and insults thrown his way for being gay.

By third grade, his classmates at the Catholic school he attended on Staten Island were calling him "faggot" and "queer." And the initial reactions of shocked surprise and tears eventually gave way to fury and fighting back. Signorile began responding to angry words with his fists. "Worse yet," he explains in *Queer in America*, "I was going after *other* kids who'd been called faggots too, so that I could prove that I agreed they were freaks and distance myself from them. I became a queer-basher to prove I wasn't queer."

Signorile went on to Brooklyn College and then to Syracuse University to study journalism. He came out as gay, at least socially with friends, if not to his family, and after graduation, moved to New York City, where he began working as a "planter," sending celebrity tidbits to the gossip columnists.

He describes his life in Manhattan in the early 1980s as "truly fantastical"—five or six nights a week of parties, gallery openings, premieres, and nightclubbing, which also gave Signorile access to the gossipy factoids desired by the columnists he worked for. Being gay, he reports in his book, was "an enormous asset" because it gave him access to information not available to his straight colleagues. At the same time, however, he became aware that the one thing that was not covered—in fact was actively hidden—was the fact of any famous person being gay.

But deep in the background, behind the frantic fun and the endless quest for "fabulousness," there was AIDS. Though Signorile first heard about a "gay disease" in 1982, he was able to keep the terrible reality away and the party whirling until 1987, even as memorial services became as much a part of the circuit as the parties.

It was at his first meeting of ACT UP (the AIDS Coalition to Unleash Power) that Signorile first tapped into the fear and anger that he had kept bottled up. That anger exploded at the first demonstration he attended, against an anti-gay cardinal giving a speech at St. Peter's Church. Intending merely to watch, Signorile found himself yelling across the packed church, "He is no man of God—he is the Devil!" then being handcuffed and carried away.

While Signorile became an active member of ACT UP, it was as the writer of his weekly "Gossip Watch" column for *Outweek* that he caught the world's attention. Bringing together his insider's knowledge of celebrity gossip and a passionate conversion to AIDS activism, Signorile became what Cheryl Lavin in the *Chicago Tribune* called "the bad boy of gay journalism. He's the angry voice that won't shut up. His writing is personal and nasty, passionate and brutal."

Signorile explains in *Queer in America*, "ACT UP's rhetoric and shrill tactics fueled many of my early columns,... creating a powerful persona, one whose trademark was upper-case invective."

> YOU SLIMY, SELF-LOATHING HYPOCRITICAL MONSTERS. YOU GO TO YOUR PARTIES, YOU WHIRL WITH BIGOTS AND MURDERERS, YOU LIE AND ENGAGE IN COVER-UPS, YOU SELL YOUR SOULS—MEANWHILE WE'RE DYING,

wrote Signorile addressing the closeted gossip columnists he had known so well. The piece then went on to name them.

The list of people outed by Signorile in his column included magazine mogul Malcolm Forbes, columnist Liz Smith, former Secretary of Defense Pete Williams, and entertainment executives David Geffen and Barry Diller. "To me outing is just reporting, honest reporting," Signorile explained to Lavin. He even balks at the term "outing," which was coined by *Time* magazine's William Henry III, a staunch critic of the practice. Writes Signorile, "We don't have a special word for any other action that deals with revelation of truth.... So why should there be a specific term for this?"

Since 1994, Signorile's tone has become more measured and the spectrum of gay issues he covers more varied, ranging from anti-gay hate crimes to same-sex marriage. In his coverage of the alarming breakdown in safer sex practices among gay men, he has been personally revealing and controversial in his opinions. "In moments of profound carelessness," he wrote in an op-ed piece in the *New York Times* in February 1995, "I have also engaged in unsafe sex. Now I find myself uncertain about my HIV status, yet fearful of being tested." Signorile then questions some of the basic tenets of the safer-sex education efforts of many AIDS organizations and focuses on some of the reasons gay men, both positive and negative, engage in unsafe sex. "Ten years ago, the gay community was fighting off hatemongers who were intent on locking up HIV-positive people. Now it seems that some of what we did for those who are positive was at the expense of those who are desperately trying to remain negative."

In May 1996 Signorile was working on his third book, scheduled for publication by HarperCollins in April 1997. Expanding on some of the themes in his *Out* columns, and based on interviews with hundreds of men across the country, it will look at how gay men are re-examining sex, love, friendship, family, spirituality, and growing older.

Current Address: c/o Random House, 201 East 50th Street, 11th Floor, New York, New York 10022. E-mail: angel@pipline.com.

References:

Graham, Renee. "The Prince of Outing," in *Boston Globe,* 13 July 1993: Living section, 25.

Lavin, Cheryl. "The Light in the Closet," in *Chicago Tribune,* 8 June 1993: Tempo section, 1.

Signorile, Michelangelo. "HIV-Positive, and Careless," in *New York Times,* February 1995.

———. *Queer in America: Sex, the Media, and the Closets of Power.* New York: Random House, 1995.

—Ira N. Brodsky

Barbara Smith

1946-

African-American writer and activist

For over three decades, African-American writer and activist Barbara Smith has been at the forefront of advocacy for African-American, women's, and lesbian and gay rights issues. She has edited major groundbreaking anthologies by black women, co-authored several books, and was a founding publisher of Kitchen Table/Women of Color Press. She has written essays, poems, and short stories underscoring the underrepresentation of black women writers in particular; the lack of recognition of the contributions of black lesbian educators, writers and activists; and the invisibility of black women in general. In a short story called "Home," her contribution to the 1983 black feminist anthology *Home Girls,* which she also edited, Smith wrote: "Loving doesn't terrify me. Loss does. The women I need are literally disappearing from the face of the earth. It has already happened."

A Feminist Legacy

Barbara Smith was born in the poor, urban Central Area of Cleveland, Ohio, on 16 November 1946. "There is nothing more important to me than home," she says in the introduction to *Home Girls*. When you examine the strong, hardworking female characters that were her role-models in childhood, you begin to see why. Smith and her twin sister were raised by their mother, grandmother, and a great-aunt who had been the first in the family to move north from rural Georgia in the late 1920s. The sisters shared a bedroom with their grandmother; another larger room was for the aunt, though they seldom saw her because she was a live-in cook for a white family across town. Their mother slept on a daybed downstairs because she worked full-time and would be up and out of the house every morning before anyone else. When the girls were six, they moved in with another great-aunt whose husband eventually left because, according to Smith in *Girls,* "she was too wrapped up in her family." "I was surrounded by women who appeared able to do everything," Smith noted. "They cleaned, cooked, washed, ironed, sewed, made soap, canned, held jobs, took care of business downtown, sang, read, and taught us to do the same." Smith's mother died when she was just nine years old.

Self-Image Problems

At the same time though (and with no small irony), Smith says she learned as much about black feminism from these women's failings as from their strengths. As she daily witnessed the humiliation they suffered because they had been born black and female in a white man's world, she "inherited fear and shame from them as well as hope." "These conflicting feelings about being a black woman still do battle inside me," she says in *Girls,* "this conflict makes my commitment real."

Smith's mother had been the only one of three children to finish college. Though she fought for certification as a teacher within Cleveland's public-school system, she preferred to work as a nurse's aide and a cashier at a local supermarket rather than teach in the demoralizing ghetto schools, which were the only ones open to her. "I [remember] telling a white woman therapist about my mother being a college graduate and the kinds of jobs she had had," Smith told Patricia Bell-Scott in *Ms* magazine in 1995, "and having this therapist tell me that my mother obviously had a self-image problem. The diagnosis was that I had a similar problem—no self-confidence." What this therapist and other well-meaning whites do not comprehend, Smith asserts, is that there were and still are many African Americans with college degrees forced to take jobs well below their qualifications and desires, and that low self-esteem is not the cause but the result of their situation.

A Natural Activist

Smith says she started to notice the unfairness around her at about the age of eight. She had an endless list of questions, including: Why were there no black people on television? Why were all the teachers white? Why was there anxiety in the air that she and her sister could feel whenever they ventured out of their neighborhood? Why did department store clerks ignore her? "I'm kind of a natural activist," she explained to Bell-Scott. In the early 1960s, while still in high school, Smith attended her first demonstration, a protest against the death of a white minister who had laid down in front of construction equipment ready to break ground for a new segregated elementary school. Whether the workers had rolled over him by design or by accident was never made clear. It is this devotion to activism above all else that kept Smith from pursuing an academic career, though she loves teaching, and has even robbed her of precious time to write. She told Bell-Scott, "black feminism has always meant to me that I have a responsibility to help build and provide resources for other women of color; and a commitment to struggle requires certain sacrifices."

Belief in Interconnectedness

Smith received her Bachelors degree from Mount Holyoke College in South Hadley, Massachusetts in 1969 and her Masters from the University of Pittsburgh in 1971. She began teaching at the University of Massachusetts in 1976. In 1977 she presented her groundbreaking and controversial essay "Toward a Black Feminist Criticism" at a National Conference of Afro-American Writers. It shocked many of the attendees because it publicly addressed for the first time the subject of black lesbianism as an integral part of the black literary tradition. In her essay, Smith explored lesbian relationships in classic black novels. She implied that the silence surrounding writings by black women—and black lesbians in particular—had made impossible any recognition of their roles in literary scholarship. And finally, she underscored the importance of applying feminist analysis to writings by black lesbians overall. As writer Ann Louise Keating observes in *The Gay and Lesbian Literary Heritage,* Smith "maintains that because issues concerning lesbianism and lesbian oppression emerged during the late 1960s and early 1970s from within the developing women's movement, writers' views of lesbianism are directly related to feminist issues."

Over the next decade, Smith expanded her examination to include discussions of the racial, sexual, and/or religious stereotyping and prejudice all women of color experience. In 1979, she co-edited with Lorraine Bell a black women's issue of *Conditions: Five,* which added issues of reproductive rights, sterilization, and violence against women to the mix. In 1981, she contributed to *This Bridge Called My Back: Writings by Radical Women of Color,* and was a founder along with writers Audre Lorde and Cherrie Moraga of Kitchen Table/Women of Color Press, established to publish this work and others on women's issues which mainstream publishers found too radical. *Bridge* set precedent in that it examined prejudice within the women's movement itself. The book went on to win the American Book Award from the Before Columbus Foundation and still enjoys widespread popularity among both women of color and in women's studies courses across the country.

Eventually, as she told *Ms,* Smith "came to identify as a black feminist, a lesbian, and a socialist." She was a co-founder of the Combahee River Collective (1974-1981) which sponsored a series of retreats that brought together black women writers who believed in the interconnectedness of strategies for social change. "We understood that dealing with sexual politics didn't mean that you weren't a race woman," she told *Ms,* "and that speaking out about homophobia didn't mean that you didn't want to end poverty."

In 1982, Smith also co-edited an innovative compilation of black women's studies brilliantly titled *All the Women Are White, All the Blacks Are Men, but Some of Us Are Brave.* There Smith, along with fellow editors Gloria T. Hull and Patricia Bell-Scott, presented groundbreaking essays by writers such as Alice Walker and Michele Russell that dispel myths about black women, confront racism, and represent a search for solidarity among all feminists. One of the long-suppressed issues that Smith raises is that of women's liberation being the sole purview of white female intellectuals. "White women [should not] work on racism to do a favor for someone else.... Racism distorts and lessens (everyone's) lives," she says in her essay on "Racism and Women's Studies." She carries this essential connection further by stressing how the political theory of feminism needs to be, by definition, a struggle by all women to free all women, lesbians included.

Home Girls and Home Truths

In 1982 Smith received the Outstanding Woman of Color Award for her writing, education, and activism, and in 1983 she added to this the Women Educators Curriculum Award. It was also in 1983 that Smith saw the publication of her celebratory collection of writings by 34 black lesbians living in the United States and the Caribbean, *Home Girls: A Black Feminist Anthology.* In that book, Smith called for a "return to the fold" for these women, a recognition of their contributions not only by people of their own race, but by the white-dominated, "heterosexually enforced" world of feminism. *Home Girls* is still immensely popular, both as a women's studies text and as an educational sourcebook for the wider culture. Smith's destruction of myths about black women and the substitution of clear knowledge are at the core of her ideology here. Black women are not already liberated, Smith contends, just because "we have had to take on responsibilities that our oppression gives us no choice but to handle."

Invisible Sister

Smith continues to be a very visible presence in the fight for what Keating calls "a positive, self-affirming history and tradition (of the roles) black lesbian artists have played in shaping African-American literature and criticism." The proliferation of writings by and about African-American lesbians is in part a response to Smith's call for their recognition and respect. Today, African-American lesbian writers are imbuing their work—"at the juncture of several divergent literary traditions," according to Keating—with even more celebratory self-expression and homegirl metaphors in an effort to overcome their historic grievances with self-love and respect. And yet, in the gay and lesbian community, Smith admits to still feeling like the "invisible sister." "At the twenty-fifth anniversary of Stonewall," she told Bell-Scott, "the underrepresentation of people of color was demoralizing.... Very few lesbians and gay men of color, including myself, are ever invited to the leadership summits called by white gay leaders. Being omitted from a meeting or invitation list might at first seem like a small thing, but the larger issue is about the disenfranchisement of women and men of color within the movement."

It's all part of the push to mainstream, and thus disempower, the gay and lesbian movement in the United States, according to Smith. This mentality is troubling for Smith because, as she says in *Ms,* "I want a nonhierarchical, nonexploitive society in which profit is not the sole motivation for every single decision made by the government or individuals.... What am I, as a black woman, going to be doing at this table—carry a tray? ... A place at the table? Not likely. It really doesn't work for me."

The fight for inclusion and against homophobia would be most righteously and effectively led by black women, according to Smith.

And yet, too may black women's organizations fear the inevitability of being labeled and dismissed as lesbians. Or perhaps they are still subscribing to the pernicious myth that "people of color need to deal with the 'larger struggle'," as outlined by Smith in *Home Girls*.

Roadblocks like these, a well as encounters with black lesbian feminists who support her work but refuse to come out publicly, remind Smith of Audre Lorde's book *Sister Outsider*, as she told *MS* in 1995. "It's an oxymoron because a sister is obviously someone inside the family, close, a home girl. But the sister with the lesbian feminist politics ... is also an outsider."

Now self-described as mid-way in life and career, she confesses to longtime friend Bell-Scott that she has a growing appreciation for simple acts of "self-care—like a daytime nap, eating on time, and sitting quietly after a bout of running around." Nevertheless, Barbara Smith is still leading the fight for empowerment—the battle to give us back something of ourselves. Currently, and true to form, she is completing another revolutionary, first-of-its-kind endeavor, a book about the history of African-American lesbians and gays.

"Almost all of my writing has been about empowerment and about trying to say to people of color, to women, to lesbians and gay men that you are really worth something, you are important, you have a history to be proud of. There is no reason to be ashamed." And there is certainly no reason to be ashamed of Barbara Smith as she continues to advocate for us all.

Current Address: Director, Kitchen Table Women of Color, P.O. Box 908, Latham, New York 12110.

References:

Bell-Scott, Patricia. "Reflections of Home Girl," in *Ms,* 2 January 1995: 59-63.

Hull, Gloria T., Bell-Scott, Patricia, and Smith, Barbara, eds. *All the Women Are White, All the Blacks Are Men, but Some of Us Are Brave*. Old Westbury, New York: The Feminist Press, 1982.

Smith, Barbara, ed. *Home Girls: A Black Feminist Anthology*. New York: Kitchen Table/Women of Color Press, 1983.

Summers, Claude J. *The Gay and Lesbian Literary Heritage*. New York: Henry Holt, 1995.

—Jerome Szymczak

Bessie Smith

1894?-1937

African-American singer

And if the Blues don't kill me,
they'll thrill me through and through.

—"Love Me Daddy Blues"

When Thomas Edison, head of the world's first recording company, first heard Bessie Smith's voice during a talent audition, he jotted down these words in his file: "Voice n.g. 4/21/24"—inauspicious beginnings for the woman who would be later dubbed "The Empress of the Blues" and become one of the highest paid black performers in the country, garnering $2,000 a week in her prime.

Smith was born in Chattanooga, Tennessee, probably on 15 April 1894 (the date has never been verified, but this was what appeared on her 1923 application for a marriage license). One fictional account of Smith's life has her growing up in Chattanooga's poor, colored section called Tannery Flats, an area noted not only for its poverty, but for the pollution attributable to the leather tannery nearby. It is clear that she lived in abject circumstances at best. Her father, William Smith, was a Baptist preacher who died shortly after Bessie's birth. By the time Bessie was eight or nine, her mother Laura had died as well, leaving Smith and her remaining siblings in the care of their eldest sister Viola.

There would have been few options available to Smith, even in the best of circumstances and hers were clearly the worst. There is some evidence that she began singing for nickels and dimes on the streets of Chattanooga as early as nine years of age, accompanied by her brother Andrew, who played the guitar.

Smith's oldest surviving brother, Clarence, had joined a traveling show as a dancer and comedian. Clarence arranged for Smith to audition with Moses Stokes' traveling show in 1912. It was during her tenure with the Stokes' show that Smith met "Ma" Rainey, "Mother of the Blues." Some accounts suggest that the openly lesbian Rainey kidnapped Smith to be in her show, later taking her as a lover. This story appears to have more legend than truth about it, however it is clear that Rainey took the young, untutored Smith under her wing, taught her the ropes of the business, and kept her out of trouble. Rainey and Smith were to remain lifelong friends.

An Escape from Poverty

The minstrel circuit was a hard, exhausting life, but for a talented girl like Smith, it was one of the few options that offered hope, if not of riches, then of survival. Minstrel shows originated from the river boats that traveled up and down the Mississippi, entertaining the patrons on board with music, dance, and burlesque numbers. When theaters opened in the south, they were confined to white audiences. The minstrel shows, or "traveling tent shows" that criss-crossed the south were primarily for black audiences. The tent shows usually set up in vacant lots, sometimes staying as long as a week, often leaving after just a single night's performance.

In spite of one early setback, when she was fired from a chorus line for being too dark, Smith toured successfully in the south for a number of years, hired initially as a dancer and later principally as a singer. Eventually she began touring with the Theater Owner's Booking Association (T.O.B.A.), a major black vaudeville circuit that was a proving ground for many black artists. Referred to euphemistically as the "Tough on Black Actors" circuit, T.O.B.A. enabled black troupes to introduce their music to northern audiences.

Smith worked in theaters scattered around the country, including the "81" Theater in Atlanta, the Standard Theater in Philadelphia, and Chicago's Grand Theater. Smith's unique blend of blues and vaudeville with a rural vocal style was popular with black audiences. By 1923, she was a seasoned performer with a distinctive delivery and a loyal following.

The early years of the 1920s must have been busy ones, unfortunately there is not much information concerning Smith's life at this time. She did marry Earl Love, who came from a prominent black Mississippi family. Little is known about him or how he and Smith met, and he died shortly after their marriage.

Good Times and Bad

The next arena for Smith to conquer was the recording industry. Between the years 1923 and 1937, Smith would bequeath a legacy of 160 records. Her early attempts at recording were not particularly encouraging, however. Edison, Emerson, Black Swan, and Okeh all turned Smith down after auditions in 1921 and 1922, citing reasons ranging from her voice was too "rich" to too "rough" to too "southern." Studios were looking for a "whiter" sound and looked more favorably on artists like the northern, fairer-skinned Ethel Waters. Smith's pronounced dialect, physical intensity, and forceful phrasing were too off-putting to the studios. There also has been some suggestion that Smith may have alienated studio executives with her aggressive, often bawdy behavior.

Smith was large in size, voice, and personality. She had a reputation for being hard drinking, raunchy, violent, and fiercely competitive. There is an uncompromising authority and conviction in Smith's voice that connects with these aspects of her personality. She was not a woman to be suffered gladly.

On stage, she was flamboyant and colorful. She wore bright costume jewelry, Birds of Paradise or ostrich plumes in her hair, and evening gowns studded with beads and rhinestones. Although critics of the time couldn't refrain from commenting on Smith's weight and so-called "homeliness," most came away enthralled by her music, and many commented on her unusual capacity to mesmerize an audience.

Columbia Records finally agreed to record Smith in 1923. Her first recording was a cover of the popular "Down-Hearted Blues," a commercial success that sold nearly 800,000 copies in 1923.

Around this time, Smith married Jack Gee, a night watchman from Philadelphia. The circumstances surrounding their first date would prove prophetic for a relationship fraught with violence and suspicion. In 1922, following a performance at Horan's Cabaret in Philadelphia, Gee was seriously wounded in a shooting incident while the couple was on their way to dinner. Over the following five weeks, Smith visited Gee every day in the hospital and they grew quite close. They moved in together soon after Gee's release from the hospital.

Although Gee initiated a relationship with Smith before she had really become successful, he would come to be viewed by many as an opportunist. It is clear that he maintained an iron grip on Smith's life in many ways. He forbade her to drink, hoarded their money in a manner that was alien to Smith herself, and flew into rages over her infidelities, real or perceived.

The couple's fights were legendary, often ending in physical abuse. And although Smith herself generally held a policy of "strike first, ask questions later," it is certain that she suffered more than her husband from these altercations. Several people who toured with Smith in the 1920s have commented on how extremely excitable both Smith and Gee were, and how Gee was known to hit Smith hard enough to knock her to the floor. In spite of Gee's controlling tendencies and the loyalty Smith felt for him throughout most of their marriage, Smith was not easily subdued and seemed to be temperamentally adverse to domesticity. She would return to the home they shared in Philadelphia, enjoying the time she spent with Gee, but treating it almost as a respite, a temporary retreat from the real life she was living. In spite of Gee's warnings and her fear of discovery, Smith continued to drink heavily and sleep with other people.

Early city blues was primarily the provenance of women; the years between 1923 and 1925 were the golden era. But as popular as the music was, it was frowned upon by the black church community. Many a blues singer got his or her start in a "jook" joint. Jook joints were "houses of wickedness or pleasure." The rough lifestyle these places embodied was reflected in the lyrics of the songs. Many dealt with the seamier undercurrents of urban society—murder, drugs, and prostitution. Many of the songs were cheerfully, often humorously sexual, perhaps epitomized in the raunchy, double-entendres of "Handyman," recorded by Alberta Hunter. Homosexuality was a fairly open and accepted fact in this world. Singers like Ma Rainey sang songs that dealt with lesbian love, either overtly or implied.

> There's two things got me puzzled, there's
> two things I don't understand;
> That's a mannish-acting woman, and a
> *skipping, twistin' woman-acting man.*
>
> —"Foolish Man Blues"

It is not clear when Smith began to have sexual relationships with women, but she was known to have had several female lovers, some of them members of her own troupe. Smith was usually, if not always, the aggressor in these relationships, and it is clear that as with everything in her life, she controlled what happened in these relationships. But her relationship with Lillian Simpson, in particular, seemed to bring out a protective, softer side. Although Gee was well aware of his wife's infidelities, and also eventually learned of her bisexuality, Smith seemed concerned that this would be more than he could stomach. She was much more cautious in these relationships for fear of Jack's retaliation, both against her as well as her lovers.

Harlem epitomized the blues of the 1920s. There was something for everyone in Harlem—high-class places that catered to white audiences only, like the Cotton Club, where the entertainment was black and the audience was white; hole-in-the-wall places for working class blacks; or speakeasies and after-hour clubs where blacks and whites mingled in a more informal atmosphere.

Smith continued to sing primarily for black audiences and she cast a disdainful eye on blacks who tried to remake themselves in the image of whites, referring to them in the southern colloquial as acting "dicty."

The mid-1920s were for Smith a professionally productive period, but her personal life was far more complicated. Her marriage to Jack Gee had always been fraught with ups and downs, but when Smith learned that Jack was using her money to finance one of his mistress's shows, it was clearly the last straw. Smith was deeply hurt by this betrayal, and things between them were never the same.

Smith's drinking had by now become a problem, at times resulting in mean-spirited, unprofessional behavior. Those who knew Smith during this period recall the contradictory sides to her personality. The woman who was known to leave her troupe stranded in towns on tour without any money was the same woman who could be generous to a fault—the sole provider for her family and a soft touch when it came to lending money to anyone in need.

Changing Times

By 1929 the popularity of the blues had begun to wane, and talking pictures were making a dent in the music industry. But Smith was given a unique opportunity that year to play the lead in a 17-minute short, *St. Louis Blues*, which offers a rare and provocative visual portrait of the legendary singer.

Although Smith was certainly not made destitute during the Depression, by the early 1930s she could no longer command the kind of fees she had in her prime. Many of the theaters had closed down and the T.O.B.A. circuit was officially dead. In 1931, Columbia Records, on the verge of bankruptcy, dropped Smith from their program, ending a nine-year relationship.

Around this time Smith began a different kind of relationship—with Richard Morgan, an old friend she had known in Birmingham, Alabama, before she was famous. In personality, Morgan was quite different from Gee; his attitude toward Smith was solicitous and non-judgmental. Morgan had made a great deal of money during prohibition times as a bootlegger. As Smith's financial circumstances became less stable, Morgan often stepped in to help her out with his own money.

By the late 1930s, blues music had become somewhat antiquated, out of sync with the vibrant, upbeat rhythms of Swing. Smith's career continued to slow down. Ever-resilient, Smith did try to adapt to the changing times; she discarded her flashy wardrobe and began to include popular songs in her repertoire. By the summer of 1937, things were looking up. She was scheduled to make a Hollywood picture; she was making records again; and she went on tour in September.

Smith's premature death in 1937 was as full of contradictions as her life. The September tour had turned into a successful show that was currently playing in the Memphis area. The next stop on tour was Darling, Mississippi. In spite of Richard Morgan's desire to stay in Memphis because of a scheduled card game, Smith insisted that he drive the two of them to Clarksdale to get a head start on the rest of the troupe. They left Memphis around 1:00 a.m. They were about 75 miles down Route 61 when they were hit by a truck. Moments later, a Dr. Hugh Smith and his fishing partner, Henry Broughton, chanced upon the scene of the accident. Smith was lying in the middle of the road. Morgan, who had not been injured, was waving his arms frantically, and Dr. Smith could see the tail lights of the retreating truck just before it disappeared from view.

Apparently the truck driver had pulled to the side of the road in order to check his tires. The shoulders were not very wide, so most of the truck was still situated in the right lane. He had just started to move back out onto the highway when he was hit by Morgan's car. It was Smith's side of the car that received the impact. As Dr. Smith began to examine her, he saw that her forearm had almost been torn loose from her upper arm at the elbow. Her ribs had also been crushed and she may have had abdominal injuries. Dr. Smith moved Smith to the side of the road to dress the wound, and sent Broughton off to call for an ambulance. During this time Smith lapsed into shock. To make matters worse, another car, approaching at a high speed, hit Dr. Smith's car, which was then parked in the middle of the road, driving it straight into Smith's car. The drivers of this car, a white couple, were now Dr. Smith's patients as well. Around this time, an ambulance and several police officers arrived on the scene and Smith was taken to the hospital, where her arm was amputated.

This is where the controversy begins. Smith was not taken to the white hospital, but to a black hospital in Clarksdale where she died; the principal cause of death was listed as shock. Although there is no evidence of this, some people believed Dr. Smith had neglected Smith by directing his medical attention to the white couple whose injuries were less severe, and some have also suggested that the black hospital did not have the resources and equipment to attend to Smith properly.

Bessie Smith

Although Dr. Smith later contended that Smith's chances of survival at either hospital were 50-50, it is clear that the truck driver should have taken Smith to the hospital immediately and that the doctor himself was remiss in not transporting Smith to the hospital in his own car, wasting valuable time in calling for an ambulance.

In the black press, Smith was depicted as a martyr, a casualty of Southern bigotry. For years after, Smith's death was attributed to her having bled to death waiting for medical aid, a notion that was later reinforced by Edward Albee's play, *The Death of Bessie Smith*. To this day, interpretations of what happened that night vary.

The Legacy

In 1970, Columbia reissued all of Smith's recordings. The accompanying publicity generated a great deal of renewed interest in the singer, and led to the discovery that her grave was as yet unmarked. Janis Joplin, a great admirer of Smith's, offered to pay half the cost of a headstone, which was unveiled on 7 August 1970.

Gunther Schuller, in his seminal book *Early Jazz*, remarked that, like a great actress, Smith mastered the illusion of improvisation. What made Smith a superior singer, Schuller said, "was a remarkable ear for and control of intonation, in all its subtlest functions; a perfectly centered, naturally produced voice (in her prime); an extreme sensitivity to word meaning and the sensory, almost physical, feeling of a word; and related to this, superb diction and what singers call projection."

Smith has been the subject of dramatic and musical theater, including Albee's play and most recently a musical production, *Bessie's Blues*, by Thomas W. Jones II. She has influenced and continues to influence countless singers, including Mahalia Jackson, Ella Fitzgerald, the great stylist Billie Holiday, and Chicago blues singers Koko Taylor and Etta James.

References:

Albee, Edward. *The Sandbox and The Death of Bessie Smith.* New York: New American Library, 1988.

Albertson, Chris. *Bessie.* New York: Stein and Day Publishers, 1972.

Dall, Christine, dir. *Wild Women Don't Have the Blues.* San Francisco: California Newsreel, 1989.

Cohn, Lawrence. *Nothing But the Blues: The Music and the Musicians.* New York: Abbeville Press, 1993.

Eberhardt, Clifford. *The Bessie Smith Story.* Chattanooga: Ebco, Inc., 1993.

Feinstein, Elaine. *Bessie Smith.* New York: Viking, 1985.

French, Mary Ann. "Bringing in 'Bessie,'" in *Washington Post,* 7 May 1995: G1.

Haskins, James. *Black Music in America: A History Through Its People.* New York: HarperCollins Publishers, 1987.

Gary, Larry. "Bessie Smith," in *Dictionary of American Negro Biography,* edited by Rayford W. Logan and Michael R. Winston. New York: W. W. Norton & Company, Inc., 1982.

Moore, Carman. *Somebody's Angel Child: The Story of Bessie Smith.* New York: Thomas Y. Crowell Company, 1969.

Schuller, Gunther. *Early Jazz.* New York: Oxford University Press, 1968.

—Lynda Schrecengost

Dame Ethel Smyth

1858-1944

British composer and writer

"I am the most interesting person I know," wrote Dame Ethel Smyth toward the end of her life in 1935, "and I don't care if anyone else thinks so." Even in an age of flamboyant personalities—Virginia Woolf, Dora Carrington, Lytton Strachey, and other Bloomsbury "buggers and Sapphists" among them—Smyth stands out. She composed operas, countless choral/orchestral works and songs, and wrote nine volumes of candid autobiography in her lifetime. She was a major player in the fight both for women's suffrage and women's rights in general—composing a popular "March of the Women" which was sung at demonstrations for decades. She was an avid traveler and sportswoman—once braving a walking tour of Greece at the age of 65 and a strenuous trek to Egypt just to examine a hermaphrodite.

Neither did she make any apologies for her love of women over the years, most notably the 47-year-old Woolf when Smyth was 71. "All my life," she wrote in one of her later memoirs, "I have found in women's affection a peculiar understanding, mothering quality that is a thing apart. My relations with certain women,... are shining threads in my life." And though she had close male companions, marriage, according to Smyth, was simply unattainable "given my life and outlook."

Ethel Smyth was the third of four children born to what she described as "a not uncommon type" English-soldier father and a "most uncommonly English" mother who had been educated in France and spoke several languages. The family bounced back and forth between India and England throughout Smyth's childhood—sojourns she claims fortified her adventurous spirit, love of travel, and eventual sacrifice of her music to "an inordinate flow of passion in three directions—sport, games and friendship."

Her older brother Johnny, Smyth wrote, "was at that time my model, my tastes being essentially boyish. I soon noticed that I could climb higher and was generally more daring than he,... which would partly account for a lack of sympathy between us." Her mother took to calling her "the stormy petrel," and Ethel took great pride in referring to herself as a "ten-month baby"—"having heard that such children are usually boys and always remarkable!" Into young adulthood, she fit in well with her family's aristocratic pastimes of sport, hunting, and entertaining.

Releasing the Divine

At 19, though, in defiance of her father's wishes, Smyth went to Leipzig, Germany, to study music. There, she "plunged joyfully into the dear old sea of German music which surged about the feet of Brahms." Here too, she was to form her first passionate attachments to other women with artistic dreams: one of composer Mendelssohn's daughters, Schuman's widow Clara, and composer Heinrich von Herzogenberg's wife Lisl, who became her unofficial guardian.

In her late twenties she met writer and philosopher Harry Brewster—part of a group of bohemian expatriates she was hanging out with in Florence—who became the librettist for some of her major compositions, including her most acclaimed opera *The Wreckers.* In her memoirs entitled *Impressions That Remained* (1919), she describes him as the only man she ever loved and the greatest single influence on her budding spirituality and career. According to Evelyn Gettone in *The Encyclopedia of Homosexuality,* "she derived [from him] a quasi-mystical Neoplatonic philosophy" that was to characterize her politics, relationships, and writings for the rest of her life. According to author Ronald Crichton, "Brewster tamed Ethel without bruising her spirit and corrected what he saw as barbarous Germanic influence with a wider appreciation of French civilization."

Smyth's first major composition—the *Mass in D Major* (1893)—was anything but traditionally religious and was praised for qualities unexpected of women composers: rich orchestration, expansive structure, and powerful musical movements. Her 1916 opera *The Boatswain's Mate* was groundbreaking in its portrayal of a strong central female character. Of her 1930 choral work *The Prison*—based on her two-month incarceration at Holloway prison for throwing a brick through a cabinet minister's window during a women's suffrage protest—she wrote: "I am striving to release that which is divine within us, and to merge it in the universally divine."

In the early 1920s—the beginning of the "second act" of her life and career—Smyth turned to her writing, largely because of a profound and growing deafness. (She always claimed to be "slow" of hearing—a notion her friend Brewster said was simply because she was deafened by what she was going to say next). *Impressions That Remained, As Time Went On* (1936), and *What Happened Next* (1940) are autobiographical works and consist largely of letters to Smyth from an impressive gallery of women who had a prominent place in her life—Mrs. E. W. Benson, the wife of the archbishop of Canterbury; Lady Ponsonby, the wife of Queen Victoria's private secretary; and Virginia Woolf, among them. Other works contain sparkling and frank portraits of Brahms, the ex-Empress Eugenia of France, and beloved fellow suffragette Emmeline Pankhurst. *A Three-Legged Tour in Greece* (1927) and *Inordinate (?) Affection* (1936) are, in turn, whimsical, insightful accounts of her "geriatric" holiday (and search for a hermaphrodite in Egypt) and her lifelong love of big English sheepdogs.

Peppered in between all these writings were book reviews, lectures, and political treatises on the status of women as artists, homemakers, and human beings unfairly denied the vote. "Because I am a militant suffragette," she wrote in 1933, "who beat out the time to *The March of the Women* from the window of my cell of Holloway Prison with a toothbrush,... I have some notoriety."

Notorious or not, Smyth's sexual passion for women was thinly shrouded (at least for public consumption) in her writings by the popular "disclaimer" of the day—namely that women of her senior stature and "spiritual intelligence" were no longer sexual beings. No doubt her Neoplatonic philosophy kept her from acknowledging her lesbian feelings openly, opting instead for the "mystically divine" good of carnal denial. But it is crucial to note that during the decade of her friendship with Woolf especially—tragically cut short by Woolf's suicide in 1941—Smyth wrote and published six of her nine books because of Woolf's avid encouragement.

Independent of the Sex Machine

Crichton says that "on the whole it seems that the greatest and most enduring of (Smyth's) 'passions' were for older women with whom, through character or circumstance or both, physical gratification was out of the question even to one of her on-coming disposition." It would seem that when she met Woolf at the age of 71, the tables were turned. Perhaps she suddenly felt "safe" from physical expressions of love due to her age (Woolf was 47), and at the same time emboldened by age to finally speak her mind. Whether they had a sexual relationship or not is almost moot in light of the unbridled love Smyth expressed for Woolf's beauty and genius.

A passage from her diary reveals her still-strong "on-coming disposition" quite revealingly. "I don't think I ever cared for anyone more profoundly," she wrote in 1933. "I met her first three years ago in 1930 and for 18 months I really thought of little else. I think this proves what I have always held—that for many women, anyhow for me, passion is independent of the sex machine. Of course when you are young, it will not be gainsaid. (Nor indeed if I am frank, did it cease to play any part with men when I should have done with all things physical ... But I have remained capable of a love as deep and absorbing as one or two major loves of my youth)."

A few weeks before her death in May of 1944, Ethel Smyth told her nurse that she thought she might die soon, "and I intend to die standing up," she added with typical tenacity. "I do not pretend there have not been times of sadness, of frustration, even of despair," she wrote in *As Time Went On* (1936), "but I never mind the sadness. It is always about the perishable self and therefore does not exist." Biographer Christopher St. John cites her own three reasons for remaining undefeated by life as "an iron constitution, a fair share of fighting spirit, and, most important of all, a small but independent income."

References:

Gettone, Evelyn. In *Encyclopedia of Homosexuality,* edited by Wayne R. Dynes. New York: Garland Publishing, 1990.

St. John, Christopher. *Ethel Smyth: A Biography.* London: Longmans, 1959.

Smyth, Ethel. *The Memoirs of Ethel Smyth,* edited by Ronald Crichton. Middlesex, England: Viking Press, 1987.

Woolf, Virginia. *The Letters of Virginia Woolf—1932-1935,* edited by Nigel Nicolson and Joanne Trautmann. New York: Harcourt Brace Jovanovich, 1979.

—Jerome Szymczak

Stephen Sondheim

1930-

American composer

A rare individual who can brilliantly write both words and music, Stephen Sondheim has become a giant of American musical theater, celebrated for his creativity, artistic daring, and integrity. His complex, unconventional musicals are not always popular with critics or audiences, but are often revived with greater success. While he has never married, the intensely private Sondheim does little to advertise his sexual preferences, and commentators on Sondheim respect his privacy.

Stephen Joshua Sondheim was born on 22 March 1930, the son of dress manufacturer Herbert Sondheim and former dress designer Helen Fox Sondheim. When he was ten, his parents divorced, and he was soon escaping from his difficult mother by spending time at the home of his friend Jimmy Hammerstein. There, he formed a bond with Jimmy's father, famed lyricist Oscar Hammerstein II, who tutored Sondheim in the art of writing musicals.

After graduating from Williams College in 1950, Sondheim received a fellowship which allowed him to study music. In 1953, he moved to Hollywood when hired by Jess Oppenheimer to write scripts for the television series *Topper*. Despite this and other television work and later collaboration with Anthony Perkins on the screenplay of *The Last of Sheila* (1973), Sondheim never writes librettos for his musicals, citing dissatisfaction with his prose.

Returning to New York, he wrote songs for a projected Broadway musical, *Saturday Night*, that was never produced, then wrote lyrics for Leonard Bernstein's *West Side Story* (1957) and Jule Styne's *Gypsy* (1959), two classic musicals whose enduring success gave him lifelong financial security.

However, wishing to write both lyrics and music, Sondheim developed a musical based on the plays of Plautus, *A Funny*

Stephen Sondheim. *Photograph by Michael le Poer Trench.*

Thing Happened on the Way to the Forum (1962), still his most accessible work. After the ill-conceived *Anyone Can Whistle* (1964), Sondheim unwisely agreed to write lyrics for Richard Rodgers's *Do I Hear a Waltz?* (1965). Their partnership proved tempestuous, perhaps because Rodgers "hate[d] homosexuality," as Oppenheimer reports (quoted in Craig Zadan's *Sondheim & Co.*). After an eccentric television musical, *Evening Primrose* (1967), Sondheim hit his stride with three musicals directed by Harold Prince which each earned Sondheim Tony Awards. In *Company* (1970), married couples ponder their friend Bobby, an attractive, thirty-five-year-old man who refuses to marry; some believe Bobby is, or must be read as, homosexual, though the play is not explicit. Guy Livingston archly commented in *Variety* that the musical was "for ladies' matinees, homos and misogynists." *Follies* (1971), surrealistically depicting the reunion of two former show girls and their husbands, was triumphantly revived as an album and television special in 1985. *A Little Night Music* (1973), based on Ingmar Bergman's film *Smiles of a Summer Night*, was lighter in tone and featured Sondheim's first hit song, "Send in the Clowns," which won a Grammy Award as Song of the Year.

Still working with Prince, though growing more adventurous, Sondheim next offered *Pacific Overtures* (1976), a Kabuki-style recounting of Japan's westernization, while a revue created without his participation, *Side by Side by Sondheim* (1976), garnered new respect for his music. *Sweeney Todd, the Demon Barber of Fleet Street* (1979) outrageously chronicled the exploits of a murderer and the woman who bakes the corpses into meat pies. Perhaps the best Sondheim/Prince musical, it was unfortunately followed by a monumental failure, *Merrily We Roll Along* (1981), their last collaboration. Sondheim then received a Pulitzer Prize for what some call his masterpiece, *Sunday in the Park with George* (1984), which depicted George Seurat's painting of his famous work and the artistic struggles of his descendant. Next came *Into the Woods* (1987), a blend of traditional fairy tales with dark overtones, and *Assassins* (1991), which offended many because of its subject matter, people who tried to murder American presidents. Reactions to *Passion* (1994), based on the film *Passione d'Amore*, were typical: critical raves and brickbats, several Tony Awards, and lackluster ticket sales.

While the theater is Sondheim's focus, he sometimes works for films, scoring *Stravinsky* (1974) and *Reds* (1981) and writing songs for *The Seven Per Cent Solution* (1976) and *Dick Tracy* (1990); a song from the latter film, "Sooner or Later," won an Oscar for Best Original Song. Other honors include membership in the American Academy and Institute of Arts and Letters—which he called "One of the few honors that I've been given that means anything to me ... because it's awarded by peers"—and a 1990 position as visiting professor of drama and musical theatre at Oxford University.

An unusual public controversy occurred in 1992 when Sondheim, amidst congressional efforts to reign in the National Endowment for the Arts because of grants to Robert Mapplethorpe and others, angrily rejected its National Medal of Arts Award because the endowment had been, he announced, "transformed into a conduit, and a symbol, of censorship and repression rather than encouragement and support." Perhaps it was not a popular gesture, but this idiosyncratic visionary has never been interested in popularity.

Current Address: c/o Flora Roberts Inc., 157 W. 57th St., New York, New York 10019.

References:

Banfield, Stephen. *Sondheim's Broadway Musicals.* Ann Arbor: University of Michigan Press, 1993.

Freedman, Samuel G. "The Creative Mind: The Words and Music of Stephen Sondheim," in *New York Times Magazine*, 1 April 1984: 22-23, 60.

Gordon, Joanne Lesley. *Art Isn't Easy: The Achievement of Stephen Sondheim.* Carbondale: Southern Illinois University Press, 1990.

Gottfried, Martin. *Sondheim.* New York: Harry N. Abrams, 1993.

Hirsch, Foster. *Harold Prince and the American Musical Theatre.* Cambridge: Cambridge University Press, 1989.

Ilson, Carol. *Harold Prince: From "Pajama Game" to "Phantom of the Opera."* Ann Arbor: UMI Research Press, 1989.

McLaughlin, Robert L. "'No One Is Alone': Society and Love in the Musicals of Stephen Sondheim," in *Journal of American Drama and Theatre*, 1991: 27-41.

Morley, Sheridan. "Side by Side with the Sondheim Art," in *Sunday Times Magazine* (London), 4 March 1990: 66-70.

Prince, Hal. *Contradictions: Notes on Twenty-Six Years in the Theatre.* New York: Dodd, Mead, & Company, 1974.

Sondheim, Stephen. "Theater Lyrics," in *Playwrights, Lyricists, Composers on Theatre,* edited by Otis L. Guernsey, Jr. New York: Dodd, Mead, & Co., 1974: 61-97.

Sondheim, Stephen, and Harold Prince. "On Collaboration between Authors and Directors," moderated by Gretchen Cryer, in *Dramatists Guild Quarterly* 16, summer, 1979: 14-35.
Zadan, Craig. *Sondheim & Co.* Second Edition, Updated. New York: Harper & Row, 1989.

—Gary Westfahl

Susan Sontag

1933-

American critic and writer

A novelist, filmmaker, literary critic, and cultural analyst, Sontag has published a dozen books and four screenplays, as well as directed stage plays. She had an eight year marriage to Philip Rieff, a cultural historian and psychologist with whom she collaborated on the book, *Freud, the Mind of the Moralist.* Although she does not address the subject of feminism often, her reason for leaving the marriage could be termed a feminist one: she needed to explore the world in a way that is not available to a married person, simply because of her commitment to another. In other words, she needed mobility in order to pursue her career. She took advantage of this mobility by living in France, England, Sweden, and Italy for the purpose of study and directorship of movies and plays.

Sontag was born on 16 January 1933 to parents whose names she does not reveal (Sontag is the name of her stepfather). Her parents were fur traders in China when she was conceived but her mother came to New York to give birth to Susan. While growing up, Sontag's father was often absent from the family home. Along with Judith, her younger sister, Susan and her mother moved to Tucson when she was six to seek relief in the treatment of her asthma. Susan was an excellent student, and skipped three grades in school. She finished high school in Hollywood when she was fifteen and enrolled at the University of California, Berkeley, the following year. Her childhood was filled with sadness and defiance: sadness at the sense of abandonment by her father and the cold distance of her mother; defiance as a reaction and defense to this abandonment.

Sontag has written that the kinds of things she thought about before age ten are the kinds of things she continues to think about, and "morality" is the word that she uses to describe them. She labels herself a "besotted aesthete," an "obsessed moralist," and a "zealot of seriousness." As a child, Sontag was precocious and self-directed in her learning. Her great discovery, one that must have mitigated some of the triviality of North Hollywood High, was an international newsstand that sold the *Partisan Review,* which she admired. She decided at that time that her goal in life was to move to New York and write for this publication.

However, instead of pursuing a career in journalism Sontag got caught up in the excitement of academia, moving from Berkeley to Chicago after her first year of teaching. Her introduction to and courtship with her husband were swift and sure: he approached her after her first day auditing his class, and ten days later they were married. Rieff introduced her to the kind of intellectual friends that she desired to have. The couple had one son, David.

Leaving the Womb: Divorce and Freelance Writing

After a year abroad in Paris at the Sorbonne (1957-58), Sontag decided that her marriage was curtailing her freedom. She said that it was, in many ways, a good marriage, but one that was too intense to allow her the room she needed to grow and change. In referring to this choice, Sontag indicated, in typically distanced, abstract diction, "somewhere along the line, one has to choose between the Life and the Project." In Sontag's mind her project was to become a respected freelance writer.

With her six-year-old son, two suitcases and thirty dollars, Sontag arrived in New York and found positions as an editor at *Commentary* and lecturer at Sarah Lawrence College and the City College of New York. Although academia was appealing because of its forum for the exchange of ideas, Sontag preferred non-academic intellectualism because of the inclusion of popular culture in its materials for evaluation and focus. It is about this time (1962) that Sontag made her famous position "against interpretation" known in a collection of essays. She favored experiencing art's sensory qualities and not worrying about its meaning. This approach enabled her to validate pornography as art, saying that it is a form of consciousness which we must not censor. To censor forms of individual consciousness, according to Sontag, is only to perpetuate our "national [American] psychosis, founded, as are all psychoses, on the efficacious denial

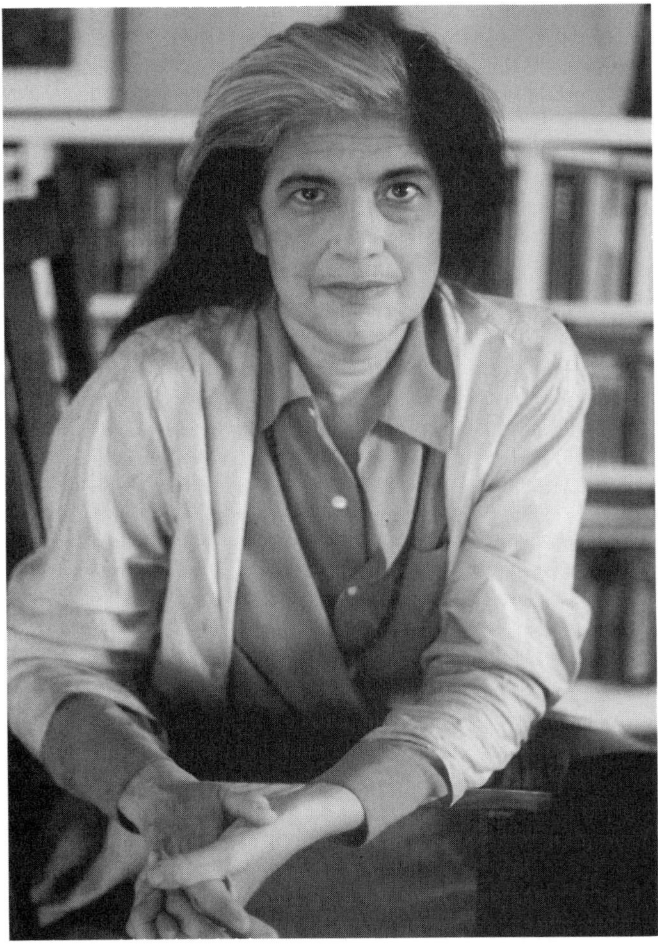

Susan Sontag

of reality." Pornography has value, according to Sontag, because it expresses consciousness, however deranged.

In the 1960s, Sontag became involved in the protest against the Vietnam War, even going so far as to say that the North Vietnamese had a more ethical society than America's. Sontag compared U.S. foreign policy to Nazi Germany's policy.

Such pronouncements were typical of Sontag's radical style. Her positions tended to create polarized reactions, in part because the content of what she said offended so-called respectable opinion, in part because her style could cause shock and pain. The combination of political and literary subjects confused some in the sixties and seventies, but should no longer come as a surprise in a decade when radical lesbians and others have let us know that "every act is a political act" because every act is about power.

Beginning in 1969, Sontag made four feature-length films. Her films were criticized for being too abstract, sacrificing dramatic content for ideas and ideologies. These opinions seem to reflect what people were also saying about her fiction. Sontag herself realized that her first love was writing and that, because of the international sets of her film projects, she felt like an expatriate, though she is quoted in *Current Biography Yearbook 1992* as explaining that she "didn't mean to become an expatriate." Wanting to return to more familiar ground, Sontag moved back to New York from Paris in 1976.

Near Death and a New Breath

After her move, a life-changing event occurred: Sontag was diagnosed with breast cancer. The doctors gave her from six months to two years to live. Clearly, they were wrong, and she has been empowered and even enriched by her struggle with death. The battle produced two books, *Illness as Metaphor* (1978) and *AIDS and Its Metaphors* (1988), in which Sontag examines the tendency of our culture to condemn the person with the disease and attach moral blame to the fact of their having contracted it. The first book was more successful than the second, perhaps not least because it dealt with first-hand experience about the illness that Sontag herself had. In contrast, her description of promiscuous gay sex life in the AIDS book offended several critics by its seeming lack of sensitivity towards either promiscuity or gayness, even while one mission of the book, she feels, is to defend gays against negative press and moralistic judgment.

It was also during the eighties that Sontag made a major shift in political affiliations. At a New York City rally for Polish solidarity in 1982, Sontag said, in her eminently quotable manner: "Communism *is* fascism—successful fascism, if you will. Not only is fascism and overt military rule probably the destiny, the future of all communist countries ... but communism is in itself a variant, the most successful variant of fascism." While this is a fact that may seem obvious to those with the retrospective vision of 1996, the intellectual left of the time was miffed, and let her know that she was considered an ideological turncoat.

Sontag returned to fiction with *The Volcano Lover* (1992), historical romance about the eighteenth-century British admiral Horatio Nelson and his mistress Edna Hamilton. Set in Naples, the book mixes natural and social history with romance and politics. Some critics feel that the book is artsy and contrived, the tone distant and boring. Others, including Sontag, believe it is her best novel.

Becoming the president of PEN in Norman Mailer's wake, in 1987, might represent the dream-come-true of the little girl who wanted to work for the *Partisan Review* or, later, become a respected free-lance writer. Sontag's reputation as impassioned, committed intellectual (with a high profile) makes this position a natural one for her. The job allows her to mix literature and radical politics and to take highly publicized stands on public issues such as South Korea's censorship policies and Khomeini's death sentence of Salman Rushdie. The accolades and equality she has been granted in the male-dominated world of American intelligentsia is something that few other women have gained.

Current Address: c/o Farrar, Straus & Giroux, Inc., 19 Union Sq. West, New York, New York 10003.

References:

Contemporary Authors: New Revision Series. Detroit: Gale, Volume 25, 1988.

Current Biography Yearbook 1992. New York: H. W. Wilson, 1992.

Dictionary of Literary Biography. Detroit: Gale, Volume 67, 1992.

Sayres, Sohnya. *Susan Sontag: The Elegiac Modernist.* New York: Routledge, 1990.

—Jill Franks

Gertrude Stein

1874-1946

American writer

Gertrude Stein is regarded as one of the most remarkable writers of the twentieth century. Reacting against the naturalistic conventions of nineteenth-century fiction, she developed an abstract manner of expression that was a counterpart in language to the work of the Post-Impressionists and Cubists in the visual arts. Her radical approach was admired and emulated by other authors of her era, including Ernest Hemingway, Thornton Wilder and Sherwood Anderson, and served as a key inspiration for many modernist writers.

A Nomadic Childhood

Born on a snowy February day in 1874, Stein was the youngest of Daniel and Amelia Stein's five children. The year after Stein's birth, her father packed up his family and moved to Vienna, Austria. Three years later the Steins were living in Paris, where Gertrude and her sister Bertha went to boarding school. In 1879 the family returned to America, and, after a short stay with relatives in Baltimore, they finally settled in California. The Steins were set apart from their neighbors by the fact that they were the only Jewish family and one of only a few wealthy families in the area.

Daniel Stein was an odd, eccentric man. He was authoritarian, moody, aggressive, and evidently unpredictable. He would one day be content with their situation, the next make drastic changes—whether in schooling, medical care, or dwelling place. Consequently his children began to dislike and often fear him. His wife was, by all accounts, withdrawn and ineffectual, and of her premature death in

1888, Stein later remarked: "We had already had the habit of doing without her." After their mother's death, life for Gertrude and her siblings became very unpleasant. Their father now became an unpredictable tyrant. Stein began to suffer from panic attacks, fearing she would break down or go mad, and eventually dropped out of high school. Her brother Leo, two years her senior, was her favorite sibling, and during this period the two became even closer; Leo would remain her mentor and close companion throughout much of her youth.

Daniel Stein died in 1891, when Gertrude was 17. Her oldest brother Michael took over as head of the household and became Gertrude's legal guardian. A year after their father's death Gertrude and her sister Bertha returned to Baltimore to live with an aunt.

Education: Academic and Sentimental

In order to be near Leo, who was then at Harvard, Stein in 1892 applied for admission to the Harvard Annex, a women's college which later became Radcliffe. Although she had not completed high school, she was accepted as a special student. At the university, Stein studied philosophy, metaphysics, English, and psychology, graduating in 1898 magna cum laude. One of her psychology professors, the noted scholar William James, became a major influence in Stein's ideas about art and literature. Under James's tutelage Stein began experimenting with a process called automatic writing, in which the conscious mind is suppressed while the unconscious mind takes control of the creative process. During this time Stein decided that she would like to become a psychologist, hoping to specialize in nervous diseases of women, and she subsequently enrolled at the Johns Hopkins Medical School in Baltimore in order to acquire the requisite medical background. After two years of academic success at Johns Hopkins, Stein began to have great difficulty with her coursework, and she eventually left without obtaining a degree.

Recent biographers have suggested that the failure of her love affair with a young feminist named May Bookstaver may have played a role in Stein's academic problems. During her medical studies, Stein had once again moved in with Leo, and together they became immersed in the Baltimore cultural milieu. In particular, they attended the salons of two wealthy sisters, Claribel and Etta Cone. (After Stein moved to Europe, she and Etta Cone engaged in a romantic affair.) There Stein met Mabel Haynes, who was at the time having an affair with Bookstaver. Stein and Bookstaver subsequently became romantically involved, and the affair—and keeping it secret from Haynes—was incredibly complicated. Bookstaver ultimately chose to stay with Haynes, and Stein was devastated. She eventually documented her emotional turmoil in the novel *Q.E.D*—her only work to deal with explicitly lesbian themes, and the book she would not allow to be published in her lifetime.

At Home in Paris

In 1903, Stein once again moved in with Leo, who had established a residence in Paris. The Steins immersed themselves in the Parisian art world and collected art—including the works of the many avant-garde painters of the era: Picasso, Matisse, Gris, and Cezanne. Soon they began their famous Saturday salons which were frequented by friends, family, and art collectors as well as artists, musicians, and writers—F. Scott Fitzgerald, Hemingway, Ezra Pound, and Lytton Strachey among them.

Gertrude Stein

At 27 rue de Fleurus, in the home that would become a part of literary history, Gertrude, at 30, found her calling. Writing would be her life. By 1907, Alice B. Toklas—coincidentally another young Jewish woman from San Francisco—would enter Stein's life and make it complete. Shortly after the two women met, Toklas became part of the Stein household. Eventually she replaced Leo as Gertrude's companion; Stein referred to the relationship as a marriage, and Toklas was very much the involved wife. She learned to type so she could transcribe Stein's work. She cooked Stein's meals and saw to it that she was undisturbed when she was writing. Together the two became the most renowned lesbian couple of the twentieth century. Their home became the cultural meeting place for Americans in Paris, as well as the site of frequent visits by artists and scholars from around the world. Stein talked painting with Picasso, who painted her portait, and argued philospohy with Bertrand Russell. Indeed, in the list of notable figures of the twentieth century, there are few who can be said never to have met or visited Stein.

A Poem Is Not a Poem

"Very few of Gertrude Stein's titles can be adequately classified into any traditional literary forms," says the biography in *Great American Writers*. "Her philosophy of composition was so idiosyncratic, her prose style so seemingly nonrational, that her writing bears little resemblance to whatever genre it purports to represent." Following example of Cubist painters, Stein sought to break the traditional story into its component pieces—that is, unrelated words—and then reassemble those words in a way that would more accurately reflect human experience. Stein had learned from James that human beings experience life not as a narrative with past, present, and future neatly divided, but as a flow of sensations, a sequence of present moments. In her mature works, Stein tried to capture this flow of awareness by reiterating ideas in slightly different forms:

> Happening and have it as happening and having it happen as happening and having to have it happen as happening, and my wife has a cow as now, my wife having a cow as now, my wife having a cow as now and having a cow as now and having a cow and having a cow now, my wife has a cow and now. My wife has a cow.

Stein employed this technique to varying degrees throughout her works. Her early writings, including *Q.E.D.* and *Three Lives,* a collection of three novella-length stories patterned after Gustave Flaubert's *Three Tales,* are somewhat more traditional in style, although they do exhibit to some extent the lack of plot development that characterized her mature works. Later works, most notably the 925-page *Making of Americans,* more fully develop this technique. Near the end of her career, Stein returned to a more conventional style of writing, producing the widely read *Autobiography of Alice B. Toklas, Everybody's Autobiography,* and *Wars I Have Seen.*

Critical response to Stein's work was at first extremely negative, with critics and the public both denouncing her works as unreadable. Gradually, however, a number of notable scholars began to explore the signicance of her aesthetic experiments, and by the 1930s critics were beginning to express admiration for her innovative approach. Stein also published a number of volumes of poetry, essays describing her aesthetic theories, and two operas.

Belated Stardom

Following the success of *The Autobiography of Alice B. Toklas,* which was published in 1933 and made Stein a celebrity in the United States and Europe, Stein was invited to make a lecture tour of the United States. Finally, she was given the opportunity to explain her writing style to readers and scholars. The tour was hugely successful; Stein was warmly received and the list of people she met with whom includes Eleanor Roosevelt, George Gershwin, Charlie Chaplin, and Dashiell Hammett.

After the lecture tour, Stein and Toklas returned to their Paris apartment. However, in 1939 they sought to escape from increasing political tensions by relocating permanently to their country home. During World War Two, both faced great danger of Nazi persecution, as Jews, lesbians, and intellectuals were among those most despised by Hitler and his minions. They were spared only by the protection influential friends. During the first World War, Stein and Toklas had actively supported French and American troops by delivering medical supplies in a truck they had purchased. Now they showed their support for the Allies by befriending American soliders. In 1946 Stein published a book of dialogues based on conversations with servicemen, *Brewsie and Willie.*

In March of 1946 Stein completed the libretto of her second opera, *The Mother of Us All,* which celebrates the life of the feminist reformer Susan B. Anthony. Stein did not live to see the opera performed. She collapsed in July of that year, and was diagnosed with inoperable abdominal cancer. She died on 27 July 1946 and was buried, still surrounded by great literary figures, in Pere Lachaise Cemetery in Paris.

Despite the literary success of her later years, Stein has never been regarded as a great author. Her autobiographical writings are valued for their lively portrait of the Paris cultural scene of the 1920s and 1930s and their witty assessments of notable figures, but the majority of her works are not widely read. However, critics acknowledge that her sophisticated aesthetic theories and experiments with language were a primary influence in the development of Modernist literature. In addition, she is widely respected for her personal courage and candor; challenging assumptions and defying tradition in a variety of ways, she provided an example of progressive thinking and behavior that continues to serve as an inspiration.

References:

Harmon, Justin, et al. *American Cultural Leaders.* Santa Barbara, California: ABC-Clio, 1993.

McGill, Frank N., ed. *Great Women Writers.* New York: Henry Holt & Co., 1994.

McGraw-Hill Encyclopedia of World Biography. New York: McGraw-Hill, 1973.

Mellow, James R. *Charmed Circle: Gertrude Stein and Company.* New York: Avon Books, 1974.

Russell, Paul. "Gertrude Stein," in *The Gay 100.* New York: Citadel Press, 1995.

Shapiro, Ann R. *Jewish American Writers.* Westport, Connecticut: Greenwood Press, 1994.

Souhami, Diane. *Gertrude and Alice.* New York: Pandora Press, 1991.

—Andrea L.T. Peterson

Lytton Strachey

1880-1932

British writer

Giles Lytton Strachey was born on 1 March 1880 in London to an upper middle class family. He received early instruction in his studies from his mother who was domineering and eager for her son to become learned, especially in literature and history. Strachey attended public schools, and in 1899 was accepted at Trinity College, Cambridge. The all-boys aspect of British public schools fostered an atmosphere where homosexuality could occur with some frequency, and the extremely thin and rather sickly (health problems were to plague him his whole life) Strachey developed an attraction for some of the more athletic, healthy boys. At Cambridge he fell in love with various companions; his most passionate attraction was to Duncan Grant. Strachey went through constant emotional turmoil of joy and sadness in these infatuations.

Strachey graduated from Cambridge in 1903, but twice failed to win a post-graduate fellowship there. He soon joined the staff of the *Spectator* and wrote essays, literary criticism, and drama reviews. In 1912 his first book, *Landmarks of French Literature*, was published which surveyed various periods of French writing and commented—at times perceptively, at other times sketchily—on the work of some of the most famous writers of each literary era.

Strachey fell in love with the painter Henry Lamb and continued his writing career. He conceived the idea of short biographical portraits of several famous English Victorian figures. This project was to result in his most famous book, *Eminent Victorians*, published in 1918. The volume featured biographical studies of Cardinal Manning, Dr. Thomas Arnold, Florence Nightingale, and General Charles George Gordon. The book introduced into literature a new type of biography. Previous biographical studies were lengthy, staid, generally appreciative, matter-of-fact recordings of details with little vigor and sparkling appeal. Strachey enlivened his studies with selected quotations by and about his subject, by psychological theorizing about their thoughts and behavior and by intermingling these materials with social and historical events. He is especially selective in the details he relates, humanizing the individuals portrayed, and making considerable use of irony. Much of his approach was based on debunking Victorian propriety and conventions, frequently revealing or conjecturing about the less praiseworthy aspects of his subjects. In so doing he did in several instances present wrong-headed and questionable theories and interpretations. All of the character analyses are conveyed in a lively, vigorous style with considerable use of effective metaphors and similes, balanced structure, and precise word choice. It has been said by several critics, with ample justification, that his biographies read like novels. Not only are the overall portraits particularly fascinating, but many individual episodes are particularly engrossing. Dr. Arnold's delivering his stirring weekly sermons to the boys at Rugby, the shattering account of the wounded and dying soldiers in the Crimean war, and General Gordon's activities in China especially stamp themselves indelibly on the readers' minds and yet perfectly blend with the complete portraits. *Eminent Victorians* was an instant success and established Strachey as the creator of a "new biography" form. To this day it remains his most famous book.

Strachey followed this work with *Queen Victoria* (1921). In this biography he continued the same technique of mixing historical details with psychological analysis. Although he was antagonistic to the restrictions of the Victorian Period, his portrayal of Victoria and Albert is essentially sympathetic. He gives the queen and her consort a vivid human dimension; and even if some of his interpretations are questionable, he teases the reader to meditate on ambiguities and uncertainties of behavior. The characters come fully alive, and Strachey's wit and winning style impel the biography forward at a bright and brisk pace.

In the meantime, Strachey had become a member of the "Bloomsbury Group" of writers, artists, and intellectuals and met Dora Carrington, with whom he established a close relationship. Although they each carried on sexual affairs with each other's knowledge and Carrington eventually was married briefly, their relationship was so intense that when Strachey died, Carrington committed suicide less than two months later.

In his last years, Strachey began a liaison with Roger Senhouse. This affair distracted him and slowed the writing of his last significant biography, *Elizabeth and Essex*, which was published in 1928. This study presented Strachey with a more difficult problem than the previous biographies because so little information was available about the inner thoughts of his subjects. The complex relationship between the powerful queen and her dashing courtier and warrior, who was over thirty years her junior, is presented in a poetic prose designed to capture the more exuberant, romantic, and imaginative era of the sixteenth century.

Lytton Strachey. ***Photograph by E. O. Hoppé.***

In addition to the change in prose style, Strachey's *Elizabeth and Essex* displays other differences from his earlier biographies. Strachey, as several critics have stressed, seems to instill more of his personal feelings into this book. He sees part of himself in both his subjects. He also brings more obviously fictional analysis into the biography so that much of the theorizing of mental states appears much less persuasive. Furthermore, he has been both praised and blamed for his introduction of Freudian analysis into his interpretation of the Queen's character and actions. The narrative drive, however, does not flag, and the tragedy of Essex remains forcefully in the reader's thoughts.

Strachey's three biographies guarantee him a significant place in this genre. His personal life, as he often admitted, was frequently in emotional turmoil, and he suffered considerably by the unreliable devotion of those to whom he was attracted and by the undesired termination of various liaisons. Over the last fifteen years of his life, it was the mental and emotional faithfulness and closeness of Carrington which brought him considerable comforting solace.

References:

Beerbohm, Max. *Lytton Strachey.* Cambridge: Cambridge University Press, 1943.

Ferns, John. *Lytton Strachey.* Boston: Twayne, 1988.
Holroyd, Michael. *Lytton Strachey: A Critical Biography, Vol. I: The Unknown Years 1880-1910.* New York: Holt, Rinehart and Winston, 1967.
———. *Lytton Strachey: A Critical Biography, Vol. II: The Years of Achievement.* New York: Holt, Rinehart and Winston, 1968.
Iyengar, K. R. *Lytton Strachey: A Critical Study.* London: Chatto & Windus, 1939.
Johnstone, J. K. *The Bloomsbury Group: A Study of E.M. Forster, Lytton Strachey, Virginia Woolf and Their Circle.* London: Secker & Warburg, 1954.
Kallich, Martin. *The Psychological Milieu of Lytton Strachey.* New Haven: College & University Press, 1961.
Sanders, C. R. *Lytton Strachey: His Mind and Art.* New Haven: Yale University Press, 1957.

—Paul A. Doyle

Gerry E. Studds

1937–

American politician

Congressman Gerry Studds, who announced his retirement in October 1995, served 12 terms in the United States House of Representatives, representing southeastern Massachusetts in the Congress since 1973. The first openly gay member of Congress, he has been a leader in the area of HIV and women's health, civil rights, and the environment.

Gerry E. Studds was born on 12 May 1937 in Mineola, New York, the son of a Long Island architect. He spent most of his youth in Cohasset, Massachusetts. He graduated from Yale University in 1959 and earned his master's degree in teaching two years later. Studds held a number of Washington jobs in the early 1960s, including working as a foreign service officer with the U.S. Department of State in 1961. He served on President Kennedy's White House staff for the Domestic Peace Corps, acting as congressional liaison for the Domestic Peace Corps Task Force, chaired by Attorney General Robert F. Kennedy. Studds turned eventually to teaching, holding a position at a boarding school in New Hampshire. His opposition to the war in Vietnam prompted him to return to politics in 1967, when he enlisted in Eugene J. McCarthy's presidential campaign. He launched his first campaign for Congress in 1970.

Congressional Censure

Perhaps Studds' most remarkable achievement is his political resiliency, even in the face of scandal. In 1983, the House censured Studds for sexual misconduct stemming from a sexual relationship he had with a 17-year-old male congressional page in the 1970s. The charge originated from a 16-month investigation of alleged sexual misconduct and drug use by the Committee on Standards of Official Conduct. It was the first time a House member had been censured for sexual misconduct. Studds responded to the charges, and in a statement on the House floor publicly acknowledged his homosexuality. In a prepared statement he said, "I do not believe that a relationship which was mutual and voluntary; without coercion; without any preferential treatment express or implied; without harassment of any kind; which was private; and which occurred 10 years ago constitutes 'improper conduct' within the meaning of House Resolution 518...."

Studds admitted to "an error in judgment," and stated at the height of the controversy that his sexual preference had nothing to do with his ability to do his job.

Although there was some initial fallout from the censure—it briefly cost Studds his base of legislative power, the chairmanship of the Coast Guard and Navigation Subcommittee on Merchant Marine—he emerged from the scandal relatively unscathed.

Rather than go into retreat following the censure, Studds returned home and embarked on a round of town meetings. He waited until early 1984, after the controversy had subsided, to announce he would run again for office.

Studds' disclosure of his homosexuality gained him a new constituency in the gay community, allowing him to play a more active role in gay issues. Studds was returned to his seat by a solid majority and restored to his committee assignments.

A 1985 profile in the *Boston Globe* characterized Studds as a bit of a renegade, occasionally aloof, and an often caustic critic of Congress. Studds seemed somewhat wistful when he recalled his first term in Congress, a time when there seemed to be weightier and more provocative issues to address such as Vietnam and civil rights, and bemoaned the gutless and undisciplined Congress of the 1980s, with its infusion of "humorless ideologues."

Fishing and maritime policy have always been top priority for Studds, and the Merchant Marine and Fisheries Committee, abol-

Gerry E. Studds

ished by Republicans in 1995, was the place where Studds' leadership was most keenly felt. It allowed him to play an active role in the passage of a number of major pieces of environmental legislation, including the Marine Mammal Protection Act and the establishment of the International 200-mile fisheries conservation zone, his most noteworthy achievement.

As a member of the Subcommittee on Health and Environment, Studds has been a strong advocate of health care reform, and has pressed forcefully for expanded federal funding for HIV/AIDS research, prevention and care. In 1987, he became the first member of Congress to send a copy of Surgeon General Koop's "Report on AIDS" to every household in his district—a step which ultimately helped convince the Reagan administration to allow a nationwide mailing. Studds authored a 1992 law to ensure the availability of Taxol, a drug which is used to treat breast and ovarian cancer, and was an early leader in the fight to lift the ban on lesbians and gay men in the military. In 1994 he joined Senator Edward Kennedy in introducing the Employment Non-Discrimination Act, which would prohibit sexual orientation discrimination in the workplace.

Studds drew some press again in 1993 when he objected to the scheduled appearance of Gary Bauer, former policy advisor in the Reagan White House, at a U.S. Coast Guard prayer breakfast. Bauer, a conservative who had spoken out against lifting the ban on homosexuals in the military, was also believed by Studds to have dragged his feet when it came to taking action on AIDS. Studds felt that Bauer's appearance at the prayer breakfast was inappropriate, but his aversion may have gone back as far as the 1983 censure, when Bauer suggested Studds should resign. Bauer's invitation to speak was retracted and the breakfast eventually canceled.

A Chapter Closes

Studds had been considering leaving congress since the summer of 1992 when his district was redrawn, but decided to stay through President Clinton's first term. The Republican takeover of congress in 1995 may have been the last straw. He was one of a number of Democrats who decided to leave the House in 1996, and he is quoted as saying that the Republican program left him "somewhere between incredulous and nauseous" (*Washington Post*, 29 October 1995). In personal statements he has stressed, however, that his decision was not related to recent political developments.

On 28 October 1995, in an open meeting on Martha's Vineyard, Studds announced his resignation in typically eloquent fashion: "Since embarking on this improbable journey, I have been very conscious that each of us is allotted only so many hours and so many days on this earth. Together, we have worked our hearts out; together, we have overcome odds and obstacles that would have discouraged most others; and together, you and I have strived to make many things better than we found them.... Never has an elected representative been so blessed by the beauty of his District and by the decency and common sense of his constituents."

Current Address: U.S. House of Representatives, 237 Cannon House Office Bureau, Washington, D.C., 20515.

References:

Babcock, Charles R. "Rep. Studds of Massachusetts Will Not Seek Reelection," in *Washington Post*, 29 October 1995: A31.

Congressional Record—House, 14 July 1983: 19167.

Duncan, Philip D. and Christine C. Lawrence. *Politics in America 1996: The 104th Congress*. Washington, D.C.: Congressional Quarterly, Inc., 1995.

Ehrenhalt, Alan, Renee Amrine, and Philip D. Duncan. *Politics in America: The 100th Congress*. Washington, D.C.: Congressional Quarterly, Inc., 1987.

Hentoff, Nat. "Gerry Studds: Chairman with an Animus," in *Washington Post*, 13 March 1993: A21.

Patterson, Eugene, ed. *Congressional Quarterly Almanac: 98th Congress Ist Session ... 1983*. Washington, D.C.: Congressional Quarterly, Inc., 1984.

Press Materials from the Office of Congressman Gerry E. Studds, 1995, 1996.

Robinson, John. "Studds' Stature High Despite '83 Censure," in *Boston Globe*, 24 November 1985: 1 & 28.

Vobejda, Barbara. "Coast Guard Entangled by Gay Issue," in *Washington Post*, 6 February 1993: A12.

—Lynda Schrecengost

John Addington Symonds

1840-1893

British historian, critic, and poet

Trapped between Victorian prudery and his intense erotic devotion to his own sex, John Addington Symonds was a classic case of a brilliant man of letters forced to repress his homosexuality. He was also an early example of a gay man who struggled to realize and live what he came to believe was his natural sexual orientation. In addition, he achieved real literary distinction.

Privilege and Conflict

Born into the family of Dr. J. A. Symonds, the most eminent physician in the west of England, young John Addington was a sickly infant, and his whole life was plagued with illnesses, especially pulmonary ones. Nevertheless, the boy was nurtured well in the cultivated home he loved at Clifton, an elevated suburb of the port city of Bristol. After his mother died of scarlet fever when he was four, the lad was devoted to his sister Charlotte and was even more influenced by his Non-conformist father.

Although John was uncomfortable with most boys of his age, with their rough and tumble games, he was drawn to them also. This attraction-repulsion syndrome was strengthened at Harrow and found expression in a sudden romantic attachment to a chorister named Willie Dyer, who had an exquisite voice. This late adolescent affair, intensely idealized and quite likely never consummated sexually, set a lifelong pattern between himself and younger males. However, physical expression also entered such relationships in his early adulthood.

Rigid and oppressive societal disapproval complicated Symonds' feelings about same sex love, especially if one partner was older than the other. While schools such as Harrow were virtually hotbeds of such affairs, most often between a dominant, demanding older youth and a neophyte, there occurred at Harrow an incriminating event so shocking that many besides Symonds were astonished, distressed, and repelled.

John Addington Symonds

Dr. Henry Vaughn was the headmaster of the school and most highly regarded. Called "the restorer of Harrow," he recreated the school, bringing enrollment from 60 to 415 in his fifteen-year tenure. Thus it was incredulous disbelief that Symonds felt when a Harrow friend, Alfred Pretor, revealed to him a number of love letters that Vaughn had written to him. Symonds told his father of Vaughn's letters, all the while agonizing because he knew he shared his headmaster's orientation.

Dr. Symonds summoned Vaughn to Clifton, revealed his knowledge, and urged Vaughn to resign. The headmaster complied. While a public school scandal was avoided, and Vaughn became vicar of Doncaster, Symonds' guilty feelings about his homosexuality and its possible consequences were magnified.

At eighteen, Symonds went up to Balliol College, Oxford, where his intellectual life was deepened through rigorous colloquies with his peers and acquaintance with such famous scholars as Benjamin Jowett, the authority on Greek literature. Though Symonds' years at Oxford were marked with attainments, he was still tormented by his homosexual obsessions and aborted romances.

An Attempt at Conventionality

Resolved to escape such obsessions and take on a more stable, conventional sexual nature, Symonds set about finding a suitable marriage partner. He found her in Catherine North, the daughter of the member of Parliament from Hastings. In England and in trips to the continent of Europe, the relationship of the two deepened, with Symonds even enduring neuralgia from sitting beside an icy Swiss stream while his intended sketched the landscape. Though never passionate in his feelings toward her, Symonds developed real respect for Catherine. She reciprocated. They were married in 1864.

Four daughters were born of this union, but Symonds' sexual orientation was by no means converted to heterosexuality. Rather, he repeated his pattern of falling in love with younger men. A typical example was Norman Moor, a sixth form boy at Clifton College. Moor was an unusually intelligent youth who attracted Symonds immediately. Their relationship became intimate, and Catherine's jealousy grew. Nevertheless, because she had never found fulfillment in their sexual relationship and felt child bearing to be outright odious, the couple's sexual relationship ceased, though their mutual respect sustained their marriage.

Because Symonds was so subject to chest diseases, it became increasingly desirable for him to live in a healthier climate than dank England. Almost by accident, he discovered Davos, an Alpine town in eastern Switzerland, where the air was clear. From 1877, he lived in Davos the greater part of the time, but he also had a residence in Venice.

Writing Success

Recovering his stamina, Symonds devoted himself to study and writing. Before he came to Switzerland, he had completed the first two volumes of *The Renaissance in Italy*, and periodically, from 1875 to 1886, five more volumes were added. Primarily a cultural history concentrating on the revival of learning and the evolving aesthetics of the period, it is presented in a series of extended essays written in a fluent, picturesque style. Though thought by some today to be dated, the study is still Symonds' monument.

Adding to both the bulk and the luster of his work, Symonds produced critical biographies of Percy Shelley, Ben Jonson, Sir Phillip Sydney, and Michaelangelo, whose sonnets he translated. An influential critic of the day, Churton Collins of the *Contemporary Review*, declared to Symonds, "There is not a single man born since 1840 who holds such a place in literature that you do ... In ten years time, your influence and status will be enormous."

Beginning in 1881, Symonds composed two works on his concept of male homosexuality in collaboration with two early sexologists, Havelock Ellis and the German, Carl Ulrichs. *A Problem in Greek Ethics* and *A Problem in Modern Ethics* were privately printed and distributed to carefully selected people.

The Greek concept represented that ancient culture's acceptance of pederasty as a socially useful combination of sexual affection and mentoring. His own concept espoused a similarly institutionalized arrangement. While reactions were mixed, the combined works stand as an extraordinarily enlightened early expression of a sexual orientation that has been increasingly recognized as natural. Among those receiving the books was Walt Whitman, who was called by Symonds "the most Hellenic of Americans." Whitman's refusal to endorse Symonds' views was a major disappointment.

Spurred on by a surprising number of testimonials from gay men who had read the texts, Symonds moved to alter sex-related legislation, especially the harsh Labouchere Amendment to the Sexual Offenses Act, the most punitive of all European sex laws.

Symonds collaborated with Ellis on the book *Sexual Inversion*. Though the majority of the public considered the publication obscene, a more enlightened minority accepted its central thesis, that the homosexual should be left free to live his own life unhampered by fear of legal or social persecution. The Wolfenden Report of 1957 reiterated this thesis.

In the dozen years before his death in 1893, Symonds developed the most completely evolved love of his life. On one of his impulsive visits to his beloved Venice, his good friend and eventual biographer Horatio Brown pointed out a strikingly handsome gondolier clad in a white uniform. A few nights later, Symonds arranged a rendezvous and persuaded the twenty-four year old man to come with him to his rooms at the Casa Alberti. So began Symonds' passionate liaison with Angelo Fusato.

Angelo was basically heterosexual and indeed married during his relationship with Symonds, a step made possible by Symonds' financial help. Nevertheless, the two men's intimacy was sustained. Symonds even took Angelo to England in 1892 and made it quite clear to the relatives and friends he visited that accommodations must be made for Angelo.

Though Symonds worked prodigiously at Davos, it was becoming clear that he was physically weakening. Again in Italy in the spring of 1893, Symonds indulged in his favorite way of knowing a city, a solitary walk through the dark streets of Rome. He returned complaining of a sore throat, and it was soon obvious that he had contracted influenza, epidemic in the city at that time. While he lay dying, boisterous festivity was raging outside in celebration of the silver anniversary of the king and queen. He slipped peacefully into death on 19 April 1893.

References:

Grosskurth, Phyllis. *The Woeful Victorian.* New York: Holt, Rhinehart and Winston, 1964.

Grosskurth, Phyllis, ed. *The Memoirs of John Addington Symonds.* New York: Random House, 1984.

Symonds, John Addington. *Studies of the Greek Poets.* 3rd. ed, London: Charles and Adam Black, 1893.

—Marvin S. Shaw

T

Peter Ilich Tchaikovsky

1840-1893

Russian composer

Peter Ilich Tchaikovsky was the most subjective of artists. His emotional life as a homosexual imbued his music, which expressed an amazing range of textures and depth of feeling while always maintaining touches of lightness and delicacy. Even during his lifetime, Tchaikovsky won wide renown on three continents as a composer of some of the most accessible classical music ever composed, with such compositions as the ballets *Swan Lake* and *The Nutcracker*, the Fantasy Overture *Romeo and Juliet*, and the *1812 Overture*. Despite his fame, many facts about Tchaikovsky's personal experiences have been elusive due to censorship, tampering, or destruction of his personal papers. However, many editions of letters and diaries still exist, thus enabling Alexander Poznansky, the author of *Tchaikovsky: The Quest for the Inner Man*, to accurately reconstruct many details of the composer's life.

Tchaikovsky was the second of six children born to Ilya Petrovich Tchaikovsky and his second wife, Aleksandra. Ilya was the prosperous manager of the ironworks at Votinsk in the Ural Mountains when Peter was born on 7 May 1840. Peter's mother Aleksandra, the daughter of a French emigré, had already born a son, Nikolay, two years earlier. Peter loved Nikolay, but was fonder of his younger siblings, Aleksandra, Ippolit, and especially the twins, Anatoly and Modest. Peter, whose effortless charm made him the favorite son and brother in the family circle, cherished his family and shared their sorrows and joys throughout his life.

Tchaikovsky was no great child prodigy. The fact that he showed perfect pitch and could easily improvise tunes was not unusual in his musical family. His mother was an accomplished singer and harpist, and his father possessed an automated orchestrina which played *Don Giovanni* by Mozart, Tchaikovsky's favorite composer. He showed extreme vulnerability towards everything, including music, which often sent him into uncontrollable fits of sobbing. Some claim that it was homosexual repression that resulted in Tchaikovsky's long history of neurotic behavior, but it was merely an inherited susceptibility: his grandfather, Andrey d'Assier, had suffered from nervous attacks similar to epilepsy.

Preparing for a Civil Service Career

A career as a civil servant was the future planned out for Tchaikovsky, who, in 1850 entered the Imperial School of Jurisprudence in St. Petersburg. He received both his secondary and higher education there. He could barely tolerate being separated from his beloved mother whose death from cholera in 1854 was the first experience of shattering grief in his life.

Peter Ilich Tchaikovsky

Life was harsh, and discipline meted out swiftly at the school of Jurisprudence, but Tchaikovsky always remained a favorite, not only of his fellow pupils but also of the administration. He was even considered one of the most handsome students. He developed lifelong friendships with fellow pupils Aleksey Apukhtin, the gay lyric poet, and Prince Vladimir Meschersky, who later became advisor to the last two tsars and was publicly reviled for his unconcealed homosexual practices. Tchaikovsky experienced his first intimate relationship with schoolmate Sergey Kireev, to whom he dedicated one of his first songs, "My genius, my angel, my friend."

Tchaikovsky left the School of Jurisprudence in May 1859 and immediately found a position at the Department of Justice in St. Petersburg. His duties were light and he devoted plenty of energy to night life. He frequented the homosexual circles of Apukhtin and Meschersky, where he charmed his new social acquaintances as he had his family and schoolmates. He entertained friends at parties with his scandalous impersonations of famous prima ballerinas. "He knew how to make the unacceptable permissible," exclaimed his homosexual brother Modest in *The Life and Letters of Peter Ilich Tchaikovsky*.

The Civil Servant Becomes the Composer

Tchaikovsky's career in the civil service came to an abrupt halt in 1862 when he was passed over for a promotion. The 22-year-old Tchaikovsky decided to develop his musical talents, although he had serious misgivings about his abilities. He enrolled at the new St. Petersburg Conservatory in September 1862, where his musical progress under the tutelage of the great composer Anton Rubinstein was deemed no less than remarkable. In August of 1865, Johann Strauss the younger conducted Tchaikovsky's orchestral piece *Characteristic Dances* (later known as "Dances of the Chambermaids" in the opera *The Voyevode*) for the public at Pavlosk near St. Petersburg. This was an auspicious debut for the young composer who had yet to graduate from the conservatory in December.

After Tchaikovsky completed his education in St. Petersburg, he began teaching music theory at the just-founded Moscow Conservatory in 1866. The conservatory's director was Anton Rubinstein's brother Nikolay, a brilliant conductor and pianist who developed a fatherly affection for Tchaikovsky. The strain of teaching while simultaneously working on his first critical success, the First Symphony in G Minor, *Winter Dreams*, led to Tchaikovsky's first nervous breakdown in July of 1866.

The following fall, Tchaikovsky began a long, emotionally turbulent relationship with a private pupil, the young, rich, and temperamental Vladimir Shilovsky. Shilovsky totally captivated the composer, who often accompanied him on trips abroad. Shilovsky's marriage would contribute to their estrangement in 1877. Tchaikovsky dedicated his famous Humoresque for piano to Shilovsky. Tchaikovsky became briefly infatuated in 1868 with Desirée Artôt, an older and somewhat stout Belgian soprano with the Paris Opéra, whom the composer considered a goddess of song. Their relationship, however, ended abruptly when rumors of homosexuality reached the ears of Artôt's mother.

Tchaikovsky had produced 30 compositions, including two operas and a symphony, by 1871 when the 12-year-old servant Aleksey Sofronov came into his life. Aleksey, affectionately called Aloysha, took on the roles of Tchaikovsky's servant, nurse, travelling companion, and friend. By 1877, he had become his master's lover as well. Aloysha eventually married, but he remained Tchaikovsky's faithful servant until the composer's death.

In 1875, the homosexual composer Camille Saint-Saens met Tchaikovsky while visiting Moscow. They both discovered their shared fondness for impersonating female dancers and became fast friends. Word reached Tchaikovsky in early 1876 that his music was stirring enthusiasm in America. This news stimulated his creative muse, and he quickly composed the Third String Quartet in E-flat Minor and began working on his first ballet, *Swan Lake*.

Women Enter Tchaikovsky's Life in 1877

In March 1877 the composer received an admiring letter from Nadezhda von Meck. This was the beginning of a passionate, spiritual bond that would span the next 13 years. Mrs. von Meck, who became Tchaikovsky's financial benefactress, was the fabulously rich, eccentric widow of a railroad tycoon and mother of 11 children. She kept an entourage of musicians about her, one of which was the young Claude Debussy. Tchaikovsky, however, was her ideal of a musician and a human being—so much so, that she feared the reality of his presence. The two agreed never to meet. In the prolific correspondence between them, Tchaikovsky never broached the subject of his homosexuality, although he poured out his soul to Mrs. von Meck in all other respects. The open-minded benefactress, however, kept abreast of all the homosexual rumors involving her beloved ideal. She amicably, yet mysteriously, ended her relationship with Tchaikovsky three years before his death.

Tchaikovsky turned to matrimony as a way to dispel rumors of homosexuality and surmount his inclinations. Up to this point, the composer had thought that his sexual preferences might somehow be reversible. Antonina Mulykova, a conservatory student, began writing the composer love letters in early 1877 while he was composing his most famous opera, *Eugene Onegin*. She threatened suicide if he did not return her affections. Tchaikovsky acquiesced to Antonina and morosely wed her on 6 July.

As Poznansky reports, Tchaikovsky described to Mrs. von Meck his marriage as a period of "unspeakable moral torments." From his pretty bride, whom he found physically repulsive, he exacted the promise that she cherish him only as a brother. He felt guilty for deceiving her only in order to disguise himself. Suffering under the strain, he took refuge in alcohol and allegedly attempted suicide by immersing himself in cold water in order to catch pneumonia.

Tchaikovsky travelled to St. Petersburg in September to oversee a production of his opera *Vakula the Smith*. Once away from Antonina, he suffered a complete nervous collapse, lapsing into unconsciousness for several days. His doctor sent him to Switzerland to recuperate. A separation was announced in October. In a letter to his brother Anatoly, Tchaikovsky confessed that marriage had taught him that it was fruitless to want to be other than what he was by nature. Antonina never divorced Tchaikovsky, but hounded him constantly for money, which he readily paid to be rid of her. In 1896 she was confined to an insane asylum after having had three illegitimate children which she abandoned to orphanages.

The Fourth Symphony Emerges from Marital Anguish

Tchaikovsky transformed the torments of his marriage and nervous breakdown into his Fourth Symphony in F Minor, which he dedicated to Mrs. von Meck. Poznansky relates that the composer told Mrs. von Meck that he completed this symphony in the aftermath of "a series of unbearable agonies of anguish and despair that had all but driven me to utter madness and ruin." Tchaikovsky described to his benefactress that the symphony's principal theme dealt with implacable Fate, "which hangs over the head like the sword of Damocles and steadily and continually poisons the soul." Modern music scholars have written much about the homosexual elements of this autobiographical composition. In her book *Feminine Endings*, Susan McClary suggests that the symphony's unusual modulatory chord progression of "feminine" thirds—as opposed to "masculine" fifths—is evidence of Tchaikovsky's homosexuality. In his article "Aspects of Sexuality and Structure in the Later Symphonies of Tchaikovsky," Timothy L. Jackson asserts that these minor thirds rise aggressively, resulting in "homosexual" tritones which deviate from "heterosexual" diatonic harmony.

Tchaikovsky quit teaching at the Moscow Conservatory in 1878. Mrs. von Meck's allowance afforded him more free time to compose. He retreated to Switzerland where he composed the opera *The Maid of Orléans*. In 1879 he travelled to Kamenka to visit his sister Aleksandra and her seven children, including eight-year-old Vladimir, whom the family called Bob. Tchaikovsky became increasingly infatuated with Bob as he grew older. Tchaikovsky and

Aleksandra unfortunately drifted apart due to her alcoholism and morphine addiction, which would eventually kill her and her oldest daughter Tatyana as well. Tchaikovsky was in Rome working on his *Capriccio italien* in January of 1880 when he learned of the passing of his elderly father, for whom he wept a great deal.

Apukhtin had once introduced the Grand Duke Konstantin Konstantinovich to Tchaikovsky, and in 1881 the two met again in Rome. Tchaikovsky intended to join the Grand Duke and his two cousins, the younger brothers of Tsar Alexander II, on a trip to Athens and Jerusalem, but the dreadful news of the tsar's assassination spoiled their plans. Tchaikovsky became a favorite of the new tsar, Alexander III, for whom he wrote the *Coronation March*. Seven years later, the composer started receiving a generous lifetime pension from the tsar.

A Love Triangle Ends in Suicide

Weary of constant travel, Tchaikovsky rented a house near Klin, where he remained for most of 1885. During this time, he created his *Manfred* Symphony and began working on the opera *The Sorceress*. He travelled to Tblisi, Georgia in 1886 to visit his brother Anatoly and his wife, Praskoyva. There he met a young artillery officer named Ivan Verinovsky, who took an immediate liking to the composer and rarely left his side. A few days after Tchaikovsky's departure, Verinovsky committed suicide. This episode haunted the composer long afterward, and he blamed his sister-in-law for the incident. The coquettish Praskoyva hinted at a love triangle many decades later when she bragged about stealing one of the famous composer's lovers.

A series of European tours in the late 1880s made Tchaikovsky's fame widespread. The composer developed a warm affection for the youthful pianist featured on these tours, although it is unlikely that their relationship was sexual. Tchaikovsky had a penchant for collecting young male protégés who admired him and flirted with him, but they ultimately wanted only the great composer's help in promoting their careers.

In April of 1891, Tchaikovsky embarked on an American tour. He received an ecstatic reception in New York, where he was surprised to discover that he was more famous than in Europe. He directed his *Coronation March* at the grand opening ceremonies of Carnegie Hall, and extended his tour to other eastern cities. Tchaikovsky felt welcome in America, but, as Poznansky points out, he missed his nephew Bob terribly, to whom he wrote: "Bob! I adore you. Do you remember, I told you that even greater than my joy at beholding you with my own eyes is my suffering when I am without you!"

By 1892 Tchaikovsky was attended by his "Fourth Suite," a retinue of young men, including Bob, a few cousins, and protégés, who provided the composer with insouciant eroticism that took his mind off unpleasant matters, such as the fact that his ballet *The Nutcracker* received bad initial reviews. It was to Bob that he lovingly dedicated his latest composition, the Sixth Symphony *Pathétique*. This symphony became Tchaikovsky's masterpiece, but he kept its theme a mystery. Some scholars claim that this subjectively imbued work was inspired by Tchaikovsky's homoerotic passion for Bob.

Untimely Death Sparks Baseless Rumors

In high spirits, the composer arrived in St. Petersburg in October of 1893. He took up residence in the apartments of his brother Modest, who had become a prominent playwright, and occupied himself with preparations for the première of his Sixth Symphony. He succumbed to the cholera epidemic that was attacking the city. Surrounded by Bob, Modest, Aloysha, and the "Fourth Suite," Tchaikovsky died on 25 October after a four-day battle with death. The Tsar bore all the costs of the elaborate funeral which took place three days later. Most of St. Petersburg turned out to pay their respects. Mrs. von Meck, who would die three months later, sent an expensive wreath.

Tchaikovsky's untimely death was met by shock and disbelief. Many did not want to admit that the famous, beloved composer had died from such an inelegant disease as cholera. Tchaikovsky's homosexuality had long been a source of whispers among the intelligentsia, and now his death fanned the flames of idle gossip. One widely held rumor purported that Tchaikovsky had been discovered in a homosexual affair with a member of the imperial family and chose suicide rather than be tried for sodomy. This rumor became a popular myth which is still repeated in sensational biographies today.

In a letter to Mrs. von Meck in 1880, which Poznansky quotes, Tchaikovsky predicted that one day people "will try to penetrate the intimate world of my feelings and thoughts, everything that all my life I have so carefully hidden from the touch of the crowd." Although many records of his thoughts and feelings did not survive, his music still exists as the best revelation of his subjective inner life. After all, Tchaikovsky himself did once proclaim that he appeared in his music as God had created him.

References:

Jackson, Timothy L. "Aspects of Sexuality and Structure in the Later Symphonies of Tchaikovsky," *Music Analysis*, March 1995.

McClary, Susan. *Feminine Endings: Music, Gender, and Sexuality*. Minneapolis: University of Minnesota Press, 1991.

Poznansky, Alexander. *Tchaikovsky: The Quest for the Inner Man*. New York: Schirmer Books, 1991.

Tchaikovsky, M. J. *The Life and Letters of Peter Ilich Tchaikovsky*, edited from the Russian by Rosa Newmarch. New York: Dodd and Mead, 1905.

—Seán Henry

Martha Carey Thomas

1857-1935

American educator, activist, and feminist

To enable future generations of women to delight in the joys of knowledge and experience professional careers, M. Carey Thomas fought for feminism. One of the most prominent American educators and women's activists at the turn to the twentieth century, Thomas gained fame as the founding dean and second president of the single-sex Bryn Mawr College in Pennsylvania.

Martha Carey Thomas

Born on 2 January 1857 in Baltimore, Maryland, Martha Carey Thomas was the first of the ten children of James Carey Thomas, a physician, and Mary Whitall Thomas, the first president of the Baltimore chapter of the Woman's Christian Temperance Union and the sister of the reformer Hannah Whitall Smith. The family, financially comfortable but by no means wealthy, belonged to the Gurneyite Quaker sect.

The Quaker principle of equality of the sexes in religion helped shape Thomas's feminism as she was growing up. Encouraged by her family to view herself as the equal of any man, Thomas established a lifelong pattern of refusing to accept subordination. A fire during her youth also had a lasting impact. Horribly burned at the age of seven, by a kitchen accident that set her dress on fire, Thomas lost her faith in God when her prayers for healing were never answered. During her long recovery, she also began to read voraciously and developed a passionate love for literature.

Minnie, as Thomas was nicknamed during her childhood, attended various Quaker schools while growing up including Howland Institute near Ithaca, New York. Convinced that a life of the mind could not be compatible with the child-bearing responsibilities of marriage, Thomas resolved never to wed. She set about developing a scholarly career, a rare dream for a Victorian woman.

After graduation from Howland, and against her father's wishes, Thomas enrolled in the newly coeducational Cornell University in 1875. Having dropped her first name for a more elegant one, the woman now known as M. Carey Thomas received a bachelor's degree in 1877. Later that year, Thomas entered Johns Hopkins University, intent on obtaining a graduate degree, but she was not permitted to attend classes with men and withdrew a year later. Leaving the United States for Europe, Thomas studied in Leipzig, Germany. When professors at Leipzig refused to examine a woman for the doctorate degree, Thomas transferred to the University of Zurich in Switzerland. In 1882, she became the first woman and the first foreigner to obtain that school's doctorate *summa cum laude*. She returned home in glory, and with the hope of a prominent role in the formation of the new Quaker women's college being planned for Bryn Mawr, Pennsylvania.

Appointed to a post at Bryn Mawr in 1883, Thomas became the first dean of an American women's college to hold a doctorate. The school officially opened in 1885 and, by 1892, Thomas was president in all but title. Named president in 1894, she boosted the scholarly reputation of the college by seeking only the ablest scholars for the faculty, recruiting Woodrow Wilson among others. She encouraged non-traditional attitudes among the undergraduates and strongly supported academic and professional careers for women, famously stating, as Helen Lefkowitz Horowitz reports in her 1994 book *The Power and Passion of M. Carey Thomas* that "our failures only marry."

Education of Women, published in 1900, established Thomas's international reputation as the leading authority on the higher education of women. Recognizing the importance of women's roles in Progressive-era social reform, Thomas also found time to contribute to the building of the Johns Hopkins University School of Medicine and the Bryn Mawr Summer School for Women Workers.

While in Europe, Thomas had lived with Mamie Gwinn and this arrangement continued at Bryn Mawr, with the two openly sharing a home on the college campus until Gwinn married in 1904. (Gertrude Stein immortalized their messy breakup in her story *Fernhurst*.) While involved with Gwinn, Thomas had pursued a relationship with Mary Garrett, a philanthropist and heiress to the Baltimore and Ohio Railroad fortune. After Gwinn and Thomas separated, Garrett and Thomas became a couple, living together at the college until Garrett's death in 1915. That Thomas was a lesbian is well-established. Analyzing Thomas's reading, Horowitz argues, that the Bryn Mawr president was well aware of the possibilities for physical love between women and of the medically oriented literature on sexuality that began to appear in the late nineteenth century.

Retiring from the college in 1922, Thomas succumbed to heart failure on 2 December 1935. Her ashes are buried in the cloister of Bryn Mawr's library and her papers remain housed at the school. A forceful woman, and not always a likeable one, Thomas is notable for managing to carve out a large role for women in the world of academia. Her accomplishments and her struggles for female independence in a man's world demand respect.

References:

Horowitz, Helen Lefkowitz. *The Power and Passion of M. Carey Thomas*. New York: Alfred A. Knopf, 1994.

Sicherman, Barbara. "Reading and Ambition: M. Carey Thomas and Female Heroism," *American Quarterly*, March 1993.

—Caryn E. Neumann

Alice B. Toklas

1877-1967

American memoirist and publisher

American writer Alice B. Toklas, devoted lover and self-acknowledged "wife" of the 20th-century writer and literary innovator Gertrude Stein, lived most of her adult life in Europe, primarily in Paris. Despite Toklas' life-long efforts to promote Stein's works and her genius, Toklas did not make her own literary contribution until after Stein's death. Toklas' memoirs are replete with reminiscences of Stein, their life together, and the writers, artists, and intellectuals whom they befriended. Her work affords a unique view of the pre-World War I Paris of Picasso and Matisse and the post-war "lost generation" of Ernest Hemingway, F. Scott Fitzgerald, and other American expatriates who flocked to the Stein-Toklas literary salon.

Alice Babette Toklas was born in San Francisco on 30 April 1877, the first child and only daughter of Ferdinand and Emma Levinsky Toklas, a prosperous, upper-middle-class Jewish couple. Ferdinand, a successful entrepreneur, provided a comfortable living for his family and the best private schools for Toklas. In 1890, the family moved to Seattle to be closer to Ferdinand's businesses. Toklas, in the hopes of becoming a concert pianist, entered the music conservatory at the University of Washington in 1893. A year later, Toklas had to withdraw from school and return with her family to San Francisco to care for her ailing mother. After her mother died in 1897, Toklas assumed the role of housekeeper to three generations of male relatives.

The Discovery of an All-Consuming Passion

It was not until ten years later, in 1907, when Toklas was 30 years old that she escaped the drudgery of her home life to travel to Paris. Not long after her arrival, Toklas met the writer and intellectual Gertrude Stein and was immediately and profoundly attracted. Linda Simon asserts in her book *The Biography of Alice B. Toklas* that Toklas was tormented about her lesbianism in the years before meeting Stein. Although Toklas had associated with young men, all her romantic relationships had been with women. As a lesbian searching for reassurances about her sexual identity, help was non-existent in turn-of-the-century post-Victorian society. Toklas left

Alice B. Toklas (right) with Gertrude Stein

for Paris convinced that she was destined to a lifetime of loneliness. In 1908, a few months after their first meeting, Stein professed her love and eternal devotion to Toklas, who immediately reciprocated. Both agreed to an exclusive relationship with Stein unabashedly choosing the role of "husband" and Toklas agreeing to be "wife."

Mindful of society's rejection of homosexuality, the couple revealed to no one the nature of their relationship though they did nothing to hide their absorption in each other. Toklas provided Stein with the unconditional approval, love, and care which she craved. And, in addition to the menial tasks of running a household, Toklas edited and typed Stein's manuscripts, served as an uncritical sounding board, and acted as manager, publicist, and agent as well as devoted, faithful lover. Although Toklas impressed their friends and acquaintances as being unassuming and willing to remain in the background, she wielded the power in the relationship. As Toklas' friend, Annette Rosenshine observed in her memoirs, "Alice had a thirst for fame." Success was indeed the one demand Toklas made of Stein.

Although Stein's and Toklas' romance is one of the most legendary lesbian relationships of the 20th century, during their years together, they were not publicly perceived as a lesbian couple. Stein celebrated their sexual relationship in prose and poetry, however, revealing the love, unbridled passion, joy, and fun inherent in their physical union. Contemporary readers have no trouble identifying the erotic, lesbian content of much of Stein's works. But at the time of the publication of *Tender Buttons* (1914) and the poem "Lifting Belly" (1953), Stein's intentionally cryptic iconography, which was intended to disguise the lesbian subject matter, baffled many readers.

Launches Small Press and Becomes Author in Her Own Right

Although Stein's works were increasingly published by small press magazines and publishers during the mid-1920s, major publishers continued to reject her work. It annoyed Toklas that the young male writers whom Stein had nurtured—Hemingway, Fitzgerald, Sherwood Anderson—were much more successful than she. In 1930, this frustration led Toklas to dedicate herself to becoming director, managing editor, distributor, and publicist of her own small press, which would be solely dedicated to publishing Stein's works. This enterprise was strictly Toklas' effort. Stein contributed only the name of the press, Plain Edition, and her books to be published, including *Lucy Church Amiably, How to Write,* and several other collected works.

As Toklas pushed Stein to produce, so Stein urged Toklas to write her memoirs. In Stein's 1933 bestseller *The Autobiography of Alice B. Toklas* (which is neither Toklas' autobiography or biography), Stein records Toklas' reluctance to add writing to her list of duties. "I am a pretty good housekeeper and a pretty good gardener ... and a pretty good secretary and a pretty good editor ... and I have to do them all at once and I find it difficult to add being a pretty good author." But after Stein's death in 1946, Toklas dealt with her grief by promoting and supervising the publication of Stein's works and by writing her memoirs.

While Toklas' articles and books are ostensibly autobiographical, they focus solely on her memories of Stein and their friends. As Diana Souhami explains in her book *Gertrude and Alice,* "Alice did not want her memoirs to reveal anything about herself." In a letter to Carl Van Vechten, Stein's and Toklas' close friend and Stein's promoter, Toklas wrote, "We are agreed that the reminiscences should be centered on Baby [Gertrude] and her work ... I am nothing but the memory of her." *The Alice B. Toklas Cookbook* (1954) and *Aromas and Flavors of Past and Present* (1958) combine anecdotes and reminiscences of Stein, their circle, and another passion shared with Stein—good food. In 1963, at the age of 86, Toklas' memoir was published. *What Is Remembered* focuses on the highlights of her years with Stein, especially their relationships with artists, writers, and other celebrities. In her final years, Toklas was plagued by severe financial problems and failing eyesight. She died on 7 March 1967 and was buried next to Stein in Pere Lachaise, Paris.

What is fascinating about Toklas' life is that the more Toklas tried to conceal herself in her all-consuming commemoration of Stein's genius, the more she revealed herself. Her memoirs display her sharp, acrid wit, her astute understanding of people and their behavior, and her joy in the simple pleasures of everyday life. And, finally, what Toklas could never hide was the profundity of her love and her own extraordinary immersion in the life of Gertrude Stein.

References:

"Alice B. Toklas," in *Feminist Companion to Literature in English: Women Writers from the Middle Ages to the Present,* edited by Virginia Blair, and others. New Haven, Connecticut: Yale University Press, 1990.

Burns, Edward, ed. *Staying on Alone: Letters of Alice B. Toklas.* New York: Liveright, 1973.

"Gertrude Stein," in *Gay and Lesbian Literary Heritage: A Reader's Companion to the Writers and Their Works, from Antiquity to the Present,* edited by Claude J. Summers. New York: Henry Holt, 1995.

Simon, Linda. *The Biography of Alice B. Toklas.* New York: Doubleday, 1977.

Souhami, Diana. *Gertrude and Alice.* New York: Pandora Press/HarperCollins, 1991.

Townsend, Janis. "Alice B. Toklas," in *American Women Writers, Volume IV,* edited by Linda Maniero. New York: Ungar, 1994.

—Judith E. Harper

Daniel C. Tsang

1949-

Asian-American librarian, writer, and activist

Daniel C. Tsang, a librarian, educator, journalist, and activist, was born on 27 October 1949 in Hong Kong. Tsang received his BA in 1971 from the University of the Redlands and received his MA in Political Science in 1973 and Masters in Library Science in 1977, both from the University of Michigan.

Tsang has devoted his professional career to being a librarian, though always with radical ends. In 1977, Tsang worked at the Institute for Social Research at the University of Michigan. From 1978 to 1980, he was hired under a U.S. Office of Education Grant to work as Research Librarian on the Alternative Acquisitions Project at Temple University Libraries' Contemporary Culture Collection. During the same years, he was founder and curator of Philadelphia's lesbian/gay Lavender Archives. In 1980, Tsang left Temple for the Community College of Philadelphia, where he worked as a reference librarian. From 1983 through 1986, Tsang held the position of Adult librarian at the Free Library of Philadelphia. In 1986, he left Philadelphia for the University of California at Irvine.

Tsang's career as a librarian has dovetailed with his writing and research interests. Most of his publications have been journalistic or bibliographic in nature. Tsang's specific research topics have included the lesbian/gay Asian press, the alternative press, Asian queers, lesbian/gay archives and special collections libraries, sex in cyberspace, police surveillance of people of color and intergenerational relationships.

As an author, Tsang has published articles in *Amerasia Journal*, *Asian Week*, *Far Eastern Economic Review*, *Frontiers*, *Fuse*, Boston's *Gay Community News*, London's *Gay News*, *The Guide*, *Journal of Homosexuality*, *Liberation News Service*, *Los Angeles Times*, *The Public Eye*, *Rice Paper*, and *Seven Days*. In the late 1970s, Tsang worked as a reporter for the *Michigan Free Press*. In 1981 he edited an anthology titled *The Age Taboo: Gay Male Sexuality, Power and Consent* which was published concurrently by Boston's Alyson Publications and London's Gay Men's Press. For *The Age Taboo*—the first anthology on man/boy love—Tsang reported on the formation of the North American Man/Boy Love Association and racism within gay male communities. *The Age Taboo* was part of what lesbian/sex radical cultural historian Gayle Rubin has called "an indigenous political theory of ... [gay male] sexual cultures" which cropped up in the late 1970s. Tsang also edited the radical gay political journal *Midwest Gay Academic Journal*, which in 1979 became *Gay Insurgent: A Gay Left Journal*. In the early 1990s, Tsang advised *Rice Paper*, University of California-Irvine's Asian alternative independent quarterly. Tsang currently serves on the editorial boards of *Journal of Homosexuality* and *Paidika*.

Throughout Tsang's professional career, he has been active in a wide range of political causes. During the late 1960s, Tsang was heavily involved in the anti-war movement and student organizing. While at the University of Michigan from 1971 through 1977, Tsang was involved with the Gay Liberation Front as well as the Gay Academic Union. He also helped organize a month-long strike in 1975 by the University of Michigan's graduate student union, a strike which fought for a sexual preference non-discrimination policy. In 1975, Tsang came out as gay in *Bridge*, an Asian American publication. It was the first such coming out essay, and it marked the beginning of his involvement with the queer Asian community. In 1979, Tsang marched with other Asian queers through Washington, D.C.'s Chinatown to join the first Gay and Lesbian March on Washington.

Currently, Tsang lives in southern California, where he works as a social science bibliographer and lecturer at the University of California at Irvine, and hosts a weekly radio interview program, *Subversity*, on KUCI, 88.9 FM. Tsang is also founder and Research Director of the Alternative Research Center (website: http://sun3.lib.uci.edu/~dtsang/arc.htm) an independent center housing a library and archives strong containing documents on sexual politics, police surveillance of people of color and declassified government documents on the gay political movement.

Since moving back to southern California in 1986, Tsang's writing has increasingly focused on the ways that law enforcement policies Asians, the rise in hate crimes against Asians in California, and the evolution of University of California educational policies.

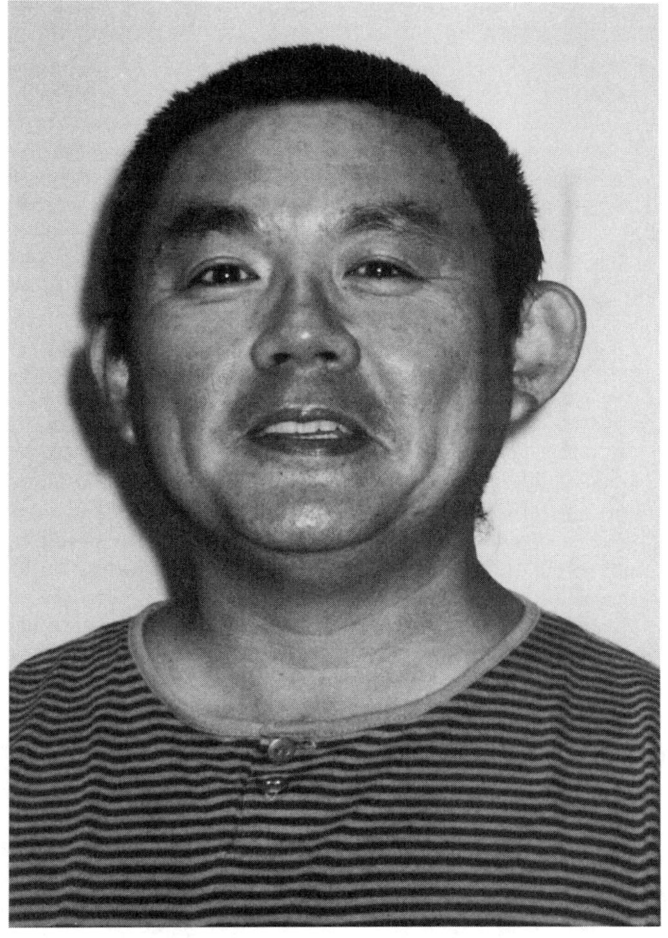

Daniel C. Tsang. ***Photograph by Charles MA.***

Tsang's political work has garnered him considerable public attention, including a 1994 biographical sketch in the *Los Angeles Times*. In September of 1993, Tsang co-founded the Alliance Working for Asian Rights and Empowerment (AWARE). AWARE focuses on increased police targeting of Asian young people in Orange County for supposed gang membership.

Throughout his professional and activist career, Tsang has combined a range of activities. In insisting upon the need to archive the present and the recent past, Tsang will leave future scholars of lesbian/gay history better able to document their research. In making explicit the political character of archival work, Tsang has merged profession and activism in a manner few community-based cultural workers are able to balance.

Current Address: Department of Political Science, University of California, Irvine, Irvine, California 92717-0002. E-mail: dtsang@uci.edu.

References:

Reyes, Davis. "UCI Lecturer, Mentor Out 'To Change Society,'" *Los Angeles Times*, 14 March 1994.

Rubin, Gayle, with Judith Butler. "Sexual Traffic," *differences*, vol. 6, nos. 2 and 3, 1994.

Tsang, Daniel, ed. *The Age Taboo: Gay Male Sexuality, Power and Consent.* Boston: Alyson Publications, 1981.

—Alex Robertson Textor

Kitty Tsui

1952-

Asian-American writer

Kitty Tsui makes a dynamic career from her identity as a Chinese-American lesbian. Her life and work thus far provide an essential corrective to minority politics, both by defining ethnic difference within the lesbian community and by modelling sexual difference within the Asian American community. Tsui is an award-winning chronicler of the rich complexities of balancing more than one identity.

Kitty Tsui. ***Photograph by Robin R. Roller.***

Born in Hong Kong in 1952, Kitty Tsui spent her childhood in California, receiving a B.A. in Creative Writing from San Francisco State University. She currently lives in the midwest with her beloved Hungarian Vizsla dog, Meggie Too.

Tsui's poetry and prose have been published in over 35 anthologies, including *Asian American Sexualities: Dimensions of the Gay and Lesbian Experience* (1995), *Lesbian Erotics* (1995), *Chloe Plus Olivia* (1994), and *Making Waves: Asian Women United of California* (1989). She is the recipient of the CLAGS 1995 Ken Dawson Award for research in gay and lesbian history and was listed in the 1990 Lambda Book Report as one of the 50 most influential people in gay and lesbian literature. She has been featured in three films, *Women of Gold* (1990), *Framing Lesbian Fashion* (1992), and *Cut Sleeve* (1992).

Although known primarily for her writing and activism within the Asian Pacific Lesbian Movement, Tsui is also a competitive body-builder, winning a bronze medal at the Gay Games in San Francisco in 1986 and a gold medal in Vancouver in 1990.

Tsui is the author of three books to date: *The Words of a Woman Who Breathes Fire* (1983), a book of poems, prose, and dramatic pieces; *Breathless* (1995), erotica for lesbians; and a historical novel, *Bak Sze, White Snake* (not yet published). These books point to her versatility in terms of genre, while she remains committed to a politics of inclusion and tolerance in the lesbian community.

The Words of a Woman Who Breathes Fire, written in the 1980s tradition of identity politics, focuses on ethnic and class differences among urban lesbians. Tsui struggles for self-definition in these poems, as a Chinese-American woman who loves women and as a writer who refuses to be encumbered by literary stylistic traditions. In the first poem, "It's In The Name," the speaker condemns the dominant culture's (including non-Asian women) confusion of Asian women with each other—"it happens all the time. /orientals so hard to tell apart" (1). The book's conclusion, however, is more upbeat, with "A Celebration Of Who I Am," and an inter-generational dramatic monologue of two women's voices, "Poa Poa is Living Breathing Light."

Because her female and Chinese heritage is so central to Tsui, she includes several poems honoring her grandmother, whose struggles as an immigrant actress and Cantonese opera singer mirror the poet's own creative efforts. *The Words of A Woman ...* is dedicated to Tsui's grandmother, Kwan Ying Lin, "[her] first and closest connection." The poem "Chinatown Talking Story" describes her grandmother's American career: "the gold mountain men said/when kwan ying lin/went on stage/even the electric fans stopped." Kwan, too, loved women and left her husband to live with another actress. Other poems describe her family's ignorance concerning her love for women; for example, in "A Chinese Banquet," Tsui is unable to invite her lover home for a traditional meal because the category "same-sex lover" does not exist for her parents. However, Tsui insists that Chinese women come with strength: "born into the/skin of yellow women/we are born/into the armor of warriors."

A large part of Tsui's fight is for lesbian autonomy. Her second book, *Breathless*, continues the theme of inclusivity. This collection of erotica covers many varieties of lesbian sexual desire, from charged glances to sex toys to sado-masochism to cutting. While some stories involve violence and are not for the faint-hearted reader, many are also simply funny along with being sexy. One story in particular, "the foodie club," contains sensual descriptions of exotic (and erotic) edibles, leaving the reader to imagine whatever sexual activities go with them. Another story, "rain," describes two old women, long-time partners, who rediscover their sexual selves.

Breathless combines questions of love, commitment, loyalty, and loneliness with raw bodies doing amazing, and, depending on your perspective, horrifying or titillating, things.

As Tsui writes in an early poem, "este poema is for the crazywoman/who lets me wear her favorite blue shirt/and takes my tongue into her mouth/and massages it." For Kitty Tsui, we are all potential crazy women, if we can learn to celebrate each other and ourselves as she does.

Current Address: 4100 North Marine Drive, #15C, Chicago, Illinois 60613-2324.

References:

Tsui, Kitty. *Breathless*. Ithaca: Firebrand Books, 1996.

———. *The Words of a Woman Who Breathes Fire*. Duluth: Spinsters, Ink., 1983.

—Catherine A. Wiley

Alan Turing

1912-1954

British mathematician

British mathematician Alan Turing was one of the great forerunners in the development of electronic digital computers. More than 40 years after his death, computer scientists still refer to his papers. His seminal contributions to the field of mathematics cannot be understated.

Alan Mathison Turing was born on 23 June 1912 in London, England, to Julius Mathias Turing and Ethel Sara Stoney. Julius Turing's post with the British Civil Service sent him and his wife to India, so Alan, who remained in England, was raised by a retired military couple in London. He attended the Sherbourne School where his mathematical ability became apparent and later went on to Kings College in Cambridge. In 1935, he was awarded a fellowship for his dissertation "On Gaussian Error Function" and received a Smith's prize for the same paper in 1936.

The Turing Machine and Beyond

Turing did graduate work at Princeton University from 1936 to 1938. There he worked closely with Alonzo Church and other scientists and there he ultimately made one of his most significant contributions to the study of mathematics—his 1937 paper "On Computable Numbers with an Application to the Entscheidungs Problem." This paper explored the question of whether or not all mathematical problems could, in principle, be solved. Interestingly, the paper demonstrated that, in fact, some problems could not be.

In a footnote, Turing referred to his hypothetical "Turing Machine" which he envisioned would read a series of numbers—ones and zeroes—from a tape. These ones and zeroes described the steps that were required either to solve a problem or perform a task. The machine's job was to read the steps, perform them in sequence, and come up with the correct answer. Turing's theory, now taken for granted in the computer age, was revolutionary at the time. His machine served as the model for, and actually defined what we know today as, the electronic digital computer.

Turing's work at Princeton resulted in several more important papers, in particular "Systems Logic Based on Ordinals" published in 1939. This seminal work was elaborated upon, adapted, relied upon, and highly regarded by his colleagues. For some it provided a foundation for their own work, for others, a verification of their findings.

Turing returned to Kings College in 1939, and shortly thereafter, the outbreak of World War II caused a disruption in his research. For the next seven years, he was posted to the Communications Department of the British Foreign Office where he served as a cryptographer, taking part in the top secret ULTRA Project. There, with the assistance of a device called COLOSSUS, he helped decipher the German military codes which eventually lead to the Allies victory. For his work at the Foreign Office, Turing was awarded the Order of the British Empire (OBE) in 1946. At the close of the war, Turing joined the staff of the National Physical Laboratory (NPL) and resumed his research. During his time at the NPL, he worked on the design of an automatic computing engine, but left the NPL before its completion.

In 1948 he was offered a lectureship at Cambridge which he declined. Instead, he became a reader at the University of Manchester and served as the Director of Manchester Automatic Digital Machine (MADAM), one of the first electronic digital computers. He strongly believed that by the end of the century machines that could replicate the human mind would be created. He worked wholeheartedly toward this end with MADAM, creating the operating manual for it and becoming a committed user of the machine in his own research.

By 1950, when mechanical computing devices were being assigned more complex tasks, Turing found himself questioning the very ability to think. His 1950 paper, "Computing Machinery and Intelligence," addressed the question: Do computers possess intelligence? As a result, he developed the Turing Test, which connected an interrogator via teletype to either a computer or a person. The interrogator asked questions and determined, based on the replies, whether the subject was a human or a machine. When the interrogator could not distinguish whether the subject was man or machine, Turing maintained that "artificial intelligence" had been achieved. For his work, he was made a Fellow of the Royal Society in 1951.

As an outcropping of his interest in machines, Turing's interest in applying mathematical mechanical theory to the biological problem of life-forms developed. His findings from this research are documented in "The Chemical Basis for Morphogenesis" (1952). His hypothesis was that small variations in the initial conditions of first-order systems of differential equations will result in appreciable deviations at later stages. Based on his findings, he could account for asymmetry in both mathematical and biological forms.

According to John M. Kowalik in his fall 1995 essay "Alan Turing," Turing believed in "the close relation between nature and math. Turing's ultimate goal was to merge the already established biological theory with mathematics and computers to create his intelligent, multi-purpose machine." He was not, however, able to achieve this goal in his lifetime and a number of papers on his work in the field of biology remained unfinished at the time of his death in 1954.

Not much is known about Turing's personal life—aside from the possibility of a relationship with a school chum who died suddenly of tuberculosis in 1930 and a later affair with a young street person, Arnold Murray. Murray's exploits brought him—and ultimately his relationship with Turing—to the attention of the police. As a result, Turing was arrested in 1952: homosexuality was a felony in England at the time. He was tried and convicted of "gross indecency," under the same law as was Oscar Wilde a half century earlier. In lieu of serving time, Turing was sentenced to a year's probation and was given the female hormone estrogen—an experimental treatment which was the equivalent of a chemical castration.

In June of 1954 Turing, just 42 years old, died of cyanide poisoning. Although he left no note, his death from consuming a cyanide-laced apple is almost universally believed to be suicide. His mother alone believed his death was accidental, but she could not convince the authorities to rule it as such.

With his death one of the brilliant analytical minds of the mid-20th century, a forerunner of technocrats to come, was lost. One can only imagine what he might have accomplished had he not died so young.

—Andrea L.T. Peterson

Karl Heinrich Ulrichs

1825-1895

German sexologist, activist, journalist, and poet

Karl Heinrich Ulrichs has been largely forgotten, but he played an early role in the fight for gay rights in Germany. In his full-scale study entitled *The Life and Works of Karl Heinrich Ulrichs: Pioneer of the Modern Gay Movement*, Hubert Kennedy asserts that Ulrichs was the "first self-proclaimed homosexual." The word *homosexual*, however, did not exist when Ulrichs sought to liberate his fellow *Urnings* (his term for homosexuals) from social and legal oppression. Some lawbooks still claimed pederasty as a source of famine and pestilence when Ulrichs set out to justify Urning sexuality scientifically, ethically, and legally in his series of twelve controversial booklets published between 1864 and 1879. These consciousness-raising writings provided gays with a sense of self-identity as a community and oppressed minority for the very first time in history.

Karl Heinrich Ulrichs was born on 28 August 1825 near Aurich in East Friesland close to Germany's North Sea coast. East Friesland was then part of the kingdom of Hanover. Karl's father Hermann Heinrich Ulrichs was an architect in the service of the Hanoverian government. His wife Elise Heinrichs Ulrichs bore him three children: Louise, born in 1819, Karl, and Ulrike Henriette, born in 1828.

Ulrichs was already aware of his special nature at a young age. He detested snowball fights with other boys and preferred the company of his sister's playmates. At age nine, he even fell in love with "Eduard," a fellow pupil at school. His acknowledged effeminacy and attraction to males at such a young age convinced him that his sexuality was inborn, and therefore not sinful. Ulrichs' father died in 1835 from internal injuries sustained in a fall, and his mother moved her young family to Burgdorf, near the city of Hanover. Ulrichs was tutored there by his grandfather, Johann Heinrich Heinrichs, until September 1839. Afterwards, he attended the *Gymnasium* (German high school) in Detmold (1839-1842) and Celle (1842-1844). In Celle, Ulrichs first discovered his lifelong predilection for soldiers, and Kennedy reports that young Ulrichs fantasized about a handsome soldier who "burned like fire" climbing through his bedroom window.

Enters the Legal Profession

In the fall of 1844, Ulrichs began his studies at the University of Göttingen and transferred to the University of Berlin in 1846. At both institutions he distinguished himself in Latin studies, a subject which won him renown later in life. In 1847 he returned to Burgdorf to study for an examination which gained him entry into the Hanover's state service as a jurist. Ulrichs soon became dissatisfied with state service and was not well liked by his conservative superiors because of his speeches promoting liberal, democratic ideas.

Ulrichs moved from post to post in his new career, and, in 1851 during his stay in Achim near Bremen, had his first bittersweet romance with a young cavalry officer. This was only the first of several love affairs with military men. In 1852 Ulrichs was promoted to *Assessor* ("assistant judge"), but he quit the state's service voluntarily in 1854 when a colleague discovered certain facts about Ulrichs' personal nature and threatened to make his job very unpleasant. Ulrichs never revealed the exact circumstances of his resignation, but vigorously attacked entrapment and persecution of homosexuals a decade later in his pamphlets.

Although his mother left him a small inheritance upon her death in 1856, Ulrichs almost always suffered financial hardships throughout his life. In 1859 he took up free-lance journalism as a source of income. He copiously contributed 132 articles between 1862 and 1863 to the *Allgemeine Zeitung*, one of the most influential newspapers of the time. He reported about the *Allgemein deutscher Schützenfest* ("All-German Shooting Festival") in July of 1862. An event intertwined with this assignment marked a major turning point in Ulrichs' life.

Johann Baptist von Schweitzer, secretary of the Schützenfest's central committee, was arrested after the festival on morals charges. He supposedly committed an indecent act with a boy under 14 years old, although the boy was never found to testify against him. Ulrichs put together a written defense for Schweitzer, but it was not used in his case. Schweitzer was only imprisoned for two weeks, but his reputation in Frankfurt was forever ruined. This was Ulrichs' first of many attempts to personally defend one of his comrades in nature before the courts and attack the unfairness of anti-homosexual laws. Unfortunately, the courts always refused to hear Ulrichs' appeals. An undeterred Ulrichs took his defense of homosexuality to the German public instead. But before he took this bold step, he informed his family.

"Comes Out" with Homosexual Theories

Through a series of letters to his family in 1862, Ulrichs "came out" with his own scientific theories defending his sexuality. He described heterosexual and homosexual males respectively as *Dionäer* ("Dionians") and *Uranier* ("Uranians"), names which hark back to the heavenly and earthly origins of the Greek goddess of love, Aphrodite, which Plato discussed in his *Symposium*. Ulrichs averred that Uranians were so different from Dionians and women that they constituted a "third sex." Using data about hermaphroditism from medical journals, Ulrichs declared to his family that Uranians prenatally developed a female love drive in the same way that hermaphrodites congenitally developed physical characteristics of the opposite sex.

In an age before genetics, Ulrichs theorized that the interplay of passive and dominant male and female sexual germs governed the sex and sexuality of the human fetus. He posited that Uranians were influenced by a dominant female germ governing spiritual development, but that a dominant male germ controlled their physical characteristics. Ulrichs made it quite clear to his shocked, but tolerant family that he intended to publish these theories: "To justify myself, and to do it completely, is nothing less than my life's work."

Ulrichs wrote his first two pamphlets simultaneously in 1863. In deference to his family, he published them under the pseudonym "Numa Numantius" in 1864. The first was *"Vindex." Social-juridical Studies on Sexual Love Between Men*, and the second was entitled *"Inclusa." Anthropological Studies on Sexual Love Between Men*. The preceding Latin catch titles refer to Latin mottos prefacing each pamphlet. Ulrichs germanized the terms *Uranier* and *Dionäer* as *Urning* and *Dioning* for publication and opened *Vindex* (Liberator) as follows in this translation by Kennedy:

> The class of Urnings is perhaps strong enough now to assert its right to equality and equal treatment.... Fortified with the shield of the justice of their cause, they must bravely dare to come out of their previous reserve and isolation. Herewith let the ice be broken.

In *Vindex*, Ulrichs addressed the persecutors of Urnings. He argued that inborn Urning existence was a riddle of nature which should be investigated scientifically, and not solved by the lashing out of blind justice, as had been the case with heretics, Jews, and witches. *Inclusa* (Confinement), which was an elaboration of his sexual germ theory, was so titled because Ulrichs believed that Urnings had a female spirit trapped in a male body, and thus were only attracted to heterosexual Dionings. Ulrichs' initial exposure to other Urnings was rather limited, so he thought that they were all more or less like himself (he preferred "straight" soldiers, considered himself effeminate, and associated with a small circle of Urning "sisters" with nicknames such as "Madonna" or "Queen of the Night"). Ulrichs adjusted his sexual theories in future publications in order to accommodate the many expressions of Urning love as he learned about them.

German Police Confiscate Pamphlets

These first two booklets were widely distributed and created quite a stir. In May of 1864 the Saxon police confiscated 1,128 copies of *Inclusa* from the Mathes Press in Leipzig. Authorities forbade the booklets in Prussia and confiscated all available copies in Berlin. Ulrichs, however, was so encouraged by warm letters from Urnings expressing thanks for fighting for their rights and opening their eyes to the truth about themselves, that he made plans for three more booklets which were published in 1865.

"Vindicta." The Struggle for Liberation from Persecution appeared in February and directly addressed the Urnings. In *Vindicta* (Liberation), Ulrichs declared himself their liberator. He asserted that anti-homosexual laws were the result of erroneous scientific conclusions and expressed the hopes that lawmakers and the oppressive majority would not prejudice themselves against new scientific discoveries about Urnings. *"Formatrix." Anthropological Studies on Urning Love* was an expansion of his scientific theories expressed in *Inclusa*. Here he acknowledged the existence of the bisexual *Uranodioning* and the Urning's female counterpart, the lesbian *Urningin*. For the first time, he admitted that mutual attraction might even occur between Urnings and categorized Urnings into two types: the active *Mannling* and the passive *Weibling*. *"Ara spei." Moral-philosophical and Social-philosophical Studies about Urning Love* was the last booklet Ulrichs published in 1865. In *Ara spei* (Altar to hope), he spoke out against the Dioning world order and its oppression of both Urnings and women.

Ulrichs always sought to enlist scientific approval for his cause, and encouraged one of the most prominent medical experts of his time, Richard von Krafft-Ebing, to read his five booklets. Krafft-Ebing agreed with Ulrichs wholeheartedly that the Urning condition was inborn, but twisted this concept in his studies of sexual psychopathology to claim that Urnings were products of biological degeneracy. The degeneration theory, which Krafft-Ebing popularized, became distorted and eventually led to the persecution of such "degenerates" as the mentally incompetent, Jews, and homosexuals during the Nazi regime.

In 1865 Ulrichs attempted to found an Urning union, intending to "to bring Urnings out of their previous isolation and unite them into a compact mass bound together in solidarity" (Kennedy). If it had been successful, it would have been the first organization ever to promote homosexual interests. No meeting ever took place, but Ulrichs sent a copy of the proposed union's by-laws to the Austro-Hungarian writer Karl Maria Kurtzbeny (who, five years later, invented the initially unpopular terms *homosexual* and *heterosexual*).

Arrested for Political Defiance

When the Prussian regime annexed Hanover in 1866, Ulrichs publicly declared himself an adversary of Prussian subjugation. He was arrested in January of 1867 for his political defiance, compounded by the fact that Urning literature was found in his home, and was imprisoned for almost five months. Ulrichs left his Hanoverian homeland in July of 1867, never to return. He took up residence in the Bavarian city of Würzburg.

From that point on, Ulrichs dropping the pseudonym "Numa Numantius" from his writings and published the next six booklets under his own name. *"Gladius furens." The Natural Riddle of Urning Love, and Deception as Lawgiver*, and *"Memnon." The Sexual Nature of Men-loving Urnings* appeared in 1868. *Memnon* was by far the most thorough of his scientific investigations. He streamlined his sexual germ theory and came to the conclusion that all humans started out from the same hermaphrodite embryo and were therefore deserving of God's grace, despite their varieties of inborn sexual drives.

The public reaction to *Memnon* was as negative as ever. Karl Marx, the father of Socialism, sent a copy of *Memnon* to his collaborator Friedrich Engels, who feared that pederasts might one day find political power in the state. In 1869, when a Berlin nobleman named Zastrow allegedly raped a five-year-old boy, a copy of *Memnon* was found in Zastrow's possession and he claimed to be a follower of Ulrichs' in the sensationalized court proceedings that followed. This was a severe blow to Ulrichs' cause. Discussions to repeal anti-homosexual laws in Prussia were underway during the Zastrow trial, but the trial's publicity wreaked such a negative influence that homosexuality remained a crime in Germany until 1969.

In 1869, Ulrichs published *"Incubus." Blood Lust and Urning Love*, which discussed deplorable cases of "gay baiting" which had come to his attention. Ulrichs expressed doubts about Zastrow's guilt in *"Argonauticus." Zastrow and the Urnings in the Barracks of Ultramontanism, Pietistism and Free-thinking* (the title was inspired by his contempt for Prussia), which was an expanded edition of *Incubus*.

Publishes First Gay Magazine

In January of 1870 Ulrichs published *Prometheus*, the first ever gay magazine. Unfortunately, only one edition was printed. Included were biographical sketches of famous Urnings in history, a list of known extorters of Urnings, and Ulrichs' defense of same-sex marriage. In that same year, Ulrichs also appealed directly to the Austrian and Prussian legislatures in *"Araxes." A Call for Setting Urning Nature Free from Penal Law.*

When Germany was united under the Prussian yoke in 1871, Ulrichs believed that Bavaria's King Ludwig II played too prominent a role in this development. As a protest, he left Bavarian Würzburg in 1872 and moved to Stuttgart, the capital of Württemberg, where in 1875 he published a volume of poetry, *Auf Bienchens Flügeln* (On the wings of a bee), which contained 279 short poems covering a wide range of topics, including homosexuality.

Ulrichs published one last pamphlet in 1879, *"Critical Arrows." A Report about the Punishment of Urning Love.* Here Ulrichs outlined the few instances when Urning sex should be punished, such as in the case of pedophilia or when violence was involved. *Critical Arrows* was warmly praised by Ulrichs' friend Paul Heyse, who later won the Nobel Prize for Literature in 1910.

Emigrates to Italy in Frustration

Depressed by the fact that his fatherland had paid no heed to his fight for Urning justice, Ulrichs emigrated to Italy, where he spent his remaining years as a private tutor of French, English, Latin and Greek. He finally settled in L'Aquila. Between 1889 and 1895 he edited and published *Aludae* (Larks), a journal which brought him international fame among Latin scholars and an honorary degree from the University of Naples. In 1891 he received a visit from the gay poet John Addington Symonds, who campaigned for legal reform of homosexual laws in England. Ulrichs' last publication, which appeared in 1894, was *Matrosengeschichten* (Sailor stories), a collection of four short stories, the best known of which is "Manor," a homosexual vampire tale which has been reprinted several times. On 14 July 1895 Ulrichs passed away peacefully after suffering from acute kidney inflammation.

Ulrichs fought for the Urning cause and died with little hope that his work would be carried on, but his groundbreaking efforts for homosexual rights inspired those who followed him, especially Magnus Hirschfeld, who published a new edition of Ulrichs' twelve booklets in 1897, collectively titled *Investigations into the Riddle of Love between Men.* Hirschfeld declared that posterity would one day remember Ulrichs as one the noblest of those who in the struggle for homosexual equality helped "truth and charity gain their rightful place." Hirschfeld founded the Scientific Humanitarian Committee in 1897, the first true organization in the gay emancipation movement, and brought the work Ulrichs had started into the twentieth century.

References:

Kennedy, Hubert. *The Life and Works of Karl Heinrich Ulrichs: Pioneer of the Modern Gay Movement.* Boston: Alyson Publications, Inc., 1988.

Ulrichs, Karl Heinrichs. *Forschungen über das Rätsel der mannmännlichen Liebe* [Investigations into the riddle of love between men], edited by Magnus Hirschfeld. Leipzig: Spohr, 1898. Reprint. New York: Arno Press, 1975.

—Seán Henry

Urvashi Vaid

1958-

Indian-American activist and writer

Urvashi Vaid is well-known in the United States as a veteran activist in gay, lesbian, and feminist movements. Her long commitment to civil rights began in her college days, when she became vocal in conferences and protests, as well as being involved in volunteer work and organizing for feminist and civil rights issues. More recently, from 1986 to 1992, she was the Public Information Director and Executive Director of the National Gay and Lesbian Task Force (NGLTF). In 1994, *Time* magazine listed her in "The Fifty"—their directory of America's most promising leaders, age 40 and under, who had the ambition, vision, and community spirit to lead America into the new millennium.

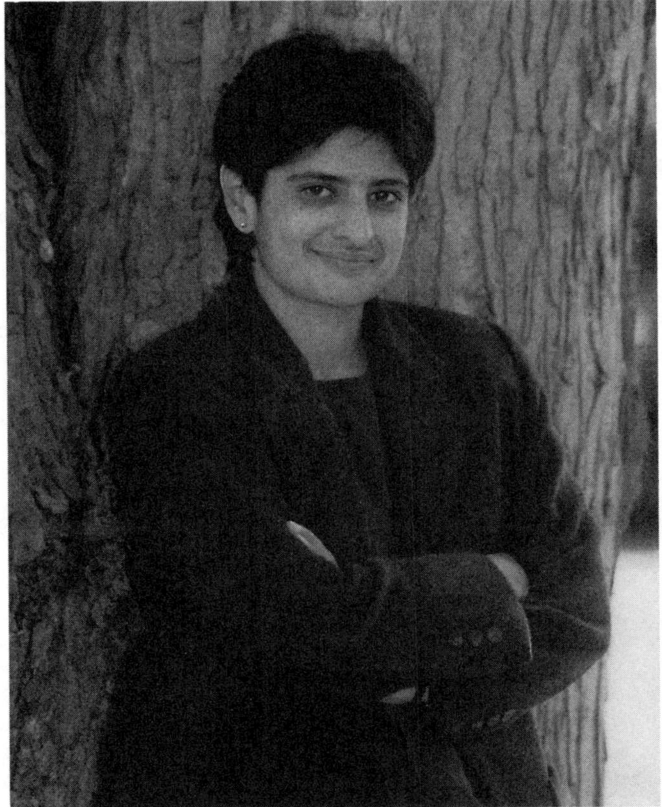

Urvashi Vaid

Although Urvashi Vaid was born in India in 1958, she immigrated to the United States in 1966 along with her family. Vaid was part of the second wave of Indian migration to the United States and was raised with a middle-class ethos in Potsdam, New York. Her parents were literary writers and teachers—her mother was a teacher and poet and her father, a novelist, who taught literature and writing at the State University at Potsdam. In high school Vaid had not heard about gay liberation, however, she considered herself "pro-civil rights, anti-war, and a women's libber" (Preface, *Virtual Equality*). Her first passion was for rock and roll music, but simultaneously, she began to acquire the tools for activism. Vaid's involvement in activism grew substantially throughout the coming years. In college, at Vassar, she was involved with anti-apartheid groups, was part of protests against financial cutbacks to education, and also participated in women's music concert groups. In 1979, at the age of 21, Vaid had joined the women's movement in Boston. At the same time, the First National March on Washington for Gay and Lesbian Rights took place. Moreover, she became an active participant in the civil disobedience protests at the Seabrook nuclear plant in New Hampshire as part of the LUNA Group (Lesbians United in Non-Nuclear Action).

In 1980, while attending Law school at North Eastern University, Vaid proclaimed her homosexuality to her parents through her sister. These years were a crucially formative period for her political awareness of gay and lesbian visibility while she volunteered for the non-profit newspaper *Gay Community News*. In 1983, during the Reaganite era, Vaid worked as an attorney for the National Prison project of the American Civil Liberties Union (ACLU) and continued the musical work she began in 1977 with Roadwork. Her involvement with the ACLU heightened the awareness of the treatment of prisoners with HIV and AIDS. It was during this time that Vaid met Jeff Levi of the National Gay Task Force who would influence her to consider gay rights activism as something she could focus on full-time. By 1987, when the Second National March for Gay Rights took place in Washington, she left the ACLU and became active in media-organizing, strategising and policy making as well as employed as the Public Information Director of the National Gay and Lesbian Task Force (NGLTF). In a movement largely dominated by gay white men, Vaid became the first woman of color and the first Indian-American to direct the NGLTF. At the helm of the NGLTF, Vaid hoped to broaden the movement's base by asking for self-reflections that could include class, gender, and race issues. She left the NGLTF, both for personal and political reasons, after working there for six-and-a-half years. In 1995, after a sabbatical time to "think and feel" in her home in Provincetown, her book *Virtual Equality* was published. The book has had mostly positive reviews and Vaid herself has spoken of enthusiastic crowds gathered in gay, lesbian, and independent bookstores when she was on her six-week book tour in January of 1996 (interview in *Sojourner*). In her book, she explains her decision to leave NGLTF as grounded in a need to spend more quality time with her lover and soulmate, Kate Clinton, as well as to re-look at and re-think where her visions for the gay and lesbian movement would best be realized.

Virtual Equality thus emerges as a consideration of the gay and lesbian movement as it approaches its sixth decade of political activism. Vaid finds that their goals of "cultural visibility, political representation and civil rights" have yet to be fully realized. She examines the disappointment gays and lesbians feel when "unprecedented cultural possibility" is followed by the "persistence of prejudice and stigmatization" that they have challenged for decades. To Vaid this is much like a state of "virtual equality," since although there is a perception that gays and lesbians have achieved freedom, this freedom rests on a simulated reality. There is an appearance of acceptance by straight America, however, it is ironic in that it possesses the promised trappings of equality and progress and actually belies what it cannot move beyond—its virtual foundations. Vaid explores this prevailing state of the gay/lesbian movement by looking candidly at its strengths and problems, its involvement in electoral politics and its responses to mainstreaming. She asks probing questions of the movement's guiding principles and looks at possibilities and crisis areas for future leadership. As a lesbian and leader of color, she herself experienced a big share of criticism and attack from within the gay and lesbian movement for some of her views and actions; for example, there were severe critiques of her decision to protest the American involvement in the Gulf War, and her decision to support direct action strategies in Washington. One of the chapters in her book focuses on leadership conundrums, detailing ambivalences and divisions regarding what is expected of leaders in the movement. All the chapters of this book show Vaid's presence, experience, hopes and disappointments as an activist, organizer, policy-maker and strategist for gay and lesbian socio-cultural visibility. She acknowledges some of her own limitations, while also critiquing some of the working ideologies inside the movement. Her tone is action-oriented: there is a pragmatic immediacy conveyed through lists, outlines, overviews, names of people and organizations, definitions, explanations, things done and those needing to be done. She urges those working in the movement to blend out, instead of mostly blending in, and to reach out on the micro and macro levels, mobilizing families and friends as much as national campaigns. Her suggestions include creating discussions groups, focusing commitments, mentoring, pooling resources, reading, exploring and discovering groups in local areas, and being politically aware of multiple levels of differences and commonalities. Vaid's vision of the movement is one that would be multi-issue oriented—which in turn allowing for allies and coalitions by including race, class and gender issues alongside issues of sexual orientation. There are echoes of her vision shown through her speech for the March on Washington in 1993, and in her "After Identity" (May 1993) where she called for the end of bigotry, racism, domestic violence, sexism, and hate along with the call to end homophobia. However, her book is sometimes contradictory or unclear about the issues of commonalities and differences, and how to resolve the problems of sorting through multilevel issues when identity politics gets fissured along these lines.

Vaid's current project includes starting a much-needed think tank named "The Center for Progressive Renewal" (CPR) in order to brainstorm, strategise, and vocalize for gay and lesbian rights. She continues to ask questions and think of ways to facilitate working together in the movement that would making for meaningful and productive action.

Current Address: c/o Doubleday, Inc., 1540 Broadway, New York, New York 10036-4094.

References:

"The Fifty: *Time*'s Roster for the Twenty-First Century," in *Time* (New York), 5 December 1994: 48-65.

Rizzo, Cynthia. Interview with Urvashi Vaid, in *Sojourner: The Women's Forum*, January 1996: 26-27.

———. Review of *Virtual Equality,* in *Sojourner: The Women's Forum,* January 1996: 25-26.
Vaid, Urvashi. 1993 March on Washington Speech, in *Out in All Directions: The Almanac of Gay and Lesbian America,* edited by Lynn Witt, Sherry Thomas, and Eric Marcus. New York: Warner, 1995: 456-459.
———. "After Identity," in *The New Republic* (New York), 10 May 1993: 28.
———. *Virtual Equality: The Mainstreaming of Gay and Lesbian Liberation.* New York: Anchor, 1995.

—Marian Gracias

Carl Van Vechten

1888-1964

American photographer and writer

On numerous counts, Carl Van Vechten stands out in American twentieth-century culture as the very symbol of a generation which combined a rapidly accumulated sophistication, an eager exploitation of the century's newly discovered freedoms, deeply felt social concerns and multiple talents to achieve a rich life and outstanding accomplishments. That he created so much along with the realizations of an active bisexual orientation marks him as truly distinctive.

Van Vechten's evolution from a white-bread Middle Westerner to an international bon vivant began in Cedar Rapids, Iowa. Proceeding through the University of Chicago to New York, he honed his writing skills as a music and dance critic for the *New York Times* and as drama critic for the *New York Press.* New York immersed him in the giddy party circus, where he met and became friends with the leading lights of high society and the arts world, including: George Gershwin, Lincoln Kirstein, and Ethel Waters.

Then declaring that his "intellectual arteries had hardened too much for more criticism," Van Vechten turned to more imaginative writing. One quick result was *In the Garrett* (1920), a collection of short pieces concentrating on such figures as Havelock Ellis, Sir Arthur Sullivan, Isaac Albeniz, and Oscar Hammerstein. But it was with *Peter Whiffle: His LIfe and Works* that Van Vechten struck his characteristic metier. This pseudo-biographical novel depicted the creation of a refined dilettante's temperament and wittily exposed the manners and morals of the author's era of elegant decadence. The work became highly popular and was followed by similar best-sellers in *The Tattoed Countess* (1924) and *Spider Boy* (1918), a satire on Hollywood.

However, Van Vechten had also established himself as a writer of social sensitivity, with the ironically titled *Nigger Heaven* (1926). Though the work was roundly condemned by the blacks who were a part of what was becoming known as the Harlem Renaissance, and has never lost the onus of the word "nigger" itself, it is still a realistic and sympathetic depiction of black life and the struggles of black artists. It was during this time that Van Vechten became friends with the black, gay poet Langston Hughes.

Though *Nigger Heaven* is part sociological tract and intellectual history, it is primarily a dramatic novel. Within a story that examines various social strata in Harlem, there is the love story of Byron

Carl Van Vechten

Kasson, a young writer, and librarian Mary Love. Mary has also been wooed by the gambler Randolph Pettijohn, but she rejects him. Both Byron and Pettijohn are attracted by the glamorous entertainer Lasca Sartoris, further disappointing Mary. At the climax, Lasca keeps both dangling, and in a fit of rage, Pettijohn shoots and kills her. Desperate, Byron goes to Lasca's dressing room, also intent on killing her in an attempt to win back Mary. He arrived after Pettijohn has killed her and is discovered by the police, who charge him with the murder. *Nigger Heaven* was not to be equalled as a powerful depiction of black life until Ralph Ellison's *Invisible Man* in 1952.

In the midst of his gathering fame, Van Vechten married Fania Marinoff, a dark, petite actress who was soon recognized as a splendid social complement to her husband. Though they had no children, their marriage endured, while others in their social set burst asunder.

Though he still worked sporadically in writing, most notably in editing *The Selected Writings of Gertrude Stein,* preserving her unpublished works after her death in 1946, Van Vechten became increasingly focused on photography from 1932 onward. While he published many of his photographs in conventional periodicals, and though they remain insightful portraits and intriguing historical artifacts, especially of such scenes as speakeasies, it is "Boy Crazy" which is the most engrossing. Basically, "Boy Crazy" is an artful series of beefcake photos, replete with a lot of fellatio and anal intercourse. Van Vechten was most adroit at combining the classic pose with sexiness, as he demonstrated in "Nude Dancer on the Beach" and "Hugh Laing as St. Sebastian."

These scrapbooks are entirely characteristic of an American artist who was bold enough to be himself always and talented enough to present his vision of the world with compassion, candor, wit, and style.

References:

Duberman, Martin et al. *Hidden from History.* New York: New American Library, 1989.

Elliot, Emory. *Columbia Literary History of the U.S.* New York: Columbia University Press, 1988.

Leuders, Edward. *Carl Van Vechten and the Twenties.* Albuquerque, New Mexico: University of New Mexico Press, 1955.

Mauribu, Saul. *The Photography of Carl Van Vechten.* New York: Bobbs-Merril, 1978.

Weinberg, Jonathan. "'Boy Crazy,' Carl Van Vechten's Queer Collection," in *The Yale Journal of Criticism,* vol. 7, no. 2, 1994.

—Marvin Shaw

Gore Vidal

1925-

American writer

For 50 years, Gore Vidal has been one of America's most prolific and provocative writers. Best known as a novelist, he is also a distinguished essayist and has written numerous plays, screenplays, television scripts, stories, and poems. An acknowledged "homosexualist"—the term he coined and prefers—Vidal has sometimes created gay characters and addressed gay issues, but sexual orientation is only one of his many concerns.

Eugene Luther Gore Vidal was born on 3 October 1925, at West Point, New York, the son of Eugene Vidal, West Point professor and later director of the Bureau of Air Commerce, and Nina Gore Vidal. During an unsettled childhood, he grew close to his grandfather, Oklahoma Senator Thomas Gore, who first inspired his lifelong interest in politics. When Vidal was nine, his parents divorced, and Nina married Hugh Auchincloss; when they also divorced, Auchincloss married Jacqueline Kennedy's mother, making the Kennedys one of the many aristocratic families that Vidal was related to or acquainted with. Despite his background, Vidal has regularly rallied against the American elite class and its pernicious control over American society.

At one prep school, Vidal had an intimate relationship with Jimmy Trimble. Trimble was later killed in World War II, and subsequently eulogized in Vidal's memoir *Palimpsest* (1995) as the major love of his life. After graduating from Exeter, Vidal served in the United States Army during World War II in the Aleutian Islands, an experience that provided material for his first novel, *Williwaw* (1946), published when he was 19. Impressively self-educated, Vidal never bothered to attend college and, after briefly working in New York as an editor for E. P. Dutton in 1946, devoted himself to writing novels. Although *In a Yellow Wood* (1947) briefly touched upon homosexuality, wasn't until his remarkable third novel, *The City and the Pillar* (1948), that the topic came to the forefront. Vidal broke new ground in making his protagonist, a young gay man, a thoroughly normal person despite his sexual orientation; its lurid conclusion, the hero's murder of a former male lover who had spurned him, was changed in a 1965 revision to a forcible rape.

After publishing *The City and the Pillar,* Vidal believes he was blacklisted by the critical establishment and, for whatever reason, his next novels—*The Season of Comfort* (1949), *A Search for the King: A Twelfth-Century Legend* (1950), *Dark Green, Bright Red* (1950), *The Judgment of Paris* (1952), and *Messiah* (1954)—were not greatly successful. Vidal lived in Guatemala from 1947 to 1949, then went to Europe, where he associated with Tennessee Williams and other celebrities. Since 1950, he has lived with Howard Austen, but Vidal says the relationship is not sexual, as Vidal preferred sex with anonymous young strangers.

Having purchased a home in New York, and needing more money, Vidal wrote three detective novels as Edgar Box—*Death in the Fifth Position* (1952), *Death Before Bedtime* (1953), and *Death Likes It Hot* (1954)—and began writing for television,

Gore Vidal

moving to Hollywood in 1955. In addition to scripts for anthology series such as *Studio One, Suspense,* and *Omnibus,* Vidal also wrote screenplays—*The Catered Affair* (1956), *I Accuse!* (1958), and *Suddenly, Last Summer* (1959)—and while uncredited, worked extensively on *Ben-Hur* (1959), suggesting a gay subtext to director William Wyler. In 1957, he adapted his television script, the science-fiction satire *Visit to a Small Planet* (1955), as a successful Broadway play (but had nothing to do with the 1960 film), and wrote a few other plays, notably *The Best Man* (1960), which he adapted as a film in 1964.

While in Hollywood, Vidal became a celebrity of sorts, serving as on-screen narrator of his 1960 teleplay, *The Indestructible Mr. Gore,* about his grandfather, then making guest appearances on numerous television programs and hosting a syndicated panel discussion show, *The Hot Seat,* in 1964. He was noted for heated televised exchanges with William F. Buckley—when they were commentators during the 1968 political conventions—and Norman Mailer—on *The Dick Cavett Show.* Beginning in 1962, Vidal spent most of his time in Rome, becoming a permanent resident of Italy in 1971 (while maintaining a home in California), so he was less visible on the Hollywood scene; still, he appeared on the soap-opera spoof *Mary Hartman, Mary Hartman* in 1976 and, more recently, in the films *Bob Roberts* (1992) and *With Honors* (1994). He also worked on a television documentary about Venice that generated his book *Vidal in Venice* (1985).

Vidal's other moments in the public eye have been as a politician. He first ran an unsuccessful campaign as the Democratic candidate for a New York seat in the United States House of Representatives in 1960. From 1961 to 1963, he served, at President Kennedy's request, on the President's Advisory Committee on the Arts (though he did no work for it); in the early 1970s, he was involved with two left-wing political parties, the New Party and the People's Party; and in 1982, he competed in the Democratic primary for a California seat in the United States Senate.

Despite continuing work for the theater—*Weekend* (1968), *An Evening with Richard Nixon* (1972)—and films—*The Last of the Mobile Hot-Shots* (1971), *Caligula* (1980), *Dress Gray* (1986), *The Palermo Connection* (1991)—and despite his flirtations with politics, Vidal has worked primarily on novels since 1964. These include *Two Sisters: A Memoir in the Form of a Novel* (1970), his most autobiographical fiction, and two massive reconsiderations of classical Greece and Rome, *Julian* (1964) and *Creation* (1981). *Washington, D.C.* (1967) launched a series of interrelated novels chronicling American political history: they are, in order of internal chronology, *Burr* (1973), *Lincoln* (1984), *1876* (1976), *Empire* (1987), *Hollywood* (1990), and the aforementioned *Washington, D.C.* These meticulously researched, charming, and cynical novels have proven to be Vidal's most popular and critically acclaimed works. Finally, there are what Vidal calls his "inventions"—wildly imaginative and satirical novels. The first, and most notorious, was *Myra Breckinridge* (1968), a novel that some condemned as pornography, told of the adventures of a gay man who became a woman. Its sequel, *Myron* (1974), transported the protagonist, now male again, to Hollywood in the 1940s. *Kalki* (1978) described the end of the world brought on by a messiah figure, while *Live from Golgotha: The Gospel According to Gore Vidal* (1992) depicted time-travelling television crews and reporters descending upon Jesus Christ's crucifixion. *Duluth* (1982), Vidal's favorite novel and perhaps his best "invention," assails modern American culture as encapsulated in a surrealistic Duluth which simultaneously borders on Canada and Mexico.

No discussion of Vidal can neglect his innumerable, often brilliant essays, collected in *Rocking the Boat* (1962), *Sex, Death and Money* (1968), *Reflections upon a Sinking Ship* (1969), *Homage to Daniel Shays: Collected Essays, 1952-1972* (1972), *Matters of Fact and Fiction* (1977), *The Second American Revolution and Other Essays* (1982, winner of the National Book Critics Circle Award for criticism), *Armageddon? Essays, 1983-1987* (1987), *At Home: Essays 1982-1988* (1989), *A View from the Diner's Club: Essays, 1987-1991* (1991), *Screening History* (1992), *The Decline and Fall of the American Empire* (1992), and *United States: Essays 1952-1992* (1992, winner of the National Book Award for nonfiction). A statement in "Writing Plays for Television" (in *Homage to Daniel Shays*)—"I am at heart a propagandist, a tremendous hater, a tiresome nag, complacently positive that there is no human problem which could not be solved if people would simply do as I advise"—is sometimes taken as Vidal's credo. But, a subsequent reference to "this sort of intensity, no matter how idiotic" also reveals his ironic, sometimes self-deprecating, wit. Vidal complains that he lives in an era that ignores its writers, but his enormous energy, passion, and creativity have made him a difficult writer to ignore.

Current Address: c/o Random House, 201 E. 50th St., New York, New York 10022.

References:

Abbott, Steven and Thom Willenbecher. "Gore Vidal: The *Gay Sunshine* Interview," in *Gay Sunshine,* Winter 1975/76: 20-25.

Austen, Roger. "Gore Vidal and His All-Male Eden," in *Playing the Game: The Homosexual Novel in America.* Indianapolis and New York: Bobbs-Merrill, 1977: 118-125.

Dick, Bernard F. *The Apostate Angel: A Critical Study of Gore Vidal.* New York: Random House, 1974.

Kieman, Robert F. *Gore Vidal.* New York: Frederick Ungar, 1982.

Mitzel, John, and Steven Abbot. *Myra & Gore: A New View of Myra Breckinridge and a Candid Interview with Gore Vidal: A Book for Vidalophiles.* Dorchester, Massachusetts: Manifest Destiny Books, 1974.

Parini, Jay, ed. *Gore Vidal: Writer Against the Grain.* New York: Columbia University Press, 1992.

Ross, Mitchell S. "Gore Vidal," in *The Literary Politicians.* Garden City, New York: Doubleday & Company, 1978: 247-300.

Stanton, Robert J. *Gore Vidal: A Primary and Secondary Bibliography.* Boston: G. K. Hall, 1978.

Summers, Claude J. "'The Cabin and the River,' Gore Vidal's *The City and the Pillar,*" in *Gay Fictions: Wilde to Stonewall: Studies in a Male Homosexual Literary Tradition.* New York: Continuum, 1990: 112-129.

Vidal, Gore. *Palimpsest: A Memoir.* New York: Random House, 1995.

———. *Vidal in Venice,* edited by George Armstrong, photographs by Tore Gill. New York: Summit Books, 1985.

White, Ray Lewis. *Gore Vidal.* Boston: Twayne, 1968.

—Gary Westfahl

Rosa von Praunheim

1942-

German filmmaker

Rosa von Praunheim would be proud to be called the "bully of European gay cinema." He delights in the cinematic fight, the opportunity to provoke action from anger while, at the same time, eliciting no small shock value. In his 1979 film *Army of Lovers*, for example, he directly challenged the liberal political correctness of his former film-school colleagues by having them film him having sex, and then actually filming them filming him in order to break the comfortable distance for both the documentary filmmaker and the moviegoer. Even his name, Rosa, according to author Keith Kelly, was "taken to force people to question sexual branding, his dress [almost always entirely in black], his public attitude [baiting his audiences through insult if necessary], and most of all, his films, are, in effect, weapons of confrontation."

Von Praunheim was born Holger Mischwitki in Riga, Latvia at the opening of World War II. As a teenager, he studied art in Berlin and had aspirations to paint, but soon opted for the more immediate confrontational opportunities that filmmaking provided. Through the 1960s, he worked as an assistant to gay filmmakers Gregory J. Markopoulos and Werner Schroeter, made several Super-8 and 16mm short films, a few features for German television, and released his first film to deal with a gay theme called *Sisters of the Revolution* in 1969.

Sisters of the Revolution established von Praunheim's oeuvre as what author Richard Dyer has called the "zap and analysis" approach to film. It is ostensibly the story of a group of militant homosexuals fighting for feminist rights, with much of the text taken directly from political pamphlets. In this sense, von Praunheim is using a critique of traditional male/female relationships to point out the way these are mimicked by gays. "It is necessary to understand oppression in one's private life not as private but as politico-economic," one of the men says to a woman in the film, according to Dyer. Two leathermen are later shown leading a man in chains who pleads, arms outstretched, directly to the camera: "I don't want to be a bunny, just because I am sensitive and in need of love."

What informs von Praunheim's sexual politics, therefore, is provocation—particularly to complacent gay men who refuse to challenge traditional conventional/societal norms he believes are too often merely adopted to ease our way into the mainstream. In *Images in the Dark*, author Raymond Murray calls him a "natural Brechtian ... less concerned with dramatic involvement and more interested in provoking an unsuspecting audience."

This is not to say his politics lack compassion, however much they force audience interpretation. In *It is not the Homosexual Who is Perverted, but the Situation in Which He Lives* (1970), for example, one particularly bitchy, stereotypically gay character invokes his gay brothers, according to Dyer, to "love them and [don't] just deal with them as competitors." Though this film paints a very unflattering portrait of gay life—joyless promiscuity, predatoriness, lack of solidarity—and it was roundly criticized by many gay groups for these portrayals, most agree that the title holds the message, namely that it is the majority heterosexual society which should be indicted for perverting gays.

Through the 1970s and 1980s, von Praunheim's films continued to be as much "zap" as theory—designed to provoke anger and therefore start people thinking. *Army of Lovers or Revolt of the Perverts* (1979) documented the progress of several gay-rights groups, and included controversial interviews with a gay Nazi, a porn star, and "sexual outlaws" (like novelist John Rechy), who insist that gay liberation is indeed *all* about sex and promiscuity.

In *A Virus Knows No Morals* (1986), the filmmaker's gallows humor is given all the rope it needs when it looks at: sex-club owners who refuse to enforce safe-sex for fear of having freedoms crushed, members of the press all too ready to create stories where there are none, and hospital workers so bored and inured of the AIDS crisis that they roll dice to see who will die next. It was with this film that the adjectives "courageous" and "subversive" were added to the milder "confrontational" in describing von Praunheim's films.

Interspersed amongst his more political works are more drama-driven documentaries—*Red Love* (1982), *City of Lost Souls* (1983), *Horror Vacui* (1984), *Anita: Dances of Vice* (1987), and *Dolly, Lotte and Maria* (1988)—which variously examine the eccentric, outlandish lives of transsexuals, housewives as wannabe sexual-politicos, and washed-up stage and screen performers. They have been critiqued as either totally tedious or the ultimate in political camp. There are few middle-of-the-road reviews when it comes to von Praunheim—not unlike the best (and worst) of Warhol/Morrissey/Waters—and all of which, of course, feeds into the controversy he strives for.

In 1990, von Praunheim collaborated with journalist Phil Zwicker to produce a two-part documentary on the response of New York's artistic community to AIDS. The results—*Silence=Death* and *Positive*—have been called his most accessible films, a shot in the arm of hope bolstered by interviews with members of ACT-UP, Queer Nation, and the Gay Men's Health Crisis. Upon its release in the United States, the *Village Voice* called the documentary "a call to arms... raw, involving eloquence ... seething with rage and disbelief." In 1992, *I Am My Own Woman* signaled a gentler brand of defiance for von Praunheim. In it, he allows 65-year-old transvestite Charlotte von Mahlsdorf to tell her story of gender-bending politics over the years, from the oppression of Nazis and East German officials to her award of the prestigious Federal Order of Merit Cross by West Germany for her courage and fortitude. "The movie finds its real strength," notes reviewer Lawrence Frascella, "in [Mahlsdorf's] modesty.... For that reason alone the film emerges as a portrait of a gay hero."

Modesty aside, von Praunheim has recently released an autobiographical account of his own brand of gay heroism, this time in the form of a book titled *Fifty Years of Perversity*. And gay moviegoers looking to have their political complacency tweaked should look for his latest video, *Nerviosa*, where von Praunheim gets shot in the opening sequence and his life is examined by a sleazy reporter for the remainder (like a queer *Citizen Kane*).

References:

Dyer, Richard. *Now You See It—Studies on Lesbian and Gay Film*. New York: Routledge Press, 1990.

Frascella, Lawrence. In *Advocate*, 23 May 1993.

Kelly, Keith. "The Sexual Politics of Rosa von Praunheim," in *Millennium Film Journal*, 1979.

Murray, Raymond. *Images in the Dark—An Encyclopedia of Gay and Lesbian Film and Video.* Philadelphia: TLA Publications, 1994.

—Jerome Szymczak

Tom Waddell

1937-1987

American physician and athlete

Tom Waddell is best known as the founder of the Gay Games, a quadrennial celebration of sports and the arts in dozens of categories conceived in 1982. Yet Waddell was also a world-class athlete, a gay activist, a father, and a doctor specializing in infectious diseases who himself succumbed to AIDS in 1987. "Waddell believed passionately in the concept of the Gay Games," wrote Dick Schapp in a 1987 *Sports Illustrated* profile of Waddell. "[They were] a chance to shatter homosexual stereotypes, a chance to dignify and motivate homosexual athletes, and a chance to bridge the gap that had long existed between gay men and women."

He was born Thomas Hubacher, the son of a bus driver and a delicatessen manager in Paterson, New Jersey. His parents divorced when he was in his early teens, and after a brief stint living with his father, he moved in with and took the last name of a local couple he was close to, Hazel and Gene Waddell. The Waddells had been vaudeville comics and acrobats, and from them Tom gained a love for gymnastics and ballet.

In high school, he excelled in sports, fearing he was the only one among his peers with homosexual feelings. "I liked who I was," he told Schapp, "but I didn't want to be this bizarre social and physical outcast.... and I realized the way I was going to [make friends] was through an athletic capacity." Tom actually dreamed of becoming a dancer, but was too frightened of the inevitability of then being called a "faggot" in 1950s America.

Waddell's record-setting in track and field earned him a scholarship to Springfield College, where he further distinguished himself in gymnastics and football. He did indulge in a few furtive homosexual encounters off campus, but generally maintained close relationships with women. Looking back, he realized he had been in love with his gymnastics co-captain Don Marshman, though their feelings were never physically expressed.

Don and Tom were inseparable. They became known as the "Gold Dust Twins" for their abilities on the flying rings. One afternoon during practice, however, tragedy struck. Don lost his grip during a particularly fast move, hit the mat head first, snapped his neck, and died in Tom's arms. That was when Tom switched his studies to medicine, which had been Don's major.

When Waddell graduated from Springfield in 1959, he took a summer job at a children's camp in the Berkshires and again fell in love with a man: 63-year-old socialist Friedrich Engels Menaker who ran a nearby intellectual/radical "think-camp" for adults called "The Farm." "He was brilliant, charismatic, manipulative, compassionate, demanding," Tom told Schapp. He changed Waddell from the conservative, Republican jock that he was to a radical, caring

Tom Waddell

intellectual—but he warned Waddell never to admit he was a homosexual. They remained friends till Menaker's death in 1985 at the age of ninety.

Waddell received his medical degree in 1965, completed his internship, was drafted into the army, managed to avoid going to Vietnam by announcing he was morally opposed to it, was surprisingly reassigned to Walter Reed Army Medical Center in Washington D.C. (ironically to study tropical diseases), and by 1967 was in training for the decathlon in the 1968 Olympics.

The fact that a thirty-year-old man was training for such an event was impressive enough, but here he was taking only three months to do so (standard training time is at least four years) and aligning himself with the U.S. Olympic Team's "fist-in-the-air" black caucus. (Perhaps this at least partly explains why the U.S. Olympic Committee so rabidly pursued legal action against Waddell and the use of the word "Olympics" to describe the Gay Games he was to organize more than a decade later.) In the end, Waddell placed an impressive sixth in the decathlon and broke five personal records.

He continued to train, but dreams of a 1972 Olympic run were shattered by a knee injury. Yet, with his confidence and medical career intact, he was "so out," according to Schapp, "that he and his lover Charles Deaton became the first gay couple to be featured in *People* magazine." Between 1976 and 1981, Waddell shuttled between London, Los Angeles, Beirut and Dubai as medical director for the Los Angeles-based Whittaker Corporation.

By 1981, a triad of events conspired to keep Waddell settled in San Francisco—he was inspired by the idea of organizing a "Gay Olympics," he met fellow athlete Sara Lewinstein and they decided to have a child, and he met and fell in love with Gay Games public-relations man and fundraiser Zohn Artman.

Waddell was passionate about the notion of organized gay and lesbian athletic events that, as he told the *Advocate* in 1986, were "conceived as a new idea in the meaning of sport based on inclusion rather than exclusion." Anyone would be allowed to compete, regardless of race, gender, religion, athletic ability, or (even) sexual orientation. Moreover, athletes would participate as individual members on behalf of cities and towns rather than their respective countries, avoiding the often-divisive nationalistic competitiveness of the Olympic Games themselves.

On 28 August through 5 September 1982, Tom Waddell's dream-come-true marched out proudly onto the field at Kezar Stadium in San Francisco. Some 1300 gay men and lesbians from over 24 countries competed in track and field, swimming, wrestling, bowling, diving, cycling, softball, soccer, tennis, and basketball. A concurrent "procession of the arts" likewise featured over twenty dance, theater, and performance exhibits.

There was, of course, a "fly in the ointment" in the form of a last-minute U.S. Olympic Committee injunction against the organizers' use of the word "Olympic" in the name for the Gay Games (they were originally to be called simply the "Gay Olympic Games"). At first, everyone thought the U.S.O.C. was merely grandstanding. True, Congress had granted the U.S.O.C. exclusive rights to the word "Olympic" in 1978, but since then the committee had allowed everything from the "Rat Olympics" to the "Police Olympics" to proceed without so much as a peep.

Right up to the tortuous end of Waddell's life in June of 1987, the U.S.O.C. doggedly pursued their sadistic suit. They even filed to recover legal fees (over $100,000) by placing a lien against Waddell's house. A few weeks before he died, the U.S. Supreme Court ruled five-to-four in favor of the committee's exclusive right to the use of the word "Olympic" and ordered that damages be paid.

But Tom was a champion to the finish. The year previous, he had seen Gay Games II grow to attract over 3,400 athletes in 17 events, and had witnessed a male-to-female ratio of 3:2 (as compared to a 4:1 ration at the 1984 Olympics in Los Angeles). He had even won a gold medal in the javelin competition just weeks after his AIDS diagnosis. Even the U.S. Supreme Court could not dampen Waddell's spirit. For him it was never really a defeat because, as he told Schapp, "the mere fact that the case had gone to the Supreme Court had exposed the pettiness and silliness of the U.S.O.C.'s position." Self-pity was never part of his style. Just thirty-six hours before his death in 1987, surrounded by his four-year-old daughter and countless friends, he took himself off all his medications, folded his hands in his lap, and simply said (as those who knew him had heard him say so many times before) "Well, this should be interesting."

References:

Bluestein, Ron. "Papa Games in Profile—Dr. Tom Waddell," in *Advocate*, 23 December 1986.

Schapp, Dick. "The Death of an Athlete," in *Sports Illustrated*, 27 July 1987.

Waddell, Tom and Dick Schapp. *Gay Olympian—The Life and Death of Dr. Tom Waddell.* New York: Alfred A. Knopf, 1996.

—Jerome Szymczak

Andy Warhol

1928-1987

American artist

After the death of Pablo Picasso in 1973, Andy Warhol ranked as the world's most famous contemporary artist. His numerous paintings entered major collections and museums everywhere. Moreover, his films—though not frequently screened after an initial flurry of interest—were important historically, marking a breakthrough in public attention to the underground cinema and enlarging the possibilities of sexual frankness. Warhol's career evolved in tandem with New York City's changing cultural scene, reflecting both its grit and glamour: grit, as seen in the fascination with the street people that marked his earlier career, glamour, as he hobnobbed with the rich and famous. He helped to shape a major change in the status of how art was regarded, so that it became less an elite preoccupation of professionals and connoisseurs and more a matter of publicity and marketing. Not everyone welcomed these changes, and some critics questioned whether the intrinsic quality of Warhol's art matched its hype.

Andrew Warhola, Jr., was born into a working-class family of Ruthenian origin on 6 August 1928, in Forest City, Pennsylvania. After completing art school at the Carnegie Institute of Technology in Pittsburgh, he settled in New York City in 1949, changing his name to Andy Warhol. Earning his living producing commercial art, he also essayed more personal work in the blotted-line technique, which fascinated him because of its impersonal quality. In those early New York years Warhol struck up a friendship with two other artists who shared both his sexual orientation and his general outlook on art, Jasper Johns and Robert Rauschenberg.

The beginning of Warhol's fame coincided with the emergence of the Pop Art trend in the 1960s. In this vein, Warhol created the multiple Campbell's Soup cans and Brillo boxes that became his signature. These works reflected the concepts of mass production and replication of images fostered by modern technology.

Warhol gradually acquired a varied and colorful entourage: everyone seemed welcome in his vast New York City loft, "the Factory," where his assistants scurried to execute works at his behest. In the 1960s, Warhol diversified his activities by producing a large number of films, only a few of which reached the public. Early titles, such as *Blow Job* (1963) and *My Hustler* (1965), were little more than home movies, but they proved timely, and succeeded in enlarging boundaries of the permissible. Then, in collaboration with Paul

Morrissey, Warhol attempted more ambitious movies that met commercial production criteria. Typically, these featured the gorgeous but empty figure of the hunk Joe Dallessandro.

Not only was Warhol reshaping the art forms of painting and film, but he had become a celebrity, a focal point for the new urban sensibility. His manifold activities blended almost seamlessly with Manhattan's Downtown scene, which was characterized by drug use, sexual freedom, and cultural anarchism. At the same time the rapturous reception accorded even his most casual productions signaled a momentous change in the rapidly expanding art world. The new art scene drew crowds of enthusiastic, green recruits, more interested in being trendy than deeply knowledgeable. Moreover, as contemporary art became increasingly popular, the inevitable simplifications of journalism were fed back into the art world. The new trends bore the imprint of the "glitterati" rather than of serious intellectuals. Creative personalities yielded to the temptation of believing their own press releases. Yet Warhol always retained a sense of irony and fun; on occasion, for example, he sent a look-alike to impersonate him at lectures and gallery openings.

The outstanding characteristic of Warhol's works is their seeming blankness and absence of specifiable emotional tone. Although he drew his subject matter from the world of mass consumption, it is impossible to tell whether Warhol is celebrating or reviling this aspect of capitalism.

The indeterminacy of affect in Warhol's art has several possible sources. Some writers and artists in nineteenth-century France, such as the novelist Gustave Flaubert and the painter Edouard Manet, had espoused an ideal of inscrutable detachment. This approach took a different form in the twentieth-century artist Marcel Duchamp, who fused it with the world of industrialized mass production. It is also possible that Warhol learned from the German playwright Bertolt Brecht, who stressed the alienation principle as a distancing device in the theater. Finally, given the interest in Zen and other Eastern religions in the United States after World War II, esoteric ideas questioning the stability of personality probably entered into the mix.

Although Warhol said that he preferred sex on the screen or in the pages of a book to experiencing the real thing, he made no secret of his homosexual preferences. Yet the artist seemed rarely to act on them. Despite being surrounded by scandal, Warhol himself could not be detected in the throes of any messy relationship; he was in fact married to his art. On 5 June 1968, Valerie Solanas, a deranged former associate, shot Warhol in his loft. The artist never fully recovered from the effects of the attack. After this setback he became more selective in his choice of friends, gravitating to the world of the wealthy and fashionable. A year after the shooting he launched a chic periodical, *Interview,* which chronicled the doings of those in the public eye.

Warhol's emergence marks an important aspect of the interface between homosexuality and creativity in the United States. The years after World War II were in some ways the most repressive ones the United States has ever experienced with regard to sexual nonconformity. Paradoxically, the emergence of such major creative talents as William Burroughs, Alan Ginsberg, Gore Vidal, and Tennessee Williams, all of whose work centered on their sexual and gender identity, occurred during this period.

In his youth, Warhol perceived the need to don a mask to conceal his true nature from the world. His enduring project of self-fashioning and his artistic blankness were coping strategies for survival in America's most vocally homophobic era. Ironically, the very qualities of his art which the mainstream idolized stemmed from the harsh impact on a sensitive adolescent of a society that proclaimed that it had no room for nonconformity. Warhol created a mythology, extending at times to personal "disinformation," as part of his life project of forging a surrogate persona that would mediate between his real life, which was often surprisingly banal, and his creative works.

Andy Warhol

On 22 February 1987, Warhol died in a New York hospital after gall-bladder surgery. His will established the Andy Warhol Foundation for the Visual Arts. Today, a representative collection of his work is on permanent display at the Andy Warhol Museum in his hometown of Pittsburgh.

With the emergence of postmodernism, Warhol's combination of commercial and high art themes, as well as the elusiveness of his public persona, acquired vast topical interest. However they may ultimately be judged, Warhol's art and fame are indispensable components of late twentieth-century culture.

References:

Colacello, Bob. *Holy Terror: Andy Warhol Close Up.* New York: HarperCollins, 1990.

Doyle, Jonathan, Jonathan Flatley, and José Esteban Muñoz, eds. *Pop Out Queen, Warhol.* Durham: Duke University Press, 1996.
McShine, Kynaston, ed. *Andy Warhol: A Retrospective.* New York: Museum of Modern Art, 1989.
Smith, Patrick S. *Andy Warhol's Art and Films.* Ann Arbor, Michigan: UMI Press, 1986.

—Wayne R. Dynes

John Waters

1946-

American filmmaker

John Waters has been dubbed the King of Puke, the Pope of Trash, the Vizier of Vulgarity, the Titan of Terrible Taste, and the Lord High Poohbah of Repulsion (according to *Rolling Stone* magazine). His films, which in fact exhibit varying degrees of bad taste and have recently become more mainstream, have earned him a huge cult following as well as a measure of sometimes grudging critical respect. With imagination and wit, Waters subverts traditional societal norms, and yet, as he himself notes, his films are basically moral stories in which "the bitter people are punished and those who are happy with themselves win."

John Waters. *Photograph by Greg Gorman.*

Born and raised in Baltimore, Waters attended Catholic schools, and it was there that he met his muse, Divine, at a time when the future 300-pound transvestite was just Glenn Milstead, another misfit hanging out. Waters produced his first film in 1963 at the age of 17. It was entitled *Hag in a Black Leather Jacket* and cost $30. After being thrown out of the New York University film school for smoking pot, Waters returned to Baltimore to form Dreamland Productions, which produced *Roman Candles* (1966), *Eat Your Makeup* (Divine as Jackie Kennedy, 1968), *Mondo Trasho* (Divine has a divine revelation and is committed, 1969) and *Multiple Maniacs* (Divine as a murdering carnival owner, 1970). Early Waters films were done in laundromats ("because the lighting was good") and in alleys ("so we could run away"). During the filming of *Mondo Trasho,* Waters and four of his actors were arrested for conspiracy to commit indecent exposure.

In 1972, Waters produced his most notorious film, and the one that made him an underground hero, *Pink Flamingos* (Divine competing for title of "Filthiest Person Alive.") Originally screened at the University of Baltimore, the film later played in a Boston pornography theater and at midnight showings in small theaters in New York City. With its bizarre cast of characters and shocking final scene, in which Divine eats dog droppings, *Pink Flamingos* became one of the most popular and profitable underground films of the 1970s, although a Florida Grand Jury declared that it was too depraved to be shown in their state. It was later selected as part of the Museum of Modern Art's bicentennial program "American Film Comedy."

Next on the film roster came *Female Trouble* (Divine is executed by electric chair, 1975), and *Desperate Living* (a lesbian melodrama, the only early Waters film without Divine). *Polyester* (Divine and Tab Hunter as psychopathic lovers, 1981) started Waters's cautious foray into mainstream America, garnering a good review from the *New York Times* and other mainstream media.

After the publication of his autobiography, *Shock Value* (1981) Waters went on the lecture circuit, talking to audiences all over the world about his peculiar take on reality. A series of his magazine articles was published in book form in 1986, entitled *Crackpot: The Obsessions of John Waters.* During the early 1980s, Waters also taught a class in filmmaking at a maximum security prison in Baltimore. He later reported that he felt a great rapport with the inmates, being as much at odds with the system as they were but having been fortunate enough to find a healthier way of expressing his opposition.

All of Waters's film have been made with small budgets, and even the commercial releases *Hairspray* (Divine convincing as a 1960s mother and Ricki Lake as her rock-and-roll crazed daughter, 1988) and *Crybaby* (Johnny Depp as another mooning rocker, 1990), which was backed by Imagine Films, were modestly budgeted by Hollywood standards. It was *Hairspray* that finally won him a measure of mainstream approval, and when *Crybaby* was made diehard Waters fans were sure he had sold out because the film was acceptable to those not in his cult. He became so famous his home city declared a John Waters Day (February 16th, for the world premiere of *Hairspray*) and commentators began to claim that he had invented a new film genre—horror/comedy. Another measure of his acceptance is that his next film, *Serial Mom* (1994), about a murderous suburban housewife who maintains a flawless Donna Reed existence while practicing her unusual hobby, starred Kathleen Turner.

Filmmakers have a high failure rate, and many projects which seem promising never make it past the development stage. Yet

Waters has had great success in getting his ideas to the public in finished form, particularly since for most of his career his offerings have been pretty far out on the edge. A sequel to *Pink Flamingos* died after Waters tried to raise funding for two years with no success and one of the leading actresses in the original died of cancer. But the script was published as part of a book entitled *Trash Trio* (Random House, 1988). A proposed film called *Glamourpuss* was turned down by seventeen studios before Waters gave up on it, but he could be back with it later.

Waters lives alone in a large old house in his native Baltimore (where all his films have been set) with his extensive collections of strange memorabilia, and occasionally in his little Greenwich Village apartment.

Current Address: c/o Bill Block, ICM, 8942 Wilshire Blvd., Beverly Hills, California 90211.

References:

"Camping Out in Hollywood," in *Interview* (New York), April 1994.
"Cool Waters," in *Premiere* (London), April 1994.
"The Domestication of John Waters," in *American Film* (New York), April 1990.
Dowd, Maureen. "John Waters: Misfits' Messiah," in *Rolling Stone* (New York), 17 May 1990.
"High Water Marks," in *Entertainment Weekly* (New York), 29 April 1994.
Interview (New York), February 1990.
"John Waters: The Sick Man of Cinema," in *People Weekly* (New York), 14 March 1989.
"Kink-Meister," in *New York Times Magazine,* 7 April 1991.
New York, 28 January 1991.
People Weekly (New York), 28 January 1991.
"Prowling for Books with John Waters," in *People Weekly* (New York), 18 April 1994.
"Trumpism Is Out, but Dork-Knobs Will be In," in *Fortune* (New York), 26 March 1990.
Waters, John. *Crackpot: The Obsessions of John Waters.* New York: MacMillan, 1986.
"The Weird World of John Waters," in *Theatre Crafts* (New York), May 1990.
"What Hath John Waters Wrought?," in *People Weekly* (New York), 1 September 1989.

—Debora Hill

Edmund White

1940-

American writer

Author Edmund White is a master stylist best known for his widely acclaimed novels, many of them semi-autobiographical treatments of gay society that combine the best features of fiction and nonfiction. Proclaimed by *Newsweek* to be "unquestionably the foremost American gay novelist," White belongs to that group of writers whose literary reputation transcends such simplistic labels. As William Goldstein explains in *Publishers Weekly*: "To call Edmund White merely a gay writer is to oversimplify his work and his intentions. Although that two-word label ... aptly sums up White's status, the first word no doubt helps obscure the fact that the second applies just as fittingly."

Still, White is best known for the themes of gay life in America as portrayed in novels such as *A Boy's Own Story* and *The Beautiful Room Is Empty*. And he told *Publishers Weekly* that he is "happy to be considered a gay writer.... Since gay people have very little political representation, we have no gay spokespeople. What happens is that there is an enormous pressure placed on gay novelists because they are virtually the *only* spokespeople."

Edmund White was born in Cincinnati on 13 January 1940, the son of a chemical engineer and a psychologist. His parents divorced when he was seven years old, and he and his sister spent many years alternating living with both parents—his father in Ohio and his mother in Chicago. He recalls being aware of his homosexuality early in life but told Leonard Schulman of *Time* magazine: "I didn't want to be gay. I wanted to be normal, to have a wife and kids." At the age of fourteen, he informed his father of his sexual orientation and asked him to pay for therapy. White spent several unhappy years in therapy before finding a gay psychologist, who helped him come to terms with his sexuality.

White excelled in his studies in Chinese at the University of Michigan, from which he graduated in 1962, having earned the prestigious Hopwood Award in 1961 and 1962 for fiction and drama. After graduation, he moved to New York's Greenwich Village and began working as an editor in the book division of Time, Inc., a position he would hold until 1970. But by the age of fifteen, he had already written his first novel (not surprisingly, about a boy coming to terms with his homosexuality), and it was to writing that White aspired. His play *The Blue Boy in Black* was produced Off-Broadway in 1963, and throughout the sixties he concentrated on writing novels.

White's first published novel, *Forgetting Elena* (1973), relates the tale of an amnesia victim struggling to determine his own identity and the identities of those around him. It was applauded by critics for its satiric and insightful look at social interaction, as well as for its elegant prose. This impressive debut brought White acceptance in literary circles that included Susan Sontag and Richard Howard and gained him many notable admirers, including master novelists Vladimir Nabokov and Gore Vidal.

His next novel, *Nocturnes for the King of Naples* (1978) also won acclaim for its discerning treatment of human values and relationships. As John Yohalem wrote in the *New York Times Book Review*, "*Nocturnes* is a series of apostrophes to a nameless, evidently famous dead lover, a man who awakened the much younger, also nameless narrator ... to the possibility of sexual friendship." J. D. McClatchy, in a *Shenandoah* review, calls White "a superior stylist of both erotic theology and plangent contrition. And his special gift is his ability to empty out our stale expectations from genres ... and types ... and to reimagine them in a wholly intriguing and convincing manner."

Caracole, White's 1985 novel, goes back to an earlier century and revives a more elaborate fictional form in its tale of two country lovers forcibly separated who turn to sexual escapades in a large city. The resulting story is a "a puzzling melange of comic opera and sleek sensuality," according to Christopher Lehmann-Haupt of

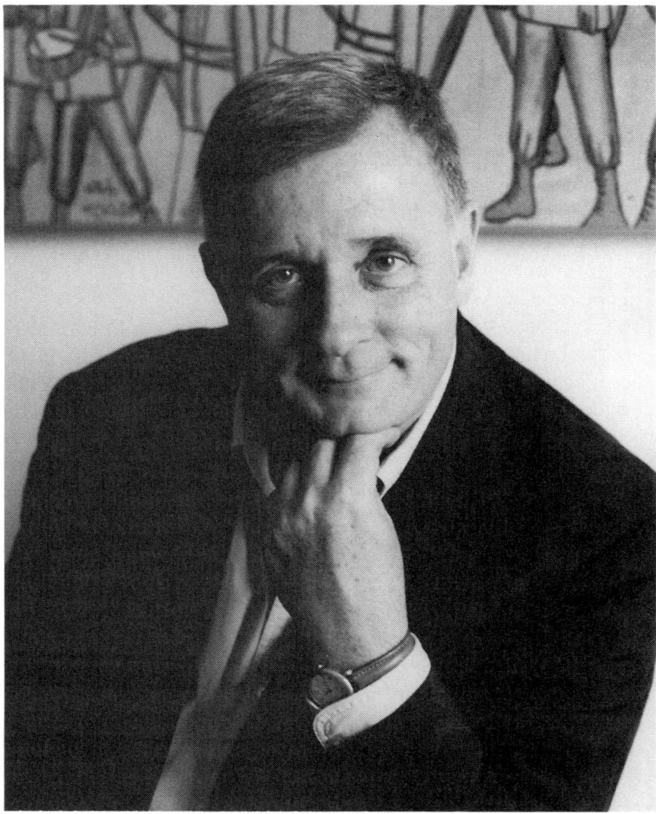

Edmund White. ***Photograph by Jerry Bauer.***

the *New York Times*. And in the *New York Times Book Review*, David R. Slavitt describes the work as "a grand fantasy.... Shrewdness and self-awareness ooze from every intricate sentence, every linguistic arabesque and hothouse epigram."

Even though all of the novels received high praise from critics and good response from the public, it is the semi-autobiographical *A Boy's Own Story* that is often cited as White's best work. This first person-narrative of a gay boy's adolescence during the 1950s was described by a *Harper's* reviewer as "a poignant combination of [fiction and nonfiction] written with the flourish of a master stylist." Lehmann-Haupt of the *New York Times* found that "this is not exclusively a homosexual boy's story. It is any boy's story, to the marvelous degree that it evokes the inchoate longing of late childhood and adolescence." More than one reviewer has called *A Boy's Own Story* a "classic" work. Comparing White to James Baldwin, Herman Wouk, and Mary McCarthy, *Washington Post* writer Thomas M. Disch called the work "the strongest bid to date by a gay writer to do for his minority experience what the writers above did for theirs—offer it as a representative, all-American instance."

White followed this success with a sequel, *The Beautiful Room Is Empty*, which, although generally well received, did not quite reach the level of acclaim that was awarded *A Boy's Own Story*. One explanation for this might be the somewhat less sympathetic narrator than that of the earlier novel. Here, the narrator alternately revels in his homosexuality and rejects himself for it. Psychoanalysis and increasing surrender to sensual activity escalates the young man's battle for self acceptance. Though his sexuality troubles him, the excitement and audacity of his experiences with gay men in public restrooms seems a needed respite from the blandness of his suburban life. Sometimes the adolescent makes bold moves, as when he shouts, "Gay is good!" in a Greenwich Village demonstration. At other times, he acts out his self-loathing, as when he seduces his music teacher and then betrays him to the authorities. In an interview in Larry McCaffery's *Alive and Writing*, White commented: "To have my boy turn out so creepy seemed to be a way of alienating some gay commissars.... You can't show somebody in a deforming period, like the 1950s in America, and then show him as happy, healthy, the perfect role model."

White discussed those earlier, more repressive times of the 1950s and 1960s in a *Paris Review* interview: "I was writing gay books well before gay liberation and before there was a recognized gay reading public. One actually existed, although no publisher was aware of it. There was also a tremendous amount of self-repression among gay editors. A gay editor would turn down a gay book because if he admitted to liking it he would have to defend it at an editorial meeting, and that might lead other people to suspect *he* was gay." As attitudes about homosexuality began to change, the publishing world became more receptive to books by gay writers. Now, White admits to being thrilled by the recognition he has received. "I know I'll always be doing this," he told the *Publishers Weekly* interviewer, "and I know that I'll never make a living from my writing; but that's fine. It's enough to be published."

Concurrent with his career as an author, White has taught creative writing at several East Coast universities, including Johns Hopkins, Columbia, Yale, and Brown. His reviews and profiles appear frequently in *Vogue* and other magazines. He also writes travel articles and reports on contemporary trends in art and politics. Continuing his role as a social historian on the homosexual experience in America, White has written several intensely personal articles on the impact of AIDS on gay life and gay writers. In the early 1980s, he became one of the founders of the Gay Men's Health Crisis and says that he has lost some forty friends to AIDS. In 1985 White himself tested positive for HIV.

In "Residence on Earth: Living with AIDS in the '80s," an article he wrote for *Life* magazine, White observed: "Ten years ago gay men were perceived as playboys who put their selfish pleasures above family or community duties and responsibilities. Now they're seen as victims who have responded to a tragedy with dignity and courage. Above all, the lesbian and gay community is recognized as a *community*, one that is often angry and militant, generally well disciplined, always concerned."

Current Address: Department of English, Brown University, Providence, Rhode Island 02912.

References:

Authors and Artists for Young Adults, Volume 7. Detroit: Gale Research, 1991.

Baylis, Jamie. Review of *A Boy's Own Story,* in *Harper's*, October 1982: 75-76.

Clemons, Walter. "Gay Rites: A Tour Coast to Coast," in *Newsweek*, 11 February 1980: 92-93.

Disch, Thomas M. "Memories of a Homosexual Boyhood," in *Washington Post Book World*, 17 October 1982: 1.

Elgrably, Jordan. "The Art of Fiction CV: Edmund White," in *Paris Review*, fall 1988: 46-80.

Goldstein, William. "Publishers Weekly Interviews: Edmund White," in *Publishers Weekly*, 24 September 1982: 6-8.
Lehmann-Haupt, Christopher. Review of *A Boy's Own Story*, in *New York Times*, 17 December 1982: 26.
———. Review of *Caracole*, in *New York Times*, 9 September 1985: 19.
McCaffery, Larry. *Alive and Writing: Interviews*. University of Illinois Press, 1987.
McClatchy, J. D. "Baroque Inventions," in *Shenandoah*, fall 1978: 97-98.
Schulman, Leonard. "Profile: Imagining Other Lives," in *Time*, 30 July 1990: 58-60.
Slavitt, David R. Review of *Caracole*, in *New York Times Book Review*, 15 September 1985: 15.
White, Edmund. "Residence on Earth: Living with AIDS in the '80s," in *Life*, fall 1989: 135.
Yohalem, John. "Apostrophes to a Dead Lover," in *New York Times Book Review*, 10 December 1978: 12.

Walt Whitman

1819-1892

American writer

Walt Whitman's effusive lyrics perfectly mirrored the exuberance and variance that characterized the young maturity of the Republic. During his lifetime and for some years afterwards, rumors of his sexual unorthodoxy mingled in an uneasy alliance with his growing reputation. During the first half of the twentieth century, however, established critics found an intolerable dissonance in the very thought that the "good gray poet" could be a "pervert," and sought to heterosexualize him. With Edward F. Grier's editing of his *Notebooks and Unpublished Prose Manuscripts* in the definitive New York University Press edition (1984) doubts have been banished. To Professor Grier's patient work all subsequent interpretations, including this one, are profoundly indebted. Scholars have found no truth in the "whopper," which the poet perpetrated in a panicky moment to his gay admirer Arthur Addington Symonds, of six illegitimate children in the south. Despite his occasional toying with the truth, today Whitman's reputation stands higher than ever. He was a great liberator of form and a guide to changing one's life—always, as he would insist, if one wanted to do so.

From Working-Class Journeyman to World Figure

Walter Whitman was born on 31 May 1819 at a farm at West Hills, Long Island. In 1823 the family moved to Brooklyn, where the future poet attended public schools. As an adult, Whitman himself tried teaching school, but found his pupils loutish and unresponsive. Beginning in 1831 he made his living mainly by working for various newspapers in Brooklyn and Manhattan as a printer and editor. Eventually, he was forced out of this profession because of his uncompromising support for the Free Soil cause. He then took up carpentry.

Throughout this career dancing, however, he was able to place occasional poems and stories—generally of little distinction—in the press. In 1855 Whitman self-published the first edition of *Leaves of Grass*, which elicited an enthusiastic letter from Ralph Waldo Emerson. Towards the end of the decade he wrote poetry infused with homoerotic sentiment that he never surpassed and rarely equaled.

In December 1862 he traveled to northern Virginia to be with a brother who was a soldier in the Union Army. Impressed by the spectacle of the Civil War, he relocated to Washington, D.C., where he mainly resided until 1873. Whitman found work as a clerk in a government office while also volunteering as a male nurse in military hospitals.

In 1865 he met a former Confederate soldier, Peter Doyle, who had become a streetcar conductor. Whitman's affection was returned, and the two formed a close bond. The relationship, which extended over many years, went to the core of Whitman's being. He was to have other favorite boys, but none made such an impression as Doyle.

In 1873 Walt Whitman suffered a paralytic stroke and moved in with his brother in Camden, New Jersey, where he was to live for the rest of his life. During this period, the poet developed an intense relationship with a boy in his late teens, Harry Stafford. Throughout 1875-77 the poet was visited by Anne Gilchrist and Edward Carpenter, from England, and Richard Maurice Bucke, from Canada, initiating a stream of admirers coming from far-away places. Profiting from an improvement in his health, he made a journey westward as far as Colorado (1879); the following year he visited his supporter Bucke in Ontario, Canada. During the last years of his life he was attended by a secretary, Horace Traubel, who carefully recorded his views. In 1891 he prepared the final issue, the "death-bed edition," of *Leaves of Grass* for publication. He died in Camden on 26 March 1891.

The Self-Realization of a Poet and Thinker

Whitman's literary career was slow to develop. In fact, there was little evidence of distinction until he began to write fragments of what was to become *Leaves of Grass* in various notebooks. The earliest of his jottings are somewhat jejune speculations. Beginning in 1857 he recorded the names of young men encountered while cruising through Brooklyn and Manhattan. Then in 1862 he included the names of wounded soldiers he met in Civil War hospitals. Laconically noted, the names are rarely repeated. More commonly, these contacts were with working-class men. The later lists of soldiers are somewhat more effusive. There can be little doubt that most of these were, or were intended to be, sexual liaisons.

In 1847 Whitman seems to have had a mystical experience in which he and his soul lay on the grass, fusing in a directly sensual manner. While presented as an allegory, the poem, "Song of Myself," clearly draws on memories of an erotic male-male encounter involving oral sex:

> I mind how we once lay such a transparent summer morning,
> How you settled your head athwart my hips and gently turn'd over upon me,
> and parted the shirt from my bosom-bone, and plunged your tongue to my bare-stripped heart,
> And reach'd till you felt my beard, and reach'd till you held my feet.

Taken in its allegorical application, this wording clearly shows Whitman's monism, his sense of the union of body and soul.

Certainly, it is hard to disagree with the assertion that *Leaves Grass* is in some sense of mystic's journal. Through successive revisions and additions, this book came to embrace his entire poetic oeuvre.

Leaves of Grass first appeared in 1855 with twelve untitled sections. The "Song of Myself" (to use the title Whitman later gave it) is the longest and most significant. Seeing his work in print as a single volume whetted the poet's appetite for publication. Accordingly, there followed the second edition (1857), boasting thirty-two items. The third, in 1860, had 156. The process of accretion continued through various editions until 1881.

The 1860 inclusion of the "Calamus" sequence, suffused with homoeroticism, was a major landmark. These poems clearly grow out of a particular relationship, in which he sought eternal union with another man. This union was not to last, such is the way of the world but to his, and our, immense benefit Whitman kept the poems.

Whitman exercised caution in describing his erotic activities—appropriately enough considering the era in which he lived. Then too, it simply never occurred to him that posterity would be so interested in the matter; evidently, he believed that his poetry, the distillation of experience, was all one needed to know. One must remember that in this period, embraces and kisses, together with mutual masturbation, sufficed for many participants in male-male sexual experience.

Whitman may also have had some experience with women. There is evidence that he had some sort of relationship with two women, one possibly an actress, the other a French entertainer. Opinion is divided as to whether the heterosexual sentiments expressed in the "Children of Adam" sequence are as convincing as those found in "Calamus." To many readers it seems that he inserted this heterosexual material for symmetry's sake and to blunt suspicions. For similar reasons, it seems he tended to say "he and she," "him and her."

For his time Whitman's attitude towards women was enlightened. He recognized that they were sexual beings, and he could feel sympathy for a streetwalker.

In fact it was his explicitness about male-female sex that shocked his early readers. In his own day only a few gay men in Britain and some readers in Germany responded to what is now unmistakable to any reader who can honestly grapple with what he or she is reading. Homoerotic imagery dominates the second and third sections of "Song of Myself." The same is true of the subsequent discussion of the body and soul, which culminates in the intercourse between the two in the fifth section. Also noteworthy is the sweep of eroticism from section 24 to the climax of fulfillment in male intercourse in section 29.

Very different from the philosophical and self-reflective passages of "Song of Myself" and the passionate sexuality though unconnected sexuality in "Children of Adam," the "Calamus" poems demonstrate not only Whitman's mastery of the lyric form as against the longer ode or rhapsody, but also differ in their obviously personal nature. The object of the poet's interest has never been identified, yet the poems convey the searing experience of being a lover. In "Out of the Cradle Endlessly Rocking" (1860), the despairing loss of a lover is recreated through the disappearance of the female of a pair of nesting mocking birds.

Whitman's poetry underwent considerable change after the Civil War. For a time he considered the 1860 edition to be final, expecting that later poems would form a new, more spiritual, book. But he dropped this plan and declined to attempt a new book. Instead he wove his new poems into a loose autobiographical cycle centering on the Civil War.

As early as 1856 he had dubbed homosexuality "adhesiveness," a term taken from the then-popular pseudoscience of phrenology. The term homosexuality, coined in 1869 in Germany, was not yet available, and it is doubtful whether Whitman would have used it if he had known it. In *Democratic Vistas* (1871) Whitman in effect contrasts homosexuality with heterosexuality ("amative love"): "[it] is to the development, identification, and general prevalence of that fervid comradeship (the adhesive love at least rivaling the amative love hitherto possessing imaginative literature, if not going beyond it), that I look for the counterbalance and offset of materialistic and vulgar American Democracy, and for the spiritualization thereof.... I say Democracy infers such loving comradeship, as its inevitable twin or counterpart, without which it will be incomplete, in vain, and incapable of perpetuating itself."

It is evident that for Whitman adhesiveness signified not only friendship but the capacity for "manly love." Grandly, he saw this as not merely a personal matter, but a governing principle of society. It was his aim to rank not merely as the prophet of an idealized democracy, but of a transformed society in which each person could fulfill his or her own sexual nature with dignity and companionship.

Whitman's Image and Message

Outside the English-speaking world, the first country to rally massively to Whitman was Germany, where no fewer than three editions of *Leaves of Grass* appeared between 1899 and 1909. Inspired by the German homosexual emancipation movement, Eduard Bertz was the first to discuss Whitman's homosexual orientation in a serious and detailed way.

It was probably in Germany just after the turn of the century that the great American dance innovator Isadora Duncan (1978-1927) discovered Whitman. She strove to incorporate his ideas in her performances and in the opinion of some was widely successful. As the critic Max Eastman remarked in 1942, she was "a winged apostle to the whole world of Walt Whitman's vision of a poised and free-bodied and free-souled humanity, carrying his thought to hears that never heard of him."

Walt Whitman's message resounded abroad, including such diverse countries as Portugal, Chile, and India, where sensitive persons were seeking to escape from the bonds of stifling traditional culture. Whitman performed a similar service in the United States after World War II, when the beat writers were seeking not only a new literary style but a new way of life. The title of Jack Kerouac's *On the Road* (1957) might almost be a mantra for Whitman enthusiasts, and the poet appears in person in several poems by Allen Ginsberg.

As these examples show, Walt Whitman's influence has transcended the sphere of literary study—where, of course, he has been assiduously cultivated. Today, perhaps, this breadth is especially true, for first and foremost he was a challenger of established gender arrangements. His example authorized a broader concept of masculinity in which a wide range of emotional feeling would be encouraged. More generally, he successfully merged his creative work and his life, forecasting one of the aims of gay liberation as it emerged after the Stonewall riots of 1969.

If Whitman were alive today, what sort of role model would he make for gay people? A tentative effort has been made to claim him for intergenerational pairing. It is true that he was attracted chiefly to men in their late teens and early twenties. But in an era in which these men were already expected to shoulder adult responsibilities the gap in age would have been less significant.

In his sexual liaisons Whitman was most strongly attracted to working-class men, often with little education and a rural background. Superficially, this resembles the "prince-and-pauper" syndrome of upper-class English homosexuals like John Addington Symonds and E. M. Forster. However, Whitman had himself sprung from the working class and had educated himself. He may have cherished the hope that his camerados would do the same.

Perhaps Whitman would feel greatest affinity with the "bear" subculture today, which consists of men who cultivate a rough-hewn masculine appearance and lifestyle. Walt Whitman prided himself on his "unbuttoned" casualness.

Yet he was more complex than these descriptions would indicate. One of Whitman's greatest loves was opera, and rhythms derived from its lyrical melodies and soaring emotions infuse his work. In this way, Whitman was even a forerunner of another common gay type today, the "opera queen."

These posited affinities are too restrictive, for Whitman speaks to straights as well as gays, to women as well as men. In the late twentieth-century gay men could have no better ambassador.

References:

Allen, Gay Wilson. *The Solitary Singer*. New ed. Chicago: University of Chicago Press, 1985.

Allen, Gay Wilson and Ed Folsom, eds. *Walt Whitman & the World*. Iowa City: University of Iowa Press, 1995.

Faner, Robert D. *Walt Whitman & Opera*. Carbondale: Southern Illinois University Press, 1951.

Folsom, Ed, ed. *Walt Whitman: The Centennial Essays*. Iowa City: University of Iowa Press, 1994.

Fone, Byrne R. S. *Masculine Landscapes: Walt Whitman and the Homoerotic Text*. Carbondale: Southern Illinois Press, 1992.

Greenspan, Ezra, ed. *The Cambridge Companion to Walt Whitman*. New York: Cambridge University Press, 1995.

Grünzweig, Walter. *Constructing the German Walt Whitman*. Iowa City: University of Iowa Press, 1995.

Killingsworth, M. Jimmie. *Whitman's Poetry of the Body: Sexuality, Politics, and the Text*. Chapel Hill: University of North Carolina Press, 1989.

Martin, Robert K. *The Homosexual Tradition in American Poetry*. Austin: University of Texas Press, 1981.

Moon, Michael. *Disseminating Whitman: Revision and Corporeality in Leaves of Grass*. Cambridge, Massachusetts: Harvard University Press, 1991.

Perlman, Jim, Ed Folson, and Don Campion, eds. *Walt Whitman: The Measure of His Song*. Minneapolis: The Holy Cow Press, 1981.

Shively, Charley. *Calamus Lovers: Walt Whitman's Working Class Camerados*. San Francisco: Gay Sunshine Press, 1987.

———. *Drum Beats: Walt Whitman's Civil War Boy Lovers*. San Francisco: Gay Sunshine Press, 1989.

—Wayne R. Dynes

Oscar Wilde

1854-1900

British writer

Oscar Wilde was born in Dublin on 16 October 1854 into the upper classes of Victorian society—one of the most rigidly directed societies the world has ever known. His mission in life was to break through the barriers of this society in every possible way. Wilde's father, Sir William Wilde, was a medical doctor and a renowned surgeon, eminent archeologist and writer. His mother, Jane Francesca Elgee, was the daughter of a lawyer who became a famous fighter for Irish independence while in her teens. She went on to become a political writer and novelist. Wilde's full name was Oscar Fingal O'Flahertie Wills Wilde. Oscar is taken from Irish folklore—the son of Ossian, the third-century Irish warrior bard. Fingal was the name of Ossian's father and also the hero of the bard's poems. However, Oscar could also have been named for the King of Sweden, who was his godfather.

That he had a strange childhood for the times is clear, as he was constantly surrounded by many rumors about the odd practices in the Wilde household. Although the family had the requisite number of servants for the age, the Wilde house always seemed to be disordered and dirty, and Sir William was known to be personally filthy. One scandal erupted when Oscar was away at school. It came about because of Sir William's mistress, Mary Travers, who, when he

Oscar Wilde

attempted to leave her, accused him of raping her. The case reached the courts and was a favored society item for some months after.

College, Friends, and Influences

At school, Wilde suffered the disorientation that many homosexuals feel as children. He had few friends as a child, but showed his brilliance early. When he was seventeen Wilde was awarded a scholarship to Trinity College, Dublin. There he met his first mentor, John Pentland Mahaffy, who was a Junior Fellow while still in his thirties. Wilde also met Edward Carson, who would become his life-long rival, while at Trinity. Wilde won a Foundation Scholarship in classics in 1873 and the Berkeley Gold Medal for Greek in 1874, beating out Carson in both. Carson would wait a long time for his revenge, but it would prove vicious when it came.

In 1874 Wilde won a scholarship to Oxford, and there became a follower of the aesthete John Ruskin. Walter Pater became his second mentor, and Wilde fell deeply into the study of aestheticism and hedonism—strange subjects for a university, but very popular disciplines in the late Victorian era. Wilde was already becoming known as a flamboyant dresser and conversational wit, and he took naturally to Pater's doctrine that pleasure and physical sensation were to be pursued for no other purpose than the experience.

In the summer of 1875 Wilde toured Northern Italy. His first poem was written while he was in Rome. Intended to be the first of a series of poems about Italy, it was entitled "Graffiti d'Italia I. San Miniato." Only one other poem was ever written for the series: "II. Arona, Lago Maggiore." Wilde began to write poetry for publication in 1876, and in 1878 he won the Newgate Prize for an epic poem called "Ravenna." It was printed by the university in a limited, paper-bound edition, and became Wilde's first published book. When asked what he had planned for his life after Oxford, Wilde remarked in prophetic fashion:

> God knows; I won't be an Oxford don anyhow. I'll be a poet, a writer, a dramatist. Somehow or other I'll be famous, and if not famous, I'll be notorious.

The Early London Years and a Trip to America

Wilde next went to London and joined a group of writers and artists who constituted the "Gay Young Things" of the time. Among them was Lily Langtry, for whom Wilde wrote the poem "The New Helen." Wilde's first play, *Vera* (about Nihilism in Russia), was canceled at the last moment due to political reasons, and the only book he published before 1881 was one of his collected poetry, bound at this own expense. Though Wilde had become famous as a wit and society ornament, he was very low on funds. In 1881 Wilde and friend Frank Miles were forced to give up their luxurious rooms in Salisbury Street and move to an apartment in Tite Street, where he would remain until 1895.

At the end of 1881, Wilde left London and embarked on a lecture tour of the United States, beginning in New York. The tour was financed by F. W. Morse, manager of Richard D'Oyly Carte. Wilde was hoping to raise funds to launch a production of *Vera.* He was badly received, particularly by the press, which lampooned him at every opportunity. The concept of aestheticism was too foreign to the earthy Americans of the 1880s, and Wilde was often used as a cartoon figure or in advertisements. One, for a clothing manufacturer, stated, "Wild Oscar, the Ass-thete, buys his clothes of our establishment." Wilde kept his sense of humor throughout the tour, and while American men mocked and satirized him, American women adored him.

Marriage, Family, and the London Gay Scene

Shortly after his return to England Wilde left for Paris, where he met Robert Sherard, the man who would eventually write three biographies about Wilde's life. *The Duchess of Padua,* a five-act tragedy commissioned by American actress Mary Anderson in 1881, was finished, but Anderson refused it and it was only produced in Germany, without any notable success.

Wilde returned to London in 1883 and was so desperate for money that he pawned his Berkeley Gold Medal. He embarked on a lecture tour of England, having grown weary of the London social set. In November of that year he became engaged to Constance Lloyd, daughter of a famous Irish lawyer. They were married on 29 May 1884 and went to Paris for a honeymoon. The Wildes returned to London and a house in Chelsea. Most of Constance's dowry was used to remodel and lavishly decorate the house, and they were constantly short of money. In 1885 Wilde became the book reviewer for the *Pall Mall Gazette* and the drama critic at the *Dramatic Review.* In June of 1885 his elder son Cyril was born.

It was in 1886 that Wilde became active in the London gay scene. He met Alfred Taylor through Robert Ross, and was introduced to some male prostitutes at Taylor's home in Bloomsbury. Wilde's first documented homosexual affair was with a valet named Charles Parker. Parker would reappear in Wilde's life as one of the prosecution witnesses in the 1895 trials.

Continued Literary Activities

In 1887 Wilde was appointed editor of a monthly magazine, first entitled the *Lady's World* and changed five months later to the *Woman's World.* Wilde also wrote a column for the magazine entitled "Literary Notes." He resigned in 1889 and the magazine folded the following year. During his tenure with the magazine he also wrote and published short stories including "The Canterville Ghost." He also wrote fairy stories that were published in 1888 in a book version entitled *The Happy Prince and Other Tales.* In 1887 his second son, Vyvyan, was born.

Wilde published four books in 1891, including: *A House of Pomegranates, Lord Arthur Savile's Crime, Intentions,* and *The Picture of Dorian Gray,* which became his most famous novel (it had appeared in a condensed version the previous year, in *Lippincott's Monthly Magazine*). Wilde received a large measure of criticism for *Intentions,* which contained four long essays. But it was *The Picture of Dorian Gray* that attracted the most abuse at the hands of the media. The book was a damning account of the hypocrisy of Victorian England, and because it did not follow the established pattern of the popular fiction of the day, many readers and critics found it incomprehensible.

From 1892 until 1895, Wilde enjoyed enormous success. His first successful play, *Lady Windermere's Fan,* was presented in 1892 at the St. James theater to enormous critical acclaim. Wilde was finally making a comfortable living for his family, and after that success he went to Paris, where he wrote *Salome.* Sarah Bernhardt had already started rehearsals on the play when it was refused a license due to an outdated law that stated Biblical characters could not be represented on the public stage in England. The play was published in France, and was also published in England with illustrations by Aubrey Beardsley.

At this time, Wilde announced in a London newspaper that he would renounce his British citizenship and become a French citizen. Unfortunately, given the events that would soon shape his life, he never did so, but began work on another play instead. This was *A Woman of No Importance,* which was produced in April of 1893 at the Haymarket Theatre. It was also an enormous success. That year his poem *The Sphynx* was published in book form.

In 1894 Wilde wrote what would be his last two plays, *An Ideal Husband* and *The Importance of Being Earnest.* The latter is a universal favorite and is still produced today. Faint hints to the disasters to come were in the wind: the Marquess of Queensberry was threatening to disgrace and ruin Wilde due to his friendship with the Marquess' son, Lord Alfred Bruce Douglas. In truth, the Marquess was a cruel and brutal tyrant who hated his son because he was the only person brave enough to defy him, and he had already conceived the idea of disgracing Douglas before Wilde entered the picture.

An Ideal Husband was produced in January of 1895 at the Haymarket Theatre. The Prince of Wales attended the opening night and congratulated Wilde on its success. While his last and most enduring play, *The Importance of Being Earnest,* was in rehearsal, Wilde and Douglas went to Algiers. The play opened at the St. James Theatre on Valentine's Day 1895 and was a great success. Wilde had reached the heights; while *Earnest* was playing at the St. James, *Husband* was still playing to sold-out crowds at the Haymarket and the Lyceum in New York. Wilde was besieged with entreaties for new plays, and had several in the works when the axe fell.

Trials, Conviction, Imprisonment, and Exile

Although the Marquess of Queensberry didn't have a nonpersonal reason for doing so, he left Wilde a card at his club, accusing him of "posing as" a sodomite (though he spelled the word incorrectly). Wilde decided to prosecute him. He applied for a warrant for the Marquess' arrest under a charge of criminal libel. When asked if there was a possibility that Wilde was a homosexual, he denied it. While awaiting the trial date Wilde went to Monte Carlo with Douglas, while the Marquess collected evidence to bolster his own charge. This was where Edward Carson got his revenge on his old rival by assisting the Marquess to bring to ruin.

The Marquess was acquitted, and shortly after that Wilde was arrested. He was refused bail and thus was unable to prepare a defense, since much of the evidence against him had been fabricated. While he was in jail he was declared bankrupt as the Marquess had claimed all of Wilde's monetary assets and the house in Tite Street against the court costs of the first case. The first trial ended with the jury unable to agree, and another trial was set for three weeks later. This time Wilde's bail was paid by Douglas, whose entire family was estranged from him by this time. In the second trial Wilde was found guilty and sentenced to two years at hard labor. The judge who sentenced Wilde claimed that homosexual acts were the worst a man could commit—worse than even rape or murder. No charge was ever brought against Douglas, although there was much more foundation for a case, as it had been he who convinced Wilde to sue the Marquess.

While Wilde was in jail he was denied books, paper and pens. Toward the end of his sentence when he was finally allowed these supplies, he wrote his last prose work, *De Profundis.* Wilde was released in May of 1897 and left for France that evening, and never returned to England. He stayed at Dieppe under an assumed name, in the company of two friends, Robert Ross and Reginald Turner. He blamed Douglas in large part for his downfall: Douglas and his father had been so bent on destroying one another they dragged Wilde into the middle of their private war and he wound up being the casualty. While in Dieppe he wrote a long letter to the *Daily Chronicle* in London about prison life. This letter was responsible, in large part, for the passing of the Prisons Act of 1898, which created widespread reform.

When Ross and Turner returned to England, Wilde moved to the small coastal village of Berneval. It was there he wrote *The Ballad of Reading Gaol.* He was reunited with Douglas here and they went to Italy together. His wife joined them there. Wilde wanted her to remain with him, but he would give her no assurance that his affair with Douglas was over. Before they could be truly reconciled, Constance died, in 1898.

Wilde did no more work, and returned to Paris where he died on 30 November 1900, one day after joining the Catholic church. The official cause of death was "cerebral meningitis"—he had been suffering from severe headaches since his imprisonment.

Aftereffects

Wilde's two sons never saw him again after 1895. Constance had adopted the name Holland and legally changed her sons' name after Wilde's imprisonment. The younger son, Vyvyan Holland, wrote a biography of his father entitled *Oscar Wilde and His World* in 1960.

Sixty years after Wilde was convicted, Sir Travers Humphreys, a British judge who had been a junior barrister during the Wilde trials, wrote: "Reflecting upon the events of nearly sixty years ago, one fact is plain beyond argument. The prosecution of Oscar Wilde never should have been brought."

Wilde has remained one of the most admired, read, and performed writers of all time. His poetry, essays, and children's books are reprinted regularly, and in the 1990s all his children's books were recorded on tape. *The Importance of Being Earnest* remains his favorite and best-known stage play, and is regularly performed all over the globe.

References:

Ellmann, Richard. *Four Dubliners.* Washington, D.C.: Library of Congress, 1986.

Holland, Vyvyan. *Oscar Wilde and His World.* New York: Charles Scribner's Sons, 1960.

Laver, James. *Writers and Their Work: Oscar Wilde.* London: The British Council and The National Book League/Longmans, Green & Co., 1954.

Miller, Robert Keith. *Oscar Wilde.* Frederick Ungar Publishing Co., 1982.

Pearson, Hesketh. *Oscar Wilde: His Life and Wit.* Harper & Brothers, 1946.

—Debora Hill

Gale Wilhelm

1908-1991

American writer

Gale Wilhelm's writing career is an extraordinary example of a successful lesbian writer in the American mass market. Her novels, six in all, were published at major publishing companies and reprinted several times from 1936 until 1985. They received favorable reviews in several national magazines at the time of their publication. Only two of her six novels featured lesbian relationships, and interestingly, they are the two with the longest printing history.

Gale Wilhelm was born 26 April 1908 in Eugene, Oregon, to Ethel Gale Brewer and Wilson Price Wilhelm. She received her education in Oregon, Idaho, and Washington. She lived briefly in New York but spent the greater part of her life in California.

She published poetry in *Overland Magazine* and short stories in *Literary America*, *Colliers* and *Yale Review*. In 1935, she moved to New York for a year to work with Kenneth Houston as the associate editor of *Literary America*, a small experimental magazine. She was given an honorary membership to the Mark Twain Society in 1943.

She submitted the manuscript of her first novel, *We Too Are Drifting*, to Random House in 1934. Although it was initially rejected, it was later accepted and published by them in 1935. It was printed and reprinted several times from 1934 to 1975. In 1984, Naiad Press published it again and included a biographical introduction written by Barbara Grier.

In this novel, Jan Morale, a woodcut artist and self-identified lesbian, is initially involved with a married woman and then falls in love with Victoria who is engaged to be married. The novel ends sadly, as Victoria chooses to marry rather than stay with Jan.

Her third novel, *Torchlight to Valhalla*, was published by Random House in 1938. An edition by Lion books in 1953 titled *The Strange Path* features a cover which reads "Her choice: normal marriage or lesbian love?" Its most recent printing by the Naiad Press in 1985 includes a foreword by Wilhelm herself.

Morgen, the principle character, struggles through much of the novel with compulsory heterosexuality and her feelings for Royal, an aggressive male suitor. It is not until the final few pages of the novel that Morgen rejects Royal and begins a very happy relationship with Toni, a woman with whom she had been in love with for years.

Only Wilhelm's first and third novels were overtly lesbian, but all of them are subversive in that they feature a woman grappling with sexual, cultural, political and psychological norms imposed upon her. Each of the women in her novels has to struggle with the limited choices open to her.

In *No Letters for the Dead* (1936) Paula suffers the loss of her only child and the imprisonment of Koni, her lover and the child's father who has been implicated in his wife's death. When Paula moves to California to be near him, she cannot find work and ends up living unhappily as a prostitute.

Marion, in *The Time Between* (1942), balances her own business, the suicide of a grieving sister-in-law suffering from hysteria, the care of her young nephew left by her sister-in-law and marriage to her second husband, a war hero home on leave.

In *Bring Home the Bride* (1940), Carol and her lover get married, but each one struggles with a secret. His is that he has an hysterical mother who literally lives in an attic. Hers is not only that she is not a virgin, but that her previous lover is her husband's father.

The complex mother daughter relationships in *Never Let Me Go* (1945) show a range of women's experiences including wealth, employment, marriage and hysteria.

At the time of the Naiad Press editions of Wilhelm's lesbian novels, Barbara Grier began an extensive search which led Grier to learn about Wilhelm's relationship with Helen Page, a woman with whom she lived for several years. She also learned that these two women were friends with Carl Sandburg. Grier kept in contact with her until Wilhelm's death on 11 July 1991.

References:

Grier, Barbara. "Introduction," in *We Too Are Drifting*. Tallahassee: Naiad Press, 1984.

Warfel, Harry. *American Novelists of Today*. New York: American Book Company, 1951.

Wilhelm, Gale. *Bring Home the Bride*. New York: William Morrow & Co., 1940.

———. "California Drypoints," in *Literary America*. New York: Galleon Press, 1934-36.

———. "Introduction," in *Writing for the Experimental Market*. New York: Literary America, 1936.

———. *Never Let Me Go*. Cleveland: World Publishing Company, 1946.

———. *No Letters for the Dead*. New York: Random House, 1936.

———. *The Time Between*. New York: William Morrow & Co., 1942.

———. *Torchlight to Valhalla*. Tallahassee: The Naiad Press, 1985.

—Danielle M. DeMuth

Tennessee Williams

1911-1983

American writer

Although his writing career spanned more than four decades, it was between the mid-1940s and the mid-1960s, that American playwright Tennessee Williams did the bulk of—and his most noteworthy—writing. His dozens of plays, most famous among them *The Glass Menagerie, A Streetcar Named Desire, Cat on a Hot Tin Roof,* and *The Night of the Iguana,* enjoyed lengthy runs in New York and earned Williams a number of prestigious awards. His plays and subsequent movie versions starred some of the greatest stage and screen stars of all time, including Elizabeth Taylor and Marlon Brando. In addition, he wrote dozens of other plays, short stories, works of short fiction, essays—including a tribute to D. H. Lawrence—and memoirs.

On 26 March 1911, Thomas Lanier Williams was born in Columbus, Mississippi, to Cornelius Coffin and Edwina Dakin Williams.

He would later be nicknamed "Tennessee"—a name that would stick. He was the second of three children.

As a young woman, his older sister Rose suffered from a number of emotional disorders, and was eventually diagnosed as schizophrenic. Williams was very fond of his sister and was greatly concerned for her welfare. Although her emotional decline was difficult for him to observe, he later wrote about her mental illness. Williams believed himself to be physically frail as a result of a near fatal bout with diphtheria when he was a child. He also believed that he had suffered irreparable heart damage.

Williams kept his own company as a young boy. He was often ridiculed by other children as well as his own father, who tormented the younger Williams with the nickname "Miss Nancy," for being less than masculine. Instead of making friends, Williams remained isolated.

The third Williams child, a boy named Dakin, was born after the family moved from Columbus to St. Louis, Missouri, when Thomas was eight. It wasn't long before the general malaise and unhappiness in young Thomas Lanier's life would lead him to writing as an escape. He entered his writing in contests and often won prizes. These early writings also gleaned him formerly lacking recognition among his peers and adults.

A Commitment to Writing

Williams' first published work appeared in the magazine *Smart Set* in 1927. The story, "Can a Good Wife Be a Good Sport" won third place in the *Smart Set* contest.

In college at the University of Missouri, Williams discovered alcohol—another way to cure life's ills or at least help him to escape from them. This early attempt at college was thought to be a failure and Williams returned home where his father found him work in a shoe factory. The emptiness of his life and the tedium of his work led to a nervous breakdown in 1935.

It was while the 24-year-old Williams was recuperating from this breakdown in Memphis with his grandparents that he discovered drama. Determined that writing would be his career, Williams returned to college—Washington University, this time—where he began writing more seriously, and became involved with a small, local theatrical group. Unable to watch his sister Rose's deterioration, he decided to leave St. Louis. He entered the University of Iowa where he studied, wrote, and eventually earned a Bachelor's Degree in 1938. After graduation Williams took a year off during which time he wandered around the country, experiencing life and gathering material for his writing.

In 1939, "The Field of Blue Children," a short story published in the magazine *Story*, was the first work to appear under the name Tennessee Williams. From this time on, Tennessee Williams was the name under which Thomas Lanier Williams would be published.

It wasn't long before Williams caught the eye of literary agent Audrey Wood and one of the most valuable friendships in Williams' life began. Wood was quite impressed with Williams' talent. She took him on as a client and secured grants and scholarships that made it possible for him to write and see several works produced.

The Struggling Playwright Has a Hit

Williams' first hopeful production, *Battle of Angels*, turned out to be a disaster. The play never completed its run in Boston, closing after just two weeks, and never made it to New York. Williams

Tennessee Williams

returned to the South discouraged. He spent a brief time in New Orleans, but soon returned to New York where he worked at relatively menial jobs—usher, elevator operator, waiter-entertainer. Much material for future short stories and one-act plays was accumulated during this transient stage in Williams' life.

Financial woes were especially severe for Williams during this period and it was around this time that Wood secured him a scriptwriting contract with MGM. This, too, was a relative disaster when Williams was kept on and paid but advised not to return to the office. He used this time to rework *The Gentleman Caller*, the script MGM had rejected, renaming it *The Glass Menagerie*.

In 1945, *The Glass Menagerie* turned out to be Williams' first major success. The play's Broadway run lasted for almost two years and it was chosen for the New York Drama Critics Circle Award.

Relationships with Carson McCullers and Frank Merlo

Williams chronicled the low period of depression and isolation following the success of *The Glass Menagerie* in "On a Streetcar Named Desire"—an essay which later served as the introduction to the 1947 play of the same name. *Streetcar*, the play, would earn Williams another New York Drama Critics Circle Award, a Donaldson Award, and a Pulitzer Prize (the first of two).

In 1946, Williams spent the summer on Nantucket with novelist Carson McCullers. This summer relationship with McCullers was the second critical relationship in Williams' life. The two admired and supported one another and spent long mornings sharing the same table as they wrote together. Williams believed that McCullers was the best American novelist of the twentieth century. Her admiration of him was equally great.

Just two years later, in 1948, *American Blues: Five Short Plays,* the collection for which Williams was given a special Group Theater Award, was published. In 1950, his first attempt at longer fiction, the short novel *The Roman Spring of Mrs. Stone* was published. In 1961, *Roman Spring* was made into a motion picture starring Vivien Leigh and Warren Beatty.

During this time the third vital relationship in Williams' adult life began. It was also his major intimate relationship. Not until the publication of his memoirs in 1975 would he actually acknowledge the homosexuality that had characterized his life for more than a decade. Prior to 1948, a number of short- and even shorter-term relationships, some of value to Williams others not, served to stave off Williams' insatiable appetites.

Williams had met Frank Merlo a number of summers earlier, but in 1948 the two men were reunited. Merlo, of Italian descent, would bring Italy to Williams and eventually bring Williams to Italy. Williams' time in Italy provided him with rich details for later work, especially *The Rose Tattoo.*

Although their relationship was not exclusive, Williams and Merlo lived and travelled together from 1948 until Merlo's death from lung cancer in 1963. The two had only been together a short time when Williams dedicated *The Rose Tattoo*, which opened in 1951 "To Frank in return for Sicily." (Also of note in 1951 was the publication of Williams' "I Rise in Flame, Cried the Phoenix"—a dramatized tribute to D. H. Lawrence.)

Making a Comeback

Cat On a Hot Tin Roof opened in March of 1955. It was something of a comeback for the playwright whose last remarkable work was *A Streetcar Named Desire* more than seven years earlier. *Cat on a Hot Tin Roof* brought Williams another New York Drama Critics Circle Award and his second Pulitzer prize.

Depression and despondency led Williams to psychoanalysis in 1957. He suffered from hypochondria, claustrophobia, fears of suffocation, and a growing dependency on alcohol. His father had died in 1957 and grandfather two years earlier in 1955. Dealing with these losses, combined with the increasing tensions of daily life, was beginning to overwhelm him.

Freudian analysis, and much reading about it filled Williams' time. *Suddenly Last Summer* emerged from this period in his life. Not surprisingly, it was judged by many to be Williams' most shocking play. In spite of how "shocking" the play was, it was still a box-office success and while it earned no awards, it did enjoy a lengthy run of more than 200 performances.

Williams enjoyed his last major recognition as a playwright in 1961. *The Night of the Iguana*, which opened in late December, earned him a fourth and final Drama Critics Circle Award. Despite the lack of success after *Night of the Iguana*, Williams continued to write and his plays were still being produced. But, in 1963 Merlo succumbed to cancer and Williams slipped into another severe depression, increased drug use, and greater alcohol dependency.

Memoirs was published in 1975. According to Sally Boyd, Williams was more concerned with "truth than fact" and penned a predictably "unchronological, often stream of consciousness recollection of the playwright's childhood, friendships, professional associations, periods of mental distress, successes and failures, heavily laced with detailed accounts of his sexual experiences."

Something Cloudy, Something Clear was Williams' last New York play. It is a frankly autobiographical account of Williams' relationship with Merlo and his understanding of himself. It was written in 1982, just a year before Williams' death. Viewed negatively by many, there are some among his critics who believe it to be the best work of Williams' last two decades.

A Career of Note

In addition to the four New York Drama Critics Circle Awards and two Pulitzer Prizes, Williams also received a Group Theater Award for *American Blues: Five Short Plays* (1939); an Academy of Arts and Letters Award in 1944; the Sidney Howard Memorial Award and Sign Magazine Annual Award for *The Glass Menagerie*; and the Kennedy Honors Award in 1979. In 1952, he was elected to the National Institute of Arts and Letters and was later elected to the Theater Hall of Fame in 1979. Among the medals he was awarded are the Brandeis University Creative Arts Medal (1964-64), The National Institute of Arts and Letters Gold Medal (1969), and the first centennial medal of the Cathedral of St. John the Divine (1973).

Williams' career is clearly marked by extraordinary successes and monumental failures. Regardless, it cannot be denied that he enriched the world in which he lived. Nor can it be argued that his body of work earned him recognition as a major figure in mid-twentieth century drama.

References:

Boyd, Sally. "Tennessee Williams," in *Concise Dictionary of American Literary Biography: The New Consciousness, 1941-1968.* Detroit: Gale Research Inc., 1987: 533.

Falk, Signi Lenea. *Tennessee Williams.* New York: Twayne, 1978.

Williams, Dakin and Shepherd Mead. *Tennessee Williams: An Intimate Biography.* New York: Arbor House, 1983.

—Andrea L. T. Peterson

Cris Williamson

1947-

American musician

Cris Williamson is among the best-known, most highly respected musicians of the late twentieth century. Williamson as a singer, songwriter, pianist, teacher, and guitarist has been at the forefront of women's and alternative music for over twenty years. In fact, it was because of Williamson's observation of women and their decreasing opportunities for involvement in producing, engineering, and playing music that Olivia Records was founded in 1973. A year later Williamson recorded her album *The Changer and the Changed,* which is currently the number one best-selling women's music album of all time.

Mary Cristine Williamson was born in Deadwood, South Dakota, in 1947 to Virginia Drake Williamson (now Virginia Drake

Reedy) and C. E. ("Woody") Williamson. Virginia Williamson worked as a registered nurse and then as a college registrar, while Woody worked for the Forest Service as a district ranger and later as a range and wildlife biologist. Williamson describes her early childhood as fairly devoid of "electrical input" and points to the absence of radio and television in her childhood home as the reason for her ability to imagine "almost anything." Claiming her childhood was "sort of a nineteenth century life," Williamson remembers singing cowboy songs with her father, community square dancing, and family singing around the piano. Throughout her life, Williamson has maintained a deep personal connection to the Native American spirituality and respect for the earth she learned during her formative years in Wyoming and Colorado. Both her music and her discussions of it reflect her sense of the world as common space and its inhabitants as members of a common family.

Between the ages of 16 and 18, Williamson recorded three albums for the Wyoming-based independent label, Avanti. After earning a B.A. in 1969, Williamson set out to teach English, but moved instead to San Francisco to pursue a career in music. The Ampex label released her first album, *Cris Williamson*, in 1971, then promptly closed its record division. However, with 17 albums to her credit, Williamson ultimately attained superstar status in women's music. Among the terms most commonly used to describe her work are "inspirational," "melodic," "honest," and "healing." Fans flock to her concerts—some to listen and share her music with her, some to feel the healing power often attributed to her performances, others to catch a glimpse of the artist whose work they have always known. Though Williamson's music, like other music produced by women's labels, does not get a lot of radio airplay, it did help pave the way for popular lesbian artists like k. d. lang and Melissa Etheridge.

The Changer and the Changed has sold over 300,000 copies, continuing to sell well, now as a compact disc. "Lumiere," Williamson's science fiction fable for children, won a Parent's Choice Award. Williamson also received a Cable Car Award for outstanding recording artist in 1983 and one in 1990 and a Cable Car Board of Directors Award for 15 years of outstanding contribution to women's music. Most recently, she received the first GLAMA Michael Callen Award for outstanding service to the gay and lesbian community. On three separate occasions, Williamson has performed to sold-out audiences at Carnegie Hall—stories of which have become legendary among women's music fans.

In 1993, Williamson and Tret Fure, her musical and romantic partner of 15 years, released *Postcards from Paradise.* The album features Williamson's "In the Best Interest of the Children," a song originally written in the late 1970s for a film about lesbian mothers and child custody, but which now provides the name for the foundation the women have established to help raise consciousness about and funds for research on pediatric AIDS. Part of the album's proceeds go to ITBIC, which sponsors yearly fundraising efforts, events that are part of Massachusetts Pediatric AIDS Awareness Week, and Camp Colors, a summer camp for children with AIDS.

In the 22 years since the appearance of *The Changer and the Changed,* Williamson's personal changes have occurred in the public's view. As a result, her relationship with her fans, though most often marked by devotion, has sometimes been tumultuous; some found the changes in her music troubling, while others felt that she could have been more consistently open about her lesbianism. Williamson, true to form, refused to bow to such demands, following instead her own sense of direction and revealing her personal self only when she felt comfortable doing so. In 1989, when Toni Armstrong, Jr. asked Williamson about her lesbianism, she responded, "No one knows if I am or not," but in a 1993 interview for the *Advocate,* she comfortably acknowledged both her lesbianism and her long-standing relationship with her partner, Tret Fure. She also said that when *Changer* was popular she was "dreadfully unhappy," but then added that today, she feels like "an old, wonderful child."

Cris Williamson. *Photgraph by Irene Young.*

Current Address: Via the internet and "The Cris Williamson & Tret Fure Homepage" at http://www.hypernet.com/CRIS &Tret.html.

References:

Alarik, Scott. "Williamson's Past," in *Boston Globe,* 18 April 1991: 6, 8.

Armstrong, Toni. "Cris Williamson," in *Hotwire,* September 1989, no. 5: 2-6.

———. "Cris Williamson at Carnegie Hall," in *Hotwire,* September 1991, no. 7: 37, 41.

Mackey, Heather. "Cris Crossing Generations," in *Advocate,* 5 October 1993: 61-63.

Post, Laura. "Olivia Artists," in *Hotwire,* July 1988, no. 4: 32, 53.

Williamson, Cris. Internet interview with Michelle Gibson. March 1996.

———. "Music and the Ancient Art of Healing," in *Women in American Music.* Santa Cruz: University of California, Kresge College, 1975.

—Michelle Gibson

Jeanette Winterson

1959-

British writer

Jeanette Winterson is generally recognized as one of Britain's most interesting and innovative novelists. She has challenged the conventions of the novel form, claiming that her writing is closer to poetry than the traditional novel. Her first book, *Oranges Are Not the Only Fruit*, won the Whitbread Prize for best first novel in 1985, and was adapted for BBC TV by Winterson herself in 1990. Partly based upon her own early life and yet not, she insists, straightforwardly autobiographical, *Oranges* put representations of sexual love between young women openly onto the agenda. Winterson is a lesbian and a writer who celebrates and describes love between women, and between those whose sexuality is shifting or indeterminate: she has a corresponding passion for language and a firm belief in the transforming power of art. "Words," she says in a BBC TV interview, "are weapons and also love affairs."

"There's no such thing as autobiography, there's only art and lies," says one of the characters in Winterson's latest book, *Art and Lies*. Asked whether *Oranges* is autobiographical, she replies in the preface "No not at all and yes of course." This obviously makes things difficult for the biographer, as only Winterson herself knows which details and events are true (at least to her own memory of them), which exaggerated, and which purely invented. She herself says that the world of her childhood has become a fictional world, and that it is one she cannot revisit as it really was.

Jeanette Winterson. ***Photograph by Polly Borlands.***

Winterson was born in Lancashire and, like the heroine of *Oranges* who shares her name, was adopted as a baby by a couple who wanted a child to dedicate to God. They belonged to an evangelical Pentecostal church, and her fictional powerful and terrifying mother believed she had a mission to convert the "heathen," and that her daughter would also become a missionary. Jeanette thus grows up believing she is special, and learns from her mother that it is possible to change the world. Winterson believes in this possibility through the power of art, instead of through the coercion of religious conversion. Like the fictional Jeanette, she was a successful preacher as a teenager and still speaks with fluency and persuasiveness. The chapters of *Oranges* are named after chapters of the Bible—one of the few books in the Winterson household, and the book which inspired her love of language. The narrative of *Oranges* is also interwoven with fairy-tales, some adapted, some invented, one of the means by which the young child understands and remakes the world: Jeanette knows the story of *Beauty and the Beast*, but in reality, she realizes, men turn into pigs when you marry them, not the other way around. *Oranges* is also striking for the way in which it represents lesbian love. Jeanette falls in love and makes love with her friend Melanie as if it is the most natural thing in the world: there is no sense of conflict or guilt.

Although Winterson dissociates herself from political lesbianism, she may here be making the point that for many women, loving other women is the only imaginable possibility, not the result of a political choice or the failure of relationships with men. "What makes life difficult for homosexuals is not their perversity but other people's," she writes in the Preface to *Oranges*, and her sexual choice does, of course, bring her into direct conflict with her church and family. In the book, and even more shockingly and violently in the TV adaptation, the "demon" of "Unnatural Passion" is (unsuccessfully) exorcised from the body of the young girl.

Like the fictional Jeanette, Winterson broke with her family, worked for an undertaker embalming corpses and in a mental hospital, and finally gained a place at Oxford University. After graduating she worked briefly as a theatre assistant and for Pandora Press, where Philippa Brewster, who remains her editor and a close friend, encouraged her in writing *Oranges*. The success of the novel meant that she was then able to dedicate herself to writing.

Oranges was followed in 1985 by a comic novel, *Boating for Beginners*, and in 1986 by the manual *Fit for the Future: For Women Who Want to Live Well*, now out of print.

Winterson really established herself with her next two books, *The Passion* (which won the 1987 John Llewellyn Rhys Memorial Prize) and *Sexing the Cherry* (1989). In these books Winterson breaks free from the conventions of realism and the everyday. *The Passion* is set during the Napoleonic Wars and tells the story of the relationship between Henri, chief chicken-cook to Napoleon and the web-footed adventuress Villanelle. Their relationship is played out in Venice in a shifting network of gender and sexual identities; Michele Roberts describes it as "completely charming ... with the intensity of a fairytale, the cool beauty of the unanalysed dream." The chief characters in *Sexing the Cherry* are the huge Dog-Woman who lives on the banks of the Thames and her adopted son Jordan whom she rescues from the river as a baby. Living in the seventeenth century, they have twentieth-century counterparts through whom Winterson voices her concern for the destruction of the environment and the instability of adolescent sexual identity. The book challenges commonly accepted notions of time, history, and gender in a way that is complex and literary but also light and playful: fruit-grafting is used as the central metaphor for gender transformation, and Jordan pursues the ideal of mysterious femininity through the fairy-tale of the Twelve Dancing Princesses.

Although Winterson claims to want to reach a wide audience, her next two books, *Written on the Body* and *Art and Lies*, are full of literary allusion and quotation and move further away from conventional narrative. *Written on the Body* is a love story, narrated by a lover whose gender is undisclosed: his/her lover, Louise, suffers from leukemia, and the central sections of the book consist of a poetic meditation on the anatomy of the lover's body. *Art and Lies* is narrated by three characters: the cancer doctor Handel, the lesbian poet Sappho, and the female painter Picasso, sexually abused by her brutish brother. Although their lives do gradually interconnect, there is very little plot, and the pleasures of this text are to be found in what Michele Roberts describes as Winterson's ability to "mint shining images in a few golden lines." Through the voice of Sappho, Winterson meditates on the power of the word:

> The word will find me out; I speak therefore I am. To match the silent eloquence of the created world I have had to learn to speak. Language, that describes it, becomes me. Careful then, what I become, by my words you will know me. The word passed down through time time returned through the word.

"By my words you will know me": but something is known of Winterson's private life. She lives with her partner Peggy Reynolds in London and Gloucestershire, loves cats and gardening, and reads for five hours a day (almost nothing written after 1940, and no newspapers). She describes her life as a "daily ecstacy," and sees her writing not only as her passion but as a duty in its ability to "quicken the dead places" and "unlock locked lives."

Current Address: c/o Jonathan Cape, 20 Vauxhall Bridge Road, SW1V 2SA, England.

References:

BBC TV interview, "Face to Face" with Jeremy Isaacs, 1994.

Roberts, Michele. "Words Are Not the Only Art," in *The Independent on Sunday*, 19 June 1994.

Turner, Jenny. "Preacher Woman," in *The Guardian Weekend*, 18 June 1994.

Winterson, Jeanette. *Art and Lies*. London: Jonathan Cape, 1994.

———. *Art Objects: Essays on Ecstacy and Effrontery*. London, Jonathan Cape, 1995.

———. *Boating for Beginners*. London: Methuen, 1985.

———. *Oranges Are Not the Only Fruit*. London: Pandora Press, 1985.

———. *The Passion*. London: Bloomsbury, 1987.

———. *Sexing the Cherry*. London: Bloomsbury, 1989.

———. *Written on the Body*. London: Jonathan Cape, 1992.

—Nicola King

Monique Wittig

1935-

French writer and scholar

"Lesbians" according to Monique Wittig are not "women" since the latter term exists only as a meaningful term in heterosexual thought and economic systems. To underline this point, Wittig compares women to slaves and draws upon the inherent power relationship that removes slave from the realm of person. As one of the few French feminists who has made a considerable mark in the United States, Wittig's theoretical model for lesbian identity places her at the forefront of lesbian theory and queer studies.

Wittig was born in France in 1935; her father was the poet Henri Dubois. She attended the Sorbonne where she studied Oriental languages during the turbulent years of the 1960s and worked at the Bibliothèque Nationale and in publishing. By the end of that decade Wittig had not only established herself as a major novelist but had also become a key figure of the MLF (Women's Liberation Movement) as the voice of the group Féministes Révolutionnaires. She had also gained a certain infamy for her participation in an attempt to place a wreath for the wife of the unknown soldier at the Arc de Triomphe. The MLF was not, however, entirely harmonious. Differing political and theoretical stances gave rise to acerbic debates and open hostility, occasionally ended in shouting matches in which Wittig participated. These differences precipitated her departure to the United States in 1976. The late 1970s and 1980s, as Wittig held various teaching posts at American universities, saw an increase in her theoretical writings on language and feminism as well as an entry into a new genre—theater. In the interim, she completed a doctoral dissertation. Currently, she holds a position at the University of Arizona and actively lectures around the country where she continues to spark heated debates over her writings. She has just completed a new work, *The Girl*.

Wittig first made her mark on the French and American literary scene in 1964 with her novel *The Opoponax*. The title refers to the non-standard spelling of a plant used in perfume making. The book received the prestigious Prix Medicis and garnered high praise from writers and critics on both continents. Although it is generally considered the most accessible and least "feminist" of her works, the themes—language and lesbian subjectivity—and the experiments in style that become Wittig's signatures are clearly present in the text. The novel presents a decentered point of view, depending on the pronoun *on* which can be translated both as the neutral "one" and the subjective "we." The story itself while moving freely from character to character ultimately deals with a girls' boarding school romance. But contrary to the expectations of that genre, Wittig refuses to play out the story line to its traditional conclusion (girl loses girl to boy) and ends with the romance. The reworking of familiar genre or text that dominates Wittig's fiction, plays an integral part in her rebellion against a phallocentric construction of society.

Les Guérillières (1969) represents a shift in form and an extension of Wittig's political thought. She rewrites the classical epic through the inscription of *elles* (the feminine plural pronoun that Wittig deploys to erase the universalized male *ils*). The phallus is replaced by an exaltation of the clitoris and the vulva. However, the society of *elles* goes beyond the limiting view of redefining themselves in sexual terms. They become the warriors, *guérillières* (a word Wittig created from the French for male *guerillas*) who overthrow the patriarchy. Wittig presents a Utopian vision of a new Amazonian society, grounded in peace rather than war. The symbolic naming with which the novel ends typifies Wittig's desire to release language from its patriarchal origins and found a discourse capable of including women's experiences.

The Lesbian Body (*Le Corps lesbien*, 1973) may be seen as an answer to the strain of French feminist thought developed by Hélène Cixous. Whereas Cixous posits a type of "writing the body" grounded in the feminine, Wittig rejects what she considers a type of mistakenly mythologized essentialism linked to a heterosexist and phallocentic society. The title provides a clue to Wittig's project: *le corps*, gendered masculine, becomes lesbian. This "lesbian body" consists of a poem cycle in which the characters *j/e* and *tu* share an all-consuming and violent passion. In the course of their sexual encounters, the myth of idealized female body of conventional lyric poetry, explodes in an intense physicality. The lovers tear each others flesh; *j/e* describes in graphic detail their love-making and the body of the lover, inside and out. Wittig chose the separated *j/e* to signify women's alienation from language and perhaps the violence of their entry into it. Thus the lyricism of *The Lesbian Body*, modeled on the "Song of Songs," prevents a disturbing, highly charged erotic vision, only reconciled at the end of the cycle when the *j/e* becomes part of society of *amantes*.

In collaboration with Sande Zeig, Wittig has produced two works. *Brouillon pour un dictionnaire des amantes* (1976), translated by Wittig and Zeig as *Lesbian Peoples: Material for a Dictionary* in 1973 and the play *Le Voyage sans fin*, performed in English as *The Constant Journey* in 1985. The dictionary takes up the task of reinventing words to liberate them from their male-oriented definitions. Thus words which have traditional negative connotations—for example *witch*—are recuperated. Illustrations for meaning come predominantly from women writers and the words of those male writers chosen appear as disjointed fragments. However, a striking feature of the dictionary is that throughout Zeig and Wittig do not so much attack men as they simply write them out of the historical linguistic model or feminize them as in the case of Pascale. The message of the *Brouillon*, a call for a return to collective society, parallels that of *Les Guérillières* and *Le Corps lesbien*. The *Voyage sans fin* recounts the travels of a female Don Quixote. Indeed, all the characters of the play are female. Quichotte herself is an idealist, on a quest to become worthy of her beloved and in the process becomes a writer. While the play reprises rather than develops the themes found in Wittig's writings, on the level of performance and stagecraft it is both bold and innovative in its conception. All elements of the spectacle—color, music, movement, language—become interrelated. A particularly striking feature of the production is the disjuncture of visual image (here, the gestures of the mime) and sound, a technique Wittig borrowed from cinema. Both of these collaborative works reflect as well a tendency towards humor, absent from many of Wittig's earlier texts.

In *Across the Acheron* (*Virgile, non*, 1985), Wittig recasts Dante's allegorical quest in a parody both comic and serious. Many similarities exist between Quichotte and narrator, who can be seen as a sort of stand-in for Wittig herself. The text stresses the notion of women's responsibility (including, of course, that of the narrator). The juxtaposition of Dante's classical and biblical references with frequent scenes of contemporary America, not unusual as a technique of appropriation, epitomizes Wittig's own admixture of European and American culture. Here, as in other of her works, Paradise, once reached takes the form a collective lesbian society.

Wittig remains active in the areas of theory and practice. Her ground-breaking theoretical essays, among them "One is Not Born a Women," "The Mark of Gender," and "The Category of Sex" appeared in the 1992 collection, *The Straight Mind*. These works have become classics in contemporary lesbian and feminist theory. She continues to produce literary works that provide illustrations for the theories she has elaborated. As a lesbian—and not a woman—Wittig must be counted among the most influential and important writers today.

Current Address: c/o Beacon Press, 25 Beacon Street, Boston, Massachusetts 02108.

References:

Crowder, Diane Griffin. "Monique Wittig," in *French Women Writers: A Bio-Bibliographical Source Book,* edited by Eva Martin Sartori and Dorothy Wayne Zimmerman. New York: Greenwood Press, 1991.

Ostrovsky, Erika. *A Constant Journey: The Fiction of Monique Wittig.* Carbondale: Southern Illinois University Press, 1991.

Wittig, Monique. *The Straight Mind.* Boston: Beacon Press, 1992.

—Edith J. Benkov

Merle Woo

1941-

Asian-American educator and writer

Merle Woo's poetry and essays have been widely published in gay/lesbian, feminist, Asian, and socialist periodicals and anthologies. She is a leader in Radical Women and the Freedom Socialist Party, two socialist feminist organization, and gained national attention in her battles against employment discrimination at the University of California at Berkeley. Since 1990, as a breast cancer survivor, she has written and organized against this epidemic, in addition to her previous multi-issue radical politics.

Born in San Francisco, California on 24 October 1941 to Helene and Richard Woo, Merle Woo learned early about racism against Asian Americans. In "Letter to Ma," published in *This Bridge Called My Back: Writings by Radical Women of Color,* Woo writes to her mother about her father: "When those two white cops said, 'Hey, fat boy, where's our meat?' he left me standing there on Grant Avenue, while he hurried over to his store to get it; they kept complaining, never satisfied.... I didn't know that he spent a year and a half on Angel Island; that we could never have our right names; that he lived in constant fear of being deported; that, like you, he worked two full-time jobs most of his life; that he was mocked and ridiculed because he speaks 'broken English.' And Ma, I was so ashamed after that experience when I was only six years old that I never held his hand again."

While Richard Woo came from southern China, Helene Chang was born in Los Angeles. Her father was a ginseng salesman and traveling Methodist minister. The Chang family emigrated back to Shanghai while Helene was still a child, then at age 10, because she was a girl, her parents sent Helene back to U.S. by herself to be raised in an orphanage. Richard Woo is her second husband. Though neither Richard nor Helene Woo were Catholic, Helene sent Merle to Catholic schools which she hoped would be of higher quality than the public schools.

Woo was married and the mother of two small children (Emily, born in 1963, and Paul, born in 1967) when she witnessed the Third World student strikes at San Francisco State University in 1968 and 1969. It was the beginning of many changes in her life. Woo writes in the anthology *Tilting the Tower*: "When I saw the success of the Third World student movement, that radicalized me faster than dropping Catholicism, faster than becoming a lesbian. That fast! What changed me was becoming conscious in a lightning flash that my education had been full of lies and censorship. I realized I had never read anything by people of color."

After Woo completed her Masters in English at San Francisco State in 1969, she began teaching in the Educational Opportunity Program, a new program at SFSU created as a result of the student strikes. In attempting to teach English to students of color, Woo became increasingly aware that there were few teaching materials relevant to her student's lives. By 1973 Woo was teaching specific classes in Third World literature and in 1977 she proposed and taught the first Third World women's literature class in Women Studies.

It was during these years that Woo realized that she was alcoholic. She writes of those years in "Letter to Ma": "You gave me, physically, what you never had, but there was a spiritual, emotional legacy you passed down which was reinforced by society: self-contempt because of our race, our sex, our sexuality. For deeply ingrained in me, Ma, there has been that strong, compulsive force to sink into self-contempt, passivity, and despair. I am sure that my fifteen years of alcohol abuse have not been forgotten by either of us, nor my suicidal depressions." Woo sees 1975 as the turning point in her claiming control over her self-destructive compulsions. Three years later she came out as a lesbian.

After almost a decade's experience at SFSU, the University of California at Berkeley hired Woo as a lecturer in the Asian American Studies Program in the Ethnic Studies Department in 1978. The next four years saw Woo publishing in *Hanai,* a publication of the Asian American Studies Program, *Bridge,* an Asian American periodical from New York and *This Bridge Called My Back,* the landmark anthology first released in 1981. Woo won high marks from her students during these years but in 1982 the University declined to renew Woo's contract, citing the brand-new "four-year rule" which limited lecturers to a maximum of four year's employment.

Woo argued that her termination was the result of her outspoken politics as a lesbian feminist, unionist, student rights advocate, and leader in the Freedom Socialist Party and Radical Women, which she had joined in 1980. She told Jil Clark of *Gay Community News,* "The four-year rule was simply a pretext used to silence my criticism and outspoken politics." The American Federation of Teachers argued Woo's case before an administrative law judge who agreed with Woo and ordered the rehiring of Woo, who had been the only Berkley lecturer fired under that rule. When the University appealed the decision and stalled on the rehirings, Woo sued in federal and state courts for reinstatement. The University settled the case out of court in 1984 and rehired Woo with back pay on a 2-year contract.

The situation repeated itself in 1986 when Woo's contract was again not renewed despite widespread support from students. While Woo accepted a lecturer position in women studies at San Francisco State, she also filed a union grievance charging discrimination on the basis of her race, gender, sexual orientation, and political ideology. Arbitration resulted in a decision in Woo's favor, followed by university stalling and Woo considering a lawsuit. Fate intervened in 1990 when she was diagnosed with breast cancer. Woo was already well-acquainted with the disease, especially through the illness and death in 1987 of Karen Brodine, a leader in the Merle Woo Defense Committee, Radical Women and the Freedom Socialist Party. She dropped her case rather than spend her potentially few remaining years in litigation.

In her essay, "The Politics of Breast Cancer" published in *The Very Inside: An Anthology of Writing by Asian and Pacific Islander Lesbian and Bisexual Women,* Woo reveals some of the complexity of this gendered disease: "I have felt so ambivalent about my double mastectomy. I was glad to have my right breast removed six months after the mastectomy on the left side: I felt symmetrical again and relief that I didn't have to wear a prosthesis ... [to prevent] throw[ing] out the alignment of the spine because the weight of the remaining breast pulling the spine to its side."

"And although I panicked because there were large cancerous tumors and knew that I could die, I rather liked having no breasts. I go back and forth on it: On one hand I feel ugly with these two asymmetrical scars slashed across my chest, and on the other, my breasts were so large, that I felt ugly with them. The image of the petite Asian women was not ever lost on me.... I hated myself because I had large breasts."

Despite her own battle against cancer, Woo's passion for social justice has not wavered throughout the institutionalization of ethnic studies, women's studies and gay/lesbian studies. She sums up her political assessment of the 1990s in her essay "Forging Our Future, Building Our Roots": "The right wing is going to come down on women, and the right wing is going to come down on lesbians and gays, and we are going to be on the front line. But who is going to stand up for us on the campuses and in the community if we don't ourselves become multi-issue? If we don't ourselves address race and sex as they connect up with heterosexism and class? ... These issues are lesbian and gay issues, and I want to see them discussed in the classroom and dealt with in the streets!"

References:

Clark, Jil. "Woo Sues University for Reinstatement, Pay," in *Gay Community News,* 16 April 1983.

Woo, Merle. "Forging the Future, Remembering Our Roots: Building Multicultural, Feminist Lesbian and Gay Studies," in *Tilting the Tower: Lesbians Teaching Queer Subjects,* edited by Linda Garber. New York: Routledge, 1994.

———. "Letter to Ma," in *This Bridge Called My Back: Writings by Radical Women of Color,* edited by Cherrie Moraga and Gloria Anzaldúa. Albany: Kitchen Table: Women of Color Press, 1981.

———. "The Politics of Breast Cancer," in *The Very Inside: An Anthology of Writing by Asian and Pacific Islander Lesbian and Bisexual Women,* edited by Sharon Lim-Hing. Toronto: Sister Vision: Black and Women of Color Press, 1994.

—Loie B. Hayes

Virginia Woolf

1882-1941

British writer

One of the most notable and prolific Modernist writers, Virginia Woolf wrote nine novels, one play, over five volumes of essays, portraits, memoirs, and reviews, more than fourteen volumes of diaries and letters, and forty-six short stories. In her novels, Woolf evolved a way of writing that demands engagement from a reader with a novel's structure as well as with its content. From the moment she began writing, Woolf had a literary career plan: to reshape the novel as it was then known. Each of her novels exists as a testament to Virginia Woolf's self-conscious evolution as an experimental writer.

Early Life and Home Schooling

Adeline Virginia Stephen came into the world on 25 January 1882 in London at 22 Hyde Park Gate, Kensington. Her parents, Leslie and Julia Duckworth Stephen, already had six children and were eventually to have one more after Virginia. Leslie Stephen had a daughter from his first marriage; Julia Duckworth Stephen had three children from her first marriage.

The family belonged to the upper-middle class and to the prestigious London literary community. Leslie Stephen, a prolific literary critic, held honorary doctorates from numerous universities including Oxford and Cambridge. Julia Duckworth Stephen, a nurse, worked committedly with the sick and the poor throughout her life. Although privileged, Woolf's parents were industrious and prodigious workers. This model of self-discipline greatly influenced her habits of writing.

Reading also influenced Woolf's writing. Having grown up in a largely literary household, Woolf had free run of her father's library. She read voluminous amounts of material and she always kept an arduous reading schedule for herself.

Virginia chronicled her reading as well as her thoughts about her writing in diaries from the time she was fifteen years old. In her mind, reading and writing worked together to create an ever-evolving art form.

Woolf's education occurred mostly at home. Her father informally guided her intellectual growth through reading. He also provided her with private tutors. Woolf never attended school, a situation she deplores in her feminist tract, *A Room of One's Own.* In this text, she creates an imaginary figure, Judith Shakespeare, who, as sister to William Shakespeare, would never have been able to pursue her genius:

> Shakespeare himself went, very probably—his mother was an heiress—to the grammar school, where he may have learnt Latin—Ovid, Virgil Horace—and the elements of grammar and logic.... Very soon he got work in the theatre, became a successful actor, and lived at the hub of the universe, meeting everybody, knowing everybody.... Meanwhile his extraordinarily gifted sister, let us suppose remained at home. She was as adventurous, as imaginative, as agog to see the world as he was. But she was not sent to school. She had no chance of learning grammar and logic, let alone of reading Horace and Virgil. She picked up a book now and then, one of her brother's perhaps, and read a few pages. But then her parents came in and told her to mend the stockings or mind the stew and not moon about the books and papers.

Woolf Gains Attention as Novelist

The Hogarth Press, owned and managed by Virginia and her husband, Leonard Woolf, published her *Jacob's Room* in 1922. In *Jacob's Room*, Woolf experiments with such modernist attributes of writing as fragmentation, internal monologue, and centering of multiple "main" characters. In particular, Woolf explores the necessity of precisely formed characters to the flow of a novel. Jacob only vaguely grows or develops into a fully formed character, instead, he remains just out of sight in the novel. Jacob's mother vies for attention as main character in the beginning of the text, but she too seems effervescent throughout the book.

Jacob's Room, although received in a lukewarm fashion by critics, brought Virginia Woolf into contact with the literary circle that was to become so important to her intellectual, social, and emotional life: Lady Colefax, Lady Londonderry, Lord David Cecil, Vita Sackville-West, and H. G. Wells.

Mrs. Dalloway Takes on James Joyce and Lesbianism

With her next novel, *Mrs. Dalloway* (1925), Woolf takes the reader on a single day's journey through perceptions of various characters. Clearly influenced by James Joyce's *Ulysses*, Woolf's "single-day novel" begins with preparations for Clarissa Dalloway's party and dutifully concludes with all the characters gathered at the party. *Mrs. Dalloway* interrogates many significant Modernist issues: the impact of technology on daily life, the impact of World War I on the collective psyche, the value of institutions such as marriage, the intricacies of emotional commitments, and the anxiety produced by alienation of people from one another. While writing this novel, Woolf fully realized one of her most acclaimed writing techniques—her "tunneling process," which allows her to portray the exterior of a character and then to move inside the character's mind and emotions. This narrative force brings psychological depth to each character.

Mrs. Dalloway also houses one of Woolf's earliest homoerotically suggestive scenarios. The description of Clarissa Dalloway and Sally Seton's relationship with each other as young women clearly alludes to a lesbian attraction:

> Take Sally Seton; her relation in the old days with Sally Seton. Had not that, after all, been love? ... all that evening she could not take her eyes off Sally. It was an extraordinary beauty of the kind she most admired, dark, large-eyed, with that quality which, since she hadn't got it herself, she always envied—a sort of abandonment.... The strange thing, on looking back, was the purity, the integrity, of her feeling for Sally. It was not like one's feeling for a man ... she could remember standing in her bedroom at the top of the house holding the hotwater can in her hands and saying aloud, "She is beneath this roof.... She is beneath this roof!" ... Then came the most exquisite moment of her whole life passing a stone urn with flowers in it. Sally stopped; picked a flower; kissed her on the lips. The whole world might have turned upside down.

This novel anticipates the sexuality of Orlando and the relationship between Chloe and Olivia in *A Room of One's Own*. Woolf plants no other kiss so firmly between two women.

By February 1926, Woolf had a new novel fully underway. *To the Lighthouse* (1927), a novel written in three parts, explores the idea of a "coherent center" made so infamous by Modernist writers. Woolf's greatest artistic achievement in this novel is her depiction of the ideological struggle outlined by feminism—the struggle between Mrs. Ramsay, mother extraordinaire, and Lily Briscoe, single woman/artist. Woolf's text evolves from centering Mrs. Ramsay in the first section to centering Lily Briscoe in the third. Yet, the novel defies any sense of hierarchical maneuvering of the single artist person as more important to life in this time. Instead Woolf opts for a complex interweaving of feminist gains and sentimental losses. *To the Lighthouse* stands as testimony to the person artist's achievements.

Orlando and Vita Sackville-West

Since 1923, when Woolf had met Vita Sackville-West, a new sense of her sexual self had been growing:

> The fact that Vita seemed drawn to her ... was flattering, for Vita was just the kind of masterful, mothering woman who could make Virginia feel cared for and secure: nor, inveterate snob that she was, could she be immune to the attraction of Vita's aristocratic background. (Alexander, 154)

Vita Sackville-West is the source of Woolf's next novel, *Orlando*. Although one might argue that all of Woolf's novels vary drastically one from another, the artistic process and esthetic goals have often emerged in similar ways. *Orlando* differs in many ways, predominantly in its sense of humor. *Orlando* is a tremendously witty text. In it Woolf uses comic understatement to feature the ways in which various societies construct sexual mores. The main character, Orlando, based loosely on Sackville-West, begins the text as a man, slips through time periods, over the course of 400 years, and just as easily slips through genders. Woolf asks her readers to consider the question, "What exactly constitutes gender throughout time?" This novel encourages the reader to notice the absurdity and the historical arbitrariness of gender role prescriptions. As well, the novel pays tribute throughout to Woolf's greatest passion, Vita Sackville-West.

The sales of *Orlando* far exceeded any other Woolf text—more than 8,000 copies in the first half year. These sales led to more and more prestige and some rather momentous speaking engagements. In October 1928 she was invited to lecture at Newnham and Girton, Cambridge's two women's colleges. Her preparations for these two engagements produced the lecture notes that were to become *A Room of One's Own*.

A Room of One's Own Starts Controversy

Gilbert and Gubar describe *A Room of One's Own* as "a luminous extended essay on 'women and fiction' which is, as most literary historians would agree, the first major achievement of feminist criticism in the English language." Critic Nigel Nicolson sees the essay as mere complaint:

> The professions *were* opening to women: to give but one example of the trend, both Virginia's doctors in middle and later life were women. The Universities *were* open to them. In 1927 there were 8,000 women students in higher education, equal in status to the men at all Universities except Cambridge.... She drew most of her examples from the past, but presented them in such a way as to suggest that they were still equally relevant. (Alexander, 157)

Virginia Woolf

To Woolf, these examples were equally relevant. She stood before these women as one who had never attended school formally, and she stood before them in the present. She had been asked as a successful writer to speak about what women needed to write, and she responded by discussing her own artistic impediments. Woolf's life was not at all removed from Nicolson's idea of the past. The more important point is that *A Room of One's Own* has never ceased to be a controversial text worthy of debate and long discussion.

In this text Woolf argues that women need education, a private room to work in, and enough money to live independently to write fiction. The Shakespeare's sister excerpt, already discussed in this essay, is one of three most often-cited passages from the tract. The second, the "Chloe liked Olivia" passage, facilitates two discussions: one of lesbianism in literature and one about women's relationships (of any type) as represented in literature:

> I may tell you that the very next words I read were these—"Chloe liked Olivia ..." Do not start. Do not blush. Let us admit in the privacy of our own society that these things sometimes happen. Sometimes women do like women.

This passage infers a lesbian relationship, but as it continues, Woolf suggests that male writers poorly represent a wide range of relationships between women. Woolf argues in this passage that women in literature simply exist to compete with other women for men. She claims that a new and interesting plot would entail women "liking" other women.

A third famous excerpt, the androgyny passage, has sparked debate regarding the exact definition of androgyny as well as its importance to creativity:

> I went on amateurishly to sketch a plan of the soul so that in each of us two powers preside, one male, one female; and in the man's brain, the man predominates over the woman, and in the woman's brain, the woman predominates over the man. The normal and comfortable state of being is that when the two live in harmony together, spiritually cooperating. If one is a man, still the woman part of the brain must have effect; and a woman must also have intercourse with the man in her. Coleridge perhaps meant this when he said that a great mind is androgynous. It is when this fusion takes place that the mind is fully fertilized and uses all its faculties.

Perhaps because *A Room of One's Own* dares to depict the relationship between sexuality, its representations, and the creation of women's art, the text has sparked debate from a range of literary scholars. Carolyn Heilbrun writes, "It has been Virginia Woolf's peculiar destiny to be declared annoyingly feminine by male critics at the same time that she has been dismissed by women interested in the sexual revolution as not really eligible to be drafted into their ranks" (*Critical Essays,* 74).

A Room of One's Own has become famous in feminist literary circles for its ability to name precisely women's inequitable treatment regarding education and financial support. However, in recent years, feminist scholars such as Elaine Showalter have criticized *A Room of One's Own* for its naive insistence on an equality gained only by running away from being a woman. In *Sexual/Textual Politics*, Toril Moi argues that some feminist scholars have unjustly criticized Woolf for this so-called "sin" of running away when often these transcendent places such as "androgyny" afford the only calm "places" of change to which women may turn (Moi, 2).

The publication of this text, although a highlight for many late twentieth century readers, marks the beginning, most critics agree, of Woolf's most tremendous bouts with depression.

Virginia Woolf Battles Depression

Woolf's biographers trace her bouts with depression to a variety of psychological issues predominantly related to death and sexuality: inappropriate sexual advances made by her stepbrothers Gerald and George Duckworth, the death of her mother, the death of stepsister Stella Duckworth in childbirth, the long-term mental illness of elder half-sister Laura, the sorrowful—yet liberating—death of her father, and brother Thoby's death from typhoid fever.

Alexander writes that "the sexual act was terrifying to her [Woolf], and was linked with her madness. In her novels, when she depicts sexuality, she often sees it in terms of the threatening or the sordid, and ugly act carried on in darkness."

Psychological readings afford much elucidation of Woolf's condition, but many other threats also fed the depression that ultimately killed Woolf: the burden of the Hogarth Press, a profound political disagreement between Virginia and Leonard over her book *Three Guineas*, the threat of Hitler, the beginning of World War II in 1939, the bombing of their London house in 1940, the constant noise of the German planes flying over head, the sour receipt of her latest biography *Roger Fry*, and Leonard's planning of a double suicide for them should the Germans finally invade Britain.

By March 1941, Woolf's depression became insurmountable. She was not eating and she was hearing voices. She unsuccessfully tried to drown herself on 18 March. Ten days later, Virginia Woolf loaded her pockets with rocks and drowned herself.

Woolf's Legacy

Virginia Woolf's greatest influence on Modernism has been "the modern novel." As Morris Beja writes, "No one aimed more unashamedly at creating 'the Art Novel' than Virginia Woolf" (*Critical Essays,* 1). In addition, we cannot overlook Woolf's contribution to feminism, to the representation of women's varied relationships in literature, and to lesbian literature. She has given us Sally Seton, Clarissa Dalloway, Orlando, Chloe and Olivia, and Judith Shakespeare.

References:

Alexander, Peter F. *Leonard and Virginia Woolf: A Literary Partnership*. New York: St. Martin's Press, 1992.

Beja, Morris. "Introduction," in *Critical Essays on Virginia Woolf.* Boston: G. K. Hall, 1985.

Gilbert, Sandra M., and Susan Gubar. *The Norton Anthology of Literature by Women*. New York: W. W. Norton, 1985.

Heilbrun, Carolyn. "Woolf and Androgyny," in *Critical Essays on Virginia Woolf.* 1985.

Moi, Toril. *Sexual/Textual Politics: Feminist Literary Theory*. New York: Routledge, 1985.

Woolf, Virginia. *Jacob's Room*. 1922.

———. *Mrs. Dalloway*. 1925.

———. *Orlando*. 1928.

———. *A Room of One's Own*. New York: Harcourt Brace Jovanovich, 1929.

———. *To the Lighthouse*. 1927.

—Renee R. Curry

Marguerite Yourcenar

1903-1987

American writer, scholar, and critic

Marguerite Yourcenar's over 70-year-career of published writing was crowned in 1980 when the French Academy bowed to her undeniable accomplishments and to overwhelming public opinion in her favor: it abandoned its 350-year all-male tradition to elect her as one of the "Immortals." Her over forty books, including novels, poetry, plays, essays, and translations from several languages, won her many international prizes, the Legion of Honor, and also publication in the Pléïade series, one reserved for classics: a rare distinction for a living author.

Marguerite Yourcenar was born to Michel Cleenewerck de Crayencour and Fernande de Cartier de Marchienne in Brussels, Belgium, on 8 June 1903, but her father immediately registered her as a French citizen. Death claimed her mother ten days later. Yourcenar's only sibling was a half-brother, Michel de Crayencour, the son of a previous marriage of her mother. Her ancestors in both families, whose histories are traced in Yourcenar's autobiographical series, *Labyrinthe du monde*, were prominent in Flanders, although on different sides of the present-day Franco-Belgian border.

Marguerite Yourcenar

Life with Father

Yourcenar spent her earliest years in Mont-Noir, a chateau, home to her cordially detested grandmother and her father who, though almost 50, undertook her upbringing. A woman's influence was limited to staff and her father's mistresses—one of them, a childhood friend, and perhaps lover, of Yourcenar's mother became the author's model in life. Yourcenar learned to love the countryside and later to appreciate museums and culture in Paris. Her education came from tutors, her father, with whom she read aloud and discussed literature, and, primarily, from her own reading. She learned Latin and Greek, taught herself Italian, and learned English in England where she and her father spent a year after escaping across the English Channel at the outbreak of World War I.

A teenage book, subsidized by her father, caught the attention of Nobelist Rabindranath Tagore. It was signed Marg Yourcenar. The first name hid the author's sex and the second was an anagram of Crayencour, that she and her father invented together.

She spent the 1920s traveling with him especially in the south of France and Italy, where the Roman emperor Hadrian attracted her and modern Fascism repelled her. She studied family history for a projected novel. All were to have a crucial place in her career.

The year 1929 was a turning point for Yourcenar. She published her first novel, *Alexis*, in the form of a letter written by a scrupulous young homosexual to explain why he was leaving his wife to pursue his music. Her father died, leaving her without and intellectual companion and almost without money. Her half-brother lost her maternal inheritance in the stock market crash, and her father's lavish lifestyle, mistresses, and gambling had depleted his fortune.

Life on the Road

Still, Yourcenar calculated that she could afford ten to twelve years of luxurious leisure, learning to live and to write. While she was extremely reticent about her private life, Josyane Savigneau's biography, *Marguerite Yourcenar: Inventing a Life*, describes a liking for alcohol and a love of conquests.

Yourcenar traveled and lived in several countries, especially Greece, France, and Italy; produced nine books, and experienced two of the great passions of her life. The first was "the man I loved," whom Savigneau identifies as André Fraigneau, her companion in Greece and editor at Grasset, a man who loved men. He inspired the lyrical *Fires* where many voices—most mythical, most women—exalt all forms of love: homosexual, heterosexual, bi-sexual and spiritual. She also traveled with André Embiricos to Turkey, but it was at the Hotel Wagram, in Paris, a meeting place for women, that she met Grace Frick, an American academic, the second passion and her long-time companion.

Poverty and War—Fame and Fortune

With 1939 came the end of her funds, the end of the fragile peace in Europe, and the end of *Coup de grâce*, (named for Frick), a tragic novel about a young woman who loves a homosexual man who loves her brother. It, along with *Fires*, was Yourcenar's means of exorcising her hopeless love. Without money, without a job, unable to return to Greece, and perhaps needing the devotion offered by Frick, she accepted her invitation for a six-month lecture tour in the United States and sailed in November of 1939.

It was the low-point of her life. Yourcenar mourned Europe's fall; earned her living teaching, which she loathed; and tolerated life in a small, conservative, town. She wrote little but re-read the classics. She also became a U.S. citizen, recovered a trunk containing an early version of *Memoirs of Hadrian*, and rediscovered her career. Everyone applauded Hadrian, model prince and lover of the boy, Antinoüs. By 1951 Yourcenar, now an international celebrity, shared a permanent home on Mt. Desert Island, Maine, with Grace, who would devote the rest of her life to Yourcenar, serving as her companion, translator, chronicler, secretary, and business manager.

The 1950s found Yourcenar traveling and re-writing early works. One featured her next great historical hero, Zeno, the alchemist of *The Abyss*, which won the Prix Fémina. Like Hadrian he was bisexual; unlike him, he was condemned for liberal ideas not tolerated by church authorities. Another led to a volume of poetry.

In the 1960s she protested the Vietnam war, rediscovered nature, and became an environmentalist. Her publications now included volumes of theater and essays.

Almost 70, Yourcenar continued her writing unabated, though Frick's illness prevented travel. Radio interviews increased, as an eager public demanded more details of her life and ideas. She was elected to the Royal Belgian Academy and completed her translations of Greek poetry and the first two volumes of her autobiography.

Tragedy

Two major events marked Yourcenar's last decade. Frick died after a long illness only weeks before Yourcenar's election to the French Academy. Despite increasing pressure from the media, and a voluminous correspondence, Yourcenar continued to work, publishing the last of her great novels, *Two Lives and a Dream*, and essays. She resumed her travels—adding Africa and Asia—this time with Jerry Wilson, a young American and "dear friend." He, too, pre-deceased her, dying of AIDS in 1986. It was the last great tragedy of her life.

Still suffering from the effects of an automobile accident in Kenya in 1984 and from the heart disease that had troubled her for years, Yourcenar almost finished her autobiography—fifty pages remained—and was planning two events abroad when, in November of 1987, she suffered the massive stroke from which she would die a month later.

In addition to her original works, she translated other writers, among them: many ancient Greek poets, Virginia Woolf, Constantin Cavafy, Yukio Mishima, and James Baldwin.

In her life and her work, Yourcenar defied convention—and won. Criticized for too much re-writing, she became an acknowledged stylist and academician. She persisted with her choice of subject—not allowing scandalized critics to deter her from creating characters, often with unisex names, who love and suffer with any partner they choose—as long as theirs is an unselfish devotion—but refusing to apply "labels." She lived with what she loved, ignoring quarrels of the literary scene; her works live on as testimony.

References:

Savigneau, Josyane. *Marguerite Yourcenar: Inventing a Life*, Joan Howard, trans. Chicago University Press, 1993.

Yourcenar, Marguerite. *Essais et mémoires*. Paris: Gallimard, 1991.

———. *Oeuvres romanesques*. Paris: Gallimard, 1982.

—C. Frederick Farrell, Jr. and Edith R. Farrell

Babe Didrikson Zaharias

1911-1956

American athlete

Babe Didrikson Zaharias—or "the Babe" as she was popularly known—was one of the most gifted and versatile American sportswomen of all time. The legend of this "Texas tornado" and her dominance over fellow athletes in a variety of sports endures even forty years after her death. Early in life, she excelled in track and field events, winning two gold medals and a silver at the 1932 Olympics. She went on to compete outstandingly in basketball, baseball, tennis, bowling, and especially golf, becoming, according to biographers William Johnson and Nancy Williamson in *"Whatta-Gal": The Babe Didrikson Story,* "a one-woman book-of-records who dominated a quarter century of American sports." She was named Female Athlete of the Year six times by the Associated Press, and Female Athlete of the Half-Century as well. Even after being stricken with cancer in 1953, Babe continued to compete and win titles, becoming a courageous model of determination and championship in the battle against disease.

Though the American public adored Babe's soft-spoken honesty and wit, and cheered her every success, the press would often attack what they called her "unladylike bravado" and pursuance of "inappropriate" sports. But Babe was quick to use her "tomboyishness" to her advantage. "A consummate self-promoter and gender trickster," wrote biographer Susan Cayleff in *Babe: The Life and Legend of Babe Didrikson Zaharias,* "Babe ably used her androgyny and her powerful athleticism to promote herself." In the process, she firmly established women's rightful place in sports competition beyond the cultural context of traditional "women's games."

Although she was already married, Babe met and quickly fell in love with protege and "buddy" Betty Dodd in 1950, a woman twenty years her junior, who lived with her and husband George Zaharias until Babe's death in 1956. Given the era, their sexual relationship was never publicly acknowledged, but it was common knowledge among close friends that they were primary partners.

A Need for Worship

Mildred Ella Didriksen was born in 1911 to Norwegian immigrant parents who had settled in Port Arthur, Texas just a few years previous. She was the second youngest of seven children. Her mother was a champion skier and ice-skater in her native land, and her father was something of a roustabout sailor and laborer.

Throughout her life, Babe admitted to cagey manipulation of both her name—changed to Didrikson so she wouldn't be labeled "a Swede"—and her birth date. On her 1932 Olympics application, for example, she wrote that she was born in 1913 in an effort to render her athletic accomplishments all the more dazzling for her youthfulness. According to Cayleff, "if a twenty-year-old excelling at the Olympics in 1932 was heralded, then an eighteen-year-old—or better yet a seventeen-year-old—might be worshipped!"

As a young girl, Babe was streetwise and competitive, with a reputation as a ruffian that lasted well through high school. Her parents never discouraged her "rock-em-sock-em" behavior, perhaps recognizing it, like she did, as a way out of her working-class poverty and a rebellion against the expectations of gentility that were the southern female standard. The fact that she was likewise built for it—tall, tough, dark and lean—didn't hurt. "I played with boys rather than girls," she said in her 1955 autobiography, *This Life I've Led.* "I preferred baseball, football, foot-racing and jumping with the boys, to hop-scotch and jacks and dolls, which were about the only things girls did."

But her rejection of standard female roles also signaled a lifelong effort on the part of peers, the public, and the press to label her. The Texas tomboy who "straddled the fence" between acceptable gender behavior chose early on to wear the monikers society bestowed upon her like a badge of courage. But she was likewise saddled with a yearning need for acceptance. She became a charmer as well as a survivor—sewing her own often ridiculously frilly clothes in an effort to assert her "femininity," for example, and cultivating a clear vision of her life's goal. "I knew exactly what I wanted to be when I grew up," she wrote in 1955. "My goal was to be the greatest athlete that ever lived."

Babe Zaharias

Conquering World Records

In high school, Didrikson was high-scorer on the girl's basketball team in both her junior and senior years, an accomplishment which brought her to the attention of Dallas-based coach Melvin J. McCombs. His company, Employers Casualty Insurance, sponsored women's semiprofessional sports teams founded on the notion that athletes were more efficient and accurate in their work. Because Babe could also type and take shorthand, she was soon brought on board, excelling both as a secretary and in basketball, baseball, diving, tennis, and track and field.

Even at the tender age of 19 she overtrained. In softball, she was an undisputed power-hitter. On the track, she often practiced from sunup to sundown, matching the women's 5-foot, 3-inch world high-jump record of the time and being rewarded by her coach with chocolate sodas. She was also just learning how to play golf, and would often hit up to 1500 balls in the course of a ten-hour day, playing till her hands were blistered and bleeding. By 1930, she was selected for the All-American team of the Women's National Basketball League and led her team to the national championship by scoring 106 points in five tournament games. "Babe's goals were perfectionist, striking, and unrelenting," Cayleff notes. "We don't see a young athlete striving solely for steady improvement or personal bests. We see a woman with a consuming hunger attacking—and determined to conquer—world records."

Babe's dedication was to pay off handsomely at the 1932 Olympic Games in Los Angeles. She shattered records in all her events and was variously described in the press as the "Iron-Woman," the "Amazing Amazon," and "Whatta Gal Didrikson." She got her first gold medal in the javelin, breaking both the Olympic and the world record (as well as tearing some cartilage) in her first throw. Her second win was in the 80-meter hurdles, where she again broke both records, and moved on to claim a silver medal in the high jump.

The Games also solidified Babe's prowess in the eyes of the world. She had broken *world* records in a year where even the men had only topped *Olympic* ones. Yet, for all the adoration, Babe's pedestal was to prove a mixed blessing. From here on in, dethroning Babe became, according to Cayleff, "a contest within a contest" for athletes (and the press). "There was winning the event," she wrote, "achieving a personal best—and then there was beating Babe."

"Gender Heresy" and Big Bucks

Following her Olympic victories, the press had a field day with Babe's sexual identity. According to biographers Johnson and Williamson, she was "seen by many reporters and members of the public as a freak ... an aberration ... a living put-down to all things feminine." Thrust into the world spotlight, Babe was experiencing a particularly venomous backlash for what Johnson and Williamson quoted the press as calling the "gender heresy" of just being herself. She hated the standard trappings of femininity—once telling a reporter she did not wear girdles, bras, and the like because she was no "sissy."

She was also defying norms beyond mere physicality. She was unmarried, self-supporting, and earning big bucks through a series of endorsements, stunts, and sideshows by the time she was 21. She carved her own way right through the standard economic dependence and austerity most other depression-era women were experiencing. Though her economic fortunes were to swing dramatically throughout her life, her Employer's Casualty income alone had her earning three times the average income of American men at the time and six times that of American women.

By 1934, Babe's fortunes were growing along with her self-styled caricature. She was boxing, golfing, playing billiards, pitching baseballs to, and even running down the gridiron with sports celebrities. She was turning on the Texas drawl and charm extra thick for the press—all in her ongoing grab for money and fame, and a deeper desire to be loved for who she was. She was still the brunt of controversy, often remarking how she hated "those darn old women reporters" for constantly asking her about marriage, even for asking her if she'd like to coach girls someday. "I'd rather train boys," she said in her autobiography, "they're easier to handle."

Concessions to Conformity

In her need for acceptance, Babe was allowing the popular cultural attitude toward both women and sports to creep into her consciousness. As she grew tired of defending her "butch persona" and sought to reinvent her career as a professional lady golfer, she likewise latched on to all things feminine and frilly—attitudes that included the search for a husband and admitting that perhaps women's participation in sports should be limited after all.

Concessions to conformity aside, she began calculating the money she could make in exhibition golf matches with the male pros, which would also pack the galleries with fans and get her back in the papers. But golf was also another "personal-best" challenge. "Most things come natural to me," she said in 1933, "and golf was the first thing that ever gave me much trouble."

By 1935, Babe was averaging an impressive $15,000 a year from golf matches and sporting-goods endorsements. And it was through golf that Babe finally gained control of the new, more feminine image she wanted to mold. As she said in *This Life I've Led,* golf was "a game of coordination, rhythm, and grace. Women have this to a much higher degree than men, as dancing shows." Friend and golf-promoter Bertha Bowen is "credited" for her efforts at "feminizing" Babe during this period—taking her to Neiman-Marcus for new clothes, teaching her how to apply makeup, even getting her to play golf in a girdle—once and only once by all accounts—under specific pressure to do so from the Texas Women's Golf Association.

During this period, Babe was also busy consciously creating a more heterosexual past, right down to an adolescent recognition of gender boundaries she never really had. She invented past boyfriends for the press, and altered her advice to aspiring young female athletes to reflect heterosexual expectations. "I'm afraid that the only real first class advice I can give," she said in her autobiography, "is get toughened up by playing boys' games, but don't get tough."

Her newly discovered enthusiasm for such decidedly "feminine" ideals are at least partly explained by her "late" adoption of them herself (she was in her mid-twenties), and the press and public were certainly breathing a collective sigh of relief. But, according to Cayleff, "Babe's successful ascension to femininity is [falsely] hailed as an applaudable accomplishment, not the tumultuous, contrived, and limiting self-molding that it really was ... the toll taken on self-esteem, individuality, and difference is ignored."

The Cost of Companionship

Babe met "Gorgeous George" Zaharias when they played golf together at the Los Angeles Open in 1938, and they were married soon afterwards. He was a professional wrestler known for his stuntsmanship on the mat—a "gladiator of camp" by some accounts. According to Cayleff, their marriage was more calculated than the love-at-first sight they both claimed. "He was a caricature of manliness," Cayleff wrote, "tough, ferocious, powerful ... [it] contrasted favorably with Babe's attempted womanliness. They were working-class sports entertainers who reflected mainstream sensibilities: individualism, the will to succeed, and materialism. The two performers had found one another. There was more than a little of each in the other."

All of which perhaps explains their seemingly affectionate union, at least for the first few years. Babe was quickly domesticated and George took charge of her career. Biographers speculate that she was ready to relinquish some control over her globe-trotting professional life for some companionship—and all the cooking, curtain-making, and country-clubbing fit in with Babe's desire to "feminize" as well as move "up" socially. Ironically, George was to push her to travel and grab a buck on the golf circuit whenever she could, which made for lengthy separations.

From 1938 to 1950, Babe Zaharias—now a "proper" contented housewife in the eyes of the public—pursued a life designed to dominate the fairways and greens of the world. She went professional in 1948—it was time to cash in. She played with celebrities like Katharine Hepburn and Cary Grant as well as major sports figures of the time. She signed a lifetime contract with Wilson Sporting Goods to promote, among other things, a golf dress and shoes with removable spikes "sensible for gals who want comfort with grooming," according to her autobiography. She was even named a woman of the year by the Associated Press in 1947, along with Hollywood stars Helen Hayes and Ingrid Bergman.

In 1950, George and Babe bought the Tampa Golf and Country Club and settled there in a huge converted clubhouse. Babe was finally achieving the secure, settled domesticity she wanted and more of the upward mobility she craved. George, on the other hand, was dragging her down. He had grown fat—over 400 pounds by the early 1950s—and was often on the road for weeks at a time "seeing to his business interests." Babe began to yearn for someone to truly share her life and home with.

When she met Betty Dodd at an amateur golf tournament in 1950—a woman described by biographer Cayleff as "a nineteen-year-old with a captivating smile and eye-catching red hair and freckles"—Babe found the partner she had longed for. Dodd quickly moved in with Babe and George, and enjoyed, according to Cayleff, "a mutually enriching and satisfying intimate relationship" until Babe's death in 1956. Any sexual relationship was never openly acknowledged, but friends could not help but notice the two women's intimacy. "I had such admiration for this fabulous person," Dodd told biographers Johnson and Williamson. "I never wanted to be away from her even when she was dying of cancer. I loved her. I would've done anything for her."

The Toughest Competition

By the end of the golf circuit in late 1952, Babe was plagued by chronic fatigue. The new year saw her game heading steadily downhill, and having noticed blood in her stool a few months earlier, she confided her fears to Dodd alone. She was diagnosed with colon cancer in the spring of 1953, and though the press immediately pounced to announce her career was over, she blithely made up her mind to battle this disease in the same manner she had fought for every victory in her life—with sheer stamina. In the process, she once again won the hearts of her beloved public. "All my life I'd been competing—competing to win," she said in her book. "I came to realize that in its way, this cancer was the toughest competition I'd faced yet."

Babe eventually had a colostomy and, as her marriage to George was all but officially over, she relied on Dodd for everything. Interestingly, George's jealousy of Dodd was tempered by his need of her. "As time went by," Dodd told Johnson and Williamson, "he couldn't afford to be [jealous] anymore. Because he wouldn't do anything for Babe ... he needed me." Six months after the operation, the indomitable "Texas tomboy" considered herself out of the rough and was back on the golfing circuit, placing sixth in the nation in 1953 and tying for first in 1954.

Even when fighting cancer, Babe was a champion. Her lifelong, mutually exploitive relationship with the press made for a very public demise. "Her personality, coupled with the media's packaging of her illness," says Cayleff, "coalesced to make her symbolic ... as the one who could beat what others couldn't." In the end, though, Babe lost the battle, wasting-away to a mere 76 pounds, and dying in September of 1956 at the age of 45. Dodd kept her promise to Babe to avoid the funeral and instead, according to Johnson and Williamson, "fell into a week-long slumber aimed at recuperating, remembering, and forgetting."

Lesbian Legacy

In 1995, Cayleff noted that, whether she was out or not, lesbians of the 1940s and 1950s certainly looked to Babe for the same "signs" that sportswomen like Martina Navratilova show the world today. Babe might have chosen to speak out for herself and a generation of lesbians like her, but she too was a product of her times—obsessed with normalcy and acceptance above all else. This sublimation of self-acceptance may indeed have been a loss for lesbian women yearning for a voice but, according to Cayleff, her "silence does not make her less of a person. It simply makes her a survivor of a generation and a culture constrained by unrealistic images of men and women and sometimes violent homophobia." In the end, her need for silence and conformity teaches us volumes about mid-century homophobia and self-preservation, just as her outstanding public victories point up the joy of winning—and the essence of achieving one's personal best.

References:

Cayleff, Susan E. *Babe: The Life and Legend of Babe Didrikson Zaharias.* Chicago: University of Illinois Press, 1995.

Johnson, William O., and Nancy P. Williamson. *"Whatta-Gal": The Babe Didrikson Story.* Boston: Little, Brown and Company, 1975.

Zaharias, Babe Didrikson. *This Life I've Led.* New York: A. S. Barnes, 1955.

—Jerome Szymczak

Franco Zeffirelli

1923-

Italian film director and stage designer

As a filmmaker and stage designer, Franco Zeffirelli has scores of worldwide productions to his credit—mostly Shakespearean or operatic—that have been called either brilliant or extravagant to a fault, and sometimes both. His personal life and politics have been equally controversial, from his conservative politics to his religious fundamentalism to his reluctantly admitted sexuality. Zeffirelli drew fire from all sides, for instance, when he vehemently opposed Martin Scorsese's *The Last Temptation of Christ* in 1988, blaming the "Jews of Hollywood" for its blasphemy. He has also cited, in his 1986 autobiography, the sacrifice his mother made of her life for "her little bastard" as solidifying his stand against abortion. In 1994, he was elected to the Italian parliament on a strident right-wing platform. And when he came out to interviewer Edward

Franco Zeffirelli

Guthmann in the *Advocate* in June 1983, he said, in part, that he hated "to call certain human beings 'gay' [because] I see already a movement or a category ... I don't like that at all."

But perhaps Zeffirelli was fated to an operatic life. He was born in Florence on 12 February 1923 amid much scandal—the illegitimate son of a respected fashion designer (whose lawyer husband was in and out of sanitariums most of his later life with incurable tuberculosis) and her fabric supplier (himself married). "A name had to be invented for me," Zeffirelli says in the opening pages of his autobiography. Of the invention of such a name, he offers the following: "My mother was fond of a Mozart aria in *Cosi fan tutte* which mentions the *Zeffiretti,* the little breezes ... but this was misspelleded in the register and came out as the previously unheard-of Zeffirelli."

After studying architecture and art at the University of Florence and Academia di Belle Arti, Zeffirelli began his career in film as an assistant to some of the greatest Italian directors of this century—Antonioni, Rosselini, De Sica—and also briefly tried his hand at acting (as the "new" Montgomery Clift) under the mentorship—and, it was assumed, more intimate tutelage—of Luchino Visconti (*Death in Venice*). In the 1940s, Zeffirelli established himself as a talented stage designer for Visconti's extravagant operas, and throughout the 1950s staged his own lavish productions of opera (often featuring soprano Maria Callas) and theater (mostly Shakespeare).

Zeffirelli carried his stage-designing reputation for vivid eroticism amid opulent sets and costumes right into the second half of the century when he gained notoriety (in the United States especially) as a film director. *The Taming of the Shrew* (1967), *Romeo and Juliet* (1968), *Brother Sun and Sister Moon* (1972), *La Traviata* (1983), *Otello* (1986), *Hamlet* (1990), and even the made-for-TV *Jesus of Nazareth* (1977) are most memorable for their lush photography, lovely lyricism, and romantic portraits well beyond the mere filming of a stage play. According to Raymond Murray in *Images in the Dark,* Zeffirelli's films have the ability to lift the viewer "out of the doldrums of everyday reality and into a world of beauty, love, and tragedy." But, there were also the incredible bombs to account for, including: *Endless Love* (1981), *The Champ* (1979), and the never-released *Young Toscanini* (with Elizabeth Taylor). True to form, Zeffirelli blames the short-sighted avarice of the Hollywood "machine" for his failures. "How on earth had I allowed this to happen," he says in his autobiography, "I who had directed Callas, Magnani and Olivier, the operas of Puccini Verdi, etc., who had handled tempestuous superstars like Elizabeth Taylor and Richard Burton [both in *The Taming of the Shrew*], who had made a box-office hit out of Shakespeare?"

Zeffirelli's personal life and politics have remained as non-emblematic as his career. When he came out in the *Advocate* article—albeit rather academically (and some say, schizophrenically)—he clearly stated that he did not like to talk about his sexual inclinations, that people were not "special" because they liked one thing better than another in bed, and that calling certain human beings gay "ghettoized" the concept to everyone's detriment. At the same time, however, and to his credit he alluded to a gay sensibility by telling Edward Guthmann that "it happens that people who have to go through this particular sexual syndrome are forced to refine certain receptive instruments in the mind and soul: they become much more sensitive, more ready to talk and to deal with things of the spirit. They suffer more than the normal person. I think it is not easy to be a gay. I know this. You have to go through a very, very anguishing time."

In the spring of 1994, Zeffirelli augmented his controversial life by being elected to the Italian parliament as a member of the right-wing Freedom Alliance party, representing the Sicilian town of Catania. As he told *New Perspectives Quarterly,* the Freedom Alliance party represents the beginnings of "direct democracy" in Italy, a repossession of "personal destiny from the ruling/political classes." When asked how such politics affect a "man of the image" like himself, Zeffirelli casts an eye toward the future:

> The image is the reality of our times.... Now television creates prime ministers and presidents. That is progress. It will be the future of politics everywhere. And after the image, something else will come because man is restless and will continue to invent new ways of expressing himself and of disseminating information.

Current Address: Via Lucio Volumni 37, 00178 Rome, Italy.

References:

Guthmann, Edward. In *The Advocate,* June 1983.

Murray, Raymond. *Images in the Dark: An Encyclopedia of Gay & Lesbian Film and Video.* Philadelphia: TLA Publications, 1995.

New Perspectives Quarterly (Los Angeles, California), Summer 1994: 11, 51-53.

Rutledge, Leigh. *The Gay Book of Lists.* Boston: Alyson Publications, 1987.

———. *The Gay Decades.* Boston: Alyson Publications, 1992.

Vernoff, Edward and Rina Shore. *International Directory of 20th-Century Biography.* New York: New American Library, 1987.

Zeffirelli, Franco. *An Autobiography.* New York: Weidenfeld & Nicolson, 1986.

—Jerome Szymczak

NATIONALITY INDEX

American
Berenice Abbott
Roberta Achtenberg
Peter Adair
Jane Addams
Alvin Ailey
Edward Albee
Paula Gunn Allen
Dorothy Allison
Margaret Anderson
Susan B. Anthony
Gloria Anzaldua
Virginia M. Apuzzo
Gregg Araki
Dorothy Arzner
Sara Josephine Baker
James Baldwin
Benjamin Banneker
Ann Bannon
Djuna Barnes
Natalie Clifford Barney
Deborah A. Batts
Joseph Beam
Bishop Carl Bean
Alison Bechdel
Arthur Bell
Miriam Ben-Shalom
Ruth Benedict
Michael Bennett
Gladys Bentley
Nancy K. Bereano
Ruth Bernhard
Leonard Bernstein
Elizabeth Bishop
Emily Blackwell
Marc Blitzstein
Kate Bornstein
John Boswell
Beth Brant
Susie Bright
Romaine Brooks
Rita Mae Brown
Charlotte Bunch
Glenn Burke
Charles Busch
Paul Cadmus
John Cage
Pat Califia
Michael Callen
Margarethe Cammermeyer
Truman Capote
Willa Cather
June Chan
Debra Chasnoff
George Chauncey
Meg Christian
Chrystos
Roy Cohn
Blanche Wiesen Cook
Aaron Copland
Tee A. Corinne
Midge Costanza
Margaret Cruikshank
George Cukor
Countee Cullen
Merce Cunningham
Mary Daly
Mercedes de Acosta
Samuel R. Delany
John D'Emilio
Barbara Deming
Michael Denneny
Emily Dickinson
Divine
Melvin Dixon
Judy Dlugacz
Alix Dobkin
Martin Duberman
Melissa Etheridge
Lillian Faderman
Harvey Fierstein
Barney Frank
Sally Gearhart
Allen Ginsberg
Barbara Gittings
Jewelle Gomez
Marga Gomez
Paul Goodman
Judy Grahn
Barbara Grier
Angelina Emily Weld Grimke
Marilyn Hacker
Barbara J. Hammer
Lorraine Hansberry
Keith Haring
Bertha Harris
Harry Hay
Essex Hemphill
Gilbert Herdt
Rock Hudson
Holly Hughes
Langston Hughes
Alberta Hunter
Christopher Isherwood
James Ivory
Henry James
Karla Jay
JEB
Sarah Orne Jewett
Jasper Johns
Bill T. Jones
Cleve Jones
Frank Kameny
Arnie Kantrowitz
Jonathan Ned Katz
Willyce Kim
Billie Jean King
Irena Klepfisz
David Kopay
Sharon Kowalski
Larry Kramer
Sheila James Kuehl

Eva Le Gallienne
W. Dorr Legg
Edmonia Lewis
Liberace
Lisa Ben
Audre Lorde
Greg Louganis
JoAnn Loulan
Susan M. Love
Amy Lowell
Charles Ludlam
Phyllis Ann Lyon
Robert Mapplethorpe
Del Martin
Johnny Mathis
Leonard P. Matlovich, Jr.
Carson McCullers
Herman Melville
Gian Carlo Menotti
Harvey Milk
Edna St. Vincent Millay
June Millington
Agnes Moorehead
Cherrie Moraga
Dee Mosbacher
Martina Navratilova
Holly Near
Joan Nestle
Elaine Noble
Jean O'Leary
Pat Parker
Michelle Parkerson
Reverend Troy D. Perry
Charles Pierce
Deb Price
Gertrude "Ma" Rainey
Toshi Reagon
Adrienne Rich
Marlon Riggs
Eleanor Roosevelt
Gayle Rubin
Muriel Rukeyser
RuPaul
Vito Russo
Bayard Rustin
Assotto Saint
George Santayana
José Sarria
May Sarton
Sarah Schulman
Carol Seajay
Randy Shilts
Charles Shively
Michelangelo Signorile
Barbara Smith
Bessie Smith
Stephen Sondheim
Susan Sontag
Gertrude Stein
Gerry E. Studds
Martha Carey Thomas
Karen Thompson
Alice B. Toklas
Daniel C. Tsang
Kitty Tsui
Urvashi Vaid
Carl Van Vechten
Gore Vidal
Tom Waddell
Andy Warhol
John Waters
Edmund White
Walt Whitman
Gale Wilhelm
Tennessee Williams
Cris Williamson
Merle Woo
Marguerite Yourcenar
Babe Didrikson Zaharias

Argentinian
Manuel Puig

Australian
Dennis Altman

Austrian
Anna Freud

Belgian
Chantal Akerman

British
W. H. Auden
Francis Bacon
Sir Cecil Beaton
Anne Bonny
Benjamin Britten
Edward Carpenter
Quentin Crisp
E. M. Forster
Sir John Gielgud
Gluck
Duncan Grant
Radclyffe Hall
David Hockney
Derek Jarman
Elton John
Isaac Julien
John Maynard Keynes
Anne Lister
Christopher Marlowe
Sir Ian McKellen
Florence Nightingale
Walter Pater
Mary Read
Mary Renault
Vita Sackville-West
Dame Ethel Smyth
Lytton Strachey

John Addington Symonds
Alan Turing
Oscar Wilde
Jeanette Winterson
Virginia Woolf

Canadian
Elizabeth Arden
Elsa Gidlow
k. d. lang
Jane Rule

Cuban
Reinaldo Arenas

Danish
Hans Christian Andersen

French
Rosa Bonheur
Colette
Michel Foucault
Jean Genet
André Gide
Marcel Proust
Arthur Rimbaud
Paul Verlaine
Monique Wittig

German
Rainer Werner Fassbinder
Frederick II
Magnus Hirschfeld
Karl Heinrich Ulrichs
Rosa von Praunheim

Greek
Plato
Sappho

Indian
Ismail Merchant
Pratibha Parmar

Irish
Ladies of Llangollen

Israeli
Marcia Freedman

Italian
Caravaggio
Leonardo da Vinci
Michelangelo Buonarroti
Franco Zeffirelli

Japanese
Yukio Mishima

Macedonian
Alexander the Great

Mexican
Sor Juana Inés de la Cruz

Roman
Hadrian

Russian
Sergei Diaghilev
Rudolf Nureyev
Peter Ilich Tchaikovsky

South African
Simon Nkoli

Spanish
Pedro Almodovar
Federico García Lorca

Swedish
Christina
Greta Garbo
Dag Hammarskjold

West Indian
Ron Buckmire

OCCUPATION INDEX

Activists
Susan B. Anthony
Gloria Anzaldua
Virginia M. Apuzzo
Joseph Beam
Arthur Bell
Miriam Ben-Shalom
Kate Bornstein
Susie Bright
Rita Mae Brown
Ron Buckmire
Charlotte Bunch
Pat Califia
Margarethe Cammermeyer
June Chan
Chrystos
John D'Emilio
Barbara Deming
Alix Dobkin
Michel Foucault
Marcia Freedman
Sally Gearhart
Barbara Gittings
Jewelle Gomez
Judy Grahn
Harry Hay
Karla Jay
Frank Kameny
Arnie Kantrowitz
Jonathan Ned Katz
David Kopay
Sharon Kowalski
Larry Kramer
W. Dorr Legg
Lisa Ben
Audre Lorde
Susan M. Love
Amy Lowell
Phyllis Ann Lyon
Del Martin
Leonard P. Matlovich, Jr.
Sir Ian McKellen
Harvey Milk
Cherrie Moraga
Martina Navratilova
Holly Near
Simon Nkoli
Elaine Noble
Jean O'Leary
Reverend Troy D. Perry
Gayle Rubin
Vito Russo
Bayard Rustin
José Sarria
Carol Seajay
Charles Shively
Barbara Smith
Martha Carey Thomas
Karen Thompson
Daniel C. Tsang
Karl Heinrich Ulrichs
Urvashi Vaid

Actors
Charles Busch
Divine
Harvey Fierstein
Greta Garbo
Sir John Gielgud
Rock Hudson
Sheila James Kuehl
Eva Le Gallienne
Sir Ian McKellen
Agnes Moorehead
Holly Near
Charles Pierce

AIDS activists/educators
Michael Callen
Cleve Jones
Simon Nkoli

Anthropologists
Ruth Benedict
Gilbert Herdt

Architects
Michelangelo Buonarroti

Archivists
Joan Nestle

Artists
Francis Bacon
Paul Cadmus
Tee A. Corinne
Duncan Grant
Keith Haring
David Hockney
Holly Hughes
Derek Jarman
Leonardo da Vinci
Andy Warhol

Astronomers
Benjamin Banneker
Frank Kameny

Athletes
Glenn Burke
Billie Jean King
David Kopay
Greg Louganis
Martina Navratilova
Tom Waddell
Babe Didrikson Zaharias

Business professionals
Elizabeth Arden
Judy Dlugacz
Anne Lister

Cartoonists
Alison Bechdel

Choreographers
Alvin Ailey
Michael Bennett
Merce Cunningham
Bill T. Jones

Composers
Leonard Bernstein
Marc Blitzstein
Benjamin Britten
John Cage
Aaron Copland
Gian Carlo Menotti
Dame Ethel Smyth
Stephen Sondheim
Peter Ilich Tchaikovsky

Conductors
Leonard Bernstein

Critics
Samuel R. Delany
Pratibha Parmar
Susan Sontag
John Addington Symonds
Marguerite Yourcenar

Dancers
Alvin Ailey
Merce Cunningham
Bill T. Jones
Rudolf Nureyev

Designers
Sir Cecil Beaton

Diplomats
Dag Hammarskjold
Eleanor Roosevelt

Economists
John Maynard Keynes

Editors
Nancy K. Bereano
Beth Brant
Michael Denneny
Barbara Grier
Karla Jay
Irena Klepfisz
Lisa Ben

Educators
Charlotte Bunch
Margaret Cruikshank
Melvin Dixon
Martin Duberman
Lillian Faderman
Sally Gearhart
Jewelle Gomez
Paul Goodman
Karla Jay
Audre Lorde
Michelle Parkerson
Adrienne Rich
Jane Rule
Charles Shively
Martha Carey Thomas
Daniel C. Tsang
Merle Woo

Female impersonators
Divine
Charles Pierce
RuPaul
José Sarria

Film historians
Vito Russo

Filmmakers
Peter Adair
Chantal Akerman
Pedro Almodovar
Gregg Araki
Dorothy Arzner
Michael Bennett
Debra Chasnoff
George Cukor
Rainer Werner Fassbinder
Barbara J. Hammer
James Ivory
Derek Jarman
JEB
Isaac Julien
Eva Le Gallienne
Ismail Merchant
Dee Mosbacher
Michelle Parkerson
Pratibha Parmar
Marlon Riggs
Rosa von Praunheim
John Waters
Franco Zeffirelli

Healthcare professionals
Sara Josephine Baker
Emily Blackwell
Margarethe Cammermeyer
Magnus Hirschfeld
Susan M. Love
Florence Nightingale
Tom Waddell

Historians
John Boswell
George Chauncey
Blanche Wiesen Cook
John D'Emilio

Michel Foucault
Jonathan Ned Katz
John Addington Symonds

Humanitarians
Eleanor Roosevelt

Impresarios
Sergei Diaghilev

Inventors
Leonardo da Vinci

Journalists
Djuna Barnes
Arthur Bell
Deb Price
Randy Shilts
Michelangelo Signorile
Daniel C. Tsang
Karl Heinrich Ulrichs

Lawyers/law professionals
Deborah A. Batts
Roy Cohn

Lecturers
JoAnn Loulan

Librarians
Daniel C. Tsang

Mathematicians
Benjamin Banneker
Ron Buckmire
Alan Turing

Mental health professionals
Anna Freud
JoAnn Loulan
Dee Mosbacher

Military personnel
Miriam Ben-Shalom
Leonard P. Matlovich, Jr.

Monarchs/heads of state
Alexander the Great
Christina
Frederick II
Hadrian

Musicians
Elton John
Liberace
June Millington
Toshi Reagon
Cris Williamson

Painters
Rosa Bonheur
Romaine Brooks
Caravaggio
Gluck
Jasper Johns
Michelangelo Buonarroti

Performers
Kate Bornstein
Michael Callen
Quentin Crisp
Marga Gomez
Holly Hughes
Lisa Ben
Charles Ludlam
Assotto Saint

Philosophers
Mary Daly
Michel Foucault
Sor Juana Inés de la Cruz
Plato
George Santayana

Photographers
Berenice Abbott
Sir Cecil Beaton
Ruth Bernhard
JEB
Robert Mapplethorpe
Carl Van Vechten

Pirates
Anne Bonny
Mary Read

Playwrights
Edward Albee
Djuna Barnes
Charles Busch
Mercedes de Acosta
Harvey Fierstein
Lorraine Hansberry
Sor Juana Inés de la Cruz
Federico García Lorca
Charles Ludlam
Christopher Marlowe
Manuel Puig

Policy analysts
John D'Emilio

Political strategists
Bayard Rustin

Politicians
Roberta Achtenberg
Midge Costanza
Barney Frank
Sheila James Kuehl
Harvey Milk

Elaine Noble
Gerry E. Studds

Publishers
Margaret Anderson
Nancy K. Bereano
Judy Grahn
Barbara Grier
Carol Seajay
Alice B. Toklas

Religious leaders
Bishop Carl Bean
Sor Juana Inés de la Cruz
Reverend Troy D. Perry

Researchers
Gayle Rubin

Scholars
Paula Gunn Allen
W. Dorr Legg
Gayle Rubin
Monique Wittig
Marguerite Yourcenar

Scientists
June Chan
Leonardo da Vinci

Sculptors
Edmonia Lewis
Michelangelo Buonarroti

Sex educators/sexologists
Susie Bright
JoAnn Loulan
Karl Heinrich Ulrichs

Singers
Gladys Bentley
Meg Christian
Alix Dobkin
Melissa Etheridge
Alberta Hunter
Elton John
k. d. lang
Johnny Mathis
Holly Near
Gertrude "Ma" Rainey
RuPaul
Bessie Smith

Social reformers
Jane Addams

Songwriters
Michael Callen
Meg Christian
Alix Dobkin
Melissa Etheridge
Alberta Hunter
Elton John
Lisa Ben
Holly Near

Stage designers
Franco Zeffirelli

Theatrical producers
Charles Ludlam

Theologians
Mary Daly

Writers
Jane Addams
Paula Gunn Allen
Dorothy Allison
Dennis Altman
Hans Christian Andersen
Margaret Anderson
Gloria Anzaldua
Reinaldo Arenas
W. H. Auden
James Baldwin
Ann Bannon
Djuna Barnes
Natalie Clifford Barney
Joseph Beam
Sir Cecil Beaton
Alison Bechdel
Michael Bennett
Elizabeth Bishop
Kate Bornstein
Beth Brant
Susie Bright
Rita Mae Brown
Charlotte Bunch
Pat Califia
Truman Capote
Edward Carpenter
Willa Cather
Chrystos
Colette
Countee Cullen
Mercedes de Acosta
Samuel R. Delany
Barbara Deming
Emily Dickinson
Melvin Dixon
Martin Duberman
Lillian Faderman
E. M. Forster
Marcia Freedman
Sally Gearhart
Jean Genet
André Gide
Elsa Gidlow
Allen Ginsberg
Jewelle Gomez
Marga Gomez

Paul Goodman
Judy Grahn
Angelina Emily Weld Grimke
Marilyn Hacker
Radclyffe Hall
Bertha Harris
Essex Hemphill
Langston Hughes
Christopher Isherwood
Henry James
Derek Jarman
Karla Jay
Sarah Orne Jewett
Bill T. Jones
Sor Juana Inés de la Cruz
Arnie Kantrowitz
Willyce Kim
Irena Klepfisz
Larry Kramer
Anne Lister
Ladies of Llangollen
Federico García Lorca
Audre Lorde
JoAnn Loulan
Amy Lowell
Phyllis Ann Lyon
Christopher Marlowe
Del Martin
Carson McCullers
Sir Ian McKellen
Herman Melville
Michelangelo Buonarroti
Edna St. Vincent Millay
Yukio Mishima
Cherrie Moraga
Joan Nestle
Florence Nightingale
Pat Parker
Michelle Parkerson
Walter Pater
Marcel Proust
Manuel Puig
Mary Renault
Adrienne Rich
Arthur Rimbaud
Eleanor Roosevelt
Muriel Rukeyser
Jane Rule
Vita Sackville-West
Assotto Saint
George Santayana
Sappho
May Sarton
Sarah Schulman
Carol Seajay
Barbara Smith
Dame Ethel Smyth
Susan Sontag
Gertrude Stein
Lytton Strachey
John Addington Symonds
Alice B. Toklas
Kitty Tsui
Karl Heinrich Ulrichs
Urvashi Vaid
Carl Van Vechten
Paul Verlaine
Gore Vidal
Edmund White
Walt Whitman
Oscar Wilde
Gale Wilhelm
Tennessee Williams
Jeanette Winterson
Monique Wittig
Merle Woo

GENERAL SUBJECT INDEX

Aberrance
Pat Califia

Abusive relationships
Truman Capote
Chrystos
Tee A. Corinne
Greg Louganis

Acceptance
Plato
Gerry E. Studds

Activism, gay and lesbian
Joseph Beam
Bishop Carl Bean
Arthur Bell
Miriam Ben-Shalom
Kate Bornstein
Susie Bright
Ron Buckmire
Charlotte Bunch
Margarethe Cammermeyer
June Chan
Blanche Wiesen Cook
Midge Costanza
John D'Emilio
Barbara Deming
Martin Duberman
Sally Gearhart
Barbara Gittings
Jewelle Gomez
Lorraine Hansberry
Keith Haring
Bertha Harris
Harry Hay
Magnus Hirschfeld
Christopher Isherwood
Karla Jay
Cleve Jones
Frank Kameny
Arnie Kantrowitz
David Kopay
W. Dorr Legg
Lisa Ben
Audre Lorde
Susan M. Love
Phyllis Ann Lyon
Del Martin
Ian McKellen
Harvey Milk
Martina Navratilova
Holly Near
Simon Nkoli
Elaine Noble
Rudolf Nureyev
Jean O'Leary
Pat Parker
Michelle Parkerson
Pratibha Parmar
Troy D. Perry
Deb Price
Toshi Reagon
Mary Renault
Gayle Rubin
Jane Rule
Vito Russo
Assotto Saint
José Sarria
Sarah Schulman
Carol Seajay
Charles Shively
Michelangelo Signorile
Barbara Smith
Dame Ethel Smyth
Susan Sontag
Gerry E. Studds
Daniel C. Tsang
Kitty Tsui
Karl Heinrich Ulrichs
Urvashi Vaid
Tom Waddell
Merle Woo

Actors and actresses
Chantal Akerman
Sir Cecil Beaton
Charles Busch
Quentin Crisp
Mercedes de Acosta
Divine
Harvey Fierstein
Greta Garbo
John Gielgud
Harry Hay
Rock Hudson
Holly Hughes
Sheila James Kuehl
Eva Le Gallienne
Liberace
Greg Louganis
Charles Ludlam
Ian McKellen
Agnes Moorehead
Charles Pierce
RuPaul

Adolescence and sexuality
Edmund White

Adoption
Debra Chasnoff

Ageism/aging
Muriel Rukeyser

AIDS
Peter Adair
Dennis Altman
Virginia M. Apuzzo

Joseph Beam
Bishop Carl Bean
Michael Callen
Debra Chasnoff
Roy Cohn
Barney Frank
Keith Haring
Gilbert Herdt
Rock Hudson
Elton John
Bill T. Jones
Cleve Jones
Arnie Kantrowitz
Larry Kramer
Greg Louganis
Charles Ludlam
Robert Mapplethorpe
Leonard P. Matlovich, Jr.
Rudolf Nureyev
Jean O'Leary
Marlon Riggs
Vito Russo
Assotto Saint
José Sarria
Randy Shilts
Michelangelo Signorile
Susan Sontag
Gerry E. Studds
Urvashi Vaid
Rosa von Praunheim
Tom Waddell
Edmund White
Cris Williamson

Alcohol and alcoholism
Susan B. Anthony
Truman Capote
Meg Christian
Tee A. Corinne
Carson McCullers
Elaine Noble
Arthur Rimbaud
Paul Verlaine
Tennessee Williams

Alienation
Alvin Ailey
Pedro Almodovar
Gregg Araki
James Baldwin
Bishop Carl Bean
Bertha Harris
Andy Warhol

American Civil Liberties Union (ACLU)
Margarethe Cammermeyer
Sharon Kowalski
Leonard P. Matlovich, Jr.
Karen Thompson
Urvashi Vaid

American Library Association, Gay and Lesbian Task Force
Barbara Gittings

Androgyny
Hans Christian Andersen
Dorothy Arzner
Willa Cather
Christina
Quentin Crisp

Anthropology
Dennis Altman
Ruth Benedict
Gilbert Herdt

Antiwar movement
Barbara Deming
Michael Denneny
Sergei Diaghilev
Paul Goodman
JEB
Susan Sontag
Lytton Strachey
Daniel C. Tsang
Marguerite Yourcenar

Aristocrats
Sir Cecil Beaton

Art
Berenice Abbott
Francis Bacon
Natalie Clifford Barney
Sir Cecil Beaton
Alison Bechdel
Ruth Bernhard
Rosa Bonheur
Romaine Brooks
Caravaggio
Tee A. Corinne
Gluck
Duncan Grant
Barbara J. Hammer
Keith Haring
David Hockney
Derek Jarman
JEB
Jasper Johns
Bill T. Jones
Leonardo da Vinci
Edmonia Lewis
Robert Mapplethorpe
Michelangelo Buonarroti
Gertrude Stein
Alice B. Toklas
Carl Van Vechten
Tom Waddell
Andy Warhol

Art, visual
Berenice Abbott
Pedro Almodovar
Francis Bacon
Sir Cecil Beaton
Ruth Bernhard
Rosa Bonheur
Romaine Brooks
Paul Cadmus
Tee A. Corinne
Barbara J. Hammer
Keith Haring
David Hockney
Derek Jarman
JEB
Jasper Johns
Leonardo da Vinci
Robert Mapplethorpe
Michelangelo Buonarroti
Pratibha Parmar
Carl Van Vechten
Andy Warhol

Athletics
Glenn Burke
Billie Jean King
David Kopay
Greg Louganis
Martina Navratilova
Tom Waddell
Babe Didrikson Zaharias

Autobiography/biography
Peter Adair
Chantal Akerman
Margaret Anderson
Margarethe Cammermeyer
Aaron Copland
Martin Duberman
Langston Hughes
Henry James
Arnie Kantrowitz
Billie Jean King
David Kopay
Liberace
Greg Louganis
JoAnn Loulan
Yukio Mishima
Holly Near
Troy D. Perry
Muriel Rukeyser
Vita Sackville-West
George Santayana
May Sarton
Dame Ethel Smyth
Gertrude Stein
Lytton Strachey
John Addington Symonds
Alice B. Toklas
Daniel C. Tsang
Carl Van Vechten
Rosa von Praunheim
John Waters
Edmund White
Tennessee Williams
Jeanette Winterson
Marguerite Yourcenar
Babe Didrikson Zaharias
Franco Zeffirelli

Ballet
Alvin Ailey
Paul Cadmus
Bill T. Jones
Rudolf Nureyev
Peter Ilich Tchaikovsky

Bars
Arthur Bell

Bathhouses
Arthur Bell
Larry Kramer

Beat generation (literature)
Allen Ginsberg

Bisexuality
Chantal Akerman
Djuna Barnes
Sir Cecil Beaton
Michael Bennett
Rita Mae Brown
Caravaggio
June Chan
Christina
Colette
John Maynard Keynes
Billie Jean King
Carson McCullers
Agnes Moorehead
Rudolf Nureyev
Gertrude "Ma" Rainey
Carl Van Vechten

"Boston marriage"
Willa Cather
Sarah Orne Jewett

Buddhism
Allen Ginsberg

Butch/femme
Dorothy Allison
Rosa Bonheur
Holly Hughes
Ladies of Llangollen
Joan Nestle
Manuel Puig
Babe Didrikson Zaharias

Capital crime, homosexuality as
Reinaldo Arenas

Cartoons
Alison Bechdel
Oscar Wilde

Catholicism, Roman
Virginia M. Apuzzo
Mary Daly
Sor Juana Inés de la Cruz
Jean O'Leary

Celibacy
Dag Hammarskjold

Censorship
David Hockney
Joan Nestle
Manuel Puig
Jane Rule
Susan Sontag
Peter Ilich Tchaikovsky

Children's literature
Hans Christian Andersen
Oscar Wilde

Christianity
Troy D. Perry
Jane Rule

Clergy
Bishop Carl Bean
Troy D. Perry

Closet
Berenice Abbott
Ann Bannon
Sir Cecil Beaton
Elizabeth Bishop
Emily Blackwell
Paul Cadmus
Aaron Copland
George Cukor
Countee Cullen
Michel Foucault
Johnny Mathis
Agnes Moorehead
Deb Price

Coming out
James Baldwin
Deborah A. Batts
Joseph Beam
Sir Cecil Beaton
Alison Bechdel
Nancy K. Bereano
Leonard Bernstein
Marc Blitzstein
Rita Mae Brown
Glenn Burke
Pat Califia
Margarethe Cammermeyer
Truman Capote
Debra Chasnoff
Margaret Cruikshank
Michael Denneny
Sergei Diaghilev
Barbara Grier
Frank Kameny
Jonathan Ned Katz
Billie Jean King
David Kopay
Phyllis Ann Lyon
Del Martin
Johnny Mathis
Ian McKellen
Harvey Milk
Dee Mosbacher
Simon Nkoli
Deb Price
Bayard Rustin
Michelangelo Signorile

Communism
Roy Cohn
Aaron Copland
Alix Dobkin
Harry Hay
Rudolf Nureyev

Community, gay
Gilbert Herdt
W. Dorr Legg
Lisa Ben
Charles Ludlam
Martina Navratilova
Joan Nestle
Adrienne Rich
Jane Rule
Randy Shilts
Gerry E. Studds
Daniel C. Tsang
Kitty Tsui
Rosa von Praunheim

Composers
Leonard Bernstein
Marc Blitzstein
Benjamin Britten
Elton John
Gian Carlo Menotti
Dame Ethel Smyth
Stephen Sondheim
Peter Ilich Tchaikovsky

Congress, U.S.
Barney Frank
Frank Kameny
Elaine Noble
Gerry E. Studds

Dance
Alvin Ailey

Michael Bennett
John Cage
Merce Cunningham
Bill T. Jones
Rudolf Nureyev
Assotto Saint

Death
Ruth Benedict
Harvey Milk
Yukio Mishima

Decadence
Christopher Marlowe

Decriminalization
Frank Kameny

Demonstration, pickets, etc.
Debra Chasnoff
George Chauncey
Paul Goodman
Lorraine Hansberry

Deviance and deviation
Pat Califia

Diaries
André Gide
Sarah Orne Jewett
Anne Lister
Audre Lorde
Florence Nightingale
Dame Ethel Smyth
Peter Ilich Tchaikovsky
Virginia Woolf

Discrimination
Gerry E. Studds
Daniel C. Tsang
Merle Woo

Drama
Edward Albee
W. H. Auden
Kate Bornstein
Truman Capote
Mercedes de Acosta
Martin Duberman
Rainer Werner Fassbinder
Harvey Fierstein
Jean Genet
André Gide
Angelina Emily Weld Grimke
Lorraine Hansberry
Holly Hughes
Sor Juana Inés de la Cruz
Jonathan Ned Katz
Larry Kramer
Federico García Lorca
Christopher Marlowe
Carson McCullers
Yukio Mishima
Cherrie Moraga
Bayard Rustin
Stephen Sondheim
Lytton Strachey
Kitty Tsui
Gore Vidal
Rosa von Praunheim
Edmund White
Oscar Wilde
Tennessee Williams
Virginia Woolf
Marguerite Yourcenar

Drugs
Glenn Burke
Truman Capote
Allen Ginsberg
Keith Haring
Johnny Mathis
Elaine Noble
Arthur Rimbaud
Paul Verlaine
Andy Warhol

Education
Debra Chasnoff
Sally Gearhart
Karla Jay
W. Dorr Legg
Audre Lorde
Simon Nkoli
Michelle Parkerson
Walter Pater
Adrienne Rich
Marlon Riggs
Eleanor Roosevelt
Gayle Rubin
Muriel Rukeyser
Jane Rule
Bayard Rustin
Vita Sackville-West
Sappho
May Sarton
Charles Shively
Barbara Smith
Stephen Sondheim
Susan Sontag
John Addington Symonds
Martha Carey Thomas
Daniel C. Tsang
Alan Turing
Edmund White
Walt Whitman
Cris Williamson
Monique Wittig
Merle Woo

Effeminacy
Francis Bacon

George Cukor

Encoding/oblique or masked references
Alexander the Great
Hans Christian Andersen
George Cukor
Countee Cullen
Dag Hammarskjold
Henry James

Eroticism
Natalie Clifford Barney
Susie Bright
Paul Cadmus
Pat Califia
Caravaggio
Chrystos
Tee A. Corinne
Michelangelo Buonarroti
Plato
Walt Whitman

Essays
Dorothy Allison
Dennis Altman
Gloria Anzaldua
W. H. Auden
E. M. Forster
Essex Hemphill
Audre Lorde
Walter Pater
Gayle Rubin
Barbara Smith
Susan Sontag
Lytton Strachey
John Addington Symonds
Alice B. Toklas
Daniel C. Tsang
Urvashi Vaid
Gore Vidal
Oscar Wilde
Tennessee Williams
Merle Woo
Virginia Woolf
Marguerite Yourcenar

Expatriate community
Djuna Barnes
Alberta Hunter
Edmonia Lewis
Susan Sontag
Gertrude Stein
Alice B. Toklas
Gore Vidal

Family/societal relationships
Roberta Achtenberg
Jane Addams
Alvin Ailey
Edward Albee
Natalie Clifford Barney
Sharon Kowalski
Marcel Proust
Adrienne Rich
Muriel Rukeyser
Sappho
Karen Thompson
Cris Williamson
Monique Wittig

Fashion
Elizabeth Arden
Sir Cecil Beaton

Feminism
Susan B. Anthony
Gloria Anzaldua
Virginia M. Apuzzo
Dorothy Arzner
Rita Mae Brown
Charlotte Bunch
Meg Christian
Colette
Tee A. Corinne
Mary Daly
Mercedes de Acosta
Barbara Deming
Alix Dobkin
Lillian Faderman
Marcia Freedman
Sally Gearhart
Judy Grahn
Bertha Harris
Holly Hughes
Karla Jay
Sarah Orne Jewett
Jonathan Ned Katz
Sheila James Kuehl
Edmonia Lewis
June Millington
Holly Near
Joan Nestle
Michelle Parkerson
Pratibha Parmar
Muriel Rukeyser
Carol Seajay
Barbara Smith
Dame Ethel Smyth
Martha Carey Thomas
Urvashi Vaid
Monique Wittig
Merle Woo
Virginia Woolf

Fiction (genre)
Samuel R. Delany
Langston Hughes
Willyce Kim
Michelle Parkerson

Fiction (novels)
Edward Albee
Paula Gunn Allen

Dorothy Allison
Dennis Altman
Margaret Anderson
Reinaldo Arenas
James Baldwin
Ann Bannon
Djuna Barnes
Natalie Clifford Barney
Rita Mae Brown
Truman Capote
Willa Cather
Colette
Samuel R. Delany
Melvin Dixon
E. M. Forster
Jean Genet
André Gide
Paul Goodman
Radclyffe Hall
Bertha Harris
Christopher Isherwood
Henry James
Larry Kramer
Carson McCullers
Herman Melville
Yukio Mishima
Walter Pater
Marcel Proust
Manuel Puig
Mary Renault
Jane Rule
Vita Sackville-West
George Santayana
May Sarton
Sarah Schulman
Susan Sontag
Gertrude Stein
Kitty Tsui
Carl Van Vechten
Gore Vidal
Oscar Wilde
Gale Wilhelm
Jeanette Winterson
Monique Wittig
Virginia Woolf
Marguerite Yourcenar

Fiction (short stories)

Reinaldo Arenas
Willa Cather
E. M. Forster
Sarah Orne Jewett
Lisa Ben
Carson McCullers
Herman Melville
Yukio Mishima
Walter Pater
Carol Seajay
Barbara Smith
Gertrude Stein
Gore Vidal
Oscar Wilde
Gale Wilhelm
Tennessee Williams
Virginia Woolf

Film

Peter Adair
Chantal Akerman
Pedro Almodovar
Gregg Araki
Dorothy Arzner
Rita Mae Brown
Truman Capote
Debra Chasnoff
Aaron Copland
George Cukor
Divine
Rainer Werner Fassbinder
Greta Garbo
Barbara J. Hammer
Harry Hay
James Ivory
Derek Jarman
JEB
Isaac Julien
Larry Kramer
Eva Le Gallienne
Ismail Merchant
Dee Mosbacher
Michelle Parkerson
Pratibha Parmar
Charles Pierce
Manuel Puig
Marlon Riggs
RuPaul
Vito Russo
Stephen Sondheim
Susan Sontag
Rosa von Praunheim
Andy Warhol
John Waters
Tennessee Williams
Franco Zeffirelli

Film criticism

Arthur Bell
Vito Russo
Susan Sontag

First Amendment

Margaret Anderson

Folklore, legend, myth

Hans Christian Andersen

Gay and lesbian rights

Virginia M. Apuzzo
Reinaldo Arenas
James Baldwin
Bishop Carl Bean
Ron Buckmire

Pat Califia
Chrystos
Roy Cohn
Midge Costanza
Barney Frank
Barbara Gittings
Jewelle Gomez
Judy Grahn
David Hockney
Frank Kameny
Arnie Kantrowitz
Sharon Kowalski
Sheila James Kuehl
W. Dorr Legg
Lisa Ben
Audre Lorde
Susan M. Love
Leonard P. Matlovich, Jr.
Ian McKellen
Martina Navratilova
Jean O'Leary
Pat Parker
Troy D. Perry
Deb Price
Mary Renault
Gayle Rubin
Jane Rule
Vito Russo
José Sarria
Randy Shilts
Charles Shively
Barbara Smith
Dame Ethel Smyth
Susan Sontag
Gerry E. Studds
John Addington Symonds
Karen Thompson
Kitty Tsui
Karl Heinrich Ulrichs
Urvashi Vaid
Gore Vidal
Rosa von Praunheim
Tom Waddell
Merle Woo

Gay and Lesbian Rights Task Force, National
John D'Emilio

Gay and lesbian studies/history
Peter Adair
John Boswell
George Chauncey
Margaret Cruikshank
John D'Emilio
Martin Duberman
Lillian Faderman
Michel Foucault
Judy Grahn
Harry Hay
Essex Hemphill
Gilbert Herdt
Karla Jay
Arnie Kantrowitz
Jonathan Ned Katz
W. Dorr Legg
Joan Nestle
Deb Price
Gayle Rubin
Vito Russo
José Sarria
Randy Shilts
Charles Shively
Daniel C. Tsang
Kitty Tsui
Edmund White
Monique Wittig

Gender studies
Gilbert Herdt
Magnus Hirschfeld
Pratibha Parmar

Government
Roberta Achtenberg
Alexander the Great
Virginia M. Apuzzo
Reinaldo Arenas
Roy Cohn
Barney Frank
Hadrian
Dag Hammarskjold
Cleve Jones
Frank Kameny
Sheila James Kuehl
Ian McKellen
Harvey Milk
Elaine Noble
Gerry E. Studds

Greece, ancient
Alexander the Great
André Gide
Plato
Sappho

Heterosexuality
Christina
Langston Hughes
Walter Pater
Marcel Proust

History, American
Jane Addams
Susan B. Anthony
George Chauncey
Blanche Wiesen Cook
Martin Duberman

History, world
Alexander the Great
Christina

Margaret Cruikshank
Frederick II
Hadrian
Sor Juana Inés de la Cruz
John Addington Symonds

Homophobia
Ruth Benedict
Judy Grahn
Arnie Kantrowitz
Jonathan Ned Katz
Sharon Kowalski
Sheila James Kuehl
Christopher Marlowe
Dee Mosbacher
Elaine Noble
Pratibha Parmar
Randy Shilts
Barbara Smith
Karen Thompson

Human rights
Roberta Achtenberg
Jane Addams
Michel Foucault
Florence Nightingale
Eleanor Roosevelt
Bayard Rustin
May Sarton
Charles Shively
Barbara Smith
Susan Sontag
Gerry E. Studds
Martha Carey Thomas
Kitty Tsui
Urvashi Vaid
Merle Woo

Humor/satire
Pedro Almodovar
Alison Bechdel
Charles Busch
Marga Gomez
John Waters
Oscar Wilde
Virginia Woolf

Identity
Dennis Altman
Gilbert Herdt
Adrienne Rich
Vita Sackville-West

Insanity
Anne Lister
Tennessee Williams
Virginia Woolf

Institutional repression/oppression
Martha Carey Thomas

Interracial
Isaac Julien
W. Dorr Legg

Jazz
Alvin Ailey
Alberta Hunter
k. d. lang

Journalism--print/broadcast
Djuna Barnes
Arthur Bell
Blanche Wiesen Cook
Arnie Kantrowitz
Lisa Ben
Audre Lorde
Phyllis Ann Lyon
Del Martin
Deb Price
Marcel Proust
Eleanor Roosevelt
Muriel Rukeyser
Vita Sackville-West
Sarah Schulman
Carol Seajay
Randy Shilts
Michelangelo Signorile
Daniel C. Tsang
Karl Heinrich Ulrichs
Andy Warhol
Walt Whitman
Oscar Wilde

Judaism
Irena Klepfisz

Language and linguistics
Mary Daly
Eleanor Roosevelt

Law
Roberta Achtenberg
Deborah A. Batts
Roy Cohn
Frank Kameny
Sheila James Kuehl
Peter Ilich Tchaikovsky
Karl Heinrich Ulrichs

Letters, correspondence
Ladies of Llangollen
Florence Nightingale
Deb Price
George Santayana
May Sarton
Peter Ilich Tchaikovsky
Karl Heinrich Ulrichs
Virginia Woolf

Liberation, gay
John D'Emilio

Frank Kameny
Arnie Kantrowitz
Jonathan Ned Katz
David Kopay
Phyllis Ann Lyon
Del Martin
Harvey Milk
Simon Nkoli
Pat Parker
Urvashi Vaid
Rosa von Praunheim
Walt Whitman

Lifestyle
Peter Adair
Dorothy Arzner

Literature
Paula Gunn Allen
Margaret Anderson
Paul Goodman
Marilyn Hacker
Amy Lowell
Marcel Proust
Mary Renault
Arthur Rimbaud
Assotto Saint
John Addington Symonds
Paul Verlaine
Walt Whitman
Virginia Woolf

Literature, gay
Michael Denneny
Sergei Diaghilev
Martin Duberman

Literary criticism
Paula Gunn Allen
Margaret Anderson
Samuel R. Delany
Melvin Dixon
Judy Grahn
Arnie Kantrowitz
Jonathan Ned Katz
Herman Melville
Arthur Rimbaud
Susan Sontag
Lytton Strachey
Paul Verlaine
Virginia Woolf

Literary movements
Margaret Anderson
Amy Lowell
Joan Nestle

Love
James Baldwin
Marilyn Hacker
Plato
Arthur Rimbaud
Paul Verlaine
Walt Whitman
Jeanette Winterson

Marriage, homosexual and lesbian
Barbara Grier
Sharon Kowalski
Audre Lorde
Michelangelo Signorile
Karen Thompson

Medicine, science, technology
Sara Josephine Baker
Benjamin Banneker
Emily Blackwell
Margarethe Cammermeyer
Magnus Hirschfeld
Isaac Julien
Leonardo da Vinci
JoAnn Loulan
Susan M. Love
Dee Mosbacher
Florence Nightingale
Elaine Noble
Pat Parker
Gerry E. Studds
Alan Turing
Karl Heinrich Ulrichs
Tom Waddell
Merle Woo

Memoirs
Peter Adair
Jane Addams
Alvin Ailey
Dag Hammarskjold
Bertha Harris
Henry James
JoAnn Loulan
Eleanor Roosevelt
May Sarton
Dame Ethel Smyth
Alice B. Toklas
Gore Vidal
Virginia Woolf

Military--gays and lesbians
Miriam Ben-Shalom
Margarethe Cammermeyer
Barney Frank
Leonard P. Matlovich, Jr.
Harvey Milk
Cherrie Moraga
Randy Shilts
Tom Waddell

Minorities
Alvin Ailey
Paula Gunn Allen
Dorothy Allison

Gloria Anzaldua
James Baldwin
Benjamin Banneker
Deborah A. Batts
Joseph Beam
Bishop Carl Bean
Gladys Bentley
Beth Brant
June Chan
Chrystos
Countee Cullen
Essex Hemphill
Langston Hughes
Alberta Hunter
Bill T. Jones
Willyce Kim
Harvey Milk
Randy Shilts
Kitty Tsui
Karl Heinrich Ulrichs

Music
Leonard Bernstein
John Cage
Meg Christian
Aaron Copland
Judy Dlugacz
Alix Dobkin
Melissa Etheridge
Elton John
k. d. lang
Liberace
Johnny Mathis
June Millington
Holly Near
Gertrude "Ma" Rainey
Toshi Reagon
Bessie Smith
Dame Ethel Smyth
Stephen Sondheim
Peter Ilich Tchaikovsky
Cris Williamson

Musicians
Bishop Carl Bean
Gladys Bentley
Michael Callen
Meg Christian
Alix Dobkin
Melissa Etheridge
Harry Hay
Alberta Hunter
Elton John
k. d. lang
Liberace
June Millington
Holly Near
Gertrude "Ma" Rainey
Toshi Reagon
Bessie Smith
Cris Williamson

Mysticism, occultism
Edward Carpenter
Arnie Kantrowitz

Mythology
Beth Brant
Andy Warhol

Nature/natural world
Alan Turing
Marguerite Yourcenar

Nonfiction
Jane Addams
Dennis Altman
Susan B. Anthony
Elizabeth Arden
Truman Capote
Marcia Freedman
Larry Kramer
W. Dorr Legg
JoAnn Loulan
Susan M. Love
Yukio Mishima
Cherrie Moraga
Joan Nestle
Plato
Adrienne Rich
Eleanor Roosevelt
Sarah Schulman
Carol Seajay
Gertrude Stein
John Addington Symonds
Monique Wittig

Opera
Benjamin Britten
David Hockney
Bill T. Jones
Gian Carlo Menotti
Dame Ethel Smyth
Gertrude Stein
Peter Ilich Tchaikovsky
Walt Whitman
Franco Zeffirelli

Oppression
Bishop Carl Bean
Benjamin Britten
Chrystos
Cherrie Moraga
Karl Heinrich Ulrichs

Parents of gays and lesbians
Sharon Kowalski
Karen Thompson

Pederasty
Caravaggio
Countee Cullen
André Gide

Michelangelo Buonarroti
Plato
John Addington Symonds
Karl Heinrich Ulrichs

Philosophy

Jane Addams
John Cage
Edward Carpenter
Mary Daly
Michel Foucault
Harry Hay
Plato
George Santayana
Susan Sontag

Poetry

Edward Albee
Paula Gunn Allen
Dorothy Allison
Gloria Anzaldua
Reinaldo Arenas
W. H. Auden
Djuna Barnes
Elizabeth Bishop
Beth Brant
Rita Mae Brown
Chrystos
Countee Cullen
Mercedes de Acosta
Emily Dickinson
Melvin Dixon
Jean Genet
Elsa Gidlow
Allen Ginsberg
Jewelle Gomez
Judy Grahn
Angelina Emily Weld Grimke
Marilyn Hacker
Radclyffe Hall
Essex Hemphill
Langston Hughes
Derek Jarman
Sor Juana Inés de la Cruz
Willyce Kim
Irena Klepfisz
Federico García Lorca
Audre Lorde
Amy Lowell
Christopher Marlowe
Michelangelo Buonarroti
Edna St. Vincent Millay
Cherrie Moraga
Pat Parker
Adrienne Rich
Arthur Rimbaud
Muriel Rukeyser
Vita Sackville-West
Assotto Saint
George Santayana
Sappho
May Sarton
Charles Shively
Barbara Smith
Gertrude Stein
John Addington Symonds
Kitty Tsui
Karl Heinrich Ulrichs
Paul Verlaine
Gore Vidal
Walt Whitman
Oscar Wilde
Gale Wilhelm
Merle Woo
Marguerite Yourcenar

Politics, political and social history

Roberta Achtenberg
Alexander the Great
Susan B. Anthony
Virginia M. Apuzzo
Deborah A. Batts
Edward Carpenter
Debra Chasnoff
Roy Cohn
Midge Costanza
John D'Emilio
Barney Frank
Hadrian
Dag Hammarskjold
Lorraine Hansberry
Phyllis Ann Lyon
Del Martin
Harvey Milk
Holly Near
Florence Nightingale
Simon Nkoli
Elaine Noble
Troy D. Perry
Eleanor Roosevelt
Bayard Rustin
José Sarria
Susan Sontag
Gerry E. Studds
John Addington Symonds
Rosa von Praunheim
Franco Zeffirelli

Pornography

Dorothy Allison
Gregg Araki
Susie Bright
Pat Califia
Barbara J. Hammer
Joan Nestle
Gayle Rubin
Susan Sontag

Prejudice

Benjamin Banneker
Lorraine Hansberry
Gertrude "Ma" Rainey

Barbara Smith
Bessie Smith

Press
Alice B. Toklas
Daniel C. Tsang
Karl Heinrich Ulrichs

Prisons
Simon Nkoli
John Waters
Oscar Wilde

Prostitution, hustling
Quentin Crisp

Psychiatry
Frank Kameny
JoAnn Loulan
Dee Mosbacher

Psychology
Michel Foucault
Anna Freud

Publishing
Michael Denneny
Sergei Diaghilev
Barbara Grier

Race relations, multiculturalism
Lorraine Hansberry
Harry Hay
Essex Hemphill
Langston Hughes
Isaac Julien
Audre Lorde
Joan Nestle
Pratibha Parmar
Mary Renault
Adrienne Rich
Bayard Rustin
Kitty Tsui
Urvashi Vaid
Monique Wittig

Racism
Ruth Benedict
Beth Brant
Melvin Dixon
Angelina Emily Weld Grimke
Leonard P. Matlovich, Jr.
Pat Parker
Pratibha Parmar
Gertrude "Ma" Rainey
Mary Renault
Bayard Rustin
Barbara Smith
Bessie Smith
Daniel C. Tsang
Urvashi Vaid
Carl Van Vechten

Religion, spirituality
James Baldwin
Bishop Carl Bean
Mary Daly
Mercedes de Acosta
Radclyffe Hall
Harry Hay
Christopher Isherwood
Sor Juana Inés de la Cruz
Jean O'Leary
Troy D. Perry
Toshi Reagon
Franco Zeffirelli

Rock & roll music
Melissa Etheridge
Elton John
k. d. lang

Role, sexual and gender
Phyllis Ann Lyon
Del Martin
Marcel Proust
Alice B. Toklas

Rome, ancient
Edward Carpenter
André Gide
Hadrian

Royalty
Christina
Frederick II
Peter Ilich Tchaikovsky

Sadism/sadomasochism
Pat Califia
Robert Mapplethorpe

San Francisco
Roberta Achtenberg
John D'Emilio
Cleve Jones
Harvey Milk

Sculpture
Leonardo da Vinci
Edmonia Lewis
Michelangelo Buonarotti

Sexism
Pratibha Parmar

Sexual ambiguity/ambivalence
Caravaggio
Edward Carpenter
Mercedes de Acosta

Manuel Puig
Rosa von Praunheim
Jeanette Winterson

Sexual health, safety
Pat Califia
Michael Callen
Edward Carpenter
Tee A. Corinne
JoAnn Loulan
Phyllis Ann Lyon
Del Martin

Sexual identity
Martin Duberman
Gilbert Herdt
Magnus Hirschfeld
Pratibha Parmar
Kitty Tsui
Rosa von Praunheim
Jeanette Winterson
Monique Wittig
Babe Didrikson Zaharias

Sexuality, gender roles
Reinaldo Arenas
Natalie Clifford Barney
Kate Bornstein
Marilyn Hacker
Radclyffe Hall
Gilbert Herdt
Magnus Hirschfeld
Anne Lister
Arthur Rimbaud
Gayle Rubin
Alice B. Toklas
Paul Verlaine
Rosa von Praunheim
Jeanette Winterson
Monique Wittig
Babe Didrikson Zaharias

Singers
Gladys Bentley
Michael Callen
Meg Christian
Melissa Etheridge
Alberta Hunter
k. d. lang
Lisa Ben
Johnny Mathis
Holly Near
Charles Pierce
Gertrude "Ma" Rainey
Toshi Reagon
RuPaul
Bessie Smith
Cris Williamson

Slavery
Essex Hemphill
Benjamin Banneker

Social commentary
Peter Adair
Edward Albee
Lorraine Hansberry
Marcel Proust
Adrienne Rich
Marlon Riggs
Vito Russo
Sappho
Sarah Schulman
Barbara Smith
Susan Sontag
Daniel C. Tsang
Carl Van Vechten

Sociology
Jane Addams
Dennis Altman
Edward Carpenter
Michel Foucault
Dag Hammarskjold
Harry Hay

Stereotypes
Harvey Fierstein
Charles Ludlam
Marcel Proust
Marlon Riggs
Vito Russo
Rosa von Praunheim

Stonewall Rebellion, 1969
George Chauncey
Michael Denneny
Sergei Diaghilev
Martin Duberman

Subculture
Gregg Araki
Andy Warhol
John Waters

Suicide
Bishop Carl Bean
Alan Turing

Television
Liberace
Holly Near
Michelle Parkerson
Vito Russo
Stephen Sondheim
Gore Vidal

Theater
Edward Albee
W. H. Auden
Harvey Fierstein

John Gielgud
Marga Gomez
Lorraine Hansberry
David Hockney
Holly Hughes
Eva Le Gallienne
Charles Ludlam
Holly Near
Charles Pierce
RuPaul
Sarah Schulman
Bessie Smith
Stephen Sondheim
Peter Ilich Tchaikovsky
Gore Vidal
Andy Warhol
Edmund White
Oscar Wilde
Tennessee Williams
Virginia Woolf
Marguerite Yourcenar
Franco Zeffirelli

Third sex
Rosa Bonheur
Lillian Faderman

Translations
Melvin Dixon

Transsexuals
Kate Bornstein
Marguerite Yourcenar

Transvestism
Francis Bacon
Arthur Bell
Gladys Bentley
Rosa Bonheur
Anne Bonny
Charles Busch
Willa Cather
Quentin Crisp
Divine
Lillian Faderman
Mary Read
John Waters

Travel and exploration
Judy Dlugacz
Dame Ethel Smyth
Marguerite Yourcenar

Venereal disease
Anne Lister

Violence
Arthur Rimbaud
Paul Verlaine

War
Alexander the Great
Hadrian

Women's studies
Chantal Akerman
Paula Gunn Allen
Susan B. Anthony
Karla Jay
Adrienne Rich
Gayle Rubin
Vita Sackville-West
Martha Carey Thomas
Monique Wittig

World War II
Ruth Benedict

Youth
Gilbert Herdt

NOTES ON CONTRIBUTORS

ALBUCHER, Ronald C., M.D. Psychiatrist involved in patient care and education issues at Ann Arbor VA Medical Center and University of Michigan. **Essay:** Roy Cohn.

ANDERSON, Andrew A. Associate professor of Spanish, University of Michigan, Ann Arbor. Author of *Lorca's Late Poetry: A Critical Study,* 1990; *García Lorca: "La zapatera prodigiosa,"* 1991; editor of Federico García Lorca's books, *Antología poética,* 1986, *Diván del Tamarit. Llanto por Ignacio Sánchez Mejías. Seis poemas galegos. Poemas sueltos,* 1988, and *Cartas reunidas,* in press. Frequent contributor of articles on García Lorca to scholarly journals in U.S., Canada, Great Britain, France, and Spain. **Essay:** Federico García Lorca.

ANDERSON, Shelley. Writer; contributor of short stories to anthologies published in the U.S. and U.K.; author of nonfiction, including *Out in the World: International Lesbian Organizing,* 1991; and *Lesbian Rights Are Human Rights,* 1995. **Essay:** Samuel R. Delany.

ARNOLD, Lee. Library director, Historical Society of Pennsylvania. Contributor of reviews and essays on gay and lesbian studies, women's studies, AIDS, and genealogy to periodicals. **Essays:** Michael Callen; Elaine Noble.

BARRIE, Cecily M. Freelance reviewer and managing editor of *Atlantis: A Women's Studies Journal,* published by Institute for the Study of Women, Mount Saint Vincent University, Halifax, Nova Scotia. **Essay:** Elizabeth Arden.

BENKOV, Edith J. Professor of French, San Diego State University, California; specializes in Medieval and Renaissance literature and feminist criticism; contributor of articles on Crétien de Troyes, Marie de France, Christine de Pizan, Louise Labé, and Medieval theatre to numerous periodicals. **Essays:** Chantal Akerman; Arthur Rimbaud and Paul Verlaine; Monique Wittig.

BILY, Cynthia A. Writing instructor and freelance writer in Adrian, Michigan. **Essays:** Sara Josephine Baker; Greta Garbo.

BRANDENBURG, Sandra. Freelance writer. **Essays:** k. d. lang; Edna St. Vincent Millay.

BREEN, Margaret Soenser. Freelance writer. **Essay:** Jane Rule.

BRODSKY, Ira N. Playwright and editor in New York City; freelance writer; has written previously for St. James Press. **Essays:** Kate Bornstein; Charles Busch; Harvey Fierstein; Michelangelo Signorile.

BURTON, Peter. Commissioning editor, Millivres Books, Brighton, East Sussex, England; literary editor, *Gay Times* (London); author of *Rod Stewart: An Authorised Biography,* 1977; *Parallel Lives: A Memoir,* 1985; *Talking To ... in Conversation with Writers Writing on Gay Themes,* 1991; *Amongst the Aliens: Some Aspects of a Gay Life*; and *The Art of Gay Love,* 1995; co-author of *The Boy from Beirut and Other Stories,* 1982; *Vale of Tears: A Problem Shared,* 1992; and *Drag: A History of Female Impersonation in the Performing Arts,* 1994. **Essays:** Marc Blitzstein; Benjamin Britten.

BUSHALLOW-WILBUR, Lara. Freelance writer. **Essay:** Michael Bennett.

CANNON, Liz. Freelance writer. **Essay:** Holly Near.

CERRITO, Joann. Writer and editor specializing in biographical reference sources in literature and the arts. Editor of *Nineteenth-Century Literature Criticism, Modern Arts Criticism,* and *Contemporary Artists.* **Essays:** Margarethe Cammermeyer; Eleanor Roosevelt.

CHRISTENSEN, Peter G. Teacher, University of Wisconsin—Milwaukee and Milwaukee Institute of Art and Design. Received Ph.D. in comparative literature from State University of New York at Binghamton; area of specialty is twentieth-century fiction. Author of articles on Vernon Lee, D. H. Lawrence, Lawrence Durrell, and John Cowper Powys. **Essay:** Walter Pater.

CHURCHILL, Mary C. Instructor in women studies, University of Colorado at Boulder. Specializes in the study of Native American women, religious traditions, and literature. **Essay:** Paula Gunn Allen.

CLANCY, Laurie. Reader of English, La Trobe University, Bundoora, Victoria, Australia. Author of *A Reader's Guide to Australian Fiction,* 1992, as well as three novels, two collections of short stories, and various critical works. Contributor of reviews and articles to Australian journals on a variety of literary topics, including popular writing. **Essays:** Dennis Altman; Yukio Mishima.

CROCKER, Elizabeth Hutchinson. Freelance writer. **Essay:** Jewelle Gomez.

CURRY, Renee R. Associate professor of literature and writing, California State University, San Marcos. Contributor of articles on lesbian women writers such as Elizabeth Bishop and May Sarton to periodicals; edited collection of cultural studies essays, *States of Rage: Emotional Eruption, Violence, and Social Change,* New York University Press, 1996. **Essays:** Marilyn Hacker; Virginia Woolf.

DAY, Susie. Freelance writer. **Essays:** Debra Chasnoff; Barbara Deming; Alix Dobkin.

DeMATIO, Joseph E. Editor, *Automobile Magazine,* Ann Arbor, Michigan; graduate of University of Michigan. **Essay:** Larry Kramer.

DeMUTH, Danielle M. Associated with Women's Studies Program, University of Toledo and is active in creating change for women on campus. Graduate student pursuing Ph.D. emphasizing rhetoric and composition, 20th century women's fiction, and women's studies at University of Toledo. Received bachelor's degree in psychology and English from Heidelberg College. **Essays:** Marcia Freedman; Dee Mosbacher; Carol Seajay; Gale Wilhelm.

DICKINSON, Peter. Completing Ph.D. in Department of English, University of British Columbia, Vancouver, Canada. Written widely in the areas of contemporary Canadian literature and lesbian and gay studies. **Essays:** Gregg Araki; Beth Brant.

DOYLE, Paul A. Instructor at various colleges; presently professor of English, Nassau Community College, State University of New York. Author and editor of eighteen books, including *A Concordance to the Collected Poems of James Joyce; Sean O'Faolain* and *Liam O'Flaherty* (both in Twayne's English Authors Series); *Paul Vincent Carroll: A Critical Introduction; Henry David Thoreau: Studies and Commentaries; Liam O'Flaherty: An Annotated Bibliography; Guide to Basic Information Sources in English Literature;* and *An Evelyn Waugh Companion.* Contributor of articles to more than 80 journals and periodicals, including *South Atlantic Quarterly, Twentieth Century Literature, James Joyce Quarterly, Dublin Review,* and *English Literature in Transition.* **Essay:** Lytton Strachey.

DYNES, Wayne R. Professor at Hunter College of the City University of New York; cofounder of New York chapter of Gay Academic Union, 1973; compiled and annotated *Homosexuality: A Research Guide;* editor-in-chief of multiple-award-winning *Encyclopedia of Homosexuality;* coeditor of *Studies in Homosexuality,* Garland Publishing, 1992. **Essays:** John Boswell; Edward Carpenter; E. M. Forster; Michel Foucault; André Gide; Magnus Hirschfeld; W. Dorr Legg; Leonardo da Vinci; Christopher Marlowe; Plato; Andy Warhol; Walt Whitman.

EAGAN, Joseph M. Head of the Government Reference Service, Enoch Pratt Free Library, Baltimore, Maryland. Mounted library exhibit, "Stonewall and After: 25 Years of Gay and Lesbian Books, 1969-1994," 1994. **Essays:** Joseph Beam; Arthur Bell; Melvin Dixon; Martin Duberman; Reverend Troy D. Perry; Randy Shilts.

ECKSTEIN-SOULE, Carolyn. Administrative professional specializing in human resources management, Michigan State University; part-time teacher, Lansing Community College. Coauthor of management column for *The Voice,* the bi-monthly publication of Michigan Nursery and Landscape Association. Received M.B.A. from Michigan State University, 1983. **Essays:** Pedro Almodovar; Divine.

EDMUNDS, Jean. Freelance writer. **Essays:** Bishop Carl Bean; Gian Carlo Menotti; Pratibha Parmar.

ELERT, Nicolet V. Editor, freelance writer, and artist. Editor of Volume 1, *Films,* of the *International Dictionary of Films and Filmmakers* series. **Essays:** Berenice Abbott; Keith Haring; Robert Mapplethorpe.

FARRELL, C. Frederick, Jr. Professor of French and chair of Division of the Humanities, University of Minnesota, Morris. Translator and editor of books, including *Les Visages de la mort, Air and Dreams* by Gaston Bachelard and *The New Cineas* by Emeric Crucé. Author of *Marguerite Yourcenar in Counterpoint;* also author of numerous textbooks and of articles on Louise Labé and François Mauriac. **Essay:** Marguerite Yourcenar.

FARRELL, Edith R. Professor of French, University of Minnesota, Morris. Author, editor, and translator of books, including *Marguerite Yourcenar in Counterpoint*; *Les Visages de la mort*; *The Alms of Alcippe and Other Poems* by Marguerite Yourcenar; *Water and Dreams* by Gaston Bachelard; *Air and Dreams* by Gaston Bachelard; *Louise Labé's Complete Works;* and *The New Cineas* by Emeric Crucé; also author of textbooks and articles on François Mauriac. **Essay:** Marguerite Yourcenar.

FITZPATRICK, Laurie. Senior arts editor for *Art and Understanding* magazine; contributor of art criticism and features to *Philadelphia Gay News*; currently assembling collection of short stories. Received M.F.A. from Tyler School of Art in 1989; painter in oils and creator of prints. Born in 1962, in Ancon Canal Zone, and has traveled extensively throughout the United States; currently resides in Philadelphia, Pennsylvania. **Essays:** Emily Blackwell; June Chan; Merce Cunningham; Edmonia Lewis; Johnny Mathis; Michelle Parkerson.

FRANCIS, Brian. Feature writer for *Xtra!,* Canada's largest gay and lesbian publication. Currently residing in Toronto, Canada. **Essay:** JoAnn Loulan.

FRANKS, Jill. Assistant professor of English, Austin Peay State University, Tennessee; instructor, University of British Columbia, Rutgers University, and University of Massachusetts. Specializes in modern British, contemporary Canadian, and African American literatures; novelist. **Essays:** Rita Mae Brown; Anna Freud; Susan Sontag.

GARCIA-JOHNSON, Ronie. Graduate student, University of Michigan, Ann Arbor; freelance writer. **Essay:** Sor Juana Inés de la Cruz.

GARNES, David. Former English teacher; reference librarian, University of Connecticut, Storrs. Contributor to *Connecticut Poets on AIDS; Liberating Minds: The Stories and Professional Lives of Gay, Lesbian and Bisexual Librarians; A Loving Testimony: Remembering Loved Ones Lost to AIDS;* and *Gay & Lesbian Literature.* **Essays:** Alexander the Great; Christina; Amy Lowell.

GIBSON, Michelle. Assistant professor of English and women's studies, University College, University of Cincinnati. Active in Conference on College Composition and Communication and co-chair of group's Caucus for Lesbian and Gay Professionals. Currently doing work on survivors of child abuse and their responses to personal writing assignments; involved in a number of workshops and presentations on child abuse; author of article on child abuse in *Writing on the Edge;* also published poetry and articles about American literature. **Essays:** Charles Shively; Cris Williamson.

GILMORE, Chris. Freelance writer. **Essay:** Hans Christian Andersen.

GOAD, Craig M. Teacher of writing and literature, Northwest Missouri State University; resides in Maryville, Missouri. Wrote both M.A. thesis and Ph.D. dissertation on Truman Capote; currently working on a book about the later years of Capote's career. **Essay:** Truman Capote.

GRACIAS, Marian. Born in India; currently completing Ph.D. in English, University of British Columbia, Vancouver, Canada. Research interests include literature from India and the South Asian diaspora, as well as gender and cultural studies. **Essay:** Urvashi Vaid.

GREENBLATT, R. Ellen. Freelance writer. **Essays:** Nancy K. Bereano; Ron Buckmire; Michael Denneny; Barbara Gittings; Barbara Grier; Deb Price.

HAMER, Diane E. Associate editor of *Harvard Gay & Lesbian Review*; office manager, Schlesinger Library, Radcliffe College. **Essay:** Charlotte Bunch.

HARPER, Judith E. Freelance writer and independent scholar in Greater Boston area. Specializes in 19th century American social, literary, and women's history. Contributor to *Feminist Writers,* St. James Press, 1996; *Scribner's American Biography;* and *Historical Encyclopedia of World Slavery,* ABC-Clio. Member, National Coalition of Independent Scholars. **Essays:** Jane Addams; Susan B. Anthony; Alice B. Toklas.

HARRIS, Laura Alexandra. Teacher, Women's Studies Department, California State University, San Marcos. Currently completing dissertation, *Women Writing Resistance: Bodies, Class, and Race in the Harlem Renaissance.* **Essay:** Gladys Bentley.

HAYES, Loie B. Editor and publisher of nonfiction political books for South End Press. Author of essays, including "Pregnant Butch?," published in *Sojourner,* the feminist monthly from Boston. **Essays:** Simon Nkoli; Merle Woo.

HELFRICH, Karen. Freelance writer. **Essays:** Djuna Barnes; Holly Hughes; Sarah Schulman.

HENRY, Seán. South Carolinian native currently pursuing Ph.D in German literature and instructor of undergraduate German courses, University of Kansas. Received B.A. in German in 1991, and M.A. degree in German literature in 1995. Lecturer on Franz Kafka at various graduate school symposiums. Research includes work on two gay German lyric poets, August von Platen and Stephan George. **Essays:** Peter Ilich Tchaikovsky; Karl Heinrich Ulrichs.

HILL, Debora. Freelance writer. **Essays:** Liberace; RuPaul; John Waters; Oscar Wilde.

HODGE, Jon. Doctoral candidate at Tufts University writing dissertation on obsessional neurosis in Victorian literature. **Essay:** Quentin Crisp.

JONES, Robert F. Freelance writer. **Essays:** Sir Cecil Beaton; Leonard Bernstein; John Maynard Keynes.

JURGENS, Jane. Reference librarian, Northeastern Illinois University, Chicago; member of Gay and Lesbian Task Force, American Library Association. **Essay:** Colette.

KATTELMAN, Beth A. Doctoral candidate in theater, Ohio State University. Editor of journal *Theatre Studies,* 1993-95. Contributor to *The Gay and Lesbian Literary Heritage,* edited by Claude J. Summers, Henry Holt, 1995, and *The Journal of Dramatic Theory and Criticism.* Currently conducting research on gender issues as they relate to the character of the hard-boiled female detective. **Essay:** Charles Ludlam.

KATZ, Judith. Freelance writer. **Essays:** Alison Bechdel; Irena Klepfisz; Agnes Moorehead.

KING, Nicola. Teacher of literature, LSU College of Higher Education, Southampton, England. Ph.D. from Southamptom University; doctoral research was on the representation of memory in recent fiction and autobiography; has written widely on contemporary fiction. **Essay:** Jeanette Winterson.

KOHL, Judith C. Professor emeritus of English and humanities, Duchess Community College; visiting professor, Vassar College. Taught contemporary drama, recent American literature, contemporary international literature, and autobiographies of marginalized Americans. Contributor of reviews to library journals; also contributor to numerous biographical encyclopedias. **Essays:** Natalie Clifford Barney; Ruth Benedict; Blanche Wiesen Cook; Henry James; Audre Lorde.

KRSTOVIĆ, Jelena. Freelance writer, editor, and translator. **Essay:** Sappho.

LEVINE, David. Freelance writer and editor living in New York City; writer on gay and lesbian related topics. **Essays:** Virginia M. Apuzzo; Paul Goodman; Cleve Jones; Charles Pierce.

LOCKARD, Ray Anne. Freelance writer. **Essay:** Tee A. Corinne.

LOUTZENHEISER, Lisa W. Graduate student in educational policy studies, University of Wisconsin—Madison. Previously teacher of sexuality, computers, and social studies at alternative high school in California. **Essays:** Margaret Cruikshank; Mary Daly.

LUTES, Michael A. Reference librarian, University of Notre Dame. Contributor to *Gay & Lesbian Literature,* St. James Press, 1994, and *Encyclopedia of AIDS,* Garland Press, 1996; also contributor to numerous gay and lesbian magazines and professional journals. Served on the American Library Association's Gay, Lesbian, and Bisexual Book Awards Committee; judge for Lambda Book Report's Lammy Awards. **Essays:** Barney Frank; Greg Louganis; Harvey Milk.

MARIE, Jacquelyn. Women's Studies Librarian, University of Santa Cruz, California. Contributor of articles on Gloria Anzaldua for *Gay & Lesbian Literature;* and on Kamala Das and Suniti Namjoshi for *Feminist Writers.* **Essays:** Alvin Ailey; Meg Christian.

McNAB, James P. Professor of French, University of North Carolina at Wilmington. Author of book on Raymond Radiguet, for G. K. Hall, 1984; contributor of articles on Cocteau and Radiguet to periodicals; associate editor, *French Review.* Interests include Rimbaud's legacy in the United States, French popular culture, and the connections between painting and literature. **Essays:** Sergei Diaghilev; Allen Ginsberg; Rudolf Nureyev.

MILLEN, Dianne. Researcher and writer with a particular interest in issues relating to women's participation in science, feminist analyses of science, and lesbian/bisexual women's experiences. Editor of numerous student publications relating to lesbigay issues/sexual health and women's issues. Currently writing Ph.D. on women's career experiences in science. **Essay:** Billie Jean King.

MILLER, D. Quentin. Freelance writer and part-time English instructor. Ph.D. in English from University of Connecticut. Has written on James Baldwin, Ernest Hemingway, James Joyce,

Cormac McCarthy, Tim O'Brien, John Updike, and Edith Wharton. **Essay:** James Baldwin.

MORY, Robert N. Freelance writer, technical writer, editor, and college teacher. Associate editor, *Middle English Dictionary*, University of Michigan, Ann Arbor, Michigan. Publications include studies of language history, linguistics, gay history and literature, and medical history. **Essays:** Frederick II; Dag Hammarskjold.

MUSBACH, Tom. Freelance writer. **Essay:** Frank Kameny.

NELSON-McDERMOTT, Catherine. Currently completing Ph.D. at University of Alberta, working on the political nature of Bloomsbury's orientalism. Written on Monique Wittig, Erna Brodber, and verbal and physical violence against women. **Essay:** Vita Sackville-West.

NEUMANN, Caryn E. Doctoral student in women's history at Ohio State University. Author of articles, including "Grounded: American Women Aviators in the Great War" in *Over the Front,* summer 1995, and "The End of Gender Solidarity: A History of the Women's Organization for Prohibition Reform, 1929-1933," forthcoming. **Essays:** Angelina Emily Weld Grimke; Martha Carey Thomas.

O'CONNOR, Michael E. New York based writer and actor. Contributor of poetry to *Mouth of the Dragon, Fag Rag,* and *James White Review;* contributor of articles to *Playbill, New York Magazine, QW,* and *Blueboy.* Editor, Mavety Media Group and Amethyst Press; assistant to composer Aaron Copland for four years. Former Columbia University swimmer, awarded six medals at Gay Games IV. **Essays:** Aaron Copland; David Kopay.

OMOSUPE, Ekua. Teacher of writing, women's studies, and American literature, Cabrillo College. With partner, Maria Davila, co-owner of ethnic arts, crafts, and jewelry business, Makua Productions. Poetry editor for *Sinister Wisdom;* contributor of poems and essays to numerous journals and anthologies, including *Wedded Wife to Lesbian Lives,* Crossing Press, 1995. **Essay:** Pat Parker.

ORTEGA, Teresa. Freelance writer and critic; contributor to numerous publications, including *South Atlantic Quarterly, Sinister Wisdom, Lambda Book Report, Lesbian Review of Books,* and *New World: Young Latino Writers.* Currently at work on a novel. **Essay:** Marga Gomez.

PERCY, William Armstrong, III. Professor of history, University of Massachusetts, Boston. Author of *Pederasty and Pedagogy in Archaic Greece;* coauthor of *The Age of Recovery: Europe During the Fifteenth Century*; "Homosexuality" in *The Handbook of Medieval Sexuality*, and *Outing: Shattering the Conspiracy of Silence.* **Essay:** Michelangelo Buonarroti.

PETERSON, Andrea L.T. Freelance writer. **Essays:** Roberta Achtenberg; Edward Albee; Margaret Anderson; Dorothy Arzner; Miriam Ben-Shalom; George Chauncey; Elsa Gidlow; Sir John Gielgud; Bertha Harris; Essex Hemphill; JEB; Elton John; Jasper Johns; Eva Le Galliene; Sir Ian McKellen; Toshi Reagon; Gayle Rubin; Assoto Saint; Gertrude Stein; Alan Turing; Tennessee Williams.

PINARSKI, Annmarie. Freelance writer. **Essays:** Dorothy Allison; Karla Jay.

PRICE, Joanna. Lecturer in American studies, Liverpool John Moores University, Great Britain. Currently writing a book about Bobbie Ann Mason; involved in a project researching the relation between consumer culture, gender, and mourning as represented by contemporary American fiction. **Essay:** Adrienne Rich.

RIDINGER, Robert B. Marks. Associate professor, Universities Libraries, Northern Illinois University. Compiler of *An Index to "The Advocate," the National Gay Newsmagazine, 1967-1982,* 1983, and *The Homosexual and Society: An Annotated Bibliography,* 1990; poet. **Essays:** Sally Gearhart; Arnie Kantrowitz.

ROCHMAN, Susan L. Freelance journalist based in Ithaca, New York; frequently covers women's health, gay and lesbian, and prison-related issues. Contributor to publications, including *The Advocate, Curve, American Health,* and *On the Issues.* **Essay:** Susan M. Love.

RUFF, Shawn Stewart. Editor of *Go the Way Your Blood Beats,* and *Beautifully Furious*, a forthcoming collection of essays on international lesbian and gay literary figures from the African diaspora; also editor of *aRude Magazine.* **Essay:** Bill T. Jones.

RUSSELL, Sue. Poet and critic; has written extensively on 20th century lesbian and gay poets. Contributor to publications, including *Kenyon Review, Lambda Book Report, Voice Literary Supplement*, and *Women's Review of Books.* **Essay:** Elizabeth Bishop.

SADLER, Geoff. Freelance writer. **Essays:** Lorraine Hansberry; Carson McCullers; Gertrude "Ma" Rainey.

SCHRECENGOST, Lynda. Freelance writer and editor based in Washington, D.C. area. Specializes in promotional and educational publications; currently working on a book project for Coopers & Lybrand Consulting. **Essays:** Hadrian; May Sarton; Bessie Smith; Gerry E. Studds.

SHAW, Marvin S. Retired teacher of English, Skyline College, San Bruno, California; coauthor of *A Viewer's Guide to Art,* 1991; frequent contributor to San Francisco *Bay Area Reporter,* and *The Advocate.* **Essays:** Paul Cadmus; Phyllis Ann Lyon and Del Martin; John Addington Symonds; Carl Van Vechten.

SHIVELY, Charles. Professor of American studies, University of Massachusetts, Boston; active in gay presses; author of *Nuestra Señora de Los Dolores,* 1975; *Calamus Lovers, Walt Whitman's Working Class Camerados,* 1987; *A History of the Conception of Death in America, 1650-1860,* 1988; and *Drum Beats, Walt Whitman's Civil War Boy Lovers,* 1989. **Essays:** Reinaldo Arenas; Countee Cullen; Harry Hay; Langston Hughes; Manuel Puig.

SHREVE, Jack. Teacher of English and Spanish, Allegany College of Maryland. Book review editor of the translation journal, *Delos;* contributor of book reviews to numerous magazines and journals, including *James White Review;* also contributor of articles to *Gay and Lesbian Literature,* St. James Press; author of textbook, *College Vocabulary Development.* **Essays:** Caravaggio; Herman Melville; George Santayana.

SPELLMAN, Bryan D. Administrative officer, School of Fine Arts and faculty member, Creative Pulse Program, University of Montana—Missoula. Ph.D. from University of California-Berkeley, 1986. Current areas of scholarly interest include French novelist Yves Navarre, the psychology of creativity, and mind-body connections; active in Montana gay politics; served as founding board member and president of Out In Montana. **Essays:** Jean Genet; Marcel Proust.

SUMMERS, Claude J. William E. Stirton Professor in the Humanities and professor of English, University of Michigan—Dearborn. Author of books, including studies of Christopher Isherwood and E. M. Forster; *Gay Fictions: Wilde to Stonewall; Homosexuality in Renaissance and Enlightenment England: Literary Representation in Historical Context,* and *The Gay and Lesbian Literary Heritage.* **Essay:** Christopher Isherwood.

SUTHERLAND, Fraser. Poet, critic, and lexicographer in Toronto, Canada. Author of ten books, including *John Glassco: An Essay and Bibliography,* 1984, and *Jonestown: A Poem,* 1996. **Essay:** Mary Renault.

SZACHNOWSKI, Lucya. Freelance writer and journalist in London, England. Studied at University of Kent at Canterbury and has degree in drama and comparative literary studies. **Essays:** Anne Bonney and Mary Read; Radclyffe Hall; Anne Lister.

SZYMCZAK, Jerome. Freelance writer. **Essays:** Gloria Anzaldua; Benjamin Bannecker; Ann Bannon; Rosa Bonheur; Romaine Brooks; Glenn Burke; Chrystos; Mercedes de Acosta; Rainer Werner Fassbinder; Gluck; Judy Grahn; Barbara J. Hammer; Gilbert Herdt; Alberta Hunter; Derek Jarman; Sarah Orne Jewett; Isaac Julien; Willyce Kim; Sharon Kowalski and Karen Thompson; Ladies of Llangollen; Ismail Merchant and James Ivory; Cherrie Moraga; Martina Navratilova; Joan Nestle; Florence Nightingale; Marlon Riggs; Muriel Rukeyser; Vito Russo; Bayard Rustin; José Sarria; Barbara Smith; Dame Ethel Smyth; Rosa von Praunheim; Tom Waddell; Babe Didrikson Zaharias; Franco Zeffirelli.

TEXTOR, Alex Robertson. Freelance writer. **Essays:** John D'Emilio; Daniel C. Tsang.

TREDELL, Nicolas. Freelance writer. **Essays:** W. H. Auden; Francis Bacon; John Cage; Emily Dickinson; David Hockney.

TURNBAUGH, Douglas Blair. Delegate for the U.S. to the Conseil International de la Danse/UNESCO; member of National Arts Club's Creative Writing Program. Contributor to numerous periodicals, including *New York* and *Atlantic;* author of *Duncan Grant and the Bloomsbury Group,* Lyle Stuart, 1987; *Private: The Erotic Art of Duncan Grant,* Gay Mens Press, 1989; *Strip Show: Paintings by Patrick Angus,* Editions Aubrey Walter, 1992; and *Sergei Diaghilev: The Quest for Love,* Chelsea House. Recipient of Poland's Nijinsky Medal and Russia's Diaghilev Medal. **Essay:** Duncan Grant.

VOOS, Richard. Freelance writer. **Essays:** Ruth Bernhard; Midge Costanza; Judy Dlugacz.

WALD, Jonathan. Contributor of theater and film commentaries to *American Theatre Magazine, San Francisco Bay Times, InsideOut Magazine,* and on PlanetOut's queer online service; award-winning screenwriter; contributor of poetry to books, including *Badboy Book of Erotic Poetry.* **Essays:** Susie Bright; Pat Califia.

WATSTEIN, Sarah. Associate librarian for public services, Jacqueline Greenan Wexler Library, Hunter College of the City University of New York; compiler of bibliographies; coauthor of *AIDS and Women: A Sourcebook,* 1990; contributor to *Feminist Bookstores News, Body Positive,* and *Visibilities.* **Essays:** Peter Adair; Lisa Ben; June Millington; Jean O'Leary.

WESTFAHL, Gary. Freelance writer. **Essays:** George Cukor; Rock Hudson; Sheila James Kuehl; Stephen Sondheim; Gore Vidal.

WHITE, Tracy. Occasional writing instructor, gymnastics coach, and author. Graduated from Oakland University in Rochester, Michigan with a degree in mathematics and English. **Essay:** Leonard P. Matlovich, Jr.

WILEY, Catherine A. Freelance writer. **Essays:** Lillian Faderman; Kitty Tsui.

WILSON, Anna. Freelance writer. **Essay:** Willa Cather.

WRIGHT, Les K. Assistant professor of humanities and English, Mount Ida College; founding member of the Gay and Lesbian Historical Society of Northern California; curator of the Bear History Project. In 1995 appointed cochair of the Committee on Lesbian and Gay History, serving as newsletter editor and membership secretary. Editor of *The Bear Book,* Haworth Press, 1997. **Essay:** Jonathan Ned Katz.

Photo Acknowledgments

Photographs in *Gay & Lesbian Biography* have been used with the permission of the following organizations and individuals:

AP/Worldwide Photos: Bernice Abbott, Dorothy Allison, Pedro Almodovar, Gregg Araki, Dorothy Arzner, Arthur Bell, John Boswell, Michael Callen, George Cukor, Merce Cunningham, Barbara Deming, Anna Freud, Cleve Jones, Susan Love, Charles Ludlam, Elaine Noble, Jean O'Leary, Charles Pierce, Mary Renault, Carol Seajay, Randy Shilts, Michelangelo Signorile, Susan Sontag, Urvashi Vaid, Carl Van Vechten, Tom Waddell, Franco Zeffirelli

The Bettmann Archive: W. H. Auden, Ruth Benedict, Rosa Bonheur, John Cage, Edward Carpenter, Sergei de Diaghilev, Hadrian, Dag Hammarskjold, Magnus Hirschfeld, Rock Hudson, Alberta Hunter, Ian McKellen, J. A. Symonds, Tennessee Williams

Corbis-Bettmann: Alexander the Great, Djuna Barnes, Cecil Beaton, Paul Cadmus, Frederick II, André Gide, Sarah Orne Jewett, Eva Le Gallienne, Michelangelo Buonarroti

Reuters/Bettmann: Roberta Achtenberg, Melissa Etheridge

Reuters/Corbis-Bettmann: Greg Louganis

UPI/Bettmann: Benjamin Banneker, Quentin Crisp, Divine, Greta Garbo, John Gielgud, Radclyffe Hall, Johnny Mathis, Leonard Matlovich, Vita Sackville-West, Alice B. Toklas

UPI/Corbis-Bettmann: Michael Bennett, Marc Blitzstein, Roy Cohn, Rainer Werner Fassbinder, Michael Foucalt, Barney Frank, John Maynard Keynes, Liberace, Robert Mapplethorpe, Gian Carlo Menotti, Agnes Moorehead, Gerry E. Studds, Martha Carey Thomas

National Gay and Lesbian Task Force Policy Institute: John D'Emilio

Daniel Nicoletta: Harry Hay

Rick Gerharter Photography: José Sarria

The editors would also like to thank the many entrants and contributors who supplied photographs for this volume.